PAROCHIAL AND PLAIN SERMONS

PAROCHIAL AND PLAIN SERMONS

JOHN HENRY NEWMAN

IGNATIUS PRESS   SAN FRANCISCO

Previously published in eight volumes
by Longman, Green, and Company
London and New York, 1891

Permission to reproduce George Richmond's
illustration of John Henry Newman
was kindly granted by
The Friends of Cardinal Newman
The Birmingham Oratory

Cover design by Roxanne Mei Lum

Reprinted 1997 Ignatius Press, San Francisco
All rights reserved
ISBN 978-0-89870-638-3 (HC)
ISBN 978-1-68149-373-2 (eBook)
Library of Congress catalogue number 97-70808
Printed in the United States of America ⬭∞

CONTENTS

III

IV

VII

VIII

FOREWORD

NEWMAN is generally known today, by Catholics and others, as "Cardinal Newman". However, he came to the purple only eleven years before the end of a life of ninety years, which he had started as a brilliant young Protestant, strongly tempted by scepticism. Being not quite sixteen he converted to a deeply committed life of dedication to God in Christ. Educated at Oxford, he would, for some years, feel inclined to a missionary vocation. Ordained to the priesthood in the Anglican church, he would eventually devote his time to a combination of parochial ministry, educational responsibilities as a fellow and tutor of Oriel College, and personal firsthand theological research, especially in the field of patristics, that is, studies of the first great masters of Christian thinking: the Fathers of the Church, as they are called.

In a church such as the Church of England in the 1830s, divided between a liberalism which meant more or less extreme rationalism and the "enthusiasm" of the late followers of the Wesleyan revival, he was—if not exactly to initiate—soon to become the main leader of a movement to rediscover and revitalize the early tradition of the Christian Church. Meeting with a growing opposition of the authorities of the English church, he would be led to reconsider his ecclesiastical situation and come to the conclusion that the church of the apostles and the Fathers, founded by and upon Christ, did not survive except in the Catholic Church, in communion with the See of Rome.

After a prolonged period of inner conflict, resolved only by prayer in an ascetical retreat, he would convert to Rome. Once a Catholic priest, he was to begin the first Oratory in England, a society of priests founded by Saint Philip Neri, first in Birmingham.

There, after attempting, in spite of numerous difficulties, to found a Catholic university in Dublin, at the request of the bishops of Ireland, he would retire and instead found a grammar school for preparing young Catholic laymen to receive a full academic education without losing their faith.

In the meantime, he would be occupied in deep reflection and research concerning the problems facing the Church as well as the individual Catholic in the modern world. The boldness of his approach would soon make him again an object of suspicion in the Church he had entered, while some of his former fellow Anglicans, such as Kingsley, were raising against him the accusation of having betrayed genuine Christianity to a contemptible and dishonest survival of medieval corruption.

His *Apologia* in response to Kingsley, which was immediately recognized as a masterpiece even to most prejudiced readers, in addition to winning him again the love and respect of Anglicans and Protestants in general, secured him at least the gratitude of the more intelligent among Catholics, whether lay or cleric. It would nonetheless require the lofty mind of a Leo XIII to acknowledge the quality of his thinking and the profoundly Christian character of his personality, and therefore to promote him to the cardinalate.

All through his long life, Newman was mostly misunderstood by the authorities, little known and still less appreciated by the majority of Catholics. Yet he had both spiritual and intellectual influence upon honest agnostics like Matthew Arnold, or unpopular but sound Catholic scholars like Lord Acton. This led to an immense correspondence, only lately fully edited. At the same time he managed to write a number of volumes touching on all the aspects of Catholic theology and spirituality with constant reference to the cultural situation of the day, and an often prophetic insight into what was to be the evolution of human society at large in the coming century.

Already as an Anglican, he had treated the problem of authority in the church and the role of the laity, in his *Prophetical Office of the Church*. Later, when a Catholic authority himself he revised and enlarged it under the new title of *Via Media*. There also, he had given a quite outstanding example of what would be long after called "ecumenism", and still more directly in his *Lectures on Justification* he would explore in depth, with an exceptional lucidity, the basic problem of Protestantism versus Catholicism.

Also, on the subject of modern conflict of faith and reason, after his *Oxford University Sermons*, which are mainly devoted to that topic, he was to produce, at the end of his life, his slowly matured *Essay in Aid of a Grammar of Assent*.

More broadly, his *Idea of a University* (the only lasting result of what he called, with a dry humor, "my campaign in Ireland") elaborated a full analysis of the relation between culture and the Christian religion.

And more specifically, in the midst of the international controversy on the decrees of Vatican I, in his *Letter to the Duke of Norfolk*, he would give a most delicately balanced treatment of the problem created by the encounter of political and ecclesiastical authority.

Behind the critical acumen of the theologian and philosopher, in Newman's treatment of any problem, there is always the penetrating historical sense already in evidence in his early work on *The Arians of the Fourth Century*, later exhibited in a charming manner in his three volumes of *Historical Sketches*, but showing his full mastership above all in his famous *Essay on the Development of Christian Doctrine*: not in the least an apology of change for the sake of changing but a most careful delineation between change which means real growth and change which is only corruption.

Of all his immense work, however, we can say that we find the seeds and at least an incipient development in the eight volumes of his *Parochial and Plain Sermons*, preached, on Sundays and feast-days, in the pulpit of his Anglican parish, Saint Mary the Virgin, at Oxford. These sermons are given here, for the first time in a single volume, as perhaps the least technical but the most lasting expression of his own gradual discovery of all the fullness of the appeal as well as the challenge addressed to all men by Catholic truth and Catholic life, inseparable as they are within genuine Christianity.

There, above all, he himself will be found, with his intellectual power, his poetical vision, as well as his moral and spiritual integrity. Nothing can constitute for us, still today, and maybe today more than ever, such an introduction to what Christianity may give to and expect from our surrender to its call in the midst of a world no longer pretending to be Christian, but, indeed, presenting us at last with a full realization of what an atrocious kind of paganism only a world boasting of having become post-Christian could produce.

In my book *Newman's Vision of Faith*, I have tried to show in detail how the *Parochial and Plain Sermons*, by the treatment of their main themes, lead to all of Newman's most important works, and given some precise suggestions for following these themes all through the *Sermons* themselves.

LOUIS BOUYER
San Francisco, 1986

CHRONOLOGY

1801: Born in London on February 21.
1816: Converted to a fully committed Christian life at Ealing
      School.
1822: Elected fellow of Oriel.
1825: Became a priest of the Church of England.
1828: Became vicar of Saint Mary the Virgin, Oxford.
1833–1841: The Oxford movement.
1841: Retired to Littlemore (a village near Oxford).
1845: Converted to the Catholic Church.
1847: Ordained to the Catholic priesthood.
1848: Established the Oratory in Birmingham.
1852–1858: Founded Dublin Catholic University.
1858: Returned to England, founded the Birmingham
      Oratory School.
1864: Wrote his *Apologia*.
1879: Made a cardinal.
1890: Died in Birmingham on August 11.

PREFACE

THE SERMONS here republished were written and preached at various periods between the years 1825 and 1843.

The first six volumes are reprinted from the six volumes of *Parochial Sermons*; the seventh and eighth formed the fifth volume of *Plain Sermons, by Contributors to the Tracts for the Times*, which was the contribution of its Author to that Series.

All the Sermons are reprinted from the last Editions of the several volumes, published from time to time by the Messrs. Rivington.

They made, in their day, partly through their publication, but yet more, probably, through their living effect upon those who heard them, a deep and lasting impression for good on the Communion for whose especial benefit they were designed; they exercised an extensive influence very far beyond it; and their republication will awaken in many minds vivid and grateful recollections of their first appearance.

They met, at that time, very real and great moral, intellectual, and spiritual needs of man,—in giving depth and precision and largeness to his belief and apprehension of the mysteries of God, and seriousness and accuracy to his study and knowledge of himself, of his own nature, with its manifold powers, capacities, and responsibilities, and of his whole relation to the supernatural and unseen. They found a response in the hearts and minds and consciences of those to whom they were addressed, in marvellous proportion to the affectionate and stirring earnestness with which their Author appealed to the conscious or dormant sense of their needs, and his zealous and energetic endeavours, under God's blessing, to show, in every variety of light, how the grand central Verities of the Christian Dispensation, entrusted as the good "Deposit," to the Church, were revealed and adapted to supply them.

Many things, indeed, contained in these volumes have become, from the very readiness of their first acceptance, and from their gradual reception into the current of religious thought, so familiar, that it requires some retrospect of the time previous to their appearance to appreciate the original freshness with which they brought out the fundamental Articles of the Christian Faith, and their bearing on the formation of the Christian character; and to understand the degree in which they have acted, like leaven, on the mind and language and literature of the Church in this Country, and have marked an era in her history.

But, besides their relation to the past, it will be seen in their republication how the spirit which dictated them pierced here and there through the cloud which hung over the future, and how the Author warned us, with somewhat of prophetic forecast, of impending trials and conflicts, and of perplexities and dangers, then only dimly seen or unheeded, of which it has been reserved to the present generation to witness the nearer approach. It might seem to have been his calling at once to warn us of them, and to provide, as best he might, words of guidance and support, and consolation and encouragement under them —an anchor of the soul in the coming storm.

They are republished in the fervent hope and belief that like good to that which, by God's blessing, they have done before, they may, by His mercy, if we be not unworthy of it, do yet again under other circumstances.

To many of this generation they will appear in much of their original freshness; and to all with the greater power and reality, from the saddening aspect of the times, and the appalling prospects before us; replete as they are with those "many secrets of religion which are not perceived till they be felt, and are not felt, but in the day of great calamity."

In conclusion it is right, though scarcely necessary to observe, that the republication of these Sermons by the Editor is not to be considered as equivalent to a re-assertion by their Author of all that they contain; inasmuch as, being printed entire and unaltered, except in the most insignificant particulars, they cannot be free from passages which he certainly now would wish were otherwise, or would, one may be sure, desire to see altered or omitted.

But the alternative plainly lies between publishing all or nothing, and it appears more to the glory of God and for the cause of religion, to publish all, than to destroy the acceptableness of the Volumes to those for whom they were written by any omissions and alterations.

W. J. Copeland
Farnham Rectory, Essex
May 15, 1868

I

To the
REV. E. B. PUSEY, B.D.,
Canon of Christ Church,
and Regius Professor of Hebrew in the
University of Oxford,
this volume
is inscribed,
in affectionate acknowledgement
of the blessing
of his long friendship and example.
March 1, 1834.

HOLINESS NECESSARY
FOR FUTURE BLESSEDNESS

"Holiness, without which no man shall see the Lord."
—Heb. xii. 14.

I N this text it has seemed good to the Holy Spirit to convey a
chief truth of religion in a few words. It is this circumstance
which makes it especially impressive; for the truth itself is declared in one form or other in every part of Scripture. It is told
us again and again, that to make sinful creatures holy was the
great end which our Lord had in view in taking upon Him our
nature, and thus none but the holy will be accepted for His sake
at the last day. The whole history of redemption, the covenant
of mercy in all its parts and provisions, attests the necessity of
holiness in order to salvation; as indeed even our natural conscience bears witness also. But in the text what is elsewhere
implied in history, and enjoined by precept, is stated doctrinally, as a momentous and necessary fact, the result of some
awful irreversible law in the nature of things, and the inscrutable determination of the Divine Will.

Now some one may ask, "Why is it that holiness is a necessary qualification for our being received into heaven? why is it
that the Bible enjoins upon us so strictly to love, fear, and obey
God, to be just, honest, meek, pure in heart, forgiving, heavenly-minded, self-denying, humble, and resigned? Man is confessedly weak and corrupt; *why* then is he enjoined to be so
religious, so unearthly? *why* is he required (in the strong language of Scripture) to become 'a new creature'? Since he is by
nature what he is, would it not be an act of greater mercy in
God to save him altogether without this holiness, which it is so
difficult, yet (as it appears) so necessary for him to possess?"

Now we have no right to ask this question. Surely it is quite
enough for a sinner to know, that a way has been opened
through God's grace for his salvation, without being informed
why that way, and not another way, was chosen by Divine

Wisdom. Eternal life is "the *gift* of God." Undoubtedly He
may prescribe the terms on which He will give it; and if He has
determined holiness to be the way of life, it is enough; it is not
for us to inquire why He has so determined.

Yet the question may be asked reverently, and with a view to
enlarge our insight into our own condition and prospects; and
in that case the attempt to answer it will be profitable, if it be
made soberly. I proceed, therefore, to state one of the reasons,
assigned in Scripture, why present holiness is necessary, as the
text declares to us, for future happiness.

To be holy is, in our Church's words, to have "the true circumcision of the Spirit;" that is, to be separate from sin, to hate
the works of the world, the flesh, and the devil; to take pleasure
in keeping God's commandments; to do things as He would
have us do them; to live habitually as in the sight of the world to
come, as if we had broken the ties of this life, and were dead
already. Why cannot we be saved without possessing such a
frame and temper of mind?

I answer as follows: That, even supposing a man of unholy
life were suffered to enter heaven, *he would not be happy there*; so
that it would be no mercy to permit him to enter.

We are apt to deceive ourselves, and to consider heaven a
place like this earth; I mean, a place where every one may
choose and take his own pleasure. We see that in this world,
active men have their own enjoyments, and domestic men have
theirs; men of literature, of science, of political talent, have
their respective pursuits and pleasures. Hence we are led to act
as if it will be the same in another world. The only difference we
put between this world and the next, is that *here*, (as we know
well,) men are *not always sure*, but there, we suppose they *will be
always sure*, of obtaining what they seek after. And accordingly
we conclude, that *any man*, whatever his habits, tastes, or manner of life, if *once admitted* into heaven, would be happy there.
Not that we altogether deny, that some preparation is necessary
for the next world; but we do not estimate its real extent and
importance. We think we can reconcile ourselves to God when
we will; as if nothing were required in the case of men in general, but some temporary attention, more than ordinary, to our
religious duties,—some strictness, during our last sickness, in
the services of the Church, as men of business arrange their letters and papers on taking a journey or balancing an account.
But an opinion like this, though commonly acted on, is refuted
as soon as put into words. For heaven, it is plain from Scripture,
is not a place where many different and discordant pursuits can

be carried on at once, as is the case in this world. Here every man can do his *own* pleasure, but there he must do *God's* pleasure. It would be presumption to attempt to determine the employments of that eternal life which good men are to pass in God's presence, or to deny that state which eye hath not seen, nor ear heard, nor mind conceived, may comprise an infinite variety of pursuits and occupations. Still so far we are distinctly told, that that future life will be spent in God's *presence*, in a sense which does not apply to our present life; so that it may be best described as an endless and uninterrupted worship of the Eternal Father, Son, and Spirit. "They serve Him day and night in His temple, and He that sitteth on the throne shall dwell among them. . . . The Lamb which is in the midst of the throne shall feed them, and shall lead them unto living fountains of waters." Again, "The city had no need of the sun, neither of the moon to shine in it, for the glory of God did lighten it, and the Lamb is the light thereof. And the nations of them which are saved shall walk in the light of it, and the kings of the earth do bring their glory and honour into it."[1] These passages from St. John are sufficient to remind us of many others.

Heaven then is not like this world; I will say what it is much more like,—*a church*. For in a place of public worship no language of this world is heard; there are no schemes brought forward for temporal objects, great or small; no information how to strengthen our worldly interests, extend our influence, or establish our credit. These things indeed may be right in their way, so that we do not set our hearts upon them; still (I repeat), it is certain that we hear nothing of them in a church. Here we hear solely and entirely of *God*. We praise Him, worship Him, sing to Him, thank Him, confess to Him, give ourselves up to Him, and ask His blessing. And *therefore*, a church is like heaven; viz. because both in the one and the other, there is one single sovereign subject—religion—brought before us.

Supposing, then, instead of it being said that no irreligious man could serve and attend on God in heaven (or see Him, as the text expresses it), we were told that no irreligious man could worship, or spiritually see Him in church; should we not at once perceive the meaning of the doctrine? viz. that, were a man to come hither, who had suffered his mind to grow up in its own way, as nature or chance determined, without any deliberate habitual effort after truth and purity, he would find no real pleasure here, but would soon get weary of the place; because,

[1] Rev. vii.15, 17; xxi.23, 24.

in this house of God, he would hear only of that one subject which he cared little or nothing about, and nothing at all of those things which excited his hopes and fears, his sympathies and energies. If then a man without religion (supposing it possible) were admitted into heaven, doubtless he would sustain a great disappointment. Before, indeed, he fancied that he could be happy there; but when he arrived there, he would find no discourse but that which he had shunned on earth, no pursuits but those he had disliked or despised, nothing which bound him to aught else in the universe, and made him feel at home, nothing which he could enter into and rest upon. He would perceive himself to be an isolated being, cut away by Supreme Power from those objects which were still entwined around his heart. Nay, he would be in the presence of that Supreme Power, whom he never on earth could bring himself steadily to think upon, and whom now he regarded only as the destroyer of all that was precious and dear to him. Ah! he could not *bear* the face of the Living God; the Holy God would be no object of joy to him. "Let us alone! What have we to do with thee?" is the sole thought and desire of unclean souls, even while they acknowledge His majesty. None but the holy can look upon the Holy One; without holiness no man can endure to see the Lord.

When, then, we think to take part in the joys of heaven without holiness, we are as inconsiderate as if we supposed we could take an interest in the worship of Christians here below without possessing it in our measure. A careless, a sensual, an unbelieving mind, a mind destitute of the love and fear of God, with narrow views and earthly aims, a low standard of duty, and a benighted conscience, a mind contented with itself, and unresigned to God's will, would feel as little pleasure, at the last day, at the words, "Enter into the joy of thy Lord," as it does now at the words, "Let us pray." Nay, much less, because, while we are in a church, we may turn our thoughts to other subjects, and contrive to forget that God is looking on us; but that will not be possible in heaven.

We see, then, that holiness, or inward separation from the world, is necessary to our admission into heaven, because heaven is *not* heaven, is not a place of happiness *except* to the holy. There are bodily indispositions which affect the taste, so that the sweetest flavours become ungrateful to the palate; and indispositions which impair the sight, tinging the fair face of nature with some sickly hue. In like manner, there is a moral malady which disorders the inward sight and taste; and no man labouring under it is in a condition to enjoy what Scripture calls "the fulness of joy in God's presence, and pleasures at His right hand for evermore."

Nay, I will venture to say more than this;—it is fearful, but it is right to say it;—that if we wished to imagine a punishment for an unholy, reprobate soul, we perhaps could not fancy a greater than to *summon it to heaven*. Heaven would be hell to an irreligious man. We know how unhappy we are apt to feel at present, when alone in the midst of strangers, or of men of different tastes and habits from ourselves. How miserable, for example, would it be to have to live in a foreign land, among a people whose faces we never saw before, and whose language we could not learn. And this is but a faint illustration of the loneliness of a man of earthly dispositions and tastes, thrust into the society of saints and angels. How forlorn would he wander through the courts of heaven! He would find no one like himself; he would see in every direction the marks of God's holiness, and these would make him shudder. He would feel himself always in His presence. He could no longer turn his thoughts another way, as he does now, when conscience reproaches him. He would know that the Eternal Eye was ever upon him; and that Eye of holiness, which is joy and life to holy creatures, would seem to him an Eye of wrath and punishment. God cannot change His nature. Holy He must ever be. But while He is holy, no unholy soul can be happy in heaven. Fire does not inflame iron, but it inflames straw. It would cease to be fire if it did not. And so heaven itself would be fire to those, who would fain escape across the great gulf from the torments of hell. The finger of Lazarus would but increase their thirst. The very "heaven that is over their head" will be "brass" to them.

And now I have partly explained why it is that holiness is prescribed to us as the condition on our part for our admission into heaven. It seems to be necessary from the very nature of things. We do not see how it could be otherwise. Now then I will mention two important truths which seem to follow from what has been said.

1. If a certain character of mind, a certain state of the heart and affections, be necessary for entering heaven, our *actions* will avail for our salvation, chiefly as they tend to produce or evidence this frame of mind. Good works (as they are called) are required, not as if they had any thing of merit in them, not as if they could of themselves turn away God's anger for our sins, or purchase heaven for us, but because they are the means, under God's grace, of strengthening and showing forth that holy

principle which God implants in the heart, and without which (as the text tells us) we cannot see Him. The more numerous are our acts of charity, self-denial, and forbearance, of course the more will our minds be schooled into a charitable, self-denying, and forbearing temper. The more frequent are our prayers, the more humble, patient, and religious are our daily deeds, this communion with God, these holy works, will be the means of making our hearts holy, and of preparing us for the future presence of God. Outward acts, done on principle, create inward habits. I repeat, the separate acts of obedience to the will of God, good works as they are called, are of service to us, as gradually severing us from this world of sense, and impressing our hearts with a heavenly character.

It is plain, then, what works are not of service to our salvation;—all those which either have no effect upon the heart to change it, or which have a bad effect. What then must be said of those who think it an easy thing to please God, and to recommend themselves to Him; who do a few scanty services, call these the walk of faith, and are satisfied with them? Such men, it is too evident, instead of being themselves profited by their acts, such as they are, of benevolence, honesty, or justice, may be (I might even say) injured by them. For these very acts, even though good in themselves, are made to foster in these persons a bad spirit, a corrupt state of heart; viz. self-love, self-conceit, self-reliance, instead of tending to turn them from this world to the Father of spirits. In like manner, the mere outward acts of coming to church, and saying prayers, which are, of course, duties imperative upon all of us, are really serviceable to those only who do them in a heavenward spirit. Because such men only use these good deeds to the improvement of the heart; whereas even the most exact outward devotion avails not a man, if it does not improve it.

2. But observe what follows from this. If holiness be not merely the doing a certain number of good actions, but is an inward character which follows, under God's grace, from doing them, how far distant from that holiness are the multitude of men! They are not yet even obedient in outward deeds, which is the first step towards possessing it. They have even to learn to practise good works, as the means of changing their hearts, which is the end. It follows at once, even though Scripture did not plainly tell us so, that no one is able to prepare himself for heaven, that is, make himself holy, in a short time;—at least we do not see how it is possible; and this, viewed merely as a deduction of the reason, is a serious thought. Yet, alas! as there are

persons who think to be saved by a few scanty performances, so there are others who suppose they may be saved all at once by a sudden and easily acquired faith. Most men who are living in neglect of God, silence their consciences, when troublesome, with the promise of repenting some future day. How often are they thus led on till death surprises them! But we will suppose they *do* begin to repent when that future day comes. Nay, we will even suppose that Almighty God were to forgive them, and to admit them into His holy heaven. Well, but is nothing more requisite? are they in a fit state to *do Him service in heaven*? is not this the very point I have been so insisting on, that they are *not* in a fit state? has it not been shown that, even if admitted there without a change of heart, they would find no pleasure in heaven? and is a change of heart wrought in a day? Which of our tastes or likings can we change at our will in a moment? Not the most superficial. Can we then at a word change the whole frame and character of our minds? Is not holiness the result of many patient, repeated efforts after obedience, gradually working on us, and first modifying and then changing our hearts? We dare not, of course, set bounds to God's mercy and power in cases of repentance late in life, even where He has revealed to us the general rule of His moral governance; yet, surely, it is our duty ever to keep steadily before us, and act upon, those general truths which His Holy Word has declared. His Holy Word in various ways warns us, that, as no one will find happiness in heaven, who is not holy, so no one can learn to be so, in a short time, and when he will. It implies it in the text, which names a qualification, which we know in matter of fact does ordinarily take time to gain. It propounds it clearly, though in figure, in the parable of the wedding garment, in which inward sanctification is made a condition distinct from our acceptance of the proffer of mercy, and not negligently to be passed over in our thoughts as if a necessary consequence of it; and in that of the ten virgins, which shows us that we must meet the bridegroom with the oil of holiness, and that it takes time to procure it. And it solemnly assures us in St. Paul's Epistles, that it is possible so to presume on Divine grace, as to let slip the accepted time, and be sealed even before the end of life to a reprobate mind.[2]

I wish to speak to you, my brethren, not as if aliens from God's mercies, but as partakers of His gracious covenant in Christ; and for this reason in especial peril, since those only can

[2] Heb. vi.4–6; x.26–29. *Vide* also 2 Pet. ii.20, 22.

incur the sin of making void His covenant, who have the privilege of it. Yet neither on the other hand do I speak to you as wilful and obstinate sinners, exposed to the imminent risk of forfeiting, or the chance of having forfeited, your hope of heaven. But I fear there are those, who, if they dealt faithfully with their consciences, would be obliged to own that they had not made the service of God their first and great concern; that their obedience, so to call it, has been a matter of course, in which the heart has had no part; that they have acted uprightly in worldly matters chiefly for the sake of their worldly interest. I fear there are those, who, whatever be their sense of religion, still have such misgivings about themselves, as lead them to make resolve to obey God more exactly some future day, such misgivings as convict them of sin, though not enough to bring home to them its heinousness or its peril. Such men are trifling with the appointed season of mercy. To obtain the gift of holiness is the work of *a life*. No man will ever be perfect here, so sinful is our nature. Thus, in putting off the day of repentance, these men are reserving for a few chance years, when strength and vigour are gone, that WORK for which a *whole* life would not be enough. That work is great and arduous beyond expression. There is much of sin remaining even in the best of men, and "if the righteous scarcely be saved, where shall the ungodly and the sinner appear?"[3] Their doom may be fixed any moment; and though this thought should not make a man despair to-day, yet it should ever make him tremble for to-morrow.

Perhaps, however, others may say:—"We know something of the power of religion—we love it in a measure—we have many right thoughts—we come to church to pray; this is a proof that we are prepared for heaven:—we are safe, and what has been said does not apply to us." But be not you, my brethren, in the number of these. One principal test of our being true servants of God is our wishing to serve Him better; and be quite sure that a man who is contented with his own proficiency in Christian holiness, is at best in a dark state, or rather in great peril. If we are really imbued with the grace of holiness, we shall abhor sin as something base, irrational, and polluting. Many men, it is true, are contented with partial and indistinct views of religion, and mixed motives. Be you content with nothing short of perfection; exert yourselves day by day to grow in knowledge and grace; that, if so be, you may at length attain to the presence of Almighty God.

[3] 1 Pet iv.18.

Lastly; while we thus labour to mould our hearts after the pattern of the holiness of our Heavenly Father, it is our comfort to know, what I have already implied, that we are not left to ourselves, but that the Holy Ghost is graciously present with us, and enables us to triumph over, and to change our own minds. It is a comfort and encouragement, while it is an anxious and awful thing to know that God works in and through us.[4] We are the instruments, but we are only the instruments, of our own salvation. Let no one say that I discourage him, and propose to him a task beyond his strength. All of us have the gifts of grace pledged to us from our youth up. We know this well; but we do not use our privilege. We form mean ideas of the difficulty, and in consequence never enter into the greatness of the gifts given us to meet it. Then afterwards, if perchance we gain a deeper insight into the work we have to do, we think God a hard master, who commands much from a sinful race. Narrow, indeed, is the way of life, but infinite is His love and power who is with the Church, in Christ's place, to guide us along it.

[4] Phil ii.12, 18.

THE IMMORTALITY OF THE SOUL

"What shall a man give in exchange for his soul?"
—Matt. xvi.26.

I SUPPOSE there is no tolerably informed Christian but considers he has a correct notion of the difference between our
religion and the paganism which it supplanted. Every one, if
asked what it is we have gained by the Gospel, will promptly
answer, that we have gained the knowledge of our immortality,
of our having souls which will live for ever; that the heathen did
not know this, but that Christ taught it, and that His disciples
know it. Every one will say, and say truly, that this was the great
and solemn doctrine which gave the Gospel a claim to be heard
when first preached, which arrested the thoughtless multitudes, who were busied in the pleasures and pursuits of this life,
awed them with the vision of the life to come, and sobered
them till they turned to God with a true heart. It will be said,
and said truly, that this doctrine of a future life was the doctrine
which broke the power and the fascination of paganism. The
poor benighted heathen were engaged in all the frivolities and
absurdities of a false ritual, which had obscured the light of nature. They knew God, but they forsook Him for the inventions
of men; they made protectors and guardians for themselves;
and had "gods many and lords many."[1] They had their profane
worship, their gaudy processions, their indulgent creed, their
easy observances, their sensual festivities, their childish extravagances, such as might suitably be the religion of beings
who were to live for seventy or eighty years, and then die once
for all, never to live again. "Let us eat and drink, for to-morrow
we die," was their doctrine and their rule of life. "To-morrow
we die;"—this the Holy Apostles admitted. They taught so far
as the heathen; "To-morrow we die;" but then they added,
"And after death *the judgment*;"—judgment upon the eternal

[1] 1 Cor. viii.5.

soul, which lives in spite of the death of the body. And this was the truth, which awakened men to the necessity of having a better and deeper religion than that which had spread over the earth, when Christ came,—which so wrought upon them that they left that old false worship of theirs, and it fell. Yes! though throned in all the power of the world, a sight such as eye had never before seen, though supported by the great and the many, the magnificence of kings, and the stubbornness of people, it fell. Its ruins remain scattered over the face of the earth; the shattered works of its great upholder, that fierce enemy of God, the Pagan Roman Empire. Those ruins are found even among themselves, and show how marvellously great was its power, and therefore how much more powerful was that which broke its power; and this was the doctrine of the immortality of the soul. So entire is the revolution which is produced among men, wherever this high truth is really received.

I have said that every one of us is able fluently to speak of this doctrine, and is aware that the knowledge of it forms the fundamental difference between our state and that of the heathen. And yet, in spite of our being able to speak about it and our "form of knowledge"[2] (as St. Paul terms it), there seems scarcely room to doubt, that the greater number of those who are called Christians in no true sense realize it in their own minds at all. Indeed, it is a very difficult thing to bring home to us, and to feel, that we have souls; and there cannot be a more fatal mistake than to suppose we see what the doctrine means, as soon as we can use the words which signify it. So great a thing is it to understand that we have souls, that the knowing it, taken in connexion with its results, is all one with *being serious*, i.e. truly religious. To discern our immortality is necessarily connected with fear and trembling and repentance, in the case of every Christian. Who is there but would be sobered by an actual sight of the flames of hell fire and the souls therein hopelessly enclosed? Would not all his thoughts be drawn to that awful sight, so that he would stand still gazing fixedly upon it, and forgetting every thing else; seeing nothing else, hearing nothing, engrossed with the contemplation of it; and when the sight was withdrawn, still having it fixed in his memory, so that he would be henceforth dead to the pleasures and employments of this world, considered in themselves, thinking of them only in their reference to that fearful vision? This would be the overpowering effect of such a disclosure, whether it actually led a

[2] Rom. ii.20.

man to repentance or not. And thus absorbed in the thought of
the life to come are they who really and heartily receive the
words of Christ and His Apostles. Yet to this state of mind, and
therefore to this true knowledge the multitude of men called
Christians are certainly strangers; a thick veil is drawn over
their eyes; and in spite of their being able to talk of the doctrine,
they are as if they never had heard of it. They go on just as the
heathen did of old: they eat, they drink; or they amuse themselves in vanities, and live in the world, without fear and without sorrow, just as if God had not declared that their conduct in
this life would decide their destiny in the next; just as if they
either had no souls, or had nothing or little to do with the saving of them, which was the creed of the heathen.

Now let us consider what it is to bring home to ourselves that
we have souls, and in what the especial difficulty of it lies; for
this may be of use to us in our attempt to realize that awful
truth.

We are from our birth apparently dependent on things about
us. We see and feel that we could not live or go forward without
the aid of man. To a child this world is every thing: he seems to
himself a part of this world,—a part of this world, in the same
sense in which a branch is part of a tree; he has little notion of
his own separate and independent existence: that is, he has no
just idea he has a soul. And if he goes through life with his notions unchanged, he has no just notion, even to the end of life,
that he has a soul. He views himself merely in his connexion
with this world, which is his all; he looks to this world for his
good, as to an idol; and when he tries to look beyond this life, he
is able to discern nothing in prospect, because he has no idea of
any thing, nor can fancy any thing, *but* this life. And if he is
obliged to fancy something, he fancies this life over again; just
as the heathen, when they reflected on those traditions of another life, which were floating among them, could but fancy
the happiness of the blessed to consist in the enjoyment of the
sun, and the sky, and the earth, as before, only as if these were
to be more splendid than they are now.

To understand that we have souls, is to feel our separation
from things visible, our independence of them, our distinct existence in ourselves, our individuality, our power of acting for
ourselves this way or that way, our accountableness for what we
do. These are the great truths which lie wrapped up indeed
even in a child's mind, and which God's grace can unfold there
in spite of the influence of the external world; but at first this
outward world prevails. We look off from self to the things

around us, and forget ourselves in them. Such is our state,—a depending for support on the reeds which are no stay, and over-looking our real strength,—at the time when God begins His process of reclaiming us to a truer view of our place in His great system of providence. And when He visits us, then in a little while there is a stirring within us. The unprofitableness and feebleness of the things of this world are forced upon our minds; they promise but cannot perform, they disappoint us. Or, if they do perform what they promise, still (so it is) they do not satisfy us. We still crave for something, we do not well know what; but we are sure it is something which the world has not given us. And then its changes are so many, so sudden, so silent, so continual. It never leaves changing; it goes on to change, till we are quite sick at heart:—then it is that our reli-ance on it is broken. It is plain we cannot continue to depend upon it, unless we keep pace with it, and go on changing too; but this we cannot do. We feel that, while it changes, we are one and the same; and thus, under God's blessing, we come to have some glimpse of the meaning of our independence of things temporal, and our immortality. And should it so happen that misfortunes come upon us, (as they often do,) then still more are we led to understand the nothingness of this world; then still more are we led to distrust it, and are weaned from the love of it, till at length it floats before our eyes merely as some idle veil, which, notwithstanding its many tints, cannot hide the view of what is beyond it;—and we begin, by degrees, to per-ceive that there are but two beings in the whole universe, our own soul, and the God who made it.

Sublime, unlooked-for doctrine, yet most true! To every one of us there are but two beings in the whole world, himself and God; for, as to this outward scene, its pleasures and pursuits, its honours and cares, its contrivances, its personages, its king-doms, its multitude of busy slaves, what are they to us? noth-ing—no more than a show:—"The world passeth away and the lust thereof." And as to those others nearer to us, who are not to be classed with the vain world, I mean our friends and relations, whom we are right in loving, these, too, after all, are nothing to us here. They cannot really help or profit us; we see them, and they act upon us, only (as it were) at a distance, through the medium of sense; they cannot get at our souls; they cannot en-ter into our thoughts, or really be companions to us. In the next world it will, through God's mercy, be otherwise; but here we enjoy, not their presence, but the anticipation of what one day shall be; so that, after all, they vanish before the clear vision we have, first, of our own existence, next of the presence of the great God in us, and over us, as our Governor and Judge, who dwells in us by our conscience, which is His representative.

And now consider what a revolution will take place in the mind that is not utterly reprobate, in proportion as it realizes this relation between itself and the most high God. We never in this life can fully understand what is meant by our living for ever, but we can understand what is meant by this world's *not* living for ever, by its dying never to rise again. And learning this, we learn that we owe it no service, no allegiance; it has no claim over us, and can do us no material good nor harm. On the other hand, the law of God written on our hearts bids us serve Him, and partly tells us how to serve Him, and Scripture completes the precepts which nature began. And both Scripture and conscience tell us we are answerable for what we do, and that God is a righteous Judge; and, above all, our Saviour, as our visible Lord God, takes the place of the world as the Only-begotten of the Father, having shown Himself openly, that we may not say that God is hidden. And thus a man is drawn forward by all manner of powerful influences to turn from things temporal to things eternal, to deny himself, to take up his cross and follow Christ. For there are Christ's awful threats and warnings to make him serious, His precepts to attract and elevate him, His promises to cheer him, His gracious deeds and sufferings to humble him to the dust, and to bind his heart once and for ever in gratitude to Him who is so surpassing in mercy. All these things act upon him; and, as truly as St. Matthew rose from the receipt of custom when Christ called, heedless what bystanders would say of him, so they who, through grace, obey the secret voice of God, move onward contrary to the world's way, and careless what mankind may say of them, as understanding that they have souls, which is the one thing they have to care about.

I am well aware that there are indiscreet teachers gone forth into the world, who use language such as I have used, but mean something very different. Such are they who deny the grace of baptism, and think that a man is converted to God all at once. But I have no need now to mention the difference between their teaching and that of Scripture. Whatever their peculiar errors are, so far as they say that we are by nature blind and sinful, and must, through God's grace, and our own endeavours, learn that we have souls and rise to a new life, severing ourselves from the world that is, and walking by faith in what is unseen and future, so far they say true, for they speak the words of Scripture;

which says, "Awake thou that sleepest, and arise from the dead, and Christ shall give thee light. See then that ye walk circumspectly, not as fools, but as wise, redeeming the time, because the days are evil; wherefore be ye not unwise, but understanding what the will of the Lord is."[3]

Let us, then, seriously question ourselves, and beg of God grace to do so honestly, whether we are loosened from the world; or whether, living as dependent on it and not on the Eternal Author of our being, we are in fact taking our portion with this perishing outward scene, and ignorant of our having souls. I know very well that such thoughts are distasteful to the minds of men in general. Doubtless many a one there is, who, on hearing doctrines such as I have been insisting on, says in his heart, that religion is thus made gloomy and repulsive; that he would attend to a teacher who spoke in a less severe way; and that in fact Christianity was not intended to be a dark burdensome law, but a religion of cheerfulness and joy. This is what young people think, though they do not express it in this argumentative form. They view a strict life as something offensive and hateful; they turn from the notion of it. And then, as they get older and see more of the world, they learn to defend their opinion, and express it more or less in the way in which I have just put it. They hate and oppose the truth, as it were upon principle; and the more they are told that they have souls, the more resolved they are to live as if they had not souls. But let us take it as a clear point from the first, and not to be disputed, that religion must ever be difficult to those who neglect it. All things that we have to learn are difficult at first; and our duties to God, and to man for His sake, are peculiarly difficult, because they call upon us to take up a new life, and quit the love of this world for the next. It cannot be avoided; we must fear and be in sorrow, before we can rejoice. The Gospel must be a burden before it comforts and brings us peace. No one can have his heart cut away from the natural objects of its love, without pain during the process and throbbings afterwards. This is plain from the nature of the case; and, however true it be, that this or that teacher may be harsh and repulsive, yet he cannot materially alter things. Religion is in itself at first a weariness to the worldly mind, and it requires an effort and a self-denial in every one who honestly determines to be religious.

But there are other persons who are far more hopeful than those I have been speaking of, who, when they hear repentance

---

[3] Eph. v. 14–17.

and newness of life urged on them, are frightened at the thought of the greatness of the work; they are disheartened at being told to do so much. Now let it be well understood, that to realize our own individual accountableness and immortality, of which I have been speaking, is not required of them all at once. I never said a person was not in a hopeful way who did not thus fully discern the world's vanity and the worth of his soul. But a man is truly in a very desperate way who does not wish, who does not try, to discern and feel all this. I want a man on the one hand to confess his immortality with his lips, and on the other, to live as if he tried to understand his own words, and then he is in the way of salvation; he is in the way towards heaven, even though he has not yet fully emancipated himself from the fetters of this world. Indeed none of us (of course) are entirely loosened from this world. We all use words, in speaking of our duties, higher and fuller than we really understand. No one entirely realizes what is meant by his having a soul; even the best of men is but in a state of progress towards the simple truth; and the most weak and ignorant of those who seek after it cannot but be in progress. And therefore no one need be alarmed at hearing that he has much to do before he arrives at a right view of his own condition in God's sight, i.e. at *faith*; for we all have much to do, and the great point is, are we willing to do it?

Oh that there were such an heart in us, to put aside this visible world, to desire to look at it as a mere screen between us and God, and to think of Him who has entered in beyond the veil, and who is watching us, trying us, yes, and blessing, and influencing, and encouraging us towards good, day by day! Yet, alas, how do we suffer the mere varying circumstances of every day to sway us! How difficult it is to remain firm and in one mind under the seductions or terrors of the world! We feel variously according to the place, time, and people we are with. We are serious on Sunday, and we sin deliberately on Monday. We rise in the morning with remorse at our offences and resolutions of amendment, yet before night we have transgressed again. The mere change of society puts us into a new frame of mind; nor do we sufficiently understand this great weakness of ours, or seek for strength where alone it can be found, in the Unchangeable God. What will be our thoughts in that day, when at length this outward world drops away altogether, and we find ourselves where we ever have been, in His presence, with Christ standing at His right hand!

On the contrary, what a blessed discovery is it to those who make it, that this world is but vanity and without substance;

and that really they are ever in their Saviour's presence. This is a thought which it is scarcely right to enlarge upon in a mixed congregation, where there may be some who have not given their hearts to God; for why should the privileges of the true Christian be disclosed to mankind at large, and sacred subjects, which are his peculiar treasure, be made common to the careless liver? He knows his blessedness, and needs not another to tell it him. He knows in whom he has believed; and in the hour of danger or trouble he knows what is meant by that peace, which Christ did not explain when He gave it to His Apostles, but merely said it was not as the world could give.

"Thou wilt keep him in perfect peace whose mind is stayed on Thee, because he trusteth in Thee. Trust ye in the Lord for ever, for in the Lord Jehovah is everlasting strength."[4]

[4] Is. xxvi.3, 4.

KNOWLEDGE OF GOD'S WILL
WITHOUT OBEDIENCE

"If ye know these things, happy are ye if ye do them."
—John xiii.17.

THERE never was a people or an age to which these words could be more suitably addressed than to this country at this time; because we know more of the way to serve God, of our duties, our privileges, and our reward, than any other people hitherto, as far as we have the means of judging. To us then especially our Saviour says, "If ye know these things, happy are ye if ye do them."

Now, doubtless, many of us think we know this very well. It seems a very trite thing to say, that it is nothing to *know* what is right, unless we *do* it; an old subject about which nothing new can be said. When we read such passages in Scripture, we pass over them as admitting them without dispute; and thus we contrive practically to forget them. Knowledge is nothing compared with doing; but the *knowing* that knowledge is nothing, we make to be *something*, we make it count, and thus we cheat ourselves.

This we do in parallel cases also. Many a man instead of *learning* humility in practice, confesses himself a poor sinner, and next *prides* himself upon the confession; he ascribes the glory of his redemption to God, and then becomes in a manner *proud* that he is redeemed. He is proud of his so-called humility.

Doubtless Christ spoke no words in vain. The Eternal Wisdom of God did not utter His voice that we might at once catch up His words in an irreverent manner, think we understand them at a glance, and pass them over. But His word endureth for ever; it has a depth of meaning suited to all times and places, and hardly and painfully to be understood in any. They, who think they enter into it easily, may he quite sure they do not enter into it at all.

Now then let us try, by His grace, to make the text a living word to the benefit of our souls. Our Lord says, "If ye know, happy are ye, if ye do." Let us consider *how* we commonly read Scripture.

We read a passage in the Gospels, for instance, a parable perhaps, or the account of a miracle; or we read a chapter in the Prophets, or a Psalm. Who is not struck with the beauty of what he reads? I do not wish to speak of those who read the Bible only now and then, and who will in consequence generally find its sacred pages dull and uninteresting; but of those who study it. Who of such persons does not see the beauty of it? for instance, take the passage which introduces the text. Christ had been washing His disciples' feet. He did so at a season of great mental suffering; it was just before He was seized by His enemies to be put to death. The traitor, His familiar friend, was in the room. All of His disciples, even the most devoted of them, loved Him much less than they thought they did. In a little while they were all to forsake Him and flee. This He foresaw; yet He calmly washed their feet, and then He told them that He did so by way of an example; that they should be full of lowly services one to the other, as He to them; that he among them was in fact the highest who put himself the lowest. This He had said before; and His disciples must have recollected it. Perhaps they might wonder in their secret hearts *why* He repeated the lesson; they might say to themselves, "We have heard this before." They might he surprised that His significant action, His washing their feet, issued in nothing else than a precept already delivered, the command to be humble. At the same time they would not be able to deny, or rather they would deeply feel, the beauty of His action. Nay, as loving Him (after all) above all things, and reverencing Him as their Lord and Teacher, they would feel an admiration and awe of Him; but their minds would not rest sufficiently on the *practical* direction of the instruction vouchsafed to them. They knew the truth, and they admitted it; they did not observe what it was they lacked. Such may be considered their frame of mind; and hence the force of the text, delivered primarily against Judas Iscariot, who knew and sinned deliberately against the truth; secondarily referring to all the Apostles, and St. Peter chiefly, who promised to be faithful, but failed under the trial; lastly, to us all, all of us here assembled, who hear the word of life continually, know it, admire it, do all but obey it.

Is it not so? is not Scripture altogether pleasant except in its strictness? do not we try to persuade ourselves, that to *feel* religiously, to confess our love of religion, and to be able to talk of religion, will stand in the place of careful obedience, of that *self-denial* which is the very substance of true practical religion? Alas! that religion which is so delightful as a vision, should be so distasteful as a reality. Yet so it is, whether we are aware of the fact or not.

1. The multitude of men even who profess religion are in this state of mind. We will take the case of those who are in better circumstances than the mass of the community. They are well educated and taught; they have few distresses in life, or are able to get over them by the variety of their occupations, by the spirits which attend good health, or at least by the lapse of time. They go on respectably and happily, with the same general tastes and habits which they would have had if the Gospel had not been given them. They have an eye to what the world thinks of them; are charitable when it is expected. They are polished in their manners, kind from natural disposition or a feeling of propriety. Thus their religion is based upon self and the world, a mere *civilization*; the same (I say), as it would have been in the main, (taking the state of society as they find it,) even supposing Christianity were not the religion of the land. But it is; and let us go on to ask, how do they in consequence feel towards it? They accept it, they add it to what they *are*, they ingraft it upon the selfish and worldly habits of an unrenewed heart. They have been taught to revere it, and to believe it to come from God; so they admire it, and accept it as a rule of life, so far forth as it agrees with the carnal principles which govern them. So far as it does *not* agree, they are blind to its excellence and its claims. They overlook or explain away its precepts. They in no sense obey *because* it commands. They do right when they *would* have done right had it not commanded; however, they speak well of it, and think they understand it. Sometimes, if I may continue the description, they adopt it into a certain refined elegance of sentiments and manners, and then the irreligion is all that is graceful, fastidious, and luxurious. They love religious poetry and eloquent preaching. They desire to have their feelings roused and soothed, and to secure a variety and relief in that eternal subject which is unchangeable. They tire of its simplicity, and perhaps seek to keep up their interest in it by means of religious narratives, fictitious or embellished, or of news from foreign countries, or of the history of the prospects or successes of the Gospel; thus perverting what is in itself good and innocent. This is their state of mind at best; for more commonly they think it enough merely to show some slight regard for the subject of religion; to attend its services on the

Lord's day, and then only once, and coldly to express an approbation of it. But of course every description of such persons can
be but general; for the shades of character are so varied and
blended in individuals, as to make it impossible to give an accurate picture, and often very estimable persons and truly good
Christians are partly infected with this bad and earthly spirit.

2. Take again another description of them. They have perhaps turned their attention to the means of promoting the happiness of their fellow-creatures, and have formed a system of
morality and religion of their own; then they come to Scripture. They are much struck with the high tone of its precepts,
and the beauty of its teaching. It is true, they find many things
in it which they do not understand or do not approve; many
things they would not have said themselves. But they pass these
by; they fancy that these do not apply to the present day,
(which is an easy way of removing any thing we do not like,)
and *on the whole* they receive the Bible, and they think it highly
serviceable for the lower classes. Therefore, they recommend
it, and support the institutions which are the channels of teaching it. But as to their own case, it never comes into their minds
to apply its precepts seriously to themselves; they know them
already, they consider. They *know* them and that is enough; but
as for *doing* them, by which I mean, going forward to obey
them, with an unaffected earnestness and an honest faith *acting
upon* them, receiving them as they are, and not as their own previously formed opinions would have them be, they have nothing of this right spirit. They do not contemplate such a mode of
acting. To recommend and affect a moral and decent conduct
(on *whatever* principles) seems to them to be enough. The spread
of knowledge bringing in its train a selfish temperance, a selfish
peaceableness, a selfish benevolence, the morality of expedience, this satisfies them. They care for none of the truths of
Scripture, *on the ground* of their being in Scripture; these
scarcely become more valuable in their eyes for being there
written. They do not obey *because* they are told to obey, on
faith; and the need of this divine principle of conduct they do
not comprehend. Why will it not answer (they seem to say) to
make men good in one way as well as another? "Abana and
Pharpar, rivers of Damascus, are they not better than all the
waters of Israel?" as if all the knowledge and the training that
books ever gave had power to unloose one sinner from the
bonds of Satan, or to effect more than an outward reformation,
an *appearance* of obedience; as if it were not a far different principle, a principle independent of knowledge, above it and

before it, which leads to *real* obedience, that principle of divine
faith, given from above, which has life in itself, and has power
really to use knowledge to the soul's welfare; in the hand of
which knowledge is (as it were) the torch lighting us on our
way, but not teaching or strengthening us to walk.

3. Or take another view of the subject. Is it not one of the
most common excuses made by the poor for being irreligious,
that they have had no education? as if to know much was a
necessary step for right practice. Again, they are apt to think it
enough to know and to talk of religion, to make a man religious. Why have you come hither to-day, my brethren?—not
as a matter of course, I will hope; not merely because friends
or superiors told you to come. I will suppose you have come to
church *as a religious act*; but beware of supposing that all is done
and over by the act of coming. It is not enough to be *present*
here; though many men act as if they forgot they must attend
to what is going on, as well as come. It is not enough to listen
to what is preached; though many think they have gone a
great way when they do this. You *must pray*; now this is very
hard in itself to any one who tries (and this is the reason why
so many men prefer the sermon to the prayers, because the
former is merely the getting *knowledge*, and the latter is to do a
deed of obedience): you must *pray*; and this I say is very
difficult, because our thoughts are so apt to wander. But even
this is not all;—you must, as you pray, really intend to *try to
practise* what you pray for. When you say, "Lead us not into
temptation," you must in good earnest mean to avoid in your
daily conduct those temptations which you have already suffered from. When you say, "Deliver us from evil," you must
mean to struggle against that evil in your hearts, which you are
conscious of, and which you pray to be forgiven. This is difficult; still more is behind. You must actually carry your good
intentions into effect during the week, and in truth and reality
war against the world, the flesh, and the devil. And any one
here present who falls short of this, that is, who thinks it
enough to come to church to *learn* God's will, but does not
bear in mind to do it in his daily conduct, be he high or be he
low, know he mysteries and all knowledge, or be he unlettered
and busily occupied in active life, he is a fool in His sight, who
maketh the wisdom of this world foolishness. Surely he is but
a trifler, as substituting a formal outward service for the religion of the heart; and he reverses our Lord's words in the text,
"because he knows these things, most unhappy is he, because
he does them not."

4. But some one may say, "It is so very *difficult* to serve God, it is so much against my own mind, such an effort, such a strain upon my strength to bear Christ's yoke, I must give it over, or I must delay it at least. Can nothing be taken instead? I acknowledge His law to be most holy and true, and the accounts I read about good men are most delightful. I wish I were like them with all my heart; and for a little while I feel in a mind to set about imitating them. I have begun several times, I have had seasons of repentance, and set rules to myself; but for some reason or other, I fell back after a while, and was even worse than before. I know, but I cannot do. O wretched man that I am!"

Now to such an one I say, You are in a much more promising state than if you were contented with yourself, and thought that knowledge was every thing, which is the grievous blindness which I have hitherto been speaking of; that is, you are in a better state, if you do not feel too much comfort or confidence in your confession. For *this* is the fault of many men; they make such an acknowledgment as I have described a *substitute* for real repentance; or allow themselves, after making it, to *put off* repentance, as if they could be suffered to give a word of promise which did not become due (so to say) for many days. You are, I admit, in a better state than if you were satisfied with yourself, *but you are not in a safe state.* If you were now to die, you would have no hope of salvation: no hope, that is, if your own showing be true, for I am taking your own words. Go before God's judgment-seat, and there plead that you know the Truth and have not done it. This is what you frankly own;—how will it there be taken? "Out of thine own month will I judge thee," says our Judge Himself, and who shall reverse His judgment? Therefore such an one must make the confession with great and real terror and shame, if it is to be considered a promising sign in him; else it is mere hardness of heart. For instance: I have heard persons say lightly (every one must have heard them) that they own it would be a wretched thing indeed for them or their companions to be taken off suddenly. The young are especially apt to say this; that is, before they have come to an age to be callous, or have formed excuses to overcome the natural true sense of their conscience. They say they hope some day to repent. This is their own witness against themselves, like that bad prophet at Bethel who was constrained with his own mouth to utter God's judgments while he sat at his sinful meat. But let not such an one think that he will receive any thing of the Lord: he does not speak in faith.

When, then, a man complains of his hardness of heart or

weakness of purpose, let him see to it whether this complaint is more than a mere pretence to quiet his conscience, which is frightened at his putting off repentance; or, again, more than a mere idle word, said half in jest and half in compunction. But, should he be earnest in his complaint, then let him consider he has no need to complain. Every thing is plain and easy to the earnest; it is the double-minded who find difficulties. If you hate your own corruption in sincerity and truth, if you are really pierced to the heart that you do not do what you know you should do, if you *would* love God if you could, then the Gospel speaks to you words of peace and hope. It is a very different thing indolently to say, "I would I were a different man," and to close with God's offer to make you different, when it is put before you. Here is the test between earnestness and insincerity. You say you wish to be a different man; Christ takes you at your word, so to speak; He offers to make you different. He says, "I will take away from you the heart of stone, the love of this world and its pleasures, if you will submit to My discipline." Here a man draws back. No; he cannot bear to *lose* the love of the world, to part with his present desires and tastes; he cannot *consent* to be changed. After all he is well satisfied at the bottom of his heart to remain as he is, only he wants his conscience taken out of the way. Did Christ offer to do this for him, if He would but make bitter sweet and sweet bitter, darkness light and light darkness, *then* he would hail the glad tidings of peace;—till then he needs Him not.

But if a man is in earnest in wishing to get at the depths of his own heart, to expel the evil, to purify the good, and to gain power over himself, so as to do as well as know the Truth, what is the difficulty?—a matter of time indeed, but not of uncertainty is the recovery of such a man. So simple is the rule which he must follow, and so trite, that at first he will be surprised to hear it. God does great things by plain methods; and men start from them through pride, *because* they are plain. This was the conduct of Naaman the Syrian. Christ says, "Watch and pray;" herein lies our cure. To watch and to pray are surely in our power, and by these means we are certain of getting strength. You feel your weakness; you fear to be overcome by temptation: then keep out of the way of it. This is watching. Avoid society which is likely to mislead you; flee from the very shadow of evil; you cannot be too careful; better be a little too strict than a little too easy,—it is the safer side. Abstain from reading books which are dangerous to you. Turn from bad thoughts when they arise, set about some business, begin conversing with some friend, or say to yourself the Lord's Prayer reverently. When you are urged by temptation, whether it be by the threats of the world, false shame, self-interest, provoking conduct on the part of another, or the world's sinful pleasures, urged to be cowardly, or covetous, or unforgiving, or sensual, shut your eyes and think of Christ's precious blood-shedding. Do not dare to say you cannot help sinning; a little attention to these points will go far (through God's grace) to keep you in the right way. And again, pray as well as watch. You must know that you can do nothing of yourself; your past experience has taught you this; therefore look to God for the will and the power; ask Him earnestly in His Son's name; seek His holy ordinances. Is not *this* in your power? Have you not power at least over the limbs of your body, so as to attend the means of grace constantly? Have you literally not the power to come hither; to observe the Fasts and Festivals of the Church; to come to His Holy Altar and receive the Bread of Life? Get yourself, at least, to do this; to put out the hand, to take His gracious Body and Blood; this is no arduous work;— and you say you really *wish* to gain the blessings He offers. What would you have more than a free gift, vouchsafed "without money and without price?" So, make no more excuses; murmur not about your own bad heart, your knowing and resolving, and not doing. Here is your remedy.

Well were it if men could be persuaded to be in earnest; but few are thus minded. The many go on with a double aim, trying to serve both God and mammon. Few can get themselves to do what is right, *because* God tells them; they have another aim; they desire to please self or men. When they can obey God without offending the bad Master that rules them, then, and then only, they obey. Thus religion, instead of being the *first* thing in their estimation, is but the second. They differ, indeed, one from another what to put foremost: one man loves to be at ease, another to be busy, another to enjoy domestic comfort: but they agree in converting the truth of God, which they know to be Truth, into a mere instrument of secular aims; not discarding the Truth, but degrading it.

When He, the Lord of hosts, comes to shake terribly the earth, what number will He find of the remnant of the true Israel? We live in an educated age. The false gloss of a mere worldly refinement makes us decent and amiable. We all know and profess. We think ourselves wise; we flatter each other; we make excuses for ourselves when we are conscious we sin, and thus we gradually lose the consciousness that we are sinning. We think our own times superior to all others. "Thou blind

Pharisee!" This was the fatal charge brought by our blessed
Lord against the falsely enlightened teachers of His own day. As
then we desire to enter into life, let us come to Christ continually for the two foundations of true Christian faith,—humbleness of mind and earnestness!

SECRET FAULTS

"Who can withstand his errors? Cleanse Thou me
from secret faults."—Ps. xix.12.

STRANGE as it may seem, multitudes called Christians go
through life with no effort to obtain a correct knowledge of
themselves. They are contented with general and vague impressions concerning their real state; and, if they have more than
this, it is merely such accidental information about themselves
as the events of life force upon them. But exact systematic
knowledge they have none, and do not aim at it.

When I say this is *strange*, I do not mean to imply that to know
ourselves is *easy*; it is very difficult to know ourselves even in
part, and so far ignorance of ourselves is not a strange thing. But
its strangeness consists in this, viz. that men should profess to
receive and act upon the great Christian doctrines, while they
are thus ignorant of themselves, considering that self-knowledge is a necessary condition for understanding them. Thus it is
not too much to say that all those who neglect the duty of habitual self-examination are using words without meaning. The
doctrines of the *forgiveness* of sins, and of a *new birth* from sin,
cannot be understood without some right knowledge of the
nature of sin, that is, of our own heart. We may, indeed, assent
to a form of words which declares those doctrines; but if such a
mere assent, however sincere, is the same as a real *holding of*
them, and belief in them, then it is equally possible to believe in
a proposition the terms of which belong to some foreign language, which is obviously absurd. Yet nothing is more common
than for men to think that because they are familiar with
words, they understand the ideas they stand for. Educated persons despise this fault in illiterate men who use hard words as if
they comprehended them. Yet they themselves, as well as others, fall into the same error in a more subtle form, when they
think they understand terms used in morals and religion, because such are common words, and have been used by them all
their lives.

Now (I repeat) unless we have some just idea of our hearts

and of sin, we can have no right idea of a Moral Governor, a
Saviour or a Sanctifier, that is, in professing to believe in Them,
we shall be using words without attaching distinct meaning to
them. Thus self-knowledge is at the root of all real religious
knowledge; and it is in vain,—worse than vain,—it is a deceit
and a mischief, to think to understand the Christian doctrines
as a matter of course, merely by being taught by books, or by
attending sermons, or by any outward means, however excellent, taken by themselves. For it is in proportion as we search
our hearts and understand our own nature, that we understand
what is meant by an Infinite Governor and Judge; in proportion
as we comprehend the nature of disobedience and our actual
sinfulness, that we feel what is the blessing of the removal of
sin, redemption, pardon, sanctification, which otherwise are
mere words. God speaks to us primarily in our hearts. Self-
knowledge is the key to the precepts and doctrines of Scripture.
The very utmost any outward notices of religion can do, is to
startle us and make us turn inward and search our hearts; and
then, when we have experienced what it is to read ourselves, we
shall profit by the doctrines of the Church and the Bible.

Of course self-knowledge admits of degrees. No one perhaps,
is *entirely* ignorant of himself; and even the most advanced
Christian knows himself only "in part." However, most men
are contented with a slight acquaintance with their hearts, and
therefore a superficial faith. This is the point which it is my
purpose to insist upon. Men are satisfied to have numberless
secret faults. They do not think about them, either as sins or as
obstacles to strength of faith, and live on as if they had nothing
to learn.

Now let us consider attentively the strong presumption that
exists, that we all have serious secret faults; a fact which, I believe, all are ready to confess in general terms, though few like
calmly and practically to dwell upon it; as I now wish to do.

1. Now the most ready method of convincing ourselves of
the existence in us of faults unknown to ourselves, is to consider how plainly we see the secret faults of others. At first sight
there is of course no reason for supposing that we differ materially from those around us; and if we see sins in them which *they*
do not see, it is a presumption that they have their own discoveries about ourselves, which it would surprise us to hear. For
instance: how apt is an angry man to fancy that he has the command of himself! The very charge of being angry, if brought
against him, will anger him more; and, in the height of his dis-
composure, he will profess himself able to reason and judge

with clearness and impartiality. Now, it may be his turn another day, for what we know, to witness the same failing in us;
or, if we are not naturally inclined to violent passion, still at
least we may be subject to other sins, equally unknown to ourselves, and equally known to him as his anger was to us. For
example: there are persons who act mainly from self-interest at
times when they conceive they are doing generous or virtuous
actions; they give freely, or put themselves to trouble, and are
praised by the world, and by themselves, as if acting on high
principle; whereas close observers can detect desire of gain,
love of applause, shame, or the mere satisfaction of being busy
and active, as the principal cause of their good deeds. This may
be our condition as well as that of others; or, if it be not, still a
parallel infirmity, the bondage of some other sin or sins, which
others see, and we do not.

But, say there is no human being sees sin in us, of which we
are not aware ourselves, (though this is a bold supposition to
make,) yet why should man's accidental knowledge of us limit
the extent of our imperfections? Should all the world speak
well of us, and good men hail us as brothers, after all there is a
Judge who trieth the hearts and the reins. He knows our real
state; have we earnestly besought Him to teach us the knowledge of our own hearts? If we have not, that very omission is a
presumption against us. Though our praise were throughout
the Church, we may be sure He sees sins without number in
us, sins deep and heinous, of which we have no idea. If man
sees so much evil in human nature, what must God see? "If our
heart condemn us, God is greater than our heart, and knoweth
all things." Not *acts* alone of sin does He set down against us
daily, of which we know nothing, but the thoughts of the
heart too. The stirrings of pride, vanity, covetousness, impurity, discontent, resentment, these succeed each other through
the day in momentary emotions, and are known to Him. We
know them not, but how much does it concern us to know
them!

2. This consideration is suggested by the first view of the
subject. Now reflect upon the *actual disclosures* of our hidden
weakness, which accidents occasion. Peter followed Christ
boldly, and suspected not his own heart, till it betrayed him in
the hour of temptation, and led him to deny his Lord. David
lived years of happy obedience while he was in private life.
What calm, clear-sighted faith is manifested in his answer to
Saul about Goliath:—"The Lord that delivered me out of the
paw of the lion, and out of the paw of the bear, He will deliver

me out of the hand of this Philistine".[1] Nay, not only in retired
life, in severe trial, under ill usage from Saul, he continued
faithful to his God; years and years did he go on, fortifying his
heart, and learning the fear of the Lord; yet power and wealth
weakened his faith, and for a season overcame him. There was a
time when a prophet could retort upon him, "Thou art the
man"[2] whom thou condemnest. He had kept his principles in
words, but lost them in his heart. Hezekiah is another instance
of a religious man bearing *trouble* well, but for a season falling
back under the temptation of prosperity; and that, after extraordinary mercies had been vouchsafed to him.[3] And if these
things be so in the case of the favoured saints of God, what (may
we suppose) is our own real spiritual state in His sight? It is a
serious thought. The warning to be deduced from it is this:—
Never to think we have a due knowledge of ourselves till we
have been exposed to various kinds of temptations, and tried on
every side. Integrity on one side of our character is no voucher
for integrity on another. We cannot tell how we should act if
brought under temptations different from those which we have
hitherto experienced. This thought should keep us humble.
We are sinners, but we do not know how great. He alone knows
who died for our sins.

   3. Thus much we cannot but allow; that we do not know
ourselves in those respects in which we have not been tried. But
farther than this; What if we do not know ourselves even where
we *have* been tried, and found faithful? It is a remarkable circumstance which has been often observed, that if we look to
some of the most eminent saints of Scripture, we shall find
their recorded errors to have occurred in those parts of their
duty in which each had had most trial, and generally showed
obedience most perfect. *Faithful* Abraham through want of
faith denied his wife. Moses, the *meekest* of men, was excluded
from the land of promise for a passionate word. The *wisdom* of
Solomon was seduced to bow down to idols. Barnabas again,
the *son of consolation*, had a sharp contention with St. Paul. If
then men, who knew themselves better than we doubtless
know ourselves, had so much of hidden infirmity about them,
even in those parts of their character which were most free from
blame, what are we to think of ourselves? and if our very virtues
be so defiled with imperfection, what must be the unknown
multiplied circumstances of evil which aggravate the guilt of
our sins? This is a third presumption against us.

[1] 1 Sam. xvii.37.   [2] 2 Sam. xii.7.   [3] 2 Kings xx.12–19.

4. Think of this too. No one begins to examine himself, and to pray to know himself (with David in the text), but he finds within him an abundance of faults which before were either entirely or almost entirely unknown to him. That this is so, we learn from the written lives of good men, and our own experience of others. And hence it is that the best men are ever the most humble; for, having a higher standard of excellence in their minds than others have, and knowing themselves better, they see somewhat of the breadth and depth of their own sinful nature, and are shocked and frightened at themselves. The generality of men cannot understand this; and if at times the habitual self-condemnation of religious men breaks out into words, they think it arises from affectation, or from a strange distempered state of mind, or from accidental melancholy and disquiet. Whereas the confession of a good man against himself, is really a witness against all thoughtless persons who hear it, and a call on them to examine their own hearts. Doubtless the more we examine ourselves, the more imperfect and ignorant we shall find ourselves to be.

5. But let a man persevere in prayer and watchfulness to the day of his death, yet he will never get to the bottom of his heart. Though he know more and more of himself as he becomes more conscientious and earnest, still the full manifestation of the secrets there lodged, is reserved for another world. And at the last day who can tell the affright and horror of a man who lived to himself on earth, indulging his own evil will, following his own chance notions of truth and falsehood, shunning the cross and the reproach of Christ, when his eyes are at length opened before the throne of God, and all his innumerable sins, his habitual neglect of God, his abuse of his talents, his misapplication and waste of time, and the original unexplored sinfulness of his nature, are brought clearly and fully to his view? Nay, even to the true servants of Christ, the prospect is awful. "The righteous," we are told, "will scarcely be saved." [4] Then will the good man undergo the full sight of his sins, which on earth he was labouring to obtain, and partly succeeded in obtaining, though life was not long enough to learn and subdue them all. Doubtless we must all endure that fierce and terrifying vision of our real selves, that last fiery trial of the soul [5] before its acceptance, a spiritual agony and second death to all who are not then supported by the strength of Him who died to bring them safe through it, and in whom on earth they have believed.

[4] 1 Pet. iv.18.   [5] 1 Cor. iii.13.

My brethren, I appeal to your reason whether these presumptions are not in their substance fair and just. And if so, next I appeal to your consciences, whether they are new to you; for if you have not even thought about your real state, nor even know how little you know of yourselves, how can you in good earnest be purifying yourselves for the next world, or be walking in the narrow way?

And yet how many are the chances that a number of those who now hear me have no sufficient knowledge of themselves, or sense of their ignorance, and are in peril of their souls! Christ's ministers cannot tell who are, and who are not, the true elect: but when the difficulties in the way of knowing yourselves aright are considered, it becomes a most serious and immediate question for each of you to entertain, whether or not he is living a life of self-deceit, and thinking far more comfortably of his spiritual state than he has any right to do. For call to mind the impediments that are in the way of your knowing yourselves, or feeling your ignorance, and then judge.

1. First of all, self-knowledge does not come as a matter of course; it implies an effort and a work. As well may we suppose, that the knowledge of the languages comes by nature, as that acquaintance with our own heart is natural. Now the very effort of steadily reflecting, is itself painful to many men; not to speak of the difficulty of reflecting correctly. To ask ourselves *why* we do this or that, to take account of the principles which govern us, and see whether we act for conscience' sake or from some lower inducement, is painful. We are busy in the world, and what leisure time we have we readily devote to a less severe and wearisome employment.

2. And then comes in our self-love. We *hope* the best; this saves us the trouble of examining. Self-love answers for our safety. We think it sufficient caution to allow for certain possible unknown faults at the utmost, and to take them *into* the reckoning when we balance our account with our conscience: whereas, if the truth were known to us, we should find we had nothing but debts, and those greater than we can conceive, and ever increasing.

3. And this favourable judgment of ourselves will especially prevail, if we have the misfortune to have uninterrupted health and high spirits, and domestic comfort. Health of body and mind is a great blessing, if we can bear it; but unless chastened by watchings and fastings,[6] it will commonly seduce a man into

6 2 Cor. xi.27.

the notion that he is much better than he really is. Resistance to our acting rightly, whether it proceed from within or without, tries our principle; but when things go smoothly, and we have but to wish, and we can perform, we cannot tell how far we do or do not act from a sense of duty. When a man's spirits are high, he is pleased with every thing; and with himself especially. He can act with vigour and promptness, and he mistakes this mere constitutional energy for strength of faith. He is cheerful and contented; and he mistakes this for Christian peace. And, if happy in his family, he mistakes mere natural affection for Christian benevolence, and the confirmed temper of Christian love. In short, he is in a dream, from which nothing could have saved him except deep humility, and nothing will ordinarily rescue him except sharp affliction.

Other accidental circumstances are frequently causes of a similar self-deceit. While we remain in retirement from the world, we do not know ourselves; or after any great mercy or trial, which has affected us much, and given a temporary strong impulse to our obedience; or when we are in keen pursuit of some good object, which excites the mind, and for a time deadens it to temptation. Under such circumstances we are ready to think far too well of ourselves. The world is away; or, at least, we are insensible to its seductions; and we mistake our merely temporary tranquillity, or our over-wrought fervour of mind, on the one hand for Christian peace, on the other for Christian zeal.

4. Next we must consider the force of habit. Conscience at first warns us against sin; but if we disregard it, it soon ceases to upbraid us; and thus sins, once known, in time become secret sins. It seems then (and it is a startling reflection), that the more guilty we are, the less we know it; for the oftener we sin, the less we are distressed at it. I think many of us may, on reflection, recollect instances, in our experience of ourselves, of our gradually forgetting things to be wrong which once shocked us. Such is the force of habit. By it (for instance) men contrive to allow themselves in various kinds of dishonesty. They bring themselves to affirm what is untrue, or what they are not sure is true, in the course of business. They overreach and cheat; and still more are they likely to fall into low and selfish ways without their observing it, and all the while to continue careful in their attendance on the Christian ordinances, and bear about them a form of religion. Or, again, they will live in self-indulgent habits; eat and drink more than is right; display a needless pomp and splendour in their domestic arrangements, without any misgiving; much less do they think of simplicity of manners

and abstinence as Christian duties. Now we cannot suppose they *always* thought their present mode of living to be justifiable, for *others* are still struck with its impropriety; and what others now feel, doubtless they once felt themselves. But such is the force of habit. So again, to take as a third instance, the duty of stated private prayer; at first it is omitted with compunction, but soon with indifference. But it is not the less a sin because we do not feel it to be such. Habit has made it a *secret* sin.

5. To the force of habit must be added that of custom. Every age has its own wrong ways; and these have such influence, that even good men, from living in the world, are unconsciously misled by them. At one time a fierce persecuting hatred of those who erred in Christian doctrine has prevailed; at another, an odious over-estimation of wealth and the means of wealth; at another an irreligious veneration of the mere intellectual powers; at another, a laxity of morals: at another, disregard of the forms and discipline of the Church. The most religious men, unless they are especially watchful, will feel the sway of the fashion of their age; and suffer from it, as Lot in wicked Sodom, though unconsciously. Yet their ignorance of the mischief does not change the nature of their sin;—sin it still is, only custom makes it *secret* sin.

6. Now what is our chief guide amid the evil and seducing customs of the world?—obviously, the Bible. "The world passeth away, but the word of the Lord endureth for ever." [7] How much extended, then, and strengthened, necessarily must be this secret dominion of sin over us, when we consider how little we read Scripture! Our conscience gets corrupted,—true; but the words of truth, though effaced from our minds, remain in Scripture, bright in their eternal youth and purity. Yet, we do not study Scripture to stir up and refresh our minds. Ask yourselves, my brethren, what do you know of the Bible? Is there any one part of it you have read carefully, and as a whole? One of the Gospels, for instance? Do you know very much more of your Saviour's works and words than you have heard read in church? Have you compared His precepts, or St. Paul's, or any other Apostle's, with your own daily conduct, and prayed and endeavoured to act upon them? If you have, so far is well; go on to do so. If you have not, it is plain you do not possess, for you have not sought to possess, an adequate notion of that perfect Christian character which it is your duty to aim at, nor an adequate notion of your actual sinful state; you are in the number

[7] Is. xl.8; 1 Pet. i.24, 25; 1 John ii.17.

of those who "come not to the light, lest their deeds should be reproved."

These remarks may serve to impress upon us the difficulty of knowing ourselves aright, and the consequent danger to which we are exposed, of speaking peace to our souls, when there is no peace.

Many things are against us; this is plain. Yet is not our future prize worth a struggle? Is it not worth present discomfort and pain to accomplish an escape from the fire that never shall be quenched? Can we endure the thought of going down to the grave with a load of sins on our head unknown and unrepented of? Can we content ourselves with such an unreal faith in Christ, as in no sufficient measure includes self-abasement, or thankfulness, or the desire or effort to be holy? for how can we feel our need of His help, or our dependence on Him, or our debt to Him, or the nature of His gift to us, unless we know ourselves? How can we in any sense be said to have that "mind of Christ," to which the Apostle exhorts us, if we cannot follow Him to the height above, or the depth beneath; if we do not in some measure discern the cause and meaning of His sorrows, but regard the world, and man, and the system of Providence, in a light different from that which His words and acts supply? If you receive revealed truth merely through the eyes and ears, you believe words, not things; you deceive yourselves. You may conceive yourselves sound in faith, but you know nothing in any true way. Obedience to God's commandments, which implies knowledge of sin and of holiness, and the desire and endeavour to please Him, this is the only practical interpreter of Scripture doctrine. Without self-knowledge you have no root in yourselves personally; you may endure for a time, but under affliction or persecution your faith will not last. This is why many in this age (and in every age) become infidels, heretics, schismatics, disloyal despisers of the Church. They cast off the form of truth, because it never has been to them more than a form. They endure not, because they never have tasted that the Lord is gracious; and they never have had experience of His power and love, because they have never known their own weakness and need. This *may* be the future condition of some of us, if we harden our hearts to-day,—*apostasy*. Some day, even in this world, we may be found openly among the enemies of God and of His Church.

But, even should we be spared this present shame, what will it ultimately profit a man to profess without understanding? to *say* he has faith, when he has not works?[8] In that case we shall remain in the heavenly vineyard, stunted plants, without the principle of growth in us, barren; and, in the end, we shall be put to shame before Christ and the holy Angels, "as trees of withering fruits, twice dead, plucked up by the roots," even though we die in outward communion with the Church.

To think of these things, and to be alarmed, is the first step towards acceptable obedience; to be at ease, is to be unsafe. We must know what the evil of sin is hereafter, if we do not learn it here. God give us all grace to choose the pain of present repentance before the wrath to come!

[8] James ii.14.

SELF-DENIAL THE TEST
OF RELIGIOUS EARNESTNESS

"Now it is high time to awake out of sleep."
—Rom. xiii.11.

B Y "sleep," in this passage, St. Paul means a state of insensibility to things as they really are in God's sight. When we
are asleep, we are absent from this world's action, as if we were
no longer concerned in it. It goes on without us, or, if our rest
be broken, and we have some slight notion of people and occurrences about us, if we hear a voice or a sentence, and see a face,
yet we are unable to catch these external objects justly and
truly; we make them part of our dreams, and pervert them till
they have scarcely a resemblance to what they really are; and
such is the state of men as regards religious truth. God is ever
Almighty and All-knowing. He is on His throne in heaven, trying the reins and the hearts; and Jesus Christ, our Lord and Saviour, is on His right hand; and ten thousand Angels and Saints
are ministering to Him, rapt in the contemplation of Him, or
by their errands of mercy connecting this lower world with His
courts above; they go to and fro, as though upon the ladder
which Jacob saw. And the disclosure of this glorious invisible
world is made to us principally by means of the Bible, partly by
the course of nature, partly by the floating opinions of mankind, partly by the suggestions of the heart and conscience;—
and all these means of information concerning it are collected
and combined by the Holy Church, which heralds the news
forth to the whole earth, and applies it with power to individual
minds, partly by direct instruction, partly by her very form and
fashion, which witnesses to them; so that the truths of religion
circulate through the world almost as the light of day, every
corner and recess having some portion of its blessed rays. Such
is the state of a Christian country. Meanwhile, how is it with
those who dwell in it? The words of the text remind us of their
condition. They are *asleep*. While the Ministers of Christ are

using the armour of light, and all things speak of Him, they "walk" not "becomingly, as in the day." Many live altogether as though the day shone not on them, but the shadows still endured; and far the greater part of them are but very faintly sensible of the great truths preached around them. They see and hear as people in a dream; they mix up the Holy Word of God with their own idle imaginings; if startled for a moment, still they soon relapse into slumber; they refuse to be awakened, and think their happiness consists in continuing as they are.

Now I do not for an instant suspect, my brethren, that you are in the sound slumber of Sin. This is a miserable state, which I should hope was, on the whole, the condition of few men, at least in a place like this. But, allowing this, yet there is great reason for fearing that very many of you are not wide awake: that though your dreams are disturbed, yet dreams they are; and that the view of religion which you think to be a true one, is not that vision of the Truth which you would see were your eyes open, but such a vague, defective extravagant picture of it as a man sees when he is asleep. At all events, however this may be, it will be useful (please God) if you ask yourselves, one by one, the question, *"How do I know* I am in the right way? *How do I know* that I have real faith, and am not in a dream?"

The circumstances of these times render it very difficult to answer this question. When the world was against Christianity it was comparatively easy. But (in one sense) the world is now *for it.* I do not mean there are not turbulent lawless men, who would bring all things into confusion, if they could; who hate religion, and would overturn every established institution which proceeds from, or is connected with it. Doubtless there are very many such, but from such men religion has nothing to fear. The truth has ever flourished and strengthened under persecution. But what we have to fear is the opposite fact, that all the rank, and the station, and the intelligence, and the opulence of the country is professedly with religion. We have cause to fear from the very circumstance that the institutions of the country are based upon the acknowledgment of religion as true. Worthy of all honour are they who so based them! Miserable is the guilt which lies upon those who have attempted, and partly succeeded, in shaking that holy foundation! But it often happens that our most bitter are not our most dangerous enemies; on the other hand, greatest blessings are the most serious temptations to the unwary. And our danger, at present, is this, that a man's having a general character for religion, reverencing the Gospel and professing it, and to a certain point obeying it, so fully promotes his temporal interests, that it is difficult for him to make out for himself whether he really acts on faith, or from a desire of this world's advantages. It is difficult to find *tests* which may bring home the truth to his mind, and probe his heart after the manner of Him who, from His throne above, tries it with an Almighty Wisdom. It can scarcely be denied that attention to their religious duties is becoming a fashion among large portions of the community,—so large, that, to many individuals, these portions are in fact *the world*. We are, every now and then, surprised to find persons to be in the observance of family prayer, of reading Scripture, or of Holy Communion, of whom we should not have expected beforehand such a profession of faith; or we hear them avowing the high evangelical truths of the New Testament, and countenancing those who maintain them. All this brings it about, that it is our interest in this world to profess to be Christ's disciples.

And further than this, it is necessary to remark, that, in spite of this general profession of zeal for the Gospel among all respectable persons at this day, nevertheless there is reason for fearing, that it is not altogether the real Gospel that they are zealous for. Doubtless we have cause to be thankful whenever we see persons earnest in the various ways I have mentioned. Yet, somehow, after all, there is reason for being dissatisfied with the character of the religion of the day; dissatisfied, first, because oftentimes these same persons are very inconsistent;— often, for instance, talk irreverently and profanely, ridicule or slight things sacred, speak against the Holy Church, or against the blessed Saints of early times, or even against the favoured servants of God, set before us in Scripture; or *act* with the world and the worse sort of men, even when they do not speak like them; attend to them more than to the Ministers of God, or are very lukewarm, lax, and unscrupulous in matters of conduct, so much so, that they seem hardly to go by principle, but by what is merely expedient and convenient. And then again, putting aside our judgment of these men as individuals, and thinking of them as well as we can (which of course it is our duty to do), yet, after all, taking merely the multitude of them as a symptom of a state of things, I own I am suspicious of any religion that is a people's religion, or an age's religion. Our Saviour says, "Narrow is the way." This, of course, must not be interpreted without great caution; yet surely the whole tenor of the Inspired Volume leads us to believe that His Truth will not be heartily received by the many, that it is against the current of human feeling and opinion, and the course of the world, and so far forth as it *is* received by a man, will be opposed by himself, i.e. by his old nature which remains about him, next by all others, so far forth as they have not received it. "The light shining in darkness" is the token of true religion; and, though doubtless there are seasons when a sudden enthusiasm arises in favour of the Truth (as in the history of St. John the Baptist, in whose "light" the Jews "were willing for a season to rejoice,"[1] so as even "to be baptized of him, confessing their sins"[2]), yet such a popularity of the Truth is *but* sudden, comes at once and goes at once, has no regular growth, no abiding stay. It is error alone which grows and is received heartily on a large scale. St. Paul has set up his warning against our supposing Truth will ever be heartily accepted, whatever show there may be of a general profession of it, in his last Epistle, where he tells Timothy, among other sad prophecies, that "evil men and seducers shall wax worse and worse."[3] Truth, indeed, has that power in it, that it forces men to profess it in words; but when they go on to act, instead of obeying *it*, they substitute some idol in the place of it. On these accounts, when there is much talk of religion in a country, and much congratulation that there is a general concern for it, a cautious mind will feel anxious lest some counterfeit be, in fact, honoured instead of it: lest it be the dream of man rather than the verities of God's word, which has become popular, and lest the received form have no more of truth in it than is just necessary to recommend it to the reason and conscience:—lest, in short, it be Satan transformed into an angel of light, rather than the Light itself, which is attracting followers.

If, then, this be a time (which I suppose it is) when a general profession of religion is thought respectable and right in the virtuous and orderly classes of the community, this circumstance should not diminish your anxiety about your own state before God, but rather (I may say) increase it; for two reasons, first, because you are in danger of doing right from motives of this world; next, because you may, perchance, be cheated of the Truth, by some ingenuity which the world puts, like counterfeit coin, in the place of the Truth.

Some, indeed, of those who now hear me, are in situations where they are almost shielded from the world's influence, whatever it is. There are persons so happily placed as to have religious superiors, who direct them to what is good only, and who are kind to them, as well as pious towards God. This is their happiness, and they must thank God for the gift; but it is

---

[1] John v.35.   [2] Matt. iii.6   [3] 2 Tim. iii.13.

their temptation too. At least they are under one of the two temptations just mentioned; good behaviour is, in their case, not only a matter of duty, but of interest. If they obey God, they gain praise from men as well as from Him; so that it is very difficult for them to know whether they do right for conscience' sake, or for the world's sake. Thus, whether in private families, or in the world, in all the ranks of middle life, men lie under a considerable danger at this day, a more than ordinary danger, of self-deception, of being asleep while they think themselves awake.

How then shall we try ourselves? Can any tests be named which will bring certainty to our minds on the subject? No indisputable tests can be given. We cannot know for certain. We must beware of an impatience about knowing what our real state is. St. Paul himself did not know till the last days of his life (as far as we know), that he was one of God's elect who shall never perish. He said, "I know nothing by myself yet am I not hereby justified;"[4] i.e. though I am not conscious to myself of neglect of duty, yet am I not therefore confident of my acceptance? Judge nothing before the time. Accordingly he says in another place, "I keep under my body, and bring it into subjection, lest that by any means, when I have preached to others, I myself should be a castaway."[5] And yet though this absolute certainty of our election unto glory be unattainable, and the desire to obtain it an impatience which ill befits sinners, nevertheless a comfortable hope, a sober and subdued belief that God has pardoned and justified us for Christ's sake (blessed be His name!), is attainable, according to St. John's words, "If our heart condemn us not, then have we confidence toward God."[6] And the question is, how are we to attain to this, under the circumstances in which we are placed? In what does it consist?

Were we in a heathen land (as I said just now) it were easy to answer. The very profession of the Gospel would almost bring evidence of true faith, as far as we could have evidence; for such profession among Pagans is almost sure to involve persecution. Hence it is that the Epistles are so full of expressions of joy in the Lord Jesus, and in the exulting hope of salvation. Well might they be confident who had suffered for Christ. "Tribulation worketh patience, and patience experience, and experience hope."[7] "Henceforth let no man trouble me, for I bear in my body the marks of the Lord Jesus."[8] "Always bearing about

[4] 1 Cor. iv.4.   [5] 1 Cor. ix.27.   [6] 1 John iii.21.
[7] Rom. v.3, 4.   [8] Gal. vi.17.

in the body the dying of the Lord Jesus; that the life also of Jesus might be made manifest in our body." [9] "Our hope of you is stedfast, knowing that as ye are partakers of the suffering, so shall ye be also of the consolation." [10] These and such like texts belong to those only who have witnessed for the truth like the early Christians. They are beyond *us*.

This is certain; yet since the nature of Christian obedience is the same in every age, it still brings with it, as it did then, an evidence of God's favour. We cannot indeed make ourselves as sure of our being in the number of God's true servants as the early Christians were, yet we may possess our degree of certainty, and by the same kind of evidence, the evidence of *self-denial*. This was the great evidence which the first disciples gave, and which we can give still. Reflect upon our Saviour's plain declarations, "Whosoever will come after Me, let him deny himself, and take up his cross and follow Me." [11] "If any man come to Me, and hate not his father and mother, and wife, and children, and brethren, and sisters, yea, and his own life also, he cannot be My disciple. And whosoever doth not bear his cross and come after Me, he cannot be My disciple." [12] "If thy hand offend thee, cut it off . . . if thy foot offend thee, cut it off . . . if thine eye offend thee, pluck it out: . . . it is better for thee to enter into life maimed . . . halt . . . with one eye than to be cast into hell." [13]

Now without attempting to explain perfectly such passages as these, which doubtless cannot be understood without a fulness of grace which is possessed by very few men, yet at least we learn thus much from them, that a rigorous self-denial is a chief duty, nay, that it may be considered the test whether we are Christ's disciples, whether we are living in a mere dream, which we mistake for Christian faith and obedience, or are really and truly awake, alive, living in the day, on our road heavenwards. The early Christians went through self-denials in their very profession of the Gospel; *what are our self-denials*, now that the profession of the Gospel is not a self-denial? In what sense do we fulfil the words of Christ? have we any distinct notion what is meant by the words "taking up our cross?" in what way are we acting, in which we should not act, supposing the Bible and the Church were unknown to this country, and religion, as existing among us, was *merely* a fashion of this world? What are we doing, which we have reason to trust is done for Christ's sake who bought us?

[9] 2 Cor. iv.10.   [10] 2 Cor. i.7.   [11] Mark viii.34.
[12] Luke xiv.26, 27.   [13] Mark ix.43–47.

You know well enough that works are said to be the fruits and evidence of faith. That faith is said to be dead which has them not. Now what works have we to show of such a kind as to give us "confidence," so that we may "not be ashamed before Him at His coming?" [14]

In answering this question I observe, first of all, that, according to Scripture, the self-denial which is the test of our faith must be daily. "If any man will come after Me, let him deny himself, and take up his cross *daily* and follow Me." [15] It is thus St. Luke records our Saviour's words. Accordingly, it seems that Christian obedience does not consist merely in a few occasional efforts, a few accidental good deeds, or certain seasons of repentance, prayer, and activity; a mistake, which minds of a certain class are very apt to fall into. This is the kind of obedience which constitutes what the world calls a great man, i.e. a man who has some noble points, and every now and then acts heroically, so as to astonish and subdue the minds of beholders, but who in private life has no abiding personal religion, who does not regulate his thoughts, words, and deeds, according to the law of God. Again, the word *daily* implies, that the self-denial which is pleasing to Christ consists in little things. This is plain, for opportunity for great self-denials does not come every day. Thus to take up the cross of Christ is no great action done once for all, it consists in the continual practice of small duties which are distasteful to us.

If, then, a person asks how he is to know whether he is dreaming on in the world's slumber, or is really awake and alive unto God, let him first fix his mind upon some one or other of his besetting infirmities. Every one who is at all in the habit of examining himself, must be conscious of such within him. Many men have more than one, all of us have some one or other; and in resisting and overcoming such, self-denial has its first employment. One man is indolent and fond of amusement, another man is passionate or ill-tempered, another is vain, another has little control over his tongue; others are weak, and cannot resist the ridicule of thoughtless companions; others are tormented with bad passions, of which they are ashamed, yet are overcome. Now let every one consider what his weak point is; in that is his trial. His trial is not in those things which are easy to him, but in that one thing, in those several things, whatever they are, in which to do his duty is against his nature. Never think yourself safe because you do

---

[14] 1 John ii.28.   [15] Luke ix.23.

your duty in ninety-nine points; it is the hundredth which is to
be the ground of your self-denial, which must evidence, or
rather instance and realize your faith. It is in reference to this
you must watch and pray; pray continually for God's grace to
help you, and watch with fear and trembling lest you fall. Other
men may not know what these weak points of your character
are, they may mistake them. But you may know them; you may
know them by *their* guesses and hints, and your own observation, and the light of the Spirit of God. And oh, that you may
have strength to wrestle with them and overcome them! Oh,
that you may have the wisdom to care little for the world's religion, or the praise you get from the world, and your agreement
with what clever men, or powerful men, or many men, make
the standard of religion, compared with the secret consciousness that you are obeying God in little things as well as great, in
the hundredth duty as well as in the ninety-nine! Oh, that you
may (as it were) sweep the house diligently to discover what
you lack of the *full* measure of obedience! for be quite sure, that
this apparently small defect will influence your whole spirit and
judgment in all things. Be quite sure that your judgment of persons, and of events, and of actions, and of doctrines, and your
spirit towards God and man, your faith in the high truths of the
Gospel, and your knowledge of your duty, all depend in a
strange way on this strict endeavour to observe the whole law,
on this self-denial in those little things in which obedience *is* a
self-denial. Be not content with a warmth of faith carrying you
over many obstacles even in your obedience, forcing you past
the fear of men, and the usages of society, and the persuasions
of interest; exult not in your experience of God's past mercies,
and your assurance of what He has already done for your soul, if
you are conscious you have neglected the one thing needful, the
"one thing" which "thou lackest,"—daily self-denial.

But, besides this, there are other modes of self-denial to try
your faith and sincerity, which it may be right just to mention.
It may so happen that the sin you are most liable to, is not called
forth every day. For instance: anger and passion are irresistible
perhaps when they come upon you, but it is only at times that
you are provoked, and then you are off your guard; so that the
occasion is over, and you have failed, before you were well aware
of its coming. It is right then almost to *find out* for yourself daily
self-denials; and this because our Lord bids you take up your
cross daily, and because it proves your earnestness, and because
by doing so you strengthen your general power of self-mastery,
and come to have such an habitual command of yourself, as will

be a defence ready prepared when the season of temptation comes. Rise up then in the morning with the purpose that (please God) the day shalt not pass without its self-denial, with a self-denial in innocent pleasures and tastes, if none occurs to mortify sin. Let your very rising from your bed be a self-denial; let your meals be self-denials. Determine to yield to others in things indifferent, to go out of your way in small matters, to inconvenience yourself (so that no direct duty suffers by it), rather than you should not meet with your daily discipline. This was the Psalmist's method, who was, as it were, "punished all day long, and chastened every morning."[16] It was St. Paul's method, who "kept under," or bruised "his body, and brought it into subjection."[17] This is one great end of fasting. A man says to himself, "How am I to know I am in earnest?" I would suggest to him, Make some sacrifice, do some distasteful thing, which you are not actually obliged to do, (so that it be lawful,) to bring home to your mind that in fact you do love your Saviour: that you do hate sin, that you do hate your sinful nature, that you have put aside the present world. Thus you will have an evidence (to a certain point) that you are not using mere words. It is easy to make professions, easy to say fine things in speech or in writing, easy to astonish men with truths which they do not know, and sentiments which rise above human nature. "But thou, O servant of God, flee these things, and follow after righteousness, godliness, faith, love, patience, meekness." Let not your words run on; force every one of them into action as it goes, and thus, cleansing yourself from all pollution of the flesh and spirit, perfect holiness in the fear of God. In dreams we sometimes move our arms to see if we are awake or not, and so we are awakened. This is the way to keep your heart awake also. Try yourself daily in little deeds, to prove that your faith is more than a deceit.

I am aware all this is a hard doctrine; hard to those even who assent to it, and can describe it most accurately. There are such imperfections, such inconsistencies in the heart and life of even the better sort of men, that continual repentance must ever go hand in hand with our endeavours to obey. Much we need the grace of Christ's blood to wash us from the guilt we daily incur; much need we the aid of His promised Spirit! And surely He will grant all the riches of His mercy to His true servants; but as surely He will vouchsafe to none of us the power to believe in Him, and the blessedness of being one with Him, who are not as earnest in obeying Him as if salvation depended on themselves.

[16] Ps. lxxiii.14.   [17] 1 Cor. ix.27.

THE SPIRITUAL MIND

"The kingdom of God is not in word, but in power."
—1 Cor. iv.20.

How are we the better for being members of the Christian Church? This is a question which has ever claims on our attention; but it is right from time to time to examine our hearts with more than usual care, to try them by the standard of that divinely enlightened temper in the Church, and in the Saints, the work of the Holy Ghost, called by St. Paul "the spirit." I ask then, how are we the better for being Christ's disciples? what reason have we for thinking that our lives are very different from what they would have been if we had been heathens? Have we, in the words of the text, received the kingdom of God in word or in power? I will make some remarks in explanation of this question, which may (through God's grace) assist you, my Brethren, in answering it.

1. Now first, if we would form a just notion how far we are influenced by the power of the Gospel, we must evidently put aside every thing which we do merely in imitation of others, and not from religious principle. Not that we can actually separate our good words and works into two classes, and say, what is done from faith, and what is done only by accident, and in a random way; but without being able to draw the line, it is quite evident that so very much of our apparent obedience to God arises from mere obedience to the world and its fashions; or rather, that it is so difficult to say what *is* done in the spirit of faith, as to lead us, on reflection, to be very much dissatisfied with ourselves, and quite out of conceit with our past lives. Let a person merely reflect on the number and variety of bad or foolish thoughts which he suffers, and dwells on in private, which he would be ashamed to put into words, and he will at once see, how very poor a test his outward demeanour in life is of his real holiness in the sight of God. Or again, let him consider the number of times he has attended public worship as a matter of course because others do, and without seriousness of

mind; or the number of times he has found himself unequal to temptations when they came, which beforehand he and others made light of in conversation, blaming those perhaps who had been overcome by them, and he must own that his outward conduct shapes itself unconsciously by the manners of those with whom he lives, being acted upon by external impulses, apart from any right influence proceeding from the heart. Now, when I say this, am I condemning all that we do without thinking expressly of the duty of obedience at the *very time* we are doing it? Far from it; a religious man, in proportion as obedience becomes more and more easy to him, *will* doubtless do his duty unconsciously. It will be *natural* to him to obey, and therefore he will do it naturally, i. e. without effort or deliberation. It is difficult things which we are obliged to think about before doing them. When we have mastered our hearts in any matter (it is true) we no more think of the duty while we obey, than we think how to walk when we walk, or by what rules to exercise any art which we have thoroughly acquired. *Separate acts* of faith aid us only while we are *unstable*. As we get strength, but one extended act of faith (so to call it) influences us all through the day, and our whole day is but one act of obedience also. Then there is no minute distribution of our faith among our particular deeds. Our will runs parallel to God's will. This is the very privilege of confirmed Christians; and it is comparatively but a sordid way of serving God, to be thinking when we do a deed, "if I do not do this, I shall risk my salvation; or, if I do it, I have a chance of being saved;"—*comparatively* a grovelling way, for it is the best, the only way for sinners such as we are, to *begin* to serve God in. Still as we grow in grace, we throw away childish things; then we are able to stand upright like grown men, without the props and aids which our infancy required. This is the noble manner of serving God, to do good without thinking about it, without any calculation or reasoning, from love of the good, and hatred of the evil;—though cautiously and with prayer and watching, yet so generously, that if we were suddenly asked why we so act, we could only reply "because it is our way," or "because Christ so acted;" so spontaneously as not to know so much that we *are* doing right, as that we are *not* doing wrong; I mean, with more of instinctive fear of sinning, than of minute and careful appreciation of the *degrees* of our obedience. Hence it is that the best men are ever the most humble; as for other reasons, so especially because they *are accustomed* to be religious. They surprise *others*, but not themselves; they surprise others at their very calmness and freedom from thought about themselves. This is to have a great mind, to have within us that "princely heart of innocence"[1] of which David speaks. Common men see God at a distance; in their attempts to be religious they feebly guide themselves as by a distant light, and are obliged to calculate and search about for the path. But the long practised Christian, who, through God's mercy, has brought God's presence near to him, the elect of God, in whom the Blessed Spirit dwells, he does not look out of doors for the traces of God; he is moved by God dwelling in him, and needs not but act on instinct. I do not say there is any man altogether such, for this is an angelic life; but it is the state of mind to which vigorous prayer and watching tend.

How different is this high obedience from that random unawares way of doing right, which to so many men seems to constitute a religious life The excellent obedience I have been describing is obedience *on habit*. Now the obedience I condemn as untrue, may be called obedience *on custom*. The one is of the heart, the other of the lips; the one is in power, the other in word; the one cannot be acquired without much and constant vigilance, generally not without much pain and trouble; the other is the result of a mere passive imitation of those whom we fall in with. Why need I describe what every man's experience bears witness to? Why do children learn their mother tongue, and not a foreign language? Do they think about it? Are they better or worse for acquiring one language and not another? Their character, of course, is just what it would have been otherwise. How then are we better or worse, if we have but in the same passive way admitted into our minds certain religious opinions; and have but accustomed ourselves to the words and actions of the world around us? Supposing we had never heard of the Gospel, should we not do just what we do, even in a heathen country, were the manners of the place, from one cause or another, as decent and outwardly religious? This is the question we have to ask ourselves. And if we are conscious to ourselves that we are not greatly concerned about the question itself, and have no fears worth mentioning of being in the wrong, and no anxiety to find what is right, is it not evident that we are living to the world, not to God, and that whatever virtue we may actually have, still the Gospel of Christ has come to us not in power, but in word only?

I have now suggested one subject for consideration concerning our reception of the kingdom of God; viz. to inquire whether we have received it more than *externally*; but,

---

[1] *Christian Year*, Sixth Sunday after Trinity.

2. I will go on to affirm that we may have received it in a higher sense than in word merely, and yet in no real sense in *power*; in other words, that our obedience may be in some sort religious, and yet hardy deserve the title of Christian. This may be at first sight a startling assertion. It may seem to some of us as if there were no difference between being religious and being Christian; and that to insist on a difference is to perplex people. But listen to me. Do you not think it possible for men to do their duty, i.e. be religious, in a heathen country? Doubtless it is. St. Peter says, that in every nation he that feareth God and worketh righteousness is accepted with Him.[2] Now are such persons, therefore, Christians? Certainly *not*. It would seem, then, it is possible to fear God and work righteousness, yet without being Christians; for (if we would know the truth of it) to be a Christian is to do this, and to do *much more* than this. Here, then, is a fresh subject for self-examination. Is it not the way of men to dwell with satisfaction on their good deeds, particularly when, for some reason or other, their conscience smites them? Or when they are led to the consideration of death, then they begin to turn in their minds how they shall acquit themselves before the judgment-seat. And then it is they feel a relief in being able to detect, in their past lives, any deeds which may be regarded in any sense religious. You may hear some persons comforting themselves that they never harmed any one; and that they have not given in to an openly profligate and riotous life. Others are able to say more; they can speak of their honesty, their industry, or their general conscientiousness. We will say they have taken good care of their families; they have never defrauded or deceived any one; and they have a good name in the world; nay, they have in one sense lived in the fear of God. I will grant them this and more; yet possibly they are not altogether Christians in their obedience. I will grant that these virtuous and religious deeds are really fruits of faith, not external merely, done without thought, but proceeding from the heart. I will grant they are really praiseworthy, and, when a man from want of opportunity knows no more, really acceptable to God; yet they determine nothing about his having received the Gospel of Christ in power. Why? for the simple reason that they are *not enough*. A Christian's faith and obedience is built on all this, but is only built on it. It is not the same as it. To be Christians, surely it is not enough to be that which we are enjoined to be, and must be, even without Christ; not

[2] Acts x.3.

enough to be no better than good heathens; not enough to be, in some slight measure, just, honest, temperate, and religious. We must indeed be just, honest, temperate, and religious, before we can rise to Christian graces, and to *be* practised in justice and the like virtues is the way, the ordinary way, in which we receive the fulness of the kingdom of God; and, doubtless, any man who despises those who try to practise them (I mean conscientious men, who notwithstanding have not yet clearly seen and welcomed the Gospel system), and slightingly calls them "mere moral men" in disparagement, such a man knows not what spirit he is of, and had best take heed how he speaks against the workings of the inscrutable Spirit of God. I am not wishing to frighten these imperfect Christians, but to lead them on; to open their minds to the greatness of the work before them, to dissipate the meagre and carnal views in which the Gospel has come to them, to warn them that they must never be contented with themselves, or stand still and relax their efforts but must go on *unto perfection*; that till they are much more than they are at present, they have received the kingdom of God in word, not in power; that they are not spiritual men, and can have no comfortable sense of Christ's presence in their souls; for to whom much is given, of him is much required.

What is it, then, that they lack? I will read several passages of Scripture which will make it plain. St. Paul says, "If any man be in Christ, he is a new creature: old things are passed away; behold, all things are become new." Again: "The life which I now live in the flesh, I live by the faith of the Son of God, who loved me and gave Himself for me." "The love of Christ constraineth us." "Put on, therefore, as the elect of God, holy and beloved, bowels of mercies, kindness, humbleness of mind, meekness, longsuffering, forbearing one another, and forgiving another, if any man have a quarrel against any, even as Christ forgave you, so also do ye; and above all these things, put on charity, which is the bond of perfectness. And let the peace of God rule in your hearts, to the which also ye are called in one body, and be ye thankful. Let the word of Christ dwell in you richly in all wisdom." "God hath sent forth the Spirit of His Son into your hearts." Lastly, our Saviour's own memorable words, "If any man will come after Me, let him deny himself, and take up his cross daily and follow Me." [3] Now it is plain that this is a very different mode of obedience from any which natural reason and conscience tell us of;—different, *not in its nature*,

---

[3] 2 Cor. v.14, 17; Gal. ii.20; Col. iii.12–16; Gal iv.6; Luke ix.23.

but *in its excellence and peculiarity*. It is much more than honesty, justice, and temperance; and *this* is to be a Christian. Observe in what respect it is different from that lower degree of religion which we may possess without entering into the mind of the Gospel. First of all in its faith; which is placed, not simply in God, but in God as manifested in Christ, according to His own words, "Ye believe in God, believe also in Me." [4] Next, we must adore Christ as our Lord and Master, and love Him as our most gracious Redeemer. We must have a deep sense of our guilt, and of the difficulty of securing heaven; we must live as in His presence, daily pleading His cross and passion, thinking of His holy commandments, imitating His sinless pattern, and depending on the gracious aids of His Spirit; that we may really and truly be servants of Father, Son, and Holy Ghost, in whose name we were baptized. Further, we must, for His sake, aim at a noble and unusual strictness of life, perfecting holiness in His fear, destroying our sins, mastering our whole soul, and bringing it into captivity to His law, denying ourselves lawful things, in order to do Him service, exercising a profound humility, and an unbounded, never-failing love, giving away much of our substance in religious and charitable works, and discountenancing and shunning irreligious men. This is to be a Christian; a gift easily described, and in a few words, but attainable only with fear and much trembling; promised, indeed, and in a measure accorded at once to every one who asks for it, but not secured till after many years, and never in this life fully realized. But be sure of this, that every one of us, who has had the opportunities of instruction and sufficient time, and yet does not in some good measure possess it, every one, who, when death comes, has not gained his portion of that gift which it requires a course of years to gain, and which he might have gained, is in a peril so great and fearful, that I do not like to speak about it. As to the notion of a partial and ordinary fulfilment of the duties of honesty, industry, sobriety, and kindness, "availing" [5] him, it has no Scriptural encouragement. We must stand or fall by another and higher rule. We must have become what St. Paul calls "new creatures;" [6] that is, we must have lived and worshipped God as the redeemed of Jesus Christ, in all faith and humbleness of mind, in reverence towards His word and ordinances, in thankfulness, in resignation, in mercifulness, gentleness, purity, patience, and love.

Now, considering the obligation of obedience which lies

[4] John xiv.1.   [5] Gal. vi.15.   [6] Gal. vi.15.

upon us Christians, in these two respects, first, as contrasted with a mere outward and nominal profession, and next contrasted with that more ordinary obedience which is required of those even who have not the Gospel, how evident is it that we are far from the kingdom of God! Let each in his own conscience apply this to himself. I will grant he has *some* real Christian principle in his heart; but I wish him to observe how *little* that is likely to be. Here is a thought not to keep us from rejoicing in the Lord Christ, but to make us "rejoice with trembling,"[7] wait diligently on God, pray Him earnestly to teach us more of our duty, and to impress the love of it on our hearts, to enable us to obey both in that free spirit, which can act right without reasoning and calculation, and yet with the caution of those who know their salvation depends on obedience in little things, from love of the truth as manifested in Him who is the Living Truth come upon earth, "the Way, the Truth, and the Life."[8]

With others we have no concern; we do not know what their opportunities are. There may be thousands in this populous land who never had the means of hearing Christ's voice fully, and in whom virtues short of evangelical will hereafter be accepted as the fruit of faith. Nor can we know the *hearts* of *any* men, or tell what is the degree in which they have improved their talents. It is enough to keep to ourselves. We dwell in the full light of the Gospel, and the full grace of the Sacraments. We ought to have the holiness of Apostles. There is no reason except our own wilful corruption, that we are not by this time walking in the steps of St. Paul or St. John, and following them as they followed Christ. What a thought is this! Do not cast it from you, my brethren, but take it to your homes, and may God give you grace to profit by it!

[7] Ps. ii.11.   [8] John xiv.6.

SINS OF IGNORANCE AND WEAKNESS

"Let us draw near with a true heart in full assurance of faith,
having our hearts sprinkled from an evil conscience,
and our bodies washed with pure water."—Heb. x.22.

Among the reasons which may be assigned for the observance of prayer at stated times, there is one which is very
obvious, and yet perhaps is not so carefully remembered and
acted upon as it should be. I mean the necessity of sinners
cleansing themselves from time to time of the ever-accumulating guilt which loads their consciences. We are ever sinning;
and though Christ has died once for all to release us from our
penalty, yet we are not pardoned once for all, but according as,
and whenever each of us supplicates for the gift. By the prayer
of faith we appropriate it; but only for the time, not for ever.
Guilt is again contracted, and must be again repented of and
washed away. We cannot by one act of faith establish ourselves
for ever after in the favour of God. It is going beyond His will to
be impatient for a final acquittal, when we are bid ask only for
our *daily* bread. We are still so far in the condition of the Israelites; and though we do not offer sacrifice, or observe the literal
washings of the Law, yet we still require the periodical renewal
of those blessings which were formerly conveyed in their degree
by the Mosaic rites; and though we gain far more excellent gifts
from God than the Jews did, and by more spiritual ordinances,
yet means of approaching Him we still need, and continual
means to keep us in the justification in which baptism first
placed us. Of this the text reminds us. It is addressed to Christians, to the regenerate; yet so far from their regeneration having cleansed them once for all, they are bid ever to sprinkle the
blood of Christ upon their consciences, and renew (as it were)
their baptism, and so continually appear before the presence of
Almighty God.

Let us now endeavour to realize a truth, which few of us will
be disposed to dispute as far as words go.

1. First consider our present condition, as shown us in Scrip-

ture. Christ has not changed this, though He has died; it is as it was from the beginning,—I mean our actual state as men. We have Adam's nature in the same sense as if redemption had not come to the world. It *has* come to all the world, but the world is not changed thereby as a whole,—that change is not a work done and over in Christ. We are changed *one by one*; the race of man is what it ever was, guilty;—what it was before Christ came; with the same evil passions, the same slavish will. The history of redemption, if it is to be effectual, must begin from the beginning with every individual of us, and be carried on through our own life. It is not a work done ages before we were born. We cannot profit by the work of a Saviour, though He be the Blessed Son of God, so as to be saved thereby without our own working; for we are moral agents, we have a will of our own, and Christ must be formed in us, and turn us from darkness to light, if God's gracious purpose, fulfilled upon the cross, is to be in our case more than a name, an abused, wasted privilege. Thus the world, viewed as in God's sight, can never become wiser or more enlightened than it has been. We cannot mount upon the labours of our forefathers. We have the same nature that man ever had, and we must begin from the point man ever began from, and work out our salvation in the same slow, persevering manner.

(1.) When this is borne in mind, how important the Jewish Law becomes to us Christians! important in itself, over and above all references contained in it to that Gospel which it introduced. To this day it fulfils its original purpose of impressing upon man his great guilt and feebleness. Those legal sacrifices and purifications which are now all done away, are still evidence to us of a fact which the Gospel has not annulled,—our corruption. Let no one lightly pass over the Book of Leviticus, and say it only contains the ceremonial of a national law. Let no one study it merely with a critic's eye, satisfied with connecting it in a nicely arranged system with the Gospel, as though it contained prophecy only. No; it speaks to us. Are we better than the Jews? is our nature less unbelieving, sensual, or proud, than theirs? Surely man is at all times the same being, as even the philosophers tell us. And if so, that minute ceremonial of the Law presents us with a picture of our daily life. It impressively testifies to our continual sinning, by suggesting that an expiation is needful in all the most trivial circumstances of our conduct; and that it is at our peril if we go on carelessly and thoughtlessly, trusting to our having been once accepted,—whether in baptism,—or (as we think) at a certain season of repentance, or (as we may fancy) at the very time of the death of Christ (as if then the whole race of man were really and at once pardoned and exalted),—or (worse still) if we profanely doubt that man has ever fallen under a curse, and trust idly in the mercy of God, without a feeling of the true misery and infinite danger of sin.

Consider the ceremony observed on the great day of atonement, and you will see what was the sinfulness of the Israelites, and therefore of all mankind, in God's sight. The High Priest was taken to represent the holiest person of the whole world. The nation itself was holy above the rest of the world; from it a holy tribe was selected; from the holy tribe, a holy family; and from that family, a holy person. This was the High Priest, who was thus set apart as the choice specimen of the whole human race; yet even he was not allowed, under pain of death, to approach even the mercy-seat of God, except once a year: nor then in his splendid robes, nor without sacrifices for the sins of himself and the people, the blood of which he carried with him into the holy place.

Or consider the sacrifices necessary according to the Law for sins of ignorance;[1] or again, for the mere touching any thing which the Law pronounced unclean, or for bodily disease,[2] and hence learn how sinful our ordinary thoughts and deeds must be, represented to us as they are by these outward ceremonial transgressions. Not even their thanksgiving might the Israelites offer without an offering of blood to cleanse it; for our corruption is not merely in this act or that, but in our *nature*.

(2.) Next, to pass from the Jewish law, you will observe that God tells us expressly in the history of the fall of Adam, what the legal ceremonies implied; that it *is* our very nature which is sinful. Herein is the importance of the doctrine of original sin. It is very humbling, and as such the only true introduction to the preaching of the Gospel. Men can without trouble be brought to confess that they sin, i.e. that they commit sins. They know well enough they are not perfect; nay, that they do nothing in the best manner. But they do not like to be told that the race from which they proceed is degenerate. Even the indolent have pride here. They think they *can* do their duty, *only do not choose to do it*; they like to believe (though strangely indeed, for they condemn themselves while they believe it), they like to believe that they do not want assistance. A man must be far gone in degradation and has lost even that false independence

---

[1] Levit. v.   [2] Levit. v.2, 6; xiv.1–32.

of mind which is often a substitute for real religion in leading to exertion, who while living in sin, steadily and contentedly holds the opinion that he is born *for* sin. And much more do the industrious and active dislike to have it forced upon their minds, that, do what they will, they have the taint of corruption about all their doings and imaginings. We know how ashamed men are of being low born, or discreditably connected. This is the sort of shame forced upon every son of Adam. "Thy first father hath sinned:" this is the legend on our forehead which even the sign of the Cross does no more than blot out, leaving the mark of it. This is our shame; but I notice it here, not so much as a humbling thought, as with a view of pressing upon your consciences the necessity of appearing before God at stated seasons, in order to put aside the continually-renewed guilt of your nature. Who will dare go on day after day in neglect of earnest prayer, and the Holy Communion, while each day brings its own fearful burden, coming as if spontaneously, springing from our very nature, but not got rid of without deliberate and direct acts of faith in the Great Sacrifice which has been set forth for its removal?

(3.) Further, look into your own souls, my brethren, and see if you cannot discern some part of the truth of the Scripture statement, which I have been trying to set before you. Recollect the bad thoughts of various kinds which come into your minds like darts; for these will be some evidence to you of the pollution and odiousness of your nature. True, they proceed from your adversary, the Devil; and the very circumstance of your experiencing them is in itself no proof of your being sinful, for even the Son of God, your Saviour, suffered from the temptation of them. But you will scarcely deny that they are received by you so freely and heartily, as to show that Satan tempts you through your nature, not against it. Again, let them be ever so external in their first coming, do you not make them your own? Do you not detain them? or do you impatiently and indignantly shake them off? Even if you reject them, still do they not answer Satan's purpose in inflaming your mind at the instant, and so evidence that the matter of which it is composed is corruptible? Do you not, for instance, dwell on the thought of wealth and splendour till you covet these temporal blessings? or do you not suffer yourselves, though for a while, to be envious, or discontented, or angry, or vain, or impure, or proud? Ah! who can estimate the pollution hence, of one single day; the pollution of touching merely that dead body of sin which we put off indeed at our baptism, but which is tied about us while we live here, and is the means of our Enemy's assaults upon us! The taint of death is upon us, and surely we shall be stifled by the encompassing plague, unless God from day to day vouchsafes to make us clean.

2. Again, reflect on the *habits* of sin which we superadded to our evil nature before we turned to God. Here is another source of continual defilement. Instead of checking the bad elements within us, perhaps we indulged them for years; and they truly had their fruit unto death. Then Adam's sin increased, and multiplied itself within us; there was a change, but it was for the worse, not for the better; and the new nature we gained, far from being spiritual, was twofold more the child of hell than that with which we were born. So when, at length, we turned back into a better course, what a complicated work lay before us, to unmake ourselves! And however long we have laboured at it, still how much unconscious, unavoidable sin, the result of past transgression, is thrown out from our hearts day by day in the energy of our thinking and acting! Thus, through the sins of our youth, the power of the flesh is exerted against us, as a second creative principle of evil, aiding the malice of the Devil; Satan from without,—and our hearts from within, not passive merely and kindled by temptation, but *devising* evil, and speaking hard things against God with articulate voice, whether we will or not! Thus do past years rise up against us in present offences; gross inconsistencies show themselves in our character; and much need have we continually to implore God to forgive us our past transgressions, which still live in spite of our repentance, and act of themselves vigorously against our better mind, feebly influenced by that younger principle of faith, by which we fight against them.

3. Further, consider how many sins are involved in our obedience, I may say from the mere necessity of the case; that is, from not having that more vigorous and clear-sighted faith which would enable us accurately to discern and closely to follow the way of life. The case of the Jews will exemplify what I mean. There were points of God's perfect Law which were not urged upon their acceptance, because it was foreseen that they would not be able to receive them as they really should be received, or to bring them home practically to their minds, and obey them simply and truly. We, Christians with the same evil hearts as the Jews had, and most of us as unformed in holy practice, have, nevertheless, a perfect Law. We are bound to take and use all the precepts of the New Testament, though it stands to reason that many of them are, in matter of fact, quite above

the comprehension of most of us. I am speaking of the actual state of the case, and will not go aside to ask why, or under what circumstances God was pleased to change His mode of dealing with man. But so it is; the Minister of Christ has to teach His sinful people a perfect obedience, and does not know how to set about it, or how to insist on any precept, so as to secure it from being misunderstood and misapplied. He sees men are acting upon low motives and views, and finds it impossible to raise their minds all at once, however clear his statements of the Truth. He feels that their good deeds might be done in a much better manner. There are numberless small circumstances about their mode of doing things, which offend him, as implying poverty of faith, superstition, and contracted carnal notions. He is obliged to leave them to themselves with the hope that they may improve generally, and outgrow their present feebleness; and is often perplexed whether to praise or blame them. So is it with all of us, Ministers as well as people; it is so with the most advanced of Christians while in the body, and God sees it. What a source of continual defilement is here; not an omission merely of what might be added to our obedience, but a cause of positive offence in the Eyes of Eternal Purity! Who is not displeased when a man attempts some great work which is above his powers? and is it an excuse for his miserable performance that the work is above him? Now this is our case; we are bound to serve God with a perfect heart; an exalted work, a work for which our sins disable us. And when we attempt it, necessary as is our endeavour, how miserable must it appear in the eyes of the Angels! how pitiful our exhibition of ourselves; and, withal, how sinful! since did we love God more from the heart, and had we served Him from our youth up, it would not have been with us as it is. Thus our very calling, as creatures, and again as elect children of God, and freemen in the Gospel, is by our sinfulness made our shame; for it puts us upon duties, and again upon the use of privileges, which are above us. We attempt great things with the certainty of failing, and yet the necessity of attempting; and so *while* we attempt, need continual forgiveness for the *failure* of the attempt. We stand before God as the Israelites at the passover of Hezekiali, who *desired* to serve God according to the Law, but could not do so accurately from lack of knowledge; and we can but offer, through our Great High Priest, our sincerity and earnestness instead of exact obedience, as Hezekiah did for them. "The good Lord pardon every one, that *prepareth his heart* to seek God, the Lord God of his fathers, though he be not cleansed according to the purification of the sanctuary;"[3] not performing, that is, the full duties of his calling.

And if such be the deficiencies, even of the established Christian, in his ordinary state, how great must be those of the penitent, who has but lately begun the service of God? or of the young, who are still within the influence of some unbridled imagination, or some domineering passion? or of the heavily depressed spirit, whom Satan binds with the bonds of bodily ailment, or tosses to and fro in the tumult of doubt and indecision? Alas! how is their conscience defiled with the thoughts, nay the words of every hour! and how inexpressibly needful for them to relieve themselves of the evil that reigns upon their heart, by dweling near to God in full assurance of faith, and washing away their guilt in the Expiation which He has appointed!

What I have said is a call upon you, my brethren, in the first place, to daily private prayer. Next, it is a call upon you to join the public services of the Church, not only once a week, but whenever you have the opportunity; knowing well that your Redeemer is especially present where two or three are gathered together. And, further, it is an especial call upon you to attend upon the celebration of the Lord's Supper, in which blessed ordinance we really and truly gain that spiritual life which is the object of our daily prayers. The Body and Blood of Christ give power and efficacy to our daily faith and repentance. Take this view of the Lord's Supper; as the appointed means of obtaining the great blessings you need. The daily prayers of the Christian do but spring from, and are referred back to, his attendance on it. Christ died once, long since: by communicating in His Sacrament, you renew the Lord's death; you bring into the midst of you that Sacrifice which took away the sins of the world; you appropriate the benefit of it, while you eat it under the elements of bread and wine. These outward signs are simply the means of an hidden grace. You do not expect to sustain your animal life without food; be but as rational in spiritual concerns as you are in temporal. Look upon the consecrated elements as *necessary*, under God's blessing, to your continual sanctification; approach them as the salvation of your souls. Why is it more strange that God should work through means for the health of the soul, than that He should ordain them for the preservation of bodily life, as He certainly has done? It is unbelief to think it matters not

[3] 2 Chron. xxx.18, 19.

to your spiritual welfare whether you communicate or not. And it is worse than unbelief, it is utter insensibility and obduracy, not to discern the state of death and corruption into which, when left to yourselves, you are continually falling back. Rather thank God, that whereas you are sinners, instead of His leaving you the mere general promise of life through His Son, which is addressed to all men, He has allowed you to take that promise to yourselves one by one, and thus gives you a humble hope that He has chosen you out of the world unto salvation.

Lastly, I have all along spoken as addressing true Christians, who are walking in the narrow way, and have hope of heaven. But these are the "few." Are there none here present of the "many" who walk in the broad way, and have upon their heads all their sins, from their baptism upwards? Rather, is it not probable that there are persons in this congregation, who, though mixed with the people of God, are really unforgiven, and if they now died, would die in their sins? First, let those who neglect the Holy Communion ask themselves whether this is not their condition; let them reflect whether among the signs by which it is given us to ascertain our state, there can be, to a man's own conscience, a more fearful one than this, that he is omitting what is appointed, as the ordinary means of his salvation. This is a plain test, about which no one can deceive himself. But next, let him have recourse to a more accurate search into his conscience; and ask himself whether (in the words of the text) he "draws near to God with a true heart," i.e. whether in spite of his prayers and religious services, there be not some secret, unresisted lusts within him, which make his devotion a mockery in the sight of God, and leave him in his sins; whether he be not in truth thoughtless, and religious only as far as his friends make him seem so,—or light-minded and shallow in his religion, being ignorant of the depths of his guilt, and resting presumptuously on his own innocence (as he thinks it) and God's mercy;—whether he be not set upon gain, obeying God only so far as *His* service does not interfere with the service of mammon;—whether he be not harsh, evil-tempered,—unforgiving, unpitiful, or high-minded,—self-confident, and secure;—or whether he be not fond of the fashions of this world, which pass away, desirous of the friendship of the great, and of sharing in the refinements of society;—or whether he be not given up to some engrossing pursuit, which indisposes him to the thought of his God and Saviour.

Any *one* deliberate habit of sin incapacitates a man for receiving the gifts of the Gospel. All such states of mind as these are fearful symptoms of the *existence* of some such wilful sin in our hearts; and in proportion as we trace these symptoms in our conduct, so much we dread, lest we be reprobate.

Let us then approach God, all of us confessing that we do not know ourselves; that we are more guilty than we can possibly understand, and can but timidly hope, not confidently determine, that we have true faith. Let us take comfort in our being still in a state of grace, though we have no certain pledge of salvation. Let us beg Him to enlighten us, and comfort us; to forgive us all our sins, teaching us those we do not see, and enabling us to overcome them.

GOD'S COMMANDMENTS NOT GRIEVOUS

"This is the love of God, that we keep His commandments; and His commandments are not grievous."—1 John v.3.

I T must ever be borne in mind, that it is a very great and arduous thing to attain to heaven. "Many are called, few are chosen." "Strait is the gate, and narrow is the way." "Many will seek to enter in, and shall not be able." "If any man come to Me and hate not his father and mother, and wife and children, and brethren and sisters, yea, and his own life also, he cannot be My disciple." [1] On the other hand, it is evident to any one who reads the New Testament with attention, that Christ and His Apostles speak of a religious life as something easy, pleasant, and comfortable. Thus, in the words I have taken for my text:— "This is the love of God, that we keep His commandments; and His commandments are not grievous." In like manner our Saviour says, "Come unto Me . . . and I will give you rest. . . . My yoke is easy, and My burden is light." [2] Solomon, also, in the Old Testament, speaks in the same way of true wisdom:—"Her ways are ways of pleasantness, and all her paths are peace. She is a tree of life to them that lay hold upon her: and happy is every one that retaineth her. . . . When thou liest down, thou shalt not be afraid: yea, thou shalt lie down, and thy sleep shall be sweet." [3] Again, we read in the prophet Micah: "What doth the Lord require of thee, but to do justly, and to love mercy, and to walk humbly with thy God?" [4] as if it were a little and an easy thing so to do.

Now I will attempt to show how it is that these apparently opposite declarations of Christ and His Prophets and Apostles are fulfilled to us. For it may be objected by inconsiderate persons that we are (if I may so express it) *hardly treated*; invited to come to Christ and receive His light yoke, promised an easy and

[1] Matt. xxii.14; vii.14; Luke xiii.24; xiv.26.
[2] Matt. xi.28–30.   [3] Prov. iii.17–24.   [4] Micah vi.8.

happy life, the joy of a good conscience, the assurance of pardon, and the hope of Heaven; and then, on the other hand, when we actually come, as it were, rudely repulsed, frightened, reduced to despair by severe requisitions and evil forebodings. Such is the objection,—not which any *Christian* would bring forward; for we, my brethren, know too much of the love of our Master and only Saviour in dying for us, seriously to entertain for an instant any such complaint. We have at least faith enough for this (and it does not require a great deal), viz. to believe that the Son of God, Jesus Christ, is not "yea and nay, but in Him is yea. For all the promises of God in Him are yea, and in Him Amen, unto the glory of God by us." [5] It is for the very reason that none of us can seriously put the objection, that I allow myself to state it strongly; to urge it being in a Christian's judgment absurd, even more than it would be wicked. But though none of *us* really feel as an objection to the Gospel, this difference of view under which the Gospel is presented to us, or even as a difficulty, still it may be right (in order to our edification) that we should see how these two views of it are reconciled. We must understand *how* it is *both* severe *and* indulgent in its commands, and both arduous and easy in its obedience, in order that we may understand it at all. "His commandments are not grievous," says the text. How is this?—I will give one answer out of several which might be given.

Now it must be admitted, first of all, as matter of fact, that they *are* grievous to the great mass of Christians. I have no wish to disguise a fact which we do not need the Bible to inform us of, but which common experience attests. Doubtless even those common elementary duties, of which the prophet speaks, "doing justly, loving mercy, and walking humbly with our God," are to most men *grievous*.

Accordingly, men of worldly minds, finding the true way of life unpleasant to walk in, have attempted to find out other and easier roads; and have been accustomed to argue, that there must be another way which suits them better than that which religious men walk in, for the very reason that Scripture declares that Christ's commandments are *not* grievous. I mean, you will meet with persons who say, "After all it is not to be supposed that a strict religious life is so necessary as is told us in church; else how should any one be saved? nay, and Christ assures us His yoke is easy. Doubtless we shall fare well enough, though we are not so earnest in the observance of our duties as

[5] 2 Cor. i.19, 20.

we might be; though we are not regular in our attendance at public worship; though we do not honour Christ's ministers and reverence His Church as much as some men do; though we do not labour to know God's will, to deny ourselves, and to live to His glory, as entirely as the strict letter of Scripture enjoins." Some men have gone so far as boldly to say, "God will not condemn a man merely for taking a little pleasure;" by which they mean, leading an irreligious and profligate life. And many there are who virtually maintain that we may live to the world, so that we do so decently, and yet live to God; arguing that this world's blessings are given us by God, and therefore may lawfully he used;—that to use lawfully is to use moderately and thankfully;—that it is wrong to take gloomy views, and right to be innocently cheerful, and so on; which is all very true thus stated, did they not apply it unfairly, and call that use of the world *moderate* and *innocent*, which the Apostles would call being *conformed* to the world, and serving mammon instead of God.

And thus, before showing you what is meant by Christ's commandments not being grievous, I have said what is not meant by it. It is *not* meant that Christ dispenses with strict religious obedience; the whole language of Scripture is against such a notion. "Whosoever shall break one of these least commandments, and shall teach men so, he shall be called the least in the kingdom of heaven." [6] "Whosoever shall keep the whole law, and yet offend in one point, he is guilty of all." [7] Whatever is meant by Christ's yoke being easy, Christ does not encourage sin. And again, whatever is meant, still I repeat, as a matter of fact, most men find it *not* easy. So far must not be disputed. Now then let us proceed, in spite of this admission, to consider how He fulfils His engagements to us, that His ways are ways of pleasantness.

1. Now, supposing some superior promised you any gift in a particular way, and you did not follow his directions, would *he* have broken his promise, or you have voluntarily excluded yourselves from the advantage? Evidently you would have brought about your own loss; you might, indeed, think his offer not worth accepting, burdened (as it was) with a condition annexed to it, still you could not in any propriety say that *he* failed in his engagement. Now when Scripture promises us that its commandments shall be easy, it couples the promise with the injunction that we should seek God *early*. "I love them that love Me, and those that seek Me *early* shall find Me." [8] Again: "Re-

[6] Matt. v. 19.   [7] James ii. 10.   [8] Prov. viii. 17.

member now thy Creator in the days of thy youth."[9] These are Solomon's words; and if you require our Lord's own authority, attend to His direction about the children: "Suffer the little children to come unto Me, and forbid them not, for of *such* is the kingdom of God."[10] Youth is the time of His covenant with us, when He first gives us His Spirit; first giving *then*, that we may *then* forthwith begin our return of obedience to Him; not then giving it that we may delay our thank-offering for twenty, thirty, or fifty years! Now it is obvious that obedience to God's commandments is ever easy, and almost without effort to those who begin to serve Him from the beginning of their days; whereas those who wait a while, find it grievous in proportion to their delay.

For consider how gently God leads us on in our early years, and how very gradually He opens upon us the complicated duties of life. A child at first has hardly any thing to do but to obey his parents; of God he knows just as much as they are able to tell him, and he is not equal to many thoughts either about Him or about the world. He is almost passive in their hands who gave him life; and, though he has those latent instincts about good and evil, truth and falsehood, which all men have, he does not know enough, he has not had experience enough from the contact of external objects, to elicit into form and action those innate principles of conscience, or to make himself conscious of the existence of them.

And while on the one hand His range of duty is very confined, observe how he is assisted in performing it. First, he has no bad habits to hinder the suggestions of his conscience: indolence, pride, ill-temper, do not then act as they afterwards act, when the mind has accustomed itself to disobedience, as stubborn, deep-seated impediments in the way of duty. To obey requires an effort, of course; but an effort like the bodily effort of the child's rising from the ground, when he has fallen on it; not the effort of shaking off drowsy sleep; not the effort (far less) of violent bodily exertion in a time of sickness and long weakness: and the first effort made, obedience on a second trial will be easier than before, till at length it will be easier to obey than not to obey. A good habit will be formed, where otherwise a bad habit would have been formed. Thus the child, we are supposing, would begin to have a character; no longer influenced by every temptation to anger, discontent, fear, and obstinacy, in the same way as before; but with something of firm principle in

[9] Eccles. xii.1.   [10] Mark x.14.

his heart to repel them in a defensive way, as a shield repels darts. In the mean time the circle of his duties would enlarge; and, though for a time the issue of his trial would be doubtful to those who (as the Angels) could see it, yet, should he, as a child, consistently pursue this easy course for a few years, it may be, his ultimate salvation would be actually secured, and might be predicted by those who could see his heart, though he would not know it himself. Doubtless new trials would come on him; bad passions, which he had not formed a conception of, would assail him; but a soul thus born of God, in St. John's words, "sinneth not; but he that is begotten of God keepeth himself, and that wicked one toucheth him not." [11] "His seed remaineth in him: and he cannot sin, because he is born of God." [12] And so he would grow up to man's estate, his duties at length attaining their full range, and his soul being completed in all its parts for the due performance of them. This *might* be the blessed condition of every one of us, did we but follow from infancy what we know to be right; and in Christ's early life (if we may dare to speak of Him in connexion with ourselves), it *was* fulfilled while He increased day by day sinlessly in wisdom as in stature, and in favour with God and man. But my present object of speaking of this gradual growth of holiness in the soul, is (not to show what we might be, had we the heart to obey God), but to show *how easy* obedience would in that case be to us; consisting, as it would, in no irksome ceremonies, no painful bodily discipline, but in the free-will offerings of the *heart*, of the heart which had been gradually, and by very slight occasional efforts, trained to love what God and our conscience approve.

Thus Christ's commandments, viewed *as He enjoins them on us*, are not grievous. They *would* be grievous if put upon us all at once; but they are *not* heaped on us, according to *His* order of dispensing them, which goes upon an harmonious and considerate plan; by little and little, first one duty, then another, then both, and so on. Moreover, they come upon us, while the safeguard of virtuous principle is forming naturally and gradually in our minds by our very deeds of obedience, and is following them as their reward. Now, if men will not take their duties in Christ's order, but are determined to delay obedience, with the intention of setting about their duty some day or other, and then making up for past time, is it wonderful that they find it grievous and difficult to perform? that they are overwhelmed with the arrears of their great work, that they are entangled

[11] 1 John v.18.   [12] 1 John iii.9.

and stumble amid the intricacies of the Divine system which has progressively enlarged upon them? And is Christ under obligation to stop that system, to recast His providence, to take these men out of their due place in the Church, to save them from the wheels that are crushing them, and to put them back again into some simple and more childish state of trial, where (though they cannot have less to unlearn) they, at least, may for a time have less to do?

2. All this being granted, it still may be objected, since (as I have allowed) the commandments of God *are* grievous to the generality of men, where is the use of saying what men *ought* to be, when we know what they *are*? and how is it fulfilling a promise that His commandments *shall not* be grievous, by informing us that they *ought not* to be? It is one thing to say that the Law is in itself holy, just, and good, and quite a different thing to declare it is not *grievous* to sinful man.

In answering this question, I fully admit that our Saviour spoke of man *as he is*, as a sinner, when He said His yoke should be easy to him. Certainly, He came not to call righteous men, but sinners. Doubtless we are in a very different state from that of Adam before his fall; and doubtless, in spite of this, St. John says that even to fallen man His commandments are not grievous. On the other hand, I grant, that if man *cannot* obey God, obedience *must* be grievous; and I grant too (of course) that man by nature *cannot* obey God. But observe, nothing has here been said, nor by St. John in the text, of man as by nature born in sin; but of man as a *child of grace*, as Christ's purchased possession, who goes *before* us with His mercy, puts the blessing first, and then adds the command; regenerates us, and *then* bids us obey. Christ bids us do nothing that we cannot do. He repairs the fault of our nature, even before it manifests itself in act. He cleanses us from original sin, and rescues us from the wrath of God by the sacrament of baptism. He gives us the gift of His Spirit, and then He says, "What doth the Lord require of thee, but to do justly, and to love mercy, and to walk humbly with thy God?" and is *this* grievous?

When, then, men allege their bad nature as an excuse for their *dislike of* God's commandments, if, indeed, they are heathens, let them be heard, and an answer may be given to them even as such. But with heathens we are not now concerned. These men make their complaint as *Christians*, and as Christians they are most unreasonable in making it; God having provided a remedy for their natural incapacity in the gift of His Spirit. Hear St. Paul's words; "If through the offence of one many be dead, much more the grace of God, and the gift by grace, which is by one man, Jesus Christ, hath abounded unto many. . . . Where sin abounded, grace did much more abound: that as sin hath reigned unto death, even so might grace reign through righteousness unto eternal life, by Jesus Christ our Lord." [13]

And there *are* persons, let it never be forgotten, who have so followed God's leading providence from their youth up, that to them His commandments not only are not grievous, but never have been: and that there *are* such, is the condemnation of all who are not such. They have been brought up "in the nurture and admonition of the Lord;" [14] and they now live in the love and "the peace of God, which passeth all understanding." [15] Such are they whom our Saviour speaks of, as "just persons, which need no repentance." [16] Not that they will give that account of themselves, for they are full well conscious in their own hearts of sins innumerable, and habitual infirmity. Still, in spite of stumblings and falls in their spiritual course, they have on the whole persevered. As children they served God on the whole; they disobeyed, but they recovered their lost ground; they sought God and were accepted. Perhaps their young faith gave way for a time altogether; but even then they contrived with keen repentance, and strong disgust at sin, and earnest prayers, to make up for lost time, and keep pace with the course of God's providence. Thus they have *walked* with God, not indeed step by step with Him; never before Him, often loitering, stumbling, falling to sleep; yet in turn starting and "*making haste to keep His commandments,*" "running, and prolonging not the time." Thus they proceed, not, however, of themselves, but as upheld by His right hand, and guiding their steps by His Word; and though they have nothing to boast of, and know their own unworthiness, still they are witnesses of Christ to all men, as showing what man *can* become, and what all Christians ought to be; and at the last day, being found meet for the inheritance of the saints in light, they "condemn the world," as Noah did and become "heirs of the righteousness which is by faith," according to the saying, "This is the victory that overcometh the world, even our faith." [17]

And now to what do the remarks I have been making tend, but to this?—to humble every one of us. For, however faithfully we have obeyed God, and however early we began to do so, surely we might have begun sooner than we did, and might

[13] Rom. v.15–21.   [14] Eph. vi.4.   [15] Phil. iv.7.
[16] Luke xv.7.   [17] 1 John v.4.

have served Him more heartily. We cannot but be conscious of this. Individuals among us may be more or less guilty, as the case may be; but the best and worst among us here assembled, may well unite themselves together so far as this, to confess they have "erred and strayed from God's ways like lost sheep," "have followed *too much* the devices and desires of their own hearts," have "no health" in themselves as being "miserable offenders." Some of us may be nearer Heaven, some further from it; some may have a good hope of salvation, and others, (God forbid! but it may be), others *no* present hope. Still let us unite now as one body in confessing (to the better part of us such confession will be the more welcome, and to the worst it is the more needful), in confessing ourselves sinners, deserving God's anger, and having no hope except "according to His promises declared unto mankind in Christ Jesus our Lord." He who first generated us and then gave His commandments, and then was so ungratefully deserted by us, He again it is that must pardon and quicken us after our accumulated guilt, if we are to be pardoned. Let us then trace back in memory (as far as we can) our early years; what we were when five years old, when ten, when fifteen, when twenty! what our state would have been as far as we can guess it, had God taken us to our account at any age before the present. I will not ask how it would go with us, were we *now* taken; we will suppose the best.

Let each of us (I say) reflect upon his own most gross and persevering neglect of God at various seasons of his past life. How considerate He has been to us! How did He shield us from temptation! how did He open His will gradually upon us, as we might be able to bear it![18] how has He done all things well, so that the spiritual work might go on calmly, safely, surely! How did He lead us on, duty by duty, as if step by step upwards, by the easy rounds of that ladder whose top reaches to Heaven? Yet how did we thrust ourselves into temptation! How did we refuse to come to Him that we might have life! how did we daringly sin against light! And what was the consequence? that our work grew beyond our strength; or rather that our strength grew less as our duties increased; till at length we gave up obedience in despair. And yet then He still tarried and was merciful unto us; He turned and looked upon us to bring us into repentance; and we for a while were moved. Yet, even then our wayward hearts could not keep up to their own resolves: letting go again the heat which Christ gave them, as if made of stone, and

[18] 1 Cor. x.13.

not of living flesh. What could have been done more to His vineyard, that He hath not done in it?[19] "O My people (He seems to say to us), what have I done unto thee? and wherein have I weaned thee? testify against Me. I brought thee up out of the land of Egypt, and redeemed thee out of the house of servants; . . . what doth the Lord require of thee, but justice, mercy, and humbleness of mind?"[20] He hath showed us what is good. He has borne and carried us in His bosom, "lest at any time we should dash our foot against a stone."[21] He shed His Holy Spirit upon us that we might love Him. And "*this* is the love of God, that we keep His commandments, and His commandments are not grievous." Why, then, have they been grievous to us? Why have we erred from His ways, and hardened our hearts from His fear? Why do we this day stand ashamed, yea, even confounded, because we bear the reproach of our youth?

Let us then turn to the Lord, while yet we may. Difficult it will be in proportion to the distance we have departed from Him. Since every one might have done more than he has done, every one has suffered losses he never can make up. We have made His commands grievous to us: we must bear it; let us not attempt to explain them away because they *are* grievous. We never can wash out the stains of sin. God may forgive, but the sin has had its work, and its memento is set up in the soul. God sees it there. Earnest obedience and prayer will gradually remove it. Still, what miserable loss of time is it, in our brief life, to be merely undoing (as has become necessary) the evil which we have done, instead of going on to perfection! If by God's grace we shall be able in a measure to sanctify ourselves in spite of our former sins, yet how much more *should* we have attained, had we always been engaged in His service!

These are bitter and humbling thoughts, but they are good thoughts if they lead us to repentance. And this leads me to one more observation, with which I conclude.

If any one who hears me is at present moved by what I have said, and feels the remorse and shame of a bad conscience, and forms any sudden good resolution, let him take heed to follow it up at once by *acting upon* it. I earnestly beseech him so to do. For this reason;—because if he does not, he is beginning a habit of inattention and insensibility. God moves us in order to make the beginning of duty *easy*. If we do not attend, He *ceases* to move us. Any of you, my brethren, who will not take advantage

---

[19] Is. v.4.   [20] Micah vi.3–8.   [21] Ps. xci.12.

of this considerate providence, if you will not turn to God now with a *warm* heart, you will hereafter be obliged to do so (if you do so at all) *with a cold heart*;—which is much harder. God keep you from this!

THE RELIGIOUS USE OF
EXCITED FEELINGS

*"The man out of whom the devils were departed besought Him that
he might be with Him; but Jesus sent him away, saying,
Return to thine own house, and show how great things God hath
done unto thee."*—Luke viii.38, 39.

IT was very natural in the man whom our Lord had set free
from this dreadful visitation, to wish to continue with Him.
Doubtless his mind was transported with joy and gratitude;
whatever consciousness he might possess of his real wretchedness while the devils tormented him, now at least, on recovering his reason, he would understand that he had been in a very
miserable state, and he would feel all the lightness of spirits and
activity of mind, which attend any release from suffering or
constraint. Under these circumstances he would imagine himself to be in a new world; he had found deliverance; and what
was more, a Deliverer too, who stood before him. And whether
from a wish to be ever in His Divine presence, ministering to
Him, or from a fear lest Satan would return, nay, with sevenfold power, did he lose sight of Christ, or from an undefined
notion that all his duties and hopes were now changed, that his
former pursuits were unworthy of him, and that he must follow
up some great undertakings with the new ardour he felt glowing within him;—from one or other, or all of these feelings
combined, he besought our Lord that he might be with Him.
Christ imposed this attendance as a command on others; He
bade, for instance, the young ruler follow Him; but He gives
opposite commands, according to our tempers and likings; He
thwarts us, that He may try our faith. In the case before us He
suffered not, what at other times He had bidden. "Return to
thine own house," He said, or as it is in St. Mark's Gospel, "Go
home to thy friends, and tell them how great things the Lord
hath done for thee, and hath had compassion on thee." [1] He

---

[1] Mark v.19.

directed the current of his newly-awakened feelings into another channel; as if He said, "Lovest thou Me? this do; return
home to your old occupations and pursuits. You did them ill
before, you lived to the world; do them well now, live to Me.
Do your duties, little as well as great, heartily for My sake; go
among your friends; show them what God hath done for thee;
be an example to them, and teach them."[2] And further, as He
said on another occasion, " Show thyself to the priest, and offer
the gift that Moses commanded, for a testimony unto them,"[3]
—show forth that greater light and truer love which you now
possess in a conscientious, consistent obedience to all the ordinances and rites of your religion.

Now from this account of the restored demoniac, his request,
and our Lord's denial of it, a lesson may be drawn for the use of
those who, having neglected religion in early youth, at length
begin to have serious thoughts, try to repent, and wish to serve
God better than hitherto, though they do not know how to set
about it. We know that God's commandments are pleasant, and
"rejoice the heart," if we accept them in the order and manner
in which He puts them upon us; that Christ's yoke, as He has
promised, is (on the whole) very easy, if we submit to it
betimes; that the practice of religion is full of comfort to those
who, being first baptized with the Spirit of grace, receive
thankfully His influences as their minds open, inasmuch as they
are gradually and almost without sensible effort on their part,
imbued in all their heart, soul, and strength, with that true
heavenly life which will last for ever.

But here the question meets us, "But what are those to do
who *have* neglected to remember their Creator in the days of
their youth, and so have lost all claim on Christ's promise, that
His yoke shall be easy, and His commandments not grievous?" I
answer, that of course they must not be surprised if obedience is
with them a laborious up-hill work all their days; nay, as having
been "once enlightened, and partaken of the Holy Ghost" in
baptism, they would have no right to complain even though "it
were impossible for them to renew themselves again unto repentance." But God is more merciful than this just severity;
merciful not only above our deservings, but even above His
own promises. Even for those who have neglected Him when
young, He has found (if they will avail themselves of it) some
sort of remedy of the difficulties in the way of obedience which
they have brought upon themselves by sinning; and what this

---

[2] Col. iii.17.   [3] Matt. viii.4.

remedy is, and how it is to be used, I proceed to describe in connexion with the account in the text.

The help I speak of is the excited feeling with which repentance is at first attended. True it is, that all the passionate emotion, or fine sensibility, which ever man displayed, will never by itself make us change our ways, and do our duty. Impassioned thoughts, high aspirations, sublime imaginings, have no strength in them. They can no more make a man obey consistently, than they can move mountains. If any man truly repent, it must be in consequence, not of these, but of a settled conviction of his guilt, and a deliberate resolution to leave his sins and serve God. Conscience, and Reason in subjection to Conscience, *these* are those powerful instruments (under grace) which change a man. But you will observe, that though Conscience and Reason lead us to resolve on and to attempt a new life, they cannot at once make us *love* it. It is long practice and habit which make us love religion; and in the beginning, obedience, doubtless, is very grievous to habitual sinners. Here then is the use of those earnest, ardent feelings of which I just now spoke, and which attend on the first exercise of Conscience and Reason,—to take away from the *beginnings* of obedience its *grievousness*, to give us an impulse which may carry us over the first obstacles, and send us on our way rejoicing. Not as if all this excitement of mind were to last (which cannot be), but it will do its office in thus setting us off; and then will leave us to the more sober and higher comfort resulting from that real *love* for religion, which obedience itself will have by that time begun to form in us, and will gradually go on to perfect.

Now it is well to understand this fully, for it is often mistaken. When sinners at length are led to think seriously, strong feelings generally precede or attend their reflections about themselves. Some book they have read, some conversation of a friend, some remarks they have heard made in church, or some occurrence or misfortune, rouses them. Or, on the other hand, if in any more calm and deliberate manner they have commenced their self-examination, yet in a little time the very view of their manifold sins, of their guilt, and of their heinous ingratitude to their God and Saviour, breaking upon them, and being new to them, strikes, and astonishes, and then agitates them. Here, then, let them know the *intention* of all this excitement of mind in the order of Divine providence. It will not continue; it arises from the novelty of the view presented to them. As they become accustomed to religious contemplations, it will wear away. It is not religion itself, though it is accidentally connected with it, and may be made a means of leading them into a sound religious course of life. It is graciously intended to be a set-off in their case against the first distastefulness and pain of doing their duty; it must be used as such, or it will be of no use at all, or worse than useless. My brethren, bear this in mind (and I may say this generally,—not confining myself to the excitement which attends repentance,—of all that natural emotion prompting us to do good, which we involuntarily feel on various occasions), it is given you in order that you may find it easy to obey at starting. Therefore obey *promptly*; make use of it whilst it lasts; it waits for no man. Do you feel natural pity towards some case which reasonably demands your charity? or the impulse of generosity in a case where you are called to act a manly self-denying part? Whatever the emotion may be, whether these or any other, do not imagine you will always feel it. Whether you avail yourselves of it or not, still any how you will feel it less and less, and, as life goes on, at last you will not feel such sudden vehement excitement at all. But this is the difference between seizing or letting slip these opportunities;—if you avail yourselves of them for acting, and yield to the impulse so far as conscience tells you to do, you have made a leap (so to say) across a gulf, to which your ordinary strength is not equal; you will have secured the beginning of obedience, and the further steps in the course are (generally speaking) far easier than those which first determine its direction. And so, to return to the case of those who feel any accidental remorse for their sins violently exerting itself in their hearts, I say to them, Do not loiter; go home to your friends, and repent in *deeds* of righteousness and love; hasten to commit yourselves to certain definite *acts* of obedience. Doing is at a far greater distance from intending to do than you at first sight imagine. Join them together while you can; you will be depositing your good feelings into your heart itself by thus making them influence your conduct; and they will "spring up into fruit." This was the conduct of the conscience-stricken Corinthians, as described by St. Paul; who rejoiced "not that they were made *sorry* (not that their feelings merely were moved), but that they sorrowed *to change of mind*. . . . For godly sorrow (he continues) worketh repentance to salvation not to be repented of; but the sorrow of the world worketh death." [4]

But now let us ask, how do men usually conduct themselves in matter of fact, when under visitings of conscience for their

[4] 2 Cor. vii.9, 10.

past sinful lives? They are far from thus acting. They look upon the turbid zeal and feverish devotion which attend their repentance, not as in part the corrupt offspring of their own previously corrupt state of mind, and partly a gracious natural provision, only temporary, to encourage them to set about their reformation, but as the substance and real excellence of religion. They think that to be thus agitated is to be religious; they indulge themselves in these warm feelings for their own sake, resting in them as if they were then engaged in a religious exercise, and boasting of them as if they were an evidence of their own exalted spiritual state; not *using them* (the one only thing they ought to do), using them as an incitement to *deeds* of love, mercy, truth, meekness, holiness. After they have indulged this luxury of feeling for some time, the excitement of course ceases; they do not feel as they did before. This (I have said) might have been anticipated, but they do not understand it so. See then their unsatisfactory state. They have lost an opportunity of overcoming the first difficulties of active obedience, and so of fixing their conduct and character, which may never occur again. This is one great misfortune; but more than this, what a perplexity they have involved themselves in! Their warmth of feeling is gradually dying away. Now they think that in it true religion consists; therefore they believe that they are losing their faith, and falling into sin again.

And this, alas! *is* too often the case; they *do* fall away, for they have no root in themselves. Having neglected to turn their feelings into principles by acting upon them, they have no inward strength to overcome the temptation to live as the world, which continually assails them. Their minds have been acted upon as water by the wind, which raises waves for a time, then ceasing, leaves the water to subside into its former stagnant state. The precious opportunity of improvement has been lost; "and the latter end is worse with them than the beginning." [5]

But let us suppose, that when they first detect this declension (as they consider it), they are alarmed, and look around for a means of recovering themselves. What do they do? Do they at once begin those practices of lowly obedience which alone can prove them to be Christ's at the last day? such as the government of their tempers, the regulation of their time, self-denying charity, truth-telling sobriety. Far from it; they despise this plain obedience to God as a mere unenlightened morality, as they call it, and they seek for potent stimulants to sustain their

[5] 2 Pet. ii.20.

minds in that state of excitement which they have been taught to consider the essence of a religious life, and which they cannot produce by the means which before excited them. They have recourse to new doctrines, or follow strange teachers, in order that they may dream on in this their artificial devotion, and may avoid that conviction which is likely sooner or later to burst upon them, that emotion and passion are in our power indeed to repress, but not to *excite*; that there is a limit to the tumults and swellings of the heart, foster them as we will; and, when that time comes, the poor, mis-used soul is left exhausted and resourceless. Instances are not rare in the world of that fearful, ultimate state of hard-heartedness which then succeeds; when the miserable sinner believes indeed as the devils may, yet not even with the devils' trembling, but sins on without fear.

Others, again, there are, who, when their feelings fall off in strength and fervency, are led to despond; and so are brought down to fear and bondage, when they might have been rejoicing in cheerful obedience. These are the better sort, who, having something of true religious principle in their hearts, still are misled in part,—so far, that is, as to rest in their feelings as tests of holiness; therefore they are distressed and alarmed at their own tranquillity, which they think a bad sign, and, being dispirited, lose time, others outstripping them in the race.

And others might be mentioned who are led by this same first eagerness and zeal into a different error. The restored sufferer in the text wished to be with Christ. Now it is plain, all those who indulge themselves in the false devotion I have been describing, may be said to be desirous of thus keeping themselves in Christ's immediate sight, instead of returning to their own home, as He would have them, that is, to the common duties of life: and they do this, some from weakness of faith, as if He could not bless them, and keep them in the way of grace, though they pursued their worldly callings; others from an ill-directed love of Him. But there are others, I say, who, when they are awakened to a sense of religion, forthwith despise their former condition altogether, as beneath them; and think that they are now called to some high and singular office in the Church. These mistake their duty as those already described neglect it; they do not waste their time in mere good thoughts and good words, as the others, but they are impetuously led on to *wrong acts*, and that from the influence of those same strong emotions which they have not learned to use aright or direct to their proper end. But to speak of these now at any length would be beside my subject.

To conclude;—let me repeat and urge upon you, my brethren, the lesson which I have deduced from the narrative of which the text forms part. Your Saviour calls you from infancy to serve Him, and has arranged all things well, so that His service shall be perfect freedom. Blessed above all men are they who heard His call then, and served Him day by day, as their strength to obey increased. But further, are you conscious that you have more or less neglected this gracious opportunity, and suffered yourselves to be tormented by Satan? See, He calls you a second time; He calls you by your roused affections once and again, ere He leave you finally. He brings you back for the time (as it were) to a second youth by the urgent persuasions of excited fear, gratitude, love, and hope. He again places you for an instant in that early, unformed state of nature when habit and character were not. He takes you out of yourselves, robbing sin for a season of its in-dwelling hold upon you. Let not those visitings pass away "as the morning cloud and the early dew." [6] Surely, you must still have occasional compunctions of conscience for your neglect of Him. Your sin stares you in the face; your ingratitude to God affects you. Follow on to know the Lord, and to secure His favour by *acting* upon these impulses; by them He pleads with you, as well as by your conscience; they are the instruments of His spirit, stirring you up to seek your true peace. Nor be surprised, though you obey them, that they die away; they have done their office, and if they die, it is but as blossom changes into the fruit, which is far better. They *must* die. Perhaps you will have to labour in darkness afterwards, out of your Saviour's sight, in the home of your own thoughts, surrounded by sights of this world, and showing forth His praise among those who are cold-hearted. Still be quite sure that resolute, consistent obedience, though unattended with high transport and warm emotion, is far more acceptable to Him than all those passionate longings to live in His sight, which look more like religion to the uninstructed. At the very best these latter are but the graceful beginnings of obedience, graceful and becoming in children but in grown spiritual men indecorous, as the sports of boyhood would seem in advanced years. Learn to live by faith, which is a calm, deliberate, rational principle, full of peace and comfort, and sees Christ, and rejoices in Him, though sent away from His presence to labour in the world. You will have your reward. He will "see you again, and your heart shall rejoice, and your joy no man taketh from you."

[6] Hosea vi.4.

PROFESSION WITHOUT PRACTICE

"When there were gathered together an innumerable multitude of people, insomuch that they trode one upon another, He began to say unto His disciples first of all, Beware ye of the leaven of the Pharisees, which is hypocrisy."—Luke xii.1.

HYPOCRISY is a serious word. We are accustomed to consider the hypocrite as a hateful, despicable character, and an uncommon one. How is it, then, that our Blessed Lord, when surrounded by an innumerable multitude, began *first of all*, to warn His disciples against hypocrisy, as though they were in especial danger of becoming like those base deceivers, the Pharisees? Thus an instructive subject is opened to our consideration, which I will now pursue.

I say, we are accustomed to consider the hypocrite as a character of excessive wickedness, and of very rare occurrence. That hypocrisy is a great wickedness need not be questioned; but that it is an uncommon sin, is not true, as a little examination will show us. For what is a hypocrite? We are apt to understand by a hypocrite, one who makes a profession of religion for secret ends, without practising what he professes; who is malevolent, covetous, or profligate, while he assumes an outward sanctity in his words and conduct, and who does so deliberately and without remorse, deceiving others, and not at all self-deceived. Such a man, truly, would be a portent, for he seems to disbelieve the existence of a God who sees the heart. I will not deny that in some ages, nay, in all ages, a few such men have existed. But this is not what our Saviour seems to have meant by a hypocrite, nor were the Pharisees such.

The Pharisees, it is true, said one thing and did another; but they were not aware that they were thus inconsistent; they deceived *themselves* as well as others. Indeed, it is not in human nature to deceive others for any long time, without in a measure deceiving ourselves also. And in most cases we contrive to deceive ourselves as much as we deceive others. The Pharisees boasted they were Abraham's children, not at all understanding, not knowing what was implied in the term. They were not really included under the blessing given to Abraham, and they wished the world to believe they were; but then they also themselves *thought* that they were, or, at least, with whatever misgivings, they were, on the whole, persuaded of it. They had deceived themselves as well as the world; and therefore our Lord sets before them the great and plain truth, which, simple as it was, they had forgotten. "If ye were Abraham's children, ye would do the works of Abraham." [1]

This truth, I say, they had *forgotten*;—for doubtless, they once knew it. There was a time doubtless, when in some measure they knew themselves, and what they were doing. When they began (each of them in his turn) to deceive the people, they were *not*, at the moment, *self*-deceived. But by degrees they forgot,—because they did not care to retain it in their knowledge,—they forgot that to be blessed like Abraham, they must be holy like Abraham; that outward ceremonies avail nothing without inward purity, that their thoughts and motives must be heavenly. Part of their duty they altogether ceased to know; another part they might still know indeed, but did not value as they ought. They became ignorant of their own spiritual condition; it did not come home to them, that they were supremely influenced by worldly objects; that zeal for God's service was but a secondary principle in their conduct, and that they loved the praise of men better than God's praise. They went on merely talking of religion, of heaven and hell, the blessed and the reprobate, till their discourses became but words of course in their mouths, with no true meaning attached to them; and they either did not read Holy Scripture at all, or read it without earnestness and watchfulness to get at its real sense. Accordingly, they were scrupulously careful of paying tithe even in the least matters, of mint, anise, and cummin, while they omitted the weightier matters of the Law, judgment, mercy, and faith; and on this account our Lord calls them "*blind* guides,"—not bold impious deceivers, who *knew* that they were false guides, but *blind*. [2] Again, they were *blind*, in thinking that, had they lived in their fathers' days, they would not have killed the prophets as their fathers did. They did not know themselves; they had unawares deceived themselves as well as the people. Ignorance of their own ignorance was their punishment and the evidence of their sin. "If ye were blind," our Saviour says to them, if you were simply blind, and conscious you were so, and

[1] John viii.39.   [2] Matt. xxiii.24.; Luke xi.39–52.

distressed at it, "ye should have no sin; but now ye say, We
see,"—they did not even know their blindness—"therefore
your sin remaineth." [3]

This then is hypocrisy;—not simply for a man to deceive others, knowing all the while that he *is* deceiving them, but to deceive himself *and* others at the same time, to aim at their praise
by a religious profession, without perceiving that he loves their
praise more than the praise of God, and that he is professing far
more than he practises. And if this be the true Scripture meaning of the word, we have some insight (as it appears) into the
reasons which induced our Divine Teacher to warn His Disciples in so marked a way against hypocrisy. An innumerable
multitude was thronging Him, and His disciples were around
Him. Twelve of them had been appointed to minister to Him as
His especial friends. Other seventy had been sent out from Him
with miraculous gifts; and, on their return, had with triumph
told of their own wonderful doings. All of them had been addressed by Him as the salt of the earth, the light of the world,
the children of His kingdom. *They* were mediators between
Him and the people at large, introducing to His notice the sick
and heavy-laden. And now they stood by Him, partaking in His
popularity, perhaps glorying in their connexion with the
Christ, and pleased to be gazed upon by the impatient crowd.
Then it was that, instead of addressing the multitude, He spoke
first of all to His disciples, saying, "Beware of the leaven of the
Pharisees, which is hypocrisy;" as if He had said, "What is the
chief sin of My enemies and persecutors? not that they openly
deny God, but that they love a profession of religion for the
sake of the praise of men that follows it. They like to contrast
themselves with other men; they pride themselves on being a
little flock, to whom life is secured in the midst of reprobates;
they like to stand and be admired amid their religious performances, and think to be saved, not by their own personal holiness, but by the faith of their father Abraham. All this delusion
may come upon you also, if you forget that you are hereafter to
be tried one by one at God's judgment-seat, according to your
works. At present, indeed, you are invested in My greatness,
and have the credit of My teaching and holiness: but 'there is
nothing covered that shall not be revealed, neither hid, that
shall not be known,' at the last day."

This warning against hypocrisy becomes still more needful
and impressive, from the greatness of the Christian privileges as

[3] John ix.41. *Vide* James i.22.

contrasted with the Jewish. The Pharisees boasted they were Abraham's children; we have the infinitely higher blessing which fellowship with Christ imparts. In our infancy we have all been gifted with the most awful and glorious titles, as children of God, members of Christ, and heirs of the kingdom of heaven. We have been honoured with the grant of spiritual influences, which have overshadowed and rested upon us, making our very bodies temples of God; and when we came to years of discretion, we were admitted to the mystery of a heavenly communication of the Body and Blood of Christ. What is more likely, considering our perverse nature, than that we should neglect the duties, while we wish to retain the privileges of our Christian profession? Our Lord has sorrowfully foretold in His parables what was to happen in His Church; for instance, when He compared it to a net which gathered of every kind, but was not inspected till the end, and then emptied of its various contents, good and bad. Till the day of visitation the visible Church will ever be full of such hypocrites as I have described, who live on under her shadow, enjoying the name of Christian, and vainly fancying they will partake its ultimate blessedness.

Perhaps, however, it will be granted that there are vast numbers in the Christian world thus professing without adequately practising; and yet denied, that such a case is enough to constitute a hypocrite in the Scripture sense of the word; as if a hypocrite were one who professes himself to be what he is not, *with some bad motive*. It may be urged that the Pharisees had an *end* in what they did, which careless and formal Christians have not. But consider for a moment; what was the motive which urged the Pharisees to their hypocrisy? surely that they might be seen of men, have glory of men.[4] This is our Lord's own account of them. Now who will say that the esteem and fear of the world's judgment, and the expectation of worldly advantages, do not at present most powerfully influence the generality of men in their profession of Christianity? so much so, that it is a hard matter, and is thought a great and noble act for men who live in the public world to do what they believe to be their duty to God, in a straightforward way, should the opinion of society about it happen to run counter to them. Indeed, there hardly has been a time since the Apostles' day, in which men were more likely than in this age to do their good deeds to be seen of men, to lay out for human praise, and therefore to shape their actions by the world's rule rather than God's will. We ought to

[4] Matt. vi.2, 5.

be very suspicious, every one of us, of the soundness of our faith and virtue. Let us consider whether we should act as strictly as we now do, were the eyes of our acquaintance and neighbours withdrawn from us. Not that a regard to the opinion of others is a bad motive; in subordination to the fear of God's judgment, it is innocent and allowable, and in many cases a duty to admit it; and the opportunity of doing so is a gracious gift given from God to lead us forward in the right way. But when we *prefer* man's fallible judgment to God's unerring command, then it is we are wrong,—and in two ways; both *because* we prefer it, and because, being fallible, it will mislead us; and what I am asking you, my brethren, is, not whether you merely regard man's opinion of you (which you ought to do), but whether you set it before God's judgment, which you assuredly should not do, and which if you do, you are like the Pharisees, so far as to be hypocrites, though you may not go so far as they did in their hollow self-deceiving ways.

1. That even decently conducted Christians are most extensively and fearfully ruled by the opinion of society about them, instead of living by faith in the unseen God, is proved to my mind by the following circumstance;—that according as their rank in life makes men independent of the judgment of others, so the profession of regularity and strictness is given up. There are two classes of men who are withdrawn from the judgment of the community; those who are above it, and those who are below it;—the poorest class of all, which has no thought of maintaining itself by its own exertions, and has lost shame; and what is called (to use a word of this world) high fashionable society, by which I mean not the rich necessarily, but those among the rich and noble who throw themselves out of the pale of the community, break the ties which attach them to others, whether above or below themselves, and then live to themselves and each other, their ordinary doings being unseen by the world at large. Now since it happens that these two ranks, the outlaws, as they may be called, of public opinion, are (to speak generally) the most openly and daringly profligate in their conduct, how much may be thence inferred about the influence of a mere love of reputation in keeping us *all* in the right way! It is plain, as a matter of fact, that the great mass of men are protected from gross sin by the forms of society. The received laws of propriety and decency, the prospect of a loss of character, stand as sentinels, giving the alarm, long before their *Christian* principles have time to act. But among the poorest and rudest class, on the contrary, such artificial

safeguards against crime are unknown; and (observe, I say) it is among them and that other class I have mentioned, that vice and crime are most frequent. Are we, *therefore*, better than they? Scarcely. Doubtless their temptations are greater, which alone prevents our boasting over them; but, besides, do we not rather gain from the sight of their more scandalous sins a grave lesson and an urgent warning for ourselves, a call on us for honest self-examination? for we are of the same nature, with like passions with them; we may be better than they, but our mere seeming so is no proof that we are. The question is, whether, in spite of our greater apparent virtue, we should not fall like them, if the restraint of society were withdrawn; i.e. whether we are not in the main hypocrites like the Pharisees, professing to honour God, while we honour Him only so far as men require it of us?

2. Another test of being like or unlike the Pharisees may be mentioned. Our Lord warns us against hypocrisy in three respects,—in doing our alms, in praying, and in fasting. "When thou doest thine alms, do not sound a trumpet before thee, as the hypocrites do in the synagogues and in the streets, that they may have glory of men. . . . When thou prayest thou shalt not be as the hypocrites are for they love to pray standing in the synagogues and in the corners of the streets, that they may be seen of men. . . . When ye fast, be not, as the hypocrites, of a sad countenance, for they disfigure their faces, that they may appear unto men to fast."[5] Here let us ask ourselves, first about our alms, whether we be not like the hypocrites. Doubtless some of our charity must be public, for the very mentioning our name encourages others to follow our example. Still I ask, is much of our charity also *private*? is as much private as is public? I will not ask whether *much more* is done in secret than is done before men, though this, if possible, ought to be the case. But at least, if we think in the first place of our public charities, and only in the second of the duty of private alms-giving, are we not plainly like the hypocritical Pharisees?

The manner of our *prayers* will supply us with a still stronger test. We are here assembled in worship. It is well. Have we really been praying as well as seeming to pray? have our minds been actively employed in trying to form in us the difficult habit of prayer? Further, are we as regular in praying in our closet to our Father which is in secret, as in public?[6] Do we feel any great remorse in omitting our morning and evening

---

[5] Matt. vi.2–16.   [6] Matt. vi.6.

prayers, in saying them hastily and irreverently? And yet should not we feel excessive pain and shame, and rightly, at the thought of having committed any *open* impropriety in church? Should we, for instance, be betrayed into laughter or other light conduct during the service, should we not feel most acutely ashamed of ourselves, and consider we had disgraced ourselves, notwithstanding our habit of altogether forgetting the next moment any sinful carelessness at prayer in our closet? Is not this to be as the Pharisees?

Take, again, the case of fasting. Alas! most of us, I fear, do not think at all of fasting. We do not even let it enter our thoughts, nor debate with ourselves, whether or not it be needful or suitable for us to fast, or in any way mortify our flesh. Well, this is *one* neglect of Christ's words. But again, neither do we disfigure our outward appearance to *seem* to fast, which the Pharisees did. Here we seem to differ from the Pharisees. Yet, in truth, this very apparent difference is a singular confirmation of our real likeness to them. Austerity gained them credit; it would gain us none. It would gain us little more than mockery from the world. The age is changed. In Christ's time the show of fasting made men appear saints in the eyes of the many. See then what we do. We keep up the outward show of almsgiving and public worship,—observances which (it so happens) the world approves. We have dropped the show of fasting, which (it so happens) the world at the present day derides. Are we quite sure that if fasting were in honour, we should not begin to hold fasts, as the Pharisees? Thus we seek the praise of men. But in all this, how are we, in any good measure, following *God's* guidance and promises?

We see, then, how seasonable is our Lord's warning to us, His disciples, first of all, to beware of the leaven of the Pharisees, which is hypocrisy: professing without practising. He warns us against it as *leaven*, as a subtle insinuating evil which will silently spread itself throughout the whole character, if we suffer it. He warns us, His disciples, lovingly considerate for us, lest we make ourselves a scorn and derision to the profane multitude, who throng around to gaze curiously, or malevolently, or selfishly, at His doings. *They* seek Him, not as adoring Him for His miracles' sake, but, if so be that they can obtain any thing from Him, or can please their natural tastes while they profess to honour Him; and in time of trial they desert Him. They make a gain of godliness, or a fashion. So He speaks not to *them*, but to us, His little flock, His Church, to whom it has been His

Father's good pleasure to give the kingdom;[7] and He bids us take heed of falling, as the Pharisees did before us, and like them coming short of our reward. He warns us that the pretence of religion never deceives beyond a little time; that sooner or later, "whatsoever we have spoken in darkness shall be heard in the light, and that which we have spoken in the ear in closets, shall be proclaimed upon the housetops." Even in this world the discovery is often made. A man is brought into temptation of some sort or other, and having no root in himself falls away, and gives occasion to the enemies of the Lord to blaspheme. Nay, this will happen to him without himself being aware of it; for though a man begins to deceive others before he deceives himself, yet he does not deceive them so long as he deceives himself. Their eyes are at length opened to him, while his own continue closed to himself. The world sees through him, detects, and triumphs in detecting, his low motives and secular plans and artifices, while he is but very faintly sensible of them himself, much less has a notion that others clearly see them. And thus he will go on professing the highest principles and feelings, while bad men scorn him, and insult true religion in his person.

Do not think I am speaking of one or two men, when I speak of the scandal which a Christian's inconsistency brings upon his cause. The Christian world, so called, what is it practically, but a witness for Satan rather than a witness for Christ? Rightly understood, doubtless the very disobedience of Christians witnesses for Him who will overcome whenever He is judged. But is there any *antecedent* prejudice against religion so great as that which is occasioned by the lives of its professors? Let us ever remember, that all who follow God with but a half heart, strengthen the hands of His enemies, give cause of exultation to wicked men, perplex inquirers after truth, and bring reproach upon their Saviour's name. It is a known fact, that unbelievers triumphantly maintain that the greater part of the English people is on *their side*; that the disobedience of professing Christians is a proof, that (whatever they say) yet in their hearts they are unbelievers too. This we ourselves perhaps have heard said; and said, not in the heat of argument, or as a satire, but in sober earnestness, from real and full persuasion that it is true; that is, the men who have cast off their Saviour, console themselves with the idea, that their neighbours, though too timid or too indolent openly to do so, yet in secret, or at least in their real character, do the same. And witnessing this general inconsis-

[7] Luke xii.32.

tency, they despise them as unmanly, cowardly, and slavish, and hate religion as the origin of this debasement of mind. "The people who in this country call themselves Christians (says one of these men), with few exceptions, are *not* believers; and every man of sense, whose bigotry has not blinded him, must see that persons who are evidently devoted to *worldly gain*, or *worldly vanities*, or *luxurious enjoyments*, though still preserving a little *decency*, while they *pretend* to believe the infinitely momentous doctrines of Christianity, are performers in a *miserable farce*, which is beneath contempt." Such are the words of an open enemy of Christ; as though he felt *he* dared confess his unbelief, and despised the mean hypocrisy of those around him. His argument, indeed, will not endure the trial of God's judgment at the last day, for no one is an unbeliever but by his own fault. But though no excuse for him, it is their condemnation. What, indeed, will they plead before the Throne of God, when, on the revelation of all hidden deeds, this reviler of religion attributes his unbelief in a measure to the sight of *their* inconsistent conduct? When he mentions this action or that conversation, this violent or worldly conduct, that covetous or unjust transaction, or that self-indulgent life, as partly the occasion of his falling away? "Woe unto the world (it is written), because of scandals; for it must needs be that scandals come, but woe to the man *by whom* the scandal cometh!"[8] Woe unto the deceiver and self-deceived! "His hope shall perish; his hope shall be cut off, and his trust shall be a spider's web: he shall lean upon his house, but it shall not stand; he shall hold it fast, but it shall not endure."[9] God give us grace to flee from this woe while we have time! Let us examine ourselves, to see if there be any wicked way in us; let us aim at obtaining some comfortable assurance that we are in the narrow way that leads to life. And let us pray God to enlighten us, and to guide us, and to give us the will to please Him, and the power.

[8] Matt. xviii.7.   [9] Job viii.13–15.

PROFESSION WITHOUT HYPOCRISY

*"As many of you as have been baptized into Christ
have put on Christ."*—Gal. iii.27.

I T is surely most necessary to beware, as our Lord solemnly
bids us, of the leaven of the Pharisees, which is hypocrisy.
We may be infected with it, even though we are not conscious
of our insincerity; for they did not *know* they were hypocrites.
Nor need we have any definite bad object plainly before us, for
they had none,—only the vague desire to be seen and honoured
by the world, such as may influence us. So it would seem, that
there are vast multitudes of Pharisaical hypocrites among baptized Christians; i.e. men professing without practising. Nay,
so far we may be called hypocritical, one and all; for no Christian on earth altogether lives up to his profession.

But here some one may ask, whether in saying that hypocrisy
is professing without practising, I am not, in fact, overthrowing
all external religion from the foundation, since all creeds, and
prayers, and ordinances, go beyond the real belief and frame of
mind of even the best Christians. This is even the ground which
some men actually take. They say that it is wrong to baptize,
and call Christians, those who have not yet shown themselves
to be really such. "As many as are baptized into Christ, put on
Christ;" so says the text, and these men argue from it, that till
we have actually put on Christ, that is, till we have given our
heart to Christ's service, and in our degree become holy as He
is holy, it can do no good to be baptized into His name. Rather
it is a great evil, for it is to become hypocrites. Nay, really
humble, well-intentioned men, feel this about themselves.
They shrink from retaining the blessed titles and privileges
which Christ gave them in infancy, as being unworthy of them;
and they fear lest they are really hypocrites like the Pharisees,
after all their better thoughts and exertions.

Now the obvious answer to this mistaken view of religion is
to say, that, on the showing of such reasoners, no one at all
ought to be baptized in any case, and called a Christian; for no

one *acts up* to his baptismal profession; no one believes, worships, and obeys duly, the Father, Son, and Holy Ghost, whose servant he is made in baptism. And yet the Lord *did* say, "Go, baptize all nations;" clearly showing us, that a man may be a fit subject for baptism, though he does not in fact practise every thing that he professes, and therefore, that any fears we may have, lest men should be in some sense like the Pharisees, must not keep us from making them Christians.

But I shall treat the subject more at length, in order that we may understand what kind of disobedience is really hypocrisy, and what is not, lest timid consciences should be frightened. Now men profess without feeling and doing, or are hypocrites, in nothing so much as in their prayers. This is plain. Prayer is the most directly religious of all our duties; and our falling short of our duty, is, then, most clearly displayed. Therefore I will enlarge upon the case of prayer, to explain what I do *not* mean by hypocrisy. We then use the most solemn words, either without attending to what we are saying, or (even if we do attend) without worthily entering into its meaning. Thus we seem to resemble the Pharisees; a question in consequence arises, whether, this being the case, we should go on repeating prayers which evidently do not suit us. The men I just now spoke of, affirm that we ought to leave them off. Accordingly, such persons in their own case first give up the Church prayers, and take to others which they think will suit them better. Next, when these disappoint them, they have recourse to what is called extempore prayer; and afterwards perhaps, discontented in turn with this mode of addressing Almighty God, and as unable to fix their thoughts as they were before, they come to the conclusion that they ought not to pray, except when specially moved to prayer by the influence of the Holy Spirit.

Now, in answer to such a manner of reasoning and acting, I would maintain that no one is to be reckoned a Pharisee or hypocrite in his prayers who *tries* not to be one,—who aims at knowing and correcting himself and who is accustomed to pray, though not perfectly, yet not indolently or in a self-satisfied way; however lamentable his actual wanderings of mind may be, or, again, however poorly he enters into the meaning of his prayers, even when he attends to them.

1. First take the case of not being *attentive* to the prayers. Men, it seems, are tempted to leave off prayers because they cannot follow them, because they find their thoughts wander when they repeat them. I answer, that to pray attentively is a *habit*. This must ever be kept in mind. No one *begins* with having

his heart thoroughly in them; but by trying, he is enabled to attend more and more, and at length, after many trials and a long schooling of himself, to fix his mind steadily on them. No one (I repeat) *begins* with being attentive. Novelty in prayers is the cause of persons being attentive in the outset, and novelty is out of the question in the Church prayers, for we have heard them from childhood, and knew them by heart long before we could understand them. No one, then, when he first turns his thoughts to religion, finds it easy to pray; he is irregular in his religious feelings; he prays more earnestly at some times than at others; his devotional seasons come by fits and starts; he cannot account for his state of mind, or reckon upon himself; he frequently finds that he is more disposed for prayer at any time and place than those set apart for the purpose. All this is to be expected; for no habit is formed at once; and before the flame of religion in the heart is purified and strengthened by long practice and experience, of course it will be capricious in its motions, it will flare about (so to say) and flicker, and at times seem almost to go out.

However, impatient men do not well consider this; they overlook or are offended at the necessity of humble, tedious practice to enable them to pray attentively, and they account for their coldness and wanderings of thought in any way but the true one. Sometimes they attribute this inequality in their religious feelings to the arbitrary coming and going of God's Holy Spirit; a most irreverent and presumptuous judgment, which I should not mention, except that men *do* form it, and therefore it is necessary to state in order to condemn it. Again, sometimes they think that they shall make themselves attentive all at once by bringing before their minds the more sacred doctrines of the Gospel, and thus rousing and constraining their souls. This does for a time; but when the novelty is over, they find themselves relapsing into their former inattention, without apparently having made any advance. And others, again, when discontented with their wanderings during prayer, lay the fault on the prayers themselves as being too long. This is a common excuse, and I wish to call your attention to it.

If any one alleges the *length* of the Church prayers as a reason for his not keeping his mind fixed upon them, I would beg him to ask his conscience whether he sincerely believes this to be at bottom the real cause of his inattention? Does he think he should attend *better* if the prayers were shorter? This is the question he has to consider. If he answers that he believes he *should* attend more closely in that case, then I go on to ask, whether he attends more closely (as it *is*) to the first part of the service than to the last; whether his mind is his own, regularly fixed on what he is engaged in, for any time in any part of the service? Now, if he is obliged to own that this is not the case, that his thoughts are wandering in all parts of the service, and that even during the Confession, or the Lord's Prayer, which come first, they are not his own, it is quite clear that it is not the *length* of the service which is the real cause of his inattention, but his being deficient in *the habit* of being attentive. If, on the other hand, he answers that he can fix his thoughts for a time, and during the early part of the service, I would have him reflect that even this degree of attention was not always his own, that *it* has been the work of time and practice; and, if by trying he has got so far, by trying he may go on and learn to attend for a still longer time, till at length he is able to keep up his attention through the whole service.

However, I wish chiefly to speak to such as are dissatisfied with themselves, and despair of attending properly. Let a man once set his heart upon learning to pray, and strive to learn, and no failures he may continue to make in his manner of praying are sufficient to cast him from God's favour. Let him but persevere, not discouraged at his wanderings, not frightened into a notion he is a hypocrite, not shrinking from the honourable titles which God puts on him. Doubtless he should be humbled at his own weakness, indolence, and carelessness; and he should feel (he cannot feel too much) the guilt, alas! which he is ever contracting in his prayers by the irreverence of his inattention. Still he must not leave off his prayers, but go on looking towards Christ his Saviour. Let him but be in earnest, striving to master his thoughts, and to be serious, and all the guilt of his incidental failings will be washed away in his Lord's blood. Only let him not be contented with himself; only let him not neglect to *attempt* to obey. What a simple rule it is, to try to be attentive in order to be so! and yet it is continually overlooked; that is, we do not *systematically* try, we do not make a point of attempting and attempting over and over again in spite of bad success; we attempt only now and then, and our best devotion is merely when our hearts are excited by some accident which may or may not happen again.

So much on inattention to our prayers, which, I say, should not surprise or frighten us, which does not prove us to be hypocrites unless we acquiesce in it; or oblige us to leave them off, but rather to learn to attend to them.

2. I proceed, secondly, to remark on the difficulty of *entering into* the meaning of them, when we *do* attend to them.

Here a tender conscience will ask, "How is it possible I *can* rightly use the solemn words which occur in the prayers?" A tender conscience *alone* speaks thus. Those confident objectors whom I spoke of just now, who maintain that set prayer is necessarily a mere formal service in the generality of instances, a service in which the heart has no part, they are silent here. They do not feel *this* difficulty, which is the real one; they use the most serious and awful words lightly and without remorse, as if they really entered into the meaning of what is, in truth, beyond the intelligence of Angels. But the humble and contrite believer, coming to Christ for pardon and help, perceives the great strait he is in, in having to address the God of heaven. This perplexity of mind it was which led convinced sinners in former times to seek refuge in beings short of God; not as denying God's supremacy, or shunning Him, but discerning the vast distance between themselves and Him, and seeking some resting places by the way, some Zoar, some little city near to flee unto,[1] because of the height of God's mountain, up which the way of escape lay. And then gradually becoming devoted to those whom they trusted, Saints, Angels, or good men living, and copying them, their faith had a fall, and their virtue trailed upon the ground, for want of props to rear it heavenward. We Christians, sinners though we be like other men, are not allowed thus to debase our nature, or to defraud ourselves of God's mercy; and though it be very terrible to speak to the living God, yet speak we must, or die; tell our sorrows we must, or there is no hope; for created mediators and patrons are forbidden us, and to trust in an arm of flesh is made a sin.

Therefore let a man reflect, whoever from tenderness of conscience shuns the Church as above him (whether he shuns her services, or her sacraments), that, awful as it is to approach Christ, to speak to Him, to "eat His flesh and drink His blood," and to live in Him, *to whom shall he go?* See what it comes to. Christ is the only way of salvation open to sinners. Truly we *are* children, and cannot suitably feel the words which the Church teaches us, though we say them after her, nor feel duly reverent at God's presence! Yet let us but know our own ignorance and weakness; and we are safe. God accepts those who thus come in faith, bringing nothing as their offering, but a confession of sin. And this is the highest excellence to which we ordinarily attain; to understand our own hypocrisy, insincerity, and shallowness of mind,—to own, while we

[1] Gen. xix.20.

pray, that we cannot pray aright,—to repent of our repent-ings,—and to submit ourselves wholly to His judgment, who could indeed be extreme with us, but has already shown His loving-kindness in bidding us to pray. And, while we thus con-duct ourselves, we must learn to feel that God knows all this before we say it, and far better than we do. He does not need to be informed of our extreme worthlessness. We must pray in the spirit and the temper of the extremest abasement, but we need not search for adequate words to express this, for in truth no words are bad enough for our case. Some men are dissatisfied with the confessions of sin we make in Church, as not being strong enough; but none *can* be strong enough; let us be satisfied with sober words, which have been ever in use; it will be a great thing if we enter into *them*. No need of searching for impassioned words to express our repentance, when we do not rightly enter even into the most ordinary expressions.

Therefore, when we pray let us not be as the hypocrites, mak-ing a show; nor use vain repetitions with the heathen; let us compose ourselves, and kneel down quietly as to a work far above us, preparing our minds for our own imperfection in prayer, meekly repeating the wonderful words of the Church our Teacher, and desiring with the Angels to look into them. When we call God our Father Almighty, or own ourselves mis-erable offenders, and beg Him to spare us, let us recollect that, though we are using a strange language, yet Christ is pleading for us in the same words with full understanding of them, and availing power; and that, though we know not what we should pray for as we ought, yet the Spirit itself maketh intercession for us with plaints unutterable. Thus feeling God to be around us and in us, and therefore keeping ourselves still and collected, we shall serve Him acceptably, with reverence and godly fear; and we shall take back with us to our common employments the assurance that He is still gracious to us, in spite of our sins, not willing we should perish, desirous of our perfection, and ready to form us day by day after the fashion of that divine im-age which in baptism was outwardly stamped upon us.

I have spoken only of our prayers, and but referred to our general profession of Christianity. It is plain, however, what has been said about praying, may be applied to all we do and say as Christians. It is true that we profess to be saints, to be guided by the highest principles, and to be ruled by the Spirit of God. We have long ago promised to believe and obey. It is also true that we cannot do these things aright; nay, even with God's help (such is our sinful weakness), still we fall short of our duty.

Nevertheless we must not cease to profess. We must not put off from us the wedding garment which Christ gave us in baptism. We may still rejoice in Him without being hypocrites, that is, if we labour day by day to make that wedding garment our own; to fix it on us and so incorporate it with our very selves, that death, which strips us of all things, may be unable to tear it from us, though as yet it be in great measure but an outward garb, covering our own nakedness.

I conclude by reminding you, how great God's mercy is in thus allowing us to clothe ourselves in the glory of Christ from the first, even before we are worthy[2] of it. I suppose there is nothing so distressing to a true Christian as to have to *prove himself* such to others; both as being conscious of his own numberless failings, and from his dislike of display. Now Christ has anticipated the difficulties of his modesty. He does not allow such an one to speak for himself; He speaks for him. He introduces each of us to His brethren, not as we are in ourselves, fit to be despised and rejected on account of "the temptations which are in our flesh," but "as messengers of God, even as Christ Jesus." It is our happiness that we need bring nothing in proof of our fellowship with Christians, besides our baptism. This is what a great many persons do not understand; they think that none are to be accounted fellow-Christians but those who evidence themselves to be such to their fallible understandings; and hence they encourage others, who wish for their praise, to practise all kinds of display, as a seal of their regeneration. Who can tell the harm this does to the true modesty of the Christian spirit? Instead of using the words of the Church, and speaking to God, men are led to use their own words, and make man their judge and justifier.[3] They think it necessary to tell out their secret feelings, and to enlarge on what God has done to their own souls in particular. And thus making themselves really answerable for all the words they use, which are altogether their own, they do in this case become hypocrites; they do say more than they can in reality feel. Of course a religious man will naturally, and unawares, out of the very fulness of his heart, show his deep feeling and his conscientiousness to his near friends; but when to do so is made a matter of *necessity*, an *object* to be aimed at, and is an *intentional* act, then it is that hypocrisy must, more or less, sully our faith. "As many of you as have been baptized into Christ, have put on Christ;" this is the Apostle's decision. "There is

---

[2] Matt. xxii.8; Col. i.10.   [3] 1 Cor. iv.3–5.

neither Jew nor Greek, there is neither bond nor free, there is neither male nor female; for ye are all one in Christ Jesus." The Church follows this rule, and bidding us keep quiet, speaks for us; robes us from head to foot in the garments of righteousness, and exhorts us to live henceforth to God. But the disputer of this world reverses this procedure; he strips off all our privileges, bids us renounce our dependence on the Mother of saints, tells us we must each be a Church to himself, and must show himself to the world to be by himself and in himself the elect of God, in order to prove his right to the privileges of a Christian.

Far be it from us thus to fight against God's gracious purposes to man, and to make the weak brother perish, for whom Christ died! [4] Let us acknowledge all to be Christians, who have not by open word or deed renounced their fellowship with us, and let us try to lead them on into all truth. And for ourselves, let us endeavour to enter more and more fully into the meaning of our own prayers and professions; let us humble ourselves for the very little we do, and the poor advance we make; let us avoid unnecessary display of religion; let us do our duty in that state of life to which God has called us. Thus proceeding, we shall, through God's grace, form within us the glorious mind of Christ. Whether rich or poor, learned or unlearned, walking by this rule, we shall become, at length, true saints, sons of God. We shall be upright and perfect, lights in the world, the image of Him who died that we might be conformed to His likeness.

[4] 1 Cor. viii.11.

PROFESSION WITHOUT OSTENTATION

*"Ye are the light of the world. A city that is set on an hill
cannot be hid."*—Matt. v.14.

OUR Saviour gives us a command, in this passage of His Sermon on the Mount, to manifest our religious profession
before all men. "Ye are the light of the world," He says to His
disciples; "A city that is set on a hill cannot be hid. Neither do
men light a candle and put it under a bushel, but on a candlestick; and it giveth light unto all that are in the house. Let your
light so shine before men, that they may see your good works,
and glorify your Father which is in heaven." Yet presently He
says, "When thou doest alms . . . when thou prayest . . . when
ye fast . . . appear not unto men . . . but unto thy Father which
is in secret."[1] How are these commands to be reconciled? how
are we at once to *profess* ourselves Christians, and yet hide our
Christian words, deeds, and self-denials?

I will now attempt to answer this question; that is, to explain
how we may be witnesses to the world for God, and yet without
pretension, or affectation, or rude and indecent ostentation.

1. Now, first, much might be said on that mode of witnessing Christ which consists in conforming to His Church. He
who simply did what the Church bids him do (if he did no
more), would witness a good confession to the world, and one
which cannot be hid; and at the same time, with very little, if
any, personal display. He does only what he is told to do; he
takes no responsibility on himself. The Apostles and Martyrs
who founded the Church, the Saints in all ages who have
adorned it, the Heads of it now alive, all these take from him
the weight of his profession, and bear the blame (so to call it)
of seeming ostentatious. I do not say that irreligious men will
not *call* such an one boastful, or austere, or a hypocrite; that is

[1] Matt. vi.2–18.

not the question. The question is, whether in *God's* judgment he *deserves* the censure; whether he is not as Christ would have him, *really and truly* (whatever the world may say) joining humility to a bold outward profession; whether he is not, in thus acting, preaching Christ without hurting his own pureness, gentleness, and modesty of character. If indeed a man stands forth *on his own ground*, declaring himself as an individual a witness for Christ, then indeed he *is* grieving and disturbing the calm spirit given us by God. But God's merciful providence has saved us this temptation, and forbidden us to admit it. He bids us unite together in one, and to shelter our personal profession under the authority of the general body. Thus, while we show ourselves as lights to the world far more effectively than if we glimmered separately in the lone wilderness without communication with others, at the same time we do so with far greater secrecy and humility. Therefore it is, that the Church does so many things for us, appoints Fasts and Feasts, times of public prayer, the order of the sacraments, the services of devotion at marriages and deaths, and all accompanied by a fixed form of sound words; in order (I say) to remove from us individually the burden of a high profession, of implying great things of ourselves by inventing for ourselves solemn prayers and praises,—a task far above the generality of Christians, to say the least, a task which humble men will shrink from, lest they prove hypocrites, and which will hurt those who *do* undertake it, by making them rude-spirited and profane. I am desirous of speaking on this subject as a matter of *practice*; for I am sure, that if we wish really and in fact to spread the knowledge of the Truth, we shall do so far more powerfully as *well* as purely, by keeping together, than by witnessing one by one. Men are to be seen adopting all kinds of strange ways of giving glory (as they think) to God. If they would but follow the Church; come together in prayer on Sundays and Saints' days, nay, every day; honour the rubric by keeping to it obediently, and conforming their families to the *spirit* of the Prayer Book, I say that on the whole they would practically do vastly more good than by trying new religious plans, founding new religious societies, or striking out new religious views. I put out of account the greater blessing they might expect to find in the way of duty, which is the first consideration.

2. One way of professing without display has been mentioned;—obeying the Church. Now in the next place, consider how great a profession, and yet a profession how unconscious

and modest, arises from the mere ordinary manner in which any strict Christian lives. Let this thought be a satisfaction to uneasy minds which fear lest they are not confessing Christ, yet dread to display. Your *life* displays Christ without your intending it. You cannot help it. Your *words and deeds* will show on the long run (as it is said), where your treasure is, and your heart. Out of the abundance of your heart your mouth speaketh words "seasoned with salt." We sometimes find men who aim at doing their duty in the common course of life, *surprised* to hear that they are ridiculed, and called hard names by careless or worldly persons. This is as it should be; it is as it should be, that they are *surprised* at it. If a private Christian sets out with *expecting* to make a disturbance in the world, the fear is, lest he be not so humble-minded as he should be. But those who go on quietly in the way of obedience, and yet are detected by the keen eye of the jealous, self-condemning, yet proud world, and who on discovering their situation, first shrink from it and are distressed, then look to see if they have done aught wrongly, and after all are sorry for it, and but slowly and very timidly (if at all) learn to rejoice in it, these are Christ's flock. These are they who follow Him who was meek and lowly of heart, His elect, in whom He sees His own image reflected. Consider how such men show forth their light in a wicked world, yet unconsciously. Moses came down from the mount, and "wist not that the skin of his face shone" as one who had held intercourse with God. But "when Aaron and all the children of Israel saw Moses, behold, the skin of his face shone; and they were afraid to come nigh him." [2] Who can estimate the power of our separate words spoken in season! How many of them are recollected and cherished by this person or that, which we have forgotten, and bear fruit! How do our good deeds excite *others* to rivalry in a good cause, as the Angels perceive though we do not! How are men thinking of us we never heard of or saw but once, and in far countries unknown! Let us for a moment view this pleasing side of our doings, as well as the sad prospect of our evil communications. Doubtless, our prayers and alms are rising as a sweet sacrifice, pleasing to God;[3] and pleasing to Him, not only as an office of devotion, but of charity towards all men. Our businesses and our amusements, our joys and our sorrows, our opinions, tastes, studies, views and principles, are drawn *one* way heavenward. Be we high or low, in our place we can serve, and in consequence glo-

---

[2] Exod. xxxiv.29, 30.   [3] Acts x.4.

rify, Him who died for us. "A little maid," who was "brought away captive out of the land of Israel, and waited on Naaman's wife,"[4] pointed out to the great captain of the host of the king of Syria the means of recovery from his leprosy, and "his *servants*" spoke good words to him afterwards, and brought him back to his reason when he would have rejected the mode of cure which the prophet prescribed. This may quiet impatient minds, and console the over-scrupulous conscience. "Wait on God and be doing good," and you must, you cannot but be showing your light before men as a city on a hill.

3. Still it is quite true that there are circumstances under which a Christian is bound openly to express his opinion on religious subjects and matters; and this is the real difficulty, viz. how to do so without display. As a man's place in society is here or there, so it is more or less his duty to speak his mind freely. We must never countenance sin and error. Now the more obvious and modest way of discountenancing evil is by silence, and by separating from it; for example, we are bound to keep aloof from deliberate and open sinners. St. Paul expressly tells us, "not to keep company, if any man that is called a brother (i.e. a Christian) be a fornicator, or covetous, or an idolater, or a railer, or a drunkard, or an extortioner; with such an one, no not to eat."[5] And St. John gives us the like advice with respect to heretics. "If there come any unto you, and bring not this doctrine (i.e. the true doctrine of Christ), receive him not into your house, neither bid him God speed; for he that biddeth him God speed is partaker of his evil deeds."[6] It is plain that such conduct on our part requires no great display, for it is but conforming to the rules of the Church; though it *is* often difficult to know on what occasions we ought to adopt it, which is another question.

A more difficult duty is that of passing judgment (as a Christian is often bound to do) on events of the day and public men. It becomes his duty, in proportion as he has station and influence in the community, in order that he may persuade others to think as he does. Above all, clergymen are bound to form and pronounce an opinion. It is sometimes said, in familiar language, that a clergyman should have nothing to do with politics. This is true, if it be meant that he should not aim at secular objects, should not side with a political party as such, should not be ambitious of popular applause, or the favour of great men, should not take pleasure and lose time in business

[4] 2 Kings v.2.   [5] 1 Cor. v.11.   [6] 2 John 10, 11.

of this world, should not be covetous. But if it means that he
should not express an opinion and exert an influence one way
rather than another, it is plainly unscriptural. Did not the
Apostles, with all their reverence for the temporal power,
whether Jewish or Roman, and all their separation from
worldly ambition, did they not still denounce their rulers as
wicked men, who had crucified and slain the Lord's Christ?[7]
and would they have been as a city on a hill if they had not
done so? *If*, indeed, this world's concerns could be altogether
disjoined from those of Christ's Kingdom, then indeed all
Christians (laymen as well as clergy) should abstain from the
thought of temporal affairs, and let the worthless world pass
down the stream of events till it perishes; but if (as is the case)
what happens in *nations* must affect the cause of *religion* in those
nations, since the Church may be seduced and corrupted by
the world, and in the world there are myriads of souls to be
converted and saved, and since a Christian nation is bound to
become part of the Church, therefore it is our duty to stand as
a beacon on a hill, to cry aloud and spare not, to lift up our
voice like a trumpet, and show the people their transgression,
and the house of Jacob their sins.[8] And all this may be done
without injury to our Christian gentleness and humbleness,
though it is difficult to do it. We need not be angry nor use
contentious words, and yet may firmly give our opinion, in
proportion as we have the means of forming one, and be zealous towards God in all active good service, and scrupulously
and pointedly keep aloof from the bad men whose evil arts we
fear.

Another and still more difficult duty is that of personally rebuking those we meet with in the intercourse of life who sin in
word or deed, and testifying before them in Christ's name; that
is, it is difficult at once to be unassuming and zealous in such
cases. We know it is a plain and repeated precept of Christ to
tell others of their faults for charity's sake; but how is this to be
done without seeming, nay, without being arrogant and severe?
There are persons who are anxious to do their duty to the full,
who fear that they are deficient in this particular branch of it,
and deficient from a blameable backwardness, and the dread of
giving offence; yet, on the other hand, they feel the painfulness
of rebuking another, and (to use a common word) the awk-
wardness of it. Such persons must consider that, though to rebuke is a duty, it is not a duty belonging at once to all men; and

---

[7] Acts ii.23; iii.13–17; iv.27; xiii.27.   [8] Is. lviii.1

the perplexity which is felt about it often arises from the very impropriety of attempting it in the particular case. It is improper, as a general rule, in the young to witness before the old, otherwise than by their silence. Still more improper is it in inferiors to rebuke their superiors; for instance, a child his parent, of course; or a private person his natural and divinely-appointed governour. When we assume a character not suited to us, of course we feel awkward; and although we may have done so in honesty and zeal (however ill-tutored), and so God may in mercy accept our service, still He, at the same time, rebukes us by our very feeling of perplexity and shame. As for such as rudely blame another, and that a superior, and feel no pain at doing so, I have nothing to say to such men, except to express my earnest desire that they may be led into a more Christian frame of mind. They do not even feel the difficulty of witnessing for God without display.

It is to be considered, too, that to do the part of a witness for the truth, to warn and rebuke, is not an elementary duty of a Christian. I mean, that our duties come in a certain order, some before others, and that this is not one of the first of them. Our first duties are to repent and believe. It would be strange, indeed, for a man, who had just begun to think of religion, to set up for "some great one," to assume he was a saint and a witness, and to exhort others to turn to God. This is evident. But as time goes on, and his religious character becomes formed, then, while he goes on to perfection in all his duties, he takes upon himself, in the number of these, to witness for God by word of mouth. It is difficult to say *when* a man has leave openly to rebuke others; certainly not before he has considerable humility; the test of which may be the absence of a feeling of triumph in doing it, a consciousness that he is no better by nature than the person he witnesses before, and that his actual sins are such as to deserve a severe rebuke were they known to the world; a love towards the person reproved, and a willingness to submit to deserved censure in his turn. In all this I am speaking of laymen. It is a clergyman's duty to rebuke by virtue of his office. And then, after all, supposing it be clearly our duty to manifest our religious profession in this pointed way before another, in order to do so modestly we must do so kindly and cheerfully, as gently as we can; doing it as little as we can help; not making matters worse than they are, or showing our whole Christian stature (or what we think to be such), when we need but put out a hand (so to say) or give a glance. And above all (as I have already said), acting as if we thought, nay, really thinking, that it may be the offender's turn some day to rebuke us; not putting ourselves above him, feeling our great imperfections, and desirous he should rebuke us, should occasion require it, and in prospect thanking him; acting, that is, in the spirit in which you warn a man in walking against rugged ground, which may cause him a fall, thinking him bound by your friendly conduct to do the like favour to you. As to grave occasions of witnessing Christ, they will seldom occur, except a man thrust himself into society where he never ought to have been, by neglecting the rule, "Come ye out, and be separate;" and then he has scarcely the right to rebuke, having committed the first fault himself. This is another cause of our perplexity in witnessing Christ before the world. We make friends of the sinful, and then they have the advantage over us.

To conclude.—The question is often raised, whether a man can do his duty simply and quietly, without being thought ostentatious by the world. It is no great matter to himself whether he is thought so or not, if he has not provoked the opinion. As a general rule, I would say the Church itself is always hated and calumniated by the world, as being in duty bound to make a bold profession. But whether individual members of the Church are so treated, depends on various circumstances in the case of each. There *are* persons, who, though very strict and conscientious Christians, are yet praised by the world. These are such, as having great meekness and humility, are not so prominent in station or so practically connected with the world as to offend it. Men admire religion, while they can gaze on it as a picture. They think it lovely in books: and as long as they can look upon Christians at a distance, they speak well of them. The Jews in Christ's time built the sepulchres of the prophets whom their fathers killed; then they themselves killed the Just One. They "reverenced" the Son of God before He came, but when their passions and interests were stirred by His coming, then they said, "This is the Heir; come, let us kill Him, and the inheritance shall be ours." [9] Thus Christians in active life thwarting (as they do) the pride and selfishness of the world, are disliked by the world, and have "all manner of evil said against them falsely for Christ's sake." [10] Still, even under these circumstances, though they must not shrink from the attack on a personal account, it is still their duty to shelter themselves, as far as they can, under the name and authority of the Holy Church; to keep to its ordinances and rules; and, if they are

[9] Mark xii.7.   [10] Matt. v.11.

called to suffer for the Church, rather to be drawn forward to
the suffering in the common course of duty, than boldly to take
upon them the task of defending it. There is no cowardice in
this. Some men are placed in posts of danger, and to these danger comes in the way of duty; but others must not intrude into
their honourable office. Thus in the first age of the Gospel, our
Lord told His followers to flee from city to city, when persecuted; and even the heads of the Church, in the early persecutions, instead of exposing themselves to the fury of the
heathen, did their utmost to avoid it. We are a suffering people
from the first; but while, on the one hand, we do not defend
ourselves illegally, we do not court suffering on the other. We
must witness and glorify God, as lights on a hill, through evil
report and good report; but the evil and the good report is not
so much of our own making as the natural consequence of our
Christian profession.

Who can tell God's will concerning this tumultuous world,
or how He will dispose of it? He is tossing it hither and thither
in His fury, and in its agitation He troubles His own people also.
Only, this we know for our comfort. Our light shall never go
down; Christ set it upon a hill, and hell shall not prevail against
it. The Church will witness on to the last for the Truth, chained
indeed to this world, its evil partner, but ever foretelling its
ruin, though not believed, and in the end promised a far different recompense. For in the end the Lord Omnipotent shall
reign, when the marriage of the Lamb shall come at length, and
His wife shall make herself ready; and to her shall be granted
"fine linen, clean and white; for the fine linen is the righteousness of saints." [11] True and righteous are His judgments; He
shall cast death and hell into the lake of fire, and avenge His
own elect which cry day and night unto Him!

"Blessed are they which are called unto the marriage supper
of the Lamb." May all we be in the number, confessing Christ in
this world, that He may confess us before His Father in the last
day!

---

[11] Rev. xix.6–8.

PROMISING WITHOUT DOING

"A certain man had two sons; and he came to the first, and said, Son,
go work to-day in my vineyard. He answered and said, I will not; but
afterward he repented, and went. And he came to the second, and said
likewise. And he answered and said, I go, Sir; and went not."
—Matt. xxi.28–30.

Our religious professions are at a far greater distance from our acting upon them, than we ourselves are aware. We know generally that it is our duty to serve God, and we resolve we will do so faithfully. We are sincere in thus generally desiring and purposing to be obedient, and we think we are in earnest; yet we go away, and presently, without any struggle of mind or apparent change of purpose, almost without knowing ourselves what we do,—we go away and do the very contrary to the resolution we have expressed. This inconsistency is exposed by our Blessed Lord in the second part of the parable which I have taken for my text. You will observe, that in the case of the first son, who said he would not go work, and yet did go, it is said, "afterward he repented;" he underwent a positive change of purpose. But in the case of the second, it is merely said, "he answered, I go, Sir; and went not;"—for here there was *no* revolution of sentiment, nothing deliberate; he merely acted according to his habitual frame of mind; he did *not* go work, because it was contrary to his general character to work; only he did not know this. He said, "I go, Sir," sincerely, from the feeling of the moment; but when the words were out of his mouth, then they were forgotten. It was like the wind blowing against a stream, which seems for a moment to change its course in consequence, but in fact flows down as before.

To this subject I shall now call your attention, as drawn from the latter part of this parable, passing over the case of the repentant son, which would form a distinct subject in itself. "He answered and said, I go, Sir; and went not." We promise to serve God: we do not perform; and that not from deliberate faithlessness in the particular case, but because it is our nature, our *way* not to obey, and we do not know this; we do not know ourselves, or what we are promising. I will give several instances of this kind of weakness.

1. For instance; that of mistaking good feelings for real religious principle. Consider how often this takes place. It is the case with the young necessarily, who have not been exposed to temptation. They have (we will say) been brought up religiously, they wish to be religious, and so are objects of our love and interest; but they think themselves far more religious than they really are. They suppose they hate sin, and understand the Truth, and can resist the world, when they hardly know the meaning of the words they use. Again, how often is a man incited by circumstances to utter a virtuous wish, or propose a generous or valiant deed, and perhaps applauds himself for his own good feeling, and has no suspicion that he is not able to act upon it! In truth, he does not understand where the real difficulty of his duty lies. He thinks that the characteristic of a religious man is his having correct notions. It escapes him that there is a great interval between feeling and acting. He takes it for granted he can do what he wishes. He knows he is a free agent, and can on the whole do what he will; but he is not conscious of the load of corrupt nature and sinful habits which hang upon his will, and clog it in each particular exercise of it. He has borne these so long, that he is insensible to their existence. He knows that in little things, where passion and inclination are excluded, he can perform as soon as he resolves. Should he meet in his walk two paths, to the right and left, he is sure he can take which he will at once, without any difficulty; and he fancies that obedience to God is not much more difficult than to turn to the right instead of the left.

2. One especial case of this self-deception is seen in delaying repentance. A man says to himself, "Of course, if the worst comes to the worst, if illness comes, or at least old age, I can repent." I do not speak of the dreadful presumption of such a mode of quieting conscience (though many persons really use it who do not speak the words out, or are aware that they act upon it), but, merely, of the ignorance it evidences concerning our moral condition, and our power of willing and doing. If men can repent, why do they not do so at once? they answer, that "they intend to do so hereafter;" i.e. they do *not* repent because they *can*. Such is their argument; whereas, the very fact that they do not now, should make them suspect that there is a greater difference between intending and doing than they know of.

So very difficult is obedience, so hardly won is every step in our Christian course, so sluggish and inert our corrupt nature, that I would have a man disbelieve he can do one jot or tittle beyond what he has already done; refrain from borrowing aught on the hope of the future, however good a security for it he seems to be able to show; and never take his good feelings and wishes in pledge for one single untried deed. Nothing but *past* acts are the vouchers for *future*. Past sacrifices, past labours, past victories over yourselves,—these, my brethren, are the tokens of the like in store, and doubtless of greater in store; for the path of the just is as the shining, growing light.[1] But trust nothing short of these. "Deeds, not words and wishes," this must be the watchword of your warfare and the ground of your assurance. But if you have done nothing firm and manly hitherto, if you are as yet the coward slave of Satan, and the poor creature of your lusts and passions, never suppose you will one day rouse yourselves from your indolence. Alas! there are men who walk the road to hell, always the while looking back at heaven, and trembling as they pace forward towards their place of doom. They hasten on as under a spell, shrinking from the consequences of their own deliberate doings. Such was Balaam. What would he have given if words and feelings might have passed for deeds! See how religious he was so far as profession goes! How did he revere God in speech! How piously express a desire to die the death of the righteous! Yet he died in battle among God's *enemies*; not suddenly overcome by temptation, only on the other hand, not suddenly turned to God by his good thoughts and fair purposes. But in this respect the power of sin differs from any literal spell or fascination, that we are, after all, willing slaves of it, and shall answer for following it. If "our iniquities, like the wind, take us away,"[2] yet we can help this.

Nor is it only among beginners in religious obedience that there is this great interval between promising and performing. We can never answer how we shall act under new circumstances. A very little knowledge of life and of our own hearts will teach us this. Men whom we meet in the world turn out, in the course of their trial, so differently from what their former conduct promised, they view things so differently *before* they were tempted and *after*, that we, who see and wonder at it, have abundant cause to look to ourselves, not to be "high-minded," but to "fear." Even the most matured saints, those who imbibed in largest measure the power and fulness of Christ's Spirit, and

[1] Prov. iv.18.   [2] Is. lxiv.6.

worked righteousness most diligently in their day, could they have been thoroughly scanned even by man, would (I am persuaded) have exhibited inconsistencies such as to surprise and shock their most ardent disciples. After all, one good deed is scarcely the pledge of another, though I just now said it was. The best men are uncertain; they are great, and they are little again; they stand firm, and then fall. Such is human virtue;— reminding us to call no one master on earth, but to look up to our sinless and perfect Lord; reminding us to humble ourselves, each within himself, and to reflect what we must appear to God, if even to ourselves and each other we seem so base and worthless and showing clearly that all who are saved, even the least inconsistent of us, can be saved only by faith, not by works.

3. Here I am reminded of another plausible form of the same error. It is a mistake concerning what is meant by faith. We know Scripture tells us that God accepts those who lave faith in Him. Now the question is, What *is* faith, and how can a man tell that he *has* faith? Some persons answer at once and without hesitation, that "to have faith is to feel oneself to be nothing, and God every thing; it is to be convinced of sin, to be conscious one cannot save oneself, and to wish to be saved by Christ our Lord; and that it is, moreover, to have the love of Him warm in one's heart, and to rejoice in Him, to desire His glory, and to resolve to live to Him and not to the world." But I will answer with all due seriousness, as speaking on a serious subject, that this is *not* faith. Not that it is not necessary (it is very necessary) to be convinced that we are laden with infirmity and sin, and without health in us, and to look for salvation solely to Christ's blessed sacrifice on the cross; and we may well be thankful if we are thus minded; but that a man may feel all this that I have described, vividly, and still not yet possess one particle of true religious faith. Why? Because there is an immeasurable distance between feeling right and doing right. A man may have all these good thoughts and emotions, yet (if he has not yet hazarded them to the experiment of practice) he cannot promise himself that he has any sound and permanent principle at all. If he has not yet acted upon them, we have no voucher, barely on *account* of them, to believe that they are any thing but words. Though a man spoke like an angel, I would not believe him, on the mere ground of his speaking. Nay, till he acts upon them, he has not even evidence to himself that he has true living faith. Dead faith (as St. James says) profits no man. Of course; the Devils have it. What, on the other hand is *living*

faith? Do fervent thoughts make faith *living*? St. James tells us otherwise. He tells us *works*, deeds of obedience, are the life of faith. "As the body without the spirit is dead, so faith without works is dead also."[3] So that those who think they really believe, because they have in word and thought surrendered themselves to God, are much too hasty in their judgment. They have done something, indeed, but not at all the most difficult part of their duty, which is to surrender themselves to God in deed and act. They have as yet done nothing to show they will not, after saying "I go," the next moment "go not;" nothing to show they will not act the part of the self-deceiving disciple, who said, "Though I die with Thee, I will not deny Thee," yet straightway went and denied Christ thrice. As far as we know any thing of the matter, justifying faith has no existence independent of its particular definite acts. It may be described to be the temper under which men obey; the humble and earnest desire to please Christ which causes and attends on actual services. He who does one little deed of obedience, whether he denies himself some comfort to relieve the sick and needy, or curbs his temper, or forgives an enemy, or asks forgiveness for an offence committed by him, or resists the clamour or ridicule of the world—such an one (as far as we are given to judge) evinces more true faith than could be shown by the most fluent religious conversation, the most intimate knowledge of Scripture doctrine, or the most remarkable agitation and change of religious sentiments. Yet how many are there who sit still with folded hands, dreaming, doing nothing at all, thinking they have done every thing, or need do nothing, when they merely have had these good *thoughts*, which will save no one!

My object has been, as far as a few words can do it, to lead you to some true notion of the depths and deceitfulness of the heart, which we do not really know. It is easy to speak of human nature as corrupt in the general, to admit it in the general, and then get quit of the subject; as if the doctrine being once admitted, there was nothing more to be done with it. But in truth we can have no real apprehension of the doctrine of our corruption, till we view the structure of our minds, part by part; and dwell upon and draw out the signs of our weakness, inconsistency, and ungodliness, which are such as can arise from nothing else than some strange original defect in our moral nature.

1. Now it will be well if such self-examination as I have suggested leads us to the habit of constant dependence upon the

[3] James ii.26.

Unseen God, in whom "we live and move and have our being." We are in the dark about ourselves. When we act, we are groping in the dark, and may meet with a fall any moment. Here and there, perhaps, we see a little; or, in our attempts to influence and move our minds, we are making experiments (as it were) with some delicate and dangerous instrument, which works we do not know how, and may produce unexpected and disastrous effects. The management of our hearts is quite above us. Under these circumstances it becomes our comfort to look up to God. "Thou, God, seest me!" Such was the consolation of the forlorn Hagar in the wilderness. He knoweth whereof we are made, and He alone can uphold us. He sees with most appalling distinctness all our sins, all the windings and recesses of evil within us; yet it is our only comfort to know this, and to trust Him for help against ourselves. To those who have a right notion of their weakness, the thought of their Almighty Sanctifier and Guide is continually present. They believe in the necessity of a spiritual influence to change and strengthen them, not as a mere abstract doctrine, but as a practical and most consolatory truth, daily to be fulfilled in their warfare with sin and Satan.

2. And this conviction of our excessive weakness must further lead us to try ourselves continually in little things, in order to prove our own earnestness; ever to be suspicious of ourselves, and not only to refrain from promising much, but actually to put ourselves to the test in order to keep ourselves wakeful. A sober mind never enjoys God's blessings to the full; it draws back and refuses a portion to show its command over itself. It denies itself in trivial circumstances, even if nothing is gained by denying, but an evidence of its own sincerity. It makes trial of its own professions; and if it has been tempted to say any thing noble and great, or to blame another for sloth or cowardice, it takes itself at its word, and resolves to make some sacrifice (if possible) in little things, as a price for the indulgence of fine speaking, or as a penalty on its censoriousness. Much would be gained if we adopted this rule even in our professions of friendship and service one towards another; and never said a thing which we were not willing to do.

There is only one place where the Christian allows himself to profess openly, and that is in Church. Here, under the guidance of Apostles and Prophets, he says many things boldly, as speaking after them, and as before Him who searcheth the reins. There can be no harm in professing much directly to God, because, *while* we speak, we know He sees through our professions, and takes them for what they really are, *prayers*. How much, for instance, do we profess when we say the Creed! and in the Collects we put on the full character of a Christian. We desire and seek the best gifts, and declare our strong purpose to serve God with our whole hearts. By doing this, we remind ourselves of our duty; and withal, we humble ourselves by the taunt (so to call it) of putting upon our dwindled and unhealthy forms those ample and glorious garments which befit the upright and full-grown believer.

Lastly, we see from the parable, what is the course and character of human obedience on the whole. There are two sides of it. I have taken the darker side; the case of profession without practice, of saying "I go, Sir," and of not going. But what is the brighter side? Nothing better than to say, "I go not," and to repent and go. The more *common* condition of men is, not to know their inability to serve God, and readily to answer for themselves; and so they quietly pass through life, as if they had nothing to fear. Their best estate, what is it, but to rise more or less in rebellion against God, to resist His commandments and ordinances, and then poorly to make up for the unbelief they have done, by repenting and obeying? Alas! to be alive as a Christian, is nothing better than to struggle against sin, to disobey and repent. There has been but One amongst the sons of men who has said and done *consistently*; who said, "I come to do Thy will, O God," and without delay or hindrance did it. He came to show us what human nature might become, if carried on to its perfection. Thus He teaches us to think highly of our nature as viewed in Him; not (as some do) to speak evil of our nature and exalt ourselves personally, but while we acknowledge *our own* distance from heaven, to view our *nature* as renewed in Him, as glorious and wonderful beyond our thoughts. Thus He teaches us to be hopeful; and encourages us while conscience abases us. Angels seem little in honour and dignity, compared with that nature which the Eternal Word has purified by His own union with it. Henceforth, we dare aspire to enter into the heaven of heavens, and to live for ever in God's presence, because the first-fruits of our race is already there in the Person of His Only-begotten Son.

RELIGIOUS EMOTION

*"But he spake the more vehemently, If I should die with Thee, I
will not deny Thee in any wise."*—Mark xiv.31.

IT is not my intention to make St. Peter's fall the direct subject
of our consideration to-day, though I have taken this text;
but to suggest to you an important truth, which that fall, together with other events at the same season, especially enforces;
viz. that violent impulse is not the same as a firm *determination*,—that men may have their religious feelings roused, without being on that account at all the more likely to obey God in
practice, rather the less likely. This important truth is in various ways brought before our minds at the season sacred to the
memory of Christ's betrayal and death. The contrast displayed
in the Gospels between His behaviour on the one hand, as the
time of His crucifixion drew near, and that both of His disciples
and of the Jewish populace on the other, is full of instruction, if
we will receive it; *He* steadily fixing His face to endure those
sufferings which were the atonement for our sins, yet without
aught of mental excitement or agitation; His disciples and the
Jewish multitude first protesting their devotion to Him in vehement language, then, the one deserting Him, the other even
clamouring for His crucifixion. He entered Jerusalem in triumph; the multitude cutting down branches of palm-trees, and
strewing them in the way, as in honour of a king and conqueror.[1] He had lately raised Lazarus from the dead; and so
great a miracle had given Him great temporary favour with the
populace. Multitudes flocked to Bethany to see Him and
Lazarus;[2] and when He set out for Jerusalem where He was to
suffer, they, little thinking that they would soon cry "Crucify
Him," went out to meet Him with the palm-branches, and hail-
ing Him as their Messiah, led Him on into the holy city. Here
was an instance of a *popular* excitement. The next instance of
excited feeling is found in that melancholy self-confidence of
St. Peter, contained in the text. When our Saviour foretold

---

[1] Matt. xxi.8; John xii.13.　　　　　　[2] John xii.1–18.

Peter's trial and fall, Peter at length "spake the more vehemently, If I should die with Thee, I will not deny Thee in any wise." Yet in a little while both the people and the Apostle abandoned their Messiah; the ardour of their devotion had run its course.

Now it may, perhaps, appear, as if the circumstance I am pointing out, remarkable as it is, still is one on which it is of little use to dwell, in addressing a mixed congregation, on the ground that most men feel too *little* about religion. And it may be thence argued, that the aim of Christian teaching rather should be to rouse them from insensibility, than to warn them against excess of religious feeling. I answer, that to mistake mere transient emotion, or mere good thoughts, for obedience, is a far commoner deceit than at first sight appears. How many a man is there, who, when his conscience upbraids him for neglect of duty, comforts himself with the reflection that he has never treated the subject of religion with open scorn,—that he has from time to time had serious thoughts,—that on certain solemn occasions he has been affected and awed,—that he has at times been moved to earnest prayer to God,—that he has had accidentally some serious conversation with a friend! This, I say, is a case of frequent occurrence among men called Christian. Again, there is a further reason for insisting upon this subject. No one (it is plain) can be religious without having his heart in his religion; his affections must be actively engaged in it; and it is the aim of all Christian instruction to promote this. But if so, doubtless there is great danger lest a perverse use should be made of the affections. In proportion as a religious duty is difficult, so is it open to abuse. For the very reason, then, that I desire to make you earnest in religion, must I also warn you against a counterfeit earnestness, which often misleads men from the plain path of obedience, and which most men are apt to fall into just on their first awakening to a serious consideration of their duty. It is not enough to bid you to serve Christ in faith, fear, love, and gratitude; care must be taken that it is the faith, fear, love, and gratitude of a sound mind. That vehement tumult of zeal which St. Peter felt before his trial failed him under it. That open-mouthed admiration of the populace at our Saviour's miracle was suddenly changed to blasphemy. This may happen now as then; and it often happens in a way distressing to the Christian teacher. He finds it is far easier to interest men in the subject of religion (hard though this be), than to rule the spirit which he has excited. His bearers, when their attention is gained, soon begin to think he does not go far enough; then they seek means which he will not supply, of encouraging and indulging their mere feelings to the neglect of humble practical efforts to serve God. After a time, like the multitude, they suddenly turn round to the world, abjuring Christ altogether, or denying Him with Peter, or gradually sinking into a mere form of obedience, while they still think themselves true Christians, and secure of the favour of Almighty God.

For these reasons I think it is as important to warn men against impetuous feelings in religion, as to urge them to give their heart to it. I proceed therefore to explain more fully what is the connexion between strong emotions and sound Christian principle, and how far they are consistent with it.

Now that perfect state of mind at which we must aim, and which the Holy Spirit imparts, is a deliberate preference of God's service to every thing else, a determined resolution to give up all for Him; and a love for Him, not tumultuous and passionate, but such love as a child bears towards his parents, calm, full, reverent, contemplative, obedient. Here, however, it may be objected, that this is not always possible: that we cannot help feeling emotion at times; that even to take the case of parents and children, a man is at certain times thrown out of that quiet affection which he bears towards his father and mother, and is agitated by various feelings; again, that zeal, for instance, though a Christian virtue, is almost inseparable from ardour and passion. To this I reply, that I am not describing the state of mind to which any one of us has *attained*, when I say it is altogether calm and meditative, but that which is the *perfect* state, that which we should aim at. I know it is often impossible, for various reasons, to avoid being agitated and excited; but the question before us is, whether we should *think highly* of violent emotion, whether we should encourage it. Doubtless it is no sin to feel at times passionately on the subject of religion; it is natural in some men, and under certain circumstances it is praiseworthy in others. But these are accidents. As a general rule, the more religious men become, the calmer they become; and at all times the religious principle, viewed by itself, is calm, sober, and deliberate.

Let us review some of the accidental circumstances I speak of.

1. The natural tempers of men vary very much. Some men have ardent imaginations and strong feelings; and adopt, as a matter of course, a vehement mode of expressing themselves. No doubt it is impossible to make all men think and feel alike. Such men of course may possess deep-rooted principle. All I

would maintain is, that their ardour does not of itself make their faith deeper and more genuine; that they must not think themselves better than others on account of it; that they must be aware of considering it a proof of their real earnestness, instead of narrowly searching into their conduct for the satisfactory *fruits* of faith.

2. Next, there are, besides, particular occasions on which excited feeling is natural, and even commendable; but not for its own sake, but *on account* of the peculiar circumstances under which it occurs. For instance, it is natural for a man to feel especial remorse at his sins when he first begins to think of religion; he *ought* to feel bitter sorrow and keen repentance. But all such emotion evidently is not the highest state of a Christian's mind; it is but the first stirring of grace in him. A sinner, indeed, can do no better; but in proportion as he learns more of the power of true religion, such agitation will wear away. What is this but saying, that change of mind is only the inchoate state of a Christian? Who doubts that sinners are bound to repent and turn to God? yet the Angels have no repentance; and who denies their peacefulness of soul to be a higher excellence than ours? The woman who had been a sinner, when she came behind our Lord wept much, and washed His feet with tears.[3] It was well done in her; she did what she could; and was honoured with our Saviour's praise. Yet it is clear this was not a permanent state of mind. It was but the first step in religion, and would doubtless wear away. It was but the accident of a season. Had her faith no deeper root than this emotion, it would soon have come to an end, as Peter's zeal.

In like manner, whenever we fall into sin, (and how often is this the case!) the truer our faith is, the more we shall for the time be distressed, perhaps agitated. No doubt; yet it would be a strange procedure to make much of this disquietude. Though it is a bad sign if we do not feel it (according to our mental temperament), yet if we do, what then? It argues no high Christian excellence; I repeat it, it is but the virtue of a very imperfect state. Bad is the best offering we can offer to God after sinning. On the other hand, the more consistent our habitual obedience, the less we shall be subject to such feelings.

3. And further, the accidents of life will occasionally agitate us:—affliction and pain; bad news; though here, too, the Psalmist describes the higher excellence of the mind, viz. the calm confidence of the believer, who "will not be afraid of any

[3] Luke vii.38.

evil tidings, *for* his heart standeth fast, and believeth in the Lord."[4] Times of persecution will agitate the mind; circumstances of especial interest in the fortunes of the Church will cause anxiety and fear. We see the influence of some of these causes in various parts of St. Paul's Epistles. Such emotion, however, is not the essence of true faith, though it accidentally accompanies it. In times of distress religious men will speak more openly on the subject of religion, and lay bare their feelings; at other times they will conceal them. They are neither better nor worse for so doing.

Now all this may be illustrated from Scripture. We find the same prayers offered, and the same resolutions expressed by good men, sometimes in a calm way, sometimes with more ardour. How quietly and simply does Agur offer his prayer to God! "Two things have I required of Thee; deny me them not before I die. Remove far from me vanity and lies; give me neither poverty nor riches; feed me with food convenient for me." St. Paul, on the other hand, with greater fervency, because he was in more distressing circumstances, but with not more acceptableness on that account in God's sight, says, "I have learned in whatsoever state I am, therewith to be content. I know both how to be abased, and I know how to abound;" and so he proceeds. Again, Joshua says, simply but firmly, "As for me and my house, we will serve the Lord." St. Paul says as firmly, but with more emotion, when his friends besought him to keep away from Jerusalem:—"What mean ye to weep and to break mine heart? for I am ready not to be bound only, but also to die at Jerusalem for the name of the Lord Jesus." Observe how calm Job is in his resignation: "The Lord gave, and the Lord hath taken away; blessed be the name of the Lord." And on the other hand, how calmly that same Apostle expresses his assurance of salvation at the close of his life, who, during the struggle, was accidentally agitated:—"I am now ready to be offered. . . . I have kept the faith. Henceforth there is laid up for me a crown of righteousness."[5]

These remarks may suffice to show the relation which excited feelings bear to true religious principle. They are sometimes natural, sometimes suitable; but they are not religion itself. They come and go. They are not to be counted on, or encouraged; for, as in St. Peter's case, they may supplant true

[4] Ps. cxii.7.

[5] Prov. xxx.7, 8; Phil. iv.11, 12; Josh. xxiv.15; Acts xxi.13; Job i.21; 2 Tim. iv.6–8.

faith, and lead to self-deception. They will gradually lose their place within us as our obedience becomes confirmed;—partly because those men are kept in perfect peace, and sheltered from all agitating feelings, whose minds are stayed on God;[6]—partly because these feelings themselves are fixed into habits by the power of faith, and instead of coming and going, and agitating the mind from their suddenness, they are permanently retained so far as there is any thing good in them, and give a deeper colour and a more energetic expression to the Christian character.

Now, it will be observed, that in these remarks I have taken for granted, as not needing proof, that the highest Christian temper is free from all vehement and tumultuous feeling. But, if we wish some evidence of this, let us turn to our Great Pattern, Jesus Christ, and examine what was the character of that perfect holiness which He alone of all men ever displayed.

And can we find any where such calmness and simplicity as marked His devotion and His obedience? When does He ever speak with fervour or vehemence? Or, if there be one or two words of His in His mysterious agony and death, characterized by an energy which we do not comprehend, and which sinners must silently adore, still how conspicuous and undeniable is His composure in the general tenour of His words and conduct! Consider the prayer He gave us; and this is the more to the purpose, for the very reason that He has given it as a model for our worship. How plain and unadorned is it! How few are the words of it! How grave and solemn the petitions! What an entire absence of tumult and feverish emotion! Surely our own feelings tell us it could not be otherwise. To suppose it otherwise were an irreverence towards Him.—At another time when He is said to have "rejoiced in spirit," His thanksgiving is marked with the same undisturbed tranquility. "I thank Thee, O Father, Lord of heaven and earth, that Thou hast hid these things from the wise and prudent, and hast revealed them unto babes. Even so, Father, for so it seemed good in Thy sight."—Again, think of His prayer in the garden. He then was in distress of mind beyond our understanding. Something there was, we know not what, which weighed heavy upon Him. He prayed He might be spared the extreme bitterness of His trial. Yet how subdued and how concise is His petition! "Abba, Father, all things are possible unto Thee: take away this cup from Me; nevertheless, not what I will, but what Thou wilt."[7] And this is but

---

[6] Is. xxvi.3.   [7] Luke x.21; Mark xiv.36.

one instance, though a chief one, of that deep tranquility of mind, which is conspicuous throughout the solemn history of the Atonement. Read the thirteenth chapter of St. John, in which He is described as washing His disciples' feet, Peter's in particular. Reflect upon His serious words addressed at several times to Judas who betrayed Him; and His conduct when seized by His enemies, when brought before Pilate, and lastly, when suffering on the cross. When does He set us an example of passionate devotion, of enthusiastic wishes, or of intemperate words?

Such is the lesson our Saviour's conduct teaches us. Now let me remind you how diligently we are taught the same by our own Church. Christ gave us a prayer to guide us in praying to the Father; and upon this model our own Liturgy is strictly formed. You will look in vain in the Prayer Book for long or vehement Prayers; for it is only upon occasions that agitation of mind is right, but there is ever a call upon us for seriousness, gravity, simplicity, deliberate trust, deepseated humility. Many persons, doubtless, think the Church prayers, for this very reason, cold and formal. They do not discern their high perfection, and they think they could easily write better prayers. When such opinions are advanced, it is quite sufficient to turn our thoughts to our Saviour's precept and example. It cannot be denied that those who thus speak, ought to consider our Lord's prayer defective; and sometimes they are profane enough to think so, and to confess they think so. But I pass this by. Granting for argument's sake His *precepts* were intentionally defective, as delivered before the Holy Ghost descended, yet what will they say to His *example*? Can even the fullest light of the Gospel revealed after His resurrection, bring us His followers into the remotest resemblance to our Blessed Lord's holiness? yet how calm was He, who was perfect man, in His own obedience!

To conclude:—Let us take warning from St. Peter's fall. Let us not promise much; let us not talk much of ourselves; let us not be high-minded, nor encourage ourselves in impetuous bold language in religion. Let us take warning, too, from that fickle multitude who cried, first Hosanna, then Crucify. A miracle startled them into a sudden adoration of their Saviour;—its effect upon them soon died away. And thus the especial mercies of God sometimes excite us for a season. We feel Christ speaking to us through our consciences and hearts; and we fancy He is assuring us we are His true servants, when He is but calling on us to receive Him. Let us not be content with

saying "Lord, Lord," without "doing the thing which He says."
The husbandman's son who said, "I go, Sir," yet went not to
the vineyard, gained nothing by his fair words. One secret act of
self-denial, one sacrifice of inclination to duty, is worth all the
mere good thoughts, warm feelings, passionate prayers, in
which idle people indulge themselves. It will give us more comfort on our deathbed to reflect on one deed of self-denying
mercy, purity, or humility, than to recollect the shedding of
many tears, and the recurrence of frequent transports, and
much spiritual exultation. These latter feelings come and go;
they may or may not accompany hearty obedience; they are
never tests of it; but good actions are the fruits of faith, and
assure us that we are Christ's; they comfort us as an evidence of
the Spirit working in us. By them we shall be judged at the last
day; and though they have no worth in themselves, by reason of
that infection of sin which gives its character to every thing we
do, yet they will be accepted for His sake, who bore the agony
in the garden, and suffered as a sinner on the cross.

RELIGIOUS FAITH RATIONAL

"He staggered not at the promise of God through unbelief; but was strong in faith, giving glory to God: and being fully persuaded that, what He had promised, He was able also to perform."
—Rom. iv.20, 21.

THERE are serious men who are in the habit of describing Christian Faith as a feeling or a principle such as ordinary persons cannot enter into; a something strange and peculiar in its very nature, different in kind from every thing that affects and influences us in matters of this world, and not admitting any illustration from our conduct in them. They consider that, because it is a spiritual gift, and heavenly in its origin, it is therefore altogether superhuman; and that to compare it with any of our natural principles or feelings, is to think unworthily of it. And thus they lead others, who wish an excuse for their own irreligious lives, to speak of Christian Faith as extravagant and irrational, as if it were a mere fancy or feeling, which some persons had and others had not; and which, accordingly, could only, and would necessarily, be felt by those who were disposed that certain way. Now, that the *object* on which Faith fixes our thoughts, that the doctrines of Scripture are most marvellous and exceeding in glory, unheard and unthought of elsewhere, is quite true; and it is also true that no mind of man will form itself to a habit of Faith without the preventing and assisting influences of Divine Grace. But it is not at all true that Faith itself, i. e. Trust, is a strange principle of action; and to say that it is irrational is even an absurdity. I mean such a Faith as that of Abraham, mentioned in the text, which led him to believe God's word when opposed to his own experience. And it shall now be my endeavour to show this.

To hear some men speak (I mean men who scoff at religion), it might be thought we never acted on Faith or Trust, except in religious matters, whereas we are acting on trust every hour of our lives. When faith is said to be a religious principle, it is (I repeat) the things believed, not the act of believing them, which is peculiar to religion. Let us take some examples.

It is obvious that we trust to our *memory*. We do not now witness what we saw yesterday; yet we have no doubt it took place in the way we *remember*. We recollect clearly the circumstances of morning and afternoon. Our confidence in our memory is so strong that a man might reason with us all day long, without persuading us that we slept through the day, or that we returned from a long journey, when our memory deposes otherwise. Thus we have faith in our memory; yet what is irrational here?

Again, even when we use reasoning, and are convinced of any thing by reasoning, what is it but that we trust the general soundness of our reasoning powers? From knowing one thing we think we can be sure about another, even though we do not see it. Who of us would doubt, on seeing strong shadows on the ground, that the sun was shining out, though our face happened to be turned the other way? Here is faith without sight but there is nothing against reason here, unless reason can be against itself.

And what I wish you particularly to observe is, that we continually trust our memory and our reasoning powers in this way, though *they often deceive us*. This is worth observing, because it is sometimes said that we cannot be *certain* that our faith in religion is not a mistake. I say our memory and reason often deceive us; yet no one says it is therefore absurd and irrational to continue to trust them; and for this plain reason, because *on the whole* they are true and faithful witnesses, because it is only *at times* that they mislead us; so that the chance is, that they are right in this case or that, which happens to be before us; and (again) because in all practical matters we are obliged to dwell upon not what *may be possibly*, but what is *likely* to be. In matters of daily life, we have no time for fastidious and perverse fancies about the minute chances of our being deceived. We are obliged to act at once, or we should cease to live. There is a chance (it cannot be denied) that our food to-day may be poisonous,—we cannot be quite certain,—but it looks the same and tastes the same, and we have good friends round us; so we do not abstain from it, for all this chance, though it is real. This necessity of acting promptly is our happiness in this world's matters; in the concerns of a future life, alas! we have time for carnal and restless thoughts about possibilities. And this is our *trial*; and it will be our condemnation, if with the experience of the folly of such idle fancyings about what may be, in matters of this life, we yet indulge them as regards the future. If it be said, that we sometimes do distrust our reasoning powers, for instance, when they lead us to some unexpected conclusion, or again our memory, when another's memory contradicts it, this only shows that there are things which we should be weak or hasty in believing; which is quite true. Doubtless there is such a fault as credulity, or believing too readily and too much (and this, in religion, we call superstition); but this neither shows that *all* trust is irrational, nor again that trust is necessarily irrational, which is founded on what is but likely to be, and may be denied without an actual absurdity. Indeed, when we come to examine the subject, it will be found that, strictly speaking, we know little more than that we exist, and that there is an Unseen Power whom we are bound to obey. Beyond this we must *trust*; and first our senses, memory, and reasoning powers; then other authorities:—so that, in fact, almost all we do, every day of our lives, is on trust, i.e. *faith*.

But it may be said, that belief in these informants, our senses, and the like, is not what is commonly meant by faith;—that to trust our senses and reason is in fact nothing more than to trust ourselves;—and though these do sometimes mislead us, yet they are so continually about us, and so at command, that we can use them to correct each other; so that on the whole we gain from these the truth of things quite well enough to act upon;— that on the other hand it is a very different thing from this to trust another person; and that faith, in the Scripture sense of the word, is trusting another, and therefore is not proved to be rational by the foregoing illustrations.

Let us, then, understand faith in this sense of *reliance on the words of another*, as opposed to trust in oneself. This is the common meaning of the word, I grant;—as when we contrast it to sight and to reason; and yet what I have already said has its use in reminding men who are eager for demonstration in matters of religion, that there are difficulties in matters of sense and reasoning also. But to proceed as I have proposed.—It is easy to show, that, even considering faith as trust in another, it is no irrational or strange principle of conduct in the concerns of this life.

For when we consider the subject attentively, how few things there are which we can ascertain for ourselves by our own senses and reason! After all, what *do* we know without trusting others? We know that we are in a certain state of health, in a certain place, have been alive for a certain number of years, have certain principles and likings, have certain persons around us, and perhaps have in our lives travelled to certain places at a distance. But what do we know more? Are there not towns (we will say) within fifty or sixty miles of us which we have never seen, and which, nevertheless, we fully believe to be as we have heard them described? To extend our view;—we know that land stretches in every direction of us, a certain number of miles, and then there is sea on all sides; that we are in an island. But who has seen the land all around, and has proved for himself that the fact is so? What, then, convinces us of it? the *report of others*,—this trust, this faith in testimony which, when religion is concerned, then, and only then, the proud and sinful would fain call irrational.

And what I have instanced in one set of facts, which we believe, is equally true of numberless others, of almost all of those which we think we know.

Consider how men in the business of life, nay, all of us, confide, are obliged to confide, in persons we never saw, or know but slightly; nay, in their hand-writings, which, for what we know, may be *forged*, if we are to speculate and fancy what *may be*. We act upon our trust in them implicitly, because common sense tells us, that with proper caution and discretion, faith in others is perfectly safe and rational. Scripture, then, only bids us act in respect to a future life, as we are every day acting at present. Or, again, how certain we all are (when we think on the subject) that we must sooner or later die. No one seriously thinks he can escape death; and men dispose of their property and arrange their affairs, confidently contemplating, not indeed the exact time of their death, still death as sooner or later to befall them. Of course they do; it would be most irrational in them not to expect it. Yet observe, *what proof* has any one of us that he shall die? because other men die? how does he know that? has he seen them die? he can know nothing of what took place before he was born, nor of what happens in other countries. How little, indeed, he knows about it at all, except that it is a *received fact*, and except that it would, in truth, be idle to doubt what mankind as a *whole* witness, though each individual has only his proportionate share in the universal testimony! And, further, we constantly believe things even against our own judgment; i. e. when we think our informant likely to know more about the matter under consideration than ourselves, which is the precise case in the question of religious faith. And thus from reliance on others we acquire knowledge of all kinds, and proceed to reason, judge, decide, act, form plans for the future. And in all this (I say) *trust* is at the bottom; and this the world calls *prudence* (and rightly); and not to trust and act upon trust, *imprudence*, or (it may be) headstrong folly, or *madness*.

But it is needless to proceed; the world could not go on without trust. The most distressing event that can happen to a state is (we know) the spreading of a want of confidence between man and man. Distrust, *want of faith*, breaks the very bonds of human society. Now, then, shall we account it only rational for a man, when he is ignorant, to believe his fellow-man, nay, to yield to another's judgment as better than his own, and yet think it *against reason* when one, like Abraham, gives ear to the Word of God, and sets the promise of God above his own shortsighted expectation? Abraham, it is true, rested in hope beyond hope, in the hope afforded by a Divine promise beyond that hope suggested by nature. He had fancied he never should have a son, and God promised him a son. But might he not well address those self-wise persons who neglect to walk in the steps of his faith, in the language of just reproof? "If we receive the witness of *men*" (he might well urge with the Apostle), "the witness of *God* is greater."[1] Therefore, he "staggered not at the promise of God through unbelief, but was strong in faith, giving glory to God, and being fully persuaded that what He had promised He was able also to perform."

But it may be objected; "True, if we *knew for certain* God had spoken to us as He did to Abraham, it were then madness indeed in us to disbelieve Him; but it is not *His voice* we hear, but *man's* speaking in His name. The Church tells us, that God has revealed to man His will; and the Ministers of the Church point to a book which they say is holy, and contains the words of God. How are we to know whether they speak truth or not? To believe this, is it according to reason or against it?"

This objection brings us to a very large and weighty question, though I do not think it is, generally speaking, a very practical one; viz. what are our reasons for believing the Bible came from God? If any one asks this in a scoffing way, he is not to be answered; for he is profane, and exposes himself to the curse pronounced by St. Paul upon the haters of the Lord Jesus. But if a man inquires sincerely, wishing to find the truth, waiting on God humbly, yet perplexed at knowing or witnessing the deeds of scorners and daring blasphemers, and at hearing their vain reasonings, and not knowing what to think or say about them, let him consider the following remarks, with which I conclude.

Now, first, whatever such profane persons may say about their willingness to believe, if they could find reason,—however willing they may profess themselves to admit that we daily

---

[1] 1 John v.9.

take things on trust, and that to act on faith is in itself quite a rational procedure,—though they may pretend that they do not quarrel with being required to believe, but say that they do think it hard that better evidence is not given them for believing what they are bid believe undoubtingly, viz. the divine authority of the Bible,—in spite of all this, depend upon it, (in a very great many cases), they *do* murmur at being required to believe, they *do* dislike being bound to act without seeing, they *do* prefer to trust themselves to trusting God, even though it *could* be plainly proved to them that God was in truth speaking to them. Did they see God, did He show Himself as He will appear at the last day, still they would be faithful to their own miserable and wretched selves, and would be practically disloyal to the authority of God. Their conduct shows this. Why otherwise do they so frequently scoff at religious men, as if timid and narrow-minded, merely because they fear to sin? Why do they ridicule such conscientious persons as will not swear, or jest indecorously, or live dissolutely? Clearly, it is their very faith itself they ridicule; not their believing on false grounds, but their believing at all. Here they show what it is which rules them within. They do not like the tie of religion, they do not like dependence. To trust another, much more to trust him implicitly, is to acknowledge oneself to be his inferior; and this man's proud nature cannot bear to do. He is apt to think it unmanly, and to be ashamed of it; he promises himself liberty by breaking the chain (as he considers it) which binds him to his Maker and Redeemer. You will say, why then do such men trust each other if they are so proud? I answer, that they cannot help it; and, again, that while they trust, they are trusted in turn; which puts them on a sort of equality with others. Unless this mutual dependence takes place, it is true, they cannot bear to be bound to trust another, to depend on him. And this is the reason that such men are so given to cause tumults and rebellion in national affairs. They set up some image of freedom in their minds, a freedom from the shackles of dependence, which they think their natural right, and which they aim to gain for themselves; a liberty, much like that which Satan aspired after, when he rebelled against God. So, let these men profess what they will, about their not finding fault with Faith on its own account, they do dislike it. And it is therefore very much to our purpose to accustom our minds to the fact, on which I have been insisting, that almost every thing we do is grounded on mere trust in others. We are from our birth dependent creatures, utterly dependent;—dependent immediately on man; and that visible dependence reminds us forcibly of our truer and fuller dependence upon God.

Next, I observe, that these unbelieving men, who use hard words against Scripture, condemn themselves out of their own mouth;—in this way. It is a mistake to suppose that our obedience to God's will is merely founded on our belief in the word of such persons as tell us Scripture came from God. We obey God primarily because we actually feel His presence in our consciences bidding us obey Him. And this, I say, confutes these objectors on their own ground; because the very reason they give for their unbelief is, that they trust their own sight and reason, because their own, more than the words of God's Ministers. Now, let me ask, if they trust their senses and their reason, why do they not trust their conscience too? Is not conscience their own? Their conscience is as much a part of themselves as their reason is; and it is placed within them by Almighty God in order to balance the influence of sight and reason; and yet they will not attend to it; for a plain reason,— they love sin,—they love to be their own masters, and therefore they will not attend to that secret whisper of their hearts, which tells them they are *not* their own masters, and that sin is hateful and ruinous.

Nothing shows this more plainly than their conduct, if ever you appeal to their conscience in favour of your view of the case. Supposing they are using profane language, murmurings, or scoffings at religion; and supposing a man says to them, "You *know* in your heart you should not do so;" how will they reply? They immediately get angry; or they attempt to turn what is said into ridicule; any thing will they do, except answer by *reasoning*. No; their boasted argumentation then fails them. It flies like a coward before the slight stirring of conscience; and their passions, these are the only champions left for their defence. They in effect say, "We do so, because we like it;" perhaps they even *avow* this in so many words. "He feedeth on ashes; a deceived heart hath turned him aside, that he cannot deliver his soul, nor say, Is there not a lie in my right hand?" [2]

And are such the persons whom any Christian can in any degree trust? Surely faith in them would be of all conceivable confidences the most irrational, the most misplaced. Can we allow ourselves to be perplexed and frightened at the words of those who carry upon them the tokens of their own inconsistency, the mark of Cain? Surely not; and as that first rebel's

[2] Is. xliv.20.

mark was set on him, "lest any finding him should kill him," in like manner their presence but reminds us thereby to view them with love, though most sorrowfully, and to pray earnestly, and do our utmost (if there is ought we can do), that they may be spared the second death;—to look on them with awe, as a land cursed by God, the plain of Siddim or the ruins of Babel, but which He, for our Redeemer's sake, is able to renew and fertilize.

For ourselves, let us but obey God's voice in our hearts, and I will venture to say we shall have no doubts practically formidable about the truth of Scripture. Find out the man who strictly obeys the law within him, and yet is an unbeliever as regards the Bible, and then it will be time enough to consider all that variety of proof by which the truth of the Bible is confirmed to us. This is no practical inquiry for *us*. Our doubts, if we have any, will be found to arise after *disobedience*; it is bad company or corrupt books which lead to unbelief. It is sin which quenches the Holy Spirit.

And if we but obey God strictly, in time (through His blessing) faith will become like sight; we shall have no more difficulty in finding what will please God than in moving our limbs, or in understanding the conversation of our familiar friends. This is the blessedness of confirmed obedience. Let us aim at attaining it; and in whatever proportion we now enjoy it, praise and bless God for His unspeakable gift.

THE CHRISTIAN MYSTERIES

"How can these things be?"—John iii.9.

THERE is much instruction conveyed in the circumstance, that the Feast of the Holy Trinity immediately succeeds that of Whit Sunday. On the latter Festival we commemorate the coming of the Spirit of God, who is promised to us as the source of all spiritual knowledge and discernment. But lest we should forget the nature of that illumination which He imparts, Trinity Sunday follows, to tell us what it is not; not a light accorded to the reason, the gifts of the intellect; inasmuch as the Gospel has its mysteries, its difficulties, and secret things, which the Holy Spirit does not remove.

The grace promised us is given, not that we may know more, but that we may do better. It is given to influence, guide, and strengthen us in performing our duty towards God and man; it is given to us as creatures, as sinners, as men, as immortal beings, not as mere reasoners, disputers, or philosophical inquirers. It teaches what we are, whither we are going, what we must do, how we must do it; it enables us to change our fallen nature from evil to good, "to make ourselves a new heart and a new spirit." But it tells us nothing for the *sake* of telling it; neither in His Holy Word, nor through our consciences, has the Blessed Spirit thought fit so to act. Not that the desire of knowing sacred things for the sake of knowing them is wrong. As knowledge about earth, sky, and sea, and the wonders they contain, is in itself valuable, and in its place desirable, so doubtless there is nothing sinful in gazing wistfully at the marvellous providences of God's moral governance, and wishing to understand them. But still God has not given us such knowledge in the Bible, and therefore to look into the Bible for such knowledge, or to expect it in any way from the inward teaching of the Holy Ghost, is a dangerous mistake, and (it may be) a sin. And since men are apt to prize knowledge above holiness, therefore it is most suitably provided, that Trinity Sunday should succeed Whit Sunday; to warn us that the enlightening vouchsafed to us is not an understanding of "all mysteries and all knowledge," but that love or charity which is "the fulfilling of the Law."

And in matter of fact there have been very grievous mistakes respecting the nature of Christian knowledge. There have been at all times men so ignorant of the object of Christ's coming, as to consider mysteries inconsistent with the light of the Gospel. They have thought the darkness of Judaism, of which Scripture speaks, to be a state of intellectual ignorance; and Christianity to be, what they term, a "rational religion." And hence they have argued, that no doctrine which was *mysterious*, i.e. too deep for human reason, or inconsistent with their self-devised notions, could be contained in Scripture; as if it were honouring Christ to maintain that when He said a thing, He could not have meant what He said, because *they* would not have said it. Nicodemus, though a sincere inquirer, and (as the event shows) a true follower of Christ, yet at first was startled at the mysteries of the Gospel. He said to Christ, "How can these things be?" He felt the temptation, and overcame it. But there are others who are altogether offended and fall away on being exposed to it; as those mentioned in the sixth chapter of St. John's Gospel, who went back and walked no more with Him.

The Feast of Trinity succeeds Pentecost; the light of the Gospel does not remove mysteries in religion. This is our subject. Let us enlarge upon it.

1. Let us consider such difficulties of religion, as press upon us independently of the Scriptures. Now we shall find the Gospel has not removed these; they remain as great as before Christ came.—How excellent is this world! how very good and fair is the face of nature! how pleasant it is to walk into the green country, and "to meditate in the field at the eventide!" [1] As we look around, we cannot but be persuaded that God is most good, and loves His creatures; yet amid all the splendour we see around us, and the happy beings, thousands and ten thousands, which live in the air and water, the question comes upon us, "But *why is there pain in the world?*" We see that the brutes prey on each other, inflicting violent, unnatural deaths. Some of them, too, are enemies of man, and harm us when they have an opportunity. And man tortures others unrelentingly, nay, condemns some of them to a life of suffering. Much more do pain and misery show themselves in the history of man;—the numberless diseases and casualties of human life, and our sorrows of mind;—then, further, the evils we inflict on each other, our

[1] Gen. xxiv.63.

sins and their awful consequences. Now why does God permit so much evil in His own world? This is a difficulty, I say, which we feel at once, before we open the Bible; and which we are quite unable to solve. We open the Bible; the fact is acknowledged there, but it is not explained at all. We are told that sin entered the world *through the Devil*, who tempted Adam to disobedience; so that God created the world good, *though* evil is in it. But why He thought fit to *suffer* this, we are not told. We know no more on the subject than we did before opening the Bible. It was a mystery before God gave His revelation, it is as great a mystery now; and doubtless for this reason, because knowledge about it would do us no good, it would merely satisfy curiosity. It is not practical knowledge.

2. Nor, again, are the difficulties of Judaism removed by Christianity. The Jews were told, that if they put to death certain animals, they should be admitted by way of consequence into God's favour, which their continual transgressions were ever forfeiting. Now there was something mysterious here. How should the death of unoffending creatures make God gracious to the Jews? They could not tell, of course. All that could be said to the point was, that in the daily course of human affairs the unoffending constantly suffer instead of the offenders. One man is ever suffering for the fault of another. But this experience did not lighten the difficulty of so mysterious a provision. It was still a mystery that God's favour should depend on the death of brute animals. Does Christianity solve this difficulty? No; it continues it. The Jewish sacrifices indeed are done away, but still there remains One Great Sacrifice for sin, infinitely higher and more sacred than all other conceivable sacrifices. According to the Gospel message, Christ has voluntarily suffered, "the just for the unjust, to bring us to God." Here is the mystery continued. Why was this suffering necessary to procure for us the blessings which we were in ourselves unworthy of? We do not know. We should not be better men for knowing why God did not pardon us without Christ's death; so He has not told us. One suffers for another in the ordinary course of things; and under the Jewish Law, too; and in the Christian scheme; and why all this, is still a mystery.

Another difficulty to a thoughtful Israelite would arise from considering the state of the heathen world. Why did not Almighty God bring all nations into His Church, and teach them, by direct revelation, the sin of idol-worship? He would not be able to answer. God had chosen one nation. It is true the same principle of preferring one to another is seen in the system of the whole world. God gives men unequal advantages, comforts, education, talents, health. Yet this does not satisfy us, *why* He has thought fit to do so at all. Here, again, the Gospel recognizes and confirms the mysterious fact. *We* are born in a Christian country, others are not; *we* are baptized; *we* are educated; others are not. We are favoured *above* others. But why? We cannot tell; no more than the Jews could tell why they were favoured;—and for this reason, because to know it is nothing to us; it would not make us better men to know it. It is intended that we should look to ourselves, and rather consider why we have privileges given us, than why others have not the same. Our Saviour repels such curious questions more than once. "Lord, and what shall this man do?"[2] St. Peter asked about St. John. Christ replied, "If I will that he tarry till I come, *what is that to thee? Follow thou Me.*"

Thus the Gospel gives us no advantages in respect to mere *barren knowledge*, above the Jew, or above the unenlightened heathen.

3. Nay, we may proceed to say, further than this, *that it increases our difficulties*. It is indeed a remarkable circumstance, that the very revelation that brings us *practical and useful knowledge* about our souls, in the very *act of doing* so, nay (as it would seem), in *consequence of* doing so, brings us mysteries. We gain spiritual light at the price of intellectual perplexity; a blessed exchange doubtless, (for which is better, to be well and happy within ourselves, or to know what is going on at the world's end?) still at the price of perplexity. For instance, how infinitely important and blessed is the news of eternal happiness? but we learn in connexion with this joyful truth, that there is a *state of endless misery* too. Now, how great a mystery is this! yet the difficulty goes hand in hand with the spiritual blessing. It is still more strikingly to the point to refer to the message of mercy itself. We are saved by the death of Christ; but who is Christ? Christ is the Very Son of God, Begotten of God and One with God from everlasting, God incarnate. This is our inexpressible comfort, and a most sanctifying truth if we receive it rightly; but how stupendous a mystery is the incarnation and sufferings of the Son of God! Here, not merely do the good tidings and the mystery go together, as in the revelation of eternal life and eternal death, but the very doctrine which is the mystery, brings the comfort also. Weak, ignorant, sinful, desponding, sorrowful man, gains the knowledge of an infinitely merciful Protec-

---

[2] John xxi.21, 22.

tor, a Giver of all good, most powerful, the Worker of all righteousness within him; at what price? at the price of a mystery. "The Word was made flesh, and dwelt among us, and we beheld His glory;" and He laid down His life for the world. What rightly disposed mind but will gladly make the exchange, and exclaim, in the language of one whose words are almost sacred among us, "Let it be counted folly, or frenzy, or fury whatsoever; it is our comfort and our wisdom. We care for no knowledge in the world but this, that man hath sinned, and God hath suffered; that God hath made Himself the Son of Man, and that men are made the righteousness of God." [3]

The same singular connexion between religious light and comfort, and intellectual darkness, is also seen in the doctrine of the Trinity. Frail man requires pardon and sanctification; can he do otherwise than gratefully devote himself to, and trust implicitly in, his Redeemer and his Sanctifier? But if our Redeemer were not God, and our Sanctifier were not God, how great would have been our danger of preferring creatures to the Creator! What a source of light, freedom, and comfort is it, to know we cannot love Them too much, or humble ourselves before Them too reverently, for both Son and Spirit are separately God! Such is the *practical* effect of the doctrine; but what a mystery also is therein involved! What a source of perplexity and darkness (I say) to the reason, is the doctrine which immediately results from it! for if Christ be by Himself God, and the Spirit be by Himself God, and yet there be but One God, here is plainly something altogether beyond our comprehension; and, though we might have antecedently supposed there were numberless truths relating to Almighty God which we could neither know nor understand, yet certain as this is, it does not make this mystery at all less overpowering when it *is* revealed.

And it is important to observe, that this doctrine of the Trinity *is not proposed in Scripture as a mystery*. It seems then that, as we draw forth many remarkable facts concerning the natural world which do not lie on its surface, so by meditation we detect in Revelation this remarkable principle, which is not openly propounded, *that religious light is intellectual darkness*. As if our gracious Lord had said to us; "Scripture does not aim at making mysteries, but they are as shadows brought out by the Sun of Truth. When you knew nothing of revealed light, you knew not revealed darkness. Religious truth requires you should be told *something*, your own imperfect nature prevents

[3] Hooker on Justification.

your knowing *all*; and to know *something*, and *not all*,—*partial knowledge*,—must of course perplex; doctrines imperfectly revealed must be mysterious."

4. Such being the necessary mysteriousness of Scripture doctrine, how can we best turn it to account in the contest which we are engaged in with our evil hearts? Now we are given to see how to do this in part, and, as far as we see, let us be thankful for the gift. It seems, then, that difficulties in revelation are especially given to prove *the reality of our faith*. What shall separate the insincere from the sincere follower of Christ? When the many own Christ with their lips, what shall try and discipline His true servant, and detect the self-deceiver? Difficulties in revelation mainly contribute to this end. They are stumbling-blocks to proud and unhumbled minds, and were intended to be such. Faith is unassuming, modest, thankful, obedient. It receives with reverence and love whatever God gives, when convinced it is His gift. But when men do not feel rightly their need of His redeeming mercy, their lost condition and their inward sinfulness, when, in fact, they do not seek Christ in good earnest, in order to gain something, and do something, but as a matter of curiosity, or speculation, or form, *of course* these difficulties will become great objections in the way of their receiving His word simply. And I say these difficulties were intended to be such by Him who "scattereth the proud in the imagination of their hearts." St. Peter assures us, that that same corner-stone which is unto them that believe "*precious*," is "unto them which be disobedient, a stone of stumbling, and a rock of offence," "whereunto also (he adds) *they were appointed*."[4] And our Lord's conduct through His ministry is a continued example of this. He spoke in parables,[5] that they might see and hear, yet not understand,—a righteous detection of insincerity; whereas the same difficulties and obscurities, which offended irreligious men, would but lead the humble and meek to seek for more light, for information as far as it was to be obtained, and for resignation and contentedness, where it was not given. When Jesus said, ". . . Except ye eat the flesh of the Son of Man, and drink His blood, ye have no life in you . . . Many of His disciples . . . said, This is a hard saying: who can hear it? . . . and from that time many . . . went back, and walked no more with Him. . . . Then said Jesus unto the twelve, Will ye also go away? Then Simon Peter answered Him, Lord, to whom shall we go? Thou hast the words of eternal life." Here

[4] 1 Pet. ii.7, 8.   [5] *Vide* Mark iv.11–25, etc.

is the trial of faith, a *difficulty*. Those "that believe not" fall
away; the true disciples remain firm, for they feel their *eternal
interests* at stake, and ask the very plain and practical, as well as
affectionate question, "*To whom* shall we go,"[6] if we leave
Christ?

At another time our Lord says, "I thank Thee, O Father,
Lord of heaven and earth, that Thou hast hid these things
from the wise and prudent (those who trust reason rather than
Scripture and conscience), and hast revealed them unto babes
(those who humbly walk by faith). Even so, Father, for so it
seemed good in Thy sight."[7]

5. Now what do we gain from thoughts such as these? Our
Saviour gives us the conclusion, in the words which follow a
passage I have just read. "Therefore said I unto you, that no
man can come unto Me, except it were given him of My Father." Or, again, "No man can come to Me, except the Father,
which hath sent Me, draw him." Therefore, if we feel the necessity of coming to Christ, yet the difficulty, let us recollect
that the gift of coming is in God's hands, and that we must pray
Him to give it to us. Christ does not merely tell us, that we
cannot come of ourselves (though this He does tell us), but He
tells us also with whom the power of coming is lodged, with His
Father,—that we may seek it of Him. It is true, religion has an
austere appearance to those who never have tried it; its doctrines full of mystery, its precepts of harshness; so that it is uninviting, offending different men in different ways, but in some
way offending all. When then we feel within us the risings of
this opposition to Christ, proud aversion to His Gospel, or a
low-minded longing after this world, let us pray God to draw
us; and though we cannot move a step without Him, at least let
us try to move. He looks into our hearts and sees our strivings
even before we strive, and He blesses and strengthens even our
feebleness. Let us get rid of curious and presumptuous thoughts
by going about our business, whatever it is; and let us mock and
baffle the doubts which Satan whispers to us by *acting* against
them. No matter whether we believe doubtingly or not, or
know clearly or not, so that we act upon our belief. The rest
will follow in time; part in this world, part in the next. Doubts
may pain, but they cannot harm, unless we give way to them;
and that we *ought not* to give way, our conscience tells us, so that
our course is plain. And the more we are in earnest to "work out
our salvation," the less shall we care to know how those things

[6] John vi.53–68.   [7] Matt. xi.25, 26.

really are, which perplex us. At length, when our hearts are in our work, we shall be indisposed to take the trouble of listening to curious truths (if they are but curious), though we might have them explained to us. For what says the Holy Scripture? that of speculations "there is no end," and they are "a weariness of the flesh;" but that we must "fear God and keep His commandments; for this is the whole duty of man." [8]

[8] Eccles. xii. 12, 13.

THE SELF-WISE INQUIRER

"Let no man deceive himself. If any man among you seemeth to be wise in this world, let him become a fool, that he may be wise. For the wisdom of this world is foolishness with God. For it is written, He taketh the wise in their own craftiness."—1 Cor. iii.18, 19.

A MONG the various deceptions against which St. Paul warns us, a principal one is that of a *false wisdom*; as in the text. The Corinthians prided themselves on their intellectual acuteness and knowledge; as if any thing could equal the excellence of Christian love. Accordingly, St. Paul writing to them says, "Let no man deceive himself. If any man among you seemeth to be wise in this world" (i.e. has the reputation of wisdom in the world), "let him become a fool (what the world calls a fool), that he may (really) be wise." "For," he proceeds (just as real wisdom is foolishness in the eyes of the world, so in turn), "the wisdom of this world is foolishness with God."

This warning of the Apostle against *our trusting our own wisdom*, may lead us, through God's blessing, to some profitable reflections to-day.

The world's wisdom is said to be *foolishness* in God's sight; and the end of it error, perplexity, and then ruin. "He taketh the wise in their own craftiness." Here is one especial reason why professed inquirers after Truth do not find it. They seek it in a wrong way, by a vain wisdom, which leads them away from the Truth, however it may seem to promise success.

Let us then inquire what is this *vain wisdom*, and then we shall the better see how it leads men astray.

Now, when it is said that to trust our own notions is a wrong thing and a vain wisdom, of course this is not meant of all our own notions whatever; for we must trust our own notions in one shape or other, and some notions which we form are right and true. The question, therefore, is, what is that *evil* trusting to ourselves, that sinful self-confidence, or self-conceit, which is called in the text the "wisdom of the world," and is a chief cause of our going wrong in our religious inquiries?

These are the notions which we may trust *without* blame; viz. such as come to us by way of our Conscience, for such come from God. I mean our certainty that there is a right and a wrong, that some things ought to be done, and other things not done; that we have duties, the neglect of which brings remorse; and further, that God is good, wise, powerful, and righteous, and that we should try to obey Him. All these notions, and a multitude of others like these, come by natural conscience, i.e. they are impressed on all our minds from our earliest years without our trouble. They do not proceed from the mere exercise of our minds, though it is true they are strengthened and formed thereby. They proceed from God, whether within us or without us; and though we cannot trust them so implicitly as we can trust the Bible, because the truths of the Bible are actually preserved in writing, and so cannot be lost or altered, still, as far as we have reason to think them true, we may rely in them, and make much of them, without incurring the sin of self-confidence. These notions which we obtain without our exertion will never make us proud or conceited, because they are ever attended with a sense of sin and guilt, from the remembrance that we have at times transgressed and injured them. To trust them is not the false wisdom of the world, or foolishness, because they come from the Allwise God. And far from leading a man into error, they will, if obeyed, of a certainty lead him to a firm belief in Scripture; in which he will find all those vague conjectures and imperfect notions about Truth, which his own heart taught him, abundantly sanctioned, completed, and illustrated.

Such then are the opinions and feelings of which a man is not proud. What are those of which he is likely to be proud? those which he obtains, *not* by nature, but by his own industry, ability, and research; those which he possesses and others not. Every one is in danger of valuing himself for what he does; and hence truths (or fancied truths) which a man has obtained for himself after much thought and labour, such he is apt to make much of, and to rely upon; and this is the source of that vain wisdom of which the Apostle speaks in the text.

Now (I say) this confidence in our own reasoning powers not only leads to pride, but to "*foolishness*" also, and destructive error, because it will oppose itself to Scripture. A man who fancies he can find out truth by himself, disdains revelation. He who thinks he *has* found it out, is *impatient* of revelation. He fears it will interfere with his own imaginary discoveries, he is unwilling to consult it; and when it does interfere, then he is angry. We hear much of this proud rejection of the truth in the Epistle from which the text is taken. The Jews felt anger, and the Greeks disdain, at the Christian doctrine. "The Jews required a sign (according to their preconceived notions concerning the Messiah's coming), and the Greeks seek after wisdom (some subtle train of reasoning), but we preach Christ crucified, unto the Jews a stumbling-block, and to the Greeks foolishness."[1] In another place the Apostle says of the misled Christians of Corinth, "Now ye are full" of your own notions, "now ye are rich, ye have reigned as kings *without us*;"[2] i. e. you have prided yourself on a wisdom, "without," separate from, the truth of Apostolic doctrine. Confidence, then, in our own reasoning powers leads to (what St. Paul calls) foolishness, by causing in our hearts an indifference towards, or a distaste for Scripture information.

But, besides thus keeping us from the best of guides, it also makes us fools, because it is a confidence in a *bad* guide. Our reasoning powers are very weak in all inquiries into moral and religious truth. Clear-sighted as reason is on other subjects, and trustworthy as a guide, still in questions connected with our duty to God and man it is very unskilful and equivocating. After all, it barely reaches the same great truths which are authoritatively set forth by Conscience and by Scripture; and if it be used in religious inquiries, without reference to these divinely-sanctioned informants, the probability is, it will miss the Truth altogether. Thus the (so-called) wise will be taken in their own craftiness. All of us, doubtless, recollect our Lord's words, which are quite to the purpose; "I thank Thee, O Father, Lord of heaven and earth, because Thou hast hid these things from the *wise and prudent* (those who trust in their own intellectual powers), and hast revealed them unto *babes*,"[3] those, i. e. that act by faith and for conscience sake.

The false wisdom, then, of which St. Paul speaks in the text, is a trusting our own powers for arriving at religious truth, instead of taking what is divinely provided for us, whether in nature or revelation. This is the way of the world. In the world, Reason is set against Conscience, and usurps its power; and hence men become "wise in their own conceits," and "leaning to their own understandings," "err from the truth." Let us now review some particulars of this contest between our instinctive sense of right and wrong, and our weak and conceited reason.

It begins within us, when childhood and boyhood are past;

---

[1] 1 Cor. i.22, 23.   [2] 1 Cor. iv.8.   [3] Matt. xi.25.

and the time comes for our entrance into life. Before that time we trusted our divinely-enlightened sense of duty and our right feeling implicitly; and though (alas!) we continually transgressed, and thereby impaired this inward guide, at least we did not question its authority. *Then* we had that original temper of faith, wrought in us by baptism, the spirit of little children, without which our Lord assures us, none of us, young or old, can enter the kingdom of heaven.[4]

But when our minds became more manly, and the world opened upon us, then in proportion to the intellectual gifts with which God had honoured us, came the temptation of unbelief and disobedience. Then came reason, led on by passion, to war against our better knowledge. We were driven into the wilderness, after our Lord's manner, by the very Spirit given us, which exposed us to the Devil's devices, before the time or power came of using the gift in God's service. And how many of the most highly endowed then fall away under trials which the sinless Son of God withstood! He feels for all who are tempted, having Himself suffered temptation; yet what a sight must He see, and by what great exercise of mercy must the Holy Jesus endure, the bold and wicked thoughts which often reign the most triumphantly in the breasts of those (at least for a time) whom He has commissioned by the abundance of their talents to be the especial ministers of His will!

A murmuring against that religious service which is perfect freedom, complaints that Christ's yoke is heavy, a rebellious rising against the authority of Conscience, and a proud arguing against the Truth, or at least an endurance of doubt and scoffing, and a light, unmeaning use of sceptical arguments and assertions, these are the beginnings of apostasy. Then come the affectation of originality, the desire to appear manly and independent, and the fear of the ridicule of our acquaintance, all combining to make us first speak, and then really think evil of the supreme authority of religion. This gradual transgression of the first commandment of the Law is generally attended by a transgression of the fifth. In our childhood we loved both religion and our home; but as we learn to despise the voice of God, so do we first affect, and then feel, an indifference towards the opinions of our superiors and elders. Thus our minds become gradually hardened against the purest pleasures, both divine and human.

As this progress in sin continues, our disobedience becomes its own punishment. In proportion as we lean to our own

[4] Matt. xviii.3.

understanding, we are driven to do so for want of a better guide. Our first true guide, the light of innocence, is gradually withdrawn from us; and nothing is left for us but to "grope and stumble in the desolate places," by the dim, uncertain light of reason. Thus we are taken in our own craftiness. This is what is sometimes called *judicial blindness*; such as Pharaoh's, who, from resisting God's will, at length did not know the difference between light and darkness.

How far each individual proceeds in this bad course, depends on a variety of causes, into the consideration of which I need not enter. Some are frightened at themselves, and turn back into the right way before it is too late. Others are checked; and though they do not see God with all their heart, yet are preserved from any strong and full manifestation of the evil principles which lurk within them; and others are kept in a correct outward form of religion by the circumstances in which they are placed. But there are others, and these many in number, perhaps in all ranks of life, who proceed onwards in evil; and I will go on to describe in part their condition,—the condition, that is, of those in whom intellectual power is fearfully unfolded amid the neglect of moral truth.

The most common case, of course, is that of those who, with their principles thus unformed, or rather unsettled, become engaged, in the ordinary way, in the business of life. Their first simplicity of character went early. The violence of passion followed, and was indulged; and it is gone, too, leaving (without their suspecting it) most baneful effects on their mind; just as some diseases silently change the constitution of the body. Lastly, a vain reason has put into disorder their notions about moral propriety and duty, both as to religion and the conduct of life. It is quite plain, that, having nothing of that faith which "overcomes the world," they must be overcome by it. Let it not be supposed I am speaking of some strange case which does not concern us; for what we know, it concerns some of us most nearly. The issue of our youthful trial in good and evil, probably has had somewhat of a decided character one way or the other; and we may be quite sure that, if it has issued in evil, we shall not know it. Deadness to the voice of God, hardness of heart, is one of the very symptoms of unbelief. God's judgments, whether to the world or the individual, are not loudly spoken. The decree goes forth to build or destroy; Angels hear it; but we go on in the way of the world as usual, though our souls may have been, at least for a season, abandoned by God. I mean, that it is not at all unlikely that, in the case of some of those who now hear me, a great part of their professed faith is a mere matter of *words*, not *ideas and principles*; that what opinions they really hold by any exertion of their own minds, have been reached by the mere exercise of their intellect, the random and accidental use of their mere reasoning powers, whether they be strong or not, and are not the result of habitual, firm, and progressive obedience to God, not the knowledge which an honest and good heart imparts. Our religious notions may lie on the mere surface of our minds, and have no root within them; and (I say) from this circumstance, that the indulgence of early passions, though forgotten now, and the misapplication of reason in our youth, have left an indelibly evil character upon our heart, a judicial hardness and blindness. Let us think of this; it may be the state of those who have had to endure only ordinary temptations, from the growth of that reasoning faculty with which we are all gifted.

But when that gift of reason is something especial,—dear, brilliant, or powerful,—then our danger is increased. The first sin of men of superior understanding is to *value* themselves upon it, and look down upon others. They make intellect the measure of praise and blame; and instead of considering a common *faith* to be the bond of union between Christian and Christian, they dream of some other fellowship of civilization, refinement, literature, science, or general mental illumination, to unite gifted minds one with another. Having thus cast down moral excellence from its true station, and set up the usurping empire of mere reason, next, they place a value upon all truths exactly in proportion to the possibility of proving them by means of that mere reason. Hence, moral and religious truths are thought little of by them, because they fall under the province of *Conscience* far more than of the intellect. Religion sinks in their estimation, or becomes of no account; they begin to think all religions alike; and no wonder, for they are like men who have lost the faculty of discerning colours, and who never, by any exercise of reason, can make out the difference between white and black. As to the code of morals, they acknowledge it in a measure, that is, so far as its dicta can be *proved* by reasoning, by an appeal to sight, and to expedience, and without reference to a natural sense of right and wrong as the sanction of these informants. Thinking much of intellectual advancement, they are much bent on improving the world by making *all men* intellectual; and they labour to convince themselves, that as men grow in knowledge they will grow in virtue.

As they proceed in their course of judicial blindness, from

undervaluing they learn to *despise* or to *hate* the authority of Conscience. They treat it as a weakness, to which all men indeed are subject,—they themselves in the number,—especially in seasons of sickness, but of which they have cause to be ashamed. The notions of better men about an over-ruling Providence, and the Divine will, designs, appointments, works, judgments, they treat with scorn, as irrational; especially if (as will often be the case) these notions are conveyed in incorrect language, with some accidental confusion or intellectual weakness of expression.

And all these inducements to live by sight and not by faith are greatly increased, when men are engaged in any pursuit which properly *belongs* to the intellect. Hence sciences conversant with experiments on the material creation, tend to make men forget the existence of spirit and the Lord of spirits.

I will not pursue the course of infidelity into its worst and grossest forms; but it may be instructive, before I conclude, to take the case of such a man as I have been describing, when under the influence of some relentings of conscience towards the close of his life.

This is a case of no unfrequent occurrence; that is, it must frequently happen that the most hardened conscience is at times visited by sudden compunctions, though generally they are but momentary. But it sometimes happens, further than this, that a man, from one cause or other, feels he is not in a safe state, and struggles with himself, and the struggle terminates in a manner which affords a fresh illustration of the working of that wisdom of the world which in God's sight is foolishness.

How shall a sinner, who has formed his character upon unbelief, trusting sight and reason rather than Conscience and Scripture, how shall he begin to repent? What must he do? Is it possible he can overcome himself, and new make his heart in the end of his days? It is possible,—not with man, but with God, who gives grace to all who ask for it; but in only one way, *in the way of His commandments*, by a slow, tedious, toilsome self-discipline; slow, tedious, and toilsome, that is, to one who has been long hardening himself in a dislike of it, and indulging himself in the rapid flights and easy victories of his reason. There is but one way to heaven; the narrow way; and he who sets about to seek God, though in old age, must enter it at the same door as others. He must retrace his way, and begin again with the very beginning as if he were a boy. And so proceeding,—labouring, watching, and praying,—he seems likely, after all, to make but little progress during the brief remnant of his life; both because the time left to him is short, and because he has to undo while he does a work;—he has to overcome that resistance from his old stout will and hardened heart, which in youth he would not have experienced.

Now it is plain how humbling this is to his pride: he wishes to be saved; but he cannot stoop to be a penitent all his days: to beg he is ashamed. Therefore he looks about for other means of finding a safe hope. And one way among others by which he deceives himself, is this same idea that he may gain religious knowledge merely by his reason.

Thus it happens, that men who have led profligate lives in their youth, or who have passed their days in the pursuit of wealth, or in some other excitement of the world, not unfrequently settle down into *heresies* in their latter years. Before, perhaps, they professed nothing, and suffered themselves to be called Christians and members of the Church; but at length, roused to inquire after truth, and forgetting that the pure in heart alone can see God, and therefore that they must begin by a *moral* reformation, by self-denial, they inquire merely by the way of reasoning. No wonder they err; they cannot understand any part of the Church's system whether of doctrine or discipline; yet they *think* themselves judges; and they treat the most sacred ordinances and the most solemn doctrines, with scorn and irreverence. Thus "the last state of such men is worse than the first." In the words of the text, they ought to have become fools, that they might have been in the end really wise; but they prefer another way, and are taken in their own craftiness.

May we ever bear in mind, that the "fear of the Lord is the beginning of wisdom;" [5] that obedience to our conscience, in all things, great and small, is the way to know the Truth; that pride hardens the heart, and sensuality debases it; and that all those who live in pride and sensual indulgence, can no more comprehend the way of the Holy Spirit, or know the voice of Christ, than the devils who believe with a dead faith and tremble!

"Blessed are they that do His commandments, that they may have right to the tree of life, and may enter in through the gates into the city" where there is "no need of the sun, neither of the moon to shine in it; for the glory of God doth lighten it, and the Lamb is the light thereof." [6]

[5] Prov. i.7.
[6] Rev. xxi.23; xxii.14.

OBEDIENCE THE REMEDY
FOR RELIGIOUS PERPLEXITY

"Wait on the Lord, and keep His way, and He shall exalt thee to inherit the land."—Ps. xxxvii.34.

THE Psalm from which I have taken my text, is written with a view of encouraging good men who are in perplexity,—and especially perplexity concerning God's designs, providence, and will. "Fret not thyself;" this is the lesson it inculcates from first to last. This world is in a state of confusion. Unworthy men prosper, and are looked on as the greatest men of the time. Truth and goodness are thrown into the shade; but wait patiently,— peace, be still; in the end, the better side shall triumph,—the meek shall inherit the earth.

Doubtless the Church is in great darkness and perplexity under the Christian dispensation, as well as under the Jewish. Not that Christianity does not explain to us the most important religious questions, which it does to our great comfort; but that, from the nature of the case, imperfect beings, as we are, must always be, on the whole, in a state of darkness. Nay, the very doctrines of the New Testament themselves bring with them their own peculiar difficulties; and, till we learn to quiet our minds, and to school them into submission to God, we shall probably find more perplexity than information even in what St. Paul calls "the light of the glorious Gospel of Christ." [1] Revelation was not given us to satisfy doubts, but to make us better men; and it is as we become better men, that it becomes light and peace to our souls; though even to the end of our lives we shall find difficulties both in it and in the world around us.

I will make some remarks to-day on the case of those who, though they are in the whole honest inquirers in religion, yet are more or less in perplexity and anxiety, and so are discouraged.

---

[1] 2 Cor. iv.4.

The use of difficulties to all of us in our trial in this world is obvious. Our faith is variously assailed by doubts and difficulties, in order to prove its sincerity. If we really love God and His Son, we shall go on in spite of opposition, even though, as in the case of the Canaanitish woman, He seem to repel us. If we are not in earnest, difficulty makes us turn back. This is one of the ways in which God separates the corn from the chaff, gradually gathering each, as time goes on, into its own heap, till the end comes, when "He will gather the wheat into His garner, but the chaff He will burn with fire unquenchable." [2]

Now, I am aware that to some persons it may sound strange to speak of *difficulties* in religion, for they find none at all. But though it is true, that the earlier we begin to seek God in earnest, the less of difficulty and perplexity we are likely to endure, yet this ignorance of religious difficulties in a great many cases, I fear, arises from ignorance of religion itself. When our hearts are not in our work, and we are but carried on with the stream of the world, continuing in the Church because we find ourselves there, observing religious ordinances merely because we are used to them, and professing to be Christians because others do, it is not to be expected that we should know what it is to feel ourselves wrong, and unable to get right,—to feel doubt, anxiety, disappointment, discontent; whereas, when our minds are awakened, and we see that there is a right way and a wrong way, and that we have much to learn, when we try to gain religious knowledge from Scripture, and to apply it to our selves, then from time to time we are troubled with doubts and misgivings, and are oppressed with gloom.

To all those who are perplexed in any way soever, who wish for light but cannot find it, one precept must be given,—*obey*. It is obedience which brings a man into the right path; it is obedience keeps him there and strengthens him in it. Under all circumstances, whatever be the cause of his distress,—obey. In the words of the text, "Wait on the Lord, and keep His way, and He shall exalt thee."

Let us apply this exhortation to the case of those who have but lately taken up the subject of religion at all. Every science has its difficulties at first; why then should the science of living well be without them? When the subject of religion is new to us, it is strange. We have heard truths all our lives without feeling them duly; at length, when they affect us, we cannot believe them to be the same we have long known. We are thrown out of

[2] Luke iii.17.

our fixed notions of things; an embarrassment ensues; a general painful uncertainty. We say, "Is the Bible true? Is it possible?" and are distressed by evil doubts, which we can hardly explain to ourselves, much less to others. No one can help us. And the relative importance of present objects is so altered from what it was, that we can scarcely form any judgment upon them, or when we attempt it, we form a wrong judgment. Our eyes do not accommodate themselves to the various distances of the objects before us, and are dazzled; or like the blind man restored to sight, we "see men as trees, walking." [3] Moreover, our judgment of persons, as well as of things, is changed; and, if not every where changed, yet at first every where suspected by ourselves. And this general distrust of ourselves is the greater the longer we have been already living in inattention to sacred subjects, and the more we now are humbled and ashamed of ourselves. And it leads us to take up with the first religious guide who offers himself to us, whatever be his real fitness for the office.

To these agitations of mind about what is truth and what is error, is added an anxiety about ourselves, which, however sincere, is apt to lead us wrong. We do not feel, think, and act as religiously as we could wish; and while we are sorry for it, we are also (perhaps) somewhat *surprised* at it, and impatient at it,—which is natural but unreasonable. Instead of reflecting that we are just setting about our recovery from a most serious disease of long standing, we conceive we ought to be able to trace the course of our recovery by a sensible improvement. This same impatience is seen in persons who are recovering from bodily indisposition. They gain strength slowly, and are better perhaps for some days, and then worse again; and a slight relapse dispirits them. In the same way, when we begin to seek God in earnest, we are apt, not only to be humbled (which we ought to be), but to be discouraged at the slowness with which we are able to amend, in spite of all the assistances of God's grace. Forgetting that our proper title at very best is that of penitent sinners, we seek to rise all at once into the blessedness of the sons of God. This impatience leads us to misuse the purpose of self-examination; which is principally intended to inform us of our sins, whereas we are disappointed if it does not at once tell us of our improvement. Doubtless, in a length of time we shall be conscious of improvement too, but the object of ordinary self-examination is to find out whether we are in

[3] Mark viii.24.

earnest, and again, what we have done wrong, in order that we may pray for pardon, and do better. Further, reading in Scripture how exalted the thoughts and spirit of Christians should be, we are apt to forget that a Christian spirit is the growth of time; and that we cannot force it upon our minds, however desirable and necessary it may be to possess it; that by giving utterance to religious sentiments we do not become religious, rather the reverse; whereas, if we strove to obey God's will in all things, we actually should be gradually training our hearts into the fulness of a Christian spirit. But not understanding this, men are led to speak much and expressly upon sacred subjects, as if it were a duty to do so, and in the hope of its making them better; and they measure their advance in faith and holiness, not by their power of obeying God in practice, mastering their wills, and becoming more exact in their daily duties, but by the warmth and energy of their religious feelings. And, when they cannot sustain these to that height which they consider almost the characteristic of a true Christian, then they are discouraged, and tempted to despair. Added to this, sometimes their old sins, reviving from the slumber into which they have been cast for a time, rush over their minds, and seem prepared to take them captive. They cry to God for aid, but He seems not to hear them, and they know not which way to look for safety.

Now such persons must be reminded first of all, of the greatness of the work which they have undertaken, viz. the sanctification of their souls. Those, indeed, who think this an easy task, or (which comes to the same thing) who think that, though hard in itself, it will be easy to them, for God's grace will take all the toil of it from them, such men of course must be disappointed on finding by experience the force of their original evil nature, and the extreme slowness with which even a Christian is able to improve it. And it is to be feared that this disappointment in some cases issues in a belief that it is *impossible* to overcome our evil selves; that bad we are, bad we must be; that our innate corruption lies like a load in our hearts, and no more admits of improvement than a stone does of light and thought; and, in consequence, that all we have to do, is to believe in Christ who is to save us, and to dwell on the thoughts of His perfect work for us,—that this is all we can do,—and that it is presumption as well as folly to attempt more.

But what says the text? "Wait on the Lord and keep His way." And Isaiah? "They that wait upon the Lord shall *renew* their strength; they shall mount up with wings like eagles; they shall

run, and not be weary; and they shall walk, and not faint."[4]
And St. Paul? "I can do all things through Christ which
strengtheneth me."[5] The very fruit of Christ's passion was the
gift of the Holy Spirit, which was to enable us to do what otherwise we could not do—"*to work out our own salvation*".[6]—Yet,
while we must aim at this, and feel convinced of our ability to
do it at length through the gifts bestowed on us, we cannot do it
rightly without a deep settled conviction of the exceeding difficulty of the work. That is, not only shall we be tempted to
negligence, but to impatience also, and thence into all kinds of
unlawful treatments of the soul, if we be possessed by a notion
that religious discipline soon becomes easy to the believer, and
that the heart is speedily changed. Christ's "yoke is easy:"[7]
true, to those who are accustomed to it, not to the unbroken
neck. "Wisdom is very unpleasant to the unlearned (says the
son of Sirach), he that is without understanding will not remain with her." "At the first she will walk with him by crooked
ways, and bring fear and dread upon him, and torment him
with her discipline, until she may trust his soul and try him by
her laws. Then will she return the straight way unto him, and
comfort him, and show him her secrets."[8]

Let, then, every beginner make up his mind to suffer disquiet
and perplexity. He cannot complain that it should be so; and
though he should be deeply ashamed of himself that it is so (for
had he followed God from a child, his condition would have
been far different, though, even then perhaps, not without
some perplexities), still he has no cause to be surprised or discouraged. The more he makes up his mind manfully to bear
doubt, struggle against it, and meekly to do God's will all
through it, the sooner this unsettled state of mind will cease,
and order will rise out of confusion. "Wait on the Lord," this is
the rule; "keep His way," this is the manner of waiting. Go
about your duty; mind little things as well as great. Do not
pause, and say, "I am as I was; day after day passes, and still no
light;" go on. It is very painful to be haunted by wandering
doubts, to have thoughts shoot across the mind about the reality of religion altogether, or of this or that particular doctrine
of it, or about the correctness of one's own faith, and the safety
of one's own state. But it must be right to serve God; we have a
voice within us answering to the injunction in the text, of waiting on Him and keeping His way. David confesses it. "When

---

[4] Is. xl.31.   [5] Phil. iv.13.   [6] Phil. ii.12.
[7] Matt. xi.30.   [8] Eccles. vi.20; iv.17, 18.

Thou saidst, Seek ye My face; my heart said unto Thee, Thy face, Lord, will I seek."[9]—And surely such obedient waiting upon Him will obtain His blessing. "*Blessed* are they that keep His commandments." And besides this express promise, even if we had to seek for a way to understand His perfect will, could we conceive one of greater promise than that of beginning with little things, and so gradually making progress? In all other things is not this the way to perfection? Does not a child learn to walk short distances at first? Who would attempt to bear great weights before he had succeeded with the lesser? It is from God's great goodness that our daily constant duty is placed in the performance of small and comparatively easy services. To be dutiful and obedient in ordinary matters, to speak the truth, to be honest, to be sober, to keep from sinful words and thoughts, to be kind and forgiving,—and all this for our Saviour's sake,— let us attempt *these* duties first. *They* even will be difficult,—the least of them; still they are much easier than the solution of the doubts which harass us, and they will by degrees give us a prac- tical knowledge of the Truth.

To take one instance, out of many which might be given: sup- pose we have any perplexing, indescribable doubts about the Divine power of our Blessed Lord, or concerning the doctrine of the Trinity; well, let us leave the subject and turn to do God's will. If we do this in faith and humility, we shall in time find that, while we have been obeying our Saviour's precepts, and imitating His conduct in the Gospels, our difficulties have been removed, though it may take time to remove them; and though we are not, during the time, sensible of what is going on. There may, indeed, be cases in which they are never removed en- tirely,—and in which doubtless some great and good object is secured by the trial; but we may fairly and safely look out for a more comfortable issue. And so as regards all our difficulties. "Wait on the Lord, and keep His way." His word is sure; we may safely trust it. We shall gain light as to general doctrines by embodying them in those particular instances in which they become ordinary duties. But it too often happens, that from one cause or other men do not pursue this simple method of gradually extricating themselves from error.—They seek some new path which promises to be shorter and easier than the lowly and the circuitous way of obedience. They wish to arrive at the heights of Mount Zion without winding round its base; and at first (it must be confessed) they seem to make greater

[9] Ps. xxvii.8.

progress than those who are content to wait, and work righteousness. Impatient of "sitting in darkness, and having no light," and of completing the Prophet's picture of a saint in trouble, "by fearing the Lord, and obeying the voice of His servant," [10] they expect to gain speedy peace and holiness by means of new teachers, and by a new doctrine.

Many are misled by confidence in themselves. They look back at the first seasons of their repentance and conversion, as if the time of their greatest knowledge; and instead of considering that their earliest religious notions were probably the most confused and mixed with error, and therefore endeavouring to separate the good from the bad, they consecrate all they then felt as a standard of doctrine to which they are bound to appeal; and as to the opinion of others, they think little of it, for religion being a new subject to themselves, they are easily led to think it must be a new and untried subject to others also, especially, since the best men are often the least willing to converse, except in private, on religious subjects, and still more averse to speak of them to those who they think will not value them rightly.

But, leaving the mention of those who err from self-confidence, I would rather lament over such as are led away from the path of plain simple obedience by a compliance with the views and wishes of those around them. Such persons there are all through the Church, and ever have been. Such perhaps have been many Christians in the communion of the Church of Rome; who, feeling deeply the necessity of a religious life, yet strive by means different from those which God has blessed, to gain His favour. They begin religion at the very end of it, and make those observances and rules the chief means of pleasing Him, which in fact should be but the spontaneous acts of the formed Christian temper. And others among ourselves are bound by a similar yoke of bondage, though it be more speciously disguised, when they subject their minds to certain unscriptural rules, and fancy they must separate in some self-devised way from the world, and that they must speak and act according to some arbitrary and novel form of doctrine, which they try to set before themselves, instead of endeavouring to imbue their hearts with that free, unconstrained spirit of devotion, which lowly obedience in ordinary matters would imperceptibly form within them. How many are there, more or less such, who love the Truth, and would fain do God's will, who

[10] Is. i.10.

yet are led aside and walk in bondage, while they are promised superior light and freedom! They desire to be living members of the Church, and they anxiously seek out whatever they can admire in the true sons of the Church but they feel forced to measure every thing by a certain superstitious standard which they revere,—they are frightened at shadows,—and thus they are, from time to time, embarrassed and perplexed, whenever, that is, they cannot reconcile the conduct and lives of those who are really, and whom they wish to believe eminent Christians, with that false religious system which they have adopted.

Before concluding, I must notice one other state of mind in which the precept of "waiting on God and keeping His way," will avail, above all others, to lead right a doubting and perplexed mind.

It sometimes happens, from ill health or other cause, that persons fall into religious despondency. They fancy that they have so abused God's mercy that there is no hope for them; that once they knew the Truth, but that now it is withdrawn from them; that they have had warnings which they have neglected, and now they are left by the Holy Spirit, and given over to Satan. Then, they recollect divers passages of Scripture, which speak of the peril of falling away, and they apply these to their own case. Now I speak of such instances, only so far as they can be called ailments of the mind,—for often they must be treated as ailments of the body. As far as they are mental, let us observe how it will conduce to restore the quiet of the mind, to attend to the humble ordinary duties of our station, that walking in God's way, of which the text speaks. Sometimes, indeed, persons thus afflicted increase their disorder by attempting to console themselves by those elevated Christian doctrines which St. Paul enlarges on; and others encourage them in it. But St. Paul's doctrine is not intended for weak and unstable minds.[11] He says himself: "We speak wisdom among them that *are perfect*;" not to those who are (what he calls) "babes in Christ."[12] In proportion as we gain strength, we shall be able to understand and profit by the full promises of the Christian covenant; but those who are confused, agitated, restless in their minds, who busy themselves with many thoughts, and are overwhelmed with conflicting feelings, such persons are, in general, made more restless and more unhappy (as the experience of sick beds may show us), by holding out to them doctrines and assurances which they cannot rightly apprehend. Now, not to speak of

[11] 2 Pet. iii.16.   [12] 1 Cor. ii.6; iii.1.

that peculiar blessing which is promised to obedience to God's will, let us observe how well it is calculated, by its natural effect, to soothe and calm the mind. When we set about to obey God, in the ordinary businesses of daily life, we are at once interested by realities which withdraw our minds from vague fears and uncertain indefinite surmises about the future. Without laying aside the thoughts of Christ (the contrary), still we learn to view Him in His tranquil providence, before we set about contemplating His greater works, and we are saved from taking an unchristian thought for the morrow, while we are busied in present services. Thus our Saviour gradually discloses Himself to the troubled mind; not as He is in heaven, as when He struck down Saul to the ground, but as He was in the days of His flesh, eating and conversing among His brethren, and bidding us, in imitation of Him, think no duty beneath the notice of those who sincerely wish to please God.

Such afflicted inquirers, then, after truth, must be exhorted to keep a guard upon their feelings, and to control their hearts. They say they are terrified lest they should be past hope; and they will not be persuaded that God is all-merciful, in spite of all the Scriptures say to that effect. Well, then, I would take them on their own ground. Supposing their state to be as wretched as is conceivable, can they deny it is their duty *now* to serve God? Can they do better than try to serve Him? Job said, "Though He slay me, yet will I trust in Him." [13] They say they do not *wish* to serve God,—that they want a heart to serve Him. Let us grant (if they will have it so), that they are most obdurate; still they are alive,—they must be doing something, and can they do aught better than try to quiet themselves, and be resigned, and to do right rather than wrong, even though they are persuaded that it does not come from their heart, and is not acceptable to God? They say they dare not ask for God's grace to assist them. This is doubtless a miserable state: still, since they must act in some way, though they cannot do what is really good without His grace, yet, at least, let them do what seems like truth and goodness. Nay, though it is shocking to set before their minds such a prospect, yet even were they already in the place of punishment, will they not confess, it would be the best thing they could do, to commit then as little sin as possible? Much more, then, *now*, when, even if they have no hope, their heart at least is not so entirely hardened as it will be then.

[13] Job xiii. 15.

It must not be for an instant supposed I am admitting the possibility of a person being rejected by God, who has any such right feelings in his mind. The anxiety of the sufferers I have been describing, shows they are still under the influence of Divine grace, though they will not allow it; but I say this, to give another instance in which a determination to obey God's will strictly in ordinary matters tends, through His blessing, to calm and comfort the mind, and to bring it out of perplexity into the clear day.

And so in various other cases which might be recounted. Whatever our difficulty be, this is plain. "Wait on the Lord, and keep His way, and He shall exalt thee." Or in our Saviour's words: "He that hath My commandments and keepeth them, he it is that loveth Me, and he that loveth Me shall be loved of My Father, and I will love him, and will manifest Myself to him." "Whosoever shall do and teach these least commandments, shall be called great in the kingdom of heaven." "Whosoever hath, to him shall be given, and he shall have more abundance." [14]

[14] John xiv.21; Matt. v.19; xiii.12.

TIMES OF PRIVATE PRAYER

"Thou, when thou prayest, enter into thy closet, and when thou hast shut thy door, pray to thy Father which is in secret; and thy Father which seeth in secret shall reward thee openly."—Matt. vi.6.

HERE is our Saviour's own sanction and blessing vouchsafed to private prayer, in simple, clear, and most gracious words. The Pharisees were in the practice, when they prayed by themselves, of praying in *public*, in the corners of the streets; a strange inconsistency according to our notions, since in our language prayer by oneself is even called *private* prayer. Public private prayer, this was their self-contradictory practice. Warning, then, His disciples against the particular form of hypocrisy in which the self-conceit of human nature at that day showed itself, our Lord promises in the text His Father's blessing on such humble supplications as were really addressed to Him, and not made to gain the praise of men. Those who seek the unseen God (He seems to say), seek Him in their hearts and hidden thoughts, not in loud words, as if He were far off from them. Such men would retire from the world into places where no human eye saw them, there to meet Him humbly and in faith, who is "about their path, and about their bed, and spieth out all their ways." And He, the Searcher of hearts, would reward them openly. Prayers uttered in secret, according to God's will, are treasured up in God's Book of Life. They seem, perhaps, to have sought an answer here, and to have failed. Their memory perishes even in the mind of the petitioner, and the world never knew of them. But God is ever mindful, and in the last day, when the books are opened, they shall be disclosed and rewarded before the whole world.

Such is Christ's gracious promise in the text, acknowledging and blessing, in His condescension, those devotional exercises which were a duty even before Scripture enjoined them and changing into a privilege that work of faith, which, though bidden by conscience, and authorized by reason, yet before He revealed His mercy, is laden, in every man's case who attempts it, with guilt, remorse, and fear. It is the Christian's unspeakable privilege, and his alone, that he has at all times free access to the throne of grace through the mediation of his Lord and Saviour.

But, in what I shall now say concerning prayer, I shall not consider it as a privilege, but as a duty; for till we have some experience of the duties of religion, we are incapable of entering duly into the privileges; and it is too much the fashion of the day to view prayer chiefly as a mere privilege, such a privilege as it is inconsiderate indeed to neglect, but only inconsiderate, not sinful; and optional to use.

Now, we know well enough that we are bound to be in one sense in prayer and meditation all the day long. The question then arises, are we to pray in any other way? Is it enough to keep our minds fixed upon God through the day, and to commune with Him in our hearts, or is it necessary, over and above this habitual faith, to set apart particular times for the more systematic and earnest exercise of it? Need we pray at certain times of the day in a set manner? *Public* worship, indeed, from its very nature, requires *places*, *times*, and even set *forms*. But *private* prayer does not necessarily require set *times*, because we have no one to consult but ourselves, and we are always with ourselves; nor *forms*, for there is no one else whose thoughts are to keep pace with ours. Still, though set times and forms of prayer are not absolutely *necessary* in private prayer, yet they are highly expedient; or rather, times are actually commanded us by our Lord in the text, "Thou, *when* thou prayest, enter into thy closet, and when thou hast shut thy door, pray to thy Father which is in secret; and thy Father which seeth in secret shall reward thee openly."

In these words certain *times* for private prayer, over and above the secret thought of God which must ever be alive in us, are clearly enjoined; and the practice of good men in Scripture gives us an example in confirmation of the command. Even our Saviour had His peculiar seasons of communing with God. *His* thoughts indeed were one continued sacred service offered up to His Father; nevertheless, we read of His going up "into a mountain apart to pray," and again, of His "continuing all night in prayer to God."[1] Doubtless, you well recollect that solitary prayer of His, before His passion, thrice repeated, "that the cup might pass from Him." St. Peter too, as in the narrative of the conversion of Cornelius, the Roman centurion, in the tenth chapter of the Acts, went up upon the house-top to pray about the sixth hour; then God visited him. And Nathanael

[1] Matt. xiv.23; Luke vi.12.

seems to have been in prayer under the fig-tree, at the time our Saviour saw him, and Philip called him.[2] I might multiply instances from Scripture of such "Israelites without guile;" which are of course applicable to us, because, though they were under a Divine government in many respects different from the Christian, yet *personal* religion is the same at all times; "the just" in every dispensation "shall live by faith," and whatever reasons there were then for faith to display and maintain itself by stated prayer, remain substantially the same now. Let two passages suffice. The Psalmist says, "*Seven* times a day do I praise Thee, because of Thy righteous judgments."[3] And Daniel's practice is told us on a memorable occasion: "Now when Daniel knew that the writing was signed (the impious decree, forbidding prayer to any but king Darius for thirty days), he went into his house, and his windows being open in his chamber toward Jerusalem, he kneeled upon his knees *three times* a day, and prayed, and gave thanks before his God, *as he did aforetime*."[4]

It is plain, then, besides the devotional temper in which we should pass the day, more solemn and direct acts of worship, nay, *regular and periodical*, are required of us by the precept of Christ, and His own example, and that of His Apostles and Prophets under both covenants.

Now it is necessary to insist upon this duty of observing private prayer at stated times, because amid the cares and hurry of life men are very apt to neglect it: and it is a much more important duty than it is generally considered, even by those who perform it.

It is important for the two reasons which follow.

1. It brings religious subjects before the mind in regular course. Prayer *through* the day, is indeed the characteristic of a Christian spirit, but we may be sure that, in most cases, those who do not pray at stated times in a more solemn and direct manner, will never pray well at other times. We know in the common engagements of life, the importance of collecting and arranging our thoughts calmly and accurately before proceeding to any important business, in order to the right performance of it; and so in that one really needful occupation, the care of our eternal interests, if we would have our minds composed, our desires subdued, and our tempers heavenly through the day, we must, before commencing the day's employment, stand still awhile to look into ourselves, and commune with our hearts, by way of preparing ourselves for the trials and duties on

[2] John i.48. [3] Ps. cxix.164. [4] Dan. vi.10.

which we are entering. A like reason may be assigned for evening prayer, viz. as affording us a time of looking back on the day past, and summing up (as it were) that account, which, if *we* do not reckon, at least God has reckoned, and written down in that book which will be produced at the Judgment; a time of confessing sin, and of praying for forgiveness, of giving thanks for what we have done well, and for mercies received, of making good resolutions in reliance on the help of God, and of sealing up and setting sure the day past, at least as a stepping-stone of good for the morrow. The precise times indeed of private prayer are no where commanded us in Scripture; the most obvious are those I have mentioned, morning and evening. In the texts just now read to you, you heard of praying three times a day, or seven times. All this depends of course on the opportunities of each individual. Some men have not leisure for this; but for morning and evening prayer all men can and should *make* leisure.

Stated times of private prayer, then, are useful as impulses (so to say) to the continuous devotion of the day. They instruct us and engage us in what is ever our duty. It is commonly said, that what is every one's business is practically no one's; this applies here. I repeat it, if we leave religion as a subject of thought for all hours of the day equally, it will be thought of in none. In all things it is by small beginnings and appointed channels that an advance is made to extensive works. Stated times of prayer put us in that posture (as I may call it) in which we ought ever to be; they urge us forward in a heavenly direction, and then the stream carries us on. For the same reason it is expedient, if possible, to be solemn in the forms of our private worship, in order to impress our minds. Our Saviour *kneeled* down, fell on His face, and prayed,[5]—so did His Apostles;[6] and so did the Saints of the Old Testament. Hence many persons are accustomed (such as have the opportunity) to set apart a particular place for their private devotions; still for the same reason, to compose their mind,—as Christ tells us in the text, to enter into our closet.

2. I now come to the second reason for stated private prayer. Besides its tending to produce in us lasting religious impressions, which I have already enlarged upon, it is also a more direct means of gaining from God an answer to our requests. He has so sanctioned it in the text:—"Shut thy door, and pray to thy Father which seeth in secret, and He shall reward thee

---

[5] Matt. xxvi.39; Luke xxii.41.   [6] Acts xx.36; xxi.5; Eph. iii.14.

openly." We do not know *how* it is that prayer receives an answer from God at all. It is strange, indeed, that weak man should have strength to move God; but it is our privilege to know that we *can* do so. The whole system of this world is a history of man's interfering with Divine decrees; and if we have the melancholy power of baffling His good-will, to our own ruin (an awful, an incomprehensible truth!), if, when He designs our eternal salvation, we can yet annul our heavenly election, and accomplish our eternal destruction, much more have we the power to move Him (blessed be His name!) when He, the Searcher of hearts, discerns in us the mind of that Holy Spirit, which "maketh intercession for the saints according to His will." And, as He has thus promised an answer to our poor prayers, so it is not more strange that prayers offered up at particular times, and in a particular way, should have especially prevailing power with Him. And the reason of it may be as follows. It is faith that is the appointed means of gaining all blessings from God. "All things are possible to him that believeth." [7] Now, at stated times, when we gather up our thoughts to pray, and draw out our petitions in an orderly and clear manner, the act of faith is likely to be stronger and more earnest; then we realize more perfectly the presence of that God whom we do not see, and Him on whom once all our sins were laid, who bore the weight of our infirmities and sickness once for all, that in all our troubles we might seek Him, and find grace in time of need. Then this world is more out of sight, and we more simply appropriate those blessings, which we have but to claim humbly and they are really ours.

Stated times of prayer, then, are necessary; first, as a means of making the mind sober, and the general temper more religious; secondly, as a means of exercising earnest faith, and thereby of receiving a more certain blessing in answer, than we should otherwise obtain.

Other reasons, doubtless, may be given; but these are enough, not only as containing subject for thought which may be useful to us, but besides, as serving to show how wise and merciful those Divine provisions really are, which our vain minds are so apt to question. All God's commands, indeed, ought to be received at once upon faith, though we saw no reason for them. It is no excuse for a man's disobeying them, even if he thinks he sees reasons against them; for God knows better than we do. But in great condescension He has allowed us to see here and

[7] Mark ix.23.

there His reasons for what He does and enjoins; and we should treasure up these occasional notices as memorials against the time of temptation, that when doubt and unbelief assail us, and we are perplexed at His revealed word, we may call to mind those former instances in our own experience, where what at first seemed strange and hard, on closer consideration was found to have a wise end.

Now the duty of having stated times of private prayer is one of those observances, concerning which we are apt to entertain the unbelieving thoughts I have been describing. It seems to us to be a form, or at least a light matter, to observe or omit; whereas in truth, such creatures are we, there is the most close and remarkable connexion between small observances and the permanence of our chief habits and practices. It is easy to see why it is irksome; because it presses upon us and is inconvenient. It is a duty which claims our attention continually, and its irksomeness leads our hearts to rebel; and then we proceed to search for reasons to justify our own dislike of it. Nothing is more difficult than to be disciplined and regular in our religion. It is very easy to be religious by fits and starts, and to keep up our feelings by artificial stimulants; but regularity seems to trammel us, and we become impatient. This is especially the case with those to whom the world is as yet new, and who can do as they please. Religion is the chief subject which meets them, which enjoins regularity; and they bear it only so far as they can make it like things of this world, something curious, or changeable, or exciting. Satan knows his advantage here. He perceives well enough that stated private prayer is the very emblem and safeguard of true devotion to God, as impressing on us and keeping up in us a rule of conduct. He who gives up regularity in prayer has lost a principal means of reminding himself that spiritual life is obedience to a Lawgiver, not a mere feeling or a taste. Hence it is that so many persons, especially in the polished ranks of society, who are out of the way of temptation to gross vice, fall away into a mere luxurious self-indulgent devotion, which they take for religion; they reject every thing which implies self-denial, and regular prayer especially. Hence it is that others run into all kinds of enthusiastic fancies; because, by giving up set private prayer in written forms, they have lost the chief rule of their hearts. Accordingly, you will hear them exclaim against regular prayer (which is the very medicine suited to their disease) as a formal service, and maintain that times and places and fixed words are beneath the attention of a spiritual Christian. And others, who are exposed to the seductions of sin, altogether fall away from the same omission. Be sure, my brethren, whoever of you is persuaded to disuse his morning and evening prayers, is giving up the armour which is to secure him against the wiles of the Devil. If you have left off the observance of them, you may fall any day;—and you will fall without notice. For a time you will go on, seeming to yourselves to be the same as before; but the Israelites might as well hope to lay in a stock of manna as you of grace. You pray God for your daily bread, your bread day by day; and if you have not prayed for it this morning, it will profit you little that you prayed for it yesterday. You did then pray and you obtained,— but not a supply for two days. When you have given over the practice of stated prayer, you gradually become weaker without knowing it. Samson did not know he had lost his strength till the Philistines came upon him; you will think yourselves the men you used to be, till suddenly your adversary will come furiously upon you, and you will as suddenly fall. You will be able to make little or no resistance. This is the path which leads to death. Men first leave off private prayer; then they neglect the due observance of the Lord's day (which is a stated service of the same kind); then they gradually let slip from their minds the very idea of obedience to a fixed eternal law; then they actually allow themselves in things which their conscience condemns; then they lose the direction of their conscience, which being ill used, at length refuses to direct them. And thus, being left by their true inward guide, they are obliged to take another guide, their reason, which by itself knows little or nothing about religion; then, this their blind reason forms a system of right or wrong for them, as well as it can, flattering to their own desires, and presumptuous where it is not actually corrupt. No wonder such a scheme contradicts Scripture, which it is soon found to do; not that they are certain to perceive this themselves; they often do not know it, and think themselves still believers in the Gospel, while they maintain doctrines which the Gospel condemns. But sometimes they perceive that their system is contrary to Scripture; and then, instead of giving it up, they give up Scripture, and profess themselves unbelievers. Such is the course of disobedience, beginning in (apparently) slight omissions, and ending in open unbelief; and all men who walk in the broad way which leads to destruction are but at different stages of it, one more advanced than another, but all in one way. And I have spoken of it here, in order to remind you how intimately it is connected with the neglect of set private prayer; whereas, he who is strict in the observance of prayer morning and evening, praying with his heart as well as his lips, can hardly go astray, for every morning and evening brings him a monitor to draw him back and restore him.

Beware then of the subtlety of your Enemy, who would fain rob you of your defence. Do not yield to his bad reasonings. Be on your guard especially, when you get into novel situations or circumstances which interest and delight you, lest they throw you out of your regularity in prayer. Any thing new or unexpected is dangerous to you. Going much into mixed society, and seeing many strange persons, taking share in any pleasant amusements, reading interesting books, entering into a new line of life, forming some new acquaintance, the sudden prospect of any worldly advantage, travelling; all these things and such like, innocent as they are in themselves, and capable of a religious use, become means of temptation if we are not on our guard. See that you are not *unsettled* by them; this is the danger; fear becoming *unsettled*. Consider that stability of mind is the chief of virtues, for it is Faith. "Thou wilt keep him in perfect peace, whose mind is stayed on Thee, because he trusteth in Thee;"[8] this is the promise. But "the wicked are like the troubled sea when it cannot rest, whose waters cast up mire and dirt; there is no peace, saith my God, to the wicked."[9] Nor to the wicked only, in our common sense of the word "wicked," but to none is there rest, who in any way leave their God, and rove after the goods of this world. Do not indulge visions of earthly good, fix your hearts on higher things, let your morning and evening thoughts be points of rest for your mind's eye, and let those thoughts be upon the narrow way, and the blessedness of heaven, and the glory and power of Christ your Saviour. Thus will you be kept from unseemly risings and fallings, and steadied in an equable way. Men in general will know nothing of this; they witness not your private prayers, and they will confuse you with the multitude they fall in with. But your friends and acquaintances will gain a light and a comfort from your example; they will see your good works, and be led to trace them to their true secret source, the influences of the Holy Ghost sought and obtained by prayer. Thus they will glorify your heavenly Father, and in imitation of you will seek Him; and He who seeth in secret, shall at length reward you openly.

[8] Is. xxvi.3.   [9] Is. lvii.20, 21.

FORMS OF PRIVATE PRAYER

"Lord, teach us to pray, as John also taught his disciples."
—Luke xi.1.

THESE words express the natural feelings of the awakened mind, perceiving its great need of God's help, yet not understanding well what its particular wants are, or how they are to be relieved. The disciples of John the Baptist, and the disciples of Christ, waited on their respective Masters for instruction *how to pray*. It was in vain that the duty of repentance was preached to the one, and of faith to the other; in vain that God's mercies and His judgments were set before them, and their own duties; they seemed to have all that was necessary for making prayers for themselves, yet they could not; their hearts were full, but they remained dumb; they could offer no petition except to *be taught* to pray; they knew the Truth, but they could not use it. So different a thing is it to be instructed in religion, and to have so mastered it in practice that it is altogether our own.

Their need has been the need of Christians ever since. All of us in childhood, and most men ever after, require direction how to pray; and hence the use of *Forms of prayer*, which have always obtained in the Church. John taught his disciples; Christ gave the Apostles the prayer which is distinguished by the name of the *Lord's Praye*r; and after He had ascended on high, the Holy Spirit has given us excellent services of devotion by the mouth of those blessed Saints, whom from time to time He has raised up to be overseers in the Church. In the words of St. Paul, "We know not what we should pray for as we ought;"[1] but "the Spirit helpeth our infirmities;" and that, not only by guiding our thoughts, but by directing our words.

This, I say, is the origin of *Forms of prayer*, of which I mean to speak to-day; viz. these two undeniable truths, first, that all men have the same spiritual wants, and, secondly, that they cannot of themselves express them.

Now it has so happened, that in these latter times self-wise

[1] Rom. viii.26.

reasoners have arisen who have questioned the use of Forms of prayer, and have thought it better to pray out of their own thoughts at random, using words which come into their minds at the time they pray. It may be right, then, that we should have some reason at hand for our use of those Forms, which we have adopted because they were handed down to us. Not, as if it were not quite a *sufficient* reason for using them, that we have received them, and (in St. Paul's words) that "neither we nor the Churches of God have known any other custom,"[2] and that the best of Christians have ever used them; for this *is* an abundantly satisfactory reason;—nor again, as if we could hope by reasons ever so good, to persuade those who inquire of us, which most likely we shall not be able to do; for a man is far gone in extravagance who deliberately denies the use of Forms, and is likely to find our reasons as difficult to receive as the practice we are defending;—so that we can only say of such men, after St. Paul's manner, "if any man be ignorant, let him be ignorant," there is no help for it. But it may be useful to show you *how* reasonable the practice is, in order that you yourselves may turn it to better account; for when we know why we do a thing, we are likely (the same circumstances being supposed) to do it more comfortably than when we obey ignorantly.

Now, I suppose no one is in any difficulty about the use of Forms of prayer in *public* worship; for common sense almost will tell us, that when many are to pray together *as one* man, if their thoughts are to go together, they *must* agree beforehand what is to be the subject of their prayers, nay, what the *words* of their prayers, if there is to be any certainty, composure, ease, and regularity, in their united devotions. To be present at extempore prayer, is to *hear prayers*. Nay, it might happen, or rather often would happen, that we did not understand what was said; and then the person praying is scarcely praying "in a tongue understanded of the people" (as our Article expresses it); he is rather interceding *for* the people, than praying *with* them, and leading their worship. In the case, then, of *public* prayer the need of Forms is evident; but it is not at first sight *so* obvious that in *private* prayer also we need use written Forms, instead of praying *extempore* (as it is called); so I proceed to show the use of them.

1. Let us bear in mind the precept of the wise man. "Be not rash with thy mouth, and let not thine heart be hasty to utter any thing before God; for God is in heaven, and thou upon

[2] 1 Cor. xi.16.

earth; therefore let thy words be few."[3] Prayers framed at the moment are likely to become *irreverent*. Let us consider for a few moments before we pray, into whose presence we are entering,—the presence of God. What need have we of humble, sober, and subdued thoughts as becomes *creatures*, sustained hourly by His bounty;—as becomes *lost sinners* who have no right to speak at all, but must submit in silence to Him who is holy;—and still more, as grateful *servants of Him* who bought us from ruin at the price of His own blood; meekly sitting at His feet like Mary to learn and to do His will, and like the penitent at the great man's feast, quietly adoring Him, and doing Him service without disturbance, washing His feet (as it were) with our tears, and anointing them with precious ointment, as having sinned much and needing a large forgiveness. Therefore, to avoid the irreverence of many or unfit words and rude half-religious thoughts, it is necessary to pray from book or memory, and not at random.

It may he objected, that this reason for using Forms proves too much; viz. that it would be wrong ever to do without them; which is an over-rigorous bond upon Christian liberty. But I reply, that reverence in our prayers will be sufficiently secured, if at our stated seasons for prayer we make use of Forms. For thus a tone and character will be imparted to our devotion throughout the day; nay, even the very petitions and ejaculations will be supplied, which we need. And much more will our souls be influenced by the power of them, at the very time we are using them; so that, should the occasion require, we shall find ourselves able to go forward naturally and soberly into such additional supplications, as are of too particular or private a nature, to admit of being written down in set words.

2. In the next place, Forms of prayer are necessary to guard us against the irreverence of *wandering* thoughts. If we pray without set words (read or remembered), our minds will stray from the subject; other thoughts will cross us, and we shall pursue them; we shall lose sight of His presence whom we are addressing. This wandering of mind is in good measure prevented, under God's blessing, by Forms of prayer. Thus a chief use of them is that of *fixing the attention*.

3. Next, they are useful in securing us from the irreverence of *excited thoughts*. And here there is room for saying much; for, it so happens, Forms of prayer are censured for the very circumstance about them which is their excellence. They are accused

[3] Eccles. v.2.

of impeding the current of devotion, when, in fact, that (so called) current is in itself faulty, and ought to be checked. And those persons (as might be expected) are most eager in their opposition to them, who require more than others the restraint of them. They sometimes throw their objection into the following form, which it may be worth while to consider. They say, "If a man is in earnest, he will soon find words; there is no need of a set Form of prayer. And if he is not in earnest, a Form can do him no good." Now that a man who is in earnest will soon find words, is true or not true, according to what is meant by being in earnest. It is true that at certain times of strong emotion, grief or joy, remorse or fear, our religious feelings outrun and leave behind them any Form of words. In such cases, not only is there no *need* of Forms of prayer, but it is perhaps impossible to write *Forms* of prayer for Christians agitated by such feelings. For each man feels in his own way,—perhaps no two men exactly alike;—and we can no more write down *how* men ought to pray at such times, than we can give rules how they should weep or be merry. The better men they are, of course the better they will pray in such a trying time; but you cannot make them better; they must be left to themselves. And, though good men have before now set down in writing Forms of prayer for persons so circumstanced, these were doubtless meant rather as patterns and helps, or as admonitions and (if so be) quietings of the agitated mind, than as prayers which it was expected would be used literally and entirely in their detail. As a general rule, Forms of prayer should not be written in strong and impassioned language; but should be calm, composed, and short. Our Saviour's own prayer is our model in this respect. How few are its petitions! how soberly expressed! how reverently and at the same time how deep are they, and how comprehensive!—I readily grant, then, that there *are* times when the heart outruns any written words; as the jailor cried out, "What shall I do to be saved?" Nay, rather I would maintain that set words should not attempt to imitate the impetuous workings to which all minds are subject at times in this world of change (and therefore religious minds in the number), lest one should seem to encourage them.

Still the question is not at all settled; granting there *are* times when a thankful or a wounded heart bursts through all Forms of prayer, yet these are not *frequent*. To be excited is not the *ordinary* state of the mind, but the extraordinary, the now and then state. Nay, more than this, it *ought not* to be the common state of the mind; and if we are encouraging within us this excitement, this unceasing rush and alternation of feelings, and think that this, and this only, is being in earnest in religion, we are harming our minds, and (in one sense) I may even say grieving the peaceful Spirit of God, who would silently and tranquilly work His Divine work in our hearts. This, then, is an especial *use* of Forms of prayer, *when* we are in earnest, as we ought always to be; viz. to keep us from self-willed earnestness, to still emotion, to calm us, to remind us what and where we are, to lead us to a purer and serener temper, and to that deep unruffled love of God and man, which is really the fulfilling of the law, and the perfection of human nature.

Then, again, as to the usefulness of Forms, if we are *not* in earnest,—this also is true or not, as we may take it. For there are degrees of earnestness. Let us recollect, the power of praying, being a habit, must be acquired, like all other habits, by practice. In order at length to pray well, we must begin by praying ill, since ill is all we can do. Is not this plain? Who, in the case of any other work, would wait till he could do it perfectly, before he tried it? The idea is absurd. Yet those who object to Forms of prayer on the ground just mentioned, fall into this strange error. If, indeed, we could pray and praise God like the Angels, we might have no need of Forms of prayer; but Forms are to teach those who pray poorly to pray better. They are helps to our devotion, as teaching us what to pray for and how, as St. John and our Lord taught their disciples; and, doubtless, even the *best* of us prays *but* poorly, and *needs* the help of them. However, the persons I speak of, think that prayer is nothing else but the bursting forth of strong feeling, not the action of a habit, but an emotion, and, therefore, *of course* to such men the very notion of *learning* to pray seems absurd. But this indulgence of emotion is in truth founded on a mistake, as I have already said.

4. Further, Forms are useful to *help our memory*, and to set before us at once, completely, and in order, what we have to pray for. It does not follow, that when the heart is really full of the thought of God, and alive to the reality of things unseen, then it is easiest to pray. Rather, the deeper insight we have into His Majesty and our innumerable wants, the less we shall be able to draw out our thoughts into words. The publican could only say, "God be merciful to me a sinner;" this was enough for his *acceptance*; but to offer such a scanty service was not to exercise the *gift* of prayer, the privilege of a ransomed and exalted son of God. He whom Christ has illuminated with His grace, is heir of all things. He has an interest in the world's multitude of matters. He has a boundless sphere of duties

within and without him. He has a glorious prospect before him. The saints shall hereafter judge the world; and shall they not *here* take cognizance of its doings? are they not in one sense counsellors and confidential servants of their Lord, intercessors at the throne of grace, the secret agents by and for whom He guides His high Providence, and carries on the nations to their doom? And in their own persons is forgiveness merely and acceptance (extreme blessings as these are) the scope of their desires? else might they be content with the publican's prayer. Are they not rather bidden to go on to perfection, to use the spirit given them, to enlarge and purify their own hearts, and to draw out the nature of man into the fulness of its capabilities after the image of the Son of God? And for the thought of all these objects at once, who is sufficient? Whose mind is not overpowered by the view of its own immense privilege, so as eagerly to seek for words of prayer and intercession, carefully composed according to the number and the nature of the various petitions it has to offer? so that he who prays without plan, is in fact losing a great part of the privilege with which his Baptism has gifted him.

5. And further, the use of a Form as a help to the memory is still more obvious, when we take into account the engagements of this world with which most men are surrounded. The cares and businesses of life press upon us with a reality which we cannot overlook. Shall we trust the matters of the next world to the chance thoughts of our own minds, which come this moment, and go the next, and may not be at hand when the time of employing them arrives, like unreal visions, having no substance and no permanence? This world is Satan's efficacious Form, it is the instrument through which he spreads out in order and attractiveness his many snares; and these doubtless will engross us, unless we also give Form to the spiritual objects towards which we pray and labour. How short are the seasons which most men have to give to prayer? Before they can collect their memories and minds, their leisure is almost over, even if they have the power to dismiss the thoughts of this world, which just before engaged them. Now Forms of prayer do this *for* them. They keep the ground occupied, that Satan may not encroach upon the seasons of devotion. They are a standing memorial, to which we can recur as to a temple of God, finding every thing in order for our worship as soon as we go into it, though the time allotted us at morning and evening be ever so circumscribed.

6. And this use of Forms in prayer becomes great, beyond power of estimating, in the case of those multitudes of men,

who, after going on well for a while, fall into sin. If even conscientious men require continual aids to be reminded of the next world, how extreme is the need of those who try to forget it! It cannot be denied, fearful as it is to reflect upon it, that far the greater number of those who come to manhood, for a while (at least) desert the God who has redeemed them; and, then, if in their earlier years they have learned and used no prayers or psalms by which to worship Him, what is to keep them from blotting altogether from their minds the thought of religion? But here it is that the Forms of the Church have ever served her children, both to restrain them in their career of sin, and to supply them with ready utterance on their repentance. Chance words and phrases of her services adhere to their memories, rising up in moments of temptation or of trouble, to check or to recover them. And hence it happens, that in the most irreligious companies a distinction is said to be observable between those who have had the opportunity of using our public Forms in their youth, and those whose religious impressions have not been thus happily fortified; so that, amid their most reckless mirth, and most daring pretence of profligacy, a sort of secret reverence has attended the wanderers, restraining them from that impiety and profaneness in which the others have tried to conceal from themselves the guilt and peril of their doings.

And again on their repentance (should they be favoured with so high a grace), what friends do they seem to find amid their gloom in the words they learned in their boyhood,—a kindly voice, aiding them to say what they otherwise would not know how to say, guiding and composing their minds upon those objects of faith which they ought to look to, but cannot find of themselves, and so (as it were) interceding for them with the power of the blessed Spirit, while nature can but groan and travail in pain! Sinners as they are by their own voluntary misdeeds, and with a prospect of punishment before them, enlightened by but few and faint gleams of hope, what shall keep them from feverish restlessness, and all the extravagance of fear, what shall soothe them into a fixed, resigned waiting for their Judge, and such lowly efforts to obey Him, however poorly, as become a penitent, but those words, long buried in their minds, and now rising again as if with the life of their uncorrupted boyhood? It requires no great experience of sick beds to verify the truth of this statement. Blessed, indeed, is the power of those formularies, which thus succeed in throwing a sinner for a while out of himself, and in bringing before him the scenes of his youth, his guardian friends now long departed, their ways and their teaching, their pious services, and their peaceful end; and though all this is an excitement, and lasts but for a season, yet, if improved by him, it may be converted into an habitual contemplation of persons and deeds which now live to God, though removed hence,—if improved by his acting upon it, it will become an abiding motive to seek the world to come, an abiding persuasion, warning him from the works of darkness, and raising him to the humble hope of future acceptance with his Saviour and Judge.

7. Such is the force of association in undoing the evil of past years, and recalling us to the innocence of children. Nor is this all we may gain from the prayers we use, nor are penitent sinners the only persons who can profit by it. Let us recollect for how long a period our prayers have been the standard Forms of devotion in the Church of Christ, and we shall gain a fresh reason for loving them, and a fresh source of comfort in using them. I know different persons will feel differently here, according to their different turn of mind; yet surely there are few of us, if we dwelt on the thought, but would feel it a privilege to use, as we do (for instance, in the Lord's Prayer), the very petitions which Christ spoke. He gave the prayer and used it. His Apostles used it; all the Saints ever since have used it. When we use it we seem to join company with them. Who does not think himself brought nearer to any celebrated man in history, by seeing his house, or his furniture, or his handwriting, or the very books that were his? Thus does the Lord's Prayer bring us near to Christ, and to His disciples in every age. No wonder, then, that in past times good men thought this Form of prayer so sacred, that it seemed to them impossible to say it too often, as if some especial grace went with the use of it. Nor can we use it too often; it contains in itself a sort of plea for Christ's listening to us; we cannot, so that we keep our thoughts fixed on its petitions, and use our minds as well as our lips when we repeat it. And what is true of the Lord's Prayer, is in its measure true of most of those prayers which our Church teaches us to use. It is true of the Psalms also, and of the Creeds; all of which have become sacred, from the memory of saints departed who have used them, and whom we hope one day to meet in heaven.

One caution I give in conclusion as to using these thoughts. Beware lest your religion be one of sentiment merely, not of practice. Men may speak in a high imaginative way of the ancient Saints and the Holy Apostolic Church, without making the fervour or refinement of their devotion bear upon their conduct. Many a man likes to be religious in graceful language;

he loves religious tales and hymns, yet is never the better Christian for all this. The works of every day, these are the tests of our glorious contemplations, whether or not they shall be available to our salvation; and he who does one deed of obedience for Christ's sake, let him have no imagination and no fine feeling, is a better man, and returns to his home justified rather than the most eloquent speaker, and the most sensitive hearer, of the glory of the Gospel, if such men do not practise up to their knowledge.

THE RESURRECTION OF THE BODY

*"Now that the dead are raised, even Moses showed at the bush,
when he calleth the Lord the God of Abraham, and the God of Isaac,
and the God of Jacob. For He is not a God of the dead, but of the
living; for all live unto Him."*—Luke xx.37, 38.

THESE words of our Saviour show us how much more there
is in Scripture than at first sight appears. God spoke to
Moses in the burning bush, and called Himself the "God of
Abraham;" and Christ tells us, that in this simple announcement was contained the promise that Abraham should rise
again from the dead. In truth, if we may say it with reverence,
the All-wise, All-knowing God cannot speak without meaning
many things at once. He sees the end from the beginning; He
understands the numberless connexions and relations of all
things one with another. Every word of His is full of instruction, looking many ways; and though it is not often given to us
to know these various senses, and we are not at liberty to attempt lightly to imagine them, yet, as far as they are told us, and
as far as we may reasonably infer them, we must thankfully accept them. Look at Christ's words, and this same character of
them will strike you; whatever He says is fruitful in meaning,
and refers to many things. It is well to keep this in mind when
we read Scripture; for it may hinder us from self-conceit, from
studying it in an arrogant critical temper, and from *giving over*
reading it, as if we had got from it all that can be learned.

Now let us consider in what sense the text contains a promise
of a resurrection, and see what instruction may be gained from
knowing it.

When God called Himself the God of Abraham, Isaac, and
Jacob, He implied that those holy patriarchs were still alive,
though they were no more seen on earth. This may seem evident at first sight; but it may be asked, how the text proves that
their *bodies* would live; for, if their *souls* were still living, that
would be enough to account for their being still called in the
Book of Exodus servants of God. This is the point to be considered. Our Blessed Lord seems to tell us, that in some sense or

other Abraham's *body* might be considered still alive as a pledge of his resurrection, though it was dead in the common sense in which we apply the word. His announcement is, Abraham *shall* rise from the dead, because in truth, he *is* still alive. He cannot in the end be held under the power of the grave, more than a sleeping man can be kept from waking. Abraham is still alive in the dust, though not risen thence. He is alive because all God's saints live to Him, though they seem to perish.

It may seem a paradox to say, that our bodies, even when dead, are still alive; but since our Lord seems to countenance us in saying so, I will say it, though a strange saying, because it has an instructive meaning. We are apt to talk about our bodies as if we knew how or what they really were; whereas we only know what our eyes tell us. They seem to grow, to come to maturity, to decay; but after all we know no more about them than meets our senses, and there is, doubtless, much which God sees in our material frames, which we cannot see. We have no direct cognizance of what may be called the substantive existence of the body, only of its accidents. Again, we are apt to speak of *soul and body*, as if we could distinguish between them, and knew much about them; but for the most part we use words without meaning. It is useful indeed to make the distinction, and Scripture makes it; but after all, the Gospel speaks of our nature, in a religious sense, *as one*. Soul and body make up one man, which is born once, and never dies. Philosophers of old time thought the soul indeed might live for ever, but that the body perished at death; but Christ tells us otherwise, He tells us the body will live for ever. In the text He seems to intimate that it never really dies; that we lose sight indeed of what *we* are accustomed to see, but that God still sees the elements of it which are not exposed to our senses.

God graciously called Himself *the God of Abraham*. He did not say the God of Abraham's soul, but simply of *Abraham*. He blest Abraham, and He gave him eternal life; not to his soul only without his body, but to Abraham as one man. And so He is *our* God, and it is not given us to distinguish between what He does for our different natures, spiritual and material. These are mere words; each of us may feel himself to be one, and that one being, in all its substantial parts, and attributes, will never die.

You will see this more clearly by considering what our Saviour says about the blessed Sacrament of His Supper. He says He will give us His flesh to eat.[1] How is this done? we do not

---

[1] John vi.51.

know. He gives it under the outward symbols of bread and wine. But in what real sense is the consecrated bread His body? It is not told us, we may not inquire. We say indeed *spiritually*, *sacramentally*, *in a heavenly way*; but this is in order to impress on our minds religious, and not carnal notions of it. All we are concerned to know is, *the effect* upon us of partaking this blessed food. Now observe what He tells us about that. "Except ye eat the flesh of the Son of man and drink His blood, ye have no life in you. Whoso eateth My flesh, and drinketh My blood, hath eternal life, and I will *raise him up at the last day*." [2] Now there is no distinction made here between soul and body. Christ's blessed Supper is food to us altogether, *whatever* we are, soul, body, and all. It is the seed of eternal life within us, the food of immortality, to "preserve our body and soul unto everlasting life." [3] The forbidden fruit wrought in Adam unto death; but this is the fruit which makes us live for ever. Bread sustains us in this *temporal* life; the consecrated bread is the means of *eternal* strength for soul and body. Who could live this visible life without earthly food? And in the same general way the Supper of the Lord is the "*means*" of our living for ever. We have no reason for thinking we shall live for ever unless we eat it, no more than we have reason to think our temporal life will be sustained without meat and drink. God *can*, indeed, sustain us, "not by bread alone;" but this is His *ordinary* means, which His will has made such. He can sustain our immortality without the Christian Sacraments, as He sustained Abraham and the other saints of old time; but under the Gospel these are His *means*, which He appointed at His will. We eat the sacred bread, and our bodies become sacred; they are not ours; they are Christ's; they are instinct with that flesh which saw not corruption; they are inhabited by His Spirit; they become immortal; they die but to appearance, and for a time; they spring up when their sleep is ended, and reign with Him for ever.

The inference to be drawn from this doctrine is plain. Among the wise men of the heathen, as I have said, it was usual to speak slightingly and contemptuously of the mortal body; they knew

[2] John vi.53, 54.

[3] "In the Supper of the Lord there is no vain ceremony, no bare sign, no untrue figure of a thing absent; but as the Scripture says, . . . the communion of the Body and Blood of the Lord, in a marvellous incorporation, which by the operation of the Holy Ghost . . . is through faith wrought in the souls of the faithful, whereby not only their souls live to eternal life, but they surely trust to win their bodies a resurrection to immortality."—*Homily on the Sacrament*, Part I.

no better. They thought it scarcely a part of their real selves, and fancied they should be in a better condition without it. Nay, they considered it to be the cause of their sinning; as if the soul of man were pure, and the material body were gross, and defiled the soul. *We* have been taught the truth, viz. that sin is a disease of *our minds*, of ourselves; and that the whole of us, not body alone, but soul and body, is naturally corrupt, and that Christ has redeemed and cleansed whatever we are, sinful soul and body. Accordingly *their* chief hope in death was the notion they should be rid of their body. Feeling they were sinful, and not knowing how, they laid the charge on their body; and knowing they were badly circumstanced here, they thought death perchance might be a change for the better. Not that they rested on the hope of returning to a God and Father, but they thought to be unshackled from the earth, and able to do what they would. It was consistent with this slighting of their earthly tabernacle, that they burned the dead bodies of their friends, not burying them as we do, but consuming them as a mere worthless case of what had been precious, and was then an in-cumbrance to the ground. Far different is the temper which the glorious light of the Gospel teaches us. Our bodies shall rise again and live for ever; they may not be irreverently handled. *How* they will rise we know not; but surely if the word of Scrip-ture be true, the body from which the soul has departed shall come to life. There are some truths addressed solely to our faith, not to our reason; not to our reason, because we know so little about "the power of God" (in our Saviour's words), that we have nothing to reason *upon*. One of these, for instance, is the presence of Christ in the Sacrament. We *know* we eat His Body and Blood; but it is our wisdom not curiously to ask how or whence, not to give our thoughts range, but to take and eat and profit thereby. This is the secret of gaining the blessing promised. And so, as regards the resurrection of the dead, we have no means or ground of argument. We cannot determine in what exact sense our bodies on the resurrection will be the same as they are at present, but we cannot harm ourselves by taking God's declaration simply, and acting upon it. And it is as believ-ing this comfortable truth, that the Christian Church put aside that old irreverence of the funeral pile, and consecrated the ground for the reception of the saints that sleep. We deposit our departed friends calmly and thoughtfully, in faith; not ceasing to love or remember that which once lived among us, but mark-ing the place where it lies, as believing that God has set His seal upon it, and His Angels guard it. His Angels, surely, guard the bodies of His servants; Michael the Archangel, thinking it no unworthy task to preserve them from the powers of evil.[4] Especially those like Moses, who fall "in the wilderness of the people," whose duty has called them to danger and suffering, and who die a violent death, these too, if they have eaten of that incorruptible bread, are preserved safe till the last day. There are, who have not the comfort of a peaceful burial. They die in battle, or on the sea, or in strange lands, or, as the early believers, under the hands of persecutors. Horrible tortures, or the mouths of wild beasts, have ere now dishonoured the sacred bodies of those who had fed upon Christ; and diseases corrupt them still. This is Satan's work, the expiring efforts of his fury, after his overthrow by Christ. Still, as far as we can, *we* repair these insults of our Enemy, and tend honourably and piously those tabernacles in which Christ has dwelt. And in this view, what a venerable and fearful place is a Church, in and around which the dead are deposited! Truly it is chiefly sacred, as being the spot where God has for ages manifested Himself to His servants; but add to this the thought, that it is the actual resting-place for those very servants, through successive times, who still live unto Him. The dust around us will one day become animate. We may ourselves be dead long before, and not see it. We ourselves may elsewhere be buried, and, should it be our exceeding blessedness to rise to life eternal, we may rise in other places, far in the east or west. But, as God's word is sure, what is sown is raised; the earth to earth, ashes to ashes, dust to dust, shall become glory to glory, and life to the living God, and a true incorruptible image of the spirit made perfect. Here the saints sleep, here they shall rise. A great sight will a Christian country then be, if earth remains what it is; when holy places pour out the worshippers who have for generations kept vigil therein, waiting through the long night for the bright coming of Christ! And if this be so, what pious composed thoughts should be ours when we enter Churches! God indeed is every where, and His Angels go to and fro; yet can they be more worthily employed in their condescending care of man, than where good men sleep? In the service of the Communion we magnify God together with Angels and Archangels, and all the company of heaven. Surely there is more meaning in this than we know of; what a "dreadful" place would this appear, if our eyes were opened as those of Elisha's servant! "This is none other than the house of God, and this is the gate of heaven."

[4] Jude 9.

On the other hand, if the dead bodies of Christians are honourable, so doubtless are the living; *because* they have had their blessedness when living, *therefore* have they in their sleep. He who does not honour his own body as something holy unto the Lord, may indeed revere the dead, but it is then a mere superstition, not an act of piety. To reverence holy places (right as it is) will not profit a man unless he reverences *himself*. Consider what it is to be partaker of the Body and Blood of Christ. We pray God, in our Church's language, that "our sinful bodies may become clean through His body;" and we are promised in Scripture, that our bodies shall be *temples of the Holy Ghost*. How should we study, then, to cleanse them from all sin, that they may be true members of Christ! We are told that the peril of disease and death attends the unworthy partaking of the Lord's Supper. Is this wonderful, considering the strange sin of receiving it into a body disgraced by wilful disobedience? All that defiles it, intemperance or other vice, all that is unbecoming, all that is disrespectful to Him who has bought our bodies with a price, must be put aside.[5] Hear St. Paul's words, "Christ being raised from the dead, dieth no more . . . likewise reckon ye also yourselves to be dead unto sin . . . let not sin therefore reign in your mortal body, that ye should obey it in the lusts thereof."[6] "If the Spirit of Him who raised up Jesus from the dead dwell in you, He that raised up Christ from the dead shall also quicken your mortal bodies by His indwelling Spirit. . . . If ye, through the Spirit, do mortify the deeds of the body, ye shall live."[7]

Work together with God, therefore, my brethren, in this work of your redemption. While He feeds you, prepare for the heavenly feast; "discern the Lord's body" when it is placed before you, and suitably treasure it afterwards. Lay up year by year this seed of life within you, believing it will one day bear fruit. "Believe that ye receive it, and ye shall have it."[8] Glorious, indeed, will be the spring time of the Resurrection, when all that seemed dry and withered will bud forth and blossom. The glory of Lebanon will be given it, the excellency of Carmel and Sharon; the fir tree for the thorn, the myrtle tree for the briar; and the mountains and the hills shall break forth before us in singing. Who would miss being of that company? Wretched men they will then appear, who now for a season enjoy the pleasures of sin. Wretched, who follow their own selfish will, instead of walking by faith, who are now idle, instead of trying

[5] 1 Cor. vi.20.
[7] Rom. viii.11.
[6] Rom. vi.9–12.
[8] Mark xi.24.

to serve God, who are set upon the world's vanities, or who scoff at religion, or who allow themselves in known sin, who live in anger, or malice, or pride, or covetousness, who do not continually strive to become better and holier, who are afraid to profess themselves Christians and take up their cross and follow Christ. May the good Lord make us all willing to follow Him! may He rouse the slumberers, and raise them to a new life here, that they may inherit His eternal kingdom hereafter!

WITNESSES OF THE RESURRECTION

*"Him God raised up the third day, and showed Him openly; not to
all the people, but unto witnesses chosen before of God, even to us
who did eat and drink with Him after He rose from the dead."*
—Acts x.40, 41.

IT might have been expected, that, on our Saviour's rising
again from the dead, He would have shown Himself to very
great numbers of people, and especially to those who crucified
Him; whereas we know from the history, that, far from this
being the case, He showed Himself only to chosen witnesses,
chiefly His immediate followers; and St. Peter avows this in the
text. This seems at first sight strange. We are apt to fancy the
resurrection of Christ as some striking visible display of His
glory, such as God vouchsafed from time to time to the Israelites in Moses' day; and considering it in the light of a public
triumph, we are led to imagine the confusion and terror which
would have overwhelmed His murderers, had He presented
Himself alive before *them*. Now, thus to reason, is to conceive
Christ's kingdom of *this* world, which it is not; and to suppose
that then Christ came to judge the world, whereas that judgment will not be till the last day, when in very deed those
wicked men *shall* "look on Him whom they have pierced."

But even without insisting upon the spiritual nature of
Christ's kingdom, which seems to be the direct reason why
Christ did not show Himself to all the Jews after His resurrection, other distinct reasons may be given, instructive too. And
one of these I will now set before you.

This is the question, "Why did not our Saviour show Himself after His resurrection to all the people? why only to witnesses chosen before of God?" and this is my answer: "Because
this was the most effectual means of propagating His religion
through the world."

After His resurrection, He said to His disciples, "Go, convert
all nations:"[1] this was His especial charge. If, then, there are

[1] Matt. xxviii.19.

grounds for thinking that, by showing Himself to a few rather than to many, He was more surely advancing this great object, the propagation of the Gospel, this is a sufficient reason for our Lord's having so ordained; and let us thankfully receive His dispensation, as He has given it.

1. Now consider what would have been the probable effect of a public exhibition of His resurrection. Let us suppose that our Saviour had shown Himself as openly as before He suffered; preaching in the Temple and in the streets of the city; traversing the land with His Apostles, and with multitudes following to see the miracles which He did. What would have been the effect of this? Of course, what it had already been. His former miracles had not effectually moved the body of the people; and, doubtless, this miracle too would have left them as it found them, or worse than before. They might have been more startled at the time; but why should this amazement last? When the man taken with a palsy was suddenly restored at His word, the multitude were all amazed, and glorified God, and were filled with fear, saying, "We have seen strange things to-day." [2] What *could* they have said and felt more than this, when "one rose from the dead"? In truth, this is the way of the mass of mankind in all ages, to be influenced by sudden fears, sudden contrition, sudden earnestness, sudden resolves, which disappear as suddenly. Nothing is done effectually through untrained human nature; and such is ever the condition of the multitude. Unstable as water, it cannot excel. One day it cried Hosanna; the next, Crucify Him. And, had our Lord appeared to them *after* they had crucified Him, of course they would have shouted Hosanna once more; and when He had ascended out of sight, then again they would have persecuted His followers. Besides, the miracle of the Resurrection was much more exposed to the cavils of unbelief than others which our Lord had displayed; than that, for instance, of feeding the multitudes in the wilderness. Had our Lord appeared in public, yet few could have touched Him, and certified themselves it was He Himself. Few, comparatively, in a great multitude could so have seen Him both before and after His death, as to be adequate witnesses of the reality of the miracle. It would have been open to the greater number of them still to deny that He *was* risen. This is the very feeling St. Matthew records. When He appeared on a mountain in Galilee to His apostles and others, as it would seem (perhaps the five hundred brethren mentioned by St.

[2] Luke v.26.

Paul), "*some doubted*" whether it were He. How could it be otherwise? these had no means of ascertaining that they really saw *Him* who had been crucified, dead, and buried. Others, admitting it was Jesus, would have denied that He ever died. Not having seen Him dead on the cross, they might have pretended He was taken down thence before life was extinct, and so restored. This supposition would be a sufficient excuse to those who *wished* not to believe. And the more ignorant part would fancy they had seen a *spirit* without flesh and bones as man has. They would have resolved the miracle into a magical illusion, as the Pharisees had done before, when they ascribed His works to Beelzebub; and would have been rendered no better or more religious by the sight of Him, than the common people are now-a-days by tales of apparitions and witches.

Surely so it would have been; the chief priests would not have been moved at all; and the populace, however they had been moved at the time, would not have been lastingly moved, not practically moved, not so moved as to proclaim to the world what they had heard and seen, as to preach the Gospel. This is the point to be kept in view: and consider that the very reason *why* Christ showed Himself at all was in order to raise up *witnesses* to His resurrection, ministers of His word, founders of His Church; and how in the nature of things could a populace ever become such?

2. Now, on the other hand, let us contemplate the means which His Divine Wisdom actually adopted with a view of making His resurrection subservient to the propagation of His Gospel.—He showed Himself openly, not to all the people, but unto witnesses chosen before of God. It is, indeed, a *general* characteristic of the course of His providence to make the few the channels of His blessings to the many; but in the instance we are contemplating, a few were selected, because only a few *could* (humanly speaking) be made instruments. As I have already said, to be witnesses of His resurrection it was requisite to have known our Lord intimately before His death. This was the case with the Apostles; but this was not enough. It was necessary they should be certain it was He Himself, the very same whom they before knew. You recollect how He urged them to handle Him, and be sure that they could testify to His rising again. This is intimated in the text also; "witnesses chosen before of God, even to us who did eat and drink with Him after He rose from the dead." Nor were they required merely to know Him, but the thought of Him was to be stamped upon their minds as the one master-spring of their whole course of life for the

future. But men are not easily wrought upon to be faithful advocates of any cause. Not only is the multitude fickle: but the best men, unless urged, tutored, disciplined to their work, give way; untrained nature has no principles.

It would seem, then, that our Lord gave His attention to a few, because, if the few be gained, the many will follow. To these few He showed Himself again and again. These He restored, comforted, warned, inspired. He formed them into Himself, that they might show forth His praise. This His gracious procedure is opened to us in the first words of the Book of the Acts. "To the Apostles whom He had chosen He showed Himself alive after His passion by many infallible proofs; being seen of them forty days, and speaking of the things pertaining to the kingdom of God." Consider, then, if we may state the alternative reverently, *which* of the two seems the more likely way, even according to a human wisdom, of forming preachers of the Gospel to all nations,—the exhibition of the Resurrection to the Jewish people generally, or this intimate private certifying of it to a few? And remember that, as far as we can understand, the two procedures were inconsistent with each other; for that period of preparatory prayer, meditation, and instruction, which the Apostles passed under our Lord's visible presence for forty days, was to them what it could not have been, had they been following Him from place to place in public, supposing there had been an object in this, and mixing in the busy crowds of the world.

3. I have already suggested, what is too obvious almost to insist upon, that in making a select few the ministers of His mercy to mankind at large, our Lord was but acting according to the general course of His providence. It is plain every great change is effected by the few, not by the many; by the resolute, undaunted, zealous few. True it is that societies sometimes fall to pieces by their own corruption, which is in one sense a change without special instruments chosen or allowed by God; but this is a dissolution, not a work. Doubtless, much may be *undone* by the many, but nothing is *done* except by those who are specially trained for action. In the midst of the famine Jacob's sons stood looking one upon another, but did nothing. One or two men, of small outward pretensions, but with their hearts in their work, these do great things. These are prepared, not by sudden excitement, or by vague general belief in the truth of their cause, but by deeply impressed, often repeated instruction; and since it stands to reason that it is easier to teach a few than a great number, it is plain such men always will be few. Such as

these spread the knowledge of Christ's resurrection over the idolatrous world. Well they answered the teaching of their Lord and Master. Their success sufficiently approves to us His wisdom in showing Himself to them, not to all the people.

4. Remember, too, this further reason why the witnesses of the Resurrection were few in number; viz. because they were on the side of *Truth*. If the witnesses were to be such as really loved and obeyed the Truth, there *could not* be many chosen. Christ's cause was the cause of light and religion, therefore His advocates and ministers were necessarily few. It is an old proverb (which even the heathen admitted), that "the many are bad." Christ did not confide His Gospel to the many; had He done so, we may even say, that it would have been at first sight a presumption against its coming from God. What was the chief work of His whole ministry, but that of choosing and separating *from* the multitude those who should be fit recipients of His Truth? As He went the round of the country again and again, through Galilee and Judea, He tried the spirits of men the while; and rejecting the baser sort who "honoured Him with their lips while their hearts were far from Him," He specially chose twelve. The many He put aside for a while as an adulterous and sinful generation, intending to make one last experiment on the mass when the Spirit should come. But His twelve He brought near to Himself at once, and taught them. Then He sifted them, and one fell away; the eleven escaped as though by fire. *For* these eleven especially He rose again; He visited *them* and taught *them* for forty days; for in *them* He saw the fruit of the "travail of His soul and was satisfied;" in them "He saw His seed, He prolonged His days, and the pleasure of the Lord prospered in His hand." These were His witnesses, for they had the love of the Truth in their hearts. "I have chosen you," He says to them, "and ordained you that ye should go and bring forth fruit, and that your fruit should remain." [3]

So much then in answer to the question, Why did not Christ show Himself to the whole Jewish people after His resurrection. I ask in reply, what would have been the use of it? a mere passing triumph over sinners whose judgment is reserved for the next world. On the other hand, such a procedure would have interfered with, nay, defeated, the real object of His rising again, the propagation of His Gospel through the world by *means of His own intimate friends and followers.* And further, this preference of the few to the many seems to have been necessary

[3] John xv.16.

from the nature of man, since all great works are effected, not by a multitude, but by the deep-seated resolution of a few;—nay, necessary too from man's depravity, for, alas! popular favour is hardly to be expected for the cause of Truth. And our Lord's instruments were few, if for no other reason, yet at least for this, because more were not to be found, because there were but few faithful Israelites without guile in Israel according to the flesh.

Now, let us observe how much matter, both for warning and comfort, is supplied by this view. We learn from the picture of the *infant* Church what that Church has been ever since, that is, as far as man can understand it. Many are called, few are chosen. We learn to reflect on the great danger there is, lest we be not in the number of the chosen, and are warned to "watch and pray that we enter not into temptation," to "work out our salvation with fear and trembling," to seek God's mercy in His Holy Church, and to pray to Him ever that He would "fulfil in us the good pleasure of His will," and complete what He once began.

But, besides this, we are comforted too; we are comforted, as many of us as are living humbly in the fear of God. Who those secret ones are, who in the bosom of the visible Church live as saints fulfilling their calling, God only knows. We are in the dark about it. We may indeed know much about ourselves, and we may form somewhat of a judgment about those with whom we are well acquainted. But of the general body of Christians we know little or nothing. It is our duty to consider them as Christians, to take them as we find them, and to love them; and it is no concern of ours to debate about their state in God's sight. Without, however, entering into this question concerning God's secret counsels, let us receive this truth before us for a practical purpose; that is, I speak to *all who* are conscious to themselves that they wish and try to serve God, whatever their progress in religion be, and whether or not they dare apply to themselves, or in whatever degree, the title of Christian in its most sacred sense. All who obey the Truth are on the side of the Truth, and the Truth will prevail. Few in number but strong in the Spirit, despised by the world, yet making way while they suffered, the twelve Apostles overturned the power of darkness, and established the Christian Church. And let all "who love the Lord Jesus Christ in sincerity" be quite sure, that weak though they seem, and solitary, yet the "foolishness of God is wiser than men, and the weakness of God is stronger than men." The many are "deceitful," and the worldly-wise are "vain;" but he "that feareth the Lord, the same shall be praised." The most excellent gifts of the intellect last but for a season. Eloquence and wit, shrewdness and dexterity, these plead a cause well and propagate it quickly, but it dies with them. It has no root in the hearts of men, and lives not out a generation. It is the consolation of the despised Truth, that its works endure. Its words are few, but they live. Abel's faith to this day, "yet speaketh." [4] The blood of the Martyrs is the seed of the Church. "Fret not thyself" then "because of evil doers, neither be thou envious against the workers of iniquity. For they shall soon be cut down like the grass, and wither as the green herb. Trust in the Lord and do good . . . delight thyself also in Him, and He shall give thee the desires of thy heart; commit thy way unto the Lord, trust also in Him, and He shall bring it to pass. . . . He shall bring forth thy righteousness as the light, and thy judgment as the noon-day. . . . A little that a righteous man hath is better than the riches of *many* wicked. For the arms of the wicked shall be broken, but the Lord upholdeth the righteous. . . . I have seen the wicked in great power, and spreading himself like a green bay-tree, yet he passed away, and, lo! he was not; yea, I sought him, and he could not be found." [5] The heathen world made much ado when the Apostles preached the Resurrection. They and their associates were sent out as lambs among wolves; but they prevailed.

We, too, though we are not witnesses of Christ's actual resurrection, are so spiritually. By a heart awake from the dead, and by affections set on heaven, we can as truly and without figure witness that Christ liveth, as they did. He that believeth on the Son of God hath the witness in himself. Truth bears witness by itself to its Divine Author. He who obeys God conscientiously, and lives holily, forces all about him to believe and tremble before the unseen power of Christ. To the world indeed at large he witnesses not; for few can see him near enough to be moved by his manner of living. But to his neighbours he manifests the Truth in proportion to their knowledge of him; and some of them, through God's blessing, catch the holy flame, cherish it, and in their turn transmit it. And thus in a dark world Truth still makes way in spite of the darkness, passing from hand to hand. And thus it keeps its station in high places, acknowledged as the creed of nations, the multitude of which are ignorant, the while, on what it rests, how it came there, how it keeps its

4 Heb. xi.4.   5 Ps. xxxvii.1–6, 16, 17, 35, 36.

ground; and despising it, think it easy to dislodge it. But "the Lord reigneth." He is risen from the dead, "His throne is established of old; He is from everlasting. The floods have lifted up their voice, the floods lift up their waves. The Lord on high is mightier than the noise of many waters, yea, than the mighty waves of the sea. His testimonies are very sure; holiness becometh His house for ever." [6]

Let these be our thoughts whenever the prevalence of error leads us to despond. When St. Peter's disciple, Ignatius, was brought before the Roman emperor, he called himself Theophorus; and when the emperor asked the feeble old man why he so called himself, Ignatius said it was because he carried Christ in his breast. He witnessed there was but One God, who made heaven, earth, and sea, and all that is in them, and One Lord Jesus Christ, His Only-begotten Son, "whose kingdom (he added) be my portion!" The emperor asked, "His kingdom, say you, who was crucified under Pilate?" "His (answered the Saint) who crucified my sin in me, and who has put all the fraud and malice of Satan under the feet of those who carry Him in their hearts: as it is written, 'I dwell in them and walk in them.'"

Ignatius was one against many, as St. Peter had been before him; and was put to death as the Apostle had been;—but he handed on the Truth, in his day. At length we have received it. Weak though we be, and solitary, God forbid we should not in our turn hand it on; glorifying Him by our lives, and in all our words and works witnessing Christ's passion, death, and resurrection!

[6] Psalm xciii.2–5.

CHRISTIAN REVERENCE

"Serve the Lord with fear, and rejoice with trembling."
—Ps. ii. 11.

W HY did Christ show Himself to so few witnesses after He rose from the dead? Because *He was a King*, a King exalted upon God's "Holy hill of Zion;" as the Psalm says which contains the text. Kings do not court the multitude, or show themselves as a spectacle at the will of others. They are the rulers of their people, and have their state as such, and are reverently waited on by their great men: and when they show themselves, they do so out of their condescension. They act by means of their servants, and must be *sought* by those who would gain favours from them.

Christ, in like manner, when exalted as the Only-begotten Son of God, did not mix with the Jewish people, as in the days of His humiliation. He rose from the grave in secret, and taught in secret for forty days, because "the government was upon His shoulder." He was no longer a servant washing His disciples' feet, and dependent on the wayward will of the multitude. He was the acknowledged Heir of all things. His throne was established by a Divine decree; and those who desired His salvation, were bound to *seek* His face. Yet not even by those who sought was He at once found. He did not permit the world to approach Him rashly, or curiously to gaze on Him. Those only did He call beside Him who had been His friends, who loved Him. Those only He bade "ascend the hill of the Lord," who had "clean hands and a pure heart, who had not worshipped vanity nor sworn deceitfully." These drew near, and "saw the Lord God of Israel," and so were fitted to bear the news of Him to the people at large. *He* remained "in His holy temple;" *they* from Him proclaimed the tidings of His resurrection, and of His mercy, His free pardon offered to all men, and the promises of grace and glory which His death had procured for all who believe.

Thus are we taught to serve our risen Lord with fear, and rejoice with trembling. Let us pursue the subject thus opened upon us.—Christ's second sojourn on earth (after His resurrection) was *in secret*. The time had been when He "preached openly in the synagogues," and in the public ways; and openly wrought miracles such as man never did. Was there to be no end of His labours in our behalf? His *death* "finished" them; afterwards He taught His *followers* only. Who shall complain of His withdrawing Himself at last from the world, when it was of His own spontaneous loving-kindness that He ever showed Himself at all?

Yet it must be borne in mind, that even before He entered into His glory, Christ spoke and acted as a King. It must not be supposed that, even in the days of His flesh, He could forget who He was, or "behave Himself unseemly" by any weak submission to the will of the Jewish people. Even in the lowest acts of His self-abasement, still He showed His greatness. Consider His conduct when He washed St. Peter's feet, and see if it were not calculated (assuredly it was) to humble, to awe, and subdue the very person to whom He ministered. When He taught, warned, pitied, prayed for, His ignorant hearers, He never allowed them to relax their reverence or to overlook His condescension. Nay, He did not allow them to praise Him aloud, and publish His acts of grace; as if what is called popularity would be a dishonour to His holy name, and the applause of men would imply their right to censure. The world's praise is akin to contempt. Our Lord delights in the tribute of the secret heart. Such was His conduct in the days of His flesh. Does it not interpret His dealings with us after His resurrection? He who was so reserved in His communications of Himself, even when He came to minister, much more would withdraw Himself from the eyes of men when He was exalted over all things.

I have said, that even when a servant, Christ spoke with the authority of a king; and have given you some proof of it. But it may be well to dwell upon this. Observe then, the difference between His promises, stated doctrinally and generally, and His mode of addressing those who came actually before Him. While He announced God's willingness to forgive *all* repentant sinners, in all the fullness of loving-kindness and tender mercy, yet He did not use supplication to these persons or those, whatever their number or their rank might be. He spoke as one who knew He had great favours to confer, and had nothing to gain from those who received them. Far from urging them to accept His bounty, He showed Himself even backward to confer it, inquired into their knowledge and motives, and cautioned them against entering His service without counting the cost of it. Thus sometimes He even repelled men from Him.

For instance: When there went "great multitudes with Him . . . He turned and said unto them, If any man come to Me, and hate not his father and mother, and wife and children, and brothers and sisters, yea, and his own life also, he cannot be My disciple." These were not the words of one who courted popularity. He proceeds;—"Which of you intending to build a tower, sitteth not down first, and counteth the cost, whether he have sufficient to finish it? . . . So likewise, whosoever he be of you, that forsaketh not all that he hath, he cannot be My disciple." [1] On the other hand, observe His conduct to the powerful men, and the learned Scribes and Pharisees. There are persons who look up to human power, and who are pleased to associate their names with the accomplished and cultivated of this world. Our blessed Lord was as inflexible towards these, as towards the crowds which followed Him. They asked for a sign; He named them "an evil and adulterous generation," who refused to profit by what they had already received. [2] They asked Him, whether He did not confess Himself to be One with God; but He, rather than tell such proud disputers, seemed even to abandon His own real claim, and made His former clear words ambiguous. [3] Such was the King of Israel in the eyes of the multitude and of their rulers; a "hard saying," a "rock of offence even to the disobedient," who came to Him "with their lips, while their hearts were far from Him." Continue this survey to the case of individuals, and it will still appear, that, loving and merciful as He was most abundantly, yet still He showed both His power and His grace with reserve, even to them, as well as to the fickle many, or the unbelieving Pharisees.

One instance is preserved to us of a person addressing Him, with some notions, indeed, of His greatness, but in a light and careless tone. The narrative is instructive from the mixture of good and bad which the inquirer's character displays. [4] He was young, and wealthy, and is called "a ruler;" yet was anxious for Christ's favour. So far was well. Nay, he "came running and kneeling to Him." And he *seemed* to address Him in what would generally be considered as respectful terms: "Good Master," he said. Yet our Saviour saw in his conduct a deficiency;—"One thing thou lackest:" viz. *devotion* in the true sense of the word,—a giving himself up to Christ. This young man seems to have considered religion as an easy work, and thought he could live as the world, and yet serve God acceptably. In consequence,

---

[1] Luke xiv.25–33.   [2] Matt. xii.39; xxi.23–27.   [3] John x.30–37.
[4] Matt. xix.16–22; Mark x.17–22; Luke xviii.18–23.

we may suppose, he had little right notion of the dignity of a Messenger from God. He did not associate the Ministers of religion with awful prospects beyond the grave, in which he was interested; nor *reverence* them accordingly, though he was not without some kind of *respect* for them. Doubtless he thought he was *honouring* our Lord when he had called Him "*Good Master*;" and would have been surprised to hear his attachment to sacred subjects and appointments called in question. Yet our Saviour rejected such half homage, and rebuked what even seemed piously offered.—"*Why* callest thou Me good?" He asked; "There is none good but One, that is, God:" as if He said, "Observest thou *what* words thou art using as if words of course? '*Good Master*'—am I accounted by thee as a teacher of man's creation, and over whom man has power, and to be accosted by a form of honour, which, through length of time, has lost its meaning; or am I acknowledged to come and have authority from Him who is the only source of goodness?" Nor did our Lord relax His severity even after this reproof. Expressly as it is told us, "*He loved him*," and spoke to him therefore in great compassion and mercy, yet He strictly charged him to sell all he had and give it away, if he would show he was in earnest, and He sent him away "sorrowful."

You may recollect, too, our Lord's frequent inquiry into *the faith* of those who came to Him. This arose, doubtless, from the same rule,—a regard to His own Majesty as a King. "If thou canst believe, all things are possible to him that believeth." [5] He did not work miracles as a mere display of power; or allow the world profanely to look on as at some exhibition of art. In this respect, as in others, even Moses and Elias stand in contrast with Him. Moses wrought miracles before Pharaoh to rival the magicians of Egypt. Elijah challenged the prophets of Baal to bring down fire from heaven. The Son of God deigned not to exert His power before Herod, after Moses' pattern; nor to be judged by the multitude, as Elijah. He subdued the power of Satan at His own appointed seasons; but when the Devil tempted Him and demanded a miracle in proof of His Divinity, He would do none.

Further, even when an inquirer showed earnestness, still He did not try to gain him over by smooth representations of His doctrine. He declared, indeed, the general characteristic of His doctrine, "My yoke is easy;" but "He made Himself strange and spake roughly" to those who came to Him. Nicodemus was an-

[5] Mark ix.23.

other ruler of the Jews, who sought Him, and he professed his belief in His miracles and Divine mission. Our Saviour answered in these severe words;—"Verily, verily, I say unto thee, Except a man be born again, he cannot see the kingdom of God."

Such was our Saviour's conduct even during the period of His ministry; much more might we expect it to be such, when He had risen from His state of servitude, and such we find it.

No man saw Him rise from the grave. His Angels indeed beheld it; but His earthly followers were away, and the heathen soldiers were not worthy. They saw, indeed, the great Angel, who rolled away the stone from the opening of the tomb. This was Christ's servant; but Him they saw not. *He* was on His way to see His own faithful and mourning followers. To these He had revealed His doctrine during His humiliation, and called them "His friends."[6] First of all, He appeared to Mary Magdalene in the garden itself where He had been buried; then to the other women who ministered unto Him; then to the two disciples travelling to Emmaus; then to all the Apostles separately; besides, to Peter and to James; and to Thomas in the presence of them all. Yet not even these, His friends, had free access to Him. He said to Mary, "Touch Me not." He came and left them according to His own pleasure. When they saw Him, they felt an awe which they had not felt during His ministry. While they doubted if it were He, "None of them," St. John says, "durst ask Him, Who art Thou? believing that it was the Lord."[7] However, as kings have their days of state, on which they show themselves publicly to their subjects, so our Lord appointed a meeting of His disciples, when they might see Him. He had determined this even before His crucifixion; and the Angels reminded them of it. "He goeth before you into Galilee; there shall ye see Him, as He said unto you."[8] The place of meeting was a mountain; the same (it is supposed) as that on which He had been transfigured; and the number who saw Him there was five hundred at once, if we join St. Paul's account to that in the Gospels. At length, after forty days, He was taken from them; He ascended up, "and a cloud received Him out of their sight."

Are *we* to feel less humble veneration for Him now, than His Apostles then? Though He is our Saviour, and has removed all slavish fear of death and judgment, are we, therefore, to make light of the prospect before us, as if we were sure of that reward which He bids us struggle for? Assuredly, we are still to "serve

[6] Matt. xiii.11; John xv.15.   [7] John xxi.12.   [8] Mark xvi.7.

the Lord with fear, and rejoice with reverence,"—to "kiss the Son, lest He be angry, and so we perish from the right way, if His wrath be kindled, yea but a little." In a Christian's course, *fear and love must go together*. And this is the lesson to be deduced from our Saviour's withdrawing from the world after His resurrection. He showed His love for men by dying for them, and rising again. He maintained His honour and great glory by retiring from them when His merciful purpose was attained, that they might seek Him if they would find Him. He ascended to His Father out of our sight. Sinners would be ill company for the exalted King of Saints. When we have been duly prepared to see Him, we shall be given to approach Him.

In heaven, love will absorb fear; but in this world, fear and love must go together. No one can love God aright without fearing Him; though many fear Him, and yet do not love Him. Self-confident men, who do not know their own hearts, or the reasons they have for being dissatisfied with themselves, do not fear God, and they think this bold freedom is to love Him. Deliberate sinners fear but cannot love Him. But devotion to Him consists in love and fear, as we may understand from our ordinary attachment to each other. No one really loves another, who does not feel a certain reverence towards him. When friends transgress this sobriety of affection, they may indeed continue associates for a time, but they have broken the bond of union. It is mutual respect which makes friendship lasting. So again, in the feelings of inferiors towards superiors. Fear must go before love. Till he who has authority shows he has it and can use it, his forbearance will not be valued duly; his kindness will look like weakness. We learn to contemn what we do not fear; and we cannot love what we contemn. So in religion also. We cannot understand Christ's mercies till we understand His power, His glory, His unspeakable holiness, and our demerits; that is, until we first fear Him. Not that fear comes first, and then love; for the most part they will proceed together. Fear is allayed by the love of Him, and our love sobered by our fear of Him. Thus He draws us on with encouraging voice amid the terrors of His threatenings. As in the young ruler's case, He loves us, yet speaks harshly to us that we may learn to cherish mixed feelings towards Him. He hides Himself from us, and yet calls us on, that we may hear His voice as Samuel did, and, believing, approach Him with trembling. This may seem strange to those who do not study the Scriptures, and to those who do not know what it is earnestly to seek after God. But in proportion as the state of mind is strange, so is there in it, therefore, untold and surpassing pleasure to those who partake it. The bitter and the sweet, strangely tempered, thus leave upon the mind the lasting taste of Divine truth, and satisfy it; not so harsh as to be loathed; nor of that insipid sweetness which attends enthusiastic feelings, and is wearisome when it becomes familiar. Such is the feeling of conscience too, God's original gift; how painful! yet who would lose it? "I opened my mouth and panted, for I longed for Thy commandments."[9] This is David's account of it. Ezekiel describes something of the same feeling when the Spirit lifted him up and took him away, "and he went in bitterness, in the heat of his spirit," "the hand of the Lord" being "strong upon him."[10]

Now how does this apply to us here assembled? Are we in danger of speaking or thinking of Christ irreverently? I do not think we are in any immediate danger of deliberate profaneness; but we are in great danger of this, viz. first, of allowing ourselves to appear profane, and secondly, of gradually becoming irreverent, while we are pretending to be so. Men do not begin by *intending* to dishonour God; but they are afraid of the ridicule of others: they are ashamed of appearing religious; and thus are led to pretend that they are worse than they really are. They say things which they do not mean; and, by a miserable weakness, allow actions and habits to be imputed to them which they dare not really indulge in. Hence, they affect a liberty of speech which only befits the companions of evil spirits. They take God's name in vain, to show that they can do what devils do, and they invoke the evil spirit, or speak familiarly of all that pertains to him, and deal about curses wantonly, as though they were not fire-brands,—as if acknowledging the Author of Evil to be their great master and lord. Yes! he *is* a master who allows himself to be served without trembling. It is his very art to lead men to be at ease with him, to think lightly of him, and to trifle with him. He will submit to their ridicule, take (as it were) their blows, and pretend to be their slave, that he may ensnare them. *He* has no dignity to maintain, and he waits his time when his malice shall be gratified. So it has ever been all over the earth. Among all nations it has been his aim to make men laugh at him; going to and fro upon the earth, and walking up and down in it, hearing and rejoicing in that light perpetual talk about him which is his *worship*.

Now, it is not to be supposed that all this careless language

9 Ps. cxix.131.   10 Ezek. iii.14.

196   CHRISTIAN REVERENCE

can be continued without its affecting a man's heart at last; and
this is the second danger I spoke of. Through a false shame, we
disown religion with our lips, and next our words affect our
thoughts. Men at last become the cold, indifferent, profane
characters they professed themselves to be. They think contemptuously of God's Ministers, Sacraments, and Worship;
they slight His Word, rarely looking into it, and never studying
it. They undervalue all religious profession, and judging of others by themselves, impute the conscientious conduct they witness to bad motives. Thus they are in heart infidels; though
they may not formally be such, and may attempt to disguise
their own unbelief under pretence of objecting to one or other
of the doctrines or ordinances of religion. And should a time of
temptation come, when it would be *safe* to show themselves as
they really are, they will (almost unawares) throw off their profession of Christianity, and join themselves to the scoffing
world.

And how must Christians, on the other hand, treat such
heartless men? They have our Lord's example to imitate. Not
that they dare precisely follow the conduct of Him who had no
sin. They dare not assume to themselves any honour on their
own account; and they are bound, especially if they are His
Ministers, to humble themselves as the Apostles did, and "going out to the highways and hedges (as it were) compel" [11] men
to be saved. Yet, while they use greater earnestness of entreaty
than their Lord, they must not forget His dignity the while,
who sends them. He manifested His love towards us, "in deed
and in truth," and we, His Ministers, declare it in word; yet for
the very reason that it is so abundant, we must in very gratitude learn reverence towards Him. We must not take advantage (so to say) of His goodness; or misuse the powers
committed to us. Never must we solicitously press the truth
upon those who do not profit by what they already possess. It
dishonours Christ, while it does the scorner harm, not good. It
is casting pearls before swine. We must wait for all opportunities of being useful to men, but beware of attempting too much
at once. We must impart the Scripture doctrines, in measure
and season, as they can bear them; not being eager to recount
them all, rather, hiding them from the world. Seldom must we
engage in controversy or dispute; for it lowers the sacred truths
to make them a subject for ordinary debate. Common propriety suggests rules like these at once. Who would speak freely

[11] Luke xiv.23.

about some revered friend in the presence of those who did not value him? or who would think he could with a few words overcome their indifference towards him? or who would hastily dispute about him when his hearers had no desire to be made love him?

Rather, shunning all intemperate words, let us show our light before men by our *works*. Here we must be safe. In doing justice, showing mercy, speaking the truth, resisting sin, obeying the Church,—in thus glorifying God, there can be no irreverence. And, above all let us look at home, check all bad thoughts, presumptuous imaginings, vain desires, discontented murmurings, self-complacent reflections, and so in our hearts ever honour Him in secret, whom we reverence by open profession.

May God guide us in a dangerous world; and deliver us from evil. And may He rouse to serious thought, by the power of His Spirit, all who are living in profaneness or unconcern.

THE RELIGION OF THE DAY

*"Let us have grace, whereby we may serve God acceptably with
reverence and godly fear. For our God is a consuming fire."*
—Heb. xii.28, 29.

I N every age of Christianity, since it was first preached, there
has been what may be called a *religion of the world*, which so
far imitates the one true religion, as to deceive the unstable and
unwary. The world does not oppose religion *as such*. I may say, it
never has opposed it. In particular, it has, in all ages, acknowledged in one sense or other the Gospel of Christ, fastened on
one or other of its characteristics, and professed to embody this
in its practice; while by neglecting the other parts of the holy
doctrine, it has, in fact, distorted and corrupted even that portion of it which it has exclusively put forward, and so has contrived to explain away the whole;—for he who cultivates only
one precept of the Gospel to the exclusion of the rest, in reality
attends to no part at all. Our duties *balance* each other; and
though we are too sinful to perform them all perfectly, yet we
may in some measure be performing them all, and preserving
the balance on the whole; whereas, to give ourselves only to this
or that commandment, is to incline our minds in a wrong direction, and at length to pull them down to the earth, which is the
aim of our adversary, the Devil.

It is his *aim* to break our strength; to force us down to the
earth,—to bind us there. The world is his instrument for this
purpose; but he is too wise to set it in open opposition to the
Word of God. No! he affects to be a prophet like the prophets
of God. He calls his servants also prophets; and they mix with
the scattered remnant of the true Church, with the solitary
Micaiahs who are left upon the earth, and speak in the name of
the Lord. And in one sense they speak the truth; but it is not the
whole truth; and we know, even from the common experience
of life, that half the truth is often the most gross and mischievous of falsehoods.

Even in the first age of the Church, while persecution still
raged, he set up a counter religion among the philosophers of

the day, partly like Christianity, but in truth a bitter foe to it; and it deceived and made shipwreck of the faith of those who had not the love of God in their hearts.

Time went on, and he devised a second idol of the true Christ, and it remained in the temple of God for many a year. The age was rude and fierce. Satan took the darker side of the Gospel: its awful mysteriousness, its fearful glory, its sovereign inflexible justice; and here *his* picture of the truth ended, "God is a consuming fire;" so declares the text, and we know it. But we know more, viz. that God is love also; but Satan did not add this to his religion, which became one of *fear*. The religion of the world was then a fearful religion. Superstitions abounded, and cruelties. The noble firmness, the graceful austerity of the true Christian were superseded by forbidding spectres, harsh of eye, and haughty of brow; and these were the patterns or the tyrants of a beguiled people.

What is Satan's device in this day? a far different one; but perhaps a more pernicious. I will attempt to expose it, or rather to suggest some remarks towards its exposure, by those who think it worth while to attempt it; for the subject is too great and too difficult for an occasion such as the present, and, after all, no one can detect falsehood for another;—every man must do it for himself; we can but *help* each other.

What is the world's religion now? It has taken the brighter side of the Gospel, its tidings of comfort, its precepts of love; all darker, deeper views of man's condition and prospects being comparatively forgotten. This is the religion *natural* to a civilized age, and well has Satan dressed and completed it into an idol of the Truth. As the reason is cultivated, the taste formed, the affections and sentiments refined, a general decency and grace will of course spread over the face of society, quite independently of the influence of Revelation. That beauty and delicacy of thought, which is so attractive in books, then extends to the conduct of life, to all we have, all we do, all we are. Our manners are courteous; we avoid giving pain or offence; our words become correct; our relative duties are carefully performed. Our sense of propriety shows itself even in our domestic arrangements, in the embellishments of our houses, in our amusements, and so also in our religious profession. Vice now becomes unseemly and hideous to the imagination, or, as it is sometimes familiarly said, "out of taste." Thus elegance is gradually made the test and standard of virtue, which is no longer thought to possess an intrinsic claim on our hearts, or to exist, *further than* it leads to the quiet and comfort of others.

Conscience is no longer recognized as an independent arbiter of actions, its authority is explained away; partly it is superseded in the minds of men by the so-called moral sense, which is regarded merely as the love of the beautiful; partly by the rule of expediency, which is forthwith substituted for it in the details of conduct. Now conscience is a stern, gloomy principle; it tells us of guilt and of prospective punishment. Accordingly, when its terrors disappear, then disappear also, in the creed of the day, those fearful images of Divine wrath with which the Scriptures abound. They are explained away. Every thing is bright and cheerful. Religion is pleasant and easy; benevolence is the chief virtue; intolerance, bigotry, excess of zeal, are the first of sins. Austerity is an absurdity;—even firmness is looked on with an unfriendly, suspicious eye. On the other hand, all open profligacy is discountenanced; drunkenness is accounted a disgrace; cursing and swearing are vulgarities. Moreover, to a cultivated mind, which recreates itself in the varieties of literature and knowledge, and is interested in the ever-accumulating discoveries of science, and the ever-fresh accessions of information, political or otherwise, from foreign countries, religion will commonly seem to be dull, from want of novelty. Hence excitements are eagerly sought out and rewarded. New objects in religion, new systems and plans, new doctrines, new preachers, are necessary to satisfy that craving which the so-called spread of knowledge has created. The mind becomes morbidly sensitive and fastidious; dissatisfied with things as they are, desirous of a change *as such*, as if alteration must of itself be a relief.

Now I would have you put Christianity for an instant out of your thoughts; and consider whether such a state of refinement as I have attempted to describe, is not that to which men might be brought, quite independent of religion, by the mere influence of education and civilization; and then again, whether, nevertheless, this mere refinement of mind is not more or less all that is called religion at this day. In other words, is it not the case, that Satan has so composed and dressed out what is the mere natural produce of the human heart under certain circumstances, as to serve his purposes as the counterfeit of the Truth? I do not at all deny that this spirit of the world uses words, and makes professions, which it would not adopt except for the suggestions of Scripture; nor do I deny that it takes a general colouring from Christianity, so as really to be modified by it, nay, in a measure enlightened and exalted by it. Again, I fully grant that many persons in whom this bad spirit shows itself, are but partially infected by it, and at bottom, good Christians, though imperfect. Still, after all, here is an existing teaching, only partially evangelical, built upon worldly principle, yet pretending to be the Gospel, dropping one whole side of the Gospel, its austere character, and considering it enough to be benevolent, courteous, candid, correct in conduct, delicate,—though it includes no true fear of God, no fervent zeal for His honour, no deep hatred of sin, no horror at the sight of sinners, no indignation and compassion at the blasphemies of heretics, no jealous adherence to doctrinal truth, no especial sensitiveness about the particular means of gaining ends, provided the ends be good, no loyalty to the Holy Apostolic Church, of which the Creed speaks, no sense of the authority of religion as external to the mind: in a word, no seriousness,—and therefore is neither hot nor cold, but (in Scripture language) *lukewarm*. Thus the present age is the very contrary to what are commonly called the dark ages; and together with the faults of those ages we have lost their virtues. I say their virtues; for even the errors then prevalent, a persecuting spirit, for instance, fear of religious inquiry, bigotry, these were, after all, but perversions and excesses of *real virtues*, such as zeal and reverence; and we, instead of limiting and purifying them, have taken them away root and branch. Why? because we have not acted from a love of the Truth, but from the influence of the Age. The old generation has passed, and its character with it; a new order of things has arisen. Human society has a new framework, and fosters and developes a new character of mind; and this new character is made by the enemy of our souls, to resemble the Christian's obedience as near as it may, its likeness all the time being but accidental. Meanwhile the Holy Church of God, as from the beginning, continues her course heavenward; despised by the world, yet influencing it, partly correcting it, partly restraining it, and in some happy cases reclaiming its victims, and fixing them firmly and for ever within the lines of the faithful host militant here on earth, which journeys towards the City of the Great King. God give us grace to search our hearts, lest we be blinded by the deceitfulness of sin! lest we serve Satan transformed into an Angel of light, while we think we are pursuing true knowledge; lest, over-looking and ill-treating the elect of Christ here, we have to ask that awful question at the last day, while the truth is bursting upon us, "Lord, *when* saw we Thee a stranger and a prisoner?" when saw we Thy sacred Word and Servants despised and oppressed, "and did not minister unto Thee?" [1]

[1] Matt. xxv.44.

Nothing shows more strikingly the power of the world's religion, as now described, than to consider the very different classes of men whom it influences. It will be found to extend its sway and its teaching both over the professedly religious and the irreligious.

1. Many religious men, rightly or not, have long been expecting a millennium of purity and peace for the Church. I will not say, whether or not with reason, for good men may well differ on such a subject. But, any how, in the case of those who have expected it, it has become a temptation to take up and recognize the world's religion as I have already delineated it. They have more or less identified their vision of Christ's kingdom with the elegance and refinement of mere human civilization; and have hailed every evidence of improved decency, every wholesome civil regulation, every beneficent and enlightened act of state policy, as signs of their coming Lord. Bent upon achieving their object, an extensive and glorious diffusion and profession of the Gospel, they have been little solicitous about the *means* employed. They have countenanced and acted with men who openly professed unchristian principles. They have accepted and defended what they considered to be reformations and ameliorations of the existing state of things, though injustice must be perpetrated in order to effect them, or long cherished rules of conduct, indifferent perhaps in their origin but consecrated by long usage, must be violated. They have sacrificed Truth to expedience. They have strangely imagined that bad men are to be the immediate instruments of the approaching advent of Christ; and (like the deluded Jews not many years since in a foreign country) they have taken, if not for their Messiah (as the Jews did), at least for their Elijah, their reforming Baptist, the Herald of the Christ, children of this world, and sons of Belial, on whom the anathema of the Apostle lies from the beginning, declaring, "If any man love not the Lord Jesus Christ, let him be Anathema Maran-atha."[2]

2. On the other hand, the form of doctrine, which I have called the religion of the day, is especially adapted to please men of sceptical minds, the opposite extreme to those just mentioned, who have never been careful to obey their conscience, who cultivate the intellect without disciplining the heart, and who allow themselves to speculate freely about what religion *ought to be*, without going to Scripture to discover what it really is. Some persons of this character almost consider religion itself

[2] 1 Cor. xvi.22.

to be an obstacle in the advance of our social and political well-being. But they know human nature requires it; therefore they select the most *rational* form of religion (so they call it) which they can find. Others are far more seriously disposed, but are corrupted by bad example or other cause. But they *all* discard (what they call) gloomy views of religion; they all trust themselves more than God's word, and thus may be classed together; and are ready to embrace the pleasant consoling religion natural to a polished age. They lay much stress on works on *Natural Theology*, and think that all religion is contained in these; whereas, in truth, there is no greater fallacy than to suppose such works to be in themselves in any true sense religious at all. Religion, it has been well observed, is something *relative to us*; a system of commands and promises from God *towards* us. But how are we concerned with the sun, moon, and stars? or with the laws of the universe? how will they teach us our *duty*? how will they speak to *sinners*? They do not speak to sinners at all. They were created *before* Adam fell. They "declare the *glory* of God," but not His *will*. They are all perfect, all harmonious; but that brightness and excellence which they exhibit in their own creation, and the Divine benevolence therein seen, are of little moment to fallen man. We see nothing there of God's *wrath*, of which the conscience of a sinner loudly speaks. So that there cannot be a more dangerous (though a common) device of Satan, than to carry us off from our own secret thoughts, to make us forget our own hearts, which tell us of a God of justice and holiness, and to fix our attention merely on the God who made the heavens; who is *our* God indeed, but not God as manifested to us sinners, but as He shines forth to His Angels, and to His elect hereafter.

When a man has so far deceived himself as to trust his destiny to what the heavens tell him of it, instead of consulting and obeying his conscience, what is the consequence? that at once he misinterprets and perverts the whole tenor of Scripture. It cannot be denied that, pleasant as religious observances are declared in Scripture to be to the holy, yet to men in general they are said to be difficult and distasteful; to all men *naturally* impossible, and by few fulfilled even with the assistances of grace, on account of their wilful corruption. Religion is pronounced to be against nature, to be against our original will, to require God's aid to make us love and obey it, and to be commonly refused and opposed in spite of that aid. We are expressly told, that "strait is the gate and narrow the way that leads to life, and few there be that find it;" that we must "*strive*" or struggle "to enter in at the strait gate," for that "many shall *seek* to enter in," but that is not enough, they merely seek and therefore do not find; and further, that they who do not obtain everlasting life, "shall go into everlasting punishment." [3] This is the dark side of religion; and the men I have been describing cannot bear to think of it. They shrink from it as too terrible. They easily get themselves to believe that those strong declarations of Scripture do not belong to the present day, or that they are figurative. They have no language within their heart responding to them. Conscience has been silenced. The only information they have received concerning God has been from Natural Theology, and that speaks only of benevolence and harmony; so they will not credit the plain word of Scripture. They seize on such parts of Scripture as seem to countenance their own opinions; they insist on its being commanded us to "rejoice evermore;" and they argue that it is our duty to solace ourselves here (in moderation, of course) with the goods of this life, —that we have only to be thankful while we use them,—that we need not alarm ourselves,—that God is a merciful God,— that amendment is quite sufficient to atone for our offences,— that though we have been irregular in our youth, yet that is a thing gone by,—that we forget it, and therefore God forgets it,—that the world is, on the whole, very well disposed towards religion,—that we should avoid enthusiasm,—that we should not be over serious,—that we should have large views on the subject of human nature,—and that we should love all men. This indeed is the creed of shallow men, in *every* age, who reason a little, and feel not at all, and who think themselves enlightened and philosophical. Part of what they say is false, part is true, but misapplied; but why I have noticed it here, is to show how exactly it fits in with what I have already described as the peculiar religion of a civilized age; it fits in with it equally well as does that of the (so called) religious world, which is the opposite extreme.

One further remark I will make about these professedly rational Christians; who, be it observed, often go on to deny the mysteries of the Gospel. Let us take the text:—"Our God is a consuming fire." Now supposing these persons fell upon these words, or heard them urged as an argument against their own doctrine of the unmixed satisfactory character of our prospects in the world to come, and supposing they did not know what part of the Bible they occurred in, what would they say?

[3] Matt. vii.14; Luke xiii.24; Matt. xxv.46.

Doubtless they would confidently say that they applied only to the Jews,—and not to Christians; that they only described the Divine Author of the Mosaic Law;[4] that God formerly spoke in terrors to the Jews, because they were a gross and brutish people, but that civilization has made us quite other men; that our *reason*, not our *fears*, is appealed to, and that the Gospel is love. And yet, in spite of all this argument, the text occurs in the Epistle to the Hebrews, written by an Apostle of Christ.

I shall conclude with stating more fully what I mean by the dark side of religion; and what judgment ought to be passed on the superstitious and gloomy.

Here I will not shrink from uttering my firm conviction, that it would be a gain to this country, were it vastly more superstitious, more bigoted, more gloomy, more fierce in its religion, than at present it shows itself to be. Not, of course, that I think the tempers of mind herein implied desirable, which would be an evident absurdity; but I think them infinitely more desirable and more promising than a heathen obduracy, and a cold, self-sufficient, self-wise tranquillity. Doubtless, peace of mind, a quiet conscience, and a cheerful countenance are the gift of the Gospel, and the sign of a Christian; but the same effects (or, rather, what appear to be the same) may arise from very different causes. Jonah slept in the storm,—so did our Blessed Lord. The one slept in an evil security: the Other in the "peace of God which passeth all understanding." The two states cannot be confounded together, they are perfectly distinct; and as distinct is the calm of the man of the world from that of the Christian. Now take the case of the sailors on board the vessel; they cried to Jonah, "What meanest thou, O sleeper?"—so the Apostles said to Christ; "Lord, we perish." This is the case of the superstitious; they stand between the false peace of Jonah and the true peace of Christ; they are better than the one, though far below the Other. Applying this to the present religion of the educated world, full as it is of security and cheerfulness, and decorum, and benevolence, I observe that these appearances may arise either from a great deal of religion, or from the absence of it; they may be the fruits of shallowness of mind and a blinded conscience, or of that faith which has peace with God through our Lord Jesus Christ. And if this alternative be proposed, I might leave it to the common sense of men to decide (if they could get themselves to think seriously) to which of the two the temper of the age is to be referred. For myself I cannot

[4] Deut. iv.24.

doubt, seeing what I see of the world, that it arises from the sleep of Jonah; and it is therefore but a dream of religion, far inferior in worth to the well-grounded alarm of the superstitious, who are awakened and see their danger, though they do not attain so far in faith as to embrace the remedy of it.

Think of this, I beseech you, my brethren, and lay it to heart, as far as you go with me, as you will answer for having heard it at the last day. I would not willingly be harsh: but knowing "that the world lieth in wickedness," I think it highly probable that you, so far as you are in it (as you must be, and we all must be in our degree), are, most of you, partially infected with its existing error, that shallowness of religion, which is the result of a blinded conscience; and, therefore, I speak earnestly to you. Believing in the existence of a general plague in the land, I judge that you probably have your share in the sufferings, the voluntary sufferings, which it is spreading among us. The fear of God is the beginning of wisdom; till you see Him to be a consuming fire, and approach Him with reverence and godly fear, as being sinners, you are not even in sight of the strait gate. I do not wish you to be able to point to any particular time when you renounced the world (as it is called), and were converted; this is a deceit. Fear and love must go together; always fear, always love, to your dying day. Doubtless;—still you must know what it is to sow in tears here, if you would reap in joy hereafter. Till you know the weight of your sins, and that not in mere imagination, but in practice, not so as merely to confess it in a formal phrase of lamentation, but daily and in your heart in secret, you cannot embrace the offer of mercy held out to you in the Gospel, through the death of Christ. Till you know what it is to fear with the terrified sailors or the Apostles, you cannot sleep with Christ at your Heavenly Father's feet. Miserable as were the superstitions of the dark ages, revolting as are the tortures now in use among the heathen of the East, better, far better is it, to torture the body all one's days, and to make this life a hell upon earth, than to remain in a brief tranquillity here, till the pit at length opens under us, and awakens us to an eternal fruitless consciousness and remorse. Think of Christ's own words: "What shall a man give in exchange for his soul?" Again, He says, "Fear Him, who after He hath killed, hath power to cast into hell; yea, I say unto you, fear Him." Dare not to think you have got to the bottom of your hearts; you do not know what evil lies there. How long and earnestly must you pray, how many years must you pass in careful obedience, before you have any right to lay aside sorrow, and to rejoice in the

Lord? In one sense, indeed, you may take comfort from the first; for, though you dare not yet anticipate you are in the number of Christ's true elect, yet from the first you know He desires your salvation, has died for you, has washed away your sins by baptism, and will ever help you; and this thought must cheer you while you go on to examine and review your lives, and to turn to God in self-denial. But, at the same time, you never can be sure of salvation, while you are here; and therefore you must always fear while you hope. Your knowledge of your sins increases with your view of God's mercy in Christ. And this is the true Christian state, and the nearest approach to Christ's calm and placid sleep in the tempest;—not perfect joy and certainty in heaven, but a deep resignation to God's will, a surrender of ourselves, soul and body, to Him; hoping indeed, that we shall be saved, but fixing our eyes more earnestly on Him than on ourselves; that is, acting for His glory, seeking to please Him, devoting ourselves to Him in all manly obedience and strenuous good works; and, when we do look within, thinking of ourselves with a certain abhorrence and contempt as being sinners, mortifying our flesh, scourging our appetites, and composedly awaiting that time when, if we be worthy, we shall be stripped of our present selves, and new made in the kingdom of Christ.

SCRIPTURE A RECORD OF
HUMAN SORROW

*"There is at Jerusalem by the sheepmarket a pool, which is called in
the Hebrew tongue Bethesda, having five porches. In these lay a
great multitude of impotent folk, of blind, halt, withered,
waiting for the moving of the water."*—John v.2, 3.

WHAT a scene of misery this pool of Bethesda must have
presented! of pain and sadness triumphing unto death!
the "blind, halt, withered, and impotent," persuaded by the
hope of cure to disclose their sufferings in the eye of day in one
large company. This pool was endued, at certain times, with a
wonderful virtue by the descent of an Angel into it, so that its
waters effected the cure of the first who stepped into it, whatever was his disease. However, I shall not speak of this wonderful pool; nor of our Saviour's miracle, wrought there upon the
man who had no one to put him in before the rest, when the
water was troubled, and who had been for thirty-eight years
afflicted with his infirmity. Without entering into these subjects, let us take the text as it stands in the opening of the chapter which contains it, and deduce a lesson from it.

There lay about the pool "a great multitude of impotent
folk, of blind, halt, and withered." This is a painful picture,
such as we do not like to dwell upon,—a picture of a chief kind
of human suffering, bodily disease; one which suggests to us
and typifies all other suffering,—the most obvious fulfilment
of that curse which Adam's fall brought upon his descendants.
Now it must strike every one who thinks at all about it, that the
Bible is full of such descriptions of human misery. We know it
also abounds in accounts of human sin; but not to speak of
these, it abounds in accounts of human distress and sufferings,
of our miserable condition, of the vanity, unprofitableness, and
trials of life. The Bible begins with the history of the curse pronounced on the earth and man; it ends with the book of Revelation, a portion of Scripture fearful for its threats, and its

prediction of judgments; and whether the original curse on Adam be now removed from the world or not, it is certain that God's awful curses, foretold by St. John, are on all sides of us. Surely, in spite of the peculiar promises made to the Church in Christ our Saviour, yet as regards the world, the volume of inspiration is still a dreary record, "written within and without with lamentations, and mourning, and woe." And further, you will observe that it seems to drop what might be said in favour of this life, and enlarges on the unpleasant side of it. The history passes quickly from the Garden of Eden, to dwell on the sufferings which followed, when our first parents were expelled thence; and though, in matter of fact, there are traces of paradise still left among us, yet it is evident, Scripture says little of them in comparison of its accounts of human misery. Little does it say concerning the innocent pleasures of life; of those temporal blessings which rest upon our worldly occupations, and make them easy; of the blessings which we derive from "the sun and moon, and the everlasting hills," from the succession of the seasons and the produce of the earth;—little about our recreations and our daily domestic comforts;—little about the ordinary occasions of festivity and mirth which occur in life, and nothing at all about those various other enjoyments which it would be going too much into detail to mention. Human tales and poems are full of pleasant sights and prospects; they make things better than they are, and portray a sort of imaginary perfection; but Scripture (I repeat) seems to abstain even from what might be said in praise of human life as it is. We read, indeed, of the feast made when Isaac was weaned, of Jacob's marriage, of the domestic and religious festivities of Job's family; but these are exceptions in the tenor of the Scripture history. "Vanity of vanities, all is vanity;" "man is born to trouble:" these are its customary lessons. The text is but a specimen of the descriptions repeated again and again throughout Scripture of human infirmity and misery.

So much is this the case, that thoughtless persons are averse to the Scripture narrative for this very reason. I do not mean bad men, who speak hard, presumptuous words against the Bible, and in consequence expose themselves to the wrath of God; but I speak of *thoughtless* persons; and of these there are many, who consider the Bible a gloomy book, and on that account seldom look into it, saying that it makes them melancholy. Accordingly, there have been attempts made on the other hand to hide this austere character of Scripture, and make it a bright interesting picture of human life. Its stories have before now been profanely embellished in human language, to suit the taste of weak and cowardly minds. All this shows, that in the common opinion of mankind, the Bible does not take a pleasant sunshine view of the world.

Now why have I thus spoken of this general character of the sacred history?—in order to countenance those who complain of it?—let it not be imagined;—far from it. God does nothing without some wise and good reason, which it becomes us devoutly to accept and use. He has not given us this dark view of the world without a cause. In truth, this view is the ultimate *true* view of human life. But this is not all; it is a view which it concerns us much to know. It concerns us (I say) much to be told that this world is, after all, in spite of first appearances and partial exceptions, a dark world; else we shall be obliged to learn it (and, sooner or later, we must learn it) by sad *experience*; whereas, if we are forewarned, we shall unlearn false notions of its excellence, and be saved the disappointment which follows them. And therefore it is that Scripture omits even what might be said in praise of this world's pleasures;—not denying their value, such as it is, or forbidding us to use them religiously, but knowing that we are sure to find them out for ourselves without being told of them, and that our danger is on the side, not of undervaluing, but of overvaluing them; whereas, by being told of the worldly vanity, *at first*, we shall learn (what else we should only attain *at last*), not indeed to be gloomy and discontented, but to bear a sober and calm heart under a smiling cheerful countenance. This is one chief reason of the solemn character of the Scripture history; and if we keep it in view, so far from being offended and frightened away by its notes of sorrow, because they grate on the ear at first, we shall stedfastly listen to them, and get them by heart, as a gracious gift from God sent to us, as a remedy for all dangerous overflowing joy in present blessings, in order to save us far greater pain (if we use the lesson well), the pain of actual disappointment, such as the overthrow of vainly cherished hopes of lasting good upon earth, will certainly occasion.

Do but consider what is the consequence of ignorance or distrust of God's warning voice, and you will see clearly how merciful He is, and how wise it is to listen to Him. I will not suppose a case of gross sin, or of open contempt for religion; but let a man have a general becoming reverence for the law and Church of God, and an unhesitating faith in his Saviour Christ, yet suppose him so to be taken with the goods of this world, as (without his being aware of it) to give his heart to them. Let him have many good feelings and dispositions; but let him love his earthly pursuits, amusements, friends, too well;—by which I mean, so well as to forget that he is bound to live in the spirit of Abraham's faith, who gave up home, kindred, possessions, all his eye ever loved, at God's word,—in the spirit of St. Paul's faith, who "counted all things but loss for the excellency of the knowledge of Christ Jesus his Lord," and to win His favour "suffered the loss of all things." How will the world go with a man thus forgetful of his true interests? For a while all will be enjoyment;—if at any time weariness comes, he will be able to change his pleasure, and the variety will relieve him. His health is good and his spirits high, and easily master and bear down all the accidental troubles of life. So far is well; but, as years roll on, by little and little he will discover that, after all, he is not, as he imagined, possessed of any real substantial good. He will begin to find, and be startled at finding, that the things which once pleased, please less and less, or not at all. He will be unable to recall those lively emotions in which he once indulged; and he will wonder why. Thus, by degrees, the delightful visions which surrounded him will fade away, and in their stead, melancholy forms will haunt him, such as crowded round the pool of Bethesda. Then will be fulfilled the words of the wise man. The days will have come, "when thou shalt say, I have no pleasure in them; the sun and the light and the moon and the stars shall be darkened, and the clouds return after the rain; then they who look out of the window shall be darkened, the doors shall be shut in the streets, all the daughters of music shall be brought low, fears shall be in the way, and desire shall fail." [1] Then a man will begin to be restless and discontented, for he does not know how to amuse himself. Before, he was cheerful only from the natural flow of his spirits, and when such cheerfulness is lost with increasing years, he becomes evil-natured. He has made no effort to change his heart,—to raise, strengthen, and purify his faith,—to subdue his bad passions and tempers. Now their day is come; they have sprung up and begin to domineer. When he was in health, he thought about his farm, or his merchandize, and lived to himself; he laid out his strength on the world, and the world is nothing to him, as a worthless bargain (so to say), seeing it is nothing worth to one who cannot take pleasure in it. He had no habitual thought of God in the former time, however he might have a general reverence for His name; and

[1] Eccles. xii. 1–5.

now he dreads Him, or (if the truth must be said) even begins to hate the thought of Him. Where shall he look for succour? Perhaps, moreover, he is a burden to those around him; they care not for him,—he is in their way. And so he will lie year after year, by the pool of Bethesda, by the waters of health, with no one helping him;—unable to advance himself towards a cure, in consequence of his long habits of sin, and others passing him by, perhaps unable to help one who obstinately refuses to be comforted. Thus he has at length full personal, painful experience, that this world is really vanity or worse, and all this because he would not believe it from Scripture.

Now should the above description appear overcharged, should it be said that it supposes a man to be possessed of more of the pleasures of life than most men have, and of keener feelings,—should it be said that most men have little to enjoy, and that most of those who have much go on in an ordinary tranquil way, and take and lose things without much thought, not pleased much in their vigorous days, and not caring much about the change when the world deserts them,—then I must proceed to a more solemn consideration still, on which I do not like to dwell, but would rather leave it for your own private reflection upon it. There is a story in the Gospels of a man who was taken out of this life before he had turned his thoughts heaven-ward, and in another world he lift up his eyes being in torments. Be quite sure that every one of us, even the poorest and the most dull and insensible, is far more attached to this world than he can possibly imagine. We get used to the things about us, and forget they are necessary for our comfort. Every one, when taken out of this world, would miss a great deal that he was used to depend on, and would in consequence be in great discomfort and sorrow in his new abode, as a stranger in an unknown place; every one, that is, who had not, while on earth, made God his Father and Protector,—that Great God who alone will there be found. We do not, then, mend the matter at all in supposing a man not to find out the world's vanity here; for, even should the world remain his faithful friend, and please him with its goods, to his dying day, still that world will be burnt up at the day of his resurrection; and even had he little of its comforts here, that little he will then miss. Then all men, small and great, will know it to be vanity, and feel their infinite loss if they have trusted it, when all the dead stand before God.

Let this suffice on the use we must make of the solemn view which the Scripture takes of this life. Those disclosures are intended to save us pain, by preventing us from enjoying the world unreservedly; that we may use not abusing it.

Nor let it seem as if this view of life must make a man melancholy and gloomy. There are, it is true, men of ill-constituted minds, whom it has driven out of the world; but, rightly understood, it has no such tendency. The great rule of our conduct is to take things as they come. He who goes out of his way as shrinking from the varieties of human life which meet him, has weak faith, or a strangely perverted conscience,—he wants elevation of mind. The true Christian rejoices in those earthly things which give joy, but in such a way as not to care for them when they go. For no blessings does he care much, except those which are immortal, knowing that he shall receive all such again in the world to come. But the least and the most fleeting, he is too religious to contemn, considering them God's gift; and the least and most fleeting, thus received, yield a purer and deeper, though a less tumultuous joy. And if he at times refrains, it is lest he should encroach upon God's bounty, or lest by a constant use of it he should forget how to do without it.

Our Saviour gives us a pattern which we are bound to follow. He was a far greater than John the Baptist, yet He came, not with St. John's outward austerity,—condemning the *display* of strictness or gloominess, that we, His followers, might fast the more in private, and be the more austere in our secret hearts. True it is, that such self-command, composure, and inward faith, are not learned in a day; but if they were, why should this life be given us? It is given us as a very preparation time for obtaining them. Only look upon the world in this light;—its sights of sorrows are to calm you, and its pleasant sights to try you. There is a bravery in thus going straightforward, shrinking from no duty little or great, passing from high to low, from pleasure to pain, and making your principles strong without their becoming formal. Learn to be as the Angel, who could descend among the miseries of Bethesda, without losing his heavenly purity or his perfect happiness. Gain healing from troubled waters. Make up your mind to the prospect of sustaining a certain measure of pain and trouble in your passage through life; by the blessing of God this will prepare you for it,—it will make you thoughtful and resigned without interfering with your cheerfulness. It will connect you in your own thoughts with the Saints of Scripture, whose lot it was to be patterns of patient endurance; and this association brings to the mind a peculiar consolation. View yourselves and all Christians as humbly following the steps of Jacob, whose days were few and evil; of David, who in his best estate was as a shadow that declineth, and was withered like grass; of Elijah, who despised soft raiment and sumptuous fare; of forlorn Daniel, who led an Angel's life; and be lighthearted and contented, *because* you are thus called to be a member of Christ's pilgrim Church. Realize the paradox of making merry and rejoicing in the world because it is *not* yours. And if you are hard to be affected (as many men are), and think too little about the changes of life, going on in a dull way without hope or fear, feeling neither your need nor the excellence of religion; then, again, meditate on the mournful histories recorded in Scripture, in order that your hearts may be opened thereby and roused. Read the Gospels in particular; you there find accounts of sick and afflicted persons in every page as mementos. Above all, you there read of Christ's sufferings, which I am not now called upon to speak of; but the thought of which is far more than enough to make the world, bright as it may be, look dark and miserable in itself to all true believers, even if the record of *them* were the only sorrowful part of the whole Bible.

And now I conclude, bidding you think much of the Scripture history in the light in which I have put it,—that you may not hereafter find that you have missed one great benefit which it was graciously intended to convey.

CHRISTIAN MANHOOD

"When I was a child, I spake as a child, I understood as a child,
I thought as a child; but when I became a man,
I put away childish things."—1 Cor. xiii.11.

WHEN our Lord was going to leave the world and return to His Father, He called His disciples orphans; children, as it were, whom He had been rearing, who were still unable to direct themselves, and who were soon to lose their Protector; but He said, "I will not leave you comfortless orphans, I will come to you;"[1] meaning to say, He would come again to them in the power of His Holy Spirit, who should be their present all-sufficient Guide, though He Himself was away. And we know, from the sacred history, that when the Holy Spirit came, they ceased to be the defenceless children they had been before. He breathed into them a divine life, and gifted them with spiritual manhood, or *perfection*, as it is called in Scripture. From that time forth, they put away childish things; they spake, they understood, they thought, as those who had been taught to govern themselves; and who, having "an unction from the Holy One, knew all things."

That such a change was wrought in the Apostles, according to Christ's promise, is evident from comparing their conduct *before* the day of Pentecost, when the Holy Spirit descended on them, and *after*. I need not enlarge on their wonderful firmness and zeal in their Master's cause afterwards. On the other hand, it is plain from the Gospels, that before the Holy Ghost came down, that is, while Christ was still with them, they were as helpless and ignorant as children; had no clear notion what they ought to seek after, and how; and were carried astray by their accidental feelings and their long-cherished prejudices.— What was it but to act the child, to ask how many times a fellow-Christian should offend against us, and we forgive him, as St. Peter did? or to ask to see the Father, with St. Philip? or to propose to build tabernacles on the mount, as if they were not

[1] John xiv.18.

215

to return to the troubles of the world? or to dispute who should be the greatest?[2] or to look for Christ's restoring at that time the temporal kingdom to Israel?[3] Natural as such views were in the case of half-instructed Jews, they were evidently unworthy of those whom Christ had made His, that He might "present them perfect" before the throne of God.

Yet the first disciples of Christ at least put off their Vanities once for all, when the Spirit came upon them; but as to ourselves, the Spirit has long since been poured upon us, even from our earliest years; yet it is a serious question, whether multitudes of us, even of those among us who make a profession of religion, are even so far advanced in a knowledge of the Truth as the Apostles were before the day of Pentecost. It may be a profitable employment to-day to consider this question, as suggested by the text,—to inquire how far we have proceeded in putting off such childish things as are inconsistent with a manly, honest profession of the Gospel.

Now, observe, I am not inquiring whether we are plainly living in sin, in wilful disobedience; nor even whether we are yielding through thoughtlessness to sinful practices and habits. The condition of those who act against their conscience, or who act without conscience, that is, lightly and carelessly, is far indeed from bearing any resemblance to that of the Apostles in the years of their early discipleship. I am supposing you, my brethren, to be on the whole followers of Christ, to profess to obey Him; and I address you as those who seem to themselves to have a fair hope of salvation. I am directing your attention, not to your sins, not to those faults and failings which you know to be such, and are trying to conquer, as being confessedly evil in themselves, but to such of your views, wishes, and tastes, as resemble those which the Apostles cherished, true believers though they were, before they attained their manhood in the Gospel: and I ask, how far you have dismissed these from your minds as vain and trifling; that is, how far you have made what St. Paul in the text seems to consider the first step in the true spiritual course of a Christian, on whom the Holy Ghost has descended.

1. For example, Let us consider our love of the pleasures of life. I am willing to allow there is an innocent love of the world, innocent in itself. God made the world, and has sanctioned the general form of human society, and has given us abundant plea-

[2] Matt. xvii.4; xviii.1; xx.20; John xiv.8.
[3] Acts i.6.

sures in it; I do not say *lasting* pleasures, but still, while they are present, really pleasures. It is natural that the young should look with hope to the prospect before them. They cannot help forming schemes what they will do when they come into active life, or what they would wish to be, had they their choice. They indulge themselves in fancyings about the future, which they know at the time cannot come true. At other times they confine themselves to what is possible; and then their hearts burn, while they dream of quiet happiness, domestic comfort, independence. Or, with bolder views, they push forward their fortunes into public life, and indulge ambitious hopes. They fancy themselves rising in the world, distinguished, courted, admired; securing influence over others, and rewarded with high station. James and John had such a dream when they besought Christ that they might sit at His side in the most honourable places in His kingdom.

Now such dreams can hardly be called sinful in themselves, and without reference to the particular case; for the gifts of wealth, power, and influence, and much more of domestic comfort, come from God, and may be religiously improved. But, though not directly censurable, they are *childish*; childish either in themselves, or at least when cherished and indulged; childish in a Christian, who has infinitely higher views to engross his mind; and, as being childish, excusable only in the young. They *are* an offence when retained as life goes on; but in the young we may regard them after the pattern of our Saviour's judgment upon the young man who was rich and noble. He is said to have "loved him;" pitying (that is) and not harshly denouncing the anticipations which he had formed of happiness from wealth and power, yet withal not concealing from him the sacrifice of all these which he must make, "if he would be perfect," that is, a man, and not a mere child in the Gospel.

2. But there are other childish views and habits besides, which must be put off while we take on ourselves the full profession of a Christian; and these, not so free from intrinsic guilt as those which have been already noticed;—such as the love of display, greediness of the world's praise, and the love of the comforts and luxuries of life. These, though wrong tempers of mind, still I do not now call by their hardest names, because I would lead persons, if I could, rather to turn away from them as unworthy a Christian, with a sort of contempt, outgrowing them as they grow in grace, and laying them aside as a matter of course, while they are gradually learning to "set their affections on things above, not on things of the earth."

Children have evil tempers and idle ways which we do not
deign to speak seriously of. Not that we, in any degree, approve
them or endure them on their own account; nay, we punish
some of them; but we bear them *in* children, and look for their
disappearing as the mind becomes more mature. And so in religious matters there are many habits and views, which we bear
with in the unformed Christian, but which we account disgraceful and contemptible should they survive that time when
a man's character may be supposed to be settled. Love of display
is one of these; whether we are vain of our abilities, or our
acquirements, or our wealth, or our personal appearance;
whether we discover our weakness in talking much, or in love
of managing, or again in love of dress. Vanity, indeed, and conceit are always disagreeable, for the reason that they interfere
with the comfort of other persons, and vex them; but I am here
observing, that they are *in themselves* odious, when discerned in
those who enjoy the full privileges of the Church, and are by
profession men in Christ Jesus, odious from their inconsistency
with Christian faith and earnestness.

And so with respect to the love of worldly comforts and luxuries (which, unhappily, often grows upon us rather than disappears, as we get old), whether or not it be natural in youth, at
least, it is (if I may so say) *shocking* in those who profess to be
"perfect," if we would estimate things aright; and this from its
great incongruity with the spirit of the Gospel. Is it not something beyond measure strange and monstrous (if we could train
our hearts to possess a right judgment in all things), to profess
that our treasure is not here, but in heaven with Him who is
ascended thither, and to own that we have a cross to bear after
Him, who first suffered before He triumphed; and yet to set
ourselves *deliberately* to study our own comfort as some great and
sufficient end, to go much out of our way to promote it, to
sacrifice any thing considerable to guard it, and to be downcast
at the prospect of the loss of it? Is it possible for a true son of the
Church militant, while "the ark, and Israel, and Judah abide in
tents," and the "servants of his Lord are encamped in the open
field," to "eat and drink" securely, to wrap himself in the furniture of wealth, to feed his eyes with the "pride of life," and
complete for himself the measure of this world's elegancies?

Again, all timidity, irresolution, fear of ridicule, weakness of
purpose, such as the Apostles showed when they deserted
Christ, and Peter especially when he denied Him, are to be
numbered among the tempers of mind which are childish as
well as sinful; which we must learn to despise,—to be ashamed

at ourselves if we are influenced by them, and, instead of thinking the conquest of them a great thing, to account it as one of
the very first steps towards being but an ordinary true believer;
just as the Apostles, in spite of their former discipleship, only
commenced (surely) their Christian course at the day of Pentecost, and then took to themselves a good measure of faith, boldness, zeal, and self-mastery, not as some great proficiency and
as a boast, but as the very condition of their being Christians at
all, as the elements of spiritual life, as a mere outfitting, and a
small attainment indeed in that extended course of sanctification through which the Blessed Spirit is willing to lead every
Christian.

Now in this last remark I have given a chief reason for dwelling on the subject before us. It is very common for Christians to
make much of what are but petty services; first to place the very
substance of religious obedience in a few meagre observances,
or particular moral precepts which are easily complied with,
and which they think fit to call giving up the world; and then to
make a great vaunting about their having done what, in truth,
every one who is not a mere child in Christ ought to be able to
do, to congratulate themselves upon their success, ostentatiously to return thanks for it, to condemn others who do not
happen to move exactly along the very same line of minute
practices in detail which they have adopted, and in consequence
to forget that, after all, by such poor obedience, right though it
be, still they have not approached even to a distant view of that
point in their Christian course, at which they may consider
themselves, in St. Paul's words, to have "attained" a sure hope
of salvation; just as little children, when they first have strength
to move their limbs, triumph in every exertion of their newly-
acquired power, as in some great victory. To put off idle hopes
of earthly good, to be sick of flattery and the world's praise, to
see the emptiness of temporal greatness, and to be watchful
against self-indulgence,—these are but the beginnings of religion; these are but the preparation of heart, which religious earnestness implies; without a good share of them, how can a
Christian move a step? How could Abraham, when called of
God, have even set out from his native place, unless he had left
off to think much of this world, and cared not for its ridicule?
Surely these attainments are but our first manly robe, showing
that childhood is gone; and, if we feel the love and fear of
the world still active within our hearts, deeply must we be
humbled, yes, and alarmed; and humbled even though but the
traces remain of former weaknesses. But even if otherwise,

what thank have we? See what the Apostles were, by way of contrast, and then you will see what is the true life of the Spirit, the substance and full fruit of holiness. To love our brethren with a resolution which no obstacles can overcome, so as almost to consent to an anathema on ourselves, if so be we may save those who hate us,—to labour in God's cause against hope, and in the midst of sufferings,—to read the events of life, as they occur, by the interpretation which Scripture gives them, and that, not as if the language were strange to us, but to do it promptly,—to perform all our relative daily duties most watchfully,—to check every evil thought, and bring the whole mind into captivity to the law of Christ,—to be patient, cheerful, forgiving, meek, honest, and true,—to persevere in this good work till death, making fresh and fresh advances towards perfection—and after all, even to the end, to confess ourselves unprofitable servants, nay, to feel ourselves corrupt and sinful creatures, who (with all our proficiency) would still be lost unless God bestowed on us His mercy in Christ;—these are some of the difficult realities of religious obedience, which we must pursue, and which the Apostles in high measure attained, and which we may well bless God's holy name, if He enables us to make our own.

Let us then take it for granted, as a truth which cannot be gainsaid, that to break with the world, and make religion our first concern, is only to cease to be children; and, again, that in consequence, those Christians who have come to mature years, and yet do not even so much as this, are "in the presence of the Angels of God" an odious and unnatural spectacle, a mockery of Christianity. I do not say what such men are in God's sight, and what are their prospects for the next world, for that is a fearful thought,—and we ought to be influenced by motives far higher than that mere slavish dread of future punishment to which such a consideration would lead us.

But here some one may ask, whether I am not speaking severely in urging so many sacrifices at the beginning of true Christian obedience. In conclusion, then, I observe, in the first place, that I have not said a word against the moderate and thankful enjoyment of this life's goods, *when* they actually come in our way; but against the wishing earnestly for them, seeking them, and preferring them to God's righteousness, which is commonly done. Further, I am not excluding from the company of Christians all who cannot at once make up their minds thus vigorously to reject the world, when its goods are dangerous, inexpedient, or unsuitable; but excluding them from the company of mature, manly Christians. Doubtless our Lord deals gently with us. He has put His two Sacraments apart from each other. Baptism first admits us to His favour; His Holy Supper brings us among His perfect ones. He has put from fourteen to twenty years between them, in the ordinary course of things, that we may have time to count the cost, and make our decision calmly. Only there must be no standing still,— there cannot be; time goes slowly, yet surely, from birth to the age of manhood, and in like manner, our minds, though slowly formed to love Christ, must still be forming. It is when men are mature in years, and yet are "children in understanding," then they are intolerable, because they have exceeded their season, and are out of place. Then it is that ambitious thoughts, trifling pursuits and amusements, passionate wishes and keen hopes, and the love of display, are directly sinful, because they are by that time deliberate sins. While they were children, "they spake as children, understood, thought as children;" but when they became men, "it was high time to awake out of sleep;" and "put away childish things." And if they have continued children instead of "having their senses exercised to discriminate between the excellent and the base," alas! what deep repentance must be theirs, before they can know what true peace is!—what self-reproach and sharp self-discipline, before their eyes can be opened to see effectually those truths which are "spiritually discerned!"

So much on the case of those who neglect to grow betimes into the hope of their calling. As to the young themselves, it is plain that nothing I have said can give encouragement to them to acquiesce in their present incomplete devotion of themselves to God, because it will be as much as they can do, even with their best efforts, to make their growth of wisdom and of stature keep pace with each other. And if there be any one who, as thinking the enjoyments of youth must soon be relinquished, deliberately resolves to make the most of them before the duties of manhood come upon him, such an one, in doing so, is rendering it impossible for him to give them up, when he is called to do so. As for those who allow themselves in what, even in youth, is clearly sinful,—the deliberate neglect of prayer, profaneness, riotous living, or other immorality,—the case of such persons has not even entered into my mind, when I spoke of youthful thoughtlessness. They, of course, have no "inheritance in the kingdom of Christ and of God."

But if there be those among us, and such there well may be, who, like the young ruler, "worshipping Christ," and "loved" by Him, and obeying His commandments from their youth up, yet cannot but be "sorrowful" at the thought of giving up their pleasant visions, their childish idolatries, and their bright hopes of earthly happiness, such I bid be of good cheer, and take courage. What is it your Saviour requires of you, more than will also be exacted from you by that hard and evil master, who desires your ruin? Christ bids you give up the world; but will not, at any rate, the world soon give up you? Can you keep it, by being its slave? Will not he, whose creature of temptation it is, the prince of the world, take it from you, whatever he at present promises? What does your Lord require of you, but to look at all things as they really are, to account them merely as His instruments, and to believe that good is good because He wills it, that He can bless as easily by hard stone as by bread, in the desert as in the fruitful field, if we have faith in Him who gives us the true bread from heaven? Daniel and his friends were princes of the royal house of David; they were "children well-favoured, and skilful in all wisdom, cunning in knowledge, and understanding science;" [4] yet they had faith to refuse even the literal meat and drink given them, because it was an idol's sacrifice, and God sustained them without it. For ten days of trial they lived on pulse and water; yet "at the end," says the sacred record, "their countenances appeared fairer and fatter in flesh than all the children which did eat the portion of the king's meat." Doubt not, then, His power to bring you through any difficulties, who gives you the command to encounter them. He has showed you the way; He gave up the home of His mother Mary to "be about His Father's business," and now He but bids you take up after Him the cross which He bore for you, and "fill up what is wanting of His afflictions in your flesh." Be not afraid,—it is but a pang now and then, and a struggle; a covenant with your eyes, and a fasting in the wilderness, some calm habitual watchfulness, and the hearty effort to obey, and all will be well. Be not afraid. He is most gracious, and will bring you on by little and little. He does not show you whither He is leading you; you might be frightened did you see the whole prospect at once. Sufficient for the day is its own evil. Follow His plan; look not on anxiously; look down at your present footing "lest it be turned out of the way," but speculate not about the future. I can well believe that you have hopes now, which you cannot give up, and even which support you in your present course. Be it so; whether

4 Dan. i.4.

they will be fulfilled, or not, is in His hand. He may be pleased to grant the desires of your heart; if so, thank Him for His mercy; only be sure, that all will be for your highest good, and "as thy days, so shall thy strength be. There is none like unto the God of Jeshurun, who rideth upon the heaven in thy help, and in His excellency on the sky. The eternal God is thy refuge, and underneath are the everlasting arms." [5] He knows no variableness, neither shadow of turning; and when we outgrow our childhood, we but approach, however feebly, to His likeness, who has no youth nor age, who has no passions, no hopes, nor fears, but who loves truth, purity, and mercy, and who is supremely blessed, because He is supremely holy.

Lastly, while we thus think of Him, let us not forget to be up and doing. Let us beware of indulging a mere barren faith and love, which dreams instead of working, and is fastidious when it should be hardy. This is only spiritual childhood in another form; for the Holy Ghost is the Author of active good works, and leads us to the observance of all lowly deeds of ordinary obedience as the most pleasing sacrifice to God.

[5] Deut. xxxiii.25–27.

II

To

JOHN WILLIAM BOWDEN, ESQ.

etc. etc.

in the cheerful conviction

that the English Church amid many defections

still holds her influence

over an attached and zealous laity,

this volume

is inscribed,

by his affectionate friend,

J. H. N.

Feb. 21, 1835.

THE WORLD'S BENEFACTORS

(The Feast of St. Andrew the Apostle)

*"One of the two which heard John speak, and followed Him, was
Andrew, Simon Peter's brother."*—John i.40.

WITH this Festival we begin our year,—thus ushering in,
with a few weeks of preparation, the day of Christ's
Nativity. St. Andrew, whom we now commemorate, has been
placed first of the Apostles, because (as far as Scripture informs
us) he was the first among them who found the Messiah, and
sought to be His disciple. The circumstances which preceded
his call are related in the passage of the Gospel from which the
text is taken. We are there informed that it was John the Baptist
who pointed out to him his Saviour. It was fitting that the forerunner of Christ should be the instrument of leading to Him
the first-fruits of his Apostles.

St. Andrew, who was already one of St. John's disciples, was
attending on his master with another, when, as it happened,
Jesus passed by. The Baptist, who had from the first declared his
own subordinate place in the dispensation which was then
opening, took this occasion of pointing out to his two disciples
Him in whom it centred. He said, "Behold the Lamb of God;"
this is He of whom I spake, whom the Father has chosen and
sent, the true sacrificial Lamb, by whose sufferings the sins of
the world will be expiated. On hearing this, the two disciples
(Andrew, I say, being one of them) straightway left John and
followed Christ. He turned round and asked them, "What seek
ye?" They expressed their desire to be allowed to wait upon His
teaching; and He suffered them to accompany Him home, and
to pass that day with Him. What He said to them is not told us;
but St. Andrew received such confirmation of the truth of the
Baptist's words that in consequence he went after his own
brother to tell him what he had found. "He first findeth his
own brother Simon, and saith unto him, We have found the
Messias . . . and he brought him to Jesus."

St. John the Evangelist, who has been guided to preserve various notices concerning the separate Apostles which are not contained in the first three Gospels, speaks of Andrew in two other places; and introduces him under circumstances which show that, little as is known of this Apostle now, he was, in fact, very high in the favour and confidence of his Lord. In his twelfth chapter he describes Andrew as bringing to Christ certain Greeks who came up to Jerusalem to worship and who were desirous of seeing Him. And, what is remarkable, these strangers had first applied to St. Philip, who, though an Apostle himself, instead of taking upon him to introduce them, had recourse to his fellow-townsman, St. Andrew, as if, whether from age or intimacy with Christ, a more suitable channel for furthering their petition. "Philip cometh, and telleth Andrew; and again, Andrew and Philip tell Jesus."

These two Apostles are also mentioned together in the sixth chapter of the same Gospel, at the consultation which preceded the miracle of the loaves and fishes; and there again Andrew is engaged, as before, in the office of introducing strangers to Christ. "There is a lad here," he says to his Lord, a lad who, perhaps, had not courage to come forward of himself, "which hath five barley loaves and two small fishes."

The information afforded by these passages, of St. Andrew's especial acceptableness to Christ among the Apostles, is confirmed by the only place in the other Gospels, beside the catalogue, in which his name occurs. After our Lord had predicted the ruin of the Temple, "Peter, James, John, and *Andrew* asked Him privately, Tell us when shall these things be?"[1] and it was to these four that our Saviour revealed the signs of His coming, and of the end of the world. Here St. Andrew is represented as in the especial confidence of Christ; and associated too with those Apostles whom He is known to have selected from the Twelve, on various occasions, by tokens of His peculiar favour.

Little is known of St. Andrew in addition to these inspired notices of him. He is said to have preached the Gospel in Scythia; and he was at length martyred in Achaia. His death was by crucifixion; that kind of cross being used, according to the tradition, which still goes by his name.

Yet, little as Scripture tells us concerning him, it affords us enough for a lesson, and that an important one. These are the facts before us. St. Andrew was the first convert among the Apostles; he was especially in our Lord's confidence; thrice is he

---

[1] Mark xiii.3.

described as introducing others to Him; lastly, he is little known in history, while the place of dignity and the name of highest renown have been allotted to his brother Simon, whom he was the means of bringing to the knowledge of his Saviour.

Our lesson, then, is this; that those men are not necessarily the most useful men in their generation, nor the most favoured by God, who make the most noise in the world, and who seem to be principals in the great changes and events recorded in history; on the contrary, that even when we are able to point to a certain number of men as the real instruments of any great blessings vouchsafed to mankind, our relative estimate of them, one with another, is often very erroneous: so that, on the whole, if we would trace truly the hand of God in human affairs, and pursue His bounty as displayed in the world to its original sources, we must unlearn our admiration of the powerful and distinguished, our reliance on the opinion of society, our respect for the decisions of the learned or the multitude, and turn our eyes to private life, watching in all we read or witness for the true signs of God's presence, the graces of personal holiness manifested in His elect; which, weak as they may seem to mankind, are mighty through God, and have an influence upon the course of His Providence, and bring about great events in the world at large, when the wisdom and strength of the natural man are of no avail.

Now, first, observe the operation of this law of God's government, in respect to the introduction of those temporal blessings which are of the first importance in securing our well-being and comfort in the present life. For example, who was the first cultivator of corn? Who first tamed and domesticated the animals whose strength we use, and whom we make our food? Or who first discovered the medicinal herbs which, from the earliest times, have been our resource against disease? If it was mortal man, who thus looked through the vegetable and animal worlds, and discriminated between the useful and the worthless, his name is unknown to the millions whom he has benefited. It is notorious, that those who first suggest the most happy inventions, and open a way to the secret stores of nature, —those who weary themselves in the search after Truth, who strike out momentous principles of action, who painfully force upon their contemporaries the adoption of beneficial measures, or, again, who are the original cause of the chief events in national history, are commonly supplanted, as regards celebrity and reward, by inferior men. Their works are not called after them; nor the arts and systems which they have given the

world. Their schools are usurped by strangers; and their maxims of wisdom circulate among the children of their people,
forming, perhaps, a nation's character, but not embalming in
their own immortality the names of their original authors.

Such is the history of the social and political world and the
rule discernible in it is still more clearly established in the world
of morals and religion. Who taught the Doctors and Saints of
the Church, who, in their day, or in after times, have been the
most illustrious expounders of the precepts of right and wrong,
and, by word and deed, are the guides of our conduct? Did Almighty Wisdom speak to them through the operation of their
own minds, or rather, did it not subject them to instructors
unknown to fame, wiser perhaps even than themselves? Andrew followed John the Baptist, while Simon remained at his
nets. Andrew first recognised the Messiah among the inhabitants of despised Nazareth; and he brought his brother to Him.
Yet to Andrew Christ spake no word of commendation which
has been allowed to continue on record; whereas to Simon,
even on his first coming, He gave the honourable name by
which he is now designated, and afterwards put him forward as
the typical foundation of His Church. Nothing indeed can
hence be inferred, one way or the other, concerning the relative
excellence of the two brothers; so far only appears, that, in the
providential course of events, the one was the secret beginner,
and the other the public instrument, of a great divine work. St.
Paul, again, was honoured with the distinction of a miraculous
conversion, and was called to be the chief agent of the propagation of the Gospel among the heathen; yet to Ananias, an otherwise unknown saint, dwelling at Damascus, was committed the
high office of conveying the gifts of pardon and the Holy Ghost
to the Apostle of the Gentiles.

Providence thus acts daily. The early life of all men is private;
it is as children, generally, that their characters are formed to
good or evil; and those who form them to good, their truest and
chief benefactors, are unknown to the world. It has been remarked, that some of the most eminent Christians have been
blessed with religious mothers, and have in after life referred
their own graces to the instrumentality of their teaching. Augustine has preserved to the Church the history of his mother
Monica; but in the case of others, even the name is denied to us
of our great benefactress, whosoever she was, and sometimes,
doubtless, the circumstance of her service altogether.

When we look at the history of inspiration, the same rule
still holds. Consider the Old Testament, which "makes us wise

unto salvation." How great a part of it is written by authors
unknown! The book of Judges, the second of Samuel, the
books of Kings, Chronicles, Esther, and Job, and great part of
the book of Psalms. The last instance is the most remarkable of
these. "Profitable" beyond words as is the instruction conveyed to us in every word of Scripture, yet the Psalms have
been the most directly and visibly useful part of the whole volume, having been the prayer-book of the Church ever since
they were written; and have done more (as far as we dare
judge) to prepare souls for heaven, than any of the inspired
books, except the Gospels. Yet the authors of a large portion
of them are altogether unknown. And so with the Liturgies
which have been the possession of the Christian Church from
the beginning; who were those matured and exalted Saints
who left them to us? Nay, in the whole system of our worship,
who are the authors of each decorous provision and each edifying custom? Who found out the musical tunes, in which our
praises are offered up to God, and in which resides so wondrous a persuasion "to worship and fall down, and kneel before the Lord our Maker?" Who were those religious men, our
spiritual fathers in the "Catholic faith," who raised of old time
the excellent fabrics all over the country, in which we worship, though with less of grateful reverence for their memory
than we might piously express? Of these greatest men in every
age, there is "no memorial;" they "are perished as though they
had never been, and become as though they had never been
born."

Now I know that reflections of this kind are apt to sadden and
vex us; and such of us particularly as are gifted with ardent and
enthusiastic minds, with a generous love of what is great and
good, and a noble hatred of injustice. These men find it difficult to reconcile themselves to the notion that the triumph of
the Truth, in all its forms, is postponed to the next world. They
would fain anticipate the coming of the righteous Judge: nay,
perhaps they are somewhat too favourably disposed towards the
present world, to acquiesce without resistance in a doctrine
which testifies to the corruption of its decisions, and the worthlessness of its honours. But that it is a truth, has already been
showed almost as matter of fact, putting the evidence of Scripture out of consideration; and if it be such, it is our wisdom, as
it will become our privilege, to accustom our minds to it, and to
receive it, not in word merely, but in seriousness.

Why indeed should we shrink from this gracious law of
God's present providence in our own case, or in the case of

those we love, when our subjection to it does but associate us
with the best and noblest of our race, and with beings of nature
and condition superior to our own? Andrew is scarcely known
except by name; while Peter has ever held the place of honour
all over the Church; yet Andrew brought Peter to Christ. And
are not the blessed Angels unknown to the world? and is not
God Himself, the Author of all good, hid from mankind at
large, partially manifested and poorly glorified, in a few scattered servants here and there? and His Spirit, do we know
whence It cometh, and whither It goeth? and though He has
taught men whatever there has been of wisdom among them
from the beginning, yet when He came on earth in visible form,
even then it was said of Him, "The world knew Him not." His
marvellous providence works beneath a veil, which speaks but
an untrue language; and to see Him who is the Truth and the
Life, we must stoop underneath it, and so in our turn hide ourselves from the world. They who present themselves at kings'
courts, pass on to the inner chambers, where the gaze of the
rude multitude cannot pierce; and we, if we would see the King
of kings in His glory, must be content to disappear from the
things that are seen. Hid are the saints of God; if they are
known to men, it is accidentally, in their temporal offices, as
holding some high earthly station, or effecting some mere civil
work, not as saints. St. Peter has a place in history, far more as a
chief instrument of a strange revolution in human affairs, than
in his true character, as a self-denying follower of his Lord, to
whom truths were revealed which flesh and blood could not
discern.

How poor spirited are we, and what dishonour we put upon
the capabilities and the true excellence of our nature, when we
subject it to the judgment and disposal of all its baser specimens, to the rude and ignorant praise, and poor recompensing
of carnal and transgressing man! How shall the flesh be at all a
judge of the spirit? or the sinner of God's elect? Are we to look
downwards, not upwards? Shall we basely acknowledge the
right of the Many, who tread the broad way, to be the judges of
holiness, which comes from God, and appeals to Him? And
does not the eye of faith discern witnesses of our conduct, ever
present, and far worthier of our respect, than even a world of
the ungodly? Is man the noblest being in the creation? Surely
we, as well as our Divine Lord, are "seen of Angels;" nay, and
ministered unto by them, much as they excel us in strength! St.
Paul plainly tells us, that it is God's purpose that "His manifold
wisdom should be known to the heavenly principalities and

powers, through the Church." [2] When we are made Christians, we are baptized "into that within the veil," we are brought near to an innumerable company of Angels; and, resembling them in their hidden condition, share their sympathy and their services. Therefore, the same Apostle exhorts Timothy to persevere in obedience, not only by the thought of God, but by that of the Angels; and surely we ought to cultivate the habitual feeling, that they see us in our most private deeds, and most carefully guarded solitudes.

It is more than enough for a sinful mortal to be made a fellow-worker and fellow-worshipper with the Blessed Spirits, and the servant and the son of God Most High. Rather let us try to realize our privilege, and withal humble ourselves at our want of faith. We are the elect of God, and have entrance "through the gates into the" heavenly "City," while we "do His commandments," [3] following Christ as Andrew did, when pointed out to us by His preachers and ministers. To those who thus "follow on to know" Him, He manifests Himself, while He is hid from the world. They are near Him, as His confidential servants, and are the real agents in the various providences which occur in the history of nations, though overlooked by their annalists and sages. They bring before Him the temporal wants of men, witnessing His marvellous doings with the barley loaves and fishes; they, too, lead strangers before Him for His favourable notice, and for His teaching. And, when He brings trouble and distress upon a sinful people, they have truest knowledge of His will, and can best interpret His Works; for they had lived in contemplation and prayer, and while others praise the goodly stones and buildings of the external Temple, have heard from Him in secret how the end shall be. Thus they live; and when they die, the world knows nothing of its loss, and soon lets slip what it might have retained of their history; but the Church of Christ does what she can, gathering together their relics, and honouring their name, even when their works cannot be found. But those works have followed them; and, at the appearing of their Lord in judgment, will be at length displayed before all the world, and for His merits eternally rewarded in His heavenly kingdom.

---

[2] Eph. iii.10.　　　　　[3] Rev. xxii.14.

FAITH WITHOUT SIGHT

(The Feast of St. Thomas the Apostle)

*"Thomas, because thou hast seen Me, thou hast believed; blessed are
they that have not seen, and yet have believed."*—John xx.29.

S T. THOMAS is the Apostle who doubted of our Lord's resurrection. This want of faith has given him a sort of character
in the minds of most people, which is referred to in the Collect
for the day. Yet we must not suppose that he differed greatly
from the other Apostles. They all, more or less, mistrusted
Christ's promises when they saw Him led away to be crucified.
When He was buried, their hopes were buried with Him; and
when the news was brought them, that He was risen again, they
all disbelieved it. On His appearing to them, He "upbraided
them with their unbelief and hardness of heart."[1] But, as St.
Thomas was not present at this time, and only heard from his
fellow Apostles that they had seen the Lord, his time of perplexity and darkness lasted longer than theirs. At the news of
this great miracle, he expressed his determination not to believe
unless he himself saw Christ, and was allowed to touch Him.
And thus, by an apparently accidental circumstance, Thomas is
singled out from his brethren, who at first disbelieved as well as
he, as if he were an especial instance of unbelief. None of them
believed till they saw Christ, except St. John, and he too hesi-
tated at first. Thomas was convinced latest, because he saw
Christ latest. On the other hand, it is certain that, though he
disbelieved the good news of Christ's resurrection at first, he
was no coldhearted follower of his Lord, as appears from his
conduct on a previous occasion, when he expressed a desire to
share danger, and to suffer with Him. When Christ was setting
out for Judaea to raise Lazarus from the dead, the disciples said,
"Master, the Jews of late sought to stone Thee, and goest Thou
thither again?"[2] When He remained in His intention, Thomas
said to the rest, "Let us also go, that we may die with Him."

---

[1] Mark xvi.14.   [2] John xi.8.

This journey ended, as His Apostles foreboded, in their Lord's death; they indeed escaped, but it was at the instance of Thomas that they hazarded their lives with Him.

St. Thomas then loved his Master, as became an Apostle, and was devoted to His service; but when He saw Him crucified, his faith failed for a season with that of the rest. At the same time we need not deny that his especial doubts of Christ's resurrection were not altogether owing to circumstances, but in a measure arose from some faulty state of mind. St. John's narrative itself, and our Saviour's speech to him, convey an impression that he was more to blame than the rest. His standing out alone, not against one witness only, but against his ten fellow disciples, besides Mary Magdalene and the other women, is evidence of this; and his very strong words, "Except I shall see in His hands the print of the nails, and put my finger into the print of the nails, and thrust my hand into His side, I will not believe." [3] And it is observable that, little as we know of St. Thomas, yet the one remaining recorded speech of his (before Christ's crucifixion), intimates something of the same doubting perplexed state of mind. When Christ said He was going to His Father, and by a way which they all knew, Thomas interposed with an argument: "Lord, we know not whither Thou goest, and how can we know the way?" [4] that is, we do not see heaven, or the God of heaven, how can we know the way thither? He seems to have required some sensible insight into the unseen state, some infallible sign from heaven, a ladder of Angels like Jacob's, which would remove anxiety by showing him the end of the journey at the time he set out. Some such secret craving after certainty beset him. And a like desire arose within him on the news of Christ's resurrection. Being weak in faith, he suspended his judgment, and seemed resolved not to believe anything, till he was told everything. Accordingly, when our Saviour appeared to him, eight days after His appearance to the rest, while He allowed Thomas his wish, and satisfied his senses that He was really alive, He accompanied the permission with a rebuke, and intimated that by yielding to his weakness, He was withdrawing from him what was a real blessedness. "Reach hither thy finger, and behold my hands; and reach hither thy hand, and thrust it into my side: and be not faithless, but believing. And Thomas answered and said unto Him, My Lord and my God. Jesus saith unto him,

[3] John xx.25.   [4] John xiv.5.

Thomas, because thou hast seen Me, thou hast believed: blessed are they that have not seen, and yet have believed." [5]

However, after all, we are not so much concerned with considerations respecting the natural disposition and temper of the Blessed Apostle, whom we to-day commemorate, as with the particular circumstance in which his name occurs, and with our Saviour's comment upon it. All His disciples minister to Him; and, as in other ways, so also in giving occasion for the words of grace which proceed from His mouth. They minister to Him even in their weaknesses, which are often brought to light in Scripture, not hidden as Christian friends would hide in piety, that so He may convert them into instruction and comfort for His Church. Thus Martha's over-earnestness in household duties had drawn from Him a sanction for a life of contemplation and prayer; and so, in the history before us, the over-caution of St. Thomas has gained for us His promise of especial blessing on those who believe without having seen. I proceed to make some remarks on the nature of this believing temper, and why it is blessed.

It is scarcely necessary to observe, that what our Saviour says to Thomas so clearly and impressively, He has implied, in one way or other, all through His ministry; the blessedness of a mind that believes readily. His demand and trial of faith in the case of those who came for His miraculous aid, His praise of it where found, His sorrow where it was wanting, His warnings against hardness of heart; all are evidence of this. "Verily I say unto you, I have not found so great faith, no, not in Israel." "Daughter, be of good comfort; thy faith hath made thee whole." "Thy faith hath saved thee; go in peace." "An evil and adulterous generation seeketh after a sign." "O fools, and slow of heart to believe all that the prophets have spoken." [6] These will remind us of a multitude of similar passages in especial praise of faith. St. Paul pursues the line of doctrine thus begun by his Lord. In three Epistles he sets before us the peculiar place faith holds among the evidences of a religious mind: and each time refers to a passage in the Prophets, in order to show that he was bringing in no new doctrine, but only teaching that which had been promulged from the beginning. In consequence, in our ordinary language we speak of religion being built upon faith, not upon reason; on the other hand, it is as common for those who scoff at religion to object this very doctrine against

---

[5] John xx.27–29.

[6] Matt. viii.10; ix.22; Luke vii.50; Matt. xii.39; Luke xxiv.25.

us; as if, in so saying, we had almost admitted that Christianity was not true. Let us then consider how the case stands.

Every religious mind, under every dispensation of Providence, will be in the habit of looking out of and beyond self, as regards all matters connected with its highest good. For a man of religious mind is he who attends to the rule of conscience, which is born with him, which he did not make for himself, and to which he feels bound in duty to submit. And conscience immediately directs his thoughts to some Being exterior to himself, who gave it, and who evidently is superior to him; for a law implies a lawgiver, and a command implies a superior. Thus a man is at once thrown out of himself, by the very Voice which speaks within him; and while he rules his heart and conduct by his inward sense of right and wrong, not by the maxims of the external world, still that inward sense does not allow him to rest in itself, but sends him forth again from home to seek abroad for Him who has put His Word in him. He looks forth into the world to seek Him who is not of the world, to find behind the shadows and deceits of this shifting scene of time and sense, Him whose Word is eternal, and whose Presence is spiritual. He looks out of himself for that Living Word to which he may attribute what has echoed in his heart; and being sure that it is to be found somewhere, he is predisposed to find it, and often thinks he has found it when he has not. Hence, if truth is not at hand, he is apt to mistake error for truth, to consider as the presence and especial work of God what is not so; and thinking anything preferable to scepticism, he becomes (what is sometimes imputed to him by way of reproach) superstitious. This, you may suppose, is the state of the better sort of persons in a heathen country. They are not vouchsafed the truer tokens of God's power and will, which we possess; so they fancy where they cannot find, and, having consciences more acute than their reasoning powers, they pervert and misuse even those indications of God which are provided for them in nature. This is one cause of the false divinities of pagan worship, which are tokens of guilt in the worshipper, not (as we trust) when they could know no better, but when they have turned from the light, not liking "to retain God in their knowledge." And if this is the course of a religious mind, even when it is not blessed with the news of divine truth, much more will it welcome and gladly commit itself to the hand of God, when allowed to discern it in the Gospel. Such is faith as it exists in the multitude of those who believe, arising from their sense of the presence of God, originally certified to them by the inward voice of conscience.

On the other hand, such persons as prefer this world to the leadings of God's Spirit within them, soon lose their perception of the latter, and lean upon the world as a god. Having no pre-sentiment of any Invisible Guide, who has a claim to be fol-lowed in matters of conduct, they consider nothing to have a substance but what meets their senses, are contented with this, and draw their rules of life from it. They truly are in no danger of being superstitious or credulous; for they feel no antecedent desire or persuasion that God may have made a revelation of Himself in the world; and when they hear of events supernatu-ral, they come to the examination of them as calmly and dispas-sionately as if they were judges in a court of law, or inquiring into points of science. They acknowledge no especial interest in the question proposed to them; and they find it no effort to use their intellect upon it as rigidly as if it were some external in-strument which could not be swayed. Here then we see two opposite characters of mind, the one credulous (as it would be commonly called), the latter candid, well-judging, and saga-cious; and it is clear that the former of the two is the religious temper rather than the latter. In this way then, if in no other, faith and reason are opposed; and to believe much is more blessed than to believe little.

But this is not all. Everyone who tries to do God's will, is sure to find he cannot do it perfectly. He will feel himself to be full of imperfection and sin; and the more he succeeds in regulating his heart, the more he will discern its original bitterness and guilt. Here is an additional cause of a religious man's locking out of himself. He knows the evil of his nature, and forebodes God's wrath as its consequence; and when he looks around him, he sees it reflected from within upon the face of the world. He fears; and, in consequence, seeks about for some means of propitiating his Maker, for some token, if so be, of God's re-lenting. He cannot stay at home; he cannot rest in himself; he wanders about from very anxiety; he needs some one to speak peace to his soul. Should a man come to him professing to be a messenger from heaven, he is at once arrested and listens; and, whether such profession be actually true or false, yet his first desire is that it may be true. Those, on the contrary, who are without this sense of sin, can bear the first news of God's having spoken to man, without being startled. They can patiently wait till the body of evidence is brought out before them, and then receive or reject, as reason may determine for them.

Further still, let us suppose two persons of strong mind, not easily excitable, sound judging and cautious; and let them be equally endowed in these respects. Now there is an additional reason why, of these two, he who is religious will believe more and reason less than the irreligious; that is, if a man's acting upon a message is the measure of his believing it, as the common sense of the world will determine. For in any matter so momentous and practical as the welfare of the soul, a wise man will not wait for the fullest evidence before he acts; and will show his caution, not in remaining uninfluenced by the existing report of a divine message, but by obeying it though it might be more clearly attested. If it is but fairly probable that rejection of the Gospel will involve his eternal ruin, it is safest and wisest to act as if it were certain. On the other hand, when a man does not make the truth of Christianity a practical concern, but a mere matter of philosophical or historical research, he will feel himself at leisure (and reasonably on his own grounds) to find fault with the evidence. When we inquire into a point of history, or investigate an opinion of science, we do demand decisive evidence; we consider it allowable to wait till we obtain it, to remain undecided; in a word, to be *sceptical*. If religion be not a practical matter, it is right and philosophical in us to be sceptics. Assuredly higher and fuller evidence of its truth might be given us; and, after all, there are a number of deep questions concerning the laws of nature, the constitution of the human mind, and the like, which must be solved before we can feel perfectly satisfied. And those whose hearts are not "tender,"[7] as Scripture expresses it,—that is, who have not a vivid perception of the Divine Voice within them, and of the necessity of His existence from whom it issues,—do not feel Christianity as a practical matter, and let it pass accordingly. They are accustomed to say that death will soon come upon them, and solve the great secret for them without their trouble,—that is, they wait for sight: not understanding, or being able to be made to comprehend, that their solving this great problem without sight is the very end and business of their mortal life: according to St. Paul's decision, that faith is "the substance," or the realizing, "of things hoped for," "the evidence," or the making trial of, the acting on, the belief of "things not seen."[8] What the Apostle says of Abraham is a description of all true faith; it goes out not knowing *whither* it goes. It does not crave or bargain to see the end of the journey; it does not argue with St. Thomas, in the days of his ignorance, "we know not whither, and how can we know the way?" it is persuaded that it has quite enough

[7] 2 Kings xxii.19.   [8] Heb. xi.1.

light to walk by, far more than sinful man has a right to expect, if it sees one step in advance; and it leaves all knowledge of the country over which it is journeying, to Him who calls it on.

And this blessed temper of mind, which influences religious men in the greater matter of choosing or rejecting the Gospel, extends itself also into their reception of it in all its parts. As faith is content with but a little light to begin its journey by, and makes it much by acting upon it, so also it reads, as it were, by twilight, the message of truth in its various details. It does not stipulate that the text of Scripture should admit of rigid and laboured proofs of its doctrines; it has the practical wisdom to consider that the Word of God must have mainly one, and one only sense, and to try, as well as may be, to find out what that sense is, whether the evidence of it be great or little, and not to quarrel with it if it is not overpowering. It keeps steadily in view that Christ *speaks* in Scripture, and receives His words as if it *heard* them, as if some superior and friend spoke them, one whom it wished to please; not as if it were engaged upon the dead letter of a document, which admitted of rude handling, of criticism and exception. It looks off from self to Christ; and instead of seeking impatiently for some personal assurance, is set by obedience, saying, "Here am I; send me." And in like manner towards every institution of Christ, His Church, His Sacraments, and His Ministers, it acts not as a disputer of this world, but as the disciple of Him who appointed them. Lastly, it rests contented with the revelation made to it; it has "found the Messias," and that is enough. The very principle of its former restlessness now keeps it from wandering. When "the Son of God is come, and hath given us an understanding to know the true God," wavering, fearfulness, superstitious trust in the creature, pursuit of novelties, are signs, not of faith, but of unbelief. [9]

Much might be added in conclusion, by way of applying what has been said to the temper of our own day, in which men around us are apt almost to make it a boast that "theirs is a rational religion." Doubtless, this happens to be the case; but it is no necessary mark of a true religion that it is rational in the common sense of the word; nor is it any credit to a man to have resolved only to take up with what he considers rational. The true religion is in part altogether above reason, as in its Mysteries; and so again, it might have been introduced into the world without that array of Evidences, as they are called, which our

[9] *Vide* Cant. iii. 1–4.

reason is able, and delights to draw out; yet it would not on that account have been less true. As far as it is above reason, as far as it has extended into any countries without sufficient proof of its divinity, so far it cannot be called rational. Indeed, that it is at all level to the reason, is rather a privilege granted by Almighty God, than a point which may be insisted on by man; and unless received as an unmerited boon, may become hurtful to us. If this remark be in any measure true, we know what to think of arguing against the doctrines of the Gospel on the ground of their being irrational, or of attempting to refute the creed of others by ridiculing articles of it as unaccountable and absurd, or of thinking that the superstitious have advanced a step towards the truth when they have plunged into infidelity, or of accounting it wrong to educate children in the Catholic faith, lest they should not have the opportunity of choosing for themselves in mature years. Dismissing such thoughts from the mind let us rather be content with the words of the Apostle. "The preaching of the cross," he says, "is to them that perish, foolishness; but unto us which are saved, it is the power of God. For it is written, I will destroy the wisdom of the wise, and will bring to nought the understanding of the prudent. Where is the wise? where is the scribe? where is the disputer of this world? Hath not God made foolish the wisdom of this world? For after that in the wisdom of God the world by wisdom knew not God, it pleased God, by the foolishness of preaching, to save them that believe." [10]

[10] 1 Cor. i.18–21.

THE INCARNATION

(The Feast of the Nativity of Our Lord)

"The Word was made flesh, and dwelt among us."—John i.14.

Thus does the favoured Apostle and Evangelist announce to us that Sacred Mystery, which we this day especially commemorate, the incarnation of the Eternal Word. Thus briefly and simply does he speak as if fearing he should fail in fitting reverence. If any there was who might seem to have permission to indulge in words on this subject, it was the beloved disciple, who had heard and seen, and looked upon, and handled the Word of Life; yet, in proportion to the height of his privilege, was his discernment of the infinite distance between him and his Creator. Such too was the temper of the Holy Angels, when the Father "brought in the First-begotten into the world:"[1] they straightway worshipped Him. And such was the feeling of awe and love mingled together, which remained for a while in the Church after Angels had announced His coming, and Evangelists had recorded His sojourn here, and His departure; "there was silence as it were for half an hour."[2] Around the Church, indeed, the voices of blasphemy were heard, even as when He hung on the cross; but in the Church there was light and peace, fear, joy, and holy meditation. Lawless doubtings, importunate inquirings, confident reasonings were not. An heartfelt adoration, a practical devotion to the Ever-blessed Son, precluded difficulties in faith, and sheltered the Church from the necessity of speaking.

He who had seen the Lord Jesus with a pure mind, attending Him from the Lake of Gennesareth to Calvary, and from the Sepulchre to Mount Olivet, where He left this scene of His humiliation; he who had been put in charge with His Virgin Mother, and heard from her what she alone could tell of the Mystery to which she had ministered; and they who had heard it from his mouth, and those again whom these had taught, the

---

[1] Heb. i.6.   [2] Rev. viii.1.

first generations of the Church, needed no explicit declarations concerning His Sacred Person. Sight and hearing superseded the multitude of words; faith dispensed with the aid of lengthened Creeds and Confessions. There was silence. "The Word was made flesh;" "I believe in Jesus Christ His only Son our Lord;" sentences such as these conveyed everything, yet were officious in nothing. But when the light of His advent faded, and love waxed cold, then there was an opening for objection and discussion, and a difficulty in answering. Then misconceptions had to be explained, doubts allayed, questions set at rest, innovators silenced. Christians were forced to speak against their will, lest heretics should speak instead of them.

Such is the difference between our own state and that of the early Church, which the present Festival especially brings to mind. In the New Testament we find the doctrine of the Incarnation announced clearly indeed, but with a reverent brevity. "The Word was made flesh." "God was manifest in the flesh." "God was in Christ." "Unto us a Child is born,—the mighty God." "Christ, over all, God, blessed for ever." "My Lord and my God." "I am Alpha and Omega, the beginning and the ending,—the Almighty." "The Son of God, the brightness of His glory, and the express image of His person."[3] But we are obliged to speak more at length in the Creeds and in our teaching, to meet the perverse ingenuity of those who, when the Apostles were removed, could with impunity insult and misinterpret the letter of their writings.

Nay, further, so circumstanced are we, as to be obliged not only thus to guard the Truth, but even to give the reason of our guarding it. For they who would steal away the Lord from us, not content with forcing us to measures of protection, even go on to bring us to account for adopting them; and demand that we should put aside whatever stands between them and their heretical purposes. Therefore it is necessary to state clearly, as I have already done, why the Church has lengthened her statements of Christian doctrine. Another reason of these statements is as follows: time having proceeded, and the true traditions of our Lord's ministry being lost to us, the Object of our faith is but faintly reflected on our minds, compared with the vivid picture which His presence impressed upon the early Christians. True is it the Gospels will do very much by way of realizing for us the incarnation of the Son of God, if studied in

[3] 1 Tim. iii.16; 2 Cor. v.19; Is. ix.6; Rom. ix.5; John xx.28; Rev. i.8; Heb. i.2, 3.

faith and love. But the Creeds are an additional help this way. The declarations made in them, the distinctions, cautions, and the like, supported and illuminated by Scripture, draw down, as it were, from heaven, the image of Him who is on God's right hand, preserve us from an indolent use of words without apprehending them, and rouse in us those mingled feelings of fear and confidence, affection and devotion towards Him, which are implied in the belief of a personal advent of God in our nature, and which were originally derived to the Church from the very sight of Him.

And we may say further still, these statements—such, for instance, as occur in the Te Deum and Athanasian Creed—are especially suitable in divine worship, inasmuch as they kindle and elevate the religious affections. They are hymns of praise and thanksgiving; they give glory to God as revealed in the Gospel, just as David's Psalms magnify His Attributes as displayed in nature, His wonderful works in the creation of the World, and His mercies towards the house of Israel.

With these objects, then, it may be useful, on today's Festival, to call your attention to the Catholic doctrine of the Incarnation.

The Word was from the beginning, the Only-begotten Son of God. Before all worlds were created, while as yet time was not, He was in existence, in the bosom of the Eternal Father, God from God, and Light from Light, supremely blessed in knowing and being known of Him, and receiving all divine perfections from Him, yet ever One with Him who begat Him. As it is said in the opening of the Gospel: "In the beginning was the Word, and the Word was with God, and the Word was God." If we may dare conjecture, He is called the Word of God, as mediating between the Father and all creatures; bringing them into being, fashioning them, giving the world its laws, imparting reason and conscience to creatures of a higher order, and revealing to them in due season the knowledge of God's will. And to us Christians He is especially the Word in that great mystery commemorated to-day, whereby He became flesh, and redeemed us from a state of sin.

He, indeed, when man fell, might have remained in the glory which He had with the Father before the world was. But that unsearchable Love, which showed itself in our original creation, rested not content with a frustrated work, but brought Him down again from His Father's bosom to do His will, and repair the evil which sin had caused. And with a wonderful condescension He came, not as before in power, but in weak-

ness, in the form of a servant, in the likeness of that fallen creature whom He purposed to restore. So He humbled Himself;
suffering all the infirmities of our nature in the likeness of sinful flesh, all but a sinner,—pure from all sin, yet subjected to all
temptation,—and at length becoming obedient unto death,
even the death of the cross.

I have said that when the Only-begotten Son stooped to take
upon Him our nature, He had no fellowship with sin. It was
impossible that He should. Therefore, since our nature was corrupt since Adam's fall, He did not come in the way of nature,
He did not clothe Himself in that corrupt flesh which Adam's
race inherits. He came by miracle, so as to take on Him our
imperfection without having any share in our sinfulness. He
was not born as other men are; for "that which is born of the
flesh is flesh." [4]

All Adam's children are children of wrath; so our Lord came
as the Son of Man, but not the son of sinful Adam. He had no
earthly father; He abhorred to have one. The thought may not
be suffered that He should have been the son of shame and
guilt. He came by a new and living way; not, indeed, formed
out of the ground, as Adam was at the first, lest He should miss
the participation of our nature, but selecting and purifying
unto Himself a tabernacle out of that which existed. As in the
beginning, woman was formed out of man by Almighty power,
so now, by a like mystery, but a reverse order, the new Adam
was fashioned from the woman. He was, as had been foretold,
the immaculate "seed of the woman," deriving His manhood
from the substance of the Virgin Mary; as it is expressed in the
articles of the Creed, "conceived by the Holy Ghost, born of
the Virgin Mary."

Thus the Son of God became the Son of Man; mortal, but
not a sinner; heir of our infirmities, not of our guiltiness; the
offspring of the old race, yet "the beginning of the" new "creation of God." Mary, His mother, was a sinner as others, and
born of sinners; but she was set apart, "as a garden inclosed, a
spring shut up, a fountain sealed," to yield a created nature to
Him who was her Creator. Thus He came into this world, not
in the clouds of heaven, but born into it, born of a woman; He,
the Son of Mary, and she (if it may be said), the mother of God.
Thus He came, selecting and setting apart for Himself the elements of body and soul; then, uniting them to Himself from
their first origin of existence, pervading them, hallowing them

[4] John iii.6.

by His own Divinity, spiritualizing them, and filling them with light and purity, the while they continued to be human, and for a time mortal and exposed to infirmity. And, as they grew from day to day in their holy union, His Eternal Essence still was one with them, exalting them, acting in them, manifesting Itself through them, so that He was truly God and Man, One Person,—as we are soul and body, yet one man, so truly God and man are not two, but One Christ. Thus did the Son of God enter this mortal world; and when He had reached man's estate, He began His ministry, preached the Gospel, chose His Apostles, suffered on the cross, died, and was buried, rose again and ascended on high, there to reign till the day when He comes again to judge the world. This is the All-gracious Mystery of the Incarnation, good to look into, good to adore; according to the saying in the text, "The Word was made flesh,—and dwelt among us."

The brief account thus given of the Catholic doctrine of the Incarnation of the Eternal Word, may be made more distinct by referring to some of those modes mentioned in Scripture, in which God has at divers times condescended to manifest Himself in His creatures, which come short of it.

1. God was in the Prophets, but not as He was in Christ. The divine authority, and in one sense, name, may be given to His Ministers, considered as His representatives. Moses says to the Israelites, "Your murmurings are not against us, but against the Lord." And St. Paul, "He therefore that despiseth, despiseth not man, but God." [5] In this sense, Rulers and Judges are sometimes called gods, as our Lord Himself says.

And further, the Prophets were inspired. Thus John the Baptist is said to have been filled with the Holy Ghost from his mother's womb. Zacharias was filled with the Holy Ghost, and prophesied. In like manner the Holy Ghost came on the Apostles at Pentecost and at other times; and so wonderfully gifted was St. Paul, that "from his body were brought unto the sick handkerchiefs or aprons, and the diseases departed from them, and the evil spirits went out of them." [6] Now the characteristic of this miraculous inspiration was, that the presence of God came and went. Thus we read, in the afore-mentioned and similar narratives, of the Prophet or Apostle being *filled* with the Spirit on particular occasions; as again of "the Spirit of the Lord departing from Saul," and an evil spirit troubling him. Thus this divine inspiration was so far parallel to demoniacal

[5] Exod. xvi.8; 1 Thess. iv.8.   [6] Acts xix.12.

possession. We find in the Gospels the devil speaking with the voice of his victim, so that the tormentor and the tormented could not be distinguished from each other. They seemed to be one and the same, though they were not; as appeared when Christ and His Apostles cast the devil out. And so again the Jewish Temple was in one sense inhabited by the presence of God, which came down upon it at Solomon's Prayer. This was a type of our Lord's manhood dwelt in by the Word of God as a Temple; still, with this essential difference, that the Jewish Temple was perishable, and again the Divine Presence might recede from it. There was no real unity between the one and the other; they were separable. But Christ says to the Jews of His own body, "Destroy this Temple and I will raise it in three days;" implying in these words such an unity between the Godhead and the manhood, that there could be no real separation, no dissolution. Even when His body was dead, the Divine Nature was one with it; in like manner it was one with His soul in paradise. Soul and body were really one with the Eternal Word,—not one in name only,—one never to be divided. Therefore Scripture says that He rose again "according to the Spirit of holiness;" and "that it was not possible that He should be holden of death." [7]

2. Again, the Gospel teaches us another mode in which man may be said to be united with Almighty God. It is the peculiar blessedness of the Christian, as St. Peter tells us, to be "partaker of the Divine Nature." [8] We believe, and have joy in believing, that the grace of Christ renews our carnal souls, repairing the effects of Adam's fall. Where Adam brought in impurity and unbelief, the power of God infuses faith and holiness. Thus we have God's perfections communicated to us anew, and, as being under immediate heavenly influences, are said to be one with God. And further, we are assured of some real though mystical fellowship with the Father, Son, and Holy Spirit, in order to this: so that both by a real presence in the soul, and by the fruits of grace, God is one with every believer, as in a consecrated Temple. But still, inexpressible as is this gift of Divine Mercy, it were blasphemy not to say that the indwelling of the Father in the Son is infinitely above this, being quite different in kind; for He is not merely of a divine nature, divine by participation of holiness and perfection, but Life and Holiness itself, such as the Father is,—the Co-eternal Son incarnate, God clothed with our nature, the Word made flesh.

[7] Rom. i.4; Acts ii.24; 2 Pet. i.4.
[8] Exod. iii.2; Acts vii.35–38; Exod. xix.3; xx.1.

3. And lastly, we read in the Patriarchal History of various appearances of Angels so remarkable that we can scarcely hesitate to suppose them to be gracious visions of the Eternal Son. For instance; it is said that "the Angel of the Lord appeared unto" Moses "in a flame of fire out of the midst of a bush;" yet presently this supernatural Presence is called "the Lord," and afterwards reveals His name to Moses, as "the God of Abraham, Isaac, and Jacob." On the other hand, St. Stephen speaks of Him as "the Angel which appeared to Moses in the bush." Again, he says soon after, that Moses was "in the Church in the wilderness with the Angel which spake to him in the mount Sinai;" yet in the book of Exodus we read, "Moses went up unto God, and the Lord called unto him out of the mountain;" "God spake all these words saying;"[9] and the like. Now, assuming, as we seem to have reason to assume, that the Son of God is herein revealed to us as graciously ministering to the Patriarchs, Moses, and others, in angelic form, the question arises, what was the nature of this appearance? We are not informed, nor may we venture to determine; still, any how, the Angel was but the temporary outward form which the Eternal Word assumed, whether it was of a material nature, or a vision. Whether or no it was really an Angel, or but an appearance existing only for the immediate purpose, still, any how, we could not with propriety say that our Lord "took upon Him the nature of Angels."

Now these instances of the indwelling of Almighty God in a created substance, which I have given by way of contrast to that infinitely higher and mysterious union which is called the Incarnation, actually supply the senses in which heretics at various times have perverted our holy and comfortable doctrine, and which have obliged us to have recourse to Creeds and Confessions. Rejecting the teaching of the Church, and dealing rudely with the Word of God, they have ventured to deny that "Jesus Christ is come in the flesh," pretending He merely showed Himself as a vision or phantom;—or they have said that the Word of God merely dwelt in the man Christ Jesus, as the Shechinah in the Temple, having no real union with the Son of Mary (as if there were two distinct Beings, the Word and Jesus, even as the blessed Spirit is distinct from a man's soul);—or that Christ was called God for His great spiritual perfections, and that He gradually attained them by long practice. All these are words not to be uttered, except to show what the true doctrine is, and what is the meaning of the language of the Church con-

[9] Exod. iii.2; Acts vii.35–38; Exod. xix.3; xx.1.

cerning it. For instance, the Athanasian Creed confesses that Christ is "God of the substance of the Father, begotten before the worlds, perfect God," lest we should consider His Divine Nature, like ours, as merely a nature resembling God's holiness: that He is "Man of the substance of His Mother, born in the world, perfect man," lest we should think of Him as "not come in the flesh," a mere Angelic vision; and that "although He be God and man, yet He is not two, but one Christ," lest we should fancy that the Word of God entered into Him and then departed, as the Holy Ghost in the Prophets.

Such are the terms in which we are constrained to speak of our Lord and Saviour, by the craftiness of His enemies and our own infirmity; and we intreat His leave to do so. We intreat His leave, not as if forgetting that a reverent silence is best on so sacred a subject; but, when evil men and seducers abound on every side, and our own apprehensions of the Truth are dull, using zealous David's argument, "Is there not a cause" for words? We intreat His leave, and we humbly pray that what was first our defence against pride and indolence, may become an outlet of devotion, a service of worship. Nay, we surely trust that He will accept mercifully what we offer in faith, "doing what we can;" though the ointment of spikenard which we pour out is nothing to that true Divine Glory which manifested itself in Him, when the Holy Ghost singled Him out from other men, and the Father's voice acknowledged Him as His dearly beloved Son. Surely He will mercifully accept it, if faith offers what the intellect provides; if love kindles the sacrifice, zeal fans it, and reverence guards it. He will illuminate our earthly words from His own Divine Holiness, till they become saving truths to the souls which trust in Him. He who turned water into wine, and (did He so choose) could make bread of the hard stone, will sustain us for a brief season on this mortal fare. And we, while we make use of it, will never so forget its imperfection, as not to look out constantly for the True Beatific Vision; never so perversely remember that imperfection as to reject what is necessary for our present need. The time will come, if we be found worthy, when we, who now see in a glass darkly, shall see our Lord and Saviour face to face; shall behold His countenance beaming with the fulness of Divine Perfections, and bearing its own witness that He is the Son of God. We shall see Him as He is.

Let us then, according to the light given us, praise and bless Him in the Church below, whom Angels in heaven see and adore. Let us bless Him for His surpassing loving-kindness in taking upon Him our infirmities to redeem us, when He dwelt in the innermost love of the Everlasting Father, in the glory which He had with Him before the world was. He came in lowliness and want; born amid the tumults of a mixed and busy multitude, cast aside into the outhouse of a crowded inn, laid to His first rest among the brute cattle. He grew up, as if the native of a despised city, and was bred to a humble craft. He bore to live in a world that slighted Him, for He lived in it, in order in due time to die for it. He came as the appointed Priest, to offer sacrifice for those who took no part in the act of worship; He came to offer up for sinners that precious blood which was meritorious by virtue of His Divine Anointing. He died, to rise again the third day, the Sun of Righteousness, fully displaying that splendour which had hitherto been concealed by the morning clouds. He rose again, to ascend to the right hand of God, there to plead His sacred wounds in token of our forgiveness, to rule and guide His ransomed people, and from His pierced side to pour forth His choicest blessings upon them. He ascended, thence to descend again in due season to judge the world which He has redeemed.—Great is our Lord, and great is His power, Jesus the Son of God and Son of man. Ten thousand times more dazzling bright than the highest Archangel, is our Lord and Christ. By birth the Only-begotten and Express Image of God; and in taking our flesh, not sullied thereby, but raising human nature with Him, as He rose from the lowly manger to the right hand of power,—raising human nature, for Man has redeemed us, Man is set above all creatures, as one with the Creator, Man shall judge man at the last day. So honoured is this earth, that no stranger shall judge us, but He who is our fellow, who will sustain our interests, and has full sympathy in all our imperfections. He who loved us, even to die for us, is graciously appointed to assign the final measurement and price upon His own work. He who best knows by infirmity to take the part of the infirm, He who would fain reap the full fruit of His passion, He will separate the wheat from the chaff, so that not a grain shall fall to the ground. He who has given us to share His own spiritual nature, He from whom we have drawn the life's blood of our souls, He our brother will decide about His brethren. In that His second coming, may He in His grace and loving pity remember us, who is our only hope, our only salvation!

MARTYRDOM

(The Feast of St. Stephen the Martyr)

"They were stoned, they were sawn asunder, were tempted, were slain with the sword."—Heb. xi.37.

S T. STEPHEN, who was one of the seven Deacons, is called the Protomartyr, as having first suffered death in the cause of the Gospel. Let me take the opportunity of his festival to make some remarks upon martyrdom generally.

The word Martyr properly means "a *witness*," but is used to denote exclusively one who has suffered *death* for the Christian faith. Those who have witnessed for Christ without suffering death, are called *Confessors*; a title which the early Martyrs often made their own, before their last solemn confession unto death, or Martyrdom. Our Lord Jesus Christ is the chief and most glorious of Martyrs, as having "before Pontius Pilate witnessed a good confession;"[1] but we do not call Him a Martyr, as being much more than a Martyr. True it is, He died for the Truth; but that was not the chief purpose of his death. He died to save us sinners from the wrath of God. He was not only a Martyr; He was an Atoning Sacrifice.

He is the supreme object of our love, gratitude, and reverence. Next to Him we honour the noble army of Martyrs; not indeed comparing them with Him, "who is above all, God blessed for ever," or as if they in suffering had any part in the work of reconciliation, but because they have approached most closely to His pattern of all His servants. They have shed their blood for the Church, fulfilling the text, "He laid down His life for us, and we ought to lay down our lives for the brethren."[2] They have followed His steps, and claim our grateful remembrance. Had St. Stephen shrunk from the trial put upon him, and recanted to save his life, no one can estimate the consequences of such a defection. Perhaps (humanly speaking) the cause of the Gospel would have been lost; the Church might

---

[1] 1 Tim. vi.13.   [2] 1 John iii.16.

have perished; and, though Christ had died for the world, the world might not have received the knowledge or the benefits of His death. The channels of grace might have been destroyed, the Sacraments withdrawn from the feeble and corrupt race which has such need of them.

Now it may be said, that many men suffer pain, as great as Martyrdom, from disease, and in other ways: again, that it does not follow that those who happened to be martyred were always the most useful and active defenders of the faith; and therefore, that in honouring the Martyrs, we are honouring with especial honour those to whom indeed we *may* be peculiarly indebted (as in the case of Apostles), but nevertheless who may have been but ordinary men, who happened to stand in the most exposed place, in the way of persecution, and were slain as if by chance, because the sword met them first. But this, it is plain, would be a strange way of reasoning in any parallel case. We are grateful to those who have done us favours, rather than to those who might or would, if it had so happened. We have no concern with the question, whether the Martyrs were the best of men or not, or whether others would have been Martyrs too, had it been allowed them. We are grateful to those who were such, from the plain matter of fact that they were such, that they did go through much suffering, in order that the world might gain an inestimable benefit, the light of the Gospel.

But in truth, if we could view the matter considerately, we shall find that (as far as human judgment can decide on such a point), the Martyrs of the primitive times were, as such, men of a very elevated faith; not only our benefactors, but far our superiors. The utmost to which any such objection as that I have stated, goes, is this; to show that others who were not martyred, might be equal to them (St. Philip the Deacon, for instance, equal to his associate St. Stephen), not that those who were martyred were not men eminently gifted with the Spirit of Christ. For let us consider what it was then to be a Martyr.

1. First, it was to be a *voluntary* sufferer. Men, perhaps, suffer in various diseases more than the martyrs did, but they cannot help themselves. Again, it has frequently happened that men have been persecuted for their religion without having expected it, or being able to avert it. These in one sense indeed are martyrs; and we naturally think affectionately of those who have suffered in our cause, whether voluntarily or not. But this was not the case with the primitive martyrs. They knew beforehand clearly enough the consequences of preaching the Gospel; they had frequent warnings brought home to them of the suf-

ferings in store for them, if they persevered in their labours of brotherly love. Their Lord and Master had suffered before them; and, besides suffering Himself, had expressly *foretold their* sufferings; "If they have persecuted Me, they will also persecute you."[3] They were repeatedly warned and strictly charged by the chief priests and rulers, not to preach in Christ's name. They had experience of lesser punishments from their adversaries in earnest of the greater; and at length they saw their brethren, one by one, slain for persevering in their faithfulness to Christ. Yet they continued to keep the faith, though they might be victims of their obedience any day.

All this must be considered when we speak of their sufferings. They lived under a continual trial, a daily exercise of faith, which we, living in peaceable times, can scarcely understand. Christ had said to His Apostles, "Satan hath desired to have you, that he may sift you as wheat."[4] Consider what is meant by sifting, which is a continued agitation, a shaking about to separate the mass of corn into two parts. Such was the early discipline inflicted on the Church. No mere sudden stroke came upon it; but it was solicited day by day, in all its members, by every argument of hope and fear, by threats and inducements, to desert Christ. This was the lot of the martyrs. Death, their final suffering, was but the consummation of a life of anticipated death. Consider how distressing anxiety is; how irritating and wearing it is to be in constant excitement, with the duty of maintaining calmness and steadiness in the midst of it; and how especially inviting any prospect of tranquillity would appear in such circumstances; and then we shall have some notion of a Christian's condition, under a persecuting heathen government. I put aside for the present the peculiar reproach and contempt which was the lot of the primitive Church, and their actual privations. Let us merely consider them as *harassed*, shaken as wheat in a sieve. Under such circumstances, the stoutest hearts are in danger of failing. They could steel themselves against certain definite sufferings, or prepare themselves to meet one expected crisis; but they yield to the incessant annoyance which the apprehension or persecution, and the importunity of friends inflict on them. They sigh for peace; they gradually come to believe that the world is not so wrong as some men say it is, and that it is possible to be over-strict and over-nice. They learn to temporize and to be double-minded. First one falls, then another; and such instances come as an

---

[3] John xv.20.   [4] Luke xxii.31.

additional argument for concession to those that remain firm as yet, who of course feel dispirited, lonely, and begin to doubt the correctness of their own judgment; while, on the other hand, those who have fallen, in self-defence become their tempters. Thus the Church is sifted, the cowardly falling off, the faithful continuing firm, though in dejection and perplexity. Among these latter are the martyrs; not accidental victims, taken at random, but the picked and choice ones, the elect remnant, a sacrifice well pleasing to God, because a costly gift, the finest wheat flour of the Church: men who have been warned what to expect from their profession, and have had many opportunities of relinquishing it, but have "borne and had patience, and for Christ's name sake have laboured, and have not fainted."[5] Such was St. Stephen, not entrapped into a confession and slain (as it were) in ambuscade, but boldly confronting his persecutors, and, in spite of circumstances that foreboded death, awaiting their fury. And if martyrdom in early times was not the chance and unexpected death of those who happened to profess the Christian faith, much less is it to be compared to the sufferings of disease, be they greater or not. No one is maintaining that the mere undergoing pain is a great thing. A man cannot help himself when in pain; he cannot escape from it, be he as desirous to do so as he may. The devils bear pain against their will. But to be a martyr, is to feel the storm coming, and willingly to endure it at the call of duty, for Christ's sake, and for the good of the brethren; and this is a kind of firmness which we have no means of displaying at the present day, though our deficiency in it may be, and is continually evidenced, as often as we yield (which is not seldom) to inferior and ordinary temptations.

2. But, in the next place, the suffering itself of Martyrdom was in some respects peculiar. It was a death, cruel in itself, publicly inflicted: and heightened by the fierce exultation of a malevolent populace. When we are in pain, we can lie in peace by ourselves. We receive the sympathy and kind services of those about us; and if we like it, we can retire altogether from the sight of others, and suffer without a witness to interrupt us. But the sufferings of martyrdom were for the most part public, attended with every circumstance of ignominy and popular triumph, as well as with torture. Criminals indeed are put to death without kindly thoughts from bystanders; still, for the most part, even criminals receive commiseration and a sort of respect. But the early Christians had to endure "the shame"

[5] Rev. ii.3.

after their Master's pattern. They had to die in the midst of enemies who reviled them, and in mockery, bid them (as in Christ's case) come down from the cross. They were supported on no easy couch, soothed by no attentive friends; and considering how much the depressing power of pain depends on the imagination, this circumstance alone at once separates their sufferings widely from all instances of pain in disease. The unseen God alone was their Comforter, and this invests the scene of their suffering with supernatural majesty, and awes us when we think of them. "Yea, though I walk through the valley of the shadow of death, I will fear no evil; *for Thou art with me.*" [6] A Martyrdom is a season of God's especial power in the eye of faith, as great as if a miracle were visibly wrought. It is a fellowship of Christ's sufferings, a commemoration of His death, a representation filling up in figure, "that which is behind of His afflictions, for his Body's sake, which is the Church." [7] And thus, being an august solemnity in itself, and a kind of sacrament, a baptism of blood, it worthily finishes that long searching trial which I have already described as being its usual forerunner in primitive times.

I have spoken only of the early martyrs, because this Festival leads me to do so; and besides, because, though there have been martyrs among us since, yet, from the time that kings have become nursing fathers to the Church, the history of confessors and martyrs is so implicated with state affairs, that their conduct is not so easily separable *by us* from the world around them, nor are we given to know them so clearly: though this difficulty of discerning them should invest their memory with peculiar interest when we do discern them, and their connexion with civil matters, far from diminishing the high spiritual excellence of such true sons of the Church, in some respects even increases it.

To conclude.—It is useful to reflect on subjects such as that I have now laid before you, in order to humble ourselves. "We have not resisted unto blood, striving against sin." [8] What are our petty sufferings, which we make so much of, to their pains and sorrows, who lost their friends, and then their own lives for Christ's sake; who were assaulted by all kinds of temptations, the sophistry of Antichrist, the blandishments of the world, the terrors of the sword, the weariness of suspense, and yet fainted not? How far above ours are both their afflictions, and their consolations under them! Now I know that such reflections are

[6] Ps. xxiii.4.   [7] Col. i.24.   [8] Heb. xii.4.

at once, and with far deeper reason, raised by the thought of the sufferings of Christ Himself; but commonly, His transcendent holiness and His depth of woe do not immediately affect us, from their very greatness. We sum them up in a few words, and we speak without understanding. On the other hand, we rise somewhat towards the comprehension of them, when we make use of that heavenly ladder by which His saints have made their way towards Him. By contemplating the lowest of His true servants, and seeing how far any one of them surpasses ourselves, we learn to shrink before His ineffable purity, who is infinitely holier than the holiest of His creatures; and to confess ourselves with a sincere mind to be unworthy of the least of all His mercies. Thus His Martyrs lead us to Himself, the chief of Martyrs and the King of Saints.

May God give us grace to receive these thoughts into our hearts, and to display the fruit of them in our conduct! What are we but sinful dust and ashes, grovellers who are creeping on to heaven, not with any noble sacrifice for Christ's cause, but without pain, without trouble, in the midst of worldly blessings! Well;—but He can save in the humblest paths of life, and in the most tranquil times. There is enough for us to do, far more than we fulfil, in our own ordinary course. Let us strive to be more humble, faithful, merciful, meek, self-denying than we are. Let us "crucify the flesh with the affections and lusts."[9] This, to be sure, is sorry martyrdom; yet God accepts it for His Son's sake. Notwithstanding, after all, if we get to heaven, surely we shall be the lowest of the saints there assembled; and if all are unprofitable servants, we verily shall be the most unprofitable of all.

[9] Gal. v.24.

LOVE OF RELATIONS AND FRIENDS

(The Feast of St. John the Evangelist)

"Beloved, let us love one another, for love is of God."—1 John iv.7.

S T. JOHN the Apostle and Evangelist is chiefly and most
familiarly known to us as "the disciple whom Jesus loved."
He was one of the three or four who always attended our
Blessed Lord, and had the privilege of the most intimate intercourse with Him; and, more favoured than Peter, James, and
Andrew, he was His bosom friend, as we commonly express
ourselves. At the solemn supper before Christ suffered, he took
his place next Him, and leaned on His breast. As the other three
communicated between the multitude and Christ, so St. John
communicated between Christ and them. At that Last Supper,
Peter dared not ask Jesus a question himself, but bade John put
it to Him,—who it was that should betray Him. Thus St. John
was the private and intimate friend of Christ. Again, it was to
St. John that our Lord committed His Mother, when He was
dying on the cross; it was to St. John that He revealed in vision
after His departure the fortunes of His Church.

Much might be said on this remarkable circumstance. I say
remarkable, because it might be supposed that the Son of God
Most High could not have loved one man more than another; or
again, if so, that He would not have had only one friend, but, as
being All-holy, He would have loved all men more or less, in
proportion to their holiness. Yet we find our Saviour had a private friend; and this shows us, first, how entirely He was a man,
as much as any of us, in His wants and feelings; and next, that
there is nothing contrary to the spirit of the Gospel, nothing
inconsistent with the fulness of Christian love, in having our
affections directed in an especial way towards certain objects,
towards those whom the circumstances of our past life, or some
peculiarities of character, have endeared to us.

There have been men before now, who have supposed Christian love was so diffusive as not to admit of concentration upon
individuals; so that we ought to love all men equally. And many

there are, who, without bringing forward any theory, yet consider practically that the love of many is something superior to the love of one or two; and neglect the charities of private life, while busy in the schemes of an expansive benevolence, or of effecting a general union and conciliation among Christians. Now I shall here maintain, in opposition to such notions of Christian love, and with our Saviour's pattern before me, that the best preparation for loving the world at large, and loving it duly and wisely, is to cultivate an intimate friendship and affection towards those who are immediately about us.

It has been the plan of Divine Providence to ground what is good and true in religion and morals, on the basis of our good natural feelings. What we are towards our earthly friends in the instincts and wishes of our infancy, such we are to become at length towards God and man in the extended field of our duties as accountable beings. To honour our parents is the first step towards honouring God; to love our brethren according to the flesh, the first step towards considering all men our brethren. Hence our Lord says, we must become as little children, if we would be saved; we must become in His Church, as men, what we were once in the small circle of our youthful homes.—Consider how many other virtues are grafted upon natural feelings. What is Christian high-mindedness, generous self-denial, contempt of wealth, endurance of suffering, and earnest striving after perfection, but an improvement and transformation, under the influence of the Holy Spirit, of that natural character of mind which we call romantic? On the other hand, what is the instinctive hatred and abomination of sin (which confirmed Christians possess), their dissatisfaction with themselves, their general refinement, discrimination, and caution, but an improvement, under the same Spirit, of their natural sensitiveness and delicacy, fear of pain, and sense of shame? They have been chastised into self-government, by a fitting discipline, and now associate an acute sense of discomfort and annoyance with the notion of sinning. And so of the love of our fellow Christians and of the world at large, it is the love of kindred and friends in a fresh shape; which has this use, if it had no other, that it is the natural branch on which a spiritual fruit is grafted.

But again, the love of our private friends is the only preparatory exercise for the love of all men. The love of God is not the same thing as the love of our parents, though parallel to it; but the love of mankind in general should be in the main the same habit as the love of our friends, only exercised towards different objects. The great difficulty in our religious duties is their extent. This frightens and perplexes men,—naturally; those especially, who have neglected religion for a while, and on whom its obligations disclose themselves all at once. This, for example, is the great misery of leaving repentance till a man is in weakness or sickness; he does not know how to set about it. Now God's merciful Providence has in the natural course of things narrowed for us at first this large field of duty; He has given us a clue. We are to begin with loving our friends about us, and gradually to enlarge the circle of our affections, till it reaches all Christians, and then all men. Besides, it is obviously impossible to love all men in any strict and true sense. What is meant by loving all men, is, to feel well-disposed to all men, to be ready to assist them, and to act towards those who come in our way, as if we loved them. We cannot love those about whom we know nothing; except indeed we view them in Christ, as the objects of His Atonement, that is, rather in faith than in love. And love, besides, is a habit, and cannot be attained without actual *practice*, which on so large a scale is impossible. We see then how absurd it is, when writers (as is the manner of some who slight the Gospel) talk magnificently about loving the whole human race with a comprehensive affection, of being the friends of all mankind, and the like. Such vaunting professions, what do they come to? that such men have certain benevolent *feelings* towards the world,—feelings and nothing more;—nothing more than unstable feelings, the mere offspring of an indulged imagination, which exist only when their minds are wrought upon, and are sure to fail them in the hour of need. This is not to love men, it is but to talk about love.—The real love of man *must* depend on practice, and therefore, must begin by exercising itself on our friends around us, otherwise it will have no existence. By trying to love our relations and friends, by submitting to their wishes, though contrary to our own, by bearing with their infirmities, by overcoming their occasional waywardness by kindness, by dwelling on their excellences, and trying to copy them, thus it is that we form in our hearts that root of charity, which, though small at first, may, like the mustard seed, at last even overshadow the earth. The vain talkers about philanthropy, just spoken of, usually show the emptiness of their profession, by being morose and cruel in the private relations of life, which they seem to account as subjects beneath their notice. Far different indeed, far different (unless it be a sort of irreverence to contrast such dreamers with the great Apostle, whose memory we are to-day celebrating), utterly the reverse of this fictitious benevolence was his elevated and enlightened sympathy for all men. We know he is celebrated for his declarations about Christian love. "Beloved, let us love one another, for love is of God. If we love one another, God dwelleth in us, and His love is perfected in us. God is love, and he that dwelleth in love dwelleth in God, and God in him."[1] Now did he begin with some vast effort at loving on a large scale? Nay, he had the unspeakable privilege of being the *friend of Christ*. Thus he was taught to love others; first his affection was concentrated, then it was expanded. Next he had the solemn and comfortable charge of tending our Lord's Mother, the Blessed Virgin, after His departure. Do we not here discern the secret sources of his especial love of the brethren? Could he, who first was favoured with his Saviour's affection, then trusted with a son's office towards His Mother, could he be other than a memorial and pattern (as far as man can be), of love, deep, contemplative, fervent, unruffled, unbounded?

Further, that love of friends and relations, which nature prescribes, is also of use to the Christian, in giving form and direction to his love of mankind at large, and making it intelligent and discriminating. A man, who would fain begin by a general love of all men, necessarily puts them all on a level, and, instead of being cautious, prudent, and sympathising in his benevolence, is hasty and rude; does harm, perhaps, when he means to do good, discourages the virtuous and well-meaning, and wounds the feelings of the gentle. Men of ambitious and ardent minds, for example, desirous of doing good on a large scale, are especially exposed to the temptation of sacrificing individual to general good in their plans of charity. Ill-instructed men, who have strong abstract notions about the necessity of showing generosity and candour towards opponents, often forget to take any thought of those who are associated with themselves; and commence their (so-called) liberal treatment of their enemies by an unkind desertion of their friends. This can hardly be the case, when men cultivate the private charities, as an introduction to more enlarged ones. By laying a foundation of social amiableness, we insensibly learn to observe a due harmony and order in our charity; we learn that all men are not on a level; that the interests of truth and holiness must be religiously observed; and that the Church has claims on us before the world. We can easily afford to be liberal on a large scale, when we have no affections to stand in the way. Those who have not accustomed themselves to love their neighbours whom they have

[1] 1 John iv.7, 12, 16.

seen, will have nothing to lose or gain, nothing to grieve at or rejoice in, in their larger plans of benevolence. They will take no interest in them for their own sake; rather, they will engage in them, because expedience demands, or credit is gained, or an excuse found for being busy. Hence too we discern how it is, that private virtue is the only sure foundation of public virtue; and that no national good is to be expected (though it may now and then accrue), from men who have not the fear of God before their eyes.

I have hitherto considered the cultivation of domestic affections as the *source* of more extended Christian love. Did time permit, I might now go on to show, besides, that they involve a real and difficult exercise of it. Nothing is more likely to engender selfish habits (which is the direct opposite and negation of charity), than *independence* in our worldly circumstances. Men who have no tie on them, who have no calls on their daily sympathy and tenderness, who have no one's comfort to consult, who can move about as they please, and indulge the love of variety and the restless humours which are so congenial to the minds of most men, are very unfavourably situated for obtaining that heavenly gift, which is described in our Liturgy, as being "the very bond of peace and of all virtues." On the other hand, I cannot fancy any state of life more favourable for the exercise of high Christian principle, and the matured and refined Christian spirit (that is, where the parties really seek to do their duty), than that of persons who differ in tastes and general character, being obliged by circumstances to live together, and mutually to accommodate to each other their respective wishes and pursuits.—And this is one among the many providential benefits (to those who will receive them) arising out of the Holy Estate of Matrimony; which not only calls out the tenderest and gentlest feelings of our nature, but, where persons do their duty, must be in various ways more or less a state of self-denial.

Or, again, I might go on to consider the private charities, which have been my subject, not only as the sources and as the discipline of Christian love, but further, as the *perfection of it*; which they are in some cases. The Ancients thought so much of friendship, that they made it a *virtue*. In a Christian view, it is not quite this; but it is often accidentally a special *test* of our virtue. For consider:—let us say that this man, and that, not bound by any very necessary tie, find their greatest pleasure in living together; say that this continues for years, and that they love each other's society the more, the longer they enjoy it. Now observe what is implied in this. Young people, indeed, readily love each other, for they are cheerful and innocent; more easily yield to each other, and are full of hope;—types, as Christ says, of His true converts. But this happiness does not last; their tastes change. Again, grown persons go on for years as friends; but these do not live together; and, if any accident throws them into familiarity for a while, they find it difficult to restrain their tempers and keep on terms, and discover that they are best friends at a distance. But what is it that can bind two friends together in intimate converse for a course of years, but the participation in something that is Unchangeable and essentially Good, and what is this but religion? Religious tastes alone are unalterable. The Saints of God continue in one way, while the fashions of the world change; and a faithful indestructible friendship may thus be a test of the parties, so loving each other, having the love of God seated deep in their hearts. Not an infallible test certainly; for they may have dispositions remarkably the same, or some engrossing object of this world, literary or other; they may be removed from the temptation to change, or they may have a natural sobriety of temper, which remains contented wherever it finds itself. However, under certain circumstances, it is a lively token of the presence of divine grace in them; and it is always a sort of symbol of it, for there is at first sight something of the nature of virtue in the very notion of constancy, dislike of change being not only the characteristic of a virtuous mind, but in some sense a virtue itself.

And now I have suggested to you a subject of thought for to-day's Festival,—and surely a very practical subject, when we consider how large a portion of our duties lies at home. Should God call upon us to preach to the world, surely we must obey His call; but at present, let us do what lies before us. Little children, let us love one another. Let us be meek and gentle; let us think before we speak; let us try to improve our talents in private life; let us do good, not hoping for a return, and avoiding all display before men. Well may I so exhort you at this season, when we have so lately partaken together the Blessed Sacrament which binds us to mutual love, and gives us strength to practise it. Let us not forget the promise we then made, or the grace we then received. We are not our own; we are bought with the blood of Christ; we are consecrated to be temples of the Holy Spirit, an unutterable privilege, which is weighty enough to sink us with shame at our unworthiness, did it not the while strengthen us by the aid itself imparts, to bear its extreme costliness. May we live worthy of our calling, and realize in our own persons the Church's prayers and professions for us!

THE MIND OF LITTLE CHILDREN

(The Feast of the Holy Innocents)

"Except ye be converted, and become as little children, ye shall not enter into the kingdom of Heaven."—Matt. xviii.3.

T HE longer we live in the world, and the further removed we are from the feelings and remembrances of childhood (and especially if removed from the sight of children), the more reason we have to recollect our Lord's impressive action and word, when He called a little child unto Him, and set him in the midst of His disciples, and said, "Verily I say unto you, Except ye be converted, and become as little children, ye shall not enter into the kingdom of Heaven. Whosoever, therefore, shall humble himself as this little child, the same is greatest in the kingdom of Heaven." And in order to remind us of this our Saviour's judgment, the Church, like a careful teacher, calls us back year by year upon this day from the bustle and fever of the world. She takes advantage of the Massacre of the Innocents recorded in St. Matthew's Gospel, to bring before us a truth which else we might think little of; to sober our wishes and hopes of this world, our high ambitious thoughts, or our anxious fears, jealousies, and cares, by the picture of the purity, peace, and contentment which are the characteristics of little children.

And, independently of the benefit thus accruing to us, it is surely right and meet thus to celebrate the death of the Holy Innocents: for it was a blessed one. To be brought near to Christ, and to suffer for Christ, is surely an unspeakable privilege; to suffer anyhow, even unconsciously. The little children whom He took up in his arms, were not conscious of His loving condescension; but was it no privilege when He blessed them? Surely this massacre had in it the nature of a Sacrament; it was a pledge of the love of the Son of God towards those who were included in it. All who came near Him, more or less suffered by approaching Him, just as if earthly pain and trouble went out of Him, as some precious virtue for the good of their souls;—and these infants in the number. Surely His very presence was a

Sacrament; every motion, look, and word of His conveying
grace to those who would receive it: and much more was fellowship with Him. And hence in ancient times such barbarous
murders or Martyrdoms were considered as a kind of baptism, a
baptism of blood, with a sacramental charm in it, which stood
in the place of the appointed Laver of regeneration. Let us then
take these little children as in some sense Martyrs, and see what
instruction we may gain from the pattern of their innocence.

There is very great danger of our becoming coldhearted, as
life goes on: afflictions which happen to us, cares, disappointments, all tend to blunt our affections and make our feelings
callous. That necessary self-discipline, too, which St. Paul enjoins Timothy to practise, tends the same way. And, again, the
pursuit of wealth especially; and much more, if men so far
openly transgress the word of Almighty God, as to yield to the
temptations of sensuality. The glutton and the drunkard bru-
talize their minds, as is evident. And then further, we are often
smit with a notion of our having become greater and more considerable persons than we were. If we are prosperous, for instance, in worldly matters, if we rise in the scale of (what is
called) society, if we gain a name, if we change our state by
marriage, or in any other way, so as to create a secret envy in the
minds of our companions, in all these cases we shall be exposed
to the temptation of *pride*. The deference paid to wealth or talent commonly makes the possessor artificial, and difficult to
reach; glossing over his mind with a spurious refinement,
which deadens feeling and heartiness. Now, after all, there is in
most men's minds a secret instinct of reverence and affection
towards the days of their childhood. They cannot help sighing
with regret and tenderness when they think of it; and it is graciously done by our Lord and Saviour, to avail Himself (so to
say) of this principle of our nature, and, as He employs all that
belongs to it, so to turn this also to the real health of the soul.
And it is dutifully done on the part of the Church to follow the
intimation given her by her Redeemer and to hallow one day
every year, as if for the contemplation of His word and deed.

If we wish to affect a person and (if so be) humble him, what
can we do better than appeal to the memory of times past, and
above all to his childhood! Then it was that he came out of the
hands of God, with all lessons and thoughts of Heaven freshly
marked upon him. Who can tell how God makes the soul, or
how He new-makes it? We know not. We know that, besides
His part in the work, it comes into the world with the taint of
sin upon it; and that even regeneration, which removes the

curse, does not extirpate the root of evil. Whether it is created in Heaven or hell, how Adam's sin is breathed into it, together with the breath of life, and how the Spirit dwells in it, who shall inform us? But this we know full well,—we know it from our own recollection of ourselves, and our experience of children,—that there is in the infant soul, in the first years of its regenerate state, a discernment of the unseen world in the things that are seen, a realization of what is Sovereign and Adorable, and an incredulity and ignorance about what is transient and changeable, which mark it as the fit emblem of the matured Christian, when weaned from things temporal, and living in the intimate conviction of the Divine Presence. I do not mean of course that a child has any formed principle in his heart, any habits of obedience, any true discrimination between the visible and the unseen, such as God promises to reward for Christ's sake, in those who come to years of discretion. Never must we forget that, in spite of his new birth, evil is within him, though in its seed only; but he has this one great gift, that he seems to have lately come from God's presence, and not to understand the language of this visible scene, or how it is a temptation, how it is a veil interposing itself between the soul and God. The simplicity of a child's ways and notions, his ready belief of everything he is told, his artless love, his frank confidence, his confession of helplessness, his ignorance of evil, his inability to conceal his thoughts, his contentment, his prompt forgetfulness of trouble, his admiring without coveting; and, above all, his reverential spirit, looking at all things about him as wonderful, as tokens and types of the One Invisible, are all evidence of his being lately (as it were) a visitant in a higher state of things. I would only have a person reflect on the earnestness and awe with which a child listens to any description or tale; or again, his freedom from that spirit of proud independence, which discovers itself in the soul as time goes on. And though, doubtless, children are generally of a weak and irritable nature, and all are not equally amiable, yet their passions go and are over like a shower; not interfering with the lesson we may gain to our own profit from their ready faith and guilelessness.

The distinctness with which the conscience of a child tells him the difference between right and wrong should also be mentioned. As persons advance in life, and yield to the temptations which come upon them, they lose this original endowment, and are obliged to grope about by the mere reason. If they debate whether they should act in this way or that, and

there are many considerations of duty and interest involved in
the decision, they feel altogether perplexed. Really, and truly,
not from self-deception, but really, they do not know how they
ought to act; and they are obliged to draw out arguments, and
take a great deal of pains to come to a conclusion. And all this,
in many cases at least, because they have lost, through sinning,
a guide which they originally had from God. Hence it is that St.
John, in the Epistle for the day, speaks of Christ's undefiled servants as "following the Lamb whithersoever He goeth." They
have the minds of children, and are able by the light within
them to decide questions of duty at once, undisturbed by the
perplexity of discordant arguments.

In what has already been said, it has been implied how striking a pattern a child's mind gives us of what may be called a
church temper. Christ has so willed it, that we should get at the
Truth, not by ingenious speculations, reasonings, or investiga-
tions of our own, but by teaching. The Holy Church has been
set up from the beginning as a solemn religious fact, so to call
it,—as a picture, a revelation of the next world, as itself the
Christian Dispensation, and so in one sense the witness of its
own divinity, as is the Natural World. Now those who in the
first place receive her words, have the minds of children, who
do not reason, but obey their mother; and those who from the
first refuse, as clearly fall short of children, in that they trust
their own powers for arriving at truth, rather than informants
which are external to them.

In conclusion, I shall but remind you of the difference, on the
other hand, between the state of a child and that of a matured
Christian; though this difference is almost too obvious to be
noticed. St. John says, "He that *doeth* righteousness is righteous,
even as He is righteous;" and again, "Every one that doeth righteousness is born of Him." [1] Now it is plain a child's innocence
has no share in this higher blessedness. He is but a type of what
is at length to be fulfilled in him. The chief beauty of his mind
is on its mere surface; and when, as time goes on, he attempts to
act (as is his duty to do), instantly it disappears. It is only while
he is still, that he is like a tranquil water, reflecting heaven.
Therefore, we must not lament that our youthful days are gone,
or sigh over the remembrances of pure pleasures and contemplations which we cannot recall; rather, what we were when
children, is a blessed *intimation*, given for our comfort, of what
God will make us, if we surrender our hearts to the guidance of

[1] 1 John iii.7; ii.29.

His Holy Spirit,—a prophecy of good to come,—a foretaste of what will be fulfilled in heaven. And thus it is that a child is a pledge of immortality; for he bears upon him in figure those high and eternal excellences in which the joy of heaven consists, and which would not be thus shadowed forth by the All-gracious Creator, were they not one day to be realized. Accordingly, our Church, for the Epistle for this Festival, selects St. John's description of the Saints in glory.

As then we would one day reign with them, let us in this world learn the mind of little children, as the same Apostle describes it: "My little children, let us not love in word, neither in tongue; but in deed and in truth." "Beloved, let us love one another: for love is of God; and every one that loveth is born of God, and knoweth God. He that loveth not knoweth not God; for God is love." [2]

[2] 1 John iii. 18; iv. 7, 8.

CEREMONIES OF THE CHURCH

(The Feast of the Circumcision of Our Lord)

*"Suffer it to be so now: for thus it becometh us
to fulfil all righteousness."*—Matt. iii.15.

WHEN our Lord came to John to be baptized, He gave this reason for it, "Thus it becometh us to fulfil all righteousness;" which seems to mean,—"It is becoming in Me, the expected Christ, to conform in all respects to all the rites and ceremonies of Judaism, to everything hitherto accounted sacred and binding." Hence it was that He came to be baptized, to show that it was not His intention in any way to dishonour the Established Religion, but to fulfil it even in those parts of it (such as Baptism) which were later than the time of Moses; and especially to acknowledge thereby the mission of John the Baptist, His forerunner. And those ordinances which Moses himself was commissioned to appoint, had still greater claim to be respected and observed. It was on this account that He was circumcised, as we this day commemorate; in order, that is, to show that He did not renounce the religion of Abraham, to whom God gave circumcision, or of Moses, by whom it was embodied in the Jewish Law.

We have other instances in our Lord's history, besides those of His circumcision and baptism, to show the reverence with which He regarded the religion which He came to fulfil. St. Paul speaks of Him as "born of a woman, born under the Law,"[1] and it was His custom to observe that Law, like any other Jew. For instance, He went up for the feasts to Jerusalem; He sent the persons He had cured to the priests, to offer the sin-offering commanded by Moses; He paid the Temple-tax; and again, He attended as "a custom" the worship of the synagogue, though this had been introduced in an age long after Moses; and He even bade the multitudes obey the Scribes and Pharisees in all lawful things, as those who sat in Moses' place.[2]

[1] Gal. iv.4. [2] Matt. xxiii.2, 3.

Such was our Saviour's dutiful attention to the religious system under which He was born; and that, not only so far as it was directly divine, but further, where it was the ordinance of uninspired though pious men, where it was but founded on ecclesiastical authority. His Apostles followed His pattern; and this is still more remarkable,—because after the Holy Spirit had descended, at first sight it would have appeared that all the Jewish ordinances ought at once to cease. But this was far from being the doctrine of the Apostles. They taught, indeed, that the Jewish rites were no longer of any use in obtaining God's favour; that Christ's death was now set forth as the full and sufficient Atonement for sin, by that Infinite Mercy who had hitherto appointed the blood of the sacrifices as in some sort means of propitiation: and, besides, that every convert who turned from Christ back to Moses, or who imposed the Jewish rites upon his brethren as necessary to salvation, was grievously erring against the Truth. But they neither abandoned the Jewish rites themselves, nor obliged any others to do so who were used to them. Custom was quite a sufficient reason for retaining them; every Christian was to remain in the state in which he was called; and in the case of the Jew, the practice of them did not necessarily interfere with a true and full trust in the Atonement which Christ had offered for sin.

St. Paul, we know, was the most strenuous opposer of those who would oblige the Gentiles to become Jews, as a previous step to their becoming Christians. Yet, decisive as he is against all attempts to force the Gentiles under the rites of Law, he never bids the Jews renounce them, rather he would have them retain them; leaving it for a fresh generation, who had not been born under them, to discontinue them, so that the use of them might gradually die away. Nay, he himself circumcised Timothy, when he chose him for his associate; in order that no offence might be given to the Jews.[3] And how fully he adhered to the Law in his own person, we learn from the same inspired history; for instance, we hear of his shaving his head, as having been under a vow,[4] according to the Jewish custom.

Now from this obedience to the Jewish Law, enjoined and displayed by our Blessed Lord and His Apostles, we learn the great importance of retaining those religious forms to which we are accustomed, even though they are in themselves indifferent, or not of Divine origin; and, as this is a truth which is not well

---

[3] Acts xvi.1–3. [4] Acts xviii.18.

understood by the world at large, it may be of use to make some observations upon it.

We sometimes meet with men, who ask *why* we observe these or those ceremonies or practices; why, for example, we use Forms of prayer so cautiously and strictly? or why we persist in kneeling at the Sacrament of the Lord's Supper? why in bowing at the name of Jesus? or why in celebrating the public worship of God only in consecrated places? why we lay such stress upon these things? These, and many such questions may be asked, and all with this argument: "They are indifferent matters; we do not read of them in the Bible."

Now the direct answer to this objection is, that the Bible was never *intended* to enjoin us these things, but *matters of faith*; and that though it happens to mention our practical duties, and some points of form and discipline, still, that it does not set about telling us what to do, but chiefly what to believe; and that there are many duties and many crimes which are not mentioned in Scripture, and which we must find out by our own understanding, enlightened by God's Holy Spirit. For instance, there is no prohibition of suicide, duelling, gaming, in Scripture; yet we know them to be great sins; and it would be no excuse in a man to say that he does not find them forbidden in Scripture, because he may discover God's will in this matter independently of Scripture. And in like manner, various matters of form and discipline are binding, though Scripture says nothing about them; for we learn the duty in another way. No matter how we learn God's will, whether from Scripture, or Antiquity, or what St. Paul calls "Nature," so that we can be sure it *is* His will. Matters of faith, indeed, He reveals to us by inspiration, because they are supernatural: but matters of moral duty, through our own conscience and divinely-guided reason; and matters of form, by tradition and long usage, which bind us to the observance of them, though they are not enjoined in Scripture. This, I say, is the proper answer to the question, "Why do you observe rites and forms which are not enjoined in Scripture?" though, to speak the truth, our chief ordinances *are* to be found there, as the Sacraments, Public Worship, the Observance of the Lord's-day, Ordination, Marriage, and the like. But I shall make another answer, which is suggested by the event commemorated this day, our Lord's conforming to the Jewish Law in the rite of circumcision; and my answer is this.

Scripture tells us what to believe, and what to aim at and maintain, but it does not tell us *how* to do it; and as we cannot do it at all unless we do it in this manner, or that, in fact we must add something to what Scripture tells us. For example, Scripture tells us to meet together for prayer, and has connected the grant of the Christian blessings on God's part, with the observance of *union* on ours; but since it does not tell us the times and places of prayer, the Church *must* complete that which Scripture has but enjoined generally. Our Lord has instituted two Sacraments, Baptism and the Lord's Supper; but has not told us, except generally, with what forms we are to administer them. Yet we *cannot* administer them without some sort of prayers; whether we use always the same, or not the same, or unpremeditated prayers. And so with many other solemn acts, such as Ordination, or Marriage, or Burial of the Dead, it is evidently pious, and becomes Christians to perform them decently and in faith; yet how is this to be done, unless the Church sanctions Forms of doing it?

The Bible then may be said to give us the *spirit* of religion; but the Church must provide the body in which that spirit is to be lodged. Religion must be realized in particular acts, in order to its continuing alive. Religionists, for example, who give up the Church rites, are forced to recall the strict Judaical Sabbath. There is no such thing as abstract religion. When persons attempt to worship in this (what they call) more spiritual manner, they end, in fact, in not worshipping at all. This frequently happens. Every one may know it from his own experience of himself. Youths, for instance (and perhaps those who should know better than they), sometimes argue with themselves, "What is the need of praying statedly morning and evening? why use a form of words? why kneel? why cannot I pray in bed, or walking, or dressing?" they end in not praying at all. Again, what will the devotion of the country people be, if we strip religion of its external symbols, and bid them seek out and gaze upon the Invisible? Scripture gives the *spirit*, and the Church the *body*, to our worship; and we may as well expect that the spirits of men might be seen by us without the intervention of their bodies, as suppose that the Object of faith can be realized in a world of sense and excitement, without the instrumentality of an outward form to arrest and fix attention, to stimulate the careless, and to encourage the desponding. But observe what follows:—who would say our bodies are not part of ourselves? We may apply the illustration; for in like manner the forms of devotion are parts of devotion. Who can in practice separate his view of body and spirit? for example, what a friend would he be to us who should treat us ill, or deny us food, or imprison us; and say, after all, that it was our body he ill-treated, and not our soul? Even so, no one can really respect religion, and insult its forms. Granting that the forms are not immediately from God, still long use has made them divine *to us*; for the spirit of religion has so penetrated and quickened them, that to destroy them is, in respect to the multitude of men, to unsettle and dislodge the religious principle itself. In most minds usage has so identified them with the notion of religion, that the one cannot be extirpated without the other. Their faith will not bear transplanting. Till we have given some attention to the peculiarities of human nature, whether from watching our own hearts, or from experience of life, we can scarcely form a correct estimate how intimately great and little matters are connected together in all cases; how the circumstances and accidents (as they might seem) of our habits are almost conditions of those habits themselves. How common it is for men to have *seasons* of seriousness, how exact is their devotion during them, how suddenly they come to an end, how completely all traces of them vanish, yet how comparatively trifling is the cause of the relapse, a change of place or occupation, or a day's interruption of regularity in their religious course! Consider the sudden changes in opinion and profession, religious or secular, which occur in life, the proverbial fickleness of the multitude, the influence of watchwords and badges upon the fortunes of political parties, the surprising falls which sometimes overtake well-meaning and really respectable men, the inconsistencies of even the holiest and most perfect, and you will have some insight into the danger of practising on the externals of faith and devotion. Precious doctrines are strung, like jewels, upon slender threads.

Our Saviour and His Apostles sanction these remarks, in their treatment of those Jewish ceremonies, which have led me to make them. St. Paul calls them weak and unprofitable, weak and beggarly elements.[5] So they were in themselves, but to those who were used to them, they were an edifying and living service. Else, why did the Apostles observe them? Why did they recommend them to the Jews whom they converted? Were they merely consulting for the prejudices of a reprobate nation? The Jewish rites were to disappear; yet no one was bid forcibly to separate himself from what he had long used, lest he lost his sense of religion also. Much more will this hold good with forms such as ours, which so far from being abrogated by the Apostles, were introduced by them or their immediate suc-

[5] Heb. vii.18; Gal. iv.9.

cessors; and which, besides the influence they exert over us from long usage, are, many of them, witnesses and types of precious gospel truths; nay, much more, possess a sacramental nature, and are adapted and reasonably accounted to convey a gift, even where they are not formally sacraments by Christ's institution. Who for instance, could be hard-hearted and perverse enough to ridicule the notion that a father's blessing may profit his children, even though Christ and His Apostles have not in so many words declared it?

Much might be said on this subject, which is a very important one. In these times especially, we should be on our guard against those who hope, by inducing us to lay aside our forms, at length to make us lay aside our Christian hope altogether. This is why the Church itself is attacked, because it is the living form, the visible body of religion; and shrewd men know that when it goes, religion will go too. This is why they rail at so many usages as superstitious; or propose alterations and changes, a measure especially calculated to shake the faith of the multitude. Recollect, then, that things indifferent in themselves become important to us when we are used to them. The services and ordinances of the Church are the outward form in which religion has been for ages represented to the world, and has ever been known to us. Places consecrated to God's honour, clergy carefully set apart for His service, the Lord's-day piously observed, the public forms of prayer, the decencies of worship, these things, viewed as a whole, are *sacred* relatively to us, even if they were not, as they are, divinely sanctioned. Rites which the Church has appointed, and with reason,—for the Church's authority is from Christ,—being long used, cannot be disused without harm to our souls. Confirmation, for instance, may be argued against, and undervalued; but surely no one who in the common run of men wilfully resists the Ordinance, but will thereby be *visibly* a worse Christian than he otherwise would have been. He will find (or rather others will find for him, for he will scarcely know it himself), that he has declined in faith, humility, devotional feeling, reverence, and sobriety. And so in the case of all other forms, even the least binding in themselves, it continually happens that a speculative improvement is a practical folly, and the wise are taken in their own craftiness.

Therefore, when profane persons scoff at our forms, let us argue with ourselves thus—and it is an argument which all men, learned or unlearned, can enter into: "These forms, even were they of mere human origin (which learned men say is *not* the case, but even if they were), are at least of as spiritual and edifying a character as the rites of Judaism. Yet Christ and His Apostles did not even suffer these latter to be irreverently treated or suddenly discarded. Much less may we suffer it in the case of our own; lest, stripping off from us the badges of our profession, we forget there is a faith for us to maintain, and a world of sinners to be eschewed."

THE GLORY OF
THE CHRISTIAN CHURCH

(The Feast of the Epiphany)

*"Arise, shine; for thy light is come, and the glory of the Lord
is risen upon thee."*—Is. lx.1.

O UR Saviour said to the woman of Samaria, "The hour
cometh, when ye shall neither in this mountain, nor yet at
Jerusalem, worship the Father."[1] And upon to-day's Festival I
may say to you in His words on another occasion, "This day is
this scripture fulfilled in your ears." This day we commemorate
the opening of the door of faith to the Gentiles, the extension
of the Church of God through all lands, whereas, before
Christ's coming, it had been confined to one nation only. This
dissemination of the Truth throughout the world had been the
subject of prophecy. "Enlarge the place of thy tent, and let
them stretch forth the curtains of thine habitations: spare not,
lengthen thy cords, and strengthen thy stakes; for thou shalt
break forth on the right hand and on the left; and thy seed shall
inherit the Gentiles, and make the desolate cities to be inhabited."[2] In these words the Church is addressed as Catholic,
which is the distinguishing title of the Christian Church, as
contrasted with the Jewish. The Christian Church is so constituted as to be able to spread itself out in its separate branches
into all regions of the earth; so that in every nation there may be
found a representative and an offshoot of the sacred and gifted
Society, set up once for all by our Lord after His resurrection.

This characteristic blessing of the Church of Christ, its
Catholic nature, is a frequent subject of rejoicing with St. Paul,
who was the chief instrument of its propagation. In one Epistle
he speaks of Gentiles being "fellow heirs" with the Jews, "and
of the same body, and partakers of His promise in Christ by the
Gospel." In another he enlarges on "the mystery now made

[1] John iv.21.   [2] Is. liv.2, 3.

manifest to the saints," viz. "Christ among the Gentiles, the hope of glory." [3]

The day on which we commemorate this gracious appointment of God's Providence, is called the Epiphany, or bright manifestation of Christ to the Gentiles; being the day on which the wise men came from the East under guidance of a star, to worship Him, and thus became the first-fruits of the heathen world. The name is explained by the words of the text, which occur in one of the lessons selected for to-day's service, and in which the Church is addressed. "Arise, shine; for thy light is come, and the glory of the Lord is risen upon thee. For, behold, the darkness shall cover the earth, and gross darkness the people: but the Lord shall arise upon thee, and His glory shall be seen upon thee. And the Gentiles shall come to thy light, and kings to the brightness of thy rising. . . . Thy people also shall be all righteous: they shall inherit the land for ever, the branch of My planting, the work of My hands, that I may be glorified." [4]

That this and other similar prophecies had their measure of fulfilment when Christ came, we all know; when His Church, built upon the Apostles and Prophets, wonderfully branched out from Jerusalem as a centre into the heathen world round about, and gathering into it men of all ranks, languages, and characters, moulded them upon one pattern, the pattern of their Saviour, in truth and righteousness. Thus the prophecies concerning the Church were fulfilled at that time in two respects, as regards its sanctity and its Catholicity.

It is often asked, have these prophecies had then and since their perfect accomplishment? Or are we to expect a more complete Christianizing of the world than has hitherto been vouchsafed it? And it is usual at the present day to acquiesce in the latter alternative, as if the inspired predictions certainly meant more than has yet been realized.

Now so much, I think, is plain on the face of them, that the Gospel is to be preached in all lands, before the end come: "This gospel of the kingdom shall be preached in all the world for a witness unto all nations and then shall the end come." [5] Whether it has been thus preached is a question of fact, which must be determined, not from the prophecy, but from history; and there we may leave it. But as to the other expectation, that a time of greater purity is in store for the Church, that is not easily to be granted. The very words of Christ just quoted, so

---

[3] Eph. iii.6; Col. i.26, 27.   [4] Is. lx.2–3, 21.   [5] Matt. xxiv.14.

far from speaking of the Gospel as tending to the conversion of the world at large, when preached in it, describe it only as a *witness* unto all the Gentiles, as if the many would not obey it. And this intimation runs parallel to St. Paul's account of the Jewish Church, as realizing faith and obedience only in a residue out of the whole people; and is further illustrated by St. John's language in the Apocalypse, who speaks of the "redeemed from among men" being but a remnant, "the first-fruits unto God and to the Lamb." [6]

However, I will readily allow that at first we shall feel a reluctance in submitting to this opinion, with such passages before us as that which occurs in the eleventh chapter of Isaiah's prophecy, where it is promised, "They shall not hurt nor destroy in all My holy mountain; for the earth shall be full of the knowledge of the Lord, as the waters cover the sea." I say it is natural, with such texts in the memory, to look out for what is commonly called a Millennium. It may be instructive then upon this day to make some remarks in explanation of the state and prospects of the Christian Church in this respect.

Now the system of this world depends, in a way unknown to us, both on God's Providence and on human agency. Every event, every course of action, has two faces; it is divine and perfect, and it belongs to man and is marked with his sin. I observe next, that it is a peculiarity of Holy Scripture to represent the world on its providential side; ascribing all that happens in it to Him who rules and directs it, as it moves along, tracing events to His sole agency, or viewing them only so far forth as He acts in them. Thus He is said to harden Pharaoh's heart, and to hinder the Jews from believing in Christ; wherein is signified His absolute sovereignty over all human affairs and courses. As common is it for Scripture to consider Dispensations, not in their actual state but as His agency would mould them, and so far as it really does succeed in moulding them. For instance: "God, who is rich in mercy, for His great love wherewith He loved us, even when we were dead in sins, hath quickened us together with Christ." [7] This is said as if the Ephesians had no traces left in their hearts of Adam's sin and spiritual death. As it is said afterwards, "Ye were sometimes darkness, but now are ye light in the Lord." [8]

In other words, Scripture more commonly speaks of the Divine *design* and *substantial work*, than of the *measure* of fulfilment

[6] Rom. xi.5; Rev. xiv.4.   [7] Eph. ii.4, 5.   [8] Eph. v.8.

which it receives at this time or that; as St. Paul expresses, when he says that the Ephesians were chosen, that they "*should* be holy and unblameable before Him in love." Or it speaks of the *profession* of the Christian; as when he says, "As many of you as have been baptized in Christ, have put on Christ;"—or of the *tendency* of the Divine gift in a long period of time, and of its *ultimate fruits*; as in the words, "Christ loved the Church, and gave Himself for it, that He might sanctify and cleanse it with the washing of water by the word, that He might present to Himself a glorious Church, not having spot, or wrinkle, or any such thing, but that it should be holy and without blemish," [9] in which baptism and final salvation are viewed as if indissolubly connected. This rule of Scripture interpretation admits of very extensive application and I proceed to illustrate it.

The principle under consideration is this: that, whereas God is one, and His will one, and His purpose one, and His work one; whereas all He is and does is absolutely perfect and complete, independent of time and place, and sovereign over creation, whether inanimate or living, yet that in His actual dealings with this world that is, in all in which we see His Providence (in that man is imperfect, and has a will of his own, and lives in time, and is moved by circumstances), He seems to work by a process, by means and ends, by steps, by victories hardly gained, and failures repaired, and sacrifices ventured. Thus it is only when we view His dispensations at a distance, as the Angels do, that we see their harmony and their unity; whereas Scripture, anticipating the end from the beginning, places at their very head and first point of origination all that belongs to them respectively in their fulness.

We find some exemplification of this principle in the call of Abraham. In every age of the world it has held good that the just shall live by faith; yet it was determined in the deep counsels of God, that for a while this truth should be partially obscured, as far as His revelations went; that man should live by sight, miracles and worldly ordinances taking the place of silent providences and spiritual services. In the latter times of the Jewish Law the original doctrine was brought to light, and when the Divine Object of faith was born into the world, it was authoritatively set forth by His Apostles as the basis of all acceptable worship. But observe, it had been already anticipated in the instance of Abraham; the evangelical covenant, which was not to be preached till near two thousand years afterwards,

[9] Eph. i.4; Gal. iii.27; Eph. v.25–27.

was revealed and transacted in his person. "Abraham believed God, and it was counted unto him for righteousness." "Abraham rejoiced to see My day; and he saw it, and was glad." [10] Nay, in the commanded sacrifice of his beloved son, was shadowed out the true Lamb which God had provided for a burnt offering. Thus in the call of the Patriarch, in whose Seed all nations of the earth should be blessed, the great outlines of the Gospel were anticipated; in that he was called in uncircumcision, that he was justified by faith, that he trusted in God's power to raise the dead, that he looked forward to the day of Christ, and that he was vouchsafed a vision of the Atoning Sacrifice on Calvary.

We call these notices *prophecy*, popularly speaking, and doubtless such they are to us, and to be received and used thankfully; but more properly, perhaps, they are merely instances of the harmonious movement of God's word and deed, His sealing up events from the first, His introducing them once and for all, though they are but gradually unfolded to our limited faculties, and in this transitory scene. It would seem that at the time when Abraham was called, both the course of the Jewish dispensation and the coming of Christ were (so to say) realized; so as, in one sense, to be actually done and over. Hence, in one passage, Christ is called "the Lamb slain from the foundation of the world;" in another, it is said, that "Levi paid tithes" to Melchizedek, "in Abraham." [11]

Similar remarks might be made on the call and reign of David, and the building of the second Temple. [12]

---

[10] Rom iv.3; John viii.56.

[11] Rev. xiii.8; Heb. vii.9.

[12] In the instance of the first [Temple] there clearly is not the same combination of the Mystical sense with the Temporal. The prediction joined with the building of Solomon's Temple is of a simple kind; perhaps it relates purely and solely to the proper Temple itself. But the second Temple rises with a different structure of prophecy upon it. Haggai, Zechariah, and Malachi have each delivered some symbolical prediction, connected with it, or with its priesthood and worship. Why this difference in the two cases? I think the answer is clear; it is a difference obviously relating to the nearer connexion which the second Temple has with the Gospel. When God gave them their first Temple, it was doomed to fall, and rise again, *under* and *during* their first economy. The elder prophecy, therefore, was directed to the proper history of the first Temple. But when He gave them their second Temple, Christianity was then nearer in view; through that second edifice lay the Gospel prospect. Its restoration, therefore, was marked by a kind of prophecy, which had its vision towards the Gospel.—Davison on Prophecy, Discourse vi, part 4.

In like manner the Christian Church had in the day of its nativity all that fulness of holiness and peace named upon it, and sealed up to it, which beseemed it, viewed as God's design,—viewed in its essence, as it is realized at all times and under whatever circumstances,—viewed as God's work without man's co-operation,—viewed as God's work in its tendency, and in its ultimate blessedness; so that the titles given it upon earth are a picture of what it will be absolutely in heaven. This might also be instanced in the case of the Jewish Church, as in Jeremiah's description: "I remember thee, the kindness of thy youth, the love of thine espousals, when thou wentest after Me in the wilderness, in a land that was not sown. Israel was holiness unto the Lord, and the first-fruits of His increase." [13] As to the Christian Church, one passage descriptive of its blessedness from its first founding has already been cited; to which I add the following by way of specimen: "The Gentiles shall see thy righteousness, and all kings thy glory; and thou shalt be called by a new name, which the mouth of the Lord shall name. Thou shalt also be a crown of glory in the hand of the Lord, and a royal diadem in the hand of thy God. . . . As the bridegroom rejoiceth over the bride, so shall thy God rejoice over thee." "The mountains shall depart, and the hills be removed; but My kindness shall not depart from thee, neither shall the covenant of My peace be removed, saith the Lord that hath mercy on thee. All thy children shall be taught of the Lord, and great shall be the peace of thy children." "Behold, I have graven thee upon the palms of My hands; thy walls are continually before Me. . . . Lift up thine eyes round about, and behold; all these gather themselves together, and come to thee. As I live, saith the Lord, thou shalt surely clothe thee with them all, as with an ornament, and bind them on thee as a bride doeth." "Violence shall no more be heard in thy land, wasting nor destruction within thy borders; but thou shalt call thy walls salvation, and thy gates praise." [14] In these passages, which in their context certainly refer to the time of Christ's coming, an universality and a purity are promised to the Church, which have their fulfilment only in the course of its history, from first to last, as foreshortened and viewed as one whole.

Consider, again, the representations given us of Christ's Kingdom. First, it is called the "Kingdom of *Heaven*," though on earth. Again, in the Angels' hymn, it is proclaimed "on

[13] Jer. ii.2, 3.
[14] Is. lxii.3, 5; liv.10, 13; xlix.16, 18; lx.18.

earth peace," in accordance with the prophetic description of the Messiah as "the Prince of Peace;" though He Himself, speaking of the earthly, not the Divine side of His dispensation, said, He came "not to send peace on earth, but a sword." [15] Further, consider Gabriel's announcement to the Virgin concerning her Son and Lord: "He shall be great, and shall be called the Son of the Highest; and the Lord God shall give unto Him the throne of His father David; and He shall reign over the house of Jacob for ever, and of His kingdom there shall be no end." Or, as the same Saviour had been foretold by Ezekiel: "I will set up one Shepherd over them, and He shall feed them. . . . I will make with them a covenant of peace, and will cause the evil beasts to cease out of the land: and they shall dwell safely in the wilderness, and sleep in the woods. And I will make them and the places round about My hill a blessing; and I will cause the shower to come down in his season; there shall be showers of blessing." [16] It is observable that in the two passages last cited, the Christian Church is considered as merely the continuation of the Jewish, as if the Gospel existed in its germ even under the Law.

Now it is undeniable, and so blessed a truth that one would not wish at all to question it, that when Christ first came, His followers were in a state of spiritual purity, far above anything which we witness in the Church at this day. That glory with which her face shone, as Moses' of old time, from communion with her Saviour on the holy Mount, is the earnest of what will one day be perfected; it is a token held out to us in our dark age, that His promise stands sure, and admits of accomplishment. They continued in "gladness and singleness of heart, praising God, and having favour with all the people." Here was a pledge of eternal blessedness, the same in kind as a child's innocence is a forerunner of a holy immortality; and as the baptismal robe of the fine linen, clean and white, which is the righteousness of saints;—a pledge like the typical promises made to David, Solomon, Cyrus, or Joshua the high-priest. Yet at the same time the corruptions in the early Church, Galatian misbelief, and Corinthian excess, show too clearly that her early glories were not more than a pledge, except in the case of individuals,—a pledge of God's purpose, a witness of man's depravity.

The same interpretation will apply to the Scripture account of the Elect People of God, which is but the Church of Christ

[15] Matt. x.34.
[16] Luke i.32, 33; Ezek. xxxiv.23, 25, 26.

under another name. On them, upon their election, are bestowed, as on a body, the gifts of justification, holiness, and final salvation. The perfections of Christ are shed around them;
His image is reflected from them; so that they receive His name
as being in Him, and beloved of God in the Beloved. Thus in
their election are sealed up, to be unrolled and enjoyed in due
season, the successive privileges of the heirs of light. In God's
purpose—according to His *grace*—in the *tendency* and ultimate
effects of His dispensation—to be called and chosen is to be
saved. "Whom He did foreknow, He also did predestinate;
whom He did predestinate, them He also called; whom He
called, them He also justified; whom He justified, them He also
glorified." [17] Observe, the whole scheme is spoken of as of a
thing past; for in His deep counsel He contemplated from everlasting the one entire work, and, having decreed it, it is but a
matter of time, of sooner or later, when it will be realized. As
the Lamb was slain from the foundation of the world, so also
were His redeemed gathered in from the first according to His
foreknowledge; and it is not more inconsistent with the solemn
announcement of the text just cited, that some once elected
should fall away (as we know they do), than that an event
should be spoken of in it as past and perfect, which is incomplete and future. All accidents are excluded, when He speaks;
the present and the to come, delays and failures, vanish before
the thought of His perfect work. And hence it happens that the
word "elect" in Scripture has two senses, standing both for
those who are called *in order* to salvation, and for those who at
the last day shall be the *actually resulting fruit* of that holy call. For
God's Providence moves by great and comprehensive laws; and
His word is the mirror of His designs, not of man's partial success in thwarting His gracious will.

The Church then, considered as one army militant proceeding forward from the house of bondage to Canaan, gains the
victory, and accomplishes what is predicted of her, though
many soldiers fall in the battle. While, however, they remain
within her lines, they are included in her blessedness so far as to
be partakers of the gifts flowing from election. And hence it is
that so much stress is to be laid upon the duty of united worship; for thus the multitude of believers coming together, claim
as one man the grace which is poured out upon the one undivided body of Christ mystical. "Where two or three are gathered together in His name, He is in the midst of them;" nay

[17] Rom. viii.29, 30.

THE GLORY OF THE CHRISTIAN CHURCH 285

rather, blessed be His name! He is so one with them, that they are not their own, lose for the time their earth-stains, are radiant in His infinite holiness, and have the promise of His eternal favour. Viewed as one, the Church is still His image as at the first, pure and spotless, His spouse all-glorious within, the Mother of Saints; according to the Scripture, "My dove, My undefiled is but one; she is the only one of her mother, she is the elect one of her that bare her. . . . Thou art all fair, My love; there is no spot in thee." [18]

And what is true of the Church as a whole, is represented in Scripture as belonging also in some sense to each individual in it. I mean, that as the Christian body was set up in the image of Christ, which is gradually and in due season to be realized within it, so in like manner each of us, when made a Christian, is entrusted with gifts, which centre in eternal salvation. St. Peter says, we are "saved" through baptism; St. Paul, that we are "saved" according to God's mercy by "the washing of regeneration;" our Lord joins together water and the Spirit; St. Paul connects baptism with putting on Christ; and in another place with being "sanctified and justified in the name of the Lord Jesus, and by the Spirit of our God." [19] To the same purport are our Lord's words: "He that heareth My word, and believeth on Him that sent Me, *hath* everlasting life, and shall not come into condemnation, but *is passed* from death unto life." [20]

These remarks have been made with a view of showing the true sense in which we must receive, on the one hand, the prophetic descriptions of the Christian Church; on the other, the grant of its privileges, and of those of its separate members. Nothing is more counter to the spirit of the Gospel than to hunger after signs and wonders; and the rule of Scripture interpretation now given, is especially adapted to wean us from such wanderings of heart. It is our duty, rather it is our blessedness, to walk by faith; therefore we will take the promises (with God's help) in faith; we will believe they are fulfilled, and enjoy the fruit of them before we see it. We will fully acknowledge, as being firmly persuaded, that His word cannot return unto Him void; that it has its mission, and must prosper so far as substantially to accomplish it. We will adore the Blessed Spirit as coming and going as He listeth, and doing wonders daily which the world

[18] Cant. vi.9; iv.7.

[19] 1 Pet. iii.21; Tit. iii.5; John iii.5; Gal. iii.27; 1 Cor. vi.11.

[20] John v.24.

knows not of. We will consider Baptism and the other Christian Ordinances effectual signs of grace, not forms and shadows, though men abuse and profane them; and particularly, as regards our immediate subject, we will unlearn, as sober and serious men, the expectation of any public displays of God's glory in the edification of His Church, seeing she is all-glorious *within*, in that inward shrine, made up of faithful hearts, and inhabited by the Spirit of grace. We will put off, so be it, all secular, all political views of the victories of His kingdom. While labouring to unite its fragments, which the malice of Satan has scattered to and fro, to recover what is cast away, to purify what is corrupted, to strengthen what is weak, to make it in all its parts what Christ would have it, a Church Militant, still (please God) we will not reckon on any visible fruit of our labour. We will be content to believe our cause triumphant, when we see it apparently defeated. We will silently bear the insults of the enemies of Christ, and resign ourselves meekly to the shame and suffering which the errors of His followers bring upon us. We will endure offences which the early Saints would have marvelled at, and Martyrs would have died to redress. We will work with zeal, but as to the Lord and not to men; recollecting that even Apostles saw the sins of the Churches they planted; that St. Paul predicted that "evil men and seducers would wax worse and worse;" and that St. John seems even to consider extraordinary unbelief as the very sign of the times of the Gospel, as if the light increased the darkness of those who hated it. "Little children, it is the last time; and as ye have heard that Antichrist shall come, even now are there many Antichrists, whereby we know that it is the last time." [21]

Therefore we will seek within for the Epiphany of Christ. We will look towards His holy Altar, and approach it for the fire of love and purity which there burns. We will find comfort in the illumination which Baptism gives. We will rest and be satisfied in His ordinances and in His word. We will bless and praise His name, whenever He vouchsafes to display His glory to us in the chance-meeting of any of His Saints, and we will ever pray Him to manifest it in our own souls.

[21] 2 Tim. iii.13; 1 John ii.18.

ST. PAUL'S CONVERSION VIEWED IN REFERENCE TO HIS OFFICE

(The Feast of the Conversion of St. Paul)

"I am the least of the Apostles, that am not meet to be called an Apostle, because I persecuted the Church of God. But by the grace of God I am what I am: and His grace which was bestowed upon me was not in vain; but I laboured more abundantly than they all: yet not I, but the grace of God which was with me."—1 Cor. xv.9, 10.

TO-DAY we commemorate, not the whole history of St. Paul, nor his Martyrdom, but his wonderful Conversion. Every season of his life is full of wonders, and admits of a separate commemoration; which indeed we do make, whenever we read the Acts of the Apostles, or his Epistles. On this his day, however, that event is selected for remembrance, which was the beginning of his wonderful course; and we may profitably pursue (please God) the train of thought thus opened for us.

We cannot well forget the manner of his conversion. He was journeying to Damascus with authority from the chief priests to seize the Christians, and bring them to Jerusalem. He had sided with the persecuting party from their first act of violence, the martyrdom of St. Stephen; and he continued foremost in a bad cause, with blind rage endeavouring to defeat what really was the work of Divine power and wisdom. In the midst of his fury he was struck down by a miracle, and converted to the faith he persecuted. Observe the circumstances of the case. When the blood of Stephen was shed, Saul, then a young man, was standing by, "consenting unto his death," and "kept the raiment of them that slew him." [1] Two speeches are recorded of the Martyr in his last moments; one, in which he prayed that God would pardon his murderers,—the other his witness, that he saw the heavens opened, and Jesus on God's right hand. His prayer was wonderfully answered. Stephen saw his Saviour; the

[1] Acts xxii.20.

next vision of that Saviour to mortal man was vouchsafed to that very young man, even Saul, who shared in his murder and his intercession.

Strange indeed it was; and what would have been St. Stephen's thoughts could he have known it! The prayers of righteous men avail much. The first Martyr had power with God to raise up the greatest Apostle. Such was the honour put upon the first-fruits of those sufferings upon which the Church was entering. Thus from the beginning the blood of the Martyrs was the seed of the Church. Stephen, one man, was put to death for saying that the Jewish people were to have exclusive privileges no longer; but from his very grave rose the favoured instrument by whom the thousands and ten thousands of the Gentiles were brought to the knowledge of the Truth!

1. Herein then, first, is St. Paul's conversion memorable; that it was a triumph over the enemy. When Almighty God would convert the world, opening the door of faith to the Gentiles, who was the chosen preacher of His mercy? Not one of Christ's first followers. To show His power, He put forth His hand into the very midst of the persecutors of His Son, and seized upon the most strenuous among them. The prayer of a dying man is the token and occasion of that triumph which He had reserved for Himself. His strength is made perfect in weakness. As of old, He broke the yoke of His people's burden, the staff of their shoulder, the rod of their oppressor.[2] Saul made furiously for Damascus, but the Lord Almighty "knew his abode, and his going out and coming in, and his rage against Him;" and "because his rage against Him, and his tumult, came up before Him," therefore, as in Sennacherib's case, though in a far different way, He "put His hook in his nose, and His bridle in his lips, and turned him back by the way by which he came."[3] He "spoiled principalities and powers, and made a show of them openly,"[4] triumphing over the serpent's head while his heel was wounded. Saul, the persecutor, was converted, and preached Christ in the synagogues.

2. In the next place, St. Paul's conversion may be considered as a suitable introduction to the office he was called to execute in God's providence. I have said it was a triumph over the enemies of Christ; but it was also an expressive emblem of the nature of God's general dealings with the race of man. What are we all but rebels against God, and enemies of the Truth? what were the Gentiles in particular at that time, but "alien-

[2] Is. ix.4.   [3] Is. xxxvii.28, 29.   [4] Col. ii.15.

ated" from Him, "and enemies in their mind by wicked works?"[5] Who then could so appropriately fulfil the purpose of Him who came to call sinners to repentance, as one who esteemed himself the least of the Apostles, that was not meet to be called an Apostle, because he had persecuted the Church of God? When Almighty God in His infinite mercy purposed to form a people to Himself out of the heathen, as vessels for glory, first He chose the instrument of this His purpose as a brand from the burning, to be a type of the rest. There is a parallel to this order of Providence in the Old Testament. The Jews were bid to look unto the rock whence they were hewn.[6] Who was the especial Patriarch of their nation?—Jacob. Abraham himself, indeed, had been called and blessed by God's mere grace. Yet Abraham had remarkable faith. Jacob, however, the immediate and peculiar Patriarch of the Jewish race, is represented in the character of a sinner, pardoned and reclaimed by Divine mercy, a wanderer exalted to be the father of a great nation. Now I am not venturing to describe him as he really was, but as he is represented to us; not personally, but in that particular point of view in which the sacred history has placed him; not as an individual, but as he is typically, or in the way of doctrine. There is no mistaking the marks of his character and fortunes in the *history*, designedly (as it would seem) recorded to humble Jewish pride. He makes his own confession, as St. Paul afterwards: "I am not worthy of the least of all Thy mercies."[7] Every year, too, the Israelites were bid to bring their offering, and avow before God, that "a Syrian ready to perish was their father."[8] Such as was the father, such (it was reasonable to suppose) would be the descendants. None would be "greater than their father Jacob,"[9] for whose sake the nation was blest.

In like manner St. Paul is, in one way of viewing the Dispensation, the spiritual father of the Gentiles; and in the history of his sin and its most gracious forgiveness, he exemplifies far more than his brother Apostles his own Gospel; that we are all guilty before God, and can be saved only by His free bounty. In his own words, "for this cause obtained he mercy, that in him first Jesus Christ might show forth all *long-suffering, for a pattern* to them which should hereafter believe on Him to life everlasting."[10]

3. And, in the next place, St. Paul's previous course of life rendered him, perhaps, after his conversion, more fit an instru-

[5] Col. i.21.   [6] Is. li.1   [7] Gen. xxxii.10.
[8] Deut. xxvi.5.   [9] John iv.12.   [10] 1 Tim. i.16.

ment of God's purposes towards the Gentiles, as well as a more striking specimen of it. Here it is necessary to speak with caution. We know that, whatever were St. Paul's successes in the propagation of the Gospel, they were in their source and nature not his, but through "the grace of God which was with him." Still, God makes use of human means, and it is allowable to inquire reverently what these were, and why St. Paul was employed to convert the Heathen world rather than St. James the Less, or St. John. Doubtless his intellectual endowments and acquirements were among the circumstances which fitted him for his office. Yet, may it not be supposed that there was something in his previous religious history which especially disciplined him to be "all things to all men?" Nothing is so difficult as to enter into the characters and feelings of men who have been brought up under a system of religion different from our own and to discern how they may be most forcibly and profitably addressed, in order to win them over to the reception of Divine truths, of which they are at present ignorant. Now St. Paul had had experience in his own case, of a state of mind very different from that which belonged to him as an Apostle. Though he had never been polluted with Heathen immorality and profaneness, he had entertained views and sentiments very far from Christian, and had experienced a conversion to which the other Apostles (as far as we know) were strangers. I am far indeed from meaning that there is aught favourable to a man's after religion in an actual unsettlement of principle, in his lapsing into infidelity, and then returning again to religious belief. This was not St. Paul's case; *he* underwent no radical change of religious principle. Much less would I give countenance to the notion, that a previous immoral life is other than a grievous permanent hindrance and a curse to a man, after he has turned to God. Such considerations, however, are out of place, in speaking of St. Paul. What I mean is, that his awful rashness and blindness, his self-confident, headstrong, cruel rage against the worshippers of the true Messiah, then his strange conversion, then the length of time that elapsed before his solemn ordination, during which he was left to meditate in private on all that had happened, and to anticipate the future,—all this constituted a peculiar preparation for the office of preaching to a lost world, dead in sin. It gave him an extended insight, on the one hand, into the ways and designs of Providence, and, on the other hand, into the workings of sin in the human heart, and the various modes of thinking in which the mind is actually trained. It taught him not to despair of the worst sinners, to be sharp-sighted in detecting the sparks of faith amid corrupt habits of life, and to enter into the various temptations to which human nature is exposed. It wrought in him a profound humility, which disposed him (if we may say so) to bear meekly the abundance of the revelations given him; and it imparted to him a practical wisdom how to apply them to the conversion of others, so as to be weak with the weak, and strong with the strong, to bear their burdens, to instruct and encourage them, to "strengthen his brethren," to rejoice and weep with them; in a word, to be an earthly *Paraclete*, the comforter, help, and guide of his brethren. It gave him to know in some good measure the *hearts of men*; an attribute (in its fulness) belonging to God alone, and possessed by Him in union with perfect purity from all sin; but which in us can scarcely exist without our own melancholy experience, in some degree, of moral evil in ourselves, since the innocent (it is their privilege) have not eaten of the tree of the knowledge of good and evil.

4. Lastly, to guard against misconception of these last remarks, I must speak distinctly on a part of the subject only touched upon hitherto, viz. on St. Paul's spiritual state before his conversion. For, in spite of what has been said by way of caution, perhaps I may still be supposed to warrant the maxim sometimes maintained, that the greater sinner makes the greater saint.

Now, observe, I do not allege that St. Paul's previous sins made him a more spiritual Christian afterwards, but rendered him *more fitted for a particular purpose* in God's providence,—more fitted, when converted, to reclaim others; just as a knowledge of languages (whether divinely or humanly acquired) fits a man for the office of missionary, without tending in any degree to make him a better man. I merely say, that if we take two men *equally* advanced in faith and holiness, that one of the two would preach to a variety of men with the greater success who had the greater experience in his own religious history of temptation, the war of flesh and spirit, sin, and victory over sin; though, at the same time, at first sight it is of course unlikely that he who had experienced all these changes of mind *should* be equal in faith and obedience to the other who had served God from a child.

But, in the next place, let us observe, how very far St. Paul's conversion is, in a matter of fact, from holding out any encouragement to those who live in sin, or any self-satisfaction to those who have lived in it; as if their present or former disobedience could be a gain to them.

Why was mercy shown to Saul the persecutor; he himself gives us the reason, which we may safely make use of. "I obtained mercy, because I did it ignorantly in unbelief." [11] And why was he "enabled" to preach the Gospel? "Because Christ counted him faithful." We have here the reason more clearly stated even than in Abraham's case, who was honoured with special Divine revelations, and promised a name on the earth, because God "knew him, that he would command his children and his household after him, to keep the way of the Lord, to do justice and judgment." [12] Saul was ever faithful, according to his notion of "the way of the Lord." Doubtless he sinned deeply and grievously in persecuting the followers of Christ. Had he known the Holy Scriptures, he never would have done so; he would have recognised Jesus to be the promised Saviour, as Simeon and Anna had, from the first. But he was bred up in a human school, and paid more attention to the writings of men than to the Word of God. Still, observe, he differed from other enemies of Christ in this, that he kept a clear conscience, and habitually obeyed God according to his knowledge. God speaks to us in two ways, in our hearts and in His Word. The latter and clearer of these informants St. Paul knew little of; the former he could not but know in his measure (for it was within him), and he obeyed it. That inward voice was but feeble, mixed up and obscured with human feelings and human traditions; so that what his conscience told him to do, was but partially true, and in part was wrong. Yet still, believing it to speak God's will, he deferred to it, acting as he did afterwards when he "was not disobedient to the heavenly vision," which informed him Jesus was the Christ. [13] Hear his own account of himself:—"I have lived in all good conscience before God until this day." "After the most straitest sect of our religion, I lived a Pharisee." "Touching the righteousness which is in the Law, blameless." [14] Here is no ease, no self-indulgent habits, no wilful sin against the light,—nay, I will say, no pride. That is though he was doubtless influenced by much sinful self-confidence in his violent and bigoted hatred of the Christians, and though (as well as even the best of us) he was doubtless liable to the occasional temptations and defilements of pride, yet, taking pride to mean, open rebellion against God, warring against God's authority, setting up reason against God, this he had not. He "verily thought within himself that he

[11] 1 Tim. i.12, 13.   [12] Gen. xviii.19.   [13] Acts xxvi.19.
[14] Acts xxiii.1; xxvi.5; Phil. iii.6.

ought to do many things contrary to the name of Jesus of Nazareth." Turn to the case of Jews and Gentiles who remained unconverted, and you will see the difference between them and him. Think of the hypocritical Pharisees, who professed to be saints, and were sinners "full of extortion, excess, and uncleanness;"[15] believing Jesus to be the Christ, but not confessing Him, as "loving the praise of men more than the praise of God."[16] St. Paul himself gives us an account of them in the second chapter of his Epistle to the Romans. Can it be made to apply to his own previous state? Was the name of God blasphemed among the Gentiles through him?—On the other hand, the Gentile reasoners sought a vain wisdom.[17] These were they who despised religion and practical morality as common matters, unworthy the occupation of a refined and cultivated intellect. "Some mocked, others said, We will hear thee again of this matter."[18] They prided themselves on being above vulgar prejudices,—on being indifferent to the traditions afloat in the world about another life,—on regarding all religions as equally true and equally false. Such a hard, vain-glorious temper our Lord solemnly condemns, when He says to the Church at Laodicea, "I would thou wert cold or hot."

The Pharisees, then, were breakers of the Law; the Gentile reasoners and statesmen were infidels. Both were proud, both despised the voice of conscience. We see, then, from this review, the kind of sin which God pities and pardons. All sin, indeed, when repented of He will put away; but pride hardens the heart against repentance, and sensuality debases it to a brutal nature. The Holy Spirit is quenched by open transgressions of conscience and by contempt of His authority. But, when men err in ignorance, following closely their own notions of right and wrong, though these notions are mistaken,—great as is their sin, if they might have possessed themselves of truer notions (and very great as was St. Paul's sin, because he certainly might have learned from the Old Testament far clearer and diviner doctrine than the tradition of the Pharisees), yet such men are not left by the God of all grace. God leads them on to the light in spite of their errors in faith, if they continue strictly to obey what they believe to be His will. And, to declare this comfortable truth to us, St. Paul was thus carried on by the providence of God, and brought into the light by a miracle; that we may learn, by a memorable instance of His grace, what He

[15] Matt. xxiii.25, 27.   [16] John xii.43.
[17] 1 Cor. i.22.   [18] Acts xvii.32.

ever does, though He does not in ordinary cases thus declare it openly to the world.

Who has not felt a fear lest he be wandering from the true doctrine of Christ? Let him cherish and obey the holy light of conscience within him, as Saul did; let him carefully study the Scriptures, as Saul did not; and the God who had mercy even on the persecutor of His saints, will assuredly shed His grace upon him, and bring him into the truth as it is in Jesus.

SECRECY AND SUDDENNESS OF DIVINE VISITATIONS

(The Feast of the Purification of
the Blessed Virgin Mary)

"The kingdom of God cometh not with observation."
—Luke xvii.20.

WE commemorate on this day the Presentation of Christ in the Temple according to the injunction of the Mosaic Law, as laid down in the thirteenth chapter of the Book of Exodus and the twelfth of Leviticus. When the Israelites were brought out of Egypt, the first-born of the Egyptians (as we all know) were visited by death, "from the first-born of Pharaoh that sat on his throne, unto the first-born of the captive that was in the dungeon; and all the first-born of cattle."[1] Accordingly, in thankful remembrance of this destruction, and their own deliverance, every male among the Israelites who was the first-born of his mother, was dedicated to God; likewise, every first-born of cattle. Afterwards, the Levites were taken, as God's peculiar possession, instead of the first-born:[2] but still the first-born were solemnly brought to the Temple at a certain time from their birth, presented to God, and then redeemed or bought off at a certain price. At the same time certain sacrifices were offered for the mother, in order to her purification after childbirth; and therefore to-day's Feast, in memory of Christ's Presentation in the Temple, is commonly called the Purification of the Blessed Virgin Mary.

Our Saviour was born without sin. His Mother, the Blessed Virgin Mary, need have made no offering, as requiring no purification. On the contrary, it was that very birth of the Son of God which sanctified the whole race of woman, and turned her curse into a blessing. Nevertheless, as Christ Himself was minded to "fulfil all righteousness," to obey all ordinances of

---

[1] Exod. xii.29.   [2] Numb. iii.12, 13.

the covenant under which He was born, so in like manner His Mother Mary submitted to the Law, in order to do it reverence.

This, then, is the event in our Saviour's infancy which we this day celebrate; His Presentation in the Temple when His Virgin Mother was ceremonially purified. It was made memorable at the time by the hymns and praises of Simeon and Anna, to whom He was then revealed. And there were others, besides these, who had been "looking for redemption in Jerusalem," who were also vouchsafed a sight of the Infant Saviour. But the chief importance of this event consists in its being a fulfilment of prophecy. Malachi had announced the Lord's visitation of His Temple in these words, "The Lord whom ye seek shall suddenly come to His Temple;" words which, though variously fulfilled during His ministry, had their first accomplishment in the humble ceremony commemorated on this day. And, when we consider the grandeur of the prediction, and how unostentatious this accomplishment was, we are led to muse upon God's ways, and to draw useful lessons for ourselves. This is the reflection which I propose to make upon the subject of this Festival.

I say, we are to-day reminded of the noiseless course of God's providence,—His tranquil accomplishment, in the course of nature, of great events long designed; and again, of the suddenness and stillness of His visitations. Consider what the occurrence in question consists in. A little child is brought to the Temple, as all first-born children were brought. There is nothing here uncommon or striking, so far. His parents are with him, poor people, bringing the offering of pigeons or doves, for the purification of the mother. They are met in the Temple by an old man, who takes the child in his arms, offers a thanksgiving to God, and blesses the parents; and next are joined by a woman of a great age, a widow of eighty-four years, who had exceeded the time of useful service, and seemed to be but a fit prey for death. She gives thanks also, and speaks concerning the child to other persons who are present. Then all retire.

Now, there is evidently nothing great or impressive in this; nothing to excite the feelings, or interest the imagination. We know what the world thinks of such a group as I have described. The weak and helpless, whether from age or infancy, it looks upon negligently and passes by. Yet all this that happened was really the solemn fulfilment of an ancient and emphatic prophecy. The infant in arms was the Saviour of the world, the rightful heir, come in disguise of a stranger to visit His own house. The Scripture had said, "The Lord whom ye seek shall suddenly come to His Temple: but who may abide the day of His coming, and who may stand when He appeareth?" He had now taken possession. And further, the old man who took the child in his arms, had upon him the gifts of the Holy Ghost, had been promised the blessed sight of his Lord before his death, came into the Temple by heavenly guidance, and now had within him thoughts unutterable, of joy, thankfulness, and hope, strangely mixed with awe, fear, painful wonder, and "bitterness of spirit." Anna too, the woman of fourscore and four years, was a prophetess; and the bystanders, to whom she spoke, were the true Israel, who were looking out in faith for the predicted redemption of mankind, those who (in the words of the prophecy) "sought" and in prospect "delighted" in the "Messenger" of God's covenant of mercy. "The glory of this latter House shall be greater than of the former," [3] was the announcement made in another prophecy. Behold the glory; a little child and his parents, two aged persons, and a congregation without name or memorial. "The kingdom of God cometh not with observation."

Such has ever been the manner of His visitations, in the destruction of His enemies as well as in the deliverance of His own people;—silent, sudden, unforeseen, as regards the world, though predicted in the face of all men, and in their measure comprehended and waited for by His true Church. Such a visitation was the flood; Noah a preacher of righteousness, but the multitude of sinners judicially blinded. "They did eat, they drank, they married wives, they were given in marriage, until the day that Noe entered into the ark, and the flood came and destroyed them all." Such was the overthrow of Sodom and Gomorrah. "Likewise as it was in the days of Lot; they did eat, they drank, they bought, they sold, they planted, they builded; but the same day that Lot went out of Sodom, it rained fire and brimstone from heaven, and destroyed them all." [4] Again, "The horse of Pharaoh went in with his chariots and with his horsemen into the sea, and the Lord brought again the waters of the sea upon them." [5] The overthrow of Sennacherib was also silent and sudden, when his vast army least expected it: "The Angel of the Lord went forth, and smote in the camp of the Assyrians a hundred fourscore and five thousand." [6] Belshazzar and Babylon were surprised in the midst of the king's great feast to his thousand lords. While Nebuchadnezzar boasted, his reason

[3] Haggai ii.9.   [4] Luke xvii.27–29.
[5] Exod. xv.19.   [6] Is. xxxvii.36.

was suddenly taken from him. While the multitude shouted with impious flattery at Herod's speech, then "the Angel of the Lord smote him, because he gave not God the glory." [7] Whether we take the first or the final judgment upon Jerusalem, both visitations were foretold as sudden. Of the former, Isaiah had declared it should come "*suddenly*, at an instant;" [8] of the latter, Malachi, "The Lord whom ye seek shall *suddenly* come to His Temple." And such, too, will be His final visitation of the whole earth: men will be at their work in the city and in the field, and it will overtake them like a thunder-cloud. "Two women shall be grinding together; the one shall be taken, and the other left. Two men shall be in the field; the one shall be taken, and the other left." [9]

And it is impossible that it should be otherwise, in spite of warnings ever so clear, considering how the world goes on in every age. Men, who are plunged in the pursuits of active life, are no judges of its course and tendency on the whole. They confuse great events with little, and measure the importance of objects, as in perspective, by the mere standard of nearness or remoteness. It is only at a distance that one can take in the out-lines and features of a whole country. It is but holy Daniel, soli-tary among princes, or Elijah the recluse of Mount Carmel, who can withstand Baal, or forecast the time of God's prov-idences among the nations. To the multitude all things con-tinue to the end, as they were from the beginning of the creation. The business of state affairs, the movements of soci-ety, the course of nature, proceed as ever, till the moment of Christ's coming. "The sun was risen upon the earth," bright as usual, on that very day of wrath in which Sodom was de-stroyed. Men cannot believe their own time is an especially wicked time; for, with Scripture unstudied and hearts un-trained in holiness, they have no standard to compare it with. They take warning from no troubles or perplexities, which rather carry them away to search out the earthly causes of them, and the possible remedies. They consider them as condi-tions of this world, necessary results of this or that state of soci-ety. When the power of Assyria became great (we might suppose), the Jews had a plain call to repentance. Far from it; they were led to set power against power: they took refuge against Assyria in Egypt, their old enemy. Probably they rea-soned themselves into what they considered a temperate, en-lightened, cheerful view of national affairs; perhaps they might

[7] Acts xii.23.   [8] Is. xxx.13.   [9] Luke xvii.35, 36.

consider the growth of Assyria as an advantage rather than otherwise, as balancing the power of Egypt, and so tending to their own security. Certain it is, we find them connecting themselves first with one kingdom, and then with the other, as men who could read (as they thought) "the signs of the times," and made some pretences to political wisdom. Thus the world proceeds till wrath comes upon it and there is no escape. "To-morrow;" they say, "shall be as this day, and much more abundant." [10]

And in the midst of this their revel, whether of sensual pleasure, or of ambition, or of covetousness, or of pride and self-esteem, the decree goes forth to destroy. The decree goes forth in secret; Angels hear it, and the favoured few on earth; but no public event takes place to give the world warning. The earth was doomed to the flood one hundred and twenty years before the "decree brought forth," [11] or men heard of it. The waters of Babylon had been turned, and the conqueror was marching into the city, when Belshazzar made his great feast. Pride infatuates man, and self-indulgence and luxury work their way unseen,—like some smouldering fire, which for a while leaves the outward form of things unaltered. At length the decayed mass cannot hold together, and breaks by its own weight, or on some slight and accidental external violence. As the Prophet says: "This iniquity shall be to you as a breach ready to fall, swelling out (or bulging) in a high wall, whose breaking cometh *suddenly at an instant.*" The same inward corruption of a nation seems to be meant in our Lord's words, when He says of Jerusalem: "Wheresoever the carcase is, there will the eagles be gathered together." [12]

Thoughts such as the foregoing are profitable at all times; for in every age the world is profane and blind, and God hides His providence, yet carries it forward. But they are peculiarly apposite now, in proportion as the present day bears upon it more marks than usual of pride and judicial blindness. Whether Christ is at our doors or not, but a few men in England may have grace enough safely to conjecture; but that He is calling upon us all to prepare as for His coming, is most evident to those who have religious eyes and ears. Let us then turn this Festival to account, by taking it as the Memorial-day of His visitations. Let us from the events it celebrates, lay up deep in our hearts the recollection, how mysteriously little things are in this world connected with great; how single moments, improved or wasted, are the salvation or ruin of all-important

[10] Is. lvi.12.   [11] Zeph. ii.2.   [12] Matt. xxiv.28.

interests. Let us bear the thought upon us, when we come to worship in God's House, that any such season of service may, for what we know, be wonderfully connected with some ancient purpose of His, announced before we were born, and may have its determinate bearing on our eternal welfare; let us fear to miss the Saviour, while Simeon and Anna find Him. Let us remember that He was not manifested again in the Temple, except once, for thirty years, while a whole generation, who were alive at His first visitation, died off in the interval. Let us carry this thought into our daily conduct; considering that, for what we know, our hope of salvation may in the event materially depend on our avoiding this or that momentary sin. And further, from the occurrences of this day let us take comfort, when we despond about the state of the Church. Perhaps we see not God's tokens; we see neither prophet nor teacher remaining to His people; darkness falls over the earth, and no protesting voice is heard. Yet, granting things to be at the very worst, still, when Christ was presented in the Temple, the age knew as little of it as it knows of His providence now. Rather, the worse our condition is, the nearer to us is the Advent of our Deliverer. Even though He is silent, doubt not that His army is on the march towards us. He is coming through the sky, and has even now His camp upon the outskirts of our own world. Nay, though He still for a while keep His seat at His Father's right hand, yet surely He sees all that is going on, and waits and will not fail His hour of vengeance. Shall He not hear His own elect, when they cry day and night to Him? His Services of prayer and praise continue, and are scorned by the multitude. Day by day, Festival by Festival, Fast after Fast, Season by Season, they continue according to His ordinance, and are scorned. But the greater His delay, the heavier will be His vengeance, and the more complete the deliverance of His people.

May the good Lord save His Church in this her hour of peril; when Satan seeks to sap and corrupt where he dare not openly assault! May He raise up instruments of His grace, "not ignorant of the devices" of the Evil One, with seeing eyes, and strong hearts, and vigorous arms to defend the treasure of the faith once committed to the Saints, and to arouse and alarm their slumbering brethren! "For Sion's sake will I not hold my peace, and for Jerusalem's sake I will not rest, until the righteousness thereof go forth as brightness, and the salvation thereof as a lamp that burneth. . . . Ye that make mention of the Lord, keep not silence, and give Him no rest, till He establish, and till He make Jerusalem a praise in the earth. . . . Go through, go through the gates: prepare ye the way of the people; cast up, cast up the highway, gather out the stones, lift up a standard for the people." [13] Thus does Almighty God address His "watchmen on the walls of Jerusalem;" and to the Church herself He says, to our great comfort: "No weapon that is formed against thee shall prosper, and every tongue that shall rise against thee in judgment thou shalt condemn. This is the heritage of the servants of the Lord, and their righteousness is of Me, saith the Lord." [14]

---

[13] Is. lxii.1, 6, 7, 10.   [14] Is. liv.17.

DIVINE DECREES

(The Feast of St. Matthias the Apostle)

"Hold that fast which thou hast, that no man take thy crown."
—Rev. iii.11.

THIS is the only Saint's day which is to be celebrated with
mingled feelings of joy and pain. It records the fall as well
as the election of an Apostle. St. Matthias was chosen in place of
the traitor Judas. In the history of the latter we have the warning recorded in very deed, which our Lord in the text gives us in
word, "Hold that fast which thou hast, that no man take thy
crown." And doubtless many were the warnings such as this,
addressed by our Lord to the wretched man who in the end betrayed Him. Not only did He call him to reflection and repentance by the hints which He let drop concerning him during
the Last Supper, but in the discourses previous to it He may be
supposed to have intended a reference to the circumstances of
His apostate disciple. "Watch ye, therefore," He said, "lest
coming suddenly, He find you sleeping."—I called Judas just
now *wretched*; for we must not speak of sinners, according to the
falsely charitable way of some, styling them *unfortunate* instead
of wicked, lest we thus learn to excuse sin in ourselves. He was
doubtless *inexcusable*, as we shall be, if we follow his pattern; and
he must be viewed, not with pity, but with fear and awe.

The reflection which rises in the mind on a consideration of
the election of St. Matthias, is this: how easily God may effect
His purposes without us, and put others in our place, if we are
disobedient to Him. It often happens that those who have long
been in His favour grow secure and presuming. They think
their salvation certain, and their service necessary to Him who
has graciously accepted it They consider themselves as personally bound up with His purposes of mercy manifested in the
Church; and so marked out that, if they could fall, His word
would fail. They come to think they have some peculiar title or
interest in His promises, over and above other men (however
derived, it matters not, whether from His eternal decree, or, on

the other hand, from their own especial holiness and obedience), but practically such an interest that the very supposition that they can possibly fall offends them. Now, this feeling of self-importance is repressed all through the Scriptures, and especially by the events we commemorate to-day. Let us consider this subject.

Eliphaz the Temanite thus answers Job, who in his distress showed infirmity, and grew impatient of God's correction. "Can a man be profitable unto God, as he that is wise may be profitable unto himself? Is it any pleasure to the Almighty, that thou art righteous? or is it gain to Him, that thou makest thy ways perfect?"[1] And the course of His providence, as recorded in Scripture, will show us that, in dealing with us His rational creatures, He goes by no unconditional rule, which makes us absolutely His from the first; but, as He is "no respecter of persons," so on the other hand righteousness and judgment are the basis of His throne; and that whoso rebels, whether Archangel or Apostle, at once forfeits His favour; and this, even for the sake of those who do not rebel.

Not long before the fall and treachery of Judas, Christ pronounced a blessing, as it seemed, upon all the twelve Apostles, the traitor included. "Ye which have followed Me, in the regeneration when the Son of Man shall sit in the throne of His glory, ye shall also sit upon twelve thrones, judging the twelve tribes of Israel."[2] Who would not have thought from this promise, taken by itself and without reference to the eternal Rule of God's government, which is always understood, even when not formally enunciated, that Judas was sure of eternal life? It is true our Saviour added, as if with an allusion to him, "many that are first shall be last;" yet He said nothing to undeceive such as might refuse to consult and apply the fundamental law of His impartial providence. All His twelve Apostles seemed, from the letter of His words, to be predestined to life; nevertheless, in a few months, Matthias held the throne and crown of one of them.— And there is something remarkable in the circumstance itself, that our Lord *should* have made up their number to a full twelve, after one had fallen; and, perhaps, there may be contained in it some symbolical allusion to the scope of His decrees, which we cannot altogether enter into. Surely, had He willed it, eleven would have accomplished His purpose as well as twelve. Why, when one had fallen, should He accurately fill up the perfect number? Yet not only in the case of the Apostles, but in that of

---

[1] Job xxii.2, 3.   [2] Matt. xix.28.

the tribes of Israel also, if He rejects one, He divides another
into two.[3] Why is this, but to show us, as it would appear, that in
this election of us, He does not look at us as mere *individuals*, but
as a body, as a certain definite whole, of which the parts may
alter in the process of disengaging them from this sinful
world,—with reference to some glorious and harmonious design upon *us*, who are the immediate objects of His bounty, and
shall be the fruit of His love, if we are faithful? Why, but to
show us that He could even find other Apostles to suffer for
Him,—and, much more, servants to fill His lower thrones,
should we be wanting and transgress His strict and holy law?

This is but one instance, out of many, in the revealed history
of His moral government. He was on the point of exemplifying
the same Rule in the case of the Israelites, when Moses stayed
His hand. God purposed to consume them, when they rebelled,
and instead to make of Moses' seed a great nation. This happened twice.[4] The second time, God declared what was His end
in view, in fulfilling which the Israelites were but His instruments. "I have pardoned according to thy word; but as truly as
I live, *all the earth shall be filled with the glory of the Lord.*" Again, on
the former occasion, He gave the Rule of His dealings with
them. Moses wished for the sake of his people to be himself
excluded from the land of promise: "If thou wilt forgive their
sin:—and if not, blot me, I pray Thee, out of Thy book which
Thou hast written. And the Lord said unto Moses, *Whosoever
hath sinned against Me, him* will I blot out of My book." So clearly
has He shown us from the beginning, that His own glory is the
End, and justice the essential *Rule*, of His providence.

Again, Saul was chosen, and thought himself secure. His
conduct evinced the self-will of an independent monarch, instead of one who felt himself to be a mere instrument of God's
purposes, a minister of His glory, under the obligation of a law
of right and wrong, and strong only as wielded by Him who
formed him. So, when he sinned, Samuel said to him: "Thou
hast done foolishly: thou hast not kept the commandment of
the Lord thy God. . . . for *now would the Lord have established* thy
kingdom upon Israel for ever. But now thy kingdom shall not
continue: the Lord hath sought Him a man after His own
heart."[5] And again, "The Lord hath rent the kingdom of Israel
from thee this day, and hath given it to a neighbour of thine,
that is better than thou."[6]

---

[3] Rev. vii.   [4] Exod. xxxii.32, 33; Numb. xiv.20, 21.
[5] 1 Sam. xiii.13, 14.   [6] 1 Sam. xv.28.

In like manner, Christ also, convicting the Jews out of their own mouth: "He will miserably destroy those wicked men, and will *let out His vineyard unto other husbandmen*, which shall render Him the fruits in their seasons."[7] Consider how striking an instance the Jews formed, when the Gospel was offered them, of the general Rule which I am pointing out. They were rejected. How hard they thought it, St. Paul's Epistles show. They did not shrink from declaring, that, if Jesus were the Christ, and the Gentiles made equal with them, God's promise was broken; and you may imagine how forcibly they might have pleaded the prophecies of the Old Testament, which seemed irreversibly to assign honour and power (not to say *temporal* honour and power) to the Israelites *by name*. Alas! they did not seek out and use the one clue given them for their religious course, amid all the mysteries both of Scripture and the world,—the one solemn *Rule* of God's dealings with His creatures. They did not listen for that small still voice, running under all His dispensations, most clear to those who would listen, amid all the intricacies of His providence and His promises. Impressed though it be upon the heart by nature, and ever insisted on in Revelation, as the basis on which God has established all His decrees, it was to them a hard saying. St. Paul retorts it on their consciences, when they complained. "God," he says "will render to every man according to his deeds. To them who by patient continuance in well-doing seek for glory and honour and immortality, eternal life; *but* unto them that are contentious, and do not obey the Truth, but obey unrighteousness, indignation and wrath; —tribulation and anguish upon every soul of man that doeth evil, of the Jew first, and also of the Gentile; but glory, honour, and peace, to every man that worketh good, to the Jew first, and also to the Gentile: for *there is no respect of persons with God*."[8]

Such was the unchangeable Rule of God's government, as it is propounded by St. Paul in explanation of the Jewish election, and significantly prefixed to his discourse upon the Christian. Such as was the Mosaic, such also is the Gospel Covenant, made without respect of persons; rich, indeed, in privilege and promise far above the Elder Dispensation, but bearing on its front the same original avowal of impartial retribution,—"peace to every man that worketh good," "wrath to the disobedient;" predestining to glory, characters not persons, pledging the gift of perseverance not to individuals, but to a body of which the separate members might change. This is the doctrine set before

---

[7] Matt. xxi.41.   [8] Rom. ii.6–11.

us by that Apostle to whom was revealed in an extraordinary
way the nature of the Christian Covenant, its peculiar blessedness, gifts, and promises. The New Covenant was, so far, not
unlike the Old, as some reasoners in these days would maintain.

We are vouchsafed a further witness to it in the favoured
Evangelist, who finally closed and perfected the volume of
God's revelations, after the death of his brethren. "Behold, I
come quickly, and My reward is with Me, to give every man
according as his work shall be. . . . Blessed are they that do His
commandments, *that they may have right* to the tree of life, and
may enter in through the gates into the city." [9]

And a third witness that the Christian Election is, like the
Jewish, conditional, is our Lord's own declaration, which He
left behind Him with His Apostles when He was leaving the
world, as recorded by the same Evangelist. "If a man *abide not in
Me*," He said, "he is cast forth as a branch, and is withered; and
men gather them and cast them into the fire, and they are
burned." And, lest restless and reluctant minds should shelter
their opposition to this solemn declaration under some supposed obscurity in the expression of "abiding in Him," and say
that none abide in Him but the predestined, He adds, for the
removal of all doubt, "*If ye keep my commandments*, ye shall abide
in my love." [10]

Lastly, in order to complete the solemn promulgation of His
Eternal Rule, He exemplified it, while He spoke it, in the instance of an Apostle. He knew whom He had chosen; that they
were "not all clean," that "one of them was a devil;" yet He
chose all twelve, as if to show that souls chosen for eternal life
might fall away. Thus, in the case of the Apostles themselves, in
the very foundation of His Church, He laid deep the serious
and merciful warning, if we have wisdom to lay it to heart, "Be
not high-minded, but fear;" for, if God spared not Apostles,
neither will He spare thee!

What solemn overpowering thoughts must have crowded on
St. Matthias, when he received the greetings of the eleven
Apostles, and took his seat among them as their brother! His
very election was a witness against himself if he did not fulfil it.
And such surely will ours be in our degree. We take the place of
others who have gone before, as Matthias did; we are "baptized
for the dead," filling up the ranks of soldiers, some of whom,
indeed, have fought a good fight, but many of whom in every
age have made void their calling. Many are called, few are cho-

[9] Rev. xxii.12, 14.   [10] John xv.16.

sen. The monuments of sin and unbelief are set up around us. The casting away of the Jews was the reconciling of the Gentiles. The fall of one nation is the conversion of another. The Church loses old branches, and gains new. God works according to His own inscrutable pleasure; He has left the East, and manifested Himself Westward. Thus the Christian of every age is but the successor of the lost and of the dead. How long we of this country shall be put in trust with the Gospel, we know not; but while we have the privilege, assuredly we do but stand in the place of Christians who have either utterly fallen away, or are so corrupted as scarcely to let their light shine before men. We are at present witnesses of the Truth; and our very glory is our warning. By the superstitions, the profanities, the indifference, the unbelief of the world called Christian, we are called upon to be lowly-minded while we preach aloud, and to tremble while we rejoice. Let us then, as a Church and as individuals, one and all, look to Him who alone can keep us from falling. Let us with single heart look up to Christ our Saviour, and put ourselves into His hands, from whom all our strength and wisdom is derived. Let us avoid the beginnings of temptation; let us watch and pray lest we enter into it. Avoiding all speculations which are above us, let us follow what tends to edifying. Let us receive into our hearts the great truth, that we who have been freely accepted and sanctified as members of Christ, shall hereafter be judged by our works, done in and through Him; that the Sacraments unite us to Him, and that faith makes the Sacraments open their hidden virtue, and flow forth in pardon and grace. Beyond this we may not inquire. How it is one man perseveres and another falls, what are the exact limits and character of our natural corruption,—these are over-subtle questions; while we know for certain, that though we can do nothing of ourselves, yet that salvation is in our own power, for however deep and far-spreading is the root of evil in us, God's grace will be sufficient for our need.

THE REVERENCE DUE TO
THE VIRGIN MARY

(The Feast of the Annunciation of
the Blessed Virgin Mary)

"From henceforth all generations shall call me blessed."
—Luke i.48.

To-day we celebrate the Annunciation of the Virgin Mary; when the Angel Gabriel was sent to tell her that she was to be the Mother of our Lord, and when the Holy Ghost came upon her, and overshadowed her with the power of the Highest. In that great event was fulfilled her anticipation as expressed in the text. All generations have called her blessed.[1] The Angel began the salutation; he said, "Hail, thou that art highly favoured; the Lord is with thee; blessed[2] art thou among women." Again he said, "Fear not, Mary, for thou hast found favour with God; and, behold, thou shalt conceive in thy womb, and bring forth a Son, and shalt call His name Jesus. He shall be great, and shall be called the Son of the Highest." Her cousin Elizabeth was the next to greet her with her appropriate title. Though she was filled with the Holy Ghost at the time she spake, yet, far from thinking herself by such a gift equalled to Mary, she was thereby moved to use the lowlier and more reverent language. "She spake out with a loud voice, and said, *Blessed art thou* among women, and blessed is the fruit of thy womb. And whence is this to me, that the mother of my Lord should come to me?" . . . . Then she repeated, "Blessed is she that believed; for there shall be a performance of those things which were told her from the Lord." Then it was that Mary gave utterance to her feelings in the Hymn which we read in the Evening Service. How many and complicated must they have been! In her was now to be fulfilled that promise which the world had been looking out for during thousands of years. The

[1] μακαριοῦσι.   [2] εὐλογημένη.

308

Seed of the woman, announced to guilty Eve, after long delay, was at length appearing upon earth, and was to be born of her. In her the destinies of the world were to be reversed, and the serpent's head bruised. On her was bestowed the greatest honour ever put upon any individual of our fallen race. God was taking upon Him her flesh, and humbling Himself to be called her offspring;—such is the deep mystery! She of course would feel her own inexpressible unworthiness; and again, her humble lot, her ignorance, her weakness in the eyes of the world. And she had moreover, we may well suppose, that purity and innocence of heart, that bright vision of faith, that confiding trust in her God, which raised all these feelings to an intensity which we, ordinary mortals, cannot understand. *We* cannot understand them; we repeat her hymn day after day,—yet consider for an instant in how different a mode *we* say it from that in which she at first uttered it. *We* even hurry it over, and do not think of the meaning of those words which came from the most highly favoured, awfully gifted of the children of men. "My soul doth magnify the Lord, and my spirit hath rejoiced in God my Saviour. For He hath regarded the low estate of His handmaiden: for, behold, from henceforth all generations shall call me blessed. For He that is mighty hath done to me great things; and holy is His name. And His mercy is on them that fear Him from generation to generation."

Now let us consider in what respects the Virgin Mary is Blessed; a title first given her by the Angel, and next by the Church in all ages since to this day.

1. I observe, that in her the curse pronounced on Eve was changed to a blessing. Eve was doomed to bear children in sorrow; but now this very dispensation, in which the token of Divine anger was conveyed, was made the means by which salvation came into the world. Christ might have descended from heaven, as He went back, and as He will come again. He might have taken on Himself a body from the ground, as Adam was given; or been formed, like Eve, in some other divinely-devised way. But, far from this, God sent forth His Son (as St. Paul says), "made of a woman." For it has been His gracious purpose to turn *all* that is ours from evil to good. Had He so pleased, He might have found, when we sinned, other beings to do Him service, casting us into hell; but He purposed to save and to change *us*. And in like manner all that belongs to us, our reason, our affections, our pursuits, our relations in life, He needs nothing put aside in His disciples, but all sanctified. Therefore, instead of sending His Son from heaven, He sent Him forth as

the Son of Mary, to show that all our sorrow and all our corruption can be blessed and changed by Him. The very punishment of the fall, the very taint of birth-sin, admits of a cure by the coming of Christ.

2. But there is another portion of the original punishment of woman, which may be considered as repealed when Christ came. It was said to the woman, "Thy husband shall rule over thee;" a sentence which has been strikingly fulfilled. Man has strength to conquer the thorns and thistles which the earth is cursed with, but the same strength has ever proved the fulfilment of the punishment awarded to the woman. Look abroad through the Heathen world, and see how the weaker half of mankind has everywhere been tyrannized over and debased by the strong arm of force. Consider all those Eastern nations, which have never at any time reverenced it, but have heartlessly made it the slave of every bad and cruel purpose. Thus the serpent has triumphed,—making the man still degrade himself by her who originally tempted him, and her, who then tempted, now suffer from him who was seduced. Nay, even under the light of revelation, the punishment on the woman was not removed at once. Still (in the words of the curse), her husband ruled over her. The very practice of polygamy and divorce, which was suffered under the patriarchal and Jewish dispensation proves it.

But when Christ came as the seed of the woman, He vindicated the rights and honour of His mother. Not that the distinction of ranks is destroyed under the Gospel; the woman is still made inferior to man, as he to Christ; but the slavery is done away with. St. Peter bids the husband "give honour unto the wife, *because* the weaker, in that both are heirs of the grace of life."[3] And St. Paul, while enjoining subjection upon her, speaks of the especial blessedness vouchsafed her in being the appointed entrance of the Saviour into the world. "Adam was first formed, then Eve; and Adam was not deceived, but the woman being deceived was in the transgression." But "notwithstanding, she shall be saved through the Child-bearing;"[4] that is, through the birth of Christ from Mary, which was a blessing, as upon all mankind, so peculiarly upon the woman. Accordingly, from that time, Marriage has not only been restored to its original dignity, but even gifted with a spiritual privilege, as the outward symbol of the heavenly union subsisting betwixt Christ and His Church.

---

[3] 1 Pet. iii.7.   [4] 1 Tim. ii.15.

Thus has the Blessed Virgin, in bearing our Lord, taken off or lightened the peculiar disgrace which the woman inherited for seducing Adam, sanctifying the one part of it, repealing the other.

3. But further, she is doubtless to be accounted blessed and favoured in herself, as well as in the benefits she has done us. Who can estimate the holiness and perfection of her, who was chosen to be the Mother of Christ? If to him that hath, more is given, and holiness and Divine favour go together (and this we are expressly told), what must have been the transcendent purity of her, whom the Creator Spirit condescended to overshadow with His miraculous presence? What must have been her gifts, who was chosen to be the only near earthly relative of the Son of God, the only one whom He was bound by nature to revere and look up to; the one appointed to train and educate Him, to instruct Him day by day, as He grew in wisdom and in stature? This contemplation runs to a higher subject, did we dare follow it; for what, think you, was the sanctified state of that human nature, of which God formed His sinless Son; knowing as we do, "that which is born of the flesh is flesh," and that "none can bring a clean thing out of an unclean?" [5]

Now, after dwelling on thoughts such as these, when we turn back again to the Gospels, I think every one must feel some surprise, that we are not told more about the Blessed Virgin than we find there. After the circumstances of Christ's birth and infancy, we hear little of her. Little is said in praise of her. She is mentioned as attending Christ to the cross, and there committed by Him to St. John's keeping; and she is mentioned as continuing with the Apostles in prayer after His ascension; and then we hear no more of her. But here again in this silence we find instruction, as much as in the mention of her.

1. It suggests to us that Scripture was written, not to exalt this or that particular Saint, but to give glory to Almighty God. There have been thousands of holy souls in the times of which the Bible history treats, whom we know nothing of because their lives did not fall upon the line of God's public dealings with man. In Scripture we read not of all the good men who ever were, only of a few, viz. those in whom God's name was especially honoured. Doubtless there have been many widows in Israel, serving God in fastings and prayers, like Anna; but she only is mentioned in Scripture, as being in a situation to glorify the Lord Jesus. She spoke of the Infant Saviour "to all them

[5] 1 John iii.6; Job xiv.4.

that looked for redemption in Jerusalem." Nay, for what we know, faith like Abraham's, and zeal like David's have burned in the breasts of thousands whose names have no memorial; because, I say, Scripture is written to show us the course of God's great and marvellous providence, and we hear of those Saints only who were the instruments of His purposes, as either introducing or preaching His Son. Christ's favoured Apostle was St. John, His personal friend; yet how little do we know of St. John compared with St. Paul;—and why? because St. Paul was the more illustrious propagator and dispenser of His Truth. As St. Paul himself said, that he "knew no man after the flesh," [6] so His Saviour, with somewhat a similar meaning, has hid from us the knowledge of His more sacred and familiar feelings, His feelings towards His Mother and His friend. These were not to be exposed, as unfit for the world to know,—as dangerous, because not admitting of being known, without a risk lest the honour which those Saints received through grace should eclipse in our minds the honour of Him who honoured them. Had the blessed Mary been more fully disclosed to us in the heavenly beauty and sweetness of the spirit within her, true, *she* would have been honoured, *her* gifts would have been clearly seen; but, at the same time, the Giver would have been somewhat less contemplated, because no design or work of His would have been disclosed in her history. She would have seemingly been introduced for *her* sake, not for His sake. When a Saint is seen working *towards* an end appointed by God, we *see* him to be a mere instrument, a servant though a favoured one; and though we admire him, yet, after all, we glorify God in him. We pass on *from* him to the work to which he ministers. But, when any one is introduced, full of gifts, yet without visible and immediate subserviency to God's designs, such a one seems revealed for his own sake. We should rest, perchance, in the thought of him, and think of the creature more than the Creator. Thus it is a dangerous thing, it is too high a privilege, for sinners like ourselves, to know the best and innermost thoughts of God's servants. We cannot bear to see such men in their own place, in the retirement of private life, and the calmness of hope and joy. The higher their gifts, the less fitted they are for being seen. Even St. John the Apostle was twice tempted to fall down in worship before an Angel who showed him the things to come. And, if he who had seen the Son of God was thus overcome by the creature, how is it possible we could bear

[6] 2 Cor. v. 16.

to gaze upon the creature's holiness in its fulness, especially as we should be more able to enter into it, and estimate it, than to comprehend the infinite perfections of the Eternal Godhead? Therefore, many truths are, like the "things which the seven thunders uttered,"[7] "sealed up" from us. In particular, it is in mercy to us that so little is revealed about the Blessed Virgin, in mercy to our weakness, though of her there are "many things to say," yet they are "hard to be uttered, seeing we are dull of hearing."[8]

2. But, further, the more we consider who St. Mary was, the more dangerous will such knowledge of her appear to be. Other saints are but influenced or inspired by Christ, and made partakers of Him mystically. But, as to St. Mary, Christ derived His manhood from her, and so had an especial unity of nature with her; and this wondrous relationship between God and man it is perhaps impossible for us to dwell much upon without some perversion of feeling. For, truly, she is raised above the condition of sinful beings, though by nature a sinner; she is brought near to God, yet is but a creature, and seems to lack her fitting place in our limited understandings, neither too high nor too low. We cannot combine, in our thought of her, all we should ascribe with all we should withhold. Hence, following the example of Scripture, we had better only think of her with and for her Son, never separating her from Him, but using her name as a memorial of His great condescension in stooping from heaven, and not "abhorring the Virgin's womb." And this is the rule of our own Church, which has set apart only such Festivals in honour of the Blessed Mary, as may also be Festivals in honour of our Lord; the Purification commemorating His presentation in the Temple, and the Annunciation commemorating His Incarnation. And, with this caution, the thought of her may be made most profitable to our faith; for nothing is so calculated to impress on our minds that Christ is really partaker of our nature, and in all respects man, save sin only, as to associate Him with the thought of her, by whose ministration He became our brother.

To conclude. Observe the lesson which we gain for ourselves from the history of the Blessed Virgin; that the highest graces of the soul may be matured in private, and without those fierce trials to which the many are exposed in order to their sanctification. So hard are our hearts, that affliction, pain, and anxiety are sent to humble us, and dispose us towards a true faith in the

---

[7] Rev. x.4.   [8] Heb. v.11.

heavenly word, when preached to us. Yet it is only our extreme obstinacy of unbelief which renders this chastisement necessary. The aids which God gives under the Gospel Covenant, have power to renew and purify our hearts, without uncommon providences to discipline us into receiving them. God gives His Holy Spirit to us silently; and the silent duties of every day (it may be humbly hoped) are blest to the sufficient sanctification of thousands, whom the world knows not of. The Blessed Virgin is a memorial of this; and it is consoling as well as instructive to know it. When we quench the grace of Baptism, then it is that we need severe trials to restore us. This is the case of the multitude, whose best estate is that of chastisement, repentance, supplication, and absolution, again and again. But there are those who go on in a calm and unswerving course, learning day by day to love Him who has redeemed them, and overcoming the sin of their nature by His heavenly grace, as the various temptations to evil successively present themselves. And, of these undefiled followers of the Lamb, the Blessed Mary is the chief. Strong in the Lord, and in the power of His might, she "staggered not at the promise of God through unbelief;" she believed when Zacharias doubted,—with a faith like Abraham's she believed and was blessed for her belief, and had the performance of those things which were told her by the Lord. And when sorrow came upon her afterwards, it was but the blessed participation of her Son's sacred sorrows, not the sorrow of those who suffer for their sins.

If we, through God's unspeakable gift, have in any measure followed Mary's innocence in our youth, so far let us bless Him who enabled us. But so far as we are conscious of having departed from Him, let us bewail our miserable guilt. Let us acknowledge from the heart that no punishment is too severe for us, no chastisement should be unwelcome (though it is a sore thing to learn to welcome pain), if it tend to burn away the corruption which has propagated itself within us. Let us count all things as gain, which God sends to cleanse away the marks of sin and shame which are upon our foreheads. The day will come at length, when our Lord and Saviour will unveil that Sacred Countenance to the whole world, which no sinner ever yet could see and live. Then will the world be forced to look upon Him, whom they pierced with their unrepented wickednesses; "all faces will gather blackness." [9] Then they will discern, what they do not now believe, the utter deformity of

[9] Joel ii.6.

sin; while the Saints of the Lord, who seemed on earth to bear but the countenance of common men, will wake up one by one after His likeness, and be fearful to look upon. And then will be fulfilled the promise pledged to the Church on the Mount of Transfiguration. It will be "good" to be with those whose tabernacles might have been a snare to us on earth, had we been allowed to build them. We shall see our Lord, and His Blessed Mother, the Apostles and Prophets, and all those righteous men whom we now read of in history, and long to know. Then we shall be taught in those Mysteries which are now above us. In the words of the Apostle, "Beloved, now are we the sons of God, and it doth not yet appear what we shall be but we know that, when He shall appear, we shall be like Him, for we shall see Him as He is: and every man that hath this hope in Him, purifieth himself, even as He is pure." [10]

---

[10] 1 John iii.2, 3. On the subject of this Sermon, *vide* Bishop Bull's Sermon on Luke i.48, 49.

CHRIST, A QUICKENING SPIRIT

(The Feast of the Resurrection of Our Lord)

*"Why seek ye the living among the dead? He is not here,
but is risen."*—Luke xxiv.5, 6.

S UCH is the triumphant question with which the Holy Angels put to flight the sadness of the women on the morning
of Christ's resurrection. "O ye of little faith," less faith than
love, more dutiful than understanding, why come ye to anoint
His Body on the third day? Why seek ye the Living Saviour in
the tomb? The time of sorrow is run out; victory has come,
according to His Word, and ye recollect it not. "He is not here,
but is risen!"

These were deeds done and words spoken eighteen hundred
years since; so long ago, that in the world's thought they are as
though they never had been; yet they hold good to this day.
Christ is to us now, just what He was in all His glorious Attributes on the morning of the Resurrection; and we are blessed
in knowing it, even more than the women to whom the Angels
spoke, according to His own assurance, "Blessed are they that
have not seen, and yet have believed."

On this highest of Festivals, I will attempt to set before you
one out of the many comfortable subjects of reflection which it
suggests.

1. First, then, observe how Christ's resurrection harmonizes
with the history of His birth. David had foretold that His "soul
should not be left in hell" (that is, the unseen state), neither
should "the Holy One of God see corruption." And with a reference to this prophecy, St. Peter says, that it "was not possible
that He should be holden of death"[1] as if there were some hidden inherent vigour in Him, which secured His manhood from
dissolution. The greatest infliction of pain and violence could
only destroy its powers for a season; but nothing could make it
decay. "Thou wilt not suffer Thy *Holy* One to see corruption;"

---

[1] Ps. xvi.10; Acts ii.24, 27, τὸν ὅσιον.

so says the Scripture, and elsewhere calls Him the "*Holy* child Jesus." [2] These expressions carry our minds back to the Angels' announcement of His birth, in which His incorruptible and immortal nature is implied. "That *Holy* Thing" which was born of Mary, was "the Son," not of man, but "of God." Others have all been born in sin, "after Adam's own likeness, in His image," [3] and, being born in sin, they are heirs to corruption. "By one man sin entered into the world, and death," and all its consequences, "by sin." Not one human being comes into existence without God's discerning evidences of sin attendant on his birth. But when the Word of Life was manifested in our flesh, the Holy Ghost displayed that creative hand by which, in the beginning, Eve was formed; and the Holy Child, thus conceived by the power of the Highest, was (as the history shows) immortal even in His mortal nature, clear from all infection of the forbidden fruit, so far as to be sinless and incorruptible. Therefore, though He was liable to death, "it was impossible He should be *holden*" of it. Death might overpower, but it could not keep possession; "it had no dominion over Him." [4] He was, in the words of the text, "*the Living* among the dead."

And hence His rising from the dead may be said to have evinced His divine original. He was "*declared* to be the Son of God with power, according to the Spirit of Holiness;" that is, His essential Godhead, "by the resurrection of the dead." [5] He had been condemned as a blasphemer by the Jewish rulers, "because He made Himself the Son of God;" and He was brought to the death of the Cross, not only as a punishment, but as a practical refutation of His claim. He was challenged by His enemies on this score: "If thou be the Son of God, come down from the cross." Thus His crucifixion was as though a trial, a new experiment on the part of Satan, who had before tempted Him, whether he was like other men, or the Son of God. Observe the event. He was obedient unto death, fulfilling the law of that disinherited nature which He had assumed; and in order, by undergoing it, to atone for our sins. So far was permitted by God's "determinate counsel and foreknowledge;" but there the triumph of His enemies, so to account it, ended,— ended with what was necessary for our redemption. He said, "It is finished;" for His humiliation was at its lowest depth when He expired. Immediately some incipient tokens showed themselves, that the real victory was with Him; first, the earthquake

[2] Acts iv.27, τὸν ἅγιον. [3] Gen. v.3.
[4] Rom. vi.9. [5] Rom. i.4.

and other wonders in heaven and earth. These even were enough to justify His claim in the judgment of the heathen centurion; who said at once, "Truly this *was* the Son of God." Then followed His descent into hell, and triumph in the unseen world, whatever that was. Lastly, that glorious deed of power on the third morning which we now commemorate. The dead arose. The grave could not detain Him who "had life in Himself." He rose as a man awakes in the morning, when sleep flies from him as a thing of course. Corruption had no power over that Sacred Body, the fruit of a miraculous conception. The bonds of death were broken as "green withes," witnessing by their feebleness that He was the Son of God.

Such is the connexion between Christ's birth and resurrection; and more than this might be ventured concerning His incorrupt nature, were it not better to avoid all risk of trespassing upon that reverence with which we are bound to regard it. Something might be said concerning His personal appearance, which seems to have borne the marks of one who was not tainted with birth-sin. Men could scarce keep from worshipping Him. When the Pharisees sent to seize Him, all the officers, on His merely acknowledging Himself to be Him whom they sought, fell backwards from His presence to the ground. They were scared as brutes are said to be by the voice of man. Thus, being created in God's image, He was the second Adam; and much more than Adam in His secret nature, which beamed through His tabernacle of flesh with awful purity and brightness even in the days of His humiliation. "The first man was of the earth, earthy; the second man was the Lord from heaven." [6]

2. And if such was His visible Majesty, while He yet was subject to temptation, infirmity, and pain, much more abundant was the manifestation of His Godhead, when He was risen from the dead. Then the Divine Essence streamed forth (so to say) on every side, and environed His Manhood, as in a cloud of glory. So transfigured was His Sacred Body, that He who had deigned to be born of a woman, and to hang upon the cross, had subtle virtue in Him like a spirit, to pass through the closed doors to His assembled followers; while, by condescending to the trial of their senses, He showed that it was no mere spirit, but He Himself, as before, with wounded hands and pierced side, who spoke to them. He manifested Himself to them, in this His exalted state, that they might be His witnesses to the people; witnesses of those separate truths which man's reason cannot

[6] 1 Cor. xv.47.

combine, that He had a real human body, that it was partaker in the properties of His Soul, and that it was inhabited by the Eternal Word. They handled Him,—they saw Him come and go, when the doors were shut,—they felt, what they could not see, but could witness even unto death, that He was "their Lord and their God;"—a triple evidence, first, of His Atonement; next of their own Resurrection unto glory; lastly, of His Divine Power to conduct them safely to it. Thus manifested as perfect God and perfect man, in the fulness of His sovereignty, and the immortality of His holiness, He ascended up on high to take possession of His kingdom. There He remains till the last day, "Wonderful, Counsellor, The Mighty God, The Everlasting Father, The Prince of Peace."[7]

3. He ascended into heaven, that He might plead our cause with the Father; as it is said, "He ever liveth to make intercession for us."[8] Yet we must not suppose, that in leaving us He closed the gracious economy of His Incarnation, and withdrew the ministration of His incorruptible Manhood from His work of loving mercy towards us. "The Holy One of God" was ordained, not only to die for us, but also to be "the beginning" of a new "creation" unto holiness, in our sinful race; to refashion soul and body after His own likeness, that they might be "raised up together, and sit together in heavenly places in Christ Jesus." Blessed for ever be His Holy Name! before He went away, He remembered our necessity, and completed His work, bequeathing to us a special mode of approaching Him, a Holy Mystery, in which we receive (we know not how) the virtue of that Heavenly Body, which is the life of all that believe. This is the blessed Sacrament of the Eucharist, in which "Christ is evidently set forth crucified among us;" that we, feasting upon the Sacrifice, may be "partakers of the Divine Nature." Let us give heed lest we be in the number of those who "discern not the Lord's Body," and the "exceeding great and precious promises" which are made to those who partake it. And since there is some danger of this, I will here make some brief remarks concerning this great gift; and, pray God that our words and thoughts may accord to its unspeakable sacredness.

Christ says, "As the Father hath life in Himself, so hath He given also to the Son to have life in Himself;" and afterwards He says, "Because I live, ye shall live also."[9] It would seem then, that as Adam is the author of death to the whole race of men, so is Christ the Origin of immortality. When Adam ate the for-

[7] Is. ix.6.   [8] Heb. vii.25.   [9] John v.26; xiv.10.

bidden fruit, it was as a poison spreading through his whole
nature, soul and body; and thence through every one of his descendants. It was said to him, when he was placed in the garden,
"In the day that thou eatest thereof, thou shalt surely die;" and
we are told expressly, "in Adam *all* die." We all are born heirs to
that infection of nature which followed upon his fall. But we
are also told, "As in Adam all die, even so in Christ shall all be
made alive;" and the same law of God's providence is maintained in both cases. Adam spreads poison; Christ diffuses life
eternal. Christ communicates life to us, one by one, by means
of that holy and incorrupt nature which He assumed for our
redemption; how, we know not; still, though by an unseen,
surely by a real communication of Himself. Therefore St. Paul
says, that "the last Adam was made" not merely "a living soul,"
but "a *quickening*" or life-giving "Spirit," as being "the Lord
from heaven." [10] Again, in His own gracious words, He is "the
Bread of life." "The Bread of God is He which cometh down
from heaven, and giveth life unto the world;" or, as He says
more plainly, "I am the Bread which came down from heaven;"
"I am that Bread of life;" "I am the living Bread which came
down from heaven; if any man eat of this bread, he shall live for
ever: and the Bread that I will give is My flesh, which I will give
for the life of the world." And again, still more clearly, "Whoso
eateth My flesh, and drinketh My blood, hath eternal life; and I
will raise him up at the last day." [11] Why should this communion with Him be thought inedible, mysterious and sacred
as it is, when we know from the Gospel how marvellously He
wrought, in the days of His humiliation, towards those who
approached Him? We are told on one occasion, "the whole
multitude sought to touch Him; for there went *virtue* out of
Him, and healed them all." Again, when the woman with the
issue of blood touched Him, He "immediately knew that virtue
had gone out of Him." [12] Such grace was invisible, known only
by the cure it effected, as in the case of the woman. Let us not
doubt, though we do not sensibly approach Him, that He can
still give us the virtue of His purity and incorruption, as He has
promised, and in a more heavenly and spiritual manner, than
"in the days of His flesh;" in a way which does not remove the
mere ailments of this temporal state, but sows the seed of eternal life in body and soul. Let us not deny Him the glory of His

---

[10] Gen. ii.17; 1 Cor. xv.22, 45, 47.   [11] John vi.33–54.
[12] Luke vi.19; Mark v.30. *Vide* Knox on the Eucharist, Remains,
vol. ii.

life-giving holiness, that diffusive grace which is the renovation
of our whole race, a spirit quick and powerful and piercing, so
as to leaven the whole mass of human corruption, and make it
live. He is the first-fruits of the Resurrection: we follow Him
each in his own order, as we are hallowed by His inward presence. And in this sense, among others, Christ, in the Scripture
phrase, is "formed in us;" that is, the communication is made to
us of His new nature, which sanctifies the soul, and makes the
body immortal. In like manner we pray in the Service of the
Communion that "our sinful bodies may be made clean by His
body, and our souls washed through His most precious blood;
and that we may evermore dwell in Him and He in us."

Such then is our risen Saviour in Himself and towards us:—
conceived by the Holy Ghost; holy from the womb; dying, but
abhorring corruption; rising again the third day by His own
inherent life; exalted as the Son of God and Son of man, to raise
us after Him; and filling us incomprehensibly with His immortal nature, till we become like Him; filling us with a spiritual
life which may expel the poison of the tree of knowledge, and
restore us to God. How wonderful a work of grace! Strange it
was that Adam should be our death, but stranger still and very
gracious, that God Himself should be our life, by means of that
human tabernacle which He has taken on Himself.

O blessed day of the Resurrection, which of old time was
called the Queen of Festivals, and raised among Christians an
anxious, nay contentious diligence duly to honour it! Blessed
day, once only passed in sorrow, when the Lord actually rose,
and the disciples believed not; but ever since a day of joy to the
faith and love of the Church! In ancient times, Christians all
over the world began it with a morning salutation. Each man
said to his neighbour, "Christ is risen;" and his neighbour answered him, "Christ is risen indeed, and hath appeared unto
Simon." Even to Simon, the coward disciple who denied Him
thrice, Christ is risen; even to us, who long ago vowed to obey
Him, and have yet so often denied Him before men, so often
taken part with sin, and followed the world, when Christ called
us an other way. "Christ is risen indeed, and hath appeared to
Simon!" to Simon Peter the favoured Apostle, on whom the
Church is built, Christ has appeared. He has appeared to His
Holy Church first of all, and in the Church He dispenses blessings, such as the world knows not of. Blessed are they if they
knew their blessedness, who are allowed, as we are, week after
week, and Festival after Festival, to seek and find in that Holy
Church the Saviour of their souls! Blessed are they beyond

language or thought, to whom it is vouchsafed to receive those
tokens of His love, which cannot otherwise be gained by man,
the pledges and means of His special presence, in the Sacrament
of His Supper; who are allowed to eat and drink the food of
immortality, and receive life from the bleeding side of the Son
of God! Alas! by what strange coldness of heart, or perverse superstition is it, that any one called Christian keeps away from
that heavenly ordinance? Is it not very grievous that there
should be any one who fears to share in the greatest conceivable
blessing which could come upon sinful men? What in truth is
that fear, but unbelief, a slavish sin-loving obstinacy, if it leads a
man to go year after year without the spiritual sustenance
which God has provided for him? Is it wonderful that, as time
goes on, he should learn deliberately to doubt of the grace
therein given? that he should no longer look upon the Lord's
Supper as a heavenly feast, or the Lord's Minister who consecrates it as a chosen vessel, or that Holy Church in which he
ministers as a Divine Ordinance, to be cherished as the parting
legacy of Christ to a sinful world? Is it wonderful that seeing he
sees not, and hearing he hears not; and that, lightly regarding
all the gifts of Christ, he feels no reverence for the treasure-
house wherein they are stored?

But we, who trust that so far we are doing God's will, inasmuch as we are keeping to those ordinances and rules which His
Son has left us, we may humbly rejoice in this day, with a joy
the world cannot take away, any more than it can understand.
Truly, in this time of rebuke and blasphemy, we cannot but be
sober and subdued in our rejoicing; yet our peace and joy may
be deeper and fuller even for that very seriousness. For nothing
can harm those who bear Christ within them. Trial or temptation, time of tribulation, time of wealth, pain, bereavement,
anxiety, sorrow, the insults of the enemy, the loss of worldly
goods, nothing can "separate us from the love of God, which is
in Christ Jesus our Lord." [13] This the Apostle told us long since;
but we, in this age of the world, over and above his word, have
the experience of many centuries for our comfort. We have his
own history to show us how Christ within us is stronger than
the world around us, and will prevail. We have the history of all
his fellow-sufferers, of all the Confessors and Martyrs of early
times and since, to show us that Christ's arm "is not shortened,
that it cannot save;" that faith and love have a real abiding-place
on earth; that, come what will, His grace is sufficient for His

[13] Rom. viii.39.

Church, and His strength made perfect in weakness; that, "even to old age, and to hoar hairs, He will carry and deliver" her; that, in whatever time the powers of evil give challenge, Martyrs and Saints will start forth again, and rise from the dead, as plentiful as though they had never been before, even "the souls of them that were beheaded for the witness of Jesus, and for the Word of God, and which had not worshipped the beast, neither his image, neither had received his mark upon their foreheads, or in their hands." [14]

Meantime, while Satan only threatens, let us possess our hearts in patience; try to keep quiet; aim at obeying God, in all things, little as well as great; do the duties of our calling which lie before us, day by day; and "take no thought for the morrow, for sufficient unto the day is the evil thereof." [15]

---

[14] Rev. xx.4.   [15] Matt. vi.34.

SAVING KNOWLEDGE

(Monday in Easter Week)

*"Hereby do we know that we know Him, if we keep His
commandments."*—1 John ii.3.

To know God and Christ, in Scripture language, seems to
mean to live under the conviction of His presence, who is
to our bodily eyes unseen. It is, in fact, to have faith, according
to St. Paul's account of faith, as the substance and evidence of
what is invisible. It is faith, but not faith such as a Heathen
might have, but Gospel faith; for only in the Gospel has God so
revealed Himself, as to allow of that kind of faith which may be
called, in a special manner, knowledge. The faith of Heathens
was *blind*; it was more or less a moving forward in the darkness,
with hand and foot;—therefore the Apostle says, "if haply they
might *feel* after Him." [1] But the Gospel is a *manifestation*, and
therefore addressed to the eyes of our mind. Faith is the same
principle as before, but with the opportunity of acting through
a more certain and satisfactory sense. We recognise objects by
the eye at once; but not by the touch. We know them when we
see them, but scarcely till then. Hence it is, that the New Testament says so much on the subject of spiritual knowledge. For
instance, St. Paul prays that the Ephesians may receive "the
spirit of wisdom and revelation in the knowledge of Christ, the
eyes of their understanding being enlightened;" and he says,
that the Colossians had "put on the new man, which is renewed
in knowledge, after the image of Him that created him." St.
Peter, in like manner, addresses his brethren with the salutation
of "Grace and peace, through the knowledge of God, and of
Jesus our Lord;" according to the declaration of our Lord Himself, "This is life eternal, to know Thee, the only true God, and
Jesus Christ whom Thou hast sent." [2] Not of course as if Christian faith had not still abundant exercise for the other senses (so

---

[1] Acts xvii.27.
[2] Eph. i.17, 18; Col. iii.10; 2 Pet. i.2; John xviii.3.

to call them) of the soul; but that the eye is its peculiar sense, by which it is distinguished from the faith of Heathens, nay, I may add, of Jews.

It is plain what is the object of spiritual sight which is vouchsafed us in the Gospel,—"God manifest in the Flesh." He who was before unseen has shown Himself in Christ; not merely displayed His glory, as (for instance) in what is called a providence, or visitation, or in miracles, or in the actions and character of inspired men, but really He Himself has come upon earth, and has been seen of men in human form. In the same kind of sense, in which we should say we saw a servant of His, Apostle or Prophet, though we could not see his soul, so man has seen the Invisible God; and we have the history of His sojourn among His creatures in the Gospels.

To know God is life eternal, and to believe in the Gospel manifestation of Him is to know Him; but how are we to "know that we know Him?" How are we to be sure that we are not mistaking some dream of our own for the true and clear Vision? How can we tell we are not like gazers upon a distant prospect through a misty atmosphere, who mistake one object for another? The text answers us clearly and intelligibly; though some Christians have recourse to other proofs of it, or will not have patience to ask themselves the question. They say they are quite certain that they have true faith; for faith carries with it its own evidence, and admits of no mistaking, the true spiritual conviction being unlike all others. On the other hand, St. John says, "Hereby do we know that we know Him, if we keep His commandments." Obedience is the test of Faith.

Thus the whole duty and work of a Christian is made up of these two parts, Faith and Obedience; "looking unto Jesus," the Divine Object as well as Author of our faith, and acting according to His will. Not as if a certain frame of mind, certain notions, affections, feelings, and tempers, were not a necessary condition of a saving state; but, so it is, the Apostle does not insist upon it, as if it were sure to follow, if our hearts do but grow into these two chief objects, the view of God in Christ and the diligent aim to obey Him in our conduct.

I conceive that we are in danger, in this day, of insisting on neither of these as we ought regarding all true and careful consideration of the Object of faith, as barren orthodoxy, technical subtlety, and the like, and all due earnestness about good works as a mere cold and formal morality; and, instead, making religion, or rather (for this is the point) making the test of our being religious, to consist in our having what is called a spiritual state of heart, to the comparative neglect of the Object from which it must arise, and the works in which it should issue. At this season, when we are especially engaged in considering the full triumph and manifestation of our Lord and Saviour, when He was "declared to be the Son of God with power, by the resurrection from the dead," it may be appropriate to make some remarks on an error which goes far to deprive us of the benefit of His condescension.

St. John speaks of knowing Christ and of keeping His commandments, as the two great departments of religious duty and blessedness. To know Christ is (as I have said) to discern the Father of all, as manifested through His Only-begotten Son Incarnate. In the natural world we have glimpses, frequent and startling, of His glorious Attributes; of His power, wisdom, and goodness; of His holiness, His fearful judgments, His long remembrance of evil, His long-suffering towards sinners, and His strange encompassing mercy at times when we least looked for it. But to us mortals, who live for a day, and see but an arm's length, such disclosures are like reflections of a prospect in a broken mirror; they do not enable us in any comfortable sense to know God. They are such as faith may use indeed, but hardly enjoy. This then was one among the benefits of Christ's coming, that the Invisible God was then revealed in the form and history of man, revealed in those respects in which sinners most required to know Him, and nature spoke least distinctly, as a Holy yet Merciful Governor of His creatures. And thus the Gospels, which contain the memorials of this wonderful grace, are our principal treasures. They may be called the text of the Revelation; and the Epistles, especially St. Paul's, are as comments upon it, unfolding and illustrating it in its various parts, raising history into doctrine, ordinances into sacraments, detached words or actions into principles, and thus everywhere dutifully preaching His Person, work, and will. St. John is both Prophet and Evangelist, recording and commenting on the Ministry of his Lord. Still, in every case, He is the chief Prophet of the Church, and His Apostles do but explain His words and actions; according to His own account of the guidance promised to them, that it should "glorify" Him. The like service is ministered to Him by the Creeds and doctrinal expositions of the early Church, which we retain in our Services. They speak of no ideal being, such as the imagination alone contemplates, but of the very Son of God, whose life is recorded in the Gospels. Thus every part of the Dispensation tends to the manifestation of Him who is its centre.

Turning from Him to ourselves, we find a short rule given us,
"If ye love Me, keep My commandments." "He that saith he
abideth in Him, ought himself also so to walk, even as He
walked." "If ye then be risen with Christ, seek those things
which are above, where Christ sitteth on the right hand of
God."[3] This is all that is put upon us, difficult indeed to perform, but easy to understand; all that is put upon us,—and for
this plain reason, because Christ has done everything else. He
has freely chosen us, died for us, regenerated us, and now ever
liveth for us; what remains? Simply that we should do as He has
done to us, showing forth His glory by good works. Thus a correct (or as we commonly call it), an orthodox faith and an obedient life, is the whole duty of man. And so, most surely, it has
ever been accounted. Look into the records of the early
Church, or into the writings of our own revered bishops and
teachers, and see whether this is not the sum total of religion,
according to the symbols of it in which children are catechized,
the Creed, the Lord's Prayer, and the Ten Commandments.

However, it is objected that such a view of religious duty encourages self-deception; that a man who does no more than
believe aright, and keep God's commandments, is what is called
a formalist; that his heart is not interested in the matter, his
affections remain unrenewed; and that, till a change takes place
there, all the faith and all the obedience which mind can conceive are but external, and avail nothing; that to his heart therefore we must make our appeal, that we must bid him search
himself, examine his motives, look narrowly lest he rest upon
himself, and be sure that his feelings and thoughts are spiritual
before he takes to himself any comfort. The merits of this view
of religion shall be considered hereafter; at present, let us take it
merely in the light of an objection to what has been already
stated. I ask then in reply, how is a man to know that his motives
and affections are right except by their fruits? Can they possibly
be their own evidence? Are they like colours, which a man
knows at once without test or calculation? Is not every feeling
and opinion, of one colour or another, fair or unpleasant, in
each man's own judgment, according to the centre light which
is set up in his soul? Is not the light that is in a man sometimes
even darkness, sometimes twilight, and sometimes of this hue
or that, tinging every part of himself with its own peculiarity?
How then is it possible that a man can duly examine his feelings
and affections by the light within him? how can he accurately

[3] John xiv.15; 1 John ii.6; Col. iii.1.

decide upon their character, whether Christian or not? It is necessary then that he go out of himself in order to assay and ascertain the nature of the principles which govern him; that is, he must have recourse to his works, and compare them with Scripture, as the only evidence to himself, whether or not his heart is perfect with God. It seems, therefore, that the proposed inquiry into the workings of a man's mind means nothing at all, comes to no issue, leaves us where it found us, unless we adopt the notion (which is seldom however openly maintained), that religious faith is its own evidence.

On the other hand, deeds of obedience are an intelligible evidence, nay, the sole evidence possible, and, on the whole, a satisfactory evidence of the reality of our faith. I do not say that this or that good work tells anything; but a course of obedience says much. Various deeds, done in different departments of duty, support and attest each other. Did a man act merely a bold and firm part, he would have cause to say to himself, "Perhaps all this is mere pride and obstinacy." Were he merely yielding and forgiving,—he might be indulging a natural indolence of mind. Were he merely industrious,—this might consist with ill-temper, or selfishness. Did he merely fulfil the duties of his temporal calling,—he would have no proof that he had given his heart to God at all. Were he merely regular at Church and Holy Communion,—many a man is such who has a lax conscience, who is not scrupulously fair-dealing, or is censorious, or niggardly. Is he what is called a domestic character, amiable, affectionate, fond of his family? let him beware lest he put wife and children in the place of God who gave them. Is he only temperate, sober, chaste, correct in his language? it may arise from mere dulness and insensibility, or may consist with spiritual pride. Is he cheerful and obliging? it may arise from youthful spirits and ignorance of the world. Does he choose his friends by a strictly orthodox rule? he may be harsh and uncharitable; or, is he zealous and serviceable in defending the Truth? still he may be unable to condescend to men of low estate, to rejoice with those who rejoice, and to weep with those who weep. No one is without some good quality or other: Balaam had a scruple about misrepresenting God's message, Saul was brave, Joab was loyal, the Bethel Prophet reverenced God's servants, the witch of Endor was hospitable; and therefore, of course, no one good deed or disposition is the criterion of a spiritual mind. Still, on the other hand, there is no one of its characteristics which has not its appropriate outward evidence; and in proportion as these external acts are multiplied and varied, so does the evidence of it become stronger and more consoling. General conscientiousness is the only assurance we can have of possessing it; and at this we must aim, determining to obey God consistently, with a jealous carefulness about all things, little and great. This is, in Scripture language, to "serve God with a perfect heart;" as you will see at once, if you compare the respective reformations of Jehu and Josiah. As far then as a man has reason to hope that he is *consistent*, so far may he humbly trust that he has true faith. To be consistent, to "walk in all the ordinances of the Lord blameless," is his one business; still, all along looking reverently towards the Great Object of faith, the Father, the Son, and the Holy Ghost, Three Persons, One God, and the Son Incarnate for our salvation. Certainly he will have enough to direct his course by, with God in his eye, and his work in his hand, though he forbear curious experiments about his sensations and emotions; and, if it be objected that an evidence from works is but a cold comfort, as being at best but faint and partial, I reply, that, after all, it is more than sinners have a right to ask,—that if it be little at first, it grows with our growth in grace,—and moreover, that such an evidence, more than any other, throws us in faith upon the loving kindness and meritorious sufferings of our Saviour. Surely, even our best doings have that taint of sinfulness pervading them, which will remind us ever, while we regard them, where our True Hope is lodged. Men are satisfied with themselves, not when they attempt, but when they neglect the details of duty. Disobedience blinds the conscience; obedience makes it keen-sighted and sensitive. The more we *do*, the more shall we trust in Christ; and that surely is no morose doctrine, which, after giving us whatever evidence of our safety can be given, leads us to soothe our selfish restlessness, and forget our fears, in the vision of the Incarnate Son of God.

Lastly, it may be objected, that, since many deeds of obedience are themselves acts of the mind, to do them well we must necessarily examine our feelings; that we cannot pray, for instance, without reflecting on ourselves as we use the words of prayer, and keeping our thoughts upon God; that we cannot repress anger or impatience, or cherish loving and forgiving thoughts, without searching and watching ourselves. But such an argument rests on a misconception of what I have been saying. All I would maintain is, that our duty lies in acts,—acts of course of every kind, acts of the mind, as well as of the tongue, or of the hand; but anyhow, it lies mainly in acts; it does not directly lie in moods or feelings. He who aims at praying well, loving sincerely, disputing meekly, as the respective duties occur, is wise and religious; but he who aims vaguely and generally at being in a spiritual frame of mind, is entangled in a deceit of words, which gain a meaning only by being made mischievous. Let us do our duty as it presents itself; this is the secret of true faith and peace. We have power over our deeds, under God's grace; we have no direct power over our habits. Let us but secure our actions, as God would have them, and our habits will follow. Suppose a religious man, for instance, in the society of strangers; he takes things as they come, discourses naturally, gives his opinion soberly, and does good according to each opportunity of good. His heart is in his work, and his thoughts rest without effort on his God and Saviour. This is the way of a Christian; he leaves it to the ill-instructed to endeavour after a (so-called) spiritual frame of mind amid the bustle of life, which has no existence except in attempt and profession. True spiritual-mindedness is unseen by man, like the soul itself, of which it is a quality; and as the soul is known by its operations, so it is known by its fruits.

I will add too, that the office of self-examination lies rather in detecting what is bad in us than in ascertaining what is good. No harm can follow from contemplating our sins, so that we keep Christ before us, and attempt to overcome them; such a review of self will but lead to repentance and faith. And, while it does this, it will undoubtedly be moulding our hearts into a higher and more heavenly state;—but still indirectly;—just as the mean is attained in action or art, not by directly contemplating and aiming at it, but negatively, by avoiding extremes.

To conclude. The essence of Faith is to look out of ourselves; now, consider what manner of a believer he is who imprisons himself in his own thoughts, and rests on the workings of his own mind, and thinks of his Saviour as an idea of his imagination, instead of putting self aside, and living upon Him who speaks in the Gospels.

So much then, by way of suggestion, upon the view of Religious Faith, which has ever been received in the Church Catholic, and which, doubtless, is saving. To-morrow I propose to speak more particularly of that other system, to which these latter times have given birth.

SELF-CONTEMPLATION

(Tuesday in Easter Week)

"Looking unto Jesus, the Author and Finisher of our faith."
—Heb. xii.2.

S URELY it is our duty ever to look off ourselves, and to look
unto Jesus, that is, to shun the contemplation of our own
feelings, emotions, frame and state of mind, as if that were the
main business of religion, and to leave these mainly to be secured in their fruits. Some remarks were made yesterday upon
this "more excellent" and Scriptural way of conducting ourselves, as it has ever been received in the Church; now let us
consider the merits of the rule for holy living, which the fashion of this day would substitute for it.

Instead of looking off to Jesus, and thinking little of ourselves, it is at present thought necessary, among the mixed
multitude of religionists, to examine the heart with a view of
ascertaining whether it is in a spiritual state or no. A spiritual
frame of mind is considered to be one in which the heinousness
of sin is perceived, our utter worthlessness, the impossibility of
our saving ourselves, the necessity of some Saviour, the sufficiency of our Lord Jesus Christ to be that Saviour, the unbounded riches of His love, the excellence and glory of His
work of Atonement, the freeness and fulness of His grace, the
high privilege of communion with Him in prayer, and the desirableness of walking with Him in all holy and loving obedience; all of them solemn truths, too solemn to be lightly
mentioned, but our hearty reception of which is scarcely
ascertainable by a direct inspection of our feelings. Moreover, if
one doctrine must be selected above the rest as containing the
essence of the truths, which (according to this system) are thus
vividly understood by the spiritual Christian, it is that of the
necessity of renouncing our own righteousness for the righteousness provided by our Lord and Saviour; which is considered, not as an elementary and simple principle (as it really is),
but as rarely and hardly acknowledged by any man, especially

repugnant to a certain (so-called) pride of heart, which is supposed to run through the whole race of Adam, and to lead every man instinctively to insist even before God on the proper merit of his good deeds; so that, to trust in Christ, is not merely the work of the Holy Spirit (as all good in our souls is), but is the especial and critical event which marks a man, as issuing from darkness, and sealed unto the privileges and inheritance of the sons of God. In other words, the doctrine of Justification by Faith is accounted to be the one cardinal point of the Gospel; and it is in vain to admit it readily as a clear Scripture truth (which it is), and to attempt to go on unto perfection; the very wish to pass forward is interpreted into a wish to pass over it, and the test of believing it at all, is in fact to insist upon no doctrine but it. And this peculiar mode of inculcating that great doctrine of the Gospel is a proof (if proof were wanting) that the persons who adopt it are not solicitous even about *it* on its own score merely, considered as (what is called) a dogma, but as ascertaining and securing (as they hope) a certain state of heart. For, not content with the simple admission of it on the part of another, they proceed to divide faith into its kinds, living and dead, and to urge against him, that the Truth may be held in a carnal and unrenewed mind, and that men may speak without real feelings and convictions. Thus it is clear they do not contend for the doctrine of Justification as a truth external to the mind, or article of faith, any more than for the doctrine of the Trinity. On the other hand, since they use the same language about dead and living faith, however exemplary the life and conduct be of the individual under their review, they as plainly show that neither are the fruits of righteousness in their system an evidence of spiritual-mindedness, but that a something is to be sought for in the frame of mind itself. All this is not stated at present by way of objection, but in order to settle accurately what they mean to maintain. So now we have the two views of doctrine clearly before us:—the ancient and universal teaching of the Church, which insists on the Objects and fruits of faith, and considers the spiritual character of that faith itself sufficiently secured, if these are as they should be; and the method, now in esteem, of attempting instead to secure directly and primarily that "mind of the Spirit," which may savingly receive the truths, and fulfil the obedience of the Gospel. That such a spiritual temper is indispensable, is agreed on all hands. The simple question is, whether it is formed by the Holy Spirit immediately acting upon our minds, or, on the other hand, by our own particular acts (whether of faith or obedience), prompted, guided, and prospered by Him; whether it is ascertainable otherwise than by its fruits; whether such frames of mind as *are* directly ascertainable and profess to be spiritual, are not rather a delusion, a mere excitement, capricious feeling, fanatic fancy, and the like.—So much then by way of explanation.

1. Now, in the first place, this modern system certainly does disparage the revealed doctrines of the Gospel, however its more moderate advocates may shrink from admitting it. Considering a certain state of heart to be the main thing to be aimed at, they avowedly make the "truth as it is in Jesus," the definite Creed of the Church, secondary in their teaching and profession. They will defend themselves indeed from the appearance of undervaluing it, by maintaining that the existence of right religious affections is a security for sound views of doctrine. And this is abstractedly true;—but not true in the use they make of it: for they unhappily conceive that they can ascertain in each other the presence of these affections; and when they find men possessed of them (as they conceive), yet not altogether orthodox in their belief, then they relax a little, and argue that an admission of (what they call) the strict and technical niceties of doctrine, whether about the Consubstantiality of the Son or the Hypostatic Union, is scarcely part of the definition of a spiritual believer. In order to support this position, they lay it down as self-evident, that the main purpose of revealed doctrine is to affect the heart,—that that which does not seem to affect it does not affect it,—that what does not affect it, is unnecessary,—and that the circumstance that this or that person's heart seems rightly affected, is a sufficient warrant that such Articles as he may happen to reject, may safely be universally rejected, or at least are only accidentally important. Such principles, when once become familiar to the mind, induce a certain disproportionate attention to the doctrines connected with the work of Christ, in comparison of those which relate to His Person, from their more immediately interesting and exciting character; and carry on the more speculative and philosophical class to view the doctrines of Atonement and Sanctification as the essence of the Gospel, and to advocate them in the place of those "Heavenly Things" altogether, which, as theologically expressed, they have already assailed; and of which they now openly complain as mysteries for bondsmen, not Gospel consolations. The last and most miserable stage of this false wisdom is, to deny that in matters of doctrine there is any one sense of Scripture such, that it is true and all others false; to make the Gospel of Truth (so far) a revelation of

words and a dead letter; to consider that inspiration speaks merely of divine operations, not of Persons; and that that is truth to each, which each man thinks to be true, so that one man may say that Christ is God, another deny His pre-existence, yet each have received the Truth according to the peculiar constitution of his own mind, the Scripture doctrine having no real independent substantive meaning. Thus the system under consideration tends legitimately to obliterate the great Objects brought to light in the Gospel and to darken what I called yesterday the eye of faith,—to throw us back into the vagueness of Heathenism, when men only felt after the Divine Presence, and thus to frustrate the design of Christ's Incarnation, so far as it is a manifestation of the Unseen Creator.

2. On the other hand, the necessity of obedience in order to salvation does not suffer less from the upholders of this modern system than the articles of the Creed. They argue, and truly, that if faith is living, works must follow; but mistaking a following *in order of conception* for a following *in order of time*, they conclude that faith ever comes first, and works afterwards; and therefore, that faith must first be secured, and that, by some means in which works have no share. Thus, instead of viewing works as the concomitant development and evidence, and instrumental cause, as well as the subsequent result of faith, they lay all the stress upon the direct creation, in their minds, of faith and spiritual-mindedness, which they consider to consist in certain emotions and desires, because they can form abstractedly no better or truer notion of those qualities. Then, instead of being "careful to maintain good works," they proceed to take it for granted, that since they have attained faith (as they consider), works will follow without their trouble as a matter of course. Thus the wise are taken in their own craftiness; they attempt to reason, and are overcome by sophisms. Had they kept to the Inspired Record, instead of reasoning, their way would have been clear; and, considering the serious exhortations to keeping God's commandments, with which all Scripture abounds, from Genesis to the Apocalypse, is it not a very grave question, which the most charitable among Churchmen must put to himself, whether these random expounders of the Blessed Gospel are not risking a participation in the woe denounced against those who preach any other doctrine besides that delivered unto us, or who "take away from the words of the Book" of revealed Truth?

3. But still more evidently do they fall into this last imputation, when we consider how they are obliged to treat the Sacred

Volume altogether, in order to support the system they have adopted. Is it too much to say that, instead of attempting to harmonize Scripture with Scripture, much less referring to Antiquity to enable them to do so, they either drop altogether, or explain away, whole portions of the Bible, and those most sacred ones? How does the authority of the Psalms stand with their opinions, except at best by a forced figurative interpretation? And our Lord's discourses in the Gospels, especially the Sermon on the Mount, are they not virtually considered as chiefly important to the persons immediately addressed, and of inferior instructiveness to us now that the Spirit (as it is profanely said) is come? In short, is not the rich and varied Revelation of our merciful Lord practically reduced to a few chapters of St. Paul's Epistles, whether rightly (as they maintain) or (as we should say) perversely understood? If then the Romanists have added to the Word of God, is it not undeniable that there is a school of religionists among us who have taken from it?

4. I would remark, that the immediate tendency of these opinions is to undervalue ordinances as well as doctrines. The same argument evidently applies; for, if the renewed state of heart is (as it is supposed) attained, what matter whether Sacraments have or have not been administered? The notion of invisible grace and invisible privileges is, on this supposition, altogether superseded; that of communion with Christ is limited to the mere exercise of the affections in prayer and meditation,—to sensible effects; and he who considers he has already gained this one essential gift of grace (as he calls it), may plausibly inquire, after the fashion of the day, why he need wait upon ordinances which he has anticipated in his religious attainments,—which are but means to an end, which *he* has not to seek, even if they be not outward forms altogether,—and whether Christ will not accept at the last day all who believe, without inquiring if they were members of the Church, or were confirmed, or were baptized, or received the blessing of mere men who are "earthen vessels."

5. The foregoing remarks go to show the utterly unevangelical character of the system in question; unevangelic in the full sense of the word, whether by the Gospel be meant the inspired document of it, or the doctrines brought to light through it, or the Sacramental Institutions which are the gift of it, or the theology which interprets it, or the Covenant which is the basis of it. A few words shall now be added, to show the inherent mischief of the system as such; which I conceive to lie in its necessarily involving a continual self-contemplation and reference to

self, in all departments of conduct. He who aims at attaining
sound doctrine or right practice, more or less looks out of himself; whereas, in labouring after a certain frame of mind, there
is an habitual reflex action of the mind upon itself. That this is
really involved in the modern system, is evident from the very
doctrine principally insisted on by it; for, as if it were not
enough for a man to look up simply to Christ for salvation, it is
declared to be necessary that he should be able to recognise this
in himself, that he should define his own state of mind, confess
he is justified by faith alone, and explain what is meant by that
confession. Now, the truest obedience is indisputably that
which is done from love of God, without narrowly measuring
the magnitude or nature of the sacrifice involved in it. He who
has learned to give names to his thoughts and deeds, to appraise
them as if for the market, to attach to each its due measure of
commendation or usefulness, will soon involuntarily corrupt
his motives by pride or selfishness. A sort of self-approbation
will insinuate itself into his mind: so subtle as not at once to be
recognised by himself,—an habitual quiet self-esteem, leading
him to prefer his own views to those of others, and a secret, if
not avowed persuasion, that he is in a different state from the
generality of those around him. This is an incidental, though of
course not a necessary evil of religious journals; nay, of such
compositions as Ministerial duties involve. They lead those
who write them, in some respect or other, to a contemplation
of self. Moreover, as to religious journals, useful as they often
are, at the same time I believe persons find great difficulty,
while recording their feelings, in banishing the thought that
one day these good feeling will be known to the world, and are
thus insensibly led to modify and prepare their language as if for
a representation. Seldom indeed is any one in the *practice* of contemplating his better thoughts or doings without proceeding to
display them to others; and hence it is that it is so easy to discover a conceited man. When this is encouraged in the sacred
province of religion, it produces a certain unnatural solemnity
of manner, arising from a wish to be, nay, to appear spiritual,
which is at once very painful to beholders, and surely quite at
variance with our Saviour's rule of anointing our head and
washing our face, even when we are most self-abased in heart.
Another mischief arising from this self-contemplation is the
peculiar kind of selfishness (if I may use so harsh a term) which
it will be found to foster. They who make self instead of their
Maker the great object of their contemplation will naturally
exalt themselves. Without denying that the glory of God is the

great end to which all things are to be referred, they will be led to connect indissolubly His glory with their own certainty of salvation; and this partly accounts for its being so common to find rigid predestinarian views, and the exclusive maintenance of justification by Faith in the same persons. And for the same reason, the Scripture doctrines relative to the Church and its offices will be unpalatable to such persons; no one thing being so irreconcileable with another, as the system which makes a man's thoughts centre in himself, with that which directs them to a fountain of grace and truth, on which God has made him dependent.

And as self-confidence and spiritual pride are the legitimate results of these opinions in one set of persons, so in another they lead to a feverish anxiety about their religious state and prospects, and fears lest they are under the reprobation of their All-merciful Saviour. It need scarcely be said that a contemplation of self is a frequent attendant, and a frequent precursor of a deranged state of the mental powers.

To conclude. It must not be supposed from the foregoing remarks that I am imputing all the consequences enumerated to every one who holds the main doctrine from which they legitimately follow. Many men zealously maintain principles which they never follow out in their own minds, or after a time silently discard, except as far as words go, but which are sure to receive a full development in the history of any school or party of men which adopts them. Considered thus, as the characteristics of a school, the principles in question are doubtless antichristian; for they destroy all positive doctrine, all ordinances, all good works; they foster pride, invite hypocrisy, discourage the weak, and deceive most fatally, while they profess to be the especial antidotes to self-deception. We have seen these effects of them two centuries since in the history of the English Branch of the Church; for what we know, a more fearful triumph is still in store for them. But, however that may be, let not the watchmen of Jerusalem fail to give timely warning of the approaching enemy, or to acquit themselves of all cowardice or compliance as regards it. Let them prefer the Old Commandment, as it has been from the beginning, to any novelties of man, recollecting Christ's words, "Blessed is he that watcheth, and keepeth his garments, lest he walk naked, and they see his shame."[1]

---

[1] Rev. xvi. 15.

RELIGIOUS COWARDICE

(The Feast of St. Mark the Evangelist)

"Lift up the hands which hang down, and the feeble knees."
—Heb. xii.12.

THE chief points of St. Mark's history are these:—first that he was sister's-son to Barnabas, and taken with him and St. Paul on their first apostolical journey; next, that after a short time he deserted them and returned to Jerusalem; then, that after an interval, he was St. Peter's assistant at Rome, and composed his Gospel there principally from the accounts which he received from that Apostle; lastly, that he was sent by him to Alexandria, in Egypt, where he founded one of the strictest and most powerful churches of the primitive times.

The points of *contrast* in his history are as follows:—that first he abandoned the cause of the Gospel as soon as danger appeared; afterwards, he proved himself, not merely an ordinary Christian, but a most resolute and exact servant of God, founding and ruling that strictest Church of Alexandria.

And the *instrument* of this change was, as it appears the influence of St. Peter, a fit restorer of a timid and backsliding disciple.

The *encouragement* which we derive from these circumstances in St. Mark's history, is, that the feeblest among us may through God's grace become strong. And the *warning* to be drawn from it is, to distrust ourselves; and again, not to despise weak brethren, or to despair of them, but to bear their burdens and help them forward, if so be we may restore them. Now, let us attentively consider the subject thus brought before us.

Some men are naturally impetuous and active; others love quiet and readily yield. The over-earnest must be sobered, and the indolent must be roused. The history of Moses supplies us with an instance of a proud and rash spirit, tamed down to an extreme gentleness of deportment. In the greatness of the change wrought in him, when from a fierce, though honest, avenger of his brethren, he became the meekest of men on the

earth, he evidences the power of faith, the influence of the
Spirit on the heart. St. Mark's history affords a specimen of the
other, and still rarer change, from timidity to boldness. Difficult as it is to subdue the more violent passions, yet I believe it to
be still more difficult to overcome a tendency to sloth, cowardice, and despondency. These evil dispositions cling about a
man, and weigh him down. They are minute chains, binding
him on every side to the earth, so that he cannot even turn himself or make an effort to rise. It would seem as if right principles
had yet to be planted in the indolent mind; whereas violent and
obstinate tempers had already something of the nature of firmness and zeal in them, or rather what will become so with care,
exercise, and God's blessing. Besides, the events of life have a
powerful influence in sobering the ardent or self-confident
temper. Disappointments, pain, anxiety, advancing years, bring
with them some natural wisdom as a matter of course; and,
though such tardy improvement bespeaks but a weak faith, yet
we may believe that the Holy Ghost often blesses these means,
however slowly and imperceptibly. On the other hand, these
same circumstances do but increase the defects of the timid and
irresolute, who are made more indolent, selfish, and fainthearted by advancing years, and find a sort of sanction of their
unworthy caution in their experience of the vicissitudes of life.

St. Mark's change, therefore, may be considered even more
astonishing in its nature than that of the Jewish Lawgiver. "By
faith," he was "out of weakness made strong," and becomes a
memorial of the more glorious and marvelous gifts of the last
and spiritual Dispensation.

Observe in what St. Mark's weakness lay. There is a sudden
defection, which arises from self-confidence. Such was St.
Peter's. He had trusted too much to his mere good feelings; he
was honest and sincere, and he thought that he could do what
he wished to do. How far apart from each other are to wish and
to do! yet we are apt to confuse them. Sometimes indeed earnest desire of an object will by a sudden impulse surmount difficulties, and succeed without previous practice. Enthusiasm
certainly does wonders in this way; just as men of weakly
frames will sometimes from extreme excitement inflict blows
of incredible power. And sometimes eagerness sets us on beginning to exert ourselves; and, the first obstacles being thus removed, we go on as a matter of course with comparatively small
labour. All this, being from time to time witnessed, impresses
us with a conviction, unknown to ourselves, that a sanguine
temper is the main condition of success in any work. And

when, in our lonely imaginings, we fancy ourselves taking a strenuous part in some great undertaking, or when we really see others playing the man, so very easy does heroism seem to be, that we cannot admit the possibility of our failing, should circumstances call us to any difficult duty. St. Peter thought that he could preserve his integrity, because he wished to do so; and he fell, from ignorance of the difficulty of doing what he wished.

In St. Mark's history, however, we have no evidence of self-confidence; rather, we may discern in it the state of multitudes at the present day, who proceed through life with a certain sense of religion on their minds, who have been brought up well and know the Truth, who acquit themselves respectably while danger is at a distance, but disgrace their profession when brought into any unexpected trial. His mother was a woman of influence among the Christians at Jerusalem; his mother's brother, Barnabas, was an eminent Apostle. Doubtless he had received a religious education; and, as being the friend of Apostles and in the bosom of the pure Church of Christ, he had the best models of sanctity before his eyes, the clearest teaching, the fullest influences of grace. He was shielded from temptation. The time came when his real proficiency in faith and obedience was to be tried. Paul and Barnabas were sent forth to preach to the Heathen; and they took Mark with them as an attendant. First they sailed to Cyprus, the native place of Barnabas: they travelled about it, and then crossed over to the main land. This seems to have been their first entrance upon an unknown country. Mark was discouraged at the prospect of danger, and returned to Jerusalem.

Now, who does not see that such a character as this, such a trial, and such a fall, belong to other days, besides those of the Apostles? Or rather, to put the question to us more closely, who will deny that there are multitudes in the Church at present, who have no evidence to themselves of more than that passive faith and virtue, which in Mark's case proved so unequal even to a slight trial? Who has not some misgivings of heart, lest, in times such as these, when Christian firmness is so little tried, his own loyalty to his Saviour's cause be perchance no truer or firmer than that of the sister's-son of a great Apostle? When the Church is at peace, as it has long been in this country, when public order is preserved in the community, and the rights of person and property secured, there is extreme danger lest we judge ourselves by what is without us, not by what is within. We take for granted we are Christians, because we have been taught aright, and are regular in our attendance upon the Christian ordinances. But, great privilege and duty as it is to use the means of grace, reading and prayer are not enough; nor, by themselves will they ever make us real Christians. They will give us right knowledge and good feelings, but not firm faith and resolute obedience. Christians, such as Mark, will abound in a prosperous Church; and, should trouble come, they will be unprepared for it. They have so long been accustomed to external peace that they do not like to be persuaded that danger is at hand. They settle it in their imagination that they are to live and die undisturbed. They look at the world's events, as they express it, *cheerfully*, and argue themselves into self-deception. Next, they make concessions, to fulfil their own predictions and wishes; and surrender the Christian cause, that unbelievers may not commit themselves to an open attack upon it. Some of them are men of cultivated and refined taste; and these shrink from the rough life of pilgrims, to which they are called, as something strange and extravagant. They consider those who take a simpler view of the duties and prospects of the Church to be enthusiastic, rash, and intemperate, or perverse-minded. To speak plainly, a state of persecution is not (what is familiarly called) their *element*; they cannot breathe in it. Alas! how different from the Apostle, who had learned in whatsoever state he was, therewith to be content, and who was all things to all men. If then there be times when we have grown thus torpid from long security, and are tempted to prefer the treasures of Egypt to the reproach of Christ, what can we do, what ought we to do, but to pray God in some way or other to try the very heart of the Church, and to afflict us here rather than hereafter? Dreadful as is the prospect of Satan's temporary triumph, fierce as are the horsehoofs of his riders, and detestable as is the cause for which they battle, yet better such anguish should come upon us, than that the recesses of our heritage should be the hiding-places of a self-indulgent spirit and the schools of luke-warmness. May God arise and shake terribly the earth (though it be an awful prayer), *rather* than the double-minded should lie hid among us, and souls be lost by present ease! Let Him arise, if there be no alternative, and chasten us with His sweet discipline, as our hearts may best bear it; bringing our sins out in this world, that we be not condemned in the day of the Lord; shaming us here, reproving us by the mouth of His servants, then restoring us, and leading us on by a better way to a truer and holier hope! Let Him winnow us, till the chaff be clean removed! though, in thus invoking Him, we know not what we ask, and, feeling the end itself to be good, yet cannot worthily estimate the fearfulness of that chastisement which we so freely speak about. Doubtless we do not, cannot measure the terrors of the Lord's judgments; we use words cheaply. Still, it cannot be wrong to use them, seeing they are the best offering we can make to God; and, so that we beg Him the while to lead us on, and give us strength to bear the trial according as it opens upon us. So may we issue Evangelists for timid deserters of the cause of truth; speaking the words of Christ, and showing forth His life and death; rising strong from our sufferings, and building up the Church in the strictness and zeal of those who despise this life except as it leads to another.

Lastly, let us not, from an excited fancy and a vain longing after the glories of other days, forget the advantages which we have. No need to have the troubles of Apostles in order to attain their faith. Even in the quietest times we may rise to high holiness, if we improve the means given us. Trials come when we forget mercies,—to remind us of them, and to fit us to enjoy and use them suitably.

THE GOSPEL WITNESSES

(The Feast of St. Philip and St. James, the Apostles)

"In the mouth of two or three witnesses shall every word be established."—2 Cor. xiii.1.

IT has pleased Almighty God, in His great mercy, to give us accumulated evidence of the truth of the Gospel; to send out His Witnesses again and again, Prophet after Prophet, Apostle after Apostle, miracle after miracle, that reason might be brought into captivity, as well as faith rewarded, by the fulness of His revelations. The double Festival which we are now celebrating, reminds us of this. Our Service is this day distinguished by the commemoration of two Apostles, who are associated together in our minds in nothing except in their being Apostles, in both of them being Witnesses, separate Witnesses of the life, death, and resurrection of Christ. Thus this union, however originating, of the Feast Days of Apostles, who are not especially connected in Scripture, will serve to remind us of the diversity and number of the Witnesses by whom one and the same Sacred Truth has been delivered to us.

But, further than this. Even the twelve Apostles, many as they were, form not the whole company of the Witnesses vouchsafed to us. In order more especially to confirm to us, that the Word has really become incarnate, and has sojourned among men, another distinct Witness is vouchsafed to us in the person of St. Paul. What could be needed beyond the preaching of the Twelve? they all were attendants upon Christ, they had heard His words, they had imbibed His Spirit; and, as agreeing one and all in the matter of their testimony, they afforded full evidence to those who required it, that, though their Master wrote not His Gospel for us with His own finger, nevertheless we have it whole and entire. Yet He did more than this. When the time came for publishing it to the world at large, while He gradually initiated their minds into the full graciousness of the New Covenant, as reaching to Gentile as well as Jew, He raised up to Himself, by direct miracle and inspiration, a fresh and independent Witness of it from among His persecutors; so that from that time the Dispensation had (as it were) a second beginning, and went forward upon a twofold foundation, the teaching, on the one hand, of the Apostles of the Circumcision, and of St. Paul on the other. Two schools of Christian doctrine forthwith existed,—if I may use the word "school," to denote a difference, not of doctrine itself, but of history, between the Apostles. Of the Gentile school, were St. Luke, St. Clement, and others, followers of St. Paul. Of the School of the Circumcision, St. Peter, and still more, St. John; St. James, and we may add, St. Philip. St. James is known to belong to the latter, in his history as Bishop of Jerusalem; and, though little is known of St. Philip, yet what is known of him indicates that he too is to be ranked with St. John, whom he followed (as history informs us), in observing the Jewish rule of celebrating the Easter Feast, and not the tradition of St. Peter and St. Paul. I propose upon this Festival to set before you some considerations which arise out of this view of the Scripture history.

Christianity was, and was not, a new religion, when first preached to the world; it seemed to supersede, but it was merely the fulfilment, the due development and maturity, of the Jewish Law, which, in one sense, vanished away, in another, was perpetuated for ever. This need not be proved here; I will but refer you, by way of illustration, to the language of Prophecy, as (for instance) to the forty-ninth chapter of the Book of Isaiah, in which the Jewish Church is comforted in her afflictions by the promise of her propagation and triumphs (that is, in her Christian form) among the Gentiles. "Zion said, The Lord hath forsaken me, and my Lord hath forgotten me. Can a woman forget her sucking child, that she should not have compassion on the son of her womb? Yea, they may forget, yet will I not forget thee. . . . Lift up thine eyes round about, and behold; all these gather themselves together, and come to thee. As I live, saith the Lord, thou shalt surely clothe thee with them all, as with an ornament, and bind them on thee as a bride doth. . . . The children which thou shalt have, after thou hast lost the other, shall say again in thine ears, The place is too strait for me, give place to me that I may dwell. Then shalt thou say in thine heart, Who hath begotten me these, seeing I have lost my children, and am desolate, a captive, and removing to and fro? . . . . Behold, I will lift up Mine hand to the Gentiles, and set up My standard to the people; . . . and kings shall be thy nursing-fathers, and their queens thy nursing-mothers." The Jewish Church, then, was not superseded, though the Nation was; it merely changed into the Christian, and thus was at once the same, and not the same, as it had been before.

Such being the double aspect of God's dealings towards His Church, when the time came for His exhibiting it in its new form as a Catholic, not a local Institution, he was pleased to make a corresponding change in the internal ministry of the Dispensation; imposing upon St. Paul the particular duty of formally delivering and adapting to the world at large that Old Essential Truth, the guardianship of which He had already committed to St. James and St. John. In consequence of this accidental difference of office, superficial readers of Scripture have sometimes spoken as if there were some real difference between the respective doctrines of those favoured Instruments of Providence. Unbelievers have objected that St. Paul introduced a new religion, such as Jesus never taught; and, on the other hand, there are Christians who maintain that St. Paul's doctrine is peculiarly the teaching of the Holy Ghost, and intended to supersede both our Lord's recorded words, and those of His original followers. Now a very remarkable circumstance it certainly is, that Almighty God has thus made two beginnings to His Gospel; and, when we have advanced far enough in sacred knowledge to see how they harmonize together, and concur in that wonderful system, which Primitive Christianity presents, and which was built on them both, we shall find abundant matter of praise in this Providential arrangement. But at first there doubtless is something which needs explanation: for we see, in matter of fact, that different classes of religionists do build their respective doctrines upon the one foundation and on the other, upon the Gospels and upon St. Paul's Epistles; the more enthusiastic upon the latter, the cold, proud, and heretical, upon the former; and though we may be quite sure that no part of Scripture favours either coldness or fanaticism, and, in particular, may zealously repel the impiety, as well as the daring perverseness, which would find countenance for an imperfect Creed in the heavenly words of the Evangelists, yet the very fact that hostile parties do agree in dividing the New Testament into about the same two portions, is just enough at first sight to show that there *is* some difference or other, whether in tone or doctrine, which needs accounting for.

This state of the case, whether a difficulty or not, may, I conceive, any how be turned into an evidence in behalf of the truth of Christianity. Some few remarks shall here be made to explain my meaning; nor is it superfluous to direct attention to the subject; for, though points of evidence seldom avail to the conversion of unbelievers, they are always edifying and instructive to Christians, as confirming their faith, and filling them with admiration and praise of God's marvellous works, which have more and more the stamp of Truth upon them, the deeper we examine them. This was the effect produced on the Apostles' minds by their own miracles, and on the Saints in the Apocalypse by the sight of God's judgments; prompting them to cry out in awe and thankfulness, "Lord, Thou art God, which hast made Heaven and earth!" "Great and marvellous are Thy works, Lord God Almighty; just and true are Thy ways, Thou King of Saints."[1]

My remark then is simply this;—that supposing an essential unanimity of teaching can be shown to exist between the respective writings of St. Paul and his brethren, then the existing difference, whatever it is, whether of phraseology, of subject, or of historical origin, in a word, the difference of school, only makes that agreement the more remarkable, and after all, only guarantees them as two independent Witnesses to the same Truth. Now to illustrate this argument.

I suppose the points of difference between St. Paul and the Twelve will be considered to be as follows:—that St. Paul, on his conversion, "conferred not with flesh and blood,"[2] neither went up to Jerusalem to them which were Apostles before him;—that, on the face of Scripture, there appears some sort of difference in viewing the Dispensation between St. Paul and the original Apostles; that St. Paul on one occasion "withstood Peter to the face," and says that "those who seemed to be somewhat," referring apparently to James and John, "in conference added nothing to him;"[3] and St. Peter, on the other hand, observes, that in St. Paul's Epistles there "are some things hard to be understood;" while St. James would even seem to qualify St. Paul's doctrine concerning the pre-eminence of faith;[4]—that St. James, not to mention St. John, was stationary, having taken on himself a local episcopate, while St. Paul was subjected to what are now called missionary labours, and laid the foundation of churches without undertaking the government of any of them;—that St. Paul speaks with especial earnestness concerning the abolition of the Jewish Law, and the admission of the Gentiles into the Church, subjects not prominently put forward by the other Apostles;—

---

[1] Acts iv.24; Rev. xv.3.   [2] Gal. i.16, 17.
[3] Gal. ii.6, 11.   [4] 2 Pet. iii.16; James ii.14–26.

that St. Paul declares distinctly and energetically, that we are elected to salvation by God's free grace, and justified by faith,[5] and traces out, in the way of system, all Christian holiness and spiritual-mindedness from this beginning; whereas, St. James says we are justified by works,[6] St. John that we shall be "judged according to our works," and St. Peter that "the Father judgeth according to every man's work, without respect of persons,"[7] phrases which are but symbols of the general character of their own and of our Lord's teaching;—lastly, that there is more expression of kindled and active affections towards God and towards man in St. Paul's writings than in those of his brethren. This is not the place to explain what needs explaining in this list of contrasts; nor indeed is there any real difficulty at all (I may say) in reconciling the one side with the other, where the heart is right and the judgment fairly clear and steady. It has often been done most satisfactorily. But let us take them as they stand, prior to all explanation; let a disputer make the most of them. So much at least is proved that St. Paul and St. James were two independent witnesses (whether concordant or not) of the Gospel doctrines, which is abundantly confirmed by all those circumstances which objectors sometimes enlarge upon, St. Paul's peculiar education, connexions and history. Take these differences at the worst, and then on the other hand take account of the wonderful agreement after all in opinion, manner of thought, feeling, and conduct, nay, in religious vocabulary, between the two Schools (as I have called them),—most wonderful, considering that the very idea of the Christian system in all its parts was virtually a new thing in the particular generation in which it was promulgated,—and if it does not impress us with the conviction that an Unseen Hand, a Divine Presence, was in the midst of it, controlling the human instruments of His work, and ruling it that they should and must agree in speaking His Word, in spite of whatever differences of natural disposition and education, surely we may as well deny the agency of the Creator, His power, wisdom, and goodness, in the appointments of the material world.—The following are some instances of the kind of agreement I speak of.

1. Take the New Testament, as we have received it. It deserves notice, that in spite of what partisans would desire, after all we cannot divide its contents between the two Schools

[5] Rom. v.1.   [6] James ii.24.
[7] Rev. xx.13; 1 Pet. i.17.

under consideration. Admitting there were two principles at work in the development of the Christian Church, they are inextricably united as regards the documents of faith; so that the modern parties in question, whether their particular view be right or wrong, are at least attempting a return to a state prior to the existence of the New Testament. Consider the Epistle to the Hebrews,—which would be sufficient evidence, were there no other, of the identity of St. Paul's doctrine with St. James's. Be as disputatious as you will about its author, still it comes at least from the School of St. Paul, if not from that Apostle himself. The parallelisms between it and his acknowledged writings forbid any other supposition. Now look through it from beginning to end, observe well its exhortations to obedience, its warnings against apostasy, its solemn announcement of the terrors of the Gospel, and further, its honourable treatment of the Jewish Law, which it sets forth as fulfilled (following our Saviour's doctrine), not disrespectfully superseded by the Gospel, and then say whether this Epistle alone be not a wonderful monument of the essential unity of the Gospel creed among all its original disseminators. Again, consider the Epistles to Timothy and Titus, which are confessedly St. Paul's, and try to discriminate, if you can, between the ethical character which they display, and that of St. James's Epistle. Next observe the position of St. Luke's writings in the Inspired Volume, an Evangelist following the language of St. Matthew, yet the associate of St. Paul. Examine the speeches of St. Paul in the Book of Acts, and consider whether he is not at once the Apostle of the Gentiles, and the fellow-disciple of those who had attended our Lord's Ministry.[8] Consider, too, the history of St. Peter, and see whether the revelations made to him in order to the conversion of Cornelius, do not form a link between "St. Paul's Gospel" and that of his earlier brethren. Lastly, count up the particular parts of St. Paul's writings, in which that Apostle may be supposed to speak a different doctrine from the rest, and determine their extent and number. Are there much more than nine chapters of his Epistle to the Romans, four of that to the Galatians, three in the Ephesians, a passage in the Colossians, and a few verses in the Philippians? Are there not in other chapters of these very Epistles clear and explicit statements, running counter to these supposed peculiarities, agreeing with St. James, and so protesting (as it were) against those who would put asunder Apostles whom God has joined together? These shall be pres-

[8] *Vide, e.g.* Acts xx.25; xxviii.31.

ently instanced; but for the moment concede the whole of the Epistles just mentioned,—yet you cannot make more than five out of fourteen, which is the whole number of his Epistles; and these, however sacred and authoritative, are not after all of greater prominence and dignity than some of the remaining nine. It would appear then, from the very face of the New Testament, that the differences between St. Paul's doctrine and that of his brethren, (whatever they were), admitted of an amalgamation, as far as Christian Teaching went, from the moment when that office was first exercised in the Church.

2. In the case of the original Apostles, the intention of delivering and explaining their Divine Master's teaching cannot be mistaken. Now, of course, St. Paul, professing to preach Christ's Gospel, could not but avow such an intention also; but it should be noticed, considering that he was not with our Lord on earth, how he devotes himself to the sole thought of Him; that is, it *would* be remarkable, were not St. Paul divinely chosen and called, as we believe him to have been. Simon Magus professed to be a Christian, yet his aim was that of exalting himself. It was quite possible for St. Paul to have acknowledged Christ generally as his Master, and still not practically to have preached Christ. Yet how full he is of his Saviour! He could not be more so, if he had attended Him all through His ministry. The thought of Christ is the one thought in which he *lives*; it is the fervent love, the devoted attachment, the zeal and reverence of one who had "heard and seen, and looked upon and handled, the Word of life."[9] What a remarkable attestation is here to the Sovereignty of the Unseen Saviour! What was Paul, and what was James, "but ministers," by whom the world believed on Him? They clearly were nothing beyond this. This is a striking fulfilment of our Lord's declaration concerning the ministration of the Spirit; "He shall glorify Me."[10] St. John records it; St. Paul exemplifies it.

It is remarkable too, how St. Paul concurs with the other Apostles in referring to our Lord's words and actions, though much opportunity for this does not occur in his writings; that is, it is plain, that he was not exalting a mere name or idea, any more than the rest, but a Person, a really existing Master. For instance, St. John says, "That which we have seen and heard, declare we unto you;" and St. Peter, "This voice which came from heaven we heard, when we were with Him in the Holy Mount;" again, "We are witnesses of all things which He

[9] 1 John i.1.   [10] John xvi.14.

did." [11] In like manner St. Paul enumerates, as his "Gospel," not mere principles of religion, but the facts of Christ's life, recurring to that very part of the Dispensation, in which he was inferior to his brethren. "I delivered unto you first of all, that which I also received, how that Christ died for our sins according to the Scriptures, . . . was buried, . . . rose again the third day, and that He was seen of Cephas, then of the Twelve, after that . . . of about five hundred brethren at once . . . after that . . . of James, then of all the Apostles;" he adds, with expressions of self-abasement, "And last of all, He was seen of me." [12] Again in his directions for administering the Lord's Supper, he refers carefully to our Lord's manner of ordaining it as recorded in the Gospels; again, in the seventh chapter of the same Epistle, there would seem a repeated reference to our Lord's words in the Gospel; "unto the married I command, yet not I, but the Lord." In the same chapter the verse beginning, "This I speak for your own profit," has been supposed with reason to refer to St. Luke's account of Martha's complaint of Mary, and our Lord's speech thereupon. In his first Epistle to Timothy, he alludes to our Lord's appearance before Pilate. In his farewell address to the elders of Ephesus he has preserved one of His sayings which the Gospels do not contain; "It is more blessed to give than to receive." [13] And in the Epistle to the Hebrews reference is made to Christ's agony in the garden.

3. The doctrine of the Incarnation, or the Gospel Economy, as embracing the two great truths of the Divinity of Christ and the Atonement, was not (as far as we know) clearly revealed, during our Lord's ministry. Yet, observe how close is St. Paul's agreement with St. John. "The Word was with God, and the Word was God, and the Word was made flesh."—"Christ Jesus, being in the form of God, thought it not robbery to be equal with God; yet humbled Himself, being made in the likeness of men." St. John calls Christ "the Only-begotten Son in the bosom of the Father;" and St. Paul, "the First-begotten." St. John says, that He hath "declared the Father," and, in His own sacred words, that "he that hath seen Him, hath seen the Father;" St. Paul declares that He is "the Image of the Invisible God,"—"the brightness of His glory, and the express Image of His Person." St. John says, "All things were made by Him;" St. Paul, that "By Him God made the worlds." Further, St. John says, "The blood of Jesus Christ cleanseth us from all sin;"—St.

---

[11] 1 John i.3; 2 Pet. i.18; Acts x.39.
[12] 1 Cor. xv.3–8.   [13] Acts xx.35.

Paul, that "in Him we have redemption through His blood, even the forgiveness of sins;"—St. John, that "if any man sin, we have an Advocate with the Father, Jesus Christ the righteous;"—St. Paul, that He "is even at the right hand of God, and also maketh intercession for us;"—St. John, that "He is the propitiation not for our sins only, but also for those of the whole world;"—St. Paul, that He has "reconciled" Jew and Gentile "in one body by the cross." [14]

Now, considering the mysteriousness of these doctrines, the probability that there would be some diversity of teaching, in the case of two different minds, and the actual differences existing among various sects at the time, I must consider this exact accordance between St. John and St. Paul (men to all appearance as unlike each other by nature as men could be) to be little short of a demonstration of the reality of the divine doctrines to which they witness. "The testimony of two men is true;" and still more clearly so in this case, supposing (what unbelievers may maintain, but they alone) that any rivalry of schools existed between these holy Apostles.

4. To continue our review. St. John and St. Paul both put forward the doctrine of Regeneration, both connect it with Baptism, both denounce the world as sinful and lost. They both teach the peculiar privilege of Christians, as God's adopted children, and make the grant of this and all other privileges, depend on faith. [15] Now the ideas and the terms employed are peculiar; and, after all allowance for what might have been anticipated by former dispensations and existing schools of religion, yet, could it be shown that ever so much of this doctrine was already familiar to the Jewish Church, this does not account for the unanimity with which they respectively adopt and modify it. I add some parallel texts on this part of the subject. St. John delivers our Saviour's prediction: "If I depart, I will send the Comforter unto you; He will guide you into all truth;"—St. Paul, "God hath revealed (the mysteries of the Gospel) unto us by His Spirit;"—"All these (gifts) worketh that one and the self-same Spirit, dividing to every man severally as He will." St. Paul says, "He which stablisheth us with you in Christ, and hath anointed us, is God;"—St. John, "Ye have an unction from the Holy One." St. John, in accordance with the

[14] John i.1, 14; Phil. ii.5–8; John i.18; Heb. i.6; John i.18; xiv.9; Col. i.15; Heb. i.3; John i.3; Heb. i.2; 1 John i.7; Col. i.14; 1 John ii.1; Rom. viii.34; 1 John ii.2; Eph. ii.16.

[15] John iii.3–5, 16, 19; 1 John iii.1; v.19; Rom. iii.19; v.1, 2; viii.14, 15; Tit. iii.5, etc.

teaching of his Lord, declares, "There is a sin unto death; I do not say that a man shall pray for it;" and St. Paul, that "it is impossible for those who were once enlightened, if they shall fall away, to renew them again unto repentance." [16]

5. We all recollect St. Paul's praise of charity as the fulfilling of the Law, and the characteristic precept of the Gospel. Yet is not the pre-eminent importance of it as clearly set forth by St. John, when he says, "We know that we have passed from death unto life, because we love the brethren," and the nature of it by St. James in his description of "the wisdom that is from above?" Again, it is observable, that our Lord's precept, adopted from the Law, of loving our neighbour as ourselves, is handed down at once by St. Paul and St. James. [17]

6. We know that an especial stress is laid by our Lord on the duty of Almsgiving. St. John and St. James follow Him in so doing; [18] and St. Paul likewise. That Apostle's words, in the Galatians, are especially in point here, as expressly acknowledging this agreement between himself and his brethren. "When James, Cephas, and John, who seemed to be pillars, perceived the grace that was given unto me, they gave to me and Barnabas the right hand of fellowship, that we should go unto the heathen, and they unto the circumcision; *only they would that we should remember the poor; the same which I also was forward to do.*" [19]

7. Self-denial, mortification of life, bearing our cross, are especially insisted on by Christ. St. Paul delivers clearly and strongly the same doctrine, declaring that he himself was "crucified with Christ," and "died daily." [20] The duty of Fasting may here be mentioned, as one in which St. Paul unhesitatingly enters into and enforces our Lord's religious system.

8. I need not observe how urgent and constant is St. Paul in his exhortations to Intercession; yet, St. James equals him in his short Epistle, which contains a passage longer and more emphatic than any which can be found in St. Paul. [21] Again, both Apostles insist on the practice of sacred Psalmody as a duty. St. James, "Is any afflicted? let him pray. Is any merry? let him sing psalms." St. Paul, "Speaking to each other in psalms and hymns, and spiritual songs." [22]

---

[16] John xvi.7, 13; 1 Cor. ii.10; xii.11; 2 Cor. i.21; 1 John ii.21; v.16; Heb. vi.4–6.

[17] 1 John iii.14; James iii.17; Rom. xiii.9; James ii.8.

[18] 1 John iii.17; James ii.15, 16.

[19] Gal. ii.9, 10.   [20] Gal. ii.20; 1 Cor. xv.31.

[21] Eph. vi.18; 1 Thess. v.17; James v.14–18.

[22] James v.13; Eph. v.19.

9. St. Paul makes much of the Holy Eucharist; nay, to him the Church is indebted for the direct and clear proof we possess of the sacramental virtue of that Ordinance. Far different is the conduct of innovators; who are impatient of nothing more than of ordinances which they find established. He also recognises the obligation of the Lord's day,[23] he being the Apostle who denounces, as other Jewish rites, so also the Sabbath.

10. St. Jude bids us "contend earnestly for the faith once delivered to the Saints." In like manner, St. Paul enjoins Timothy to "hold fast the form of sound words, which he had heard of him;" and Titus, to "hold fast the faithful word as he had been taught, that he might be able by sound doctrine both to exhort and to convince the gainsayers."[24] St. Paul bids us "speak the Truth in love;" St. John says, he "loves Gaius in the Truth."[25]

11. It is observable that our Lord speaks of His Gospel being preached, not chiefly as a means of converting, but as a witnesss against the world. This is confessedly a remarkable ground to be taken by the Founder of a new religion. "The Gospel of the kingdom shall be preached in all the world, for a witness unto all nations."[26] Accordingly, He Himself witnessed even before the heathen Pilate, "To this end was I born, and for this cause came I into the world, that I should bear witness unto the Truth."[27] Yet, surely, it is still more remarkable, that the Apostle of the Gentiles should take up precisely the same view, even referring to our Lord's Confession before Pilate, when giving Timothy his charge to preach the Truth, declaring, that the Gospel is "a savour of death unto death," as well as "of life unto life," and foretelling the growth of "evil men and seducers" after his departure.[28]

12. Observe the agreement of sentiment in the following texts: St. James, taught by his Lord and Master, says, "Be ye doers of the word, and not hearers only, deceiving your own selves." St. Paul nearly in the same words, "Not the hearers of the law are just before God, but the doers of the law shall be justified."[29] Again, did we not know whence the following passages come, should we not assign them to St. James? "God will render to every man according to his deeds; to them, who by patient continuance in well-doing, seek for glory, and honour,

---

[23] Acts xx.7; 1 Cor. xvi.2.   [24] Jude 3; 2 Tim. i.13; Tit. i.9.
[25] Eph. iv.15; 3 John 1.   [26] Matt. xxiv.14; xviii.37.
[27] John xviii.37.
[28] 1 Tim. vi.13; 2 Cor. ii.16; 2 Tim. iii.13.
[29] James i.22; Rom. ii.13.

and immortality, eternal life; but unto them that are contentious, and do not obey the truth, but obey unrighteousness, indignation, and wrath . . . . for there is no respect of persons
with God." This, as well as the text just cited, is to be found in
the opening of that Epistle, in which St. Paul appears most to
differ from St. James; now observe how he closes it. "Why dost
thou judge thy brother? And why dost thou set at nought thy
brother? For we shall all stand before the judgment-seat of
Christ. . . . Every one of us shall give account of himself to
God." Again, in another Epistle: "We must all be made manifest before the judgment-seat of Christ; that every one may receive the things done in his body, according to that he hath
done, whether it be good or bad. Knowing therefore the terror
of the Lord, we persuade men."[30]

13. St. John, after our Lord's example, implies especial praise
upon those who follow an unmarried life, involving the letter
in the spirit, as is frequent in Scripture.[31] "These are they which
were not defiled with women, for they are virgins; these are
they which follow the Lamb whithersoever He goeth." St. Paul
gives more direct praise to the same state, and gives the same
reason for its especial blessedness; "He that is unmarried careth

[30] Rom. ii.6–8; xiv.10–12; 2 Cor. v.10, 11.

[31] *Vide* Hosea xiii.14; John xi.23, 40; xiii.8; xviii.9. And especially, as
being a parallel case, Matt. xviii.3–6, and so again, Matt. x.38; Rev.
vii.14.—The parallel is instructively brought out in separate passages in
the "Christian Year:"

> "Yet in that throng of selfish hearts untrue,
>   Thy sad eye rests upon Thy faithful few,
>   Children *and* childlike souls are there," etc.—*Advent.*

> . . .

> "There hangs a radiant coronet,
>   All gemm'd with pure and living light,
>   Too dazzling for a sinner's sight,
>   Prepares for virgin souls, and them
>   Who seek the martyr's diadem,
>   *Nor deem*, who, to that bliss aspire,
>   Must win their way through blood and fire," etc.
>   *Wednesday before Easter.*

In other words, Childhood, Virginity, Martyrdom, are made in Scripture at once the Types and Standards of religious Perfection, as they are
represented in the three Saints' Days following Christmas-Day,—St.
Stephen's, St. John's, and Holy Innocents'. So again, Poverty, Luke
vi.20; xii.33; Matt. xi.5, with Matt. v.3. But this rule of interpretation,
and the light it throws upon Gospel duties and the Christian character,
cannot be more than alluded to in a note.

for the things that belong to the Lord, how he may please the Lord. . . . I speak this for your own profit . . . . that ye may attend upon the Lord without distraction." [32]

14. St. Paul says, "Be careful for nothing, but in every thing by prayer and supplication with thanksgiving, let your requests be made known unto God;" St. Peter in like manner, "Casting all your care upon Him, for He careth for you." Both after our Lord's exhortation, "Be not careful for the morrow, for the morrow shall take care for the things of itself." [33]

15. Lastly, as Christ foretells the approaching visitations of the Jewish Church, and the necessity of looking out for them, so St. Peter declares, "The end of all things is at hand; be ye therefore sober, and watch unto prayer." St. James, "Be ye also patient, stablish your hearts, for the coming of the Lord draweth nigh." [34] And St. Paul in like manner, "Let your moderation be known unto all men; the Lord is at hand."

These instances may suffice by way of pointing out the argument for the truth of Christianity, which, as I conceive, lies in the *historical* difference existing between the respective schools of St. Paul and St. James. Such a difference there is, as every one must grant: I mean that St. Paul did, as a matter of fact, begin his preaching upon his own independent revelations. And thus, however we may be able (as assuredly every Christian is gradually able, in proportion to his diligence and prayer) to reconcile and satisfy himself as regards St. Paul's apparent discordances in doctrine from the rest of the Apostles, so much after all must remain, just enough, that is, to build the foregoing argument upon. At the same time, as if to ensure even the historical harmony of the whole Dispensation, we are allowed to set against our information concerning this separate origin of the two Apostolical Schools, the following facts; first, that St. Paul ever considered himself ecclesiastically subordinate to the Church at Jerusalem, and to St. James, as the Book of Acts shows us; next, that St. John, the beloved disciple, who "was in Christ before him," was appointed to outlive him, and, as a faithful Steward, to seal up, avouch, and deliver over inviolate to the Church after him, the pure and veritable teaching of his Lord.

As to the point of *doctrinal* agreement and difference which I have been employed in ascertaining, it is scarcely necessary to

[32] Rev. xiv.4; 1 Cor. vii.32, 35.
[33] Phil. iv.6; 1 Pet. v.7; Matt. vi.34.
[34] 1 Pet. iv.7; Phil. iv.5; James v.8.

observe, that beyond controversy the agreement is in essentials—the nature and office of the Mediator, the gifts which He vouchsafes to us, and the temper of mind and the duties required of a Christian; whereas the difference of doctrine between them, even admitting there is a difference, relates only at the utmost to the Divine counsels, the sense in which the Jewish law is abolished, and the condition of justification, whether faith or good works. I would not (God forbid!) undervalue these or any other questions on which inspiration has spoken; it is our duty to search diligently after every jot and tittle of the Truth graciously revealed to us, and to maintain it: but I am here speaking as to an unbeliever, and he must confess, that viewing the Gospel Creed in what may be called its historical proportions, a difference of opinion as to these latter subjects cannot detract from that real and substantial agreement of System, visible in the course of doctrine which the Two Witnesses respectively deliver.

Next, speaking as a Christian, who will admit neither inconsistency to exist between the inspired documents of faith, nor points of trivial importance in the revelation, I observe notwithstanding, that the foregoing argument affords us additional certainty respecting the characteristic doctrines as well as the truth of Christianity. An agreement between St. Paul and St. John in behalf of a certain doctrine is an agreement not of mere texts, but of separate Witnesses, an evidence of the prominence of the doctrine delivered in the Gospel system. In this way, if in no other, we learn the momentous character of some particular tenets of revelation which heretics have denied, as the Eternity, or, again, the Personality of the Divine Word.

Further, we are thus permitted more clearly to ascertain the main outlines of the Christian *character*; for instance, that love is its essence,—its chief characteristics, resignation, and composure of mind, neither anxious for the morrow, nor hoping from this world—and its duties, almsgiving, self-denial, prayer and praise.

Lastly, the very circumstance that Almighty God has chosen this mode of introducing the Gospel into the world, I mean, this employment of a double agency, opens a wide field of thought, had we light to trace out the parallel providences which seem to lie amid the intricacies of His dealings with mankind. As it is, we can but gaze with the Apostle in wonder and adoration upon the mystery of His counsels. "O the depth of the riches both of the wisdom and knowledge of God! how unsearchable are His judgments, and His ways past finding out!

For who hath known the mind of the Lord? Or who hath been His counsellor? Or who hath first given to Him, and it shall be recompensed unto him again? For of Him, and through Him, and to Him, are all things: to whom be glory for ever. Amen."[35]

---

[35] Rom. xi.33–36.

MYSTERIES IN RELIGION

(The Feast of the Ascension of Our Lord)

"It is Christ that died, yea rather, that is risen again, Who is even
at the right hand of God, Who also maketh intercession for us."
—Rom. viii.34.

THE Ascension of our Lord and Saviour is an event ever to be commemorated with joy and thanksgiving, for St. Paul tells us in the text that He ascended to the right hand of God, and there makes intercession for us. Hence it is our comfort to know, that "if any man sin, we have an Advocate with the Father, Jesus Christ the righteous, and He is the propitiation for our sins." [1] As the Jewish High Priest, after the solemn sacrifice for the people on the great day of Atonement, went into the Holy of Holies with the blood of the victim, and sprinkled it upon the Mercy-Seat, so Christ has entered into Heaven itself to present (as it were) before the Throne that sacred Tabernacle which was the instrument of His passion,—His pierced hands and wounded side,—in token of the atonement which He has effected for the sins of the world.

Wonder and awe must always mingle with the thankfulness which the revealed dispensation of mercy raises in our minds. And this, indeed, is an additional cause of thankfulness, that Almighty God has disclosed to us enough of His high Providence to raise such sacred and reverent feelings. Had He merely told us that He had pardoned us, we should have had overabundant cause for blessing and praising Him; but in showing us somewhat of the means, in vouchsafing to tell what cannot wholly be told, in condescending to abase heavenly things to the weak and stammering tongues of earth, He has enlarged our gratitude, yet sobered it with fear. We are allowed with the Angels to obtain a glimpse of the mysteries of Heaven, "to rejoice with trembling." Therefore, so far from considering the Truths of the Gospel as a burden, because they are beyond our

[1] 1 John ii.1, 2.

understanding, we shall rather welcome them and exult in them, nay, and feel an antecedent stirring of heart towards them, for the very reason that they are above us. Under these feelings I will attempt to suggest to you on the present Festival some of the incentives to wonder and awe, humility, implicit faith, and adoration, supplied by the Ascension of Christ.

1. First, Christ's Ascension to the right hand of God is marvellous, because it is a sure token that heaven is a certain fixed place, and not a mere state. That bodily presence of the Saviour which the Apostles handled is not here; it is elsewhere,—it is in heaven. This contradicts the notions of cultivated and speculative minds, and humbles the reason. Philosophy considers it more rational to suppose that Almighty God, as being a Spirit, is in every place; and in no one place more than another. It would teach, if it dare, that heaven is a mere state of blessedness; but, to be consistent, it ought to go on to deny, with the ancient heretics, referred to by St. John, that "Jesus Christ is come in the flesh," and maintain that His presence on earth was a mere vision; for, certain it is, He who appeared on earth went up from the earth, and a cloud received Him out of His Apostles' sight. And here again an additional difficulty occurs, on minutely considering the subject. Whither did He go? beyond the sun? beyond the fixed stars? Did He traverse the immeasurable space which extends beyond them all? Again, what is meant by *ascending*? Philosophers will say there is no difference between *down* and *up*, as regards the sky; yet, whatever difficulties the word may occasion, we can hardly take upon us to decide that it is a mere popular expression, consistently with the reverence due to the Sacred Record.

And thus we are led on to consider, how different are the character and effect of the Scripture notices of the structure of the physical world, from those which philosophers deliver. I am not deciding whether or not the one and the other are reconcileable; I merely say their respective *effect* is different. And when we have deduced what we deduce by our reason from the study of visible nature, and then read what we read in His inspired word, and find the two apparently discordant, *this* is the feeling I think we ought to have on our minds;—not an impatience to do what is beyond our powers, to weigh evidence, sum up, balance, decide, and reconcile, to arbitrate between the two voices of God,—but a sense of the utter nothingness of worms such as we are; of our plain and absolute incapacity to contemplate things *as they really are*; a perception of our emptiness, before the great Vision of God; of our "comeliness being turned into corruption, and our retaining no strength;" a conviction, that what is put before us, in nature or in grace, though true in such a full sense that we dare not tamper with it, yet is but an intimation useful for particular purposes, useful for practice, useful in its department, "until the day-break and the shadows flee away," useful in such a way that both the one and the other representation may at once be used, as two languages, as two separate approximations towards the Awful Unknown Truth, such as will not mislead us in their respective provinces. And thus while we use the language of science, without jealousy, for scientific purposes, we may confine it to these; and repel and reprove its upholders, should they attempt to exalt it and to "stretch it beyond its measure." In its own limited round it has its use, nay, may be made to fill a higher ministry, and stand as a proselyte under the shadow of the temple; but it must not dare profane the inner courts, in which the ladder of Angels is fixed for ever, reaching even to the Throne of God, and "Jesus standing on the right hand of God."

I will but remind you on this part of the subject, that our Lord is to come from heaven "in like manner" as He went; that He is to come "in clouds," that "every eye shall see Him," and "all tribes of the earth wail because of Him." Attempt to solve this prediction, according to the received theories of science, and you will discover their shallowness. They are unequal to the depth of the problem.

2. I have made the foregoing remark in order to impress upon you the mystery with which we are encompassed all about, such as not merely to attach to one or two truths of religion, but extending to almost every sacred fact, and to every action of our lives. With the same view, let me observe upon the doctrine which accompanies the fact of the Ascension. Christ, we are told, has gone up on high "to present Himself before the face of God for us." He has "entered by His own blood once for all into the Holy Place, having effected eternal redemption." "He ever liveth to make intercession for those who come unto God by Him; He hath a priesthood which will not pass from Him." "We have such an High Priest, who is set on the right hand of the throne of the Majesty in the heavens; a Minister of the Sanctuary, and of the true Tabernacle, which the Lord pitched, and not man." [2]

These and similar passages refer us to the rites of the Jewish law. They contain notice of the type, but what is the Antitype?

[2] Heb. ix.12, 24, 25; vii.24, 25; viii.1, 2.

We can give no precise account of it. For consider; *why* was it that Christ ascended on high? With what object? What is His work? What is the meaning of His interceding for us in heaven? We know that, whatever He does, it is the gracious reality of the Mosaic figure. The High Priest entering with the atoning blood into the Holiest, was a representation of Christ's gracious deed in our behalf. But what is that deed? We know what the shadow is; what is the substance? The death of Christ answers to the Jewish rite of Atonement; how does He vouchsafe to fulfil the rite of Intercession? Instead of explaining, Scripture does but continue to answer us in the language of the type; even to the last it veils His deed under the ancient figure.[3] Shall we therefore explain away its language as merely figurative, which (as the word is now commonly understood) is next to saying it has no meaning at all? Far from it. Clouds and darkness are round about Him. We are not given to see into the secret shrine in which God dwells. Before Him stand the Seraphim, veiling their faces. Christ is within the veil. We must not search curiously what is His present office, what is meant by His pleading His sacrifice, and by His perpetual intercession for us. And, since we do not know, we will studiously keep to the figure given us in Scripture: we will not attempt to interpret it, or change the wording of it, being wise above what is written. We will not neglect it, because we do not understand it. We will hold it as a Mystery, or (what was anciently called) a Truth Sacramental; that is, a high invisible grace lodged in an outward form, a precious possession to be piously and thankfully guarded for the sake of the heavenly reality contained in it. Thus much we see in it, the pledge of a doctrine which reason cannot understand, viz. of the influence of the prayer of faith upon the Divine counsels. The Intercessor directs or stays the hand of the Unchangeable and Sovereign Governor of the World; being at once the meritorious cause and the earnest of the intercessory power of His brethren. "Christ rose again for our justification," "The effectual fervent prayer of a righteous man availeth much," are both infinite mercies, and deep mysteries.

3. Further still, consider our Saviour's words:—"It is expedient for you that I go away: for if I go not away, the Comforter will not come unto you." He does not tell us, why it was that His absence was the condition of the Holy Spirit's presence. "If I depart," He says, "I will send Him unto you." "I will pray the

---

[3] Rev. viii.3, 4.

Father, and He shall give you another Comforter, that He may abide with you for ever." [4] To the same purpose are the following texts: "He that believeth on Me, the works that I do shall he do also; and greater works than these shall he do, *because* I go unto My Father." "If ye loved Me, ye would rejoice, because I said, I go unto the Father; for My Father is greater than I." "Touch Me not; for I am not yet ascended to My Father; but go to My brethren, and say unto them, I ascend unto My Father and your Father, and to My God and your God." [5] Now, proud and curious reason might seek to know why He could not "pray the Father," without going to Him; why He must depart in order to send the Spirit. But faith, without asking for one ray of light more than is given, muses over the wonderful system of Providence, as seen in this world, which is ever connecting events, between which man sees no necessary bond. The whole system of what is called cause and effect, is one of mystery; and this instance, if it may be called one, supplies abundant matter of praise and adoration to a pious mind. It suggests to us, equally with the topics which have already come before us, how very much our knowledge of God's ways is but on the surface. What are those deep hidden reasons why Christ went and the Spirit came? Marvellous and glorious, beyond our understanding! Let us worship in silence; meanwhile, let us jealously maintain this, and every other portion of our Creed, lest, by dropping jot or tittle, we suffer the truths concealed therein to escape from us.

Moreover, this departure of Christ, and coming of the Holy Ghost, leads our minds with great comfort to the thought of many lower dispensations of Providence towards us. He, who, according to His inscrutable will, sent first His Co-equal Son, and then His Eternal Spirit, acts with deep counsel, which we may surely trust, when He sends from place to place those earthly instruments which carry on His purposes. This is a thought which is particularly soothing as regards the loss of friends; or of especially gifted men, who seem in their day the earthly support of the Church. For what we know, their removal hence is as necessary for the furtherance of the very objects we have at heart, as was the departure of our Saviour.

Doubtless, "it is expedient" they should be taken away; otherwise some great mercy will not come to us. They are taken away perchance to other duties in God's service, equally ministrative to the salvation of the elect, as earthly service.

---

[4] John xvi.7; xiv.16.   [5] John xiv.12, 28; xx.17.

Christ went to intercede with the Father: we do not know, we may not boldly speculate,—yet, it may be, that Saints departed intercede, unknown to us, for the victory of the Truth upon earth; and their prayers above may be as really indispensable conditions of that victory, as the labours of those who remain among us. They are taken away for some purpose surely: their gifts are not lost to us; their soaring minds, the fire of their contemplations, the sanctity of their desires, the vigour of their faith, the sweetness and gentleness of their affections, were not given without an object. Yea, doubtless, they are keeping up the perpetual chant in the shrine above, praying and praising God day and night in His Temple, like Moses upon the Mount, while Joshua and his host fight with Amalek. Can they be allotted greater blessedness, than to have a station after the pattern of that Saviour who has departed hence? Has *He* no power in the world's movements because He is away? And though He is the Living and exalted Lord of all, and the government is on His shoulder, and they are but His servants, without strength of themselves, laid up moreover apart from the conflict of good and evil in the paradise of God, yet so much light as this is given us by the inspired pages of the Apocalypse, that they are interested in the fortunes of the Church. We read therein of the Martyrs crying with a loud voice, "How long, O Lord, holy and true, dost Thou not judge and avenge our blood on them that dwell on the earth?" At another time, of the Elders worshipping God, saying, "We give Thee thanks, O Lord God Almighty, which art, and wast, and art to come, because Thou hast taken to Thee Thy great power and hast reigned; and the nations were wrathful, but Thy wrath is come." And again of the Saints, saying, "Great and marvellous are Thy works, Lord God Almighty; just and true are Thy ways, Thou King of Saints. Who shall not fear Thee, O Lord, and glorify Thy name? for Thou only art holy; for all nations shall come and worship before Thee, for Thy judgments are made manifest." [6] Let us not forget that, though the prophecies of this sacred book may be still sealed from us, yet the doctrines and precepts are not; and that we lose much both in the way of comfort and instruction, if we do not use it for the purposes of faith and obedience.

What has been now said about the Ascension of our Lord comes to this; that we are in a world of mystery, with one bright Light before us, sufficient for our proceeding forward through

[6] Rev. vi.10; xi.17, 18; xv.3, 4.

all difficulties. Take away this Light, and we are utterly wretched,—we know not where we are, how we are sustained, what will become of us, and of all that is dear to us, what we are to believe, and why we are in being. But with it we have all and abound. Not to mention the duty and wisdom of implicit faith in the love of Him who made and redeemed us, what is nobler, what is more elevating and transporting, than the generosity of heart which risks everything on God's word, dares the powers of evil to their worst efforts, and repels the illusions of sense and the artifices of reason, by confidence in the Truth of Him who has ascended to the right hand of the Majesty on high? What infinite mercy it is in Him, that He allows sinners such as we are, the privilege of acting the part of heroes rather than of penitents? Who are we "that we should be able" and have opportunity "to offer so willingly after this sort?"[7] "Blessed," surely thrice blessed, "are they who have not seen, and yet have believed!" We will not wish for sight; we will enjoy our privilege; we will triumph in the leave given us to go forward, "not knowing whither we go," knowing that "this is the victory that overcometh the world, even our faith."[8] It is enough that our Redeemer liveth; that He has been on earth and will come again. On Him we venture our all; we can bear thankfully to put ourselves into His hands, our interests present and eternal, and the interests of all we love. Christ has died, "yea rather is risen again, who is even at the right hand of God, who also maketh intercession for us. Who shall separate us from His love? Shall tribulation, or distress, or persecution, or famine, or nakedness, or peril, or sword? Nay, in all these things we are more than conquerors, through Him that loved us."[9]

[7] 1 Chron. xxix.14.   [8] 1 John v.4.   [9] Rom. viii.34–37.

THE INDWELLING SPIRIT

(The Feast of Pentecost)

"Ye are not in the flesh, but in the Spirit, if so be that the Spirit of God dwell in you."—Rom. viii.9.

GOD the Son has graciously vouchsafed to reveal the Father to His creatures from without; God the Holy Ghost, by inward communications. Who can compare these separate works of condescension, either of them being beyond our understanding? We can but silently adore the Infinite Love which encompasses us on every side. The Son of God is called the Word, as declaring His glory throughout created nature, and impressing the evidence of it on every part of it. He has given us to read it in His works of goodness, holiness, and wisdom. He is the Living and Eternal Law of Truth and Perfection, that Image of God's unapproachable Attributes, which men have ever seen by glimpses on the face of the world, felt that it was sovereign, but knew not whether to say it was a fundamental Rule and self-existing Destiny, or the Offspring and Mirror of the Divine Will. Such has He been from the beginning, graciously sent forth from the Father to reflect His glory upon all things, distinct from Him, while mysteriously one with Him; and in due time visiting us with an infinitely deeper mercy, when for our redemption He humbled Himself to take upon Him that fallen nature which He had originally created after His own image.

The condescension of the Blessed Spirit is as incomprehensible as that of the Son. He has ever been the secret Presence of God within the Creation: a source of life amid the chaos, bringing out into form and order what was at first shapeless and void, and the voice of Truth in the hearts of all rational beings, tuning them into harmony with the intimations of God's Law, which were externally made to them. Hence He is especially called the "life-giving" Spirit; being (as it were) the Soul of universal nature, the Strength of man and beast, the Guide of faith, the Witness against sin, the inward Light of patriarchs and prophets, the Grace abiding in the Christian soul, and the Lord and Ruler of the Church. Therefore let us ever praise the Father Almighty, who is the first Source of all perfection, in and together with His Co-equal Son and Spirit, through whose gracious ministrations we have been given to see "what manner of love" it is wherewith the Father has loved us.

On this Festival I propose, as is suitable, to describe as scripturally as I can, the merciful office of God the Holy Ghost, towards us Christians; and I trust I may do so, with the sobriety and reverence which the subject demands.

The Holy Spirit has from the beginning pleaded with man. We read in the Book of Genesis, that, when evil began to prevail all over the earth before the flood, the Lord said, "My Spirit shall not always strive with man;"[1] implying that He had hitherto striven with his corruption. Again, when God took to Him a peculiar people, the Holy Spirit was pleased to be especially present with them. Nehemiah says, "Thou gavest also Thy Good Spirit to instruct them,"[2] and Isaiah, "They rebelled and vexed His Holy Spirit."[3] Further, He manifested Himself as the source of various gifts, intellectual and extraordinary, in the Prophets, and others. Thus at the time the Tabernacle was constructed, the Lord filled Bezaleel "with the Spirit of God, in wisdom, and in understanding, and in knowledge, and in all manner of workmanship, to devise cunning works"[4] in metal, stone, and timber. At another time, when Moses was oppressed with his labours, Almighty God vouchsafed to "take of the Spirit" which was upon him, and to put it on seventy of the elders of Israel, that they might share the burden with him. "And it came to pass, that, when the Spirit rested upon them, they prophesied, and did not cease."[5] These texts will be sufficient to remind you of many others, in which the gifts of the Holy Ghost are spoken of under the Jewish covenant. These were great mercies; yet, great as they were, they are as nothing compared with that surpassing grace with which we Christians are honoured; that great privilege of receiving into our hearts, not the mere gifts of the Spirit, but His very presence, Himself, by a real not a figurative indwelling.

When our Lord entered upon His Ministry, He acted as though He were a mere man, needing grace, and received the consecration of the Holy Spirit for our sakes. He became the Christ, or Anointed, that the Spirit might be seen to come from

---

[1] Gen. vi.3.   [2] Neh. ix.20.   [3] Is. lxiii.10.
[4] Exod. xxxi.3, 4.   [5] Numb. xi.17, 25.

God, and to pass from Him to us. And, therefore, the heavenly
Gift is not simply called the Holy Ghost, or the Spirit of God,
but the Spirit of Christ, that we might clearly understand, that
He comes to us from and instead of Christ. Thus St. Paul says,
"God hath sent forth the Spirit of His Son into your hearts;"
and our Lord breathed on His Apostles, saying, "Receive ye the
Holy Ghost;" and He says elsewhere to them, "If I depart, I will
send Him unto you."[6] Accordingly this "Holy Spirit of promise" is called "the earnest of our inheritance," "the seal and earnest of an Unseen Saviour;"[7] being the present pledge of Him
who is absent,—or rather more than a pledge, for an earnest is
not a mere token which will be taken from us when it is fulfilled, as a pledge might be, but a something in advance of what
is one day to be given in full.

This must be clearly understood; for it would seem to follow,
that if so, the Comforter who has come instead of Christ, must
have vouchsafed to come in the same sense in which Christ
came; I mean, that He has come, not merely in the way of gifts,
or of influences, or of operations, as He came to the Prophets,
for then Christ's going away would be a loss, and not a gain, and
the Spirit's presence would be a mere pledge, not an earnest;
but He comes to us as Christ came, by a real and personal visitation. I do not say we could have inferred this thus clearly by the
mere force of the above cited texts; but it being actually so revealed to us in other texts of Scripture, we are able to see that it
may be legitimately deduced from these. We are able to see that
the Saviour, when once He entered into this world, never so
departed as to suffer things to be as before He came; for He still
is with us, not in mere gifts, but by the substitution of His Spirit
for Himself, and that, both in the Church and in the souls of
individual Christians.

For instance, St. Paul says in the text, "Ye are not in the flesh,
but in the Spirit, if so be that the Spirit of God *dwell in you*."
Again, "He shall quicken even your mortal bodies by His Spirit
that *dwelleth* in you." "Know ye not that your body is the
Temple of the Holy Ghost which is in you?" "Ye are the Temple
of the Living God, as God hath said, I will dwell in them, and
walk in them." The same Apostle clearly distinguishes between
the indwelling of the Spirit, and His actual operations within
us, when he says, "The love of God is shed abroad in our hearts
by the Holy Ghost which is given unto us;" and again, "The

[6] Gal. iv.6; John xx.22; xvi.7.
[7] Eph. i.14; 2 Cor. i.22; v.5.

Spirit Himself beareth witness with our spirit that we are the children of God." [8]

Here let us observe, before proceeding, what indirect evidence is afforded us in these texts of the Divinity of the Holy Spirit. Who can be personally present at once with every Christian, but God Himself? Who but He, not merely ruling in the midst of the Church invisibly, as Michael might keep watch over Israel, or another Angel might be "the Prince of Persia,"— but really taking up His abode as one and the same in many separate hearts, so as to fulfil our Lord's words, that it was expedient that He should depart; Christ's bodily presence, which was limited to place, being exchanged for the manifold spiritual indwelling of the Comforter within us? This consideration suggests both the dignity of our Sanctifier, and the infinite preciousness of His Office towards us.

To proceed: The Holy Ghost, I have said, dwells in body and soul, as in a temple. Evil spirits indeed have power to possess sinners, but His indwelling is far more perfect; for He is all-knowing and omnipresent, He is able to search into all our thoughts, and penetrate into every motive of the heart. Therefore, He pervades us (if it may be so said) as light pervades a building, or as a sweet perfume the folds of some honourable robe; so that, in Scripture language, we are said to be in Him, and He in us. It is plain that such an inhabitation brings the Christian into a state altogether new and marvellous, far above the possession of mere gifts, exalts him inconceivably in the scale of beings, and gives him a place and an office which he had not before. In St. Peter's forcible language, he becomes "partaker of the Divine Nature," and has "power" or authority, as St. John says, "to become the son of God." Or, to use the words of St. Paul, "he is a new creation; old things are passed away, behold all things are become new." His rank is new; his parentage and service new. He is "of God," and "is not his own," "a vessel unto honour, sanctified and meet for the Master's use, and prepared unto every good work." [9]

This wonderful change from darkness to light, through the entrance of the Spirit into the soul, is called Regeneration, or the New Birth; a blessing which, before Christ's coming, not even Prophets and righteous men possessed, but which is now conveyed to all men freely through the Sacrament of Baptism.

[8] Rom. viii.9, 11; 1 Cor. vi.19; 2 Cor. vi.16; Rom. v.5; viii.16.
[9] 2 Pet. i.4; John i.12; 2 Cor. v.17; 1 John iv.4; 1 Cor. vi.19, 20; 2 Tim. ii.21.

By nature we are children of wrath; the heart is sold under sin, possessed by evil spirits; and inherits death as its eternal portion. But by the coming of the Holy Ghost, all guilt and pollution are burned away as by fire, the devil is driven forth, sin, original and actual, is forgiven, and the whole man is consecrated to God. And this is the reason why He is called "the earnest" of that Saviour who died for us, and will one day give us the fulness of His own presence in heaven. Hence, too, He is our "seal unto the day of redemption;" for as the potter moulds the clay, so He impresses the Divine image on us members of the household of God. And His work may truly be called Regeneration; for though the original nature of the soul is not destroyed, yet its past transgressions are pardoned once and for ever, and its source of evil staunched and gradually dried up by the pervading health and purity which has set up its abode in it. Instead of its own bitter waters, a spring of health and salvation is brought within it; not the mere streams of that fountain, "clear as crystal," which is before the Throne of God,[10] but, as our Lord says, "a well of water *in him*," in a man's heart, "springing up into everlasting life." Hence He elsewhere describes the heart as giving forth, not receiving, the streams of grace: "Out of his belly shall flow rivers of Living Water." St. John adds, "this spake He of the Spirit."[11]

Such is the inhabitation of the Holy Ghost within us, applying to us individually the precious cleansing of Christ's blood in all its manifold benefits. Such is the great doctrine, which we hold as a matter of faith, and without actual experience to verify it to us. Next, I must speak briefly concerning the manner in which the Gift of grace manifests itself in the regenerate soul; a subject which I do not willingly take up, and which no Christian perhaps is ever able to consider without some effort, feeling that he thereby endangers either his reverence towards God, or his humility, but which the errors of this day, and the confident tone of their advocates, oblige us to dwell upon, lest truth should suffer by our silence.

1. The heavenly gift of the Spirit fixes the eyes of our mind upon the Divine Author of our salvation. By nature we are blind and carnal; but the Holy Ghost by whom we are newborn, reveals to us the God of mercies, and bids us recognise and adore Him as our Father with a true heart. He impresses on us our Heavenly Father's image, which we lost when Adam fell, and disposes us to seek His presence by the very instinct of our

---

[10] Rev. iv.6; Ps. xlvi.4. [11] John iv.14; vii.38, 39.

new nature. He gives us back a portion of that freedom in willing and doing, of that uprightness and innocence, in which Adam was created. He unites us to all holy beings, as before we had relationship with evil. He restores for us that broken bond, which, proceeding from above, connects together into one blessed family all that is anywhere holy and eternal, and separates it off from the rebel world which comes to nought. Being then the sons of God, and one with Him, our souls mount up and cry to Him continually. This special characteristic of the regenerate soul is spoken of by St. Paul soon after the text. "Ye have received the Spirit of adoption, whereby we cry, Abba, Father." Nor are we left to utter these cries to Him, in any vague uncertain way of our own; but He who sent the Spirit to dwell in us habitually, gave us also a form of words to sanctify the separate acts of our minds. Christ left His sacred Prayer to be the peculiar possession of His people, and the voice of the Spirit. If we examine it, we shall find in it the substance of that doctrine, to which St. Paul has given a name in the passage just quoted. We begin it by using our privilege of calling on Almighty God in express words as "Our Father." We proceed, according to this beginning, in that waiting, trusting, adoring, resigned temper, which children ought to feel; looking towards Him, rather than thinking of ourselves; zealous for His honour rather than fearful about our safety; resting in His present help, not with eyes timorously glancing towards the future. His name, His kingdom, His will, are the great objects for the Christian to contemplate and make his portion, being stable and serene, and "complete in Him," as beseems one who has the gracious presence of His Spirit within him. And, when he goes on to think of himself, he prays, that he may be enabled to have towards others what God has shown towards himself, a spirit of forgiveness and loving-kindness. Thus he pours himself out on all sides, first looking up to catch the heavenly gift, but, when he gains it, not keeping it to himself, but diffusing "rivers of living water" to the whole race of man, thinking of self as little as may be, and desiring ill and destruction to nothing but that principle of temptation and evil, which is rebellion against God;—lastly, ending, as he began, with the contemplation of His kingdom, power, and glory everlasting. This is the true "Abba, Father," which the Spirit of adoption utters within the Christian's heart, the infallible voice of Him who "maketh intercession for the Saints in God's way." And if he has at times, for instance, amid trial or affliction, special visitations and comfortings from the Spirit, "plaints unutterable" within him, yearnings after the life to come, or bright and passing gleams of God's eternal election, and deep stirrings of wonder and thankfulness thence following, he thinks too reverently of "the secret of the Lord," to betray (as it were) His confidence, and, by vaunting it to the world, to exaggerate it perchance into more than it was meant to convey: but he is silent, and ponders it as choice encouragement to his soul, meaning something, but he knows not how much.

2. The indwelling of the Holy Ghost raises the soul, not only to the thought of God, but of Christ also. St. John says, "Truly our fellowship is with the Father, and with His Son Jesus Christ." And our Lord Himself, "If a man love Me, he will keep My words; and My Father will love him, and We will come unto him, and make our abode with him." [12] Now, not to speak of other and higher ways in which these texts are fulfilled, one surely consists in that exercise of faith and love in the thought of the Father and Son, which the Gospel, and the Spirit revealing it, furnish to the Christian. The Spirit came especially to "glorify" Christ; and vouchsafes to be a shining light within the Church and the individual Christian, reflecting the Saviour of the world in all His perfections, all His offices, all His works. He came for the purpose of unfolding what was yet hidden, whilst Christ was on earth; and speaks on the house-tops what was delivered in closets, disclosing Him in the glories of His transfiguration, who once had no comeliness in His outward form, and was but a man of sorrows and acquainted with grief. First, He inspired the Holy Evangelists to record the life of Christ, and directed them which of His words and works to select, which to omit; next, He commented (as it were) upon these, and unfolded their meaning in the Apostolic Epistles. The birth, the life, the death and resurrection of Christ, has been the text which He has illuminated. He has made history to be doctrine; telling us plainly, whether by St. John or St. Paul, that Christ's conception and birth was the real Incarnation of the Eternal Word,—His life, "God manifest in the Flesh,"—His death and resurrection, the Atonement for sin, and the Justification of all believers. Nor was this all: He continued His sacred comment in the formation of the Church, superintending and overruling its human instruments, and bringing out our Saviour's words and works, and the Apostles' illustrations of them into acts of obedience and permanent Ordinances, by the ministry of Saints and Martyrs. Lastly, He completes His

[12] 1 John i.3; John xiv.23.

gracious work by conveying this system of Truth, thus varied and expanded, to the heart of each individual Christian in whom He dwells. Thus He vouchsafes to edify the whole man in faith and holiness: "casting down imaginations and every high thing that exalteth itself against the knowledge of God, and bringing into captivity every thought to the obedience of Christ." [13] By His wonder-working grace all things tend to perfection. Every faculty of the mind, every design, pursuit, subject of thought, is hallowed in its degree by the abiding vision of Christ, as Lord, Saviour, and Judge. All solemn, reverent, thankful, and devoted feelings, all that is noble, all that is choice in the regenerate soul, all that is self-denying in conduct, and zealous in action, is drawn forth and offered up by the Spirit as a living sacrifice to the Son of God. And, though the Christian is taught not to think of himself above his measure, and dare not boast, yet he is also taught that the consciousness of the sin which remains in him, and infects his best services, should not separate him from God, but lead him to Him who can save. He reasons with St. Peter, "To whom should he go?" and, without daring to decide, or being impatient to be told how far he is able to consider as his own every Gospel privilege in its fulness, he gazes on them all with deep thought as the Church's possession, joins her triumphant hymns in honour of Christ, and listens wistfully to her voice in inspired Scripture, the voice of the Bride calling upon and blest in the Beloved.

3. St. John adds, after speaking of "our fellowship with the Father and His Son:" "These things write we unto you, that your joy may be full." What is fulness of joy but *peace*? Joy is tumultuous only when it is not full; but peace is the privilege of those who are "filled with the knowledge of the glory of the Lord, as the waters cover the sea." "Thou wilt keep him in perfect peace, whose mind is stayed on Thee, because he trusteth in Thee." [14] It is peace, springing from trust and innocence, and then overflowing in love towards all around him. What is the effect of mere animal ease and enjoyment, but to make a man pleased with everything which happens? "A merry heart is a perpetual feast;" and such is peculiarly the blessing of a soul rejoicing in the faith and fear of God. He who is anxious, thinks of himself, is suspicious of danger, speaks hurriedly, and has no time for the interests of others; he who lives in peace is at leisure, wherever his lot is cast. Such is the work of the Holy Spirit in the heart, whether in Jew or Greek, bond or free. He Himself

[13] 2 Cor. x. 5.   [14] Is. xxvi. 3.

perchance in His mysterious nature, is the Eternal Love whereby the Father and the Son have dwelt in each other, as ancient writers have believed; and what He is in heaven, that He is abundantly on earth. He lives in the Christian's heart, as the never-failing fount of charity, which is the very sweetness of the living waters. For where He is, "there is liberty" from the tyranny of sin, from the dread, which the natural man feels, of an offended, unreconciled Creator. Doubt, gloom, impatience have been expelled; joy in the Gospel has taken their place, the hope of heaven and the harmony of a pure heart, the triumph of self-mastery, sober thoughts, and a contented mind. How can charity towards all men fail to follow, being the mere affectionateness of innocence and peace? Thus the Spirit of God creates in us the simplicity and warmth of heart which children have, nay, rather the perfections of His heavenly hosts, high and low being joined together in His mysterious work; for what are implicit trust, ardent love, abiding purity, but the mind both of little children and of the adoring Seraphim!

Thoughts, such as these, will affect us rightly, if they make us fear and be watchful, while we rejoice. They cannot surely do otherwise; for the mind of a Christian, as I have been attempting to describe it, is not so much what we have, as what we ought to have. To look, indeed, after dwelling on it, upon the multitude of men who have been baptized in Christ's name, is too serious a matter, and we need not force ourselves to do so. We need not do so, further than to pray for them, and to protest and strive against what is evil among them; for as to the higher and more solemn thought, how persons, set apart individually and collectively, as Temples of Truth and Holiness, should become what they seem to be, and what their state is in consequence in God's sight, is a question which it is a great blessing to be allowed to put from us as not our concern. It is our concern only to look to ourselves, and to see that, as we have received the gift, we "grieve not the Holy Spirit of God, whereby we are sealed unto the day of redemption;" remembering that "if any man destroy the temple of God, him shall God destroy." This reflection and the recollection of our many backslidings, will ever keep us, please God, from judging others, or from priding ourselves on our privileges. Let us but consider how we have fallen from the light and grace of our Baptism. Were we now what that Holy Sacrament made us, we might ever "go on our way rejoicing;" but having sullied our heavenly garments, in one way or other, in a greater or less degree (God knoweth and our own consciences too in a measure), alas! the Spirit of adoption has in part receded from us, and the sense of guilt, remorse, sorrow, and penitence must take His place. We must renew our confession, and seek afresh our absolution day by day, before we dare call upon God as "our Father," or offer up Psalms and Intercessions to Him. And, whatever pain and affliction meets us through life, we must take it as a merciful penance imposed by a Father upon erring children, to be borne meekly and thankfully, and as intended to remind us of the weight of that infinitely greater punishment, which was our desert by nature, and which Christ bore for us on the Cross.

THE KINGDOM OF THE SAINTS

(Monday in Whitsun Week)

"The stone that smote the Image became a great Mountain, and filled the whole earth."—Dan. ii.35.

DOUBTLESS, could we see the course of God's dispensations in this world, as the Angels see them, we should not be able to deny that it was His unseen hand that ordered them. Even the most presumptuous sinner would find it hopeless to withstand the marks of Divine Agency in them; and would "believe and tremble." This is what moves the Saints in the Apocalypse, to praise and adore Almighty God,—the view of His wonderful works seen as a whole from first to last. "Great and marvellous are Thy works, Lord God Almighty; just and true are Thy ways, Thou King of Saints! Who shall not fear Thee, O Lord, and glorify Thy name?" [1] And perchance such a contemplation of the providences of God, whether in their own personal history, or in the affairs of their own country, or of the Church, or of the world at large, may be one of the blessed occupations of God's elect in the Intermediate State. However, even to us sinners, who have neither secured our crown like the Saints departed, much less are to be compared to the Angels who "excel in strength, that do His commandments, hearkening unto the voice of His Word," [2] even to us is vouchsafed some insight into God's providence, by means of the records of it. History and Prophecy are given us as informants, and reflect various lights upon His Attributes and Will, whether separately or in combination. The text suggests to us an especial instance of this privilege, in the view which is allowed us of the introduction and propagation of the Gospel; and it will be fitting at a Season when we are especially commemorating its first public manifestation in the Holy Ghost's descent upon the Apostles, to make some remarks upon the wonderful providence of God as seen in it.

[1] Rev. xv.3, 4.   [2] Ps. ciii.20.

The words of Daniel in the text form part of the disclosure he was inspired to make to Nebuchadnezzar, of the dream that "troubled" him. After describing the great Image, with a head of fine gold, arms of silver, belly and thighs of brass, legs of iron, and feet of iron and clay, by which were signified the four Empires which preceded the coming of Christ, he goes on to foretell the rise of Christianity in these words: "Thou sawest till that a stone was cut out without hands, which smote the Image upon his feet which were of iron and clay, and brake them to pieces. Then was the iron, the clay, the brass, the silver, and the gold, broken in pieces together, and became like the chaff;" heavy and costly as the metals were, they became as light as chaff "of the summer threshing-floors, and the wind carried them away. . . . And the stone that smote the Image became a great Mountain, and filled the whole earth."

Afterwards, he adds this interpretation: "In the days of these kings, shall the God of Heaven set up a Kingdom which shall never be destroyed; and the Kingdom shall not be left to other people, but it shall break in pieces, and consume all these kingdoms, and it shall stand for ever."

This prophecy of Daniel is fulfilled among us, at this day. We know it is so. Those four idol kingdoms are gone, and the Kingdom of Christ, made without human hands, remains, and is our own blessed portion. But to speak thus summarily, is scarcely to pay due honour to God's work, or to reap the full benefit of our knowledge of it. Let us then look into the details of this great Providence, the history of the Gospel Dispensation.

1. Observe what it was that took place. There have been many kingdoms before and since Christ came, which have been set up and extended by the sword. This, indeed, is the only way in which earthly power grows. Wisdom and skill direct its movements, but the arm of force is the instrument of its aggrandizement. And an unscrupulous conscience, a hard heart, and guilty deeds, are the usual attendants upon its growth: which is, in one form or other, but usurpation, invasion, conquest, and tyranny. It rises against its neighbours, and increases by external collisions and a visible extension. But the propagation of the Gospel was the internal development of one and the same principle in various countries at once, and therefore may be suitably called invisible, and not of this world. The Jewish nation did not "push westward, and northward, and southward;" but a spirit went out from its Church into all lands, and wherever it came, there a new Order of things forthwith arose in the bosom of strangers; arose simultaneously, independently

in each place, and recognising, but in no sense causing, the repetitions of itself which arose all around it. We know indeed that
the Apostles were the instruments, the secret emissaries (as
they might be called) of this work; but I am speaking of the
appearance of things as a heathen might regard them. Who
among the wise men or the disputers of this world will take
account of a few helpless men wandering about from place to
place, and preaching a new doctrine? It never can be believed, it
is impossible that they should be the real agents of the revolution which followed. So we maintain, and the world's philosophy must be consistent enough to agree with us. It looked down
upon the Apostles in their day; it said they could effect nothing;
let it say the same thing now in common fairness. Surely to the
philosophy of this world it must appear as absurd to ascribe
great changes to such weak vessels, as to attribute them to some
imaginary unseen agents, to the heavenly hosts whose existence
it disbelieves. As it would account the hypothesis of Angelic
interference gratuitous, so did it then, and must still pronounce
the hypothesis of the Apostolic efforts insufficient. Its own witness in the beginning becomes our evidence now.

Dismissing then the thought of the feeble and despised
preachers, who went to and fro, let us see what really happened.
In the midst of a great Empire, such as the world had never
seen, powerful and crafty beyond all former empires, more extensive, and better organized, suddenly a new Kingdom arose.
Suddenly in every part of this well-cemented Empire, in the
East and West, North and South, as if by some general understanding, yet without any sufficient system of correspondence
or centre of influence, ten thousand orderly societies, professing one and the same doctrine, and disciplined upon the same
polity, sprang up as from the earth. It seemed as though the
fountains of the great deep were broken up, and some new
forms of creation were thrown forward from below, the manifold ridges of some "great Mountain," crossing, splitting, disar-
ranging the existing system of things, levelling the hills, filling
up the valleys,—irresistible as being sudden, unforeseen, and
unprovided for,—till it "filled the whole earth." [3] This was indeed a "new thing;" and independent of all reference to prophecy, is unprecedented in the history of the world before or
since, and calculated to excite the deepest interest and amazement in any really philosophical mind. Throughout the kingdoms and provinces of Rome, while all things looked as usual,

[3] Is. xli.15, 16.

the sun rising and setting, the seasons continuing, men's passions swaying them as from the beginning, their thoughts set on their worldly business, on their gain or their pleasures, on their ambitious prospects and quarrels, warrior measuring his strength with warrior, politicians plotting, and kings banqueting, suddenly this portent came as a snare upon the whole earth. Suddenly, men found themselves encompassed with foes, as a camp surprised by night. And the nature of this hostile host was still more strange (if possible) than the coming of it. It was not a foreigner who invaded them, not a barbarian from the north, nor a rising of slaves, nor an armament of pirates, but the enemy rose up from among themselves. The first-born in every house, "from the first-born of Pharaoh on the throne, to the first-born of the captive in the dungeon," unaccountably found himself enlisted in the ranks of this new power, and estranged from his natural friends. Their brother, the son of their mother, the wife of their bosom, the friend that was as their own soul, these were the sworn soldiers of the "mighty army," that "covered the face of the whole earth."

Next, when they began to interrogate this enemy of Roman greatness, they found no vague profession among them, no varying account of themselves, no irregular and uncertain plan of action or conduct. They were all members of strictly and similarly organized societies. Every one in his own district was the subject of a new state, of which there was one visible head, and officers under him. These small kingdoms were indefinitely multiplied, each of them the fellow of the other. Wherever the Roman Emperor travelled, there he found these seeming rivals of his power, the Bishops of the Church. Further, they one and all refused to obey his orders, and the prescriptive laws of Rome, so far as religion was concerned. The authority of the Pagan Religion, which in the minds of Romans was identified with the history of their greatness, was plainly set at nought by these upstart monarchies. At the same time they professed and observed a singular patience and subjection to the civil powers. They did not stir hand or foot in self-defence; they submitted to die, nay, accounted death the greatest privilege that could be inflicted on them. And further, they avowed one and all the same doctrine clearly and boldly; and they professed to receive it from one and the same source. They traced it up through the continuous line of their Bishops to certain twelve or fourteen Jews, who professed to have received it from Heaven. Moreover, they were bound one to another by the closest ties of fellowship; the society of each place to its ruler, and their rulers one with another by an intimate alliance all over the earth. And lastly, in spite of persecution from without, and occasional dissensions from within, they so prospered, that within three centuries from their first appearance in the Empire, they forced its sovereigns to become members of their confederation; nay, nor ended there, but as the civil power declined in strength, they became its patrons instead of its victims, mediated between it and its barbarian enemies, and after burying it in peace when its hour came, took its place, won over the invaders, subdued their kings, and at length ruled as supreme; ruled, united under one head, in the very scenes of their former suffering, in the territory of the Empire, with Rome itself, the seat of the Imperial government, as a centre. I am not entering into the question of doctrine, any more than of prophecy. I am not inquiring how far this victorious Kingdom was by this time perverted from its original character; but only directing attention to the historical phenomenon. How strange then is the course of the Dispensation! Five centuries compass the rise and fall of other kingdoms; but ten were not enough for the full aggrandizement of this. Its sovereignty was but commencing, when other powers have run their course and are exhausted. And now to this day, that original Dynasty, begun by the Apostles, endures. Through all changes of civil affairs, of race, of language, of opinion, the succession of Rulers then begun, has lasted on, and still represents in every country its original founders. "Instead of its fathers, it has had children, who have been princes in all lands." Truly, this is the vision of "stone *cut out without hands*," "smiting" the idols of the world, "breaking them in pieces," scattering them "like chaff," and, in their place, "filling the whole earth." If there be a Moral Governor over the world, is there not something unearthly in all this, something which we are forced to refer to Him from its marvellousness, something which from its dignity and greatness bespeaks His hand?

2. Now, with this wonderful phenomenon before us, let us consider well the language of Christ and His Apostles. In the very infancy of their Kingdom, while travelling through the cities of Israel, or tossed to and fro as outcasts among the heathen, they speak confidently, solemnly, calmly, of its destined growth and triumph. Observe our Lord's language: "Jesus came into Galilee, preaching the Gospel of the Kingdom of God, and saying, The time is fulfilled, and the Kingdom of God is at hand; repent ye, and believe the Gospel." Again, "Thou art Peter, and upon this rock I will build My Church; and the gates

of hell shall not prevail against it." "I appoint unto you a Kingdom, as My Father hath appointed unto Me; that ye may eat
and drink at My table in My kingdom, and sit on thrones, judging the Twelve Tribes of Israel." "The Kingdom of Heaven is
like to a grain of mustard seed, which a man took and sowed in
his field; which indeed is the least of all seeds, but when it is
grown, *it is the greatest among herbs*, and becometh a tree, *so that the
birds of the air come and lodge in the branches thereof.*" Is it possible to
doubt that Christ contemplated in these words the overshad-
owing sovereignty of His Kingdom? Let it be observed that the
figure used is the same applied by Daniel to the Assyrian Empire. "The tree that thou sawest," he says to Nebuchadnezzar,
"which grew and was strong. . . . . upon whose branches the
fowls of the heaven had their habitation, it is thou, O King."
How wondrously was the parallel prophecy fulfilled, when the
mighty men of the earth fled for refuge to the Holy Church!
Again, "Go ye into all the world, and preach the Gospel to
every creature. He that believeth and is baptized shall be saved;
but he that believeth not shall be damned."[4] With what "authority" He speaks! What majestic simplicity, what unhesitating resolve, what commanding superiority is in His words!
Reflect upon them in connexion with the event.

On the other hand, consider in what language He speaks of
that disorganization of society which was to attend the establishment of His kingdom. "I am come to send fire on the earth;
and what will I, if it be already kindled? But I have a baptism to
be baptized with, and how am I straitened till it be accomplished!" "Think not that I am come to send peace on earth; I
came not to send peace, but a sword. For I am come to set a man
at variance against his father, and the daughter against her
mother, and the daughter-in-law against the mother-in-law:
and a man's foes shall be they of his own household." "The
brother shall betray the brother to death, and the father the
son; and children shall rise up against their parents, and shall
cause them to be put to death; and ye shall be hated of all men
for My name's sake. . . . . In those days, after that tribulation,
the sun shall be darkened, and the moon shall not give her light,
and the stars of heaven shall fall, and the powers of heaven shall
be shaken."[5] In the last words, whatever difficulty there may be
in the chronological arrangement, is contained a clear announcement under the recognised prophetical symbols, of the

[4] Mark i.14, 15; Matt. xvi.18; Luke xxii.29,30; Matt. xiii.31, 32; Dan.
iv.20, 22; Mark vi.15, 16.

[5] Luke xii.49, 50; Matt. x.34–36; Mark xiii.12, 13, 24, 25.

destruction, sooner or later, of existing political institutions. In like manner, observe how St. Paul takes for granted the troubles which were coming on the earth, and the rise of the Christian Church amidst them, and reasons on all this as if already realized. "Now hath He promised, saying, Yet once more I shake not the earth only, but also heaven. And this word, yet once more, signifieth the removing of those things that are shaken, as of things that are made, that those things which cannot be shaken may remain. Wherefore we receiving a Kingdom which cannot be moved, let us have grace, whereby we may serve God acceptably with reverence and godly fear." [6]

The language, of which the above is but a specimen, is the more remarkable, because neither Christ nor His Apostles looked forward to these wonderful changes with exultation, but with a deep feeling of mingled joy and sadness, as foreboding those miserable corruptions in the Church, which all Christians allow to have since taken place, though they may differ in their account of them. "Because iniquity shall abound, the love of many shall wax cold. . . . . There shall arise false Christs and false prophets, and shall show great signs and wonders; insomuch that, if it were possible, they shall deceive the very elect. Behold, I have told you before." "In the last days, perilous times shall come. For men shall be lovers of their own selves, covetous, boasters, ... traitors, heady, high-minded . . . . having a form of godliness, but denying the power thereof. . . . . Evil men and seducers shall wax worse and worse, deceiving and being deceived." [7]

Now, if we had nothing more to bring forward than the two considerations which have been here insisted on, the singular history of Christianity, and the clear and confident anticipation of it by its first preachers, we should have enough of evidence, one would think, to subdue the most difficult inquirer to a belief of its divinity. But, to-morrow we will see, please God, whether something may not be added to the above view of it.

[6] Heb. xii.26–28.
[7] Matt. xxiv.12, 24, 25; 2 Tim. iii.1–5, 18.

THE KINGDOM OF THE SAINTS

(Tuesday in Whitsun Week)

"The stone that smote the Image became a great Mountain, and filled the whole earth."—Dan. ii.35.

YESTERDAY I drew your notice to the outlines of the history of the Church, and the clear and precise anticipation of it, by our Lord and His Apostles. The Gospel Dispensation is confessedly a *singular* phenomenon in human affairs; singular, whether we consider the extent it occupies in history, the harmony of its system, the consistency of its design, its contrariety to the existing course of things, and success in spite of that contrariety, and lastly, the avowed intention of its first preachers to effect those objects, which it really has attained. They professed to be founding a Kingdom; a new Kingdom, different from any that had been before, as disclaiming the use of force,—in this world, yet not of this world,—while it was to be, notwithstanding, of an aggressive and encroaching character, an empire of conquest and aggrandizement, destroying all former powers, and itself standing for ever. Infidels often object to us, that our interpretation of the Scripture prophecies concerning Christ's Kingdom is after all but allegorical, and therefore evasive. Not so; we are on the whole willing to take our stand on their literal fulfilment. Christ preached that "the kingdom of God was at hand." He founded it and made Peter and the other Apostles His Vicegerents in it after His departure, and He announced its indefinite extension, and its unlimited duration. And, in matter of fact, it exists to this day, with its government vested in the very dynasty which His Apostles began, and its territory spread over more than the world then known to the Jews; with varying success indeed in times and places, and varying consistency and unanimity within; yet, after making every allowance for such partial failures, strictly a visible power, with a political influence founded on invisible pretensions. Thus the anticipations of its founders are unparalleled in their novelty, their boldness, and their correctness. To continue our review.

3. If the Christian Church has spread its branches high and wide over the earth, its roots are fixed as deep below the surface. The intention of Christ and His Apostles, on which I have dwelt, is itself but the accomplishment of ancient prophecy.

First, let it be observed that there was an existing belief among the heathen, at the time of its rise, that out of the East a new Empire of the world was destined to issue.[1] This rumour, however originating, was known at Rome, the then seat of dominion, and is recorded by a Roman historian. Next, it became matter (as it would seem) for heathen poetry. The most celebrated of Roman poets has foretold the coming of a new Kingdom of peace and righteousness under the rule of a divine and divinely-favoured King, who was to be born into the world. Could it be maintained that he wrote from his own imagination, not from existing traditions, this would not at all diminish the marvel, as not in any measure tending to account for it. In that case, the poet would but take his place among the Prophets. Further, if we admit St. Matthew's testimony, which we have no excuse for doubting, we must believe, that, just at the time of Christ's birth, certain Eastern Sages came to Jerusalem in search of a child, of whom they expected great things, and whom they desired to worship in His cradle. And lastly, another Eastern Sage, fourteen hundred years before, had declared, heathen though he was, and uninterested in the event, that "a Star should come out of Jacob, and a Sceptre should rise out of Israel, . . . that out of Jacob should come He that should have dominion."[2] Now, whether we may assume that this last prophecy is faithfully recorded by Moses or not, so far is clear, and not a little remarkable, that the Jewish traditions concerning the expected Empire profess to take their rise in heathen sources.[3] It is a clear coincidence with the fact, already adverted to, of the prevalence of such predictions among the heathen at the time of Christ's coming.

While such was the testimony of enemies and strangers to this destined rise of a prosperous Empire from Judæa, much more full and varied are the predictions of it delivered by the natives of that country themselves. These, as contained in our holy books, have been again and again illustrated by Christian

---

[1] *Vide* Horsley's Dissertation on the Prophecies among the Heathen.

[2] Numb. xxiv.17, 19.

[3] Gen. xlix.10, does not speak of conquest or empire, so clearly as to constitute an exception; much less Gen. xii.2, 3, and xxviii.14, which could scarcely be so interpreted, except after other and clearer prophecies.

writers, and neither need nor admit of enumeration here. I will but cite one or two passages, by way of reminding you of them. "Ask of Me, and I shall give Thee the heathen for Thine inheritance, and the uttermost parts of the earth for Thy possession. Thou shalt break them with a rod of iron; Thou shalt dash them in pieces like a potter's vessel." "Gird Thy sword upon Thy thigh, O most Mighty, with Thy glory and Thy majesty. And in Thy majesty ride prosperously, because of truth, and meekness, and righteousness: and Thy right hand shall teach Thee terrible things. Thine arrows are sharp in the heart of the King's enemies, whereby the people fall under Thee. . . . . Instead of Thy fathers shall be Thy children, whom Thou mayest make princes in all the earth." "The Lord shall send the rod of Thy strength out of Zion; rule Thou in the midst of Thine enemies. . . . . The Lord at Thy right hand shall strike through kings in the day of His wrath." "It shall come to pass in the last days, that the Mountain of the Lord's House shall be established in the top of the mountains, and shall be exalted above the hills; and all nations shall flow unto it. . . . . Out of Zion shall go forth the Law, and the Word of the Lord from Jerusalem. And He shall judge among the nations, and shall rebuke many people; and they shall beat their swords into plowshares, and their spears into pruning hooks; nation shall not lift up sword against nation; neither shall they learn war any more." "It is a light thing that Thou shouldest be My servant to raise up the tribes of Jacob, and to restore the preserved of Israel. I will also give Thee for a light to the Gentiles, that Thou shouldest be My salvation unto the end of the earth." And almost in the same words, the aged Simeon recognises in the infant Jesus the Lord's promised "salvation, a light to lighten the Gentiles, and the glory of His people Israel." [4] In these passages the prediction of bloody revolution and of peace are as strangely combined, as in our Lord's account of His Kingdom, as being at once a refuge and consolation, and a sword. Maintain, if you will, that they have not hitherto been so fully accomplished in its history as is conceivable; yet, in matter of fact, has not this twofold character of the Dispensation been in such measure realized, as substantially answers to the words of the prediction? Consider only the wars and tumults of the Middle Ages, of which the Church was the occasion, and, at the same time, its salutary influence upon the fierce and lawless soldiers who then filled the thrones of Europe. Take the Prophecy, take the History; and say fairly,

[4] Ps. ii.8, 9; xlv.3–5, 16; cx.2, 5; Is. ii.2–4; xlix.6; Luke ii.30–32.

whether, in accordance with the Scripture prospect, we do not actually find in the centuries I speak of, a political power, making vassals of the kings of the earth, humbling them beneath its feet, affording matter of endless strife, yet acting as the very bond of peace, as far as peace was really attained. How truly have "the sons of them that afflicted" the Church, "come bending unto her; and they that despised her, bowed themselves at the soles of her feet,"[5] and "the enemies of Christ been made His footstool!"

It may help us in entering into the state of the case, to consider what our surprise would be, did we, in the course of our researches into history, find any resemblance to this prophetic forecast in the annals of other kingdoms. Even one poor coincidence in the history of Rome, viz. of the anticipated and the actual duration of its greatness, does not fail to arrest our attention. We know that even before the Christian era, it was the opinion of the Roman Augurs, that the twelve vultures which Romulus had seen previous to the foundation of the city, represented the twelve centuries, assigned as the limit of its power; an anticipation which was singularly fulfilled by the event.[6] Yet what is this solitary fact to the series of varied and circumstantial prophecies which ushered in, and were fulfilled in Christianity? Extend the twelve centuries of Roman dominion to an additional half of that period, preserve its monarchical form inviolate, whether from aristocratic or popular innovation, from first to last, and trace back the predictions concerning it, through an antecedent period, nearly of the same duration, and then you will have assimilated its history—not altogether, but in one or two of its features—to the characteristics of the Gospel Dispensation. As it is, this Roman wonder only serves to assist the imagination in embracing the marvellousness of those systematic prophecies concerning Christ's kingdom, which, from their number, variety, succession, and contemporary influence, may almost be accounted in themselves, and without reference to their fulfilment, a complete and independent dispensation.

[5] Is. lx.14.
[6] *Vide* Gibbon, chap. xxxv.*fin*. The ancient prediction concerning the fortunes of Russia is a more remarkable instance. A brazen equestrian statue, which had been originally in Antioch, is said, by historians of the beginning of the twelfth century, to be "inscribed with a prophecy, how the Russians in the last days should become masters of Constantinople."—*Vide* Gibbon, chap. lv.

4. Lastly, the course of Providence co-operated with this scheme of prophecy; God's word and hand went together. The state of the Jews for the last four hundred years before Christ was a preparation deliberately carried on for that which was to follow; just as the wanderings of Abraham and his heirs, the descent into Egypt, and the captivity there, for the same period, constituted a process introductory to the establishment of the Jewish Church. Consider the nature of this preparation:—the overthrow of the nation by the Chaldeans, issued in the dispersion of its members all over the civilized world, so that in all the principal cities Jewish communities existed, which gradually attracted to their faith Gentile converts, and were in one way or other the nucleus of the Christian Church when the Gospel was at length published. Now, here, I would first direct your attention to this strange connexion, which is visible at first sight between the dispersion of the Jews and the propagation of Christianity. Does not such a manifest appearance of cause and effect look very much like an indication of design? Next, I remark that this dispersion was later than the predictions concerning the Christian Church contained in the Jewish Scriptures: which in consequence cannot be charged with borrowing the idea of it from any actual disposition of things. And further, let it be observed that the disposition arose from the apparent frustration of all their hopes; a signal instance, as it would seem, of an overruling Providence, which would not be defeated as regards its object, in spite of the failure of those instruments, in which alone a human eye could see the means of accomplishing it.

Before concluding, I must explain myself on one point which has been incidentally mentioned more than once in the foregoing remarks, viz. as to the connexion between the temporal fortunes of the Church in the Middle Ages, and the inspired predictions concerning it. It may seem, before due attention has been given to the subject, as if none but members of the Roman Communion could regard them as parts of the Divine Dispensation; I therefore observe as follows:—

There is a considerable analogy between the history of what are called the Middle Ages and that of the Israelitish monarchy. That monarchy was perversely demanded and presumptuously realized by the nation when God had not led the way; it terminated in the dissolution of the federal union of the Tribes, the corruption of the people, and the ruin of their temporal power. Nevertheless, it cannot be denied, that in one sense that kingdom was the scope of the Mosaic institutions,[7] and a fulfilment of prophecy. Its kings were many of them highly favoured in themselves, and types of the promised Saviour; and their government and subjects were singularly blessed. Consider the circumstances attendant upon the building of the Temple. This may be accounted as the most glorious event in their history, the fruit of Moses' anxieties and David's labours, the completion and resting-place of the whole Dispensation, and the pledge of the more spiritual blessedness which was to come. Connect it with Solomon's reign, its peace and prosperity,—on the other hand, with its voluptuousness, its departure from the simplicity of the Mosaic Law,—with Solomon's personal character, degenerating from faith and purity into sins which we are not given to fathom. Are we able rightly to adjust the relation between the blessings destined for Israel, and the actual prosperity and greatness of this kingdom set up in rebellion against God, so as to be able to say how far it was recognised in His counsels, how far not? Can we draw the line between God's work and man's work?

I am not maintaining that the case of the Papacy is parallel to that of the Jewish Monarchy; nay, I do not introduce the latter for the sake of the analogy at all, be it stronger or fainter; but merely in order to show that it is possible for certain events to be in some sort a fulfilment of prophecy, without considering every part of them, the manner of their accomplishment, the circumstances, the instruments, and the like, to be approved by God. The Latin ecclesiastical system of the Middle Ages may anyhow be the fulfilment of that gracious design, which would have been even more exactly accomplished, had Christians possessed faith enough to keep closely to God's revealed will. For what we know, it was intended that all the kingdoms of the earth should have been made subject to the spiritual rule of the Church. The infirmity of man defeated this purpose; but it could not so far defeat it, but some sort of fulfilment took place. The mustard plant, stopped in its natural growth, shot out irregular branches. Satan could not hinder, he could but weaken the Kingdom promised to the Saints. He could but seduce them to trust in an arm of flesh. He could but sow the seeds of decay among them, by alluring them to bow down to "Ashtoreth the goddess of the Zidonians, and Milcom the abomination of the Ammonites." Had it not been for this falling away in divers times and places, surely Christendom would

[7] Deut. xvii. 14–20.

not be in its present miserable state of disunion and feebleness; nor the prophecies respecting it have issued in any degree in defeat and disappointment. Still partial as is their fulfilment, there is more than enough, even in what is and has been, to attest in the Church the presence of that Mighty Hand, whose very failures (so to say) and losses are deeds of victory and triumph.

As for ourselves, what was the exact measure of the offences of our forefathers in the faith, when they tired of the Christian Theocracy, and clothed the Church with "the purple robe" of Caesar, it avails not to determine. Not denying their sin, still after contemplating the glories of the Temple which were contemporaneous with it, we may well bewail our present fallen state,—the Priests and Levites, and chief of the Fathers, all of us "weeping with a loud voice," though the many shout for joy,— "praising" indeed, "and giving thanks unto the Lord, because He is good, for His mercy endureth for ever toward Israel," [8]— not undervaluing the blessings we have, yet humbling ourselves as the sinful offspring of sinful parents, who from the first have resisted and frustrated the grace of God, and seeing in the present feebleness and blindness of the Church, the tokens of His righteous judgments upon us; yet withal, from His continued mercies towards us, drawing the comfortable hope, that for His Son's sake He will not forsake us in time to come, and cherishing a sure trust, that, if we "give Him no rest" by our services of prayer and good works, He will at length, even yet, though doubtless in a way which we cannot understand, "establish and make Jerusalem a praise in the earth."

[8] Ezra iii. 11, 12.

THE GOSPEL, A TRUST
COMMITTED TO US

(The Feast of the Holy Trinity)

"O Timothy, keep that which is committed to thy trust, avoiding profane and vain babblings, and oppositions of science, falsely so called; which some professing, have erred concerning the Faith."
—1 Tim. vi.20, 21.

THESE words are addressed in the first place to the Ministers of the Gospel, in the person of Timothy; yet they contain a serious command and warning for all Christians. For all of us, high and low, in our measure are responsible for the safe-keeping of the Faith. We have all an equal interest in it, no one less than another, though an Order of men has been especially set apart for the duty of guarding it. If we Ministers of Christ guard it not, it is *our* sin but it is *your* loss, my brethren; and as any private person would feel that his duty and his safety lay in giving alarm of a fire or of a robbery in the city where he dwelt, though there were ever so many special officers appointed for the purpose, so, doubtless, every one of us is bound in his place to contend for the Faith, and to have an eye to its safe custody. If indeed the Faith of Christ were vague, indeterminate, a matter of opinion or deduction, then, indeed, we may well conceive that the Ministers of the Gospel would be the only due expounders and guardians of it; then it might be fitting for private Christians to wait till they were informed concerning the best mode of expressing it, or the relative importance of this or that part of it. But this has been all settled long ago; the Gospel Faith is a definite deposit,—a treasure, common to all, one and the same in every age, conceived in set words, and such as admits of being received, preserved, transmitted. We may safely leave the custody of it even in the hands of individuals; for in so doing, we are leaving nothing at all to private rashness and fancy, to pride, debate, and strife. We are but allowing men to "contend earnestly for the Faith once delivered to the Saints;" the Faith which was put into their hands one by one at their baptism, in a form of words called the Creed, and which has come down to them in that very same form from the first ages. This Faith is what even the humblest member of the Church may and must contend for; and in proportion to his education, will the circle of his knowledge enlarge. The Creed delivered to him in Baptism will then unfold, first, into the Nicene Creed (as it is called), then into the Athanasian; and, according as his power of grasping the sense of its articles increases, so will it become his duty to contend for them in their fuller and more accurate form. All these unfoldings of the Gospel Doctrine will become to him precious as the original articles, because they are in fact nothing more or less than the one true explanation of them delivered down to us from the first ages, together with the original baptismal or Apostles' Creed itself. As all nations confess to the existence of a God, so all branches of the Church confess to the Gospel doctrine; as the tradition of men witnesses to a Moral Governor and Judge, so the tradition of Saints witnesses to the Father Almighty, and His only Son, and the Holy Ghost. And as neither the superstitions of polytheism, nor the atheistic extravagances of particular countries at particular times, practically interfere with our reception of the one message which the sons of Adam deliver; so, much less, do the local heresies and temporary errors of the early Church, and its superadded corruptions, its schismatic offshoots, or its partial defections in later ages, impair the evidence and the claim of its teaching, in the judgment of those who sincerely wish to know the Truth once delivered to it. Blessed be God! we have not to find the Truth, it is put into our hands; we have but to commit it to our hearts, to preserve it inviolate, and to deliver it over to our posterity.

This then is the meaning of St. Paul's injunction in the text, given at the time when the Truth was first published. "Keep that which is committed to thy trust," or rather, "keep the deposit;" turn away from those "profane emptinesses" which pretenders to philosophy and science bring forward against it. Do not be moved by them; do not alter your Creed for them; for the end of such men is error. They go on disputing and refining, giving new meanings, modifying received ones, still with the idea of the True Faith in their minds as the scope of their inquiries; but at length they "miss" it. They shoot on one side of it, and embrace a deceit of their own instead of it.

By the Faith is evidently meant, as St. Paul's words show, some definite doctrine; not a mere temper of mind or principle of action, much less, vaguely, the Christian cause; and accordingly, in his Second Epistle to Timothy, the Apostle mentions as his comfort in the view of death, that he had "kept the Faith." In the same Epistles he describes it more particularly as "the Form" or outline "of sound words," "the excellent deposit;" phrases which show that the deposit certainly was a series of truths and rules of some sort (whether only doctrinal, or preceptive also, and ecclesiastical), and which are accurately descriptive of the formulary since called the Apostles' Creed.[1] And these same sacred truths which Timothy had received in trust, he was bid "commit" in turn "to faithful men," who should be "able to teach others also." By God's grace, he was enabled so to commit them; and they being thus transmitted from generation to generation, have, through God's continued mercy, reached even unto us "upon whom the ends of the world are come."

I propose in what follows, to set before you the account given us in Scripture of this Apostolic Faith; being led to do so on the one hand by the Day, on which we commemorate its fundamental doctrine, and on the other, by the mistaken views entertained of it by many persons in this day, which seem to require notice.

Perhaps it may be right first to state what these erroneous opinions are; which I will do briefly. They are not novel, as scarcely any religious error can be, and assuredly what has once or twice died away in former times will come to its end in like manner once more. I do not speak as if I feared it could overcome the Ancient Truth once delivered to the Saints; but still our watchfulness and care are the means appointed for its overthrow, and are not superseded, but rather encouraged, and roused, by the anticipation of ultimate success.

It is a fashion of the day, then, to suppose that all insisting upon precise Articles of Faith is injurious to the cause of spiritual religion, and inconsistent with an enlightened view of it; that it is all one to maintain, that the Gospel requires the reception of definite and positive Articles, and to acknowledge it to be technical and formal; that such a notion is superstitious, and interferes with the "liberty wherewith Christ has made us free;" that it argues a deficient insight into the principles and ends, a narrow comprehension of the spirit of His Revelation.

[1] *Vide* also, among other passages, 1 John ii.21–27, which refers to nothing short of a definite doctrine; *e.g.* "Let that therefore abide in you, *which ye have heard* from the beginning." Again, 2 Tim. ii.18, "Who *concerning the Truth* have erred, *saying that the Resurrection is past already*, and overthrow the *faith* of some."

Accordingly, instead of accepting reverently the doctrinal
Truths which have come down to us, an attempt is made by the
reasoners of this age to compare them together, to weigh and
measure them, to analyse, simplify, refashion them; to reduce
them to system, to arrange them into primary and secondary,
to harmonize them into an intelligible dependence upon each
other. The teacher of Christianity, instead of delivering its
Mysteries, and (as far as may be) unfolding them, is taught to
scrutinise them, with a view of separating the inward holy sense
from the form of words, in which the Spirit has indissolubly
lodged them. He asks himself, what is the *use* of the message
which has come down to him? what the comparative value of
this or that part of it? He proceeds to assume that there is some
one end of his ministerial labours, such as to be ascertainable by
him, some one revealed object of God's dealings with man in
the Gospel. Then, perhaps, he arbitrarily assigns this end to be
the salvation of the world, or the conversion of sinners. Next he
measures all the Scripture doctrines by their respective sensible
tendency to effect this end. He goes on to discard or degrade
this or that sacred truth as superfluous in consequence, or of
inferior importance; and throws the stress of his teaching upon
one or other, which he pronounces to contain in it the essence
of the Gospel, and on which he rests all others which he retains.
Lastly, he reconstructs the language of theology to suit his (so-
called) improved views of Scripture doctrine.

For instance, you will meet with writers who consider that all
the Attributes and Providences of God are virtually expressed
in the one proposition, "God is Love;" the other notices of His
Unapproachable Glory contained in Scripture being but modi-
fications of this. In consequence, they are led on to deny, first,
the doctrine of eternal punishment, as being inconsistent with
this notion of Infinite Love; next, resolving such expressions as
the "wrath of God" into a figure of speech, they deny the
Atonement, viewed as a real reconciliation of an offended God
to His creatures. Or again, they say that the object of the Gospel
Revelation is merely practical, and therefore, that theological
doctrines are altogether unnecessary, mere speculations, and
hindrances to the extension of religion; or, if not purely injurious, at least requiring modification. Hence you may hear them
ask, "What is the *harm* of being a Sabellian, or Arian? how does
it affect the moral character?" Or, again, they say that the great
end of the Gospel is the union of hearts in the love of Christ and
of each other, and that, in consequence, Creeds are but fetters
on souls which have received the Spirit of Adoption; that Faith

is a mere temper and a principle, not the acceptance for Christ's sake of a certain collection of Articles. Others, again, have rested the whole Gospel upon the doctrines of the Atonement and Sanctification. And others have seemed to make the doctrine of Justification by Faith the one cardinal point, upon which the gates of life open and shut. Let so much suffice in explanation of the drift of the following remarks.

St. Paul, I repeat, bids us hold fast the faith which is entrusted to our custody; and that Faith is a "Form of sound words," an "Outline," which it is our duty, according to our opportunities, to fill up and complete in all its parts. Now, let us see how much the very text of Scripture will yield us of these elementary lines of Truth, of the unchangeable Apostolic Rule of Faith, of which we are bound to be so jealous.

Its essential doctrine of course is what St. John terms generally "the doctrine of Christ," and which, in the case of every one calling himself Christian, is the profession necessary (as he tells us) for our receiving him into our houses. St. Paul speaks in much the same compendious way concerning the Gospel Faith, when he says, "Other foundation can no man lay than that is laid, which is Jesus, the Christ." However, in an earlier passage of the same Epistle, he speaks more explicitly: "I determined not to know anything among you save Jesus Christ, and Him crucified." Thus the Crucifixion of Christ was one essential part of the outline of sound words, preached and delivered by the Apostle. In his Epistle to the Romans, he adds another article of faith: "If thou shalt confess with thy mouth the Lord Jesus, and shalt believe in thine heart that God hath raised Him from the dead, thou shalt be saved." Here then the doctrine of the Resurrection is added to that of the Crucifixion. Elsewhere he says: "There is One God, and one Mediator between God and man, the Man Christ Jesus, who gave Himself a ransom for all to be testified in due time; even whereunto I am ordained a preacher." Here Christ's Mediation and Atonement are added as doctrines of Apostolical preaching. Further, towards the end of an Epistle already quoted, he speaks still more distinctly of the Gospel which he had preached, and had delivered over to his converts; and which, he adds, all the other Apostles preached also. "I put into your hands, first of all, what had before been put into mine, how that Christ died for our sins according to the Scriptures, and that He was buried, and that He rose again the third day according to the Scriptures." [2] Here we

<hr />

[2] 2 John 9–11; 1 Cor. iii.11; ii.2; Rom. x.9; 1 Tim. ii.5–7; 1 Cor. xv.3, 4.

find an approximation to the Articles of the Creed, as the Church has ever worded them.

But the letter of Scripture gives us still further insight into the subjects of the Sacred Deposit, of which St. Paul speaks in the text. In the course of the very Epistle in which it occurs, he delivers to Timothy a more explicit "Form of sound words" than any I have cited from his writings. He writes to tell him "how to conduct himself in the Church of the Living God," which he had to govern, and how to preserve it as "the pillar and ground of the Truth;" and proceeds to remind him what that Truth is. "God was manifested in the flesh, justified in the Spirit, seen of Angels, preached unto the Gentiles, believed on in the world, received up into glory." Here is mention, among other doctrines, of the Incarnation and the Ascension. It seems then to have been an article of the original Apostles' Creed, that Christ was not a mere man, but God Incarnate. In like manner, when the Ethiopian asked to be baptized, and Philip said he might if he "believed with all his heart," this was his confession: "I believe that Jesus Christ is the Son of God." This, it should be observed, is his confession, *after* Philip had "*preached unto him Jesus.*"[3]

Now, let us pass on to the very words in which that Baptism itself was administered; words which the Eunuch might not understand indeed at the time, but which were then committed to him to feed upon in his heart by faith, and, by the influence of the grace at the same time given, gradually to enter into. Those words were first ordained by Christ Himself, as some mysterious key by which the fountains of grace might be opened upon the baptismal water,—"In the Name of the Father, and of the Son, and of the Holy Ghost;" and they show that not only the doctrine of Christ, but that of the Trinity also, formed an essential portion of the Sacred Treasure, of which the Church was ordained to be the Preacher. Lastly, in the Epistle to the Hebrews, we are presented with an enumeration of some other of the fundamental Articles of Faith which the Apostles delivered. St. Paul therein speaks of "the *foundation* of repentance from dead works, and of Faith towards God, of the doctrine of Baptisms, and of Laying on of hands, and of Resurrection of the dead, and of Eternal Judgment."[4]

Observe then, how many Articles of that Faith, which the Church has ever confessed, are incidentally brought before us

---

[3] 1 Tim. iii.15, 16; Acts viii.35-37.

[4] Matt. xxviii.19; Heb. vi.1, 2. *Vide* also 2 Tim. ii.16-18, above referred to.

as such, and delivered as such in very form, in the course of Scripture narrative and precept;—the doctrine of the Trinity; of the Incarnation of the Son of God, His Mediatorship, His Atonement for our sins on the Cross, His Death, Burial, Resurrection on the third day, and Ascension; of Pardon on Repentance, Baptism as the instrument of it, Imposition of hands, the General Resurrection and the Judgment once for all. I might also appeal to such passages as that in the First Epistle to the Corinthians, where St. Paul says, "To us there is one God the Father, ... and one Lord Jesus Christ;"[5] but I wished to confine myself to texts in which the doctrines specified are expressly introduced as portions of a Formulary or Confession, committed or accepted, whether on the part of Ministers of the Church at Ordination, or of each member of it when he was baptized.

It may be proper to add, that the history of the Primitive Church altogether concurs in this view of the nature of Gospel Faith which Scripture sets before us. I mean we have sufficient evidence that, in matter of fact, such Creeds as St. Paul's did exist in its various branches, not differing from each other, except (for instance) as the Lord's Prayer in St. Matthew's Gospel differs from St. Luke's version of it; that this one and the same Faith was committed to every Christian everywhere on his baptism; and that it was considered as the especial trust of the Church of each place and of its Bishop, as having been received by continual transmission from its original Founder, whether Apostle or Evangelist.

Enough has been already said by way of proving from Scripture how precise, positive, manifold, are the Articles of our Faith, and how St. Paul insists on this their definiteness and minuteness; enough to show that we may not slur them over, nor heap them together confusedly, nor tamper with them, with the profaneness either of carelessness or of curious disputing,—in a word, that they are *sacred*. But this sacred character of our trust may be shown by several distinct considerations, which shall now be set before you.

1. First, from the very circumstance that it *is* a trust. The plain and simple reason for our preaching and preserving the Faith, is because we have been told to do so. It is an act of mere obedience to Him who has "put us in trust with the Gospel." Our one great concern as regards it, is to deliver it over safe. This is the end in view, which all men have before them, who

are anyhow trusted in worldly matters. "It is required in stewards, that a man be found faithful." [6] Our Lord had said, that "this Gospel of the Kingdom shall be preached in all the world *as a witness* unto all nations." Accordingly, His Apostle declares, speaking of his persecutions, "None of these things move me, . . . so that I might finish . . . the Ministry which I have received of the Lord Jesus, fully to *witness* the Gospel of the grace of God." And again, when his departure is at hand, he comforts himself with the reflection, that he has "kept the Faith." [7] To keep the Faith in the world till the end, may, for what we know, be a sufficient object of our preaching and confessing, though nothing more come of it. Hence then the force of the words addressed to Timothy: "Hold fast," "keep;" "This charge I commit unto thee;" "continue thou in the things entrusted thee;" "put the brethren in remembrance;" "commit thou the same to faithful men;" "refuse profane and old wives' fables;" "shun profane vain talking;" "avoid foolish and unlearned questions." Were there no other reason for the Articles of the Creed being held sacred, their being a trust would be sufficient. Till we feel that we *have* a trust, a treasure to transmit, for the safety of which we are answerable, we have missed one chief peculiarity in our actual position. Yet did men feel this adequately, they would have little heart to indulge in the random speculations which at present are so familiar to their minds.

2. This sense of the seriousness of our charge is increased by considering, that after all we do not know, and cannot form a notion, what is the real final object of the Gospel Revelation. Men are accustomed to say, that it is the salvation of the world, which it certainly is not. If, instead of this, we say that Christ came "to purify unto Himself a peculiar people," then, indeed, we speak a great Truth; but this, though a main end of our preaching, is not its simple and ultimate object. Rather, as far as we are told at all, that object is the glory of God; but we cannot understand what is meant by this, or how the Dispensation of the Gospel promotes it. It is enough for us that we must act with the simple thought of God before us, make all ends subordinate to this, and leave the event to Him. We know, indeed, to our great comfort, that we cannot preach in vain. His heavenly word "shall not return unto Him void, but shall prosper in the thing whereto He sent it." Still it is surely our duty to preach, "whether men will hear, or whether they will forbear." We

[6] 1 Cor. iv.2.
[7] Matt. xxiv.14; Acts xx.24; 2 Tim. iv.7.

must preach, as our Lord enjoins in a text already quoted, "as a witness." Accordingly He Himself, before the heathen Pilate, "bore witness unto the truth;" and St. Paul conjures us to keep our sacred charge as in the presence of Him, who "before Pontius Pilate witnessed a good confession." Doubtless, His glory is set forth in some mysterious way in the rejection, as well as in the reception of the Gospel; and we must co-operate with Him. We must co-operate so far, as to be content to wound as well as to heal, to condemn as well as to absolve. We must not shrink from being "a savour from death unto death," as well as of "life unto life." We must stedfastly believe, however painful may be the duty, that we are in either case offering up a "sweet savour of Christ unto God, both in them that are saved, and in them that perish." We must learn to acquiesce and concur in the order of God's providence, and bear to rejoice over great Babylon and her inhabitants, when the wrath of God has fallen upon her.

This consideration is an answer to those who would limit our message to what is influential and convincing in it, and measure its divinity by its success. But I have introduced it rather to show generally, how utterly we are in the dark about the whole subject; and therefore, as being in the dark, how necessary it is to gird our garments about us, and hold fast our treasure, and hasten forward, lest we betray our trust. We have no means of knowing how far a small mistake in the Faith may carry us astray. If we do not know why it is to be proclaimed to all, though all will not hear, much less do we know why this or that doctrine is revealed, or what is the importance of it. The grant of grace in Baptism follows upon the accurate enunciation of one or two words; and if so much depends on one sacred observance, even down to the letter in which it is committed to us, why should not at least the substantial sense of other truths, nay, even the primitive wording of them, have some especial claim upon the Church's safe guardianship of them? St. Paul's Articles of Belief are precise and individual; why should we not take them as we find them? Why should we be wise above that is written? Why should we not be thankful that a work is put upon us which is so plainly within our power, to hold the Gospel Truths, to count and note them, to feed upon them, to hand them on? However, wilful and feverish minds have not the wisdom to trust Divine teaching. They persist in saying that Articles of Belief are mere formalities; and that to preach and transmit them is to miss the conversion of the heart in faith and holiness. They would rather rouse emotions, with the view (as

they hope) of changing the character. Forgetful that tempers
and states of mind are things seen by God alone, and when really spiritual are the work of His Unseen Spirit, and beyond the
power of man to insure or ascertain, they put upon themselves
what a man cannot do. They think it a light thing to be sowers
of that heavenly seed, which He shall make spring up in the
hearer's heart to life eternal. They are willing to throw it aside
as something barren and worthless, as the sand of the sea-shore;
and they desire to plant simply the flowers of grace (or what
appear such) in one another's hearts, as though under their as-
siduous culture they could take root therein. Far different is the
example set us in the services of the Church! In the Office for
Baptism the Articles of the Creed are recited one by one, that
the infant Christian may be put in charge of every jot and tittle
of the sacred Covenant, which he inherits. In the Communion
Service, in the midst of its solemn praises to the God of all
grace, when Angels and Archangels are to be summoned to join
in the Thanksgiving, Articles from the Creed are recited, as if
by way of preparation, with an exact doctrinal precision, according to the Festival celebrated,—as for instance on this day.
And in the Visitation of the Sick, he whom God seems about to
call away, is asked, not whether he has certain spiritual feelings
within him (of which he cannot judge), but, definitely and to
his great comfort, whether he believes those Articles of the
Christian Faith, one by one, which he received at Baptism, was
catechized in during his childhood, and confessed whenever he
came to worship God in Church. It is in the same spirit that the
most precise and systematic of all the Creeds, the Athanasian, is
rather, as the form of it shows, a hymn of praise to the Eternal
Trinity; it being meet and right at festive seasons to bring forth
before our God every jewel of the Mysteries entrusted to us, to
show that those of which He gave us we have lost none.

3. Lastly, the sacred character of our charge is shown most
forcibly by the sanction which attends it. What God has
guarded by an Anathema, surely claims some jealous custody
on our part. Christ says expressly, "He that believeth and is
baptized shall be saved; and he that believeth not shall be
damned." [8] It is quite clear, that in our Lord's meaning, this belief included the reception of a positive Creed, because He gave
one at the time,—that sovereign Truth, from which all others
flow, which we this day celebrate, the Faith of Father, Son, and
Holy Ghost, Three Persons, One God. This doctrine then, at

[8] Mark xvi.16.

least, is necessary to be believed by every one in order to salvation: and that certain other doctrines are also necessary, is plain
from other parts of Scripture; as, for instance, our Lord's Resurrection, from St. Paul's words to the Romans.[9] Now, this
doctrine of the Resurrection, which closed our Lord's earthly
mission, is evidently at a wide interval in the series of doctrines
from that of the Trinity in Unity, which is the foundation of
the whole Dispensation; so that a thoughtful mind, which fears
to go wrong, will see reason to conclude even from hence that
perchance the doctrines which go between the two—the Incarnation, for instance, or the Crucifixion—are also essential parts
of saving Faith. And, in fact, various passages of Scripture, as
we have already seen, occur, in which these intermediate Articles are separately made the basis of the Gospel. Again, let St.
Paul's language to the Galatians be well considered, who had
departed from the Faith in what might have seemed but a subordinate detail, the abolition of the Jewish Law. "Though we,
or an Angel from heaven," he says, "preach any other Gospel
unto you, than that which we have preached unto you, let him
be Anathema. As we said before, so say I now again, If any man
preach any other Gospel unto you than that ye have received,
let him be Anathema." [10] The state of the case then is this:—we
know that some doctrines are necessary to be believed; we are
not told how many; and we have no powers of mind adequate to
the task of solving the problem. We cannot give any sufficient
reason, beside the revealed word, why the doctrine of the Trinity itself should be essential; and if it is essential nevertheless,
why should not any other? How dangerous then is it to trifle
with any portion of the message committed to us! Surely we are
bound to guard what *may* be material in it, as carefully as if we
knew it to be so; our not knowing it, so far from being a reason
for indifference, becoming an additional motive for anxiety and
watchfulness. And, while we do not dare anticipate God's final
judgment by attaching the Anathema to individual unbelievers,
yet neither do we dare conceal any part of the doctrines
guarded by it, lest haply it should be found to lie against ourselves, who have "shunned to declare the whole counsel of
God."

To conclude.—The error against which these remarks are directed, viz. that of systematizing and simplifying the Gospel
Faith, making much of one or two articles of it, and disparaging
or dismissing the rest, is not confined to this province of

religion only. In the same spirit, sometimes the Ordinances, sometimes the Polity of the Church, are dishonoured and neglected; the Doctrine of Baptism contrasted with that of inward Sanctification, precepts of "decency and order" made light of before the command to evangelize the heathen, the injunction to "stand in the old ways" broken with a view to increase the so-called efficiency of our ecclesiastical institutions. In like manner, by one class of reasoners the Gospels are made everything, by another the Epistles. In all ages, indeed, consistent obedience is a very rare endowment; but in this cultivated age, we have undertaken to defend inconsistency on grounds of reason. On the other hand hear the words of Eternal Truth. "Whosoever shall break one of these *least* commandments, *and shall teach men so,* he shall be called the least in the Kingdom of Heaven; but whosoever shall do and teach them, the same shall be called great in the Kingdom of Heaven."[11]

[11] Matt. v.19.

SERMON 23

TOLERANCE OF RELIGIOUS ERROR

(The Feast of St. Barnabas the Apostle)

"He was a good man, and full of the Holy Ghost and of faith."
—Acts xi.24.

WHEN Christ came to form a people unto Himself to show forth His praise, He took of every kind. Highways and hedges, the streets and lanes of the city, furnished guests for His supper, as well as the wilderness of Judea, or the courts of the Temple. His first followers are a sort of type of the general Church, in which many and various minds are as one. And this is one use, if we duly improve it, of our Festivals; which set before us specimens of the Divine Life under the same diversity of outward circumstances, advantages, and dispositions, which we discern around us. The especial grace poured upon the Apostles and their associates, whether miraculous or moral, had no tendency to destroy their respective peculiarities of temper and character, to invest them with a sanctity beyond our imitation, or to preclude failings and errors which may be our warning. It left them, as it found them, men. Peter and John, for instance, the simple fishers on the lake of Gennesareth, Simon the Zealot, Matthew the busy tax-gatherer, and the ascetic Baptist, how different are these,—first, from each other,—then, from Apollos the eloquent Alexandrian, Paul the learned Pharisee, Luke the physician, or the Eastern Sages, whom we celebrate at the Feast of the Epiphany; and these again how different from the Blessed Virgin Mary, or the Innocents, or Simeon and Anna, who are brought before us at the Feast of the Purification, or the women who ministered to our Lord, Mary the wife of Cleophas, the Mother of James and John, Mary Magdalene, Martha and Mary, sisters of Lazarus; or again, from the widow with her two mites, the woman whose issue of blood was staunched, from her who poured forth tears of penitence upon His feet, and the ignorant Samaritan at the well! Moreover, the definiteness and evident truth of many of the pictures presented to us in the Gospels serve to realize to us the history, and to help our faith, while at the same time they afford us abundant instruction. Such, for instance, is the immature ardour of James and John, the sudden fall of Peter, the obstinacy of Thomas, and the cowardice of Mark. St. Barnabas furnishes us with a lesson in his own way; nor shall I be wanting in piety towards that Holy Apostle, if on this his day I hold him forth, not only in the peculiar graces of his character, but in those parts of it in which he becomes our warning, not our example.

The text says, that "he was a good man, full of the Holy Ghost and of faith." This praise of goodness is explained by his very name, Barnabas, "the Son of Consolation," which was given him, as it appears, to mark his character of kindness, gentleness, considerateness, warmth of heart, compassion, and munificence.

His acts answer to this account of him. The first we hear of him is his selling some land which was his, and giving the proceeds to the Apostles, to distribute to his poorer brethren. The next notice of him sets before us a second deed of kindness, of as amiable, though of a more private character. "When Saul was come to Jerusalem, he assayed to join himself to the disciples; but they were all afraid of him, and believed not that he was a disciple. But Barnabas took him and brought him to the Apostles, and declared how he had seen the Lord in the way, and that He had spoken to him, and how he had preached boldly at Damascus, in the name of Jesus."[1] Next, he is mentioned in the text, and still with commendation of the same kind. How had he shown that "he was a good man?" by going on a mission of love to the first converts at Antioch. Barnabas, above the rest, was honoured by the Church with this work, which had in view the encouraging and binding together in unity and strength this incipient fruit of God's grace. "When he came, and had seen the grace of God, he was glad" (surely this circumstance itself is mentioned by way of showing his character); "and exhorted them all that with purpose of heart they would cleave unto the Lord." Thus he may even be accounted the founder of the Church of Antioch, being aided by St. Paul, whom he was successful in bringing thither. Next, on occasion of an approaching famine, he is joined with St. Paul in being the minister of the Gentiles' bounty towards the poor saints of Judea. Afterwards, when the Judaizing Christians troubled the Gentile converts with the Mosaic ordinances, Barnabas was sent with the same Apostle and others from the

---

[1] Acts ix.26, 27.

Church of Jerusalem to relieve their perplexity. Thus the Scripture history of him does but answer to his name, and is scarcely more than a continued exemplification of his characteristic grace. Moreover, let the particular force of his name be observed. The Holy Ghost is called our Paraclete, as assisting, advocating, encouraging, comforting us; now, as if to put the highest honour upon the Apostle, the same term is applied to him. He is called "the Son of Consolation," or the Paraclete; and in accordance with this honourable title, we are told, that when the Gentile converts of Antioch had received from his and St. Paul's hands the Apostles' decision against the Judaizers, "they rejoiced for the *consolation*."

On the other hand, on two occasions his conduct is scarcely becoming an Apostle, as instancing somewhat of that infirmity which uninspired persons of his peculiar character frequently exhibit. Both are cases of indulgence towards the faults of others, yet in a different way; the one, an over-easiness in a matter of doctrine, the other, in a matter of conduct. With all his tenderness for the Gentiles, yet on one occasion he could not resist indulging the prejudices of some Judaizing brethren, who came from Jerusalem to Antioch. Peter first was carried away; before they came, "he did eat with the Gentiles, but when they were come, he withdrew, and separated himself, fearing them which were of the circumcision. And the other Jews dissembled likewise with him; insomuch, that Barnabas also was carried away with their dissimulation." [2] The other instance was his indulgent treatment of Mark, his sister's son, which occasioned the quarrel between him and St. Paul. "Barnabas determined to take with them," on their Apostolic journey, "John, whose surname was Mark. But Paul thought not good to take him with them, who departed from them from Pamphylia, and went not with them to the work." [3]

Now it is very plain what description of character, and what kind of lesson, is brought before us in the history of this Holy Apostle. Holy he was, full of the Holy Ghost and of faith; still the characteristics and the infirmities of man remained in him, and thus he is "unto us for an ensample," consistently with the reverence we feel towards him as one of the foundations of the Christian Church. He is an ensample and warning to us, not only as showing us what we ought to be, but as evidencing how the highest gifts and graces are corrupted in our sinful nature, if we are not diligent to walk step by step, according to the light of

[2] Gal. ii.12, 13.   [3] Acts xv.37, 38.

God's commandments. Be our mind as heavenly as it may be, most loving, most holy, most zealous, most energetic, most peaceful, yet if we look off from Him for a moment, and look towards ourselves, at once these excellent tempers fall into some extreme or mistake. Charity becomes over-easiness, holiness is tainted with spiritual pride, zeal degenerates into fierceness, activity eats up the spirit of prayer, hope is heightened into presumption. We cannot guide ourselves. God's revealed word is our sovereign rule of conduct; and therefore, among other reasons, is faith so principal a grace, for it is the directing power which receives the commands of Christ, and applies them to the heart.

And there is particular reason for dwelling upon the character of St. Barnabas in this age, because he may be considered as the type of the better sort of men among us, and those who are most in esteem. The world itself indeed is what it ever has been, ungodly; but in every age it chooses some one or other peculiarity of the Gospel as the badge of its particular fashion for the time being, and sets up as objects of admiration those who eminently possess it. Without asking, therefore, how far men act from Christian principle, or only from the imitation of it, or from some mere secular or selfish motive, yet, certainly, this age, as far as appearance goes, may be accounted in its character not unlike Barnabas, as being considerate, delicate, courteous, and generous-minded in all that concerns the intercourse of man with man. There is a great deal of thoughtful kindness among us, of conceding in little matters, of scrupulous propriety of words, and a sort of code of liberal and honourable dealing in the conduct of society. There is a steady regard for the rights of individuals, nay, as one would fain hope in spite of misgivings, for the interest of the poorer classes, the stranger, the fatherless, and the widow. In such a country as ours, there must always be numberless instances of distress after all; yet the anxiety to relieve it existing among the more wealthy classes is unquestionable. And it is as unquestionable that we are somewhat disposed to regard ourselves favourably in consequence; and in the midst of our national trials and fears, to say (nay, sometimes with real humility and piety) that we do trust that these characteristic virtues of the age may be allowed to come up as a memorial before God, and to plead for us. When we think of the commandments, we know Charity to be the first and greatest; and we are tempted to ask with the young ruler, "What lack we yet?"

I ask, then, by way of reply, does not our kindness too often degenerate into weakness, and thus become not Christian Charity, but lack of Charity, as regards the objects of it? Are we sufficiently careful to do what is right and just, rather than what is pleasant? do we clearly understand our professed principles, and do we keep to them under temptation?

The history of St. Barnabas will help us to answer this question honestly. Now I fear we lack altogether, what he lacked in certain occurrences in it, firmness, manliness, godly severity. I fear it must be confessed, that our kindness, instead of being directed and braced by principle, too often becomes languid and unmeaning; that it is exerted on improper objects, and out of season, thereby is uncharitable in two ways, indulging those who should be chastised, and preferring their comfort to those who are really deserving. We are over-tender in dealing with sin and sinners. We are deficient in jealous custody of the revealed Truths which Christ has left us. We allow men to speak against the Church, its ordinances, or its teaching, without remonstrating with them. We do not separate from heretics, nay, we object to the word as if uncharitable; and when such texts are brought against us as St. John's command, not to show hospitality towards them, we are not slow to answer that they do not apply to us. Now I scarcely can suppose any one really means to say for certain, that these commands are superseded in the present day, and is quite satisfied upon the point; it will rather be found that men who so speak, merely wish to put the subject from them. For a long while they have forgotten that there were any such commands in Scripture; they have lived as though there were not, and not being in circumstances which immediately called for the consideration of them, they have familiarized their minds to a contrary view of the matter, and built their opinions upon it. When reminded of the fact, they are sorry to have to consider it, as they perhaps avow. They perceive that it interferes with the line of conduct to which they are accustomed. They are vexed, not as if allowing themselves to be wrong, but as feeling conscious that a plausible argument (to say the least) may be maintained against them. And instead of daring to give this argument fair play, as in honesty they ought, they hastily satisfy themselves that objections may be taken against it, use some vague terms of disapprobation against those who use it, recur to, and dwell upon, their own habitual view of the benevolent and indulgent spirit of the Gospel, and then dismiss the subject altogether, as if it had never been brought before them.

Observe *how* they rid themselves of it; it is by confronting it with other views of Christianity, which they consider incompatible with it: whereas the very problem which Christian duty requires us to accomplish, is the reconciling in our conduct opposite virtues. It is not difficult (comparatively speaking) to cultivate single virtues. A man takes some one partial view of his duty, whether severe or kindly, whether of action or of meditation: he enters into it with all his might, he opens his heart to its influence, and allows himself to be sent forward on its current. This is not difficult: there is no anxious vigilance or self-denial in it. On the contrary, there is a pleasure often in thus sweeping along in one way; and especially in matters of giving and conceding. Liberality is always popular, whatever be the subject of it, and excites a glow of pleasure and self-approbation in the giver, even though it involves no sacrifice, nay, is exercised upon the property of others. Thus in the sacred province of religion, men are led on,—without any bad principle, without that utter dislike or ignorance of the Truth, or that self-conceit, which are chief instruments of Satan at this day, nor again from mere cowardice or worldliness, but from thoughtlessness, a sanguine temper, the excitement of the moment, the love of making others happy, susceptibility of flattery, and the habit of looking only one way,—led on to give up Gospel Truths, to consent to open the Church to the various denominations of error which abound among us, or to alter our Services so as to please the scoffer, the lukewarm, or the vicious. To be kind is their one principle of action; and, when they find offence taken at the Church's creed, they begin to think how they may modify or curtail it, under the same sort of feeling as would lead them to be generous in a money transaction, or to accommodate another at the price of personal inconvenience. Not understanding that their religious privileges are a trust to be handed on to posterity, a sacred property entailed upon the Christian family, and their own in enjoyment rather than in possession, they act the spendthrift, and are lavish of the goods of others. Thus, for instance, they speak against the Anathemas of the Athanasian Creed, or of the Commination Service, or of certain of the Psalms, and wish to rid themselves of them.

Undoubtedly, even the best specimens of these men are deficient in a due appreciation of the Christian Mysteries, and of their own responsibility in preserving and transmitting them; yet, some of them are such truly "good" men, so amiable and feeling, so benevolent to the poor, and of such repute among all classes, in short, fulfil so excellently the office of shining like lights in the world, and witnesses of Him "who went about doing good," that those who most deplore their failing, will still be most desirous of excusing them personally, while they feel it a duty to withstand them. Sometimes it may be, that these persons cannot bring themselves to think evil of others; and harbour men of heretical opinions or immoral life from the same easiness of temper which makes them fit subjects for the practices of the cunning and selfish in worldly matters. And sometimes they fasten on certain favourable points of character in the person they should discountenance, and cannot get themselves to attend to any but these; arguing that he is certainly pious and well-meaning, and that his errors plainly do himself no harm;—whereas the question is not about their effects on this or that individual, but simply whether they *are* errors; and again, whether they are not certain to be injurious to the mass of men, or on the long run, as it is called. Or they cannot bear to hurt another by the expression of their disapprobation, though it be that "his soul may be saved in the day of the Lord." Or perhaps they are deficient in keenness of intellectual perception as to the moral mischief of certain speculative opinions, as they consider them; and not knowing their ignorance enough to forbear the use of private judgment, nor having faith enough to acquiesce in God's word, or the decision of His Church, they incur the responsibility of serious changes. Or, perhaps they shelter themselves behind some confused notion, which they have taken up, of the peculiar character of our own Church, arguing that they belong to a tolerant Church, that it is but consistent as well as right in her members to be tolerant, and that they are but exemplifying tolerance in their own conduct, when they treat with indulgence those who are lax in creed or conduct. Now, if by the tolerance of our Church, it be meant that she does not countenance the use of fire and sword against those who separate from her, so far she is truly called a tolerant Church; but she is not tolerant of error, as those very formularies, which these men wish to remove, testify; and if she retains within her bosom proud intellects, and cold hearts, and unclean hands, and dispenses her blessings to those who disbelieve or are unworthy of them, this arises from other causes, certainly not from her principles; else were she guilty of Eli's sin, which may not be imagined.

Such is the defect of mind suggested to us by the instances of imperfection recorded of St. Barnabas; it will be more clearly understood by contrasting him with St. John. We cannot compare good men together in their points of excellence; but whether the one or the other of these Apostles had the greater share of the spirit of love, we all know that anyhow the Beloved Disciple abounded in it. His General Epistle is full of exhortations to cherish that blessed temper, and his name is associated in our minds with such heavenly dispositions as are more immediately connected with it,—contemplativeness, serenity of soul, clearness of faith. Now see in what he differed from Barnabas; in uniting charity with a firm maintenance of "the Truth as it is in Jesus." So far were his fervour and exuberance of charity from interfering with his zeal for God, that rather, the more he loved men, the more he desired to bring before them the great unchangeable Verities to which they must submit, if they would see life, and on which a weak indulgence suffers them to shut their eyes. He loved the brethren, but he "loved them in the Truth."[4] He loved them for the Living Truth's sake which had redeemed them, for the Truth which was in them, for the Truth which was the measure of their spiritual attainments. He loved the Church so honestly, that he was stern towards those who troubled her. He loved the world so wisely, that he preached the Truth in it; yet, if men rejected it, he did not love them so inordinately as to forget the supremacy of the Truth, as the Word of Him who is above all. Let it never be forgotten then, when we picture to ourselves this saintly Apostle, this unearthly Prophet, who fed upon the sights and voices of the world of spirits, and looked out heavenwards day by day for Him whom he had once seen in the flesh, that this is he who gives us that command about shunning heretics, which whether of force in this age or not, still certainly in any age is (what men now call) severe; and that this command of his is but in unison with the fearful descriptions he gives in other parts of his inspired writings of the Presence, the Law, and the Judgments of Almighty God. Who can deny that the Apocalypse from beginning to end is a very fearful book; I may say, the most fearful book in Scripture, full of accounts of the wrath of God? Yet, it is written by the Apostle of love. It is possible, then, for a man to be at once kind as Barnabas, yet zealous as Paul. Strictness and tenderness had no "sharp contention" in the breast of the Beloved Disciple; they found their perfect union, yet distinct exercise, in the grace of Charity, which is the fulfilling of the whole Law.

[4] 3 John 1.

I wish I saw any prospect of this element of zeal and holy sternness springing up among us, to temper and give character to the languid, unmeaning benevolence which we misname Christian love. I have no hope of my country till I see it. Many schools of religion and Ethics are to be found among us, and they all profess to magnify, in one shape or other, what they consider the principle of love; but what they lack is, a firm maintenance of that characteristic of the Divine Nature, which, in accommodation to our infirmity, is named by St. John and his brethren, the wrath of God. Let this be well observed. There are men who are advocates of Expedience; these, as far as they are religious at all, resolve conscience into an instinct of mere benevolence, and refer all the dealings of Providence with His creatures to the same one Attribute. Hence, they consider all punishment to be remedial, a means to an end, deny that the woe threatened against sinners is of eternal duration, and explain away the doctrine of the Atonement. There are others, who place religion in the mere exercise of the excited feelings; and these too, look upon their God and Saviour, as far (that is) as they themselves are concerned, solely as a God of love. They believe themselves to be converted from sin to righteousness by the mere manifestation of that love to their souls, drawing them on to Him; and they imagine that that same love, untired by any possible transgressions on their part, will surely carry forward every individual so chosen to final triumph. Moreover, as accounting that Christ has already done everything for their salvation, they do not feel that a moral change is necessary on their part, or rather, they consider that the Vision of revealed love works it in them spontaneously; in either case dispensing with all laborious efforts, all "fear and trembling," all self-denial in "working out their salvation," nay, looking upon such qualifications with suspicion, as leading to a supposed self-confidence and spiritual pride. Once more, there are others of a mystical turn of mind, with untutored imaginations and subtle intellects, who follow the theories of the old Gentile philosophy. These, too, are accustomed to make love the one principle of life and providence in heaven and earth, as if it were a pervading Spirit of the world, finding a sympathy in every heart, absorbing all things into itself, and kindling a rapturous enjoyment in all who contemplate it. They sit at home speculating, and separate moral perfection from action. These men either hold, or are in the way to hold, that the human soul is pure by nature; sin an external principle corrupting it; evil, destined to final annihilation; Truth attained by means of the

imagination; conscience, a taste; holiness, a passive contemplation of God; and obedience, a mere pleasurable work. It is difficult to discriminate accurately between these three schools of
opinion, without using words of unseemly familiarity; yet I
have said enough for those who wish to pursue the subject. Let
it be observed then, that these three systems, however different
from each other in their principles and spirit, yet all agree in
this one respect, viz., in overlooking that the Christian's God is
represented in Scripture, not only as a God of Love, but also as
"a consuming fire." Rejecting the testimony of Scripture, no
wonder they also reject that of conscience, which assuredly
forebodes ill to the sinner, but which, as the narrow religionist
maintains, is not the voice of God at all,—or is a mere benevolence, according to the disciple of Utility,—or, in the judgment
of the more mystical sort, a kind of passion for the beautiful and
sublime. Regarding thus "the goodness" only, and not "the severity of God," no wonder that they ungird their loins and become effeminate; no wonder that their ideal notion of a perfect
Church, is a Church which lets every one go on his way, and
disclaims any right to pronounce an opinion, much less inflict a
censure on religious error.

But those who think themselves and others in risk of an eternal curse, dare not be thus indulgent. Here then lies our want at
the present day, for this we must pray,—that a reform may
come in the spirit and power of Elias. We must pray God thus
"to revive His work in the midst of the years;" to send us a severe Discipline, the Order of St. Paul and St. John, "speaking
the Truth in love," and "loving in the Truth,"—a Witness of
Christ, "knowing the terror of the Lord," fresh from the presence of Him "whose head and hairs are white like wool, as
white as snow, and whose eyes are as a flame of fire, and out of
His mouth a sharp sword,"—a Witness not shrinking from
proclaiming His wrath, as a real characteristic of His glorious
nature, though expressed in human language for our sakes, proclaiming the narrowness of the way of life, the difficulty of attaining Heaven, the danger of riches, the necessity of taking up
our cross, the excellence and beauty of self-denial and austerity,
the hazard of disbelieving the Catholic Faith, and the duty of
zealously contending for it. Thus only will the tidings of mercy
come with force to the souls of men, with a constraining power
and with an abiding impress, when hope and fear go together.
Then only will Christians be successful in fight, "quitting
themselves like men," conquering and ruling the fury of the
world, and maintaining the Church in purity and power, when

they condense their feelings by a severe discipline, and are loving in the midst of firmness, strictness, and holiness. Then only can we prosper (under the blessing and grace of Him who is the Spirit both of love and of truth), when the heart of Paul is vouchsafed to us, to withstand even Peter and Barnabas, if ever they are overcome by mere human feelings, to "know henceforth no man after the flesh," to put away from us sister's son, or nearer relative, to relinquish the sight of them, the hope of them, and the desire of them, when He commands, who raises up friends even to the lonely, if they trust in Him, and will give us "within His walls a name better than of sons and of daughters, an everlasting name that shall not be cut off." [5]

[5] Is. lvi.4, 5.

REBUKING SIN

(The Feast of the Nativity of St. John Baptist)

"John had said unto Herod, It is not lawful for thee to have thy brother's wife."—Mark vi.18.

IN the Collect of this day, we pray God to enable us "boldly to rebuke vice" after the example of St. John the Baptist, who died a Martyr in the faithful discharge of this duty.

Herod the Tetrarch had taken his brother's wife. John the Baptist protested against so heinous a sin; and the guilty king, though he could not bring himself to forsake it, yet respected the prophet, and tried to please him in other ways; but Herodias, the proud and cruel woman whom he had married, resented his interference, and at length effected his death. I need not go through the details of this atrocious history, which are well known to every reader of the Gospels.

St. John the Baptist had a most difficult office to fulfil; that of rebuking a king. Not that it is difficult for a man of rude arrogant mind to say a harsh thing to men in power,—nay, rather, it is a gratification to such a one; but it is difficult to rebuke *well*, that is, at a right time, in a right spirit, and a right manner. The Holy Baptist rebuked Herod without making him angry; therefore he must have rebuked him with gravity, temper, sincerity, and an evident good-will towards him. On the other hand, he spoke so firmly, sharply, and faithfully, that his rebuke cost him his life.

We who now live have not that extreme duty put upon us with which St. John was laden; yet every one of us has a share in his office, inasmuch as we are all bound "to rebuke vice boldly," when we have fit opportunities for so doing. I proceed then to make some remarks upon the duty, as enforced upon us by to-day's Festival.

Now, it is plain that there are two sorts of men in the world; those who put themselves forward, and speak much; and those who retire, and from indolence, timidity, or fastidiousness do not care to express an opinion on what comes before them.

Neither of these classes will act the part of St. John the Baptist in their intercourse with others: the retiring will not rebuke vice at all; the bold and ill-mannered will take a pleasure in giving their judgment, whether they are fit judges or not, whether they ought to speak or not, and at all times proper and improper.

These self-appointed censors of vice are not to be countenanced or tolerated by any serious Christian. The subjects of their attacks are often open to censure, it is true; and should be censured, but not by them. Yet these men take upon them, on their own authority, to blame them; often, because those whose duty it is, neglect to do so; and then they flatter themselves with the notion that they are energetic champions of virtue, strenuous and useful guardians of public morals or popular rights. There is a multitude of such men in these days, who succeed the better, because they conceal their names; and are thus relieved of the trouble of observing delicacy in their manner of rebuking, escape the retaliation which the assailed party may inflict on an open assailant, and are able to dispense with such requisites of personal character and deportment as are ordinarily expected from those who assume the office of the Baptist. And, by speaking against men of note, they gratify the bad passions of the multitude; fond, as it ever is, of tales of crime, and malevolent towards the great; and thus they increase their influence, and come to be looked up to and feared.

Now such officious accusers of vice are, I say, to be disowned by all who wish to be really Christians. Every one has his place, one to obey, another to rule, a third to rebuke. It is not religious to undertake an office without a commission. John the Baptist was miraculously called to the duties of a reformer and teacher. Afterwards, an order of men was appointed for the performance of the same services; and this order remains to this day in an uninterrupted succession. Those who take upon them to rebuke vice without producing credentials of their authority, are intruding upon the office of God's Ministers. They may indeed succeed in their usurpation, they may become popular, be supported by the many, and be recognised even by the persons whom they attack; still the function of censor is from God, whose final judgment it precedes and shadows forth; and not a whole generation of self-willed men can bestow on their organ the powers of a divine ambassador. It is our part, then, anxiously to guard against the guilt of acquiescing in the claims of such false prophets, lest we fall under the severity of our Lord's prediction: "I am come in My Father's name," He says, "and ye receive Me not. If another shall come in his own name, him ye will receive." [1]

I notice this peculiarity of the Reprover's office, as founded on a Divine Commission, and the consequent sin of undertaking it without a call, for another reason. Besides these bad men, who clamour against vice for gain and envy's sake, I know there are others of a better stamp, who imagine that they ought to rebuke, when in truth they ought not; and who, on finding that they cannot do the office well, or on getting into trouble in attempting it, are perplexed and discouraged, or consider that they suffer for righteousness' sake. But our duty is commonly a far more straightforward matter than excited and over-sensitive minds are apt to suppose, that is, as far as concerns our *knowing* it; and, when we find ourselves perplexed to ascertain it, we should ask ourselves, whether we have not embarrassed our course by some unnecessary or self-willed conduct of our own. For instance, when men imagine it to be their duty to rebuke their superiors, they get into difficulties, for the simple reason, that it is and ever will be difficult to do another man's duty. When the young take upon them to set right their elders, private Christians speak against the Clergy, the Clergy attempt to direct their Bishops, or servants their masters, they will find that, generally speaking, the attempt does not succeed; and perhaps they will impute their failure to circumstances,—whereas, the real reason is, that there was no call on them to rebuke at all. There is ever, indeed, a call on them to keep from sin themselves in all things, which itself is a silent protest against whatever is wrong in high places,—and this they cannot avoid, and need not wish to avoid; but very seldom, only in extreme cases, for instance, as, when the Faith is in jeopardy, or in order to protect or rescue the simple-minded, is a man called upon in the way of duty, directly to blame or denounce his superiors.

And in truth we have quite enough to do in the way of rebuking vice, if we confine our censure to those who are the lawful subjects of it. These are our equals and our inferiors. Here, again, it is easy to use violent language towards those who are below us in station, to be arrogant, to tyrannize; but such was not St. John the Baptist's manner of reproving. He reproved under the prospect of suffering for his faithfulness; and we should never use a strong word, however true it be, without being willing to acquiesce in some penalty or other, should it so happen, as the seal of our earnestness. We must not suppose,

[1] John v.43.

that our inferiors are without power to annoy us, because they are inferior. We depend on the poor as well as on the rich. Nor, by inferiors, do I mean those merely who are in a lower rank of society. Herod was St. John's inferior; the greatest king is, in one sense, inferior to God's ministers, and is to be approached by them, with all honour indeed and loyal service, but without trepidation of mind or cowardice, without forgetting that they are servants of the Church, gifted with their power by a divine appointment. And what is true even in the instance of the King himself is much more applicable in the case of the merely wealthy or ennobled. But is it a light matter to reprove such men? And can we do so without the risk of suffering for it? Who is sufficient for these things, without the guidance and strength of Him who died to purchase for His Church this high authority?

Again, parents are bound to rebuke their children; but here the office is irksome for a different reason. It is misplaced affection, not fear, which interferes here with the performance of our duty. And besides, parents are indolent as well as overfond. They look to their home as a release from the world's cares, and cannot bear to make duties in a quarter where they would find a recreation. And they have their preferences and partialities about their children; and being alternately harsh and weakly indulgent, are not respected by them, even when they seasonably rebuke them.

And as to rebuke those who are inferior to us in the temporal appointments of Providence, is a serious work, so also, much more, does it require a ripeness in Christian holiness to rebuke our equals suitably;—and this, first, because we fear their ridicule and censure; next, because the failings of our equals commonly lie in the same line as our own, and every considerate person is aware, that, in rebuking another, he is binding himself to a strict and religious life, which we naturally shrink from doing. Accordingly, it has come to pass, that Christians, by a sort of tacit agreement, wink at each other's faults, and keep silence; whereas, if each of us forced himself to make his neighbour sensible when he did wrong, he would both benefit another, and, through God's blessing, would bind himself also to a more consistent profession. Who can say how much harm is done by thus countenancing the imperfections of our friends and equals? The standard of Christian morals is lowered; the service of God is mixed up with devotion to Mammon; and thus society is constantly tending to a heathen state. And this culpable toleration of vice is sanctioned by the manners of the present age, which seems to consider it a mark of good breeding not to be solicitous about the faith or conduct of those around us, as if their private views and habits were nothing to us; which would have more pretence of truth in it, were they merely our fellow-creatures, but is evidently false in the case of those who all the while profess to be Christians, who imagine that they gain the privileges of the Gospel by their profession, while they bring scandal on it by their lives.

Now, if it be asked, what rules can be given for rebuking vice? —I observe, that, as on the one hand to perform the office of a censor requires a maturity and consistency of principle seen and acknowledged, so is it also the necessary result of possessing it. They who reprove with the greatest propriety, from their weight of character, are generally the very men who are also best qualified for reproving. To rebuke well is a gift which grows with the need of exercising it. Not that any one will gain it without an effort on his part; he must overcome false shame, timidity, and undue delicacy, and learn to be prompt and collected in withstanding evil; but after all, his mode of doing it will depend mainly on his *general* character. The more his habitual temper is formed after the law of Christ, the more discreet, unexceptionable, and graceful will be his censures, the more difficult to escape or to resist.

What I mean is this: cultivate in your general deportment a cheerful, honest, manly temper; and you will find fault well, because you will do so in a natural way. Aim at viewing all things in a plain and candid light, and at calling them by their right names. Be frank, do not keep your notions of right and wrong to yourselves, nor, on some conceit that the world is too bad to be taught the Truth, suffer it to sin in word or deed without rebuke. Do not allow friend or stranger in the familiar intercourse of society to advance false opinions, nor shrink from stating your own, and do this in singleness of mind and love. Persons are to be found, who tell their neighbours of their faults in a strangely solemn way, with a great parade, as if they were doing something extraordinary; and such men not only offend those whom they wish to set right, but also foster in themselves a spirit of self-complacency. Such a mode of finding fault is inseparably connected with a notion that they themselves are far better than the parties they blame; whereas the single-hearted Christian will find fault, not austerely or gloomily, but in love; not stiffly, but naturally, gently, and as a matter of course, just as he would tell his friend of some obstacle in his path which was likely to throw him down, but without any absurd feeling of superiority over him, because he was able to do so. His feeling is, "I have done a good office to you, and you must in turn serve me." And though his advice be not always taken as he meant it, yet he will not dwell on the pain occasioned to himself by such a result of his interference; being conscious, that in truth there ever is much to correct in his mode of doing his duty, knowing that his intention was good, and being determined any how to make light of his failure, except so far as to be more cautious in future against even the appearance of rudeness or intemperance in his manner.

These are a few suggestions on an important subject. We daily influence each other for good or evil; let us not be the occasion of misleading others by our silence, when we ought to speak. Recollect St. Paul's words:—"Be not partaker of other men's sins: keep thyself pure." [2]

---

[2] 1 Tim. v.22.

THE CHRISTIAN MINISTRY

(The Feast of St. Peter the Apostle)

*"I say unto you, among those that are born of women there is not a
greater prophet than John the Baptist; but he that is least in the
Kingdom of God is greater than he."*—Luke vii.28.

S T. PETER's day suitably follows the day of St. John the Baptist; for thus we have a striking memento, as the text suggests, of the especial dignity of the Christian Ministry over all
previous Ministries which Almighty God has appointed. St.
John was "much more than a Prophet;" he was as great as any
messenger of God that had ever been born; yet the least in the
Kingdom of heaven, the least of Christ's Ministers, is greater
than he. And this, I observe, is a reflection especially fitted for
this Festival, because the Apostle Peter is taken in various parts
of the Gospel, as the appropriate type and representative of the
Christian ministry.[1]

Now, let us consider in what the peculiar dignity of the
Christian Minister consists. Evidently in this, that he is the representative of Christ; for, as Christ is infinitely above all other
messengers from God, he who stands in His stead, must be
superior, beyond compare, to all Ministers of religion, whether
Prophets, Priests, Lawgivers, Judges, or Kings, whom Almighty
God ever commissioned. Moses, Aaron, Samuel, and David,
were shadows of the Saviour; but the Minister of the Gospel is
His present substitute. As a type or prophecy of Grace is less
than a pledge and means, as a Jewish sacrifice is less than a Gospel sacrament, so are Moses and Elias less by office than the
representatives of Christ. This I consider to be evident, as soon
as stated; the only question being, whether there is reason for
thinking, that Christ *has*, in matter of fact, left representatives
behind Him; and this, as I proceed to show, Scripture enables us
to determine in the affirmative.

Now, in the first place, as we all know, Christ chose twelve

[1] *Vide* Matt. xvi.18, 19; Luke xxii.29, 30; John xxi.15–17.

out of His disciples, whom He called Apostles, to be His representatives even during His own ministry. And He gave them
the power of doing the wonderful works which He did Himself. Of course I do not say He gave them equal power (God
forbid!); but He gave them a certain sufficient portion of His
power. "He gave them power," says St. Luke, "and authority
over all devils, and to cure diseases; and He sent them to preach
the Kingdom of God, and to heal the sick." [2] And He expressly
made them His substitutes to the world at large; so that to receive them was to receive Himself. "He that receiveth you,
receiveth Me." [3] Such was their principal power before His passion, similar to that which He principally exercised, viz. the
commission to preach and to perform bodily cures. But when
He had wrought out the Atonement for human sin upon the
Cross, and purchased for man the gift of the Holy Ghost, then
He gave them a higher commission; and still, be it observed,
parallel to that which He Himself then assumed. *"As My Father
hath sent Me, even so send I you.* And when He had said this, He
breathed on them, and saith unto them, Receive ye the Holy
Ghost. Whose soever sins ye remit, they are remitted unto
them; and whose soever sins ye retain, they are retained." [4]
Here, then, the Apostles became Christ's representatives in the
power of His Spirit, for the remission of sins, as before they
were His representatives as regards miraculous cures, and
preaching His Kingdom.

The following texts supply additional evidence that the
Apostles were commissioned in Christ's stead, and inform us
likewise in detail of some of the particular offices included in
their commission. "Let a man so account of us, as of the *Ministers* of Christ, and *Stewards of the Mysteries* of God." "Ye received
me as an *Angel*" or heavenly Messenger "of God, even as Christ
Jesus." "We *are Ambassadors* for Christ, as though God did beseech you by us; we pray you *in Christ's stead*, be ye reconciled to
God." [5]

The Apostles then, standing in Christ's place, were consequently exalted by office far above any divine Messengers before them. We come to the same conclusion from considering
the sacred treasures committed to their custody, which (not to
mention their miraculous powers, which is beside our present
purpose) were those peculiar spiritual blessings which flow
from Christ as a Saviour, as a Prophet, Priest, and King.

[2] Luke ix.1, 2.   [3] Matt. x.40.   [4] John xx.21–23.
[5] 1 Cor. iv.1; Gal. iv.14; 2 Cor. v.20.

These blessings are commonly designated in Scripture as "the Spirit," or "the gift of the Holy Ghost." John the Baptist said of himself and Christ; "I indeed baptize you with water unto repentance; but He shall baptize you with the Holy Ghost, and with fire."[6] In this respect, Christ's ministrations were above all that had ever been before Him, in bringing with them the gift of the Holy Ghost, that one gift, one, yet multiform, sevenfold in its operation, in which all spiritual blessedness is included. Accordingly, our Lord was solemnly anointed with the Holy Ghost Himself, as an initiation into His Ministerial office. He was manifested as receiving, that He might be believed on as giving. He was thus commissioned, according to the Prophet, "to preach good tidings," "to heal the brokenhearted," "to give the oil of joy for mourning." Therefore, in like manner, the Apostles also were anointed with the same heavenly gift for the same Ministerial office. "He breathed on them, and saith unto them, Receive ye the Holy Ghost." Such as was the consecration of the Master, such was that of the Disciples; and such as His, were the offices to which they were thereby admitted.

Christ is a Prophet, as authoritatively revealing the will of God and the Gospel of Grace. So also were the Apostles; "He that heareth you, heareth Me; and he that despiseth you, despiseth Me: and he that despiseth Me, despiseth Him that sent Me;" "He that despiseth, despiseth not man, but God, who hath also given unto us His Holy Spirit."[7]

Christ is a Priest, as forgiving sin, and imparting other needful divine gifts. The Apostles, too, had this power; "Whose soever sins ye remit, they are remitted unto them; and whose soever sins ye retain, they are retained." "Let a man so account of us as . . . Stewards of the Mysteries of God."

Christ is a King, as ruling the Church; and the Apostles rule it in His stead. "I appoint unto you a Kingdom, as My Father hath appointed unto Me; that ye may eat and drink at My table in My Kingdom, and sit on thrones judging the twelve tribes of Israel."[8]

The gift, or office, cannot be named, which belongs to our Lord as the Christ, which He did not in its degree transfer to His Apostles by the communication of that Spirit, through which He Himself wrought; one of course excepted, the One great work, which none else in the whole world could sustain, of being the Atoning Sacrifice for all mankind. So far no one

---

[6] Matt. iii.11.   [7] Luke x.16; 1 Thess. iv.8.   [8] Luke xxi.29, 30.

can take His place, and "His glory He does not give to another." His Death upon the Cross is the sole Meritorious Cause, the sole Source of spiritual blessing to our guilty race; but as to those offices and gifts which flow from this Atonement, preaching, teaching, reconciling, absolving, censuring, dispensing grace, ruling, ordaining, these all are included in the Apostolic Commission, which is instrumental and representative in His absence. "As My Father hath sent Me, so send I you." His gifts are not confined to Himself. "The whole house is filled with the odour of the ointment."

This being granted, however, as regards the Apostles themselves, some one may be disposed to inquire, whether their triple office has descended to Christian Ministers after them. I say their *triple* office, for few persons will deny that some portion of their commission still remains among us. The notion that there is no divine appointment of one man above another for Ministerial duties is not a common one, and we need not refute it. But it is very common for men to believe only as far as they can see and understand; and, because they are witnesses of the process and effects of instructing and ruling, and not of (what may be called) "the ministry of reconciliation," to accept Christ's Ministers as representatives of His Prophetic and Regal, not of His Priestly authority. Assuming then their claim to inherit two portions of His Anointing, I shall confine myself to the question of their possessing the third likewise: not however with a view of proving it, but rather of removing such antecedent difficulties as are likely to prejudice the mind against it.

By a Priest, in a Christian sense, is meant an appointed channel by which the peculiar Gospel blessings are conveyed to mankind, one who has power to apply to individuals those gifts which Christ has promised us generally as the fruit of His mediation. This power was possessed by the Apostles; I am now to show that it is possessed by their successors likewise.

1. Now, first, that there is a strong line of distinction between the Apostles and other Christian Ministers, I readily grant; nay, rather I would maintain it to be so clearly marked that there is no possibility of confusing together those respects in which they resemble with those in which they differ from their brethren. The Apostles were not only Ministers of Christ, but first founders of His Church; and their gifts and offices, so far forth as they had reference to this part of their commission, doubtless were but occasional and extraordinary, and ended with themselves. They were organs of Revelation, inspired Teachers, in some respects infallible, gifted with divers tongues,

workers of miracles; and none but they are such. The duration of any gift depends upon the need which it supplies; that which has answered its purpose ends, that which is still necessary is graciously continued. Such at least seems to be the rule of a Merciful Providence. Therefore it is, that the Christian Ministry still includes in it the office of teaching, for education is necessary for every soul born into the world; and the office of governing, for "decency and order" are still necessary for the quiet and union of the Christian brotherhood. And, for the same reason, it is natural at first sight to suppose that the office of applying the gifts of grace should be continued also, while there is guilt to be washed away, sinners to be reconciled, believers to be strengthened, matured, comforted. What warrant have we from the nature of the case, for making any distinction between the ministry of teaching and the ministry of reconciliation? if one is still committed to us, why not the other also?

And it will be observed, that the only real antecedent difficulty which attaches to the doctrine of the Christian Priesthood, is obviated by Scripture itself. It might be thought that the power of remitting and retaining sins was too great to be given to sinful man over his fellows; but in matter of fact it was committed to the Apostles without restriction, though they were not infallible in what they did. "*Whose soever* sins ye remit they are remitted unto them; and *whose soever* sins ye retain, they are retained." The grant was in the very form of it *unconditional*, and left to their Christian discretion. What has once been given, may be continued. I consider this remark to be of weight in a case like the present, where the very nature of the professed gift is the only considerable reason against the fact of its bestowal.

2. But all this is on the bare antecedent view of the case. In fact, our Lord Himself has decided the question, by declaring that His presence, by means of His Apostles, *should* be with the Church to the end of the world. He promised this on the solemn occasion of His leaving them; He declared it when He bade them make converts, baptize, and teach. As well may we doubt whether it is our duty to preach and make proselytes, and prepare men for Heaven, as that His Apostolic Presence is with us, for those purposes. His words then at first sight even go to include *all* the gifts vouchsafed to His first Ministers; far from having a scanty grant of them, so large is the promise, that we are obliged to find out reasons to justify us in considering the Successors of the Apostles in any respects less favoured than themselves. Such reasons we know are to be found, and lead us

to distinguish the extraordinary gifts from the ordinary, a distinction which the event justifies; but what is there either in Scripture or in Church History to make us place the commission of reconciliation among those which are extraordinary?

3. In the next place, it is deserving of notice that this distinction between ordinary and extraordinary gifts, is really made in Scripture itself, and that among the extraordinary there is no mention made of the sacerdotal power. No one can doubt, that on the day of Pentecost the formal inauguration of the Apostles took place into their high and singular office of building the Church of Christ. They were "wise Master-builders, according to the grace given them;" and that grace was extraordinary. However, among those gifts, "tongues and visions, prophecies and wonders," their priestly power is not enumerated. On the contrary, that power had been previously conferred, according to the passage already cited, when Christ breathed on them, and gave them, through the Holy Ghost, the authority to remit and retain sins.[9] And further, I would remind you, that this is

---

[9] The following passage supplies a corroboration of the above argument, and carries it on to the doctrine of the Apostolical Succession:—
"The very first act of the Apostles after Christ was gone out of their sight, was the ordination of Matthias in the room of the traitor Judas. That ordination is related very minutely. Every particular of it is full of instruction; but at present I wish to draw attention to one circumstance more especially: namely, the *time* when it occurred. It was contrived (if one may say so) exactly to fall within *the very short interval* which elapsed between the departure of our Lord, and the arrival of the Comforter in His place: on that 'little while,' during which the Church was comparatively left alone in the world. Then it was that St. Peter rose and declared with authority, that the time was come for supplying the vacancy which Judas had made. 'One,' said he, 'must be ordained;' and without delay they proceeded to the ordination. Of course, St. Peter must have had from our Lord express authority for this step. Otherwise it would seem most natural to defer a transaction so important until the unerring Guide, the Holy Ghost, should have come among them, as they knew He would in a few days. On the other hand, since the Apostles were eminently Apostles of our Incarnate Lord, since their very being, *as* Apostles, depended entirely on their personal mission from Him (which is the reason why catalogues are given of them, with such scrupulous care, in many of the holy books): in that regard one should naturally have expected that He Himself before His departure would have supplied the vacancy by personal designation. But we see it was not His pleasure to do so. As the Apostles afterwards brought on the ordination sooner, so He had deferred it longer than might have been expected. Both ways it should seem as if there were a purpose of bringing the event within those ten days, *during which*, as I said, *the*

certainly our Church's deliberate view of the subject: for she
expressly puts into the Bishop's mouth at ordination the very
words here used by our Saviour to His Apostles. "Receive the
Holy Ghost;" "Whose soever sins ye remit, they are remitted to
them; and whose soever sins ye retain, they are retained;"
words, which it were inexpressibly profane for man to use to
man, except by a plain divine commission to do so.

4. But again, has not the Gospel Sacraments? and have not
Sacraments, as pledges and means of grace, a priestly nature? If
so, the question of the existence of a Christian Priesthood is
narrowed at once to the simple question whether it is or is not
probable that so precious an ordinance as a channel of grace
would be committed by Providence to the custody of certain
guardians. The tendency of opinions at this day is to believe
that nothing more is necessary for acceptance than faith in
God's promise of mercy; whereas it is certain from Scripture,
that the gift of reconciliation is not conveyed to individuals except through appointed ordinances. Christ has interposed
something between Himself and the soul; and if it is not inconsistent with the liberty of the Gospel that a Sacrament should
interfere, there is no antecedent inconsistency in a keeper of the
Sacrament attending upon it. Moreover, the very circumstance
that a standing Ministry has existed from the first, leads on to
the inference that that Ministry was intended to take charge of
the Sacraments; and thus the facts of the case suggest an interpretation of our Lord's memorable words, when He committed
to St. Peter "the *keys* of the Kingdom of Heaven."

I would have this Scripture truth considered attentively; viz.
that Sacraments are the channels of the peculiar Christian
privileges, and not merely (as many men think, and as the rite
of Confirmation really is) *seals* of the covenant. A man may
object, indeed, that in St. Paul's Epistle to the Romans nothing

-----

church was left to herself; left to exercise her faith and hope, much as
Christians are left now, without any *miraculous* aid or extraordinary illumination from above. Then, at that moment of the New Testament
history in which the circumstances of believers corresponded most
nearly to what they have been since miracles and inspiration ceased,—
just at that time it pleased our Lord that a fresh Apostle should be consecrated, with authority and commission as ample as the former
enjoyed. In a word, it was His will that the eleven Disciples alone, not
Himself personally, should name the successor of Judas; and that they
chose the right person, He gave testimony very soon after, by sending
His Holy Spirit on St. Matthias, as richly as on St. John, St. James, or
St. Peter."—*Tracts for the Times*, vol. ii, no. 52.

is said about channels and instruments; that faith is represented as the sole medium of justification. But I will refer him, by way of reply, to the same Apostle's speech to Festus and Agrippa, where he describes Christ as saying to him on his miraculous conversion, "Rise and stand upon thy feet; for I have appeared unto thee for this purpose, to make thee a Minister and a Witness," sending him forth, as it might appear, to preach the Gospel, without instrumentality of Ordinance or Minister. Had we but this account of his conversion, who would not have supposed, that he who was "to open men's eyes, and turn them from darkness to light," had been pardoned and accepted at once upon his faith, without rite or form? Yet from other parts of the history, we learn what is here omitted, viz. that an especial revelation was made to Ananias, lest Saul should go without baptism; and that, so far from his being justified immediately on his faith, he was bid not to tarry, but "to arise and be baptized, and *to wash away his sins* calling on the name of the Lord." [10] So dangerous is it to attempt to prove a negative from insulated passages of Scripture.

Here then we have a clear instance in St. Paul's own case, that there are priestly Services between the soul and God, even under the Gospel; that though Christ has purchased inestimable blessings for our race, yet that it is still necessary ever to apply them to individuals by visible means; and if so, I confess, that to me at least it seems more likely antecedently, that such services should have, than that they should lack, an appropriate minister. But here again we are not left to mere conjecture, as I proceed to show.

5. You well know that the benefits of the Atonement are frequently represented in Scripture under the figure of spiritual food, bread from heaven, the water that never faileth, and in more sacred language, as the communion of the Body and Blood of the Divine Sacrifice. Now, this special Christian benefit is there connected, as on the one hand with an outward rite, so on the other with certain appointed Dispensers. So that the very context of Scripture leads us on from the notion of a priestly service to that of a priesthood.

"Who then is that faithful and wise *Steward*," says Christ, "whom his Lord shall make ruler over His household, to give them their *portion of food* in due season? Blessed is that servant, whom his Lord when He cometh shall find so doing." [11] Now, I

[10] Acts xxvi.16–18; xxii.16; ix.17. *Vide* also xiii.2, 3.
[11] Luke xii.43.

infer from this passage; first, that there are, under the Gospel, especial Dispensers of the Christian's spiritual food, in other words (if the word "food"[12] may be interpreted from the parallel of the sixth chapter of St. John), Dispensers of invisible grace, or Priests;—next, that they are to continue to the Church in every age till the end, for it is said, "Blessed is he, whom his Lord, *when He cometh*, shall find so doing;"—further, that the Minister mentioned is also "Ruler over His household," as in the case of the Apostles, uniting the Regal with the Sacerdotal office;—lastly, the word "Steward," which incidentally occurs in the passage, a title applied by St. Paul to the Apostles, affords an additional reason for supposing that other like titles, such as "Ambassadors of Christ," given to the Apostles, do also belong in a true and sufficient sense to their Successors.

6. These considerations in favour of the existence of a Christian Priesthood, are strengthened by observing that the office of intercession, which though not a peculiarity, is ever characteristic of the Priestly Order, is spoken of in Scripture as a sort of prerogative of the Gospel Ministry. For instance, Isaiah, speaking of Christian times, says, "I have set watchmen upon thy walls, O Jerusalem, which shall never hold their peace day nor night. Ye that make mention of the Lord, keep not silence; and give Him no rest, till He establish, and till He make Jerusalem a praise in the earth."[13] In the Acts of the Apostles, we find Christ's ministers engaged in this sacred service, according to the prophecy. "There were in the Church that was at Antioch certain prophets and teachers, as Barnabas, and Simeon called Niger, and Lucius of Cyrene, and Manaen, foster brother to Herod the Tetrarch, and Saul. As they *ministered* to the Lord, and fasted,"[14] the Holy Ghost separated two of them for His work. This "ministering" to the Lord with fasting was surely some solemn intercessory service. And this agrees with a passage in St. James's Epistle, which seems to invest the Elders of the Church with this same privilege of the priesthood. "Is any sick among you? Let him call for the Elders of the Church, *and let them pray over him* (not pray *with* him merely), anointing him with oil in the name of the Lord; and *the prayer of faith* (not the oil merely) shall save the sick, and the Lord shall raise him up." In like manner St. Paul speaks of Epaphras as "our dear fellow-servant, who is *for* you," that is, for the Colossians to whom he is writing, "a faithful minister of Christ." Presently be explains

---

[12] $\sigma\iota\tau o\mu\acute{\epsilon}\tau\rho\iota o\nu$.   [13] Is. lxii.6, 7.   [14] Acts xiii.1, 2.

what was the service which Epaphras did for them: "*always labouring fervently for you in prayer*, that ye may stand perfect and complete in all the will of God." [15]

7. We may end these remarks by recurring to the instances of St. Peter and St. John the Baptist; who, as types of God's ordained servants, before and after His Son's coming, may serve to explain the office of ordinary Christian Ministers. Even the lowest of them is "greater than John." Now what was it that he wanted? Was it the *knowledge of Gospel doctrine*? No, surely; no words can be clearer than his concerning the New covenant. "Behold the Lamb of God, which taketh away the sin of the world." "He that cometh from above, is above all . . . He whom God hath sent speaketh the words of God, for God giveth not the Spirit by measure unto Him. The Father loveth the Son, and hath given all things into His hand. He that believeth on the Son hath everlasting life, and he that believeth not the Son shall not see life, but the wrath of God abideth on him." [16] Therefore, the Baptist lacked not the full Christian *doctrine*; what he did lack was (as he says himself) the Baptism *of the Spirit*, conveying a commission from Christ the Saviour, in all His manifold gifts, ordinary and extraordinary, Regal and Sacerdotal. John was not inferior to us Gospel Ministers in knowledge, but in power.

On the other hand, if, as I have made appear, St. Peter's ministerial office continues as regards ordinary purposes, in the persons of those who come after him, we are bound to understand our Lord's blessing, pronounced in the first instance upon him, as descending in due measure on the least of us His ministers who "keep the faith," Peter being but the representative and type of them all. "Blessed art thou, Simon Bar-jona; for flesh and blood hath not revealed it unto thee, but My Father, which is in heaven. And I say also unto thee, that thou art Peter, and upon this rock I will build My Church, and the gates of hell shall not prevail against it. And I will give unto thee the keys of the Kingdom of Heaven; and whatsoever thou shalt bind on earth shall be bound in heaven, and whatsoever thou shalt loose on earth shall be loosed in heaven." August and glorious promise! Can it be, that it is all expended on St. Peter, how great soever that noble Apostle? Is it inserted in the "everlasting Gospel," to witness merely of one long since departed? Is it the practice of the inspired word to exalt individuals? Does not the

[15] James v.14, 15; Col. i.7; iv.12.
[16] John i.29; iii.31–36.

very exuberance of the blessing resist any such niggardly use of it? Does it not flow over in spite of us, till our unbelief is vanquished by the graciousness of Him who spoke it? Is it, in short, anything but the prejudices of education, which prevent so many of us from receiving it in that fulness of grace in which it was poured out?

I say our *prejudices*,—for these surely are the cause of our inconsistency in faith; adopting, as we do, a rule of Scripture interpretation, which carries us a certain way, and stops short of the whole counsel of God, and should teach us nothing, or a great deal more. If the promises to Christ's Apostles are not fulfilled in the Church for ever after, why should the blessing attaching to the Sacraments extend after the first age? Why should the Lord's Supper be now the Communion of the Lord's Body and Blood? Why should Baptism convey spiritual privileges? Why should any part of Scripture afford permanent instruction? Why should the way of life be any longer narrow? Why should the burden of the Cross be necessary for every disciple of Christ? Why should the Spirit of adoption any longer be promised us? Why should separation from the world be now a duty? Happy indeed it is for men that they *are* inconsistent; for then, though they lose some part of a Christian's faith, at least they keep a portion. This will happen in quiet times, and in the case of those who are of mature years, and whose minds have been long made up on the subject of religion. But should a time of controversy arise, then such inconsistencies become of fearful moment as regards the multitude called Christian, who have not any decided convictions to rest upon. Inconsistency of creed is sure to attract the notice of the intellect, unless habit has reconciled the heart to it. Therefore, in a speculative age, such as our own, a religious education which involves such inconsistency, is most dangerous to the unformed Christian, who will set straight his traditionary creed by unlearning the portion of truth it contains, rather than by adding that in which it is deficient. Hence, the lamentable spectacle, so commonly seen, of men who deny the Apostolic commission proceeding to degrade the Eucharist from a Sacrament to a bare commemorative rite; or to make Baptism such a mere outward form, and sign of profession, as it would be childish or fanciful to revere. And reasonably; for they who think it superstitious to believe that particular persons are channels of grace, are but consistent in denying virtue to particular ordinances. Nor do they stop even here; for denying the grace of baptism, they proceed to deny the doctrine of original sin, for which that grace is the remedy.[17] Further, denying the doctrine of original sin, they necessarily impair the doctrine of the Atonement, and so prepare a way for the denial of our Lord's Divinity. Again, denying the power of the Sacraments on the ground of its *mysteriousness*, demanding from the very text of Scripture the fullest proof of it conceivable, and thinking little of the blessedness of "not seeing, and yet believing," they naturally proceed to object to the doctrine of the Trinity as obstructing and obscuring the simplicity (as they consider it) of the Gospel, and but indirectly deducible from the extant documents of inspiration. Lastly, after they have thus divested the divine remedies of sin, and the treatment necessary for the sinner, of their solemnity and awe, having made the whole scheme of salvation of as intelligible and ordinary a character as the repair of any accident in the works of man, having robbed Faith of its mysteries, the Sacraments of their virtue, the Priesthood of its commission, no wonder that sin itself is soon considered a venial matter, moral evil as a mere imperfection, man as involved in no great peril or misery, his duties of no very arduous or anxious nature. In a word, religion, as such, is in the way to disappear from the mind altogether; and in its stead a mere cold worldly morality, a decent regard to the claims of society, a cultivation of the benevolent affections, and a gentleness and polish of external deportment, will be supposed to constitute the entire duties of that being, who is conceived in sin, and the child of wrath, is redeemed by the precious blood of the Son of God, is born again and sustained by the Spirit through the invisible strength of Sacraments, and called, through self-denial and sanctification of the inward man, to the Eternal Presence of the Father, Son, and Holy Ghost.

Such is the course and issue of unbelief, though beginning in what the world calls trifles. Beware then, O my Brethren, of entering a way which leads to death. Fear to question what Scripture says of the Ministers of Christ, lest the same perverse spirit lead you on to question its doctrine about Himself and His Father. "Little children, it is the last time; and as ye have heard that Antichrist shall come, even now are there many Antichrists. . . . They went out from us, but they were not of us." [18] "Ye shall know them by their fruits." [19] If any man come

---

[17] *E.g.* A Dissenting Catechism has lately been published in the country for popular use, in which the doctrine of original sin is denied, by way of meeting the charge of cruelty towards children, as involved in the omission of infant baptism.

[18] 1 John ii.18, 19.   [19] Matt. vii.16.

to you, bringing any scoff against the power of Christ's Ministers, ask him what he holds concerning the Sacraments, or concerning the Blessed Trinity; look narrowly after his belief as
regards the Atonement, or Original Sin. Ascertain whether he
holds with the Church's doctrine in these points; see to it
whether at very best he does not try to evade the question, has
recourse to explanations, or professes to have no opinion at all
upon it. Look to these things, that you may see whither you are
invited. Be not robbed of your faith blindfold. Do what you do
with a clear understanding of the consequences. And if the arguments which he uses against you tend to show that your
present set of opinions is in some measure inconsistent, and
force you to see in Scripture more than you do at present, or
else less, be not afraid to add to it, rather than to detract from it.
Be quite sure that, go as far as you may, you will never, through
God's grace, be led to see more in it than the early Christians
saw; that, however you enlarge your creed, you will but carry
yourselves on to Apostolic perfection, equally removed from
the extremes of presumption and of unbelief, neither intruding
into things not seen as yet, nor denying, on the other hand,
what you cannot see.

HUMAN RESPONSIBILITY

(The Feast of St. James the Apostle)

*"To sit on My right hand and on My left is not Mine to give; but it
shall be given to them for whom it is prepared of My Father."*
—Matt. xx.23.

IN these words, to which the Festival of St. James the Greater
especially directs our minds, our Lord solemnly declares that
the high places of His Kingdom are not His to give,—which can
mean nothing else, than that the assignment of them does not
simply and absolutely depend upon Him; for that He will actually dispense them at the last day, and moreover is the meritorious cause of any being given, is plain from Scripture. I say, He
avers most solemnly that something besides His own will and
choice is necessary, for obtaining the posts of honour about His
throne; so that we are naturally led on to ask, *where* it is that this
awful prerogative is lodged. Is it with His Father? He proceeds
to speak of His Father; but neither does he assign it to Him, "It
shall be given to them for whom it is *prepared* of My Father."
The Father's foreknowledge and design are announced, not His
choice. "Whom He did foreknow, them He did predestinate."
He prepares the reward, and confers it, but upon whom? No
answer is given us, unless it is conveyed in the words which follow,—upon the humble:—"Whosoever will be great among
you, let him be your minister; and whosoever will be chief
among you, let him be your servant."

Some parallel passages may throw some further light upon
the question. In the description our Lord gives us of the Last
Judgment, He tells us He shall say to them on His right hand,
"Come, ye blessed of My Father, inherit the kingdom *prepared*
for you from the foundation of the world." Here we have the
same expression. Who then are the heirs for whom the Kingdom is prepared? He tells us expressly, those who fed the hungry and thirsty, lodged the stranger, clothed the naked, visited
the sick, came to the prisoners, for His sake. Consider again an
earlier passage in the same chapter. To whom is it that He will

say, "Enter thou into the joy of thy Lord?"—to those whom He can praise as "good and faithful servants," who have been "faithful over a few things." These two passages then carry our search just to the very point which is suggested by the text. They lead us *from* the thought of God and Christ, and throw us upon human agency and responsibility, for the solution of the question; and they finally lodge us there, *unless* indeed other texts of Scripture can be produced to lead us on further still. We know for certain that they for whom the Kingdom is prepared are the humble, the charitable, and the diligent in the improvement of their gifts; to which another text (for instance) adds the spiritually-minded:—"Eye hath not seen the things which God hath *prepared* for them that *love* Him." [1] Is this as far as we can go? Does it now depend ultimately on ourselves, or on any one else, that we come to be humble, charitable, diligent, and lovers of God?

Now, in answering this question, religious men have for many centuries differed in opinion; not indeed in the first and purest ages of the Church, but when corruptions began to steal in. In the primitive times it was always considered that, though God's grace was absolutely necessary for us from first to last,— before we believed, in order to our believing, and while we obeyed and worked righteousness, in order to our obeying,—so that not a deed, word, or thought could be pleasing to Him without it; yet, that after all the human mind had also from first to last a power of resisting grace, and thus (as the foregoing texts imply) had the ultimate determination of its own fate committed to it, whether to be saved or rejected, the responsibility of its conduct, and, if it was rejected, the whole blame of it. However, at the beginning of the fifth century, when shadows were coming over the Church, a celebrated Doctor arose, whose name must ever be honoured by us, for his numberless gifts, his diligence, and his extended usefulness, whatever judgment may be passed on certain of his opinions. He is known in the Theological Schools as the first to have given some sort of sanction to two doctrines hitherto unknown in the Church and apparently far removed from each other, as indeed are the modern Systems in which they are found. The one is the Predestinarian Hypothesis; viz. that, in spite of the text, it is God and Christ with whom the ultimate decision concerning the individual's state depends; that His grace does not merely suggest, influence, precede, and follow, but forms in the soul a new

[1] Matt. xxv.21, 34–36; 1 Cor. ii.9.

character, not by the soul's instrumentality, but immediately by Himself, and is effectual with some, not with others, at His own will, not at the individual's. The one, I say, is this Predestinarian Doctrine; and the other is the doctrine of Purgatory. With this latter I am not now concerned; and I mention it, only as a remarkable fact, that the same Teacher, highly to be venerated except where he deviates from Catholic doctrine, should have first sanctioned certain characteristics of two Systems, which lie on either side, as of the primitive, so of the present Anglican Church. Dismissing the coincidence with this remark, I proceed to make some brief observations on the ground of argument on which the Predestinarian Doctrine rests.

It is doubtless a great mystery, how it is that one man believes, and another rejects the Gospel. It is altogether a mystery; we cannot get at all beyond the fact, and must be content with our ignorance. But men of reasoning, subtle, and restless minds, have within them a temptation to inquisitiveness; they cannot acquiesce in the limits of God's revelation, and go on to assume a cause for the strange things they see when they are not told one. Thus they argue that a man's self cannot be the ultimate cause of his faith or unbelief, else there would be more first causes than God in the world: as if the same reasoning would not show that God is the Author of evil; or as if it were more intelligible, why the Divine Will should choose this man and reject that, than why an individual man should choose or reject good or evil. When then they see, as is constantly seen in life, two persons, in education the same, in circumstances the same, both baptized, both admitted to full Church privileges, one turning out well, the other ill, astonished at the mystery, they hastily say, "Here is God's secret election! God has decreed life to one, and has passed over the other; else why this difference of conduct?" when they should bow the head, and wait till the day of the revelation of all secrets. Again, they assume that the will is subjected to the influence of the reason, affections, and the like, in the same uniform way in which material bodies obey the laws of matter;—that certain inducements or a certain knowledge being presented, the mind can but act in one way; so that, its movements varying, on a given rule, according to influences from without (whether from the world or from God), every one's doom must be determined, either by the mere chance of external circumstances (which is irrational), or else certainly by the determination of God. Such are their reasonings; and it is remarkable that they should trust to reasoning and in so special a way, considering they are commonly the men who speak against human reason as fallible and corrupt, when it is brought to oppose their opinions. Such grounds of argument, then, we may dismiss at once, except in philosophical discussions; certainly when we speak as Christians.

Next, let us inquire whether there be any Scripture reason for breaking the chain of doctrine which the text suggests. Christ gives the Kingdom to those for whom it is prepared of the Father; the Father prepares it for those who love and serve Him. Does Scripture warrant us in reversing this order, and considering that any are chosen to love Him by His irreversible decree? The disputants in question maintain that it does.

1. Scripture is supposed expressly to *promise* perseverance, when men once savingly partake of grace; as where it is said, "He which hath begun a good work in you, will perform it until the day of Jesus Christ;" [2] and hence it is inferred that the salvation of the individual rests ultimately with God, and not with himself. But here I would object in the outset to applying to individuals promises and declarations made to bodies, and of a general nature. The question in debate is, not whether God carries forward bodies of men, such as the Christian Church, to salvation, but whether He has accorded any promise of indefectibility to given individuals? Those who differ from us say, that individuals are absolutely chosen to eternal life; let them then reckon up the passages in Scripture where perseverance is promised to individuals. Till they can satisfy this demand, they have done nothing by producing such a text as that just cited; which, being spoken of the body of Christians, does but impart that same kind of encouragement, as is contained in other general declarations, such as the statement about God's willingness to save, His being in the midst of us, and the like.

But let us suppose, for argument's sake, that such passages may be applied to individuals; for instance, as when Christ says, that no one "shall pluck His sheep out of His Father's hand." Now, I would maintain that here a condition is understood, as is constantly the case in Scripture, as in other writings; viz. that while the sheep "follow" Christ, and keep within the fold, none can pluck them thence. God proclaims his name to Moses, as "forgiving iniquity, and transgression, and sin, and that will by no means clear the guilty;" [3] but what would be thought of a commentator who hence inferred that the impenitent might be forgiven, and the repenting sinner fail of pardon?

[2] Phil. i.6.
[3] John x.28; Exod. xxxiv.7.

Again, "It is God which worketh in you both to will and to do of His good pleasure." [4] What is this but a declaration, that on the whole all our sanctification is from first to last God's work? how does it interfere with this, to say that we may effectually resist that work? Might it not truly be said that the cure of a sick person was wholly attributable to the physician, without denying that the former, had he so chosen, might have obstinately rejected the medicine, or that there might have been (though there was not) some malignant habit of body, which completely baffled the medical art? Does the chance of failure make it less the physician's work when there is not failure?

In truth, the two doctrines of the sovereign and overruling power of Divine grace, and man's power of resistance, need not at all interfere with each other. They lie in different provinces, and are (as it were) incommensurables. Thus St. Paul evidently accounted them; else he could not have introduced the text in question with the exhortation, "Work out" or accomplish "your own salvation with fear and trembling, *for* it is God which worketh" or acts "in you." So far was he from thinking man's distinct working inconsistent with God's continual aiding, that he assigns the knowledge of the latter as an encouragement to the former. Let me challenge then a Predestinarian to paraphrase this text. We, on the contrary, find no insuperable difficulty in it, considering it to enjoin upon us a deep awe and reverence, while we engage in those acts and efforts which are to secure our salvation from the belief that God is in us and with us, inspecting and succouring our every thought and deed. Would not the Jewish High Priest, on the Great Day of Atonement, when going through his several acts of propitiation in God's presence, without and within the Veil, "exceedingly fear and quake," lest he should fail in aught put upon Him? and shall not we, in our more blessed Covenant, knowing that God himself is within us, and in all we do, fear the more from the thought that, after all, we have our own part in the work, and must do it well, if we are to be saved? What, on the other hand, is the meaning of saying with the Predestinarian, "Work anxiously, because, in reality, you have no work to do?"

I say this, not so much by way of argument against him, as to show that a text which might be adduced in his behalf chances (so to say) to be implicated with an exhortation, such as proves that it, and therefore similar passages, cannot really be explained as he would have it; proves, that his argument from it,

[4] Phil. ii.13.

"The whole work of salvation is of God, *therefore* man has no real part in securing it," in fact runs contrary to the Apostle's own argument from his own words, "Man must exert himself, *because* God is present with him." It is quite certain that a modern Predestinarian never could have written such a sentence.

Another instructive passage of this kind is our Lord's declaration, with St. John's comment upon it, in the sixth chapter of his Gospel, "There are some of you that believe not. For Jesus *knew from the beginning* who they were that believed not, and who should betray Him. And He said, *Therefore* said I unto you, that *no man can come unto Me, unless it were given unto him of My Father.*" Here, in the plain meaning of the words, God's foreknowledge of the issue of free will in individuals is made compatible (though the manner how is not told us) with electing grace. "Whom He did foreknow, He also did predestinate."

Take again another passage. "I obtained mercy, *because* I did it ignorantly;" "I obtained mercy, *that* in me first Jesus Christ might show forth all long suffering."[5] It appears that the Apostle saw no inconsistency in preaching that *no* sinner can *claim* forgiveness, yet that those who are *less guilty* than others *obtain* it. These two doctrines do not seem to have come into collision in his mind, any more than in our own; but it is quite plain that a Predestinarian never would have introduced the first while descanting on the second.

2. In the next place, there are many passages of the following kind, which are sometimes taken to favour the Predestinarian view, and require explanation. "God hath blessed us with all spiritual blessings in heavenly places in Christ, according as He hath chosen us in Him before the foundation of the world, that we should be holy and without blame before Him in love, having predestinated us unto the adoption of children by Jesus Christ to Himself according to the good pleasure of His will." Here certainly an election is spoken of, irrespective of the conduct of the individuals who are subjects of it. Again, "By grace are ye saved through faith; and that salvation not of yourselves, it is the gift of God:"[6] and the like. But in such passages let it be observed, neither heaven nor the grace of sanctification is spoken of, but the present privilege, high indeed and peculiar to the Gospel, but only a privilege, of regeneration. This great Christian gift of course includes in it the communication of a sanctifying grace; but such a grace may be, and under circum-

[5] John vi.64, 65; 1 Tim. i.13, 16.
[6] Eph. i.3–5; ii.8.

stances has been, given without it. The Jews were aided by the Spirit of Sanctification, not of Regeneration. They were not the sons of God, as we are; whereas in every age "the just have lived by faith," and the like fruits of Sanctification. Now, where are we told that this sanctifying Grace is irrespective of the free-will of individuals? for this is the point. On the other hand, we readily grant that the grace of Regeneration is such; indeed, we grant that it is more than all that certain teachers hold Sanctification to be. It is a definite and complete gift conveyed, not gradually, but at once; or at least it has not more than a second degree, in the rite of Confirmation, wherein what is given in Baptism is sealed and secured; and moreover, it is a state distinct from every other, consisting in the Sacred Presence of the Spirit of Christ in soul and body; and lastly, it is bestowed on this man, or that, not by any rule which we can discover, but at the inscrutable decree of Him who calls into His Church whom He will. But faith, together with the other gifts of Sanctification, is not thus bestowed. In its nature it is independent of Regeneration, and, in the formal scheme of the Gospel, it is antecedent to it. It is the antecedent condition for receiving the Ordinances which convey and seal Regeneration, —Baptism and Confirmation. Hence, St. John says, "*As many as received Him*, to them gave He power to become the sons of God, even to them that believe on His Name, which were born, not of blood, nor of the will of the flesh, nor of the will of man, but of God." And St. Paul, "*Believing* in Christ, ye were *sealed with that Holy Spirit of promise*, which is the earnest of our inheritance, until the redemption of the purchased possession."[7]

It avails not, therefore, to enlarge upon the characteristics of the Christian Election, with a view of proving the irreversible decrees of God concerning the *final* salvation of individuals.

3. Lastly, there are passages which speak of God's *judicial* dealings with the heart of man; in which, doubtless, He does act absolutely at His sole will,—yet not in the beginning of His Providence towards us, but at the close. Thus He is said "to send" on men "strong *delusion* to believe a lie;" but only on those who "received not the love of the truth that they might be saved."[8] Such irresistible influences do but presuppose, instead of superseding, our own accountableness.

These three explanations then being allowed their due weight,—the compatibility of God's sovereignty over the soul, with man's individual agency; the distinction between Regen-

[7] John i.12, 13.; Eph. i.13, 14.   [8] 2 Thess. ii.10, 11.

eration and faith and obedience; and the judicial purpose of certain Divine influences upon the heart,—let us ask what does there remain of Scripture evidence in behalf of the Predestinarian doctrines? Are we not obliged to leave the mystery of human agency and responsibility as we find it? as truly a mystery in itself as that which concerns the Nature and Attributes of the Divine Mind.

Surely it will be our true happiness thus to conduct ourselves; to use our reason, in getting at the true sense of Scripture, not in making a series of deductions from it; in unfolding the doctrines therein contained, not in adding new ones to them; in acquiescing in what is told, not in indulging curiosity about the "secret things" of the Lord our God.

I conclude with the following text, which, while it is a solemn warning to us all to turn to God with a true heart, states with a force not to be explained away, what the revealed Will is, and what we are to hold respecting it. "*As I live*, saith the Lord God, I have no pleasure in the death of the wicked; but that the wicked turn from his way and live. Turn ye, turn ye from your evil ways: why will ye die, O House of Israel?" [9]

[9] Ezek. xxxiii.11.

GUILELESSNESS

(The Feast of St. Bartholomew the Apostle)

*"Jesus saw Nathanael coming to Him, and saith of him, Behold an
Israelite indeed, in whom is no guile!"*—John i.47.

S T. BARTHOLOMEW, whose Festival we celebrate to-day, has
been supposed to be the same as the Nathanael mentioned
in the text. Nathanael was one of Christ's first converts, yet his
name does not occur again till the last chapter of St. John's
Gospel, where he is mentioned in company with certain of the
Apostles, to whom Christ appeared after His resurrection.
Now, why should the call of Nathanael have been recorded in
the opening of the Gospel, among the acts of Christ in the beginning of His Ministry, unless he was an Apostle? Philip, Peter, and Andrew, who are mentioned at the same time, were
all Apostles; and Nathanael's name is introduced without pref-
ace, as if familiar to a Christian reader. At the end of the Gospel it appears again, and there too among Apostles. Besides,
the Apostles were the special witnesses of Christ, when He
was risen. He manifested Himself, "not to all the people," says
Peter, "but unto witnesses chosen before of God, even to us,
who did eat and drink with Him after He rose from the
dead." [1] Now, the occasion on which Nathanael is mentioned,
was one of these manifestations. "This is now the third time,"
says the Evangelist, "that Jesus was manifested to His disciples,
after that He was risen from the dead." It was in the presence
of Nathanael, that He gave St. Peter his commission, and foretold his martyrdom, and the prolonged life of St. John. All this
leads us to conjecture that Nathanael is one of the Apostles
under another name. Now, he is not Andrew, Peter, or Philip,
for they are mentioned in connexion with him in the first
chapter of the Gospel; nor Thomas, James, or John, in whose
company he is found in the last chapter; nor Jude (as it would
seem), because the name of Jude occurs in St. John's four-

---

[1] Acts x.41.

teenth chapter. Four Apostles remain, who are not named in his Gospel,—St. James the Less, St. Matthew, St. Simon, and St. Bartholomew; of whom St. Matthew's second name is known to have been Levi, while St. James, being related, was not at any time a stranger to our Lord, which Nathanael evidently was. If then Nathanael were an Apostle, he was either Simon or Bartholomew. Now it is observable, that, according to St. John, Philip brought Nathanael to Christ; therefore Nathanael and Philip were friends: while in the other Gospels, in the list of Apostles, Philip is associated with Bartholomew; "Simon and Andrew, James and John, Philip and Bartholomew." [2] This is some evidence that Bartholomew and not Simon is the Nathanael of St. John. On the other hand, Matthias has been suggested instead of either, his name meaning nearly the same as Nathanael in the original language. However, since writers of some date decide in favour of Bartholomew, I shall do the like in what follows.

What then do we learn from his recorded character and history? It affords us an instructive lesson.

When Philip told him that he had found the long-expected Messiah of whom Moses wrote, Nathanael (that is, Bartholomew) at first doubted. He was well read in the Scriptures, and knew the Christ was to be born in Bethlehem; whereas Jesus dwelt at Nazareth, which Nathanael supposed in consequence to be the place of His birth,—and he knew of no particular promises attached to that city, which was a place of evil report, and he thought no good could come out of it. Philip told him to come and see; and he went to see, as a humble single-minded man, sincerely desirous to get at the truth. In consequence, he was vouchsafed an interview with our Saviour, and was converted.

Now, from what occurred in this interview, we gain some insight into St. Bartholomew's character. Our Lord said of him, "Behold an Israelite indeed, in whom is no guile!" and it appears, moreover, as if, before Philip called him to come to Christ, he was engaged in meditation or prayer, in the privacy which a fig-tree's shade afforded him. And this, it seems, was the life of one who was destined to act the busy part of an Apostle; quietness without, guilelessness within. This was the tranquil preparation for great dangers and sufferings! We see who make the most heroic Christians, and are the most honoured by Christ!

[2] Matt. x.3.

An even, unvaried life is the lot of most men, in spite of occasional troubles or other accidents; and we are apt to despise it, and to get tired of it, and to long to see the world,—or, at all events, we think such a life affords no great opportunity for religious obedience. To rise up, and go through the same duties, and then to rest again, day after day,—to pass week after week, beginning with God's service on Sunday, and then to our worldly tasks,—so to continue till year follows year, and we gradually get old,—an unvaried life like this is apt to seem unprofitable to us when we dwell upon the thought of it. Many indeed there are, who do not think at all;—but live in their round of employments, without care about God and religion, driven on by the natural course of things in a dull irrational way like the beasts that perish. But when a man begins to feel he has a soul, and a work to do, and a reward to be gained, greater or less, according as he improves the talents committed to him, then he is naturally tempted to be anxious from his very wish to be saved, and he says, "What must I *do* to please God?" And sometimes he is led to think he ought to be useful on a large scale, and goes out of his line of life, that he may be doing something worth doing, as he considers it. Here we have the history of St. Bartholomew and the other Apostles to recall us to ourselves, and to assure us that we need not give up our usual manner of life, in order to serve God; that the most humble and quietest station is acceptable to Him, if improved duly—nay, affords means for maturing the highest Christian character, even that of an Apostle. Bartholomew read the Scriptures and prayed to God; and thus was trained at length to give up his life for Christ, when He demanded it.

But, further, let us consider the particular praise which our Saviour gives him. "Behold an Israelite indeed, in whom is no guile!" This is just the character which (through God's grace) they may attain most fully, who live out of the world in the private way I have been describing,—which is made least account of by man, and thought to be in the way of success in life, though our Saviour chose it to make head against all the power and wisdom of the world. Men of the world think an ignorance of its ways is a disadvantage or disgrace; as if it were somehow unmanly and weak to have abstained from all acquaintance with its impieties and lax practices. How often do we hear them say that a man must do so and so, unless he would be singular and absurd; that he must not be too strict, or indulge high-flown notions of virtue, which may be good to talk about, but are not fit for this world! When they hear of any young person resolving on being consistently religious, or being strictly honest in trade, or observing a noble purity in language and demeanour, they smile and think it very well, but that it will and must wear off in time. And they are ashamed of being innocent, and pretend to be worse than they really are. Then they have all sorts of little ways—are mean, jealous, suspicious, censorious, cunning, insincere, selfish; and think others as low-minded as themselves, only proud, or in some sense hypocritical, unwilling to confess their real motives and feelings.

To this base and irreligious multitude is opposed the Israelite indeed, in whom there is no guile. David describes his character in the fifteenth Psalm; and, taken in all its parts, it is a rare one. He asks, "Lord, who shall abide in Thy tabernacle? who shall dwell in Thy holy hill? He that walketh uprightly, and worketh righteousness, and speaketh the truth in his heart. He that backbiteth not with his tongue, nor doeth evil to his neighbour, nor taketh up a reproach against his neighbour. In whose eyes a vile person is contemned; but he honoureth them that fear the Lord. He that sweareth to his own hurt, and changeth not."

I say, it is a difficult and rare virtue, to mean what we say, to love without dissimulation, to think no evil, to bear no grudge, to be free from selfishness, to be innocent and straightforward. This character of mind is something far above the generality of men; and when realized in due measure, one of the surest marks of Christ's elect. And the instances which we may every now and then discover of it among Christians, will be an evidence to us, if evidence be wanting, that, in spite of all that grovelling minds may say about the necessity of acquaintance with the world and with sin, in order to get on well in life, yet after all, inexperienced guilelessness carries a man on as safely and more happily. For, first, it is in itself a great privilege to a rightly disposed mind, not to be sensible of the moral miseries of the world; and this is eminently the lot of the simple-hearted. They take everything in good part which happens to them, and make the best of every one; thus they have always something to be pleased with, not seeing the bad, and keenly sensible of the good. And communicating their own happy peace to those around them, they really diminish the evils of life in society at large, while they escape from the knowledge of them themselves. Such men are cheerful and contented; for they desire but little, and take pleasure in the least matters, having no wish for riches and distinction. And they are under the tyranny of no evil or base thoughts, having never encouraged what in the case of other men often spreads disorder and unholiness through their whole future life. They have no phantoms of former sins, such as remain even to the penitent, when he has subdued their realities, rising up in their minds, harassing them, for a time domineering, and leaving a sting behind them. Guileless persons are, most of all men, skilful in shaming and silencing the wicked;—for they do not argue, but take things for granted in so natural a way, that they throw back the sinner upon the recollection of those times of his youth, when he was pure from sin, and thought as they do now; and none but very hardened men can resist this sort of appeal. Men of irreligious lives live in bondage and fear; even though they do not acknowledge it to themselves. Many a one, who would be ashamed to own it, is afraid of certain places or times, or of solitude, from a sort of instinct that he is no company for good spirits, and that devils may then assail him. But the guileless man has a simple boldness and a princely heart; he overcomes dangers which others shrink from, merely because they are no dangers to him, and thus he often gains even worldly advantages, by his straightforwardness, which the most crafty persons cannot gain, though they risk their souls for them. It is true such single-hearted men often get into difficulties, but they usually get out of them as easily; and are almost unconscious both of their danger and their escape. Perhaps they have not received a learned education, and cannot talk fluently; yet they are ever a match for those who try to shake their faith in Christ by profane argument or ridicule, for the weakness of God is stronger than men.

Nor is it only among the poor and lowly that this blessed character of mind is found to exist. Secular learning and dignity have doubtless in their respective ways a powerful tendency to rob the heart of its brightness and purity; yet even in kings' courts, and the schools of philosophy, Nathanaels may be discovered. Nay, like the Apostles, they have been subjected to the world's buffetings, they have been thwarted in their day, lived in anxiety, and seemingly lost by their honesty, yet without being foiled either of its present comfort or its ultimate fruit. Such was our great Archbishop and Martyr, to whom perchance we owe it, that we who now live are still members of a branch of the Church Catholic; one of whose "greatest unpopular infirmities," according to the historian of his times, was "that he believed innocence of heart, and integrity of manners, was a guard strong enough to secure any man in his voyage through this world, in what company soever he travelled and through what ways soever he was to pass. And sure," he adds, "never any man was better supplied with that provision."

I have in these remarks spoken of guileless men as members of society, because I wished to show that, even in that respect in which they seem deficient, they possess a hidden strength, an unconscious wisdom, which makes them live above the world, and sooner or later triumph over it. The weapons of their warfare are not carnal; and they are fitted to be Apostles, though they seem to be ordinary men. Such is the blessedness of the innocent, that is, of those who have never given way to evil, or formed themselves to habits of sin; who in consequence literally do not know its power or its misery, who have thoughts of truth and peace ever before them, and are able to discern at once the right and wrong in conduct, as by some delicate instrument which tells truly because it has never been ill-treated. Nay, such may be the portion (through God's mercy) even of those who have at one time departed from Him, and then repented; in proportion as they have learned to love God, and have purified themselves, not only from sin, but from the recollections of it.

Lastly, more is requisite for the Christian, even than guilelessness such as Bartholomew's. When Christ sent forth him and his brethren into the world, He said, "Behold, I send you forth as sheep in the midst of wolves; be ye therefore wise as serpents and harmless as doves." Innocence must be joined to prudence, discretion, self-command, gravity, patience, perseverance in well-doing, as Bartholomew doubtless learned in due season under his Lord's teaching; but innocence is the beginning. Let us then pray God to fulfil in us "all the good pleasure of His goodness, and the work of faith with power;" that if it should please Him suddenly to bring us forward to great trials, as He did His Apostles, we may not be taken by surprise, but be found to have made a private or domestic life a preparation for the achievements of Confessors and Martyrs.

THE DANGER OF RICHES

(The Feast of St. Matthew the Apostle)

"Woe unto you that are rich! for ye have received your consolation."—Luke vi.24.

UNLESS we were accustomed to read the New Testament from our childhood, I think we should be very much struck with the warnings which it contains, not only against the love of riches, but the very possession of them; we should wonder with a portion of that astonishment which the Apostles at first felt, who had been brought up in the notion that they were a chief reward which God bestowed on those He loved. As it is, we have heard the most solemn declarations so continually, that we have ceased to attach any distinct meaning to them; or, if our attention is at any time drawn more closely to them, we soon dismiss the subject on some vague imagination, that what is said in Scripture had a reference to the particular times when Christ came, without attempting to settle its exact application to us, or whether it has any such application at all,—as if the circumstance, that the interpretation requires care and thought, were an excuse for giving no thought or care whatever to the settling of it.

But, even if we had ever so little concern in the Scripture denunciations against riches and the love of riches, the very awfulness of them might have seemed enough to save them from neglect; just as the flood, and the judgment upon Sodom and Gomorrah, are still dwelt upon by Christians with solemn attention, though we have a promise against the recurrence of the one, and trust we shall never be so deserted by God's grace as to call down upon us the other. And this consideration may lead a man to suspect that the neglect in question does not entirely arise from unconcern, but from a sort of misgiving that the subject of riches is one which cannot be safely or comfortably discussed by the Christian world at this day; that is, which cannot be discussed without placing the claims of God's Law and the pride of life into visible and perplexing opposition.

Let us then see what the letter of Scripture says on the subject. For instance, consider the text. "Woe unto you that are rich! for ye have received your consolation." The words are sufficiently clear (it will not be denied), as spoken of rich persons in our Saviour's day. Let the full force of the word "consolation" be observed. It is used by way of contrast to the comfort which is promised to the Christian in the list of Beatitudes. Comfort, in the fulness of that word, as including help, guidance, encouragement, and support, is the peculiar promise of the Gospel.[1] The Promised Spirit, who has taken Christ's place, was called by Him "the Comforter." There is then something very fearful in the intimation of the text, that those who have riches thereby receive their portion, such as it is, in full, instead of the Heavenly Gift of the Gospel. The same doctrine is implied in our Lord's words in the parable of Dives and Lazarus: "Son, remember thou in thy lifetime receivedst *thy* good things, and likewise Lazarus evil things; but *now* he is *comforted*, and thou art tormented." At another time He said to His disciples, "How hardly shall they that have riches enter into the kingdom of God! for it is easier for a camel to go through a needle's eye, than for a rich man to enter into the kingdom of God."[2]

Now, it is usual to dismiss such passages with the remark, that they are directed, not against those who have, but against those who trust in, riches; as if forsooth they implied no *connexion* between the having and the trusting, no warning *lest* the possession led to the idolatrous reliance on them, no necessity of fear and anxiety in the possessors, lest they should become castaways. And this irrelevant distinction is supposed to find countenance in our Lord's own language on one of the occasions above referred to, in which He first says, "How hardly shall they that *have* riches," then, "How hard is it for them that *trust* in riches, to enter into the kingdom of God;" whereas surely, He only removes His disciples' false impression, that the bare circumstance of possessing wealth was inconsistent with a state of salvation, and no more interprets *having* by *trusting* than makes *trusting* essential to *having*. He connects the two, without identifying, without explaining away; and the simple question which lies for our determination is this:—whether, considering that they who had riches when Christ came, were likely in His judgment idolatrously to trust in them, there is, or is not, reason for thinking that this likelihood varies materially in differ-

[1] Matt. v.4.   [2] Luke xvi.25; xviii.24, 25.

ent ages; and, according to the solution of this question, must we determine the application of the woe pronounced in the text to these times. And, at all events, let it be observed, it is for those who would make out that these passages do *not* apply now, to give their reasons for their opinion; the burden of proof is with them. Till they draw their clear and reasonable distinctions between the first and the nineteenth century, the denunciation hangs over the world,—that is, as much as over the Pharisees and Sadducees at our Lord's coming.

But, in truth, that our Lord meant to speak of riches as being in some sense a calamity to the Christian, is plain, not only from such texts as the foregoing, but from His praises and recommendation on the other hand of poverty. For instance, "Sell that ye have and give alms; provide yourselves bags which wax not old." "If thou wilt be perfect, go sell that thou hast, and give to the poor, and thou shalt have treasure in heaven." "Blessed be ye poor: for yours is the kingdom of God." "When thou makest a dinner or a supper, call not thy friends, nor thy brethren, neither thy kinsmen, nor thy rich neighbours . . . . but . . . . call the poor, the maimed, the lame, the blind." And in like manner, St. James: "Hath not God chosen the poor of this world rich in faith, and heirs of that kingdom which He hath promised to them that love Him?"[3] Now, I cite these texts in the way of doctrine, not of precept. Whatever be the line of conduct they prescribe to this or that individual (with which I have nothing to do at present), so far seems clear, that according to the rule of the Gospel, the absence of wealth is, as such, a more blessed and a more Christian state than the possession of it.

The most obvious danger which worldly possessions present to our spiritual welfare is, that they become practically a substitute in our hearts for that One Object to which our supreme devotion is due. They are present; God is unseen. They are means at hand of effecting what we want: whether God will hear our petitions for those wants is uncertain; or rather I may say, certain in the negative. Thus they minister to the corrupt inclinations of our nature; they promise and are able to be gods to us, and such gods too as require no service, but, like dumb idols, exalt the worshipper, impressing him with a notion of his own power and security. And in this consist their chief and most subtle mischief. Religious men are able to repress, nay extirpate sinful desires, the lust of the flesh and of the eyes,

---

[3] Luke xii.33; Matt. xix.21; Luke vi.20; xiv.12, 13.

gluttony, drunkenness, and the like, love of amusements and frivolous pleasures and display, indulgence in luxuries of whatever kind; but as to wealth, they cannot easily rid themselves of a secret feeling that it gives them a footing to stand upon, an importance, a superiority; and in consequence they get attached to this world, lose sight of the duty of bearing the Cross, become dull and dim-sighted, and lose their delicacy and precision of touch, are numbed (so to say) in their fingers' ends, as regards religious interests and prospects. To risk all upon Christ's word seems somehow unnatural to them, extravagant, and evidences a morbid excitement; and death, instead of being a gracious, however awful release, is not a welcome subject of thought. They are content to remain as they are, and do not contemplate a change. They desire and mean to serve God, nay actually do serve Him in their measure; but not with the keen sensibilities, the noble enthusiasm, the grandeur and elevation of soul, the dutifulness and affectionateness towards Christ which become a Christian, but as Jews might obey, who had no Image of God given them except this created world, "eating their bread with joy, and drinking their wine with a merry heart," caring that "their garments be always white, and their head lacking no ointment, living joyfully with the wife whom they love all the days of the life of their Vanity," and "enjoying the good of their labour."[4] Not, of course, that the due use of God's temporal blessings is wrong, but to make them the object of our affections, to allow them to beguile us from the "One Husband" to whom we are espoused, is to mistake the Gospel for Judaism.

This, then, if we may venture to say so, was some part of Our Saviour's meaning, when He connects together the having with the trusting in riches; and it is especially suitable to consider it upon this day, when we commemorate an Apostle and an Evangelist, whose history is an example and encouragement for all those who have, and fear lest they should trust. But St. Matthew was exposed to an additional temptation, which I shall proceed to consider; for he not only possessed, but he was engaged also in the pursuit of wealth. Our Saviour seems to warn us against this further danger in His description of the thorns in the parable of the Sower, as being "the care of this world and the deceitfulness of riches;" and more clearly in the parable of the Great Supper, where the guests excuse themselves, one as having "bought a piece of ground," another "five

[4] Eccles. ix.7–9; v.18.

yoke of oxen." Still more openly does St. Paul speak in his First Epistle to Timothy: "They that desire to be rich, fall into temptation and a snare, and into many foolish and hurtful lusts, which drown men in destruction and perdition. For the love of money is the root of all evil; which, while some coveted after, they have erred from the Faith, and pierced themselves through with many sorrows." [5]

The danger of *possessing* riches is the carnal security to which they lead; that of "*desiring*" and *pursuing* them, is, that an object of this world is thus set before us as the aim and end of life. It seems to be the will of Christ that His followers should have no aim or end, pursuit or business, merely of this world. Here, again, I speak as before, not in the way of precept, but of doctrine. I am looking at His holy religion as at a distance and determining what is its general character and spirit, not what may happen to be the duty of this or that individual who has embraced it. It is His will that all we do should be done, not unto men, or to the world, or to self, but to His glory; and the more we are enabled to do this simply, the more favoured we are. Whenever we act with reference to an object of this world, even though it be ever so pure, we are exposed to the temptation—(not irresistible, God forbid!) still to the temptation—of setting our hearts upon obtaining it. And therefore, we call all such objects *excitements*, as stimulating us incongruously, casting us out of the serenity and stability of heavenly faith, attracting us aside by their proximity from our harmonious round of duties, and making our thoughts converge to something short of that which is infinitely high and eternal. Such excitements are of perpetual occurrence, and the mere undergoing them, so far from involving guilt in the act itself or its results, is the great business of life and the discipline of our hearts. It is often a sin to withdraw from them, as has been the case of some perhaps who have gone into monasteries to serve God more entirely. On the other hand, it is the very duty of the Spiritual Ruler to labour for the flock committed to him, to suffer and to dare; St. Paul was encompassed with excitements hence arising, and his writings show the agitating effect of them on his mind. He was like David, a man of war and blood; and that for our sakes. Still it holds good that the essential spirit of the Gospel is "quietness and confidence;" that the possession of these is the highest gift, and to gain them perfectly our main aim.

[5] Matt. xiii.22; Luke xiv.18, 19; 1 Tim. vi.9, 10.

Consequently, however much a duty it is to undergo excitements when they are sent upon us, it is plainly unchristian, a manifest foolishness and sin, to seek out any such, whether secular or religious. Hence gaming is so great an offence; as being a presumptuous creation on our part of a serious, if not an overpowering temptation to fix the heart upon an object of this world. Hence, the mischief of many amusements, of (what is called) the fashion of the day; which are devised for the very purpose of taking up the thoughts, and making time pass easy. Quite contrary is the Christian temper, which is in its perfect and peculiar enjoyment when engaged in that ordinary, unvaried course of duties which God assigns, and which the world calls dull and tiresome. To get up day after day to the same employments, and to feel happy in them, is the great lesson of the Gospel; and, when exemplified in those who are alive to the temptation of being busy, it implies a heart weaned from the love of this world. True it is that illness of body, as well as restlessness of mind, may occasionally render such a life a burden; it is true also that indolence, self-indulgence, timidity and other similar bad habits, may adopt it by preference, as a pretext for neglecting more active duties. Men of energetic minds and talents for action are called to a life of trouble; they are the compensations and antagonists of the world's evils; still let them never forget their place; they are men of war, and we war that we may obtain peace. They are but men of war, honoured indeed by God's choice, and, in spite of all momentary excitements, resting in the depth of their hearts upon One true Vision of Christian faith; still after all they are but soldiers in the open field, not builders of the Temple, nor inhabitants of those "amiable" and specially blessed "Tabernacles" where the worshipper lives in praise and intercession, and is militant amid the unostentatious duties of ordinary life. "Martha, Martha, thou art anxious and troubled about many things; but one thing is needful, and Mary has chosen that good part which shall not be taken away from her."[6] Such is our Lord's judgment, showing that our true happiness consists in being at leisure to serve God without excitements. For this gift we especially pray in one of our Collects: "Grant, O Lord, that the course of this world may be so peaceably ordered by Thy governance, that Thy Church may joyfully serve Thee in all godly quietness."[7] Persecution, civil changes, and the like break in upon the Church's calm. The greatest privilege of a Christian is

[6] Luke x.41, 42.   [7] *Vide* 1 Tim. ii.2.

to have nothing to do with worldly politics,—to be governed and to submit obediently; and though here again selfishness may creep in, and lead a man to neglect public concerns in which he is called to take his share, yet, after all, such participation must be regarded as a duty, scarcely as a privilege, as the fulfilment of trusts committed to him for the good of others, not as the enjoyment of rights (as men talk in these days of delusion), not as if political power were in itself a good.

To return to the subject immediately before us; I say then, that it is a part of Christian caution to see that our engagements do not become pursuits. Engagements are our portion, but pursuits are for the most part of our own choosing. We may be engaged in worldly business, without pursuing worldly objects; "not slothful in business," yet "serving the Lord." In this then consists the danger of the pursuit of gain, as by trade and the like. It is the most common and widely extended of all excitements. It is one in which every one almost may indulge, nay, and will be praised by the world for indulging. And it lasts through life; in that differing from the amusements and pleasures of the world, which are short-lived, and succeed one after another. Dissipation of mind, which these amusements create, is itself indeed miserable enough: but far worse than this dissipation is the concentration of mind upon some worldly object, which admits of being constantly pursued,—and such is the pursuit of gain. Nor is it a slight aggravation of the evil, that anxiety is almost sure to attend it. A life of money-getting is a life of care; from the first there is a fearful anticipation of loss in various ways to depress and unsettle the mind; nay to haunt it, till a man finds he can think about nothing else, and is unable to give his mind to religion, from the constant whirl of business in which he is involved. It is well this should be understood. You may hear men talk as if the pursuit of wealth was the business of life. They will argue, that by the law of nature a man is bound to gain a livelihood for his family, and that he finds a reward in doing so, an innocent and honourable satisfaction, as he adds one sum to another, and counts up his gains. And perhaps they go on to argue, that it is the very duty of man since Adam's fall, "in the sweat of his face," by effort and anxiety, "to eat bread." How strange it is that they do not remember Christ's gracious promise, repealing that original curse, and obviating the necessity of any real pursuit after "the meat that perisheth!" In order that we might be delivered from the bondage of corruption, He has expressly told us that the necessaries of life shall never fail His faithful follower, any more than the meal and oil the widow-woman of Sarepta; that, while he is bound to labour for his family, he need not be engrossed by his toil,—that while he is busy, his heart may be at leisure for his Lord. "Be not anxious, saying, what shall we eat? or what shall we drink? or wherewithal shall we be clothed? For after all these things do the Gentiles seek; for your heavenly Father knoweth that ye have need of all these things. But seek ye first the kingdom of God and His righteousness; and all these things shall be added unto you." Here is revealed to us at once our privilege and our duty, the Christian portion of having engagements of this world without pursuing objects. And in accordance with our Divine Teacher are the words of the Apostle, introductory of a passage already cited. "We brought nothing into this world, and it is certain we can carry nothing out. And having food and raiment, let us therewith be content." [8] There is no excuse then for that absorbing pursuit of wealth, which many men indulge in as if a virtue, and expatiate upon as if a science. "After all these things do the Gentiles seek!" Consider how different is the rule of life left us by the Apostles. "I speak this for your own profit," says St. Paul, "that ye may attend upon the Lord, without distraction." "This I say, brethren, the time is short; it remaineth, that both they that have wives be as though they had none, and they that weep as though they wept not, and they that rejoice as though they rejoiced not, and they that buy as though they possessed not, and they that use this world as not abusing it, for the fashion of this world passeth away." "Be anxious for nothing; but in everything, by prayer and supplication with thanksgiving, let your requests be made known unto God." And St. Peter, "Casting all your anxiety upon Him, for He careth for you." [9]

I have now given the main reason why the pursuit of gain, whether in a large or small way, is prejudicial to our spiritual interests, that it fixes the mind upon an object of this world; yet others remain behind. Money is a sort of creation, and gives the acquirer, even more than the possessor, an imagination of his own power; and tends to make him idolize self. Again, what we have hardly won, we are unwilling to part with; so that a man who has himself made his wealth will commonly be penurious, or at least will not part with it except in exchange for what will reflect credit upon himself, or increase his importance. Even when his conduct is most disinterested and amiable (as in

[8] Matt. vi; 1 Tim. vi:7, 8.
[9] 1 Cor. vii.29–31, 35; Phil. iv.6; 1 Pet. v.7.

spending for the comfort of those who depend upon him), still this indulgence of self, of pride and worldliness, insinuates itself. Very unlikely therefore is it that he should be liberal towards God; for religious offerings are an expenditure without sensible return, and that upon objects for which the very pursuit of wealth has indisposed his mind. Moreover, if it may be added, there is a considerable tendency in occupations connected with gain to make a man unfair in his dealings,—that is, in a subtle way. There are so many conventional deceits and prevarications in the details of the world's business, so much intricacy in the management of accounts, so many perplexed questions about justice and equity, so many plausible subterfuges and fictions of law, so much confusion between the distinct yet approximating outlines of honesty and civil enactment, that it requires a very straightforward mind to keep firm hold of strict conscientiousness, honour, and truth, and to look at matters in which he is engaged, as he would have looked on them, supposing he now came upon them all at once as a stranger.

And if such be the effect of the pursuit of gain on an individual, doubtless it will be the same on a nation; and if the peril be so great in the one case, why should it be less in the other? Rather, considering that the tendencies of things are sure to be brought out, where time and numbers allow them fair course, is it not certain that any multitude, any society of men, whose object is gain, will on the whole be actuated by those feelings, and moulded into that character, which has been above described? With this thought before us, it is a very fearful consideration that we belong to a nation which in good measure subsists by making money. I will not pursue it; nor inquire whether the especial political evils of the day have not their root in that principle, which St. Paul calls the root of all evil, the love of money. Only let us consider the fact, that we *are* money-making people, with our Saviour's declarations before us against wealth, and trust in wealth: and we shall have abundant matter for serious thought.

Lastly, with this dreary view before us of our condition and prospects as a nation, the pattern of St. Matthew is our consolation; for it suggests that we, Christ's ministers, may use great freedom of speech, and state unreservedly the peril of wealth and gain, without aught of harshness or uncharitableness towards individuals who are exposed to it. They may be brethren of the Evangelist, who left all for Christ's sake. Nay, such there have been (blessed be God!) in every age; and in proportion to the strength of the temptation which surrounds them, is their blessedness and their praise, if they are enabled amid the "waves of the seas" and the "great wisdom of their traffic" to hear Christ's voice, to take up their cross, and follow Him.

THE POWERS OF NATURE

(The Feast of St. Michael and All Angels)

"Who maketh His Angels spirits, His ministers a flaming fire."
—Ps. civ.4.

O N to-day's Festival it well becomes us to direct our minds to the thought of those Blessed Servants of God, who have never tasted of sin; who are among us, though unseen, ever serving God joyfully on earth as well as in heaven; who minister, through their Maker's condescending will, to the redeemed in Christ, the heirs of salvation.

There have been ages of the world, in which men have thought too much of Angels, and paid them excessive honour; honoured them so perversely as to forget the supreme worship due to Almighty God. This is the sin of a dark age. But the sin of what is called an educated age, such as our own, is just the reverse: to account slightly of them, or not at all; to ascribe all we see around us, not to their agency, but to certain assumed laws of nature. This, I say, is likely to be our sin, in proportion as we are initiated into the learning of this world;—and this is the danger of many (so called) philosophical pursuits, now in fashion, and recommended zealously to the notice of large portions of the community, hitherto strangers to them,—chemistry, geology, and the like; the danger, that is, of resting in things seen, and forgetting unseen things, and our ignorance about them.

I will attempt to say what I mean more at length. The text informs us that Almighty God makes His Angels spirits or winds, and His Ministers a flame of fire. Let us consider what is implied in this.

1. What a number of beautiful and wonderful objects does Nature present on every side of us! and how little we know concerning them! In some indeed we see symptoms of intelligence, and we get to form some idea of what they are. For instance, about brute animals we know little, but still we see they have sense, and we understand that their bodily form which meets the eye is but the index, the outside token of something we do

not see. Much more in the case of men: we see them move, speak, and act, and we know that all we see takes place in consequence of their will, because they have a spirit within them, though we do not see it. But why do rivers flow? Why does rain fall? Why does the sun warm us? And the wind, why does it blow? Here our natural reason is at fault; we know, I say, that it is the *spirit* in man and in beast that makes man and beast move, but reason tells us of no spirit abiding in what is commonly called the natural world, to make it perform its ordinary duties. Of course, it is *God's* will which *sustains* it all; so does God's will enable *us* to move also, yet this does not hinder, but, in one sense we may be truly said to move ourselves: but how do the wind and water, earth and fire, move? Now here Scripture interposes, and seems to tell us, that all this wonderful harmony is the work of Angels. Those events which we ascribe to chance as the weather, or to nature as the seasons, are duties done to that God who maketh His Angels to be winds, and His Ministers a flame of fire. For example, it was an Angel which gave to the pool at Bethesda its medicinal quality; and there is no reason why we should doubt that other health-springs in this and other countries are made such by a like unseen ministry. The fires on Mount Sinai, the thunders and lightnings, were the work of Angels; and in the Apocalypse we read of the Angels restraining the four winds. Works of vengeance are likewise attributed to them. The fiery lava of the volcanoes, which (as it appears) was the cause of Sodom and Gomorrah's ruin, was caused by the two Angels who rescued Lot. The hosts of Sennacherib were destroyed by an Angel, by means (it is supposed) of a suffocating wind. The pestilence in Israel when David numbered the people, was the work of an Angel. The earthquake at the resurrection was the work of an Angel. And in the Apocalypse the earth is smitten in various ways by Angels of vengeance.[1]

Thus, as far as the Scripture communications go, we learn that the course of Nature, which is so wonderful, so beautiful, and so fearful, is effected by the ministry of those unseen beings. Nature is not inanimate; its daily toil is intelligent; its works are *duties*. Accordingly, the Psalmist says, "The heavens declare the glory of God, and the firmament showeth His handy-work." "O Lord, Thy word endureth for ever in heaven.

---

[1] John v.4; Exod. xix.16–18; Gal. iii.19; Acts vii.53; Rev. vii.1; Gen. xix.13; 2 Kings xix.35; 2 Sam. xxiv.15–17; Matt. xxviii.2; Rev. viii., ix., xvi.

Thy truth also remaineth from one generation to another; Thou hast laid the foundation of the earth, and it abideth. They continue this day according to Thine ordinance, for *all things serve Thee.*" [2]

I do not pretend to say, that we are told in Scripture what Matter is; but I affirm, that as our souls move our bodies, be our bodies what they may, so there are Spiritual Intelligences which move those wonderful and vast portions of the natural world which seem to be inanimate; and as the gestures, speech, and expressive countenances of our friends around us enable us to hold intercourse with them, so in the motions of universal Nature, in the interchange of day and night, summer and winter, wind and storm, fulfilling His word, we are reminded of the blessed and dutiful Angels. Well then, on this day's Festival, may we sing the hymn of those Three Holy Children whom Nebuchadnezzar cast into the fiery furnace. The Angels were bid to change the nature of the flame, and make it harmless to them; and they in turn called on all the creatures of God, on the Angels especially, to glorify Him. Though many hundreds of years have passed since that time, and the world now vainly thinks it knows more than it did, and that it has found the real causes of the things it sees, still may we say, with grateful and simple hearts, "O all ye works of the Lord, O ye Angels of the Lord, O ye sun and moon, stars of heaven, showers and dew, winds of God, light and darkness, mountains and hills, green things upon the earth, bless ye the Lord, praise Him, and magnify Him for ever." Thus, whenever we look abroad, we are reminded of those most gracious and holy Beings, the servants of the Holiest, who deign to minister to the heirs of salvation. Every breath of air and ray of light and heat, every beautiful prospect, is, as it were, the skirts of their garments, the waving of the robes of those whose faces see God in heaven. And I put it to any one, whether it is not as philosophical, and as full of intellectual enjoyment, to refer the movements of the natural world to them, as to attempt to explain them by certain theories of science; useful as these theories certainly are for particular purposes, and capable (in subordination to that higher view) of a religious application.

2. And thus I am led to another use of the doctrine under consideration. While it raises the mind, and gives it a matter of thought, it is also profitable as a humbling doctrine, as indeed I have already shown. Vain man would be wise, and he curiously

---

[2] Ps. xix.1; cxix.89–91.

examines the works of Nature, as if they were lifeless and sense-less; as if he alone had intelligence, and they were base inert matter, however curiously contrived at the first. So he goes on, tracing the order of things, seeking for Causes in that order, giving names to the wonders he meets with, and thinking he understands what he has given a name to. At length he forms a theory, and recommends it in writing, and calls himself a phi-losopher. Now all these theories of science, which I speak of, are useful, as classifying, and so assisting us to *recollect*, the works and ways of God and of His ministering Angels. And again, they are ever most useful, in enabling us to *apply* the course of His providence, and the ordinances of His will, to the benefit of man. Thus we are enabled to enjoy God's gifts; and let us thank Him for the knowledge which enables us to do so, and honour those who are His instruments in communicating it. But if such a one proceeds to imagine that, because he knows something of this world's wonderful order, he therefore knows *how* things really go on, if he treats the miracles of Nature (so to call them) as mere mechanical processes, continuing their course by them-selves,—as works of man's contriving (a clock, for instance) are set in motion, and go on, as it were, of themselves,—if in conse-quence he is, what may be called, irreverent in his conduct to-wards Nature, thinking (if I may so speak) that it does not hear him, and see how he is bearing himself towards it; and if, more-over, he conceives that the Order of Nature, which he partially discerns, will stand in the place of the God who made it, and that all things continue and move on, not by His will and power, and the agency of the thousands and ten thousands of His unseen Servants, but by fixed laws, self-caused and self-sustained, what a poor weak worm and miserable sinner he be-comes! Yet such, I fear, is the condition of many men nowadays, who talk loudly, and appear to themselves and others to be oracles of science, and, as far as the detail of facts goes, do know much more about the operations of Nature than any of us.

Now let us consider what the real state of the case is. Suppos-ing the inquirer I have been describing, when examining a flower, or a herb, or a pebble, or a ray of light, which he treats as something so beneath him in the scale of existence, suddenly discovered that he was in the presence of some powerful being who was hidden behind the visible things he was inspecting, who, though concealing his wise hand, was giving them their beauty, grace, and perfection, as being God's instrument for the purpose, nay whose robe and ornaments those wondrous ob-jects were, which he was so eager to analyse, what would be his thoughts? Should we but accidentally show a rudeness of manner towards our fellow-man, tread on the hem of his garment, or brush roughly against him, are we not vexed, not as if we had hurt him, but from the fear we may have been disrespectful? David had watched the awful pestilence three days, doubtless not with curious eyes, but with indescribable terror and remorse; but when at length he "lifted up his eyes and saw the *Angel* of the Lord" (who caused the pestilence) "stand between the earth and the heaven, having a drawn sword in his hand stretched out over Jerusalem, *then* David and the elders, who were clothed in sackcloth, *fell* upon their faces." [3] The mysterious, irresistible pestilence became still more fearful when the cause was known;—and what is true of the terrible, is true on the other hand of the pleasant and attractive operations of Nature. When then we walk abroad, and "meditate in the field at the eventide," how much has every herb and flower in it to surprise and overwhelm us! For, even did we know as much about them as the wisest of men, yet there are those around us, though unseen, to whom our greatest knowledge is as ignorance; and, when we converse on subjects of Nature scientifically, repeating the names of plants and earths, and describing their properties, we should do so religiously, as in the hearing of the great Servants of God, with the sort of diffidence which we always feel when speaking before the learned and wise of our own mortal race, as poor beginners in intellectual knowledge, as well as in moral attainments.

Now I can conceive persons saying all this is fanciful; but if it appears so, it is only because we are not accustomed to such thoughts. Surely we are not told in Scripture about the Angels for nothing, but for practical purposes; nor can I conceive a use of our knowledge more practical than to make it connect the sight of this world with the thought of another. Nor one more consolatory; for surely it is a great comfort to reflect that, wherever we go, we have those about us, who are ministering to all the heirs of salvation, though we see them not. Nor one more easily to be understood and felt by all men; for we know that at one time the doctrine of Angels was received even too readily. And if any one would argue hence against it as dangerous, let him recollect the great principle of our Church, that the abuse of a thing does not supersede the use of it; and let him explain, if he can, St. Paul's exhorting Timothy not only as "before God and Christ," but before "the elect Angels" also. Hence, in the

[3] 1 Chron. xxi.16.

Communion Service, our Church teaches us to join our praises with that of "Angels and Archangels, and all the Company of heaven;" and the early Christians even hoped that they waited on the Church's seasons of worship, and glorified God with her. Nor are these thoughts without their direct influence on our faith in God and His Son; for the more we can enlarge our view of the next world, the better. When we survey Almighty God surrounded by His Holy Angels, His thousand thousands of ministering Spirits, and ten thousand times ten thousand standing before Him, the idea of His awful Majesty rises before us more powerfully and impressively. We begin to see how little we are, how altogether mean and worthless in ourselves, and how high He is, and fearful. The very lowest of His Angels is indefinitely above us in this our present state; how high then must be the Lord of Angels! The very Seraphim hide their faces before His glory, while they praise Him; how shamefaced then should sinners be, when they come into His presence!

Lastly, it is a motive to our exertions in doing the will of God, to think that, if we attain to heaven, we shall become the fellows of the blessed Angels. Indeed, what do we know of the courts of heaven, but as peopled by them? and therefore doubtless they are revealed to us, that we may have something to fix our thoughts on, when we look Heavenwards. Heaven indeed is the palace of Almighty God, and of Him doubtless we must think in the first place; and again of His Son our Saviour, who died for us, and who is manifested in the Gospels, in order that we may have something definite to look forward to: for the same cause, surely, the Angels also are revealed to us, that heaven may be as little as possible an unknown place in our imaginations.

Let us then entertain such thoughts as these of the Angels of God; and while we try to think of them worthily, let us beware lest we make the contemplation of them a mere feeling, and a sort of luxury of the imagination. This world is to be a world of practice and labour; God reveals to us glimpses of the Third Heaven for our comfort; but if we indulge in these as the end of our present being, not trying day by day to purify ourselves for the future enjoyment of the fulness of them, they become but a snare of our enemy. The Services of religion, day by day, obedience to God in our calling and in ordinary matters, endeavours to imitate our Saviour Christ in word and deed, constant prayer to Him, and dependence on Him, these are the due preparation for receiving and profiting by His revelations; whereas many a man can write and talk beautifully about them, who is not at all better or nearer heaven for all his excellent words.

THE DANGER OF
ACCOMPLISHMENTS

(The Feast of St. Luke the Evangelist)

"In the hearts of all that are wise hearted, I have put wisdom."
—Exod. xxxi.6.

S T. LUKE differed from his fellow-evangelists and fellow-
disciples in having received the advantages of (what is
called) a liberal education. In this respect he resembled St. Paul,
who, with equal accomplishments, appears to have possessed
even more learning. He is said to have been a native of Antioch,
a city celebrated for the refined habits and cultivated intellect
of its inhabitants; and his profession was that of a physician or
surgeon, which of itself evidences him to have been in point of
education something above the generality of men. This is confirmed by the character of his writings, which are superior in
composition to any part of the New Testament, excepting some
of St. Paul's Epistles.

There are persons who doubt whether what are called "accomplishments," whether in literature or in the fine arts, can be
consistent with deep and practical seriousness of mind. They
think that attention to these argues a lightness of mind, and, at
least, takes up time which might be better employed; and, I
confess, at first sight they seem to be able to say much in defence
of their opinion. Yet, notwithstanding, St. Luke and St. Paul
were accomplished men, and evidently took pleasure in their
accomplishments.

I am not speaking of human learning; this also many men
think inconsistent with simple uncorrupted faith. They suppose that learning must make a man proud. This is of course a
great mistake; but of it I am not speaking, but of an over-jeal-
ousy of *accomplishments*, the elegant arts and studies, such as poetry, literary composition, painting, music, and the like; which
are considered (not indeed to make a man *proud*, but) to make
him *trifling*. Of this opinion, how far it is true, and how far not

true, I am going to speak: being led to the consideration of it by the known fact, that St. Luke was a polished writer, and yet an Evangelist.

Now, that the accomplishments I speak of have a *tendency* to make us trifling and unmanly, and therefore are to be viewed by each of us with suspicion as far as regards himself, I am ready to admit, and shall presently make clear. I allow, that in matter of fact, refinement and luxury, elegance and effeminacy, go together. Antioch, the most polished, was the most voluptuous city of Asia. But the *abuse* of good things is no argument against the things themselves; mental cultivation *may* be a divine gift, though it is abused. All God's gifts are perverted by man; health, strength, intellectual power, are all turned by sinners to bad purposes, yet they are not evil in themselves: therefore an acquaintance with the elegant arts may be a gift and a good, and intended to be an instrument of God's glory, though numbers who have it are rendered thereby indolent, luxurious, and feeble-minded.

But the account of the building of the Tabernacle in the wilderness, from which the text is taken, is decisive on this point. It is too long to read to you, but a few verses will remind you of the nature of it. "Thou shalt speak unto all that are wise hearted, whom I have filled with the spirit of wisdom, that they may make Aaron's garments to consecrate him, that he may minister unto me in the priest's office." "See I have called by name Bezaleel . . . and have filled him with the Spirit of God, in wisdom and in understanding, and in knowledge, and in all manner of workmanship, to devise cunning works, to work in gold, and in silver, and in brass, and in cutting of stones, to set them, and in carving of timber, to work all manner of workmanship." "Take ye from among you an offering unto the Lord; whosoever is of a willing heart let him bring it, an offering of the Lord, gold, and silver, and brass, and blue, and purple, and scarlet and fine linen, and goats' hair, and rams' skins dyed red, and badgers' skins, and shittim wood, and oil for the light, and spices for anointing oil, and for the sweet incense, and onyx stones, and stones to be set for the ephod, and for the breast-plate. And every wise hearted among you shall come and make all that the Lord hath commanded." [1]

How then is it, that what in itself is of so excellent, and (I may say) divine a nature, is yet so commonly perverted? I proceed to

---

[1] Exod. xxviii.3; xxxi.2–5; xxxv.5–10.

state what is the danger, as it appears to me, of being accomplished, with a view to answer this question.

Now the *danger* of an elegant and polite education is that it separates feeling and acting; it teaches us to think, speak, and be affected aright, without forcing us to practise what is right. I will take an illustration of this, though somewhat a familiar one, from the effect produced upon the mind by reading what is commonly called a romance or novel, which comes under the description of polite literature, of which I am speaking. Such works contain many good sentiments (I am taking the better sort of them): characters too are introduced, virtuous, noble, patient under suffering, and triumphing at length over misfortune. The great truths of religion are upheld, we will suppose, and enforced; and our affections excited and interested in what is good and true. But it is all fiction; it does not exist out of a book which contains the beginning and end of it. *We* have nothing *to do*; we read, are affected, softened or roused, and that is all; we cool again,—nothing comes of it. Now observe the effect of this. God has made us feel in order that we may *go on to act* in consequence of feeling; if then we allow our feelings to be excited without acting upon them, we do mischief to the moral system within us, just as we might spoil a watch, or other piece of mechanism, by playing with the wheels of it. We weaken its springs, and they cease to act truly. Accordingly, when we have got into the habit of amusing ourselves with these works of fiction, we come at length to feel the excitement without the slightest thought or tendency to act upon it; and, since it is very difficult to begin any duty *without* some emotion or other (that is, to begin on mere principles of dry reasoning) a grave question arises, how, after destroying the connexion between feeling and acting, how shall we get ourselves to act when circumstances make it our duty to do so? For instance, we will say we have read again and again, of the heroism of facing danger, and we have glowed with the thought of its nobleness. We have felt how great it is to bear pain, and submit to indignities, rather than wound our conscience; and all this, again and again, when we had no opportunity of carrying our good feelings into practice. Now, suppose at length we actually come into trial, and let us say, our feelings become roused, as often before, at the thought of boldly resisting temptations to cowardice, shall we therefore do our duty, quitting ourselves like men? rather, we are likely to talk loudly, and then run from the danger. Why?—rather let us ask, why *not*? what is to keep us from yielding? Because we *feel* aright? nay, we have again and again felt aright, and thought aright, without accustoming ourselves to act aright, and, though there was an original connexion in our minds between feeling and acting, there is none now; the wires within us, as they may be called, are loosened and powerless.

And what is here instanced of fortitude, is true in all cases of duty. The refinement which literature gives, is that of thinking, feeling, knowing and speaking, right, not of acting right: and thus, while it makes the manners amiable, and the conversation decorous and agreeable, it has no tendency to make the conduct, the practice of the man *virtuous*.

Observe, I have supposed the works of fiction I speak of to inculcate right sentiments; though such works (play-books for example) are often vicious and immoral. But even at best, supposing them well principled, still after all, at best, they are, I say, dangerous, in themselves;—that is, if we allow refinement to stand in the place of hardy, rough-handed obedience. It follows, that I am much opposed to certain *religious* novels, which some persons think so useful: that they sometimes do good, I am far from denying;—but they do more harm than good. They do harm on the whole; they lead men to cultivate the religious affections separate from religious practice. And here I might speak of that entire religious system (miscalled religious) which makes Christian faith consist, not in the honest and plain practice of what is right, but in the luxury of excited religious feeling, in a mere meditating on our Blessed Lord, and dwelling as in a reverie on what He has done for us;—for such indolent contemplation will no more sanctify a man *in fact*, than reading a poem or listening to a chant or psalm-tune.

The case is the same with the arts last alluded to, poetry and music. These are especially likely to make us unmanly, if we are not on our guard, as exciting emotions without insuring correspondent practice, and so destroying the connexion between feeling and acting; for I here mean by unmanliness the inability to do with ourselves what we wish,—the saying fine things and yet lying slothfully on our couch, as if we could not get up, though we ever so much wished it.

And here I must notice something besides in elegant accomplishments, which goes to make us over-refined and fastidious, and falsely delicate. In books, everything is made beautiful in its way. Pictures are drawn of *complete* virtue; little is said about failures, and little or nothing of the drudgery of ordinary, every-day obedience, which is neither poetical nor interesting. True faith teaches us to do numberless disagreeable things for

Christ's sake, to bear petty annoyances, which we find written down in no book. In most books Christian conduct is made grand, elevated, and splendid; so that any one, who only knows of true religion from books, and not from actual endeavours to be religious, is sure to be offended at religion when he actually comes upon it, from the roughness and humbleness of his duties, and his necessary deficiencies in doing them. It is beautiful in a picture to wash the disciples' feet; but the sands of the real desert have no lustre in them to compensate for the servile nature of the occupation.

And further still, it must be observed, that the art of composing, which is a chief accomplishment, has in itself a tendency to make us artificial and insincere. For to be ever attending to the fitness and propriety of our words, is (or at least there is the risk of its being) a kind of acting; and knowing what can be said on both sides of a subject, is a main step towards thinking the one side as good as the other. Hence men in ancient times, who cultivated polite literature, went by the name of "Sophists;" that is, men who wrote elegantly, and talked eloquently, on any subject whatever, right or wrong. St. Luke perchance might have been such a Sophist, had he not been a Christian.

Such are some of the dangers of elegant accomplishments; and they beset more or less all educated persons; and of these perhaps not the least such females as happen to have no very direct duties, and are above the drudgery of common life, and hence are apt to become fastidious and fine,—to love a luxurious ease, and to amuse themselves in mere elegant pursuits, the while they admire and profess what is religious and virtuous, and think that they really possess the character of mind which they esteem.

With these thoughts before us, it is necessary to look back to the Scripture instances which I began by adducing, to avoid the conclusion that accomplishments are positively dangerous, and unworthy a Christian. But St. Luke and St. Paul show us, that we may be sturdy workers in the Lord's service, and bear our cross manfully, though we be adorned with all the learning of the Egyptians; or rather, that the resources of literature, and the graces of a cultivated mind, may be made both a lawful source of enjoyment to the possessor, and a means of introducing and recommending the Truth to others; while the history of the Tabernacle shows that all the cunning arts and precious possessions of this world may be consecrated to a religious service, and be made to speak of the world to come.

I conclude then with the following cautions, to which the

foregoing remarks lead. First, we must avoid giving too much time to lighter occupations; and next, we must never allow ourselves to read works of fiction or poetry, or to interest ourselves in the fine arts for the mere sake of the things themselves: but keep in mind all along that we are Christians and accountable beings, who have fixed principles of right and wrong, by which all things must be tried, and have religious habits to be matured within them, towards which all things are to be made subservient. Nothing is more common among accomplished people than the habit of reading books so entirely for reading's sake, as to praise and blame the actions and persons described in a random way, according to their fancy, not considering whether they are really good or bad according to the standard of moral truth. I would not be austere; but when this is done habitually, surely it is dangerous. Such too is the abuse of poetical talent, that sacred gift. Nothing is more common than to fall into the practice of uttering fine sentiments, particularly in letter writing, as a matter of course, or a kind of elegant display. Nothing more common in singing than to use words which have a light meaning, or a bad one. All these things are hurtful to seriousness of character. It is for this reason (to put aside others) that the profession of stage-players, and again of orators, is a dangerous one. They learn to say good things, and to excite in themselves vehement feelings, about nothing at all.

If we are in earnest, we shall let nothing lightly pass by which may do us good, nor shall we dare to trifle with such sacred subjects as morality and religious duty. We shall apply all we read to ourselves; and this almost without intending to do so, from the mere sincerity and honesty of our desire to please God. We shall be suspicious of all such good thoughts and wishes, and we shall shrink from all such exhibitions of our principles, as fall short of action. We shall aim at doing right, and so glorifying our Father, and shall exhort and constrain others to do so also; but as for talking on the appropriate subjects of religious meditation, and *trying* to show piety, and to excite corresponding feelings in another, even though our nearest friend, far from doing this, we shall account it a snare and a mischief. Yet this is what many persons consider the highest part of religion, and call it spiritual conversation, the test of a spiritual mind; whereas, putting aside the incipient and occasional hypocrisy, and again the immodesty of it, I call all formal and intentional expression of religious emotions, all studied passionate discourse, *dissipation*,—dissipation the same in nature, though different in subject, as what is commonly so

called; for it is a drain and a waste of our religious and moral
strength, a general weakening of our spiritual powers (as I have
already shown); and all for what?—for the pleasure of the immediate excitement. Who can deny that this religious disorder
is a parallel case to that of the sensualist? Nay, precisely the same
as theirs, from whom the religionists in question think themselves very far removed, of the fashionable world. I mean, who
read works of fiction, frequent the public shows, are ever on the
watch for novelties, and affect a pride of manners and a
"mincing"[2] deportment, and are ready with all kinds of good
thoughts and keen emotions on all occasions.

Of all such as abuse the decencies and elegancies of moral
truth into a means of luxurious enjoyment, what would a
prophet of God say? Hear the words of the holy Ezekiel, that
stern rough man of God, a true Saint in the midst of a self-
indulgent, high-professing people: "Thou son of man, the
children of thy people still are talking against thee by the walls
and in the doors of the houses, and speak one to another, every
one to his brother, saying, Come, I pray you, and hear what is
the word that cometh forth from the Lord. And they come
unto thee as the people cometh, and they sit before thee as My
people, and they hear thy words, but they will not do them:
for with their mouth they show much love, but their heart
goeth after their covetousness. And, lo, thou art unto them as a
very lovely song of one that hath a pleasant voice, and can play
well on an instrument: for they hear thy words, but they do
them not."[3]

Or, consider St. Paul's words; which are still more impressive, because he was himself a man of learning and accomplishments, and took pleasure, in due place, in the pursuits to which
these give rise.

"Preach the word; be instant in season, out of season; reprove, rebuke, exhort, with all long-suffering and doctrine. For
the time will come when they will not endure sound doctrine;
but after their own lusts shall they heap to themselves teachers,
having itching ears. And they shall turn away their ears from
the Truth, and shall be turned unto fables." "Watch ye, stand
fast in the faith, quit you like men, be strong."[4]

[2] Is. iii.16.   [3] Ezek. xxxiii.30–32.
[4] 2 Tim. iv.2–4; 1 Cor. xvi.13.

CHRISTIAN ZEAL

(The Feast of St. Simon and St. Jude the Apostles)

"The zeal of Thine house hath eaten Me up."—John ii.17.

THE Apostles commemorated on this Festival direct our attention to the subject of Zeal, which I propose to consider, under the guidance of our Saviour's example, as suggested by the text. St. Simon is called Zelotes, which means the Zealous; a title given him (as is supposed) from his belonging before his conversion to the Jewish sect of Zealots, which professed extraordinary Zeal for the law. Anyhow, the appellation marks him as distinguished for this particular Christian grace. St. Jude's Epistle, which forms part of the service of the day, is almost wholly upon the duty of manifesting Zeal for Gospel Truth, and opens with a direct exhortation to "contend earnestly for the Faith once delivered to the Saints." The Collect also indirectly reminds us of the same duty, for it prays that all the members of the Church may be united in spirit by the Apostles' doctrine; and what are these but the words of Zeal, viz. of a love for the Truth and the Church so strong as not to allow that man should divide what God hath joined together?

However, it will be a more simple account of Zeal, to call it the earnest desire for God's honour, leading to strenuous and bold deeds in His behalf; and that in spite of all obstacles. Thus when Phinehas stood up and executed judgment in Israel, he was zealous for God. David also, in his punishment of the idolaters round about, and in preparing for the building of the Temple, showed his Zeal, which was one of his especial virtues. Elijah, when he assembled the Israelites upon Mount Carmel, and slew the prophets of Baal, was "very zealous for the Lord God of Hosts." Hezekiah besides, and Josiah, were led to their reformations in religious worship by an admirable Zeal; and Nehemiah too, after the captivity, who with the very fire and sweetness of Gospel Love set the repentant nation in order for the coming of Christ.

1. Now, Zeal is one of the elementary religious qualifications; that is, one of those which are essential in the very notion of a religious man. A man cannot be said to be in earnest in religion, till he magnifies his God and Saviour; till he so far consecrates and exalts the thought of Him in his heart, as an object of praise, and adoration, and rejoicing, as to be pained and grieved at dishonour shown to Him, and eager to avenge Him. In a word, a religious temper is one of loyalty towards God; and we all know what is meant by being loyal from the experience of civil matters. To be loyal is not merely to obey; but to obey with promptitude, energy, dutifulness, disinterested devotion, disregard of consequences. And such is Zeal, except that it is ever attended with that reverential feeling which is due from a creature and a sinner towards his Maker, and towards Him alone. It is the main principle in *all* religious service to love God above all things; now, Zeal is to love Him above all men, above our dearest and most intimate friends. This was the especial praise of the Levites, which gained for them the reward of the Priesthood, viz. their executing judgment on the people in the sin of the golden calf. "Let Thy Thummim and Thy Urim be with Thy Holy One, whom Thou didst prove at Massah, and with whom Thou didst strive at the waters of Meribah. Who said unto his father and to his mother, I have not seen him; neither did he acknowledge his brethren, nor knew his own children; for they have observed Thy word, and kept Thy covenant. They shall teach Jacob Thy Judgments, and Israel Thy Law; they shall put incense before Thee, and whole burnt sacrifice upon Thine Altar. Bless, Lord, his substance, and accept the work of his hands; smite through the loins of them that rise against him, and of them that hate him, that they rise not again." Phinehas was rewarded in like manner, after executing judgment. "Behold, I give unto him My covenant of peace. And he shall have it, and his seed after him, even the covenant of an everlasting Priesthood, because he was zealous for his God." [1] Zeal is the very consecration of God's Ministers to their office. Accordingly our Blessed Saviour, the One Great High Priest, the Antitype of all Priests who went before Him and the Lord and Strength of all who come after, began His manifestation of Himself by two acts of Zeal. When twelve years old he deigned to put before us in representation the sacredness of this duty, when He remained in the Temple "while His father and mother sought Him sorrowing," and on their finding Him,

---

[1] Deut. xxxiii.8–11; Numb. xxv.12, 13.

returned answer, "Wist ye not that I must be about My Father's business?" And again, at the opening of His public Ministry, He went into the Temple, and "made a scourge of small cords, and drove out the sheep and oxen, and overthrew the changers' tables"[2] that profaned it: thus fulfilling the prophecy contained in the text, "The Zeal of Thine house hath eaten Me up."

Being thus consumed by Zeal Himself, no wonder He should choose His followers from among the Zealous. James and John, whom He called Boanerges, the sons of Thunder, had warm hearts, when He called them, however wanting in knowledge; and felt as if an insult offered to their Lord should have called down fire from Heaven. Peter cut off the right ear of one of those who seized Him. Simon was of the sect of the Zealots. St. Paul's case is still more remarkable. He, in his attachment to the elder Covenant of God, had even fought against Christ; but he did so from earnestness, from being "zealous towards God," though blindly. He "verily thought with himself, that he *ought to do* many things contrary to the name of Jesus of Nazareth," and acted "in ignorance;"[3] so he was spared. With a sort of heavenly compassion his persecuted Lord told him, that it was "hard for him to kick against the pricks;" and turned his ignorant zeal to better account. On the same ground rests the commendation which that Apostle bestows in turn upon his countrymen, while he sorrowfully condemns their unpardonable obstinacy. "My heart's desire and prayer to God for Israel," he says, "is, that they might be saved; for I bear them record, that they have a Zeal of God, but not according to knowledge."[4] They were guilty, because they might have known what they did not know; but so far as they were zealous, they claimed from him a respectful notice, and were far better surely than those haughty scorners, the Romans, who felt no concern whether there was a God or no, worshipped one idol as readily as another, and spared the Apostles from contemptuous pity. Of these was Gallio, who "cared for none of those things" which either Jews or Christians did. Such men are abominated by our Holy Lord, who "honours them that honour Him," while "they that despised Him are lightly esteemed."[5] He signifies this judgment on the lukewarm and disloyal, in His message to the Church of Laodicea: "I know thy works, that thou art neither cold nor hot. I would thou wert cold or hot. So then, because thou art lukewarm and neither cold nor hot, I will cast

---

[2] Luke ii.48, 49; John ii.15.   [3] Acts xxvi.9; 1 Tim. i.13.
[4] Rom. x.i.   [5] 1 Sam. ii.30.

thee forth out of My mouth."[6] Thus positive misbelief is a less odious state of mind than the temper of those who are indifferent to religion, who say that one opinion is as good as the other, and contemn or ridicule those who are in earnest. Surely, if this world be a scene of contest between good and evil, as Scripture declares, "he that is not with Christ, is against Him;" and Angels who witness what is going on, and can estimate its seriousness, may well cry out, "Curse ye Meroz, curse ye bitterly the inhabitants thereof; because they came not to the help of the Lord, to the help of the Lord against the mighty."[7]

I do not deny that this view of the subject is different from that which certain principles and theories now current in the world would lead us to adopt; but this surely is no reason that it should not be true, unless indeed, amid the alternate successes of good and evil, there be any infallible token given us to ascertain the superior illumination of the present century over all those which have preceded it. In fact we have no standard of Truth at all but the Bible, and to that I would appeal. "To the Law and to the Testimony;" if the opinions of the day are conformable to it, let them remain in honour, but if not, however popular they may be at the moment, they will surely come to nought. It is the present fashion to call Zeal by the name of intolerance, and to account intolerance the chief of sins; that is, any earnestness for one opinion above another concerning God's nature, will, and dealings with man,—or, in other words, any earnestness for the Faith once delivered to the Saints, any earnestness for Revelation as such. Surely, in this sense, the Apostles were the most intolerant of men: what is it but intolerance in this sense of the word to declare, that "he that hath the Son hath life, and he that hath not the Son of God hath not life;" that "they that obey not the Gospel of our Lord Jesus Christ, shall be punished with everlasting destruction from the presence of the Lord;" that "neither fornicators, nor idolaters, nor adulterers, nor covetous, nor revilers, nor extortioners, shall inherit the kingdom of God;" that we must not even "eat" with a brother who is one of such; that we may not "receive into our houses," or "bid God speed" to any one who comes to us without the "doctrine of Christ"? Has not St. Paul, whom many seem desirous of making an Apostle of less rigid principles than his brethren, said, even about an individual, "The Lord reward him according to his works!"[8] and though we of

[6] Rev. iii.15, 16.　　　　　　　　[7] Judges v.23.

[8] 1 John v.12; 2 Thess. i.8, 9; 1 Cor. vi.9, 10; v.11; 2 John 10, 11; 2 Tim. iv.14.

this day have not the spiritual discernment which alone can warrant such a form of words about this man or that, have we not here given us a clear evidence, that there are cases in which God's glory is irreconcilable with the salvation of sinners, and when, in consequence, it is not unchristian to acquiesce in His judgments upon them? These words were deliberately written by St. Paul, in the closing days of his life, when his mind was most calm and heavenly, his hope most assured, his reward immediately in view: circumstances which render it impossible for any one who even reverences St. Paul as a man of especial holiness, to explain them away, not to insist on the argument from his inspiration.

Such is Zeal, a Christian grace to the last, while it is also an elementary virtue; equally belonging to the young convert and the matured believer; displayed by Moses at the first, when he slew the Egyptian, and by St. Paul in his last hours, while he was reaching forth his hand for his heavenly crown.

2. On the other hand, Zeal is an imperfect virtue; that is, in our fallen state, it will ever be attended by unchristian feelings, if it is cherished by itself. This is the case with many other tempers of mind which yet are absolutely required of us. Who denies that it is a duty in the returning sinner to feel abhorrence of his past offences, and a dread of God's anger? yet such feelings, unless faith accompany them, lead to an unfruitful remorse, to despair, to hardened pride; or again, to perverse superstitions. Not that humiliation is wrong in any sense or degree, but it induces collateral weaknesses or sins, from unduly exciting one side of our imperfect nature. Mercy becomes weakness, when unattended by a sense of justice and firmness: the wisdom of the serpent becomes craft, unless it be received into the harmlessness of the dove. And Zeal, in like manner, though an essential part of a Christian temper, is but a part; and is in itself imperfect, even for the very reason that it is elementary. Hence it appropriately fills so prominent a place in the Jewish Dispensation, which was intended to lay the foundations, as of Christian Faith, so of the Christian character. Whether we read the injunctions delivered by Moses against idolatry and idolaters, or trace the actual history of God's chosen servants, such as Phinehas, Samuel, Elijah, and especially David, we find that the Law was peculiarly a Covenant of Zeal. On the other hand, the Gospel brings out into its full proportions, that perfect temper of mind, which the Law enjoined indeed, but was deficient both in enforcing and creating,—Love; that is, Love or Charity, as described by St. Paul in his first Epistle to the Corinthians,

which is not merely brotherly-love (a virtue ever included in the notion of Zeal itself), but a general temper of gentleness, meekness, sympathy, tender consideration, open-heartedness towards all men, brother or stranger, who come in our way. In this sense, Zeal is of the Law, and Love of the Gospel: and Love perfects Zeal, purifying and regulating it. Thus the Saints of God go on unto perfection. Moses ended his life as "the meekest of men," though he began it with undisciplined Zeal, which led him to a deed of violence. St. John, who would call down fire from heaven, became the Apostle of Love; St. Paul, who persecuted Christ's servants, "was made all things to all men;" yet neither of them lost their Zeal, though they trained it to be spiritual.

Love, however, is not the only grace which is necessary to the perfection of Zeal; Faith is another. This, at first sight, may sound strange; for what is Zeal, it may be asked, but a result of Faith? who is zealous for that in which he does not trust and delight? Yet, it must be kept in mind, that we have need of Faith, not only that we may direct our actions to a right object, but that we may perform them rightly; it guides us in choosing the means, as well as the end. Now, Zeal is very apt to be self-willed; it takes upon itself to serve God in its own way. This is evident from the very nature of it; for, in its ruder form, it manifests itself in sudden and strong emotions at the sight of presumption or irreverence, proceeding to action almost as a matter of feeling, without having time to inquire which way is best. Thus, when our Lord was seized by the officers, Peter forthwith "drew his sword, and struck a servant of the High Priest's, and smote off his ear."[9] Patience, then, and resignation to God's will, are tempers of mind of which Zeal especially stands in need,—that dutiful Faith, which will take nothing for granted on the mere suggestion of nature, looks up to God with the eyes of a servant towards his master, and, as far as may be, ascertains His will before it acts. If this heavenly corrective be wanting, Zeal, as I have said, is self-willed in its temper: while, by using sanctions, and expecting results of this world, it becomes (what is commonly called) political. Here, again, we see the contrast between the Jewish and the Christian Dispensations. The Jewish Law being a visible system, sanctioned by temporal rewards and punishments, necessarily involved the duty of a political temper on the part of those who were under it. They were bound to aim at securing the triumph of Religion

[9] Matt. xxvi.51.

here; realizing its promises, enjoying its successes, enforcing its precepts, with the sword. This, I say, was their duty; and, as fulfilling it, among other reasons, David is called "a man after God's own heart." But the Gospel teaches us to "walk by Faith, not by sight;" and Faith teaches us so to be zealous, as still to forbear anticipating the next world, but to wait till the Judge shall come. St. Peter drew his sword, in order (as he thought) to realize at once that good work on which his heart was set, our Lord's deliverance; and, on this very account, he met with that Saviour's rebuke, who presently declared to Pilate, that His Kingdom was not of this world, else would His servants fight. Christian Zeal, therefore, ever bears in mind that the Mystery of Iniquity is to continue on till the Avenger solves it once for all; it renounces all hope of hastening His coming, all desire of intruding upon His work. It has no vain imaginings about the world's real conversion to Him, however men may acknowledge Him outwardly, knowing that "the world lies in wickedness." It has recourse to no officious modes of propagating or strengthening His truth. It does not flatter and ally itself with Samaria, in order to repress Syria. It does not exalt an Idumaean as its king, though he be willing to beautify the Temple, or has influence with the Emperors of the World. It plans no intrigues; it recognises no parties; it relies on no arm of flesh. It looks for no essential improvements or permanent reformations, in the dispensation of those precious gifts, which are ever pure in their origin, ever corrupted in man's use of them. It acts according to God's will, this time or that, as it comes, boldly and promptly; yet letting each act stand by itself as a sufficient service to him, not connecting them in one, or working them into system, further than He commands. In a word, Christian Zeal is not political.

Two reflections arise from considering this last characteristic of the virtue in question; and with a brief notice of these I will conclude.

1. First, it is too evident how grievously the Roman Schools have erred in this part of Christian duty. Let their doctrines be as pure as they would represent, still they have indisputably made their Church an instrument of worldly politics by a "zeal not according to knowledge," and failed in this essential duty of a Christian Witness, viz. in preserving the spiritual character of Christ's kingdom.[10] In saying this, I would not willingly deny

---

[10] Among the principles referred to are the following, which occur among the Dictatus Hildebrandi: "Quod liceat illi [Papae] imperatores

the great debt we owe to that Church for her faithful custody of
the Faith itself through so many centuries; nor seem unmindful
of the circumstances of other times, the gradual growth of religious error, and the external dangers which appeared to place
the cause of Christianity itself in jeopardy, and to call for extraordinary measures of defence. Much less would I speak disrespectfully of the great men, who were the agents under
Providence in various stages of that mysterious Dispensation,
and whom, however our Zeal may burn, we must in very Charity believe to be, what their works and sufferings betoken,
single-minded, self-denying servants of their God and Saviour.

2. The Roman Church then has become political; but let us
of the present day beware of running into the other extreme,
and of supposing that, because Christ's Kingdom is not based
upon this world, that it is not connected with it. Surely it was
established here for the sake of this world, and must ever act in
it, as if a part of it, though its origin is from above. Like the
Angels which appeared to the Patriarchs, it is a Heavenly Messenger in human form. In its Polity, its Public Assemblies, its
Rules and Ordinances, its Censures, and its Possessions, it is a
visible body, and, to appearance, an institution of this world. It
is no faulty zeal to labour to preserve it in the form in which
Christ gave it.

And further, it should ever be recollected, that, though the
Church is not of this world, yet we have assurance from God's
infallible word, that there are in the world temporal and present
Dispensers of His Eternal Justice. We are expressly told, that
"the powers that be are ordained of God;" that they "bear not
the sword in vain, but are ministers of God, revengers to
execute wrath upon the evil-doer," and bestow "praise" on
those who do well. Hence, as being gifted with a portion of
God's power, they hold an office of a priestly nature,[11] and are
armed with the fearful sanction, that "they that resist them,
shall receive to themselves Judgment." On this ground, religious Rulers have always felt it to be their duty to act as in God's
place for the promulgation of the Truth; and the Church, on
the other hand, has seen her obligation not only to submit to
them, in things temporal, but zealously to co-operate with
them in her own line, towards those sacred objects which they
have both in common. And thus has been happily fulfilled for

---

deponere;" "Quod a fidelitate iniquorum subditos potest absolvere."
Vide Laud against Fisher, p. 181.

[11] λειτουργοὶ Θεοῦ. Rom. xiii.1–6.

fifteen hundred years, Isaiah's prophecy, that "kings should be nursing fathers to the Church, and queens her nursing mothers." Yet, clearly, there is nothing here, either of a self-willed zeal, or political craft, in the conduct of the Church; inasmuch as she has but submitted herself thereby to the guidance of the revealed Word.

May Almighty God, for His dear Son's sake, lead us safely through these dangerous times; so that, while we never lay aside our Zeal for His honour, we may sanctify it by Faith and Charity, neither staining our garments by wrath or violence, nor soiling them with the dust of a turbulent world!

USE OF SAINTS' DAYS

(The Feast of all Saints)

*"Ye shall be Witnesses unto Me, both in Jerusalem, and in all
Judea, and in Samaria, and unto the uttermost part of the earth."*
—Acts i.8.

So many were the wonderful works which our Saviour did on earth, that not even the world itself could have contained the books recording them. Nor have His marvels been less since He ascended on high;—those works of higher grace and more abiding fruit, wrought in the souls of men, from the first hour till now,—the captives of His power, the ransomed heirs of His kingdom, whom He has called by His Spirit working in due season, and led on from strength to strength till they appear before His face in Zion. Surely not even the world itself could contain the records of His love, the history of those many Saints, that "cloud of Witnesses," whom we to-day celebrate, His purchased possession in every age! We crowd these all up into one day; we mingle together in the brief remembrance of an hour all the choicest deeds, the holiest lives, the noblest labours, the most precious sufferings, which the sun ever saw. Even the least of those Saints were the contemplation of many days,—even the names of them, if read in our Service, would outrun many settings and risings of the light,—even one passage in the life of one of them were more than sufficient for a long discourse. "Who can count the dust of Jacob, and the number of the fourth part of Israel?" [1] Martyrs and Confessors, Rulers and Doctors of the Church, devoted Ministers and Religious brethren, kings of the earth and all people, princes and judges of the earth, young men and maidens, old men and children, the first fruits of all ranks, ages, and callings, gathered each in his own time into the paradise of God. This is the blessed company which to-day meets the Christian pilgrim in the Services of the Church. We are like Jacob, when, on his

[1] Numb. xxiii.10.

journey homewards, he was encouraged by a heavenly vision. "Jacob went on his way, and the Angels of God met him; and when Jacob saw them, he said, This is God's host: and he called the name of that place Mahanaim." [2]

And such a host was also seen by the favoured Apostle, as described in the chapter from which the Epistle of the day is taken. "I beheld, and lo, a great multitude, which no man could number, of all nations, and kindreds, and people, and tongues, stood before the Lamb, clothed with white robes, and palms in their hands. . . . These are they which came out of great tribulation, and have washed their robes, and made them white in the blood of the Lamb." [3]

This great multitude, which no man could number, is gathered into this one day's commemoration, the goodly fellowship of the Prophets, the noble army of Martyrs, the Children of the Holy Church Universal, who have rested from their labours.

The reason of this disposition of things is as follows:—Some centuries ago there were too many Saints' days; and they became an excuse for idleness. Nay, worse still, by a great and almost incredible perverseness, instead of glorifying God in His Saints, Christians came to pay them an honour approaching to Divine worship. The consequence was, that it became necessary to take away their Festivals, and to commemorate them all at once in a summary way. Now men go into the contrary extreme. These Holydays, few though they be, are not duly observed. Such is the way of mankind, ever contriving to slip by their duty, and fall into one or other extreme of error. Idle or busy, they are in both cases wrong: idle, and so neglecting their duties towards man; busy, and so neglecting their duties towards God. We have little to do, however, with the faults of others;—let us then, passing by the error of idling time under pretence of observing many Holydays, rather speak of the fault of our own day, viz. of neglecting to observe them, and that, under pretence of being too busy.

Our Church abridged the number of Holydays, thinking it right to have but a few; but we account any as too much. For, taking us as a nation, we are bent on gain; and grudge any time which is spent without reference to our worldly business. We should seriously reflect whether this neglect of the appointments of religion be not a great national sin. As to individuals, I can easily understand how it is that they pass them over. A considerable number of persons (for instance) have not their time

[2] Gen. xxxii.1, 2.   [3] Rev. vii.9, 14.

at their own disposal. They are in service or business, and it is their duty to attend to the orders of their masters or employers,—which keep them from church. Or they have particular duties to keep them at home, though they are their own masters. Or, it even may be said, that the circumstances under which they find their calling, the mode in which it is exercised by others, may be a sort of reason for doing as others do. It may be such a worldly loss to them to leave their trade on a Saint's day and go to church, as to appear to them a reason in conscience for their not doing so? I do not wish to give an opinion upon this case or that, which is a matter for the individual immediately concerned. Still, I say, *on the whole*, that state of society must be defective, which renders it necessary for the Ordinances of religion to be neglected. There must be a fault *somewhere*; and it is the duty of every one of us to clear himself of his own portion of the fault, to avoid partaking in other men's sins, and to do his utmost that others may extricate themselves from the blame too.

I say this neglect of religious Ordinances is an especial fault of these latter ages. There was a time when men openly honoured the Gospel; and when, consequently, they had each of them more means of becoming religious. The institutions of the Church were impressed upon the face of society. Dates were reckoned not so much by months and seasons, as by sacred Festivals. The world kept pace with the Gospel; the arrangements of legal and commercial business were regulated by a Christian rule. Something of this still remains among us; but such customs are fast vanishing. Mere grounds of utility are considered sufficient for re-arranging the order of secular engagements. Men think it waste of time to wait upon the course of the Christian year; and they think they gain more by a business-like method, and the neatness, dispatch, and clearness in their worldly transactions consequent upon it (and this perhaps they really *do* gain, but they think they gain *more* by it), than they lose by dropping the Memorials of religion. These they really do lose; they lose those regulations which at stated times brought the concerns of another life before their minds; and, if the truth must be spoken, they often rejoice in losing what officiously interfered, as they consider, with their temporal schemes, and reminded them they were mortal.

Or view another part of the subject. It was once the custom for the churches to be open through the day, that at spare times Christians might enter them,—and be able to throw off for some minutes the cares of the world in religious exercises.

Services were appointed for separate hours in the day, to allow
of the attendance in whole or part of those who happened to be
at hand. Those who could not come, still might keep their ser-
vice-book with them; and at least repeat at times the prayers in
private which were during the passing hour offered in church.
Thus provision was made for the spiritual sustenance of Christians day by day; for that daily-needed bread which far exceeds
"the bread that perisheth." All this is now at an end. We dare
not open our churches, lest men should profane them instead of
worshipping. As for an accurately arranged Ritual, too many of
us have learned to despise it, and to consider it a form. Thus the
world has encroached on the Church; the lean kine have eaten
up the fat. We are threatened with years of spiritual famine,
with the triumph of the enemies of the Truth, and with the
stifling, or at least enfeebling of the Voice of Truth;—and why?
All because we have neglected those religious observances
through the year which the Church commands, which we are
bound to observe; while, by neglecting them, we have provided
a sort of argument for those who have wished to do them away
altogether. No party of men can keep together without stated
meetings; assemblings are, we know, the very life of political
associations. Viewing, then, the institutions of the Church
merely in a human point of view, how can we possess power as
Christians, if we do *not*, and on the other hand, what great
power we should have, if we *did*, flock to the Ordinances of religion, present a bold face to the world, and show that Christ
has still servants true to Him? That we come to church on Sundays is a help this way, doubtless; but it would be a vastly more
powerful evidence of our earnestness for the Truth, if we testified for Christ at some worldly inconvenience to ourselves,
which would be the case with some of us on other Holydays.
Can we devise a more powerful mode of preaching to men at
large, and one in which the most unlearned and most timid
among us might more easily partake, of preaching Christ as a
warning and a remembrance, than if all who loved the Lord
Jesus Christ in sincerity made it a practice to throng the
churches on the week-day Festivals and various Holy Seasons,
allowing less religious persons the while to make the miserable
gains which greater keenness in the pursuit of this world certainly does secure?

I have not yet mentioned the peculiar benefit to be derived
from the observance of Saints' days: which obviously lies in
their setting before the mind patterns of excellence for us to
follow. In directing us to these, the Church does but fulfil the

design of Scripture. Consider how great a part of the Bible is historical; and how much of the history is merely the lives of those men who were God's instruments in their respective ages. Some of them are no patterns for us, others show marks of the corruption under which human nature universally lies:—yet the chief of them are specimens of especial faith and sanctity, and are set before us with the evident intention of exciting and guiding us in our religious course. Such are, above others, Abraham, Joseph, Job, Moses, Joshua, Samuel, David, Elijah, Jeremiah, Daniel, and the like; and in the New Testament the Apostles and Evangelists. First of all, and in His own incommunicable glory, our Blessed Lord Himself gives us an example; but His faithful servants lead us on towards Him, and confirm and diversify His pattern. Now it has been the aim of our Church in her Saints' days to maintain the principle, and set a pattern, of this peculiarly Scriptural teaching.

And we, at the present day, have particular need of the discipline of such commemorations as Saints' days to recall us to ourselves. It is a fault of these times (for we have nothing to do with the faults of other times) to despise the past in comparison of the present. We can scarce open any of the lighter or popular publications of the day without falling upon some panegyric on ourselves, on the illumination and humanity of the age, or upon some disparaging remarks on the wisdom and virtues of former times. Now it is a most salutary thing under this temptation to self-conceit to be reminded, that in all the highest qualifications of human excellence, we have been far outdone by men who lived centuries ago; that a standard of truth and holiness was then set up which we are not likely to reach, and that, as for thinking to become wiser and better, or more acceptable to God than they were, it is a mere dream. Here we are taught the true value and relative importance of the various gifts of the mind. The showy talents, in which the present age prides itself, fade away before the true metal of Prophets and Apostles. Its boasted "knowledge" is but a shadow of "power" before the vigorous strength of heart which they displayed, who could calmly work moral miracles, as well as speak with the lips of inspired wisdom. Would that St. Paul or St. John could rise from the dead! How would the minute philosophers who now consider intellect and enlightened virtue all their own, shrink into nothing before those well-tempered, sharp-edged weapons of the Lord! Are not we come to this, is it not our shame as a nation, that, if not the Apostles themselves, at least the Ecclesiastical System they devised, and the Order they founded, are viewed with coldness and disrespect? How few are there who look with reverent interest upon the Bishops of the Church as the Successors of the Apostles; honouring them, if they honour, merely because they like them as individuals, and not from any thought of the peculiar sacredness of their office! Well, let it be! the End must one time come. It cannot be that things should stand still thus. Christ's Church is indestructible; and, lasting on through all the vicissitudes of this world, she must rise again and flourish, when the poor creatures of a day who opposed her, have crumbled into dust. "No weapon that is formed against her shall prosper." "Rejoice not against me, O mine enemy! when I fall, I shall arise; when I sit in darkness, the Lord shall be a light unto me." [4] In the meantime let us not forget our duty; which is, after the example of Saints, to take up our cross meekly, and pray for our enemies.

These are thoughts suitably to be impressed on us, on ending (as we do now) the yearly Festivals of the Church. Every year brings wonders. We know not any year, what wonders shall have happened before the circle of Festivals has run out again, from St. Andrew's to All Saints'. Our duty then is, to wait for the Lord's coming, to prepare His way before Him, to pray that when He comes we may be found watching; to pray for our country, for our King and all in authority under him, that God would vouchsafe to enlighten the understandings and change the hearts of men in power, and make them act in His faith and fear, for all orders and conditions of men, and especially for that branch of His Church which He has planted here. Let us not forget, in our lawful and fitting horror at evil men, that they have souls, and that they know not what they do, when they oppose the Truth. Let us not forget, that we are sons of sinful Adam as well as they, and have had advantages to aid our faith and obedience above other men. Let us not forget, that, as we are called to be Saints, so we are, by that very calling, called to suffer; and, if we suffer, must not think it strange concerning the fiery trial that is to try us, nor be puffed up by our privilege of suffering, nor bring suffering needlessly upon us, nor be eager to make out we have suffered for Christ, when we have but suffered for our faults, or not at all. May God give us grace to act upon these rules, as well as to adopt and admire them; and to say nothing for saying's sake, but to do much and say little!

---

[4] Is. liv.17; Micah vii.8.

III

To the venerable
ROBERT HURRELL FROUDE,
Archdeacon of Totnes,
the following volume,
with every feeling
of esteem and attachment,
and with a grateful remembrance
of many kindnesses received,
is respectfully inscribed.
By
the author.

The Conversion of St. Paul, 1836.

ABRAHAM AND LOT

*"Lot lifted up his eyes, and beheld all the plain of Jordan,
that it was well watered everywhere, before the Lord destroyed Sodom
and Gomorrah, even as the garden of the Lord, like the land of
Egypt, as thou comest unto Zoar. Then Lot chose him all the plain
of Jordan."*—Gen. xiii.10, 11.

THE lesson to be gained from the history of Abraham and Lot is obviously this—that nothing but a clear apprehension of things unseen, a simple trust in God's promises, and the greatness of mind thence arising, can make us act above the world—indifferent, or almost so, to its comforts, enjoyments, and friendships; or in other words, that its goods corrupt the common run even of religious men who possess them. Lot, as well as Abraham, left his own country "by faith," in obedience to God's command; yet on a further trial, in which the will of God was not so clearly signified, the one was found "without spot and blameless," the other "was saved so as by fire." Abraham became the "father of all them that believe;" Lot obscured the especial hope of his calling—impaired the privileges of his election—for a time allowed himself to resemble the multitude of men, as now seen in a Christian country, who are religious to a certain point, and inconsistent in their lives, not aiming at perfection.

His history may be divided into three parts:—first, from the time of his setting out with Abraham from Haran, to their separation; then, from his settlement in the cities of the plain (as they are called), of which Sodom was one, till his captivity and rescue; and lastly, from his return to Sodom, to his escape thence to the mountain, under the Angel's guidance, when the Scripture history loses sight of him. Let us review these in order:—

1. When Abraham and Lot first came into the land of Canaan, they had received, as it seems, no Divine direction where they were to settle. They first came to Sichem; thence they went on to the neighbourhood of Bethel; at length a famine drove them down to Egypt; and after this the history of their temptation (for so it must be called) begins.

Abraham and Lot had given up this world at the word of God; but a more difficult trial remained. Though never easy, yet it is easier to set our hearts on religion, when we have nothing else to engage them—or to take some one decided step, which throws us out of our line of life, and in a manner forces upon us what we should naturally shrink from; than to possess in good measure the goods of this world, and yet love God supremely. Many a man might make a sacrifice of his worldly interests from impulse; and then having little to unsettle him, he is enabled to hold fast his religion, and serve God consistently and acceptably. Of course men who make such sacrifices, often evidence much strength of character in making them, which doubtless was Lot's case when he left his country. But it is even a greater thing, it requires a clearer, steadier, nobler faith, to be surrounded with worldly goods, yet to be self-denying; to consider ourselves but stewards of God's bounty, and to be "faithful in all things" committed to us. In this, then, lay the next temptation which befell the two patriarchs. God gave them riches and importance. When they went down to Egypt, Abraham was honourably received by the king of the country. Soon after, it is said that Abraham had "sheep, and oxen, and he-asses, and men-servants, and maid-servants, and she-asses, and camels:" again, that "Abram was very rich in cattle, in silver, and in gold;" and presently, that "Lot also . . . . . had flocks, and herds, and tents." [1] The consequence was, that, on their return to Canaan, their households and cattle had become too numerous for one place: "The land was not able to bear them, that they might dwell together; for their substance was great, so that they could not dwell together." [2] Their servants quarrelled in consequence; each party, for instance, endeavouring to secure the richest pastures, and the best supplied wells. This discordance in the chosen family was, of course, very unseemly, as witnessed by idolaters, the Canaanites and Perizzites, who lived in the neighbourhood. Abraham accordingly proposed a friendly separation, and left it to Lot to choose what part of the country he would settle in. Here was the trial of Lot's faith; let us see how he met it. It so happened, that the most fruitful region, the plain of Jordan, was in the hands of an abandoned people, the inhabitants of Sodom, Gomorrah, and the neighbouring cities. Now, the wealth which Lot had hitherto enjoyed had been given him as a pledge of God's favour, and had its chief value as coming from Him. But surely he forgot this,

<hr>

[1] Gen. xii.16; xiii.2, 5.   [2] Gen. xiii.6.

and esteemed it for its own sake, when he allowed himself to be attracted by the richness and beauty of a guilty and devoted country. The prosperity of a wicked people could not be accounted a mark of God's love; but to look toward Sodom was to go the way of the world, and to make wealth the measure of all things, and the end of life. In the words of the text, "Lot lifted up his eyes, and beheld all the plain of Jordan, that it was well watered everywhere .... even as the garden of Eden......
And Lot chose him all the plain of Jordan ..... and pitched his tent toward Sodom. But the men of Sodom were wicked, and sinners before the Lord exceedingly." I do not see how we can deny that this was a false step in the holy patriarch, blamable in itself, and leading to most serious consequences. "I had rather be a doorkeeper in the house of my God," says the Psalmist, "than to dwell in the tents of wickedness."[3] But those who have accustomed their minds to look on worldly prosperity as highly desirable in itself, take it wherever they meet with it; now as given by God, and now, again, when not given by Him. It is not to them a point of first importance *by whom* it is given, at least not in their secret hearts: though they might, perhaps, be surprised did any one so tell them. If all this does not in its fulness apply to Lot, his history at least reminds us of what takes place daily in instances which resemble it externally. Men still consider themselves, and promise themselves to be, consistent worshippers of the One True God, while they are falling into that sin which the Apostle calls "idolatry,"—the love and worship of the creature for the Creator.

In the meantime Abraham is left without any earthly portion, but with God's presence for his inheritance: and so God witnessed it: for, as if to reward him for his disinterestedness, He renewed to him the promise already made him, of the future grant of the whole land, including even that fair portion of which Lot had temporary possession. "And the Lord said unto Abram, after that Lot was separated from him, Lift up now thine eyes, and look from the place where thou art, northward and southward and eastward and westward; for all the land which thou seest, to thee will I give it, and to thy seed for ever. And I will make thy seed as the dust of the earth, so that if a man can number the dust of the earth, then shall thy seed also be numbered. Arise, walk through the land in the length of it, and in the breadth of it, for I will give it unto thee."[4]

[3] Ps. lxxxiv.10.   [4] Gen. xiii.14–17.

2. Thus ends the first portion of the history of Abraham and Lot:—To proceed. God is so merciful that He suffers not His favoured servants to wander from Him without repeated warnings. They cannot be "as the heathen:" they are pursued with gracious visitings, as Jonah when he fled away. Lot had chosen the habitation of sinners; still he was not left to himself. A calamity was sent to warn and chasten him;—we are not told indeed that this was the intention of it, but we know even by the light of nature that all affliction is calculated to try and improve us, and so it is fair to say that this was the design of the violence and captivity to which Lot was soon exposed. Sodom, Gomorrah, and the neighbouring cities, which were subject to Chedorlaomer, king of Elam, at this time revolted from him. In consequence, their country was overrun by his forces and those of his allies; and, a battle taking place, the kings of those cities were defeated and killed, and "their goods and victuals" taken. Lot also and his property fell into their hands. Thus, independently of religious considerations, his place of abode had its disadvantage in that very fertility and opulence which he had coveted, and which attracted the notice of those whose power enabled them to be rapacious. Abraham at this time dwelt in the plain of Mamre, and on hearing the news of his kinsman's capture, he at once assembled his own followers, to the number of above three hundred men, and being joined by several princes of the country, with whom he was confederate, he pursued the plunderers, surprised them by night, routed them, and rescued Lot with his fellow-captives and all his goods.

This, I have said, was a gracious warning to Lot; not a warning only, it seems also to have been an opportunity of breaking off his connection with the people of Sodom, and removing from the sinful country. However, he did not take it as such. Nothing, indeed, is said of his return thither in this passage of the history; but in the narrative which follows shortly after, we find him still in Sodom, though not involved in the Divine vengeance inflicted upon it;—but of this more presently.

Let us first turn, by way of contrast, to Abraham. How many excuses might he have made to himself, had he so willed, for neglecting his kinsman in misfortune! Especially might he have enlarged on the danger and apparent hopelessness of the attempt to rescue him. But it is a principal characteristic of faith to be careful for others more than for self. With a small band of followers he boldly pursued the forces of the victorious kings, and succeeded in recovering his brother's son. Observe, too, his disinterested and princely spirit after the battle, in refusing part of the spoil. "I will not take from a thread even to a shoe-latchet," he said to the king of Sodom, "and I will not take any thing that is thine, lest thou shouldest say, I have made Abram rich." Besides, this might be especially necessary to mark his abhorrence of the men of Sodom and Gomorrah, and was a sort of protest against their sins. His conduct suggests a further remark:—He had been promised the land in which he now lived as a stranger;—he had valiant troops, though few in number, who, doubtless, had he so desired, might have conquered for him a sufficient portion of it. But he did not attempt it: for he knew God could bring about His design and accomplish His promise in His own good time, without his use of unlawful means. Force of arms, indeed, would not have been unlawful, had God ordered their use, as afterwards when the Israelites returned from Egypt; but it was unlawful without express command, and Abraham perhaps had to overcome a temptation in not having recourse to it. We have, in the after-history, a similar instance of forbearance in the conduct of David towards Saul. David was promised the kingdom by God Himself; Saul's life was more than once in his hands, but he thought not of the sin of doing him any harm. God could bring about His promise without his "doing evil that good might come." This is the true spirit of faith: to wait upon God, to watch for and to follow His guidance, not to attempt to go before Him.

But did Abraham return to his place without reward for his generous and self-denying conduct? Far otherwise; God mercifully renewed to him the pledge of His favour in answer to this new instance of his faith. As He had renewed the blessing when Lot at first chose the fruitful land, so He blessed him now by the mouth of a great priest and king. Lot went back to Sodom in silence;—but God spoke to Abraham by Melchizedek. "And Melchizedek, king of Salem, brought forth bread and wine, and he was the priest of the most High God; and he blessed him and said, Blessed be Abram of the most High God, possessor of heaven and earth" (who can give away kingdoms and countries as He will), "and blessed be the most High God, who hath delivered thine enemies into thy hand." Who Melchizedek was, is not told us: Scripture speaks of him as a type of Christ; but we cannot tell how far Abraham knew this, or what particular sanctity attached to his character, or what virtue to his blessing. But evidently it was a special mark of favour placed on Abraham; and the bread and wine, brought forth as refreshment after the fight, had perhaps something of the nature of a sacrament, and conveyed the pledge of mercy.

3. Now let us pass to the concluding event of Lot's history. The gain of this world is but transitory; faith reaps a late but lasting recompense. Soon the Angels of God descended to fulfil in one and the same mission a double purpose;—to take from Lot his earthly portion, and to prepare for the accomplishment of the everlasting blessings promised to Abraham; to destroy Sodom, while they foretold the approaching birth of Isaac.

The destruction of the guilty cities was at hand. "The Lord said, Because the cry of Sodom and Gomorrah is great, and because their sin is very grievous, I will go down now, and see whether they have done altogether according to the cry of it, which is come unto Me, and if not, I will know."[5] And now the greatest honour was put upon Abraham. God entrusted him with the knowledge of His secret purpose, and, in so doing, made him a second time the deliverer of Lot from ruin; strongly marking the contrast between the two, in that the weak brother owed his safety to the intercession of him, who, enjoying God's favour, was content to be without earthly portion. "And the Lord said, Shall I hide from Abraham that thing which I do? seeing that Abraham shall surely become a great and mighty nation, and all the nations of the earth shall be blessed in him? For I know him, that he will command his children and his household after him, and they shall keep the way of the Lord to do justice and judgment, that the Lord may bring upon Abraham that which He hath spoken of Him." Accordingly, Abraham was allowed to intercede for Sodom, and all who were in it. I need scarcely go through this solemn narrative, which is doubtless well known to all of us. Abraham began with asking whether fifty righteous were not remaining in the city; he found himself obliged gradually to contract the supposed remnant of good men therein, till he came down to ten, but not even ten were found to delay God's vengeance. Here he ceased his intercession, perhaps in despair, and fearing to presume upon that adorable mercy, the depths of which he had tried, but had not ascertained. He did not mention Lot by name; still God understood and answered the unexpressed desire of his heart; for we are told presently, "It came to pass, when God destroyed the cities of the plain, that God *remembered Abraham*, and sent Lot out of the midst of the overthrow, when he overthrew the cities in the which Lot dwelt."[6]

It was at eventide that two Angels came to Sodom, to rescue from it the only man (as it would seem) who had retained in his

[5] Gen. xviii.20, 21.   [6] Gen. xix.29.

mind those instincts of right and wrong which are given us by nature, who continued to acknowledge the true God, had exercised himself in faith and obedience, and had not done despite to the gracious Spirit. Multitudes of children there doubtless were in that city untainted with actual sin; these were involved in their parents' ruin, as they are now-a-days in earthquakes, conflagrations, or shipwreck. But of those who could "discern between their right hand and their left," not ten (we know for certain), and (as it may be concluded) not one had righteousness such as Lot's. "Old and young, all the people," "in every quarter," were corrupt before God, and therefore are "set forth for an example" of what the All-merciful God can do when sinners provoke Him to wrath. "We will destroy this place," the Angels said, "because the cry of them is waxen great before the face of the Lord, and the Lord hath sent us to destroy it." "And when the morning arose the Angels hastened Lot . . . and brought him forth and set him without the city: and said, Escape for thy life, look not behind thee, neither stay thou in all the plain, escape to the mountain, lest thou be consumed." Thus was Lot a second time warned and rescued; whether he was brought thereby to a more consistent righteousness, or more enlightened faith, than before, we know not. What became of him after this event, we know not; of his subsequent life and death nothing is told us, the sacred record breaks off abruptly. This alone we know, that his posterity, the Moabites and Ammonites, were the enemies of the descendants of Abraham, his friend and kinsman, the favoured servant of God; especially as seducing them to that idolatry and sensuality which the chosen family was set apart to withstand. Had not God in mercy confirmed to us, by the mouth of St. Peter, the saying of the wise man in the Apocrypha, that Lot was "righteous," we should have had cause to doubt whether he had not fallen away.

However, without forming harsh judgments concerning one whom Scripture thus honours, we may at least draw from his history a useful lesson for ourselves. Miserable will be the fate of the doubleminded, of those who love this world so well that they will not give it up, though they believe and acknowledge that God bids them do so. Not that they confess to themselves that their hearts are set upon it; they contrive to hide the fact from themselves by specious excuses, and consider themselves religious men. My brethren, do not take it for granted that your temper of mind is much superior to that which I have been describing and condemning; nay, that it is not worse than it. You, indeed, are placed in an age of the world which is conspicuous for decency, and in which there are no temptations to the more hideous forms of sin, or rather much to deter from them. But answer this one question, and then decide whether this age does not follow Lot's pattern. It would appear that he thought more of the riches than of the sins of the cities of the plain. Now, as to the temper of this country, consider fairly, is there any place, any persons, any work, which our countrymen will not connect themselves with, in the way of trade or business? For the sake of gain, do we not put aside all considerations of principle as unseasonable and almost absurd? It is not possible to explain myself on this subject without entering into details too familiar for this sacred place; but try to follow out for yourselves what I suggest in general terms. Is there any speculation in commerce which religion is allowed to interfere with? Whether Jew, Pagan, or Heretic, is to be our associate, does it frighten us ever so little? Do we care what side of a quarrel, civil, political, or international, we take, so that we gain by it? Do we not serve in war, do we not become debaters and advocates, do we not form associations and parties, with the supreme object of preserving property, or making it? Do we not support religion for the sake of peace and good order? Do we not measure its importance by its efficacy in securing these objects? Do we not support it only so far as it secures them? Do we not retrench all expenses of maintaining it which are not necessary for securing them? Should we not feel very lukewarm towards the established religion, unless we thought the security of property bound up in its welfare? Should we not easily resign ourselves to its overthrow, could it be proved to us that it endangered the State, involved the prospect of civil disturbances, or embarrassed the Government? nay, could we not even consent to that overthrow, at the price of the reunion of all parties in the nation, the pacification of turbulent districts, and the establishment of our public credit? Nay, further still, could we not easily persuade ourselves to support Antichrist, I will not say at home, but at least abroad, rather than we should lose one portion of the freights which "the ships of Tarshish" bring us? If this be the case in any good measure, how vain is it to shelter ourselves, as the manner of some is, under the notion that we are a moral, thoughtful, sober-minded, or religious people! Lot is called a "just man" by St. Peter, he is referred to as "hospitable" by St. Paul;[7] doubtless he was a confessor of the truth among the wretched inhabitants of the cities in which he dwelt; and the rays of light which those

[7] 2 Pet. ii.7, 8; Heb. xiii.2.

Apostles shed upon his history, are most cheering and acceptable, after reading the sad narrative of the Book of Genesis; still, after all, who would willingly take on himself Lot's sins, plain though it be that God had not deserted him? Surely, if we are to be saved, it is not by keeping ourselves just above the line of reprobation, and living without any anxiety and struggle to serve God with a perfect heart. Surely, if Christians are to be saved, at least their righteousness must be far other than that which merely argued some remaining grace in one who was not a Christian. Surely, if Christians are to be saved, they must have carefully unlearned the love of this world's pleasures, comforts, luxuries, honours. No one, surely, can really be a Christian, who makes his worldly interests his chief end of action. A man may be, in a measure, ill-tempered, resentful, proud, cruel, or sensual, and yet be a Christian. For passions belong to our inferior nature; they are irrational, rise spontaneously, are to be subdued by our governing principle, and (through God's grace) are ultimately, though gradually, subdued. But what shall be said when the reasoning and ruling faculty, the power that wills and controls, is turned earthward? "If the light that is in thee be darkness, how great is that darkness!"[8]

God only knows how far these remarks concern each of us. I will not dare to apply them to this man or that; but where I even might, I will rather turn away my mind from the subject. The thought is too serious, too dreadful to dwell upon. But you must do, my brethren, what I must not do. It is your duty to apply them to yourselves. Do not hesitate, as many of you as have never done so, to imagine the miserable and shocking possibility of your coming short of your hope "having loved this present world." Retire into yourselves and imagine it; in the presence of Christ your Saviour—in that presence which at once will shame you, and will encourage you to hope for forgiveness, if you earnestly turn to Him to obtain it.

[8] Matt. vi.23.

WILFULNESS OF ISRAEL IN REJECTING SAMUEL

"Be still, and know that I am God: I will be exalted among the heathen, I will be exalted in the earth."—Ps. xlvi.10.

I T was a lesson continually set before the Israelites, that they were never to presume to act of themselves, but to wait till God wrought for them, to look on reverently, and then follow His guidance. God was their All-wise King: it was their duty to have no will of their own, distinct from His will, to form no plan of their own, to attempt no work of their own. *"Be still*, and know that I am God." Move not, speak not—look to the pillar of the cloud, see how *it* moves—then follow. Such was the command.

For instance—when the Egyptians pursued the Israelites to the coast of the Red Sea, Moses said to the people, "Fear ye not, *stand still*, and see the salvation of the Lord; the Lord shall fight for you, and ye shall hold your peace." When they came to the borders of Canaan, and were frightened at the strength of its inhabitants, they were exhorted, "Dread not, neither be afraid of them. The Lord your God shall fight for you." To the same effect was the dying injunction of Joshua, "Be very courageous to keep and to do all that is written in the book of the law of Moses, that ye turn not aside therefrom to the right hand or to the left." And in a later age, when the Moabites and Ammonites made war against Jehoshaphat, the prophet Jahaziel was inspired to encourage the people in these words:—"Be not afraid nor dismayed by reason of this great multitude; for the battle is not yours, but God's. . . . Ye shall not need to fight in this battle: set yourselves, *stand ye still*, and see the salvation of the Lord with you, O Judah and Jerusalem." Once more—When Israel and Syria came against Judah, the prophet Isaiah was directed to meet Ahaz, and to say to him, "Take heed, and *be quiet*; fear not, neither be fainthearted." [1] Presumption—that is, the

---

[1] Exod. xiv.13, 14; Deut. i.29, 30; Josh. xxiii.6; 2 Chron. xx.15, 17; Is. vii.4.

determination to act of themselves, or self-will—was placed in the number of the most heinous sins. "The man that will do presumptuously, and will not hearken unto the priest that standeth to minister there before the Lord thy God, or unto the judge, even that man shall die, and thou shalt put away the evil from Israel."[2]

While, however, this entire surrender of themselves to their Almighty Creator was an especial duty enjoined on the chosen people, a deliberate and obstinate transgression of that duty is one of the especial characteristics of their history. They failed most conspicuously in that very point in which obedience was most strictly enjoined them. They were told never to act of themselves, and (as if out of mere perverseness) they were for ever acting of themselves; and, if we look through the series of their punishments, we shall find them inflicted, not for mere indolent disobedience, or for frailty under temptation, but for deliberate, shameless presumption, running forward just in that very direction in which the providence of God did *not* lead them, and from which it even prohibited them.

First, they made a molten image to worship, and this just after receiving the command to make to themselves no emblems of the Divine Majesty, and while Moses was still in the Mount. Then they would take to themselves a captain, and return to Egypt, instead of proceeding into the land of promise. When forbidden to go forward, then they at once attempted to do so. At last, when they had entered it, instead of following God's guidance, and destroying the guilty inhabitants, they adopted a plan of their own, and put their conquered enemies under tribute. Next followed their self-willed purpose of having a king like the nations around them.

It is observable, moreover, that they were the most perversely disobedient at those times when Divine mercy had aided them in some remarkable way. For instance, in the lifetime of Moses. Again, when Samuel was raised up to bring back the age of Moses, and to complete what he had begun, then they ran counter to God's design most signally; at the very time, I say, when God was visiting them in their low estate, and renewing His mercies, their very first act, on gaining a little strength, and recovering from their despair, was to reject God's government over them, and ask a king like other nations.

This is the part of their history to which I wish now particularly to draw your attention, the times of Samuel; the main

[2] Deut. xvii.12.

circumstances to be considered being these—the renewal of God's mercies to them after their backslidings; His single demand in return, that they should submit themselves to His guidance; and, lastly, their plain refusal to do so, or rather their impetuous and deliberate movement in another direction.

When Moses was nigh his death, he foretold that a prophet was one day to arise like unto him in his place, a promise which was properly fulfilled in Christ's coming, but which had a prior accomplishment in the line of prophets from Samuel down to the captivity. A period, however, of four hundred years intervened between Moses' age and this first fulfilment of the prediction. The people were at first ruled by judges. At length, in the midst of the distress which their sins had brought upon them, when the Philistines had overrun the country, God visited them according to the promise. He raised up Samuel as His first prophet, and him not as a solitary messenger of His purposes, but as the first of many hundreds in succession.

Now, let us consider the circumstances under which Samuel, the first of the prophets, was raised up. We shall find that his elevation was owing simply to God's will and power. He, like Moses, was not a warrior, yet by his prayers he saved his people from their enemies, and established them in a settled government. "Be still, and know that I am God." The principle of this command had been illustrated in the giving of the Law, and now it was enforced in the beginning of the Prophetical Dispensation, as also in later ages, after the captivity, and when Christ came, according to the words of Zechariah, "Not by might, nor by power, but by My Spirit, saith the Lord of Hosts." [3]

Observe, Samuel was born, in answer to his mother's earnest prayer for a son. Hannah, "in bitterness of soul, had prayed unto the Lord, and wept sore, and vowed a vow," viz.—that if God would give her a son, he should be dedicated to Him. This should be noticed, for Samuel was thus marked from his birth as altogether an instrument of the Lord's providing. A similar providence is observable in the case of other favoured objects and ministers of God's mercy, in order to show that that mercy is entirely of grace. Isaac was the child of Divine power, so was John the Baptist; and Moses, again, was almost miraculously saved from the murderous Egyptians in his infancy.

According to his mother's vow, Samuel was taken into the service of the temple from his earliest years; and, while yet a

[3] Zech. iv.6.

child, was made the organ of God's sentence of evil upon Eli the high priest. God called him, in the sacred time, between night and morning, "Samuel, Samuel," and pronounced through him a judgment against Eli, for his sinful indulgence towards his sons. Here, again, was a lesson to the Israelites, how entirely the prophetic spirit, with which the nation was henceforth to be favoured, was from God. Had Samuel grown to manhood before he was inspired, it would not have clearly appeared how far the work was immediately Divine; but when an untaught child was made to prophesy against Eli, the aged high priest, the people were reminded, as in the case of Moses, who was slow of speech, that it was the Lord who "made man's mouth, the dumb, or deaf, the seeing, or the blind;"[4] and that age and youth were the same with Him when His purposes required an instrument.

Samuel thus grew up to manhood, with the presages of greatness on him from the first. It is written, "Samuel grew, and the Lord was with him, and did let none of his words fall to the ground. And all Israel, from Dan even to Beersheba" (*i.e.*, from one end of the land to the other), "knew that Samuel was established to be a prophet of the Lord. And the Lord appeared again in Shiloh; for the Lord revealed Himself to Samuel in Shiloh by the word of the Lord."[5]

After this, when he was about thirty years old, the battle took place with the Philistines, in which thirty thousand Israelites fell. The ark of God was taken, and Eli, on hearing the news, fell from off his seat backward, and was killed. Thus Samuel was raised to the supreme power, in his country's greatest affliction. Still, even in his elevation, he was not allowed to do any great action himself. The ark of God was taken, yet he was not to rescue it. God so ordered it that His name "should be exalted among the heathen, and should be exalted in the earth."

The Philistines took the ark to Ashdod, and placed it in the temple of their idol, Dagon. Next morning, Dagon was found fallen on its face to the earth before it. They set it up again, and the next morning it was found broken into pieces;[6] and soon after the men of Ashdod and its neighbourhood were smitten with a Divine judgment. In consequence, they resolved to rid themselves of what they rightly considered the cause of it, and transported the ark to Gath. The men of Gath were smitten with God's anger in their turn, and in their turn sent away the ark to Ekron. The Ekronites, in their terror, hardly suffered it

---

[4] Exod. iv.11.   [5] 1 Sam. iii.19–21.   [6] 1 Sam. v.3, 4.

to approach them. But the mysterious plague still attended it; and the Ekronites, as they had justly feared, were smitten with a "deadly destruction throughout all the city." The Philistines now determined to send their spoil, as they had at first fancied it, back to Israel; but in order to try further, as it seems, the power of the God of Israel, they did as follows: They took two milch-kine, which had never been under the yoke, and shutting up their calves at home, harnessed them to the cart on which they had placed the ark. Should the kine, in spite of their natural affection for their young, go towards the Israelitish border, then, they argued, they might be sure that it was the God of Israel who had smitten them, in punishment for their capture of His holy habitation. It is written, "The kine took the straight way" towards the territory of Israel, "lowing as they went, and *turned not aside to the right hand or to the left.*" [7]

All this was a lesson to the Philistines; but the Israelites had yet theirs to learn. They had taken the ark to the battle, not in reverence, but as if it were a sort of charm, with virtue in itself, and without any command from God, presumptuously. They were first punished by losing it. When they saw the ark returning to them, they rejoiced; and the Levites took it down and offered sacrifice. So far was well, but presently, "The men of Bethshemesh . . . . looked into it;" this evidenced a want of reverence towards God's sacred dwelling-place. And God "smote of the people fifty thousand threescore and ten men; and the people lamented," and said, "Who is able to stand before this Holy Lord God?"

Thus, when Almighty God, four hundred years after the age of Moses, again visited His people, He showed Himself in various ways to be the sole Author of the blessings they received. The child Samuel, the ark of wood, the brute cattle—these were the instruments through which He manifested that He was a living God; and having thus bared His mighty arm, and bid all men "be still, and know that He was God," then at length He sent His first prophet forward to teach and reclaim the people. "Samuel spake unto all the house of Israel, saying, If ye do return unto the Lord with all your hearts, then put away the strange gods and Ashtaroth from among you, and prepare your hearts unto the Lord, and serve Him only: and He will deliver you out of the hand of the Philistines. Then the children of Israel did put away Baalim and Ashtaroth, and served the Lord only." The period during which this reforma-

[7] I Sam. vi.12.

tion was carried on seems to have been the greater part of twenty years, which was more or less a time of captivity. Towards the end of it, he gathered the Israelites together at Mizpeh, to hold a fast for their past sins; and then "he judged the children of Israel in Mizpeh." This seems to imply a more open assumption of power than any he had been hitherto directed to make. In consequence, the Philistines were alarmed, thinking perhaps the subjugated people were on the point of recovering their independence; and, assembling their forces, they marched against them. "And the children of Israel said to Samuel, Cease not to cry unto the Lord for us, that He will save us out of the hand of the Philistines. And Samuel took a sucking lamb, and offered it for a burnt-offering wholly unto the Lord: and Samuel cried unto the Lord for Israel, and the Lord heard him." The Philistines drew near to battle, while the sacrifice was offering; "but the Lord thundered with a great thunder on that day upon the Philistines, and discomfited them, and they were smitten before Israel. . . . . . Then Samuel took a stone and set it between Mizpeh and Shen, and called the name of it Ebenezer, saying, Hitherto hath the Lord helped us." This whole transaction is a fresh illustration of the text. It is added, "So the Philistines were subdued, and came no more into the coast of Israel, and the hand of the Lord was against the Philistines all the days of Samuel. And the cities which they had taken from Israel were restored." "And Samuel judged Israel all the days of his life," making circuits year by year through the land.

And now we have arrived at the point in the history, which evidences, more than any other, the perverse ingratitude of the Israelites. Just when God had rescued them from their enemies, given them peace, and by a fresh act of bounty established the prophets in the land as ministers of His word and will, when the heavenly system was just coming into operation, this was the very time they chose to rebel and run counter to His purposes. They asked for themselves a king like the nations. The immediate occasion of this request was the faulty conduct of Samuel's sons, who assisted their father in his old age, "but walked not in his ways, but turned aside after lucre, and took bribes, and perverted judgment." [8] This, however, though doubtless a grievance, surely was no excuse for them. While the Lord was their king, no lasting harm could happen to them; yet even "the elders of Israel came to Samuel, and said unto him, Behold,

[8] 1 Sam. viii.3.

thou art old, and thy sons walk not in thy ways: now make us a
king to judge us like all the nations." They added a reason
which still more clearly evidenced their obstinate unbelief—
"to judge us, and go out before us, and fight our battles." By
what strange infatuation was it that they sought for a king to
"*fight their battles*," when, through the whole course of Samuel's
government, it was so evident that God's power alone had subdued their enemies? There was one additional aggravation of
their sin; they had really been promised a king, at some future
time undetermined, by Moses himself;[9] and hence, indeed,
they probably defended their asking for one. But, in truth, that
very circumstance gave to their self-will its distinctive mark already insisted on, viz., the desire of doing things in their own
way instead of waiting God's time. The fact that God had
promised what they clamoured for, and merely claimed to
choose the time, surely ought to have satisfied them. But they
were headstrong; and He answered them according to their wilfulness. He "gave them a king in His anger." David, indeed,
succeeded, but the corruption and degradation of the people
quickly followed his death. The kingdom was divided into two;
idolatry was introduced; and at length captivity came upon
them, the loss of their country, and the dispersion or rather
annihilation of the greater part of the tribes.

In conclusion, I will make one remark by way of applying
their history to ourselves at this day. Certainly we have not, at
the present time, learned the duty of waiting and being still.
Great perils, just now, encompass our branch of the Church;
here the question comes upon us, as a body and as individuals,
what ought we to do? Doubtless to meet them with all the wisdom and prudence in our power, to use all allowable means to
avert them; but, after all, is not our main duty this: to go on
quietly and steadfastly in our old ways, as if nothing was the
matter? "When Daniel knew that the writing was signed,"
which condemned him to the lions' den, if he did what was his
plain duty, he did not look about to see whether he might not
lawfully suspend it for a time, or whether there were not other
ways of serving God not interdicted by the civil power, but "he
kneeled upon his knees three times a day, and prayed, and gave
thanks before his God, as he did aforetime." [10] It is a very painful
subject, but it is not right to shut our eyes to the fact, that
friends of the Church are far more disposed to look out for
secular and unauthorized ways of defending her, than to pro-

---

[9] Deut. xvii.14–20.   [10] Dan. vi.10.

ceed quietly in their ordinary duties, and trust to God to save her. What is the use of these feverish exertions, on all sides of us, to soothe our enemies, conciliate the suspicious or wavering, and attach to us men of name and power? Rather let our resolve be, if we are to perish, it shall be at our post of duty. We will be found in the circle of our sacred services, in prayer and praise, in fasting and alms-doing, "in quietness and confidence." All the great deliverances of the Church have been thus gained. Israel stood still and saw the Egyptians overwhelmed in the sea. Hezekiah went up unto the house of the Lord, and prayed to Him who dwelt between the Cherubim, and Sennacherib's army was destroyed. "Prayer was made without ceasing of the Church unto God for" St. Peter, and the Apostle was delivered out of prison by an Angel. The course of Providence is not materially different now. God's arm is not shortened, nay, nor so restrained that He cannot save without miracles as well as with them. He can save silently and suddenly, while things seem to go on as usual. The hearts of all are in His hand, the issues of life and death, the rise and fall of mighty men, and the distribution of gifts. Why, then, should we fear, or cast about for means of defence, who have the Lord for our God? He may indeed, if it so happen, make us His instruments, He may put arms into our hands; but even if He gives us no tokens what He is meditating, what then? At length our deliverance will come, when we expect it not; whereas we shall lose our own hope, and disorder the Church greatly, if we presume to form plans of our own by way of protecting it. Jeroboam thought he acted "wisely" when he set up the calves of gold at Dan and Bethel. Our wisdom is like his, if we venture to relax one jot or tittle of Christ's perfect law, one article of the Creed, one holy ordinance, one ancient usage, with the hope of placing ourselves in a more advantageous or less irksome position. "Our strength is to sit still;" and till we learn this far more than we seem at present to understand it, surely the hopes of the true Israel among us must be low, and with prayers for the Church's safety they will have to mingle confessions and intercessions in behalf of those who believe themselves its prudent friends and effective defenders, and are not.

SAUL

*"I gave thee a king in Mine anger, and took him away
in My wrath."*—Hosea xiii. 11.

THE Israelites seem to have asked for a king from an unthankful caprice and waywardness. The ill conduct, indeed, of Samuel's sons was the occasion of the sin, but "an evil
heart of unbelief," to use Scripture language, was the real cause
of it. They had ever been restless and dissatisfied, asking for
flesh when they had manna, fretful for water, impatient of the
wilderness, bent on returning to Egypt, fearing their enemies,
murmuring against Moses. They had miracles even to satiety;
and then, for a change, they wished a king like the nations. This
was the chief reason of their sinful demand. And further, they
were dazzled with the pomp and splendour of the heathen
monarchs around them, and they desired some one to fight
their battles, some visible succour to depend on, instead of having to wait for an invisible Providence, which came in its own
way and time, by little and little, being dispensed silently, or
tardily, or (as they might consider) unsuitably. Their carnal
hearts did not love the neighbourhood of heaven; and, like the
inhabitants of Gadara afterwards, they prayed that Almighty
God would depart from their coasts.

Such were some of the feelings under which they desired a
king like the nations; and God at length granted their request.
To punish them, He gave them a king *after their own heart*, Saul,
the son of Kish, a Benjamite; of whom the text speaks in these
terms, "I gave them a king in Mine anger, and took him away in
My wrath."

There is, in true religion, a sameness, an absence of hue and
brilliancy, in the eyes of the natural man; a plainness, austereness, and (what he considers) sadness. It is like the heavenly
manna of which the Israelites complained, insipid, and at length
wearisome, "like wafers made with honey." They complained
that "their soul was dried away:" "There is nothing at all," they
said, "beside this manna, before our eyes. . . . We remember
the fish, which we did eat in Egypt freely; the cucumbers, and

the melons, and the leeks, and the onions, and the garlick."[1] Such were the dainty meats in which their soul delighted; and for the same reason they desired a king. Samuel had too much of primitive simplicity about him to please them, they felt they were behind the world, and clamoured to be put on a level with the heathen.

Saul, the king whom God gave them, had much to recommend him to minds thus greedy of the dust of the earth. He was brave, daring, resolute; gifted, too, with strength of body as well as of mind—a circumstance which seems to have attracted their admiration. He is described in person as if one of those sons of Anak, before whose giant-forms the spies of the Israelites in the wilderness were as grasshoppers—"a choice young man, and a goodly; there was not among the children of Israel a goodlier person than he: from his shoulders and upward he was higher than any of the people."[2] Both his virtues and his faults were such as became an eastern monarch, and were adapted to secure the fear and submission of his subjects. Pride, haughtiness, obstinacy, reserve, jealousy, caprice—these, in their way, were not unbecoming qualities in the king after whom their imaginations roved. On the other hand, the better parts of his character were of an excellence sufficient to engage the affection of Samuel himself.

As to Samuel, his conduct is far above human praise. Though injuriously treated by his countrymen, who cast him off after he had served them faithfully till he was "old and grayheaded,"[3] and who resolved on setting over themselves a king against his earnest entreaties, still we find no trace of coldness or jealousy in his behaviour towards Saul. On his first meeting with him, he addressed him in the words of loyalty—"On whom is all the desire of Israel? is it not on thee, and on all thy father's house?" Afterwards, when he anointed him king, he "kissed him, and said, Is it not because the Lord hath anointed thee to be captain over His inheritance?" When he announced him to the people as their king, he said, "See ye him whom the Lord hath chosen, that there is none like him among all the people?" And, some time after, when Saul had irrecoverably lost God's favour, we are told, "Samuel came no more to see Saul until the day of his death: *nevertheless Samuel mourned for Saul.*" In the next chapter he is even rebuked for immoderate

[1] Exod. xvi; Numb. xi.5.

[2] 1 Sam. ix.2; *vide* 1 Sam. x.23.

[3] 1 Sam. xii.2.

grief—"How long wilt thou mourn for Saul, seeing I have rejected him from reigning over Israel?"[4] Such sorrow speaks favourably for Saul as well as for Samuel; it is not only the grief of a loyal subject and a zealous prophet, but, moreover, of an attached friend; and, indeed, instances are recorded, in the first years of his reign, of forbearance, generosity, and neglect of self, which sufficiently account for the feelings with which Samuel regarded him. David, under very different circumstances, seems to have felt for him a similar affection.

The higher points of his character are brought out in instances such as the following:—The first announcement of his elevation came upon him suddenly, but apparently without unsettling him. He kept it secret, leaving it to Samuel, who had made it to him, to publish it. "Saul said unto his uncle, He" (that is, Samuel) "told us plainly that the asses were found. But of the matter of the kingdom, whereof Samuel spake, *he told him not*." Nay, it would even seem he was averse to the dignity intended for him; for when the Divine lot fell upon him, he hid himself, and was not discovered by the people, without recourse to Divine assistance. The appointment was at first unpopular. "The children of Belial said, How shall this man save us? They despised him, and brought him no presents, *but he held his peace*." Soon the Ammonites invaded the country beyond Jordan, with the avowed intention of subjugating it. The people sent to Saul for relief almost in despair; and the panic spread in the interior as well as among those whose country was immediately threatened. The history proceeds:—"*Behold, Saul came after the herd out of the field*; and Saul said, What aileth the people that they weep? and they told him the tidings of the men of Jabesh. And the Spirit of God came upon Saul, and his anger was kindled greatly." His order for an immediate gathering throughout Israel was obeyed with the alacrity with which the multitude serve the strong-minded in times of danger. A decisive victory over the enemy followed; then the popular cry became, "Who is he that said, Shall Saul reign over us? bring the men, that we may put them to death. And Saul said, *There shall not a man be put to death this day*, for to-day the Lord hath wrought salvation in Israel."[5]

Thus personally qualified, Saul was, moreover, a prosperous king. He had been appointed to subdue the enemies of Israel, and success attended his arms. At the end of the fourteenth

[4] 1 Sam. ix.20; x.1, 24; xv.35; xvi.1.
[5] 1 Sam. xi.12, 13.

chapter, we read, "So Saul took the kingdom over Israel, and fought against all his enemies on every side, against Moab, and against the children of Ammon, and against Edom, and against the kings of Zobah, and against the Philistines; and whithersoever he turned himself, he vexed them. And he gathered an host, and smote the Amalekites, and delivered Israel out of the hands of them that spoiled them."

Such was Saul's character and success; his character faulty, yet not without promise; his success in arms as great as his carnal subjects could have desired. Yet, in spite of Samuel's private liking for him, and in spite of the good fortune which actually attended him, we find that from the beginning the prophet's voice is raised both against people and king in warnings and rebukes, which are omens of his destined destruction, according to the text, "I gave them a king in Mine anger, and took him away in My wrath." At the very time that Saul is publicly received as king, Samuel protests, "Ye have this day rejected your God, who Himself saved you out of all your adversities and your tribulations." [6] In a subsequent assembly of the people, in which he testified his uprightness, he says, "Is it not wheat-harvest to-day? I will call unto the Lord, and He shall send thunder and rain; that ye *may perceive and see that your wickedness is great*, in asking you a king." Again, "If ye shall still do wickedly, ye shall be consumed, both ye and your king." [7] And after this, on the first instance of disobedience, and at first sight no very heinous sin, the sentence of rejection is passed upon him: "Thy kingdom shall not continue; the Lord hath sought Him a man after His own heart." [8]

Here, then, a question may be raised—Why was Saul thus marked for vengeance from the beginning? Why these presages of misfortune, which from the first hung over him, gathered, fell in storm and tempest, and at length overwhelmed him? Is his character so essentially faulty that it must be thus distinguished for reprobation above all the anointed kings after him? Why, while David is called a man after God's own heart, should Saul be put aside as worthless?

This question leads us to a deeper inspection of his character. Now, we know, the first duty of every man is the fear of God— a reverence for His word, a love of Him, and a desire to obey Him; and, besides, it was peculiarly incumbent on the king of Israel, as God's vicegerent, by virtue of his office, to promote His glory whom his subjects had rejected.

---

[6] 1 Sam. x.19.   [7] 1 Sam. xii.17, 25.   [8] 1 Sam. xiii.14.

Now Saul "lacked this one thing." His character, indeed, is obscure, and we must be cautious while considering it; still, as Scripture is given us for our instruction, it is surely right to make the most of what we find there, and to form our judgment by such lights as we possess. It would appear, then, that Saul was never under the abiding influence of religion, or, in Scripture language, "the fear of God," however he might be at times moved and softened. Some men are inconsistent in their conduct, as Samson; or as Eli, in a different way; and yet may have lived by faith, though a weak faith. Others have sudden falls, as David had. Others are corrupted by prosperity, as Solomon. But as to Saul, there is no proof that he had any deep-seated religious principle at all; rather, it is to be feared, that his history is a lesson to us, that the "heart of unbelief" may exist in the very sight of God, may rule a man in spite of many natural advantages of character, in the midst of much that is virtuous, amiable, and commendable.

Saul, it would seem, was naturally brave, active, generous, and patient; and what nature made him, such he remained, that is, without improvement; with virtues which had no value, because they required no effort, and implied the influence of no principle. On the other hand, when we look for evidence of his faith, that is, his practical sense of things unseen, we discover instead a deadness to all considerations not connected with the present world. It is his habit to treat prophet and priest with a coldness, to say the least, which seems to argue some great internal defect. It would not be inconsistent with the Scripture account of him, even should the real fact be, that (with some general notions concerning the being and providence of God) he doubted of the divinity of the Dispensation of which he was an instrument. The circumstance which first introduces him to the inspired history is not in his favour. While in search of his father's asses, which were lost, he came to the city where Samuel was; and though Samuel was now an old man, and from childhood known as the especial minister and prophet of the God of Israel, Saul seems to have considered him as a mere diviner, such as might be found among the heathen, who, for "the fourth part of a shekel of silver," would tell him his way.

The narrative goes on to mention, that after his leaving Samuel "God gave him another heart," and on meeting a company of prophets, "the Spirit of God came upon him, and he prophesied among them." Upon this, "all that knew him beforetime" said, "What is this that is come unto the son of Kish: is Saul also among the prophets? . . . . . therefore it became a proverb." From this narrative we gather, that his carelessness and coldness in religious matters were so notorious, that, in the eyes of his acquaintance, there was a certain strangeness and incongruity, which at once struck the mind, in his being associated with a school of the prophets.

Nor have we any reason to believe, from the after history, that the divine gift, then first imparted, left any religious effect upon his mind. At a later period of his life we find him suddenly brought under the same sacred influence on his entering the school where Samuel taught; but, instead of softening him, its effect upon his outward conduct did but testify the fruitlessness of divine grace when acting upon a will obstinately set upon evil.

The immediate occasion of his rejection was his failing under a specific trial of his obedience, as set before him at the very time he was anointed. He had collected with difficulty an army against the Philistines: while waiting for Samuel to offer the sacrifice, his people became dispirited, and began to fall off and return home. Here he was doubtless exposed to the temptation of taking unlawful measures to put a stop to their defection. But when we consider that the act to which he was persuaded was no less than that of his offering sacrifice—he being neither priest nor prophet, nor having any commission thus to interfere with the Mosaic ritual—it is plain "his *forcing himself*" to do so (as he tenderly described his sin) was a direct profaneness—a profaneness which implied that he was careless about forms, which in this world will ever be essential to things supernatural, and thought it mattered little whether he acted in God's way or in his own.

After this, he seems to have separated himself from Samuel, whom he found unwilling to become his instrument, and to have had recourse to the priesthood instead. Ahijah or Ahimelech (as he is afterwards called), the high priest, followed his camp; and the ark too, in spite of the warning conveyed by the disasters which attended the presumptuous use of it in the time of Eli. "And Saul said unto Ahijah, Bring hither the ark of God;" while it was brought, a tumult which was heard in the camp of the Philistines, increased. On this interruption Saul irreverently put the ark aside, and went out to the battle.

It will be observed, that there was no professed or intentional irreverence in Saul's conduct; he was still on the whole the same he had ever been. He outwardly respected the Mosaic ritual—about this time he built his first altar to the Lord,[9] and

---

[9] 1 Sam. xiv.35.

in a certain sense seemed to acknowledge God's authority. But nothing shows he considered that there was any vast distinction between Israel and the nations around them. He was *indifferent*, and cared for none of these things. The chosen people desired a king like the nations, and such a one they received.

After this he was commanded to "go and smite the sinners, the Amalekites, and utterly destroy them and their cattle." This was a judgment on them which God had long decreed, though He had delayed it; and He now made Saul the minister of His vengeance. But Saul performed it so far only as fell in with his own inclination and purposes. He smote, indeed, the Amalekites, and "destroyed all the people with the edge of the sword"—this exploit had its glory; the best of the flocks and herds he spared, and why? to sacrifice therewith to the Lord. But since God had expressly told him to destroy them, what was this but to imply, that divine intimations had nothing to do with such matters? what was it but to consider that the established religion was but a useful institution, or a splendid pageant suitable to the dignity of monarchy, but resting on no unseen supernatural sanction? Certainly he in no sense acted in the fear of God, with the wish to please Him, and the conviction that he was in His sight. One might consider it mere pride and wilfulness in him, acting in his own way because it was his own (which doubtless it was in great measure), except that he appears to have had an eye to the feelings and opinions of men as to his conduct, though not to God's judgment. He "feared the people and obeyed their voice." Again, he spared Agag, the king of the Amalekites. Doubtless he considered Agag as "his brother," as Ahab afterwards called Ben-hadad. Agag was a king, and Saul observed towards him that courtesy and clemency which earthly monarchs observe one towards another, and rightly, when no divine command comes in the way. But the God of Israel required a king after His own heart, jealous of idolatry; the people had desired a king like the nations around them.

It is remarkable, moreover, that while he spared Agag, he attempted to exterminate the Gibeonites with the sword, who were tolerated in Israel by virtue of an oath taken in their favour by Joshua and "the princes of the congregation." This he did "*in his zeal* to the children of Israel and Judah." [10]

From the time of his disobedience in the matter of Amalek, Samuel came no more to see Saul, whose season of probation

[10] Josh. ix.2; 2 Sam. xxi.1–5.

was over. The evil spirit exerted a more visible influence upon him; and God sent Samuel to anoint David privately, as the future king of Israel. I need not trace further the course of moral degradation which is exemplified in Saul's subsequent history. Mere natural virtue wears away, when men neglect to deepen it into religious principle. Saul appears in his youth to be unassuming and forbearing; in advanced life he is not only proud and gloomy (as he ever was in a degree), but cruel, resentful, and hardhearted, which he was not in his youth. His injurious treatment of David is a long history; but his conduct to Ahimelech, the high priest, admits of being mentioned here. Ahimelech assisted David in his escape. Saul resolved on the death of Ahimelech and all his father's house.[11] On his guards refusing to execute his command, Doeg, a man of Edom, one of the nations which Saul was raised up to withstand, undertook the atrocious deed. On that day, eighty-five priests were slain. Afterwards Nob, the city of the priests, was smitten with the edge of the sword, and all destroyed, "men and women, children and sucklings, and oxen, and asses, and sheep." That is, Saul executed more complete vengeance on the descendants of Levi, the sacred tribe, than on the sinners, the Amalekites, who laid wait for Israel in the way, on their going up from Egypt.

Last of all, he finishes his bad history by an open act of apostasy from the God of Israel. His last act is like his first, but more significant. He began, as we saw, by consulting Samuel as a diviner; this showed the direction of his mind. It steadily persevered in its evil way—and he ends by consulting a professed sorceress at Endor. The Philistines had assembled their hosts; Saul's heart trembled greatly—he had no advisers or comforters; Samuel was dead—the priests he had himself slain with the sword. He hoped, by magic rites, which he had formerly denounced, to foresee the issue of the approaching battle. God meets him even in the cave of Satanic delusions—but as an Antagonist. The reprobate king receives, by the mouth of dead Samuel, who had once anointed him, the news that he is to be "taken away in God's wrath"—that the Lord would deliver Israel, with him, into the hands of the Philistines, and that on the morrow he and his sons should be numbered with the dead.[12]

The next day "the battle went sore against him, the archers hit him; and he was sore wounded of the archers."[13] "Anguish came upon him,"[14] and he feared to fall into the hands of the

[11] 1 Sam. xxii.16. [12] 1 Sam. xxviii.19.
[13] 1 Sam. xxxi.3. [14] 2 Sam. i.9.

uncircumcised. He desired his armour-bearer to draw his sword and thrust him through therewith. On his refusing, he fell upon his own sword, and so came to his end.

Unbelief and wilfulness are the wretched characteristics of Saul's history—an ear deaf to the plainest commands, a heart hardened against the most gracious influences. Do not suppose, my brethren, because I speak thus strongly, I consider Saul's state of mind to be something very unusual. God forbid it should exist in its full misery any where among us! but surely there is not any one soul here present but what may trace in itself the elements of sins like his. Let us only reflect on our hardness of heart when attending religious ordinances, and we shall understand something of Saul's condition when he prophesied. We may be conscious to ourselves of the truth of things sacred as entirely as if we saw them; we may have no misgivings about the presence of God in Church, or about the grace of the Sacraments, and yet we often feel in as ordinary and as unconcerned a mood as if we were altogether unbelievers. Again, let us reflect on our callousness after mercies received, or after suffering. We are often in worse case even than this; for to realize the unseen world in our imagination, and feel as if we saw it, may not always be in our power. But what shall be said to wilful transgression of God's commandments, such as most of us, I fear, must recollect in ourselves, even as children, when our hearts were most tender, when we least doubted about religion, were least perplexed in matters of duty, and had all the while a full consciousness of what we were doing? What, again, shall be said to those, perhaps not few in number, who sin with the purpose beforehand of repenting afterwards?

What makes our insensibility still more alarming is, that it follows the grant of the highest privileges. Saul was hardened after the Spirit of God had come on him; ours is a sin after Baptism. There is something awful in this, if we understood it; as if that peculiar hardness of heart which we experience, in spite of whatever excellences of character we may otherwise possess, like Saul—in spite of the benevolence, or fairness, or candour, or consideration, which are the virtues of this age—was the characteristic of a soul transgressing after it had "tasted the powers of the world to come," and an earnest of the second death. May this thought, through God's mercy, rouse us to a deeper seriousness than we have at present, while Christ still continues to intercede for us, and grants us time for repentance!

EARLY YEARS OF DAVID

*"Behold, I have seen a son of Jesse the Beth-lehemite, that is
cunning in playing, and a mighty valiant man, and a man of war,
and prudent in matters, and a comely person,
and the Lord is with him."*—1 Sam. xvi.18.

S UCH is the account given to Saul of David, in many respects
the most favoured of the ancient Saints. David is to be accounted the most favoured, first as being the principal type of
Christ, next as being the author of great part of the book of
Psalms, which have been used as the Church's form of devotion
ever since his time. Besides, he was a chief instrument of God's
providence, both in repressing idolatry and in preparing for the
gospel; and he prophesied in an especial manner of that Saviour
whom he prefigured and preceded. Moreover, he was the chosen king of Israel, a man after God's own heart, and blessed, not
only in himself, but in his seed after him. And, further, to the
history of his life a greater share is given of the inspired pages
than to that of any other of God's favoured servants. Lastly, he
displays in his personal character that very temper of mind in
which his nation, or rather human nature itself, is especially
deficient. Pride and unbelief disgrace the history of the chosen
people; the deliberate love of this world, which was the sin of
Balaam, and the presumptuous wilfulness which is exhibited in
Saul. But David is conspicuous for an affectionate, a thankful, a
loyal heart towards his God and defender, a zeal which was as
fervent and as docile as Saul's was sullen, and as keen-sighted
and as pure as Balaam's was selfish and double-minded. Such
was the son of Jesse the Beth-lehemite; he stands midway between Abraham and his predicted seed, Judah and the Shiloh,
receiving and transmitting the promises; a figure of the Christ,
and an inspired prophet, living in the Church even to the end of
time, in his office, his history, and his sacred writings.

Some remarks on his early life, and on his character, as
therein displayed, may profitably engage our attention at the
present time.

When Saul was finally rejected for not destroying the Amalekites, Samuel was bid go to Beth-lehem, and anoint, as future king of Israel, one of the sons of Jesse, who should be pointed out to him when he was come there. Samuel accordingly went thither and held a sacrifice; when, at his command, Jesse's seven sons were brought by their father, one by one, before the prophet; but none of them proved to be the choice of Almighty God. David was the youngest and out of the way, and it seemed to Jesse as unlikely that God's choice should fall upon him, as it appeared to Joseph's brethren and to his father, that he and his mother and brethren should, as his dreams foretold, bow down before him. On Samuel's inquiring, Jesse said, "There remaineth yet the youngest, and, behold, he keepeth the sheep." On Samuel's bidding, he was sent for. "Now he was ruddy," the sacred historian proceeds, "and withal of a beautiful countenance, and goodly to look to. And the Lord said, Arise, anoint him, for this is he." After Samuel had anointed him, "the Spirit of the Lord came upon David from that day forward." It is added, "But the Spirit of the Lord departed from Saul."

David's anointing was followed by no other immediate mark of God's favour. He was tried by being sent back again, in spite of the promise, to the care of his sheep, till an unexpected occasion introduced him to Saul's court. The withdrawing of the Spirit of the Lord from Saul was followed by frequent attacks from an evil spirit, as a judgment upon him. His mind was depressed, and a "trouble," as it is called, came upon him, with symptoms very like those which we now refer to derangement. His servants thought that music, such, perhaps, as was used in the schools of the prophets, might soothe and restore him; and David was recommended by one of them for that purpose, in the words of the text: "Behold, I have seen a son of Jesse the Beth-lehemite, that is cunning in playing, and a mighty valiant man, and a man of war, and prudent in matters, and a comely person, and the Lord is with him."

David came in the power of that sacred influence whom Saul had grieved and rejected. The Spirit which inspired his tongue guided his hand also, and his sacred songs became a medicine to Saul's diseased mind. "When the evil spirit from God was upon Saul, ... David took an harp, and played with his hand; so Saul was refreshed, and was well, and the evil spirit departed from him." Thus he is first introduced to us in that character in which he still has praise in the Church, as "the anointed of the God of Jacob, and the sweet psalmist of Israel." [1]

---

[1] 2 Sam. xxiii. 1.

Saul "loved David greatly, and he became his armour-bearer;" but the first trial of his humility and patience was not over, while many other trials were in store. After a while he was a second time sent back to his sheep; and though there was war with the Philistines, and his three eldest brethren were in the army with Saul, and he had already essayed his strength in defending his father's flocks from wild beasts, and was "a mighty valiant man," yet he contentedly stayed at home as a private person, keeping his promise of greatness to himself, till his father bade him go to his brethren to take them a present from him, and report how they fared. An accident, as it appeared to the world, brought him forward. On his arrival at the army, he heard the challenge of the Philistine champion, Goliath of Gath. I need not relate how he was divinely urged to engage the giant, how he killed him, and how he was, in consequence, again raised to Saul's favour; who, with an infirmity not inconsistent with the deranged state of his mind, seems to have altogether forgotten him.

From this time began David's public life; but not yet the fulfilment of the promise made to him by Samuel. He had a second and severer trial of patience to endure for many years; the trial of "being still" and doing nothing before God's time, though he had (apparently) the means in his hands of accomplishing the promise for himself. It was to this trial that Jeroboam afterwards showed himself unequal. He, too, was promised a kingdom, but he was tempted to seize upon it in his own way, and so forfeited God's protection.

David's victory over Goliath so endeared him to Saul, that he would not let him go back to his father's house. Jonathan too, Saul's son, at once felt for him a warm affection, which deepened into a firm friendship. "Saul set him over the men of war, and he was accepted in the sight of all the people, and also in the sight of Saul's servants." [2] This prosperous fortune however, did not long continue. As Saul passed through the cities from his victory over his enemies, the women of Israel came out to meet him, singing and dancing, and they said, "Saul hath slain his thousands, and David his ten thousands." Immediately the jealous king was "very wroth, and the saying displeased him;" his sullenness returned; he feared David as a rival; and "eyed him from that day and forward." On the morrow, as David was playing before him, as at other times, Saul threw his javelin at him. After this, Saul displaced him from his situation at his

[2] 1 Sam. xviii. 5.

court, and sent him to the war, hoping so to rid himself of him by his falling in battle; but, by God's blessing, David returned victorious.

In a second war with the Philistines, David was successful as before; and Saul, overcome with gloomy and malevolent passions, again cast at him with his javelin, as he played before him, with the hope of killing him.

This repeated attempt on his life drove David from Saul's court; and for some years after, that is, till Saul's death, he was a wanderer upon the earth, persecuted in that country which was afterwards to be his own kingdom. Here, as in his victory over Goliath, Almighty God purposed to show us, that it was *His* hand which set David on the throne of Israel. David conquered his enemy by a sling and stone, in order, as he said at the time, that all . . . . . might know "that the Lord saveth not with sword and spear; for the battle is the Lord's."[3] Now again, but in a different way, His guiding providence was displayed. As David slew Goliath without arms, so now he refrained himself and used them not, though he possessed them. Like Abraham, he traversed the land of promise "as a strange land,"[4] waiting for God's good time. Nay, far more exactly, even than to Abraham, was it given to David to act and suffer that life of faith which the Apostle describes, and by which "the elders obtained a good report." By faith he wandered about, "being destitute, afflicted, evil-entreated, in deserts, and in mountains, and in dens, and in caves of the earth." On the other hand, through the same faith, he "subdued kingdoms, wrought righteousness, obtained promises, waxed valiant in fight, turned to flight the armies of the aliens."

On escaping from Saul, he first went to Samuel to ask his advice. With him he dwelt some time. Driven thence by Saul he went to Bethlehem, his father's city, then to Ahimelech, the high priest, at Nob. Thence he fled, still through fear of Saul, to Achish, the Philistine king of Gath; and finding his life in danger there, he escaped to Adullam, where he was joined by his kindred, and put himself at the head of an irregular band of men, such as, in the unsettled state of the country, might be usefully and lawfully employed against the remnant of the heathen. After this he was driven to Hareth, to Keilah, which he rescued from the Philistines, to the wilderness of Ziph among the mountains, to the wilderness of Maon, to the strongholds of Engedi, to the wilderness of Paran. After a time he again be-

[3] 1 Sam. xvii.47.   [4] Heb. xi.9.

took himself to Achish, king of Gath, who gave him a city; and there it was that the news was brought him of the death of Saul in battle, which was the occasion of his elevation first to the throne of Judah, afterwards to that of all Israel, according to the promise of God made to him by Samuel.

It need not be denied that, during these years of wandering, we find in David's conduct instances of infirmity and inconsistency, and some things which, without being clearly wrong, are yet strange and startling in so favoured a servant of God. With these we are not concerned, except so far as a lesson may be gained from them for ourselves. We are not at all concerned with them as regards our estimate of David's character. That character is ascertained and sealed by the plain word of Scripture, by the praise of Almighty God, and is no subject for our criticism; and if we find in it traits which we cannot fully reconcile with the approbation divinely given to him, we must take it in faith to be what it is said to be, and wait for the future revelations of Him who "overcomes when He is judged." Therefore I dismiss these matters now, when I am engaged in exhibiting the eminent obedience and manifold virtues of David. On the whole his situation during these years of trial was certainly that of a witness for Almighty God, one who does good and suffers for it, nay, suffers on rather than rid himself from suffering by any unlawful act.

Now, then, let us consider what was, as far as we can understand, his especial grace, what is his gift; as faith was Abraham's distinguishing virtue, meekness the excellence of Moses, self-mastery the gift especially conspicuous in Joseph.

This question may best be answered by considering the purpose for which he was raised up. When Saul was disobedient, Samuel said to him, "Thy kingdom shall not continue: the Lord hath sought Him *a man after His own heart*, and the Lord hath commanded him to be captain over His people, because thou hast not kept that which the Lord commanded thee." [5] The office to which first Saul and then David were called was different from that with which other favoured men before them had been intrusted. From the time of Moses, when Israel became a nation, God had been the king of Israel, and His chosen servants, not delegates, but mere organs of His will. Moses did not direct the Israelites by his own wisdom, but he spake to them, as God spake from the pillar of the cloud. Joshua, again, was merely a sword in the hand of God. Samuel was but His

[5] 1 Sam. xiii.14.

minister and interpreter. God acted, the Israelites "stood still and saw" His miracles, then followed. But, when they had rejected Him from being king over them, then their chief ruler was no longer a mere organ of His power and will, but had a certain authority entrusted to him, more or less independent of supernatural direction; and acted, not so much *from* God, as *for* God, and *in the place of* God. David, when taken from the sheepfolds "to feed Jacob His people and Israel His inheritance," "fed them," in the words of the Psalm, "with a faithful and true heart; and ruled them prudently with all his power."[6] From this account of his office, it is obvious that his very first duty was that of *fidelity to Almighty God* in the trust committed to him. He had power put into his hands, in a sense in which neither Moses had it nor Samuel. He was charged with a certain office, which he was bound to administer according to his ability, so as best to promote the interests of Him who appointed him. Saul had neglected his Master's honour; but David, in this an eminent type of Christ, "came to do God's will" as a viceroy in Israel, and, as being tried and found faithful, he is especially called "a man after God's own heart."

David's peculiar excellence, then, is that of *fidelity to the trust committed to him*; a firm, uncompromising single-hearted devotion to the cause of his God, and a burning zeal for His honour.

This characteristic virtue is especially illustrated in the early years of his life which have engaged our attention. He was tried therein and found faithful; before he was put in power, it was proved whether he could obey. Till he came to the throne, he was like Moses or Samuel, an instrument in God's hands, bid do what was told him and nothing more;—having borne this trial of obedience well, in which Saul had failed, then at length he was intrusted with a sort of discretionary power, to use in his Master's service.

Observe how David was tried, and what various high qualities of mind he displayed in the course of the trial. First, the promise of greatness was given him, and Samuel anointed him. Still he stayed in the sheepfolds; and though called away by Saul for a time, yet returned contentedly when Saul released him from attendance. How difficult is it for such as know they have gifts suitable to the Church's need to refrain themselves, till God makes a way for their use! and the trial would be the more severe in David's case, in proportion to the ardour and energy of his mind; yet he fainted not under it. Afterwards for seven

[6] Ps. lxxviii.71–73.

years, as the time appears to be, he withstood the strong temptation, ever before his eyes, of acting without God's guidance, when he had the means of doing so. Though skilful in arms, popular with his countrymen, successful against the enemy, the king's son-in-law, and on the other hand grievously injured by Saul, who not only continually sought his life, but even suggested to him a traitor's conduct by accusing him of treason, and whose life was several times in his hands, yet he kept his honour pure and unimpeachable. He feared God and honoured the king; and this at a time of life especially exposed to the temptations of ambition.

There is a resemblance between the early history of David and that of Joseph. Both distinguished for piety in youth, the youngest and the despised of their respective brethren, they are raised, after a long trial, to a high station, as ministers of God's Providence. Joseph was tempted to a degrading adultery; David was tempted by ambition. Both were tempted to be traitors to their masters and benefactors. Joseph's trial was brief; but his conduct under it evidenced settled habits of virtue which he could call to his aid at a moment's notice. A long imprisonment followed, the consequence of his obedience, and borne with meekness and patience; but it was no part of his temptation, because, when once incurred, release was out of his power. David's trial, on the other hand, lasted for years, and grew stronger as time went on. His master, too, far from "putting all that he had into his hand,"[7] sought his life. Continual opportunity of avenging himself incited his passions; self-defence, and the Divine promise, were specious arguments to seduce his reason. Yet he mastered his heart—he was "still;"—he kept his hands clean and his lips guileless—he was loyal throughout—and in due time inherited the promise.

Let us call to mind some of the circumstances of his steadfastness recorded in the history.

He was about twenty-three years old when he slew the Philistine; yet, when placed over Saul's men of war, in the first transport of his victory, we are told he "behaved himself wisely."[8] When fortune turned, and Saul became jealous of him, still "David behaved himself wisely in all his ways, and the Lord was with him." How like is this to Joseph under different circumstances! "Wherefore when Saul saw that he behaved himself very wisely he was afraid of him; and all Israel and Judah loved David." Again, "And David behaved himself more wisely than

---

[7] Gen. xxxix.4.　　　　　　[8] 1 Sam. xviii.5–30.

all the servants of Saul, so that his name was much set by." Here, in shifting fortunes, is evidence of that staid, composed frame of mind in his youth, which he himself describes in the one hundred and thirty-first Psalm. "My heart is not haughty, nor mine eyes lofty. . . . . . Surely I have behaved and quieted myself, as a child that is weaned of his mother."

The same modest deportment marks his subsequent conduct. He consistently seeks counsel of God. When he fled from Saul he went to Samuel; afterwards we find him following the directions of the prophet Gad, and afterwards of Abiathar the high priest.[9] Here his character is in full contrast to the character of Saul.

Further, consider his behaviour towards Saul, when he had him in his power; it displays a most striking and admirable union of simple faith and unblemished loyalty.

Saul, while in pursuit of him, went into a cave in Engedi. David surprised him there, and his companions advised to seize him, if not to take his life. They said, "Behold the day of which the Lord said unto thee." [10] David, in order to show Saul how entirely his life had been in his power, arose and cut off a part of his robe privately. After he had done it, his "heart smote him" even for this slight freedom, as if it were a disrespect offered towards his king and father. "He said unto his men, The Lord forbid that I should do this thing unto my master, the Lord's anointed, to stretch forth mine hand against him, seeing he is the anointed of the Lord." When Saul left the cave, David followed him and cried, "My Lord the king. And when Saul looked behind him, David stooped with his face to the earth and bowed himself." He hoped that he could now convince Saul of his integrity. "Wherefore hearest thou men's words," he asked, "saying, Behold, David seeketh thy hurt? Behold, this day thine eyes have seen how that the Lord had delivered thee to-day into mine hand in the cave: and some bade me kill thee. . . . . Moreover, my father, see, yea see the skirt of thy robe in my hand: for in that I cut off the skirt of thy robe, and killed thee not, know thou and see, that there is neither evil nor transgression in mine hand, and I have not sinned against thee: yet thou huntest my soul to take it. The Lord judge between me and thee, and the Lord avenge me of thee: but mine hand shall not be upon thee. . . . . After whom is the king of Israel come out? after whom dost thou pursue? after a dead dog, after a flea. The Lord therefore judge . . . . and see, and plead my cause,

---

[9] 1 Sam. xxii.5, 20; xxiii.6.   [10] 1 Sam. xxiv.4.

and deliver me out of thine hand." Saul was for the time overcome; he said, "Is this thy voice, my son David? and Saul lifted
up his voice and wept." And he said, "Thou art more righteous
than I; for thou hast rewarded me good, whereas I have rewarded thee evil." He added, "And now, behold, I know well
that thou shalt surely be king." At another time David surprised Saul in the midst of his camp, and his companion would
have killed him; but he said, "Destroy him not, for who can
stretch forth his hand against the Lord's anointed and be guiltless?" [11] Then, as he stood over him, he meditated sorrowfully
on his master's future fortunes, while he himself refrained from
interfering with God's purposes. "Surely the Lord shall smite
him; or his day shall come to die; or he shall descend into battle
and perish." David retired from the enemy's camp; and when at
a safe distance, roused Saul's guards, and blamed them for their
negligent watch, which had allowed a stranger to approach the
person of their king. Saul was moved the second time; the miserable man, as if waking from a dream which hung about him,
said, "I have sinned; return, my son David . . . . . behold, I have
played the fool, and have erred exceedingly." He added, truth
overcoming him, "Blessed be thou, my son David; thou shalt
both do great things, and also shalt still prevail."

How beautiful are these passages in the history of the chosen
king of Israel! How do they draw our hearts towards him, as one
whom in his private character it must have been an extreme
privilege and a great delight to know! Surely the blessings of the
patriarchs descended in a united flood upon "the lion of the
tribe of Judah," the type of the true Redeemer who was to
come. He inherits the prompt faith and magnanimity of Abraham; he is simple as Isaac; he is humble as Jacob; he has the
youthful wisdom and self-possession, the tenderness, the affectionateness, and the firmness of Joseph. And, as his own especial gift, he has an overflowing thankfulness, an ever-burning
devotion, a zealous fidelity to his God, a high unshaken loyalty
towards his king, an heroic bearing in all circumstances, such as
the multitude of men see to be great, but cannot understand.
Be it our blessedness, unless the wish be presumptuous, so to
acquit ourselves in troubled times; cheerful amid anxieties, collected in dangers, generous towards enemies, patient in pain
and sorrow, subdued in good fortune! How manifold are the
ways of the Spirit, how various the graces which He imparts;
what depth and width is there in that moral truth and virtue for

[11] 1 Sam. xxvi.9.

which we are created! Contrast one with another the Scripture Saints; how different are they, yet how alike! how fitted for their respective circumstances, yet how unearthly, how settled and composed in the faith and fear of God! As in the Services, so in the patterns of the Church, God has met all our needs, all our frames of mind. "Is any afflicted? let him pray; is any merry? let him sing Psalms." [12] Is any in joy or in sorrow? there are saints at hand to encourage and guide him. There is Abraham for nobles, Job for men of wealth and merchandise, Moses for patriots, Samuel for rulers, Elijah for reformers, Joseph for those who rise into distinction; there is Daniel for the forlorn, Jeremiah for the persecuted, Hannah for the downcast, Ruth for the friendless, the Shunammite for the matron, Caleb for the soldier, Boaz for the farmer, Mephibosheth for the subject; but none is vouchsafed to us in more varied lights, and with more abundant and more affecting lessons, whether in his history or in his writings, than he whose eulogy is contained in the words of the text, as cunning in playing, and a mighty valiant man, and prudent in matters, and comely in person, and favoured by Almighty God. May we be taught, as he was, to employ the gifts, in whatever measure given us, to God's honour and glory, and to the extension of that true and only faith which is the salvation of the soul!

[12] James v. 13.

JEROBOAM

"He cried against the altar in the word of the Lord, and said,
O altar, altar, thus saith the Lord, Behold, a child shall be born unto
the house of David, Josiah by name; and upon thee shall he offer the
priests of the high places that burn incense upon thee, and men's
bones shall be burnt upon thee."—1 Kings xiii.2.

THESE words are parts of a narrative which we hear read
once a year in the Sunday Service, but which can scarcely
be understood without some attention to the history which
precedes it. It is a prophecy against the form of worship set up in
the kingdom of Israel; let us consider what this kingdom and
this worship were, and how this woe came to be uttered by a
prophet of God.

When Solomon fell into idolatry, he broke what may be
called his coronation oath, and at once forfeited God's favour.
The essential duty of a king of the chosen people was to act as
God's representative, to govern for Him. David was called a
man after God's heart, because he was thus faithful; he fulfilled
his trust. Solomon failed, failed in the very one duty which, as
king of Israel, he was bound to perform.

In consequence, a message came from Almighty God, revealing what the punishment of his sin would be. He might be considered as having forfeited his kingdom, for himself and his
posterity. For David's sake, however, this extreme sentence was
not pronounced upon him. First, since the promise had been
made to David that his son should reign after him, though that
son was the very transgressor, yet *he* was spared the impending
evil on account of the promise. As an honour to David, Solomon's reign closed without any open infliction of divine vengeance; only with the presage of it. "Forasmuch as this is done
of thee, I will surely rend the kingdom from thee, and will give
it to thy servant. Notwithstanding in thy days I will not do
it, for David thy father's sake: but I will rend it out of the hand
of thy son."[1] A still further mitigation of punishment was

[1] 1 Kings xi.11, 12.

granted, still for David's sake. It had been promised David, "I will set up thy seed after thee, and I will stablish the throne of his kingdom for ever. . . . . . If he commit iniquity, I will chasten him with the rod of men; but My mercy shall not depart away from him, as I took it from Saul, whom I put away before thee."[2] Accordingly, when Solomon had sinned, and the kingdom was rent from him, still holy David's seed was not utterly put away before a new king, as the family of Saul had fallen before David; part of the kingdom was still left to the descendants of the faithful king. "Howbeit, I will not rend away *all* the kingdom; but will give one tribe to thy son," Solomon's son, "for *David My servant's sake*." This one tribe was the tribe of Judah, David's own tribe; to which part of Benjamin was added, as being in the neighbourhood. And this kingdom, over which David's line reigned for four hundred years after him, is called the kingdom of Judah.—But with this kingdom of Judah we are not now concerned; but with that larger portion of the tribes, which was rent away from David's house, and forms what is called the kingdom of Israel.

These were the circumstances under which the division of the kingdom was made. Solomon seems to have allowed himself in tyrannical conduct towards his subjects, as well as in idolatry. On his death the people came to his son Rehoboam, at Shechem, and said, "Thy father made our yoke grievous; now therefore make thou the grievous service of thy father and his heavy yoke which he put upon us lighter, and we will serve thee." Rehoboam was rash enough to answer, after three days' deliberation, "My father made your yoke heavy, and I will add to your yoke; my father also chastised you with whips, but I will chastise you with scorpions."[3] Now every one sees that Rehoboam here acted very wrongly, and Solomon too, as I have said, had sinned grievously before him. His oppression of the people was a *sin*; yet, you will observe, the people had no right to complain. They had brought this evil on themselves; they had obstinately courted and struggled after it. They would have "a king like the nations," a despotic king; and now they had one, they were discontented. Samuel had not only earnestly and solemnly protested against this measure, as an offence against their Almighty Governor, but had actually forewarned them of the evils which despotic power would introduce among them. "He will take your sons and appoint them for himself, for his chariots, and to be his horsemen; he will set them to ear his ground

---

[2] 2 Sam. vii.12–15.   [3] 1 Kings xii.4, 14.

and to reap his harvest and to make his instruments of war. He will take your daughters to be confectionaries, and to be cooks, and to be bakers. And he will take your fields, and your vineyards, and your oliveyards, and give them to his servants." The warning ends thus: "And ye shall cry out in that day, *because of your king which ye shall have chosen you*, and the Lord will not hear you in that day." [4] These were Samuel's words beforehand. Now all this had come upon them: as they had sown, so had they reaped. And, as matters stood, their best course would have been contentment, resignation; it was their duty to bear the punishment of their national self-will. But one sin was not enough for them. They proceeded, as men commonly do, to mend (as they considered) their first sin, by a fresh one;—they rebelled against their king. "What portion have we in David?" they said, "neither have we inheritance in the son of Jesse. To your tents, O Israel—now see to thine own house, David." [5] Ten tribes out of twelve revolted from their king in that day. Here they were quite inexcusable. Even putting it out of the question that they had brought the evil on themselves, still, independently of this, their king's tyranny did not justify their sudden, unhesitating, violent rebellion. He was acting against no engagement or stipulation. Because their king did not do his duty to them, this was no reason they should not do their duty to him. Say that he was cruel and rapacious, still they might have safely trusted the miraculous providence of God, to have restrained the king by His prophets, and to have brought them safely through. This would have been the way of *faith*; but they took the matter into their own hands, and got into further difficulty. And I wish you to observe, that all the evil arose from this original fault, worked out in its consequences through centuries, viz., their having a king at all.

So much, then, for their first sin, and their second sin. To continue further the history of their downward course, we must look to the man whom they made the leader of their rebellion. This was Jeroboam.

Jeroboam, the son of Nebat, had been, during Solomon's life-time, appointed to collect the tribute from the tribe of Ephraim, the most powerful of the ten tribes; a situation which gave him influence and authority in that part of the country. The king appointed him, "seeing the young man that he was industrious." We are told, too, that he was "a mighty man of valour." [6] Thus honoured by Solomon, he abused his trust, even

---

[4] 1 Sam. viii.11–18.   [5] 1 Kings xi.16.   [6] 1 Kings xi.28.

in the king's life-time, by rebelling against him. "Jeroboam, Solomon's servant, even he lift up his hand against the king." When Solomon, in consequence, "sought to kill him," he fled to Egypt, where Shishak, the king, sheltered him. On Solomon's death he returned to his country, and at the invitation of the revolting tribes, headed their rebellion. "It came to pass when all Israel (*i.e.* the ten tribes) heard that Jeroboam was come again, that they sent and called him unto the congregation, and made him king over all Israel: there was none that followed the house of David, but the tribe of Judah only." [7]

Now, that Jeroboam was an instrument in God's hand to chastise Solomon's sin is plain; and there is no difficulty in conceiving how a wicked man, without its being any excuse to him, still may bring about the Divine purposes. But in Jeroboam's particular case there *is* this difficulty at first sight; that Almighty God had seemed to sanction his act by *promising* him, in Solomon's life-time, the kingdom of the ten tribes. The prophet Ahijah had met him, and delivered to him a message from "the Lord, the God of Israel." "I will rend the kingdom out of the hand of Solomon, and will give ten tribes *to thee*." And it was on account of this prophecy that Jeroboam "lifted up his hand against the king." On a little consideration, however, we shall find no difficulty here: for though Almighty God promised him the kingdom, He did not tell him to *gain it for himself*; and, if we must not do evil that good may come, surely we may not do evil that a promise may be fulfilled; and to "rebel against his lord" (in the words of Scripture) was a plain indisputable sin. God, who made the promise, could of course fulfil it in His own time. He did not require man's crime to bring it about. It was, of course, an insult to His holiness and power to suppose He did. Jeroboam ought to have waited patiently God's time; this would have been the part of true faith. But it had always been, as on this occasion, the sin of the Israelites, to outrun God's providence; and even when they chose to pursue His ends, to wish to work them out in their own way. They never would "be still and know that He was God," wait His word and follow His guidance. Thus, when they first took possession of the promised land, they were told to cast the nations out, and utterly destroy all that did not leave the country. They soon became weary of this, and thought they had found out a better way. They thought it wiser to spare their enemies, and form alliances with them and put them under tribute. This

[7] 1 Kings xii.20.

brought them first into idolatry, then into captivity. When Samuel rescued them, and their hopes revived, their first act was to choose a king like the nations, contrary to God's will. And Jeroboam, in this instance, as a special emblem of the whole people in the rebellion itself, had not patience to wait, and faith to trust God, that "what He had promised He was able also to perform." That it was *a trial* to Jeroboam we need not deny; of course it was. He was tried and found wanting. Had he withstood the temptation, and refrained himself till lawfully called to reign, untold blessings might have been showered on him and on his people, who, in the actual history, were all cut off for their sins. He was not the first man who had thus been tried. David had been promised Saul's kingdom, and anointed thereunto by Samuel, years before he came into possession; yet, though he was persecuted by Saul, and had his life several times in his power, still he would not lift up his hand against his king. He had the faith of his forefather Abraham, who, though promised the land he dwelt in, wandered in it as a pilgrim, without daring to occupy it; wandered on with a band of trained servants at his command, who might have gained for him a territory had he desired it, as certainly as they smote Chedorlaomer and recovered Lot and his goods. David inherited this patient faith, and through it "obtained the promise," and founded a throne in righteousness and truth. Had Jeroboam followed it, he, too, might have been the father of a line of kings; he might have been the instrument and object of God's promised favour towards the house of Joseph; satisfying, in his own person, the prophecies which Jacob and Moses[8] had delivered, and which Joshua, himself an Ephraimite, had begun to fulfil, and founding a dominion not inferior in glory to that of Judah and Jerusalem.

Jeroboam, then, is not excused, though Ahijah prophesied; but, next, let us inquire how did he act when at length seated on the throne? It is not surprising, after such a beginning, that he sinned further and more grievously. When a man begins to do wrong, he cannot answer for himself how far he may be carried on. He does not see beforehand, he cannot know where he shall find himself after the sin is committed. One false step forces him to another, for retreat is impossible. This, which occurs every day, is instanced, first, in the history of the whole people, and then, in the history of Jeroboam. For awhile, indeed, he seemed to prosper. Rehoboam, Solomon's son, had brought an

---

[8] Gen. xlix.22–26; Deut. xxxiii.13–17; cf. 1 Kings xi.38.

extraordinary force of chosen men against him; but Almighty God, willing there should be no blood shed, designing to punish Solomon's idolatry, and intending to leave Jeroboam to himself, to work out the fruit of his rebellion, and then to judge and smite him with His own arm, would not allow the war. The prophet Shemaiah was sent to Rehoboam to put an end to it, and Rehoboam obeyed.

Thus Jeroboam seemed to have everything his own way; but soon a difficulty arose which he had thought light of, if he thought of it at all. The Jewish nation was not only a kingdom, but a church, a religious as well as a political body; and Jeroboam found, before long, that in setting up a new kingdom in Israel, he must set up a new religion too.

It was ordered in the Law of Moses, that all the men throughout Israel should go up to Jerusalem to worship three times a year; but Jerusalem was, at this time, the capital of the kingdom of Judah, the rival kingdom; and Jeroboam clearly saw that if his new subjects were allowed to go up thither, they could not remain his subjects long, but would return to their former allegiance. Here, then, a second false step was necessary to complete the first; for a false step that must have been which, as it would seem, required for its protection a violation of the Law of Moses. He, doubtless, argued that he was obliged to do what he did, that he could not help himself. It is true;—sin *is* a hard master; once sold over to it, we cannot break our chain; one evil concession requires another.

"Jeroboam said in his heart, Now shall the kingdom return to the house of David: if this people go up to do sacrifice in the house of the Lord at Jerusalem, then shall the heart of this people turn again unto their lord, even unto Rehoboam, king of Judah, and they shall kill me, and go again to Rehoboam, king of Judah. Whereupon the king took counsel."[9] A melancholy counsel it was: he resolved to select places for religious worship in his own kingdom. This was against the Law, of course; but what he did was worse than this. He could not build a Temple like Solomon's, and yet he needed some visible sign of the presence of God. Almighty God had bid the Israelites take to themselves no sign of His presence, no likeness of Him; but Jeroboam thought he could not do better than set up two figures of gold, one at each end of his country, not, indeed, as representations (he would argue), but as emblems and memorials of the true God, and as marking the established place of wor-

[9] I Kings xii.26–28.

ship. It is probable that the age of Solomon, a season of peace, when the arts were cultivated and an intercourse opened with foreign nations, was a season also of a peculiar religious corruption, such as had never occurred before. All through their history, indeed, the Israelites had opposed God's will; but by this time they had learned to defend their disobedience by argument, and to transgress upon a system. Jeroboam's sins, in regard to religious worship, were not single, or inconsistent with each other, but depended on this principle—that there is no need to attend to the positive laws and the outward forms and ceremonies of religion, so that we attend to the substance. In setting up these figures of gold, it was far from his intention to oppose the worship of the One True God, the Maker of heaven and earth, the Saviour of Israel; the words he used on the occasion, and the course of the history, show this. He thought he was only altering the discipline of the Church, as we should now call it, and he might plausibly ask, What did that matter? He was but putting another emblem of God in the place of the Cherubim. He made merely such alterations as change of circumstances and the course of events rendered indispensable. He was in difficulties, and had to consider, not what was best, or what he himself should choose, had he to choose, but what was practicable.

The figure he adopted, as a memorial of Almighty God, was in the shape of an ox or calf, the same which the Israelites had set up in the wilderness. It is hardly known what is the meaning of the emblem, which, doubtless, came from Egypt. The ox is thought to be the emblem of life or strength; and, being set up as a religious monument, might be intended to signify God's creative power. But, however, this might be, it was, at any rate, a direct and open transgression of the second Commandment. "The king took counsel, and made two calves of gold, and said unto the people, It is too much for you to go up to Jerusalem; behold thy gods, O Israel, which brought thee up out of the land of Egypt. And he set the one in Bethel, and the other put he in Dan."

Even this open idolatrous worship, not merely tolerated, but established, even this was not the last sin of this unhappy man, who had begun a course of wickedness upon system, and then left it as an inheritance for others more abandoned than himself to perfect. The tribe of Levi, who were especially consecrated to religious purposes, had their possessions not in one place, but scattered up and down the country. It was not to be supposed that they, who executed judgment upon the sin of

the calf in the wilderness, would tamely suffer this renewal of
the ancient offence in a more heinous shape. They refused to
countenance the idolatrous worship, and Jeroboam, led on by
hard necessity, cast them out of the country, got possession of
their cities and lands, and put in priests of his own making in
their stead. "He made a house of high places," and "he and his
sons cast off the Levites from executing the priest's office unto
the Lord, and he ordained him priests for the high places, and
for the devils, and for the calves which he had made; priests of
the lowest of the people, which were not of the sons of Levi." [10]
And he changed the solemn feast days, and dared to offer incense, himself intruding first, for example's sake, into the sacred office.

In consequence of these impious proceedings, not only "the
priests and Levites, that were in all Israel," left his kingdom
and retired to Judea, but also, "after them, out of all the"
other "tribes, such as set their hearts to seek the Lord God of
Israel, came to Jerusalem to sacrifice unto the Lord God of
their fathers."

Truly this was an ill-omened commencement of his reign. He
had made it impossible for pious Israelites to remain in the
country. The irreligious alone held by him. Jeroboam ruled in a
country given up, as it seemed, to evil spirits. So true is it, in a
kindred sense to that in which the words were used by Samuel,
that "rebellion is as the sin of witchcraft, and stubbornness is as
iniquity and idolatry." [11]

Now, then, we come to the concluding scene of this course of
crime, perpetrated by one man—the transaction to which the
text belongs.

It was on the new feast day "which he had devised of his own
heart," and at Bethel where the idol was set up. The people
were collected from all parts of the country, and the king "offered upon the altar and burnt incense." Such was the formal
inauguration of the false religion in God's own hallowed country, answering to that sacred solemnity when Solomon offered
the prayer of dedication in the Temple. The glory of God had
come down on that chosen place in token of His favour, and
now at Bethel, which He had once specially visited in an earlier
age, He suffered not the heathen act to pass without an indication of His wrath. One of His prophets was sent from Judah to
attend the festival; but, as if he were entering a country infected

[10] 1 Kings xii.31; 2 Chron. xi.14, 15.
[11] 1 Sam. xv.23.

by the pestilence, he was bid go into no house, nor eat nor drink while he was in it, nay, he was not even to return to his home the same way by which he came, as if his feet must not touch the polluted earth twice.

When the prophet came, he uttered his message before the apostate king. It was a prophecy; a prophecy set up as a witness against the complicated sins of the people, the destiny of that rebellious and idolatrous kingdom stamped upon it in the day of its nativity. The man of God addressed the altar, as not deigning to speak to Jeroboam, and foretold its fate. He announced that, after no long time, the idolatrous power should be destroyed, and that very altar should last long enough to see its fall; for upon it, fragrant as it now was with incense, the impious priests should be sacrificed, and men's bones burned; moreover, that all this should be done by a prince of the house of Judah; thus intimating that David's royal line would outlive the revolting kingdom of Israel. "O altar, altar, thus saith the Lord, Behold, a child shall be born unto the house of David, Josiah by name; and upon thee shall he offer the priests of the high places that burn incense upon thee, and men's bones shall be burnt upon thee." To show his Divine commission, the prophet gave the word, and the altar was miraculously rent in twain, and the ashes of the sacrifice scattered on the ground. Nothing could be more public than a judgment like this, denounced from God Himself, after Rehoboam, Solomon's son, had not been allowed to take the matter into his own hands. And to make the occurrence still more impressive, two further signs were added. Jeroboam stretched forth his hand to seize the prophet; it was instantly shrivelled up, so that he could not pull it to him again. At the prophet's prayer, it was restored. The second miracle was still more awful. The prophet, wearied with his journey, was, on his return, persuaded by a bad man to eat and drink, against the express word of God declared to him. An immediate judgment followed. As he sat at table, his seducer was constrained to declare to him his punishment—that his body should not come into the sepulchre of his fathers; and as he went home, a lion, God's second instrument for its infliction, met and slew him, yet did not devour him, nor touch the ass he rode on, nor molest other passengers he met, but, fixed to the spot by miracle, he stood over the prophet's body, a sign, more truly than the idols at Dan and Bethel, of God's power, holiness, and severe justice, and suggesting, throughout all Israel, the fearful argument—"If God so punish his own children, what will be the final, though delayed, punishment of the

wicked? If the righteous scarcely be saved, where shall the ungodly and the sinner appear?" [12]

As for Jeroboam, in spite of all this, "after this thing he returned not from his evil way, but made again of the lowest of
the people priests of the high places; whosoever would, he consecrated him, and he became one of the priests of the high
places." [13] Such was his life.

At the close of his reign, he lost even his earthly prosperity.
"The Lord struck him, and he died." Such was his end.

His family was soon cut off from the throne; and after all his
wise counsels and bold plans he has left but his name and title to
posterity, "Jeroboam the son of Nebat who caused Israel to
sin." Such is his memorial.

"Cursed be the man that trusteth in man, and maketh flesh
his arm, and whose heart departeth from the Lord. For he shall
be like the heath in the desert, and shall not see when good
cometh, but shall inhabit the parched places in the wilderness,
in a salt land, and not inhabited." [14]

It requires but a very few words to show the application of
this history to the circumstances in which we find ourselves. So
strongly does it pourtray to us the existing disorders and
schisms in the Christian Church—the profane and tyrannical
usage which it meets with from the world—that the only question which can possibly arise in the mind is, whether it is
allowable to apply it, and whether, as the events are alike, their
respective character and their issue are like each other also.
This, I say, is the only question, whether we may, without
blame, judge of what we see by the light of what we read in the
history of Israel; and I wish all readers would clearly understand
that this is the only question. If the deeds of Israel and Jeroboam
may be taken as types of what has been acted under the Gospel
for centuries past, can we doubt that schism, innovation in doctrine, a counterfeit priesthood, sacrilege, and violence, are sins
so heinous and crying, that there is no judgment too great for
them, no woe which we may not expect will ultimately fall on
the systems which have been born in them, and the lineage of
their perpetrators? What other lesson can we draw from the
history but this? but that we ought to draw a lesson, is plain
from the repeated declaration of St. Paul:—"Whatsoever
things were written aforetime, were written for our teaching."
"All these things happened unto them as types, and they are
written for our admonition, upon whom the ends of the world

---

[12] 1 Pet. iv.18.   [13] 1 Kings xiii.33.   [14] Jer. xvii.5, 6.

are come." "All Scripture is given by inspiration of God, and is profitable for teaching, for reproof, for correction, for instruction in righteousness." St. Peter also and St. Jude expressly apply occurrences in the Old Testament to parallels under the Gospel.[15]

May God give us the will and the power to realize to our minds this most serious truth, and fairly to follow it out in its necessary consequences! And may He of His mercy have pity upon our poor distracted Church, rescue it from the dominion of the heathen, and grant that "the world's course may be so peaceably ordered by His governance, that" it and all branches of the One Church Catholic "may joyfully serve Him in all godly quietness!"

[15] Rom. xv.4; 1 Cor. x.11; 2 Tim. iii.16; 2 Pet. ii.1–15; Jude 5–11.

FAITH AND OBEDIENCE

"If thou wilt enter into life, keep the commandments."
—Matt. xix.17.

L ET a plain man read the Gospels with a serious and humble
mind, and as in God's presence, and I suppose he would be
in no perplexity at all about the meaning of these words. They
are clear as the day at first reading, and the rest of our Saviour's
teaching does but corroborate their obvious meaning. I conceive that if such a man, after reading them and the other similar passages which occur in the Gospels, were told that he had
not mastered the sense of them, and that in matter of fact to
attempt to enter into life by keeping the commandments, to
attempt to keep the commandments in order to enter into life,
were suspicious and dangerous modes of expression, and that
the use of them showed an ignorance of the real spirit of
Christ's doctrine, he would in despair say, "Then truly Scripture is not a book for the multitude, but for those only who
have educated and refined understandings, so as to see things in
a sense different from their obvious meaning."

Or, again, supposing one, who disbelieved our Lord's divinity, fell in with persons who did thus consider that to keep the
commandments by way of entering into life, was a sign of spiritual blindness in a man, not to say of pride and reprobation; do
you suppose there would be any possibility of their silencing
him as regards his own particular heresy, with Scripture proofs
of the sacred truth which he denied? For can the doctrine that
Christ is God, be more clearly enunciated than the precept,
that, to enter into life, we must keep the commandments? and
is it not the way to make men think that Scripture has no definite meaning at all, and that each man may fairly put his own
sense upon it, when they see our Lord's plain directions thus
explained away?

The occasion of this unreal interpretation of Scripture,
which, in fact, does exist among us to a great extent, is, that St.
Paul, in some passages of his Epistles, teaches us that we are
accepted and saved by faith; and it is argued that, since he

wrote under the guidance of the promised Spirit, his is the true Gospel mode of Speech, and that the language of Christ, the Eternal Word of God, must be drawn aside, however violently, into that certain meaning which is assumed as the only true sense of St. Paul. *How* our Divine Master's words are explained away, what ingenious refinements are used to deprive us of the plain and solemn sense which they bear on their very front, it profits not here to inquire; still no one, it may be presumed, can deny, that, whether rightly or wrongly, they *are* turned aside in a very unexpected way, unless rather they are put out of sight altogether, and forgotten, as if superseded by the Apostolic Epistles. Doubtless those Epistles are inspired by the Holy Spirit: but He was sent from Christ to glorify and illuminate the words of Christ. The two heavenly witnesses cannot speak diversely; faith will listen to them both. Surely our duty is, neither to resist the One nor the Other; but humbly to consider whether there is not some one substantial doctrine which they teach in common; and that with God's blessing I will now attempt to do.

How are we sinners to be accepted by Almighty God? Doubtless the sacrifice of Christ on the cross is the *meritorious cause* of our justification, and His Church is the *ordained instrument* of conveying it to us. But our present question relates to another subject, to *our own part* in appropriating it; and here I say Scripture makes two answers, saying sometimes "Believe, and you shall be saved," and sometimes "Keep the commandments, and you shall be saved." Let us consider whether these two modes of speech are not reconcilable with each other.

What is meant by faith? It is to feel in good earnest that we are creatures of God; it is a practical perception of the unseen world; it is to understand that this world is not enough for our happiness, to look beyond it on towards God, to realize His presence, to wait upon Him, to endeavour to learn and to do His will, and to seek our good from Him. It is not a mere temporary strong act or impetuous feeling of the mind, an impression or a view coming upon it, but it is a *habit*, a state of mind, lasting and consistent. To have faith in God is to surrender one's-self to God, humbly to put one's interests, or to wish to be allowed to put them into His hands who is the Sovereign Giver of all good.

Now, again, let me ask, what is obedience? it is the obvious mode, suggested by nature, of a creature's conducting himself in God's sight, who fears Him as his Maker, and knows that, as a sinner, he has especial cause for fearing Him. Under such circumstances he "will do what he can" to please Him, as the woman whom our Lord commended. He will look every way to see how it is possible to approve himself to Him, and will rejoice to find any service which may stand as a sort of proof that He is in earnest. And he will find nothing better as an offering, or as an evidence, than obedience to that Holy Law, which conscience tells him has been given us by God Himself; that is, he will be diligent in doing all his duty as far as he knows it and can do it.—Thus, as is evident, the two states of mind are altogether one and the same: it is quite indifferent whether we say a man seeks God in faith, or say he seeks Him by obedience; and whereas Almighty God has graciously declared He will receive and bless all that seek Him, it is quite indifferent whether we say, He accepts those who *believe*, or those who *obey*. To believe is to look beyond this world to God, and to obey is to look beyond this world to God; to believe is of the heart, and to obey is of the heart; to believe is not a solitary act, but a consistent habit of trust; and to obey is not a solitary act, but a consistent habit of doing our duty in all things. I do not say that faith and obedience do not stand for separate ideas in our minds, but they stand for nothing more; they are not divided one from the other in fact. They are but one thing viewed differently.

If it be said that a man may keep from sin and do good without thinking of God, and therefore without being religious or having faith; this is true, but nothing to the purpose. It is, alas! too true that men often do what is in itself right, not from the thought of God, but for some purpose of this world; and all of us have our best doings sullied by the intrusion of bad thoughts and motives. But all this, I say, is nothing to our present purpose; for if a man does right, *not* for religion's sake but the world's sake, though he happens to be doing right, that is, to perform outwardly good actions, this is in no sense *obedience*, which is of the *heart*. And it was obedience, not mere outward good conduct, which I said belonged to the same temper of mind as faith. And I repeat it, for by obedience is meant obedience, not to the world, but to God—and habitually to obey God, is to be constant in looking on to God—and to look on to Almighty God, is to have faith; so that to "live by faith," or "walk by faith" (according to the Scripture phrases), that is, to have a habit of faith, and to be obedient, are one and the same general character of mind;—viewed as sitting at Jesus' feet, it is called *faith*; viewed as running to do His will, it is called *obedience*.

If, again, it be said that a man may be obedient and yet proud of being so, that is, obedient, without having faith, I would maintain, on the other hand, that in matter of fact a man is proud, or (what is sometimes called) self-righteous, not when obedient, but in proportion to his disobedience. To be proud is to rest on one's-self, which they are most chargeable with who do least; but a really obedient mind is necessarily dissatisfied with itself, and looks out of itself for help, from understanding the greatness of its task; in other words, in proportion as a man obeys, is he driven to faith, in order to learn the remedy of the imperfections of his obedience.

All this is clear and obvious to every thinking man; and this view of the subject was surely present to the minds of the inspired writers of Scripture—for this reason, because they use the two words, faith and obedience, indiscriminately, sometimes declaring we shall be accepted, saved, by *believing*, sometimes by *doing our duty*. And they so interchange these two conditions of God's favour, so quickly pass to and fro from the one view to the other, as to show that in truth the two do not differ, except in idea. If these apparently *two* conditions were merely connected, not substantially one, surely the inspired writers would compare them one with the other—surely they would be consistent in appropriating distinct offices to each. But, in very truth, from the beginning to the end of Scripture, the one voice of inspiration consistently maintains, not an uniform contrast between faith and obedience, but this *one* doctrine, that the only way of salvation open to us is the *surrender* of ourselves to our Maker in all things—supreme devotion, resignation of our will, the turning with all our heart to God; and this state of mind is ascribed in Scripture sometimes to the believing, sometimes to the obedient, according to the particular passage; and it is no matter to which it is ascribed.

Now, I will cite some passages from Scripture in proof of what I have said. The Psalmist says, "Lord, who shall abide in Thy tabernacle? who shall dwell in Thy holy hill? He that walketh uprightly, and worketh righteousness, and speaketh the truth in his heart." "He that hath clean hands and a pure heart, who hath not lifted up his soul unto vanity nor sworn deceitfully." [1] Here *obedience* is described as securing a man's salvation. But, in another Psalm we read, "How great is Thy goodness which Thou hast laid up for them that fear Thee; which Thou hast wrought for them that *trust in Thee!*" [2] Here, trust or faith is the condition of God's favour. Again, in other

[1] Ps. xv. 1, 2; xxiv. 4.
[2] Ps. xxxi. 19; xxxiv. 12–14, 18, 22.

Psalms, first, "What man is he that desireth life? Keep thy tongue from evil, and thy lips from speaking guile. *Depart from evil and do good*, seek peace and pursue it." . . . . Next, it is said, "The Lord is nigh unto them that are of a *broken heart*, and saveth such as be of a *contrite spirit*." Lastly, "None of them that *trust in* Him shall be desolate." Here, obedience, repentance, and faith, are successively mentioned as the means of obtaining God's favour; and why all of them, but because they are all names for one and the same substantial character, only viewed on different sides of it, that one character of mind which is pleasing and acceptable to Almighty God? Again, the prophet Isaiah says, "Thou wilt keep him in perfect peace whose mind is stayed on Thee, because he trusteth in Thee."[3] Yet, in the preceding verse he had proclaimed, "Open ye the gates (of the heavenly city) that the righteous nation, which keepeth the Truth, may enter in." In like manner Solomon says, "By *mercy and truth* iniquity is purged:" Daniel, that "*mercy to the poor*" is a "breaking off of sin," and "an healing of error:" Nehemiah prays God to "remember him," and "not wipe out his *good deeds for the House of his God*;" yet Habakkuk says, the "just shall live by his *faith*."[4]

What honour our Saviour put on faith I need hardly remind you. He blessed Peter's confession, and, in prospect, those who, though they saw Him not on earth, as Thomas, yet believe; and in His miracles of mercy, *faith* was the condition He exacted for the exertion of His powers of healing and restoration. On one occasion He says, "*All things* are possible to him that *believeth*."[5] Yet, afterwards, in His solemn account of the last Judgment, He tells us that it is *obedience to His will* which will then receive His blessing, "Inasmuch as ye have done it unto one of the least of these My brethren, ye have done it unto Me."[6] Again, the Angel said to Cornelius, "Thy prayers and thine alms are come up for a memorial before God;" and Cornelius is described as "a devout man, and one that feared God with all his house, which gave much alms to the people and prayed to God alway."[7] Yet it is in the very same Book of Acts that we read St. Paul's words, "*Believe*, and thou shalt be saved."[8] His Epistles afford us still more striking instances of the intimate association existing in the Apostle's thoughts between believing and obeying, as though exhibitions of one and the same spiritual character of

[3] Is. xxvi.2, 3.
[4] Prov. xvi.6; Dan. iv.27; Neh. xiii.14; Hab. ii.4.
[5] Mark ix.23.   [6] Matt. xxv.40.
[7] Acts x.2.   [8] Acts xvi.31.

mind. For instance, he says that Abraham was accepted (not by ceremonial observances, but) by *faith*, yet St. James says he was accepted by works of *obedience*. The meaning is clear, that Abraham found favour in God's sight, *because he gave himself* up to Him: this is faith or obedience, whichever we please to call it. No matter whether we say, Abraham was favoured because his faith embraced God's *promises*, or because his obedience cherished God's *commands*, for God's commands are promises, and His promises commands to a heart devoted to Him; so that, as there is no substantial difference between command and promise, so there is likewise none between obedience and faith. Perhaps it is scarcely correct even to say that faith comes first and obedience follows as an inseparable second step, and that faith, as being the first step, is accepted. For not a single act of faith can be named but what has in it the nature of obedience, that is, implies the making an effort and a consequent victory. What is the faith which earns Baptism—the very faith which appropriates the free gift of grace—but an acquiescence of the reason in the Gospel Mysteries? Even the thief upon the Cross had (it would seem) to rule his reason, to struggle against sight, and to bring under pride and obstinacy, when he turned to Him as his Saviour, who seemed to mortal eyes only his fellow-sufferer. A mere confession or prayer, which might not be really an act of obedience in us, might be such in him. On the other hand, faith does not cease with the first act, but continues. It works with obedience. In proportion as a man believes, so he obeys; they come together, and grow together, and last through life. Neither are perfect; both are on the same level of imperfection; they keep pace with each other; in proportion to the imperfection of one, so is the imperfection of the other; and, as the one advances, so does the other also.

And now I have described the temper of mind which has, in every age, been acceptable to Almighty God, in its two aspects of faith and obedience. In every age "the righteous shall live by faith." And it is remarkable that these words of the prophet Habakkuk, which St. Paul quotes three several times, to show the identity of true religion under all dispensations, do also represent it under these very two characteristics, Righteousness and Faith.

Before closing the subject, however, it may be necessary, in a few words, to explain *why* it is that, in some parts of St. Paul's Epistles, a certain stress is laid upon faith over and above the other parts of a religious character, in our justification. The reason seems to be as follows: the Gospel being pre-eminently a covenant of grace, faith is so far of more excellence than other virtues, because it confesses this beyond all others. Works of obedience witness to God's just claims upon us, not to His mercy: but faith comes empty-handed, hides even its own worth, and does but point at that precious scheme of redemption which God's love has devised for sinners. Hence, it is the frame of mind especially suitable to us, and is said, in a special way, to justify us, because it glorifies God, witnessing that He accepts those and those only, who confess they are not worthy to be accepted.

On this account, faith has a certain prerogative of dignity under the Gospel. At the same time we must never forget that the more usual mode of doctrine both with Christ and His Apostles is to refer our acceptance to obedience to the commandments, not to faith; and this, as it would appear, from a merciful anxiety in their teaching, lest, in contemplating God's grace, we should forget our own duties.

To conclude. If, after all, to believe and to obey be but different characteristics of one and the same state of mind, in what a most serious error are whole masses of men involved at this day, who are commonly considered religious! It is undeniable that there are multitudes who would avow with confidence and exultation that they put obedience only in the second place in their religious scheme, as if it were rather a necessary consequence of faith than requiring a direct attention for its own sake; a something subordinate to it, rather than connatural and contemporaneous with it. It is certain, however startling it is to reflect upon it, that numbers do not in any true sense believe that they shall be judged; they believe in a coming judgment as regards the wicked, but they do not believe that all men, that they themselves personally, will undergo it. I wish from my heart that the persons in question could be persuaded to read Scripture with their own eyes, and take it in a plain and natural way, instead of perplexing themselves with their human systems, and measuring and arranging its inspired declarations by an artificial rule. Are they quite sure that in the next world they will be able to remember these strained interpretations in their greatest need? Then surely, while we wait for the Judgment, the luminous sentences of Divine Truth will come over us, first one and then another, and we shall wonder how we ever misunderstood them! Then will they confront us in their simplicity and entireness, and we shall understand that nothing can be added to them, nothing taken away. Then at length, if not before, we shall comprehend our Lord's assurance, that "He will reward every man according to his works;" St. Paul's, that "we must all appear before the Judgment-seat of Christ, that every one may receive the things done in his body, according to that he hath done, whether it be good or bad;" St. Peter's, that "He is ordained of God to be the Judge of quick and dead;" St. James's, that "a man is justified by works and not by faith only;" and St. John's, that "they are blessed that do His commandments, that they might have right to the tree of life, and may enter in through the gates into the city." [9] Whatever else may be true, these declarations, so solemnly, so repeatedly made, must hold good in their plain and obvious sense, and may not be infringed or superseded. So many testimonies combined are "an anchor of the soul, sure and steadfast," and if they mean something else than what they all say, what part of Scripture can we dare trust in future as a guide and consolation?

"O Lord, Thy Word endureth for ever in heaven!" but the expositions of men are written on the sea-shore, and are blotted out before the evening.

[9] Matt. xvi.27; 2 Cor. v.10; Acts x.42; James ii.24; Rev. xxii.14.

CHRISTIAN REPENTANCE

"Father, I have sinned against heaven and before thee, and am no more worthy to be called thy son; make me as one of thy hired servants."—Luke xv.18, 19.

THE very best that can be said of the fallen and redeemed race of Adam is, that they confess their fall, and condemn themselves for it, and try to recover themselves. And this state of mind, which is in fact the only possible religion left to sinners, is represented to us in the parable of the Prodigal Son, who is described as receiving, then abusing, and then losing God's blessings, suffering from their loss, and brought to himself by the experience of suffering. A poor service indeed to offer, but the best we can offer, to make obedience our second choice when the world deserts us, when that is dead and lost to us wherein we were held!

Let it not be supposed, because I say this, that I think that in the life-time of each one of us there is some clearly marked date at which he began to seek God, and from which he has served him faithfully. This may be so in the case of this person or that, but it is far from being the rule. We may not so limit the mysterious work of the Holy Ghost. He condescends to plead with us continually, and what He cannot gain from us at one time, He gains at another. Repentance is a work carried on at diverse times, and but gradually and with many reverses perfected. Or rather, and without any change in the meaning of the word repentance, it is a work never complete, never entire—unfinished both in its inherent imperfection, and on account of the fresh and fresh occasions which arise for exercising it. We are ever sinning, we must ever be renewing our sorrow and our purpose of obedience, repeating our confessions and our prayers for pardon. No need to look back to the first beginnings of our repentance, should we be able to trace these, as something solitary and peculiar in our religious course; we are *ever* but beginning; the most perfect Christian is to himself but a beginner, a penitent prodigal, who has squandered God's gifts, and comes to Him to be tried over again, not as a son, but as a hired servant.

In this parable, then, we need not understand the description of the returning prodigal to imply that there is a state of disobedience and subsequent state of conversion definitely marked in the life of Christians generally. It describes the state of all Christians at all times, and is fulfilled more or less, according to circumstances, in this case or that; fulfilled in one way and measure at the beginning of our Christian course, and in another at the end. So I shall now consider it, viz., as describing the *nature* of all true repentance.

1. First, observe, the prodigal son said, "I am no more worthy to be called Thy son, make me as one of Thy hired servants." We know that God's service is perfect freedom, not a servitude; but this it is in the case of those who have long served Him; at first it *is* a kind of servitude, it is a task till our likings and tastes come to be in unison with those which God has sanctioned. It is the happiness of Saints and Angels in heaven to take pleasure in their duty, and nothing but their duty; for their mind goes that one way, and pours itself out in obedience to God, spontaneously and without thought or deliberation, just as man *sins* naturally. This is the state to which we are tending if we give ourselves up to religion; but in its commencement, religion is necessarily almost a task and a formal service. When a man begins to see his wickedness, and resolves on leading a new life, he asks, *What must I do?* he has a wide field before him, and he does not know how to enter it. He must be bid to do some particular plain acts of obedience, to fix him. He must be told to go to Church regularly, to say his prayers morning and evening, and statedly to read the Scriptures. This will limit his efforts to a certain end, and relieve him of the perplexity and indecision which the greatness of his work at first causes. But who does not see that this going to Church, praying in private, and reading Scripture, must in his case be, in great measure, what is called a form and a task? Having been used to do as he would, and indulge himself, and having very little understanding or liking for religion, he cannot take pleasure in these religious duties; they will necessarily be a weariness to him; nay, he will not be able even to give his attention to them. Nor will he see the use of them; he will not be able to find they make him better though he repeat them again and again. Thus his obedience at first is altogether that of a hired servant, "The servant knoweth not what his lord doeth." [1] This is Christ's account of him. The servant is not in his lord's confidence, does not understand

---

[1] John xv.15.

what he is aiming at, or why he commands this and forbids that. He executes the commands given him, he goes hither and thither, punctually, but by the mere letter of the command. Such is the state of those who *begin* religious obedience. They do not see anything come of their devotional or penitential services, nor do they take pleasure in them; they are obliged to defer to God's word simply because it is His word; to do which implies faith indeed, but also shows they are in that condition of a servant which the prodigal felt himself to be in at best.

Now, I insist upon this, because the conscience of a repentant sinner is often uneasy at finding religion a task to him. He thinks he ought to rejoice in the Lord at once, and it is true he is often told to do so; he is often taught to begin by cultivating high affections. Perhaps he is even warned against offering to God what is termed a *formal service*. Now this is reversing the course of a Christian's life. The prodigal son judged better, when he begged to be made one of his father's servants—he knew his place. We *must begin* religion with what looks like a form. Our fault will be, not in beginning it as a form, but in continuing it as a form. For it is our duty to be ever striving and praying to *enter* into the real spirit of our services, and in proportion as we understand them and love them, they will cease to be a form and a task, and will be the real expressions of our minds. Thus shall we gradually be changed in heart from servants into sons of Almighty God. And though from the very first, we must be taught to look to Christ as the Saviour of sinners, still His very love will frighten, while it encourages us, from the thought of our ingratitude. It will fill us with remorse and dread of judgment, for we are not as the heathen, we have received privileges, and have abused them.

2. So much, then, on the condition of the repentant sinner; next, let us consider the motives which actuate him in his endeavours to serve God. One of the most natural, and among the first that arise in the mind, is that of *propitiating* Him. When we are conscious to ourselves of having offended another, and wish to be forgiven, of course we look about for some *means* of setting ourselves right with him. If it be a slight offence, our overtures are in themselves enough, the mere expression that we wish our fault forgotten. But if we have committed some serious injury, or behaved with any special ingratitude, we, for a time, keep at a distance, from a doubt how we shall be received. If we can get a common friend to mediate in our behalf, our purpose is best answered. But even in that case we are not satisfied with leaving our interests to another; we try to do

something for ourselves; and on perceiving any signs of compassion or placability in the person offended, we attempt to approach him with propitiations of our own, either very humble confession, or some acceptable service. It was under this feeling that Jacob attempted to conciliate the governor of Egypt (whom he knew not to be his son Joseph), with a present of the best fruits of the land, "a little balm, and a little honey, spices, and myrrh, nuts, and almonds." And this holds good when applied to the case of sinners desiring forgiveness from God. The marks of His mercy all around us are strong enough to inspire us with some general hope. The very fact that He still continues our life, and has not at once cast us into hell, shows that He is waiting awhile before the wrath comes upon us to the uttermost. Under these circumstances it is *natural* that the conscience-stricken sinner should look round him for some atonement with which to meet his God. And this in fact has been the usual course of religion in all ages. Whether "with burnt-offerings and calves of a year old, with thousands of rams, and ten thousands of rivers of oil, with the offering of a man's first-born for his transgression, the fruit of his body for the sin of his soul;" or, in a higher way, "by doing justly, loving mercy, and walking humbly with our God;" [2] by some means or other, repentant sinners have attempted to win God's attention and engage His favour. And this mode has, before now, been graciously accepted by God, though He generally chose the gift which He would accept. Thus Jacob was instructed to sacrifice on the altar at Bethel, after his return from Padan-aram. David, on the other hand, speaks of the more spiritual sacrifice in the fifty-first Psalm: "The sacrifices of God are a broken spirit; a broken and a contrite heart, O God, Thou wilt not despise." Such are the services of the penitent, as suggested by nature, and approved by God Himself in the Old Testament.

But now, turning to the parable of the prodigal son, we find nothing of this kind in it. There is no mention made here of any offering on his part to his father, any propitiatory work. This should be well observed. The truth is, that our Saviour has shown us in all things a more perfect way than was ever before shown to man. As He promises us a more exalted holiness, an exacter self-command, a more generous self-denial, and a fuller knowledge of truth, so He gives us a more true and noble repentance. The most noble repentance (if a fallen being can be noble in his fall), the most decorous conduct in a conscious

---

[2] Micah vi.6–8.

sinner, is an *unconditional surrender* of himself to God—not a bargaining about terms, not a scheming (so to call it) to be received back again, but an instant *surrender* of himself in the first instance. Without knowing what will become of him, whether God will spare or not, merely with so much hope in his heart as not utterly to despair of pardon, still not looking merely to *pardon* as an *end*, but rather looking to the claims of the Benefactor whom he has offended, and smitten with shame, and the sense of his ingratitude, he must *surrender himself* to his lawful Sovereign. He is a runaway offender; he must come back, as a very first step, before anything can be determined about him, bad or good; he is a rebel, and must lay down his arms. Self-devised offerings might do in a less serious matter; as an atonement for sin, they imply a defective view of the evil and extent of sin in his own case. Such is that perfect way which nature shrinks from, but which our Lord enjoys in the parable—a surrender. The prodigal son waited not for his father to show signs of placability. He did not merely approach a space, and then stand as a coward, curiously inquiring, and dreading how his father felt towards him. He made up his mind at once to degradation at the best, perhaps to rejection. He arose and went straight on towards his father, with a collected mind; and though his relenting father saw him from a distance, and went out to meet him, still his purpose was that of an instant frank submission. Such must be Christian repentance: First we must put aside the idea of finding a remedy for our sin; then, though we feel the guilt of it, yet we must set out firmly towards God, not knowing for certain that we shall be forgiven. He, indeed, meets us on our way with the tokens of His favour, and so He bears up human faith, which else would sink under the apprehension of meeting the Most High God; still, for our repentance to be Christian, there must be in it that generous temper of self-surrender, the acknowledgment that we are unworthy to be called any more His sons, the abstinence from all ambitious hopes of sitting on His right hand or His left, and the willingness to bear the heavy yoke of bond-servants, if He should put it upon us.

This, I say, is Christian repentance. Will it be said, "It is too hard for a beginner?" true: but I have not been describing the case of a beginner. The parable teaches us what the character of the true penitent is, not how men actually *at first* come to God. The longer we live, the more we may hope to *attain* this higher kind of repentance, viz., in proportion as we advance in the other graces of the perfect Christian character. The truest kind of repentance as little comes at first, as perfect conformity to any other part of God's Law. It is gained by long practice—it will come at length. The dying Christian will fulfil the part of the returning prodigal more exactly than he ever did in his former years. When first we turn to God in the actual history of our lives, our repentance is mixed with all kinds of imperfect views and feelings. Doubtless there is in it something of the true temper of simple submission; but the wish of appeasing God on the one hand, or a hard-hearted insensibility about our sins on the other, mere selfish dread of punishment, or the expectation of a sudden easy pardon, these, and such-like principles, influence us, whatever we may say or may think we feel. It is, indeed, easy enough to have good words put into our mouths, and our feelings roused, and to profess the union of utter self-abandonment and enlightened sense of sin; but to claim is not really to possess these excellent tempers. Really to gain these is a work of time. It is when the Christian has long fought the good fight of faith, and by experience knows how few and how imperfect are his best services; then it is that he is able to acquiesce, and most gladly acquiesces in the statement, that we are accepted by faith only in the merits of our Lord and Saviour. When he surveys his life at the close of it, what is there he can trust in? what act of it will stand the scrutiny of the Holy God? of course no part of it, so much is plain without saying a word. But further, what part of it even is a sufficient evidence to himself of his own sincerity and faithfulness? This is the point which I urge. How shall he know that he is still in a state of grace after all his sins? Doubtless he may have some humble hope of his acceptance. St. Paul speaks of the testimony of his conscience as consoling him; but his conscience also tells him of numberless actual sins, and numberless omissions of duty; and with the awful prospect of eternity before him, and in the weakness of declining health, how shall he collect himself to appear before God? Thus he is after all, in the very condition of the returning prodigal, and cannot go beyond him, though he has served God ever so long. He can but *surrender* himself to God, as after all, a worse than unprofitable servant, resigned to God's will, whatever it is, with more or less hope of pardon, as the case may be; doubting not that Christ is the sole meritorious Author of all grace, resting simply on Him who, "if He will, can make him clean," but not without fears about himself, because unable, as he well knows, to read his own heart in that clear unerring way in which God reads it. Under these circumstances, how vain it is to tell him of his own good deeds, and to bid him look back on his past consistent life! This reflection will rarely comfort him; and when it does, it will be the recollection of the instances of God's mercy towards him in former years which will be the chief ground of encouragement in it. No, his true stay is, that Christ came "to call sinners to repentance," that "He died for the ungodly." He acknowledges and adopts, as far as he can, St. Paul's words, and nothing beyond them, "This is a faithful saying, and worthy of all acceptation, that Christ Jesus came into the world to save *sinners*, of whom I am chief." [3]

Who shall dare approach Christ at the dreadful Day of Judgment, who has rejected the calling of His Spirit here? Who shall then dare to surrender himself to the great God, when hell is opened ready to receive him? Alas! it is only because *some* hope is left to us that we dare give ourselves up to Him *here*; *despair* ever keeps away. But then, when He takes His seat as the severe Judge of sinners, who, among His slothful disobedient servants, will willingly present himself? Surely the time of *submission* will then be over; resignation has no place among fallen spirits; they are swept away by the uncontrollable power of God. "Bind him *hand and foot*, and take him away;" [4] such will be the dreadful command. They *would* struggle if they *could*.

And in hell they will be still tormented by the worm of proud rebellious hatred of God! Not even ages will reconcile them to a hard endurance of their fate; not even the dry apathy in which unbelievers on earth take refuge, will be allowed them. There is no fatalism in the place of torment. The devils see their doom was their own fault, yet they are unable to be sorry for it. It is their *will* that is in direct energetic variance with the will of God, and they know it.

Consider this, my brethren, and lay it to heart. Doubtless you must render yourselves to God's mercy here, or else be forced away before His anger hereafter.

"To-day, while it is called to-day, harden not your hearts." [5]

[3] Matt. ix.13; Rom. v.6; 1 Tim. i.15.
[4] Matt. xxii.13.   [5] Heb. iii.7–15.

CONTRACTED VIEWS IN RELIGION

"Lo, these many years do I serve thee, neither transgressed I at any time thy commandment; and yet thou never gavest me a kid, that I might make merry with my friends."—Luke xv.29.

THERE is a general correspondence between this parable, and that in St. Matthew's gospel of the two sons whom their father bade go work in his vineyard; but they differ as regards the character of the professedly obedient son: in St. Matthew he says, "I go, sir, and went not;" in the parable before us he is of a far different class of Christians, though not without his faults. There is nothing to show that he is insincere in his profession, though in the text he complains in a very unseemly and foolish way. He bears a considerable resemblance to the labourers in the vineyard, who complained of their master; though they are treated with greater severity. The elder brother of the prodigal complained of his father's kindness towards the penitent; the labourers of the vineyard murmured against the good-man of the house for receiving and rewarding those who came late to his service as liberally as themselves. They, however, spoke in selfishness and presumption; but he in perplexity, as it would appear, and distress of mind. Accordingly, he was comforted by his father, who graciously informed him of the reason of his acting as he had done. "Son, *thou* art ever with me," he says, "and all that I have is thine. It was meet that we should make merry and be glad; for this thy brother was dead and is alive again, and was lost and is found."

Now let us try to understand the feelings of the elder brother, and to apply the picture to the circumstances in which we find ourselves at present.

First, then, in the conduct of the father, there seemed, at first sight, an evident departure from the rules of fairness and justice. Here was a reprobate son received into his favour on the first stirrings of repentance. What was the use of serving him dutifully, if there were no difference in the end between the righteous and the wicked? This is what we feel and act upon in life constantly. In doing good to the poor, for instance, a chief object is to encourage industrious and provident habits; and it is evident we should hurt and disappoint the better sort, and defeat our object, if, after all, we did not take into account the difference of their conduct, though we promised to do so, but gave those who did not work nor save all the benefits granted to those who did. The elder brother's case, then, seemed a hard one; and that, even without supposing him to feel jealous, or to have unsuitable notions of his own importance and usefulness. Apply this to the case of religion, and it still holds good. At first sight, the reception of the penitent sinner seems to interfere with the reward of the faithful servant of God. Just as the promise of pardon is abused by bad men to encourage themselves in sinning on, that grace may abound; so, on the other hand, it is misapprehended by the good, so as to dispirit them. For what is our great stay and consolation amid the perturbations of this world? The truth and justice of God. This is our one light in the midst of darkness. "He loveth righteousness, and hateth iniquity;" "just and right is He." Where else should we find rest for our foot all over the world? Consider in how mysterious a state all things are placed; the wicked are uppermost in power and name, and the righteous are subjected to bodily pain and mental suffering, as if they did not serve God. What a temptation is this to unbelief! The Psalmist felt it when he spoke of the prosperity of the wicked. "Behold, these are the ungodly, who prosper in the world; they increase in riches. Verily I have cleansed my heart in vain, and washed my hands in innocency." [1] It is to meet this difficulty that Almighty God has vouchsafed again and again to declare the unswerving rule of His government— favour to the obedient, punishment to the sinner; that there is "no respect of persons with Him;" that "the righteousness of the righteous shall be upon him, and the wickedness of the wicked shall be upon him." [2] Recollect how often this is declared in the book of Psalms. "The Lord knoweth the way of the righteous: but the way of the ungodly shall perish." "The righteous Lord loveth righteousness; His countenance doth behold the upright." "With the merciful Thou wilt show Thyself merciful; with an upright man Thou wilt show Thyself upright. With the pure Thou wilt show Thyself pure; and with the froward Thou wilt show Thyself froward. For Thou wilt save the afflicted people; but wilt bring down high looks." "Many sorrows shall be to the wicked; but he that trusteth in the Lord, mercy shall compass him about." "Do good, O Lord,

[1] Ps. lxxiii.12, 13.   [2] Rom. ii.11; Ezek. xviii.20.

unto those that be good."[3] These declarations, and numberless others like them, are familiar to us all; and why, I say, so often made, except to give us that one fixed point for faith to rest upon, while all around us is changing and disappointing us? viz., that we are quite sure of peace in the end, bad as things may now look, if we do but follow the rule of conscience, avoid sin, and obey God. Hence, St. Paul tells us that "he that cometh to God, must believe that He is a *rewarder* of them that diligently seek Him."[4] Accordingly, when we witness the inequalities of the present world, we comfort ourselves by reflecting that they will be put right in another.

Now the restoration of sinners seems to interfere with this confidence; it seems, at first sight, to put bad and good on a level. And the feeling it excites in the mind is expressed in the parable by the words of the text: "These many years do I serve Thee, neither transgressed I at any time Thy commandment," yet I never have been welcomed and honoured with that peculiar joy which Thou showest towards the repentant sinner. This is the expression of an agitated mind, that fears lest it be cast back upon the wide world, to grope in the dark without a God to guide and encourage it in its course.

The condescending answer of the Father in the parable is most instructive. It sanctions the great truth, which seemed in jeopardy, that it is *not* the same thing in the end to obey or disobey, expressly telling us that the Christian penitent is not placed on a footing with those who have consistently served God from the first. "Son, *thou* art ever with Me, and all that I have is thine:" that is, why this sudden fear and distrust? can there be any misconception on thy part because I welcome thy brother? dost thou not yet understand Me? Surely thou hast known Me too long to suppose that *thou* canst lose by his gain. *Thou* art in My confidence. I do not make any outward display of kindness towards *thee*, for it is a thing to be taken for granted. We give praise and make professions to strangers, not to friends. Thou art My heir, all that I have is thine. "O thou of little faith, wherefore didst thou doubt?" Who could have thought that it were needful to tell to thee truths which thou hast heard all thy life long? Thou art *ever* with Me; and canst thou really grudge that I should, by one mere *act* of rejoicing, show My satisfaction at the sinner's recovery, and should console him with a promise of mercy, who, before he heard of it, was sinking down under the dread of deserved punishment?

[3] Ps. i.6; xi.7; xviii.25–27; xxxii.10; cxxv.4.   [4] Heb. xi.6.

"It was *meet* that we should make merry and be glad," thou as well as thy Father.—Such is our merciful God's answer to His suspicious servants, who think He cannot pardon the sinner without withdrawing His favour from them; and it contains in it both a consolation for the perplexed believer not to distrust Him; and again, a warning to the disobedient, not to suppose that repentance makes all straight and even, and puts a man in the same place as if he had never departed from grace given.

But let us now notice the unworthy feeling which appears in the conduct of the elder brother. "He was angry, and would not go" into the house. How may this be fulfilled in our own case?

There exists a great deal of infirmity and foolishness even in the better sort of men. This is not to be wondered at, considering the original corrupt state of their nature, however it is to be deplored, repented of, and corrected. Good men are, like Elijah, "jealous for the Lord God of hosts," and rightly solicitous to see His tokens around them, the pledges of His unchangeable just government; but then they mix with such good feelings undue notions of self-importance, of which they are not aware. This seemingly was the state of mind which dictated the complaint of the elder brother.

This will especially happen in the case of those who are in the most favoured situations in the Church. All places possess their peculiar temptation. Quietness and peace, those greatest of blessings, constitute the trial of the Christians who enjoy them. To be cast on the world, and to see life (as it is called) is a vanity, and "drowns" the unstable "in destruction and perdition;" but while, on the one hand, a religious man may thrive even in the world's pestilent air and on unwholesome food, so, on the other hand, he may become sickly, unless he guards against it, from the very abundance of privileges vouchsafed to him in a peaceful lot. The elder brother had always lived at home; he had seen things go on one way, and, as was natural and right, got attached to them in that one way. But then he could not conceive that they possibly could go on in any other way; he thought he understood his Father's ways and principles far more than he did, and when an occurrence took place, for which he had hitherto met with no precedent, he lost himself, as being suddenly thrust aside out of the contracted circle in which he had hitherto walked. He was disconcerted, and angry with his Father. And so in religion, we have need to watch against that narrowness of mind, to which we are tempted by the uniformity and tranquillity of God's providence towards us. We should be on our guard lest we suppose ourselves to have such a clear knowledge of God's ways, as to rely implicitly on our own notions and feelings. Men attach an undue importance to this or that point in received opinions or practices, and cannot understand how God's blessing can be given to modes of acting to which they themselves are unaccustomed. Thus the Jews thought religion would come to an end, if the Temple were destroyed, whereas, in fact, it has spread abroad and flourished more marvellously since than ever it did before. In this perplexity of mind the Church Catholic is our divinely intended guide, which keeps us from a narrow interpretation of Scripture, from local prejudices and excitements of the day; and by its clear-sighted and consolatory teaching scatters those frightful self-formed visions which scare us.

But I have not described the extreme state of the infirmity into which the blessing of peace leads unwary Christians. They become not only over-confident of their knowledge of God's ways, but positive in their over-confidence. They do not like to be contradicted in their opinions, and are generally most attached to the very points which are most especially of their own devising. They forget that all men are at best but learners in the school of Divine Truth, and that they themselves ought to be *ever* learning, and that they may be sure of the truth of their creed, without a like assurance in the details of religious opinion. They find it a much more comfortable view, much more agreeable to the indolence of human nature, to give over seeking, and to believe they had nothing more to find. A right faith is ever eager and on the watch, with quick eyes and ears, for tokens of God's will, whether He speak in the way of nature or of grace. "I will stand upon my watch, and set me upon the tower, and will watch to see what He will say unto me, and what I shall answer when I am reproved." [5] This is that faith by which (as the Prophet continues) "the just shall live." The Psalmist also expresses this expectant temper. "Unto Thee lift I up mine eyes, O Thou that dwellest in the heavens. Behold, as the eyes of servants look unto the hand of their masters, and as the eyes of a maiden unto the hand of her mistress." [6] But as for those who have long had God's favour without cloud or storm, so it is, they grow secure. They do not feel the great gift. They are apt to presume, and so to become irreverent. The elder brother was too familiar with his Father. Irreverence is the very opposite temper to faith. "Son, thou art ever with Me, and all that I have is thine." This most gracious truth was the very

[5] Heb. ii.1.   [6] Ps. cxxiii.1, 2.

cause of his murmuring. When Christians have but a little, they are thankful; they gladly pick up the crumbs from under the table. Give them much, they soon forget it is much; and when they find it is not all, and that for other men, too, even for penitents, God has some good in store, straightway they are offended. Without denying in words their own natural unworthiness, and still having real convictions of it to a certain point, nevertheless, somehow, they have a certain secret over-regard for themselves; at least they *act* as if they thought that the Christian privileges belonged to them over others, by a sort of fitness. And they like respect to be shown them by the world, and are jealous of anything which is likely to interfere with the continuance of their credit and authority. Perhaps, too, they have pledged themselves to certain received opinions, and this is an additional reason for their being suspicious of what to them is a novelty. Hence such persons are least fitted to deal with difficult times. God works wondrously in the world; and at certain eras His providence puts on a new aspect. Religion seems to be failing, when it is merely changing its form. God seems for an instant to desert His own appointed instruments, and to be putting honour upon such as have been framed in express disobedience to His commands. For instance, sometimes He brings about good by means of wicked men, or seems to bless the efforts of those who have separated from His Holy Church more than those of His true labourers. Here is the trial of the Christian's faith, who, if the fact is so, must not resist it, lest haply he be found fighting against God, nor must he quarrel with it after the manner of the elder brother. But he must take everything as God's gift, hold fast his *principles*, not give *them* up because appearances are for the moment against them, but believe all things will come round at length. On the other hand, he must not cease to beg of God, and try to gain, the spirit of a sound mind, the power to separate truth from falsehood, and to try the spirits, the disposition to submit to God's teaching, and the wisdom to act as the varied course of affairs requires; in a word, a portion of that spirit which rested on the great Apostle, St. Paul.

I have thought it right to enlarge upon the conduct of the elder brother in the parable, because something of his character may perchance be found among ourselves. We have long had the inestimable blessings of peace and quiet. We are unworthy of the least of God's mercies, much more of the greatest. But with the blessing we have the trial. Let us then guard against abusing our happy lot, while we have it, or we may lose it for having abused it. Let us guard against discontent in any shape; and as we cannot help hearing what goes on in the world, let us guard, on hearing it, against all intemperate, uncharitable feelings towards those who differ from us, or oppose us. Let us pray for our enemies; let us try to make out men to be as good as they can fairly and safely be considered; let us rejoice at any symptoms of repentance, or any marks of good principle in those who are on the side of error. Let us be forgiving. Let us try to be very humble, to understand our ignorance, and to rely constantly on the enlightening grace of our Great Teacher. Let us be "slow to speak, slow to wrath;"—not abandoning our principles, or shrinking from the avowal of them when seasonable, or going over to the cause of error, or fearing consequences, but acting ever from a sense of duty, not from passion, pride, jealousy, or an unbelieving dread of the future; feeling gently, even when we have reason to act severely. "Son, thou art ever with Me, and all that I have is thine." What a gracious announcement, if we could realize it! and how consolatory, so far as we have reason to hope that we are following on to know God's will, and living in His faith and fear! What should alarm those who have Christ's power, or make them envious who have Christ's fulness? How ought we calmly to regard, and resolutely endure, the petty workings of an evil world, thinking seriously of nothing but of the souls that are perishing in it!

"I, even I, am He that comforteth you," says Almighty God: "who art thou, that thou shouldest be afraid of a man that shall die, and of the son of man which shall be made as grass; and forgettest the Lord thy Maker; and hast feared continually every day because of the fury of the oppressor, as if he were ready to destroy? And where is the fury of the oppressor? I am the Lord thy God: and I have put My words in thy mouth, and have covered thee in the shadow of Mine hand, that I may plant the heavens, and lay the foundations of the earth, and say unto Zion, Thou art My people." [7]

[7] Is. li. 12, 13, 15, 16.

A PARTICULAR PROVIDENCE AS REVEALED IN THE GOSPEL

"Thou God seest me."—Gen. xvi.13.

WHEN Hagar fled into the wilderness from the face of her mistress, she was visited by an Angel, who sent her back; but, together, with this implied reproof of her impatience, he gave her a word of promise to encourage and console her. In the mixture of humbling and cheerful thoughts thus wrought in her, she recognized the presence of her Maker and Lord, who ever comes to His servants in a two-fold aspect, severe because He is holy, yet soothing as abounding in mercy. In consequence, she called the name of the Lord that spake unto her, "Thou God seest me."

Such was the condition of man before Christ came, favoured with some occasional notices of God's regard for individuals, but, for the most part, instructed merely in His general Providence, as seen in the course of human affairs. In this respect even the Law was deficient, though it abounded in proofs that God was a living, all-seeing, all recompensing God. It was deficient, in comparison of the Gospel, in evidence of the really-existing relation between each soul of man and its Maker, independently of everything else in the world. Of Moses, indeed, it is said, that "the Lord spake unto him *face to face*, as a man speaketh unto his friend." [1] But this was an especial privilege vouchsafed to him only and some others, as to Hagar, who records it in the text, not to all the people. But, under the New Covenant, this distinct regard, vouchsafed by Almighty God to every one of us, is clearly revealed. It was foretold of the Christian Church; *"All* thy children shall be taught of the Lord; and great shall be the peace of thy children." [2] When the Eternal Son came on earth in our flesh, men saw their invisible Maker and Judge. He showed Himself no longer through the mere powers of nature, or the maze of human affairs, but in our own

[1] Exod. xxxiii.11.   [2] Is. liv.13.

likeness to Him. "God, who commanded the light to shine out of darkness, hath shined in our hearts, to give the light of the knowledge of the glory of God in the face of Jesus Christ;" [3] that is, in a sensible form, as a really existing individual being. And, at the same time, He forthwith began to speak to *us* as individuals. He, on the one hand, addressed each of us on the other. Thus it was in some sense a revelation face to face.

This is the subject on which I propose now to make a few remarks. And first, let me observe, it is very difficult, in spite of the revelation made us in the Gospel, to master the idea of this particular providence of God. If we allow ourselves to float down the current of the world, living as other men, gathering up our notions of religion here and there, as it may be, we have little or no true comprehension of a particular Providence. We conceive that Almighty God works on a large plan; but we cannot realize the wonderful truth that He sees and thinks of individuals. We cannot believe He is really present everywhere, that He is wherever we are, though unseen. For instance, we can understand, or think we understand, that He was present on Mount Sinai, or within the Jewish Temple, or that He clave the ground under Dathan and Abiram. But we do not in any sufficient sense believe that He is in like manner "about *our* path, and about *our* bed, and spieth out all *our* ways." [4] We cannot bring ourselves to get fast hold of the solemn fact, that He sees what is going on among ourselves at this moment; that this man falls and that man is exalted, at His silent, invisible appointment. We use, indeed, the prayers of the Church, and intercede, not only for all conditions of men, but for the King and the Nobility, and the Court of Parliament, and so on, down to individual sick people in our own parish; yet in spite of all this, we do not bring home to our minds the truth of His omniscience. We know He is in heaven, and forget that He is also on earth. This is the reason why the multitude of men are so profane. They use light words; they scoff at religion; they allow themselves to be lukewarm and indifferent; they take the part of wicked men; they push forward wicked measures; they defend injustice, or cruelty, or sacrilege, or infidelity; because they have no grasp of a truth, which nevertheless they have no intention to deny, that God sees them. There is, indeed, a self-will, and self-deceit, which would sin on even in God's visible presence. This was the sin of Balaam, who took part with the enemies of Israel for reward; and of Zimri, the son of Salu, a

---

[3] 2 Cor. iv.6.   [4] Ps. cxxxix.2.

prince of the Simeonites, on whom Phineas did judgment; and such the sin of Saul, of Judas, of Ananias and Sapphira. Alas! doubtless such is the sin of many a man now in England, unless human nature is other than it was aforetime; alas! such a sin is in a measure our own from time to time, as any one may know for certain who is used to self-examination. Yet, over and above this, certainly there is also a great deal of profane sinning from our *forgetting*, not comprehending that we are in God's presence; not comprehending, or (in other words) believing, that He sees and hears and notes down everything we do.

This, again, is often the state in which persons find themselves on falling into trouble. The world fails them, and they despair, because they do not realize to themselves the loving-kindness and the presence of God. They find no comfort in a truth which to them is not a substance but an opinion. Therefore it was that Hagar, when visited in the wilderness by the Angel, called the name of the Lord that spake unto her, "Thou God seest me!" It came as a new truth to her that, amid her trouble and her waywardness, the eye of God was upon her. The case is the same now. Men talk in a general way of the goodness of God, His benevolence, compassion, and long-suffering; but they think of it as of a flood pouring itself out all through the world, as the light of the sun, not as the continually repeated action of an intelligent and living Mind, contemplating whom it visits and intending what it effects. Accordingly, when they come into trouble, they can but say, "It is all for the best—God is good," and the like; and this does but fall as cold comfort upon them, and does not lessen their sorrow, because they have not accustomed their minds to feel that He is a merciful God, regarding them individually, and not a mere universal Providence acting by general laws. And then, perhaps, all of a sudden the true notion breaks on them, as it did upon Hagar. Some especial Providence, amid their infliction, runs right into their heart, and brings it close home to them, in a way they never experienced before, that God sees them. And then, surprised at this, which is a something quite new to them, they go into the other extreme, in proportion to their former apathy, and are led to think that they are especial objects of God's love, more than all other men. Instead of taking what has happened to them as an evidence of His particular Providence over all, as revealed in Scripture, they still will not believe a jot or tittle more than they see; and, while discovering He loves them individually, they do not advance one step, on that account, to the general truth, that He loves other men individually also. Now, had they been all along in the practice of studying Scripture, they would have been saved from both errors—their first, which was blindness to a particular Providence altogether—their second, which was a narrow-minded limiting of it to themselves, as if the world at large were rejected and reprobate; for Scripture represents this privilege as the portion of all men one by one.

I suppose it is scarcely necessary to prove to those who have allowed their minds to dwell on the Gospels, that the peculiar character of our Lord's goodness, as displayed therein, is its tenderness and its considerateness. These qualities are the very perfection of kindness between man and man; but, from the very extent and complication of the world's system, and from its Maker's being invisible, our imagination scarcely succeeds in attributing them to Him, even when our reason is convinced, and we wish to believe accordingly. His Providence manifests itself in general laws, it moves forward upon the lines of truth and justice; it has no respect of persons, rewarding the good and punishing the bad, not as individuals, but according to their character. How shall He who is Most Holy direct His love to this man or that for the sake of each, contemplating us one by one, without infringing on His own perfections? Or even were the Supreme Being a God of unmixed benevolence, how, even then, shall the thought of Him come home to our minds with that constraining power which the kindness of a human friend exerts over us? The greatest acknowledgment we can make of the kindness of a superior, is to say that he acts as if he were personally interested in us. The mass of benevolent men are kind and generous, because it is their way to be so, irrespectively of the person whom they benefit. Natural temper, a flow of spirits, or a turn of good fortune, opens the heart, which pours itself out profusely on friend and enemy. They scatter benefits as they move along. Now, at first sight, it is difficult to see how our idea of Almighty God can be divested of these earthly notions, either that His goodness is imperfect, or that it is fated and necessary; and wonderful indeed, and adorable is the condescension by which He has met our infirmity. He has met and aided it in that same Dispensation by which He redeemed our souls. In order that we may understand that in spite of His mysterious perfections He has a separate knowledge and regard for individuals, He has taken upon Him the thoughts and feelings of our own nature, which we all understand *is* capable of such personal attachments. By becoming man, He has cut short the perplexities and the discussions of our reason on the subject, as if He would grant our objections for argument's sake, and supersede them by taking our own ground.

The most winning property of our Saviour's mercy (if it is right so to speak of it), is its dependence on time and place, person and circumstance; in other words, its tender discrimination. It regards and consults for each individual as he comes before it. It is called forth by some as it is not by others, it cannot (if I may say so) manifest itself to every object alike; it has its particular shade and mode of feeling for each; and on some men it so bestows itself, as if He depended for His own happiness on their well-being. This might be illustrated, as is often done, by our Lord's tender behaviour towards Lazarus and his sisters, or His tears over Jerusalem; or by His conduct towards St. Peter, before and after his denial of Him, or towards St. Thomas when he doubted, or by His love of His mother, or of St. John. But I will direct your attention rather to His treatment of the traitor Judas; both because it is not so commonly referred to, and, also, because if there was a being in the whole world whom one might suppose to be cast out of His presence as hateful and reprobate, it was he who He foresaw would betray Him. Yet we shall find that even this wretched man was followed and encompassed by His serene though grave regard till the very hour he betrayed Him.

Judas was in darkness and hated the light, and "went to his own place;" yet he found it, not by the mere force of certain natural principles working out their inevitable results—by some unfeeling fate, which sentences the wicked to hell—but by a Judge who surveys him from head to foot, who searches him through and through, to see if there is any ray of hope, any latent spark of faith; who pleads with him again and again, and, at length abandoning him, mourns over him the while with the wounded affection of a friend rather than the severity of the Judge of the whole earth. For instance, first a startling warning a year before his trial. "Have not I chosen you twelve, and one of you is a devil?" Then, when the time was come, the lowest act of abasement towards one who was soon to betray Him, and to suffer the unquenchable fire. "He riseth from supper, and .... poureth water into a bason, and began to wash the disciples' feet," [5] and Judas in the number. Then a second warning at the same time, or rather a sorrowful lament spoken as if to Himself, "Ye are not all clean." Then openly, "Verily, verily, I say unto you, that one of you shall betray Me." "The Son of

[5] John vi.70; xiii.4, 5.

man goeth as it is written of Him; but woe unto that man by whom the Son of man is betrayed! it had been good for that man if he had not been born. Then Judas, which betrayed Him, answered and said, Master, is it I? He said unto him, Thou hast said it." Lastly, when He was actually betrayed by him, "Friend, wherefore art thou come?" "Judas" (He addresses him by name), "betrayest thou the Son of man with a kiss?" [6] I am not attempting to reconcile His divine foreknowledge with this special and prolonged anxiety, this personal feeling towards Judas; but wish you only to dwell upon the latter, in order to observe what is given us by the revelation of Almighty God in the Gospels, viz., an acquaintance with His providential regard for *individuals*, making His sun to rise on the evil as well as on the good. And, in like manner doubtless, at the last day, the wicked and impenitent shall be condemned, not in a mass, but one by one—one by one, appearing each in his own turn before the righteous Judge, standing under the full glory of His countenance, carefully weighed in the balance and found wanting, dealt with, not indeed with a weak and wavering purpose, where God's justice claims satisfaction, yet, at the same time, with all the circumstantial solicitude and awful care of one who would fain make, if He could, the fruit of His passion more numerous than it is.

This solemn reflection may be further enforced by considering our Lord's behaviour towards strangers who came to Him. Judas was His friend; but *we* have never seen Him. How will He look, and how does He look upon us? Let His manner in the Gospels towards the multitude of men assure us. All-holy, Almighty as He is, and has shown Himself to be, yet in the midst of His Divine Majesty, He could display a tender interest in all who approached Him; as if He could not cast His eyes on any of His creatures without the overflowing affection of a parent for his child, regarding it with a full satisfaction, and simply desiring its happiness and highest good. Thus, when the rich young man came to him, it is said, "And Jesus beholding him, *loved him*, and said unto him, One thing thou lackest." When the Pharisees asked a sign, "He sighed deeply in His Spirit." At another time, "He looked round about on them"—as if on every one, to see if here or there perchance there might be an exception to the general unbelief, and to condemn, one by one, those who were guilty[7]—"He looked round about on them with

---

[6] Matt. xxvi.24, 25, 50; Luke xxii.48.
[7] Mark x.21; viii.12; iii.5.

anger, being grieved for the hardness of their hearts." Again, when a leper came to Him, He did not simply heal him, but, "moved with compassion, He put forth His hand." [8]

How gracious is this revelation of God's particular providence to those who seek Him! how gracious to those who have discovered that this world is but vanity, and who are solitary and isolated in themselves, whatever shadows of power and happiness surround them! The multitude, indeed, go on without these thoughts, either from insensibility, as not understanding their own wants, or changing from one idol to another, as each successively fails. But men of keener hearts would be overpowered by despondency, and would even loathe existence, did they suppose themselves under the mere operation of fixed laws, powerless to excite the pity or the attention of Him who has appointed them. What should they do especially, who are cast among persons unable to enter into their feelings, and thus strangers to them, though by long custom ever so much friends! or who have perplexities of mind they cannot explain to themselves, much less remove, and no one to help them; or who have affections and aspirations pent up within them, because they have not met with objects to which to devote them; or who are misunderstood by those around them, and find they have no words to set themselves right with them, or no principles in common by way of appeal; or who seem to themselves to be without place or purpose in the world, or to be in the way of others; or who have to follow their own sense of duty without advisers or supporters, nay, to resist the wishes and solicitations of superiors or relatives; or who have the burden of some painful secret, or of some incommunicable solitary grief! In all such cases the Gospel narrative supplies our very need, not simply presenting to us an unchangeable Creator to rely upon, but a compassionate Guardian, a discriminating Judge and Helper.

God beholds thee individually, whoever thou art. He "calls thee by thy name." He sees thee, and understands thee, as He made thee. He knows what is in thee, all thy own peculiar feelings and thoughts, thy dispositions and likings, thy strength and thy weakness. He views thee in thy day of rejoicing, and thy day of sorrow. He sympathizes in thy hopes and thy temptations. He interests Himself in all thy anxieties and remembrances, all the risings and fallings of thy spirit. He has numbered the very hairs of thy head and the cubits of thy stat-

---

[8] *Vide* also Matt. xix.26; Luke xxii.61; Mark iii.34; i.41.

ure. He compasses thee round and bears thee in His arms; He takes thee up and sets thee down. He notes thy very countenance, whether smiling or in tears, whether healthful or sickly. He looks tenderly upon thy hands and thy feet; He hears thy voice, the beating of thy heart, and thy very breathing. Thou dost not love thyself better than He loves thee. Thou canst not shrink from pain more than He dislikes thy bearing it; and if He puts it on thee, it is as thou wilt put it on thyself, if thou art wise, for a greater good afterwards. Thou art not only His creature (though for the very sparrows He has a care, and pitied the "much cattle" of Nineveh), thou art man redeemed and sanctified, His adopted son, favoured with a portion of that glory and blessedness which flows from Him everlastingly unto the Only-begotten. Thou art chosen to be His, even above thy fellows who dwell in the East and South. Thou wast one of those for whom Christ offered up His last prayer, and sealed it with His precious blood. What a thought is this, a thought almost too great for our faith! Scarce can we refrain from acting Sarah's part, when we bring it before us, so as to "laugh" from amazement and perplexity. What is man, what are we, what am I, that the Son of God should be so mindful of me? What am I, that He should have raised me from almost a devil's nature to that of an Angel's? that He should have changed my soul's original constitution, new-made me, who from my youth up have been a transgressor, and should Himself dwell personally in this very heart of mine, making me His temple? What am I, that God the Holy Ghost should enter into me, and draw up my thoughts heavenward "with plaints unutterable?"

These are the meditations which come upon the Christian to console him, while he is with Christ upon the holy mount. And, when he descends to his daily duties, they are still his inward strength, though he is not allowed to tell the vision to those around him. They make his countenance to shine, make him cheerful, collected, serene, and firm in the midst of all temptation, persecution, or bereavement. And with such thoughts before us, how base and miserable does the world appear in all its pursuits and doctrines! How truly miserable does it seem to seek good from the creature; to covet station, wealth, or credit; to choose for ourselves, in fancy, this or that mode of life; to affect the manners and fashions of the great; to spend our time in follies; to be discontented, quarrelsome, jealous or envious, censorious or resentful; fond of unprofitable talk, and eager for the news of the day; busy about public matters which concern us not; hot in the cause of this or that interest or party;

or set upon gain; or devoted to the increase of barren knowledge! And at the end of our days, when flesh and heart fail, what will be our consolation, though we have made ourselves rich, or have served an office, or been the first man among our equals, or have depressed a rival, or managed things our own way, or have settled splendidly, or have been intimate with the great, or have fared sumptuously, or have gained a name! Say, even if we obtain that which lasts longest, a place in history, yet, after all, what ashes shall we have eaten for bread! And, in that awful hour, when death is in sight, will He, whose eye is now so loving towards us, and whose hand falls on us so gently, will He acknowledge us any more? or, if He still speaks, will His voice have any power to stir us? rather will it not repel us, as it did Judas, by the very tenderness with which it would invite us to Him?

Let us then endeavour, by His grace, rightly to understand where we stand, and what He is towards us; most tender and pitiful, yet, for all His pity, not passing by the breadth of a single hair the eternal lines of truth, holiness, and justice; He who can condemn to the woe everlasting, though He weeps and laments beforehand, and who, when once the sentence of condemnation has gone forth, will wipe out altogether the remembrance of us, "and know us not." The tares were "bound in bundles" for the burning, indiscriminately, promiscuously, contemptuously. "Let us then fear, lest a promise being left us of entering into His rest, any of us should seem to come short of it."

TEARS OF CHRIST AT
THE GRAVE OF LAZARUS

*"Jesus said, Where have ye laid him? They said unto Him,
Lord, come and see. Jesus wept. Then said the Jews,
Behold how He loved him."*—John xi.34–36.

O N first reading these words the question naturally arises in the mind—*why* did our Lord weep at the grave of Lazarus? He knew He had power to raise him, why should He act the part of those who sorrow for the dead? In attempting any answer to this inquiry, we should ever remember that the thoughts of our Saviour's mind are far beyond our comprehension. Hardly do we enter into the feelings and meaning of men like ourselves, who are gifted with any special talent; even human philosophers or poets are obscure from the depth of their conceptions. What then must be the marvellous abyss of love and understanding in Him who, though partaker of our nature, is the Son of God?

This, indeed, is evident, as a matter of fact, on the face of the Scripture record, as any one may see who will take the trouble to inspect it. It is not, for instance, the text alone which raises a question; but the whole narrative, in which it occurs, exhibits our Saviour's conduct in various lights, which it is difficult for weak creatures, such as we are, properly to blend together.

When He first received the news of Lazarus's illness, "He abode two days still in the same place where He was." Then telling His disciples that Lazarus was dead, He said He was "glad for their sake that He was not there;" and said that He would "go and awaken him out of sleep." Then, when He was come to Bethany, where Lazarus dwelt, He was so moved by the sorrow of the Jews, that "He groaned in the spirit and was troubled." Lastly, in spite of His perturbation and weeping, presently He raised Lazarus.

I say, it is remarkable that such difficulties as these should lie on the face of Scripture, quite independently of those arising from the comparison of the texts in question with the doctrine of His divine nature. We know, indeed, there are insuperable mysteries involved in the union of His divine with His human attributes, which seem incompatible with each other; for instance, how He should be ever-blessed, and yet weep—all-knowing, yet apparently ignorant; but, without entering into the consideration of the mysteries of faith, commonly so called, it is worth inquiring whether the very surface of the sacred history does not contain seeming inconsistencies, of a nature to prepare us for such other difficulties as may lie from a deeper comparison of history with doctrine.

As another instance of the discrepancy I speak of, consider our Saviour's words according to the received versions, "Sleep on now, and take your rest;" and immediately after, "Rise, let us be going." [1]

So again, "He that hath no sword, let him sell his garment and buy one;" then follows, "Lord, behold, here are two swords. And He said, It is enough;" lastly, when Peter used his sword, "Put up again thy sword into his place: for all they that take the sword shall perish with the sword." [2]

I am not saying that we cannot possibly remove any part of the seeming opposition between such passages, but only that on the whole there is quite enough in the narrative to show that He who speaks is not one whose thoughts it is easy to get possession of; that it is no light matter to put one's-self, even in part, into the position of His mind, and to state under what feelings and motives He said this or that; in a word, I wish to impress upon you, that our Saviour's words are not of a nature to be heard once and no more, but that to understand them we must feed upon them, and live in them, as if by little and little growing into their meaning.

It would be well if we understood the necessity of this more than we do. It is very much the fashion at present to regard the Saviour of the world in an irreverent and unreal way—as a mere idea or vision; to speak of Him so narrowly and unfruitfully, as if we only knew of His name; though Scripture has set Him before us in His actual sojourn on earth, in His gestures, words, and deeds, in order that we may have that on which to fix our eyes. And till we learn to do this, to leave off vague statements about His love, His willingness to receive the sinner, His imparting repentance and spiritual aid, and the like, and view Him in His particular and actual works, set before us in Scripture, surely we have not derived from the Gospels that very

[1] Matt. xxvi.45, 46.   [2] Luke xxii.36, 38; Matt. xxvi.52.

benefit which they are intended to convey. Nay, we are in some danger, perhaps, even as regards our faith; for, it is to be feared, while the thought of Christ is but a creation of our minds, it may gradually be changed or fade away, it may become defective or perverted; whereas, when we contemplate Christ as manifested in the Gospels, the Christ who exists therein, external to our own imaginings, and who is as really a living being, and sojourned on earth as truly as any of us, then we shall at length believe in Him with a conviction, a confidence, and an entireness, which can no more be annihilated than the belief in our senses. It is impossible for a Christian mind to meditate on the Gospels, without feeling, beyond all manner of doubt, that He who is the subject of them is God; but it is very possible to speak in a vague way of His love towards us, and to use the name of Christ, yet not at all to realize that He is the Living Son of the Father, or to have any anchor for our faith within us, so as to be fortified against the risk of future defection.

I will say a few words then under this impression, and with the reverent thoughts before me with which I began, by way of comment on our Saviour's weeping at Lazarus's grave; or, rather, I will suggest what each of you may, please God, improve for himself.

What led our Lord to weep over the dead, who could at a word restore him, nay, had it in purpose so to do?

1. First of all, as the context informs us, He wept from very sympathy with the grief of others. "When Jesus saw Mary weeping, and the Jews also weeping which came with her, He groaned in the spirit, and was troubled." It is the very nature of compassion or sympathy, as the word implies, to "rejoice with those who rejoice, and weep with those who weep." We know it is so with men; and God tells us He also is compassionate, and full of tender mercy. Yet we do not well know what this means, for how can God rejoice or grieve? By the very perfection of His nature Almighty God cannot show sympathy, at least to the comprehension of beings of such limited minds as ours. He, indeed, is hid from us; but if we were allowed to see Him, how could we discern in the Eternal and Unchangeable signs of sympathy? Words and works of sympathy He does display to us; but it is the very sight of sympathy in another that affects and comforts the sufferer more even than the fruits of it. Now we cannot see God's sympathy; and the Son of God, though feeling for us as great compassion as His Father, did not show it to us while He remained in His Father's bosom. But when He took flesh and appeared on earth, He showed us the Godhead in a new

manifestation. He invested Himself with a new set of attributes, those of our flesh, taking into Him a human soul and body, in order that thoughts, feelings, affections might be His, which could respond to ours and certify to us His tender mercy. When, then, our Saviour weeps from sympathy at Mary's tears, let us not say it is the love of a man overcome by natural feeling. It is the love of God, the bowels of compassion of the Almighty and Eternal, condescending to show it as we are capable of receiving it, in the form of human nature.

Jesus wept, therefore, not merely from the deep thoughts of His understanding, but from spontaneous tenderness; from the gentleness and mercy, the encompassing loving-kindness and exuberant fostering affection of the Son of God for His own work, the race of man. Their tears touched Him at once, as their miseries had brought Him down from heaven. His ear was open to them, and the sound of weeping went at once to His heart.

2. But next, we may suppose (if it is allowable to conjecture), that His pity, thus spontaneously excited, was led forward to dwell on the various circumstances in man's condition which excite pity. It was awakened, and began to look around upon the miseries of the world. What was it He saw ? He saw visibly displayed the *victory of death*; a mourning multitude—everything present which might waken sorrow except him who was the chief object of it. He was not—a stone marked the place where he lay. Martha and Mary, whom He had known and loved in their brother's company, now solitary, approached Him, first one and then the other, in far other mood and circumstance than heretofore—in deep affliction! in faith indeed and resignation, yet, apparently, with somewhat of a tender complaint: "Lord, if Thou hadst been here, my brother had not died." Such has been the judgment passed, or the doubt raised, concerning Him, in the breast of the creature in every age. Men have seen sin and misery around them, and, whether in faith or unbelief, have said, "If Thou hadst been here," if Thou hadst interfered, it might have been otherwise. Here, then, was the Creator surrounded by the works of His hands, who adored Him indeed, yet seemed to ask why He suffered what He Himself had made so to be marred. Here was the Creator of the world at a scene of death, seeing the issue of His gracious handiwork. Would not He revert in thought to the hour of creation, when He went forth from the bosom of the Father to bring all things into existence? There had been a day when He had looked upon the work of His love, and seen that it was "very

good." Whence had the good been turned to evil, the fine gold become dim? "An enemy had done this." Why it was allowed, and how achieved, was a secret with Him; a secret from all who were about Him, as it is a secret to us at this day. Here He had incommunicable thoughts with His Eternal Father. He would not tell them why it was; He chose another course for taking away their doubts and complaints. "He opened not His mouth," but He wrought wondrously. What He has done for all believers, revealing His atoning death yet not explaining it, this He did for Martha and Mary also, proceeding to the grave in silence, to raise their brother, while they complained that he had been allowed to die.

Here then, I say, were abundant sources for His grief (if we may be permitted to trace them), in the contrast between Adam, in the day in which he was created, innocent and immortal, and man as the devil had made him, full of the poison of sin and the breath of the grave; and again, in the timid complaint of His sorrowing friends that that change had been permitted. And though He was about to turn back the scene of sorrow into joy again, yet, after all, Lazarus one day must die again—He was but delaying the fulfilment of His own decree. A stone lay upon him now; and, though he was raised from the grave, yet, by His own inscrutable law, one day he must lie down again in it. It was a respite, not a resurrection.

3. Here I have suggested another thought which admits of being dwelt upon. Christ was come to do a deed of mercy, and it was a secret in His own breast. All the love which He felt for Lazarus was a secret from others. He was conscious to Himself He loved him; but none could tell but He how earnest that affection was. Peter, when his love for Christ was doubted, found a relief in an appeal to Himself: "Lord, Thou knowest all things: Thou knowest that I love Thee."[3] But Christ had no earthly friend who could be His confidant in this matter; and, as His thoughts turned on Lazarus, and His heart yearned towards him, was He not in Joseph's case, who not in grief, but from the very fulness of his soul, and his desolateness in a heathen land, when his brethren stood before him, "sought where to weep," as if his own tears were his best companions, and had in them a sympathy to soothe that pain which none could share? Was He not in the case of a parent hanging over an infant, and weeping upon it, from the very thought of its helplessness and insensibility to the love poured out upon it? But the

[3] John xxi. 17.

parent weeps from the feeling of her weakness to defend it; knowing that what is now a child must grow up and take its own course, and (whether for earthly or heavenly good) must depend, not on her, but on the Creator and on itself. Christ's was a different contemplation; yet attended with its own peculiar emotion. I mean the feeling that He *had* power to raise up Lazarus. Joseph wept, as having a secret, not only of the past, but of the future;—of good in store as well as of evil done—of good which it was in his own power to confer. And our Lord and Saviour knew that, while all seemed so dreary and hopeless, in spite of the tears and laments of his friends, in spite of the corpse four days old, of the grave and the stone which was upon it, He had a spell which could overcome death, and He was about to use it. Is there any time more affecting than when you are about to break good news to a friend who has been stricken down by tidings of ill?

4. Alas! there were other thoughts still to call forth His tears. This marvellous benefit to the forlorn sisters, how was it to be attained? at His own cost. Joseph knew he could bring joy to his brethren, but at no sacrifice of his own. Christ was bringing life to the dead by His own death. His disciples would have dissuaded Him from going into Judea, *lest* the Jews should kill Him. Their apprehension was fulfilled. He went to raise Lazarus, and the fame of that miracle was the immediate cause of His seizure and crucifixion. This He knew beforehand, He saw the prospect before Him; He saw Lazarus raised; the supper in Martha's house; Lazarus sitting at table; joy on all sides of Him; Mary honouring her Lord on this festive occasion by the outpouring of the very costly ointment upon His feet; the Jews crowding not only to see Him, but Lazarus also; His triumphant entry into Jerusalem; the multitude shouting Hosanna; the people testifying to the raising of Lazarus; the Greeks, who had come up to worship at the feast, earnest to see Him; the children joining in the general joy; and then the Pharisees plotting against Him, Judas betraying Him, His friends deserting Him, and the cross receiving Him. These things doubtless, among a multitude of thoughts unspeakable, passed over His mind. He felt that Lazarus was wakening to life at His own sacrifice; that He was descending into the grave which Lazarus left. He felt that Lazarus was to live and He to die; the appearance of things was to be reversed; the feast was to be kept in Martha's house, but the last passover of sorrow remained for Him. And He knew that this reverse was altogether voluntary with Him. He had come down from His Father's bosom to be

an Atonement of blood for all sin, and thereby to raise all believers from the grave, as He was then about to raise Lazarus;
and to raise them, not for a time, but for eternity; and now the
sharp trial lay before Him, through which He was to "open the
kingdom of heaven to all believers." Contemplating then the
fulness of His purpose while now going about a single act of
mercy, He said to Martha, "I am the Resurrection and the Life:
he that believeth in Me, though he were dead, yet shall he live,
and whosoever liveth and believeth in Me, shall never die."

Let us take to ourselves these comfortable thoughts, both in
the contemplation of our own death, or upon the death of our
friends. Wherever faith in Christ is, there is Christ Himself. He
said to Martha, "Believest thou this?" Wherever there is a heart
to answer, "Lord, I believe," there Christ is present. There our
Lord vouchsafes to stand, though unseen—whether over the
bed of death or over the grave; whether we ourselves are sinking
or those who are dear to us. Blessed be His name! nothing can
rob us of this consolation: we will be as certain, through His
grace, that He is standing over us in love, as though we saw
Him. We will not, after our experience of Lazarus's history,
doubt an instant that He is thoughtful about us. He knows the
beginnings of our illness, though He keeps at a distance. He
knows when to remain away and when to draw near. He notes
down the advances of it, and the stages. He tells truly when His
friend Lazarus is sick and when he sleeps. We all have experience of this in the narrative before us, and henceforth, so be it!
will never complain at the course of His providence. Only, we
will beg of Him an increase of faith;—a more lively perception
of the curse under which the world lies, and of our own personal demerits, a more understanding view of the mystery of
His Cross, a more devout and implicit reliance on the virtue of
it, and a more confident persuasion that He will never put upon
us more than we can bear, never afflict His brethren with any
woe except for their own highest benefit.

BODILY SUFFERING

*"I fill up that which is behind of the afflictions of Christ in my flesh
for His body's sake, which is the Church."*—Col. i.24.

Oᴜʀ Lord and Saviour Jesus Christ came by blood as well as
by water, not only as a Fount of grace and truth—the
source of spiritual light, joy, and salvation—but as a combatant
with Sin and Satan, who was "consecrated through suffering."
He was, as prophecy had marked Him out, "red in His apparel,
and His garments like Him that treadeth in the wine-fat;" or, in
the words of the Apostle, "He was clothed with a vesture
dipped in blood." It was the untold sufferings of the Eternal
Word in our nature, His body dislocated and torn, His blood
poured out, His soul violently separated by a painful death,
which has put away from us the wrath of Him whose love sent
Him for that very purpose. This only was our Atonement; no
one shared in the work. He "trod the wine-press alone, and of
the people there was none with Him." When lifted up upon the
cursed tree, He fought with all the hosts of evil, and conquered
by suffering.

Thus, in a most mysterious way, all that is needful for this
sinful world, the life of our souls, the regeneration of our nature, all that is most joyful and glorious, hope, light, peace,
spiritual freedom, holy influences, religious knowledge and
strength, all flow from a fount of blood. A work of blood is our
salvation; and we, as we would be saved, must draw near and
gaze upon it in faith, and accept it as the way to heaven. We
must take Him, who thus suffered, as our guide; we must embrace His sacred feet, and follow Him. No wonder, then, should
we receive on ourselves some drops of the sacred agony which
bedewed His garments; no wonder, should we be sprinkled
with the sorrows which He bore in expiation of our sins!

And so it has ever been in very deed; to approach Him has
been, from the first, to be partaker, more or less, in His sufferings; I do not say in the case of every individual who believes in
Him, but as regards the more conspicuous, the more favoured,
His choice instruments, and His most active servants; that is, it

has been the lot of the Church, on the whole, and of those, on the whole, who had been most like Him, as Rulers, Intercessors, and Teachers of the Church. He, indeed, alone meritoriously; they, because they have been near Him. Thus, immediately upon His birth, He brought the sword upon the infants of His own age at Bethlehem. His very shadow, cast upon a city, where He did not abide, was stained with blood. His Blessed Mother had not clasped Him to her breast for many weeks, ere she was warned of the penalty of that fearful privilege: "Yea, a sword shall pierce through thy own soul also." [1] Virtue went out of Him; but the water and the blood flowed together as afterwards from His pierced side. From among the infants He took up in His arms to bless, is said to have gone forth a chief martyr of the generation after Him. Most of His Apostles passed through life-long sufferings to a violent death. In particular, when the favoured brothers, James and John, came to Him with a request that they might sit beside Him in His kingdom, He plainly stated this connection between nearness to Him and affliction. "Are ye able," He said, "to drink of the cup that I shall drink of, and to be baptized with the baptism that I am baptized with?" [2] As if He said, "Ye cannot have the sacraments of grace without the painful figures of them. The Cross, when imprinted on your foreheads, will draw blood. You shall receive, indeed, the baptism of the Spirit, and the cup of My communion, but it shall be with the attendant pledges of My cup of agony, and My baptism of blood." Elsewhere He speaks the same language to all who would partake the benefits of His death and passion: "Whosoever doth not bear his cross, and come after Me, cannot be My disciple." [3]

Accordingly, His Apostles frequently remind us of this necessary, though mysterious appointment, and bid us "think it not strange concerning the fiery trial which is to try us, as though some strange thing happened unto us, but to rejoice in having communion with the sufferings of Christ." [4] St. Paul teaches us the same lesson in the text, in which he speaks of taking up the remnant of Christ's sorrows, as some precious mantle dropt from the Cross, and wearing it for His sake. "I rejoice in my sufferings for you, and fill up in my flesh what remains of the afflictions of Christ for His body's sake, that is, the Church." [5] And though he is speaking especially of persecution and other sufferings borne in the cause of the Gospel, yet it is our great

---

[1] Luke ii.35. [2] Matt. xx.22. [3] Luke xiv.27.
[4] 1 Pet. iv.12, 13. [5] *Vide* also 2 Cor. iv.10.

privilege, as Scripture tells us, that all pain and trouble, borne in faith and patience, will be accounted as marks of Christ, grace-tokens from the absent Saviour, and will be accepted and rewarded for His sake at the last day. It declares generally, "When thou passest through the waters, I will be with thee; and through the rivers, they shall not overflow thee: when thou walkest through the fire, thou shalt not be burned; neither shall the flame kindle upon thee." "Our light affliction, which is but for a moment, worketh for us a far more exceeding and eternal weight of glory." [6]

Thus the Gospel, which has shed light in so many ways upon the state of this world, has aided especially our view of the *sufferings* to which human nature is subjected; turning a punishment into a privilege, in the case of all pain, and especially of bodily pain, which is the most mysterious of all. Sorrow, anxiety, and disappointment are more or less connected with sin and sinners; but bodily pain is involuntary for the most part, stretching over the world by some external irresistible law, reaching to children who have never actually sinned, and to the brute animals, who are strangers to Adam's nature, while in its manifestations it is far more piteous and distressing than any other suffering. It is the lot of all of us, sooner or later; and that, perhaps in a measure which it would be appalling and wrong to anticipate, whether from disease, or from the casualties of life. And all of us at length must die; and death is generally ushered in by disease, and ends in that separation of soul and body, which itself may, in some cases, involve peculiar pain.

Worldly men put such thoughts aside as gloomy; they can neither deny nor avert the prospect before them; and they are wise, on their own principles, not to embitter the present by anticipating it. But Christians may bear to look at it without undue apprehension; for this very infliction, which most touches the heart and imagination, has (as I have said) been invested by Almighty God with a new and comfortable light, as being the medium of His choicest mercies towards us. Pain is no longer a curse, a necessary evil to be undergone with a dry submission or passive endurance—it may be considered even as a blessing of the Gospel, and being a blessing, admits of being met well or ill. In the way of nature, indeed, it seems to shut out the notion of duty, as if so masterful a discipline from without superseded the necessity or opportunity of self-mastery; but now that "Christ hath suffered in the flesh," we are bound "to arm

[6] Is. xliii.2; 2 Cor. iv.17.

ourselves with the same mind," and to obey, as He did, amid suffering.

In what follows, I shall remark briefly, first, on the natural effect of pain upon the mind; and next, upon the remedies and correctives of that effect which the knowledge of the Gospel supplies.

1. Now, as to its effect upon the mind, let it be well understood that it has no sanctifying influence in itself. Bad men are made worse by it. This should be borne in mind, lest we deceive ourselves; for sometimes we speak (at least the poor often so speak) as though present hardship and suffering were in some sense a ground of confidence in themselves as to our future prospects, whether as expiating our sins or bringing our hearts nearer to God. Nay, even the more religious among us may be misled to think that pain makes them better than it really does; for the effect of it at length, on any but very proud or ungovernable tempers, is to cause a languor and composure of mind, which looks like resignation, while it necessarily throws our reason upon the especial *thought* of God, our only stay in such times of trial. Doubtless it does really benefit the Christian, and in no scanty measure; and he may thank God who thus blesses it; only let him be cautious of *measuring* his spiritual state by the particular exercise of faith and love in his heart at the time, especially if that exercise be limited to the affections themselves, and have no opportunity of showing itself in works. St. Paul speaks of chastisement "yielding *afterwards* the peaceable fruit of righteousness,"[7] formed indeed and ripened at the moment, but manifested in due season. This may be the real fruit of the suffering of a death-bed, even though it may not have time to show itself to others before the Christian departs hence. Surely we may humbly hope that it perfects habits hitherto but partially formed, and blends the several graces of the Spirit more entirely. Such is the issue of it in *established* Christians;—but it *may* possibly effect nothing so blessed. Nay, in the case of those who have followed Christ with but a half heart, it may be a trial too strong for their feebleness, and may overpower them. This is a dreadful reflection for those who put off the day of repentance. Well does our Church pray for us: "Suffer us not, at our last hour, for any pains of death to fall from Thee!" As for unbelievers, we know how it affects them, from such serious passages of Scripture as the following: "They gnawed their tongues for pain, and blasphemed the God of

[7] Heb. xii.11.

heaven because of their pains and their sores, and repented not of their deeds."[8]

Nay, I would go so far as to say, not only that pain does not commonly improve us, but that without care it has a strong tendency to do our souls harm, viz., by making us selfish; an effect produced, even when it does us good in other ways. Weak health, for instance, instead of opening the heart, often makes a man supremely careful of his bodily ease and well-being. Men find an excuse in their infirmities for some extraordinary attention to their comforts; they consider they may fairly consult, on all occasions, their own convenience rather than that of another. They indulge their wayward wishes, allow themselves in indolence when they really might exert themselves, and think they may be fretful because they are weak. They become querulous, self-willed, fastidious, and egotistical. Bystanders, indeed, should be very cautious of thinking any particular sufferer to be thus minded, because, after all, sick people have a multitude of feelings which they cannot explain to any one else, and are often in the right in those matters in which they appear to others most fanciful or unreasonable. Yet this does not interfere with the correctness of my remark on the whole.

Take another instance under very different circumstances. If bodily suffering can be presented under distinct aspects, it is in the lassitude of a sick-bed and in the hardships of the soldier's life. Yet of the latter we find selfishness almost a proverbial characteristic. Surely the life of soldiers on service is a very school of generosity and self-neglect, if rightly understood, and is used as such by the noble and high-principled; yet here, a low and carnal mind, instead of profiting by its advantages, will yield to the temptation of referring everything that befalls it to its own comfort and profit. To secure its own interests, will become enshrined within it as its main duty, and with the greater plausibility, inasmuch as there is a sense in which it may really be so accounted. Others (it will suggest) must take care of themselves; it is a folly and weakness to think of them; there are but few chances of safety; the many must suffer, some unto death; it is wisdom to struggle for life and comfort, and to dismiss the thought of others. Alas! instances occur, every now and then, in the experience of life, which show that such thoughts and feelings are not peculiar to any one class of men, but are the actuating principles of the multitude. If an alarm of

[8] Rev. xvi. 10, 11.

danger be given amid a crowd, the general eagerness for safety leads men to act towards each other with utter unconcern, if not with frantic cruelty. There are stories told of companies of men finding themselves at sea with scanty provisions, and of the shocking deeds which followed, when each was struggling to preserve his own life.

The natural effect, then, of pain and fear, is to individualize us in our own minds, to fix our thoughts on ourselves, to make us selfish. It is through pain, chiefly, that we realize to ourselves even our bodily organs; a frame entirely without painful sensations is (as it were) one whole without parts, and prefigures that future spiritual body which shall be the portion of the Saints. And to this we most approximate in our youth, when we are not sensible that we are compacted of gross terrestrial matter, as advancing years convince us. The young reflect little upon themselves; they gaze around them, and live out of doors, and say they have souls, little understanding their words. "They rejoice in their youth." This, then, is the effect of suffering, that it arrests us: that it puts, as it were, a finger upon us to ascertain for us our own individuality. But it does no more than this; if such a warning does not lead us through the stirrings of our conscience heavenwards, it does but imprison us in ourselves and make us selfish.

2. Here, then, it is that the Gospel finds us; heirs to a visitation, which, sooner or later, comes upon us, turning our thoughts from outward objects, and so tempting us to idolize self, to the dishonour of that God whom we ought to worship, and the neglect of man whom we should love as ourselves. Thus it finds us, and it obviates this danger, not by removing pain, but by giving it new associations. Pain, which by nature leads us only to ourselves, carries on the Christian mind from the thought of self to the contemplation of Christ, His passion, His merits, and His pattern; and, thence, further to that united company of sufferers who follow Him and "are what He is in this world." He is the great Object of our faith; and, while we gaze upon Him, we learn to forget ourselves.

Surely that is not the most fearful and hateful of evils, here below, however trying to the flesh, which Christ underwent voluntarily. No one chooses evil for its own sake, but for the greater good wrought out through it. He underwent it as for ends greater than the immediate removal of it, "not grudgingly or of necessity," but cheerfully doing God's will, as the Gospel history sets before us. When His time was come, we are told, "He steadfastly set His face to go to Jerusalem." His disciples

said, "Master, the Jews of late sought to stone Thee, and goest
Thou thither again?" but He persisted. Again, He said to Judas,
"That thou doest, do quickly." He proceeded to the garden beyond Cedron, though Judas knew the place; and when the band
of officers came to seize Him, "He went forth, and said unto
them, I am He." [9] And with what calmness and majesty did He
bear His sufferings, when they came upon Him, though by His
agony in the garden He showed He fully felt their keenness!
The Psalmist, in his prediction of them, says, "I am poured out
like water, and all my bones are out of joint; my heart is like
wax, it is melted;" [10] describing, as it would seem, that sinking
of spirit and enfeebling of nerve which severe pain causes. Yet,
in the midst of distress which seemed to preclude the opportunity of obedience, He was "about His Father's business," even
more diligently than when in His childhood He asked questions
of the doctors in the Temple; not thinking to be merely passive
under the trial, but accounting it as if a great occasion for a
noble and severe surrender of Himself to His Father's will.
Thus He "learned obedience by the things that He suffered."
Consider the deep and serene compassion which led Him to
pray for those who crucified Him; His solicitous care of His
Mother; and His pardoning words addressed to the robber who
suffered with Him. And so, when He said, "It is finished," He
showed that He was still contemplating, with a clear intellect,
"the travail of His soul, and was satisfied;" and in the solemn
surrender of Himself into His Father's hand, He showed where
His mind rested in the midst of its darkness. Even when He
seemed to be thinking of Himself, and said, "I thirst," He really
was regarding the words of prophecy, and was bent on vindicat-
ing, to the very letter, the divine announcements concerning
Him. Thus, upon the Cross itself, we discern in Him the mercy
of a Messenger from heaven, the love and grace of a Saviour,
the dutifulness of a Son, the faith of a created nature, and the
zeal of a servant of God. His mind was stayed upon His Father's
sovereign will and infinite perfections, yet could pass, without
effort, to the claim of filial duty, or the need of an individual
sinner. Six out of His seven last words were words of faith and
love. For one instant a horrible dread overwhelmed Him, when
He seemed to ask why God had forsaken Him. Doubtless "that
voice was for our sakes;" as when He made mention of His
thirst; and, like the other, was taken from inspired prophecy.
Perhaps it was intended to set before us an example of a special

---

[9] Luke ix.51; John xi.8; xiii.27; xviii.2, 4, 5.   [10] Ps. xxii.14.

trial to which human nature is subject, whatever was the real and inscrutable manner of it in Him, who was all along supported by an inherent Divinity; I mean the trial of sharp agony, hurrying the mind on to vague terrors and strange inexplicable thoughts; and is, therefore, graciously recorded for our benefit, in the history of His death, "who was tempted, in all points, like as we are, yet without sin." [11]

Such, then, were our Lord's sufferings, voluntarily undergone, and ennobled by an active obedience; themselves the centre of our hopes and worship, yet borne without thought of self, towards God and for man. And who, among us, habitually dwells upon them, but is led, without deliberate purpose, by the very warmth of gratitude and adoring love, to attempt bearing his own inferior trials in the same heavenly mind? Who does not see that to bear pain well is to meet it courageously, not to shrink or waver, but to pray for God's help, then to look at it steadfastly, to summon what nerve we have of mind and body, to receive its attack, and to bear up against it (while strength is given us) as against some visible enemy in close combat? Who will not acknowledge that, when sent to us, we must make its presence (as it were) our own voluntary act, by the cheerful and ready concurrence of our own will with the will of God? Nay, who is there but must own that with Christ's sufferings before us, pain and tribulation are, after all, not only the most blessed, but even the most congruous attendants upon those who are called to inherit the benefit of them? Most congruous, I say, not as though necessary, but as most natural and befitting, harmonizing most fully, with the main Object in the group of sacred wonders on which the Church is called to gaze. Who, on the other hand, does not at least perceive that all the glare and gaudiness of this world, its excitements, its keenly-pursued goods, its successes and its transports, its pomps and its luxuries, are not in character with that pale and solemn scene which faith must ever have in its eye? What Christian will not own that to "reign as kings," and to be "full," is not his calling; so as to derive comfort in the hour of sickness, or bereavement, or other affliction, from the thought that he is now in his own place, if he be Christ's, in his true home, the sepulchre in which his Lord was laid? So deeply have His Saints felt this, that when times were peaceful, and the Church was in safety, they could not rest in the lap of ease, and have secured to themselves hardnesses, lest the world should corrupt them. They could not

[11] Heb. iv.15.

bear to see the much-enduring Paul adding to his necessary tribulations a self-inflicted chastisement of the flesh, and yet allow themselves to live delicately, and fare sumptuously every day. They saw the image of Christ reflected in tears and blood, in the glorious company of the Apostles, the goodly fellowship of the Prophets, and the noble army of Martyrs; they read in prophecy of the doom of the Church, as "a woman fed by God in the wilderness," [12] and her witnesses as "clothed in sackcloth;" and they could not believe that they were meant for nothing more than to enjoy the pleasures of this life, however innocent and moderate might be their use of them. Without deciding about their neighbours, they felt themselves called to higher things; their own sense of the duty became the sanction and witness of it. They considered that God, at least, would afflict them in His love, if they spared themselves ever so much. The thorn in the flesh, the buffetings of Satan, the bereavement of their eyes, these were their portion; and, in common prudence, were there no higher thought, they could not live out of time and measure with these expected visitations. With no superstitious alarms, or cowardly imaginations, or senseless hurrying into difficulty or trial, but calmly and in faith, they surrendered themselves into His hands, who had told them in His inspired word that affliction was to be their familiar food; till at length they gained such distaste for the luxuries of life as to be impatient of them from their very fulness of grace.

Even in these days, when the "fine gold has become dim," such has been the mind of those we most revere. [13] But such was it especially in primitive times. It was the temper, too, of those Apostles who were removed, more than their brethren, from the world's buffetings; as if the prospect of suffering afterwards were no ground of dispensation for a present self-inflicted discipline, but rather demanded it. St. James the Less was Bishop of Jerusalem, and was highly venerated for his uprightness by the unbelieving Jews among whom he lived unmolested. We are told that he drank no wine nor strong drink, nor did he eat any animal food, nor indulge in the luxury of the bath. "So often was he in the Temple on his knees, that they were thin and hard by his continual supplication." [14] Thus he kept his

[12] *Vide* Rev. xii.6; xi.3.

[13] "It is a most miserable state for a man to have everything according to his desire, and quietly to enjoy the pleasures of life. There needs no more to expose him to eternal misery."—Bishop Wilson—*Sacra Privata*, Wednesday.

[14] Euseb. Hist., ii, 23.

"loins girded about, and his lamp burning," for the blessed martyrdom which was to end his course. Could it be otherwise? How could the great Apostle, sitting at home by his Lord's decree, "nourish his heart," as he calls it, "as for the slaughter?" How could he eat, and drink, and live as other men, when "the Ark, and Israel, and Judah were in tents," encamped in the open fields, and one by one, God's chosen warriors were falling before the brief triumph of Satan! How could he be "delicate on the earth, and wanton," when Paul and Barnabas, Peter, too, and John were in stripes and prisons, in labours and perils, in hunger and thirst, in cold and nakedness! Stephen had led the army of Martyrs in Jerusalem itself, which was his own post of service. James, the brother of John, had followed him in the same city; he first of the Apostles tasting our Lord's cup, who had unwittingly asked to drink it. And if this was the feeling of the Apostles, when in temporary safety, why is it not ours, who altogether live at ease, except that we have not faith enough to realize what is past? Could we see the Cross upon Calvary, and the list of sufferers who resisted unto blood in the times that followed it, is it possible that we should feel surprise when pain overtook us, or impatience at its continuance? Is it strange though we are smitten by ever so new a plague? Is it grievous that the Cross presses on one nerve or limb ever so many years till hope of relief is gone? Is it, indeed, not possible with the Apostle to rejoice in "bearing in our body the marks of the Lord Jesus?" And much more, can we, for very shame's sake, suffer ourselves to be troubled at what is but ordinary pain, to be irritated or saddened, made gloomy or anxious by inconveniences which never could surprise or unsettle those who had studied and understood their place as servants of a crucified Lord?

Let us, then, determine with cheerful hearts to sacrifice unto the Lord our God our comforts and pleasures, however innocent, when He calls for them, whether for the purposes of His Church, or in His own inscrutable Providence. Let us lend to Him a few short hours of present ease, and we shall receive our own with abundant usury in the day of His coming. There is a Treasury in heaven stored with such offerings as the natural man abhors; with sighs and tears, wounds and blood, torture and death. The Martyrs first began the contribution, and we all may follow them; all of us, for every suffering, great or little, may, like the widow's mite, be sacrificed in faith to Him who sent it. Christ gave us the words of consecration, when He for an ensample said, "Thy will be done." Henceforth, as the

Apostle speaks, we may "glory in tribulation," as the seed of future glory.

Meanwhile, let us never forget in all we suffer, that, properly speaking, our own sin is the cause of it, and it is only by Christ's mercy that we are allowed to range ourselves at His side. We who are children of wrath, are made through Him children of grace; and our pains—which are in themselves but foretastes of hell—are changed by the sprinkling of His blood into a preparation for heaven.

THE HUMILIATION OF
THE ETERNAL SON

*"Who, in the days of His flesh, when He had offered up prayers and
supplications with strong crying and tears unto Him that was able
to save Him from death, and was heard in that He feared,
though He were a Son, yet learned He obedience
by the things which He suffered."*—Heb. v.7, 8.

T HE chief mystery of our holy faith is the humiliation of the
Son of God to temptation and suffering, as described in
this passage of Scripture. In truth, it is a more overwhelming
mystery even than that which is involved in the doctrine of the
Trinity. I say, more overwhelming, not greater—for we cannot
measure the more and the less in subjects utterly incomprehensible and divine; but with more in it to perplex and subdue our
minds. When the mystery of the Trinity is set before us, we see
indeed that it is quite beyond our reason; but, at the same time,
it is no wonder that human language should be unable to convey, and human intellect to receive, truths relating to the incommunicable and infinite essence of Almighty God. But the
mystery of the Incarnation relates, in part, to subjects more
level with our reason; it lies not only in the manner how God
and man is one Christ, but in the very fact that so it is. We think
we know of God so much as this, that He is altogether separate
from imperfection and infirmity; yet we are told that the Eternal Son has taken into Himself a creature's nature, which
henceforth became as much one with Him, as much belonged
to Him, as the divine attributes and powers which He had ever
had. The mystery lies as much in what we think we know, as in
what we do not know. Reflect, for instance, upon the language
of the text. The Son of God, who "had glory with the Father"
from everlasting, was found, at a certain time, in human flesh,
offering up prayers and supplications to Him, crying out and
weeping, and exercising obedience in suffering! Do not suppose, from my thus speaking, that I would put the doctrine before you as a hard saying, as a stumbling-block, and a yoke of

bondage, to which you must perforce submit, however unwillingly. Far be it from us to take such unthankful account of a dispensation which has brought us salvation! Those who in the Cross of Christ see the Atonement for sin, cannot choose but glory in it; and its mysteriousness does but make them glory in it the more. They boast of it before men and Angels, before an unbelieving world, and before fallen spirits; with no confusion of face, but with a reverent boldness they confess this miracle of grace, and cherish it in their creed, though it gains them but the contempt and derision of the proud and ungodly.

And as the doctrine of our Lord's humiliation is most mysterious, so the very surface of the narrative in which it is contained is mysterious also, as exciting wonder, and impressing upon us our real ignorance of the nature, manner, and causes of it. Take, for instance, His temptation. Why was it undergone at all, seeing our redemption is ascribed to His death, not to it? Why was it so long? What took place during it? What was Satan's particular object in tempting Him? How came Satan to have such power over Him as to be able to transport Him from place to place? and what was the precise result of the temptation? These and many other questions admit of no satisfactory solution. There is something remarkable too in the period of it, being the same as that of the long fasts of Moses and Elijah, and of His own abode on earth after His resurrection. A like mystery again is cast around that last period of His earthly mission. Then He was engaged we know not how, except that He appeared, from time to time, to His Apostles; of the forty days of His temptation we know still less, only that "He did eat nothing," and "was with the wild beasts." [1]

Again, there is something of mystery in the connection of His temptation with the descent of the Holy Ghost upon Him on His baptism. After the voice from heaven had proclaimed, "This is My beloved Son, in whom I am well pleased," "*immediately*," as St. Mark says, "the Spirit *driveth* Him into the wilderness." As if there were some connection, beyond our understanding, between His baptism and temptation, the first act of the Holy Spirit is forthwith to "drive Him" (whatever is meant by the word) into the wilderness. Observe, too, that it was almost from this solemn recognition, "This is My beloved Son," that the Devil took up the temptation, "*If* Thou be the Son of God, command that these stones be made bread;" [2] yet what his thoughts and designs were we cannot even conjec-

[1] Luke iv.2; Mark i.13.   [2] Matt. iv.3.

ture. All we see is a renewal, apparently, of Adam's temptation, in the person of the "second Man."

In like manner, questions might be asked concerning His descent into hell, which could as little be solved, with our present limited knowledge of the nature and means of His gracious Economy.

I bring together these various questions in order to impress upon you our depth of ignorance on the entire subject under review. The Dispensation of mercy is revealed to us in its great and blessed result, our redemption, and in one or two other momentous points. Upon all these we ought to dwell and enlarge, mindfully and thankfully, but with the constant recollection that after all, as regards the Dispensation itself, only one or two partial notices are revealed to us altogether of a great Divine Work. Enlarge upon them we ought, even because they are few and partial, not slighting what is given us, because it is not all (like the servant who buried his lord's talent), but giving it what increase we can. And as there is much danger of the narrow spirit of that slothful servant at the present day, in which is strangely combined a profession of knowing everything, with an assertion that there is nothing to know concerning the Incarnation, I propose now, by God's blessing, to set before you the Scripture doctrine concerning it, as the Church Catholic has ever received it; trading with the talent committed to us, so that when our Lord comes He may receive His own with usury.

Bearing in mind, then, that we know nothing truly about the manner or the ultimate ends of the humiliation of the Eternal Son, our Lord and Saviour, let us consider what that humiliation itself was.

The text says, "though He were a Son." Now, in these words, "the Son of God," much more is implied than at first sight may appear. Many a man gathers up, here and there, some fragments of religious knowledge. He hears one thing said in Church, he sees another thing in the Prayer-book; and among religious people, or in the world, he gains something more. In this way he gets possession of sacred words and statements, knowing very little about them really. He interprets them, as it may happen, according to the various and inconsistent opinions which he has met with, or he puts his own meaning upon them, that is, the meaning, as must needs be, of an untaught, not to say a carnal and irreverent mind. How can a man expect he shall discern and apprehend the real meaning and language of Scripture, if he has never approached it as a learner, and waited on the Divine Author of it for the gift of wisdom? By continual meditation on the sacred text, by diligent use of the Church's instruction, he will come to understand what the Gospel doctrines are; but, most surely, if all the knowledge he has be gathered from a sentence caught up here, and an argument heard there, even when he is most orthodox in word, he has but a collection of phrases, on which he puts, not the right meaning, but his own meaning. And the least reflection must show you what a very poor and unworthy meaning, or rather how false a meaning "the natural man" will put upon "the things of the Spirit of God." I have been led to say this from having used the words, "The Son of God," which, I much fear, convey, to a great many minds, little or no idea, little or nothing of a high, religious, solemn idea. We have, perhaps, a vague general notion that they mean something extraordinary and supernatural; but we know that we ourselves are called, in one sense, sons of God in Scripture. Moreover we have heard, perhaps (and even though we do not recollect it, yet may retain the impression of it), that the Angels are sons of God. In consequence, we collect just thus much from the title as applied to our Lord, that He came from God, that He was the well-beloved of God, and that He is much more than a mere man. This is all that the words convey to many men at the most; while many more refer them merely to His human nature. How different is the state of those who have been duly initiated into the mysteries of the kingdom of heaven! How different was the mind of the primitive Christians, who so eagerly and vigorously apprehended the gracious announcement, that in this title, "The Son of God," they saw and enjoyed the full glories of the Gospel doctrine! When times grew cold and unbelieving, then indeed, as at this day, public explanations were necessary of those simple and sacred words; but the first Christians needed none. They felt that in saying that Christ was the Son of God, they were witnessing to a thousand marvellous and salutary truths, which they could not indeed understand, but by which they might gain life, and for which they could dare to die.

What, then, is meant by the "Son of God?" It is meant that our Lord is the very or true Son of God, that is, His Son by nature. We are but *called* the sons of God—we are adopted to be sons—but our Lord and Saviour is the Son of God, really and by birth, and He alone is such. Hence Scripture calls Him the Only-begotten Son. "Such knowledge is too excellent for" us; yet, however high it be, we learn as from His own mouth that God is not solitary, if we may dare so to speak, but that in His own incomprehensible essence, in the perfection of His one indivisible and eternal nature, His Dearly-beloved Son has ever existed with Him, who is called the Word, and, being His Son, is partaker in all the fulness of His Godhead. "In the beginning was the Word, and the Word was with God, and the Word was God." Thus when the early Christians used the title, "The Son of God," they meant, after the manner of the Apostles when they use it in Scripture, all we mean in the Creed, when, by way of explaining ourselves, we confess Him to be "God from God, Light from Light, Very or True God from True God." For in that He is the Son of God, He must be whatever God is, allholy, all-wise, all-powerful, all-good, eternal, infinite; yet since there is only one God, he must be at the same time not separate from God, but ever one with and in Him, one indivisibly; so that it would be as idle language to speak of Him as separated in essence from His Father, as to say that our reason, or intellect, or will, was separate from our minds—as rash and profane language to deny to the Father His Only-begotten Word, in whom He has ever delighted, as to deny His Wisdom or Goodness, or Power, which also have been in and with Him from everlasting.

The text goes on to say: "Though He were a Son, yet learned He obedience by the things which He suffered." Obedience belongs to a servant, but accordance, concurrence, co-operation, are the characteristics of a Son. In His eternal union with God there was no distinction of will and work between Him and His Father; as the Father's life was the Son's life, and the Father's glory the Son's also, so the Son was the very Word and Wisdom of the Father, His Power and Co-equal Minister in all things, the same and not the same as He Himself. But in the days of His flesh, when He had humbled Himself to "the form of a servant," taking on Himself a separate will and a separate work, and the toil and sufferings incident to a creature, then what had been mere concurrence became obedience. This, then, is the force of the words, "Though He was a Son, yet had He experience of *obedience*." He took on Him a lower nature, and wrought in it towards a Will higher and more perfect than it. Further, "He learned obedience amid *suffering*," and, therefore, amid temptation. His mysterious agony under it is described in the former part of the text; which declares that "in the days of His flesh," He "offered up prayers and supplications with strong crying and tears, unto Him that was able to save Him from death, and was heard in that He feared." Or, in the words of the foregoing chapter, He "was in all points tempted like as we are, yet without sin."

I am only concerned here in setting before you the sacred truth itself, not how it was, or why, or with what results. Let us, then, reverently consider what is implied in it. "The Word was made flesh;" by which is meant, not that He selected some particular existing man and dwelt in him (which in no sense would answer to the force of those words, and which He condescends to do continually in the case of all His elect, through His Spirit), but that He became what He was not before, that He took into His own Infinite Essence man's nature itself in all its completeness, creating a soul and body, and, at the moment of creation, making them His own, so that they never were other than His, never existed by themselves or except as in Him, being properties or attributes of Him (to use defective words) as really as His divine goodness, or His eternal Sonship, or His perfect likeness to the Father. And, while thus adding a new nature to Himself, He did not in any respect cease to be what He was before. How was that possible? All the while He was on earth, when He was conceived, when He was born, when He was tempted, on the cross, in the grave, and now at God's right hand—all the time through, He was the Eternal and Unchangeable Word, the Son of God. The flesh which He had assumed was but the instrument through which He acted for and towards us. As He acts in creation by His wisdom and power, towards Angels by His love, towards devils by His wrath, so He has acted for our redemption through our own nature, which in His great mercy He attached to His own Person, as if an attribute, simply, absolutely, indissolubly. Thus St. Paul speaks— as in other places, of the love of God, and the holiness of God—so in one place expressly of "the blood of God," if I may venture to use such words out of the sacred context. "Feed the Church of God," he says to the elders of Ephesus, "which He hath purchased *with His own blood*." [3] Accordingly, whatever our Lord said or did upon earth was strictly and literally the word and deed of God Himself. Just as we speak of seeing our friends, though we do not see their souls but merely their bodies, so the Apostles, Disciples, Priests, and Pharisees, and the multitude, all who saw Christ in the flesh, saw, as the whole earth will see at the last day, the Very and Eternal Son of God.

After this manner, then, must be understood His suffering, temptation, and obedience, not as if He ceased to be what He had ever been, but, having clothed Himself with a created essence, He made it the instrument of His humiliation; He acted

[3] Acts xx.28.

in it, He obeyed and suffered through it. Do not we see among men, circumstances of a peculiar kind throw one of our own race out of himself, so that he, the same man, acts as if his usual self were not in being, and he had fresh feelings and faculties, for the occasion, higher or lower than before? Far be it from our thoughts to parallel the incarnation of the Eternal Word with such an accidental change! but I mention it, not to explain a Mystery (which I relinquished the thought of from the first), but to facilitate your *conception* of Him who is the subject of it, to help you towards contemplating Him as God and man at once, as still the Son of God though He had assumed a nature short of His original perfection. That Eternal Power, which, till then, had thought and acted as God, began to think and act as a man, with all man's faculties, affections, and imperfections, sin excepted. Before He came on earth He was infinitely above joy and grief, fear and anger, pain and heaviness; but afterwards all these properties and many more were His as fully as they are ours. Before He came on earth, He had but the perfections of God, but afterwards He had also the virtues of a creature, such as faith, meekness, self-denial. Before He came on earth He could not be tempted of evil; but afterwards He had a man's heart, a man's tears, and a man's wants and infirmities. His Divine Nature indeed pervaded His manhood, so that every deed and word of His in the flesh savoured of eternity and infinity; but, on the other hand, from the time He was born of the Virgin Mary, he had a natural fear of danger, a natural shrinking from pain, though ever subject to the ruling influence of that Holy and Eternal Essence which was in Him. For instance, we read on one occasion of His praying that the cup might pass from Him; and, at another, when Peter showed surprise at the prospect of His crucifixion, He rebuked him sharply, as if for tempting Him to murmur and disobey.

Thus He possessed at once a double assemblage of attributes, divine and human. Still he was all-powerful, though in the form of a servant; still He was all-knowing, though seemingly ignorant; still incapable of temptation, though exposed to it; and if any one stumble at this, as not a mere mystery, but in the very form of language a contradiction of terms, I would have him reflect on those peculiarities of human nature itself, which I just now hinted at. Let him consider the condition of his own mind, and see how like a contradiction it is. Let him reflect upon the faculty of memory, and try to determine whether he does or does not know a thing which he cannot recollect, or rather, whether it may not be said of him, that one self-same person, that in one sense he knows it, in another he does not know it. This may serve to appease his imagination, if it startles at the mystery. Or let him consider the state of an infant, which seems, indeed, to be without a soul for many months, which seems to have only the senses and functions of animal life, yet has, we know, a soul, which may even be regenerated. What, indeed, can be more mysterious than the Baptism of an infant? How strange is it, yet how transporting a sight, what a source of meditation is opened on us, while we look upon what seems so helpless, so reasonless, and know that at that moment it has a soul so fully formed, as on the one hand, indeed, to be a child of wrath; and, on the other (blessed be God), to be capable of a new birth through the Spirit! Who can say, if we had eyes to see, in what state that infant soul is? Who can say it has not its energies of reason and of will in some unknown sphere, quite consistently with the reality of its insensibility to the external world? Who can say that all of us, or at least all who are living in the faith of Christ, have not some strange but unconscious life in God's presence all the while we are here, seeing what we do not know we see, impressed yet without power of reflection, and this, without having a double self in consequence, and with an increase to us, not a diminution, of the practical reality of our earthly sojourn and probation? Are there not men before now who, like Elisha, when his spirit followed Gehazi, or St. Peter, when he announced the coming of Sapphira's bearers, or St. Paul, when his presence went before him to Corinth,[4] seem to range beyond themselves, even while in the flesh? Who knows where he is "in visions of the night?" And this being so, how can we pronounce it to be any contradiction that, while the Word of God was upon earth, in our flesh, compassed within and without with human virtues and feelings, with faith and patience, fear and joy, grief, misgivings, infirmities, temptations, still He was, according to His Divine Nature, as from the first, passing in thought from one end of heaven even to the other, reading all hearts, foreseeing all events, and receiving all worship as in the bosom of the Father? This, indeed, is what He suggests to us Himself in those surprising words addressed to Nicodemus, which might even be taken to imply that even His human nature was at that very time in heaven while He spoke to him. "No man hath ascended up to heaven, but He that came down from heaven, even the Son of man, *which is in heaven.*"[5]

---

[4] 2 Kings v.26; Acts v.9; 1 Cor. iv.19; v.3.
[5] John iii.13.

To conclude, if any one is tempted to consider such subjects as the foregoing, abstract, speculative, and unprofitable, I would observe, in answer, that I have taken it on the very ground of its being, as I believe, especially practical. Let it not be thought a strange thing to say, though I say it, that there is much in the religious belief, even of the more serious part of the community at present, to make observant men very anxious where it will end. It would be no very difficult matter, I suspect, to perplex the faith of a great many persons who believe themselves to be orthodox, and, indeed, are so, according to their light. They have been accustomed to call Christ God, but that is all; they have not considered what is meant by applying that title to One who was really a man, and from the vague way in which they use it, they would be in no small danger, if assailed by a subtle disputant, of being robbed of the sacred truth in its substance, even if they kept it in name. In truth, until we contemplate our Lord and Saviour, God and man, as a really existing being, external to our minds, as complete and entire in His personality as we show ourselves to be to each other, as one and the same in all His various and contrary attributes, "the same yesterday, to-day, and for ever," we are using words which profit not. Till then we do not realize that Object of faith, which is not a mere name on which titles and properties may be affixed without congruity and meaning, but has a personal existence and an identity distinct from everything else. In what true sense do we "know" Him, if our idea of Him be not such as to take up and incorporate into itself the manifold attributes and offices which we ascribe to Him? What do we gain from words, however correct and abundant, if they end with themselves, instead of lighting up the image of the Incarnate Son in our hearts? Yet this charge may too surely be brought against the theology of late centuries, which, under the pretence of guarding against presumption, denies us what is revealed; like Ahaz, refusing to ask for a sign, lest it should tempt the Lord.

Influenced by it, we have well-nigh forgotten the sacred truth, graciously disclosed for our support, that Christ is the Son of God in His Divine nature, as well as His human; we have well-nigh ceased to regard Him, after the pattern of the Nicene Creed, as "God from God, and Light from Light," ever one with Him, yet ever distinct from Him. We speak of Him in a vague way as God, which is true, but not the whole truth; and, in consequence when we proceed to consider His humiliation, we are unable to carry on the notion of His personality from heaven to earth. He who was but now spoken of as God, without mention of the Father from whom He is, is next described as if a creature; but how do these distinct notions of Him hold together in our minds? We are able indeed to continue the idea of a Son into that of a servant, though the descent was infinite, and, to our reason, incomprehensible; but when we merely speak first of God, then of man, we seem to change the Nature without preserving the Person. In truth, His Divine Sonship is that portion of the sacred doctrine on which the mind is providentially intended to rest throughout, and so to preserve for itself His identity unbroken. But when we abandon this gracious help afforded to our faith, how can we hope to gain the one true and simple vision of Him? how shall we possibly look beyond our own words, or apprehend, in any sort, what we say? In consequence we are too often led, as a matter of necessity, in discoursing of His words and works, to distinguish between the Christ who lived on earth and the Son of God Most High, speaking of His human nature and His Divine nature so separately as not to feel or understand that God is man and man is God. I am speaking of those of us who have learned to reflect, reason, and dispute, to inquire and pursue their thoughts, not of the incurious or illiterate, who are not exposed to the temptation in question; and of the former I fear I must say (to use the language of ancient theology), that they begin by being Sabellians, that they go on to be Nestorians, and that they tend to be Ebionites and to deny Christ's Divinity altogether. Meanwhile, the religious world little thinks whither its opinions are leading; and will not discover that it is adoring a mere abstract name or a vague creation of the mind for the Ever-living Son, till the defection of its members from the faith startle it, and teach it that the so-called religion of the heart, without orthodoxy of doctrine, is but the warmth of a corpse, real for a time, but sure to fail.

How long will that complicated Error last under which our Church now labours? How long are human traditions of modern date to obscure, in so many ways, the majestic interpretations of Holy Writ which the Church Catholic has inherited from the age of the Apostles? When shall we be content to enjoy the wisdom and the pureness which Christ has bequeathed to His Church as a perpetual gift, instead of attempting to draw our Creed, each for himself, as he best may, from the deep wells of truth? Surely in vain have we escaped from the superstitions of the middle ages, if the corruptions of a rash and self-trusting philosophy spread over our faith!

May God, even the Father, give us a heart and understanding

to realize, as well as to confess that doctrine into which we were baptized, that His Only-begotten Son, our Lord, was conceived by the Holy Ghost, was born of the Virgin Mary, suffered, and was buried, rose again from the dead, ascended into heaven, from whence He shall come again, at the end of the world, to judge the quick and the dead!

JEWISH ZEAL,
A PATTERN TO CHRISTIANS

*"So let all thine enemies perish, O Lord; but let them that love Him,
be as the sun when he goeth forth in his might. And the land had rest
forty years."*—Judges v.31.

WHAT a contrast do these words present to the history
which goes before them! "It came to pass," says the sacred writer, "when Israel was strong, that they put the
Canaanites to tribute, and did not utterly drive them out. Neither did Ephraim drive out the Canaanites that dwelt in Ge-
zer. . . . Neither did Zebulon drive out the inhabitants of
Kitron. . . . . Neither did Asher drive out the inhabitants of Ac-
cho. . . . . Neither did Naphtali drive out the inhabitants of
Bethshemesh."[1] What was the consequence? "And the children
of Israel did evil in the sight of the Lord and served Baalim . . . . they forsook the Lord and served Baal and Ashtaroth.
And the anger of the Lord was hot against Israel, and He delivered them into the hands of spoilers that spoiled them, and He
sold them into the hands of their enemies round about. . . . .
Whithersoever they went out, the hand of the Lord was against
them for evil, as the Lord had said, and as the Lord had sworn
unto them; and they were greatly distressed."[2] Here is the picture of indolence and unfaithfulness leading to cowardice, to
apostasy, and to national ruin.

On the other hand, consider, by way of contrast, the narrative contained in the chapter which ends with the text.
Ephraim and Benjamin, Machir and Zebulon, Issachar and
Naphtali, rousing, uniting, assailing their enemies, and conquering; conquering in the strength of the Lord. Their long
captivity was as nothing, through God's great mercy, when
they turned to Him. In vain had their enemies trod them down
to the ground; the Church of God had that power and grace
within it, that whenever it could be persuaded to shake off its

[1] Judges i.28–32.   [2] Judges ii.11–15.

lassitude and rally, it smote as sharply and as effectively as though it had never been bound with the green withs and the new ropes of the Philistines. So it was now. "Awake, awake, Deborah: awake, awake, utter a song: arise, Barak, and lead thy captivity captive, thou son of Abinoam." Such was the inspired cry of war: and it was obeyed. In consequence the Canaanites were discomfited in battle and fled; "and the land had rest forty years." Here is a picture of manly obedience to God's will—a short trial of trouble and suffering—and then the reward, *peace*.

I propose now to make some remarks upon the lesson conveyed to us in this picture, which extends indeed through the greater part of the Old Testament—the lesson to us *as individuals*; for surely it is with reference to our own duties *as individuals*, that we should read every part of Scripture.

What the Old Testament especially teaches us is this:—that zeal is as essentially a duty of all God's rational creatures, as prayer and praise, faith and submission; and, surely, if so, especially of sinners whom He has redeemed; that zeal consists in a strict attention to His commands—a scrupulousness, vigilance, heartiness, and punctuality, which bears with no reasoning or questioning about them—an intense thirst for the advancement of His glory—a shrinking from the pollution of sin and sinners—an indignation, nay impatience, at witnessing His honour insulted—a quickness of feeling when His name is mentioned, and a jealousy how it is mentioned—a fulness of purpose, an heroic determination to yield Him service at whatever sacrifice of personal feeling—an energetic resolve to push through all difficulties, were they as mountains, when His eye or hand but gives the sign—a carelessness of obloquy, or reproach, or persecution, a forgetfulness of friend and relative, nay, a hatred (so to say) of all that is naturally dear to us, when He says, "Follow me." These are some of the characteristics of zeal. Such was the temper of Moses, Phinehas, Samuel, David, Elijah; it is the temper enjoined on all the Israelites, especially in their conduct towards the abandoned nations of Canaan. The text expresses that temper in the words of Deborah: "So let all thine enemies perish, O Lord; but let them that love Him be as the sun when he goeth forth in his might."

Now, it has sometimes been said that the commands of strenuous and stern service given to the Israelites—for instance, those relative to their taking and keeping possession of the promised land—do not apply to us Christians. There can be no doubt it is not our duty to take the sword and kill the enemies of

God as the Jews were told to do; "Put up again thy sword into
his place," [3] are our Saviour's words to St. Peter. So far, then, if
this is what is meant by saying that these commands do not apply to us, so far, doubtless, it is clear they do not apply to us. But
it does not, hence, follow that the temper of mind which they
pre-suppose and foster is not required of us; else, surely, the
Jewish history is no longer profitable for doctrine, for reproof,
for correction, for instruction in righteousness. St. Peter was
blamed, not for his zeal, but for his use of the sword,

Man's duty, perfection, happiness, have always been one and
the same. He is not a different being now from what he ever
was; he has always been commanded the same duties. What was
the holiness of an Israelite is still the holiness of a Christian,
though the Christian has far higher privileges and aids for perfection. The Saints of God have ever lived by faith, and walked
in the way of justice, mercy, truth, self-mastery, and love. It is
impossible, then, that all these duties imposed on the Israelites
of driving out their enemies, and taking and keeping possession
of the promised land, should not in some sense or other apply to
us; for it is clear they were not in their case mere accidents of
obedience, but went to form a certain inward character, and as
clear is it that our heart must be as the heart of Moses or David,
if we would be saved through Christ.

This is quite evident, if we attentively examine the Jewish
history, and the Divine commands which are the principles of
it. For these commands, which some persons have said do not
apply to us, are so many and varied, and repeated at so many
and diverse times, that they certainly must have formed a peculiar character in the heart of the obedient Israelite, and were
much more than an outward form and a sort of ceremonial service. They are so abundant throughout the Old Testament,
that unless they in some way apply to us, it is difficult to see
what is its direct use, at this day, in the way of precept; and this
is the very conclusion which these same persons often go on to
draw. They are willing to rid themselves of the Old Testament,
and they say that Christians are not concerned in it, and that
the Jews were almost barbarians; whereas St. Paul tells us, that
the Jewish history is "written for our admonition and our
learning." [4]

Let us consider some of the commands I have referred to, and
the terms in which they are conveyed. For instance, that for the
extirpation of the devoted nations from the land of Canaan.

---

[3] Matt. xxvi.52.   [4] 1 Cor. x.11; Rom. xv.4.

"When the Lord thy God shall bring thee into the land whither thou goest to possess it, ... thou shalt smite" the nations that possess it, "and utterly destroy them; thou shalt make no covenant with them, nor show mercy unto them; neither shalt thou make marriages with them. . . . . Ye shall destroy their altars and break down their images, and cut down their groves, and burn down their graven images with fire. . . . . Thou shalt consume all the people which the Lord thy God shall deliver thee; thine eye shall have no pity upon them."[5]

Next observe, this merciless temper, as profane people would call it, but as well-instructed Christians say, this godly zeal, was enjoined upon them under far more distressing circumstances, viz., the transgressions of their own relations and friends. "If thy brother, the son of thy mother, or thy son, or thy daughter, or the wife of thy bosom, or thy friend which is as thine own soul, entice thee secretly, saying, Let us go and serve other gods, ... Thou shalt not consent unto him, nor hearken unto him, neither shall thine eye pity him, neither shalt thou spare, neither shalt thou conceal him. But thou shalt surely kill him. Thine hand shall be first upon him to put him to death, and afterwards the hand of all the people."[6] Now, doubtless, we at this day are not to put men to death for idolatry; but, doubtless also, whatever temper of mind the fulfilment of this command implied in the Jew, such, essentially, must be our temper of mind, whatever else it may be also; for God cannot speak two laws, He cannot love two characters—good is good, and evil is evil, and the law He gave to the Jews was, in its substance, "perfect, converting the soul; the testimony of the Lord sure, making wise the simple; the statutes of the Lord right, rejoicing the heart; the commandment of the Lord pure, enlightening the eyes; . . . . more to be desired than gold, yea than much fine gold; sweeter also than honey and the honeycomb. Moreover," as the Psalmist proceeds, "by them is thy servant taught, and in keeping of them there is great reward."[7]

A self-mastering fearless obedience was another part of this same religious temper enjoined on the Jews, and still incumbent, as I dare affirm, on us Christians. "Be ye very *courageous* to keep and to do all that is written in the book of the law of Moses."[8] It required an exceeding moral courage in the Jews to enable them to go straight forward, seduced neither by their feelings nor their reason.

[5] Deut. vii.1–5, 16.   [6] Deut. xiii.6–9.
[7] Ps. xix.7, 8, 10, 11.   [8] Josh. xxiii.6.

Nor was the severe temper under review a duty in the early ages of Judaism only. The book of Psalms was written at different times, between David's age and the captivity, yet it plainly breathes the same hatred of sin, and opposition to sinners. I will but cite one text from the hundred and thirty-ninth Psalm. "Do not I hate them, O Lord, that hate Thee? and am not I grieved with those that rise up against Thee? I hate them with perfect hatred; I count them mine enemies." And then the inspired writer proceeds to lay open his soul before God, as if conscious he had but expressed feelings which He would approve. "Search me, O God, and know my heart: try me, and know my thoughts, and see if there be any wicked way in me, and lead me in the way everlasting."

Further still, after the return from the captivity, after the Prophets had enlarged the compass of Divine Revelation, and purified and heightened the religious knowledge of the nation, still this rigid and austere zeal was enjoined and enforced in all its ancient vigour by Ezra. The Jews set about a reformation; and what was its most remarkable act? Let us attend to the words of Ezra: "The princes came to me, saying, The people of Israel, and the priests, and the Levites have not separated themselves from the people of the lands; for they have taken of their daughters for themselves and for their sons; so that the holy seed have mingled themselves with the people of those lands; yea, the hand of the princes and rulers hath been chief in this trespass." Now let me stop to ask what would most likely be the conduct of a temporizing Christian of this day, had he, in that day, been in Ezra's place? He would, doubtless, have said that such marriages were quite unjustifiable certainly, but now that they were made, there was no remedy for it; that they must be hindered in future; but in the existing instances, the evil being done could not be undone; and, besides, that great men were involved in the sin, whom it was impossible to interfere with. This he would have said, I think, though the prohibition of Moses seemed to make such marriages null and void from the first. Now, I do not say that every one ought to have done what Ezra did, for he was supernaturally directed; but would the course he adopted have ever entered into the mind of men of this day, or can they even understand or acquiesce in it, now that they know it? for what did he? "And when I heard this thing," he says, "I rent my garment and my mantle, and plucked off the hair of my head, and of my beard, and sat down astonied. Then were assembled unto me every one that trembled at the words of the God of Israel, because of the transgression of those that had been carried away, and I sat astonied until the evening sacrifice." [9] Then he offered a confession and intercession in behalf of the people; then at length he and the people came to a decision; which was no other than this—to command all persons who had married foreign wives to *put them away*. He undid the evil as well as hindered it in future. What an act of self-denying zeal was this in a multitude of people!

These are some, out of many instances, which might be brought from the Jewish history, in proof of the duty of strict and severe loyalty to God and His revealed will; and I here adduce them, first, to show that the commands involving it could not (their number and variety are so great), could not have related to a merely outward and ceremonial obedience, but must have wrought in the Jews a certain temper of mind, pleasing to God, and therefore necessary for us also to possess. Next, I deduce from that same circumstance of their number and variety, that they must be binding on us, else the Old Testament would be but a shadow of a revelation or law to the Christian.

I wish to insist on the lesson supplied merely by the Old Testament, and will not introduce into the argument the consideration of the Apostles' doctrine, which is quite in accordance with it. Yet it may be right, briefly, to refer to the sinless pattern of our Lord, and to what is told us of the holy inhabitants of heaven, in order to show that the temper of mind enjoined on the Jews belongs to those who are in a state of being superior to us, as well as to those who were living under a defective and temporary Dispensation. There was an occasion when our Lord is expressly said to have taken upon Him the zeal which consumed David. "Jesus went up to Jerusalem, and found in the Temple those that sold oxen, and sheep, and doves, and the changers of money, sitting; and when He had made a scourge of small cords, He drove them all out of the Temple, and the sheep, and the oxen; and poured out the changers' money, and overthrew the tables." Surely, unless we had this account given us by an inspired writer, we should not have believed it! Influenced by notions of our own devising, we should have said, this zealous action of our Lord's was quite inconsistent with His merciful, meek, and (what may be called) His majestic and serene temper of mind. To put aside form, to dispense with the ministry of His attendant Angels, to act before He had spoken His displeasure, to use His own hand, to hurry to and fro, to be a servant in the work of purification, surely this must have

[9] Ezra ix.3, 4.

arisen from a fire of indignation at witnessing His Father's House insulted, which we sinners cannot understand. But any how, it is but the perfection of that temper which, as we have seen, was encouraged and exemplified in the Jewish Church. That energy, decision, and severity which Moses enjoined on his people, is manifested in Christ Himself, and is, therefore, undeniably a duty of man as such, whatever be his place or attainments in the scale of human nature.

Such is the pattern afforded us by our Lord; to which add the example of the Angels which surround Him. Surely in Him is mingled "goodness and severity;" such, therefore, are all holy creatures, loving and severe. We read of their thoughts and desires in the Apocalypse, "Fear God, and give glory to Him, for the hour of His judgment is come." Again, "Thou art righteous, O Lord, which art, and wast, and shalt be, because Thou hast judged thus. For they have shed the blood of saints and prophets, and Thou hast given them blood to drink, for they are worthy." And again, "Even so, Lord God Almighty, true and righteous are Thy judgments." Once more, "Her sins have reached unto heaven, and God hath remembered her iniquities. Reward her even as she rewarded you, and double unto her double according to her works;" [10]—all which passages imply a deep and solemn acquiescence in God's judgments.

Thus a certain fire of zeal, showing itself, not by force and blood, but as really and certainly as if it did—cutting through natural feelings, neglecting self, preferring God's glory to all things, firmly resisting sin, protesting against sinners, and steadily contemplating their punishment, is a duty belonging to all creatures of God, a duty of Christians, in the midst of all that excellent overflowing charity which is the highest Gospel grace, and the fulfilling of the second table of the Law.

And such, in fact, has ever been the temper of the Christian Church; in evidence of which I need but appeal to the impressive fact that the Jewish Psalter has been the standard book of Christian devotion from the first down to this day. I wish we thought more of this circumstance. Can any one doubt that, supposing that blessed manual of faith and love had never been in use among us, great numbers of the present generation would have clamoured against it as unsuitable to express *Christian* feelings, as deficient in charity and kindness? Nay, do we not know, though I dare say it may surprise many a sober Christian to hear that it is so, that there are men at this moment who

[10] Rev. xiv.7; xvi.5–7; xviii.5, 6.

(I hardly like to mention it) wish parts of the Psalms left out of the Service as ungentle and harsh? Alas! that men of this day should rashly put their own judgment in competition with that of all the Saints of every age hitherto since Christ came— should virtually say, "Either *they* have been wrong or *we* are," thus forcing us to decide between the two. Alas! that they should dare to criticise the words of inspiration! Alas! that they should follow the steps of the backsliding Israelites, and shrink from siding with the Truth in its struggle with the world, instead of saying with Deborah, "So let all Thine enemies perish, O Lord!"

Now I shall make a few observations in conclusion, with a view of showing how meekness and charity are compatible with this austere and valiant temper of the Christian soldier.

1. Of course it is absolutely sinful to have any private enmities. Not the bitterest personal assaults upon us should induce us to retaliate. We must do good for evil, "love those who hate, bless those who curse us, and pray for those who despitefully use us." It is only when it is impossible at once to be kind to them, and give glory to God, that we may cease to act kindly towards them. When David speaks of hating God's enemies, it was under circumstances when keeping friends with them would have been a desertion of the Truth. St. James says, "Know ye not that the friendship of the world is enmity with God?"[11] and so, on the other hand, devotion to God's cause is enmity with the world. But no personal feeling must intrude itself in any case. We hate sinners, by putting them out of our sight, as if they were not, by annihilating them, in our affections. And this we must do, even in the case of our friends and relations, if God requires it. But in no case are we to allow ourselves in resentment or malice.

2. Next, it is quite compatible with the most earnest zeal, to offer kind offices to God's enemies when in distress. I do not say that a denial of these offices may not be a duty ordinarily; for it is our duty, as St. John tells us in his second Epistle, not even to receive them into our houses. But the case is very different where men are brought into extremity. God "maketh His sun to rise on the evil and on the good, and sendeth rain on the just and on the unjust."[12] We must go and do likewise, imitating the good Samaritan; and as he thought nothing of difference of nations when a Jew was in distress, in like manner we must not take account of wilful heresy, or profaneness, in such circumstances.

---

[11] James iv.4.   [12] Matt. v.45.

3. And, further, the Christian keeps aloof from sinners in order to do them good. He does so in the truest and most enlarged charity. It is a narrow and weak feeling to please a man here, and to endanger his soul. A true friend is he who speaks out, and, when a man sins, shows him that he is displeased at the sin. He who sets up no witness against his friend's sin, is "partaker of his evil deeds." [13] The Psalmist speaks in this spirit, when, after praying to God "to persecute" the ungodly "with His tempest," he adds, "fill their faces with shame, that they may seek Thy name, O Lord." [14]

Accordingly, the more zealous a Christian is, therefore is he the more charitable. The Israelite, when he entered Canaan, was told to spare neither old nor young; the weak and the infirm were to be no exception in the list of victims whose blood was to be shed. "Of the cities of these people, which the Lord thy God doth give thee for an inheritance, thou shalt save alive nothing that breatheth." [15] Accordingly, when the people fought against Sihon, they "took all his cities at that time, and utterly destroyed the men, and the women, and the little ones of every city," they "left none to remain." [16] And when Jericho was taken, "they utterly destroyed all that was in the city, both man and woman, young and old, and ox, and sheep, and ass, with the edge of the sword." [17] What an awful office was this, what an unutterably heart-piercing task, almost enough to make a man frantic, except as upheld by the power of Him who gave the command! Yet Moses, thus severely-minded to do God's will, was the meekest of men. Samuel, too, who sent Saul to slay in Amalek "man and woman, infant and suckling, ox and sheep, camel and ass," was, from his youth up, the wise and heavenly-minded guide and prophet of Israel. David, who had a fiery zeal, so as even to consume him, was (as we see by his Psalms) most tender-hearted and gentle in his feelings and thoughts. Doubtless, while the servants of God executed His judgments, they still could bend in pity and in hope over the young and old whom they slew with the sword—merciful amid their severity—an unspeakable trial, doubtless, of faith and self-mastery, and requiring a very exalted and refined spirit successfully to undergo. Doubtless, as they slew those who suffered for the sins of their fathers, their thoughts turned, first to the fall of Adam, next to that unseen state where all inequalities are righted, and they surrendered them-

[13] 2 John 11.   [14] Ps. lxxxiii.16.   [15] Deut. xx.16.
[16] Deut. ii.34.   [17] Josh. vi.21.

selves as instruments unto the Lord, of mysteriously working out good through evil.

And shall *we* faint at our far lesser trials when they bore the greater? Spared the heavy necessity of piercing with the spear of Phinehas, and of hewing Agag in Gilgal—allowed to take instead of inflicting suffering and "to make a difference" instead of an indiscriminate severity—shall we, like cowards, shrink from bearing our lighter burdens, which our Lord commands, and in which He sets us the pattern? Shall we be perversely persuaded by the appearance of amiableness or kindness in those whom God's word bids us depart from as heretics, or profligate livers, or troublers of the Church? Joseph could speak strangely to his brethren, and treat them as spies, put one of them in prison, and demand another from Canaan, while he hardly refrained himself in doing so, and his bowels yearned over them; and by turns he punished them, and wept for them. Oh, that there was in us this high temper of mingled austerity and love! Barely do we conceive of severity by itself, and of kindness by itself; but who unites them? We think we cannot be kind without ceasing to be severe. Who is there that walks through the world, wounding according to the rule of zeal, and scattering balm freely in the fulness of love; smiting as a duty, and healing as a privilege; loving most when he seems sternest, and embracing them most tenderly whom in semblance he treats roughly? What a state we are in, when any one who rehearses the plain threats of our Lord and His Apostles against sinners, or ventures to defend the anathemas of His Church, is thought unfeeling rather than merciful; when they who separate from the irreligious world are blamed as fanciful and extravagant, and those who confess the truth, as it is in Jesus, are said to be bitter, hot of head, and intemperate. Yet, with God's grace, with the history of the Old Testament before us, and the fearful recompense, to warn us, which came upon backsliding Israel, we, the Ministers of Christ, dare not keep silence amid this great error. In behalf of Christ, our Saviour and Lord, who yielded up His precious life for us, and now feeds us with His own blood, for the sake of the souls whom He has redeemed, and whom, by a false and cruel charity, the world would keep in ignorance and sin, we cannot refrain; and if His Holy Spirit be with us, as we trust He is, whatever betides, whatever is coming on this country, speak the truth we will, and overcome in our speaking we must; for He has given us to overcome!

SUBMISSION TO CHURCH AUTHORITY

"Put away from thee a froward mouth, and perverse lips put far from thee. Let thine eyes look right on, and let thine eyelids look straight before thee. Ponder the path of thy feet, and let all thy ways be established. Turn not to the right hand nor to the left: remove thy foot from evil."—Prov. iv.24–27.

PRECEPTS such as these come home with the force of truth, even to minds which fain would resist them, from their seriousness and practical wisdom, putting aside the authority of inspiration. At no time and under no circumstances are they without their application; at the present time, when religious unity and peace are so lamentably disregarded, and novel doctrines and new measures alone are popular, they naturally remind us of the duty of obedience to the Church, and of the sin of departing from it, or what our Litany prays against under the name of "heresy and schism." It may seem out of place to speak of this sin here, because those who commit it are not likely to be in Church to profit by what might be said about it; yet the commission of it affects even those who do not commit it, by making them indifferent to it. For this reason, and because it is right that even such persons as are firmest in their adherence to the Church should know why they adhere to it, I will consider some of the popular objections which are made to such adherence, by those who account it, not sinful indeed (though many go even this length), but unnecessary.

You know time was when there was but one vast body of Christians, called the Church, throughout the world. It was found in every country where the name of Christ was named; it was everywhere governed in the same way by Bishops; it was everywhere descended from the Apostles through the line of those Bishops; and it was everywhere in perfect peace and unity together, branch with branch, all over the world. Thus it fulfilled the prophecy: "Jerusalem is builded as a city that is compact together: for there are set Thrones of judgment, the

Thrones of the House of David." [1] There were, indeed, separatists and dissenters, then as now, but they were many and various, not one body like the Church; they were short-lived, had a beginning after the Apostles, and came to an end, first one and then another. But now all this beauty of Jerusalem is miserably defaced. That vast Catholic body, "the Holy Church throughout all the world," is broken into many fragments by the power of the Devil; just as some huge barrier cliff which once boldly fronted the sea is at length cleft, parted, overthrown by the waves. Some portions of it are altogether gone, and those that remain are separated from each other. We are the English Catholics; abroad are the Roman Catholics, some of whom are also among ourselves; elsewhere are the Greek Catholics, and so on. And thus we stand in this day of rebuke and blasphemy—clinging to our own portion of the Ancient Rock which the waters are roaring round and would fain overflow—trusting in God—looking for the dawn of day, which "will at length come and will not tarry," when God will save us from the rising floods, if we have courageously kept our footing where He has placed us, neither yielding to the violence of the waves which sweep over us, nor listening to the crafty invitations of those who offer us an escape in vessels not of God's building.

Now I am going to notice and refute some of the bad arguments by which the children of this world convey their invitation.

1. First they say, "Why keep so strictly to one body of Christians when there are so many other bodies also—so many denominations, so many persuasions—all soldiers of Christ, like so many different armies, all advancing in one cause against one enemy? Surely this exclusive attachment to one party," so they speak, "to the neglect of other Christians who profess a like doctrine, and only differ in forms, is the sign of a narrow and illiberal mind. Christianity is an universal gift; why then limit its possession to one set of men and one kind of Church government, instead of allowing all who choose to take it to themselves in any way they please?"

Now surely those who thus speak should begin with answering Scripture, not questioning us; for Scripture certainly recognizes but "one body" of Christians as explicitly as "one Spirit, one faith, one Lord, and one God and Father of all." [2] As far as the text of Scripture goes, it is as direct a contradiction of it to speak of more than one body as to speak of more than one

---

[1] Ps. cxxii.3, 5.   [2] Eph. iv.4–6.

Spirit. On the other hand, Scripture altogether contemplates the *existence* of persuasions, as they are fitly called, round about this one body, for it speaks of them; but it does not hint ever so faintly that, because they exist, therefore they must be acknowledged. So much the contrary, that it says, "There must be heresies," that is private persuasions, self-formed bodies, "among you, that they which are approved may be made manifest among you." Again, "A man that is a heretic," that is, one who adopts some opinion of his own in religious matters, and gets about him followers, "after the first and second admonition, reject." And again, "Mark them which cause divisions, and avoid them."[3] Now, we are of those who, in accordance with these directions, have done our best to keep clear of such human doctrines and private opinions, adhering to that one Body Catholic which alone was founded by the Apostles, and will last till the end of all things. And it is surely better thus implicitly to believe and obey God's voice in Scripture than to reason; it is more tolerable to be called narrow-minded by man, than to be pronounced self-wise and self-sufficient by God; it is happier to be thought over-scrupulous, with the Bible, than to have the world's praise for liberality without it.

But again, who is bold enough to say that "it would be a narrow and niggardly appointment, were the blessings of the Gospel stored up in one body or set of persons to the exclusion of others?" Let him see to it, how he opposes God's universal scheme of providence which we see before our eyes. Christianity is a blessing for the whole earth—granted; but it does not therefore follow (to judge from what we otherwise know of God's dealings with us) that none have been specially commissioned to dispense the blessing. Mercies given to multitudes are not less mercies because they are made to flow from particular sources. Indeed, most of the great appointments of Divine goodness are marked by this very character of what men call *exclusiveness*. God distributes numberless benefits to all men, but He does so through a few select instruments. The few are favoured for the good of the many. Wealth, power, gifts of mind, learning, all tend towards the welfare of the community; yet, for all that, they are not given at once to all, but channelled out to the many through the few. And so the blessings of the Gospel are open to the whole world, as freely given as light or fire; yet even light has had its own receptacle since the fourth day of creation, and fire has been hidden in the flinty rock, as if

[3] 1 Cor. xi.19; Tit. iii.10; Rom. xvi.17.

to show us that the light and fire of our souls are not gained without the use of means, nor except from special sources.

Again, as to the Ministerial Succession being a form, and adherence to it a form, it can only be called a form because we do not see its effects; did anything *visible* attend it, we should no longer call it a form. Did a miracle always follow a baptism or a return into the Church, who would any longer call it a form? that is, we call it a form, only so long as we refuse to walk by *faith*, which dispenses with things visible. Faith sees things not to be forms, if commanded, which seem like forms; it realizes consequences. Men ignorant in the sciences would predict no result from chemical and the like experiments; they would count them a form and a pretence. What is prayer but a form? that is, who (to speak generally) sees anything come of it? But we believe it, and so are blessed. In what sense is adherence to the Church a form in which prayer is not also? The benefit of the one is not seen, nor of the other; the one will not profit the ungodly and careless, nor will the other; the one is commanded in Scripture, so is the other. Therefore, to say that Church-union is a form, is no disparagement of it; forms are the very food of faith.

2. However, it may be argued, that, "whatever was the cause, and whatever was intended by Divine Providence, many sects there are;" and that, "if unity be a duty, as members of the Church maintain, the best, the only way to effect it now, is for them to relax their strictness and join in one with all sects upon whatever terms." I answer by asking, whether we have any *leave* so to do, any commission to alter any part of what God has appointed; whether we might not as well pretend to substitute another ordinance for Baptism as to annul the rights of the Church Catholic, and put human societies and teachers of man's creating on a level with it? Even Balaam felt what was the power of a Divine appointment. "He hath blessed," he says, "*and I cannot reverse it.*" Even holy Isaac, much as he wished it, could not change the course of the blessing once conferred, or the decree of God. He cried out concerning Jacob, "yea, and he shall be blessed;" for "it is not of him that willeth, nor of him that runneth," "not of blood, nor of the will of the flesh, nor of the will of man" "but of God that showeth mercy." "The gifts and calling of God are without repentance." [4]

Men, who have themselves separated from the Church, sometimes urge a union among all Christians in the following

---

[4] Numb. xxiii.20; Gen. xxvii.33; Rom. ix.16; John i.13; Rom. xi.29.

way: they say, "We dissent from you; yet we will cast aside our forms if you will cast aside yours. Thus there will be mutual concession. What are forms, so that our hearts are one?" Nay, but there is not, there cannot be, a like heart and spirit, from the very nature of the case, between us and them, for obedience to the Church is one part of our spirit. Those who think much of submission to her authority, as we do, plainly do differ in spirit from those who think little of it. Such persons, then, however well they mean it, yet, in fact, ask us to give up something, while they give up nothing themselves; for that is not much to give up which a man sets no value upon. All they give up is what they themselves disparage by calling it a form. They call *our* holy discipline also a form, but *we* do not: and it is *not* a mere form in our judgments, though it may be in theirs. They call it a human invention, just as they call their own; but, till we call it so also, till they have first convinced us that it is, it must be a sacrifice in us to give it up, such as they cannot possibly make. They cannot make such sacrifice, because they have made it already, or their fathers before them, when they left the Church. They cannot make it, for they have no affections to sacrifice in the matter; whereas our piety, our reverence, our faith, our love adhere to the Church of the Apostles, and could not (were desertion possible, which God forbid!) could not be torn away from it without many wounds and much anguish. Surely, then, it is craft, or over simplicity in those who differ from us thus to speak. They strip themselves of what we consider an essential of holiness, the decencies and proprieties of the Ancient Rule. Then, being unclothed, they are forced to array themselves in new forms and ordinances, as they best may; and these novelties, which their own hands have sewed together to cover them, which they never revered, and which are soon to wither, they purpose (as though) to sacrifice to us, provided we, on our part, will cast from us the Lord's own clothing, that sanctity and sobriety of order, which is the gift of Christ, the earnest of His imputed merits, the type and the effectual instrument of His work in our hearts. This, truly, would be exchanging the fine gold for brass; or, like unthankful Esau, bartering our enduring birthright for an empty and transitory benefit.

3. But the argument is continued. "Well," it may be said, "even granting that obedience to the Church be a Scripture duty, still, when there are erroneous teachers in it, surely it is a higher duty to desert them for their error's sake than to keep to them for form's sake." Now, before this question can be an-

swered, the error must be specified which this or that teacher holds. The plain and practical question we have to decide is, whether his error be such as to suspend his power of administering the Sacraments. It must be deadly indeed and monstrous to effect this; and, surely, this ministry of the Sacraments, not of the outward word—of the spirit, not of the letter—is his principal power and our principal need. It is our interest, it is our soul's interest, that we keep to those who minister divine benefits, even though they "offend in many things." And it is plainly our duty also. If they be in error, let us pray for them, not abandon them. If they sin against us, let not us sin against them. Let us return good for evil. Thus David acted even towards Saul his persecutor. He "behaved himself wisely in all his ways; and the Lord was with Him."[5] The cruelty of Saul was an extreme case; yet David's "eyes looked right on," and "he turned not to the right hand nor the left." He still honoured Saul, as put over him by Almighty God. So ought we, in St. Paul's words, to "obey them that have the rule over us, and submit ourselves." In truth, the notion that errors in a particular teacher justify separation from the Church itself, is founded in a mistake as to the very object (as it may be considered) for which teaching was committed to it. If individual teachers were infallible, there would be no need of order and rule at all. If we had a living Head upon earth, such as once our Saviour was with His disciples, teaching and directing us in all things, the visible Church might *so far* be dispensed with. But, since we have not, a form of doctrine, a system of laws, a bond of subordination connecting all in one, is the next best mode of securing the stability of sacred Truth. The whole body of Christians thus become the *trustees* of it, to use the language of the world, and, in fact, have thus age after age transmitted it down to ourselves. Thus, teachers have been bound to teach in one way not in another, as well as hearers to hear. As, then, we have a share in the advantage, let us not complain of sharing in the engagement; as we enjoy the truth at this day by the strictness of those who were before us, let us not shrink from undergoing that through which we have inherited it. If hearers break the rule of discipline, why should not teachers break the rule of faith? and if we find fault with our teacher, even while he is restrained by the Church's rule, how much greater would be our complaint when he was not so restrained? Let us not, then, be impatient of an appointment which effects so much, on the ground that it

[5] I Sam. xviii.14.

does not effect all. Let us not forget that rules presuppose the risk of error, but rather reflect whether they do not do more than they fail to do. Let us be less selfish than to think of ourselves only. Let us look out upon the whole community, the poor, the ignorant, the wayward, and the mistaken. Let us consider whether it will be prudent to become responsible for the Church's ultimately withdrawing from our land, which we shall be (as far as in us lies) by our withdrawing from it.

4. But it may be said, "Faith is not a matter of words, but of the heart. It is more than the formal doctrine, it is the temper and spirit of this or that teacher which is wrong. His creed may be orthodox, but his religion is not vital; and surely external order must not lie upon us as a burden, stifling and destroying the true inward fellowship between Christian and Christian." Now let it be carefully noted, that if order is to be preserved at all, it must be at the expense of what seems to be of more consequence, viz., the so-called communion of the heart between Christians. This peculiarity is involved in its very nature; and surely our Saviour knew this when He enjoined it. For consider a moment. True spiritual feeling, heartfelt devotion, lively faith, and the like, do not admit of being described, defined, ascertained in any one fixed way; as is implied indeed in the very objection under consideration. We form our judgment of them, whatever it be, by a number of little circumstances, of language, manner, and conduct, which cannot be put into words, which to no two beholders appear exactly the same, insomuch that if every one is to be satisfied, every one must have the power of drawing his line for himself. But if every one follow his own rule of fellowship, how can there possibly be but "one body," and in what sense are those words of the Apostle to be taken?

Again, this or that person may be more or less religious in speech and conduct; how are we to draw the line, even according to our own individual standard, and say who are to be in our Church and who out of it? Scandalous offenders indeed and open heretics might be excluded at once; but it would be far easier to say whom to put out than whom to let in, unless we let in all. From the truest believer to the very infidel there may be interposed a series of men, more or less religious, in human eyes, gradually filling up the whole interval. Even if we would infallibly decide between good and bad, life would be spent in the work; what our success really will be, may be foretold from the instances of those who attempt to do so, and who not unfrequently mistake for highly-gifted Christians men who are almost unbelievers. But, granting we have some extraordinary gift of discernment, still any how we could not see more than He sees, who implies that the faith of all of us is but immature and in its rudiments, by His very postponement of the final judgment;—so that to draw a line at all, and yet to include just all who seem religious, are things of necessity incompatible with each other.

On the other hand, forms are precise and definite. Once broken, they are altogether broken. There are no degrees of breaking them; either they are observed or they are not. It seems, then, on the whole, that if we leave the Church, in order to join what appears a less formal, a more spiritual, religion elsewhere, we break a commandment for certain, and we do not for certain secure to ourselves a benefit.

5. Lastly, it may be asked, "Are we then to keep aloof from those whom we think good men, granting that it would be better that they should be in the Church?" We need not, we must not, keep aloof. We are not bound, indeed, to court their society, but we are bound not to shrink from them when we fall in with them, except, indeed, they be the actual authors and fomenters of division. We are bound to love them and pray for them; not to be harsh with them, or revile or despise them, but to be gentle, patient, apt to teach, merciful, to make allowance, to interpret their conduct for the best. We would, if we could, be one with them in heart and in form, thinking a loving unity the glory and crown of Christian faith; and we will try all means to effect this; but we feel, and we cannot conceal it, we feel that, if we and they are to be one, they must come over to us. We desire to meet together, but it must be in the Church, not on neutral ground, or rather an enemy's, the open inhospitable waste of this world, but within that sheltered heritage whose land-marks have long since been set up. If Christ has constituted one Holy Society (which He has done); if His Apostles have set it in order (which they did), and have expressly bidden us (as they have in Scripture) not to undo what they have begun; and if (in matter of fact) their Work so set in order and so blessed is among us this very day (as it is), and we partakers of it, it were a traitor's act in us to abandon it, an unthankful slight on those who have preserved it for so many ages, a cruel disregard of those who are to come after us, nay of those now alive who are external to it and might otherwise be brought into it. We must transmit as we have received. We did not make the Church, we may not unmake it. As we believe it to be a Divine Ordinance, so we must ever protest against sepa-

ration from it as a sin. There is not a dissenter living, but, inasmuch and so far as he dissents, is in a sin. It may, in this or that instance, be a sin of infirmity, or carelessness, nay of ignorance; it may be a sin of the society to which a man belongs, not his own, a ceremonial offence, not a personal; still it is in its nature sinful. It may be mixed up with much that is good; it may be a perversion of conscience, or again, an inconsistency in him; it may be connected more or less with piety towards his forefathers; still, considered as such, it cannot but be a blemish and a disadvantage, and, if he is saved, he will be saved, not through it, but in spite of it. So far forth as he dissents, he is under a cloud; and though we too may, for what we know, have as great sins to answer for, taking his sin at the greatest, and though we pray that Christ will vouchsafe, in some excellent way, known to Himself, to "perfect, stablish, strengthen, settle," all "who love Him uncorruptly," even if separate from the glories of His Church on earth, still protest we should and must against separation itself, and wilful continuance in it, as evil—as nothing short of "the gainsaying of Core," and the true child of that sin which lost us Eden.

Nor does the sin of separation end in itself. Never suppose, my brethren, whatever the world may say, that a man is neither better nor worse, in his own faith and conduct, for separating from the Church. Of course we cannot "try the heart and the reins," or decide about individuals; still, this much seems clear, that, on the whole, deliberate insubordination is the symptom, nay, often the cause and first beginning of an unhumbled, wilful, self-dependent, contentious, jealous spirit; and, as far as any man allows himself in acts of it, so far has he upon him the tokens of pride or of coldness of heart, going before or following after. Coldness and pride—these sins are not peculiar, alas, to those who leave us; that we know full well. We all have the seeds of them within us, and it is our shame and condemnation if we do not repress them. But between us, if we be cold or proud, and those who are active in dissent, there is this clear difference—that proud reliance on self, or that cold formality, which may also be found in the Church, these, though found in it, are not fruits of it, do not rise from connection with it, but are inconsistent with it. For to obey is to be meek, not proud; and to obey, for Christ's sake, is to be zealous, not cold; whereas, wilful separation or turbulent conduct, forming religious meetings of our own, opposing our private judgment to those who have the rule over us, disaffection towards them, and the like feelings and courses, are the very effects and the sure forerunners of pride, or impatience, or restlessness, or self-will, or lukewarmness; so that these sins in members of the Church are in spite of the Church, but in separatists are involved in their separating.

"Put away from thee a froward mouth, and perverse lips put far from thee. Let thine eyes look right on, and let thine eyelids look straight before thee. Ponder the path of thy feet, and let all thy ways be established. Turn not to the right hand, nor to the left; remove thy foot from evil." What have we, private Christians, to do with hopes and fears of earth, with schemes of change, the pursuit of novelties, or dreams of reforms? The world is passing like a shadow; the day of Christ is hastening on. It is our wisdom, surely, to use what has been provided for us, instead of lusting after what we have not, asking flesh to eat, and gazing wistfully upon Egypt, or on the heathen around us. Faith has no leisure to act the busy politician, to bring the world's language into the sacred fold, or to use the world's jealousies in a divine polity, to demand rights, to flatter the many, or to court the powerful. What is faith's highest wish and best enjoyment? A dying saint shall answer. It is related of a meek and holy confessor of our own, shortly before his departure, that when, after much pain, he was asked by a friend, "What more special thing he would recommend for one's whole life?" he briefly replied, "*uniform obedience*," by which he meant, as his biographer tells us, that the happiest state of life was one in which we had not to command or direct, but *to obey solely*; not having to choose for ourselves, but having our path of duty, our mode of life, our fortunes marked out for us.[6] This lot, indeed, as is plain, cannot be the lot of all; but it is the lot of the many. Thus God pours out His blessings largely, and puts trial on the few; but men do not understand their own gain, and run into trials as being unfit for enjoyment. May He give us grace to cherish a wiser mind, to make much of our privilege, if we have it, to serve and be at rest; and, if we have it not, to covet it, and to bear dutifully as but a misfortune to a sinner, that freedom from restraint which the world boasts in as a chief good!

[6] Fell's "Life of Hammond."

CONTEST BETWEEN TRUTH AND FALSEHOOD IN THE CHURCH

"The kingdom of heaven is like unto a net, that was cast into the sea, and gathered of every kind: which, when it was full, they drew to shore, and sat down, and gathered the good into vessels, but cast the bad away."—Matt. xiii.47, 48.

IN the Apostle's age, the chief contest between Truth and Falsehood lay in the war waged by the Church against the world, and the world against the Church—the Church, the aggressor in the name of the Lord; the world, stung with envy and malice, rage and pride, retaliating spiritual weapons with carnal, the Gospel with persecution, good with evil, in the cause of the Devil. But of the conflict *within* the Church, such as it is at this day, Christians knew comparatively little. True, the Prophetic Spirit told them that "even of their ownselves should men arise, speaking perverse things, to draw away disciples after them;" that "in the last days perilous times should come."[1] Also they had the experience of their own and former times to show them, as in type, that in the Church evil will always mingle with the good. Thus, at the flood, there were eight men in the Ark, and one of them was reprobate; out of twelve Apostles, one was a devil; out of seven Deacons, one (as it is said) fell away into heresy; out of twelve tribes, one is dropped at the final sealing. These intimations, however, whether by instance or prophecy, were not sufficient to realize to them, before the event, the serious and awful truth implied in the text, viz.— that the warfare which Christ began between his little flock and the world should be in no long while transferred into the Church itself, and be carried on by members of that Church one with another.

This, I say, the early Christians did not see fulfilled, as our eyes see it; and so hard is it to possess ourselves of a true conviction about it, that even at this day, when it may be plainly seen,

[1] Acts xx.30; 2 Tim. iii.1.

men will not see it. They will not so open and surrender their minds to Divine truth, as to admit that the Holy Church has unholy members, that blessings are given to the unworthy, that "the Kingdom of Heaven is like a net that gathers of every kind." They evade this mysterious appointment in various ways. Sometimes they deny that bad men are really in God's Church, which they think consists only of good men. They have invented an Invisible Church, distinct and complete at present, and peopled by saints only,—as if Scripture said one word, anywhere, of a spiritual body existing in this world separate from, and independent of, the Visible Church; and they consider the Visible Church to be nothing but a mere part of this world, an establishment, sect, or party. Or, again, while they admit it as a Divine ordinance, they lower its standard of faith and holiness, and its privileges; and, considering the communion of saints to be but a name, and all Christians to be about alike, they effectually destroy all notions, whether of a Church or of a conflict. Thus, in one way or other, they refuse to admit the idea, contained in the text, that the dissimilitude, the enmity, and the warfare which once existed between the world and the Church, is now transferred into the Church itself.

But let us try, with God's blessing, to get a firm hold upon this truth, and see if we cannot draw some instruction from it. The text says, that "the Kingdom of Heaven," that is, the Christian Church, "is like unto a net that was cast into the sea, and gathered of every kind." Elsewhere St. Paul says, "In a great house there are not only vessels of gold and of silver, but also of wood and of earth; and some to honour, and some to dishonour." [2] Now, passages such as these admit of a very various application. I shall consider them here with reference to the contest between Truth and Falsehood in the Church.

Doubtless, in the eye of natural reason, it would be a privilege, were the enemies of Christ and of our souls separated from us, and did the trial of our faith take place on some broad questions, about which there could be no mistake; but such is not the fact "in the wisdom of God." Faith and unbelief, humbleness and pride, love and selfishness, have been from the Apostles' age united in one and the same body; nor can any means of man's device disengage the one from the other. All who are within the Church have the same privileges; they are all baptized, all admitted to the Holy Eucharist, all taught in

[2] 2 Tim. ii.20.

the Truth, all profess the Truth. At all times, indeed, there have been those who have avowed corrupt doctrine or indulged themselves in open vice; and whom, in consequence, it was easy to detect and avoid. But these are few; the great body in the Christian Church profess one and the same faith, and seem one and all to agree together. Yet, among these persons, thus apparently unanimous, is the real inveterate conflict proceeding, as from the beginning, between good and evil. Some of these are wise, some foolish. Who belong to the one, and to the other party, is hid from us, and will be hid till the day of judgment; nor are they at present individually formed upon the perfect model of good or evil; they vary one with another in the degree and mode of their holding to the one or the other; but that there are two parties in the Church, two parties, however vague and indefinite their outlines, among those who live, in one sense, as familiar friends, I mean, who eat the same spiritual Food, and profess the same Creed, is certain.

Next, what do they contend about? how and where is their conflict? The Apostles contended about the truth of the Gospel with unbelievers; their immediate successors contended, though within the Church, yet against open heresies, such as they could meet, confute, and cast out; but in after times, in our own day, now, what do the two secret parties in the Church, the elect and the false-hearted, what do they contend about?

It is difficult to answer this question suitably with the reverence due to this sacred place, in which the language of the world should not be heard. Yet, in so important a matter, one would wish to say something. That contest, which was first about the truth of the Gospel itself, next about the truth of doctrine, is now commonly about very small matters, of an every-day character, of public affairs, or domestic business, or parochial concerns, which serve as tests of our religious state quite as truly as greater things, in God's unerring judgment— serve as powerfully to form and train us for heaven or for hell.

I say, that as the early Christians were bound to "contend earnestly for the faith once delivered to the saints," so the trial of our obedience commonly lies in taking this or that side in a multitude of questions, in which there happen to be two sides, and which come before us almost continually; and, before attempting to explain what I mean, I would have you observe how parallel this state of things is to God's mode of trying and disciplining us in other respects.

For instance, how is our devotion to Christ shown? Ordinarily, not in great matters, not in giving up house and lands for

His sake, but in making little sacrifices which the world would ridicule, if it knew of them; in abridging ourselves of comforts for the sake of the poor, in sacrificing our private likings to religious objects, in going to Church at a personal inconvenience, in taking pleasure in the society of religious men, though not rich, or noble, or accomplished, or gifted, or entertaining; in matters, all of them of very little moment in themselves.

How is self-denial shown? Not in literally bearing Christ's Cross, and living on locusts and wild honey, but in such light abstinences as come in our way, in some poor efforts at fasting and the like, in desiring to be poor rather than rich, solitary or lowly rather than well-connected, in living within our income, in avoiding display, in being suspicious of comforts and luxuries; all of which are too trifling for the person observing them to think about, yet have their use in proving and improving his heart.

How is Christian valour shown? Not in resisting unto blood, but in withstanding mistaken kindness, in enduring importunity, in not shrinking from surprising and hurting those we love, in undergoing little losses, inconveniences, censures, slights, rather than betray what we believe to be God's Truth, be it ever so small a portion of it.

As then Christian devotion, self-denial, courage, are tried in this day in little things, so is Christian faith also. In the Apostles' age faith was shown in the great matter of joining either the Church, or the pagan or Jewish multitude. It is shown in this day by taking this side or that side in the many questions of opinion and conduct which come before us, whether domestic, or parochial, or political, or of whatever kind.

Take the most unlettered peasant in the humblest village; his trial lies in acting for the Church or against it in his own place. He may happen to be at work with others, or taking refreshment with others; and he may hear religion spoken against, or the Church, or the King; he may hear voices raised together in scoffing or violence; he must withstand laugh and jest, evil words and rudeness, and witness for Christ. Thus he carries on, in his day, the eternal conflict between Truth and Falsehood.

Another, in a higher class of society, has a certain influence in parish matters, in the application of charities, the appointment of officers, and the like; he, too, must act, as in God's sight, for the Truth's sake, as Christ would have him.

Another has a certain political power; he has a vote to bestow, or dependents to advise; he has a voice to raise, and substance to

contribute. Let him act for religion, not as if there were not a
God in the world.

My brethren, I must not venture to keep silence in respect to
a province of Christian duty, in which men are especially tried
at this day, and in which they especially fail.

It is sometimes said that religion is not (what is called) political. Now there is a bad sense of the word "political," and religion is nothing that is bad. But there is also a good sense of the
word, and in this sense whoever says that religion is not political
speaks as erringly, and (whether ignorantly or not) offends
with his tongue as certainly, as if in St. Paul's time a man had
said it mattered not whether he was Christian or heathen; for
what the question of Christian or no Christian was in the
Apostle's day, such are questions of politics now. It is as right to
take one side, and as wrong to take the other, now, in that multitude of matters which comes before us of a social nature, as it
was right to become a Christian in St. Paul's day, and wrong to
remain a heathen.

I am not saying *which* side is right and which is wrong, in the
ever-varying course of social duty, much less am I saying that all
religious people are on one side and all irreligious on the other
(for then would have that division between good and evil take place,
which the text and other parables assure us is not to be till the
Day of Judgment); I only say there *is* a right and a wrong, that it
is not a matter of indifference which side a man takes, that a
man will be judged hereafter for the side he takes.

When a man (for instance) says that he takes part against the
King or against the Church, because he thinks kingly power or
established Churches contrary to Scripture, I think him as far
from the truth as light is from darkness; but I understand him.
He takes a religious ground, and, whatever I may think of his
doctrine, I praise him for that. I had rather he should take a
religious ground (if in sincerity) and be against the Church,
than a worldly selfish ground, and be for it; that is, if done in
earnest, not in pretence, I think it speaks more hopefully for his
soul. I had rather the Church were levelled to the ground by a
nation, really, honestly, and seriously, thinking they did God
service in doing so (fearful indeed as the sin would be), than
that it should be upheld by a nation on the *mere* ground of maintaining property, for I think this a much greater sin. I think that
the worshipper of mammon will be in worse case before
Christ's Judgment-seat than the mistaken zealot. If a man must
be one or the other (though he ought to be neither), but if I
must choose for him, I had rather he should be Saul raging like

a wild beast against the Church, than Gallio caring for none of these things, or Demas loving the present world, or Simon trafficking with sacred gifts, or Ananias grudging Christ his substance, and seeking to be saved as cheaply as possible. There would be more chance of such a man's conversion to the Truth; and, if not converted, less punishment reserved for him at the Last Day. Our Lord says to the Church of Laodicea, "I would thou wert cold or hot. So then because thou art lukewarm, and neither cold nor hot, I will cast thee from My mouth." [3]

Men, however, generally act from mixed motives; so I do not mean that they are at once in a fearful peril, or as bad as fanatical revolutionists, for having some regard to the security of property, while they defend what is called the Church Established;—far from it, though I still think it would be better if the thought of religion absorbed all other considerations:—but I am speaking against an avowed doctrine maintained in this day, that religion has nothing to do with political matters; which will not be true till it is true that God does not govern the world, for as God rules in human affairs, so must His servants obey in them. And what we have to fear more than anything else at this time is, that persons who are sound on this point, and do believe that the concerns of the nation ought to be carried on on religious principles, should be afraid to avow it, and should ally themselves, *without protesting*, with those who deny it; lest they should keep their own opinion to themselves, and act with the kindred of Gallio, Demas, Simon, and Ananias, on some mere secular basis, the mere defence of property, the security of our institutions, considered merely as secular, the maintenance of our national greatness; forgetting that, as no man can serve two masters, God and mammon, so no man can at once be in the counsels of the servants of the two;—forgetting that the Church, in which they and others are, is a net gathering of *every* kind; that it is no proof that others are to be followed and supported in all things, because they happen to be in it and profess attachment to it; and that though we are bound to associate in a general way with all (except, indeed, such as openly break the rules of the Church, heretics, drunkards, evil livers, and the like, who ought of course to be put out of it), yet we are not bound to countenance all men in all they do, and are ever bound to oppose bad principles—bound to attempt to raise the standard of faith and obedience in that multitude of men whom, though we disapprove in many respects, we dare not af-

[3] Rev. iii.15, 16.

firm to be entirely destitute of the life of the Holy Ghost, and not to suffer friend or stranger to take part against the Truth without warning him of it according to our opportunities.

Lastly, this union of the True and the False in the Church, which I have been speaking of, has ever existed in the governing part of it as well as among the people at large. Our Saviour sets this truth before us in the twenty-third chapter of St. Matthew's gospel, in which He bids His hearers obey their spiritual rulers in all lawful things, even though they be unworthy of their office, because they hold it—obey "as unto the Lord and not to men." "The Scribes and the Pharisees sit in Moses' seat; all, therefore, whatsoever they bid you observe, that observe and do: but do not ye after their works, for they say, and do not." And no one can read, ever so little, the history of the Church since He was on earth, without perceiving that, under all the forms of obedience and subordination, of kind offices and social intercourse, which Christ enjoins, a secret contest has been carried on, in the most sacred chambers of the temple, between Truth and Falsehood;—rightly, peaceably, lovingly by some, uncharitably by others, with a strange mixture at times of right principles and defective temper, or of sincerity and partial ignorance; still, on the whole, a contest such as St. John's against Diotrephes, or St. Paul's against Ananias the High Priest, or Timothy's against Hymeneus and Alexander. Meantime, the rules of ecclesiastical discipline have been observed on both sides, as well as the professions of faith, as conditions of the contest; nevertheless, the contest has proceeded.

Now I would have every one who hears me bring what I have said home as a solemn truth to his own mind;—the solemn truth, that there is nothing indifferent in our conduct, no part of it without its duties, no room for trifling, lest we trifle with eternity. It is very common to speak of our political and social privileges as *rights*, which we may do what we like with; whereas they merely impose *duties* on us in God's sight. A man says, "I have a right to do this or that; I have a right to give my vote here or there; I have a right to further this or that measure." Doubtless, you *have* a right—you have the right of free-will—you have from your birth the birthright of being a free agent, of doing right or wrong, of saving yourself or ruining yourself; you have the right, that is, you have the power—(to speak plainly) the power to damn yourself; but (alas!) a poor consolation will it be to you in the next world, to know that your ruin was all your own fault, as brought upon you by yourself—for what you have said comes to nothing more than this; and be quite sure, men do not lose their souls by some one extraordinary act, but by a course of acts; and the careless, or rather, the self-sufficient and haughty-minded use of your political power, this way or that, at your pleasure, which is now so common, is among those acts by which men save or lose them. The young man whom Solomon speaks of, thought he had a right to indulge his lusts, or, as the rich man in the Gospel, to "take his ease, eat, drink, and be merry;" but the preacher says to him, "Rejoice, O young man in thy youth; and let thy heart cheer thee in the days of thy youth, and walk in the ways of thine heart, and in the sight of thine eyes: *but know thou, for all these things God will bring thee into judgment.*" [4]

So, again, many a man, when warned against the sin of leaving the Church, or of wandering about from one place of worship to another, says, "he has a right to do so." So it is, he has a strange notion that it is an Englishman's right to think what he will, and do what he will, in matters of religion. Nay, it *is* the right of the *whole world*, not ours alone; it *is* the attribute of all rational beings to have a right to do wrong, if they will. Yet, after all, there is but one right way, and there a hundred wrong ways. You *may* do as you will; but the first who exercised that right was the devil when he fell; and every one of us, when he does this or that in matters between himself and his God, merely because he *wills* it, and not for conscience' sake, is (so far) following the devil's pattern.

Now let us put aside these vain fancies, and look at our position steadily. Every one of us here assembled is either a vessel of mercy or a vessel of wrath fitted to destruction; or rather, I should say, *will be* such at the Last Day, and now is acting *towards* the one or the other. We cannot judge each other, we cannot judge ourselves. We only know about ourselves whether or no we are in some measure trying to serve God; we know He has loved us and "blessed us with all spiritual blessings in Christ," and desires our salvation. We know about others around us that they too have been blessed by the same Saviour, and are to be looked on as our brethren, till, by word or deed, they openly renounce their brotherhood. Still it is true that the solemn process of *separation* between bad and good is ever going on. The net has at present gathered of every kind. At the end of the world will be the final division; meanwhile there is a gradual sorting and sifting, silent but sure, towards it. It is also true that all the

[4] Eccles. xi.9.

matters which come before us in the course of life are trials of our faith, and instruments of our purification. It is also true that certain principles and actions are right and others wrong. It is true, moreover, that our part lies in finding out what is right, and observing and contending for it. And without judging of our brethren's state, and, again, without being over-earnest about little matters, it is our duty plainly to witness against others when we think them wrong, and to impress our seriousness upon them by our very manner towards them; lest we suffer sin in them, and so become partakers of it.

If all this be true, may God Himself, the Father of our Lord Jesus Christ, enable us heartily to act upon it! May He give us that honesty and simplicity of mind, which looks at things as He views them, realizes what is unseen, puts aside all the shadows and mists of pride, party-feeling, or covetousness; and not only knows and does what is right, but does it because it knows it, and that not from mere reason and on grounds of argument, but from the heart itself, with that inward and pure sense, and scrupulous fear, and keen faith, and generous devotion, which does not need arguments, except as a means of strengthening itself, and of persuading and satisfying others.

THE CHURCH VISIBLE
AND INVISIBLE

"In a great house there are not only vessels of gold and of silver,
but also of wood and of earth; and some to honour,
and some to dishonour."—2 Tim. ii.20.

IN these words St. Paul speaks of the Church as containing within it good and bad, after our Saviour's pattern, who, in the parables of the Net and of the Tares, had, from the first, announced the same serious truth. That Holy House which Christ formed in order to be the treasury and channel of His grace to mankind, over which His Apostles presided at the first, and after them others whom they appointed, was, even from their time, the seat of unbelief and unholiness as well as of true religion. Even among the Apostles themselves, one was "a devil." No wonder then that ever since, whether among the rulers or the subjects of the Church, sin has abounded, where nothing but righteousness, and peace, and joy in the Holy Ghost should have been found. It is so at this day; our eyes see it; we cannot deny it.

But, though we all see it, we do not all see it in that particular light which Scripture sheds upon it. We often account for it differently, we view it in a different relation to other truths, from that in which it really stands. In other words, we admit the fact, but adopt our own theory about it. I will explain what I mean, which will introduce a subject worth considering.

The sight of the sins of Christians has led us to speak of what are called the Visible and the Invisible Church in what seems an unscriptural way. The word Church, applied to the body of Christians in this world, means but one thing in Scripture, a visible body invested with invisible privileges. Scripture does not speak of two bodies, one visible, the other invisible, each with its own complement of members. But this is a common notion at present; and it is an erroneous, and (I will add) a dangerous notion.

It is true there are some senses in which we may allowably

talk of the Visible and Invisible Church. I am not finding fault with mere expressions; one is not bound in common discourse to use every word with scientific precision. It is allowable to speak of the Visible and of the Invisible Church, as two sides of one and the same thing, separated by our minds only, not in reality. For instance, in political matters, we sometimes speak of England as a nation and sometimes as a state; not meaning different things, but one certain identical thing viewed in a different relation. When we speak of the Nation, we take into account its variety of local rights, interests, attachments, customs, opinions; the character of its people, and the history of that character's formation. On the other hand, when we speak of the State, we imply the notion of orders, ranks, and powers, of the legislative and executive departments, and the like. In like manner, no harm can come of the distinction of the Church into Visible and Invisible, while we view it as, on the whole, but one in different aspects; as Visible, because consisting (for instance) of clergy and laity—as Invisible, because resting for its life and strength upon unseen influences and gifts from Heaven. This is not really to divide into two, any more than to discriminate (as they say) between concave and convex, is to divide a curve line; which looked at outwardly is convex, but looked at inwardly, concave.

Again, we may consider the Church in one century as different from the Church in another. We may speak of the modern Church and the ancient Church; and this without meaning that these are two bodies, merely by way of denoting difference of time. In a similar way we talk of the Jewish Church and the Christian, though really both Churches are one, only under different Dispensations. "What is meant," you will ask, "by the Church in one age being the same as the Church in another?"— plainly this, that there is no real line of demarcation between them, that the one is but the continuation of the other, and that you may as well talk of two Churches at this moment in the north and south of England, as two in different centuries. Properly speaking, the One Church is the whole body gathered together from all ages; so that the Church of this very age is but part of it, and this in the same sense in which the Church in England, again, in this day, is but part of the present Church Catholic. In the next world this whole Church will be brought together in one, whenever its separate members lived, and then, too, all its unsound and unfruitful members will be dropped, so that nothing but holiness will remain in it. Here, then, is a second sense in which we may discriminate between the Church Visible and Invisible. The body of the elect, con-templated as it will be hereafter, nay, as it already exists in Para-dise, we may, if we will, call the Church, and, since this blessed consummation takes place in the unseen world, we may call it the Invisible Church. Doubtless, we may speak of the Invisible Church in the sense of the Church in glory, or the Church in rest. There is no error in such a mode of speech. We do not make two Churches, we only view the Christian body as exist-ing in the world of spirits; and the present Church Visible, so far as it really has part and lot in the same blessedness.

Still further, we may, by a figure of speech, speak of the members of the existing Church, who are at present walking in God's faith and fear, as the Invisible Church; not meaning thereby that they constitute a separate body (which is not the case), but by a mental abstraction, separating them off in imagi-nation from the rest, speaking of them as invisible because we do not know them, and speaking of them as peculiarly the Church because they are what all Christians are intended and ought to be, and are all that would remain of the Church Vis-ible, did the Day of Judgment suddenly come. In like manner, speaking politically, we talk of the clergy as the Church: here is a parallel instance, in which a part of a body is viewed as the whole; still, who would say that the Laity are one Church by themselves, and the Clergy by themselves another?

In all these senses then, whether we speak of the Church as invisibly blest and succoured, or as triumphant hereafter, or in relation to its true members, who are its substantial support and glory, we may allowably make mention of the Invisible Church. But if we conceive of the Invisible as one, and the Visible as another, as if there were one body without spiritual privileges, of good and bad together, and another of good only, with spiri-tual privileges, surely we speak without warrant, or rather without leave of Holy Scripture.

The Church of Christ, as Scripture teaches, is a visible body, invested with, or (I may say) existing in invisible privileges. Take the analogy of the human body by way of illustration. Considering man according to his animal nature, I might speak of him as having an organized visible frame sustained by an un-seen spirit. When the soul leaves the body it ceases to be a body, it becomes a corpse. So the Church would cease to be the Church, did the Holy Spirit leave it; and it does not exist at all except in the Spirit. Or, consider the figure of a tree, which is our Lord's own instance. A vine has many branches, and they are all nourished by the sap which circulates throughout. There may be dead branches, still they are upon one and the selfsame tree. Were they as numerous as the sound ones, were they a hundred times as many, they would not form a tree by themselves. Were all the branches dead, were the stock dead, then it would be a dead tree. But any how, we could never say there were two trees. Such is the Scripture account of the Church, a living body with branches, some dead, some living; as in the text by another figure: "In a great house there are vessels; some to honour, and some to dishonour." Can any account be plainer than this is? Why divide into two, when the only reason for so dividing, viz., the improbability that good and bad should be found together, is superseded, as irrelevant, by our Lord and His Apostles themselves? Very various things are said of the Church; sometimes it is spoken of as glorious and holy, sometimes as abounding in offences and sins. It is natural, perhaps, at first sight, to invent, in consequence, the hypothesis of two Churches, as the Jews have dreamed of two Messiahs; but, I say, our Saviour has implied that it is unnecessary, that these opposite descriptions of it are not really incompatible; and if so, what reason remains for doing violence to the sacred text?

Consider these various descriptions, carefully examine them, and say, why it is not possible to adjust them together in one subject, directly we know that it is lawful to do so? Consider how they were all fulfilled in the case of the Corinthians, which is expressly given in Scripture. For instance, the Church is made up of ranks and offices. "God hath set some in the Church, first apostles, secondarily prophets, thirdly teachers, after that miracles, then gifts of healings, helps, governments, diversities of tongues." It is inhabited by the Holy Ghost: "All these worketh that one and the selfsame Spirit, dividing to every man severally as He will. For as the body is one, and hath many members, and all the members of that one body, though many, are one body; so also is Christ." Its Sacraments are the instruments which the Holy Ghost uses: "By one Spirit are we all baptized into one body, whether we be Jews or Gentiles, whether we be bond or free; and have been all made to drink into one Spirit." Yet, in spite of these precious gifts, the Church consists of bad as well as good; for the Corinthians, though "the temple of the Holy Ghost," are reproved by St. Paul for being "puffed up," "contentious," and "carnal."

Now, in answer to this account of the Church, as one, and not double, it may be objected, that "surely it is impossible that bad men can really have God's grace within them, or that the irreligious or secular can be properly called justified or elect; yet such men are outwardly in the Church, so that there are two Churches any how, an outward and an inward." Or, again, it may be said that "repentance and faith are confessedly necessary in order to enjoy the Christian privileges; those, therefore, who have not these requisites, certainly have not the privileges, that is, are not members of Christ's true Church; from which again it follows, that there certainly are two bodies, whatever words we use." It will be added, perhaps, that "Simon Magus, though he had been baptized, was unregenerate, being addressed by St. Peter as being 'in the gall of bitterness and the bond of iniquity.'" [1] On the other hand it may be argued, that "there are good men outside the Visible Church, viz., among Dissenters, who, as being good, must necessarily be in the Invisible Church; and thus there certainly are two Churches." On the whole, then, there are these two arguments to prove that the word Church has two distinct meanings in Scripture; first, that there are bad men in the Visible Church; next, that certain good men are out of it:—both being derived from *the actual state of things which we see*, which is supposed to be a legitimate comment upon the words of Scripture.

1. We will first take the objection, that bad men are in the Visible Church; what is this to prove? Let us observe. It is maintained, that "bad men cannot be members of the true Church, therefore, there is a true Church distinct from the Visible Church." But we shall be nearer the truth, if, instead of saying "bad men cannot be members of the true Church," we word it, "bad men cannot be true members of the Church." Does not this meet all that reason requires, yet without leading to the inference that the Church Visible is not the true Church? Again, it is said that "the Visible Church has not the gifts of grace, because wicked men are members of it, who, of course, cannot have them." What! must the Church be without them herself, because she is not able to impart them to wicked men? What reasoning is this? because certain individuals of a body have them not, therefore the body has them not! Surely it is possible that certain members of a body should be debarred, under circumstances, from its privileges; and this we consider to be the case with bad men.

Let us return to the instance of a tree, already used. Is a dead branch part or not part of a tree? You may decide this way or that, but you will never say, because the branch is dead, that therefore the tree has no sap. It is a dead branch of a living tree,

[1] Acts viii.23.

not a branch of a dead tree. In like manner, irreligious men are dead members of the one Visible Church, which is living and true, not members of a Church which is dead. Because they are dead, it does not follow that the Visible Church to which they belong is dead also.

Or, consider the parallel of a body politic. Are persons, who are under disabilities, members of it or not? Are convicts? Prisoners are debarred from certain rights, but they are still members of the state, and, after a while, recover what they have forfeited.

The case is the same as regards the Church. Its invisible privileges range throughout it; but there may be, on the part of individuals, obstacles or impediments which suspend *their* enjoyment of them. It is one thing to be admitted into the body, and another thing to enjoy its privileges. While men are impenitent, the grace of the Christian election does not operate in their case. And in proportion to their carelessness and profaneness do they quench the Spirit. Hence it is, that faith is necessary for our justification, as an indispensable condition, where it can be had. Simon Magus, we may securely grant, was profited nothing by his baptism; the font of regeneration was opened upon him, but his heart was closed. The blessing was put into his hand, but he had not that which alone could apprehend and apply it. It was sealed up from him and only penitence and faith could unseal it. Therefore St. Peter bids him repent, that he might receive it. He went on further in wickedness, as history informs us, and then, of course, the gift thus attached to him, but not enjoyed, would prove, at the last day, but a cause of heavier condemnation. I do not presume to say that this is the true explanation *of his case*, which is not told us, but as a mode of explaining it, and yet keeping clear of the conclusion, for the sake of which it is usually brought. If there be one such explanation, there may be others.

In like manner, when men fall into sin, *they* lose the light of God's countenance; but why should it be withdrawn from the Holy Church, for *their* individual transgressions?

There was a controversy, in early times, which illustrates still further the foregoing explanation of the difficulty. It was disputed whether the baptism administered by clergy who were heretics, and had been put out of the Church, was valid. And at length it was decided as follows: that the baptism was valid for the primary purpose of baptism, viz., that of admitting into the visible body of Christ, but that the *enjoyment* of its privileges was suspended, while the parties receiving it remained in heretical communion. On coming over to the Church Catholic, they were formally admitted by confirmation, and released from the bond under which they had hitherto lain.

If, then, I am asked what is to be thought of the state of irreligious men in the Church, I answer, that if open sinners, or heretics, or leaders in dissent, be meant they are to be put out of it by the competent authority. As to those who are not such, we cannot determine about their real condition, for we cannot see their hearts. Many may seem fair and specious to us, who are really dead in God's sight; and these, of course, cannot possess the gifts of grace any more than Simon Magus. Or they may be lukewarm, unstable, inconsistent; and may thus have forfeited, more or less, the privileges which have graciously been committed to them. But how does all this show that the Visible Church has not the true and spiritual gifts of the Gospel attached to her?

2. Now, to consider the second objection that is urged, viz., that "there are good men external to the Visible Church, therefore there is a second Church, called the Invisible." In answer, I observe, that as every one, who has been duly baptized, is, in one sense, in the Church, even though his sins since have hid God's countenance from him; so, if a man has not been baptized, be he ever so correct and exemplary in his conduct, this does not prove that he has received regeneration, which is the peculiar and invisible gift of the Church. What is Regeneration? It is the gift of a new and spiritual nature; but men have, through God's blessing, obeyed and pleased Him without it. The Israelites were not regenerated; Cornelius, the Centurion, was not regenerated, when his prayers and alms came up before God. No outward conduct, however consistent, can be a criterion, to our mortal judgments, of this unearthly and mysterious privilege. Therefore, when you bring to me the case of religious Dissenters, I rejoice at hearing of them. If they know no better, God, we trust, will accept them as He did the Shunammite. I wish, with all my heart, they partook the full blessings of the Church; but all my wishing cannot change God's appointments; and His appointment, I say, is this—that the Church Visible should be the minister, and baptism the instrument of Regeneration. But I have said not a word to imply that a man, if he knows no better, may not be exemplary in his generation without it.

So much in answer to this objection; but the same consideration throws light upon the former difficulty also, that of inconsistent men being in the Church. Regeneration, I say, is a new birth, or the giving of a new nature. Now, let it be observed, there is nothing impossible in the thing itself, though we believe it is not so, but nothing impossible in the very *notion* of a regeneration being accorded even to impenitent sinners. I do not say regeneration in its fulness, for that includes in it perfect happiness and holiness, to which it tends from the first; yet regeneration in a true and sufficient sense, in its primary qualities. For the essence of regeneration is the communication of a higher and diviner nature; and sinners may have this gift, though it would be a curse to them, not a blessing. The devils have a nature thus higher and more divine than man, yet they are not preserved thereby from evil.

And if this is the case even with sinners, much more is regeneration conceivable in the instance of children, who have done neither good nor evil. Nor does it all follow, even though they grow up disobedient, and are a scandal to the Church, that therefore the Church has not conveyed to them a great gift, an initiation into the powers of the world to come.

If, indeed, this gracious privilege ensured religious obedience, then, truly, disobedience in those who have been admitted into the Church would prove that the Church had not conveyed it to them. But, until a man is ready to maintain that the Spirit cannot be "quenched," he has no warrant for saying that it has not been given.

Now, then, after these explanations, let me ask, in what is this whole doctrine concerning the Church, which I have been giving, *inconsistent*? What *difficulty* does it present to force us to reject the plain word of Scripture about it, and to imagine a Visible Church with no privileges at all, and an Invisible Church of real Christians exclusively with them? Surely, nothing but the influence of a human system, acting on us, can make us read Scripture so perversely! and how is it a less violence to deny that the Church which the Apostles set up, and which is, in matter of fact, among us at this day, is (what Scripture says it is) the pillar and ground of the Truth, the Mother of us all, the House of God, the dwelling-place of the Holy Ghost, the Spouse of Christ, a glorious Church without spot or wrinkle or any such thing, and destined to remain even to the end of the world—how is this a less violent perversion of Scripture truth than theirs, who, when Scripture says that Christ is God, obstinately maintain He is a mere man?

I will notice in conclusion one objection which subtle minds may make to the statements now set before you. It may be said that the Church has forfeited its early privileges, by allowing itself to remain in a state of sin and disorder which Christ never intended: for instance, "that from time to time there have been great corruptions in it, especially under the ascendancy of the Papal power: that there have been very many scandalous appointments to its highest dignities, that infidels have been bishops, that men have administered baptism or ordination, not believing that grace was imparted in those sacred ordinances, and that, in particular in our own country, heretics and open sinners, whom Christ would have put out of the Church, are suffered, by a sin on the part of the Church, to remain within it unrebuked, uncondemned." This is what is sometimes said; and I confess, had we not Scripture to consult, it would be a very specious argument against the Church's present power, now at the distance of eighteen hundred years from the Apostles. It would certainly seem as if, the conditions not having been fully observed on which that power was granted, it was forfeited. But here the case of the Jewish Church affords us the consoling certainty, that God does not so visit, even though He might, and that His gifts and calling "are without repentance." [2] Christ's Church cannot be in a worse condition than that of Israel when He visited it in the flesh; yet He expressly assures us that in His day "the Scribes and Pharisees," wicked men as they were, "sat in Moses' seat," and were to be obeyed in what they taught; and we find, in accordance with this information, that Caiaphas, "because he was the high priest," had the gift of prophecy—had it, though he did not know he had it, nay, in spite of his being one of the foremost in accomplishing our Lord's crucifixion. Surely, then, we may infer, that, however fallen the Church now is from what it once was, however unconscious of its power, it still has the gift, as of old time, to convey and withdraw the Christian privileges, "to bind and to loose," to consecrate, to bless, to teach the Truth in all necessary things, to rule, and to prevail.

But if these things be so, if the Church Visible really has invisible privileges, what must we think, my brethren, of the general spirit of this day, which looks upon the Church as but a civil institution, a creation and a portion of the State? What shall be thought of the notion that it depends upon the breath of princes, or upon the enactments of human law? What, again, shall be thought of those who fiercely and rancorously oppose and revile what is really an Ordinance of God, and the place where His honour dwelleth? Even to the Jewish priest-

[2] Rom. xi.29.

hood after the blood of the Redeemer was upon it, even to it St. Paul deferred, signifying that God's high priest was not to be reviled; and if so, surely much less the rulers of a branch of the Church, which, whatever have been its sins in times past, yet is surely innocent (as we humbly and fervently trust) of any inexpiable crime. Moreover, what an unworthy part they act, who, knowing and confessing the real claims of the Church, yet allow them to be lightly treated and forgotten, without uttering a word in their behalf; who from secular policy, or other insufficient reason, bear to hear our spiritual rulers treated as mere civil functionaries, without instructing, or protesting against, or foregoing intimacy with those who despise them, nay even co-operating with them cordially, as if they could serve two masters, Christ and the world! And how melancholy is the general spectacle in this day of ignorance, doubt, perplexity, misbelief, perverseness, on the subject of this great doctrine, to say nothing of the jealousy, hatred, and unbelieving spirit with which the Church is regarded! Surely, thus much we are forced to grant, that, be the privileges vested in the Church what they may, yet, at present, they are, as to their full fruits, suspended in our branch of it by our present want of faith; nor can we expect that the glories of Christ's Kingdom will again be manifested in it, till we repent, confess "our offences and the offences of our forefathers;" and, instead of trusting to an arm of flesh, claim for the Church what God has given it, for Christ's sake, "whether men will hear, or whether they will forbear."

THE VISIBLE CHURCH
AN ENCOURAGEMENT TO FAITH

"Wherefore seeing we also are compassed about with so great a cloud
of witnesses, let us lay aside every weight, and the sin which doth
so easily beset us, and let us run with patience the race
that is set before us."—Heb. xii.1.

THE warning and consolation given by the Apostle to the Hebrews, amid their sufferings for the truth's sake, were as follows: they were to guard against unbelief, that easily-besetting sin under temptation, chiefly, and above all, by "looking unto Jesus, the Author and Finisher of faith;" but, besides this, a secondary stay was added. So glorious and holy is our Lord, though viewed in His human nature, so perfect when He was tempted, so heavenly even upon earth, that sinners, such as we are, cannot endure the sight of Him at first. Like the blessed Apostle in the book of Revelation, we "fall at His feet as dead." So, in mercy to us, without withdrawing His presence, He has included within it, His Saints and Angels, a great company of created beings, nay, of those who once were sinners, and subjects of His kingdom upon earth; that thus we may be encouraged by the example of others before us to look unto Him and live. St. Paul, in the foregoing chapter, enumerates many of the Ancient Saints who had run the course of faith; and then he says in the text, "Wherefore, let us also, being compassed about with so great a cloud of witnesses, lay aside every weight, and the sin which doth so easily beset us, and let us run with patience the race that is set before us." And presently he speaks in still more high and glowing language of the Christian Church, that august assemblage which Christ had formed of all that was holy in heaven and earth. "Ye are come unto Mount Sion, and unto the city of the living God, the heavenly Jerusalem, and to an innumerable company of Angels, to the general assembly and Church of the first-born, and to the spirits of the just made perfect, and to Jesus the Mediator of the New Covenant."

And much is needed, in every age, as a remedy against unbelief, that support which St. Paul suggested to the Hebrews in persecution, the vision of the Saints of God, and of the Kingdom of Heaven. Much is it needed, in every age, by those who have set their hearts to serve God, because they are few, and faint for company. We are told, expressly, "Broad is the way that leadeth to destruction, and many there be which go in thereat." On the other hand, "Strait is the gate, and narrow is the way, which leadeth unto life, and few there be that find it." [1] Alas! is it not discouragement enough to walk in a path of self-denial, to combat our natural lusts and high imaginations, to have the war of the flesh, that the war with the world must be added to it? Is it not enough to be pilgrims and soldiers all our days, but we must hear the mutual greetings, and exulting voices of those who choose the way of death, and must walk not only in pain but in solitude? Where is the blessing upon the righteous, where the joy of faith, the comfort of love, the triumph of self-mastery, in such dreariness and desolateness? Who are to sympathize with us in our joys and sorrows, who are to spur us on by the example of their own success? St. Paul answers us—the cloud of witnesses of former days. Let us then consider our need and its remedy.

1. Certainly it cannot be denied that, if we surrender our hearts to Christ and obey God, we shall be in the number of the few. So it has been in every age, so it will be to the end of time. It is hard, indeed, to find a man who gives himself up honestly to his Saviour. In spite of all the mercies poured upon us, yet in one way or other we are in danger of being betrayed by our own hearts, and taking up with a pretence of religion instead of the substance. Hence, in a country called Christian, the many live to the world. Nay, it would seem that as Christianity spreads, its fruit becomes less; or, at least, does not increase with its growth. It seems (some have said) as if a certain portion of truth were in the world, a certain number of the elect in the Church, and, as you increased its territory, you scattered this remnant to and fro, and made them seem fewer, and made them feel more desolate.

"Behold, I send you forth as sheep in the midst of wolves;" [2] what our Lord addressed to His Apostles is fulfilled to this day in all those who obey Him. They are sprinkled up and down the world; they are separated the one from the other, they are bid quit each other's dear society, and sent afar off to those who are

---

[1] Matt. vii.13, 14.   [2] Matt. x.16.

differently minded. Their choice of profession and employment is not their own. Outward circumstances, over which they have no control, determine their line of life; accidents bring them to this place or that place, not knowing whither they go; not knowing the persons to whom they unite themselves, they find, almost blindly, their home and their company. And in this, moreover, differing from the Apostles, and very painfully; that the Apostles knew each other, and could communicate one with another, and could form, nay, were bound to form one body; but now, those honest and true hearts, in which the good seed has profitably fallen, do not even know each other; nay, even when they think they can single out their fellows, yet are they not allowed to form a separate society with them.

They do not know each other; they do not know themselves; they do not dare take to themselves the future titles of God's elect, though they be really reserved for them; and the nearer they are towards heaven, so much the more lowly do they think of themselves. "Lord, I am not worthy that Thou shouldest come under my roof," [3] was the language of him who had greater faith than any in Israel. Doubtless, they do not know their own blessedness, nor can they single out those who are their fellows in blessedness. God alone sees the heart; now and then, as they walk their way, they see glimpses of God's work in others; they take hold of them awhile in the dark, but soon lose them; they hear their voices, but cannot find them. Some few, indeed, are revealed to them in a measure. Among those with whom their lot is cast, whom they see continually, one or two, perhaps, are given them to rejoice in, but not many even of these. For so it has pleased the Dresser of the Vineyard, who seems to have purposed that His own should not grow too thick together; and if they seem to do so, He prunes His vine, that, seeming to bear less, it may bear better. He plucks off some of the promise of the vintage; and they who are left, mourn over their brethren whom God has taken to Himself, not understanding that it is no strange providence, but the very rule of His government, to leave His servants few and solitary.

And, even when they know each other (as far as man can know man), still, as I have said, they may not form an exclusive communion together. Of course, every one will naturally live most with those whom he likes most; but it is one thing to have a preference, and quite another to draw a line of exclusion, and

[3] Matt. viii.8.

to form a select company within the Church. The Visible Church of God is that one only company which Christians know as yet; it was set up at Pentecost, with the Apostles for founders, their successors for rulers, and all professing Christian people for members. In this Visible Church the Church Invisible is gradually moulded and matured. It is formed slowly and variously by the Blessed Spirit of God, in the instance of this man and that, who belong to the general body. But all these blessed fulfilments of God's grace are as yet but parts of the Visible Church; they grow from it; they depend upon it; they do not hang upon each other; they do not form a body together; there is no Invisible Church yet formed; it is but a name as yet; a name given to those who are hidden, and known to God only, and as yet but half formed, the unripe and gradually ripening fruit which grows on the stem of the Church Visible. As well might we attempt to foretell the blossoms which will at length turn to account and ripen for the gathering, and then counting up all these and joining them together in our minds, call them by the name of a tree, as attempt now to associate in one the true elect of God. They are scattered about amid the leaves of that Mystical Vine which is seen, and receive their nurture from its trunk and branches. They live on its Sacraments and its Ministry; they gain light and salvation from its rites and ordinances; they communicate with each other through it; they obey its rulers; they walk together with its members; they do not dare to judge of this man or that man, on their right hand or their left, whether or not he is absolutely of the number of those who shall be saved; they accept all as their brethren in Christ, as partakers of the same general promises, who have not openly cast off Christ—as really brethren, till death comes, as those are who fulfil their calling most strictly.

Yet, at the same time, while in faith they love those, all around them, who are called by Christ's name, and forbear to judge about their real state in God's sight, they cannot but see much in many of them to hurt and offend them; they cannot but feel, most painfully, the presence of that worldly atmosphere which, however originating, encircles them; they feel the suffocation of those vapours in which the many are content to remain; and while they cannot trace the evil to its real authors individually, they are sure that it is an evil to be avoided and pointed out, and originating somewhere or other in the Church. Hence, in their spheres, whether high or low, the faithful few are witnesses; they are witnesses for God and Christ, in their lives, and by their protestations, without judging others, or exalting themselves. They are witnesses in various degrees, to various persons, more or less, as each needs it—differing from the multitude variously, as each of that multitude, before whom they witness, is better or worse, and as they themselves are more or less advanced in the truth; still, on the whole, they are witnesses, as light witnesses against darkness by the contrast;—giving good and receiving back evil; receiving back on themselves the contempt, the ridicule, and the opposition of the world, mixed, indeed, with some praise and reverence, reverence which does not last long, but soon becomes fear and hatred. And hence it is that religious men need some consolation to support them, which the Visible Church seems, at first sight, not to supply, when the overflowings of ungodliness make them afraid.

2. Now then, secondly, in such circumstances what shall we say? Are they but solitary witnesses, each in his place? Is the Church which they see really no consolation to them at all, except as contemplated by faith in respect of its invisible gifts? or does it, after all, really afford them some sensible stay, a vision of Heaven, of peace and purity, antagonist to the world that now is, in spite of the evil which abounds in it, and overlays it? Through God's great mercy, it is actually, in no small degree, a present and a sensible consolation, as I proceed to show.

In truth, do what he will, Satan cannot quench or darken the light of the Church. He may incrust it with his own evil creations, but even opaque bodies transmit rays, and Truth shines with its own heavenly lustre, though "under a bushel." The Holy Spirit has vouchsafed to take up His abode in the Church, and the Church will ever bear, on its front, the visible signs of its hidden privilege. Viewed at a little distance, its whole surface will be illuminated, though the light really streams from apertures which might be numbered. The scattered witnesses thus become, in the language of the text, "a cloud," like the Milky Way in the heavens.

We have, in Scripture, the records of those who lived and died by faith in the old time, and nothing can deprive us of them. The strength of Satan lies in his being seen to have the many on his side; but, when we read the Bible, this argument loses its hold over us. There we find that we are not solitary; that others, before us, have been in our very condition, have had our feelings, undergone our trials, and laboured for the prize which we are seeking. Nothing more elevates the mind than the consciousness of being one of a great and victorious company. Does not the soldier exult in his commander, and consider his triumph as his own? He is but one, yet he identifies himself with the army, and the cause in which he serves, and dwells upon the thought of victories, and those who win them, more than on casual losses and defeats. Does not a native of a powerful country feel it a joy and boast to be so? Do we not hear men glory in being born Englishmen? And they go to and fro, gazing on the works of their own days, and the monuments of their forefathers, and say to themselves that their race is a noble one. Much more fully, much more reasonably is this the boast of a Christian, and without aught of arrogant or carnal feeling. He knows, from God's Word, that he is "citizen of no mean city." He feels that his is no upstart line, but very ancient; Almighty God having purposed to bring many sons unto glory through His Son, and begetting them again, in their separate ages, to do Him service. He is one of a host, and all those blessed Saints he reads of are his brethren in the faith. He finds, in the history of the past, a peculiar kind of consolation, counteracting the influence of the world that is seen. He cannot tell who the Saints are now on earth; those yet unborn are known to God only; but the Saints of former times are sealed for heaven and are in their degree revealed to him. The spirits of the just made perfect encourage him to follow them. This is why it is a Christian's characteristic to look back on former times. The man of this world lives in the present, or speculates about the future; but faith rests upon the past and is content. It makes the past the mirror of the future. It recounts the list of faithful servants of God, to whom St. Paul refers in the text, and no longer feels sad as if it were alone. Abraham and the Patriarchs, Moses, Samuel, and the Prophets, David and the kings who walked in his steps, these are the Christian's forefathers. By degrees he learns to have them as familiar images before his mind, to unite his cause with theirs, and, since their history comforts him, to defend them in his own day. Hence he feels jealous for their honour, and when they are attacked he answers eagerly, so as to surprise those who are contented with things as they are; but, truly, he is too grateful, too affectionate, too much interested in the matter, to be complimentary and generous towards their assailants. He had rather the present day should be proved captious, than a former day mistaken.

But to return: what a world of sympathy and comfort is thus opened to us in the Communion of Saints! The heathen, who sought truth most earnestly, fainted for want of companions; every one stood by himself. They were tempted to think that all their best feelings were but an empty name, and that it mattered not whether they served God or disobeyed Him. But Christ has "gathered together the children of God that were scattered abroad," and brought them near to each other in every time and place. Are we young, and in temptation or trial? we cannot be in worse circumstances than Joseph. Are we in sickness? Job will surpass us in sufferings as in patience. Are we in perplexities and anxieties, with conflicting duties and a bewildered mind, having to please unkind superiors, yet without offending God; so grievous a trial as David's we cannot have, when Saul persecuted him. Is it our duty to witness for the truth among sinners? No Christian can at this day be so hardly circumstanced as Jeremiah. Have we domestic trials? Job, Jacob, and David, were afflicted in their children. It is easy indeed to say all this, and many a man may hear it said, and not feel moved by it, and conceive it is a mere matter of words, easy and fitting indeed to say, but a cold consolation in actual suffering. And I will own that a man cannot profit by these considerations all at once. A man, who has never thought of the history of the Saints, will gain little benefit from it on first taking up the subject when he comes into trouble. He will turn from it disappointed. He may say, "My pain or my trial is not the less because another had it a thousand years since." But the consolation in question comes not in the way of argument but by habit. A tedious journey seems shorter when gone in company, yet, be the travellers many or few, each goes over the same ground.

Such is the Christian's feeling towards all Saints, but it is especially excited by the Church of Christ and by all that belong to it. For what is that Church but a pledge and proof of God's never-dying love and power from age to age? He set it up in mercy to mankind, and its presence among us is a proof that in spite of our sins He has not yet forsaken us;—"Hitherto hath the Lord helped us." He set it up on the foundation of His Twelve Apostles, and promised that the gates of hell should not prevail against it; and its presence among us is a proof of His power. He set it up to succeed to the four monster kingdoms which then were; and it lived to see those kingdoms of the earth crumble into dust and come to nought. It lived to see society new formed upon the model of the governments which last to this day. It lives still, and it is older than them all. Much and rightly as we reverence old lineage, noble birth, and illustrious ancestry, yet the royal dynasty of the Apostles is far older than all the kingly families which are now on the earth. Every Bishop of the Church whom we behold, is a lineal descendant of St. Peter and St. Paul after the order of a spiritual birth;—a noble thought, if we could realize it! True it is that at various times the Bishops have forgotten their high rank and acted unworthily of it. So have kings and princes, yet noble they were by blood in spite of their personal errors, and the line of their family is not broken or degraded thereby. And in like manner, true though it be that the descendants of the Apostles have before now lived to this world, have fancied themselves of this world, have thought their office secular and civil, or if religious, yet at least "of men and by man," not "by Jesus Christ," have judged it much to have riches, or to sit in high places, or to have rank and consideration, or to have the fame of letters, or to be king's counsellors, or to live in courts—yet, granting the utmost, for all this they are not the less inspiring an object to a believing mind, which sees in each of them the earnest of His promise, "I will never leave thee nor forsake thee." He said, He would be with His Church: He has continued it alive to this day. He has continued the line of His Apostles onwards through every age and all troubles and perils of the world. Here then, surely, is somewhat of encouragement for us amid our loneliness and weakness. The presence of every Bishop suggests a long history of conflicts and trials, sufferings and victories, hopes and fears, through many centuries. His presence at this day is the fruit of them all. He is the living monument of those who are dead. He is the promise of a bold fight and a good confession and a cheerful martyrdom now, if needful, as was instanced in those of old time. We see their figures on our walls, and their tombs are under our feet; and we trust, nay, we are sure, that God will be to us in our day what He was to them. In the words of the Psalmist, "The Lord hath been mindful of us; He will bless us; He will bless the house of Israel; He will bless the house of Aaron." [4]

And more especially does the sight of our living Apostles bring before our thoughts the more favoured of their line, who, at different times, have fought the good fight of faith valiantly and gloriously. Blessed be God, He has given us to know them as if we had lived in their day and enjoyed their pattern and instructions. Alas! in spite of the variety of books now circulated among all classes of the community, how little is known about the Saints of past times! How is this? has Christ's Church failed in any age? or have His witnesses betrayed their trust? are they not our bone and our flesh? Have they not partaken the same spiritual food as ourselves and the same spiritual drink,

[4] Ps. cxv. 12.

used the same prayers, and confessed the same creed? If a man merely looks into the Prayer-Book, he will meet there with names, about which, perhaps, he knows and cares nothing at all. A prayer we read daily is called the prayer of St. Chrysostom; a creed is called the Creed of St. Athanasius; another creed is called the Nicene Creed; in the Articles we read of St. Augustine and St. Jerome; in the Homilies of many other such besides. What do these names mean? Sad it is, you have no heart to inquire after or celebrate those who are fellow-citizens with you, and your great benefactors! Men of this world spread each other's fame—they vaunt loudly;—you see in every street the names and the statues of the children of men, you hear of their exploits in speeches and histories; yet you care not to know concerning those to whom you are indebted for the light of Gospel truth. Truly they were in their day men of God; they were rulers and teachers in the Church; they had received by succession of hands the power first given to the Apostles and now to us. They laboured and suffered and fainted not, and their writings remain to this day. Now a person who cultivates this thought, finds therein, through God's mercy, great encouragement. Say he is alone, his faith counted a dream, and his efforts to do good a folly, what then? He knows there have been times when his opinions were those of the revered and influential, and the opinions now in repute only not reprobated because they were not heard of. He knows that present opinions are the accident of the day, and that they will fall as they have risen. They will surely fall even though at a distant date! He labours for that time; he labours for five hundred years to come. He can bear in faith to wait five hundred years, to wait for an era long, long after he has mouldered into dust. The Apostles lived eighteen hundred years since; and as far as the Christian looks back, so far can he afford to look forward. There is one Lord, one faith, one baptism, one God and Father of all, from first to last.

I referred just now to our Sacred Services; these, again, may be made to furnish a support to our faith and hope. He who comes to Church to worship God, be he high or low, enters into that heavenly world of Saints of which I have been speaking. For in the Services of worship we elicit and realize the invisible. I know, indeed, that Christ is then especially present, and vouchsafes to bless us; but I am speaking all along of the help given to us by sensible objects, and, even in this lower view, doubtless much is done for us in the course of divine worship. We read from the Bible of the Saints who have gone before us, and we make mention of them in our prayers. We thank God for them, we praise God with them, we pray God to visit us in mercy as He visited them. And every earthly thought or principle is excluded. The world no longer rules as it does abroad; no longer teaches, praises, blames, scoffs, wonders, according to its own false standard. It is merely spoken of as one of the three great enemies whom we are sworn to resist; it holds its proper place; and its doom is confidently predicted, the final victory of the Church over it. And, further, it is much more impressive to hear and to see, than to read in a book. When we read the Bible and religious books in private, there is great comfort; but our minds are commonly more roused and encouraged in Church, when we see those great truths displayed and represented which Scripture speaks of. There we see "Jesus Christ, evidently set forth, crucified among us." The ordinances which we behold, force the unseen truth upon our senses. The very disposition of the building, the subdued light, the aisles, the Altar, with its pious adornments, are figures of things unseen, and stimulate our fainting faith. We seem to see the heavenly courts, with Angels chanting, and Apostles and Prophets listening, as we read their writings in due course. And thus, even attendance on a Sunday may, through God's mercy, avail even in the case of those who have not given themselves up to Him—not to their salvation (for no one can be saved by one or two observances merely, or without a life of faith), but so far as to break in upon their dream of sin, and give them thoughts and notions which may be the germ of future good. Even to those, I say, who live to the world, the mere Sunday attendance at Church is a continual memento on their conscience, giving them a glimpse of things unseen, and rescuing them in a measure from the servitude of Mammon or of Belial. And therefore it is, that Satan's first attempt, when he would ruin a soul, is to prevail upon him to desecrate the Lord's Day. And if such is the effect of coming to Church once a week, even to an undecided or carnal mind, how much more impressive and invigorating are the Services to serious men who come daily or frequently! Surely such attendance is a safeguard, such as amulets were said to be, a small thing to all appearance, but effectual. I say it with confidence, he who observes it, will grow in time a different man from what he was, God working in him. His heart will be more heavenly and aspiring; the world will lie under his feet; he will be proof against its opinions, threats, blandishments, ridicule. His very mode of viewing things, his very voice, his manner, gait, and countenance, will speak of Heaven to those who know him well, though the many see nothing in him.

The many understand him not, and even in St. Paul or St. John would see but ordinary men. Yet at times such a one will speak effectually even to the many. In seasons of unusual distress or alarm, when men's minds faint for fear, then he will have a natural power over the world, and will seem to speak, not as an individual, but as if in him was concentrated all the virtue and the grace of those many Saints who have been his life-long companions. He has lived with those who are dead, and he will seem to the world as one coming from the dead, speaking in the name of the dead, using the language of souls dead to things that are seen, revealing the mysteries of the heavenly world, and aweing and controlling those who are wedded to this. What slight account did the centurion and the crew make of St. Paul, till a tempest had long time "lain on them," and "all hope that they should be saved was then taken away!" But then, though he had done no miracle, "he stood forth in the midst," exhorted and encouraged them, bade them take meat, acted as their priest, giving thanks to God and breaking bread in the presence of them all, and so made them "of good cheer." Such is the gift, deeply lodged and displayed at times, of those who have ascended into the third heaven. One living Saint, though there be but one, is a pledge of the whole Church Invisible. Let this thought console us as it ought to do; let it have its full influence in us, and possess us. Let us "lift up our hearts," let us "lift them up unto the Lord!"

THE GIFT OF THE SPIRIT

"We all, with open face beholding as in a glass the glory of the Lord,
are changed into the same image from glory to glory, even as by the
Spirit of the Lord."—2 Cor. iii.18.

MOSES prayed for this one thing, that he might "see God's glory;" and he was allowed to behold it in such measure, that when he came down from the Mount, "the skin of his face shone," so that the people "were afraid to come nigh him." Only to him was this privilege vouchsafed in this intimate way, and that but once; but a promise was given, that at some future time it should be extended to the whole earth. God said to him, "As truly as I live, all the earth shall be filled with the glory of the Lord," that glory which the Israelites had seen in glimpses and had profaned. Afterwards the prophets Isaiah and Habakkuk foretold, in like manner, that the earth should be filled with the Lord's glory and the knowledge of it. When Christ came, these promises were fulfilled, for "we beheld His glory," St. John says, "the glory as of the Only-begotten of the Father." [1]

In the chapter which ends with the text, St. Paul contrasts the shadows and earnests under the Law, of "the glory that should follow" Christ's coming, with that glory itself. He says that he and his brother Apostles are "not as Moses, who put a veil over his face." At length the glory of God in full measure was the privilege and birthright of all believers, who now, "in the un-veiled face of Christ their Saviour, beheld the reflection of the Lord's glory," and were "changed into His likeness from one measure of glory to another." Our Saviour's words in His last prayer for His Apostles, and for all His disciples as included under them, convey to us the same gracious truth. He says, "The glory which Thou gavest Me, I have given them." [2]

This glorious Dispensation, under which the Church now exists, is called by St. Paul, in the same chapter, "the ministra-

---

[1] Exod. xxxiv.30; Numb. xiv.21; Is. xi.9; Hab. ii.14; John i.14.
[2] John xvii.22.

tion of the Spirit;" and again in the text, we are said to be changed into the glorious image of Christ, "by the Spirit of the Lord."

And further, the Church, as being thus honoured and exalted by the presence of the Spirit of Christ, is called "the Kingdom of God," "the Kingdom of Heaven;" as, for instance, by our Lord Himself. "The Kingdom of Heaven is at hand:" "Except a man be born of water and of the Spirit, he cannot enter into the Kingdom of God."[3]

I propose now to make some remarks on this peculiar gift of the Gospel Dispensation, which, as in the foregoing passages, is spoken of as the gift of "the Spirit," the gift of "glory," and through which the Church has become what it was not before, the Kingdom of Heaven.

And here, before entering upon the subject, I would observe, that as there is a sense in which the grant of glory was made even under the Law, viz., in its miracles (as when the Israelites are condemned for having "seen the glory of the Lord and His miracles," and yet "not having hearkened to His voice"[4]), so in another point of view it belongs exclusively to the promised blessedness hereafter. Still there is a peculiar and sufficient sense in which it is ascribed to the Christian Church, and what this is, is the question now before us.

1. In the first place, some insight is given into the force of the word "glory," as our present privilege, by considering the meaning of the title "Kingdom of Heaven," which, as has been just observed, has also belonged to the Church since Christ came. The Church is called by this name as being the court and domain of Almighty God, who retreated from the earth, as far as His kingly presence was concerned, when man fell. Not that He left Himself without witness in any age, but even in His most gracious manifestations, still He conducted Himself as if in an enemy's country, "as a stranger in the land, and as a wayfaring man that turneth aside to tarry for a night."[5] But when Christ had reconciled Him to His fallen creatures, He returned according to the prophecy, "I will dwell in them, and walk in them; I will set My sanctuary in the midst of them for evermore."[6] From that time there has really been a heaven upon earth, in fulfilment of Jacob's vision. Thenceforth the Church was not a carnal ordinance, made of perishable materials, like the Jewish Tabernacle, which had been a type of the Dispensation to which

---

[3] Matt. x.7; John iii.5.   [4] Numb. xiv.22.
[5] Jer. xiv.8.   [6] 2 Cor. vi.16; Ezek. xxxvii.26.

it belonged. It became "a kingdom which cannot be moved," being sweetened, purified, and spiritualized by the pouring out of Christ's blood in it. It became once more an integral part of that unseen, but really existing world, of which "the Lord is the everlasting Light;" and it had fellowship with its blessed inhabitants. St. Paul thus describes it in his epistle to the Hebrews: "Ye are come to Mount Sion;" to the true "mountain of the Lord's House," of which the earthly Sion was a type; "and to the city of the Living God, the heavenly Jerusalem;" that is, as he elsewhere calls it, "the Jerusalem that is above," or, as he speaks in another place, "our citizenship is in heaven;" "and to an innumerable company of Angels, to the festive concourse and Church of the First-born enrolled in heaven, and to God the Judge of all, and to the spirits of the perfected Just, and to Jesus the Mediator of the New Covenant, and to the blood of sprinkling, that speaketh better things than that of Abel." [7]

Since then the Christian Church is a Heaven upon earth, it is not surprising that in some sense or other its distinguishing privilege or gift should be glory, for this is the one attribute which we ever attach to our notion of Heaven itself, according to the Scripture intimations concerning it. The glory here may be conceived of by considering what we believe of the glory hereafter.

2. Next, if we consider the variety and dignity of the gifts ministered by the Spirit, we shall, perhaps, discern in a measure, why our state under the Gospel is called a state of glory. It is not uncommon, in the present day, to divide the works of the Holy Ghost in the Church into two kinds, miraculous and moral. By *miraculous* are meant such as He manifested in the first ages of the Gospel, marvels out of the course of nature, addressed to our senses; such as the power of healing, of raising the dead, and the like; or, again, such as speaking with tongues or prophecy. On the other hand, by *moral* operations or influences are meant such as act upon our minds, and enable us to be what we otherwise could not be, holy and accepted in all branches of the Christian character; in a word, all such as issue in Sanctification, as it is called. These distinct works of the Holy Spirit, viewed in their effects, are commonly called extraordinary and ordinary, or *gifts* and *graces*; and it is usual to say, that gifts have ceased, and graces alone remain to us, and hence, to limit the present "ministration of the Spirit" to certain

[7] Heb. xii.22–24.

influences on our moral nature, to the office of changing, renewing, purifying the heart and mind, implanting a good will, imparting knowledge of our duty and power to do it, and cultivating and maturing within us all right desires and habits, and leading us to all holy works. Now, all these influences and operations certainly do belong to the "ministration of the Spirit;" but in what appropriate sense can any effects wrought in us be called "glory?" Add to them the miracles which now have ceased, and you will indeed gain a more intelligible meaning of the word, but not even then any meaning peculiar to the Gospel. The Jewish Church was gifted by a more abiding superhuman presence than the Christian, and with as overpowering miracles, yet it did not possess this privilege of glory. Again, its patriarchs and teachers rose to degrees of sanctification quite as much above our power of measuring them as those attained by Apostles and Martyrs under the Gospel; nor, to all human appearance, is the actual sanctification of the mass of Christians more true or complete than was that of the Jews: how then are we in a state of glory, and the Jewish Church not? Granting then that the gift of the Spirit mentioned in Scripture includes in it both the miracles of the first ages and the influences of grace; granting also that the sanctifying grace bestowed on each Christian is given with far greater fulness, variety, and power, than it was vouchsafed to the Jews (whether it be eventually quenched or not); granting, too, that holiness is really the characteristic of that gift which the Holy Spirit ministers now, as miracles were its outward manifestation in the first ages; still all this is not a sufficient account of it; it is not equivalent to our great Gospel privilege, which is something deeper, wider, and more mysterious, though including both miracles and graces.

In truth, the Holy Ghost has taken up His abode in the Church in a variety of gifts, as a sevenfold Spirit. For instance, is the gift of the body's immortality miraculous or moral? Neither, in the common sense of the words; yet it is a gift bestowed on us in this life, and by the power of the Holy Ghost, according to the texts, "Your body is the temple of the Holy Ghost;" and "He that raised up Christ from the dead shall also quicken your mortal bodies by His indwelling Spirit."[8] Again, is justification, or the application of Christ's merits to the soul, moral or miraculous? Neither; yet we are told that we are "washed, hallowed, justified in the name of the Lord Jesus, and by the Spirit of our God."[9] Or is the gift of the Holy Ghost in Ordination

---

[8] 1 Cor. vi.19; Rom. viii.11. [9] 1 Cor. vi.11.

miraculous or moral? It is neither the one nor the other, but a supernatural power of ministering effectually in holy things. Once more, is communion with Christ miraculous or moral? On the contrary, it is a real but mysterious union of nature with Him, according to the text, "we are members of His body, from His flesh, and from His bones." [10] Such reflections as these are calculated, perhaps, to give us somewhat of a deeper view than is ordinarily admitted, of the character of that Gift which attends on the presence of the Holy Ghost in the Church, and which is called the gift of glory. I do not say that anything that has been just said has been sufficient to define it; rather I would maintain, that it cannot be defined. It cannot be limited; it cannot be divided, and exhausted by a division. This is the very faultiness of the division into miraculous and moral, useful as this may be for particular purposes, that it professes to embrace what is in fact incomprehensible and unfathomable. I would fain keep from the same mistake; and the instances already given may serve this purpose, enlarging our view without bounding it. The gift is denoted in Scripture by the vague and mysterious term "glory;" and all the descriptions we can give of it can only, and should only, run out into a mystery.

3. Perhaps, however, it may be questioned, whether the gift of the Spirit, now possessed by us, is really called by this name; with a view of making this quite clear, I will here recite a number of passages in order, in addition to those with which I began; and while I do so, I would have you observe in what close and continual connection the "Spirit," and "glory," and "heaven," occur.

"The Spirit of glory and of God resteth upon you."

"The God of all grace, who hath called us unto His eternal glory by Christ Jesus, after that ye have suffered a while, make you perfect."

"According as His divine power hath given unto us all things that pertain unto life and godliness, through the knowledge of Him that hath called us to glory and virtue."

"Whom He did predestinate, them he also called, and whom He called, them He also justified, and whom He justified, them He also glorified."

"We speak the wisdom of God in a mystery, even the hidden wisdom which God ordained before the world unto our glory. . . . . Eye hath not seen, nor ear heard, neither have entered into the heart of man, the things which God hath prepared for them

[10] 2 Pet. i.4; Eph. v.30.

that love Him. . . . . The natural man receiveth not the things of the Spirit of God; for they are foolishness unto him, neither can he know them, because they are spiritually discerned."

"Blessed be the God and Father of our Lord Jesus Christ, who hath blessed us with all spiritual blessings in heavenly places in Christ."

[I pray] "that the God of our Lord Jesus Christ, the Father of glory, may give unto you the Spirit of wisdom and revelation in the knowledge of Him, the eyes of your understanding being enlightened, that ye may know what is the hope of His calling, and what the riches of the glory of His inheritance in the Saints, and what is the exceeding greatness of His power to us-ward who believe, according to the working of His mighty power which He wrought in Christ, when He raised Him from the dead."

"God, who is rich in mercy, for His great love wherewith He loved us, even when we were dead in sins, hath quickened us together with Christ (by grace ye are saved), and hath raised us up together, and made us sit together in heavenly places in Christ Jesus. . . . . Through Him we both have access by one Spirit unto the Father. . . . . In whom [Christ] ye also are builded together for an habitation of God through the Spirit."

[I pray] "that He would grant you according to the riches of His glory, to be strengthened with might by His Spirit in the inner man; that Christ may dwell in your hearts by faith; that ye, being rooted and grounded in love, may be able to comprehend, with all saints, what is the breadth, and length, and depth, and height, and to know the love of Christ, which passeth knowledge, that ye might be filled with all the fulness of God."

"Christ loved the Church and gave Himself for it, that He might sanctify and cleanse it with the washing of water by the word; that He might present it to Himself a glorious Church, not having spot or wrinkle, or any such thing; but that it should be holy and without blemish."

"It is impossible for those who were once illuminated, and have tasted of the heavenly gift, and were made partakers of the Holy Ghost, and have tasted the good word of God, and the powers of the world to come, if they shall fall away, to renew them again unto repentance." [11]

I would have you pay particular attention to this last passage, which, in speaking of those who thwart God's grace, runs

---

[11] I Pet. iv.14; v.10; 2 Pet. i.3; Rom. viii.30; I Cor. ii.7, 9, 14; Eph. i.3, 17–20; ii.4–6, 18, 22; iii.16–19; v.25–27; Heb. vi.4–6.

through the various characteristics or titles of that glory which they forfeit:—illumination, the heavenly gift, the Holy Ghost, the Divine Word, the powers of the world to come; which all mean the same thing, viewed in different lights, viz., that unspeakable Gospel privilege, which is an earnest and portion of heavenly glory, of the holiness and blessedness of Angels—a present entrance into the next world, opened upon our souls through participation of the Word Incarnate, ministered to us by the Holy Ghost.

Such is the mysterious state in which Christians stand, if it be right to enlarge upon it. They are in Heaven, in the world of spirits, and are placed in the way of all manner of invisible influences. "Their conversation is in heaven;" they live among Angels, and are within reach (as I may say) of the Saints departed. They are ministers round the throne of their reconciled Father, "kings and priests unto God," having their robes washed in the Lamb's blood, and being consecrated as temples of the Holy Ghost. And this being so, we have some insight into the meaning of St. Paul's anxiety that his brethren should understand "the breadth and length," "the riches" of the glorious inheritance which they enjoyed, and of his forcible declaration, on the other hand, that "the natural man" could not "discern" it.

If we now recur to our Saviour's words already cited, we shall find that all that the Apostles have told us in their Epistles is but an expansion of two short sentences of His: "Except a man be born of water and of *the Spirit*, he cannot enter into, or (as it is said just before) see the *Kingdom of God*." "The *glory* which Thou gavest me, I have given them." [12] On these texts I make the following additional remarks:—When Nicodemus doubted about our Lord's declaration, that a birth through the Spirit was the entrance into His kingdom, He said, "If I have told you earthly things, and ye believe not, how shall ye believe, if I tell you of heavenly things? And no man hath ascended up to Heaven, but He that came down from Heaven, even the Son of man *which is in Heaven*." In these words our Lord plainly discloses that in some mysterious way He, the Son of man, was really in Heaven, even while, by human eyes, He was seen to be on earth. His discourse seems to run thus:— "Are you offended at the doctrine of the new birth of the soul into the kingdom of God? High as it is, it is but an earthly truth compared with others I, as coming from Heaven, could disclose. It is mysterious how regenerate man should be a citizen of a heavenly kingdom,

[12] John iii.5; xvii.22.

but I Myself, who speak, am at this moment in Heaven too, even in this My human nature." Thus the greater Mystery of the Incarnation is made to envelope and pledge to us the mystery of the new birth. As He was in Heaven in an ineffable sense, even "in the days of His flesh," so are we, in our degree; according to the words of His prayer, that His disciples might "all be one; as Thou, Father, art in Me, and I in Thee, that they also may be one in Us." [13]

But He was pleased to reveal this high truth more explicitly on a subsequent occasion; I mean in His Transfiguration. To many persons this portion of the Sacred History may have appeared without object or meaning. It was, in one sense, a miracle; yet it had no beneficent purpose or lasting consequence, as is usual with our Lord's miracles, and it took place in private. But, surely, it is of a doctrinal nature, being nothing less than a figurative exhibition of the blessed truth contained in the texts under review, a vision of the glorious Kingdom which He set up on the earth on His coming. He said to His Apostles, "I tell you of a truth, there be some standing here which shall not taste of death till they *see the Kingdom of God.*" Then, "after six days Jesus taketh Peter, James, and John his brother, and bringeth them up into a high mountain apart, and was transfigured before them. And as He prayed the fashion of His countenance was altered, and His raiment was white and glistening. And His face did shine as the sun, and His raiment was white as the light. . . . . And behold there talked with Him two men, which were Moses and Elias, who appeared in glory. . . . . But Peter and they that were with him were heavy with sleep; and when they were awake, *they saw His glory.*" [14] Such is the Kingdom of God; Christ the centre of it, His glory the light of it, the Just made perfect His companions, and the Apostles His witnesses to their brethren. It realizes what the ancient Saints saw by glimpses—Jacob at Bethel, Moses on Sinai.

Such, then, being the especial glory and "dreadfulness" which attaches to the Christian Church, it may be asked, how far the gift is also imparted to every individual member of it? It is imparted to every member on his Baptism; as may plainly be inferred from our Lord's words, who, in His discourse with Nicodemus, makes a birth through the Spirit, which He also declares is wrought by Baptism, to be the *only* means of entering into His Kingdom; so that, unless a man is thus "born of water

[13] John xvii.21.
[14] Matt. xvii.1, etc.; Luke ix.27, etc.; cf. John i.14; 2 Pet. i.17.

and of the Spirit," he is in no sense a member of His Kingdom at all. By this new birth the Divine Shechinah is set up within him, pervading soul and body, separating him really, not only in name, from those who are not Christians, raising him in the scale of being, drawing and fostering into life whatever remains in him of a higher nature, and imparting to him, in due season and measure, its own surpassing and heavenly virtue. Thus, while he carefully cherishes the Gift, he is, in the words of the text, "changed from glory to glory, even as by the Spirit of the Lord." On the other hand, if the Gift be resisted, it gradually withdraws its presence, and being thwarted in its chief end, the sanctification of our nature, is forfeited as regards its other benefits also. Such seems to be the rule on which the Almighty Giver acts; and, could we see the souls of men, doubtless we should see them after this manner: infants just baptized bright as the Cherubim, as flames of fire rising heavenward in sacrifice to God; then as they passed from childhood to man's estate, the light within them fading or strengthening as the case may be; while of grown men the multitude, alas! might show but fearful tokens that the Lord had once been among them, only here and there some scattered witnesses for Christ remaining, and they, too, seamed all over with the scars of sin.

To conclude. It were well if the views I have been setting before you, which in the main are, I trust, those of the Church Catholic from the beginning, were more understood and received among us. They would, under God's blessing, put a stop to much of the enthusiasm which prevails on all sides, while they might tend to dispel those cold and ordinary notions of religion which are the opposite extreme. Till we understand that the gifts of grace are unseen, supernatural, and mysterious, we have but a choice between explaining away the high and glowing expressions of Scripture, or giving them that rash, irreverent, and self-exalting interpretation, which is one of the chief errors of this time. Men of awakened and sensitive minds, knowing from Scripture that the gift of the Holy Ghost is something great and unearthly, dissatisfied with the meagre conceptions of the many, yet not knowing where to look for what they need, are led to place the life of a Christian, which "is hid with Christ in God," in a sort of religious ecstasy, in a high-wrought sensibility on sacred subjects, in impassioned thoughts, a soft and languid tone of feeling, and an unnatural profession of all this in conversation. And further, from the same cause, their ignorance of the *supernatural* character of the Heavenly Gift, they attempt to measure it in each other by its sensible effects, and account none to be Christians but those whom they suppose they can ascertain to be such, by their profession, language, and carriage. On the other hand, sensible and sober-minded men, offended at such excesses, acquiesce in the notion, that the gift of the Holy Ghost was almost peculiar to the Apostles' day, that now, at least, it does nothing more than make us decent and orderly members of society; the privileges bestowed upon us in Scripture being, as they conceive, but of an external nature, education and the like, or, at the most, a pardon of our sins and admission to God's favour, unaccompanied by any actual and inherent powers bestowed upon us. Such are the consequences which naturally follow, when, from one cause or other, any of those doctrines are obscured, which have been revealed in mercy to our necessities. The mind catches at the words of life, and tries to apprehend them; and being debarred their true meaning, takes up with this or that form of error, as the case may be, in the semblance of truth, by way of compensation.

For ourselves, in proportion as we realize that higher view of the subject, which we may humbly trust is the true one, let us be careful to act up to it. Let us adore the Sacred Presence within us with all fear, and "rejoice with trembling." Let us offer up our best gifts in sacrifice to Him who, instead of abhorring, has taken up His abode in these sinful hearts of ours. Prayer, praise, and thanksgiving, "good works and alms-deeds," a bold and true confession and a self-denying walk, are the ritual of worship by which we serve Him in these His Temples. How the distinct and particular works of faith avail to our final acceptance, we know not; neither do we know how they are efficacious in changing our wills and characters, which, through God's grace, they certainly do. All we know is, that as we persevere in them, the inward light grows brighter and brighter, and God manifests Himself in us in a way the world knows not of. In this, then, consists our whole duty, first in contemplating Almighty God, as in Heaven, so in our hearts and souls; and next, while we contemplate Him, in acting towards and for Him in the works of every day; in viewing by faith His glory without and within us, and in acknowledging it by our obedience. Thus we shall unite conceptions the most lofty concerning His majesty and bounty towards us, with the most lowly, minute, and unostentatious service to Him.

Lastly, the doctrine on which I have been dwelling cannot fail to produce in us deeper and more reverent feelings towards the Church of Christ, as His especial dwelling-place. It is evident we are in a much more extraordinary state than we are at all aware of. The multitude do not understand this. So it was in Israel once. There was a time when, even at Bethel, where God had already vouchsafed a warning against such ignorance, the very children of the city "mocked" His prophet, little thinking he had with him the mantle of Elijah. In an after age, the prophet Ezekiel was bid prophesy to the people, "whether they would hear or whether they would forbear;" and, it was added, "and they, whether they will hear or whether they will forbear, yet shall know that there hath been a prophet among them." [15]

Let us not fear, therefore, to be but a few among many in our belief. Let us not fear opposition, suspicion, reproach, or ridicule. God sees us; and His Angels, they are looking on. They know we are right, and bear witness to us; and, "yet a little while, and He that cometh shall come, and will not tarry. Now the just shall live by *faith*." [16]

---

[15] 2 Kings ii.23; Ezek. ii.5, 7.   [16] Heb. v.37, 38.

REGENERATING BAPTISM

"By one Spirit are we all baptized into one body."—1 Cor. xii.13.

As there is One Holy Ghost, so there is one only visible Body of Christians which Almighty God "knows by name," and one Baptism which admits men into it. This is implied in the text, which is nearly parallel to St. Paul's words to the Ephesians: "There is one Body, and one Spirit, one Baptism." But more than this is taught us in it; not only that the Holy Ghost is in the Church, and that Baptism admits into it, but that the Holy Ghost admits by means of Baptism, that the Holy Ghost baptizes; in other words, that each individual member receives the gift of the Holy Ghost as a preliminary step, a condition, or means of his being incorporated into the Church; or, in our Saviour's words, that no one can enter, except he be regenerated in order to enter it.

Now, this is much more than many men are willing to grant, their utmost concession being, that the Church has the presence of the Holy Spirit in it, and therefore, to be in the Church is to be in that which has the presence of the Holy Spirit; that is, to be in the *way* of the Spirit (so to speak), which cannot but be a state of favour and privilege; but, that the Holy Spirit is given to infants, one by one, on their Baptism, this they will not admit. Yet, one would think words could not be plainer than the text in proof of it; however, they do not admit it.

This defective view of the Sacrament of Baptism, for so I must not shrink from calling it, shall now be considered, and considered in its connection with a popular argument for the Baptism of infants, which, most true as it is in its proper place, yet is scarcely profitable for these times, as seeming to countenance the error in question. I mean, the assumed parallel between Baptism and Circumcision.

It is undeniable that Circumcision in some important respects resembles Baptism, and may allowably, nay, usefully be referred to in illustration of it. Circumcision was the entrance into the Jewish Covenant, and it typified the renunciation of the flesh. In respects such as these it resembles Baptism; and hence it has been of service in the argument for Infant Baptism, as having been itself administered to infants. But, though it resembles Baptism in some respects, it is unlike it in others more important. When, then, it is found to be the chief and especially approved argument in favour of Infant Baptism among Christians, there is reason for some anxiety, lest this circumstance should betoken, or introduce, insufficient views of a Christian Sacrament. This remark, I fear, is applicable in the present day.

We baptize infants, in the first place, because the Church has ever done so; and, to say nothing of the duty of observing and transmitting what we have received, in the case of so great a privilege as Baptism, we should be ungrateful and insensible indeed if we did not give our children the benefit of the usage, even though Scripture said not a word on the subject, so that it said nothing the other way. But, besides, we consider we do find, in our Saviour's words, a command to bring children to Him, for His blessing. Again, He said they were to be members of His Kingdom; also, that Baptism is the only entrance, the new birth into it. We administer, then, Baptism to children as a sure *benefit* to their souls.

But, when men refuse to admit the doctrine of Baptismal Regeneration in the case of infants, then they look about how they may defend Infant Baptism, which, perhaps, from habit, good feeling, or other causes, they do not like to abandon. The ordinary and intelligible reason for the Baptism of infants, is the securing to them remission of sins, and the gift of the Holy Ghost—Regeneration: but if this sacred privilege is not given to them in Baptism, why, it may be asked, should Baptism be administered to them at all? Why not wait till they can understand the meaning of the rite, and can have faith and repentance themselves? Certainly it does seem a very intricate and unreasonable proceeding; first, to lay stress on the necessity of repentance and faith in persons to be baptized, and then to proceed to administer Baptism universally in such a way as to exclude the possibility of their having repentance and faith. I say, this would be strange and inconsistent, were not Baptism, in itself, so direct a blessing that, when parents demand it for their children, all abstract rules must, in very charity, necessarily give way. We administer it whenever we do not discover some actual obstacle in the recipient to hinder its efficacy, as we give medicine to the sick. Otherwise the objection holds; and, accordingly, clear-sighted men, who deny its regenerating power in the case of infants, often do come to the conclusion that to ad-

minister it to them is a needless and officious act, nay, a profanation of a sacred institution. It seems to them a mockery to
baptize them; the waste of an edifying rite, not to say a Sacrament, upon those who cannot understand or use it; and, to
speak the truth, they do appear reasonable and straightforward
in their inference, granting their premises. It does seem as if
those who deny the regeneration of infants ought, if they were
consistent (which happily they are not), to refrain from baptizing them. Surely, if we go by Scripture, the question is decided
at once; for no one can deny that there is much more said in
Scripture in behalf of the connection between Baptism and Divine grace, than about the duty of Infant Baptism. The passage
can scarcely be named, in the New Testament, where Baptism is
referred to, without the mention, direct or indirect, of spiritual
influences. What right have we to put asunder what God has
united? especially since, on the other hand, the text cannot be
found which plainly enjoins the Baptism of infants. If the doctrine and the practice are irreconcilable—Baptismal Regeneration and Infant Baptism—let the practice, which is not written
in Scripture, yield to the doctrine which is; and let us (if we can
bear to do so) defraud infants of Baptism, not Baptism of its
supernatural virtue. Let us go counter to Tradition rather than
to Scripture. This being the difficulty which comes upon those
who deny the Regeneration, yet would retain the Baptism of
infants, let us next see how they meet it.

We need not suppose that all I am drawing out passes
through the mind of every one who denies that infants are regenerated in Baptism: but, surely, some such processes of
thought are implied, which it may be useful to ourselves to
trace out. This being understood, I observe that the partly assumed and partly real parallel of Circumcision comes, in fact,
whether they know it or not, as a sort of refuge to those who
have taken up this intermediate position between Catholic
doctrine and heretical practice. They avail themselves of the
instance of Circumcision as a proof that a divinely-appointed
ordinance need not convey grace, even while it admits into a
state of grace; and they argue from the analogy between Circumcision and Baptism, that what was the case with the Mosaic ordinance is the case with the Christian also. Circumcision
admitted to certain privileges, to the means of grace, to teaching, and the like; Baptism, they consider, does the same and no
more. It has also the same uses as Circumcision, in teaching the
necessity of inward sanctification, and implying the original
corrupt condition of our nature. In like manner, it ought to be

administered to infants, since Circumcision was so administered under the Law.

I do not deny that this view is consistent with itself, and plausible. And it would be perfectly satisfactory, as a view, were it Scriptural. But the plain objection to it is, that Christ and His Apostles do attach a grace to the ordinance of Baptism, such as is not attached in the Old Testament to Circumcision—which is exactly that difference which makes the latter a mere rite, the former a Sacrament; and if this be so, it is nothing to the purpose to build up an argument on the assumption that the two ordinances are precisely the same.

Surely we have forgotten, in good measure, the difference between Jewish Ordinances and Christian. It was said of old time, after St. Paul, "The Law has a shadow, the Gospel an image, Heaven the reality;" or, in other words, that of those heavenly blessings which the Jewish Dispensation prefigured, the Christian imparts a portion or earnest. This, then, is the distinction between our ritual and the Mosaic. The Jewish rites had no substance of blessing in them; they were but outward signs and types of spiritual privileges. They had in them no "grace and truth." When the Divine Antitype came, they were simply and merely in the way; they did but hide from the eye of faith the reality which they had been useful in introducing. They were as the forerunners in a procession, who, after announcing their Prince's coming, must themselves retire, or they crowd his path. Nor these alone, but all mere ceremonies were then for ever unseasonable, as mere obstacles intercepting the Divine light. Yet, while Christ abolished them, considered as means of expiation or mere badges of profession, or as prophetical types of what was no longer future, He introduced another class of ordinances in their stead; Mysteries, as they are sometimes called, among which are the Sacraments, viz., rites as valueless and powerless in themselves as the Jewish, but being, what the Jewish were not, instruments of the application of His merits to individual believers. Though He now sits on the right hand of God, He has, in one sense, never left the world since He first entered it; for, by the ministration of the Holy Ghost, He is really present with us in an unknown way, and ever imparts Himself to those who seek Him. Even when visibly on earth He, the Son of Man, was still "in heaven;" and now, though He is ascended on high, He is still on earth. And as He is still with us, for all that He is in heaven, so, again, is the hour of His cross and passion ever mystically present, though it be past these eighteen hundred years. Time and space have no portion in the spiritual Kingdom which He has founded; and the rites of His Church are as mysterious spells by which He annuls them both. They are not like the Jewish ordinances, long and laborious, expensive or irksome, with aught of value or merit in themselves: they are so simple, so brief, with so little of outward substance, that the mind is not detained for a moment from Him who works by means of them, but takes them for what they really are, only so far outward as to serve for a medium of the heavenly gift. Thus Christ shines through them, as through transparent bodies, without impediment. He is the Light and Life of the Church, acting through it, dispensing of His fulness, knitting and compacting together every part of it; and these its Mysteries are not mere outward signs, but (as it were) effluences of His grace developing themselves in external forms, as Angels might do when they appeared to men. He has touched them, and breathed upon them, when He ordained them; and thenceforth they have a virtue in them, which issues forth and encircles them round, till the eye of faith sees in them no element of matter at all. Once for all He hung upon the cross, and blood and water issued from His pierced side, but by the Spirit's ministration, the blood and water are ever flowing, as though His cross were really set up among us, and the baptismal water were but an outward image meeting our senses. Thus in a true sense that water is not what it was before, but is gifted with new and spiritual qualities. Not as if its material substance were changed, which our eyes see, or as if any new nature were imparted to it, but that the lifegiving Spirit, who could make bread of stones, and sustain animal life on dust and ashes, applies the blood of Christ through it; or according to the doctrine of the text, that He, and not man, is the baptizer.

St. Paul sets this great truth before us, among other places, in the second chapter of his Epistle to the Colossians. First, he says, "In Christ dwelleth all the fulness of the Godhead bodily, and ye have fulness in Him, who is the Head of all principality and power." Here the most solemn and transporting doctrine of the Incarnation is disclosed to us, as the corner stone of the whole Church system; "the Word made flesh," being the divinely appointed Way whereby we are regenerated and saved. The Apostle then proceeds to describe the manner in which this divine fulness is imparted to us, and in so doing contrasts the Jewish ceremony of Circumcision with the spiritual Ordinance which has superseded it. "In whom also," in Christ, "ye are circumcised with a circumcision made without hands," heavenly, supernatural, invisible; "when ye strip yourselves of the body of the sins of the flesh, and receive" the true circumcision, "the circumcision of Christ, namely, buried with Him in Baptism." Thus Baptism is a spiritual Circumcision. He continues still more plainly. "Let no man *therefore* judge you in meat or in drink, or in respect of an holy day, or of the new moon, or of the Sabbath days; which are a shadow of things to come, but the body is of Christ." Now if Baptism were but an outward rite, like Circumcision, how strange a proof would it be of the Gospel's superseding *all* outward rites, to say that it enforced Baptism! He says, "Ye have Baptism, *therefore* do not think of *shadows*," as if Baptism took the place of shadows, as if it were certainly not a shadow but a substance. Again he says, "But the body is of Christ;" Circumcision is a shadow, but Baptism and the other Mysteries of the Church are "the *body*," and that because they are "of Christ." And lastly, he speaks of the duty of "holding to the Head," that is, to Christ, "from whom the whole body, being nourished and knit together by joints and bands, increaseth with a godly increase." What are these joints and bands but the Christian Ordinances and Ministrations, together with those who perform them? but observe, they are of such a nature as to subserve the "increase" of the Church.

Such is St. Paul's doctrine after Christ had died; St. John the Baptist teaches the same beforehand. "I indeed baptize you with water unto repentance, but he shall baptize you with the Holy Ghost and with fire." Doubtless there is an allusion here to the special descent of the Spirit at Pentecost; but, even taking it as such, the fulfilment of the Baptist's words then, becomes a pledge to us of the fulfilment of our Saviour's words to Nicodemus to the end of time. He who came by fire at Pentecost, will, as He has said, come by water now. But we may reasonably consider these very words of the Baptist as referring to ordinary Christian Baptism, as well as to the miraculous Baptism of the Apostles. As if he said, "Christ's Baptism shall not be mere water, as mine is. What you see of it indeed is water, but that is but the subordinate element of it; for it is water endued with high and supernatural qualities. Would it not surprise you if water burned like fire? Such, and more than such, is the mystery of that water which He shall pour out on you, having a searching and efficacious influence upon the soul itself."

Now, if any one says that such passages as this *need* not mean all I have supposed, I answer, that the question is not what they *must* mean, but what they *do* mean. I am not now engaged in proving, but in explaining the doctrine of Baptism, and in illustrating it from Scripture.

To return:—hence too the Baptismal Font is called "the washing *of regeneration*," not of mere water, "and renewing of the Holy Ghost which He hath poured out on us richly through Jesus Christ our Saviour;" and Christ is said to have "loved the Church and given Himself for it, that He might sanctify and cleanse it with the washing of water by the Word, that He might present it to Himself a glorious Church."

Further, let us consider the instances of the administration of Baptism in the Acts of the Apostles. If it be as serious a rite as I have represented, surely it must be there set forth as a great thing, and received with awe and thankfulness. Now we shall find these expectations altogether fulfilled. For instance, on the day of Pentecost, St. Peter said to the multitude, who asked what they must do, "Repent, and be baptized every one of you in the name of Jesus Christ for the remission of sins, and ye shall receive the gift of the Holy Ghost." Accordingly, "they that gladly received His word were baptized," in order to obtain these privileges; and, forthwith, we hear of their continuing "in gladness and singleness of heart, praising God." Again, when the Ethiopian Eunuch had been baptized by Philip, he "went on his way rejoicing." After St. Paul had been struck down by the Saviour whom he was persecuting, and sent to Damascus, he began to pray; but though in one sense a changed man already, he had not yet received the gift of regeneration, nor did he receive it except by the ministry of Ananias, who was sent to Him from Christ, expressly that he "might be filled with the Holy Ghost." Accordingly, Ananias said to him, "And now why tarriest thou? arise and be baptized, and wash away thy sins, calling on the name of the Lord." So again Cornelius, religious man as he was, and that doubtless by God's secret aid, yet was not received into Christ's family except by Baptism. Even the descent of the Holy Ghost upon him and his friends miraculously, while St. Peter was preaching to them, did not supersede the necessity of the Sacrament. And lastly, when the jailor at Philippi had been baptized, he "rejoiced, believing in God with all his house."[1]

These and similar passages seem to prove clearly the superiority of Baptism to Circumcision, as being a Sacrament; but if they did not, what conclusion should we have arrived at? no other than this, that Baptism is like Circumcision, but a carnal ordinance (if the words may be spoken), not a spiritual possession. See what follows. Do you not recollect how much St. Paul

---

[1] Acts ii.38–47; viii.39; ix.17; xxii.16; x.44–48; xvi.34.

says in depreciation of the rites of the Jewish Law, on the ground of their being rudiments of this world, carnal ordinances? Now if Baptism be altogether like Circumcision, can it, any more than they, have a place in the New Covenant? This was the very defect of the Mosaic Law, that it was but a form; this was one part of the bondage of the Jews, that they were put under forms, which contained in them no direct or intrinsic virtue, but had their spiritual use only as obeyed for conscience' sake, and as means of prophetic instruction. Surely this cannot be our state under the Gospel: "We," says St. Paul, "when we were children," that is, Jews, "were in bondage under the elements of the world; but when the fulness of the time was come, God sent forth His Son, made of a woman . . . . that we might receive the adoption of sons. And because ye are sons, God hath sent forth the Spirit of His Son into your hearts, crying, Abba, Father." Is it possible, then, now that the Spirit is come, we can be under dead rites and ordinances? It is plainly impossible. If Baptism then has no spiritual virtue in it, can it be intended for us Christians? If it has no regenerating power, surely they only are consistent who reject it altogether. I will boldly say it, we have nothing dead and earthly under the Gospel, and we act like the Judaizing Christians of old time if we submit to anything such; therefore they only are consistent, who, denying the virtue of Baptism, also deny its authority as a permanent ordinance of the Gospel. Surely it was but intended for the infancy of the Church, ere men were weaned from their attachment to a ritual. Surely it was but an oriental custom, edifying to those who loved a symbolical worship, but needless, nay, harmful to us; harmful as impeding the prerogative of Christian liberty, obscuring our view of the one Christian Atonement, corrupting the simplicity of our faith and trust, and profaning the dispensation of the Spirit! I repeat it, either Baptism is an instrument of the Holy Ghost, or it has no place in Christianity. We indeed, who, in accordance with the teaching of the Church Universal, believe that it is an act of the Spirit, are under no difficulty in this matter. But let those who deny it look to themselves. They are on their own principles committing the sin of the Galatians, and severing themselves from Christ. Surely if their doctrine be right, they may consider themselves addressed by St. Paul in his language to those early Judaizers, "O senseless Galatians," he would have said to them, "who hath bewitched you? Are ye so foolish, having begun in the Spirit, are ye now made perfect by the flesh? Why burden yourselves with mere ceremonies, external washings, the rudiments of the world, shadows of good things, weak, beggarly, and unprofitable elements, whereunto ye desire to be in bondage? Stand fast in the liberty wherewith Christ hath made us free, and be not entangled with the yoke of bondage. Spiritual men are delivered from formal observances. If ye be baptized, Christ shall profit you nothing; for neither Baptism availeth anything nor want of Baptism, but faith which worketh by love. Neither Baptism availeth anything nor want of Baptism, but a new creature; and as many as walk according to this rule, peace be on them and mercy, and upon the Israel of God."

Such, doubtless, is the only consistent mode of regarding and treating this sacred ordinance, if it has no power or grace in it above a Jewish rite. We should discard it. And in whatever degree we think it thus unprofitable, so far we should discard it. If we think it but a figure in the case of children, though a Sacrament to grown men, we should keep from wasting upon children what would benefit them as men. And this holds good of all the ordinances of the Church; so far as they are but outward forms, let them be abolished as parts of dead Judaism. But, praised be God! they are none of them such. They all have life. Christ has lodged virtue in His Church, and she dispenses it forth from her in all her words and works. Why will you not believe this? What do you gain by so jealous and niggardly a spirit, such "slowness of heart," but the loss of thoughts full of comfort and of majesty? To view Christ as all but visibly revealed—to look upon His ordinances, not in themselves, but as signs of His presence and power, as the accents of His love, the very form and countenance of Him who ever beholds us, ever cherishes us—to see Him thus revealed in glory day by day—is not this to those who believe it an unspeakable privilege? Is it not so great that a man might well wish it true from the excellence of it, and count them happy who are able to receive it? And when this is all plainly revealed in Scripture, when we are expressly told that Christ washes us by Water to change us into a glorious Church, that the consecrated bread is His flesh, that He is present with His ministers, and is in the midst of His Church, why should we draw back, like Thomas doubting of our Lord's resurrection? "Blessed are they that have not seen and yet have believed!" Surely, so it is; and however the world may scorn our faith, however those may despise us from whom we might expect better things, we will cheerfully bear what is a slight drawback indeed on our extreme blessedness. While they accuse us of trusting in ourselves, of trusting in our forms, and of ignorance of the Gospel, we will meekly say in our hearts,

"'Thou God, seest me:' Thou knowest that we desire to love nothing but Thee, and to trust in nothing but the cross of Christ; and that we relinquish all self-reliance, and know ourselves in ourselves to have nothing but sin and misery, and esteem these ordinances of Thine not for their own sake, but as memorials of Thee and of Thy Son—memorials which He has appointed, which He has blessed, and in which, by faith, we see Him manifested, day by day, and through which we hope to receive the imputation of those merits, once for all wrought out on the Cross, and our only effectual help in the day of account."

INFANT BAPTISM

*"Whoso shall receive one such little child in My name,
receiveth Me."*—Matt. xviii.5.

PERHAPS there are no words uttered by our Lord in the Gospels more gracious and considerate, as well as holy, just, and
good (that is, if we dare measure His words by our own sense of
them), than the encouragement given in this text, and others of
a similar character; none, more gracious and considerate, taking into account our nature and the necessary consequence of
believing the doctrines He has brought to light. He has brought
to light life and immortality; but, with immortal life, He has
also brought to light eternal death; He has revealed the awful
truth, that the soul never dies, never ceases to think and to be
conscious, to be capable of happiness or misery; that when once
a man is born into the world, neither time nor place, friend nor
enemy, Angels nor devils, can touch the living principle within
him; not even himself has any power over himself; but, as he has
begun, so he must continue to exist on to eternity. He has
taught us, that every child, from the moment of his birth, has
this prospect before him; also, that far from being sure of
heaven, he is to be put on a trial, whether He will serve God or
no; nay, not only on a trial, but on a trial not on even terms; not
a trial to which he is equal, but with a strong propensity within
him to the worse alternative, a tendency weighing him down to
earth; so that of himself, he cannot serve God acceptably, or
even repent of his unworthy service.

I say, if we knew only this, no thoughtful person could ever,
without the greatest humiliation and terror, reflect on his being
responsible for the existence of beings exposed to such miserable disadvantages. Surely, if we only knew the primary doctrines of the Gospel, viz., that man is a sinner by nature, and
though redeemed by Christ, cannot turn to Christ of his own
strength, I say, the cruelty of giving birth to poor infants, who
should inherit our nature and receive from us the birthright of
corruption, would be so great, that bowing the head to God's
appointment, and believing it to be good and true, we could but

conclude with the Apostles on one occasion, that "it were good not to marry." Our knowledge of the real condition of man in God's sight would surely lead to the breaking up of society, in proportion as it was sincerely and simply received; for what good were it to know that Christ has died for us, if we also knew that no one is by nature able to repent and believe, and knew nothing more? It would lead thoughtful men to think of their own personal salvation only, and thus to defraud Christ of the succession of believers, and the perpetual family of Saints, which is to be the salt of the earth to the end of time and the full fruit of His passion.

It is true, there is another doctrine besides those which I have stated, viz., that Christ has not only died for sinners, but also vouchsafes from above the influences of grace, to enable them to love what by nature they cannot love, and to do what they cannot do—to believe and obey. But even this would not be enough to remove the alarm and distress of the Christian parent. For, though God mercifully gives His grace to enable men to believe in His Son, yet it is as certain as the truth of Scripture itself, that He does not give His grace to *all*, but to those to whom He will. If any word of Scripture be true, it is this—that there is an election, that "it is not of him that willeth, nor of him that runneth, but of God that showeth mercy," that some men are brought near unto God, and gifted with His regenerating grace, and others not; so that, although we knew ever so much concerning the gift of the Holy Ghost, as well as concerning the meritorious death of Christ, yet, that knowledge would not tend a whit more to reconcile religious men to what they must certainly consider the cruelty, and the personal responsibility of becoming a parent.

I would say, then, that if this were all we knew on the subject, no one of any seriousness could bear the thought of adding to this world's "children of wrath," except an express divine command obliged him to do so. If even a single deliberate act of sin be (as it is) a great and fearful matter, mortal and damnable, yet what is any sin, say blasphemy, murder, idolatry, even the greatest, what would it be to the giving being to a soul intelligent, individual, accountable, fraught with all the sensibilities and affections which belong to human nature, capable of pain, immortal, and in due season manifesting a will incurably corrupt, and a heart at enmity with God, even though there were the chance that possibly it might be one of those who were elected for eternal life? There can be no doubt that if we know no more of the Gospel than I have hitherto mentioned, if we content ourselves with that half Gospel which is sometimes taken for the whole, none would be so selfish and so unfeeling as we, who could be content, for the sake of worldly comforts, a cheerful home, and the like, to surround ourselves with those, about whom, dearly as we loved them, and fervently as we might pray for them, we only knew thus much, that there was a chance—a chance of some sort that, perhaps, they might be in the number of the few whom Christ rescues from the curse of original sin.

Let us now see how His gracious words contained in the text remove the difficulty.

In truth, our Merciful Saviour has done much more for us than reveal the wonderful doctrines of the Gospel; He has enabled us to apply them. He has given us directions as well as doctrines, and while giving them has imparted to us especial encouragement and comfort. What an inactive useless world this would be, if the sun's light did not diffuse itself through the air and fall on all objects around us, enabling us to see earth and sky as well as the sun itself! Cannot we conceive nature so constituted that the sun appeared as a bright spot in the heavens, while the heavens themselves were black as in the starlight, and the earth dark as night? Such would have been our religious state, had not our Lord applied and diversified and poured to and fro, in heat and light, those heavenly glories which are concentrated in Him. He would shine upon us from above in all His high attributes and offices, as the Prophet, Priest, and King of His elect; but how should we bring home His grace to ourselves? How indeed should we gain, and know we gain, an answer to our prayers—how secure the comfortable assurance that He loves us personally, and will change our hearts, which we feel to be so earthly, and wash away our sins, which we confess to be so manifold, unless He had given us Sacraments—means and pledges of grace—keys which open the treasure-house of mercy—ordinances in which we not only ask, but receive, and know we receive, all we can receive as accountable beings (not, indeed, the certainty of heaven, for we are still in the flesh), but the certainty of God's present favour, the certainty that He is reconciled to us, will work in us and with us all righteousness, will so supply our need, that henceforth we shall lack nothing for the completion and overflowing sanctification of our defective and sinful nature, but have all, and more than all that Adam ever had in his first purity, all that the highest Archangel or Seraph ever had, when on his trial whether he would stand or fall?

For instance, in the particular case I have been considering, our gracious Lord has done much more than tell us that some souls are elected to the mercies of redemption and others not. He has not left Christians thus uncertain about their children. He has expressly assured us that children are in the number of His chosen; and, if you ask, whether all children, I reply, all children you can bring to Baptism, all children who are within reach of it. So literally has He fulfilled His promise: "Ho, every one that thirsteth, come ye to the waters, and he that hath no money come ye buy and eat; yea, come buy wine and milk without money and without price!" and again, "All that the Father giveth me shall come to Me, and him that cometh to Me, I will in no wise cast out." He has disclosed His secret election in a visible Sacrament, and thus enables Christians to bear to be, what otherwise they would necessarily shrink from being—parents. He relieves, my brethren, your anxious minds, anxious (as they must ever be) for your children's welfare, even after all the good promises of the Gospel, but unspeakably anxious before you understand *how* you are to be rid of the extreme responsibility of bestowing an eternal being upon sinful creatures whom you cannot change. With the tenderest feeling He removes your difficulty. He bids you bring them to Him from the first, and then take and educate them in His name. Like Pharaoh's daughter, He takes them up when you, their natural kin, have been forced to abandon them to inevitable death; and then He gives them back to you to nurse for His sake. "Suffer the little children to come unto Me, and forbid them not, for of such is the kingdom of God." [1] Again in the text, "Whoso shall receive one such little child in My name, receiveth Me." Observe how He speaks, as if He would give you some great and urgent encouragement; not only does He give permission, but He promises a reward to those who dedicate children to Him. He not only bids us do the very thing we wish to do, but bestows on the doing it a second blessing. He promises that if we bring children to Him for His blessing, He will bless us for bringing them; if we receive them for His sake, He will make it as if we received Himself, which is the greatest reward He could give us. Thus, while we are engaged in this work of receiving children in His name, let us recollect, to our great comfort, that we are about no earthly toil; we are taking part in a joyful solemnity, in a blessed and holy ordinance, in which our Saviour Christ not

[1] Mark x.14.

only comes to them, but is spiritually received into our own souls.

These reflections arise on the first view of the subject. However, it may be objected, that, after all, numbers fall away from God, even with the advantages of Baptism, and if so, the birth of children is not a less awful subject of contemplation now than before, nay rather more so, inasmuch as a heavier doom awaits those who sin after grace given, than those who have not received it.

But this objection surely brings us to a very different question. What I have been saying comes to this:—that a child seems by its very nature, which is corrupt and ungodly, to complain of those parents who gave it him; I mean, seems to do so in the parents' estimation, when they think of him. Their tender love towards him is humbled and distressed by this thought: "This dear and helpless object of our affection is a sinner through his parents, shapen in iniquity, conceived in sin, born a child of wrath." Now, I conceive this dreadful thought is at once removed, directly it is known that they who gave him his natural being may also bring him to a second birth, in which original sin is washed away, and such influences of grace given and promised as make it a child's own fault, if he, in the event, fails of receiving an eternal inheritance of blessedness in God's presence. They undo their own original injury. Now that Christ receives us in our infancy, no one has any ground for complaining of his fallen nature. He receives by birth a curse, but by Baptism a blessing, and the blessing is the greater; and to murmur now against his condition is all one with murmuring against his being created at all, his being created as a responsible being, which is a murmuring, not against man, but against God; for though it was man who has made our nature inclined to evil, yet, that we are beings on a trial, with moral natures, a power to do right or wrong, and a capacity of happiness or misery, is not man's work, but the Creator's. Thus parents being allowed to bestow a second birth upon their offspring, henceforth do but share and are sheltered in His responsibility (if I may dare so to speak), who is ever "justified in His sayings, and overcomes when He is judged."

However, it may be asked, how this applies to the case of the heathen? They cannot bring their children to Baptism, therefore they do incur the responsibility of giving being to souls who live and die in the wrath of God. I answer, that a man cannot be responsible for that about which he is altogether ignorant. The heathen have no knowledge of the real state of mankind, and therefore they can have none of the duties which arise out of that knowledge. None of us, not even Christians, know fully our own condition, and the consequences of our actions; else, doubtless, we should be too much overpowered to act at all. Did we see the complete consequences of any one sin, did we see how it spreads by the contagion of example and influence through the world, how many souls it injures, and what its eternal effects are, doubtless we should become speechless and motionless, as though we saw the flames of hell fire. Enough light is given us to direct us, and to make us responsible beings, not so much as to overwhelm us. We are not told the secret of our guilty nature, till we are told the means to escape from it; we are not told of God's fearful wrath, till we are told of His love in Christ. The heathen do not know of Baptism, but they do not know of original sin; for God would allot fear, faith, and hope to all men, despair to none. Again, the heathen know nothing of the eternity of future punishment, yet our Lord, in His account of the Judgment, when "*all* nations" shall be gathered before Him, does not except them from the risk of it. They know neither of eternal death nor eternal life. Let us leave the case of the heathen, about which nothing has been revealed to us; they are in the hand of God, the righteous and merciful God; "Shall not the Judge of all the earth do right?" [2]

But further, it may be objected that though Baptism is vouchsafed to the children of Christian parents, yet we are expressly assured that the few, not the many, shall be saved; so that the gift, however great, does not remove the difficulty in our way, or make it less of a risk to bring into existence those who are more likely to be among the wretched many than the blessed few. But, surely, this is a misconception of our Saviour's words. Where does He say that only few of the children *of His sincere followers* shall be saved? He says, indeed, that there will be but few out of the whole multitude of the regenerate; and the greater number of them, as we know too well, are disobedient to their calling. No wonder if their children turn out like themselves, and live to this world. But, because the mass of men abuse their privileges, which we see they do, and because we dare not entertain any sanguine hopes of the children of careless parents, how does this prove that those who do live in God's faith and fear, and are labouring and tending to be in the number of the elect few, may not cherish the confidence that their children, in like manner, will in due season obey God's calling,

[2] Gen. xviii.25.

yield to His Holy Spirit, "be made like the image of His Only-begotten Son, walk religiously in good works," and at length attain to everlasting glory? Solomon, even under the Law, assures us that, if "a child be trained up in the way he should go, when he is old he will not depart from it."[3] Much more (please God) will this be true, where the parents' prayers and the children's training are preceded by the grant of so great and present a benefit as regenerating Baptism; much more, when His Son has so graciously made the little children patterns to grown men, declaring that then, and then only, we become true members of His Kingdom when we become like them, and when, in sign of His favour "He took them up in His arms, put His hands upon them, and blessed them." Let a man consider how much is contained in the declaration, that God "hath not appointed us unto wrath, but to obtain salvation;"[4] and he will feel that he may safely trust his children to their Lord and Saviour—reluctance being no longer a serious prudence, but an unbelieving and unthankful jealousy, and the care of them no burdensome nor sorrowful toil, though an anxious one, but a labour of love, a joyful service done to Christ.

Lastly, it may still be asked what encouragement after all has been gained through Christian Baptism, which we should not have had without it, since it seems the children's hopes are to be ultimately rested not on the Sacrament administered, but on the parents' faith and prayers and careful training of them. These means, it may be objected, might and would have been used by religious men, even though they had known only of Christ's merits and gifts without direction how to convey and apply them to individuals; they would have prayed and been careful then, and so gained grace for their children, and they can do no more now. But can you indeed thus argue? What! is there no difference between asking and receiving?—for prayer is an asking and Baptism is a receiving. Is there no difference between a chance and a certainty? How many infants die in their childhood! is it no difference between knowing that a child is gone to heaven, or that he has died as he was born? But supposing a child lives, is not regeneration a real gain? does not it renew our nature, exalt us in the scale of being, give us additional powers, open upon us untold blessings, and moreover brighten in an extreme degree the prospect of our salvation, if religious training follows? I will say more. Many men die without any signs of confirmed holiness, or formed character one

---

[3] Prov. xxii.6. [4] 1 Thess. v.9.

672   INFANT BAPTISM

way or the other. We know, indeed, that privileges not improved will save no one; but we do not know, we cannot pronounce, whether in souls where there is but a little strength, yet
much conflict, and much repentance, their regeneration may
not, as in the case with children, avail them hereafter in some
secret manner which, with our present knowledge, we cannot
speak about or imagine. Surely it is not a slight benefit to have
been "made partakers of the Holy Ghost, and tasted of the
heavenly gift and the powers of the world to come." [5]

Now, I trust that these considerations may suffice, through
God's grace, to open on you a more serious view of the subject
treated of, than is often taken even by those who are not without religious thoughts upon it. I fear, indeed, that most men,
though they profess and have a regard for religion, yet have very
low and contracted notions of the dignity of their station as
Christians. To be a Christian is one of the most wondrous and
awful gifts in the world. It is, in one sense, to be higher than
Angel or Archangel. If we have any portion of an enlightened
faith, we shall understand that our state, as members of Christ's
Church, is full of mystery. What so mysterious as to be born, as
we are, under God's wrath? What so mysterious as to be redeemed by the death of the Son of God made flesh? What so
mysterious as to receive the virtue of that death one by one
through Sacraments? What so mysterious as to be able to teach
and train each other in good or evil? When a man at all enters
into such thoughts, how is his view changed about the birth of
children! in what a different light do his duties, as a parent,
break upon him! The notion entertained by most men seems to
be, that it is a pleasant thing to have a home;—this is what
would be called an innocent and praiseworthy reason for marrying;—that a wife and family are comforts. And the highest
view a number of persons take is, that it is decent and respectable to be a married man; that it gives a man a station in society,
and settles him. All this is true. Doubtless wife and children *are*
blessings from God: and it *is* praiseworthy and right to be domestic, and to live in orderly and honourable habits. But a man
who limits his view to these thoughts, who does not look at
marriage and at the birth of children as something of a much
higher and more heavenly nature than anything we see, who
does not discern in Holy Matrimony a divine ordinance, shad-
owing out the union between Christ and the Church, and does
not associate the birth of children with the Ordinance of their

[5] Heb. vi.4, 5.

new birth, such a one, I can only say, has very carnal views. It is well to go on labouring, year after year, for the bread that perisheth; and if we are well off in the world, to take interest and pleasure in our families rather than to seek amusements out of doors; it is very well, but it is not religion; and let us endeavour to make our feelings towards them more and more religious. Let us beware of aiming at nothing higher than their being educated well for this world, their forming respectable connections, succeeding in their callings, and settling well. Let us never think we have absolved ourselves from the responsibility of being their parents, till we have brought them to Christ, as in Baptism, so by religious training. Let us bear in mind ever to pray for their eternal salvation; let us "watch for their souls as those who must give account." Let us remember that salvation does not come as a matter of course; that Baptism, though administered to them once and long since, is never past, always lives in them as a blessing or as a burden: and that though we may cherish a joyful confidence that "He who hath begun a good work in them will perform it," then only have we a right to cherish it, when we are doing our part towards fulfilling it.

THE DAILY SERVICE

"Not forsaking the assembling of ourselves together, as the manner of some is, but exhorting one another; and so much the more, as ye see the Day approaching."—Heb. x.25.

THE first Christians set up the Church in continual prayer. "They persevering daily with one mind in the Temple, and breaking bread from house to house, did share their food with gladness and singleness of heart, praising God."[1] St. Paul in his Epistles binds their example upon their successors for ever. Indeed, we could not have conceived, even if he and the other Apostles had been silent, that such a solemn opening of the Gospel, as that contained in the book of Acts, was only of a temporary nature, and not rather a specimen of what was to take place among the elect people in every age, and a shadow of that perfect service which will be their blessedness in heaven. However, St. Paul removes all doubt on this subject by expressly enjoining this united and unceasing prayer in various passages of his Epistles; as for instance, "I will . . . that men pray in every place, lifting up holy hands."[2] "Persevere in prayer, and watch in the same with thanksgiving;"[3] and in the text.

But it will be said, "Times are altered; the rites and observances of the Church are local and occasional; what was a duty then, need not be a duty now, even though St. Paul happens to enjoin it on those whom he addresses. Such continual prayer was the particular form which the religion of the early Christians took, and ours has taken another form." Do not suppose, because I allow myself thus to word the objection, that I therefore, for an instant, allow that continual united prayer may religiously be considered a mere usage or fashion; but so it is treated—so, perhaps, some of us in our secret hearts have at times been tempted to imagine; that is, we have been disposed to think that public worship at intervals of a week has in it something of natural fitness and reasonableness which con-

[1] Acts ii.46, 47.   [2] 1 Tim. ii.8.   [3] Col. iv.2.

tinual weekday worship has not. Still, supposing it—granting daily worship to be a mere observance, or an usage, while Sunday worship is not—calling it by any title the most slighting and disparaging—the question returns, was this observance or usage of continual united prayer intended by the Apostles, for every age of the Church, or only for the early Christians? A precept may be but positive, not simply moral, and yet of perpetual obligation. Now, I answer confidently, that united prayer, unceasing prayer, is enjoined by St. Paul, in a passage just cited, from an Epistle which lays down rules for the government and due order of the Church to the end of time. More plausibly even might we desecrate Sunday, which he does not mention in it, than neglect continual prayer, which he does. Observe how explicitly he speaks, "I will therefore that men pray in *every place*;"—not only at Jerusalem, not only at Corinth, not only in Rome, but even in England; in England at this day, in our secluded villages, in our rich populous busy towns, whatever be the importance of those secular objects which absorb our thoughts and time.

Or, again, take the text, and consider whether it favours the notion of a change or relaxation of the primitive custom. "Not forsaking the assembling of ourselves together, as the manner of some is, but exhorting one another; and so *much the more*, as ye see the Day approaching." The increasing troubles of the world, the fury of Satan, and the madness of the people, the dismay of sun, moon, and stars, distress of nations with perplexity, men's hearts failing them for fear, the sea and the waves roaring, all these gathering tokens of God's wrath are but calls upon us for greater perseverance in united prayer. Let those men especially consider this, who say that we are but dreaming of centuries gone by, missing our mark and born out of time, when we insist on such duties and practices as are now merely out of fashion; those who point to the tumult and fever which agitates the whole nation, and say we must be busy and troubled too, in order to respond to it; who say that the tide of events has set in one way, and that we must give in to it, if we would be practical men; that it is idleness to attempt to stem a current, which it will be a great thing even to direct: that since the present age loves conversing and hearing about religion, and does not like silent thought, patient waiting, recurring prayers, severe exercises, that therefore we must obey it, and, dismissing rites and sacraments, convert the Gospel into a rational faith, so called, and a religion of the heart; let these men seriously consider St. Paul's exhortation, that we are to persevere in prayer—and that in every place—and the more, the more troubled and perplexed the affairs of this world become; not indeed omitting active exertions, but not, on that account, omitting prayer.

I have spoken of St. Paul, but, consider how this rule of "continuing in prayer" is exemplified in St. Peter's history also. He had learned from his Saviour's pattern not to think prayer a loss of time. Christ had taken him up with Him into the holy mount, though multitudes waited to be healed and taught below. Again, before His passion, He had taken him into the garden of Gethsemane; and while He prayed Himself, He called upon him likewise to "watch and pray lest he entered into temptation." In consequence, St. Peter warns us in his first Epistle, as St. Paul in the text, "The end of all things is at hand, be ye therefore sober, and watch unto prayer."[4] And, in one memorable passage of his history, he received a revelation of a momentous and most gracious truth, when he was at his prayers. Who would not have said that he was wasting his time, when he retired to the house of Simon at Joppa, for many days, and went up upon the house-top to pray, about the sixth hour? Was that, it might be asked, the part of an Apostle, whose commission was to preach the Gospel? Was he thus burying his light, instead of meeting the exigencies of the time? Yet, there God met him, and put a word in his mouth. There he learned the comfortable truth that the Gentiles were no longer common or unclean, but admissible into the Covenant of Grace. And if continual prayer was the employment of an Apostle, much more was it observed by those Christians who were less prominently called to labour. Accordingly, when St. Peter was in prison, prayers were offered for him, "without ceasing," by the Church; and to those prayers he was granted. When miraculously released, and arrived at the house of Mary, the mother of Mark, he found "many gathered together praying."[5]

Stated and continual prayer, then, and especially united prayer, is plainly the duty of Christians. And if we ask how often we are to pray, I reply, that we ought to consider prayer as a plain privilege, directly we know that it is a duty, and therefore that the question is out of place. Surely, when we know we may approach the Mercy-seat, the only further question is, whether there be anything to forbid us coming often, anything implying that such frequent coming is presumptuous and irreverent. So great a mercy is it to be permitted to come, that a humble mind

---

[4] 1 Pet. iv.7.   [5] Acts xii.12.

may well ask, "Is it a profane intrusion to come when I will?" If it be not, such a one will rejoice to come continually. Now, by way of removing these fears, Scripture contains most condescending intimations that we may come at all times. For instance, in the Lord's Prayer petition is made for *daily* bread for *this* day; therefore, our Saviour intended it should be used daily. Further, it is said, "give *us*," "forgive *us*;" therefore it may fairly be presumed to be given us as a social prayer. Thus in the Lord's Prayer itself there seems to be sanction for daily united prayer. Again, if we consider His words in the parable, twice a day at least seems permitted us, "Shall not God avenge His own elect, which cry day and night unto Him?"[6] though this is to take the words according to a very restricted interpretation. And since Daniel prayed three times a day, and the Psalmist even seven, under the Law, we may infer, that Christians, certainly, are not irreverent, nor incur the blame of using vain repetitions, though they join in many Services.

Now, I do not see what can be said in answer to these arguments, imperfect as they are compared with the whole proof that might be adduced, except that some of the texts cited may, perhaps, refer to mere secret prayer almost without words, and some speak primarily of private prayer. Yet it is undeniable, on the other hand, that united prayer, not private or secret, is principally intended in those passages of the New Testament, which speak of prayer at all; and if so, the remainder may be left to apply indirectly or not, as we chance to decide, without interfering with a conclusion otherwise drawn. If, however, it be said that family prayer is a fulfilment of the duty, without prayer in Church, I reply, that I am not at all speaking of it as a duty, but as a privilege; I do not tell men that they must come to Church, so much as declare the glad tidings that they may. This surely is enough for those who "hunger and thirst after righteousness," and humbly desire to see the face of God.

Now, I will say a few words on the manner in which the early Christians fulfilled this duty.

Quite at first, when the persecutions raged, they assembled when and where they could. At times they could but avail themselves of Christ's promise, that if two of His disciples "*agree* on earth, as touching anything that they shall ask, it shall be done for them of their Heavenly Father;" though, by small parties, and in the towns, they seem to have met together continually from the first. Gradually, as they grew stronger, or as

[6] Luke xviii.7.

they happened to be tolerated, they made full proof of their sacred privilege, and showed what was the desire of their hearts.

Their most solemn Service took place on the Lord's day, as might be expected, when the Holy Eucharist was celebrated.[7] Next to Sunday came Wednesday and Friday, when, also, assemblies for worship continued till three o'clock in the afternoon, and were observed with fasting; in some places with the Eucharist also. Saturday, too, was observed in certain branches of the Church with especial devotion, the Holy Mysteries being solemnized and other Services performed as on the Lord's day.

Next must be mentioned, the Festivals of the Martyrs, when, in addition to the sacred Services used on the Lord's day, there was read some account of the particular Martyr commemorated, with exhortations to follow his pattern.

These holydays, whether Sunday or Saint's day, were commonly ushered in by a Vigil or religious watching, as you find it noted down in the Calendar at the beginning of the Prayer-Book. These lasted through the night.

Moreover, there were the sacred Seasons; such as the forty days of Lent for fasting, and the fifty days between Easter and Whitsuntide for rejoicing.

Such was the course of special devotions in the early Church; but, besides, every day had its ordinary Services, viz., prayer morning and evening.

Besides these, might be mentioned the prayers at the canonical hours, which were originally used for private, but, at length, for united worship; viz., at the third hour, or nine in the morning, in commemoration of the Holy Ghost's descent at Pentecost at that hour; at the sixth, the time of St. Peter's vision at Joppa, in memory of our Saviour's crucifixion; and at the ninth, in memory of His death, which was the hour when St. Peter and St. John went up to the Temple and healed the lame man. It may be added, that in some places the Holy Eucharist was celebrated and partaken daily.

This is by no means a full enumeration of the sacred Services in the early Church; but it is abundantly sufficient for my purpose, which is to show how highly they valued the privilege of united prayer, and how literally they understood the words of Christ and His Apostles. I am by no means contending, that every point of discipline and order in this day must be precisely the same as it was then. Christians then had more time on their

[7] Bingham's Antiq., xiii, 9.

hands than many of us have; and certain peculiarities of the age and place might combine to allow them to do what we cannot do. Still, so far must be clear to every candid person who considers the state of the case, that they found some sort of pleasure in prayer which we do not; that they took delight in an exercise, which—(I am afraid I must say, though it seems profane even to say it)—which we should consider painfully long and tedious.

This too is worth observing of the primitive Christians, that they united social and private prayer in their Service. On holydays, for instance, when it was extended till three o'clock in the afternoon, they commenced with singing the Psalms, in the midst of which two Lessons were read, as is usual with us, commonly one from the Old and one from the New Testament. But in some places, instead of these Lessons, after every Psalm, a short space was allowed for private prayer to be made in silence, much in the way we say a short prayer on coming into and going out of Church. After the Psalms and Lessons came the Sermon, the more solemn prayers having not yet begun. Shortly after, followed the celebration of the Holy Communion, which again was introduced by a time of silence for private prayer, such as we at this day are allowed during the administration of the Sacred Elements to other communicants.

And in this way they lengthened out and varied their Services; principally, that is, by means of private prayers and psalms: so that, when no regular course of service was proceeding, yet the Church might be full of people, praying in secret and confessing their sins, or singing together psalms or hymns. Thus exactly did they fulfil the Scripture precepts—"Is any among you afflicted? let him pray; is any merry? let him sing psalms," and "Let the word of Christ dwell in you richly in all wisdom; teaching and admonishing one another in psalms and hymns and spiritual songs, singing with grace in your hearts to the Lord." [8]

I have now said enough to let you into the reasons why I lately began Daily Service in this Church. I felt that we were very unlike the early Christians, if we went on without it; and that it was my business to give you an opportunity of observing it, else I was keeping a privilege from you. If you ask, why I did not commence it before? I will rather tell you why I began just at this time. It was, that the state of public affairs was so threatening, that I could not bear to wait longer; for there seemed

[8] James v.13; Col. iii.16.

quite a call upon all Christians to be earnest in prayer, so much
the more, as they thought they saw the Day of vengeance approaching. Under these circumstances it seemed wrong to
withhold from you a privilege, for as a privilege I would entirely consider it. I wish to view it rather as a privilege than as a
duty, because then all those perplexed questions are removed at
once, which otherwise beset the mind, whether a man should
come or not. Considering it in the light of a privilege, I am not
obliged to blame a man for not coming. I say to him, If you
cannot come, then you have a great loss. Very likely you are
right in not coming; you have duties connected with your temporal calling which have a claim on you; you must serve like
Martha, you have not the leisure of Mary. Well, be it so; still
you have a loss, as Martha had while Mary was at Jesus' feet.
You have a loss; I do not say God cannot make it up to you;
doubtless He will bless every one who continues in the path of
duty. He blessed Peter in prison, and Paul on the sea, as well as
the mother of Mark, or the daughters of Philip. Doubtless,
even in your usual employments you can be glorifying your
Saviour; you can be thinking of Him; you can be thinking of
those who are met together in worship; you can be following in
your heart, as far as may be, the prayers they offer. Doubtless:
only try to realize to yourself that continual prayer and praise *is*
a privilege; only feel in good earnest, what somehow the mass
of Christians, after all, do not recognize, that "it is good to be
here"—feel as the early Christians felt when persecution hindered them from meeting, or, as holy David, when he cried
out, "My soul is athirst for God, yea, even for the Living God;
when shall I come to appear before the presence of God?"[9] feel
this, and I shall not be solicitous about your coming; you will
come if you can.

　　With these thoughts in my mind, I determined to offer to
God the Daily Service here myself, in order that all might have
the opportunity of coming before Him who would come; to
offer it, not waiting for a congregation, but independently of all
men, as our Church sanctions; to set the example, and to save
you the need of waiting for one another; and at least to give
myself, with the early Christians, and St. Peter on the house-
top, the benefit, if not of social, at least of private prayer, as
becomes the Christian priesthood. It is quite plain that far the
greater part of our Daily Service, though more fitted for a congregation than for an individual (as indeed is the Lord's Prayer

[9] Ps. xlii.2.

itself), may yet be used, as the Lord's Prayer is used, by even one person. Such is our Common Prayer viewed in itself, and our Church has in the Introduction to it expressly directed this use of it. It is there said, "All priests and deacons are to say daily the morning and evening prayer, either privately or openly, not being let by sickness, or some other urgent cause." Again, "The curate that ministereth in every parish church or chapel, being at home, and not being otherwise reasonably hindered, shall say the same in the parish church or chapel where he ministereth, and shall cause a bell to be tolled thereunto a convenient time before he begin, that people may come to hear God's word and to pray with him." Now, doubtless, there are many reasons which may render the strict observances of these rules inexpedient in this or that place or time. The very disuse of them will be a reason for reviving them very cautiously and gradually; the paucity of clergy is another reason for suspending them. Still there they remain in the Prayer-Book—obsolete they cannot become, nay, even though torn from the book in some day of rebuke (to suppose what should hardly even be supposed), they still would have power, and live unto God. If prayers were right three centuries since, they are right now. If a Christian minister might suitably offer up common prayer by himself then, surely he may do so now. If he was then the spokesman of the saints far and near, gathering together their holy and concordant suffrages, and presenting them by virtue of his priesthood, he is so now. The revival of this usage is merely a matter of place and time; and though neither our Lord nor His Church would have us make sudden alterations, even though for the better, yet certainly we ought never to forget what is abstractedly our duty, what is in itself best, what it is we have to aim at and labour towards. If authority were needed, besides our Church's own, for the propriety of Christian Ministers praying even by themselves in places of worship, we have it in the life of our great pattern of Christian faith and wisdom, Hooker. "To what he persuaded others," says his biographer, "he added his own example of fasting and prayer; and did usually every Ember week take from the parish clerk the key of the church-door, into which place he retired every day, and locked himself up for many hours; and did the like most Fridays, and other days of fasting."

That holy man, in this instance, kept his prayers to himself. He was not offering up the Daily Service; but I adduce his instance to show that there is nothing strange or unseemly in a Christian minister praying in church by himself; and if so, much less when he gives his people the opportunity of coming if they will. *This*, then, is what I felt and feel:—it is commonly said, when week-day prayers are spoken of, "You will not get a congregation, or you will get but a few;" but they whom Christ has brought near to Himself to be the Stewards of His Mysteries depend on no man; rather, after His pattern, they are to draw men after them. He prayed alone on the mountain; He prays alone (for who shall join with Him?) in His Father's presence. He is the one effectual Intercessor for sinners at the right hand of God. And what He is really, such are we in figure; what He is meritoriously, such are we instrumentally. Such are we by His grace; allowed to occupy His place visibly, however unworthily, in His absence, till He come; allowed to depend on Him, and not on our people; allowed to draw our commission from Him, not from them; allowed to be centres, about which the Church may grow, and about which it really exists, be it great or little.

Therefore, in beginning and continuing the Daily Service, I do not, will not measure the effect produced, by appearances. If we wait till all the world are worshippers, we must wait till the world is new made; but, if so, who shall draw the line, and say, how many are enough to pray together, when He has told us that His flock is little, and that where two or three are gathered together in His name, He is in the midst of them? So I account a few met together in prayer to be a type of His true Church; not actually His true Church (God forbid the presumption!) but as a token and type of it:—not *as being* His elect, one by one, for who can know whom He has chosen but He who chooses?—not *as* His elect for certain, for it may be a man's duty to be away, as Martha was in her place when serving, and only faulty when she thought censoriously of Mary;—not as His complete flock, doubtless, for that were to exclude the old, and the sick, and the infirm, and little children;—not as His select and undefiled remnant, for Judas was one of the twelve—still as the earnest and promise of His Saints, the birth of Christ in its rudiments, and the dwelling-place of the Spirit; and precious, even though but one out of the whole number, small though it be, belong at present to God's hidden ones; nay, though, as is likely to be the case, in none of them there be more than the dawn of the True Light and the goings forth of the morning.—Some, too, will come at times, as accident guides them, giving promise that they may one day be settled and secured within the sacred fold. Some will come in times of grief or compunction, others in preparation for the Holy Communion.[10] Nor is it a service for those only who are present; all men know the time, and many mark it, whose bodily presence is away. We have with us the hearts of many. Those who are conscious they are absent in the path of duty, will naturally turn their thoughts to the Church at the stated hour, and thence to God. They will recollect what prayers are then in course, and they will have fragments of them rising on their minds amid their worldly business. They will call to mind the day of the month, and the psalms used on it, and the chapters of Scripture then read out to the people. How pleasant to the wayfaring man, on his journey, to think of what is going on in his own Church! How soothing and consolatory to the old and infirm who cannot come, to follow in their thoughts, nay, with the prayers and psalms before them, what they do not hear! Shall not those prayers and holy meditations, separated though they be in place, ascend up together to the presence of God? Shall not they be with their minister in spirit, who are provoked unto prayer by his service? Shall not their prayers unite in one before the Mercy-seat, sprinkled with the Atoning Blood, as a pure offering of incense unto the Father, and an acceptable sacrifice both for the world of sinners and for His purchased Church? Who then will dare speak of loneliness and solitude, because in man's eyes there are few worshippers brought together in one place? or, who will urge it as a defect in our Service, even if that were the case? Who, moreover, will so speak, when even the Holy Angels are present when we pray, stand by us as guardians, sympathize in our need, and join us in our praises?

When thoughts such as these are set before the multitude of men, they appear to some of them strained and unnatural; to others, formal, severe, and tending to bondage. So must it be. Christ's commands will seem to be a servitude, and His privileges will be strange, till we act upon the one and embrace the other. To those who come in faith, to receive and to obey, who, instead of standing at a distance, reasoning, criticising, investigating, adjusting, hear His voice and follow Him, not knowing

[10] It may be suggested here, that week-day services (with fasting) are the appropriate attendants on weekly communion, which has lately been advocated, especially in the impressive sermons of Mr. Dodsworth. When the one observance is used without the other, either the sacredness of the Lord's day is lost, from its wanting a peculiar Service, or the Eucharist is in danger of profanation, from its frequency leading us to remissness in preparing for it.

whither they go; who throw themselves, their hearts and wills, their opinions and conduct, into His Divine System with a noble boldness, and serve Him on a venture, without experience of results, or skill to defend their own confidence by argument: who, when He says "Pray," "Continue in prayer," take His words simply, and forthwith pray, and that instantly; these men, through His great mercy and the power of the Holy Ghost working in them, will at length find persevering prayer, praise, and intercession, neither a bondage nor a barrenness. But it is in the nature of things that Christ's word must be a law *while* it is good tidings. That very message of good tidings, that Christ saves sinners, is no good tidings to those who have not a heart to abandon sin; and as no one, by nature, has this good heart, and, even under grace, no one obtains it except gradually, there must ever be a degree of bondage in the Gospel, till, by obeying the Law and creating within us a love of God and holiness, we, by little and little, enter into the meaning of His promises.

May He lead us on evermore in the narrow way, who is the One Aid of all that need, the Helper of all that flee to Him for succour, the Life of them that believe, and the Resurrection of the dead!

THE GOOD PART OF MARY

*"Martha, Martha, thou art careful and troubled about many things;
but one thing is needful: and Mary hath chosen that good part which
shall not be taken away from her."*—Luke x.41, 42.

E VERY word of Christ is good; it has its mission and its
purpose, and does not fall to the ground.[1] It cannot be that
He should ever speak transitory words, who is Himself the very
Word of God, uttering, at His good pleasure, the deep counsels
and the holy will of Him who is invisible. Every word of Christ
is good; and did we receive a record of His sayings even from
ordinary men, yet we might be sure as to whatever was thus
preserved, whether spoken to disciple or enemy, whether by
way of warning, advice, rebuke, comfort, argument, or condemnation, that nothing had a merely occasional meaning, a
partial scope and confined range, nothing regarded merely the
moment, or the accident, or the audience; but all His sacred
speeches, though clothed in a temporary garb, and serving an
immediate end, and difficult, in consequence, to disengage
from what is temporary in them and immediate, yet all have
their force in every age, abiding in the Church on earth, "enduring for ever in heaven," and running on into eternity. They
are our rule, "holy, just, and good," "the lantern of our feet and
the light of our paths," in this very day as fully and as intimately
as when they were first pronounced.

And if this had been so, though mere human diligence had
gathered up the crumbs from His table, much more sure are we
of the value of what is recorded of Him, receiving it, as we do,
not from man, but from God. The Holy Ghost, who came to
glorify Christ, and inspired the Evangelists to write, did not
trace out for us a barren Gospel; but doubtless, praised be His
name, selected and saved for us those words which were to have
an especial usefulness in after times, those words which might
be the Church's law, in faith, conduct, and discipline; not a law
written in tables of stone, but a law of faith and love, of the

[1] Basil, Const. Mon. 1.

spirit, not of the letter; a law for willing hearts, who could bear to "live by every word," however faint and low, "which proceeded from His mouth," and who out of the seeds which the Heavenly Sower scattered, could foster into life a Paradise of Divine Truth. Let us then humbly try with this thought before us, and the help of His grace, to gain some benefit from the text.

Martha and Mary were the sisters of Lazarus, who was afterwards raised from the dead. All three lived together, but Martha was mistress of the house. St. Luke mentions, in a verse preceding the text, that Christ came to a certain village, "and a certain woman, named Martha, received Him into her house." Being then at the head of a family, she had duties which necessarily engaged her time and thoughts. And on the present occasion she was especially busy, from a wish to do honour to her Lord. "Martha was cumbered about much serving." On the other hand, her sister was free from the necessity of worldly business, by being the younger. "She had a sister called Mary, which also sat at Jesus' feet, and heard His word." The same distinction, at once of duty and character, appears in the narrative of Lazarus' death and restoration, as contained in St. John's Gospel. "Then Martha, as soon as she heard that Jesus was coming, went and met Him; but Mary sat still in the house." [2] Afterwards Martha "went her way and called Mary her sister secretly, saying, The Master is come, and calleth for thee." Again, in the beginning of the following chapter, "There they made Him a supper; and Martha served. . . . . Then took Mary a pound of ointment of spikenard, very costly, and anointed the feet of Jesus, and wiped His feet with her hair." [3] In these passages the same general difference between the sisters presents itself, though in a different respect;—Martha still directs and acts, while Mary is the retired and modest servant of Christ, who, at liberty from worldly duties, loves to sit at His feet and hear His voice, and silently honours Him with her best, without obtruding herself upon His sacred presence.

To return:—"Martha was cumbered about much serving, and came to Him, and said, Lord, dost Thou not care that my sister hath left me to serve alone? bid her therefore that she help me. And Jesus answered and said unto her," in the words of the text, "Martha, Martha, thou art careful and troubled about many things; but one thing is needful: and Mary hath chosen that good part which shall not be taken away from her."

---

[2] John xi.20.   [3] John xii.2, 3.

I shall draw two observations from this incident, and our Saviour's comment on it.

1. First, it would appear from hence, on His own authority, that there are two ways of serving Him—by active business, and by quiet adoration. Not, of course, that He speaks of those who call themselves His servants and are not; who counterfeit the one or the other manner of life; either those who are "choked with the cares of this world," or those who lie idle and useless as the hard way-side, and "bring no fruit to perfection." Nor, again, as if His words implied that any Christians were called to nothing but religious worship, or any to nothing but active employment. There are busy men and men of leisure, who have no part in Him; there are others, who are not without fault, as altogether sacrificing leisure to business, or business to leisure. But putting aside the thought of the untrue and of the extravagant, still after all there remain two classes of Christians;— those who are like Martha, those like Mary; and both of them glorify Him in their own line, whether of labour or of quiet, in either case proving themselves to be not their own, but bought with a price, set on obeying, and constant in obeying His will. If they labour, it is for His sake; and if they adore, it is still from love of Him.

And further, these two classes of His disciples do not choose for themselves their course of service, but are allotted it by Him. Martha might be the elder, Mary the younger. I do not say that it is never left to a Christian to choose his own path, whether he will minister with the Angels or adore with the Seraphim; often it is: and well may he bless God if he has it in his power freely to choose that good portion which our Saviour especially praises. But, for the most part, each has his own place marked out for him, if he will take it, in the course of His providence; at least there can be no doubt *who* are intended for worldly cares. The necessity of getting a livelihood, the calls of a family, the duties of station and office, these are God's tokens, tracing out Martha's path for the many. Let me, then, dismiss the consideration of the many, and rather mention who they are who may be considered as called to the more favoured portion of Mary; and in doing so I shall more clearly show what that portion is.

First, I instance the Old, as is natural, whose season of business is past, and who seem to be thereby reminded to serve God by prayer and contemplation. Such was Anna; "she was of a great age, ... and was a widow of about fourscore and four years, which departed not from the Temple, but served God with fastings and prayers night and day."[4] Here we see both the description of person called, and the occupation itself. Further, observe, it was the promises stored in Christ the Saviour, which were the object, towards which her service had respect. When He was brought into the Temple, she "gave thanks to the Lord, and spake of Him to all them that looked for redemption in Jerusalem." Again, the same description of person, certainly the same office, is set before us in the parable of the importunate widow. "He spake a parable unto them to this end, that we ought always to pray and not to faint."[5] The widow said, "Avenge me of mine adversary." "And shall not God avenge His own elect," our Lord asks, "which cry day and night unto Him, though He bear long with them?" Add to these St. Paul's description: "Now she that is a widow indeed, and desolate, trusteth in God, and continueth in supplications and prayers night and day."[6]

Next those, who minister at the Altar, are included in Mary's portion. "Blessed is the man whom thou choosest and causest to approach unto Thee," says the Psalmist, "that He may dwell in Thy courts."[7] According to the Apostles' rule, the Deacons were to minister the worldly matters of the Church, the Evangelists were to go among the heathen, the Bishops were to govern; but the Elders were to remain, more or less, in the very bosom of the Lord's people, in the courts of His house, in the services of His worship, "executing the priest's office," as we read in the book of Acts,[8] offering up the Sacrifice of praise and thanksgiving, teaching, catechising, but not busy or troubled with the world. I do not mean that these distinct offices were never united in one person, but that they were in themselves distinct, and that the tendency of the Apostles' discipline was to separate off from the multitude of Christian Ministers certain who should serve God and the Church by giving thanks, and intercession.

And next, I may mention Children as in some respects partakers of Mary's portion. Till they go out into the world, whether into its trades or its professions, their school-time should be, in some sort, a contemplation of their Lord and Saviour. Doubtless they cannot enter into sacred subjects as steadily as is possible afterwards; they must not be unnaturally compelled to serve, and they are to be exercised in active habits of obedience, and in a needful discipline for the future; still,

---

[4] Luke ii.36, 37.   [5] Luke xviii.1.   [6] 1 Tim. v.5.
[7] Ps. lxv.4.   [8] Acts xiii.2.

after all, we must not forget that He, who is the pattern of children as well as grown men, was, at twelve years old, found in His Father's House; and that afterwards, when He came thither before His passion, the children welcomed Him with the words, "Hosanna to the Son of David," and fulfilled a prophecy, and gained His praise, in so doing.

Further, we are told, on St. Paul's authority (if that be necessary on so obvious a point), that Mary's portion is allotted, more or less, to the unmarried. I say more or less, for Martha herself, though unmarried, yet as mistress of a household, was in a measure an exception; and because servants of God, as St. Paul, may remain unmarried, not to labour less, but to labour more directly for the Lord. St. Paul's words, some have observed, almost appear to refer to the language used in the text, when read in the original Greek; which is the more likely, as St. Luke was an attendant on the Apostle and his Gospel seems to be cited elsewhere by him. As if he said, "The unmarried careth for the things of the Lord, so as to be holy both in body and in spirit. And this I speak for your own profit, that ye may sit at the Lord's feet without being cumbered."

And further still, there are vast numbers of Christians, in Mary's case, who are placed in various circumstances, and of whom no description can well be given; rich men having leisure, or active men during seasons of leisure, as when they leave their ordinary work for recreation's sake. Certainly our Lord meant that some or other of His servants should be ever worshipping Him in every place, and that not in their hearts merely, but with the ceremonial of devotion. St. Paul says, "I will therefore that men," even that sex whose especial punishment it was that they should "eat bread in the sweat of their face," "that men pray every where, *lifting up holy hands*," in common and public worship, "without wrath and doubting."[9] And we find, accordingly, that even a Roman Centurion, Cornelius, had found time, amid his military duties, to serve God continually, before he became a Christian, and was rewarded with the knowledge of the Gospel in consequence. "He prayed to God alway," we are told, and his "prayers and alms came up for a memorial before God."[10]

And last of all, in Mary's portion, doubtless, are included the souls of those who have lived and died in the faith and fear of Christ. Scripture tells us that "they rest from their labours;"[11] and in the same sacred book, that their employment is prayer

---

[9] 1 Tim. ii.8.   [10] Acts x.4.   [11] Rev. xiv.13.

and praise. While God's servants below cry to Him day and night in every place; these "serve Him day and night in His temple" above, and from their resting-place beneath the altar intercede, with loud voice, for those holy interests which they have left behind them. "How long, O Lord, holy and true, dost Thou not judge and avenge our blood on them that dwell on the earth?" "We give Thee thanks, because Thou hast taken to Thee Thy great power, and hast reigned." [12]

This then is the company of those who stand in Mary's lot;— the Aged and the Children—the Unmarried and the Priests of God—and the spirits of the just made perfect, all with one accord, like Moses on the Mount, lifting up holy hands to God, while their brethren fight, or meditating on the promises, or hearing their Saviour's teaching, or adorning and beautifying His worship.

2. Such being the two-fold character of Christian obedience, I observe, secondly, that Mary's portion is the better of the two. Our Lord does not expressly say so, but He clearly implies it: "Martha, Martha, thou art careful and troubled about many things; but one thing is needful: and Mary hath chosen that good part, which shall not be taken away from her." If His words be taken literally, they might, indeed, even mean that Martha's heart was not right with Him, which, it is plain from other parts of the history, they do not mean. Therefore, what He intimated surely was, that Martha's portion was full of snares, as being one of worldly labour, but that Mary could not easily go wrong in hers; that we may be busy in a wrong way, we cannot well adore Him except in a right one; that to serve God by prayer and praise continually, when we can do so consistently with other duties, is the pursuit of the "one thing needful," and emphatically "that good part which shall not be taken away from us."

It is impossible to read St. Paul's Epistles carefully without perceiving how faithfully they comment on this rule of our Lord's. Is it doubtful to any one, that they speak much and often of the duties of worship, meditation, thanksgiving, prayer, praise, and intercession; and in such a way as to lead the Christian, so far as other duties will allow him, to make them the ordinary employment of his life? not, indeed, to neglect his lawful calling, nor even to be content without some active efforts to do good, whether in the way of education of the young, attendance on the sick and needy, pastoral occupation,

[12] Rev. vi. 10; xi. 17.

study, or other toil, yet to devote himself to a life at Jesus' feet, and a continual hearing of His word? And is it not plainly a privilege, above other privileges, if we really love Him, to be called to this unearthly life? Consider the following passages, in addition to those already quoted, and see if they can possibly be completely realized in the life of the common run of Christians, though all, doubtless, must cultivate inwardly, and in due measure bring into outward act, the spirit which they enjoin. See if they be not illustrations of that more blessed portion with which Mary was favoured. "Continue in prayer, watching in it with thanksgiving." [13] "Let the word of Christ dwell in you richly in all wisdom; teaching and admonishing one another in psalms, and hymns, and spiritual songs, singing with grace in your hearts to the Lord." [14] "Rejoice evermore, pray without ceasing, in every thing give thanks, . . . quench not the Spirit, despise not prophesyings." [15] "I will that men pray every where, lifting up holy hands." [16] "Be not drunk with wine, wherein is excess, but be filled with the Spirit, speaking to each other in psalms, and hymns, and spiritual songs, singing and making melody in your heart to the Lord; giving thanks always, for all things, unto God our Father in the name of our Lord Jesus Christ." [17] "Stand therefore, having your loins girt about with truth, . . . taking the shield of faith, . . . and the sword of the Spirit, which is the word of God, praying always with all prayer and supplication in the Spirit, and watching thereunto with all perseverance and supplication for all the saints." [18] Thus St. Paul speaks: in like manner St. Peter, "casting all your care" (such as Martha's) "upon Him, for He is concerned for you." [19] "Abstain from wine, that you may pray;" [20] and St. James, "Is any among you afflicted? let him pray. Is any merry? let him sing psalms." [21]

These are the injunctions of the Apostles; next, observe how they were fulfilled in the early Church. Before the Comforter came down, they "all (the Apostles) *continued*," St. Paul's very word in the passages above cited, they persevered steadily, they endured, "with one accord, in prayer and supplication, with the women, and Mary the mother of Jesus, and with His brethren." And so, after Pentecost; "They *continuing*"—the same word—steadfastly enduring, "daily with one accord, in the Temple, and breaking bread from house to house, did eat their

[13] Col. iv.2. [14] Col. iii.16. [15] 1 Thess. v.16–20.
[16] 1 Tim. ii.8. [17] Eph. v.18–20. [18] Eph. vi.14–18.
[19] 1 Pet. v.7. [20] 1 Pet. iv.7. [21] James v.13.

meat with gladness and singleness of heart, praising God." [22]
That early privilege, we know, was soon taken from them as a
body. Persecution arose, and they were "scattered" [23] to and fro,
over the earth. Henceforth Martha's portion befell them. They
were full of labours, whether pleasant or painful;—pleasant,
for they had to preach the Gospel over the earth—but painful as
losing, not only earthly comforts, but, in some sort, spiritual
quietness. They were separated from the Ordinances of Divine
grace, as wanderers in a wilderness. Here and there, as they
journeyed, they met a few of their brethren, "prophets and
teachers, ministering to the Lord" at Antioch; or Philip's
daughters, "virgins, which did prophesy" [24] at Caesarea. They
met for worship in secret, fearing their enemies; and in course
of time, when the fire of persecution became fiercer, they fled
to the deserts, and there set up houses for God's service. Thus
Mary's portion was withheld from the Church for many years,
while it laboured and suffered. St. Paul himself, that great
Apostle, though he had his seasons of privilege, when he was
caught up into the third heaven, and heard the hymns of Angels, yet he, too, was a man of contention and toil. He fought
for the Truth, and so laid the foundations of the Temple. He
was "sent to preach, not to baptize." He was not allowed to
build the House of God, for he was, in figure, like David, a
"man of blood." He did but bring together into one the materials for the Sacred Building. The Order of the Ministry, the
Succession of Apostles, the Services of Worship, the Rule of
Discipline, all that is calm, beautiful, and soothing in our Holy
Religion, was brought forth piecemeal, out of his writings, by
his friends and fellow-disciples, in his own day, and in the time
after him, as the state of the Church admitted.

Accordingly, as peace was in any measure enjoyed, so the
building was carried on, here and there, at this time and that, in
the cavern, or the desert, or the mountain, where God's stray
servants lived; till a time of peace came, and by the end of three
hundred years the work was accomplished. From that time onwards to the present day, Mary's lot has been offered to vast
multitudes of Christians, if they could receive it. If they knew
their blessedness, there are numbers now, in various ranks of
society, who might enjoy the privilege of continual praise and
prayer, and a seat at Jesus' feet. Doubtless they are, after all, but
the few: for the great body of Christians have but the Lord's day,
as a day of rest, and would be deserting their duty if they lived

22 Acts i.14; ii.46.   23 Acts viii.1.   24 Acts xiii.2; xxi.9.

on other days as on it. But what is not granted to some, is granted to others, to serve God in His Temple, and be at rest. Who these favoured persons are, has already been said generally; which is all that can be said in a matter in which every one must decide for himself, according to his best light and his own peculiar case. Yet surely, without attempting to pronounce upon individuals, so far at least we may say, that if there be an age when Mary's portion is altogether let alone and decried, that age is necessarily so far a stranger to the spirit of the Gospel.

Let me then, in conclusion, ask, for our edification, whether perchance this is not such an age? I say "perchance;" because in matters of this kind, men show their motives and principles less openly than in other matters, as being of a nature more immediately lying between themselves and God. Yet, taking account of this, at least is not this an age in which few persons are in a condition, from the very state of society, to "give themselves continually to prayer" and other direct religious services? Has not the desire of wealth so eaten into our hearts, that we think poverty the worst of ills, that we think the security of property the first of blessings, that we measure all things by mammon, that we not only labour for it ourselves, but so involve in our own evil earnestness all around us, that they cannot keep from the pursuit of it though they would? Does not the frame-work of society move forward on such a plan as to enlist into the service of the world all its members, almost whether they will or no? Would not a man be thought unaspiring and unproductive, who cared not to push forward in pursuit of that which Scripture calls "the root of all evil," the love of which it calls "covetousness which is idolatry," and the possession of which it solemnly declares all but excludes a man from the kingdom of Heaven? Alas! can this be denied? And therefore, of course, the entire system of tranquil devotion, holy meditation, freedom from worldly cares, which our Saviour praises in the case of Mary, is cast aside, misunderstood, or rather missed altogether, as much as the glorious sunshine by a blind man, slandered and ridiculed as something contemptible and vain. Surely, no one, who is candid, can doubt, that, were Mary now living, did she choose on principle that state of life in which Christ found her, were she content to remain at Jesus' feet hearing His word and disengaged from this troublesome world, she would be blamed and pitied. Careless men would gaze strangely, and wise men compassionately, on such an one, as wasting her life, and choosing a melancholy, cheerless portion. Long ago was this the case. Even in holy Martha, zealous as she was and true-hearted, even in her instance we are reminded of the impatience and disdain with which those who are far different from her, the children of this world, regard such as dedicate themselves to God. Long ago, even in her, we seem to witness, as in type, the rash, unchristian way in which this age disparages devotional services. Do we never hear it said, that the daily Service of the Church is unnecessary? Is it never hinted that it is scarcely worth while to keep it up unless we get numbers to attend it, as if one single soul, if but one, were not precious enough for Christ's love and His Church's rearing? Is it never objected, that a partially-filled Church is a discouraging sight, as if, after all, our Lord Jesus had chosen the many and not the few to be His true disciples? Is it never maintained, that a Christian minister is off his post unless he is for ever labouring for the heartless many, instead of ministering to the more religious few? Alas! there must be something wrong among us; when our defenders recommend the Church on the mere plea of its activity, its popularity, and its visible usefulness, and would scarcely scruple to give us up, had we *not* the many on our side! If our ground of boasting be, that rich men, and mighty men, and many men love us, it never can be a religious boast, and may be our condemnation. Christ made His feast for "the poor, the maimed, the lame, and the blind." It is the widow and the fatherless, the infirm, the helpless, the devoted, bound together in prayer, who are the strength of the Church. It is their prayers, be they many or few, the prayers of Mary and such as Mary, who are the safety, under Christ, of those who with Paul and Barnabas fight the Lord's battles. "It is but lost labour to rise up early, to sit up late, to eat the bread of sorrows," if prayers are discontinued. It is mere infatuation, if we think to resist the enemies who at this moment are at our doors, if our Churches remain shut, and we give up to prayer but a few minutes in the day.

Blessed indeed are they whom Christ calls near to Him to be His own peculiar attendants and familiar friends; more blessed if they obey and fulfil their calling! Blessed even if they are allowed to seize intervals of such service towards Him; but favoured and honoured beyond thought, if they can, without breach of duty, put aside worldly things with full purpose of heart, renounce the pursuit of wealth, keep clear of family cares, and present themselves as a holy offering, without spot or blemish, to Him who died for them.[25] These are they who "fol-

---

[25] The life here advocated is one of which Prayer, Praise, Intercession, and other devotional services, are made the object and business, in

THE GOOD PART OF MARY

low Him whithersoever He goeth," and to them He more especially addresses those lessons of faith and resignation which are
recorded in His Gospel. "Take heed," he says, "and beware of
covetousness, for man's life consisteth not in the overabun-
dance of the things which he possesseth. Take no care for your
life, what ye shall eat, neither for the body, what ye shall put on.
Consider the lilies how they grow, they toil not, they spin not.
Seek not ye what ye shall eat or what ye shall drink, neither be
ye unsettled; for all these things do the nations of the world
seek after, and your Father knoweth that ye have need of these
things. Fear not, little flock, for it is your Father's good pleasure
to give you the Kingdom. Sell that ye have, and give alms; provide yourselves bags which wax not old, where no thief ap-
proacheth, neither moth corrupteth. Let your loins be girded
about, and your lights burning; and ye yourselves like unto men
that wait for their Lord, when He will return from the wedding. Blessed are those servants, whom the Lord, when He
cometh, shall find watching. Verily I say unto you, that He will
gird Himself"—He who on earth has let them sit at His feet
hearing His word, or let them anoint His feet with ointment,
kissing them, He in turn, as He did before His passion, by an
inexpressible condescension, "will gird Himself; and make
them to sit down to meat, and will come forth and serve them.
And if He shall come in the second watch, or come in the third
watch, and find them so, blessed are those servants. Be ye therefore ready also; for the Son of man cometh at an hour when ye
think not." [26]

----

the same sense in which a certain profession or trade is the object and
business of life to the mass of men: one in which devotion is *the* end to
which everything else gives way. This explanation will answer the
question, *how much* of each day it supposes set aside for devotion. Callings of this world do not necessarily occupy the whole, or half, or a
third of our time, but they *rule* and *dispose* of the whole of it.

[26] Luke xii.15-40.

RELIGIOUS WORSHIP
A REMEDY FOR EXCITEMENTS

*"Is any among you afflicted? let him pray. Is any merry?
let him sing psalms."*—James v.13.

S T. JAMES seems to imply in these words that there is that in
religious worship which supplies all our spiritual need,
which suits every mood of mind and every variety of circumstances, over and above the heavenly and supernatural assistance
which we are allowed to expect from it. Prayer and praise seem
in his view to be an universal remedy, a panacea, as it is called,
which ought to be used at once, whatever it be that affects us.
And, as is implied in ascribing to them this universal virtue, they
produce very opposite effects, according to our need; allaying or
carrying off the fever of the mind, as the case may be. The
Apostle is not speaking of *sin* in the text; he speaks of the *emotions* of the mind, whether joyful or sorrowful, of good and bad
spirits; and for these and all other such disturbances, prayer and
praise are a medicine. Sin indeed has its appropriate remedies
too, and more serious ones; penitence, self-abasement, self-re-
venge, mortification, and the like. But the text supposes the
case of a Christian, not of a mere penitent—not of scandalous
wickedness, but of emotion, agitation of mind, regret, longing,
despondency, mirthfulness, transport, or rapture; and in case of
such ailments it says, prayer and praise is the remedy.

Indisposition of body shows itself in a *pain* somewhere or
other;—a distress, which draws our thoughts to it, centres them
upon it, impedes our ordinary way of going on, and throws the
mind off its balance. Such too is indisposition of the soul, of
whatever sort, be it passion or affection, hope or fear, joy or
grief. It takes us off from the clear contemplation of the next
world, ruffles us, and makes us restless. In a word, it is what we
call an excitement of mind. Excitements are the indisposition
of the mind; and of these excitements in different ways the services of divine worship are the proper antidotes. How they are
so, shall now be considered.

1. Excitements are of two kinds, secular and religious: First, let us consider secular excitements. Such is the pursuit of gain, or of power, or of distinction. Amusements are excitements; the applause of a crowd, emulations, hopes, risks, quarrels, contests, disappointments, successes. In such cases the object pursued naturally absorbs the mind, and excludes all thoughts but those relating to itself. Thus a man is sold over into bondage to this world. He has one idea, and one only before him, which becomes his idol. Day by day he is engrossed by this one thing, to which his heart pays worship. It may attract him through the imagination, or through the reason; it may appeal to his heart, or to his self-interest, or to his pride; still, whether we be young or old, rich or poor, each age, each fortune is liable to its own peculiar excitement, which has power to fascinate the eye of our minds, to enervate and destroy us. Not all at once (God forbid!), but by a gradual process, till every thought of religion is lost before the contemplation of this nearer good.

The most ordinary of these excitements, at least in this country, is the pursuit of gain. A man may live from week to week in the fever of a decent covetousness, to which he gives some more specious name (for instance, desire of doing his duty by his family), till the heart of religion is eaten out of him. He may live and die in his farm or in his merchandise. Or he may be labouring for some distinction, which depends on his acquitting himself well on certain trying occasions, and requires a laborious preparation beforehand. Or he may be idly carried away by some light object of sense, which fills his mind with empty dreams and with pains which profit not. Or he may be engaged in the general business of life; be full of schemes and projects, of political manoeuvres and efforts, of hate, or jealousy, or resentment, or triumph. He may be busy in managing, persuading, outwitting, resisting other men. Again, he may be in one or other of these states, not for a life, but for a season; and this is the more general case. Anyhow, *while* he is so circumstanced, whether for a longer or a shorter season, this will hold good—viz., the thought of religion is excluded by the force of the excitement which is on him.

Now, then, observe what is the remedy. "Is any afflicted? let him pray. Is any merry? let him sing psalms." Here we see one very momentous use of prayer and praise to all of us; it breaks the current of worldly thoughts. And this is the singular benefit of stated worship, that it statedly interferes with the urgency of worldly excitements. Our daily prayer, morning and evening, suspends our occupations of time and sense. And especially the daily prayers of the Church do this. I say especially, because a man, amid the business of life, is often tempted to defraud himself of his private devotions by the pressure of engagements. He has not many minutes to give to them; and if by accident they are broken in upon, the season is gone and lost. But the public Service is of a certain length, and cannot be interrupted; and it is long enough to calm and steady the mind. Scripture must be read, psalms must be sung, prayers must be offered; every thing comes in course. I say, it is impossible (under God's blessing) for any one to attend the Daily Service of the Church "with reverence and godly fear," and a wish and effort to give his thoughts to it, and not find himself thereby sobered and brought to recollection. What kinder office is there, when a man is agitated, than for a friend to put his hand upon him by way of warning, to startle and recall him? It often has the effect of saving us from angry words, or extravagant talking, or inconsiderate jesting, or rash resolves. And such is the blessed effect of the sacred Services on Christians busied about many things; reminding them of the one thing needful, and keeping them from being drawn into the great whirlpool of time and sense.

This, let it be observed, is one important benefit arising from the institution of the Lord's day. Over and above the privilege of being allowed one day in seven for religious festivity, the Christian may accept it as a merciful break in upon his usual employments, lest they should engross him. Most men, indeed, perceive this; they will feel wearied with the dust of this world when Saturday comes, and understand it to be a mercy that they are not obliged to go on toiling without cessation. But still, there are many who, if it were not an express ordinance of religion, would feel tempted, or think it their duty, to continue their secular labours, even though the custom of society allowed them to rest. Many, as it is, are so tempted; that is, at times, when they have some pressing object in view, and think they cannot afford to lose a day: and many always—such, for instance, as are in certain professions, which are not regulated (as trade is, more or less) by times and places. And great numbers, it is to be feared, yield to the temptation; and the evil effect of it shows itself in various miserable ways, even in the overthrow of their health and reason. In all these cases, then, the weekly Services of prayer and praise come to us as a gracious relief, a pause from the world, a glimpse of the third heaven, lest the world should rob us of our hope, and enslave us to that hard master who is plotting our eternal destruction.

You see, then, how secular excitements are remedied by religious worship; viz., by breaking them up, and disabling them.

2. Next, let us consider how religious excitements are set right by the same Divine medicine.

If we had always continued in the way of light and truth, obeying God from childhood, doubtless we should know little of those swellings and tumults of the soul which are so common among us. Men who have grown up in the faith and fear of God, have a calm and equable piety; so much so, that they are often charged on that very account with being dull, cold, formal, insensible, dead to the next world. Now, it stands to reason, that a man who has always lived in the contemplation and improvement of his Gospel privileges, will not feel that agitating surprise and vehemence of joy, which he would feel, and ought to feel, if he had never known anything of them before. The jailor, who for the first time heard the news of salvation through Christ, gave evident signs of transport. This certainly is natural and right; still it is a state of excitement, and, if I might say it, all states of excitement have dangerous tendencies. Hence one never can be sure of a new convert; for, in that elevated state of mind in which he is at first, the affections have much more sway than the reason or conscience; and unless he takes care, they may hurry him away, just as a wind might do, in a wrong direction. He is balanced on a single point, on the summit of an excited mind, and he may easily fall. However, though this danger would not exist, or, at least, not commonly or seriously, did men turn to God from early youth, yet, alas! in matter of fact they do not so turn; in matter of fact they are open to the influence of excitement, when they begin to seek God; and the question is, what is then to be done with them?

Now, this advice is often given:—"Indulge the excitement; when you flag, seek for another; live upon the thought of God; go about doing good; let your light shine before men; tell them what God has done for your soul;"—by all which is meant, when we go into particulars, that they ought to fancy that they have something above all other men; ought to neglect their worldly calling, or at best only bear it as a cross; to join themselves to some particular set of religionists; to take part in this or that religious society; go to hear strange preachers, and obtrude their new feelings and new opinions upon others, at times proper and improper. I am speaking now of the temper, not of those who profess adherence to the Church, but of such as detach themselves, more or less, from its discipline; and the reason I allude to them is this. It is often said, that schism and dissent are but accidents of a religious temper; that they who fall into them, if pious, are the same in heart as Churchmen, only are divided by some outward difference of forms and circumstances. Not so; the mind of dissent, viewed in itself, is far other than the mind of Christ and His Holy Church Catholic; in whatever proportion it may or may not be realized in individuals. It is full of self-importance, irreverence, censoriousness, display, and tumult. It is right, therefore, ever to insist that it is different, lest men should be seduced into it, by being assured that it is not different.

That it is different from the mind and spirit of the early Christians at least, is quite plain from history. If there was a time, when those particular irregularities, which now are so common, were likely to abound, it was in the primitive Church. Men, who had lived all their lives in the pollutions of sin unspeakable, who had been involved in the darkness of heathenism, were suddenly brought to the light of Christian truth. Their sins were all freely forgiven them, clean washed away in the waters of Baptism. A new world of ideas was opened upon them; and the most astonishing objects presented to their faith. What a state of transport must have been theirs! We know it was so, by the account of such men in the book of Acts. The jailor "*rejoiced*, believing in God, with all his house." And what an excited and critical state was theirs! Critical and dangerous in proportion to its real blessedness; for, in proportion to the privileges we enjoy, ever will be our risk of misusing them. In spite, then, of their blessedness, they were in a state of risk, and that from the excitement of their minds. How then did they escape that enthusiasm which now prevails, that irreverence, immodesty, and rudeness? I say, if in any age that feverish spirit was likely to have prevailed, which now prevails, the early times of the Gospel was such; how is it we do not read generally of what happened in a measure and for a season in the Corinthian Church, of Christians disobeying their Rulers, saying that their own hearts were the best judges in religious matters, censuring those about them, taking teachers for themselves, and so breaking up the Church of Christ into ten thousand parts? If at any time the outward frame-work of Christianity was in jeopardy, surely it was then. How was it the ungovernable elements within it did not burst forth and shiver to pieces the vessel which contained them? How was it, that for fifteen hundred years the Church was preserved from those peculiar affections of mind and irregularities of feeling and conduct, which now torment it like an ague?

Now certainly, looking at external and second causes, the miracles had much to do in securing this blessed sobriety in the early Christians. These kept them from wilfulness and extravagance, and tempered them to the spirit of godly fear. Thus St. Paul, when converted, was not let go by himself, so to speak. His merciful Lord kept His hand upon him, and directed his every step, lest he should start aside and go astray. Thus He would not tell him all at once what to do, though St. Paul wished it; but bade him "arise, and go into the city," and there it was to be told him what he was to do. He was *led by the hand* (a fit emblem of his spiritual condition), and brought to Damascus. Then he was three days without sight, and without meat and drink. During this time he was still kept in suspense and ignorance what was to happen, and was employed in praying. Such desolateness—his darkness, fasting, and suspense—had a sobering influence. Then Ananias was sent to him to baptize him. Forthwith he began to preach Christ at Damascus, but was soon checked, thwarted, sent into Arabia out of the way, for three years. Then he returned to Damascus, and again, preaching Christ, was in no long time obliged to flee for his life. He came to Jerusalem, and began again to preach. Here first he had a difficulty in getting acknowledged by the Apostles, who were for a time afraid of him; then the Jews laid a plot to kill him. As he was praying in the Temple, Christ appeared to him, and bade him depart from Jerusalem. The brethren brought him down to Caesarea; thence he went to Tarsus. Now, who does not see in this history how the Apostle was repressed and brought under by the plain commands and providences of God, hurrying him to and fro, without saying why? After all this, many years passed before he was employed to preach to the heathen, and then only after a solemn ordination.

Thus, God's miraculous providence, awing and controlling the heart, would seem to be one especial means by which the early Christians were kept from enthusiasm; and the persecutions of the Church became another. But the more ordinary means was one which we may enjoy at this day, if we choose: the course of religious Services, the round of prayer and praise, which, indeed, was also part of St. Paul's discipline, as we have seen, and which has a most gracious effect upon the restless and excited mind, giving it an outlet, yet withal calming, soothing, directing, purifying it.

To go into details. It often happens that in a family who have been brought up together, one suddenly takes what is called a religious turn. Such a person wishes to be more religious than the rest, wishes to do something more than ordinary, but does not know exactly what to do. You will find, generally, that he joins himself to some dissenting party, mainly for this reason, to evidence to himself greater strictness. His mind is under excitement; he seems to say with St. Paul, "Lord, what wilt Thou have me to do?" This is the cause, again and again, of persons falling from the Church. And hence, a notion has got abroad that dissenting bodies have more of true religion within them than the Church; I say, for this reason, because earnest men, awaking to a sense of religion, wish to do something more than usual, and join sects and heresies as a relief to their minds, by way of ridding themselves of strong feelings, which, pent up within them, distress them. And I cannot deny, that in this way those bodies do gain, and the Church does lose, earnestly religious people, or rather those who would have been such in time; for it is, I fear, too true that, while the sects in question are in this way recruited and improved from the Church, the persons themselves, who join them, are injured. They lose the greater part of that religious light and warmth which hung about them, even though they have been hitherto careless, and but partially availed themselves of it. It is as if a living hand were to touch cold iron; the iron is somewhat warmed, but the hand is chilled. And thus the blossom of truth, the promise of real religion, is lost to the Church. Men begin well, but being seduced by their own waywardness fall away.

Here, then, if we knew how to employ them, the Services of the Church come in to soothe and guide the agitated mind. "Is any afflicted? let him pray: is any merry? let him sing psalms." Is any in a perturbed state of mind? he need not go off to strange preachers and meetings, in order to relieve himself of his uneasiness. We can give him a stricter rule of life, and a safer one. Did not our Lord make a distinction between the life of Martha and that of Mary, and without disclaiming Martha, who was troubled for His sake with the toils of life, yet praise Mary the rather, who sat at His feet? Does not St. Paul make a distinction between the duties *necessary* for a Christian, and those which are *comely and of good report*? Let restless persons attend upon the worship of the Church, which will attune their minds in harmony with Christ's law, while it unburdens them. Did not St. Paul "pray" during his three days of blindness? Afterwards he was praying in the Temple, when Christ appeared to him. Let this be well considered. We may build Houses of God without number, up and down the land, as indeed our duty is; we may multiply resident ministers; we may (with a less commendable zeal) do our utmost to please the many or the wealthy; but all this will not deprive Dissenting bodies of their virtue and charm, such as it is. Their strength is their semblance of a strictness beyond members of the Church. Till we act up to our professed principles more exactly; till we have in deed and actual practice more frequent Services of praise and prayer, more truly Catholic plans for honouring God and benefiting man; till we exhibit the nobler and more beautiful forms of Christian devotedness for the admiration and guidance of the better sort, we have, in a manner, done nothing. Surely we want something more than the material walls, we want the "spirit and truth" of the Heavenly Jerusalem, the worshippers "with one accord continuing in the Temple, with gladness and singleness of heart, praising God," persevering and prevailing in prayer, and thus, without seeking it, "having favour with all the people."

Is any one then desirous of gaining comfort to his soul, of bringing Christ's presence home to his very heart, and of doing the highest and most glorious things for the whole world? I have told him how to proceed. Let him praise God; let holy David's Psalter be as familiar words in his mouth, his daily service, ever repeated, yet ever new and ever sacred. Let him pray; especially let him intercede. Doubt not the power of faith and prayer to effect all things with God. However you try, you cannot do works to compare with those which faith and prayer accomplish in the name of Christ. Did you give your body to be burned, and all your goods to feed the poor, you could not do so much as by continual intercession. Few are rich, few can suffer for Christ; all may pray. Were you an Apostle of the Church, or a Prophet, you could not do more than you can do by the power of prayer. Go not then astray to find out new modes of serving God and benefiting man. I show you "a more excellent way." Come to our Services; come to our Litanies; throw yourself out of your own selfish heart; pour yourself out upon the thought of sin and sinners, upon the contemplation of God's Throne, of Jesus the Mediator between God and man, and of that glorious Church to which the dispensation of His merits is committed. Aspire to be what Christ would make you, His friend; having power with Him and prevailing. Other men will not pray for themselves. You may pray for them and for the general Church; and while you pray, you will find enough in the defects of your praying to remind you of your own nothingness, and to keep you from pride while you aim at perfection.

But I must draw to an end. Thus, in both ways, whether our excitements arise from objects of this world or the next, praise and prayer will be, through God's mercy, our remedy; keeping the mind from running to waste; calming, soothing, sobering, steadying it; attuning it to the will of God and the mind of the Spirit, teaching it to love all men, to be cheerful and thankful, and to be resigned in all the dispensations of Providence towards us.

Oh that we knew our own true bliss, now that Christ is come, instead of being, as we still are, for the most part, like the heathen, as sheep without a shepherd! May the good Lord fulfil His purpose towards us in His own time! Amen.

INTERCESSION

*"Praying always with all prayer and supplication in the Spirit,
and watching thereunto with all perseverance and supplication
for all saints."*—Eph. vi.18.

E VERY one knows, who has any knowledge of the Gospel,
that Prayer is one of its especial ordinances; but not every
one, perhaps, has noticed what kind of prayer its inspired teachers most carefully enjoin. Prayer for self is the most obvious of
duties, as soon as leave is given us to pray at all, which Christ
distinctly and mercifully accorded, when He came. This is plain
from the nature of the case; but He himself has given us also an
express command and promise about ourselves, to "ask and it
shall be given to us." Yet it is observable, that though prayer for
self is the first and plainest of Christian duties, the Apostles especially insist on another kind of prayer; prayer for others, for
ourselves with others, for the Church, and for the world, that it
may be brought into the Church. Intercession is the characteristic of Christian worship, the privilege of the heavenly adoption, the exercise of the perfect and spiritual mind. This is the
subject to which I shall now direct your attention.

1. First, let us turn to the express injunctions of Scripture.
For instance, the text itself: "Praying in every season with all
prayer and supplication in the Spirit, and abstaining from sleep
for the purpose, with all perseverance and supplication for all
saints." Observe the earnestness of the intercession here inculcated; "in every season," "with all supplication," and "to the
loss of sleep." Again, in the Epistle to the Colossians; "Persevere in prayer, watching in it with thanksgiving, withal praying
for us also." Again, "Brethren, pray for us." And again in detail;
"I exhort that, first of all, supplications, prayers, intercessions,
and giving of thanks, be made for all men; for kings, and all that
are in authority. I will therefore that men pray in every place."
On the other hand, go through the Epistles, and reckon up how
many exhortations occur therein to pray merely for self. You
will find there are few, or rather none at all. Even those which
seem at first sight to be such, will be found really to have in view

the good of the Church. Thus, to take the words following the text, St. Paul, in asking his brethren's prayers, seems to pray for himself: but he goes on to explain why—"that he might make known the Gospel:" or elsewhere—that "the word of the Lord might have free course and be glorified;" or, as where he says— "Let him that speaketh in an unknown tongue, pray that he may interpret," [1] for this, too, was a petition in order to the edification of the Church.

Next, consider St. Paul's own example, which is quite in accordance with his exhortations: "I cease not to give thanks for you, making mention of you in my prayers, that the God of our Lord Jesus Christ, the Father of Glory, may give unto you the Spirit of wisdom and revelation in the knowledge of Him." "I thank my God upon every remembrance of you, always in every prayer of mine for you all, making request with joy." "We give thanks to God, the Father of our Lord Jesus Christ, praying always for you." "We give thanks to God always for you all, making mention of you in our prayers." [2]

The instances of prayer, recorded in the book of Acts, are of the same kind, being almost entirely of an intercessory nature, as offered at ordinations, confirmations, cures, missions, and the like. For instance; "As they interceded before the Lord, and fasted, the Holy Ghost said, Separate Me Barnabas and Saul for the work whereunto I have called them; and when they had fasted and prayed, and laid their hands on them, they sent them away." Again, "And Peter put them all forth, and kneeled down, and prayed: and turning him to the body, said, Tabitha, arise." [3]

2. Such is the lesson taught us by the words and deeds of the Apostles and their brethren. Nor could it be otherwise, if Christianity be a social religion, as it is pre-eminently. If Christians are to live together, they will pray together; and united prayer is necessarily of an intercessory character, as being offered for each other and for the whole, and for self as one of the whole. In proportion, then, as unity is an especial Gospel-duty, so does Gospel-prayer partake of a social character; and Intercession becomes a token of the existence of a Church Catholic.

Accordingly, the foregoing instances of intercessory prayer are supplied by *Christians*. On the other hand, contrast with these the recorded instances of prayer in men who were *not* Christians, and you will find they are not intercessory. For in-

[1] Col. iv.2; 1 Thess. v.25; 1 Tim. ii.1, 2, 8; 2 Thess. iii.1; 1 Cor. xiv.3.
[2] Eph. i.16, 17; Phil. i.3, 4; Col. i.3; 1 Thess. i.2.
[3] Acts xiii.2, 3; ix.40.

stance: St. Peter's prayer on the house-top was, we know, answered by the revelation of the call of the Gentiles: viewing it
then by the light of the texts already quoted, we may conclude,
that, as was the answer, such was the prayer—that it had reference to others. On the other hand, Cornelius, not yet a Christian, was also rewarded with an answer to his prayer. "Thy
prayer is heard; call for Simon, whose surname is Peter; *he shall
tell thee what thou oughtest to do.*" Can we doubt, from these words
of the Angel, that his prayers had been offered for himself especially? Again, on St. Paul's conversion, we are told, "Behold, he
prayeth." It is plain he was praying for himself; and observe, it
was before he was a Christian. Thus, if we are to judge of the
relative prominence of religious duties by the recorded instances of the performance of them, we should say that Intercession is the kind of prayer distinguishing a Christian from
such as are not Christians.

3. But the instance of St. Paul opens upon us a second reason for this distinction. Intercession is the especial observance
of the Christian, because he alone is in a condition to offer it.
It is the function of the justified and obedient, of the sons of
God, "who walk not after the flesh but after the spirit;" not of
the carnal and unregenerate. This is plain even to natural reason. The blind man, who was cured, said of Christ, "We know
that God heareth not sinners; but, if any man *be a worshipper of
God and doeth His will*, him He heareth."[4] Saul the persecutor
obviously could not intercede like St. Paul the Apostle. He
had yet to be baptized and forgiven. It would be a presumption
and an extravagance in a penitent, before his regeneration, to
do aught but confess his sins and deprecate wrath. He has not
yet proceeded, he has had no leave to proceed, out of himself;
and has enough to do within. His conscience weighs heavy on
him, nor has he "the wings of a dove to flee away and be at
rest." We need not, I say, go to Scripture for information on so
plain a point. Our first prayers ever must be for ourselves. Our
own salvation is our personal concern; till we labour to secure
it, till we try to live religiously, and pray to be enabled to do
so, nay, and have made progress, it is but hypocrisy, or at best
it is overbold, to busy ourselves with others. I do not mean
that prayer for self always comes first in order of time, and Intercession second. Blessed be God, we were all made His children before we had actually sinned; we began life in purity and
innocence. Intercession is never more appropriate than when

[4] John ix.31.

sin had been utterly abolished, and the heart was most affectionate and least selfish. Nor would I deny, that a care for the
souls of other men may be the first symptom of a man's beginning to think about his own; or that persons, who are conscious to themselves of much guilt, often pray for those whom
they revere and love, when under the influence of fear, or in
agony, or other strong emotion, and, perhaps, at other times.
Still it is true, that there is something incongruous and inconsistent in a man's presuming to intercede, who is an habitual
and deliberate sinner. Also it is true, that most men do, more
or less, fall away from God, sully their baptismal robe, need
the grace of repentance, and have to be awakened to the necessity of prayer for self, as the first step in observing prayer of
any kind.

"God heareth not sinners;" nature tells us this; but none but
God Himself could tell us that He will hear and answer those
who are not sinners; for "when we have done all, we are unprofitable servants, and can claim no reward for our services."
But He has graciously promised us this mercy, in Scripture, as
the following texts will show.

For instance, St. James says, "The effectual fervent prayer of
a *righteous* man availeth much." St. John, "Whatsoever we ask,
we receive of Him, *because we keep* His commandments, and do
those things that are pleasing in His sight." [5] Next let us weigh
carefully our Lord's solemn announcements uttered shortly
before His crucifixion, and, though addressed primarily to His
Apostles, yet, surely, in their degree belonging to all who "believe on Him through their word." We shall find that consistent obedience, mature, habitual, lifelong holiness, is therein
made the condition of His intimate favour, and of power in Intercession. "If ye abide in Me," He says, "and My words abide
in you, ye shall ask what ye will, and it shall be done unto you.
Herein is my Father glorified, that ye bear much fruit; so shall
ye be My disciples. As the Father hath loved Me, so have I
loved you; abide ye in My love. If ye keep my commandments,
ye shall abide in My love. Ye are My friends, if ye do whatsoever I command you. Henceforth I call you not servants; for
the servant knoweth not what his lord doeth; but I have called
you friends, for all that I have heard of My Father, I have made
known unto you." [6] From this solemn grant of the peculiarly
Gospel privilege of being the "friends" of Christ, it is certain,
that as the prayer of repentance gains for us sinners Baptism

[5] James v.16; 1 John iii.22.   [6] John xv.7–15.

and justification, so our higher gift of having power with Him and prevailing, depends on our "adding to our faith virtue."

Let us turn to the examples given us of holy men under former dispensations, whose obedience and privileges were anticipations of the evangelical. St. James, after the passage already cited from his epistle, speaks of Elijah thus: "Elias was a man subject to like passions as we are, yet he prayed earnestly that it might not rain, and it rained not on the earth by the space of three years and six months." Righteous Job was appointed by Almighty God to be the effectual intercessor for his erring friends. Moses, who was "faithful in all the house" of God, affords us another eminent instance of intercessory power; as in the Mount, and on other occasions, when he pleaded for his rebellious people, or in the battle with Amalek, when Israel continued conquering as long as his hands remained lifted up in prayer. Here we have a striking emblem of that continued, earnest, unwearied prayer of men "lifting up *holy* hands," which, under the Gospel, prevails with Almighty God. Again, in the book of Jeremiah, Moses and Samuel are spoken of as mediators so powerful, that only the sins of the Jews were too great for the success of their prayers. In like manner it is implied, in the book of Ezekiel, that three such as Noah, Daniel, and Job, would suffice, in some cases, to save guilty nations from judgment. Sodom might have been rescued by ten. Abraham, though he could not save the abandoned city just mentioned, yet was able to save Lot from the overthrow; as at another time he interceded successfully for Abimelech. The very intimation given him of God's purpose towards Sodom was of course an especial honour, and marked him as the friend of God. "Shall I hide from Abraham that thing which I do, seeing that Abraham shall surely become a great and mighty nation; and all the nations of the world shall be blessed in him?" The reason follows, "*for I know him*, that he will command his children and his household after him, and they shall keep the way of the Lord to do justice and judgment, that the Lord may bring upon Abraham that which He hath spoken of him." [7]

4. The history of God's dealings with Abraham will afford us an additional lesson, which must be ever borne in mind in speaking of the privilege of the saints on earth as intercessors between God and man. I can fancy a person, from apprehension lest the belief in it should interfere with the true reception

---

[7] Gen. xviii.17–19.

of the doctrine of the Cross, perplexed at finding it in the foregoing texts so distinctly connected with obedience: I say *perplexed*, for I will not contemplate the case of those, though there are such, who, when the text of Scripture seems to them to be at variance with itself, and one portion to diverge from another, will not allow themselves to be perplexed, will not suspend their minds and humbly wait for light, will not believe that the Divine Scheme is larger and deeper than their own capacities, but boldly wrest into a factitious agreement what is already harmonious in God's infinite counsels, though not to them. I speak to perplexed persons; and would have them observe that Almighty God has, in this very instance of Abraham our spiritual father, been mindful of that other aspect under which the most highly exalted among the children of flesh must ever stand in His presence. It is elsewhere said of him, "Abraham *believed* in the Lord, and He counted it to Him for righteousness,"[8] as St. Paul points out, when he is discoursing upon the free grace of God in our redemption. Even Abraham was justified by faith, though he was perfected by works; and this being told us in the book of Genesis, seems as if an intimation to the perplexed inquirer that his difficulty can be but an apparent one—that, while God reveals the one doctrine, He is not the less careful of the other also, nor rewards His servants (though He rewards them) for works done by their own strength. On the other hand, it is a caution to us, who rightly insist on the prerogatives imparted by his grace, ever to remember that it is grace only that ennobles and exalts us in His sight. Abraham is our spiritual father; and as he is, so are his children. In us, as in him, faith must be the foundation of all that is acceptable with God. "By faith we stand," by faith we are justified, by faith we obey, by faith our works are sanctified. Faith applies to us again and again the grace of our Baptism; faith opens upon us the virtue of all other ordinances of the Gospel—of the Holy Communion, which is the highest. By faith we prevail "in the hour of death and in the day of judgment." And the distinctness and force with which this is told us in the Epistles, and its obviousness, even to our natural reason, may be the cause why less stress is laid in them on the duty of prayer for self. The very instinct of faith will lead a man to do this without set command, and the Sacraments secure its observance.—So much then, by way of caution, on the influence of faith upon our salvation, furthering it, yet not

[8] Gen. xv.6.

interfering with the distinct office of works in giving virtue to our intercession.

And here let me observe on a peculiarity of Scripture, its speaking as if separate rewards attended on separate graces, according to our Lord's words, "To him that hath more shall be given;" so that what has been said in contrasting faith and works, is but one instance under a general rule. Thus, in the Sermon on the Mount, the beatitudes are pronounced on separate virtues respectively. "Blessed are the meek, for they shall inherit the earth;" "Blessed are the pure in heart, for they shall see God;" and the rest in like manner. I am not attempting to determine what these particular graces are, what the rewards, what the aptitude of the one to the other, what the real connection between the reward and the grace, or how far one grace can be separated from another in fact. We know that all depend on one root, faith, and are but differently developed in different persons. Again, we see in Scripture that the same reward is not invariably assigned to the same grace, as if, from the intimate union between all graces, their rewards might (as it were) be lent and interchanged one with another; yet enough is said there to direct our minds to the existence of the principle itself, though we be unable to fathom its meaning and consequences. It is somewhat upon this principle that our Articles ascribe justification to faith *only*, as a symbol of the free grace of our redemption; just as in the parable of the Pharisee and Publican, our Lord would seem to impute it to self-abasement, and in His words to the "woman which was a sinner," to love as well as to faith, while St. James connects it with works. In other instances the reward follows in the course of nature. Thus the gift of wisdom is the ordinary result of trial borne religiously; courage, of endurance. In this way St. Paul draws out a series of spiritual gifts one from another, experience from patience, hope from experience, boldness and confidence from hope. I will add but two instances from the Old Testament. The commandment says, "Honour thy father and thy mother, that thy days may be long;" a promise which was signally fulfilled in the case even of the Rechabites, who were not of Israel. Again, from Daniel's history we learn that illumination, or other miraculous power, is the reward of fasting and prayer. "In those days I, Daniel, was mourning three full weeks. I ate no pleasant bread, neither came flesh nor wine in my mouth, neither did I anoint myself at all, till three whole weeks were fulfilled. . . . . . And he said unto me, Fear not, Daniel; for from the first day that thou didst set thine heart *to understand and to chasten thyself before thy God*, thy words were heard, and I am come for thy words. . . . . . Now I am come to make thee understand what shall befall thy people in the latter days." With this passage compare St. Peter's vision about the Gentiles while he prayed and fasted; and, again, our Lord's words about casting out the "dumb and deaf spirit," "This kind can come forth by nothing but by prayer and fasting." [9] It is then by a similar appointment that Intercession is the prerogative and gift of the obedient and holy.

5. Why should we be unwilling to admit what it is so great a consolation to know? Why should we refuse to credit the transforming power and efficacy of our Lord's Sacrifice? Surely He did not die for any common end, but in order to exalt man, who was of the dust of the field, into "heavenly places." He did not die to leave him as he was, sinful, ignorant, and miserable. He did not die to see His purchased possession, as feeble in good works, as corrupt, as poor-spirited, and as desponding as before He came. Rather, He died to renew him after His own image, to make him a being He might delight and rejoice in, to make him "partaker of the divine nature," to fill him within and without with a flood of grace and glory, to pour out upon him gift upon gift, and virtue upon virtue, and power upon power, each acting upon each, and working together one and all, till he becomes an Angel upon earth, instead of a rebel and an outcast. He died to bestow upon him that privilege which implies or involves all others, and brings him into nearest resemblance to Himself, the privilege of Intercession. This, I say, is the Christian's especial prerogative; and if he does not exercise it, certainly he has not risen to the conception of his real place among created beings. Say not he is a son of Adam, and has to undergo a future judgment; I know it; but he is something besides. How far he is advanced into that higher state of being, how far he still languishes in his first condition, is, in the case of individuals, a secret with God. Still every Christian is in a certain sense both in the one and in the other: viewed in himself he ever prays for pardon, and confesses sin; but viewed in Christ, he "has access into this grace wherein we stand, and rejoices in hope of the glory of God." [10] Viewed in his place in "the Church of the First-born enrolled in heaven," with his original debt cancelled in Baptism, and all subsequent penalties put aside by Absolution, standing in God's presence upright and irreprovable, accepted in the Beloved, clad in the garments of righteousness,

---

[9] Exod. xx.12; Jer. xxxv.18, 19; Dan. x.2–14; Mark ix.29.
[10] Rom. v.2.

anointed with oil, and with a crown upon his head, in royal and priestly garb, as an heir of eternity, full of grace and good works, as walking in all the commandments of the Lord blameless, such an one, I repeat it, is plainly in his fitting place when he intercedes. He is made after the pattern and in the fulness of Christ—he is what Christ is. Christ intercedes above, and he intercedes below. Why should he linger in the doorway, praying for pardon, who has been allowed to share in the grace of the Lord's passion, to die with Him and rise again? He is already in a capacity for higher things. His prayer thenceforth takes a higher range, and contemplates not himself merely, but others also. He is taken into the confidence and counsels of his Lord and Saviour. He reads in Scripture what the many cannot see there, the course of His providence, and the rules of His government in this world. He views the events of history with a divinely enlightened eye. He sees that a great contest is going on among us between good and evil. He recognizes in statesmen, and warriors, and kings, and people, in revolutions and changes, in trouble and prosperity, not merely casual matters, but instruments and tokens of heaven and of hell. Thus he is in some sense a prophet; not a servant, who obeys without knowing his Lord's plans and purposes, but even a confidential "familiar friend" of the Only-begotten Son of God, calm, collected, prepared, resolved, serene, amid this restless and unhappy world. O mystery of blessedness, too great to think of steadily, lest we grow dizzy! Well is it for those who are so gifted, that they do not for certain know their privilege; well is it for them that they can but timidly guess at it, or rather, I should say, are used, as well as bound, to contemplate it as external to themselves, lodged in the Church of which they are but members, and the gift of all saints in every time and place, without curiously inquiring whether it is theirs peculiarly above others, or doing more than availing themselves of it as any how a trust committed to them (with whatever success) to use. Well is it for them; for what mortal heart could bear to know that it is brought so near to God Incarnate, as to be one of those who are perfecting holiness, and stand on the very steps of the throne of Christ?

To conclude. If any one asks, "How am I to know whether I am advanced enough in holiness to intercede?" he has plainly mistaken the doctrine under consideration. The privilege of Intercession is a trust committed to all Christians who have a clear conscience and are in full communion with the Church. We leave secret things to God—what each man's real

advancement is in holy things, and what his real power in the
unseen world. Two things alone concern us, to exercise our
gift and make ourselves more and more worthy of it. The
slothful and unprofitable servant hid his Lord's talent in a
napkin. This sin be far from us as regards one of the greatest
of our gifts! By words and works we can but teach or influence a few; by our prayers we may benefit the whole world,
and every individual of it, high and low, friend, stranger, and
enemy. Is it not fearful then to look back on our past lives
even in this one respect? How can we tell but that our king,
our country, our Church, our institutions, and our own respective circles, would be in far happier circumstances than
they are, had we been in the practice of more earnest and serious prayer for them? How can we complain of difficulties,
national or personal, how can we justly blame and denounce
evil-minded and powerful men, if we have but lightly used
the intercessions offered up in the Litany, the Psalms, and in
the Holy Communion? How can we answer to ourselves for
the souls who have, in our time, lived and died in sin; the
souls that have been lost and are now waiting for judgment,
the infidel, the blasphemer, the profligate, the covetous, the
extortioner; or those again who have died with but doubtful
signs of faith, the death-bed penitent, the worldly, the double-
minded, the ambitious, the unruly, the trifling, the self-
willed, seeing that, for what we know, we were ordained to
influence or reverse their present destiny and have not done it?

Secondly and lastly, If so much depend on us, "What manner
of persons ought we to be, in all holy conversation and godliness!" Oh that we may henceforth be more diligent than heretofore, in keeping the mirror of our hearts unsullied and bright,
so as to reflect the image of the Son of God in the Father's presence, clean from the dust and stains of this world, from envies
and jealousies, strife and debate, bitterness and harshness, indolence and impurity, care and discontent, deceit and meanness,
arrogance and boasting! Oh that we may labour, not in our own
strength, but in the power of God the Holy Spirit, to be sober,
chaste, temperate, meek, affectionate, good, faithful, firm,
humble, patient, cheerful, resigned, under all circumstances, at
all times, among all people, amid all trials and sorrows of this
mortal life! May God grant us the power, according to His
promise, through His Son our Saviour Jesus Christ!

THE INTERMEDIATE STATE

"And white robes were given unto every one of them; and it was said unto them, that they should rest yet for a little season, until their fellow-servants also, and their brethren that should be killed as they were, should be fulfilled."—Rev. vi. 11.

I N taking these words as a text, I do not profess to give you any sufficient explanation of them. Doubtless in their full meaning they are too deep for mortal man; yet they are written for our reverent contemplation at least, and perchance may yield something, under God's blessing, even though the true and entire sense of them was lost to the Church with him who wrote them. He was admitted into the heaven of heavens, while yet in the flesh, as St. Paul before him. He saw the throne and Him who sat on it; and his words, as those of the prophets under the Law, are rather spontaneous accompaniments on what he saw, than definite and complete descriptions addressed to us. They were provided, indeed, and directed according to our need, by an overruling inspiration; but the same sacred influence also limited their range, and determined under what aspect and circumstances they should delineate the awful realities of heaven. Thus they are but shadows cast, or at best, lines or portions caught from what is unseen, and they attend upon it after the manner of the Seraphim, with wings covering their face, and wings covering their feet, in adoration and in mystery.

Now as to the text itself, it speaks of the Martyrs in their disembodied state, between death and judgment; according to the foregoing verse, "the souls of them that were slain for the word of God, and for the testimony which they held." It describes them in a state of rest; still they cry out for some relief, for vengeance upon their persecutors. They are told to wait awhile, "to rest yet for a little season," till the circle of Martyrs is completed. Meantime they receive some present earnest of the promise, by way of alleviation; "white robes were given unto every one of them."

Some men will say that this is all figurative, and means merely that the blood of the Martyrs, crying now for vengeance, will be requited on their murderers at the last day. I cannot persuade myself thus to dismiss so solemn a passage. It seems a presumption to say of dim notices about the unseen world, "they only mean this or that," as if one had ascended into the third heaven, or had stood before the throne of God. No; I see herein a deep mystery, a hidden truth, which I cannot handle or define, shining "as jewels at the bottom of the great deep,"[1] darkly and tremulously, yet really there. And for this very reason, while it is neither pious nor thankful to explain away the words which convey it, while it is a duty to use them, not less a duty is it to use them humbly, diffidently, and teachably, with the thought of God before us, and of our own nothingness.

Under these feelings I shall now attempt to comment upon the text, and with reference to the Intermediate State, of which it seems plainly to speak. But it will be best rather to use it as sanctioning and connecting our anticipations of that State, as drawn from more obvious passages of Scripture, than to venture to infer anything from it in the first instance. Also, though it directly speaks of the Martyrs, it may be profitably applied to the case of all Saints whatever; for, the Martyrs being types and first fruits of all, what is true of them, is perchance in some sense true also of their brethren; and if it be true of any, at least all antecedent objections vanish, against its being true of all, which are the chief arguments we shall have to contend with. Now let us proceed to the consideration proposed.

St. John says:—"I saw under the Altar the souls of them that were slain for the word of God, and for the testimony which they held; and they cried with a loud voice, saying, How long, O Lord, holy and true, dost Thou not judge and avenge our blood on them that dwell on the earth? And white robes were given unto every one of them, and it was said unto them, that they should rest yet for a little season, until their fellow-servants also, and their brethren that should be killed as they were, should be fulfilled."

1. Now first in this passage we are told that the Saints are *at rest*. "White robes were given unto every one of them." "It was said unto them that they should *rest* yet for a little season." This is expressed still more strongly in a later passage of the same book: "Blessed are the dead which die in the Lord *from hence-forth*. Yea, saith the Spirit, that they *may rest from their labours*." Again, St. Paul had a desire "to depart and *to be with Christ*,

---

[1] Davison on "Sacrifice."

which (he adds) is far better." And our Lord told the penitent robber, "To-day shalt thou be with Me in *paradise*." And in the parable He represents Lazarus as being "*in Abraham's bosom*;" a place of rest surely, if words can describe one.

If we had no other notice of the dead than the foregoing, it would appear quite sufficient for our need. The great and anxious question that meets us is, what is to become of us after this life? We fear for ourselves, we are solicitous about our friends, just on this point. They have vanished from us with all their amiable and endearing qualities, all their virtues, all their active powers. Where is that spirit gone, over the wide universe, up or down, which once thought, felt, loved, hoped, planned, acted in our sight, and which, wherever it goes, must carry with it the same affections and principles, desires and aims? We know how it thought, felt, and behaved itself on earth; we know that beloved mind, and it knows us, with a mutual consciousness;— and now it is taken from us, what are its fortunes?—This is the question which perplexed the heathen of old time. It is fearful to be exposed in this world to ills we know of—to the fury of the elements and the darkness of night, should we be left houseless and shelterless. But when we think how utterly ignorant we are both of the soul's nature and of the invisible world, the idea of losing friends, or departing ourselves into such gloom, is, to those who get themselves to think about it, very overpowering. Now, here Scripture meets our need, in the texts already cited. It is enough, surely, to be in Abraham's bosom, in our Saviour's presence; it is enough, after the pain and turmoil of this world, to be at rest.

Moreover, texts such as these do more than satisfy the doubts which beset the heathen; they are useful to us at the present day, in a perplexity which may easily befall us. A great part of the Christian world, as is well known, believes that after this life the souls of Christians ordinarily go into a prison called Purgatory, where they are kept in fire or other torment, till, their sins being burned away, they are at length fitted for that glorious kingdom into which nothing defiled can enter. Now, if there were any good reason for this belief, we should certainly have a very sad and depressing prospect before us:—watch and pray and struggle as we might, yet after all to have to pass from the sorrows of this life, from its weariness and its pains, into a second and a worse trial! Not that we should have any reason to complain: for our sins deserve an eternal punishment, were God severe. Still it would be a very afflicting thought, especially as regarded our deceased friends, who (if the doctrine were true) would now, at this very moment, be in a state of suffering. I do not say that to many a sinner, it would not be an infinitely less evil to suffer for a time in Purgatory, than to be cast into hell for ever; but those whom we have loved best, and revered most, are not of this number; and before going on to examine the grounds of it, every one must admit it to be a very frightful notion at least, that *they* should be kept from their rest, and confined in a prison beneath the earth. Nay, though the Bible did not positively affirm it, yet if it did not contradict it, and if the opinion itself was very general in the Church (as it is), and primitive too (as it is not), there would be enough in it reasonably to alarm us; for who could tell in such a case, but probably it might be true? This is what might have been; but, in fact, Christ has mercifully interfered, expressly to assure us that our friends are better provided for than this doctrine would make it appear.[2] He assures us that they "*rest* from their labours, and their works do follow them;" and we gather from the text, that even that loneliness and gloom which, left to themselves, they would necessarily feel, though ever so secured from actual punishment, may, in truth, be mercifully compensated. The sorrowful state is there described, in which they would find themselves when severed from the body, and waiting for the promised glory at Christ's coming, and they are represented as sustained under it, soothed, quieted, consoled. As a parent would hush a child's restlessness, cherishing it in her arms, and lulling it to sleep, or diverting it from the pain or the fright which agitates it, so the season of delay, before Christ comes in judgment, tedious in itself, and solitary, is compensated to the spirits of the just by a present gift in earnest of the future joy. "How long, O Lord, holy and true?" Such is their complaint. "And white robes were given unto every one of them; and it was said unto them, that they should rest yet for a little season," till the end.

2. Next, in this description is implied, what I have in fact already deduced from it, that departed Saints, though at rest, have not yet received their actual reward. "Their works do follow with them," not yet given in to their Saviour and Judge. They are in an incomplete state in every way, and will be so till the Day of Judgment, which will introduce them to the joy of their Lord.

[2] It ought perhaps to be added, by way of explanation, that the doctrine would of course be binding on our faith, in spite of any *primâ facie* bearing of certain texts, were it, what our formularies imply it is not, a doctrine sanctioned by the Catholic Church.

They are incomplete, inasmuch as their bodies are in the dust of the earth, and they wait for the Resurrection.

They are incomplete, as being neither awake nor asleep; I mean, they are in a state of rest, not in the full employment of their powers. The Angels are serving God actively; they are ministers between heaven and earth. And the Saints, too, one day shall judge the world—they shall judge the fallen Angels; but at present, till the end comes, they are at rest only, which is enough for their peace, enough for our comfort on thinking of them, still, incomplete, compared with what one day shall be.

Further, there is an incompleteness also as regards their place of rest. They are "under the Altar." Not in the full presence of God, seeing His face, and rejoicing in His works, but in a safe and holy treasure-house close by,—like Moses, "in a cleft of the rock,"—covered by the hand of God, and beholding the skirts of His glory. So again, when Lazarus died, he was carried to Abraham's bosom; which, however honoured and peaceful an abode, was a place short of heaven. This is elsewhere expressed by the use of the word "paradise," or the garden of Eden; which, again, though pure and peaceful, visited by Angels and by God Himself, was not heaven. No emblem could express more vividly the refreshment and sweetness of that blessed rest, than to call it the garden in which the first man was placed;—to which must be added St. Paul's account of it, that he heard in it (when he was caught up thither) "unspeakable words, which it is not lawful for a man to utter."[3] Doubtless, it is full of excellent visions and wonderful revelations. God there manifests Himself, not as on earth dimly, and by material instruments, but by those more intimate approaches which spirit admits of, and our present faculties cannot comprehend. And in some unknown way, that place of rest has a communication with this world, so that disembodied souls know what is going on below. The Martyrs, in the passage before us, cry out, "How long, O Lord, Holy and True, dost Thou not judge and avenge our blood on them that dwell on the earth?" They saw what was going on in the Church, and needed comfort from the sight of the triumph of evil. And they obtained white robes and a message of peace. Still, whatever be their knowledge, whatever their happiness, they have but lost their tabernacle of corruption, and are "unclothed," and wait to be "clothed upon," having put off "mortality," but not yet being absorbed in "life."[4]

[3] 2 Cor. xii.4.   [4] 2 Cor. v.4.

There is another word used in Scripture to express the abode of just men made perfect, which gives us the same meaning. Our Lord is said in the Creed to have "descended into *hell*," which word has a very different sense there from that which it commonly bears. Our Saviour, as we suppose, did not go to the abyss assigned to the fallen Angels, but to those mysterious mansions where the souls of all men await the judgment. That he went to the abode of blessed spirits is evident, from His words addressed to the robber on the cross, when he also called it paradise; that he went to some other place besides paradise, may be conjectured from St. Peter's saying, He "went and preached to the spirits in prison, who had once been disobedient." [5] The circumstance then that these two abodes of disembodied good and bad, are called by one name, Hades, or (as we happen to express it) hell, seems clearly to show that paradise is not the same as Heaven, but a resting-place at the foot of it. Let it be further remarked, that Samuel, when brought from the dead, in the witch's cavern, said, "Why hast thou disquieted me, to bring me *up*?" [6] words which would seem quite inconsistent with his being then already in Heaven.

Once more, the Intermediate State is incomplete as regards the happiness of the Saints. Before our Lord came, it may be supposed even to have admitted at times of a measure of disquiet, and that in the case of the greatest Saints themselves, though most surely still they were altogether "in God's hand;" for Samuel says, "Why hast thou *disquieted* me, to bring me up?" Perchance our Lord reversed this imperfection at His coming, and took with Him, even in their bodies, to heaven itself, some principal Saints of the old Covenant; according to St. Matthew's intimation. But even now, as it would appear from the text, the Blessed, in their disembodied state, admit of an increase of happiness, and receive it. "They cried out" in complaint,—and "white robes were given them;" they were soothed and bid wait awhile.

Nor would it be surprising if, in God's gracious providence, the very purpose of their remaining thus for a season at a distance from heaven, were, that they may have time for growing in all holy things, and perfecting the inward development of the good seed sown in their hearts. The Psalmist speaks of the righteous as "trees planted by the rivers of water, that bring forth their fruit in due season;" and when might this silent growth of holiness more suitably and happily take place, than when they

---

[5] 1 Pet. iii.19, 20.   [6] 1 Sam. xxviii.15.

are waiting for the Day of the Lord, removed from those trials and temptations which were necessary for its early beginnings? Consider how many men are very dark and feeble in their religious state, when they depart hence, though true servants of God as far as they go. Alas! I know that the multitude of men do not think of religion at all;—they are thoughtless in their youth, and secular as life goes on;—they find their interests lie in adopting a decent profession; they deceive themselves, and think themselves religious, and (to all appearance) die with no deeper religion than such a profession implies. Alas! there are many also, who, after careless lives, amend, yet not truly;—think they repent, but do not in a Christian way. There are a number, too, who leave repentance for their death-bed, and die with no fruits of religion at all, except with so much of subdued and serious feeling as pain forces upon them. All these, as far as we are told, die without hope. But, after all these melancholy cases are allowed for, many there are still, who, beginning well, and persevering for years, yet are even to the end but beginners after all, when death comes upon them;—many who have been in circumstances of especial difficulty, who have had fiercer temptations, more perplexing trials than the rest, and in consequence have been impeded in their course. Nay, in one sense, all Christians die with their work unfinished. Let them have chastened themselves all their lives long, and lived in faith and obedience, yet still there is much in them unsubdued,—much pride, much ignorance, much unrepented, unknown sin, much inconsistency, much irregularity in prayer, much lightness and frivolity of thought. Who can tell, then, but, in God's mercy, the time of waiting between death and Christ's coming, may be profitable to those who have been His true servants here, as a time of maturing that fruit of grace, but partly formed in them in this life—a school-time of contemplation, as this world is a discipline of active service? Such, surely, is the force of the Apostle's words, that "He that hath begun a good work in us, will perform it *until* the day of Jesus Christ," *until*, not *at*, not stopping it with death, but carrying it on to the Resurrection. And this, which will be accorded to all Saints, will be profitable to each in proportion to the degree of holiness in which he dies; for, as we are expressly told that in one sense the spirits of the just are *perfected* on their death, it follows that the greater advance each has made here, the higher will be the line of his subsequent growth between death and the Resurrection.

And all this accounts for what else may surprise us,—the especial stress the Apostles lay on the coming of Christ, as the object to which our hope must be directed. We are used in this day to look upon death as the point of victory and triumph for the Saints;—we leave the thought of them when life is over, as if then there was nothing more to be anxious about; nor in one sense is there. Then they are secure from trial, from falling; as they die, so they remain. Still, it will be found, on the whole, that death is not *the* object put forward in Scripture for hope to rest upon, but the *coming of Christ*, as if the interval between death and His coming was by no means to be omitted in the process of our preparation for heaven. Now, if the sacred writers uniformly hold out Christ's coming, but we consider death, as the close of all things, is it not plain that, in spite of our apparent agreement with them in formal statements of doctrine, there must be some hidden and undetected difference between them and ourselves, some unfounded notion on our part which we have inherited, some assumed premiss, some lurking prejudice, some earthly temper, or some mere human principle? For instance, St. Paul speaks of the Corinthians as "*waiting for the coming* of our Lord Jesus Christ." To the Philippians he says, "Our citizenship is in heaven, from whence also we *look out for the Saviour*, the Lord Jesus Christ, who shall change our vile body." In his first Epistle to the Thessalonians, he seems to make this waiting for the Last Day almost part of his definition of a true Christian; "Ye turned to God from idols, to serve the living and true God, and to *wait for His Son from heaven*." In his Epistle to Titus, "*Looking for that blessed hope and glorious appearing* of our great God and Saviour, Jesus Christ." To the Hebrews, "Unto them that *look for Him*, shall Christ appear the second time without sin unto salvation." Again, "*Ye have need of patience*, that after ye have done the will of God, ye might *receive the promise. For yet a little while*, and he that shall come will come and will not tarry." And to the Romans, "I reckon that the sufferings of this present time are not worthy to be compared with the glory which shall be revealed in us," *i.e.* at the Resurrection; "for *the earnest expectation of the creature waiteth for the manifestation of the sons of God.* . . . We ourselves groan within ourselves, *waiting for the adoption*, to wit, the redemption of our body;" and presently he adds, evidently speaking of things belonging to the unseen world, and (as we may suppose) the Intermediate State inclusively, "I am persuaded that neither death, nor life, nor Angels, nor principalities, nor powers, nor things present, nor *things to come*, nor height, nor depth, nor any other creature, shall be able to separate us from the love of God, which is in Christ Jesus our Lord." Again, "He that raised up the Lord Jesus, shall *raise up us also by Jesus*, and shall present us with you. Our light afflic-tion, which is but for a moment, worketh for us a far more ex-ceeding and eternal weight of glory; . . . *for we know that if our earthly house of this tabernacle were dissolved, we have a building of God, a house not made with hands, eternal in the heavens.*" Now, how parallel is this waiting for Christ's coming, as inculcated in the foregoing passages, to the actual conduct of the Saints as recorded in the passage of which the text forms part! "*How long, O Lord, holy and true, dost Thou not judge and avenge our blood on them that dwell on the earth? . . . . And white robes were given unto every one of them, until their fellow-servants also, and their brethren that should be killed as they were, should be fulfilled:*"—and with our Saviour's words in the Gos-pel, "Shall not God *avenge* His own elect, *which cry day and night unto Him*, though He bear long with them? I tell you that He will avenge them speedily. Nevertheless, *when the Son of man cometh*" (Christ's coming then is the "avenging" for which they cry), "when the Son of man cometh, shall He find faith on the earth."[7]

This, indeed, is our Saviour's usual doctrine as well as that of His Apostles. I mean, it is his custom to insist on two events chiefly, His first coming and His second—our regeneration and our resurrection—throwing into the background the prospect of our death, as if it were but a line of distinction (however momentous a one), not of division, in the extended course of our purification. For example: "The hour is coming, and now is, when the dead shall hear the voice of the Son of God, and they that hear shall live;"—the dead in sin; here, then, our re-generation is set forth. Then He proceeds: "The hour is com-ing in the which all that are in the graves shall hear His voice, and shall come forth; they that have done good unto the resur-rection of life, and they that have done evil unto the resurrec-tion of damnation." Here is mentioned His second coming with its attendant events. Again: "In My Father's house are many mansions: if it were not so, I would have told you. I go to prepare a place for you. And if I go and prepare a place for you, I *will come again* and receive you unto Myself, that where I am, there ye may be also." And in the parable of the talents: "A cer-tain nobleman went into a far country, to receive for himself a kingdom and to return; and he called his ten servants, and de-livered them ten pounds, and said unto them, Occupy till I

[7] 1 Cor. i.7; Phil. iii.20, 21; 1 Thess. i.9, 10; Tit. ii.13; Heb. ix.28; x.36, 37; Rom. viii.18–39; 2 Cor. iv.14–17; v.1; Luke xviii.7, 8.

come."[8] Here is mention of Christ's first and His second coming. It is not uncommon, indeed, to say, that "till I come," means "till every man's death," when in a certain sense Christ comes to him: but surely this is a mere human assumption; the time of judgment, and not till then, is the time when Christ calls His servants and takes account.

Lastly, it is the manner of Scripture to imply that all Saints make up but one body, Christ being the Head, and no real distinction existing between dead and living; as if the Church's territory were a vast field, only with a veil stretched across it, hiding part from us. This at least, I think, will be the impression left on the mind after a careful study of the inspired writers. St. Paul says, "I bow my knees unto the Father of our Lord Jesus Christ, of whom the *whole* family in heaven and earth is named," where "heaven" would seem to include paradise. Presently he declares that there is but "one body," not two, as there is but one Spirit. In another epistle he speaks of Christians in the flesh being "come to the heavenly Jerusalem, and the spirits of just men made perfect."[9] Agreeably to this doctrine, the collect for All Saints' Day teaches us, that "Almighty God has knit together His elect" (that is, both living and dead), "in *one* communion and fellowship in the mystical body of His Son."

This, then, on the whole, we may humbly believe to be the condition of the Saints before the Resurrection, a state of repose, rest, security; but again a state more like paradise than heaven—that is, a state which comes short of the glory which shall be revealed in us after the Resurrection, a state of waiting, meditation, hope, in which what has been sown on earth may be matured and completed.

I will make one remark before concluding, by way of applying what has been said to ourselves. There have been times, we know, when men thought too much of the dead. That is not the fault of this age. We now go into the opposite extreme. Our fault surely is, to think of them too little. It is a miserable thing to confess, yet surely so it is, that when a friend or relative is dead, he is commonly dismissed from the mind very shortly, as though he was not; there is no more talk of him, or reference to him, and the world goes on without him as if he had never been. Now, of course the deepest feelings are those which are silent; so I do not mean to say that friends are not thought of, because they are not talked of. How could it be? Can any form of society

[8] John v.25–29; xiv.2, 3; Luke xix.12, 13.
[9] Eph. iii.14, 15; iv.4; Heb. xii.22, 23.

or any human doctrine fetter down our hearts, and make us think and remember as it will? Can the tyranny of earth hinder our holding a blessed and ever-enduring fellowship with those who are dead, by consulting their wishes, and dwelling upon their image, and trying to imitate them, and imagining their peaceful state, and sympathizing in their "loud cry," and hoping to meet them hereafter? No, truly! we have a more glorious liberty than man can take from us, with all the sophistries of selfishness, and subtleties of the schools! I do not speak of the tender-hearted, affectionate, and thoughtful. They cannot forget the departed, whose presence they once enjoyed, and who (in Scripture language), though "absent in the body, are present with them in spirit," "joying and beholding their order and the steadfastness of their faith in Christ." [10] But I speak of the many, the rude, cold, and scornful, the worldly-minded, the gay, and the careless; whose ordinary way it is, when a friend is removed, to put aside the thought of him, and blot it out from their memories.

Let me explain what I mean by taking an instance, which is not uncommon. We will say, a parent or relative dies and leaves a man a property: he comes into it gladly; buries the dead splendidly; and then thinking he has done all, he wipes out what is past, and enters upon the enjoyment of his benefaction. He is not profuse or profligate, proud or penurious, but he thinks and acts in all respects as if he, to whom he is indebted, were annihilated from God's creation. He has no obligations. He was dependent before, but now he is independent; he is his own master; he ceases to be in the number of "little children." Like the Corinthians, "now he is full, now he is rich, he reigns as a king without" those to whom he once was forced to submit. He is the head of (what is called) an establishment. If he ever speaks of the dead, it is in a way half kind, half contemptuous, as of those who are helpless and useless, as he would speak of men still living who were in dotage or in mental incapacity. You hear even the most good-hearted and kindly (such is the force of bad example) speak in this disrespectful way of old people they knew in their youth, not meaning anything unkind by it, but still, doubtless, cherishing in themselves thereby a very subtle kind of hardness, selfishness, superciliousness, self-gratulation. Men little think what an effect all this has on their general character. It teaches them to limit their belief to what they see. They give up a most gracious means divinely provided for their

[10] 1 Cor. v.3; Col. ii.5.

entering into "that which is within the veil," and seeing beyond the grave; and they learn to be contented in uniting themselves with things visible, in connections and alliances which come to nought. Moreover, this same error casts them upon the present instead of the past. They lose their reverence for antiquity; they change the plans and works of their predecessors without scruple; they enjoy the benefactions of past ages without thankfulness, as if by a sort of right; they worship in churches for which "other men laboured," without thinking of them; they forget they have but a life-interest in what they possess, that they have received it in trust, and must transmit as they have received.

On the other hand, while the thought of the dead is thus a restraint upon us, it is also a great consolation, especially in this age of the world, when the Universal Church has fallen into errors and is divided branch against branch. What shall sustain our faith (under God's grace) when we try to adhere to the Ancient Truth, and seem solitary? What shall nerve the "watchman on the walls of Jerusalem," against the scorn and jealousy of the world, the charge of singularity, of fancifulness, of extravagance, of rashness? What shall keep us calm and peaceful within, when accused of "troubling Israel," and "prophesying evil?" What but the vision of all Saints of all ages, whose steps we follow? What but the image of Christ mystical stamped upon our hearts and memories? The early times of purity and truth have not passed away! They are present still! We are not solitary, though we seem so. Few now alive may understand or sanction us; but those multitudes in the primitive time, who believed, and taught, and worshipped, as we do, still live unto God, and, in their past deeds and their present voices, cry from the Altar. They animate us by their example; they cheer us by their company; they are on our right hand and our left, Martyrs, Confessors, and the like, high and low, who used the same Creeds, and celebrated the same Mysteries, and preached the same Gospel as we do. And to them were joined, as ages went on, even in fallen times, nay, even now in times of division, fresh and fresh witnesses from the Church below. In the world of spirits there is no difference of parties. It is our plain duty indeed here, to contend even for the details of the Truth according to our light; and surely there is a Truth in spite of the discordance of opinions. But that Truth is at length simply discerned by the spirits of the just; human additions, human institutions, human enactments, enter not with them into the unseen state. They are put off with the flesh. Greece and

Rome, England and France, give no colour to those souls which have been cleansed in the One Baptism, nourished by the One Body, and moulded upon the One Faith. Adversaries agree together directly they are dead, if they have lived and walked in the Holy Ghost. The harmonies combine and fill the temple, while discords and imperfections die away. Therefore is it good to throw ourselves into the unseen world, it is "good to be there," and to build tabernacles for those who speak "a pure language" and "serve the Lord with one consent;" not indeed to draw them forth from their secure dwelling-places, not superstitiously to honour them, or wilfully to rely on them, lest they be a snare to us, but silently to contemplate them for our edification; thereby encouraging our faith, enlivening our patience, sheltering us from thoughts about ourselves, keeping us from resting on ourselves, and making us seem to ourselves (what really we ought ever to be) only followers of the doctrine of those who have gone before us, not teachers of novelties, not founders of schools.

God grant to us all, out of the superabundant treasures of His grace, such a spirit, the spirit of mingled teachableness and zeal, of calmness in inquiry and vigour in resolve, of power, and of love, and of a sound mind!

IV

To the
REV. HUGH JAMES ROSE, B.D.,
Principal of King's College, London,
and domestic chaplain to the
archbishop of Canterbury,
who, when hearts were failing,
bade us stir up the gift that was in us,
and betake ourselves to our true Mother,
this volume
is inscribed,
by his obliged and faithful friend,
the author.

Nov. 19, 1838.

THE STRICTNESS
OF THE LAW OF CHRIST

*"Being then made free from sin, ye became the servants of
righteousness."*—Rom. vi.18.

I N the passage of which these words form a part, St. Paul insists again and again on the great truth which they declare,
that Christians are not their own, but bought with a price,
and, as being so, are become the servants or rather the slaves
of God and His righteousness; and this, upon their being rescued from the state of nature. The great Apostle is not content with speaking half the truth; he does not merely say that
we are set free from guilt and misery, but he adds, that we
have become the servants of Christ; nay, he uses a word which
properly means *slaves*. Slaves are bought and sold; we were by
nature slaves to sin and Satan; we are bought by the blood of
Christ: we do not cease to be slaves. We no longer indeed belong to our old master; but a master we have, unless slaves on
being bought become freemen. We are still slaves, but to a
new master, and that master is Christ. He has not bought us,
and then set us loose upon the world; but He has done for us
what alone could complete His first benefit, bought us to be
His servants or slaves. He has given us that only liberty which
is really such, bond-service to Himself; lest if left to ourselves,
we should fall back again, as we certainly should, to the cruel
bondage from which He redeemed us. But any how, whatever
be the consequences it involves, whatever the advantage,
whatever the trial, we did not cease to be slaves on being set
free from Satan; but we became subject to a new Master, to
Him who bought us.

This needs insisting on; for a number of persons who are
not unwilling to confess that they are slaves by nature, from
some cause or other have learned to think that they are not
bound to any real service at all, now that Christ has set them
free. Now if by the word *slavery*, some cruel and miserable
state of suffering is meant, such as human masters often inflict

on their slaves, in that sense indeed Christians are not slaves, and the word is improper to apply to them; but if by being slaves, is meant that we cannot throw up our service, change our place, and do as we will, in that sense it is literally true, that we are more than servants to Christ, we are, as the text really words it, slaves. Men often speak as if the perfection of human happiness lay in our being free to do or not to do, to choose and to reject. Now we are indeed thus free, as far as this,—that if we do not choose to be Christ's servants, we can go back to that old bondage from which He rescued us, and be slaves again to the powers of evil. But though we are free to make our situation worse, we are not free to be without service or post of any kind. It is not in man's nature to be out of all service and to be self-dependent. We may choose our master, but God or mammon we must serve. We cannot possibly be in a neutral or intermediate state. Such a state does not exist. If we will not be Christ's servants, we are forthwith Satan's; and Christ set us free from Satan only by making us His servants. Satan's kingdom touches upon Christ's, the world touches on the Church; and we cease to be Satan's property by becoming Christ's. We cannot be without a master, such is the law of our nature; yet a number of persons, as I have said, overlook it, and think their Christian liberty lies in being free from all law, even from the law of God. Such an error seems to have obtained even in St. Paul's time and is noticed in the chapter before us. Men seem to have thought that, since the law of sin was annulled, and the terrors of the law of nature removed, that therefore they were under no law at all; that their own will was their law, and that faith stood instead of obedience. In opposition to this great mistake, St. Paul reminds his brethren in the text, that when they were "made free from *sin*," they "became the servants of *righteousness*." And again, "Sin shall not have dominion over you; for ye are not under the law," that is, the law of nature, "but under grace," or (as he elsewhere expresses it), "the law of faith," or, "the law of the Spirit of life." They were not without a master, but they had a gracious and bountiful one.

He says the same in other Epistles. For instance, "He that is called, being free" (that is, free as regards this world), "is Christ's servant" or slave. "Ye are bought with a price: be not ye slaves of *men*," but, that is, be slaves of Christ. Again, after saying, "Slaves, obey in all things your masters according to the flesh," he adds, "for ye are slaves to the Lord Christ." Elsewhere he speaks of himself as "Paul a servant," or slave, as the word really means, "of Jesus Christ;" and again, as "not without law to God, but under the law to Christ." [1]

Religion then is a necessary service; of course it is a privilege too, but it becomes more and more of a privilege, the more we exercise ourselves in it. The perfect Christian state is that in which our duty and our pleasure are the same, when what is right and true is natural to us, and in which God's "service is perfect freedom." And this is the state towards which all true Christians are tending; it is the state in which the Angels stand; entire subjection to God in thought and deed is their happiness; an utter and absolute captivity of their will to His will, is their fulness of joy and everlasting life. But it is not so with the best of us, except in part. Upon our regeneration indeed, we have a seed of truth and holiness planted within us, a new law introduced into our nature; but still we have that old nature to subdue, "the old man, which is corrupt according to the deceitful lusts." [2] That is, we have a work, a conflict all through life. We have to master and bring under all we are, all we do, expelling all disorder and insubordination, and teaching and impressing on every part of us, of soul and body, its due place and duty, till we are wholly Christ's in will, affections, and reason, as we are by profession; in St. Paul's words, "casting down imaginations and every high thing that exalteth itself against the knowledge of God, and bringing into captivity every thought to the obedience of Christ." [3]

Now I may seem to have been saying what every one will at once confess. And yet, after all, nothing perhaps is so rare among those who profess to be Christians, as an assent in practice to the doctrine that they are under a law; nothing so rare as strict obedience, unreserved submission to God's will, uniform conscientiousness in doing their duty,—as a few instances will at once show.

Most Christians then will allow in general terms that they are under a law, but then they admit it with a reserve; they claim for themselves some dispensing power in their observance of the law. What I am saying is quite independent of the question, what is the *standard* of obedience which each man proposes to himself? One man puts the line of his duty higher than another; some men take a low view of it, confining it to mere personal morality; others confine it to their social obligations; others limit it by some conventional law, which is received in particu-

---

[1] 1 Cor. vii.22, 23; Col. iii.22, 24; Rom. i.1; 1 Cor. ix.21.
[2] Eph. iv.22.   [3] 2 Cor. x.5.

lar classes or circles; others include religious observances. But whether men view the law of conscience as high or low, as broad or narrow, few indeed there are who make it a rule to themselves; few there are who make their own notion of it, whatever that be, binding on themselves; few who even profess to act up to it uniformly and consistently. Inquire of the multitude of men, as you meet them in the world, and you will find that one and all think it allowable at times to put themselves above the law, even according to their own standard of it; to make exceptions and reserves, as if they were absolute sovereigns of their conscience, and had a dispensing power upon occasions.

What is the sort of man whom the world accounts respectable and religious, in a high rank or a lower? At best he is such as this. He has a number of good points in his character; but some of these he has by nature, and if others have been acquired by trouble, it is either because outward circumstances compelled him to acquire them, or that he has from nature some active principle within him, of one kind or another, which has exerted itself and brought other principles under, and rules him. He has acquired a certain self-command, because no one is respected without it. He has been forced into habits of diligence, punctuality, precision, and honesty. He is courteous and obliging; and has learned not to say all he thinks and feels, or to do all he wishes to do, on all occasions. The great mass of men of course are far from having in them so much that is really praise-worthy as this; but I am supposing the best. I am supposing then, that a man's character and station are such, that only now and then he will feel his inclinations or his interest to run counter to his duty. Such times constitute his trial; there is nothing to hinder him serving God in the ordinary course, but the proof of his sincerity lies in his conduct on these extraordinary occasions. Now this is the point to which I wish to draw attention; for these very occasions, which alone are his times of trial, are just the times on which he is apt to consider that he has a leave to dispense with the law. He dispenses with it at those very times when it is simply the law of God, without being also the law of self, and of the world. He does what is right, while the road of religion runs along the road of the world; when they part company awhile, he chooses the world, and calls his choice an exception. He does right for ninety-nine days, but on the hundredth he knowingly and wilfully does wrong; and if he does not justify, at least he absolves himself in doing it.

For instance; he *generally* comes to Church, it is his *practice*; but some urgent business at a certain time presses on him, or some scheme of pleasure tempts him:—he omits his attendance; he knows this is wrong, and says so, but it is only once in a way.

Again; he is strictly honest in his dealings; he speaks the truth, that is, it is his rule to do so; but if hard pressed, he allows himself now and then in a falsehood, particularly if it is a slight one. He knows he should not lie; he confesses it; but he thinks it cannot be helped; it is unavoidable from circumstances, as being his only way of escaping some great difficulty. In *such* a case it is, as he says, all fair, and so he gets over it; that is, in a case where he must either disobey God, or incur some temporal disadvantage.

Again; he has learned to curb his temper and his tongue; but on some unusual provocation they get the better of him. He becomes angry, says what he should not, perhaps curses and swears. Are not all men subject to be overtaken with anger or ill temper? that is not the point: the point is this,—that he does not feel compunction afterward, he does not feel he has done any thing which needs forgiveness. On the contrary, he defends himself to himself, on the plea that such language is very *unusual* with him; he does not understand that he is under a law, which he may not put himself above, which he may not dispense with.

Once more; he is in general sober and temperate; but he joins a party of friends and makes merry; he is tempted to exceed. Next day he says that it is a long time since such a thing happened to him; it is not at all his way; he hardly touches wine or the like in common. He does not understand he has any sin to repent of, because it is but once in a way.

And now, I suppose, you quite understand what I mean, and I need not say more in explanation. Such men, being thus indulgent to themselves, are indulgent to each other; they make allowance for all around them, as taking what they give freely. This is the secret of being friends with the world, to have a sympathy and a share in its sins. They who are strict with themselves are strict with the world; but where men grant themselves a certain licence of disobedience, they do not draw the line very rigidly as regards others. Conscious of what might be said against themselves, they are cautious what they say against others; and they meet them on the understanding of a mutual sufferance. They learn to say, that the private habits of their neighbours are nothing to them; and they hold intercourse

with them only as public men, or members of society, or in the
way of business, not at all as with responsible beings having
immortal souls. They desire to see and know nothing but what
is on the surface; and they call a man's personal history sacred,
because it is sinful. In their eyes, their sole duty to their neighbour is, not to offend him; whatever his morals, whatever his
creed, is nothing to them. Such are they in mature and advanced life; in youth, they are pliable as well as indulgent, they
readily fall in with the ways of the world, as they come across
them. They are, and have the praise of being, pleasant, good-
tempered, and companionable. They are not bad-principled, or
evilly disposed, or flagrantly irregular, but they are lax. They in
no sense live by rule. They have high spirits, and all the natural
amiableness which youth has to show, and they generally go
right; but, since they have no root in themselves, an accident
from within or without, the stirring of a passion, or the incitement of a friend, makes them swerve at once. They swerve, and
they have little compunction afterwards; they forget it. They
shrink from the notion of being under a law, and think religion
gloomy as imposing it. They like their own way, and without
any great extreme of sin, or at least any habits of sin, follow it.
They are orderly and well-conducted, when among well-conducted people,—at home, for instance; but they indulge themselves abroad, when temptation comes in their way. They have
the world at will; they are free; alas! what a melancholy freedom! yet in one sense a freedom it is. A religious man must
withdraw his eyes from sights which inflame his heart, recollecting our Saviour's caution; but a man of the world thinks it
no harm to gaze where he should not, because he goes no further. A religious man watches his words; but the other utters
whatever his heart prompts, and excuses himself for profane
language, on the plea that he means nothing by it. A religious
man will scruple about his society; but the other takes part in
jests and excesses, though he condemns while he shares them,
but not himself for sharing, and despises those with whom he
shares them. He can see life, as it is called. He can go among all
sorts of people, for he has no troublesome ceremonial, no rule
of religion to shackle him. Perhaps he goes abroad, and then for
a time he considers himself to be in disguise, as an unknown
person in unknown countries, permitted to fall in with all
things bad and good, as they come. Or again, he may be so circumstanced, whatever his station, as to find himself engaged in
what are called politics; and then he thinks that though truth
and religion are certainly all-commanding and all-important,

yet still the world could not go on, public business would be at
a stand, political parties would be unable to act, all that he really
loves and reveres would become but of secondary concern, if
religion refused at all times to give way ever so little. Again; a
religious man carries his religion into his conduct throughout
the day; but lax persons will do many things in private, which
they would not like to be known. They will overreach, if they
can do it without noise. They will break promises when made
to an inferior. Or, if they have time on their hands, they will be
curious and meddlesome; they will speak against others and
spread scandals. They will pry into things which do not concern them, according to their station in life. They will listen
where they have no right to listen; they will read what they
have no right to read. Or they will allow themselves in petty
thefts, where they think they do no injury, excusing themselves
on the plea that what they take will never be missed. Or in
matters of trade, they think a certain sort and degree of double-
dealing allowable, and no dishonesty. They argue with themselves as if it were not their business to be true and just, but of
others to find them out; and as if fraud and cheating did not
imply sin in the one party, but dulness in the other. If in humble
life, they think it no harm to put on an appearance; to profess
what is not strictly true, if they are to gain by it; to colour a
story; or to affect to be more religious than they are; or to pretend to agree in religion with persons from whom they hope
something; or to take up a religion if it is their interest to do so;
or to profess two or three religions at once, when any alms or
other benefit is to be given away.

These are a few out of a multitude of traits which mark an
easy religion,—the religion of the world; which would cast in
its lot with Christian truth, were not that truth so very strict,
and quarrels with it and its upholders, not as if it were not good
and right, but because it is so unbending,—because it will not
suit itself to times and emergencies, and to the private and occasional likings and tastes of individuals. This is the kind of religion which St. Paul virtually warns us against, as often as he
speaks of the Gospel as really being a law and a servitude. He
indeed glories in its being such; for, as the happiness of all creatures lies in their performing their parts well, where God has
placed them, so man's greatest good lies in obedience to God's
law and in imitation of God's perfections. But the Apostle
knew that the world would not think so, and therefore he insists on it. Therefore it is that he insists on the necessity of
Christians "*fulfilling* the righteousness of the law;" fulfilling it,

because till we aim at complete, unreserved obedience in all things, we are not really Christians at all. Hence St. James says, "Whosoever shall keep the whole law, and yet offend in one point, he is guilty of all." And our Saviour assures us that "Whosoever shall break one of these least commandments, and shall teach men so, he shall be called least in the kingdom of heaven;" and that "Except our righteousness shall exceed the righteousness of the Scribes and Pharisees," which was thus partial and circumscribed, "we shall in no case enter into the kingdom of heaven." And when the young man came to Him, saying that he had kept all the commandments, and asking what he lacked, He pointed out the "one thing" wanting in him; and when he would not complete his obedience by that one thing, but went away sorrowful, then, as if all his obedience in other points availed him nothing, Christ added, "Children, how hard is it for them that trust in riches to enter into the Kingdom of God?"[4] Let us not then deceive ourselves; what God demands of us is to fulfil His law, or at least to aim at fulfilling it; to be content with nothing short of perfect obedience,—to attempt every thing,—to avail ourselves of the aids given us, and throw ourselves, not first, but afterwards on God's mercy for our short-comings. This is, I know, at first hearing a startling doctrine; and so averse are our hearts to it, that some men even attempt to maintain that it is an unchristian doctrine. A forlorn expedient indeed, with the Bible to refer to, and its statements about the strait gate and the narrow way. Still men would fain avail themselves of it, if they could; they argue that all enforcement of religion as a service or duty is erroneous, or what they call legal, and that no observance is right but what proceeds from impulse, or what they call the heart. They would fain prove that the law is not binding on us, because Christ has fulfilled it; or because, as is the case, faith would be accepted instead of obedience in those who had not yet had time to begin fulfilling it.

Such persons appeal to Scripture, and they must be refuted, as is not difficult, from Scripture; but the multitude of men do not take so much trouble about the matter. Instead of even professing to discover what God has said, they take what they call a common-sense view of it. They maintain it is impossible that religion should really be so strict according to God's design. They condemn the notion as over-strained and morose. They profess to admire and take pleasure in religion as a whole, but

[4] Rom. viii.1–4; James ii.10; Matt. v.19, 20; Mark x.21, 24.

think that it should not be needlessly pressed in details, or, as they express it, carried too far. They complain only of its particularity, if I may use the term, or its want of indulgence and consideration in little things; that is, in other words, they like religion before they have experience of it,—in prospect,—at a distance, *till* they have to be religious. They like to talk of it, they like to see men religious; they think it commendable and highly important; but directly religion comes home to them in real particulars of whatever kind, they like it not. It suffices them to have seen and praised it; they feel it a burden whenever they feel it at all, whenever it calls upon them to do what otherwise they would not do. In a word, the state of the multitude of men is this,—their hearts are going the wrong way; and their real quarrel with religion, if they know themselves, is not that it is strict, or engrossing, or imperative, not that it goes too far, but that it is religion. It is religion itself which we all by nature dislike, not the excess merely. Nature tends towards the earth, and God is in heaven. If I want to travel north, and all the roads are cut to the east, of course I shall complain of the roads. I shall find nothing but obstacles; I shall have to surmount walls, and cross rivers, and go round about, and after all fail of my end. Such is the conduct of those who are not bold enough to give up a profession of religion, yet wish to serve the world. They try to reach Babylon by roads which run to Mount Sion. Do you not see that they necessarily must meet with thwartings, crossings, disappointments, and failure? They go mile after mile, watching in vain for the turrets of the city of Vanity, because they are on the wrong road; and, unwilling to own what they are really seeking, they find fault with the road as circuitous and wearisome. They accuse religion of interfering with what they consider their innocent pleasures and wishes. But religion is a bondage only to those who have not the heart to like it, who are not cast into its mould. Accordingly, in the verse before the text, St. Paul thanks God that his brethren had "obeyed from the *heart* that *form* of teaching, into which they had been delivered." We Christians are cast into a certain mould. So far as we keep within it, we are not sensible that it is a mould, or has an outline. It is when our hearts would overflow in some evil direction, then we discover that we are confined, and consider ourselves in prison. It is the law in our members warring against the law of the Spirit which brings us into a distressing bondage. Let us then see where we stand, and what we must do. Heaven cannot change; God is "without variableness or shadow of turning." His "word endureth for ever in heaven." His law is from everlasting to everlasting. *We* must change. We must go over to the side of heaven. Never had a soul true happiness but in conformity to God, in obedience to His will. We must become what we are not; we must learn to love what we do not love, and practise ourselves in what is difficult. We must have the law of the Spirit of life written and set up in our hearts, "that the righteousness of the law may be fulfilled in us," and that we may learn to please and to love God.

Lastly, as some men defend their want of strictness on what they consider the authority of Scripture, and others, that is, the majority, try to persuade themselves that religion cannot really be strict, whatever strong expressions or statements may be found in Scripture, others again there are, who take a more candid, but a more daring course. Instead of making excuses, such as I have been considering, they frankly admit the fact, and then go on to urge it as a valid argument against religion altogether. Instead of professing to like religion, *all but* its service, they boldly object that religion is altogether unnatural, and therefore cannot be incumbent on us. They say that it is very well for its ministers and teachers to set up a high doctrine, but that men are men, and the world is the world, and that life was not meant to be a burden, and that God sent us here for enjoyment, and that He will never punish us hereafter for following the law of our nature. I answer, doubtless this life was meant to be enjoyment; but why not a rejoicing in the Lord? We were meant to follow the law of our nature; but why of our old nature, why not of our new? Were we indeed in the state of our first nature, under the guilt and defilement of our birth-sin, then this argument might be urged speciously, though not conclusively of course then; but how does it apply to Christians? Now that God has opened the doors of our prison-house, and brought us into the kingdom of His Son, if men are still carnal men, and the world a sinful world, and the life of Angels a burden, and the law of our nature not the law of God, whose fault is it?

We Christians are indeed under the law as other men, but, as I have already said, it is the new law, the law of the Spirit of Christ. We are under grace. That law, which to nature is a grievous bondage, is to those who live under the power of God's presence, what it was meant to be, a rejoicing. When then we feel reluctant to serve God, when thoughts rise within us as if He were a hard Master, and that His promises are not attractive enough to balance the strictness of His commandments, let us recollect that we, as being Christians, are not in the flesh, but in the Spirit, and let us act upon the conviction of it. Let us go to Him for grace. Let us seek His face. Let us come where He gives grace. Let us come to the ordinances of grace, in which Christ gives His Holy Spirit, to enable us to do that which by nature we cannot do, and to be "the servants of righteousness." They who pray for His saving help to change their likings and dislikings, their tastes, their views, their wills, their hearts, do not indeed all at once gain what they seek;—they do not gain it at once asking;—they do not *perceive* they gain it while they gain it,—but if they come continually day by day to Him,—if they come humbly,—if they come in faith,—if they come, not as a trial how they shall like God's service, but throwing (as far as may be) their whole hearts and souls into their duty as a sacrifice to Him,—if they come, not seeking a sign, but determined to go on seeking Him, honouring Him, serving Him, trusting Him, whether they see light, or feel comfort, or discern their growth, or no,—such men *will* gain, though they know it not; they will find, even while they are still seeking; before they call, He will answer them, and they will in the end find themselves saved wondrously, to their surprise, how they know not, and when their crown seemed at a distance. "They that wait on the Lord;" says the Prophet, "shall renew their strength; they shall mount up with wings as eagles; they shall run and not be weary, and they shall walk and not faint." [5]

[5] Is. xl.31.

OBEDIENCE WITHOUT LOVE, AS INSTANCED IN THE CHARACTER OF BALAAM

"The word that God putteth in my mouth, that shall I speak."—
Numb. xxii.38.

WHEN we consider the Old Testament as written by divine inspiration, and preserved, beyond the time of its own Dispensation, for us Christians,—as acknowledged and delivered over to us by Christ Himself, and pronounced by St. Paul to be "profitable for doctrine, reproof, correction, and instruction in righteousness,"[1]—we ought not surely to read any portion of it with indifference, nay, without great and anxious interest. "Lord, what wilt Thou have me to do?" is the sort of inquiry which spontaneously arises in the serious mind. Christ and His Apostle cannot have put the Law and the Prophets into our hands for nothing. I would this thought were more carefully weighed than it commonly is. We profess indeed to revere the Old Testament; yet, for some reason or other, at least one considerable part of it, the historical, is regarded by the mass, even of men who think about religion, as merely historical, as a relation of facts, as antiquities; not in its divine characters, not in its practical bearings, not in reference to themselves. The notion that God speaks in it to them personally, the question, *"What* does He say?" "What must I *do?"* does not occur to them. They consider that the Old Testament concerns them only as far as it can be made typical of one or two of the great Christian doctrines; they do not consider it in its fulness, and in its literal sense, as a collection of deep moral lessons, such as are not vouchsafed in the New, though St. Paul expressly says that it is "profitable for instruction in righteousness."

If the Old Testament history generally be intended as a permanent instruction to the Church, much more, one would

[1] 2 Tim. iii.16.

think, must such prominent and remarkable passages in it as the history of Balaam. Yet I suspect a very great number of readers carry off little more from it than the impression of the miracle which occurs in it, the speaking of his ass. And not unfrequently they talk more lightly on the subject than is expedient. Yet I think some very solemn and startling lessons may be drawn from the history, some of which I shall now attempt to set before you.

What is it which the chapters in question present to us? The first and most general account of Balaam would be this;—that he was a very eminent person in his age and country, that he was courted and gained by the enemies of Israel, and that he promoted a wicked cause in a very wicked way; that, when he could do nothing else for it, he counselled the Moabites to employ their women as means of seducing the chosen people into idolatry; and that he fell in battle in the war which ensued. These are the chief points, the prominent features of his history as viewed at a distance;—and repulsive indeed they are. He took on him the office of a tempter, which is especially the Devil's office. But Satan himself does not seem so hateful near as at a distance; and when we look into Balaam's history closely, we shall find points of character which may well interest those who do not consider his beginning and his end. Let us then approach him more nearly, and forget for a moment the summary account of him, which I have just been giving.

Now first he was blessed with God's especial favour. You will ask at once, How could so bad a man be in God's favour? but I wish you to put aside reasonings, and contemplate facts. I say he was especially favoured by God; God has a store of favours in His treasure-house, and of various kinds,—some for a time, some for ever,—some implying His approbation, others not. He showers favours even on the bad. He makes His sun to rise on the unjust as well as on the just. He willeth not the death of a sinner. He is said to have loved the young ruler, whose heart, notwithstanding, was upon the world. His loving-mercy extends over all His works. How He separates in His own divine thought, kindness from approbation, time from eternity, what He does from what He foresees, we know not and need not inquire. At present He is loving to all men, as if He did not foresee that some are to be saints, others reprobates to all eternity. He dispenses His favours variously,—gifts, graces, rewards, faculties, circumstances being indefinitely diversified, nor admitting of discrimination or numbering on our part. Balaam, I say, was in His favour; not indeed for his holiness' sake, not for ever; but in a certain sense, according to His inscrutable purpose,—who chooses whom He will choose, and exalts whom He will exalt, without destroying man's secret responsibilities or His own governance, and the triumph of truth and holiness, and His own strict impartiality in the end. Balaam was favoured in an especial way above the mere heathen. Not only had he the grant of inspiration, and the knowledge of God's will, an insight into the truths of morality, clear and enlarged, such as even we Christians cannot surpass; but he was even admitted to conscious intercourse with God, such as we Christians have not. In our Sunday Services, you may recollect, we read the chapters which relate to this intercourse; and we do not read those which record the darker passages of his history. Now, do you not think that most persons, who know only so much of him as our Sunday lessons contain, form a very mild judgment about him? They see him indeed to be on the wrong side, but still view him as a prophet of God. Such a judgment is not incorrect as far as it goes; and I appeal to it, if it be what I think it is, as a testimony how highly Balaam was in God's favour.

But again, Balaam was, in the ordinary and commonly-received sense of the word, without straining its meaning at all, a very *conscientious* man. That this is so, will be plain from some parts of his conduct and some speeches of his, of which I proceed to remind you; and which will show also his enlightened and admirable view of moral and religious obligation. When Balak sent to him to call him to curse Israel, he did not make up his mind for himself, as many a man might do, or according to the suggestions of avarice and ambition. No, he brought the matter before God in prayer. He *prayed* before he did what he did, as a religious man ought to do. Next, when God forbade his going, he at once, as he ought, positively refused to go. "Get you into your land," he said, "for the Lord refuseth to give me leave to go with you." Balak sent again a more pressing message and more lucrative offers, and Balaam was even more decided than before. "If Balak," he said, "would give me his house full of silver and gold, I cannot go beyond the word of the Lord my God, to do less or more." Afterwards God gave him leave to go. "If the men come to call thee, rise up, and go with them." [2] Then, and not till then, he went.

Almighty God added, "Yet the word which I shall say unto thee, that shalt thou do." Now, in the next place, observe how strictly he obeyed this command. When he first met Balak, he

[2] Numb. xxii.

said, in the words of the text, "Lo I am come unto thee; have I now any power at all to say any thing? the word that God putteth in my mouth, that shall I speak." Again, when he was about to prophesy, he said, "Whatsoever He showeth me I will tell thee;" [3] and he did so, in spite of Balak's disappointment and mortification to hear him bless Israel. When Balak showed his impatience, he only replied calmly, "Must I not take heed to speak that which the Lord hath put in my mouth?" Again he prophesied, and again it was a blessing; again Balak was angered, and again the prophet firmly and serenely answered, "Told not I thee, saying, All that the Lord speaketh, that I must do ?" A third time he prophesied blessing; and now Balak's anger was kindled, and he smote his hands together, and bade him depart to his place. But Balaam was not thereby moved from his duty. "The wrath of a king is as messengers of death." [4] Balak might have instantly revenged himself upon the prophet; but Balaam, not satisfied with blessing Israel, proceeded, as a prophet should, to deliver himself of what remained of the prophetic burden, by foretelling more pointedly than before, destruction to Moab and the other enemies of the chosen people. He prefaced his prophecy with these unacceptable words,— "Spake I not also unto thy messengers which thou sentest unto me, saying, If Balak would give me his house full of silver and gold, I cannot go beyond the commandment of the Lord, to do either good or bad of mine own mind? but what the Lord saith, that will I speak. And now behold, I go unto my people; come, therefore, and I will advertise thee what this people shall do to thy people in the latter days." After delivering his conscience, he "rose up, and went and returned to his place."

All this surely expresses the conduct and the feelings of a high-principled, honourable, conscientious man. Balaam, I say, was certainly such, in that very sense in which we commonly use those words. He said, and he did; he professed, and he acted according to his professions. There is no inconsistency in word and deed. He obeys as well as talks about religion; and this being the case, we shall feel more intimately the value of the following noble sentiments which he lets drop from time to time, and which, if he had shown less firmness in his conduct, might have passed for mere words, the words of a maker of speeches, a sophist, moralist, or orator. "Let me die the death of the righteous, and let my last end be like his." "God is not a man that He should lie; neither the son of man, that He should repent

---

[3] Numb. xxiii.   [4] Prov. xvi. 14.

. . . Behold, I have received commandment to bless; and He hath blessed, and I cannot reverse it." "I shall see Him, but not now; I shall behold Him, but not nigh." It is remarkable that these declarations are great and lofty in their mode of expression; and the saying of his recorded by the prophet Micah is of the same kind. Balak asked what sacrifices were acceptable to God. Balaam answered, "He hath showed thee, O man, what is good; and what doth the Lord require of thee, but to do justly, and to love mercy, and to walk humbly with thy God?"[5]

Viewing then the inspired notices concerning Balaam in all their parts, we cannot deny to him the praise which, if those notices have a plain meaning, they certainly do convey, that he was an honourable and religious man, with a great deal of what was great and noble about him; a man whom any one of us at first sight would have trusted, sought out in our difficulties, perhaps made the head of a party, and any how spoken of with great respect. We may indeed, if we please, say that he fell away afterwards from all this excellence: though, after all, there is something shocking in such a notion. Nay, it is not natural even that ordinarily honourable men should suddenly change; but however this *may* be said,—it may be said he fell away; but, I presume, it *cannot* be said that he was other than a high-principled man (in the language of the world) *when* he so spoke and acted.

But now the strange thing is, that at this very time, *while* he so spoke and acted, he seems, as in one sense to be in God's favour, so in another and higher to be under His displeasure. If this be so, the supposition that he fell away will not be in point; the difficulty it proposes to solve will remain; for it will turn out that he was displeasing to God *amid* his many excellences. The passage I have in mind is this, as you will easily suppose. "God's anger was kindled, because he went" with the princes of Moab, "and the Angel of the Lord stood in the way for an adversary against him." Afterwards, when God opened his eyes, "he saw the Angel of the Lord standing in the way, and his sword drawn in his hand" . . . "And Balaam said, I have *sinned*, for I knew not that thou stoodest in the way against me; now, therefore, if it displease thee, I will get me back again." You observe Balaam said, "I have sinned," *though* he avers he did not *know* that God was his adversary. What makes the whole transaction the more strange is this,—that Almighty God had said before, "If the men come to call thee, rise up, and go with them;" and that

[5] Micah vi.8.

when Balaam offered to go back again, the Angel repeated, "Go with the men." And afterwards we find in the midst of his heathen enchantments "God met Balaam," and "put a word in his mouth;" and afterwards "the Spirit of God came unto him."

Summing up then what has been said, we seem, in Balaam's history, to have the following remarkable case, that is, remarkable according to our customary judgment of things: a man divinely favoured, visited, influenced, guided, protected, eminently honoured, illuminated,—a man possessed of an enlightened sense of duty, and of moral and religious acquirements, educated, high-minded, conscientious, honourable, firm; and yet on the side of God's enemies, personally under God's displeasure, and in the end (if we go on to that) the direct instrument of Satan, and having his portion with the unbelievers. I do not think I have materially overstated any part of this description; but if it be correct only in substance, it certainly is most fearful, after allowing for incidental exaggeration,—most fearful to every one of us, the more fearful the more we are conscious to ourselves in the main of purity of intention in what we do, and conscientious adherence to our sense of duty.

And now it is natural to ask, what is the *meaning* of this startling exhibition of God's ways? Is it really possible that a conscientious and religious man should be found among the enemies of God, nay, should be personally displeasing to Him, and that at the very time God was visiting him with extraordinary favour? What a mystery is this! Surely, if this be so, Revelation has added to our perplexities, not relieved them! What instruction, what profit, what correction, what doctrine is there in such portions of inspired Scripture?

In answering this difficulty, I observe in the first place, that it certainly is impossible, quite impossible, that a really conscientious man should be displeasing to God; at the same time it is possible to be *generally* conscientious, or what the world calls honourable and high-principled, yet to be destitute of that religious fear and strictness, which God calls conscientiousness, but which the world calls superstition or narrowness of mind. And bearing this in mind, we shall, perhaps, have a solution of our perplexities concerning Balaam.

And here I would make a remark: that when a passage of Scripture, descriptive of God's dealings with man, is obscure or perplexing, it is as well to ask ourselves whether this may not be owing to some insensibility, in ourselves or in our age, to certain peculiarities of the Divine law or government therein involved. Thus, to those who do not understand the nature and history of religious truth, our Lord's assertion about sending a sword on earth is an obscurity. To those who consider sin a light evil, the doctrine of eternal punishment is a difficulty. In like manner the history of the flood, of the call of Abraham, of the plagues of Egypt, of the wandering in the desert, of the judgment on Korah, Dathan, and Abiram, and a multitude of other occurrences, may be insuperable difficulties, except to certain states and tempers of mind, to which, on the contrary, they will seem quite natural and obvious. I consider that the history of Balaam is a striking illustration of this remark. Those whose hearts, like Josiah's, are "tender," scrupulous, sensitive in religious matters, will see with clearness and certainty what the real state of the case was as regards him; on the other hand, our difficulties about it, if we have them, are a presumption that the age we live in has not the key to a certain class of Divine providences, is deficient in a certain class of religious principles, ideas, and sensibilities. Let it be considered then whether the following remarks may not tend to lessen our perplexity.

Balaam obeyed God from a sense of its being right to do so, but not from a *desire to please Him*, not from *fear and love*. He had other ends, aims, wishes of his own, distinct from God's will and purpose, and he would have effected these if he could. His endeavour was, not to please God, but to please self without displeasing God; to pursue his own ends *as far* as was consistent with his duty. In a word, he did not give his heart to God, but obeyed Him, as a man may obey human law, or observe the usages of society or his country, as something external to himself, because he knows he ought to do so, from a sort of rational good sense, a conviction of its propriety, expediency, or comfort, as the case may be.

You will observe he *wished* to go with Balak's messengers, only he felt he *ought not* to go; and the problem which he attempted to solve was *how* to go and yet not offend God. He was quite resolved he *would* any how act religiously and conscientiously; he was too honourable a man to break any of his engagements; if he had given his word, it was sacred; if he had duties, they were imperative: he had a character to maintain, and an inward sense of propriety to satisfy; but he would have given the world to have got rid of his duties; and the question was, *how* to do so without violence; and he did not care about walking on the very brink of transgression, so that he could keep from falling over. Accordingly he was not content with *ascertaining* God's will, but he attempted to *change* it. He inquired of Him a *second time*, and this was to tempt Him. Hence, while God bade him go, His anger was kindled against him because he went.

This surely is no uncommon character; rather, it is the common case even with the more respectable and praise-worthy portion of the community. I say plainly, and without fear of contradiction, though it is a serious thing to say, that the aim of most men esteemed conscientious and religious, or who are what is called honourable, upright men, is, to all appearance, not how to please God, but how to please themselves without displeasing Him. I say confidently,—that is, if we may judge of men in general by what we see,—that they make this world the first object in their minds, and use religion as a corrective, a restraint, upon *too much* attachment to the world. They think that religion is a negative thing, a sort of moderate love of the world, a moderate luxury, a moderate avarice, a moderate ambition, and a moderate selfishness. You see this in numberless ways. You see it in the course of trade, of public life, of literature, in all matters where men have objects to pursue. Nay you see it in religious exertions; of which it too commonly happens that the chief aim is, to attain *any how* a certain definite end, religious indeed, but of man's own choosing; not, to please God, and *next*, if possible, to attain it; not, to attain it religiously, or not at all.

This surely is so plain that it is scarcely necessary to enlarge upon it. Men do not take for the object towards which they act, God's will, but certain maxims, rules, or measures, right perhaps as far as they go, but defective because they admit of being subjected to certain other ultimate ends, which are not religious. Men are just, honest, upright, trustworthy; but all this not from the love and fear of God, but from a mere feeling of obligation to be so, and in subjection to certain worldly objects. And thus they are what is popularly called moral, without being religious. Such was Balaam. He was in a popular sense a strictly moral, honourable, conscientious man; that he was not so in a heavenly and true sense is plain, if not from the considerations here insisted on, at least from his after history, which (we may presume) brought to light his secret defect, in whatever it consisted.

And here we see why he spoke so much and so vauntingly of his determination to follow God's direction. He made a great *point* of following it; his end was not to please God, but to keep straight with Him. He who loves does not act from calculation or reasoning; he does not in his cool moments reflect upon or talk of what he is doing, as if it were a great sacrifice. Much less does he pride himself on it; but this is what Balaam seems to have done.

I have been observing that his defect lay in this, that he had not a single eye towards God's will, but was ruled by other objects. But moreover, this evil heart of unbelief showed itself in a peculiar way, to which it is necessary to draw your attention, and to which I alluded just now in saying that the difficulties of Scripture often arose from the defective moral condition of our hearts.

Why did Almighty God give Balaam leave to go to Balak, and then was angry with him for going? I suppose for this reason, because his asking twice was tempting God. God is a jealous God. Sinners as we are, nay as creatures of His hands, we may not safely intrude upon Him, and make free with Him. We may not dare to do that, which we should not dare to do with an earthly superior, which we should be punished, for instance, for attempting in the case of a king or noble of this world. To rush into His presence, to address Him familiarly, to urge Him, to strive to make our duty lie in one direction when it lies in another, to handle rudely and practise upon His holy word, to trifle with truth, to treat conscience lightly, to take liberties (as it may be called) with any thing that is God's, all irreverence, profaneness, unscrupulousness, wantonness, is represented in Scripture not only as a sin, but as felt, noticed, quickly returned on God's part (if I may dare use such human words of the Almighty and All-holy God, without transgressing the rule I am myself laying down,—but He vouchsafes in Scripture to represent Himself to us in that only way in which we can attain to the knowledge of Him), I say all irreverence towards God is represented as being jealously and instantly and fearfully noticed and visited, as friend or stranger among men might resent an insult shown him. This should be carefully considered; we are apt to act towards God and the things of God as towards a mere system, a law, a name, a religion, a principle, not as against a Person, a living, watchful, present, prompt and powerful Eye and Arm. That all this is a great error, is plain to all who study Scripture; as is sufficiently shown by the death of that multitude of persons for looking into the ark—the death of the Prophet by the lion, who was sent to Jeroboam from Judah, and did not minutely obey the instructions given him—the slaughter of the children at Bethel by the bears, for mocking Elisha—the exclusion of Moses from the promised land, for smiting the rock twice—and the judgment on Ananias and Sapphira. Now Balaam's fault seems to have been of this nature. God told him distinctly not to go to Balak. He was rash enough to ask a second time, and God as a punishment gave him leave to ally himself with His enemies, and to take part against His people. With this presumptuousness and love of self in his innermost heart, his prudence, firmness, wisdom, illumination, and general conscientiousness, availed him nothing.

A number of reflections crowd upon the mind on the review of this awful history, as I may well call it; and with a brief notice of some of these I shall conclude.

1. First, we see how little we can depend, in judging of right and wrong, on the apparent excellence and high character of individuals. There *is* a right and a wrong in matters of conduct, in spite of the world; but it is the world's aim and Satan's aim to take our minds off from the indelible distinctions of things, and to fix our thoughts upon man, to make us the slaves of man, to make us dependent on his opinion, his patronage, his honour, his smiles, and his frowns. But if Scripture is to be our guide, it is quite plain that the most conscientious, religious, high-principled, honourable men (I use the words in their ordinary, not in their Scripture sense), may be on the side of evil, may be Satan's instruments in cursing, if that were possible, and at least in seducing and enfeebling the people of God. For in the world's judgment, even when most refined, a person is conscientious and consistent, who acts up to his standard, *whatever that is*, not he only who aims at taking the highest standard. This is the world's highest flight; but in its ordinary judgment, a man is conscientious and consistent, who is only inconsistent and goes against conscience in any extremity, when hardly beset, and when he must cut the knot or remain in present difficulties. That is, *he* is thought to obey conscience, who only disobeys it when it is a praise and merit to obey it. This, alas! is the way with some of the most honourable of mere men of the world, nay of the mass of (so called) respectable men. They never tell untruths, or break their word, or profane the Lord's day, or are dishonest in trade, or falsify their principles, or insult religion, except in very great straits or great emergencies, when driven into a corner; and then perhaps they force themselves, as Saul did when he offered sacrifice instead of Samuel;—they force themselves, and (as it were) undergo their sin as a sort of unpleasant self-denial or penance, being ashamed of it all the while, getting it over as quickly as they can, shutting their eyes and leaping blindfold, and then forgetting it, as something which is bitter to think about. And if memory is ever roused and annoys them, they console themselves that after all they

have only gone against their conscience now and then. This is their view of themselves and of each other, taken at advantage; and if any one come across them who has lived more out of the world than themselves, and has a truer sense of right and wrong, and who fastens on some one point in them, which to his mind is a token and warning to himself against them, such a one seems of course narrow-minded and overstrict in his notions. For instance; supposing some such man had fallen in with Balaam, and had been privy to the history of his tempting God, it is clear that Balaam's general correctness, his nobleness of demeanour, and his enlightened view of duty, would not have availed one jot or tittle to overcome such a man's repugnance to him. He would have been startled and alarmed, and would have kept at a distance, and in consequence he would have been called by the world uncharitable and bigoted.

2. A second reflection which rises in the mind has relation to the wonderful secret providence of God, while all things seem to go on according to the course of this world. Balaam did not see the Angel, yet the Angel went out against him as an adversary. He had no open denunciation of God's wrath directed against him. He had sinned, and nothing happened outwardly, but wrath was abroad and in his path. *This* again is a very serious and awful thought. God's arm is not shortened. What happened to Balaam is as if it took place yesterday. God is what He ever was; we sin as man has ever sinned. We sin without being aware of it. God is our enemy without our being aware of it; and when the blow falls, we turn our thoughts to the creature, we ill-treat our ass, we lay the blame on circumstances of this world, instead of turning to Him. "Lord, when Thy hand is lifted up, they will not see; but they shall see," in the next world if not here, "and be ashamed for their envy at the people; yea the fire of Thine enemies shall devour them." [6]

3. Here too is a serious reflection, if we had time to pursue it, that when we have begun an evil course, we cannot retrace our steps. Balaam was forced to go with the men; he offered to draw back—he was not allowed—yet God's wrath followed him. This is what comes of committing ourselves to an evil line of conduct; and we see daily instances of it in our experience of life. Men get entangled, and are bound hand and foot in unadvisable courses. They make imprudent marriages or connexions; they place themselves in dangerous situations; they engage in unprofitable or harmful undertakings. Too often

[6] Is. xxvi. 11.

indeed they do not discern their evil plight; but when they do, they cannot draw back. God seems to say, "Go with the men." They are in bondage, and they must make the best of it; being the slave of the creature, without ceasing to be the responsible servants of God; under His displeasure, yet bound to act as if they could please Him. All this is very fearful.

4. Lastly, I will but say this in addition,—God gives us warnings now and then, but does not repeat them. Balaam's sin consisted in not acting upon what was told him *once for all*. In like manner, you, my brethren, now hear what you may never hear again, and what perchance in its substance is the word of God. You may never hear it again, though with your outward ears you hear it a hundred times, because you may be impressed with it now, but never may again. You may be impressed with it now, and the impression may die away; and some time hence, if you ever think about it, you may then speak of it thus,—that the view struck you at the time, but somehow the more you thought about it, the less you liked or valued it. True; this *may* be so, and it *may* arise, as you think, from the doctrine I have been setting before you not being true and scriptural; but it *may* also arise from your having heard God's voice and not obeyed it. It may be that you have become blind, not the doctrine been disproved. Beware of trifling with your conscience. It is often said that second thoughts are best; so they are in matters of judgment, but not in matters of conscience. In matters of duty first thoughts are commonly best—they have more in them of the voice of God. May He give you grace so to hear what has been said, as you will wish to have heard, when life is over; to hear in a practical way, with a desire to profit by it, to learn God's will and to do it!

MORAL CONSEQUENCES
OF SINGLE SINS

"Be sure your sin will find you out."—Numb. xxxii.23.

THIS is one of those passages in the inspired writings, which, though introduced on a particular occasion and with a limited meaning, express a general truth, such as we seem at once to feel as being far greater than the context requires, and which we use apart from it. Moses warned the Reubenites and Gadites, that, if they, who had already been allotted their inheritance, did not assist their brethren in gaining theirs, their sin would find them out, or be visited on them. And, while he so spoke, He who spoke through him, God, the Holy Spirit, conveyed, as we believe, a deeper meaning under his words, for the edification of His Church to the end; viz., He intimated that great law of God's governance, to which all who study that governance will bear witness, that sin is ever followed by punishment. Day and night follow each other not more surely, than punishment comes upon sin. Whether the sin be great or little, momentary or habitual, wilful or through infirmity, its own peculiar punishment seems, according to the law of nature, to follow, as far as our experience of that law carries us,—sooner or later, lighter or heavier, as the case may be.

We Christians indeed are under a Dispensation of grace, and are blessed with a certain suspension of this awful law of natural religion. The blood of Christ, as St. John says, is of such wonderful efficacy as to "cleanse us from all sin;" to interpose between our sin and its punishment, and to wipe out the former before the latter has overtaken us. This inestimable benefit is applied to our souls in various ways, according to God's inscrutable pleasure; and so far as this is the case, it supersedes or reverses the law of nature which has annexed suffering to disobedience. But, however effectually and extensively it is applied, still experience assures us that it is not yet vouchsafed to us in full measure and under all circumstances. It is an undeniable fact still, that penitents, however truly such, are not secured from the present consequences of their past offences, whether outward or inward, in mind, body, or estate. And we know that there are cases in which Christians fall away and do not repent again. Nay, we have reason for saying that those who sin after grace given, are, as such, in a worse state than if they had not received it. Great, then, as are our privileges under the Gospel, they in no degree supersede the force and the serious warning of the words in the text. Still it is true, and in many frightful ways, nay more so even than before Christ died, that our sin finds us out, and brings punishment after it, in due course; just as a stone falls to the earth, or as fire burns, or as poison kills, as if by the necessary bond of cause and effect.

The text leads us to consider the consequences of a single sin, such as a breach of their engagement would have been in the Reubenites and Gadites; and to narrow the subject, I shall speak only of the moral consequences. Let us then consider the influence which single sins, past or present, may have on our present moral character in God's sight; how great it may be, will be plain from such reflections as the following:—

And first of all, it is natural to reflect on the probable influence upon us of sins committed in our childhood, and even infancy, which we never realized or have altogether forgotten. Ignorant as we may be when children begin to be responsible beings, yet we are ignorant also when they are not so; nor can we assign a date ever so early at which they certainly are not. And even the latest assignable date is very early; and thenceforward, whatever they do exerts, we cannot doubt, a most momentous influence on their character. We know that two lines starting at a small angle, diverge to greater and greater distances, the further they are produced; and surely in like manner a soul living on into eternity may be infinitely changed for the better or the worse by very slight influences exerted on it in the beginning of its course. A very slight deviation at setting out may be the measure of the difference between tending to hell and tending to heaven.

To give due weight to this thought, we should recollect that children's minds are impressible in a very singular way, such as is not common afterwards. The passing occurrences which meet them, these, whether from their novelty or other cause, rest upon their imagination, as if they had duration; and days or hours, having to them the semblance, may do the work of years. Any one, on casting his thoughts back on his first years, may convince himself of this; the character, which his childhood bears in his memory as a whole, being traceable to a few external circumstances, which lasted through a very small portion of it, a certain abode, or a visit to some particular place, or the presence of certain persons, or some one spring or summer,— circumstances which he at first cannot believe to have been so transitory as on examination he finds they certainly were.

On the other hand, let it be observed, that we are certainly ignorant of a great deal that goes on in us in infancy and childhood; I mean our illnesses and sufferings as children, which we are either not conscious of at the time, or at any rate forget soon afterwards;—which yet are of a very serious nature, and while they must have a moral cause, known or unknown, must, one would think, have a moral effect also; and while they suggest by their occurrence the possibility of other serious things going on in us also, have moreover a natural tendency to affect us in some way or other. Mysterious as it is that infants and children should suffer pain, surely it is not less so that, when they come to years of reason, they should so forget it, as hardly to be able to believe, when told of it, that they themselves were the very sufferers; yet as sicknesses and accidents then happening permanently affect their body, though they recollect nothing of them, there is no extravagance in the idea that passing sins then contracted and forgotten for ever afterwards, should so affect the soul as to cause those moral differences between man and man which, however originating, are too clear to be denied. And with this fearful thought before us of the responsibility attaching to the first years of our life, how miserable is it to reflect on the other hand that children are commonly treated as if they were not responsible, as if it did not matter what they did or were! They are indulged, humoured, spoiled, or at best neglected. Bad examples are set them; things are done or said before them, which they understand and catch up, when others least think it, and store in their minds, or act upon; and thus the indelible hues of sin and error are imprinted on their souls, and become as really part of their nature as that original sin in which they were born.

And what is true in infancy and childhood, is in its degree true in after life. Though our earliest years have especially the characteristic of being impressible by outward things, and of being unconscious or forgetful of them, yet at particular seasons afterwards, when the mind is excited, thrown out of its ordinary state, thrown for a while out of its subjection to habit, as if into that original unformed state when it was more free to choose good and evil, then in like manner it takes impressions, and those indelible ones, and withal almost unconsciously, after the manner of childhood. This is one reason why a time of trial is often such a crisis in a man's spiritual history. It is a season when the iron is heated and malleable; one or two strokes serve to fashion it as a weapon for God or for Satan. Or in other words, if a man is then taken at unawares, an apparently small sin leads to consequences in years and ages to come so fearful, that one can hardly dare contemplate them. This may serve to make us understand the shortness and apparent simplicity of the trial which is sometimes represented in Scripture as sealing the fate of those who succumb to it; Saul's trial, for instance, or Esau's; as on the other hand, indefinitely great results may follow from one act of obedience, as Joseph's in resisting his master's wife, or David's in sparing the life of Saul. Such great occasions, good or evil, occur all through life, but especially in youth; and it were well if young persons would realize that they do occur and are momentous. Alas! what would they give afterwards, when they come to repent (not to speak of that most awful season, the future judgment, when they stand before God, and are shortly to enter heaven or hell), not to have done what in a moment of excitement they did—to recall the blasphemous avowal, or the guilty deed—to be what they then were and now are not, free to serve God, free from the brand and the yoke of Satan! How will they bitterly bewail that fascination, or delirium, or sophistry, which made them what they need not have been, had they used against it the arms which Christ gave them!

But to return:—to these single or forgotten sins, such as I have described them, are not improbably to be traced the strange inconsistencies of character which we often witness in our experience of life. I mean, you meet continually with men possessed of a number of good points, amiable and excellent men, yet in one respect perhaps strangely perverted. And you cannot move them, or succeed at all with them, but must leave them as you find them. Perhaps they are weak and overindulgent towards others, perhaps they are harsh, perhaps they are obstinate, perhaps they are perversely wedded to some wrong opinion, perhaps they are irresolute and undecided,—some fault or other they have, and you lament it, but cannot mend it, and are obliged to take them for what they are, and be resigned, however you may regret. Men are sometimes so good and so great, that one is led to exclaim, Oh that they were only a little better, and a little greater!

This indeed is all the difference between being a true saint of God, and a second rate or third rate Christian. Few men are great saints. There is always a something; I am not speaking of wilful or admitted sins—sins against the conscience (they of course exclude a man altogether from any hope), but of a defect of view and principle, a perversion of character. This is the common case even with the better sort of Christians; they are deformed in stature, they are not upright, they do not walk perfectly with God. And you cannot tell why it is;—they have ever lived religiously,—they have been removed from temptation, had good training and instruction, and they fulfil their calling, are good husbands or wives, good parents, good neighbours,—still when you come to know them well, there is in them this or that great inconsistency.

This consideration moreover tends to account for the strange way in which defects of character are buried in a man. He goes on, for years perhaps, and no one ever discovers his particular failings, nor does he know them himself; till at length he is brought into certain circumstances, which bring them out. Hence men turn out so very differently from what was expected; and we are seldom able to tell beforehand of another, and scarcely ever dare we promise for ourselves, as regards the future. The proverb, for instance, says, power tries a man; so do riches, so do various changes of life. We find that after all, we do not know him, though we have been acquainted with him for years. We are disappointed, nay sometimes startled, as if he had almost lost his identity; whereas perchance it is but the coming to light of sins committed long before we knew him.

Again: single sins indulged or neglected are often the cause of other defects of character, which seem to have no connexion with them, but which after all are rather symptomatic of the former, than themselves at the bottom of the mischief. This is generally acknowledged as regards a sceptical temper of mind, which commonly is assailed by argument in vain, the root of the evil lying deeper, viz., in habits of vice, which however the guilty parties strenuously maintain to be quite a distinct matter, to relate to their conduct, and to have no influence whatever upon their reason or their opinion. And the same thing perhaps holds true in other cases; softness of mind and manner and false refinement may sometimes be the result of allowing ourselves in impure thoughts; or wanderings in prayer may have some subtle connexion with self-conceit; or passionateness may owe its power over us to indulgence, though without excess, in eating and drinking. I am not connecting these several sins together as if in the way of cause and effect, but stating a connexion which sometimes holds in matter of fact, however we account for it.

Now I will proceed to consider the existence of single sins, and the state of persons labouring under them, in another point of view. I suppose there are few persons indeed, if any, but have some besetting sin or other, some infirmity, some temptation; and in resisting this lies their trial. Now a man may be very religious *all but* this one infirmity, and this one indulged infirmity may in consequence be producing most distressing effects on his spiritual state considered both in itself and in God's sight, without his being aware of it. Suppose, for instance, that a man is naturally resentful and unforgiving. He may, in spite of this, have a great number of excellences, very high views, very deeply seated principles, very great points, great self-devotion to God's service, great faith, great sanctity. I can fancy such a person almost arguing himself out of his own conviction, that he is fostering the secret sin in question, from his consciousness of his own integrity, and his devotional spirit in the general round of his duties. There are sins which when committed, so acutely distress the mind, that they are far less dangerous to it than their intrinsic heinousness would otherwise make them. Never must we undervalue of course the extreme misery and guilt of evil thoughts which are often indulged by the young; still afterwards they fill a person with remorse, and are clamorous for his repentance, and before he repents they so burden him, that he has no ease, no satisfaction. He cannot go about his ordinary duties as before: and, while all this is felt, great as is their sinfulness, they strike no secret blow, but in a certain sense counteract their own effects. But far different is it with covetousness, conceit, ambition, or resentment, which is the particular sin I am speaking of. It may have ten thousand palliations; it may be disguised by fair names; it affects the conscience only now and then, for a moment, and that is all; the pang is soon over. The pang is momentary, but the ease and satisfaction and harmony of mind, arising from the person's exact performance of his general duties, are abiding guests within him. Whatever his duties are, this consciousness is with him: he is honest, just, temperate, self-denying; he mixes with others, and is perhaps meek and lowly, unassuming and affectionate, or, if need be, firm, clearsighted in matters of principle, zealous in conduct, pure in his motives. He enters God's house, and his heart responds to what he sees and hears there. He seems to himself to be able to say, "Thou, God, seest me!" as if he had no secret fault at all in his heart. He prays as calmly and seriously as before; he feels, as before, his heart drawn upwards by his Lord's history, or the Psalms of David. He is conscious to himself that he is not of this world. He humbly trusts that there is nothing in this world (through God's grace) that can tempt his heart from his God and Saviour. Do you not see how his imagination is affected by all this? he is in the main what he thinks he is; he thinks himself devoted to God in all active services, in all inward thoughts; and so he is. He is not wrong in thinking so; but in spite of all this, he has just one fault in a different direction,—there is a fault out of sight. He forgets, that in spite of this harmony between all within and all without for twenty-three hours of the day, there is one subject, now and then recurring, which jars with his mind,—there is just one string out of tune. Some particular person has injured him or dishonoured him, and a few minutes of each day or of each week, are given to the indulgence of harsh, unforgiving thoughts, which at first he suspected were what they really are, sinful, but which he has gradually learned to palliate, or rather account for, on other principles, to refer to other motives, to justify on religious or other grounds. Solomon says, "Dead flies cause the ointment of the apothecary to send forth a stinking savour; so doth a little folly him that is in reputation for wisdom and honour." [1] Alas! who can pretend to estimate the effect of this apparently slight transgression upon the spiritual state of any one of us? Who can pretend to say what the effect of it is in God's sight? What do the Angels think of it? What does our own guardian Angel, if one be vouchsafed us, who has watched over us, and been intimate with us from our youth up; who joyed to see how we once grew together with God's grace, but who now is in fear for us? Alas! what is the real condition of our heart itself? Dead bodies keep their warmth a short time; and who can tell but a soul so circumstanced may be severed from the grace of the Ordinances, though he partakes them outwardly, and is but existing upon and exhausting the small treasure of strength and life which is laid up within him? Nay, we know that so it really is, if the sin be deliberate and wilful; for the word of Scripture assures us that such sin shuts us out from God's presence, and obstructs the channels by which He gives us grace.

Consider again, how miserable a calamity may from such a cause be inflicted on a whole Church. The intercessions of the Saints are the life of the Church. The alms and good works, the

---

[1] Eccles. x. 1.

prayers and fastings, the purity, the strict conscientiousness, the devotion of all true believers, high and low, are our safety and protection. When Satan then would afflict her in any of her branches, he begins doubtless by attempting to rob her of that in which her strength lies. He has gained a point whenever he can entangle religious persons in some deliberate sin, when he can rouse their pride, inflame their resentment, allure their covetousness, or feed their ambitious hopes. One sin is enough: his work is done, when he can put one single obstacle in their road; and there he leaves it, satisfied. And let it be observed, this applies both to the case of individuals and of the Church itself at a given time. For what we know, at this very time Satan may have succeeded in attaching some sin upon us as a people, which is working our destruction, in spite of whatever good points we may really have besides. Love of the world's good things, for instance, may be sufficient to ruin many graces. As to individuals, the case of Achan is quite in point, as you must well recollect. His one sin, secreting from among the spoils of Jericho a goodly Babylonish garment and some gold and silver, brought defeat upon the forces of Israel, and next death upon himself, and death upon his sons and his daughters. Let us not think that God's providence is materially different now, because we do not happen to see it. The chief difference between His dealings with Jews and with Christians is surely but this: they were visible to the one, to the other invisible. We do not *see* the effects of His wrath now as then, but they are as real, and more terrible as being proportioned to the greatness of the privileges abused.

And here I will notice another instance, as it may be considered, of a disobedience in one particular only, which sometimes consists with much excellence in other respects; that of separation or alienation from the Church. When we come across persons who have seceded from the Church, or who actively oppose her, or who disbelieve some of her doctrines, it may sometimes happen that we see so much of good principle and right conduct in them, as to be perplexed, and to begin to ask ourselves whether they can be very wrong in their opinions, or whether they themselves gain any harm from them. Now here let it be observed, I am speaking of those who go counter to the truth, when they might have known better. Again, I would not have you forget that the higher gifts of grace are altogether unseen, as well as the inflictions of God's wrath; but still let us speak of what *is* seen in those who deliberately oppose the Church, I say our imagination is likely to be affected by what appears in them of faith and holiness; and much more the imagination of the persons themselves, who often have no doubt whatever that they are in God's favour. I repeat, I am speaking of those whom God sees to be wilful in their separation; and though we cannot know who are such, and therefore can pronounce judgment absolutely on no one, yet I would have all those who are thrown with persons who, being separatists, may be such, to bear in mind that their seeming to be holy and religious ever so much, does not prove they are really so, supposing they have this one secret sin chargeable upon them in God's books. Just as a man may be in good health, may have his arms and hands his own, his head clear, his mind active, and yet may just have one organ diseased, and the disease not at once appear, but be latent, and yet be mortal, bringing certain death in the event, so may it be with them. As, in the instance just now taken, a man may be upright and noble-minded, with a single purpose and a high resoluteness, kind and gentle, self-denying and charitable, and yet towards one certain individual may cherish feelings of revenge, and thereby show that some principle short of the love of God rules his heart,—so may it be with those who seem to be good men, and wilfully leave the Church. Their religious excellences, whatever these may be, are of no avail really against this or any other wilful sin.

To conclude. I have suggested but one or two thoughts on a very large subject, yet through God's mercy they may be useful. They must be useful, if they lead us to be frightened at ourselves. "Who can understand his errors?" says holy David. "Cleanse Thou me from secret faults." And how awful is the text, "Your sin will find you out!" Who can undertake to say for himself what and when have been his wilful sins, how frequently they recur, and how continually in consequence he is falling from grace! What need have we of a cleansing and a restoration day by day! What need have we of drawing near to God in faith and penitence, to seek from Him such pardon, such assurance, such strength, as He will vouchsafe to bestow! What need have we to continue in His presence, to remain under the shadow of His throne, to make use of all the means and expedients He allows us, to be steadfast in His Ordinances, and zealous in His precepts, lest we be found shelterless and helpless when He visits the earth!

Moreover, what constant prayers should we offer up to Him that He would be merciful to us in the dreadful day of judgment! It will indeed be a fearful moment when we stand before Him in the sight of men and Angels, to be judged according to our works! It will be fearful for ourselves and for all our friends. Then the day of grace will be over; prayers will not avail then, when the books are opened. Let us then plead for ourselves and for each other while it is called to-day. Let us pray Him, by the merits of His cross and passion, to have mercy on us, to have mercy on all we love, on all the Church; to pardon us, to reveal to us our sins, to give us repentance and amendment of life, to give us present grace, and to bestow on us, according to the riches of His love, future blessedness in His eternal kingdom.

ACCEPTANCE OF RELIGIOUS PRINCIPLES COMPULSORY

*"And the lord said unto the servant, Go out into
the highways and hedges, and compel them to come in,
that my house may be filled."*—Luke xiv.23.

THE Parable of the Great Supper, from which these words
are taken, is found also in St. Matthew's Gospel, with this
especial addition, that of the guests thus brought in by force,
one was found not having on a wedding garment, who in consequence was not simply dismissed as unworthy, but condemned
to punishment. "Friend, how camest thou in hither, not having
a wedding garment? and he was speechless. Then said the king
to the servants, Bind him hand and foot, and take him away,
and cast him into outer darkness: there shall be weeping and
gnashing of teeth; for many are called but few are chosen." [2]
"Friend, *how* camest thou in hither?" You may suppose he
might have answered, "I was forced in;" but our Saviour says,
"And he was speechless," and pronounces his everlasting punishment.

Surely, there is something very awful and startling in the
doctrine thus contained in the Parable. It would seem from
thence that we are compelled to accept of religious advantages,
for the use of which we are answerable, for the misuse of which
we shall be condemned. We are compelled to become Christians, yet this compulsion is not taken into account when the
day of reckoning comes. The same doctrine is implied in the
parable of the talents. The servant who hid his lord's talent,
seems to have had some such thoughts about fairness and justice, as the natural man so often indulges in now,—some idea of
being quits and even with him, if he left his gift alone,—as if he
could wash his hands (as it is said) of the whole business, and
venture neither the gain nor the loss; feeling that it was a deli-

---

[1] This Sermon was not originally written for a Parish.
[2] Matt. xxii.12–14.

cate matter that was put upon him, that there was great risk of failing, that his lord was an austere kind of man, hard to please, having his own views of right and duty, and unreasonable; and that, consequently, it was safest to keep aloof, to have no cares on any score, and so escape the danger. But here again this selfish reasoner is met by the same stern necessity, so to call it. The law of his nature is urged upon him, by the Creator of that law; a sort of uncontrollable destiny is represented as encompassing him; the destiny of accountableness, the fate of being free, the unalienable prerogative of choosing between life and death, the inevitable prospect of heaven and hell. "Out of thine own mouth will I judge thee, thou wicked servant." [3]—"Cast ye the unprofitable servant into outer darkness." [4]

And so again of Judas our Lord says, "*Woe* unto that man by whom the Son of man is betrayed. It had been good for that man if he had not been born." Yet he was born, he was suffered to betray, and he was condemned.

The same is the doctrine of the Old Testament; as, for example, in the memorable words in the prophet Ezekiel, in which Almighty God says to the Israelites, "That which cometh into your mind shall not be at all, that ye say, We will be as the heathen, as the families of the countries, to serve wood and stone; As I live, saith the Lord God, surely with a mighty hand, and with a stretched out arm, and with fury poured out, will I rule over you. . . . . And I will cause you to pass under the rod, and I will bring you into the bond of the covenant." [5]

Now, before proceeding to observe upon this very solemn and certain truth (certain if Scripture is true), I would entreat you to consider *who it is* who has propounded it in the parable in question. It is our Lord Christ. Here, as in other places, He has not left to His servants,—He has taken upon Himself (what may be called) the responsibility, I might even say the odium, of declaring startling doctrines. Consider then His words and works, as displayed in the Gospels. Is He not the author of a religion which we every day hear called, and most truly called, mild, beneficent, charitable, and cheering? Is not His own character, as the common voice of all men proclaims, most meek, gentle, considerate, and loving? Can any one read the history of His life and death without being himself convinced of the truth of this universal judgment? much more, can any one in any degree enter into the depths of the gracious doctrine of the Atonement, His expiation of sin on the Cross,

[3] Luke xix.22. [4] Matt. xxv.30. [5] Ezek. xx.32–37.

without possessing a clear assurance that there is nothing in the whole world that can be done for us which He has not done and will not do? Yet He it is who leaves us under this bond. By His sighs and tears then, by His toilsome wanderings, by His earnest speeches, by His agony and death, by all He has done, all He has suffered, He seems to entreat us to have confidence in Him; He condescends to entreat us to take on trust the truth and the equity of His words, when He declares that we are compelled to receive God's mercies, yet punished for the mis-use of them.

Now I shall enlarge somewhat upon the general state of the case, and then show how Christians are especially interested in it.

1. In the first place, consider what first of all presents itself to our thoughts, our birth into the world. Allow that this is a world of enjoyment, yet unquestionably it is a world of care and pain also. Most men will judge that the pain on the whole ex-ceeds the enjoyment on the whole. But, whether this be so or not with most men, even if there be one man in the whole world who thinks so, that is enough for my purpose. It is enough for my purpose, if only there be one person to be found, who thinks sickness, disappointment, anxiety, affliction, suf-fering, fear, to be such grievous ills, that he had rather not have been born. If this be the sentiment only of one man, that one man, it is plain, is, as regards his very existence, what the Chris-tian is relatively to his new birth, an unwilling recipient of a gift. We are not asked, whether we will choose this world, be-fore we are born into it. We are brought under the yoke of it, whether we will or no; since we plainly cannot choose or not choose before the power of choice is bestowed on us, this gift of a mortal nature.

This is one of the thoughts which to the pride of reflecting but irreligious minds is sometimes a stumbling block. Arro-gant, impatient, rebellious hearts, finding themselves possessed of this gift of life and reason, fight against what they cannot undo—they turn it against itself, and argue against it by means of it. They beat and break themselves fruitlessly against the des-tiny to which they are chained; and since they cannot annul their creation, they think to revenge themselves by blasphe-mously rising against their Creator. "Why am I made? why cannot I annihilate myself? why must I suffer?" Such as these are the questions with which they fatigue themselves; some-times even rushing out of life by self-inflicted violence, from the frantic hope that perchance they have power over their own being. And when they have committed that fatal deed, and find themselves, as assuredly they do, still sentient, conscious, independent beings, with their own thoughts and wills and tastes and judgments, who can imagine the horror that possesses them in that their new state of existence? the horror of finding themselves without bodies, without any thing to touch, any thing to turn upon, and wreak their fury upon, with nothing but themselves,—without bodies, yet living, living without aught of power over the principle of their life, which rests upon the will of Him alone, who called them into being, and whom they have blasphemed!

Or sometimes this want of resignation takes another turn. Many there are who, without thus rising against the will of God, yet will not admit that it is their duty to serve Him *under* that dispensation, whatever it is, to which He has chosen to subject them, that they are accountable for what they do, and must bring forth from within, by the power of their will, what may duly respond to the circumstances in which they stand. Accordingly, they deliberately and on principle suffer themselves to be borne down the stream of life passively, by whatever happens to them. Does temptation come to them? they yield to it; does danger? they are cowards; inducements to virtue? they are virtuous; is religion in fashion? they take up a profession; in no case entering into the simple and momentous truth, that the circumstances which come upon them, are matters external both to their own choice and their responsibility,—are but conditions appointed by Almighty God, under which they find themselves placed (why, it boots not to inquire), and which it is their wisdom to take as such, to take, use, and improve.

I have noticed these instances of want of resignation, not for their own sake, but in order to illustrate, by the contrast, that law of our birth, of which I am speaking, viz., that we are brought, without our consent being asked, into a certain state of things, into a life of suffering, and of moral discipline; and are imperatively required to obey God *under it*, as if we had brought ourselves into it, on the pain of fearful consequences, if we do not.

2. Such is our condition as men; it is the same as Christians. For instance, we are not allowed to grow up before choosing our religion. We as little choose our religion as we choose to be born. It is done for us without our having part in it. We are baptized in infancy. Our sponsors promise for us. Now considering how great on the one hand the privileges of Baptism are,

and on the other how great the risk of resisting and abusing them, this is a very serious thought. St. Paul's words about the danger of quenching the gift of grace are decisive—"It is impossible (he says) for those who were once enlightened, and have tasted of the heavenly gift, and were partakers of the Holy Ghost, and have tasted the good word of God, and the powers of the world to come, if they shall fall away, to renew them again unto repentance." [6]

Now I can fancy a person saying, who had fallen into sin, "O that I had never been baptized! O that I did not incur this great risk! O that the one Baptism once applied for the remission of sins were yet to come! O that I had not already had that cleansing once for all, and were quit of the necessity of striving continually to keep myself in the state into which I have been brought!" But this cannot be; we are Christians from our earliest years, we can decline neither the great privilege nor the responsibility of it; and, instead of shrinking from the responsibility, rather we must comfort ourselves with the privilege, with the contemplation of the fulness of the aid given us to help us in all our trials; and, thus encouraged, we must go on to co-operate with God manfully.

So again with respect to our education. We are brought up as Christians. We may not, we cannot stand aloof, and say we will keep our judgment unbiassed, and decide for ourselves. We find ourselves *Christians*; and our duty is, not to consider what we should do if we were not Christians,—not to go about disputing, sifting the evidence for Christianity, weighing this side or that,—but to act upon the rules given us, till we have reason to think them wrong, and to bring home to ourselves the truth of them, as we go on, *by* acting upon them,—by their fruits on ourselves. Heathens indeed may be bound to go into the question of evidences, but our duty is to use the talents of which we find ourselves possessed, and to essay their genuineness by deeds, not by arguments.

These are instances (such as I proposed to give) of our being forced into the possession of certain advantages or disadvantages, and being obliged to act up to this our state, to co-operate with it, according to the inward power given us, instead of drawing back from it. You see how parallel the Christian method is to that of nature. God appoints us by nature to be the sons of sinful Adam, responsible beings, with never-dying souls,—by force, as it were; and by means of the Church, in like manner, He gives us the Sacrament of the new birth, and educates us in right principles, whether we will or no.

3. But this compulsion on the part of the Church is still more urgent and extensive than I have yet mentioned, and it may be right therefore to give a few additional instances of it, in order to impress upon your minds the principle on which it is founded.

First, then, I will instance the remarkable fact, that (as it appears) whole households were baptized by the Apostles, which must include slaves as well as children. It would seem that grown persons, if dependent on the master of the house, were, on his conversion, made partakers of his privileges and his duties. This was so ordered in the Old Testament, in the case of Abraham, whose circumcision was followed, by divine command, by the circumcision of his servants with him; "all the men of his house, born in the house, and bought with money of the stranger."[7] In like manner we read in the Acts, that when Lydia was converted, not only she herself was baptized, but, almost as *a matter of course* (for such is the impression conveyed by the sacred narrative), "her household"[8] was baptized also. Again, when the jailer at Philippi is baptized, it is not only he, but "he and all his straightway." Again, in the first Epistle to the Corinthians, St. Paul speaks of having baptized "the household of Stephanas."[9] The circumstances and conditions requisite for this procedure, and the limitations by which it was guarded, need not here be considered; I wish merely to point out the principle involved in the procedure itself.

Another remarkable instance of the force which was put upon men by the early Church, will be found in the then existing usage of bringing such as had the necessary gifts to ordination, without asking their consent. The primitive Christians looked upon Ordination very differently (alas for ourselves!) very differently from this age. Now the ministerial office is often regarded as a profession of this world,—a provision, a livelihood; it is associated in men's minds with a comparatively easy, or at least not a troubled life,—with respectability and comfort, a competency, a position in society. Alas for us! we feel none of those terrors about it, which made the early Christians flee from it! But in their eyes (putting aside the risk of undertaking it in times of persecution) it was so solemn a function, that the holier a man was, the less inclined he felt to undertake it. They felt that it was in some sort to incur the responsibility of other

[7] Gen. xvii.27.   [8] Acts xvi.15, 33.   [9] 1 Cor. i.16.

men, and to be put in trust with their salvation; they felt it was scarcely possible to engage in it, without the risk of being besprinkled with the blood of ruined souls. They understood somewhat of St. Paul's language when he said that necessity was laid upon him, and woe to him unless he preached the Gospel. In consequence they shrank from the work, as though (to use a weak similitude) they had been bid dive down for pearls at the bottom of the sea, or scale some precipitous and dizzy cliff. True, they knew that abundance of heavenly aid would be given them, according to their need; but they knew also, that even if any part of the work was to be their own, though they were only called on to co-operate with God, that was in such a case fearful undertaking enough. So they literally fled away in many instances, when they were called to the sacred office; and the Church as literally took them by force, and (after the precedent of St. Paul's own conversion) laid necessity upon them.

Once more, consider the conduct of the Church from the very first time any civil countenance was extended towards it, and you will have a fresh instance of this constraining principle of which I speak. What are national conversions, such as took place in the middle ages, when kings submitted to the Gospel and their people followed, but going out into the highways and hedges, and compelling men to come in? And though we can conceive cases in which this urgency was unwisely, over-strongly, unseasonably, or too extensively applied, yet the principle of it is no other than that of the Baptism of households mentioned in the Acts. Again, what was it but this religious and charitable force (so to call it) which once guarded the true doctrine with state penalties, and made a man think twice and thrice before he rashly uttered any light words, or promulgated any heterodox tenet? a public duty, which is now altogether neglected, from the abuse of it in certain times and places, and the proneness of men on a re-action to run from one extreme into another.

4. And now let me notice, in conclusion, the light which the law of Providence I have been explaining casts upon the circumstances and mode in which one other ordinance of the Church is administered,—I mean Confirmation. Though in some respects individual Christians are always under the constraining power of the Church, yet as life goes on, they are more and more withdrawn from it; and, compared with what they were in childhood, they may at a certain time be called free men. They enjoy no longer, at least in the same sense as before, the privilege and mercy of being dependent. Confirmation is

the last act on the part of the Church before she parts with them. She blesses them, and sends them out from the home of their youth to seek their fortunes in the world. She ends her constraint of them by a blessing; she blesses them by force and lets them go. They are sent to receive it by their friends; they submit, and are then set free. O my brethren, both young and old, this is an awful thought,—a most affecting thought, indeed, to those who witness a Confirmation, but a most awful thought to those who take part in it. You who have the care of young people, see to it that you bring them to be confirmed; let not the time slip by; let them not get too old. Why? because then you cannot bring them; the time of constraint is passed; they are their own masters. But you will say that you may perhaps still have influence with your children and dependents, and can get them to come, though they be past age. O but what if we be not willing to receive them? So perchance it may be. I mean, that when a man or woman is grown, much more is required of them than before, and they less likely to be able to answer it. When persons are young, before their minds are formed, ere they have sullied their baptismal robe, and contracted bad habits, this is the time for Confirmation, which conveys to them grace whereby they may perform that "good work" which Baptism has begun in them. But when they have gone into the world,—whatever their age be, for it varies in different persons,—when they have begun the war with world, flesh, and devil, when their minds are now grown into some determinate shape, and much more when they have wilfully sinned in any gross way, are they likely to be fitly prepared for Confirmation, even if they are persuaded to offer themselves? When a grown person comes coldly, and indifferently, and merely because his friends send him to us, can we, ministers of Christ, receive him? Can we receive, as if being in a mere negative state, one who, as being of mature years, ought to be mature in his religious principles also? Beware, then, all who have the care of the young, lest you let slip the time of bringing them for God's grace, when you can bring them, for it will not return. Bring them while their hearts are tender: they may escape from you, and you may not be able to reclaim them.

On the other hand, the same considerations come home with greater force to the young themselves: it is their own concern. They who are of an age to be confirmed should come to be confirmed at once, lest they get too old to be confirmed,—I mean lest they be first confirmed in another way, a way which will keep them from this holy confirmation, lest they receive that miserable confirmation, which those have who rush into sin,—the touch of this infectious world, and the imposition of the devil's hand upon them. You do not know yourselves, my brethren; you cannot answer for yourselves; you cannot trust your own promises about yourselves; you do not know what will become of you, unless you receive the gifts of grace *when* they are offered. They are, as it were, forced upon you now. If you put them from you, doubtless you can in this case overcome that force, you can be stronger than God's mercy. You may put off this holy ordinance, because you do not at present like a strict religious life,—because you take no interest in your eternal prospects. Alas! for what you know, you will be taking a step never to be retrieved. This blessed means of grace, perchance would change your heart and will, and make you love God's service. But the season once lost will never return. Year after year may pass, and you will be further and further from God. Perhaps you will rush into open and wilful sin: perhaps not; but still without loving God at all the more. Your heart may be upon the world; you may pass through life in a cold, unbelieving, narrow spirit, with no high aims, no love of things invisible, no love of Christ your Saviour. This will be the end of your refusing the loving compulsion of Almighty God:—slavery to this world, and to the god of this world. God save us all, young and old, from this, through Jesus Christ.

RELIANCE ON RELIGIOUS OBSERVANCES

"When ye shall have done all those things which are commanded you, say, We are unprofitable servants; we have done that which was our duty to do."—Luke xvii. 10.

IF, when we have done all, we are unprofitable, what are we when we have but a part? and then again, what are we if that part itself be defective, and defiled with evil? There is no sort of question then, that if *reason* is to be judge, there can be no boasting towards God even on the part of His most matured saints and exactest servants. There can, I say, be no boasting, because whatever we do is the fruit of His grace, and because we do very little, and because, in spite of His grace, what we do is infected with sin, and because even if we did all, we should be doing no more than we are bound to do. I cannot conceive any one who fairly gave his mind to consider the matter, whatever weight he might give to this or that consideration in particular, however disposed he might be to exalt his natural powers, or his actual services, not coming after all to this conclusion—to this conclusion in the judgment of *reason*.

And yet, it will be said, there are many persons in the world who are well pleased with what they are and what they do, who are well satisfied with themselves, who think themselves in so fair a way for attaining heaven, that they need not give themselves any extraordinary trouble about it; who are what is commonly called self-righteous. Now I do not allow that those *are* self-righteous necessarily who are *called* so, because there is among us much unfair and harsh judging of the feelings and motives of others; but still after all there *is* a state of mind which is self-righteous,—I mean a state of mind in which a person has no serious fears of future judgment, and is well satisfied with himself. Certainly; but this is no objection to what I have been saying, for you will find this to arise from persons *not* thinking of God. What I said just now was, that no one who thinks seriously of Almighty God and himself, can pride himself on his services; but this is what men in general cannot bring themselves steadily to do. Self-righteous men are men who live to the world, and do not think of God. They do not think of judgment as sure to come one day or another. They have no fears for the future, because they have no prospect about the future. They are contented with the present, and with themselves, because they live in what is visible and tangible, and do not measure themselves by what is unseen and spiritual. "They, measuring themselves by themselves, and comparing themselves among themselves, are not wise . . . for not he that commendeth himself is approved, but whom the Lord commendeth."[1] Worldly men are self-righteous men.

Another class of self-righteous men are they who do not believe in the Divinity and Atonement of Christ. These men, again, do not really measure themselves by a heavenly standard and by God's judgment; they measure themselves merely by their own conscience, and their conscience is dark and blind. They have low and narrow views of duty.

Once more, men who fasten their minds on any particular object of religion short of God, become self-righteous, for they narrow the field of duty, and make this object the measure of it. Hence, whether men make benevolent schemes and exertions to be the whole of their religion, or ceremonial observances, or maintenance of true doctrine, or obedience to any other portion of God's law, they are insensibly led to be satisfied with their own doings, both because of the vivid consciousness which this prominent object creates in them, that religion is their chief employment, and because of the persuasion which readily comes on them that they duly act up to it. Such was the case of the Pharisee in the parable. And if this is true in the case of objects and observances good in themselves, much more will it happen when men place their religion in such things as are not so;—the main fault in all cases being this, that the persons in question, instead of thinking anxiously of God and His law, think only of a portion of it, which they have of themselves set apart, and make it a sort of idol. On the whole, then, what I have said is true, that in spite of the existence of self-righteous men in fact, no one can really think himself meritorious in God's sight, who comes seriously to consider himself and God, apparent exceptions being those cases in which persons do not think duly of either.

[1] 2 Cor. x.12, 18.

This I consider to be the real state of the case; however, the popular view of spiritual pride or self-righteousness is this, that those men are self-righteous, or in great danger of being so, who come often to Church, and are diligent in their moral duties. Now this is the point on which I consider that there is a great deal of unfair and uncharitable judgment among us, persons being said to be satisfied with themselves who are really not so. However, our business is, when the world blames and slanders us, not to be vexed at it, but rather to consider whether there is any foundation for it, any truth at bottom, though there be exaggeration and mistake. I conceive a person may always gain good to his own soul, gain instruction and useful suggestions, by the mistakes of the world about him. Now then let us consider, from this hint given us by ignorant and prejudiced men, whether we, who are blessed so frequently as we are with the ordinances of the Gospel, with the privilege of Prayer and Holy Communion, are or are not in any special danger of spiritual pride, or as of late years it has been called, self-righteousness.

Now of course there *is* a danger of persons becoming self-satisfied, in being regular and exemplary in devotional exercises; there is danger, which others have not, of their so attending to them as to forget that they have other duties to attend to. I mean the danger, of which I was just now speaking, of having their attention drawn off from other duties by their very attention to this duty in particular. And what is still most likely of all, persons who are regular in their devotions may be visited with passing thoughts every now and then, that they are thereby better than other people; and these occasional thoughts may secretly tend to make them self-satisfied, without their being aware of it, till they have a latent habit of self-conceit and contempt of others. Such cases certainly are possible or probable; in none of them do persons actually rely on their merit, or boastfully plead their services in God's sight; but still those services do seem to be a snare to them, leading some of them to forget how far they are from perfection on the whole, and how much they sin; leading others to forget that they have other duties also to do; and encouraging others again in a quiet, unobtrusive self-complacency, while they still acknowledge themselves to be sinners. What is done statedly forces itself upon the mind, impresses the memory and imagination, and seems to be a *substitute* for other duties; and what is contained in definite outward acts has a completeness and tangible form about it, which is likely to *satisfy* the mind. I do not deny then there is

some danger, lest persons who are frequent in devotional services should be as the Pharisees,—do nothing else, and be well
contented that they do so much. Accordingly you may hear ill-
natured persons, or scoffers, say severe things against those who
are strict in their religious observances, as if in other respects
they were *worse* than others, or were hypocritical. All this is but
the language of the world, and not to be believed; still I do not
deny that persons who are frequent in prayers and other religious exercises should be jealous over themselves, and not take
for granted they are going on right, particularly since their very
strictness is a call on them for a more exact observance of their
other duties. But all this is quite a different matter, from such
danger being an *objection* to observing devotional duties. If there
is a danger, let it be watched and prevented, but let not the observance be omitted: there are few things which are not dangerous. All things may be perverted and abused. The great lesson
set before us in the Gospel is to use the world without abusing
it, and in like manner to use *God's mercies* without abusing
them. If frequent attendance at the Lord's Table or at prayers
leads, unless we are watchful, to spiritual pride, our duty is *to be*
watchful, not to omit attendance.

However, I do not think, after all, that there *is* any very great
danger to a serious mind in the frequent use of these great privileges. Indeed, it were a strange thing to say that the simple performance of what God has told us to do *can* do harm to any but
those who have not the love of God in their hearts, and to such
persons all things are harmful; *they* pervert every thing into evil.
It is impossible (praised be God!) that earnest and humble
minds should derive any thing from Christ's ordinances but
those high and ineffable blessings which are lodged in them.
Christ's gifts are not snares, but mercies. Let us then see how
this danger, which I have allowed to exist in devotional observances, is counteracted in the case of serious minds.

1. Now, first, the evil in question (supposing it to exist) is
singularly adapted to be its own corrective. It can only do us
injury when we do not know its existence. When a man knows
and feels the intrusion of self-satisfied and self-complacent
thoughts, here is something at once to humble him and destroy
that complacency. To know of a weakness is always humbling;
now humility is the very grace needed here. To know we are
passionate, or slothful, or severe, is indeed the first step towards
removing such defects, but does not directly tend to remove
them. Knowledge of our indolence does not encourage us to
exertion, but induces despondence; but to know we are self-

satisfied is a direct blow to self-satisfaction. There is no satisfaction in perceiving that we are self-satisfied. No one can be self-righteous who knows and laments his proud thoughts; but a person may be slothful who knows and laments that he is slothful. Here then is one great safeguard against our priding ourselves on our observances. Evil thoughts do us no harm, if recognized, if repelled, if protested against by the indignation and self-reproach of the mind. It is when we do not discern them, when we admit them, when we cherish them, that they ripen into principles. And if this is true of all bad thoughts, much more is it of those now spoken of, which humble us on their detection as much as they elate us on their first entrance. I do not deny that the intrusion of such vain and foolish thoughts takes off from the comfort of our devotion, when they occur; but that is another matter. The question is not about comfort, but about mischief. It is no good reason for giving over devotional exercises, that we have not all the comfort from them which we might have.

2. But again, if religious persons are troubled with proud thoughts about their own excellence and strictness, I think it is only when they are young in their religion, and that the trial will wear off; and that for many reasons. I would not indeed speak with undue decision on such a point,—every one has his particular temptations; yet one should hardly think that any but minds very young in the faith, minds to whom religion was a new thing, would pride themselves on their performances or rest upon them,—I mean, would even have the temptation to do so; for surely it does not require much keenness of spiritual sight to see how very far our best is from what it should be. Satisfaction with our own doings, as I have said, arises from fixing the mind on some *one part* of our duty, instead of attempting the whole of it. In proportion as we narrow the field of our duties, we become able to compass them. Men who pursue only this duty or only that duty, are in danger of self-righteousness;—zealots, bigots, devotees, men of the world, sectarians, are for this reason self-righteous. For the same reason, persons beginning a religious course are self-righteous, though they often think themselves just the reverse. They consider, perhaps, all religion to be in confessing themselves sinners, and having warm feelings concerning their redemption and justification,—in having what they consider faith; and, as all this is fulfilled in them, they come to think they have attained and are sure of heaven; and all because they have so very contracted a notion of the range of God's commandments, of the rounds of

that ladder which reaches from earth to heaven. And in the same way, I admit that religious persons who for one reason or another are led to begin a greater strictness than hitherto in their devotional observances, in attending prayers or the Lord's Supper, or in fasting, or in almsgiving, are, on beginning, in some danger of becoming self-satisfied; for the same reason,— as fixing their minds on one certain portion of their duty and becoming excited about *it*; and this the more, inasmuch as the observances in question are something definite and precise, and on the other hand are evidently neglected by others.

But the remedy of the evil is obvious, and one which, since it will surely be applied by every religious person because he *is* religious, will, under God's grace, effect in no long time a cure. Try to do your *whole* duty, and you will soon cease to be well-pleased with your religious state. If you are in earnest, you will try to add to your faith virtue; and the more you effect, the less will you seem to yourself to do. On the other hand, attend prayer and the Holy Eucharist without corresponding strictness in other matters; and it is plain what will follow, from the nature of the human mind, without going to more solemn considerations. The more you neglect your daily, domestic, relative, temporal, duties, the more you will prize yourself on your (I cannot call them religious, your) formal, ceremonial observances. Thus it is plain that self-satisfaction is the feeling either of a beginner, or of a very defective and negligent Christian.

3. But this is not all. Certainly this objection, that devotional practices, such as prayer, fasting, and communicating, tend to self-righteousness, is the objection of those, or at least is just what the objection of those would be, who never attempted them. Men speak as if it was the easiest thing in the world to fast and pray, and do austerities, and as if such courses were the most seductive, easiest, pleasantest, methods of attaining heaven. I do not deny that there are certain states of society, certain ages and countries, in which they are much easier than in others; but this is true of all duties. We, for instance, of this day, find *manliness* and *candour* as easy as some eastern nations might find fasting and meditation. But that is not the question. We are what we are,—Englishmen; and for us who are active in our habits and social in our tempers, fasting and meditation have no such great attractions, and are of no such easy observance. When then an objector fears lest such observances should make him self-righteous, were he to attempt them, I do think he is over-anxious, over-confident in his own power to fulfil them; he trusts too much in his own strength already, and,

depend on it, to attempt them would make him less self-righteous, not more so. He need not be so very fearful of being too good; he may assure himself that the smallest of his Lord's commandments are to a spiritual mind solemn, arduous, and inexhaustible. Is it an easy thing to pray? It *is* easy to wait for a rush of feelings, and then to let our petitions be borne upon them; and never to attempt the duty till then; but it is not at all easy to be in the habit day after day and hour after hour, in all frames of mind, and under all outward circumstances, to bring before God a calm, collected, awakened soul. It is not at all easy to keep the mind from wandering in prayer, to keep out all intrusive thoughts about other things. It is not at all easy to realize what we are about, who is before us, what we are seeking, and what our state is. It is not at all easy to throw off the world and to understand that God and Christ hear us, that Saints and Angels are standing by us, and the devil desiring to have us. What indeed *is* after all meant, by asserting that regular and stated prayers are dangerous to a sensitive and serious mind? They are dangerous to the blind and formal; but so all things are; but where is the really serious mind that will say it is easy to take delight in stated prayer, to attend to it duly? Is not at the best our delight in it transient, and our attention irregular? Is all this satisfactory and elating?

And so again of austerities; there may be persons so constituted by nature as to take pleasure in mortifications for their own sake, and to be able to practise them adequately; and *they* certainly *are* in danger of practising them for their own sakes, not through faith, and of becoming spiritually proud in consequence: but surely it is idle to speak of this as an ordinary danger.

And so again a religious mind has a perpetual source of humiliation from *this* consciousness also, viz., how far his *actual conduct in the world* falls short of the profession which his devotional observances involve. It is not a pleasant, not an inspiring, not an elating reflection, to think that you are making a profession which you must in some measure dishonour by your daily imperfections. There is nothing flattering and soothing in the thought that you are inviting the world to criticise you, and preparing it to expect more than it will find; to say nothing of the more bitter feelings which the professions and the vows of obedience, made in Church and broken in the world, cost you when thought of in God's sight. Alas! is it at all a comfort to add to the catalogue of those sins which we must answer for in the Last Day? yet this we must do, or at least run the risk of it, if we

attempt those services which some persons would persuade us
necessarily tend to self-righteousness.

4. But, after all, what is this shrinking from responsibility,
which fears to be obedient lest it should fail, but cowardice and
ingratitude? What is it but the very conduct of the Israelites,
who, when Almighty God bade them encounter their enemies
and so gain Canaan, feared the sons of Anak, because they were
giants? To fear to do our duty lest we should become self-
righteous in doing it, is to be wiser than God; it is to distrust
Him; it is to do and to feel like the unprofitable servant who hid
his Lord's talent, and then laid the charge of his sloth on his
Lord, as being a hard and austere man. At best we are
unprofitable servants when we have done all; but if we are but
unprofitable when we do our best to be profitable, what are we,
when we fear to do our best, but unworthy to be His servants at
all? No! to *fear* the *consequences* of obedience is to be worldly-
wise, and to go by reason when we are bid go by faith. Let us
dare to do His commandments, leaving to Him to bring us
through, who has imposed them. Let us risk dangers which
cannot in truth be realized, however they threaten, since He
has bid us risk them, and will protect us in them. Let us bear,
what probably will befall us, the assaults of Satan, the sins of
infirmity, the remains of the old Adam, involuntary mistakes,
the smarting of our wounds, and the dejection and desolateness
ensuing, if it be His will. He has promised to lead us safely heavenward, in spite of all things being against us; He will keep us
from all wilful sin: but the infirmities which beset us, our ignorances, waywardnesses, weaknesses, and misconceptions, these
He still ordains should try us and humble us, should move in us
vexation of spirit and self-abasement, and should bring us day
by day to the foot of His Cross for pardon. Let us then compose
ourselves, and bear a firm and courageous heart. Let us steel
ourselves, not against self-reproach and self-hatred, but against
unmanly fear. Let us feel what we really are,—sinners attempting great things, and succeeding at best only so far as to show
that we do attempt them. Let us simply obey God's will, whatever may befall; whether it tend to elate us or to depress us,
what is that to us? He can turn all things to our eternal good. He
can bless and sanctify even our infirmities. He can lovingly
chastise us, if we be puffed up, and He can cheer us when we
despond. He can and will exalt us the more we afflict ourselves;
and we shall afflict ourselves the more, in true humbleness of
mind, the more we really obey Him. Blessed are they who in
any matter do His will; and they are thrice blessed who, in what

they are doing, are also interesting themselves, as in the case which has been under our consideration, in His special sacramental promises. Blessed indeed are they, who, while obeying God, are seeking Christ; who, while they do a duty, receive a privilege; who commemorate His death because He bids them, and while they do so gain the virtue of it in the very commemoration; who live in Him, both in the thought of Him and the possession of Him; who glory in Him who died for them, and was buried, and rose again, and now lives in their hearts; who are willing to take their part with Him, in suffering as in joy; who willingly associate themselves in that Mysterious Communion which He offers them, and which, though it brings glory in the end, brings suffering and affliction at present,—which makes them at present in a special way heirs of tears and pain and disappointment and reproach, heirs of special trials which may come upon them though they live in the most peaceful times, which may come without the world perceiving that they differ in their lot from other men, trials which work for them a far more exceeding and eternal weight of glory, and which in the present world are recompensed by the faith, humility, patience, and gentleness resulting from them.

THE INDIVIDUALITY
OF THE SOUL

"The spirit shall return unto God, who gave it."—Eccles. xii.7.

HERE we are told that upon death the spirit of man returns to God. The sacred writer is not speaking of good men only, or of God's chosen people, but of men generally. In the case of all men, the soul, when severed from the body, returns to God. God gave it: He made it, He sent it into the body, and He upholds it there; He upholds it in distinct existence, wherever it is. It animates the body while life lasts; it returns again, it relapses into the unseen state upon death. Let us steadily contemplate this truth, which at first sight we may fancy we altogether enter into. The point to be considered is this, that every soul of man which is or has been on earth, has a separate existence; and that, in eternity, not in time merely,—in the unseen world, not merely in this,—not only during its mortal life, but ever from the hour of its creation, whether joined to a body of flesh or not.

Nothing is more difficult than to realize that every man has a distinct soul, that every one of all the millions who live or have lived, is as whole and independent a being in himself, as if there were no one else in the whole world but he. To explain what I mean: do you think that a commander of an army realizes it, when he sends a body of men on some dangerous service? I am not speaking as if he were wrong in so sending them; I only ask in matter of fact, does he, think you, commonly understand that each of those poor men has a soul, a soul as dear to himself, as precious in its nature, as his own? Or does he not rather look on the body of men collectively, as one mass, as parts of a whole, as but the wheels or springs of some great machine, to which he assigns the individuality, not to each soul that goes to make it up?

This instance will show what I mean, and how open we all lie to the remark, that we do not understand the doctrine of the distinct individuality of the human soul. We class men in masses, as we might connect the stones of a building. Consider our common way of regarding history, politics, commerce, and the like, and you will own that I speak truly. We generalize, and lay down laws, and then contemplate these creations of our own minds, and act upon and towards them, as if they were the real things, dropping what are more truly such. Take another instance: when we talk of national greatness, what does it mean? Why, it really means that a certain distinct definite number of immortal individual beings happen for a few years to be in circumstances to act together and one upon another, in such a way as to be able to act upon the world at large, to gain an ascendancy over the world, to gain power and wealth, and to look like one, and to be talked of and to be looked up to as one. They seem for a short time to be some one thing: and we, from our habit of living by sight, regard them as one, and drop the notion of their being any thing else. And when this one dies and that one dies, we forget that it is the passage of separate immortal beings into an unseen state, that the whole which appears is but appearance, and that the component parts are the realities. No, we think nothing of this; but though fresh and fresh men die, and fresh and fresh men are born, so that the whole is ever shifting, yet we forget all that drop away, and are insensible to all that are added; and we still think that this whole which we call the nation, is one and the same, and that the individuals who come and go, exist only in it and for it, and are but as the grains of a heap or the leaves of a tree.

Or again, survey some populous town: crowds are pouring through the streets; some on foot, some in carriages; while the shops are full, and the houses too, could we see into them. Every part of it is full of life. Hence we gain a general idea of splendour, magnificence, opulence, and energy. But what is the truth? why, that every being in that great concourse is his own centre, and all things about him are but shades, but a "vain shadow," in which he "walketh and disquieteth himself in vain." He has his own hopes and fears, desires, judgments, and aims; he is everything to himself, and no one else is really any thing. No one outside of him can really touch him, can touch his soul, his immortality; he must live with himself for ever. He has a depth within him unfathomable, an infinite abyss of existence; and the scene in which he bears part for the moment is but like a gleam of sunshine upon its surface.

Again: when we read history, we meet with accounts of great slaughters and massacres, great pestilences, famines, conflagrations, and so on; and here again we are accustomed in an especial way to regard collections of people as if individual units. We cannot understand that a multitude is a collection of immortal souls.

I say immortal souls: each of those multitudes, not only *had* while he was upon earth, but *has* a soul, which did in its own time but return to God who gave it, and not perish, and which now lives unto Him. All those millions upon millions of human beings who ever trod the earth and saw the sun successively, are at this very moment in existence all together. This, I think, you will grant we do not duly realize. All those Canaanites, whom the children of Israel slew, every one of them is somewhere in the universe, now at this moment, where God has assigned him a place. We read, "They utterly destroyed all that was in" Jericho, "young and old." Again, as to Ai; "So it was that all that fell that day, both of men and women, were twelve thousand." Again, "Joshua took Makkedah, Libnah, Lachish, Eglon, Hebron, Debir, and smote them with the edge of the sword, and utterly destroyed all the souls that were therein." [1] Every one of those souls still lives. They had their separate thoughts and feelings when on earth, they have them now. They had their likings and pursuits; they gained what they thought good and enjoyed it; and they still somewhere or other live, and what they then did in the flesh surely has its influence upon their present destiny. They live, reserved for a day which is to come, when all nations shall stand before God.

But why should I speak of the devoted nations of Canaan, when Scripture speaks of a wider, more comprehensive judgment, and in one place appears to hint at the present state of awful waiting in which they are who were involved in it? What an overwhelming judgment was the Flood! all human beings on the earth but eight were cut off by it. That old world of souls still lives, though its material tabernacle was drowned. Scripture, I say, signifies this; obscurely indeed, yet still, as it appears, certainly. St. Peter speaks of "the spirits in prison," that is, *then* in prison, who had been "disobedient," "when once the long-suffering of God waited in the days of Noah." [2] Those many, many souls, who were violently expelled from their bodies by the waters of the deluge, were alive two thousand years afterwards, when St. Peter wrote. Surely they are alive still.

And so of all the other multitudes we any where read of.—All the Jews who perished in the siege of Jerusalem, still live; Sennacherib's army still lives; Sennacherib himself still lives; all

[1] Jos. vi, viii, x.   [2] 1 Pet. iii.20.

the persecutors of the Church that ever were, are still alive. The kings of Babylon are still alive; they are still, as they are described by the Prophet, weak indeed now, and in "hell beneath," but having an account to give, and waiting for the day of summons. All who have ever gained a name in the world, all the mighty men of war that ever were, all the great statesmen, all the crafty counsellors, all the scheming aspirants, all the reckless adventurers, all the covetous traders, all the proud voluptuaries, are still in being, though helpless and unprofitable. Balaam, Saul, Joab, Ahithophel, good and bad, wise and ignorant, rich and poor, each has his separate place, each dwells by himself in that sphere of light or darkness, which he has provided for himself here. What a view this sheds upon history! We are accustomed to read it as a tale or a fiction, and we forget that it concerns immortal beings, who cannot be swept away, who are what they were, however this earth may change.

And so again all the names we see written on monuments in churches or churchyards, all the writers whose names and works we see in libraries, all the workmen who raised the great buildings, far and near, which are the wonder of the world, they are all in God's remembrance, they all live.

It is the same with those whom we ourselves have seen, who now are departed. I do not now speak of those whom we have known and loved. These we cannot forget; we cannot rid our memory of them: but I speak of all whom we have *ever* seen; it is also true that they live. Where we know not, but live they do. We may recollect when children, perhaps, once seeing a certain person; and it is almost like a dream to us now, that we did. It seems like an accident which goes and is all over, like some creature of the moment, which has no existence beyond it. The rain falls, and the wind blows; and showers and storms have no existence beyond the time when we felt them; they are nothing in themselves. But if we have but once seen any child of Adam, we have seen an immortal soul. It has not passed away as a breeze or sunshine, but it lives; it lives at this moment in one of those many places, whether of bliss or misery, in which all souls are reserved until the end.

Or again, let us call to mind those whom we knew a little better, though not intimately:—all who died suddenly or before their time, all whom we have seen in high health and spirits, all whom we have seen in circumstances which in any way brought out their characters, and gave them some place in our memories. They are gone from our sight, but they all live still, each with his own thoughts; they are waiting for the judgment.

I think we shall see that these thoughts concerning others are not familiar to us; yet no one can say they are not just. And I think too that the thoughts concerning others, which *are* familiar to us, are not those which become believers in the Gospel; whereas these which I have been tracing, do become us, as tending to make us think less of this world, with its hopes and fears, its plans, successes, and enjoyments.

Moreover, every one of all the souls which have ever been on earth is, as I have already implied, in one of two spiritual states, so distinct from one another, that the one is the subject of God's favour, and the other under His wrath; the one on the way to eternal happiness, the other to eternal misery. This is true of the dead, and is true of the living also. All are tending one way or the other; there is no middle or neutral state for any one; though as far as the sight of the external world goes, all men seem to be in a middle state common to one and all. Yet, much as men look the same, and impossible as it is for us to say where each man stands in God's sight, there are two, and but two classes of men, and these have characters and destinies as far apart in their tendencies as light and darkness: this is the case even of those who are in the body, and it is much more true of those who have passed into the unseen state.

No thought of course is more overpowering than that every one who lives or has lived is destined for endless bliss or torment. It is far too vast for us to realize. But what especially increases the mind's confusion when it attempts to do so, is just this very thing which I have been mentioning, that there are but these two states, that every individual among us is either in one or the other,—that the states in which we individually are placed are so unspeakably contrary to each other, while we look so like each other. It is certainly quite beyond our understandings, that all we should now be living together as relatives, friends, associates, neighbours; that we should be familiar or intimate with each other, that there should be among us a general intercourse, circulation of thought, interchange of good offices, the action of mind upon mind, and will upon will, and conduct upon conduct, and yet after all that there should be a bottomless gulf between us, running among us invisibly, and cutting us off into two parties;—not indeed a gulf impassable here, God be praised!—not impassable till we pass into the next world, still really existing, so that every person we meet is in God's unerring eye either on the one side or the other, and, did He please to take him hence at once, would find himself either in paradise or in the place of torment. Our Lord observes this

concerning the Day of Judgment, "Two women shall be grinding at the mill; the one shall be taken, and the other left. Two
men shall be in the field; the one shall be taken, and the other
left."

What makes this thought still more solemn, is that we have
reason to suppose that souls on the wrong side of the line are far
more numerous than those on the right. It is wrong to speculate; but it is safe to be alarmed. This much we know, that
Christ says expressly, "Many are called, few are chosen;"
"Broad is the way that leadeth to destruction, and many there
be who go in thereat;" whereas "narrow is the way that leadeth
to life, and few there be who find it."

If then it is difficult, as I have said it is, to realize that all who
ever lived still live, it is as difficult at least to believe that they
are in a state either of eternal rest or eternal woe; that all whom
we have known and who are gone, are, and that we who still
live, were we now to die, should then at once be, either in the
one state or the other. Nay, I will say more: when we think seriously on the subject, it is almost impossible to comprehend, I do
not say that a great number, but that any person whom we see
before us, however unsatisfactory appearances may be, is really
under God's displeasure, and in a state of reprobation. So hard
is it to live by faith! People feel it to be a difficulty to have to
admit certain other doctrines of the Church, which are more or
less contrary to sight. For instance, they say as an argument
against regeneration in Baptism, "Is it possible that all who
have been baptized can have been born again, considering what
lives they lead?" They make the evidence of sight tell against a
doctrine which demands their faith. Yet, after all, is there any
thing more startling, more difficult to believe, than that any
one person, whom we see, however sinful his life, is at present
under God's eternal wrath, and would incur it if he were to die
at once, and will incur it unless he repents? This is what we
cannot bring ourselves to believe. All we commonly allow is,
that certain persons are what we call "in *danger* of hell." Now, if
by using this cautious phrase we mean merely to express, that
irreligious men may repent before death, or that men may seem
to be irreligious to us, who are not so, and therefore that it is
safer to speak of men being in danger of God's wrath than actually under it; so far is well. But we are in error if we mean, as is
often the case, to deny thereby that irreligious men, as such,
whether man can ascertain them or not, are at this very time,
not only in danger, but actually under the power of God's
wrath. Healthy men in a sickly country may be said to be in

danger of sickness; soldiers in a battle are in danger of wounds; but irreligious men not only hazard, but do lie under God's eternal curse; and when we see an irreligious man, we see one who is under it, only we speak guardedly, both as hoping that he may repent, and as feeling that we may be mistaken. But whether or not men may be what they seem, or whether or not they are to change, certain it is that every one who dies, passes at once into one or other of two states; and if he dies unsanctified and unreconciled to God, into a state of eternal misery.

How little the world at large realizes this, is shewn by the conduct of surviving friends after a loss. Let a person who is taken away have been ever so notorious a sinner, ever so confirmed a drunkard, ever so neglectful of Christian ordinances, and though they have no reason for supposing any thing hopeful was going on in his mind, yet they will generally be found to believe that he has gone to heaven; they will confidently talk of his being at peace, of his pains being at an end, of his happy release, and the like. They enlarge on these subjects; whereas their duty lies in keeping silence, waiting in trembling hope, and being resigned. Now, why is it they speak and think in this manner? Apparently because they cannot conceive it possible that he or that they should be lost. Even the worst men have qualities which endear them to those who come near them. They have human affections in some shape or other. Even the witch of Endor showed a sympathy and kindness towards her guest, which move us. Human feelings cannot exist in hell, and we cannot bring ourselves to think that they are subjects of hell who have them. And for this reason men cannot admit the bare possibility of another being lost; they reject the idea, and therefore, when a man dies, they conclude, as the only alternative, that he must be in Abraham's bosom; and they boldly say so, and they catch at some half sentence which he said duing his illness, when he was calmer or weaker, or at the ease with which he died, in confirmation of their belief.

And if it is difficult to believe that there are any persons among us at this moment in a state of spiritual death, how shall we understand, what perchance is the case, that there are many such, perhaps multitudes? how shall we persuade ourselves of the great truth that, in spite of outward appearances, human society, as we find it, is but a part of an invisible world, and is really divided into but two companies, the sons of God, and the children of the wicked one; that some souls are ministered unto by Angels, others led captive by devils; that some are "fellow-citizens of the saints," and of the invisible "household of God," and others companions of those His enemies in time past, who now are waiting in prison for the judgment.

How blessed would it be, if we really understood this! What a change it would produce in our thoughts, unless we were utterly reprobate, to understand what and where we are,—accountable beings on their trial, with God for their friend and the devil for their enemy, and advanced a certain way on their road either to heaven or to hell. No truths indeed, ever so awful, ever so fully brought home to the mind, will change it, if the love of God and of holiness be not there; but none among us, as we may humbly trust, is in this reprobate state. One wishes to think that no one has so done despite to the Spirit of grace, and so sinned against the Blood of the Covenant, as to have nothing of his regenerate nature left to him; no one among us, but, if he shut his eyes to the external world, and opened them to the world within him, contemplated his real state and prospects, and called to mind his past life, would be brought to repentance and amendment. Endeavour then, my brethren, to realize that you have souls, and pray God to enable you to do so. Endeavour to disengage your thoughts and opinions from the things that are seen; look at things as God looks at them, and judge of them as He judges. Pass a very few years and you will actually experience what as yet you are called on to believe. There will be no need of the effort of mind to which I invite you, when you have passed into the unseen state. There will be no need of shutting your eyes to this world, when this world has vanished from you, and you have nothing before you but the throne of God, and the slow but continual movements about it in preparation of the judgment. In that interval, when you are in that vast receptacle of disembodied souls, what will be your thoughts about the world which you have left! how poor will then seem to you its highest aims, how faint its keenest pleasures, compared with the eternal aims, the infinite pleasures, of which you will at length feel your souls to be capable! O, my brethren, let this thought be upon you day by day, especially when you are tempted to sin. Avoid sin as a serpent; it looks and promises well; it bites afterwards. It is dreadful in memory, dreadful even on earth; but in that awful period, when the fever of life is over, and you are waiting in silence for the judgment, with nothing to distract your thoughts, who can say how dreadful may be the memory of sins done in the body? Then the very apprehension of their punishment, when Christ shall suddenly visit, will doubtless outweigh a thousand-fold the gratification, such as it was, which you felt in committing them; and if so, what will be the proportion between it and that punishment, if after all it be actually inflicted? Let us lay to heart our Saviour's own most merciful words, "Be not afraid," He says, "of them that kill the body, and after that have no more that they can do. But I will forewarn you, whom ye shall fear. Fear Him, which, after He hath killed, hath power to cast into hell. Yea, I say unto you, Fear Him."

CHASTISEMENT AMID MERCY

"Rejoice not against me, O mine enemy; when I fall, I shall arise;
when I sit in darkness, the Lord shall be a light unto me. I will bear
the indignation of the Lord, because I have sinned against Him."
—Micah vii.8, 9.

I T very commonly happens that men, who in youth or early life live in a thoughtless way, without restraint over themselves, not indeed scoffing or objecting against religion, but running into sin more or less according to the accident of external temptations, as time goes on and they get older, or when they get settled in life, or from other causes, become more serious than they were, and turn out what is called respectable and excellent men. Nay, persons who have gone farther than this, who have led really bad lives,—been drunkards and profligates, or even unbelievers, are tamed down in the course of years, and become decent or well conducted, or even religious; nay, not only in appearance religious, but perhaps they become really good men, bent on doing their duty, and making up for what they have done wrong, so that one cannot help feeling love and respect for them. And what is the conduct of the world in such cases? It is very generous, or rather indulgent. It passes over every thing that has happened, and regards and treats them just as if they had never gone wrong. And what again is the conduct towards them of a great number of religious men? They conclude in the case of those who display a fair appearance of seriousness in their present behaviour, that God has absolutely and utterly forgiven all that has passed, as if it had never been committed; and, with that sort of liberality, in so many ways now common, so untrue, yet so easy to those who exercise it, they give away freely what is not theirs to give, and speak and act as if it lay with them to pronounce God's "absolution and remission" of the sins of others. And what effect has such treatment on those who are the subjects of it? Of course, to make them forget that they have been sinners, and to consider themselves on a level with those who have never been sinners. So that they never look back at their past lives with fear; but, rather, when they speak of the past, there is in their tone sometimes even something of tenderness and affection for their former selves;—or at best they speak of themselves in a sort of moralizing way, as they might of sinners they read of, as if it was not now *their* concern what they then were, or as if the contrast between what they were and are did but set off to advantage their present spiritual state. And thus, without going to those somewhat extreme cases, where a man almost makes his former sins a mode of entering *into* God's favour, a sort of necessary preparation for being spiritually-minded, and so far a sort of boast and glory, there are a very great many cases, I fear, where persons, religious and well-meaning, according to the ordinary standard, are little or not at all impressed with the notion that their past sins, whether from their moral consequences, or as remembered by God, are a present disadvantage to them.

This, I conceive, in one shape or other, to be a very common state of mind. For instance, I can fancy persons, especially young persons, coming into temptation, and from one cause or other, through God's mercy, escaping from it. Either the temptation went before they could make up their minds to the sin, or their minds were diverted in other ways. And I can fancy them afterwards, it is a shocking thing to say, vexed with themselves that they did not commit the sin to which they were tempted; as if it now would be over,—as if they would not in such a case be worse now than they actually are, and they would have enjoyed the "pleasures of sin for a season," but, as it is, had lost an opportunity. Now a person who so feels, clearly does not understand that sin *leaves* a burden upon the soul, which has to be got rid of. He thinks it is done and over,—the question of guilt, pollution, punishment not occurring to him. Nothing surely is more common among persons of the most various characters of mind than thus to think that God forgets sin as soon as we forget it.

Again: take another instance, applicable especially at this time. Whole bodies of men rush into sin, and while they sin, even do not allow that they sin, because each shelters himself behind the other, and thinks that what is no one person's sin is no sin at all. This of itself is a strange view of the case, yet it is very common. Men call themselves the *nation* when they sin in a body, and think that the nation, being a name, has nothing to answer for, and may do what it will; that its acts are only the "course of events," and necessary, as the motion of the earth. They do very rash acts, without the fear of God before their eyes, making large and bold changes (whether allowably or not, is not here the question; their plain fault being that they do not ask themselves whether or not it *is* allowable,—the question does not enter their minds); I say they make large changes,— they endanger God's holy religion,—they encourage scoffers and deceivers. Then, perhaps, they see they have gone too far, and they change their course; perhaps try to reverse what they have done. Now the thought never crosses them that any one has any thing to repent of; or, if they are determined to put the blame on the nation, that the nation has any thing to repent of. Accordingly, persons who hail the return of any portion of the nation to a sounder state of mind, never hint or seem to feel that a national sin has been committed, that Almighty God has books in which are set down the events of every year and day, books which will be opened at the Day of Judgment, and men judged out of them.

Further: perhaps particular *persons* have been forward in the evil course, in direct opposition to the cause of truth and holiness; and *they* change their mind and adopt another line of (what is called) politics. They are right in so doing; but no one ever seems to doubt that the change wipes out the fault, no one ever has the real kindness to hint to them that they have committed a sin: to show any recollection of the past is thought to arise, as it often does, from personal feeling, and to be impolitic and unwise. Such persons are hailed as a succour, not thoughtfully and religiously regarded as penitents.

Many other instances might be given from which it is clear that men commonly think a sin to be cancelled when it is done and over, or, in other words, that *amendment is an expiation.* If I were to give this tone of mind a name, I should call it a practical Socinianism.

Now it will be answered that the merits of our Lord Jesus Christ are sufficient to wash out all sin, and that they really do wash it out. Doubtless; but the question to be decided is, whether He has promised to apply His all-sufficient merits at once on persons doing nothing more than changing their mode of living. Surely if any truth of the Bible is clear, it is that He gives to those who ask, not to those who do not ask. Yet the fact is, as I would maintain, that men in general do not take the trouble to ask, or, in other words, to repent; but they think the change, or apparent change or improvement itself stands instead of repentance, as a sort of means, a sacramental means, imparting forgiveness by itself by its own virtue, as a work done;—or they think that the state of grace in which they are is such as to absorb (as it were) and consume all sin as fast as it springs up in the heart;—or they think that faith has this power of obliterating and annihilating sin, so that in fact there is nothing on their conscience to repent of. They consider faith as superseding repentance. Such seem to be their thoughts, as far as they have any on the subject.

But, again: it may be objected that we are told that "there is joy in heaven over one sinner that repenteth." But I reply as before, that the persons I am speaking of do not repent, unless the mere fact of amendment be repentance. We may, if we please, maintain that there is no such thing as repentance distinct from amendment; that the feeling, whatever it is, which prompts amendment, is repentance, or includes repentance; that the word repentance is, practically speaking, but a figure of speech, and means reformation. But let us speak plainly, if such is our meaning, and then we shall have to prove it from Scripture. For surely Scripture cannot be said thus to hide or dissipate repentance in other acts or courses of conduct. It surely describes it as a duty, distinct from other duties,—as a condition distinct, though of course inseparable, from other conditions, such as faith and amendment may be. We have instances of acts of faith in Scripture, and instances of acts of repentance; and it would be as reasonable to say there is no such Christian grace as faith, because it is ever joined with and lives in other graces, as to say that repentance is not a real, substantive, and independent exercise of mind, because it presupposes faith, and terminates in amendment. When St. Peter said, "Thou art the Christ, the Son of the Living God," this was an act of faith; when he "went out and wept bitterly," this was an act of repentance;—when the Prodigal Son said, "I will arise and go to my father," this was an act of faith; when he said, "Make me as one of thy hired servants," this was an act of repentance. When "the Publican did not so much as lift up his eyes unto heaven, but smote upon his breast, saying, God be merciful to me a sinner," this was an act of repentance. When the woman who had been a sinner washed our Saviour's feet with her tears and wiped them with the hairs of her head, this was an act of repentance in one who loved much. When Zacchaeus gave half his goods to the poor, and restored fourfold what he had wrongfully obtained, this was an act of repentance in one who would fain undo the past. They are acts of a mind lingering and engaged in the past, as hope is engaged in contemplating the future. It is common enough at present to speak lightly of the past, as if it *was* past and could not be helped, as if we could not reverse the past. We cannot literally reverse it; yet surely instances such as the foregoing are the acts of persons who would if they could; who, as it were, are trying to do so, and in a manner doing so from the intense feeling of their hearts. Regret, vexation, sorrow, such feelings seem to this busy, practical, unspiritual generation as idle; as something despicable and unmanly,—just as tears may be. And many men think it religious to say that such feelings argue a want of faith in Christ's merits. They *are* unbelieving, they *are* irrational, if they are nothing more than remorse, bitterness, gloom, and despondency. Such is "the sorrow of the world" which "worketh death." Yet there is a "godly sorrow" also; a positive sorrowing for sin, and a deprecation of its consequences and that quite distinct from faith or amendment; and this, so far from being a barren sorrow, "worketh," as the Apostle assures us, "repentance to salvation, not to be repented of." "Behold this selfsame thing," continues the Apostle to the Corinthians, "that ye sorrowed after a godly sort, what carefulness it wrought in you, yea what clearing of yourselves, yea what indignation, yea what fear, yea what vehement desire, yea what zeal, yea what revenge! In all things ye have approved yourselves to be clear in this matter." [1] Faith, then, neither is repentance, nor stands instead of it.

Here, however, we are met with another objection. It is said if a man be changed in heart and life, this is a plain proof that he has been revisited by God's grace; and if so, he is in God's favour, *or* in other words, his past sins are already forgiven him. I answer by denying what is here assumed; I would say, then, that a man may be in God's favour, yet his sins not absolutely forgiven; that faith brings him, that is, his person, into God's favour, yet a long repentance may be the only remedy for his past deeds; that faith brings him into God's favour at once, that he may receive grace to repent continually.

It may seem a contradiction, first to say that God loves a man, and next that some remnant of His displeasure is in store for him; but we are so profoundly ignorant of Him, whose thoughts and ways are not as ours, that if we have proof of the fact in His inspired word, it is our wisdom to believe that it is a fact, and leave difficulties to Him who in His good time will explain them. For instance; few persons, comparatively speaking, would maintain that a man once in a state of grace cannot fall away; now here in like manner, it might be asked how can God at present love one whom He has appointed to everlasting punishment? As, then, souls may be at present in God's favour,

---

[1] 2 Cor. vii.10, 11.

whom He foresees to be His impenitent enemies, and companions of devils for ever, so others also much more may be in His
favour, against whom an unsettled reckoning lies, the issue of
which is future, who have certain sins as yet unforgiven, and
certain consequences of sins as yet unprovided for. The young
man whom our Lord bade give up all and follow Him, went
away sorrowful and unforgiven; yet Christ is said to have "loved
him." Again, how is it that God is loving over all His works, yet
is angry with the wicked? His love then does not necessarily
exclude His anger, nor His favour His severity, nor His grace
His justice. How He reconciles these together we know not:
thus much we know, that those who forsake their sins, and
come to Him for grace, are in His favour, and obtain what they
need for the day; but that they are forgiven at once for all the
past, we do not know.

The following instances from Scripture seem to prove the
contrary:—When David, for example, said to Nathan, "I have
sinned against the Lord," this act of repentance was allowed to
avail for much. "Nathan said unto David, the Lord also hath
put away thy sin; *thou shalt not die.*" The extreme debt of sin was
remitted; yet the Prophet goes on to say, "Howbeit, because by
this deed thou hast given great occasion to the enemies of the
Lord to blaspheme, the child also that is born unto thee shall
surely die." [2] David then had the prospect of a punishment for
his sin after it was remitted, and what did he do in consequence? he sought to deprecate God; he exercised in acts of repentance, that life of faith and prayer which had been renewed
in him, if so be to deprecate God's wrath. As then he was not
allowed to take his restoration as a proof that God would not
punish, neither have we any ground to conclude, merely because God vouchsafes to work in us what is good, that therefore what is past will never rise up in judgment against us. It
may, or it may not: we trust, nay may cheerfully confide, that
if we go on confessing, repenting, deprecating, and making
amends, it will not: but there is no reason to suppose it will not
unless we do.

Again: Moses was excluded from the promised land for
speaking unadvisedly with his lips. Was he therefore "blotted
out of God's book?" Was he not in a justified state, though under punishment? and does not that great Saint show us how to
meet the prospect of God's judgments, when he earnestly supplicates God to pardon him what seemed so small a sin, and to

[2] 2 Sam. xii.13, 14.

let him go over Jordan? And can we have a more striking instance of this double condition in which we stand, after sinning and returning, than when so great a Saint as Moses, who was faithful in all the house of God, who saw God's face, and was the mediator for His people, yet beseeches Him, "O Lord God, ... I pray Thee, let me go over and see the good land that is beyond Jordan, that goodly mountain, and Lebanon;" and the Almighty remains still unappeased, and "will not hear" him, and says, "Let it suffice thee; speak no more unto Me of this matter?" [3] Yet Moses, though he did not gain all he would by his earnest prayer, gained something. His punishment was lightened. He was allowed to ascend Pisgah, and see the land.

Again: when the prophet from Judah had disobediently turned back to the old prophet's house, and had death denounced against him, and was met by the lion, was he at that moment in God's favour or not? Must we suppose, because he died under a judgment, that he died impenitent and unreconciled, and had his portion with Jeroboam and the worshippers of calves?

However, it may be objected to these instances, that they come from the Old Testament, that they took place before Christ came, and that little indeed is said in the New Testament about the chance of such judgments, and the necessity of such deprecation on the part of Christians. In answer, I allow that there is very little in the New Testament concerning the punishment of Christians; but then there is as little said about their sins; so that if Scripture negatives everything which it is silent about, it would be as easy to show that the Gospel does not belong at all to those who have lapsed into sin, as that punishments are not their portion, and penitential acts not their duty. As the sins of Christians are beyond the ordinary contemplation of Scripture, so are their remedies.

It will take some time to show this of the New Testament, yet it is worth attempting it from its importance. I say, then, that many as are the passages in the New Testament, which describe a state of salvation, none of them, excepting one or two, mention pardon as among the *continual* privileges of that state, or otherwise than as a gift once given on entering into it. The notion of sins in Christians, other than sins of infirmity, is, for whatever reason, scarcely contemplated in Scripture. And the few texts that speak of pardon, such as "If any man sin, we have an Advocate with the Father," do not deny that *means* are

[3] Deut. iii.24–26; *vide* also Exod. xxxii.34.

necessary to interest ourselves in that pardon; whereas there are many texts on the other hand which do allude to acts of penitence and satisfaction as necessary in order to the pardon. For instance, St. Paul, as above cited, speaks of such acts in the case of the Corinthians; and St. James as decisively of "*mercy*," *i.e.* almsgiving and the like, "rejoicing against judgment." Now to show this at length.

Now, first, I need hardly call to mind the passages in which sins are expressly declared to be forgiven when persons *first* enter into the kingdom of God. For instance, "Arise, and be baptized, and wash away thy sins,"[4] says Ananias to St. Paul before his baptism. So St. Peter to the multitude, "Repent, and be baptized every one of you in the name of Jesus Christ, for the *remission of sins*." But what was to follow? "and ye shall receive the gift of the Holy Ghost."[5] This, then, was to be their state *henceforth*, not a state of sinning, but of the Spirit of holiness; their divine birth and life were such as to need no forgiveness, in the sense in which they had needed it before. Hence in the verses which follow we read, "they continued stedfastly in the Apostles' doctrine and fellowship, and in breaking of bread and in prayers. . . . . All that believed were together, and had all things common, and sold their possessions and goods, and parted them to all men as every man had need; and they, continuing daily with one accord in the temple, and breaking bread from house to house, did eat their meat with gladness and singleness of heart, praising God, and having favour with all the people."[6] Or again, take St. Paul's description, "Being justified by faith, we have peace with God through our Lord Jesus Christ, by whom we have access by faith into this grace wherein we stand, and rejoice in hope of the glory of God; and not only so, but we glory in tribulations also, knowing that tribulation worketh patience, and patience experience." And so he proceeds enumerating the fruits of the Holy Ghost in the heart, but not a word about fresh sins and fresh forgiveness in that state; as if while we remain in the Holy Ghost, this could not be. Again, in the third chapter of the same Epistle, he speaks of "the remission of sins that *are past*," not a word of sins which are to come. In another Epistle, he says that Christ is the Mediator "for the redemption of the transgressions that were under the *first* Testament;" he does not say "under the *second*." St. Peter, in like manner, after going through the parts of a Christian character, faith, virtue, knowledge, temperance, and the like, adds,

---

[4] Acts xxii.16.   [5] Acts ii.38.   [6] Acts ii.42–47.

"He that lacketh these things is blind, and cannot see afar off, and is forgetful of the *cleansing from his former sins*."[7] Thus he reminds such a one of that former cleansing, and is silent about any second cleansing for his lack of holiness. Again, St. John addresses three classes of Christians,—beginners, the manly, and the mature; he reminds the beginners of the forgiveness of their sins, for this was the peculiar privilege of those who were just entering the kingdom—"I write unto you, little children, because your sins have been forgiven you for His Name's sake;"[8] but this is not said to the other two; no, the young men in the faith are those who "are *strong*, and the word of God abideth in them, and they *have overcome* the wicked one;" and the elders are they who "have known Him that is from the beginning." Thus is Christian life marked out,—first forgiveness, then warfare, then contemplation; whereas the chief notion, that many men now have of a saving state, is but of a warfare which is disgraced with defeat, and of a contemplation disjoined from holiness.

Far different is the Apostles' way of viewing the Christian state. We are taken from sin, not forgiven in it merely. For instance; this is St. Peter's account of our election in Christ—"Who His own self bare our sins in His own body on the tree, *that* we *being dead to sins, should live unto righteousness*; by whose stripes ye *were* healed. For ye *were* as sheep going astray, but are now returned unto the Shepherd and Bishop of your souls."[9] And St. Paul, "Who gave Himself for us, that he might redeem us from all iniquity, *and purify unto Himself a peculiar people*, zealous of good works."[10] You see that the Apostles' one broad idea of a state of salvation is one, not of sinning and being forgiven, but of holiness; though now men often consider that the *highest* excellence of a Christian is to cry out, "O wretched man that I am!" Again, "How much more shall the blood of Christ, who through the Eternal Spirit offered Himself without spot to God, purge your *conscience from* dead works *to serve* the living God?"[11] Again, in another Epistle he speaks of forgiveness emphatically as *the* forgiveness, *the* redemption, as if there were but one great forgiveness;—"In whom we have *the* redemption through His blood, *the* forgiveness of sins;"[12] and he says just before that, "He hath chosen us . . . . . that *we should be holy* and without blame before Him in love." And in another chapter, "Christ . . . . . loved the Church and gave Himself for it, that

---

[7] 2 Pet. i.9.   [8] 1 John ii.12.   [9] 1 Pet. ii.24, 25.
[10] Tit. ii.14.   [11] Heb. ix.14.   [12] Eph. i.7.

He might sanctify it, cleansing it in the *washing of water* by the word;"[13] *then* is the forgiveness, and why? The Apostle proceeds, "*That* He might present it unto Himself a *glorious* Church, not having spot or wrinkle, or any such thing, but that it should be *holy* and without blemish."

In like manner, the prayers and good wishes which the Apostles send their brethren do not contain any prayers for forgiveness. This is remarkable; they pray God to bless them, and make them more and more holy, and the like, but not to pardon their sins. Not as if Christians do not sin; I began by assuming that, alas, they do; I only say that the New Testament mainly contemplates them in a higher state, and gives little information how to treat them as we actually find them; and therefore obliges us to have recourse to the Old Testament. For instance, St. Paul prays for the Ephesians, that they may have "the spirit of *wisdom* and *revelation*," have the "eyes of their understanding *enlightened*," discern "the riches of the glory of God's inheritance," and "the exceeding greatness of His power;" may be "strengthened with *might* by His Spirit in the inner man," and be "rooted and grounded in *love*."[14] He prays for the Thessalonians that their "whole spirit and soul and body may be preserved *blameless* unto the coming of the Lord Jesus Christ;"[15] that "God which hath given us everlasting consolation, and good hope through grace, may comfort their hearts, and *stablish* them in every good word and work;"[16] that "the Lord may make them increase and abound in love one toward another . . . . . to the end that He may establish their hearts *unblameable* in holiness before God;"[17] what a strong word "unblameable" is, and "unblameable *before God!*" This was what He aimed at for them, not that they should be forgiven, but that they should not sin. Again, for the Hebrews, that God would "make them *perfect* in every good work to do His will, working in them that which is well-pleasing in His sight through Jesus Christ."[18] In like manner, St. Peter prays for his brethren, that God may "perfect, stablish, strengthen, settle them;"[19] and St. Jude exhorts them "building up themselves on their most holy faith, praying in the Holy Ghost, to *keep themselves* in the love of God, looking for the mercy of our Lord Jesus Christ unto eternal life," and gives glory to Him "who is *able* to *keep* them from falling" (he does not say to pardon, as if *that* was the end of the

---

[13] Eph. v.26.

[14] Eph. i.17–19; iii.16, 17.

[15] 1 Thess. v.23.

[16] 2 Thess. ii.16, 17.   [17] 1 Thess. iii.13.

[18] Heb. xiii.21.

[19] 1 Pet. v.10.

Gospel), "and to present them before the presence of His glory with exceeding joy." Now, considering the number of passages I have quoted, surely it is very remarkable, even before we know what is to be found in other places, even supposing a forgiveness of sins, after the one great forgiveness and like it, is mentioned somewhere else, it is very remarkable (I say) that it should not be mentioned in all these. Can we doubt that under the Gospel sins were not to be *expected*, to say the least; and, as far as these passages go, were not *provided* for in it?

But let us turn our thoughts to some more extended passages of Scripture. Consider, for instance, St. Paul's Epistle to the Ephesians, detached passages of which have already been cited. The whole of it is addressed to Christians; and though there is abundant mention of their blessedness as being such, in various ways, yet the idea of continual forgiveness does not suggest itself as one of their privileges;—just as the forgiveness of sins is not mentioned as a privilege to be enjoyed by Saints in heaven, or by the Angels, for they do not need it, in like manner, Christians are called from sin unto holiness, and at least ought not to need it. Thus in the fourth and fifth chapters there is a description of the Church in the way of precept which exactly answers to its actual state, as described in history, in the second chapter of the Acts. Christians were to be followers of God as dear children, to walk in love as Christ had loved them, to walk circumspectly, to redeem the time, to be filled with the Spirit, and to be instant in praises and thanksgivings. Grievous crimes *are* mentioned also, and we are warned against them; but how? does St. Paul for an instant suppose that a Christian, remaining a Christian, can be guilty of them? Does he say, if a Christian is unclean, or covetous, or the like, that of course he must repent indeed and amend, but still that he is safe if he has faith? Far from it; he speaks as if such sins were impossible in Christians; he does not enter into the case of a Christian who has been guilty of them. "For this *ye know*, that no fornicator, nor unclean person, nor covetous man, ... *hath any inheritance* in the kingdom of Christ and God." Therefore the Apostle warns his brethren not to be "*partakers* with the children of disobedience, for they *were* darkness, but *are* light in the Lord," in that Spirit, whose fruit is "goodness, righteousness, and truth," and in that light which detects all that is evil; for the words have been spoken over them, "Awake, thou that sleepest, and arise from the dead, and Christ shall give thee light."

Now consider, again, the sixth and eighth chapters of the Romans, which are more remarkable because they are in contrast with other parts of the Epistle. In the seventh chapter, St. Paul speaks of a state in which there was no forgiveness also; but of what state? one of spiritual death and despair; our state *by nature*. In it the absence of pardon is the cause of eternal woe, but in the Christian state it is the consequence of the gift of grace. The Apostle declares that there is no condemnation to those who are in the Spirit; why? because "the righteousness of the law *is* fulfilled in them;" how? by "the law of the Spirit of life," or (as he says in the Epistle last quoted) because the fruit of the Spirit is "goodness, righteousness, and truth." Again, in the sixth chapter, which also describes the Christian state, there is not a hint of forgiveness being a special privilege of a state of grace; but rather Christians, "being made free from sin," are said to become "the servants of *righteousness*." All this is very different from what the Apostle said in the third chapter, when speaking of our state by nature, and justification out of it. There *forgiveness of sins* is dwelt on. It is remarkable that it should *then* be dwelt on and that it should not afterwards.

Once more, consider the first chapter of St. James's Epistle. There *temptation* is spoken of, as it is by St. Paul in a passage already quoted. St. Paul speaks of it, not as causing us to fall, but as a means of our becoming holier. "We *glory* in tribulations also, knowing that tribulation worketh patience, and patience experience, and experience hope, and hope maketh *not ashamed*," [20] or as the Psalmist says, "They had an eye unto Him and were lightened, and their faces were not ashamed;" [21]— there is no shame in the Church. Such is St. Paul's view of trial to the Christian; such is St. James's also; "My brethren," he says, "count it all *joy* when ye fall into divers temptations, knowing this, that the trying of your faith worketh patience; and let patience have her perfect work." [22] Then he bids them ask of God wisdom, speaks of good gifts and perfect gifts coming from the Father of Lights, and of pure religion and undefiled; but not a word of sins to be forgiven: on the contrary, he declares that wilful sin, such as temptations may occasion, is the beginning of a course which "when finished bringeth forth death;" whereas the real Christian *overcomes* temptation, or, as St. John says, "overcomes the world," not falls under it. "Blessed is the man that endureth temptation, for when he is tried, he shall receive the *crown of life*, which the Lord hath promised to them that *love* Him;" words which singularly correspond to St. Paul's at the end of his trial, "*I have* fought a good

[20] Rom. v.3–5.   [21] Ps. xxxiv.5.   [22] James i.2–4.

fight, I have finished my course, I have kept the faith; hence-forth there is laid up for me a *crown* of righteousness, which the Lord the righteous Judge shall give me at that day; and not to me only, but unto all them also that *love* His appearing." [23] Moreover, there is this additional remark to be made about St. James's Epistle, that, whereas there are one or two passages in which he addresses, not Christians, but Jews, there he does speak at once of conversion, submission, purification, and approach to God. Now it is not strange he should speak of these things to the unregenerate; but it is strange he should not also speak of them to Christians, if he contemplated the case of Christians reducing themselves to a state like that of the unregenerate. Since, then, he, as well as the other Apostles, does not treat of an unhappy condition, which now occurs so frequently, it is not wonderful that he and they do not give its symptoms, dangers, or remedies, or enlarge, whether upon those judgments or those penitential observances, which in the case of sinners as yet unregenerate, the Gospel and the Old Testament describe.

However, I observe lastly, there *are* instances of declension both of faith and conduct in the Corinthians and Galatians. St. Paul writes to both. He arraigns and remonstrates with them. Does he give them one hint that if they believe in Christ's atoning power, those particular sins of theirs will be at once remitted?

To sum up then, and apply what I have said:—When Christians have gone wrong in any way, whether in belief or in practice, scandalously or secretly, it seems that pardon is not explicitly and definitely promised them in Scripture as a matter of course; and the mere fact that they afterwards become better men, and are restored to God's favour, does not decide the question whether they are in every sense pardoned; for David was restored and yet was afterwards punished. It is still a question whether a debt is not standing against them for their past sins, and is not now operating or to operate to their disadvantage. What its payment consists in, and how it will be exacted, is quite another question, and a hidden one. It may be such, if they die under it, as to diminish their blessedness in heaven; or it may be a sort of obstacle here to their rising to certain high points of Christian character; or it may be a hindrance to their ever attaining one or other particular Christian grace in perfection,—faith, purity, or humility; or it may prevent religion

[23] 2 Tim. iv. 7, 8.

taking deep root within them and imbuing their minds; or it
may make them more liable to fall away; or it may hold them
back from that point of attainment which is the fulfilment of
their trial; or it may forfeit for them the full assurance of hope;
or it may lessen their peace and comfort in the intermediate
state, or even delay their knowledge there of their own salvation; or it may involve the necessity of certain temporal punishments, grievous bodily disease, or sharp pain, or worldly
affliction, or an unhappy death. Such things are "secrets of the
Lord our God,"—not to be pried into, but to be acted upon. We
are all more or less sinners against His grace, many of us grievous sinners; and St. Paul and the other Apostles give us very
scanty information what the consequences of such sin are. God
may spare us, He may punish. In either case, however, our duty
is to surrender ourselves into His hands, that He may do what
He will. "It is the Lord," said pious Eli, when judgment came
on him, "let Him do what seemeth Him good." Only let us beg
of Him not to forsake us in our miserable state; to take us up
where we are, and make us obey Him under the circumstances
into which sin has brought us. Only let us beg of Him to work
all repentance and all righteousness in us, for we can do nothing
of ourselves, and to enable us to hate sin truly, and confess it
honestly, and deprecate His wrath continually, and to undo its
effects diligently, and to bear His judgments cheerfully and
manfully. Let us beg of Him the spirit of faith and hope, that we
may not repine or despond, or account Him a hard master; that
we may learn lovingly to adore the hand that afflicts us, and, as
it is said, to kiss the rod, however sharply or long it smites us;
that we may look on to the end of all things, which will not
tarry, and to the coming of Christ which will at length save us,
and not faint on the rough way, nor toss upon our couch of
thorns; in a word, that we may make the words of the text our
own, which express all that sinners repentant and suffering,
should feel, whether towards God or towards their tempter.
"Rejoice not against me, O mine enemy: when I fall, I shall
arise; when I sit in darkness, the Lord shall be a light unto me. I
will bear the indignation of the Lord, because I have sinned
against Him; until He plead my cause, and execute judgment
for me: He will bring me forth to the light, and I shall behold
His righteousness."

PEACE AND JOY
AMID CHASTISEMENT

"Though He slay me, yet will I trust in Him."—Job xiii.15.

THIS is a sentiment which often occurs in Scripture whether expressed in words or implied in the conduct of good men. It is founded on the belief that God is our sole strength, our sole refuge; that if good is in any way in store for us, it lies with God; if it is attainable, it is attained by coming to God. Though we be in evil case even after coming to Him, we are sure to be in still worse, if we keep away. If He will but allow sinners such as we are to approach Him, for that is the only question, then it is our wisdom to approach Him at once in such a way as He appoints or appears to approve. At all events, there is no one else we can go to; so that if He refuses to receive us, we are undone. And on the other hand, if He does receive us, then we must be ready to submit to His will, whatever it is towards us, pleasant or painful. Whether He punishes us or not, or how far pardons, or how far restores, or what gifts He bestows, rests with Him; and it is our part to take good or bad, as He gives it.

This is the general feeling which St. Peter seems to express in one way, when he cries out, "Lord, to whom shall we go? Thou hast the words of eternal life." It is the feeling under different circumstances and in a different tone, of the Prodigal Son, when He said, "I will arise, and go to my Father, and will say unto Him, Father, I have sinned against heaven and before thee, and am no more worthy to be called thy son; make me as one of thy hired servants." It shows itself under the form of peace and joy in the words of David: "Yea, though I walk through the valley of the shadow of death, I will fear no evil, for Thou art with me;" and it speaks in the text by the mouth of the heavily afflicted and sorely perplexed Job, "Though He slay me, yet will I trust in Him." Inquirers seeking the truth, prodigals repentant, saints rejoicing in the light, saints walking in darkness, all of them have one word on their lips, one creed in their hearts,—to "trust in the Lord for ever, for with the Lord Jehovah is everlasting strength."

There is another case different from all of these, in which it is equally our duty and wisdom thus to stay ourselves upon God; that of our being actually under punishment for our sins. Job maintained his innocence, which his friends denied, as thinking his afflictions were a judgment upon some secret wickedness now coming to light. He, on the other hand, being conscious of his integrity and sincerity in time past, could but wait in the darkness till God revealed why He chastised as a sinner, one who had been "perfect and upright, one that feared God and eschewed evil."[1] But men may often be conscious that they have incurred God's displeasure, and conscious that they are suffering it; and then their duty is still to trust in God, to acquiesce or rather to concur in His chastisements, as if they were a self-inflicted penance, and not the strokes of His rod. For God is our merciful Father, and when He afflicts His sons, yet it is not willingly; and though in one sense it is in judgment, yet in another and higher, it is in mercy. He provides that what is in itself an evil should become a good; and, while He does not supersede the original law of His just government, that suffering should follow sin, He overrules it to be a healing medicine as well as a punishment. Thus, "in wrath" He "remembers mercy." Thus St. Paul decides, quoting the words of Solomon, "My son, despise not thou the chastening of the Lord, nor faint when thou art rebuked of Him; for whom the Lord loveth He chasteneth, and scourgeth every son whom He receiveth."[2] You see he calls it a "chastisement" and a "rebuke," but still it is in "love;" and it is our duty to take it as such, and to bless and praise Him under it.

And Scripture affords us some remarkable instances of persons glorifying, or called on to glorify God, when under His hand, some of which it may be well here to mention.

One which deserves especial notice is Joshua's exhortation to Achan, who was about to be put to death for secreting a portion of the spoils of Jericho, and was thus dying apparently under the very rod, and (if any man ever), without encouragement to trust in God, or hope of profit in serving Him. "My son," Joshua says to him, "give, I pray thee, glory to the Lord God of Israel, and make confession unto Him." Thus he began; yet observe, his next words were as severe as if no duty, no consolation, were left to the offender,—despair only. He continues thus sternly, "Why hast thou troubled us? the Lord shall trouble thee this day." "And all Israel stoned him with stones,

---

[1] Job i.1.   [2] Heb. xii.5, 6.

and burned them with fire," him "and his sons and his daughters," "after they had stoned them with stones."[5]

Another remarkable instance is given us in the history of Jonah; I mean, in his address to Almighty God out of the fish's belly. It illustrates most appositely the case of a true, though erring servant of God, chastised, yet blessing God under the chastisement, and submitting himself even without any clear prospect how he was to escape from it.—"I cried," he says, "by reason of my affliction unto the Lord, and He heard me; out of the belly of hell cried I, and Thou heardest my voice. For Thou hadst cast me into the deep, in the midst of the seas, and the floods compassed me about; all Thy billows and Thy waves passed over me. Then I said, I am cast out of Thy sight; yet I will look again toward Thy Holy Temple. . . . . When my soul fainted within me, I remembered the Lord; and my prayer came in unto Thee, into Thine Holy Temple. They that observe lying vanities forsake their own mercy. But I will sacrifice unto Thee with the voice of thanksgiving; I will pay that that I have vowed. Salvation is of the Lord."[4]

Now, one should think, nothing could be more simple to understand than the state of mind described, however hard it be to realize; I mean the combined feeling that God loves us yet punishes us, that we are in His favour, yet are under, or may be brought under His rod; the feeling of mingled hope and fear, of suspense, of not seeing our way, yet having a general conviction that God will bring us on it, if we trust to Him. And this the more so, because very few indeed, or rather none at all, but must be conscious, if they get themselves to think, that they have grievously offended God at various times, in spite of all He has done for them; and that, for what they know, Christ's merits may not be so imputed to them as to exempt them from some punishment, which will demand in them the feelings I have been describing. Yet so it is, at least in this day, men find a difficulty in conceiving how Christians can have hope without certainty, sorrow and pain without gloom, suspense with calmness and confidence; how they can believe that in one sense they are in the light of God's countenance, and that in another sense they have forfeited it. I proceed then to describe a state of mind which it seems to me no one ought to misunderstand; it is so much a matter of common sense.

We will say, a man *is* a serious Christian, for of such I am speaking. He is in the habit of prayer; and he tries to serve God,

[3] Josh. vii. 19, 24, 25. [4] Jonah ii. 2–4, 7–9.

and he has, through God's mercy, the reward of such a religious course of life. He has a consciousness that God has not given him up; he has a good hope of heaven. I am not speaking of the strength of it, but more or less a good hope. He does not indeed often realize the circumstances of the future, he does not dwell upon what is to become of him; but I mean he does not look forward anxiously, feeling, as he does, around him the proofs, in which he cannot be deceived, of God's present love towards him. His being allowed to attend God's ordinances, his being enabled in a measure to do his duty, his perception of Gospel truth, his being able to accept, admire, and love high and holy views of things, all conspire to prove that at present, without going on to speculate or to calculate how he shall fare at Christ's judgment seat, at present he is in a certain true sense in God's favour. The feeling may vary from a mere trembling guess, a mere dawning and doubtful hope, to a calm though subdued confidence; still, something of this kind is the state of mind of all serious men. They are not in a state of immediate alarm, for the day of judgment is future; and for the present they are conscious somehow they are in God's hands as yet, and are thereby supported.

But now suppose a man (and this is the case of most Christians), who is conscious of some deliberate sin or sins in time past, some course of sin, or in later life has detected himself in some secret and subtle sin. Supposing it breaks on a man that he has been an overindulging father, and his children have suffered from it; or that he has been harsh, and so has alienated those who ought to have confided in him; or that he has been overfond of worldly goods, and now is suddenly overtaken with some grievous fall in consequence; or that he has on any particular occasions allowed sin in others, when he might have warned them, and they are dead and gone, and the time of retrieving matters is past; or that he has taken some false step in life, formed connexions irreligiously or the like:—what will be his state when the conviction of his sin, whatever it is, breaks upon him? Will he think himself utterly out of God's favour? I think not; he has the consciousness of his present prevailing habits of obedience, in spite of his not being so careful as he ought to be; he knows he has served God on the whole; he knows he has really desired to do God's will, though he has not striven as he ought to have done, or has been negligent in some particulars in ascertaining what that will was. Much as he may be shocked at and condemn and hate himself, much as he will humble himself, yet I do not suppose he will ordinarily *despair*.

But on the other hand, will he take up a notion that God has forgiven him? I think not either; I will not believe he has so little humility, and so much presumption. I am not speaking of ordinary men, who have no fixed principle, who take up and lay down religion as it may happen, but of *serious* men; and I will not lightly impute it to any such man that he takes up the notion of his having been absolutely forgiven for the sins of his past life. Who is to forgive him? how is he to know it? No; I see no certainty for him; he will be convinced indeed that God has not cast him out of His sight, whatever his sins have been; for he will argue, "If I were utterly reprobate, I could have no holy wish at all, or could even attempt any good work." His outward privileges, his general frame and habit of mind, assure him of so much as this; but as surely his memory tells him that he has had sins upon his conscience; he has no warrant that they are not there still; and what has come, what is to come of them, what future consequences they imply, is unknown to him. Thus he is under two feelings at once, not at all inconsistent with each other,—one of present enjoyment, another of undefined apprehension; and on looking on to the Day of Judgment, hope and fear both rise within him.

Further, let us suppose such an one actually brought into trouble, and that evidently resulting from the sin in question. For instance: supposing he has been passionate and violent, or unjust, and suppose some serious annoyance in consequence befals him from the injured party; or supposing he has neglected some obvious duty, and now the consequences of that neglect come upon him; or supposing he has in former years been imprudent in money transactions, and is under the embarrassments which they have occasioned. Now here he certainly experiences, with a clearness which he cannot explain away, a double aspect of God's providence towards him; for he sees His love and fatherly affection plainly enough, in the opportunity he still has of attending God's ordinances, and in the inward evidences of that faith, obedience, and peace, which can come from God only; on the other hand, he sees His displeasure as plainly in the visitation which comes upon him from without. I know it is sometimes said, that such trials are to the true Christian not judgments but corrections; rather they are judgments *and* corrections; surely they are merciful corrections, but they are judgments too. It is impossible but a man must consider (for example) undutiful children a punishment on him for having once neglected them, or penury a judgment on him for past extravagance, whatever may be his present attainments in obedience, greater or less; whatever his hope that God is still gracious to him in spite of past sin; whatever be his duty and his ability to turn it into a blessing. It is against common sense to say otherwise. In spite, then, of the doctrine now popular, that "as to past sin, it is over, God has forgiven it," really I do not think any truly serious lowly Christian of himself will think so, will of himself say so, though many are betrayed into such a way of speaking from want of seriousness, and many because others indulge in it. God has not absolutely forgiven the sin past; here is a proof He has not,—He is punishing it. It will be said, He has forgiven it as to its eternal consequences. Where is the proof of this? all we see is, that He is punishing it. If we argue from what we see, He has not forgiven it at all. Here a man will say, "How can He be gracious to me in other ways, unless He has been gracious so as to forgive? Is not forgiveness the first step in grace?" It *was* when we were baptized; whether it is so since must be decided from Scripture. Certainly, if we go by what our reason tells us (and I insist on what reason would say, not as if I thought Scripture spoke differently, but because persons often seem to have a great difficulty in understanding what is meant by saying that God should both be gracious to us, yet not have absolutely forgiven us), I say nothing is more compatible with reason, judging from our experience of life, than that we should have God's present favour and help without full pardon for the past. Supposing, for instance, a child has disobeyed us, and in disobeying has met with an accident. Do we at once call him to account? and not rather wait a while, till he is in a fit state to be spoken to, and when we can better decide whether or no what has befallen him be a sufficient punishment? We pass the fault over for the present, and act towards him as if we had no cause to be displeased. This is one instance out of a thousand which occur in daily life of our treating kindly, nay loving persons, with whom we are dissatisfied, and mean one day to expostulate. Surely, then, the two ideas are quite separate, of putting aside what is past and of showing kindness at present. Of course, the instance referred to is not an exact parallel to our own state in God's sight; no exact parallel can be found. We do not even know what is meant by saying that God, who sees the end from the beginning, pardons at one time rather than at another. We can but take divine truth as it is given us. We know there is one time at least when He pardons persons, whom He foresees will afterwards fall away and perish; I mean, the time of Baptism. He desires the salvation of those who ultimately come short of it. It does not follow, then, because He is still gracious to us, enables us to serve Him, and makes us love Him, that therefore we have no arrears of obedience, no debt of punishment, to be brought into account against us, when He visits. And so far from its being strange that we are in this double state in His sight, and ought to have these mingled feelings towards Him, rather it is too reasonable for us not to assent to it unless Scripture says the contrary.

But, it may be said, Scripture does say the contrary; it declares that all who repent shall be forgiven. Doubtless; but what is repentance? is repentance the work of a day? is it a mere word? is it enough to say, "I am sorry?" Consider the different frames of mind we are in hour by hour; how much we feel at one time which we do not at another. What degree or kind of feeling is enough? Considering how our hearts deceive us, is even the most passionate feeling to be trusted? Did not the Son in the Parable say, "I go sir," and went not. Do you suppose that he meant to go, or did not mean when he so promised? did he not think he was in earnest when he was not? If indeed we feel distress at having sinned, let us give God the praise; it shows that He is pleading with our hearts, it shows that He wishes us to repent, that He is bringing us to repentance: but it does not show that we have duly repented, and that He actually has forgiven us.

But it may be said, that Scripture says that faith will apply to us the merits of Christ, and thus become the instrument of washing away sins. I do not know where Scripture so says; but even if it did, I suppose it would not speak of every kind of faith, but of living faith. But how is living faith ascertained? by works;—now, who will maintain that his works can be such as to bring home to him an undoubting assurance, that he has a faith able to do this great thing?

But again, a person may say, "I have a conviction I have this faith; I feel I have; I feel I can appropriate the merits of Christ." Or again, "I have an assurance that I am forgiven." True: but where does Scripture tell us that such an assurance, without grounds for it beyond our feeling it, comes from God? where is it promised? till it is found there, we must be content not to be sure, and to fear and hope about ourselves at once.

But it may be said again, that we are told, "Ask, and ye shall receive;" if then we ask for pardon, we are pardoned. It is true; but where is it said that we shall gain it by once asking? on the contrary, are we not expressly told that we must come again and again, that we must "wait on the Lord," that we must "continue in prayer," that we must "pray and not faint," that we must be importunate in our supplications, though God seems as though He hears us not? It is quite true that if we persevere in prayer for pardon through our lives, that in spite of God's not sensibly answering, we shall at length obtain it; but this is the very state of mingled hope and fear, of peace and anxiety, of grace and of insecurity, which I have been describing. Surely, no words can express better such a waiting and persevering temper, than the words of the text, "though He slay me, yet will I trust in Him."

Once more, it may be said, and this is a far better answer than any that I have hitherto noticed, that the Sacrament of the Lord's Supper imparts to us forgiveness, and assures us of it. The benefits imparted to our souls by this Holy Sacrament are indeed most high and manifold; but that the absolute forgiveness of our past sins is not one of them, is plain in our Church's judgment from the Confession in the Service, indeed from all our Confessions. We there say, that "the remembrance of our sins is grievous, and the burden intolerable;"—now does our "remembrance" only carry us back to those sins which we have committed since we last came to this blessed ordinance, and not rather those into which we have fallen from our earliest years? and if so, is not this to confess that we are not sure of their pardon? else why are they a "burden?" Again: "for Thy Son our Lord Jesus Christ's sake forgive us all that is past;" our past sins then are not forgiven when we thus pray: does not that "past" extend back through our whole life up to infancy? If so, up to the day of our death, up to the last awful celebration of this Blessed Sacrament in our sick chamber, we confess that our sins all through our life are unforgiven, whatever be the effect, which we know cannot be little, of the grace of that Ordinance and the Absolution therein pronounced over us.

To these considerations I will add one other. We are to be *judged* at the Last Day, and "receive the things done in the body, whether they be good or bad."[5] Our sins will then be had in remembrance; therefore they are not forgiven here.

It seems clear, then, that the sins which we commit here, are not put away here,—are not put away absolutely and once for all, but are in one sense upon us till the Judgment. There is indeed one putting away of sins expressly described in Scripture, which we all received from God's mercy, when though "born in sin and the children of wrath," we were "made the children of grace." This was in Baptism, which accordingly is called in the

[5] 2 Cor. v.10.

Creed, the "One Baptism for the remission of sins." And of this great absolution Scripture speaks in many ways, calling on those who have not received it to "arise, and be baptized, and wash away their sins;" declaring there is "a fountain opened to the house of David, and to the inhabitants of Jerusalem, for sin and for uncleanness;" and promising that "though their sins be as scarlet, they shall be as white as snow; though they be red like crimson, they shall be as wool."[6] This all we have received long since; and none knows but God and His Angels,—nay, I will say, none knows but God Himself and His Only Son, and His Spirit who then is present,—how much Holy Baptism does secretly for our souls, what hidden wounds it heals, and what inbred corruption it allays; but this is past long since. We have sinned in spite of grace then given; many of us grievously; and the question now is, where do we stand, and *how* are we to gain a second pardon?

I answer, we stand in God's presence, we are in His Church, in His favour, in the way of His grace, in the way to be pardoned; and this is our great comfort on the very first view of the matter. We are not in a desperate state, we are not cast out of our Father's house; we have still privileges, aids, powers, from Him; our persons are still acceptable to Him. And this being the case, through God's great mercy, it is quite clear what our duty is, even if Scripture gave us no insight into it. Even if Scripture said nothing of the duty of importunate prayer and patient waiting, in order to obtain that which we need so much, yet our natural sense must suggest it to us. See what our condition is;— at present most happily circumstanced, in the bosom of God's choicest gifts; but with evil behind us, and that through our frailty ever increasing, and a judgment before us. Why, it is plainly our duty to make the most of our time of grace; to be earnest and constant in deprecating God's wrath; to do all we can to please Him; to bring Him of our best, not as if it had any intrinsic merit, but because it is our best; to endeavour so to cherish and bring to fruit the gifts of His grace within us, that "when we fail, they may receive us into everlasting habitations;" and, since He at present condescends to work in us "to will and to do," to aim, as St. Paul directs, at "working out our own salvation with fear and trembling," working while it is day, "before the night cometh," for "now is the accepted time, now is the day of salvation." Though we be at present punished for our sins, though we be under judgment, or, if it be in prospect,

[6] Acts xxii.16; Zech. xiii.1; Is. i.18.

though we be uncertain more or less how things will be with us, though the adversary of our souls accuse us before God, though his threatening voice sound in our ears year after year, though we feel the load of our sins and cannot throw them from our memory, nay, though it should be God's will that even to the Day of Judgment, no assurance should be given us, still, wherever we are, and whatever we are, like Jonah "in the belly of hell," with Job among the ashes, with Jeremiah in the dungeon, or like the Holy Children in the flames, let us glorify our Lord God, and trust in Him, and praise Him, and magnify Him for ever. Let us take in good part whatever sorrow He inflicts in His providence, or however long. Let us "glorify the Lord in the fires;" [7] they may circle us, but they cannot really touch us; they may threaten, but they are as yet restrained. "Hitherto hath the Lord helped us." We will sing and praise His Name. When two or three are gathered together, an interior temple, a holy shrine is formed for them, which nothing without can destroy. We will not cease to rejoice in what God has given, because He has not as yet promised us every thing. Nor will we on the other hand forget our past sins, because He allows us peace and joy in spite of them. We will remember them that He may not remember them; we will repent of them again and again, that He may forgive them; we will rejoice in the punishment of them if He punishes, thinking it better to be punished in this life than in the next; and if not yet punished, we will be prepared for the chance of it. He will give us grace according to our day, according to His gracious promise: "Fear not, for I have redeemed thee; I have called thee by thy name; thou art Mine. When thou passest through the waters, I will be with thee; and through the rivers, they shall not overflow thee; when thou walkest through the fire, thou shalt not be burnt, neither shall the flame kindle upon thee." [8]

---

[7] Is. xxiv.15.   [8] Is. xlii.1, 2.

THE STATE OF GRACE

*"Being justified by faith we have peace with God through our Lord
Jesus Christ; by whom also we have access by faith into this grace
wherein we stand, and rejoice in hope of the glory of God."*
—Rom. v.1, 2.

THERE are many men, nay the greater part of a Christian
country, who have neither hope nor fear about futurity or
the unseen world; they do not think of it at all, or bring the idea
of it home to them in any shape. They do not really understand,
or try to understand, that they are in God's presence, and must
one day be judged for what they are now doing, any more than
they see what is going on in another quarter of the world, or
concern themselves about what is to happen to them ten years
hence. The next world is far more distant from them than any
future period of this life or any other country; and consequently, they have neither hope nor fear about it, for they have
no thought about it of any kind.

There are others who feel no fear whatever, though they profess to feel much joy and transport. I cannot sympathize with
such, nor do I think St. Paul would, for he bids us "work out
our own salvation with fear and trembling;" nor St. Peter, who
bids us "pass the time of our sojourning here in fear."[1]

But there are others who seem only to fear, or to have very
little joy in religion. These are in a more hopeful state than
those who only joy and do not fear at all; yet they are not altogether in a right state. However, they are in an interesting state.
I purpose to describe it now, and to make some remarks upon it.

It is certainly the duty, as it is the privilege, of every Christian
to have his heart so fixed on Christ as to desire His coming; yet
alas! it too often happens that when we say, "Thy kingdom
come," our sins rise up before our minds, and make our words
falter. Now the persons I speak of are in so sad and uncomfortable a state of mind, as to be distressed whenever they think of
the next world. They may be well-living, serious persons, and

---

[1] Phil. ii.12; 1 Pet. i.17.

have ever been such from their youth; yet they have an indefinite sense of guilt on their minds, a consciousness of their own miserable failings and continual transgressions, such as annoys and distresses them, as a wound or sore might, when they think of Christ's coming in judgment. A sense of guilt, indeed, every one, the best of us, must have. I am not blaming *that*, but I speak of *such* a sense as hinders those who feel it from rejoicing in the Lord. They have one thought alone before their minds, the great irregularity of their lives; they come to Church, and try to attend, but their thoughts wander; the day passes, and it seems to them unprofitable. They have done God no service. Or again, they have some natural failing which breaks out from time to time, and grievously afflicts them on recollection. Perhaps they are passionate, and are ever saying what they are sorry for afterwards; or they are ill-tempered, and from time to time put every thing about them into confusion, and make every one unhappy by their gloomy looks and sullen words; or they are slothful, and with difficulty moved to do any thing, and they are ever lamenting wasted hours, and opportunities lost. The consequence is, that their religion is a course of sorrowful attempting and failing, self-reproach, and dryness of spirits. They are deeply sensible how good God is, and how wonderful His providence; they really feel very grateful, and they really put their trust where it should be put. But their faith only leads them to see that judgment is a fearful thing, and their sense of God's mercies to say, "How little grateful am I." They hear of the blessings promised to God's true servants after death, and they say, "Oh, how unprepared am I to receive them."

Now no one will fancy, I should trust, that I am saying any thing in disparagement of such feelings; they are very right and true. I only say they should not be the whole of a man's religion. He ought to have other and more cheerful feelings too. No one on earth is free from imperfection and sin, no one but has much continually to repent of; yet St. Paul bids us "rejoice in the Lord alway;" and in the text, he describes Christians as having peace with God and rejoicing in hope of His glory. Sins of infirmity, then, such as arise from the infection of our original nature, and not from deliberation and wilfulness, have no divine warrant to keep us from joy and peace in believing.

Now, then, the question is, *how* the persons in question come to have this defective kind of religion.

1. In the first place, of course, we must take into account bodily disorder, which is not unfrequently the cause of the perplexity of mind I have been describing. Many persons have an

anxious self-tormenting disposition, or depression of spirits, or
deadness of the affections, in consequence of continued or peculiar ill-health; and though it is their study, as it is their duty,
to strive against this evil as much as they can, yet it often may be
impossible to be rid of it. Of course, in such cases we can impute
no fault to them. It is God's will; He has willed in His inscrutable purpose that they should not be able to rejoice in the Gospel, doubtless for their ultimate good, to try and prove them; as
any thing else may be a trial, as ill-health itself is such. They
should not repine. It is an undeserved mercy that they have the
Gospel brought near to them at all, that they have the prospect
of heaven, be it faint or distinct; and they must be patient under
their fears, and try to serve God more strictly.

2. But, again, the uncomfortable state of mind I have described, sometimes, it is to be feared, arises, I will not say from
wilful sin, but from some habitual deficiency which might be
corrected, but is not. It is very difficult of course to draw the
line between sins which are (as it were) the direct consequences
of our old nature, and those which are more strictly and entirely our own, yet there is a class which rises above the former,
though it would be harsh to call them wilful. The sins I speak
of arise partly through frailty, partly through want of love; and
they seem just to have this effect, of dimming or quenching our
peace and joy. Such, for instance, are recurring and stated acts
of sin, such as might be foreseen and provided against. Anger,
on the contrary, may overtake a man when he least expects it.
Indolence may show itself in a difficulty or inability to fix his
mind on the subject which ought to occupy it, so that time
goes and nothing is done. Ill-temper may fall upon him like a
spell, and bind his faculties, so that his very attempts to break it
may make him seem more gloomy, untoward, and disagreeable, from the appearance of an effort and struggle. Such need
not be more than sins of infirmity. But there are sins which
happen at certain times or places, and which a man ought to
prepare for and overcome. I do not say that he must overcome
them this time or that, but he must be in a state of warfare
against them, and must be tending to overcome them. Such,
for instance, is indolence in rising from his bed. Such, again, is
a careless, irregular, or hurried way of saying private prayer.
Such is any habitual excess in eating or drinking. Such is running into temptation,—going again and again to places, or
among people, who will induce him to do what he should not,
to idle, or to jest, or to talk much. Such is extravagance in
spending money. All these laxities of conduct impress upon

our conscience a vague sense of irregularity and guilt. The absence of a vigilant walk, of exact conscientiousness in all things, of an earnest and vigorous warfare against our spiritual enemies, in a word, of strictness, this is what obscures our peace and joy. Strictness is the condition of rejoicing. The Christian is a soldier; he may have many falls; these need not hinder his joy in the Gospel; he must be humbled indeed, but not downcast; it does not prove he is not fighting; he has enemies within and without him; he has the remains of a fallen nature. But wilful sin in any shape proves that he is not an honest soldier of Christ. If it is habitual and deliberate, of course it destroys his hope; but if it be less than deliberate, and yet of the nature of wilful sin, it is sufficient, though not (we trust) to separate him at once from Christ, yet to separate him from the inward vision of Him. The same result will follow, perhaps irremediably, where men have been in past life open or habitual sinners, though they may now have repented. Penitents cannot hope to be as cheerful and joyful in faith as those who have never fallen away from God; perhaps it is not desirable they should be, and is a bad sign if they are. I do not mean to say that in the course of years, and after severe humiliation, it is not possible for a repentant sinner to feel a well-grounded peace and comfort, but he must not expect it. He must expect to be haunted with the ghosts of past sins, rising from the charnel-house, courting him to sin again, yet filling him the while with remorse; he must expect "a trembling heart, and failing of eyes, and sorrow of mind,"[2] misgivings about his safety, misgivings about the truth of religion, and about particular doctrines, painful doubts and difficulties, so that he is forced to grope in darkness or in cold and dreary twilight. I do not say there are not ways of escaping all this misery at a moment, but they are false ways; but if he continues in the true and narrow way, he will find it rough and painful; and this is his fit correction.

3. Again, where there is no room for supposing the existence of wilful sins, past or present, this fearful anxious state of mind arises very commonly from another cause in one shape or other—from not having a lively sense of our present privileges; and this is the subject to which I shall call your attention. Many indeed, finding that Scripture says great things about the joy which true Christians have in the Gospel, think it consists in their having personally and individually an assurance of their

[2] Deut. xxviii.65.

absolute predestination to eternal life; or at least of their being now in a state of salvation, such that, were they at once to die, they would be sure of heaven. Such a knowledge of course would inspire great joy if they had it; and they fancy that the joy of the Christian does arise from it. But since they have it not, and only think they have it, it is obvious what extravagances will follow from the notion instead of real benefit; what perversion of the Gospel, what rashness, presumption, self-exaltation, and intemperate conduct. Such persons of course claim the more consolatory parts of Scripture, such as the text, for themselves. They forcibly take them from more sober Christians, as if they were their own, and others had no right to them, nay, as if others had no right to explain them, to comment on them, or to have an opinion about them; as if they alone could understand them, or feel them, or appreciate them, or use them. What is the consequence? better men are robbed of their portion; their comfortable texts are gone, they acquiesce in the notion (too readily) that these texts are *not* theirs; not that they exactly allow that they belong to the enthusiastic persons who claim them, but they think they belong to no one at all, that they belonged indeed to St. Paul, and to inspired or highly-gifted men, but to no one now.

And this conclusion is strengthened by the circumstance, that men of duller and less sensitive minds are willing to give them up. There are persons highly respectable indeed, and serious, but whose religion is of a dry and cold character, with little heart or insight into the next world. They have strong sense and regular habits; their passions are not violent, their feelings not quick, and they have no imagination or restless reason to run away with their thoughts or to perplex them. They do not grieve much or joy much. They do joy and grieve, but it is in a way, in a certain line, and not the highest. They are most excellent men in their line, but they do not walk in a lofty path. There is nothing unearthly about them; they cannot be said to be worldly, yet they do not walk by things unseen; they do not discern and contemplate the next world. They are not on the alert to detect, patient in watching, keen-sighted in tracing the movements of God's secret Providence. They do not feel they are in an immense unbounded system, with a height above and a depth beneath. They think every thing is plain and easy, they have no difficulties in religion, they see no recondite and believe in no hidden meanings in Scripture, and discern no hints there sympathetic with guesses within them. Such men are used to explain away such passages as the text; to be "at peace with God," to "have access into the grace in which we stand," to "rejoice in hope of the glory of God,"—to them have little or no meaning. Their joy does not rise higher than what they call a "rational faith and hope, a satisfaction in religion, a cheerfulness, a well-ordered mind, and the like,"—all very good words, if properly used, but shallow to express the fulness of the Gospel privileges.

What with the enthusiastic, then, on the one hand, who pervert the texts in question, and with the barren-minded on the other, who explain them away, Christians are commonly left without the texts at all, and so have nothing to contemplate but their own failings; and these surely are numerous enough, and fit to make them dejected.

Observe, then, what religion becomes to them,—a system of duties with little of privilege or comfort. Not that any one would have cause to complain (God forbid!) though it had no privilege; for what can sinners claim to whom it is a great gain to be respited from hell? Not that religion can really be without privilege; for the very leave to serve God is a privilege, the very thought of God is a privilege, the very knowledge that Christ has so loved the world as to die for it is an inestimable privilege. Religion is full of privileges, involved in the very notion of it, and drawn out on the right hand and on the left, as a man walks along the path of duty. He cannot stir this way or that, but he awakens some blessed and consoling thought which cheers and strengthens him insensibly, even if it does not so present itself to him, that he can contemplate and feed upon it. However, in the religious system I speak of, the privilege of obedience *is* concealed, and the bare duty prominently put forward; the privileges are made vague and general rather than personal; and thus a man is almost reduced to the state of natural religion in which God's Law is known without His Gospel. Under such circumstances, religion becomes little more than a code of morals, the word and will of an absent God, who will one day come to judge and recompense, not the voice of a present and bountiful Saviour.

And this may in one sense be called a bondage,—a bondage, yet without thereby disparaging the excellence and perfection of God's law. Men at this day so boldly talk of the bondage of the law, that if you heard them, you would think that the being under that law was in itself a misery or an inferior state, as if obedience to God's commandments were something low and second best. But is it really so? then are the Angels in a very low state. The highest blessedness of any creature is to be under the law, the highest glory is obedience. It is our shame, not our privilege, that we do not obey as the Angels do. Men speak as if the Gospel were glorious, because it destroyed the law of obedience. No; it destroyed the Jewish law, but not the holy law of God therein contained and manifested. And if that Holy Word, which "endureth for ever in heaven," which is co-eternal with God, is a bondage to us, as it is by nature, so much the more shame for us. It is our great sinfulness, not any inherent defect in the law, which makes it a bondage; and the message of the Gospel is glorious, not because it releases us from the law, but because it enables us to fulfil it,—fulfil it (I do not say wholly and perfectly), but with a continual approximation to perfect obedience, with an obedience running on into perfection, and which in the next world will rise into and result in perfection. This is St. Paul's account of it, "Being not without law to God," he says, "but under the law to Christ."[3] Again, "Not having mine own righteousness, which is of the law," that is, that kind of obedience to the law to which he *by himself* attained, "but that which is through the faith of Christ;"[4] that high and spiritual obedience which faith in Christ, aided by the grace of Christ, enabled him to accomplish. And in another place, "The commandment which was ordained to life, I found to be unto death. . . . . The Law is holy, and the commandment holy, and just, and good. Was then that which is good made death unto me? God forbid. But sin, that it might appear sin, working death in me by that which is good, that sin by the commandment might become exceeding sinful . . . . The law is spiritual, but *I* am carnal, sold under sin." And again, "What the law could not do, in that it was weak through the flesh, God sending His own Son in the likeness of sinful flesh, and for sin, condemned sin in the flesh; that the righteousness of the law might be fulfilled in us, who walk not after the flesh but after the Spirit."[5]

When then I say that religion, considered as a law or code of morals, is a bondage, let no one suppose me to countenance that presumptuous and unchristian spirit, which seems to exult in being through Christ free (as it thinks) from the law, instead of being bound and able through Christ to obey it more perfectly. The glory of the Gospel is, not that it *destroys* the law, but that it makes it *cease* to *be* a bondage; not that it gives us freedom *from* it, but *in* it; and the notion of the Gospel which I have been describing as cold and narrow, is not that of supposing Chris-

[3] 1 Cor. ix.21.   [4] Phil. iii.9.   [5] Rom. viii.3, 4.

tianity a law, but of supposing it to be scarcely more than a law, and thus leaving us where it found us. He who thinks it but a law, will of course be fearful and miserable. The commandment of God will seem true, but to him, a helpless sinner, hard and uninviting; and though it is still his duty to try to obey, and he will do so, if he be Christ's in heart, yet he will do so sadly and sorrowfully, his memory continually embittered, and his conscience laden with fresh and fresh sins. Two thoughts alone will be before him, God's perfections and his own sinfulness; and he will feel love and gratitude indeed to his Almighty Lord and Saviour, but not joy. He will look upon the message of the Gospel as a series of *conditions*. He will consider the Gospel as a *covenant*, in which he must do his part, and God will assuredly do His. Now, salvation, doubtless, *is* conditional, and the Gospel *is* a covenant. These words are as good and as true as the word "law;" but then salvation is not *merely* conditional, nor the Gospel *merely* a covenant; and those who think so, unless they have peculiarly happy minds, will obey in a certain dry, dull, heavy way, without spring, animation, life, vigour, and nobleness. And if possessed of sensitive, gentle, affectionate minds, they will be very likely to sink into despondency and fear. And they are the prey or the mockery of every proud, self-confident boaster, who passes by on the other side, boldly proclaiming himself to be elect and safe and possessed of a joyful assurance, and that every one else, who does not make as venturesome a profession as he, is carnal and a slave of Satan, or at least in a state far, far below himself.

What then is it, that these little ones of Christ lack, who, without wilful sin, past or present, on their consciences, are in gloom and sorrow? What is the doctrine that will quicken them, and make their devotion healthy? What will brace them and nerve them, and make them lift up their heads, and will pour light and joy upon their countenance till it shines like the face of Moses when he came down from the Mount? What but the great and high doctrines connected with the Church? They are not merely taken into covenant with God; they are taken into His Church. They have not merely the promise of grace; they have its presence. They have not merely the conditional prospect of a reward; for a blessing, nay, unspeakable, fathomless, illimitable, infinite, eternal blessings are poured into their very hearts, even as a first step and an earnest from God our Saviour, of what He will do for those who love Him. They "are passed from death unto life," and are the children of God and heirs of heaven. Let us steadily contemplate this comfortable view, and we shall gain strength, and feel cheerful and joyful in spite of our sins. O fearful follower of Christ, how is it thou hast never thought of what thou art and what is in thee? Art thou not Christ's purchased possession? Has He not rescued thee from the devil, and put a new nature within thee? Did He not in Baptism cast out the evil spirit and enter into thee Himself, and dwell in thee as if thou hadst been an Archangel, or one of the Seraphim who worship before Him continually? Much and rightly as thou thinkest of thy sins, hast thou no thought, I do not say of gratitude, but of wonder, of admiration, of amazement, of awful and overpowering transport, at what thou art through grace? When Jacob woke in the morning, his first thought was not about his sins or his danger, though he rightly felt both, but about God;—he said, "How dreadful is this place! this is none other but the house of God, and this is the gate of heaven." [6] Contemplate then thyself, not in thyself, but as thou art in the Eternal God. Fall down in astonishment at the glories which are around thee and in thee, poured to and fro in such a wonderful way that thou art (as it were) dissolved into the kingdom of God, as though thou hadst nought to do but to contemplate and feed upon that great vision. This surely is the state of mind the Apostle speaks of in the text when he reminds us who are justified and at peace with God, that we have the access to His royal courts, and stand in His grace, and rejoice in hope of His glory. All the trouble which the world inflicts upon us, and which flesh cannot but feel, sorrow, pain, care, bereavement, these avail not to disturb the tranquillity and the intensity with which faith gazes upon the Divine Majesty. All the necessary exactness of our obedience, the anxiety about failing, the pain of self-denial, the watchfulness, the zeal, the self-chastisements which are required of us, as little interfere with this vision of faith, as if they were practised by another, not by ourselves. We are two or three selves at once, in the wonderful structure of our minds, and can weep while we smile, and labour while we meditate.

And if so much is given us by the first Sacrament of the Church, what, think we, is given us in the second? O, my brethren, let us raise and enlarge our notions of Christ's Presence in that mysterious Ordinance, and we shall understand how it is that the Christian, in spite of his infirmities, and not forgetting them, still may rejoice—"with joy unspeakable and full of glory." For what is it that is vouchsafed to us at the Holy

[6] Gen. xxviii.17.

Table, when we commemorate the Lord's death? It is, "Jesus Christ before our eyes evidently set forth, crucified among us."[7] Not before our bodily eyes; so far, every thing remains at the end of that Heavenly Communion as it did at the beginning. What was bread remains bread, and what was wine remains wine. We need no carnal, earthly, visible miracle to convince us of the Presence of the Lord Incarnate. We have, we trust, more faith than to need to see the heavens open, or the Holy Ghost descend in bodily shape,—more faith than to attempt, in default of sight, to indulge our reason, and to confine our notion of the Sacrament to some clear assemblage of words of our own framing. We have faith and love enough, in St. Paul's words, to "*discern* the Lord's Body." He who is at the right hand of God, manifests Himself in that Holy Sacrament as really and fully as if He were visibly there. We are allowed to draw near, to "give, take, and eat" His sacred Body and Blood, as truly as though like Thomas we could touch His hands and thrust our hand into His side. When He ascended into the Mount, "His face did shine as the sun, and His raiment was white as the light."[8] Such is the glorious presence which faith sees in the Holy Communion, though every thing looks as usual to the natural man. Not gold or precious stones, pearls of great price or gold of Ophir, are to the eye of faith so radiant as those lowly elements which He, the Highest, is pleased to make the means of conveying to our hearts and bodies His own gracious self. Not the light of the sun sevenfold is so awfully bright and overpowering, if we could see as the Angels do, as that seed of eternal life, which by eating and drinking we lay up in our hearts against the day of His coming. In spite then of all recollections of the past or fear for the future, we have a present source of rejoicing; whatever comes, weal or woe, however stands our account as yet in the books against the Last Day, this we have and this we may glory in, the present power and grace of God in us and over us, and the means thereby given us of victory in the end.

Such are the thoughts which fill the heart with joy, yet without tending in consequence to relax our obedience, for a reason already mentioned, viz. that *strictness* of life, exact conscientiousness, is the tenure of our privileges. They are ours to possess, that is our glory; they are ours to lose, that is our solicitude. We can keep them, we have not to gain them,—but we shall not keep them without fear and trembling; still we have

---

[7] Gal. iii.1.					[8] Matt. xvii.2.

them, and there is nothing to hinder our rejoicing in them while we have them. For fear has reference to the future; and that we *may* lose them to-morrow (which God forbid), but supposing it, is no reason why we should not rejoice in them to-day.

THE VISIBLE CHURCH FOR
THE SAKE OF THE ELECT

"I endure all things for the elect's sake; that they may also obtain the
salvation which is in Christ Jesus with eternal glory."
—2 Tim. ii.10.

IF we were asked what was the object of Christian preaching,
teaching, and instruction, what the office of the Church,
considered as the dispenser of the word of God, I suppose we
should not all return the same answer. Perhaps we might say
that the object of Revelation was to enlighten and enlarge the
mind, to make us act by reason, and to expand and strengthen
our powers;—or to impart knowledge about religious truth,
knowledge being power directly it is given, and enabling us
forthwith to think, judge, and act for ourselves;—or to make us
good members of the community, loyal subjects, orderly and
useful in our station, whatever it be;—or to secure, what otherwise would be hopeless, our leading a religious life; the reason
why persons go wrong, throw themselves away, follow bad
courses and lose their character being, that they have had no
education, and that they are ignorant. These and other answers
might be given; some beside, and some short of the mark. It
may be useful then to consider with what end, with what expectation, we preach, teach, instruct, discuss, bear witness,
praise, and blame; what fruit the Church is right in anticipating
as the result of her ministerial labours.

St. Paul gives us a reason in the text different from any of
those which I have mentioned. He laboured more than all the
Apostles; and why? not to civilize the world, not to smooth the
face of society, not to facilitate the movements of civil government, not to spread abroad knowledge, not to cultivate the reason, not for any great worldly object, but "for the elect's sake."
He "endured all things," all pain, all sorrow, all solitariness;
many a tear, many a pang, many a fear, many a disappointment,
many a heartache, many a strife, many a wound; he was "five
times scourged, thrice beaten with rods, once stoned, thrice in

828

shipwreck, in journeys often, in perils of waters, of robbers, of his own countrymen, of the heathen, of the city, of the wilderness, of the sea, of false brethren, in weariness and painfulness, in watchings often, in hunger and thirst, in fastings often, in cold and nakedness;"[1] and some men could have even been content so to have suffered, had they by these voluntary acts of suffering, been buying as by a price first one and then another triumph of the Gospel. If every stripe was a sinner's ransom, and every tear restored a backslider, and every disappointment was balanced with a joy, and every privation was a brother's edification, then he might have gladly endured all things, knowing that the more he suffered the more he did. And to a certain degree this effect certainly followed; the jailor after his scourging at Philippi, was converted, and washed his stripes; and his "bonds in Christ" were "manifest" at Rome, "in all the palace, and in all other places."[2] In spite, however, of such gracious compensations vouchsafed to the Apostle from time to time, still great visible effects, adequate to the extent of his suffering, were neither its result nor its motive. He sowed in abundance that he might reap in measure; he spoke to the many that he might gain the few; he mixed with the world that he might build up the Church; he "endured all things," not for the sake of all men, but "for the elect's sake," that he might be the means of bringing them to glory. This is instanced of him and the other Apostles in the book of Acts. Thus when St. Peter first preached the Gospel, on the day of Pentecost, "they were all amazed," some "mocked," but "they that gladly received the word were baptized." And when St. Paul and St. Barnabas preached at Antioch to the Gentiles, "As many as were ordained to eternal life, believed."[3] When St. Paul preached at Athens, "some mocked," others said, "We will hear thee again," but "certain men clave unto him." And when he addressed the Jews at Rome, "some believed the things which were spoken, and some believed not." Such was the view, which animated, first Christ Himself, then all His Apostles, and St. Paul in particular, to preach to all, in order to succeed with some. Our Lord "saw of the travail of His soul, and was satisfied." St. Paul, as His servant and instrument, was satisfied in like manner to endure all things for the elect's sake; or, as he says in another place, "I am made all things to all men, that I might by all means save some."[4] And such is the office of the Church in every nation

[1] 2 Cor. xi.24–27.   [2] Phil. i.13.
[3] Acts ii.12, 13; xiii.48; xvii.32–34.
[4] 1 Cor. ix.22.

where she sojourns; she attempts much, she expects and promises little.

This is a great Scripture truth, which in this busy and sanguine day needs insisting upon. There are in every age a certain number of souls in the world, known to God, unknown to us, who will obey the Truth when offered to them, whatever be the mysterious reason that they do and others do not. These we must contemplate, for these we must labour, these are God's special care, for these are all things; of these and among these we must pray to be, and our friends with us, at the Last Day. They are the true Church, ever increasing in number, ever gathering in, as time goes on; with them lies the Communion of Saints; they have power with God; they are His armies who follow the Lamb, who overcome princes of the earth, and who shall hereafter judge Angels. These are that multitude which took its beginning in St. Paul's day, for which he laboured, having his portion in it himself; for which we in our day must labour too, that, if so be, we too may have a place in it: according to the text, "He that receiveth a prophet in the name of a prophet shall receive a prophet's reward; and he that receiveth a righteous man in the name of a righteous man shall receive a righteous man's reward. And whosoever shall give to drink unto one of these little ones a cup of cold water only in the name of a disciple, verily I say unto you, he shall in no wise lose his reward." [5]

God is neither "without witness" nor without fruit, even in a heathen country:—"In every nation," says St. Peter, "he that feareth God and worketh righteousness is accepted with Him." [6] In every nation, among many bad, there are some good; and, as nations are before the Gospel is offered to them, such they seem to remain on the whole after the offer; "many are called, few are chosen." And to spend and be spent upon the many called for the sake of the chosen few, is the office of Christian teachers and witnesses.

That their office is such seems to be evident from the existing state of Christian countries from the first. Unless it be maintained that the Church has never done her duty towards the nations where she has sojourned, it must be granted that success in the hearts of the many is not promised her. Christianity has raised the tone of morals, has restrained the passions, and enforced external decency and good conduct in the world at large; it has advanced certain persons in virtuous or religious

---

[5] Matt. x.41, 42.　　　　　　[6] Acts x.35.

habits, who otherwise might have been imbued with the mere rudiments of truth and holiness; it has given a firmness and consistency to religious profession in numbers, and perhaps has extended the range of really religious practice. Still on the whole the great multitude of men have to all appearance remained, in a spiritual point of view, no better than before. The state of great cities now is not so very different from what it was of old; or at least not so different as to make it appear that the main work of Christianity has lain with the face of society, or what is called the world. Again, the highest class in the community and the lowest, are not so different from what they would be respectively without the knowledge of the Gospel, as to allow it to be said that Christianity has succeeded with the world, as the world, in its several ranks and classes. And so of its pursuits and professions; they are in character what they were, softened or restrained in their worst consequences, but still with the same substantial fruits. Trade is still avaricious, not in tendency only but in fact, though it has heard the Gospel; physical science is still sceptical as it was when heathen. Lawyers, soldiers, farmers, politicians, courtiers, nay, shame to say, the priesthood, still savour of the old Adam. Christian states move forward upon the same laws as before, and rise and fall as time goes on, upon the same internal principles. Human nature remains what it was, though it has been baptized; the proverbs, the satires, the pictures, of which it was the subject in heathen times, have their point still. In a word, taking religion to mean as it well may, the being bound by God's law, the acting under God's will instead of our own, how few are there in a country called Christian who even profess religion in this sense! how few there are who live by any other rule than that of their own ease, habit, inclination, as the case may be, on the one hand, and of external circumstances on the other! with how few is the will of God an habitual object of thought, or search, or love, or obedience! All this is so notorious that unbelievers taunt us with it. They see, and scoff at seeing, that Christians, whether the many or the educated or the old, nay, or the sacred ministry, are open to the motives, and unequal to the temptations, which prevail with human nature generally.

The knowledge of the Gospel then has not materially changed more than the surface of things; it has made clean the outside; but as far as we have the means of judging, it has not acted on a large scale upon the mind within, upon that "heart" out of which proceed the evil things "which defile a man." Nor did it ever promise it would do so. Our Saviour's words, spoken of the Apostles in the first instance, relate to the Church at large,—"I pray not for the world, but for them which Thou hast given Me, for they are Thine." In like manner St. Paul says that Christ came, not to convert the world, but "to purify unto Himself a *peculiar people*, zealous of good works;" not to sanctify this evil world, but to "deliver us *out of* this present evil world according to the will of God and our Father;"[7] not to turn the whole earth into a heaven, but to bring down a heaven upon earth. This has been the real triumph of the Gospel, to raise those beyond themselves and beyond human nature, in whatever rank and condition of life, whose wills mysteriously co-operate with God's grace, who, while God visits them, really fear and really obey God, whatever be the unknown reason why one man obeys Him and another not. It has made men saints, and brought into existence specimens of faith and holiness, which without it are unknown and impossible. It has laboured for the elect, and it has succeeded with them. This is, as it were, its token. An ordinary kind of religion, praiseworthy and re-spectable in its way, may exist under many systems; but saints are creations of the Gospel and the Church. Not that such a one need in his lifetime seem to be more than other well-living men, for his graces lie deep, and are not known and understood till after his death, even if then. But then, it may be, he "shines forth as the sun in the kingdom of his Father," figuring in his memory on earth what will be fulfilled in soul and body in heaven. And hence we are not accustomed to give to living men the *title* of saints, since *we* cannot well know, while they are among us, who have lived up to their calling and who have not. But in process of time, after death, their excellence perhaps gets abroad; and then they become a witness, a specimen of what the Gospel can do, and a sample and a pledge of all those other high creations of God, His saints in full number, who die and are never known.

There are many reasons why God's saints cannot be known all at once;—first, as I have said, their good deeds are done in secret. Next, good men are often slandered, ridiculed, ill-treated in their lifetime; they are mistaken by those, whom they offend by their holiness and strictness, and perhaps they are obliged to withstand sin in their day, and this raises about them a cloud of prejudice and dislike, which in time indeed, but not till after a time, goes off. Then again their intentions and aims are misunderstood; and some of their excellent deeds or noble

[7] John xvii.9; Tit. ii.14; Gal. i.4.

traits of character are known to some men, others to others, not all to all. This is the case in their lifetime; but after their death, when envy and anger have died away, and men talk together about them, and compare what each knows, their good and holy deeds are added up; and while they evidence their fruitfulness, also clear up or vindicate their motives, and strike the mind of survivors with astonishment and fear; and the Church honours them, thanks God for them, and "glorifies God in"[8] them. This is why the saints of God are commonly honoured, not while they live, but in their death; and if I am asked to state plainly how such a one differs from an ordinary religious man, I say in this,—that he sets before him as the one object of life, to please and obey God; that he ever aims to submit his will to God's will; that he earnestly follows after holiness; and that he is habitually striving to have a closer resemblance to Christ in all things. He exercises himself, not only in social duties, but in Christian graces; he is not only kind, but meek; not only generous, but humble; not only persevering, but patient; not only upright, but forgiving; not only bountiful, but self-denying; not only contented, but meditative and devotional. An ordinary man thinks it enough to do as he is done by; he will think it fair to resent insults, to repay injuries, to show a becoming pride, to insist on his rights, to be jealous of his honour, when in the wrong to refuse to confess it, to seek to be rich, to desire to be well with the world, to fear what his neighbours will say. He seldom thinks of the Day of Judgment, seldom thinks of sins past, says few prayers, cares little for the Church, has no zeal for God's truth, spends his money on himself. Such is an ordinary Christian, and such is not one of God's elect. For the latter is more than just, temperate, and kind; he has a devoted love of God, high faith, holy hope, over-flowing charity, a noble self-command, a strict conscientiousness, humility never absent, gentleness in speech, simplicity, modesty, and unaffectedness, an unconsciousness of what his endowments are, and what they make him in God's sight. This is what Christianity has done in the world; such is the result of Christian teaching; viz., to elicit, foster, mature the seeds of heaven which lie hid in the earth, to multiply (if it may be said) images of Christ, which, though they be few, are worth all else that is among men, and are an ample recompense and "a crown of rejoicing" for Apostles and Evangelists "in the presence of our Lord Jesus Christ at His coming."[9]

---

[8] Gal. i. 24.   [9] 1 Thess. ii. 19.

It is no triumph then for unbelievers that the Gospel has not done what it never attempted. From the first it announced what was to be the condition of the many who heard and professed it. "Many are called, few are chosen." "Broad is the way that leadeth to destruction, and many there be which go in thereat. Strait is the gate and narrow is the way which leadeth unto life, and few there be that find it." Though we laboured ever so much, with the hope of satisfying the objector, we could not reverse our Saviour's witness, and make the many religious and the bad few. We can but do what is to be done. With our utmost toil we do but reach those for whom crowns are prepared in heaven. "Whom He did foreknow, them did He predestinate." "He that is unjust, let him be unjust still; and he that is filthy, let him be filthy still; and he that is righteous, let him be righteous still; and he that is holy, let him be holy still." [10] We cannot destroy the personal differences which separate man and man; and to lay it as a fault to baptism, teaching, and other ministrations, that they cannot pass the bounds predicted in God's word, is as little reasonable as attempting to make one mind the same as another.

And if this be the case, how mistaken is the notion of the day, that the main undertaking of a Christian Church is to make men good members of society, honest, upright, industrious, and well-conducted; and that it fails of its duty, and has cause of shame unless it succeeds in doing so; and that of two religious communities, that must be the more scriptural in its tenets, of which the members are more decent and orderly!—whereas it may easily happen that a corruption of the Gospel, which sacrifices the better fruit, may produce the more abundant, men being not unwilling to compound for neglect of a strict rule by submitting to an easy one. How common is it, at this time, to debate the question, whether the plans of education pursued for the last fifty years have diminished crime or not; whether those who are convicted of offences against the law have for the most part been at school or not! Such inquiries surely are out of place, if Christian education is in question. If the Church set out by engaging to make men good members of the state, they would be very much in place; but if the great object of her Sacraments, preaching, Scriptures, and instructions, is to save the elect of God, to foster into life and rear up into perfection what is really good, not in the sight of man merely, but in the sight of God; not what is useful merely, but what is true and holy; and if

[10] Rom. viii.29; Rev. xxii.11.

to influence those who act on secondary motives require a low-
ering of the Christian standard, and if an exhibition of the truth
makes a man worse unless it makes him better, then she has
fulfilled her calling if she has saved the few; and she has done
more than her calling, so far as by God's grace she has, consistently with the higher object, restrained, softened, or sobered
the many. Much doubtless she will do in this way, but what she
does must not be by compromise or unfaithfulness. The
Church and the world cannot meet without either the world
rising or the Church falling; and the world forsooth pleads necessity, and says it cannot rise to the Church, and deems the
Church unreasonable when she will not descend instead.

The Gospel then has come to us, not merely to make us good
subjects, good citizens, good members of society, but to make
us members of the New Jerusalem, and "fellow-citizens with
the saints and of the household of God." Certainly no one is a
true Christian who is not a good subject and member of society; but neither is he a true Christian if he is nothing more than
this. If he is not aiming at something beyond the power of the
natural man, he is not really a Christian, or one of the elect.
The Gospel offers to us things supernatural. "Call unto Me,"
says Almighty God by His prophet, "and I will answer thee, and
show thee great and mighty things which thou knowest not." [11]
But, alas! the multitude of men do not enter into the force of
such an invitation, or feel its graciousness or desirableness.
They are satisfied to remain where they find themselves by nature, to be what the world makes them, to bound their conceptions of things by sight and touch, and to conceive of the Gospel
according to the thoughts, motives, and feelings which spring
up spontaneously within them. They form their religion for
themselves from what they are, and live and die in the ordinary
and common-place round of hopes and fears, pleasures and
pains. In the ordinary common-place round of *duties* indeed,
they ought to be engaged, and are bound to find satisfaction. To
be out of conceit with our lot in life, is no high feeling,—it is
discontent or ambition; but to be out of conceit with the ordinary way of *viewing* our lot, with the ordinary thoughts and
feelings of mankind, is nothing but to be a Christian. This is the
difference between worldly ambition and heavenly. It is a heavenly ambition which prompts us to soar above the vulgar and
ordinary *motives* and *tastes* of the world, the while we abide *in*
our calling; like our Saviour who, though the Son of God and

[11] Jer. xxxiii.3.

partaking of His Father's fulness, yet all His youth long was obedient to His earthly parents, and learned a humble trade. But it is a sordid, narrow, miserable ambition to attempt to *leave* our earthly lot; to be wearied or ashamed of what we are, to hanker after greatness of station, or novelty of life. However, the multitude of men go neither in the one way nor the other; they neither have the high ambition nor the low ambition. It is well they have not the low, certainly; it is well they do not aim at being great men, or heroes; but they have no temptation to do so. What they are tempted to, is to settle down in a satisfied way in the world as they find it, to sit down in the "mire and dirt" of their natural state, to immerse themselves and be absorbed in the unhealthy marsh which is under them. They tend to become part of the world, and be sucked in by it, and (as it were) changed into it; and so to lose all aspirations and thoughts, whether good or bad, after any thing higher than what they are. I do not know whether rich or poor are in greater temptation this way. Poor people, having daily wants, having their bread to earn, and raiment and shelter to provide, being keenly and earnestly and day by day pressed with the realities of pain and anxiety, seem cut off from all high thoughts. To call on a poor man to live a Seraph's life, to live above the world, and to be ambitious of perfection, seems at first sight, as things go, all one with bidding him be a man of refinement of mind or literary taste, a man of science, or a philosopher. Yet is it so? Were not the Apostles in great necessities? had not St. Paul to work for his livelihood? did they eat and drink at their will? did they know one day where they should get their meal or lay their head the next? Surely not; yet they were as expressly told as others, "Seek ye first the kingdom of God and His righteousness." [12] And then it is promised with an express reference to those anxieties about food and clothing, "And all these things shall be added unto you." This passage in our Saviour's Sermon on the Mount shows us most undeniably, that poverty must not be allowed to make us,—is no excise for our being,—what poor people so often are, anxious, fretful, close, deceitful, dullminded, suspicious, envious, or ungrateful. No; much as we ought to feel for the poor, yet, if our Saviour's words be true, there is nothing to hinder the poorest man from living the life of an Angel, living in all the unearthly contemplative blessedness of a Saint in glory, except so far as sin interferes with it. I mean, it is *sin*, and not poverty which is the hindrance.

[12] Matt. vi.33.

Such is the case with the poor; now again take the case of those who have a competency. They too are swallowed up in the cares or interests of life as much as the poor are. While want keeps the one from God by unsettling his mind, a competency keeps the other by the seductions of ease and plenty. The poor man says, "I cannot go to Church or to the Sacrament of the Lord's Supper, till I am more at ease in my mind; I am troubled, and my thoughts are not my own." The rich man does not make any excuses,—he comes; but his "heart goeth after his covet-ousness." It is not enlarged by being rid of care; but is as little loosened from what is seen, as little expatiates in the free and radiant light of Gospel day, as if that day had not been poured upon it. No; such a one may be far other than a mere man of the world,—he may be a religious man, in the common sense of the word; he may be exemplary in his conduct, as far as the social duties of life go; he may be really and truly, and not in pretence, kind, benevolent, sincere, and in a manner serious: but so it is, his mind has never been unchained to soar aloft, he does not look out with longing into the infinite spaces in which, as a Christian, he has free range. Our Lord praises those who "*hunger and thirst* after righteousness." *This* is what men in general are without. They are more or less "full, and have need of noth-ing," in religious matters; they do not feel how great a thing it is to be a Christian, and how far they fall short of it. They are contented with themselves on the whole; they are quite con-scious indeed that they do act up to their standard, but it is their standard that is low. A sort of ordinary obedience suffices them as well as the poor. A person in straitened circumstances will say, "I have enough to do to take care of my wife and children;" another says, "I have lost my husband and friends, and have enough to do to take care of myself;" bystanders say, "What a mockery to call on a starving population, to watch, fast, and pray, and aim at perfection." Well, let me turn, I say, to the rich men, and speak to them; what say the rich? *They* put aside all such hungering and thirsting after righteousness as visionary, high-flown, and what they call romantic. They have a certain definite and clear view of their duties; they think that the sum-mit of perfection is to be decent and respectable in their calling, to enjoy moderately the pleasures of life, to eat and drink, and marry and give in marriage, and buy and sell, and plant and build, and to take care that religion does not *engross* them. Alas! and is it so? is the superhuman life enjoined on us in the Gospel but a dream? is there no meaning in our own case, of the texts about the strait gate and the narrow way, and Mary's good part, and the rule of perfection, and the saying which "all cannot receive save they to whom it is given?" Holy men, certainly, do not throw themselves out of their stations. They are not gloomy, or morose, or overbearing, or restless; but still they are pursuing in their daily walk, and by their secret thoughts and actions, a conduct *above* the world. Whether rich or poor, high-born or low-born, married or single, they have never wedded themselves to the world; they have never surrendered them-selves to be its captives; never looked out for station, fashion, comfort, credit, as the end of life. They have kept up the feeling which young people often have, who at first ridicule the artificial forms and usages of society, and find it difficult to con-form themselves to its pomp and pretence. Of course it is not wise to ridicule and run counter to any thing that is in its nature indifferent; and as they have grown older they have learned this; but the feeling remains of want of sympathy with what surrounds them; whereas these are the very things which men of the world are most proud of, their appointments, and their dress, and their bearing, and their gentility, and their acquain-tance with great men, and their connexions, and their power of managing, and their personal importance.

God grant to us a simple, reverent, affectionate, temper, that we may truly be the Church's children, and fit subjects of her instructions! This gained, the rest through His grace will fol-low. This is the temper of those "little ones," whose Angels "do always behold the face" of our heavenly Father; of those for whom Apostles endured all things, to whom the Ordinances of grace minister, and whom Christ "nourisheth and cherisheth" even as His own flesh.

THE COMMUNION OF SAINTS

*"All Thy Works praise Thee, O Lord, and Thy saints give thanks
unto Thee: they show the glory of Thy kingdom,
and talk of Thy power."*—Ps. cxlv.10, 11.

IT was the great promise of the Gospel, that the Lord of all,
who had hitherto manifested Himself externally to His servants, should take up His abode in their hearts. This, as you
must recollect, is frequently the language of the Prophets; and
it was the language of our Saviour when He came on earth: "I
will love him," He says, speaking of those who love and obey
Him, "and will manifest Myself to him. . . . We will come unto
him, and make our abode with him." [1] Though He had come in
our flesh, so as to be seen and handled, even this was not
enough. Still He was external and separate; but after His ascension He descended again by and in His Spirit, and then at length
the promise was fulfilled.

There must indeed be a union between all creatures and their
Almighty Creator even for their very existence; for it is said,
"In Him we live, and move, and have our being;" and in one of
the Psalms, "When Thou lettest Thy breath go forth, they shall
be made." [2] But far higher, more intimate, and more sacred is
the indwelling of God in the hearts of His elect people;—so
intimate, that compared with it, He may well be said not to
inhabit other men at all; His presence being specified as the
characteristic privilege of His own redeemed servants.

From the day of Pentecost, to the present time, it has been
their privilege, according to the promise, "I will pray the Father, and He shall give you another Comforter, that He may
abide with you *for ever*,"—for ever: not like the Son of man, who
having finished His gracious work went away. Then it is added,
"even the *Spirit* of Truth:" that is, He who came for ever, came
as a Spirit, and, so coming, did for His own that which the visible flesh and blood of the Son of man, from its very nature,
could not do, viz., He came into the souls of all who believe,

[1] John xiv.21, 23.   [2] Ps. civ.30.

and taking possession of them, He, being One, knit them all together into one. Christ, by coming in the flesh, provided an external or apparent unity, such as had been under the Law. He formed His Apostles into a visible society; but when He came again in the Person of His Spirit, He made them all in a real sense one, not in name only. For they were no longer arranged merely in the form of unity, as the limbs of the dead may be, but they were parts and organs of one unseen power; they really depended upon, and were offshoots of that which was One; their separate persons were taken into a mysterious union with things unseen, were grafted upon and assimilated to the spiritual body of Christ, which is One, even by the Holy Ghost, in whom Christ has come again to us. Thus Christ came, not to make us one, but to die for us: the Spirit came to make us one in Him who had died and was alive, that is, to form the Church.

This then is the special glory of the Christian Church, that its members do not depend merely on what is visible, they are not mere stones of a building, piled one on another, and bound together from without, but they are one and all the births and manifestations of one and the same unseen spiritual principle or power, "*living* stones," internally connected, as branches from a tree, not as the parts of a heap. They are members of the Body of Christ. That divine and adorable Form, which the Apostles saw and handled, after ascending into heaven became a principle of life, a secret origin of existence to all who believe, through the gracious ministration of the Holy Ghost. This is the fruitful Vine, and the rich Olive tree upon and out of which all Saints, though wild and barren by nature, grow, that they may bring forth fruit unto God. So that in a true sense it may be said, that from the day of Pentecost to this hour there has been in the Church but One Holy One, the King of kings, and Lord of lords Himself, who is in all believers, and through whom they are what they are; their separate persons being but as separate developments, vessels, instruments, and works of Him who is invisible. Such is the difference between the Church before the Spirit of Christ came, and after. Before, God's servants were as the dry bones of the Prophet's vision, connected by profession, not by an inward principle; but since, they are all the organs as if of one invisible, governing Soul, the hands, or the tongues, or the feet, or the eyes of one and the same directing Mind, the types, tokens, beginnings, and glimpses of the Eternal Son of God. Hence the text, in speaking of the kingdom of Christ, enlarges upon the special office of His Saints,—"All Thy works praise Thee, O Lord, and Thy Saints give thanks unto Thee: they show the glory of Thy kingdom, and talk of Thy power, that Thy power, Thy glory, and mightiness of Thy kingdom might be known unto men."

Such is the Christian Church, a *living* body, and *one*; not a mere framework artificially arranged to *look* like one. Its being alive is what makes it one; were it dead, it would consist of as many parts as it has members; but the Living *Spirit* of God came down upon it at Pentecost, and made it *one*, by giving it *life*.

On this great day then,[3] when we commemorate the quickening or vivifying of the Church, the birth of the spiritual and new creature out of an old world "as good as dead," it will be seasonable to consider the nature and attributes of this Church, as manifested in the elect, as invisible, one, living and spiritual; or what is otherwise called the doctrine of the Communion of Saints with each other, and in the Holy Trinity, in whom their communion with each other consists. And this I the rather do, because the Communion of Saints is an article of the Creed, and therefore is not a matter of secondary importance, of doubt or speculation.

The Church then, properly considered, is that great company of the elect, which has been separated by God's free grace, and His Spirit working in due season, from this sinful world, regenerated, and vouchsafed perseverance unto life eternal. Viewed so far as it merely consists of persons *now* living in this world, it is of course a visible company; but in its nobler and truer character it is a body invisible, or nearly so, as being made up, not merely of the few who happen still to be on their trial, but of the many who sleep in the Lord. At first, indeed, in the lifetime of the Apostles, a great proportion of the whole body was in this world; that is, not taking into account those Saints, who had lived in Jewish times, and whom Christ, on His departure, made partakers of the privileges then purchased by His death for *all* believers. St. Stephen and St. James the Greater were the first distinguished Saints of the New Covenant, who were gathered in to enrich the elder company of Moses, Elias, and their brethren. But from that time they have flowed in space; and as years passed away, greater and greater has become the proportion which the assembly of spirits made perfect bears to that body militant which is its complement in God's new creation. At present, we who live are but one generation out of fifty, which since its formation have been new born into it, and endowed with spiritual life and the hope of glory. Fifty times as

[3] Preached on Whitsunday.

many Saints are in the invisible world sealed for immortality, as are now struggling on upon earth towards it; unless indeed the later generations have a greater measure of Saints than the former ones. Well then may the Church be called invisible, not only as regards her vital principle, but in respect to her members. "That which is born of the Spirit is spirit;" and since God the Holy Ghost is invisible, so is His work. The Church is invisible, because the greater number of her true children have been perfected and removed, and because those who are still on earth cannot be ascertained by mortal eye; and had God so willed, she might have had no visible tokens at all of her existence, and been as entirely and absolutely hidden from us as the Holy Ghost is, her Lord and Governor. But seeing that the Holy Ghost is our life, so that to gain life we must approach Him, in mercy to us, His place of abode, the Church of the Living God, is not so utterly veiled from our eyes as He is; but He has given us certain outward signs, as tokens for knowing, and means for entering that living Shrine in which He dwells. He dwells in the hearts of His Saints, in that temple of living stones, on earth and in heaven, which is ever showing the glory of His kingdom, and talking of His power; but since faith and love and joy and peace cannot be seen, since the company of His people are His secret ones, He has given us something outward as a guide to what is inward, something visible as a guide to what is spiritual.

Now, what is that outward visible guide, having the dispensation of what is unseen, but the Christian Ministry, which directs and leads us to the very Holy of Holies, in which Christ dwells by His Spirit? As landmarks or buoys inform the steersman, as the shadow on the dial is an index of the sun's course; so, if we would cross the path of Christ, if we would arrest His eye and engage His attention, if we would interest ourselves in the special virtue and fulness of His grace, we must join ourselves to that Ministry which, when He ascended up on high, He gave us as a relic, and let drop from Him as the mantle of Elijah, the pledge and token of his never-failing grace from age to age. "Tell me, O Thou whom my soul loveth, where Thou feedest, where Thou makest Thy flock to rest at noon; for why should I be as one that turneth aside by the flocks of Thy companions?"[4] Such is the petition, as it were, of the soul that seeks for Christ. His answer is as precise as the question. "If thou know not, O thou fairest among women, go thy way forth by the *footsteps* of the flock, and feed thy kids beside the

---

[4] Cant. i.7, 8.

shepherds' tents." Out of the Church is no salvation—I mean to say out of that great invisible company, who are one and all incorporate in the one mystical body of Christ, and quickened by one Spirit: now, by adhering to the visible Ministry which the Apostles left behind them, we approach unto what we see not, to Mount Zion, to the heavenly Jerusalem, to the spirits of the just, to the first-born elected to salvation, to Angels innumerable, to Jesus the One Mediator, and to God. This heavenly Jerusalem is the true Spouse of Christ and virgin Mother of Saints; and the visible ministry on earth, the Bishops and Pastors, together with Christians depending on them, at this or that day is *called* the Church, though really but a fragment of it, as being that part of it which is seen and can be pointed out, and as resembling it in type, and witnessing it, and leading towards it. This *invisible* body is the *true* Church, because it changes not, though it is ever increasing. What it has, it keeps and never loses; but what is visible is fleeting and transitory, and continually passes off into the invisible. The visible is ever dying for the increase of the invisible company, and is ever reproduced from out the mass of human corruption, by the virtue of the Spirit lodged in the invisible, and acting upon the world. Generation after generation is born, tried, sifted, strengthened, and perfected. Again and again the Apostles live in their successors, and their successors in turn are gathered unto the Apostles. Such is the efficacy of that inexhaustible grace which Christ has lodged in His Church, as a principle of life and increase, till He comes again. The expiring breath of His Saints is but the quickening of dead souls.

And now we may form a clearer notion than is commonly taken of the one Church Catholic which is in all lands. Properly it is not on earth, except so far as heaven can be said to be on earth, or as the dead are still with us. It is not on earth, except in such sense as Christ or His Spirit are on earth. I mean it is not locally or visibly on earth. The Church is not in time or place, but in the region of spirits; it is in the Holy Ghost; and as the soul of man is in every part of his body, yet in no part, not here nor there, yet every where; not so in any one part, head or heart, hands or feet, as not to be in every other; so also the heavenly Jerusalem, the mother of our new birth, is in all lands at once, fully and entirely as a spirit; in the East and in the West, in the North and in the South,—that is, wherever her outward instruments are to be found. The Ministry and Sacraments, the bodily presence of Bishop and people, are given us as keys and spells, by which we bring ourselves into the presence of the great company of Saints; they are as much as this, but they are no more; they are not identical with that company; they are but the outskirts of it; they are but porches to the pool of Bethesda, entrances into that which is indivisible and one. Baptism admits, not into a mere visible society, varying with the country in which it is administered, Roman here, and Greek there, and English there, but *through* the English, *or* the Greek, *or* the Roman porch into the one invisible company of elect souls, which is independent of time and place, and untinctured with the imperfections or errors of that visible porch by which entrance is made. And its efficacy lies in the inflowing upon the soul of the grace of God lodged in that unseen body into which it opens, not, in any respect, in the personal character of those who administer or assist in it. When a child is brought for Baptism, the Church invisible claims it, begs it of God, receives it, and extends to it, as God's instrument, her own sanctity. When we praise God in Holy Communion, we praise Him with the Angels and Archangels, who are the guards, and with the Saints, who are the citizens of the City of God. When we offer our Sacrifice of praise and thanksgiving, or partake of the sacred elements so offered, we solemnly eat and drink of the powers of the world to come. When we read the Psalms, we use before many witnesses the very words on which those witnesses themselves—I mean, all successive generations of that holy company,—have sustained themselves in their own day, for thousands of years past, during their pilgrimage heavenward. When we profess the Creed, it is no self-willed, arbitrary sense, but in the presence of those innumerable Saints who well remember what its words mean, and are witnesses of it before God, in spite of the heresy or indifference of this or that day. When we stand over their graves, we are in the very vestibule of that dwelling which is "all-glorious within," full of light and purity, and of voices crying, "Lord, how long?" When we pray in private, we are not solitary; others "are gathered together" with us "in Christ's Name," though we see them not, with Christ in the midst of them. When we approach the Ministry which He has ordained, we approach the steps of His throne. When we approach the Bishops, who are the centres of that Ministry, what have we before us but the Twelve Apostles, present but invisible? When we use the sacred Name of Jesus, or the Sign given us in Baptism, what do we but bid defiance to devils and evil men, and gain strength to resist them? When we protest, or confess, or suffer in the Name of Christ, what are we but ourselves types and symbols of the Cross of Christ, and of the strength of Him who died on it? When we are called to battle for the Lord, what are we who are seen, but mere outposts, the advanced guard of a mighty host, ourselves few in number and despicable, but bold beyond our numbers, because supported by chariots of fire and horses of fire round about the Mountain of the Lord of Hosts under which we stand?

Such is the City of God, the Holy Church Catholic throughout the world, manifested in and acting through what is called in each country the Church visible; which visible Church really depends solely on it, on the invisible,—not on civil power, not on princes or any child of man, not on its endowments, not on its numbers, not on any thing that is seen, unless indeed heaven can depend on earth, eternity on time, Angels on men, the dead on the living. The unseen world through God's secret power and mercy, encroaches upon this world; and the Church that is seen is just that portion of it by which it encroaches; and thus though the visible Churches of the Saints in this world seem rare, and scattered to and fro, like islands in the sea, they are in truth but the tops of the everlasting hills, high and vast and deeply-rooted, which a deluge covers.

Now these thoughts are so very foreign from the world's ordinary view of things, which walks by sight, not by faith, and never allows any thing to exist in what comes before it, but what it can touch and handle, that it is necessary to insist and enlarge upon them. The world then makes *itself* the standard of perfection and the centre of all good; and when the souls of Christians pass from it into the place of spirits, it fancies that this is *their* loss, not its own; it pities them in its way of speaking of them, and calls them by names half compassionate, half contemptuous, as if its own presence and society were some great thing. It pities them too as thinking that they do not witness the termination of what they began or saw beginning, that they are ignorant of the fortunes of their friends or of the Church, are powerless over their own schemes, or rather careless about them, as being insensible, and but shadows, and ghosts not substances; as if we who live were the real agents in the course of events, and they were attached to us only as a church-yard to a church, which it is decent to respect, unsuitable to linger in. Such is its opinion of the departed; as though *we* were in light and *they* in darkness,—we in power and influence, they in weakness,—we the living, and they the dead; yet with the views opened on us in the Gospel, with the knowledge that the One Spirit of Christ ever abides, and that those who are made one with Him are never parted from Him, and that those who die in

Him are irrevocably knit into Him and one with Him, shall we dare to think slightly of these indefectible members of Christ and vessels of future glory? Shall we presume to compare that great assemblage of the elect, perfected and at rest,—shall we weigh in the balance that glorious Church invisible, so populous in souls, so pure from sin, so rid of probation,—with ourselves, poor strugglers with the flesh and the devil, who have but the earnest not the crown of victory, whose names are not so written in the heavens, but they may be blotted out again? Shall we doubt for a moment, though St. Paul was martyred centuries upon centuries since, that he, who even while in the body was present in spirit at Corinth when he was at Ephesus, is present in the Church still, more truly alive than those who are called living, more truly and awfully an Apostle now upon a throne, than when he had fightings without and fears within, a thorn in his flesh, and a martyrdom in prospect? Shall we be as infidels to suppose that the Church is only what she seems to be, a poor, helpless, despised, and human institution, scorned by the wealthy, plundered by the violent, out-reasoned by the sophist, and patronized by the great, and not rather believe that she is serving in presence of the Eternal Throne, round which are the "four and twenty seats, and upon the seats" are "four and twenty elders sitting, clothed in white raiment," and "on their heads crowns of gold?"[5] Nay shall we not dimly recognize amid the aisles of our churches and along our cloisters, about our ancient tombs, and in ruined and desolate places, which once were held sacred, not in cold poetical fancy, but by the eye of faith,—the spirits of our fathers and brethren of every time, past and present, whose works have long been "known" to God, and whose former dwelling-places remain among us, pledges (as we trust) that He will not utterly forsake us, and make an end? Can aught mortal and earthly, force without, or treachery within, the popular voice, or any will of man, aught in the whole universe, height or depth, or any other creature, aught save the decree of God, issued for our sins, chase away our holy unseen companions from us, and level us with the grass of the field? Can all the efforts of the children of men, their accurate delineations of our outward form, their measurement of our visible territory, their summing up of our substance, their impairing of our civil rights, their numbering of our supporters, circumscribe the City of the Living God, or localize the site of Eden, and the Mountain of the Saints?

[5] Rev. iv.4.

But here it may be asked, whether such a belief in the ever-abiding presence among us of the Church invisible, in that Spirit whom all believe to be ever present with us to the end, does not interfere with our comfortable assurance that it is at rest. "Christ (it may be said) worketh hitherto as His Father worketh; and the Angels excel in strength; but human nature, even in its purest and more heavenly specimens, is unequal to this incessant watchfulness, and when it dies is said to fall asleep:—why should we not leave to it so comfortable and gracious a portion?" Now, however we answer this question, so far is certain, for we have St. Paul's authority for saying it, that in coming to the Church, we approach not God alone, nor Jesus the Mediator of the New Covenant, nor Angels innumerable, but also, as he says expressly, "the spirits of the just made perfect." And in thus speaking, he is evidently speaking neither of saints on earth nor saints after the resurrection, were it only that he designates especially "the *spirits* of the *just*." Certainly, then, the Church, in St. Paul's judgment, is made up of the dead as well as of the living; and though this be so, though the dead be present, it does not follow they are not at rest also. Such presence in the Church does not involve any labour or toil, any active interference, on the part of those who (we are told) "rest from their labours." For it is plain, though they "live unto God," and have power with Him, this does not imply that they *act*, or that they are *conscious* of their power. This holds good, through God's mercy, in the case of those who labour in the flesh, who pray and preach, work righteousness, and glorify God. They too see none of those fruits which notwithstanding do follow them. Had Noah, Daniel, and Job been in any evil city, and saved it by their righteousness from destruction, would they have known what they were enabled to do? We have no reason to say they would; for it is one thing to do good, another to see we do it.

But again it may be quite true that in one sense they are at rest, and yet in another active promoters of the Church's welfare, as by prayer; though we know not *how* they are active, or *how* they are at rest, or *how* they can be both at once. It is said that God "rested on the seventh day from all the work which He had made," yet nevertheless that He "worketh hitherto." Surely, in Him who is eternal and all-sufficient, is found absolutely and perfectly that incomprehensible union of Almighty power with everlasting repose; and what He is in fulness, He may graciously impart in its degree, and according to their capacity to His chosen. If it is no contradiction in terms that God should rest and yet work, that the Son of God should die and yet have an eternal essence, that the Son of man should be in heaven while He spoke to Nicodemus, it may be no contradiction that the soul of man should sleep in the intermediate state, and yet be awake. I say, what God has infinitely and by nature, He may bestow in part to us; and thus it may be true that though the Saints are "joyful with glory," and "rejoice in their beds," and "the praises of God" are "in their mouths," yet at the same time "a two-edged sword" is "in their hands, to be avenged of the heathen, and to rebuke the people; to bind their kings in chains and their nobles with links of iron; that they may be avenged of them, as it is written: Such honour have all His Saints." [6]

Lastly, while we thus think of the invisible Church, we are restrained by many reasons from such invocations of her separate members as are unhappily so common in other Christian countries. First, because the practice was not primitive, but an addition when the world had poured into the Church; next, because we are told to pray to God only, and invocation may easily be corrupted into prayer, and then becomes idolatrous. And further, it must be considered that though the Church is represented in Scripture as a channel of God's gifts to us, yet it is only as a body and sacramentally, not as an agent, nor in her members one by one. St. Paul does not say that we are brought near to this saint or that saint, but to all together, "to the spirits of just men made perfect;" one by one they have to undergo the Day of Judgment, but as a body they are the City of God, the immaculate Spouse of the Lamb.

Let us then stand in that lot in which God has placed us, and thank Him for what He has so mercifully, so providentially done for us. He has done all things well,—neither too much nor too little. He has neither told us to neglect the faithful servants of Christ departed, nor to pay them undue honour; but to think of them, yet not speak to them; to make much of them, but to trust solely in Him. Let us follow His rule, neither exceeding nor wanting in our duty; but according to St. Paul's injunction, "using" His gifts "without abusing" them; not ceasing to use, lest we *should* abuse, but abstaining from the abuse, while we adhere thankfully to the use.

These are inspiring thoughts for the solitary, the dejected, the harassed, the defamed, or the despised Christian; and they belong to him, if by act and deed he unites in that Communion

[6] Ps. cxlix.5–9.

which he professes. He joins the Church of God, not merely who speaks about it, or who defends it, or who contemplates it, but who loves it. He loves the unseen company of believers, who loves those who are seen. The test of our being joined to Christ is love; the test of love towards Christ and His Church, is loving those whom we actually see. "He that loveth not his brother whom he hath seen, how can he love God, whom he hath not seen?"[7] As then we would be worthy to hold communion with believers of every time and place, let us hold communion duly with those of our own day and our own neighbourhood. Let us pray God, to teach us what we are so deficient in, and save us from using words and cherishing thoughts which our actions put to shame. It is a very easy thing to say fine things, which we have no right to say. Let us feel tenderly affectioned towards all whom Christ has made His own by Baptism. Let us sympathize with them, and have kind thoughts towards them, and be warm-hearted, and loving, and simple-minded, and gentle-tempered towards them, and consult for their good, and pray for their growth in faith and holiness. "Let us not love in word, neither in tongue, but in deed and in truth." For "God is love;" and if we love one another, "God dwelleth in us, and His love is perfected in us."

[7] 1 John iv.20.

THE CHURCH A HOME
FOR THE LONELY

"Hath raised us up together, and made us sit together in heavenly
places in Christ Jesus."—Eph. ii.6.

D ID we from our youth up follow the guidings of God's
grace, we should, without reasoning and without severe
trial, understand that heaven is an object claiming our highest
love and most persevering exertions. Such doubtless is the
blessedness of some persons: such in a degree is perchance the
blessedness of many. There are those who, like Samuel, dwell in
the Temple of God holy and undefiled from infancy, and, after
the instance of John the Baptist, are sanctified by the Holy
Ghost, if not as he, from their mother's womb, yet from their
second birth in Holy Baptism. And there are others who possess
this great gift more or less, in whom the divine light has been
preserved, even though it has been latent; not quenched or
overborne by open sin, even though it has not been from the
first duly prized and cherished. Many there are, one would
hope, who keep their baptismal robes unstained, even though
the wind and storm of this world, and the dust of sloth and
carelessness for a while discolour them; till in due season they
arouse them from their dreams, and, before it is too late, give
their hearts to God. All these, whether they have followed Him
from infancy, or from childhood, or from boyhood, or from
youth, or from opening manhood, have never been wedded to
this world; they have never given their hearts to it, or vowed
obedience or done folly in things of time and sense. And therefore they are able, from the very power of God's grace, as conveyed to them through the ordinances of the Gospel, to
understand that the promise of heaven is the greatest, most
blessed promise which could be given.

Others turn from God, and fall into courses of wilful sin, and
they of course lose the divine light originally implanted; and if
they are recovered are recovered by a severer discipline. They
are recovered by finding disappointment and suffering from

850

that which they had hoped would bring them good; they learn to love God and prize heaven, not by baptismal grace, but by trial of the world; they seek the world, and they are driven by the world back again to God. The world is blessed to them, in God's good providence, as an instrument of His grace transmuted from evil to good, as if a second sacrament, doing over again what was done in infancy, and then undone. They are led to say, with St. Peter, "Lord, to whom *shall* we go?" for they have tried the world, and it fails them; they have trusted it, and it deceives them; they have leant upon it, and it pierces them through; they have sought it for indulgence, and it has scourged them for their penance. O blessed lot of those, whose wanderings though they wander, are thus overruled; that what they lose of the free gift of God, they regain by His compulsory remedies!

But almost all men, whether they are thereby moved to return to God or not, will on experience feel, and confess, and that in no long time, that the world is not enough for their happiness; and they accordingly seek means to supply their need, though they do not go to religion for it. Though they will not accept God's remedy, yet they confess that a remedy is needed, and have recourse to what they think will prove such. Though they may not love God and His holy heaven, yet they find they cannot take up with the world, or cast their lot with it wholly, much as they may wish it. This leads me to the subject which I propose to consider, as suggested by the text; viz. the need which mankind lies under of some shelter, refuge, rest, home or sanctuary from the outward world, and the shelter or secret place which God has provided for them in Christ.

By the world, I mean all that meets a man in intercourse with his fellow men, whether in public or in private, all that is new, strange, and without natural connexion with him. This outward world is at first sight most attractive and exciting to the generality of men. The young commonly wish to enter into it as if it would fulfil all their wants and hopes. They wish to enter into life, as it is called. Their hearts beat, as they anticipate the time when they shall, in one sense or other, be their own masters. At home, or at school, they are under restraint, and thus they come to look forward to the liberty of the world, and the independence of being in it, as a great good. According to their rank in life, they wish to get into service, or they wish to go into business, or they wish to be principals in trade, or they wish to enter into the world's amusements and gaieties, or they look forward with interest to some profession or employment which stirs their ambition and promises distinction.

And when their wish is gratified, for a time all things perhaps go as they would have them. There is so much novelty, and so much interest in what takes place out of doors, that they find themselves as if in a new state of existence, and in one way or other "rejoice in their youth." Happy they who are otherwise circumstanced; for there *are* a number after all who may be said to have no youth; who from weak health, or from narrow circumstances, or from unkind superiors, or from family affliction, or from other causes, though in the world, have scarcely been exposed at all to its seductions, or have seen in it any thing to delight them, or to arrest their imagination or reason. God's providence has so ordered it for them, that, whatever be their peculiar trials and temptations, these do not come from the gaieties or the occupations of life. From the first they have only had experience of the world as a hard master, and owe it nothing. But whatever be our lot, whether to have had enjoyment from the world or not, whether we have not had the temptation of it, or not felt it, or felt it and overcome it, or felt it and been overcome, all men, whether religious or not, find in no long time that the world is insufficient for their happiness, and look elsewhere for repose.

Surely this is the case on all sides of us; the outward world is found not to be enough for man, and he looks for some refuge near him, more intimate, more secret, more pure, more calm and stable. This is a main reason and a praiseworthy one, why a great number of the better sort of men look forward to marriage as the great object of life. They call it being settled, and so it is. The mind finds nothing to satisfy it in the employments and amusements of life, in its excitements, struggles, anxieties, efforts, aims, and victories. Supposing a man to make money, to get on in life, to rise in society, to gain power, whether in a higher or lower sphere, this does not suffice; he wants a home, he wants a centre on which to place his thoughts and affections, a secret dwelling-place which may soothe him after the troubles of the world, and which may be his hidden stay and support wherever he goes, and dwell in his heart, though it be not named upon his tongue. The world may seduce, may terrify, may mislead, may enslave, but it cannot really inspire confidence and love. There is no rest for us, except in quietness, confidence, and affection; and hence all men, without taking religion into account, seek to make themselves a home, as the only need of their nature, or are unhappy if they be without one. Thus they witness against the world, even though they be children of the world; witness against it equally with the holiest and most self-denying, who have by faith overcome it.

Here then Christ finds us, weary of that world in which we are obliged to live and act, whether as willing or unwilling slaves to it. He finds us needing and seeking a home, and making one, as we best may, by means of the creature, since it is all we can do. The world, in which our duties lie, is as waste as the wilderness, as restless and turbulent as the ocean, as inconstant as the wind and weather. It has no substance in it, but is like a shade or phantom; when you pursue it, when you try to grasp it, it escapes from you, or it is malicious, and does you a mischief. We need something which the world cannot give: this is what we need, and this it is which the Gospel has supplied.

I say, that our Lord Jesus Christ, after dying for our sins on the Cross, and ascending on high, left not the world as He found it, but left a blessing behind Him. He left in the world what before was not in it,—a secret home, for faith and love to enjoy, wherever they are found, in spite of the world around us. Do you ask what it is? the chapter from which the text is taken describes it. It speaks of "the foundation of the Apostles and Prophets, Jesus Christ Himself being the chief corner-stone;" of "the Building fitly framed" and "growing unto an Holy Temple in the Lord;" of "a Habitation of God through the Spirit." This is the Church of God, which is our true Home of God's providing, His own heavenly court, where He dwells with Saints and Angels, into which He introduces us by a new birth, and in which we forget the outward world and its many troubles.

The Jews had some such refuge in their own material Temple, though of course it was far inferior to that which Christ has provided. Thrice a year did all the males from every quarter go up to Jerusalem to appear before God in it; and some holy persons were even allowed to dwell in it. Such were the prophet Samuel in his youth, and Anna the prophetess in her old age; not to mention Priests and Levites, who were ever there by office. The Temple rose stately and beautiful upon Mount Zion, invited the worshipper, admitted him, hid him from the outward world, with all its miseries and offences, and brought him immediately into God's Presence. No wonder, then, that David speaks with such devout affection of it, and with such sorrow and longing when he is away. "O how amiable are Thy dwellings," he says, "Thou Lord of Hosts! My soul hath a desire and longing to enter into the courts of the Lord; my heart and my flesh rejoice in the living God. . . . . Blessed are they that dwell in Thy house; they will be alway praising Thee. . . . . One day in Thy courts is better than a thousand. I had rather be a doorkeeper in the house of my God, than to dwell in the tents of ungodliness." And again, "My soul is athirst for God, yea, even for the living God: when shall I come to appear before the presence of God?" "O send out Thy light and Thy truth, that they may lead me, and bring me unto Thy holy hill and to Thy dwelling; and that I may go unto the altar of God, even unto the God of my joy and gladness; and upon the harp will I give thanks unto Thee, O God, my God." And again, "Behold now, praise the Lord, all ye servants of the Lord: ye that by night stand in the house of the Lord, even in the courts of the house of our God. Lift up your hands in the sanctuary, and praise the Lord."[1]

Such was the Jewish Temple; but, besides other deficiencies, as being visible and material, it was confined to one place. It could not be a home for the whole world, nay not for one nation, but only for a few out of the multitude. But the Christian Temple is invisible and spiritual, and hence admits of being every where. "The kingdom of God," says our Lord, speaking of it, "cometh not with observation; neither shall they say, Lo here, or Lo there; for behold, the kingdom of God is within you." And again to the Samaritan woman, "The hour cometh, when ye shall neither in this mountain nor yet at Jerusalem, worship the Father. . . . The hour cometh, and now is, when the true worshippers shall worship the Father in Spirit and in truth; for the Father seeketh such to worship Him. God is a Spirit; and they that worship Him must worship Him in spirit and in truth."[2] "In spirit and in truth;" for unless His Presence were invisible, it could not be real. That which is seen is not real; that which is material is dissoluble; that which is in time is temporary; that which is local is but partial. But the Christian Temple is wherever Christians are found in Christ's Name; it is as fully in each place as if it were in no other; and we may enter it, and appear among its holy inmates, God's heavenly family, as really as the Jewish worshipper betook himself to the visible courts of the Temple. We see nothing; but this I repeat, is a condition necessary to its being every where. It would not be every where, if we saw it any where; we see nothing; but we enjoy every thing.

---

[1] Ps. lxxxiv.; xlii.; xliii.; cxxxiv.
[2] Luke xvii.20, 21; John iv.21–24.

And thus is it set before us in the Old Testament, whether in prophecy or by occasional anticipation. Isaiah prophesies that "it shall come to pass, that the Mountain of the Lord's House shall be established in the top of the mountains, and shall be exalted above the hills; and *all nations* shall flow into it." And it was shown by anticipation to Jacob, and Elisha's servant; to Jacob when he saw in his dream "a ladder set upon the earth, and the top of it reached to heaven, and behold the Angels of God ascending and descending on it;" and to Elisha's servant when "the Lord opened the eyes of the young man . . . . . and behold the mountain was full of horses and chariots of fire round about Elisha." [3] These were anticipations of what was to be continually, when Christ came and "opened the kingdom of heaven to all believers;" and what that opening consisted in, St. Paul tells us.—"Ye are come," he says, "unto Mount Sion, and unto the City of the Living God, the heavenly Jerusalem, and to an innumerable company of Angels, to the general assembly and church of the first-born which are written in heaven, and to God the Judge of all, and to the spirits of just men made perfect, and to Jesus the Mediator of the New Covenant, and to the blood of sprinkling." Such are the dwellers in our holy home; God Himself; Christ; the assembly of the first-born, such as the Apostles; Angels; and the spirits of the just. This being the case, no wonder the text actually speaks of the Church as heaven upon earth, saying that God "hath quickened us together with Christ, ... and hath raised us up together, and made us sit together in heavenly places in Christ Jesus."

What, then, the visible Temple was to the Jews, such and much more is the kingdom of heaven to us; it is really a refuge and hiding-place as theirs was, and shuts out the world. When men are distressed with anxiety, care, and disappointment, what do they? they take refuge in their families; they surround themselves with the charities of domestic life, and make for themselves an inner world, that their affections may have something to rest on. Such was the gift which inspired men anticipated, and we enjoy in the Christian Church. "*Hide* me," the Psalmist prays, "from the gathering together of the froward, and from the insurrection of wicked doers." Again: "Keep me as the apple of an eye; *hide* me under the shadow of Thy wings; from the ungodly that trouble me." Again; "Blessed is the man whom Thou choosest and receivest unto Thee; he shall dwell in Thy court, and shall be satisfied with the pleasures of Thy House,

[3] Is. ii.2; Gen. xxviii.12; 2 Kings vi.17.

even of Thy Holy Temple. Thou shalt show us wonderful things in Thy righteousness, O God of our salvation." And again; "One thing have I desired of the Lord, which I will require; even that I may dwell in the house of the Lord all the days of my life, to behold the fair beauty of the Lord, and to visit His Temple: for in the time of trouble He shall *hide* me in His Tabernacle, yea, in the secret place of His dwelling shall He *hide* me, and set me up upon a rock of stone." Again; "Thou art a place to *hide* me in, Thou shalt preserve me from trouble." Once more; "O how plentiful is Thy goodness, which Thou hast laid up for them that fear Thee . . . . Thou shalt *hide* them privily *by Thine own presence* from the provoking of all men; Thou shalt keep them *secretly* in Thy tabernacle from the strife of tongues. Thanks be to the Lord; for He hath shewed me marvellous great kindness in a strong city." And in like manner the Prophets; for instance, the Prophet Isaiah says, "Behold a king shall reign in righteousness, and princes shall rule in judgment, and a man shall be as an *hiding-place* from the wind, and a covert from the tempest, as rivers of water in a dry place, as the shadow of a great rock in a weary land." Again; "Thou hast been a strength to the poor, a strength to the needy in his distress, a refuge from the storm, a shadow from the heat . . . . . in this mountain shall the hand of the Lord rest." "We have a strong city; salvation will God appoint for walls and bulwarks. Open ye the gates, that the righteous nation which keepeth the truth may enter in; Thou wilt keep him in perfect peace whose mind is stayed on Thee; because he trusteth in Thee." And again; "The work of righteousness shall be peace, and the effect of righteousness quietness and assurance for ever. And My people shall dwell in a peaceable habitation, and in sure dwellings, and in quiet-resting places; when it shall hail, coming down on the forest." With which agree many texts in the New Testament, such as St. Paul's words to the Colossians, "Your life is *hid* with Christ in God."[4]

Now what has been said, little as it is to what might be brought together on the subject, may suffice to suggest to us that great privilege which we may enjoy if we seek it, of dwelling in a heavenly home in the midst of this turbulent world. The world is no helpmeet for man, and a helpmeet he needs. No one, man nor woman, can stand alone; we are so constituted by nature; and the world, instead of helping us, is an open adversary. It but increases our solitariness. Elijah cried, "I, I only am

[4] Ps. lxiv.; xvii.; lxv.; xxvii.; xxxii.; xxxi.; Is. xxxii.; xxv; xxvi; Col. iii.

left, and they seek my life to take it away." [5] How did Almighty God answer him? by graciously telling him that He had reserved to Himself a remnant of seven thousand true believers. Such is the blessed truth which He brings home to us also. We may be full of sorrows; there may be fightings without and fears within; we may be exposed to the frowns, censure, or contempt of men; we may be shunned by them; or, to take the lightest case, we may be (as we certainly shall be) wearied out by the unprofitableness of this world, by its coldness, unfriendliness, distance, and dreariness; we shall need something nearer to us. What is our resource? It is not in arm of man, in flesh and blood, in voice of friend, or in pleasant countenance; it is that holy home which God has given us in His Church; it is that everlasting City in which He has fixed His abode. It is that Mount invisible whence Angels are looking at us with their piercing eyes, and the voices of the dead call us. "Greater is He that is in us than he that is in the world;" "If God be for us, who can be against us?"

Great privilege indeed, if we did but realize its greatness! Man seeks the creature when the world distresses him; let us seek the Creator; let us "seek the Lord and His strength, seek His face evermore." Let us turn from the world, let us hide ourselves in His dwelling-place, let us shroud ourselves from the earth, and disappear in the spiritual kingdom of our God. Great benefit indeed beyond thought, thus to ally ourselves with the upper creation of God instead of taking our portion with the lower! What can we want more than this, whether to satisfy our real wants or our own feeling of them? Do we need aid and comfort? Can any thing of this world impart such strength, as He who is present in that Sanctuary which He has given us? Do we need images and ideas to occupy our minds for encouragement and comfort, as intelligible companions, which we may think of and dwell upon, and hold communion with, and be one with? What fellowship can be more glorious, more satisfying than that which we may hold with those inmates of the City of God whom St. Paul enumerates? Leave then this earthly scene, O virgin soul, though most attractive and most winning; aim at a higher prize, a nobler companionship. Enter into the tabernacle of God. "Whoso dwelleth under the defence of the Most High, shall abide under the shadow of the Almighty . . . . He shall defend thee under His wings, and thou shalt be safe under His feathers. Thou shalt not be afraid for any terror

[5] 1 Kings xix. 10.

by night, nor for the arrow that flieth by day. Thou shalt go upon the lion and adder, the young lion and the dragon shalt thou tread under thy feet." Satan may do his worst; he may afflict thee sore, he may wound thee, he may brand thee, he may cripple thee, as regards *this* world; but he cannot touch thee in things spiritual; he has no power over thee to bring thee into sin and God's displeasure. O virgin soul, let this be thy stay in the dark day. When thou art sick of the world, to whom shouldst thou go? to none short of Him who is the Heavenly Spouse of every faithful soul. Yield thyself to Him freely and without guile. "He will bring thee to the banqueting house, and His banner over thee shall be love. He will make thee to sit down under His shadow with great delight, and His fruit shall be sweet to thy taste." Thou needest covet nothing on earth; thou art full and aboundest; houses, and lands, and brethren, and parents, and wife, and children, are more than made up by "the special gift of faith, more acceptable to thy mind." [6] Though thou art in a body of flesh, a member of this world, thou hast but to kneel down reverently in prayer, and thou art at once in the society of Saints and Angels. Wherever thou art, thou canst, through God's incomprehensible mercy, in a moment bring thyself into the midst of God's holy Church invisible, and receive secretly that aid, the very thought of which is a present sensible blessing. Art thou afflicted? thou canst pray; art thou merry? thou canst sing psalms. Art thou lonely? does the day run heavily? fall on thy knees, and thy thoughts are at once relieved by the idea and by the reality of thy unseen companions. Art thou tempted to sin? think steadily of those who perchance witness thy doings from God's secret dwelling-place; hast thou lost friends? realize them by faith; art thou slandered? thou hast the praise of Angels; art thou under trial? thou hast their sympathy.

May thoughts like these, my brethren, sink deep into your hearts, and bring forth good fruit in holiness and constancy of obedience. Whatever has been your past life, whether (blessed be God) you have never trusted aught but God's sacred light within you, or whether you have trusted the world and it has failed you, God's mercies in Christ are here offered to you in full abundance. Come to Him for them; approach Him in the way He has appointed, and you shall find Him, as He has said, upon His Holy Hill of Zion. Let not your past sins keep you from Him. Whatever they be, they cannot interfere with His

[6] Wisd. iii.14.

grace stored up for all who come to Him for it. If you have in past years neglected Him, perchance you will have to suffer for it; but fear not; He will give you grace and strength to bear such punishment as He may be pleased to inflict. Let not the thought of His just severity keep you at a distance. He can make even pain pleasant to you. Keeping from Him is not to escape from His power, only from His love. Surrender yourselves to Him in faith and holy fear. He is All-merciful, though All-righteous; and though He is awful in His judgments, He is nevertheless more wonderfully pitiful, and of tender compassion above our largest expectations; and in the case of all who humbly seek Him, He will in "wrath remember mercy."

THE INVISIBLE WORLD

"While we look not at the things which are seen, but at the things which are not seen; for the things which are seen are temporal, but the things which are not seen are eternal."—2 Cor. iv.18.

THERE are two worlds, "the visible and the invisible," as the Creed speaks,—the world we see, and the world we do not see; and the world which we do not see as really exists as the world we do see. It really exists, though we see it not. The world that we see we know to exist, *because* we see it. We have but to lift up our eyes and look around us, and we have proof of it: our eyes tell us. We see the sun, moon and stars, earth and sky, hills and valleys, woods and plains, seas and rivers. And again, we see men, and the works of men. We see cities, and stately buildings, and their inhabitants; men running to and fro, and busying themselves to provide for themselves and their families, or to accomplish great designs, or for the very business' sake. All that meets our eyes forms one world. It is an immense world; it reaches to the stars. Thousands on thousands of years might we speed up the sky, and though we were swifter than the light itself, we should not reach them all. They are at distances from us greater than any that is assignable. So high, so wide, so deep is the world; and yet it also comes near and close to us. It is every where; and it seems to leave no room for any other world.

And yet in spite of this universal world which we see, there is another world, quite as far-spreading, quite as close to us, and more wonderful; another world all around us, though we see it not, and more wonderful than the world we see, for this reason if for no other, that we do not see it. All around us are number-less objects, coming and going, watching, working or waiting, which we see not: this is that other world, which the eyes reach not unto, but faith only.

Let us dwell upon this thought. We are born into a world of sense; that is, of the real things which lie round about us, one great department comes to us, accosts us, through our bodily organs, our eyes, ears, and fingers. We feel, hear, and see them; and we know they exist, because we do thus perceive them.

Things innumerable lie about us, animate and inanimate; but one particular class of these innumerable things is thus brought home to us through our senses. And moreover, while they act upon us, they make their presence known. We are sensible of them at the time, we are conscious that we perceive them. We not only see, but know that we see them; we not only hold intercourse, but know that we do. We are among men, and we know that we are. We feel cold and hunger; we know what sensible things remove them. We eat, drink, clothe ourselves, dwell in houses, converse and act with others, and perform the duties of social life; and we feel vividly that we are doing so, while we do so. Such is our relation towards one part of the innumerable beings which lie around us. They act upon us, and we know it; and we act upon them in turn, and know we do.

But all this does not interfere with the existence of that other world which I speak of, acting upon us, yet not impressing us with the consciousness that it does so. It may as really be present and exert an influence as that which reveals itself to us. And that such a world there is, Scripture tells us. Do you ask what it is, and what it contains? I will not say that all that belongs to it is vastly more important than what we see, for among things visible are our fellow-men, and nothing created is more precious and noble than a son of man. But still, taking the things which we see altogether, and the things we do not see altogether, the world we do not see is on the whole a much higher world than that which we do see. For, first of all, He is there who is above all beings, who has created all, before whom they all are as nothing, and with whom nothing can be compared. Almighty God, we know, exists more really and absolutely than any of those fellow-men whose existence is conveyed to us through the senses; yet we see Him not, hear Him not, we do but "feel after Him," yet without finding Him. It appears, then, that the things which are seen are but a part, and but a secondary part of the beings about us, were it only on this ground, that Almighty God, the Being of beings, is not in their number, but among "the things which are not seen." Once, and once only, for thirty-three years, has He condescended to become one of the beings which are seen, when He, the second Person of the Ever-blessed Trinity, was, by an unspeakable mercy, born of the Virgin Mary into this sensible world. And then He was seen, heard, handled; He ate, He drank, He slept, He conversed, He went about, He acted as other men: but excepting this brief period, His presence has never been perceptible; He has never made us conscious of His existence by means of our

senses. He came, and He retired beyond the veil: and to us individually, it is as if He had never shown Himself; we have as little
sensible experience of His presence. Yet "He liveth evermore."

And in that other world are the souls also of the dead. They
too, when they depart hence, do not cease to exist, but they
retire from this visible scene of things; or, in other words, they
cease to act towards us and before us *through our senses*. They live
as they lived before; but that outward frame, through which
they were able to hold communion with other men, is in some
way, we know not how, separated from them, and dries away
and shrivels up as leaves may drop off a tree. They remain, but
without the usual means of approach towards us, and correspondence with us. As when a man loses his voice or hand, he
still exists as before, but cannot any longer talk or write, or otherwise hold intercourse with us; so when he loses not voice and
hand only, but his whole frame, or is said to die, there is nothing
to show that he is gone, but we have lost our means of apprehending him.

Again: Angels also are inhabitants of the world invisible, and
concerning them much more is told us than concerning the
souls of the faithful departed, because the latter "rest from
their labours;" but the Angels are actively employed among us
in the Church. They are said to be "ministering spirits, sent
forth to minister for them who shall be heirs of salvation."[1] No
Christian is so humble but he has Angels to attend on him, if he
lives by faith and love. Though they are so great, so glorious, so
pure, so wonderful, that the very sight of them (if we were allowed to see them) would strike us to the earth, as it did the
prophet Daniel, holy and righteous as he was; yet they are our
"fellow-servants" and our fellow-workers, and they carefully
watch over and defend even the humblest of us, if we be
Christ's. That they form a part of our unseen world, appears
from the vision seen by the patriarch Jacob. We are told that
when he fled from his brother Esau, "he lighted upon a certain
place, and tarried there all night, because the sun had set; and
he took of the stones of that place, and put them for his pillows,
and lay down in that place to sleep."[2] How little did he think
that there was any thing very wonderful in this spot! It looked
like any other spot. It was a lone, uncomfortable place: there
was no house there: night was coming on; and he had to sleep
upon the bare rock. Yet how different was the truth! He saw but
the world that is seen; he saw not the world that is not seen; yet

---

[1] Heb. i. 14.   [2] Gen. xxviii. 11.

the world that is not seen was there. It was there, though it did not at once make known its presence, but needed to be supernaturally displayed to him. He saw it in his sleep. "He dreamed, and behold, a ladder set up on the earth, and the top of it reached up to heaven; and behold, the Angels of God ascending and descending on it. And behold, the Lord stood above it." This was the other world. Now, let this be observed. Persons commonly speak as if the other world did not exist now, but would after death. No: it exists now, though we see it not. It is among us and around us. Jacob was shown this in his dream. Angels were all about him, though he knew it not. And what Jacob saw in his sleep, that Elisha's servant saw as if with his eyes; and the shepherds, at the time of the Nativity, not only saw, but heard. They heard the voices of those blessed spirits who praise God day and night, and whom we, in our lower state of being, are allowed to copy and assist.

We are then in a world of spirits, as well as in a world of sense, and we hold communion with it, and take part in it, though we are not conscious of doing so. If this seems strange to any one, let him reflect that we are undeniably taking part in a third world, which we do indeed see, but about which we do not know more than about the Angelic hosts,—the world of brute animals. Can any thing be more marvellous or startling, unless we were used to it, than that we should have a race of beings about us whom we do but see, and as little know their state, or can describe their interests, or their destiny, as we can tell of the inhabitants of the sun and moon? It is indeed a very overpowering thought, when we get to fix our minds on it, that we familiarly use, I may say hold intercourse with creatures who are as much strangers to us, as mysterious, as if they were the fabulous, unearthly beings, more powerful than man, and yet his slaves, which Eastern superstitions have invented. We have more real knowledge about the Angels than about the brutes. They have apparently passions, habits, and a certain accountableness, but all is mystery about them. We do not know whether they can sin or not, whether they are under punishment, whether they are to live after this life. We inflict very great sufferings on a portion of them, and they in turn, every now and then, seem to retaliate upon us, as if by a wonderful law. We depend upon them in various important ways; we use their labour, we eat their flesh. This however relates to such of them as come near us: cast your thoughts abroad on the whole number of them, large and small, in vast forests, or in the water, or in the air; and then say whether the presence of such countless multitudes, so various in their natures, so strange and wild in their shapes, living on the earth without ascertainable object, is not as mysterious as any thing which Scripture says about the Angels? Is it not plain to our senses that there is a world inferior to us in the scale of beings, with which we are connected without understanding what it is? and is it difficult to faith to admit the word of Scripture concerning our connection with a world superior to us?

When, indeed, persons feel it so difficult to conceive the existence among us of the world of spirits, because they are not aware of it, they should recollect how many worlds all at once are in fact contained in human society itself. We speak of the political world, the scientific, the learned, the literary, the religious world; and suitably: for men are so closely united with some men, and so divided from others, they have such distinct objects of pursuit one from another, and such distinct principles and engagements in consequence, that in one and the same place there exist together a number of circles or (as they may be called) worlds, made up of visible men, but themselves invisible, unknown, nay, unintelligible to each other. Men move about in the common paths of life, and look the same; but there is little community of feeling between them; each knows little about what goes on in any other sphere than his own; and a stranger coming into any neighbourhood would, according to his own pursuits or acquaintances, go away with an utterly distinct or a reverse impression of it, viewed as a whole. Or again, leave for a while the political and commercial excitement of some large city, and take refuge in a secluded village; and there, in the absence of news of the day, consider the mode of life and habits of mind, the employments and views of its inhabitants; and say whether the world, when regarded in its separate portions, is not more unlike itself than it is unlike the world of Angels which Scripture places in the midst of it?

The world of spirits then, though unseen, is present; present, not future, not distant. It is not above the sky, it is not beyond the grave; it is now and here; the kingdom of God is among us. Of this the text speaks;—"We look," says St. Paul, "not at the things which are seen, but at the things which are not seen; for the things which are seen are temporal, but the things which are not seen are eternal." You see he regarded it as a practical truth, which was to influence our conduct. Not only does he speak of the world invisible, but of the duty of "looking at" it; not only does he contrast the things of time with it, but says that their belonging to time is a reason, not for looking at, but for looking off them. Eternity was not distant because it reached to the future; nor the unseen state without its influence on us, because it was impalpable. In like manner, he says in another Epistle, "Our conversation is in heaven." And again, "God hath raised us up together, and made us sit together in heavenly places in Christ Jesus." And again, "Your life is hid with Christ in God." And to the same purport are St. Peter's words, "Whom having not seen, ye love; in whom, though now ye see Him not, yet believing, ye rejoice with joy unspeakable and full of glory." And again, St. Paul speaking of the Apostles, "We are made a spectacle unto the world, and to Angels, and to men." And again in words already quoted, he speaks of the Angels as "ministering spirits sent forth to minister for them who shall be heirs of salvation." [3]

Such is the hidden kingdom of God; and, as it is now hidden, so in due season it shall be revealed. Men think that they are lords of the world, and may do as they will. They think this earth their property, and its movements in their power; whereas it has other lords besides them, and is the scene of a higher conflict than they are capable of conceiving. It contains Christ's little ones whom they despise, and His Angels whom they disbelieve; and these at length shall take possession of it and be manifested. At present, "all things," to appearance, "continue as they were from the beginning of the creation;" and scoffers ask, "Where is the promise of His coming?" but at the appointed time there will be a "manifestation of the sons of God," and the hidden saints "shall shine out as the sun in the kingdom of their Father." When the Angels appeared to the shepherds it was a sudden appearance,—"*Suddenly* there was with the Angel a multitude of the heavenly host." How wonderful a sight! The night had before that seemed just like any other night; as the evening on which Jacob saw the vision seemed like any other evening. They were keeping watch over their sheep; they were watching the night as it passed. The stars moved on,—it was midnight. They had no idea of such a thing when the Angel appeared. Such are the power and virtue hidden in things which are seen, and at God's will they are manifested. They were manifested for a moment to Jacob, for a moment to Elisha's servant, for a moment to the shepherds. They will be manifested for ever when Christ comes at the Last Day "in the glory of His Father with the holy Angels."

[3] Phil. iii.20; Eph. ii.6; Col. iii.3; 1 Pet. i.8; 1 Cor. iv.9; Heb. i.14.

Then this world will fade away and the other world will shine forth.

Let these be your thoughts my brethren, especially in the spring season, when the whole face of nature is so rich and beautiful. Once only in the year, yet once, does the world which we see show forth its hidden powers, and in a manner manifest itself. Then the leaves come out, and the blossoms on the fruit trees and flowers; and the grass and corn spring up. There is a sudden rush and burst outwardly of that hidden life which God has lodged in the material world. Well, that shows you, as by a sample, what it can do at God's command, when He gives the word. This earth, which now buds forth in leaves and blossoms, will one day burst forth into a new world of light and glory, in which, we shall see Saints and Angels dwelling. Who would think, except from his experience of former springs all through his life, who could conceive two or three months before, that it was possible that the face of nature, which then seemed so lifeless, should become so splendid and varied? How different is a tree, how different is a prospect, when leaves are on it and off it! How unlikely it would seem, before the event, that the dry and naked branches should suddenly be clothed with what is so bright and so refreshing! Yet in God's good time leaves come on the trees. The season may delay, but come it will at last. So it is with the coming of that Eternal Spring, for which all Christians are waiting. Come it will, though it delay; yet though it tarry, let us wait for it, "because it will surely come, it will not tarry." Therefore we say day by day, "Thy kingdom come;" which means,—O Lord, show Thyself; manifest Thyself; Thou that sittest between the Cherubim, show Thyself; stir up Thy strength and come and help us. The earth that we see does not satisfy us; it is but a beginning; it is but a promise of something beyond it; even when it is gayest, with all its blossoms on, and shows most touchingly what lies hid in it, yet it is not enough. We know much more lies hid in it than we see. A world of Saints and Angels, a glorious world, the palace of God, the mountain of the Lord of Hosts, the heavenly Jerusalem, the throne of God and Christ, all these wonders, everlasting, all-precious, mysterious, and incomprehensible, lie hid in what we see. What we see is the outward shell of an eternal kingdom; and on that kingdom we fix the eyes of our faith. Shine forth, O Lord, as when on Thy Nativity Thine Angels visited the shepherds; let Thy glory blossom forth as bloom and foliage on the trees; change with Thy mighty power this visible world into that diviner world, which as yet we see not; destroy what we see, that it may pass and be transformed into what we believe. Bright as is the sun, and the sky, and the clouds; green as are the leaves and the fields; sweet as is the singing of the birds; we know that they are not all, and we will not take up with a part for the whole. They proceed from a centre of love and goodness, which is God himself; but they are not His fulness; they speak of heaven, but they are not heaven; they are but as stray beams and dim reflections of His Image; they are but crumbs from the table. We are looking for the coming of the day of God, when all this outward world, fair though it be, shall perish; when the heavens shall be burnt, and the earth melt away. We can bear the loss, for we know it will be but the removing of a veil. We know that to remove the world which is seen, will be the manifestation of the world which is not seen. We know that what we see is as a screen hiding from us God and Christ, and His Saints and Angels. And we earnestly desire and pray for the dissolution of all that we see, from our longing after that which we do not see.

O blessed they indeed, who are destined for the sight of those wonders in which they now stand, at which they now look, but which they do not recognize! Blessed they who shall at length behold what as yet mortal eye hath not seen and faith only enjoys! These wonderful things of the new world are even now as they shall be then. They are immortal and eternal; and the souls who shall then be made conscious of them, will see them in their calmness and their majesty where they ever have been. But who can express the surprise and rapture which will come upon those, who then at last apprehend them for the first time, and to whose perceptions they are new! Who can imagine by a stretch of fancy the feelings of those who having died in faith, wake up to enjoyment! The life then begun, we know, will last for ever; yet surely if memory be to us then what it is now, that will be a day much to be observed unto the Lord through all the ages of eternity. We may increase indeed for ever in knowledge and in love, still that first waking from the dead, the day at once of our birth and our espousals, will ever be endeared and hallowed in our thoughts. When we find ourselves after long rest gifted with fresh powers, vigorous with the seed of eternal life within us, able to love God as we wish, conscious that all trouble, sorrow, pain, anxiety, bereavement, is over for ever, blessed in the full affection of those earthly friends whom we loved so poorly, and could protect so feebly, while they were with us in the flesh, and above all, visited by the immediate visible ineffable Presence of God Almighty, with his Only-begotten Son our Lord Jesus Christ, and His Co-equal Co-eternal Spirit, that great sight in which is the fulness of joy and pleasure for evermore,—what deep, incommunicable, unimaginable thoughts will be then upon us! what depths will be stirred up within us! what secret harmonies awakened, of which human nature seemed incapable! Earthly words are indeed all worthless to minister to such high anticipations. Let us close our eyes and keep silence.

"All flesh is grass, and all the goodliness thereof is as the flower of the field. The grass withereth, the flower fadeth, because the Spirit of the Lord bloweth upon it: surely the people is grass. The grass withereth, the flower fadeth; but the Word of our God shall stand for ever." [4]

[4] Is. xl.6–8.

THE GREATNESS AND LITTLENESS
OF HUMAN LIFE

*"The days of the years of my pilgrimage are an hundred and thirty
years: few and evil have the days of the years of my life been; and
have not attained unto the days of the years of the life of my fathers,
in the days of their pilgrimage."*—Gen. xlvii.9.

WHY did the aged Patriarch call his days few, who had
lived twice as long as men now live, when he spoke?
why did he call them evil, seeing he had on the whole lived in
riches and honour, and, what is more, in God's favour? yet he
described his time as short, his days as evil, and his life as but a
pilgrimage. Or if we allow that his afflictions were such as to
make him reasonably think cheaply of his life, in spite of the
blessings which attended it, yet that he should call it short,
considering he had so much more time for the highest purposes of his being than we have, is at first sight surprising. He
alludes indeed to the longer life which had been granted to his
fathers, and perhaps felt a decrepitude greater than theirs had
been; yet this difference between him and them could hardly
be the real ground of his complaint in the text, or more than a
confirmation or occasion of it. It was not because Abraham
had lived one hundred and seventy-five years, and Isaac one
hundred and eighty, and he himself, whose life was not yet
finished, but one hundred and thirty, that he made this
mournful speech. For it matters not, when time is gone, what
length it has been; and this doubtless was the real cause why
the Patriarch spoke as he did, not because his life was shorter
than his fathers', but because it was well nigh over. When life
is past, it is all one whether it has lasted two hundred years or
fifty. And it is this characteristic, stamped on human life in the
day of its birth, viz. that it is mortal, which makes it under all
circumstances and in every form equally feeble and despicable.
All the points in which men differ, health and strength, high
or low estate, happiness or misery, vanish before this common
lot, mortality. Pass a few years, and the longest-lived will be

gone; nor will what is past profit him then, except in its consequences.

And this sense of the nothingness of life, impressed on us by the very fact that it comes to an end, is much deepened, when we contrast it with the capabilities of us who live it. Had Jacob lived Methuselah's age, he would have called it short. This is what we all feel, though at first sight it seems a contradiction, that even though the days as they go be slow, and be laden with many events, or with sorrows or dreariness, lengthening them out and making them tedious, yet the year passes quick though the hours tarry, and time bygone is as a dream, though we thought it would never go while it was going. And the reason seems to be this; that, when we contemplate human life in itself, in however small a portion of it, we see implied in it the presence of a soul, the energy of a spiritual existence, of an accountable being; consciousness tells us this concerning it every moment. But when we look back on it in memory, we view it but externally, as a mere lapse of time, as a mere earthly history. And the longest duration of this external world is as dust and weighs nothing, against one moment's life of the world within. Thus we are ever expecting great things from life, from our internal consciousness every moment of our having souls; and we are ever being disappointed, on considering what we have gained from time past, or can hope from time to come. And life is ever promising and never fulfilling; and hence, however long it be, our days are few and evil. This is the particular view of the subject on which I shall now dwell.

Our earthly life then gives promise of what it does not accomplish. It promises immortality, yet it is mortal; it contains life in death and eternity in time; and it attracts us by beginnings which faith alone brings to an end. I mean, when we take into account the powers with which our souls are gifted as Christians, the very consciousness of these fills us with a certainty that they must last beyond this life; that is in the case of good and holy men, whose present state I say, is to them who know them well, an earnest of immortality. The greatness of their gifts, contrasted with their scanty time for exercising them, forces the mind forward to the thought of another life, as almost the necessary counterpart and consequence of this life, and certainly implied in this life, provided there be a righteous Governor of the world who does not make man for nought.

This is a thought which will come upon us not always, but under circumstances. And many perhaps of those who at first hearing may think they never felt it, may recognize what I mean, while I describe it.

I mean, when one sees some excellent person, whose graces we know, whose kindliness, affectionateness, tenderness, and generosity,—when we see him dying (let him have lived ever so long; I am not supposing a premature death; let him live out his days), the thought is forced upon us with a sort of surprise; "Surely, he is not to die yet; he has not yet had any opportunity of exercising duly those excellent gifts with which God has endowed him." Let him have lived seventy or eighty years, yet it seems as if he had done nothing at all, and his life were scarcely begun. He has lived all his days perhaps in a private sphere; he has been engaged on a number of petty matters which died with the day, and yielded no apparent fruit. He has had just enough of trial under various circumstances, to evidence, but not adequately to employ, what was in him. He has, we perhaps perceive, a noble benevolence of mind, a warmth of heart, and a beneficent temper, which, had it the means, would scatter blessings on every side; yet he has never been rich,—he dies poor. We have been accustomed to say to ourselves, "What would such a one be were he wealthy?" not as fancying he ever *will* have riches, but from feeling how he would become them; yet, when he actually does die as he lived, without them, we feel somehow disappointed,—there has been a failure,—his mind, we think, has never reached its scope,—he has had a treasure within him which has never been used. His days have been but few and evil, and have become old unseasonably, compared with his capabilities; and we are driven by a sense of these, to look on to a future state as a time when they will be brought out and come into effect. I am not attempting by such reflections to prove that there is a future state; let us take that for granted. I mean, over and above our positive belief in this great truth, we are actually driven to a belief, we attain a sort of sensible conviction of that life to come, a certainty striking home to our hearts and piercing them, by this imperfection in what is present. The very greatness of our powers makes this life look pitiful; the very pitifulness of this life forces on our thoughts to another; and the prospect of another gives a dignity and value to this life which promises it; and thus this life is at once great and little, and we rightly contemn it while we exalt its importance.

And, if this life is short, even when longest, from the great disproportion between it and the powers of regenerate man, still more is this the case, of course, where it is cut short, and death comes prematurely. Men there are, who, in a single moment of their lives, have shown a superhuman height and majesty of mind which it would take ages for them to employ on its proper objects, and, as it were, to exhaust; and who by such passing flashes, like rays of the sun, and the darting of lightning, give token of their immortality, give token to us that they are but Angels in disguise, the elect of God sealed for eternal life, and destined to judge the world and to reign with Christ for ever. Yet they are suddenly taken away, and we have hardly recognized them when we lose them. Can we believe that they are not removed for higher things elsewhere? This is sometimes said with reference to our intellectual powers; but it is still more true of our moral nature. There is something in moral truth and goodness, in faith, in firmness, in heavenly-mindedness, in meekness, in courage, in loving-kindness, to which this world's circumstances are quite unequal, for which the longest life is insufficient, which makes the highest opportunities of this world disappointing, which must burst the prison of this world to have its appropriate range. So that when a good man dies, one is led to say, "He has not half showed himself, he has had nothing to exercise him; his days are gone like a shadow, and he is withered like grass."

I say the word "disappointing"is the only word to express our feelings on the death of God's saints. Unless our faith be very active, so as to pierce beyond the grave, and realize the future, we feel depressed at what seems like a failure of great things. And from this very feeling surely, by a sort of contradiction, we may fairly take hope; for if this life be so disappointing, so unfinished, surely it is not the whole. This feeling of disappointment will often come upon us in an especial way, on happening to hear of or to witness the deathbeds of holy men. The hour of death seems to be a season, of which, in the hands of Providence, much might be *made*, if I may use the term; much might be done for the glory of God, the good of man, and the manifestation of the person dying. And beforehand friends will perhaps look forward, and expect that great things are then to take place, which they shall never forget. Yet, "how dieth the wise man? as the fool."[1] Such is the preacher's experience, and our own bears witness to it. King Josiah, the zealous servant of the Living God, died the death of wicked Ahab, the worshipper of Baal. True Christians die as other men. One dies by a sudden accident, another in battle, another without friends to see how

---

[1] Eccles. ii. 16.

he dies, a fourth is insensible or not himself. Thus the opportunity seems thrown away, and we are forcibly reminded that "the manifestation of the sons of God" [2] is hereafter; that "the earnest expectation of the creature" is but waiting for it; that this life is unequal to the burden of so great an office as the due exhibition of those secret ones who shall one day "shine forth as the sun in the kingdom of their Father." [3]

But further (if it be allowable to speculate), one can even conceive the same kind of feeling, and a most transporting one, to come over the soul of the faithful Christian, when just separated from the body, and conscious that his trial is once for all over. Though his life has been a long and painful discipline, yet when it is over, we may suppose him to feel at the moment the same sort of surprise at its being ended, as generally follows any exertion in this life, when the object is gained and the anticipation over. When we have wound up our minds for any point of time, any great event, an interview with strangers, or the sight of some wonder, or the occasion of some unusual trial, when it comes, and is gone, we have a strange reverse of feeling from our changed circumstances. Such, but without any mixture of pain, without any lassitude, dulness, or disappointment, may be the happy contemplation of the disembodied spirit; as if it said to itself, "So all is now over; this is what I have so long waited for; for which I have nerved myself; against which I have prepared, fasted, prayed, and wrought righteousness. Death is come and gone,—it is over. Ah! is it possible? What an easy trial, what a cheap price for eternal glory! A few sharp sicknesses, or some acute pain awhile, or some few and evil years, or some struggles of mind, dreary desolateness for a season, fightings and fears, afflicting bereavements, or the scorn and ill-usage of the world, how they fretted me, how much I thought of them, yet how little really they are! How contemptible a thing is human life,—contemptible in itself, yet in its effects invaluable! for it has been to me like a small seed of easy purchase, germinating and ripening into bliss everlasting."

Such being the unprofitableness of this life, viewed in itself, it is plain how we should regard it while we go through it. We should remember that it is scarcely more than an accident of our being—that it is no part of ourselves, who are immortal; that we are immortal spirits, independent of time and space, and that this life is but a sort of outward stage, on which we act

[2] Rom. viii. 19. [3] Matt. xiii. 43.

for a time, and which is only sufficient and only intended to answer the purpose of trying whether we will serve God or no. We should consider ourselves to be in this world in no fuller sense than players in any game are in the game; and life to be a sort of dream, as detached and as different from our real eternal existence, as a dream differs from waking; a serious dream, indeed, as affording a means of judging us, yet in itself a kind of shadow without substance, a scene set before us, in which we seem to be, and in which it is our duty to act just as if all we saw had a truth and reality, because all that meets us influences us and our destiny. The regenerate soul is taken into communion with Saints and Angels, and its "life is hid with Christ in God;"[4] it has a place in God's court, and is not of this world,—looking into this world as a spectator might look at some show or pageant, except when called from time to time to take a part. And while it obeys the instinct of the senses, it does so for God's sake, and it submits itself to things of time so far as to be brought to perfection by them, that, when the veil is withdrawn and it sees itself to be, where it ever has been, in God's kingdom, it may be found worthy to enjoy it. It is this view of life, which removes from us all surprise and disappointment that it is so incomplete: as well might we expect any chance event which happens in the course of it to be complete, any casual conversation with a stranger, or the toil or amusement of an hour.

Let us then thus account of our present state: it is precious as revealing to us, amid shadows and figures, the existence and attributes of Almighty God and His elect people: it is precious, because it enables us to hold intercourse with immortal souls who are on their trial as we are. It is momentous, as being the scene and means of our trial; but beyond this it has no claims upon us. "Vanity of vanities, says the Preacher, all is vanity." We may be poor or rich, young or old, honoured or slighted, and it ought to affect us no more, neither to elate us nor depress us, than if we were actors in a play, who know that the characters they represent are not their own, and that though they may appear to be superior one to another, to be kings or to be peasants, they are in reality all on a level. The one desire which should move us should be, first of all, that of seeing Him face to face, who is now hid from us; and next of enjoying eternal and direct communion, in and through Him, with our friends around us, whom at present we know only through the

[4] Col. iii.3.

medium of sense, by precarious and partial channels, which give us little insight into their hearts.

These are suitable feelings towards this attractive but deceitful world. What have we to do with its gifts and honours, who, having been already baptized into the world to come, are no longer citizens of this? Why should we be anxious for a long life, or wealth, or credit, or comfort, who know that the next world will be everything which our hearts can wish, and that not in appearance only, but truly and everlastingly? Why should we rest in this world, when it is the token and promise of another? Why should we be content with its surface, instead of appropriating what is stored beneath it? To those who live by faith, every thing they see speaks of that future world; the very glories of nature, the sun, moon, and stars, and the richness and the beauty of the earth, are as types and figures witnessing and teaching the invisible things of God. All that we see is destined one day to burst forth into a heavenly bloom, and to be transfigured into immortal glory. Heaven at present is out of sight, but in due time, as snow melts and discovers what it lay upon, so will this visible creation fade away before those greater splendours which are behind it, and on which at present it depends. In that day shadows will retire, and the substance show itself. The sun will grow pale and be lost in the sky, but it will be before the radiance of Him whom it does but image, the Sun of Righteousness, with healing on His wings, who will come forth in visible form, as a bridegroom out of his chamber, while His perishable type decays. The stars which surround it will be replaced by Saints and Angels circling His throne. Above and below, the clouds of the air, the trees of the field, the waters of the great deep will be found impregnated with the forms of everlasting spirits, the servants of God which do His pleasure. And our own mortal bodies will then be found in like manner to contain within them an inner man, which will then receive its due proportions, as the soul's harmonious organ, instead of that gross mass of flesh and blood which sight and touch are sensible of. For this glorious manifestation the whole creation is at present in travail, earnestly desiring that it may be accomplished in its season.

These are thoughts to make us eagerly and devoutly say, "Come, Lord Jesus, to end the time of waiting, of darkness, of turbulence, of disputing, of sorrow, of care." These are thoughts to lead us to rejoice in every day and hour that passes, as bringing us nearer the time of His appearing, and the termination of sin and misery. They are thoughts which ought thus to affect us; and so they would, were it not for the load of guilt which weighs upon us, for sins committed against light and grace. O that it were otherwise with us! O that we were fitted duly to receive this lesson which the world gives us, and had so improved the gifts of life, that while we felt it to be perishing, we might rejoice in it as precious! O that we were not conscious of deep stains upon our souls, the accumulations of past years, and of infirmities continually besetting us! Were it not for all this,—were it not for our unprepared state, as in one sense it may truly be called, how gladly should we hail each new month and year as a token that our Saviour is so much nearer to us than He ever has been yet! May He grant His grace abundantly to us, to make us meet for His presence, that we may not be ashamed before Him at His coming! May He vouchsafe to us the full grace of His ordinances: may He feed us with His choicest gifts: may He expel the poison from our souls: may He wash us clean in His precious blood, and give us the fulness of faith, love, and hope, as foretastes of the heavenly portion which He destines for us!

MORAL EFFECTS OF
COMMUNION WITH GOD

*"One thing have I desired of the Lord, which I will require; even that
I may dwell in the house of the Lord all the days of my life, to behold
the fair beauty of the Lord, and to visit His Temple."*
—Ps. xxvii.4.

WHAT the Psalmist desired, we Christians enjoy to the
full,—the liberty of holding communion with God in
His Temple all through our life. Under the Law, the presence of
God was but in one place; and therefore could be approached
and enjoyed only at set times. For far the greater part of their
lives, the chosen people were in one sense "cast out of the sight
of His eyes;"[1] and the periodical return to it which they were
allowed, was a privilege highly coveted and earnestly expected.
Much more precious was the privilege of continually dwelling
in His sight, which is spoken of in the text. "One thing," says
the Psalmist, "have I desired of the Lord . . . . that I may dwell
in the house of the Lord all the days of my life, to behold the fair
beauty of the Lord, and to visit His Temple." He desired to have
continually that communion with God in prayer, praise, and
meditation, to which His presence admits the soul; and this, I
say, is the portion of Christians. Faith opens upon us Christians
the Temple of God wherever we are; for that Temple is a spiritual one, and so is everywhere present. "We have access," says
the Apostle,—that is, we have admission or introduction, "by
faith into this grace wherein we stand, and rejoice in hope of
the glory of God." And hence he says elsewhere, "Rejoice in
the Lord alway, and again I say, Rejoice." "Rejoice evermore,
pray without ceasing; in every thing give thanks." And St.
James, "Is any afflicted? let him pray: is any merry? let him sing
Psalms."[2] Prayer, praise, thanksgiving, contemplation, are the
peculiar privilege and duty of a Christian, and that for their

[1] Ps. xxxi.24.
[2] Rom. v.2; Phil. iv.4; 1 Thess. v.16–18; James v.13.

own sakes, from the exceeding comfort and satisfaction they afford him, and without reference to any definite results to which prayer tends, without reference to the answers which are promised to it, from a general sense of the blessedness of being under the shadow of God's throne.

I propose, then, in what follows, to make some remarks on communion with God, or prayer in a large sense of the word; not as regards its external consequences, but as it may be considered to affect our own minds and hearts.

What, then, is prayer? It is (if it may be said reverently) *conversing* with God. We converse with our fellow-men, and then we use familiar language, because they *are* our fellows. We converse with God, and then we use the lowliest, awfullest, calmest, concisest language we can, because He *is* God. Prayer, then, is *divine* converse, differing from human as God differs from man. Thus St. Paul says, "Our conversation is in heaven,"[3]— not indeed thereby meaning converse of words only, but intercourse and manner of living generally; yet still in an especial way converse of words only, because language is the special means of all intercourse. Our intercourse with our fellow-men goes on, not by sight, but by sound, not by eyes, but by ears. Hearing is the social sense, and language is the social bond. In like manner, as the Christian's conversation is in heaven, as it is his duty, with Enoch and other Saints, *to walk with God*, so his voice is in heaven, his heart "inditing of a good matter," of prayers and praises. Prayers and praises are the mode of his intercourse with the next world, as the converse of business or recreation is the mode in which this world is carried on in all its separate courses. He who does not pray, does not claim his citizenship with heaven, but lives, though an heir of the kingdom, as if he were a child of earth.

Now, it is not surprising if that duty or privilege, which is the characteristic token of our heavenly inheritance, should also have an especial influence upon our fitness for claiming it. He who does not use a gift, loses it; the man who does not use his voice or limbs, loses power over them, and becomes disqualified for the state of life to which he is called. In like manner, he who neglects to pray, not only suspends the enjoyment, but is in a way to lose the possession, of his divine citizenship. We are members of another world; we have been severed from the companionship of devils, and brought into that invisible kingdom of Christ which faith alone discerns,—that mysterious

[3] Phil. iii.20.

Presence of God which encompasses us, which is in us, and around us, which is in our heart, which enfolds us as though with a robe of light, hiding our scarred and discoloured souls from the sight of Divine Purity, and making them shining as the Angels; and which flows in upon us too by means of all forms of beauty and grace which this visible world contains, in a starry host or (if I may so say) a milky way of divine companions, the inhabitants of Mount Zion, where we dwell. Faith, I say, alone apprehends all this; but yet there *is* something which is not left to faith, our own tastes, likings, motives, and habits. Of these we are conscious in our degree, and we can make ourselves more and more conscious; and as consciousness tells us what they are, reason tells us whether they are such as become, as correspond with, that heavenly world into which we have been translated.

I say then, it is plain to common sense that the man who has not accustomed himself to the language of heaven will be no fit inhabitant of it when, in the Last Day, it is perceptibly revealed. The case is like that of a language or style of speaking of this world; we know well a foreigner from a native. Again, we know those who have been used to kings' courts or educated society from others. By their voice, accent, and language, and not only so, by their gestures and gait, by their usages, by their mode of conducting themselves and their principles of conduct, we know well what a vast difference there is between those who have lived in good society and those who have not. What indeed is called "*good* society" is often very worthless society. I am not speaking of it to praise it; I only mean, that, as the manners which men call refined or courtly are gained only by intercourse with courts and polished circles, and as the influence of the words there used (that is, of the ideas which those words, striking again and again on the ear, convey to the mind), extends in a most subtle way over all that men do, over the turn of their sentences, and the tone of their questions and replies, and their general bearing, and the spontaneous flow of their thoughts, and their mode of viewing things, and the general maxims or heads to which they refer them, and the motives which determine them, and their likings and dislikings, hopes and fears, and their relative estimate of persons, and the intensity of their perceptions towards particular objects; so a habit of prayer, the practice of turning to God and the unseen world, in every season, in every place, in every emergency (let alone its supernatural effect of prevailing with God),—prayer, I say, has what may be called a *natural* effect, in spiritualizing and elevating the soul. A man is no longer what he was before; gradually, imperceptibly to himself, he has imbibed a new set of ideas, and become imbued with fresh principles. He is as one coming from kings' courts, with a grace, a delicacy, a dignity, a propriety, a justness of thought and taste, a clearness and firmness of principle, all his own. Such is the power of God's secret grace acting through those ordinances which He has enjoined us; such the evident fitness of these ordinances to produce the results which they set before us. As speech is the organ of human society, and the means of human civilization, so is prayer the instrument of divine fellowship and divine training.

I will give, for the sake of illustration, some instances in detail of one particular fault of mind, which among others a habit of prayer is calculated to cure.

For instance; many a man seems to have no grasp at all of doctrinal truth. He cannot get himself to think it of importance what a man believes, and what not. He tries to do so; for a time he does; he does for a time think that a certain faith is necessary for salvation, that certain doctrines are to be put forth and maintained in charity to the souls of men. Yet though he thinks so one day, he changes the next; he holds the truth, and then lets it go again. He is filled with doubts; suddenly the question crosses him, "Is it possible that such and such a doctrine *is* necessary?" and he relapses into an uncomfortable sceptical state, out of which there is no outlet. Reasonings do not convince him; he *cannot* be convinced; he has no grasp of truth. Why? Because the next world is not a reality to him; it only exists in his mind in the form of certain conclusions from certain reasonings. It is but an inference; and never can be more, never can be present to his mind, until he acts, instead of arguing. Let him but act as if the next world were before him; let him but give himself to such devotional exercises as we ought to observe in the presence of an Almighty, All-holy, and All-merciful God, and it will be a rare case indeed if his difficulties do not vanish.

Or again: a man may have a natural disposition towards caprice and change; he may be apt to take up first one fancy, then another, from novelty or other reason; he may take sudden likings or dislikings, or be tempted to form a scheme of religion for himself, of what he thinks best or most beautiful out of all the systems which divide the world.

Again: he is troubled perhaps with a variety of unbecoming thoughts, which he would fain keep out of his mind if he could. He finds himself unsettled and uneasy, dissatisfied with his condition, easily excited, sorry at sin one moment, forgetting it the next, feeble-minded, unable to rule himself, tempted to dote upon trifles, apt to be caught and influenced by vanities, and to abandon himself to languor or indolence.

Once more: he has not a clear perception of the path of truth and duty. This is an especial fault among us now-a-days: men are actuated perhaps by the best feelings and the most amiable motives, and are not fairly chargeable with insincerity; and yet there is a want of straightforwardness in their conduct. They allow themselves to be guided by expediency, and defend themselves, and perhaps so plausibly, that though you are not convinced, you are silenced. They attend to what others think, more than to what God says; they look at Scripture more as a gift to man than as a gift from God; they consider themselves at liberty to modify its plain precepts by a certain discretionary rule; they listen to the voice of great men, and allow themselves to be swayed by them; they make comparisons and strike the balance between the impracticability of the whole that God commands, and the practicability of effecting a part, and think they may consent to give up something, if they can secure the rest. They shift about in opinion, going first a little this way, then a little that, according to the loudness and positiveness with which others speak; they are at the mercy of the last speaker, and they think they observe a safe, judicious, and middle course, by always keeping a certain distance behind those who go furthest. Or they are rash in their religious projects and undertakings, and forget that they may be violating the lines and fences of God's law, while they move about freely at their pleasure. Now, I will not judge another; I will not say that in this or that given case the fault of mind in question (for any how it is a fault), does certainly arise from some certain cause which I choose to guess at: but at least there *are* cases where this wavering of mind *does* arise from scantiness of prayer; and if so, it is worth a man's considering, who is thus unsteady, timid, and dimsighted, whether this scantiness be not perchance the true reason of such infirmities in his own case, and whether a "continuing instant in prayer,"—by which I mean, not merely prayer morning and evening, but some thing suitable to his disease, something extraordinary, as medicine is extraordinary, a "redeeming of time" from society and recreation in order to pray more—whether such a change in his habits would not remove them?

For what is the very promise of the New Covenant but stability? what is it, but a clear insight into the truth, such as will enable us to know how to walk, how to profess, how to meet the circumstances of life, how to withstand gainsayers? Are we built upon a rock or upon the sand? are we after all tossed about on the sea of opinion, when Christ has stretched out His hand to us, to help and encourage us? "Thou wilt keep him in perfect peace whose mind is stayed on Thee, because he trusteth in Thee." [4] Such is the word of promise. Can we possibly have apprehensions about what man will do to us or say of us, can we flatter the great ones of earth, or timidly yield to the many, or be dazzled by talent, or drawn aside by interest, who are in the habit of divine conversations? "Ye have an unction from the Holy One," says St. John, "and ye know all things. I have not written unto you because ye know not the truth, but because ye know it, and that no lie is of the truth. . . . . The anointing which ye have received of Him abideth in you, and ye need not that any man teach you. . . . . Whosoever is born of God, doth not commit sin, for his seed remaineth in him; and he cannot sin, because he is born of God." [5] This is that birth, by which the baptized soul not only enters, but actually embraces and realizes the kingdom of God. This is the true and effectual regeneration, when the seed of life takes root in man and thrives. Such men have accustomed themselves to speak to God, and God has ever spoken to them; and they feel "the powers of the world to come" as truly as they feel the presence of this world, because they have been accustomed to speak and act as if it were real. All of us must rely on something; all must look up to, admire, court, make themselves one with something. Most men cast in their lot with the visible world; but true Christians with Saints and Angels.

Such men are little understood by the world because they are not of the world; and hence it sometimes happens that even the better sort of men are often disconcerted and vexed by them. It cannot be otherwise; they move forward on principles so different from what are commonly assumed as true. They take for granted, as first principles, what the world wishes to have proved in detail. They have become familiar with the sights of the next world, till they talk of them as if all men admitted them. The immortality of truth, its oneness, the impossibility of falsehood coalescing with it, what truth is, what it should lead one to do in particular cases, how it lies in the details of life,—all these points are mere matters of debate in the world, and men go through long processes of argument, and pride themselves on their subtleness in defending or attacking, in

[4] Is. xxvi.3.   [5] 1 John ii.20, 21, 27; iii.9.

making probable or improbable, ideas which are assumed without a word by those who have lived in heaven, as the very ground to start from. In consequence, such men are called bad disputants, inconsecutive reasoners, strange, eccentric, or perverse thinkers, merely because they do not take for granted, nor go to prove, what others do,—because they do not go about to define and determine the sights (as it were), the mountains and rivers and plains, and sun, moon, and stars, of the next world. And hence in turn they are commonly unable to enter into the ways of thought or feelings of other men, having been engrossed with God's thoughts and God's ways. Hence, perhaps, they seem abrupt in what they say and do; nay, even make others feel constrained and uneasy in their presence. Perhaps they appear reserved too, because they take so much for granted which might be drawn out, and because they cannot bring themselves to tell all their thoughts from their sacredness, and because they are drawn off from free conversation to the thought of heaven, on which their minds rest. Nay, perchance, they appear severe, because their motives are not understood, nor their sensitive jealousy for the honour of God and their charitable concern for the good of their fellow-Christians duly appreciated. In short, to the world they seem like *foreigners*. We know how foreigners strike us; they are often to *our* notions strange and unpleasing in their manners; why is this? merely *because* they are of a different country. Each country has its own manners,—one may not be better than other; but we naturally like our own ways, and we do not understand other. We do not see their meaning. We misconstrue them; we think they mean something unpleasant, something rude, or over-free, or haughty, or unrefined, when they do not. And in like manner, the world at large, not only is not Christian, but cannot discern or understand the Christian. Thus our Blessed Lord Himself was not recognized or honoured by His relatives, and (as is plain to every reader of Scripture) He often seems to speak abruptly and severely. So too St. Paul was considered by the Corinthians as contemptible in speech. And hence St. John, speaking of "what manner of love the Father hath bestowed upon us that we should be called the sons of God," adds, "therefore the world *knoweth* us not, because it knew Him not."[6] Such is the effect of divine meditations: admitting us into the next world, and withdrawing us from this; making us children of God, but withal "strangers unto our brethren, even aliens unto our mother's

[6] 1 John iii.1.

children."[7] Yea, though the true servants of God increase in meekness and love day by day, and to those who know them will seem what they really are; and though their good works are evident to all men, and cannot be denied, yet such is the eternal law which goes between the Church and the world—we cannot be friends of both; and they who take their portion with the Church, will seem, except in some remarkable cases, unamiable to the world, for the "world knoweth them not," and does not like them though it can hardly tell why; yet (as St. John proceeds) they have this blessing, that "when He shall appear, they shall be like Him, for they shall see Him as He is."[8]

And if, as it would seem, we must choose between the two, surely the world's friendship may be better parted with than our fellowship with our Lord and Saviour. What indeed have we to do with courting men, whose faces are turned towards God? We know how men feel and act when they come to die; they discharge their worldly affairs from their minds, and try to realize the unseen state. Then this world is nothing to them. It may praise, it may blame; but they feel it not. They are leaving their goods, their deeds, their sayings, their writings, their names, behind them; and they care not for it, for they wait for Christ. To one thing alone they are alive, His coming; they watch against it, if so be they may then be found without shame. Such is the conduct of dying men; and what all but the very hardened do at the last, if their senses fail not and their powers hold, that does the true Christian all life long. He is ever dying while he lives; he is on his bier, and the prayers for the sick are saying over him. He has no work but that of making his peace with God, and preparing for the judgment. He has no aim but that of being found worthy to escape the things that shall come to pass and to stand before the Son of man. And therefore day by day he unlearns the love of this world, and the desire of its praise; he can bear to belong to the nameless family of God, and to seem to the world strange in it and out of place, for so he is.

And when Christ comes at last, blessed indeed will be his lot. He has joined himself from the first to the conquering side; he has risked the present against the future, preferring the chance of eternity to the certainty of time; and then his reward will be but beginning, when that of the children of this world is come to an end. In the words of the wise man, "Then shall the righteous man stand in great boldness before the face of such as have

---

[7] Ps. lxix.8. [8] 1 John iii.2.

afflicted him, and made no account of his labours. When they see it they shall be troubled with terrible fear, and shall be amazed at the strangeness of His salvation, so far beyond all that they looked for. And they, repenting and groaning for anguish of spirit, shall say within themselves, This is he whom we had sometimes in derision and a proverb of reproach; we fools counted his life madness, and his end to be without honour. How is he numbered among the children of God, and his lot is among the saints!"[9]

[9] Wisd. v. 1–5.

CHRIST HIDDEN
FROM THE WORLD

"The light shineth in darkness;
and the darkness comprehended it not."—John i.5.

O F all the thoughts which rise in the mind when contemplating the sojourn of our Lord Jesus Christ upon earth,[1]
none perhaps is more affecting and subduing than the obscurity
which attended it. I do not mean His obscure condition, in the
sense of its being humble; but the obscurity in which He was
shrouded, and the secrecy which He observed. This characteristic of His first Advent is referred to very frequently in Scripture, as in the text, "The light shineth in darkness, and the
darkness comprehended it not;" and is in contrast with what is
foretold about His second Advent. Then "every eye shall see
Him;" which implies that all shall recognize Him; whereas,
when He came for the first time, though many saw Him, few
indeed discerned Him. It had been prophesied, "When we shall
see Him there is no beauty that we should desire Him;" and at
the very end of His ministry, He said to one of His twelve chosen friends, "Have I been so long time with you, and yet hast
thou not known Me, Philip?"[2]
I propose to set before you one or two thoughts which arise
from this very solemn circumstance, and which may, through
God's blessing, be profitable.
  1. And first, let us review some of the circumstances which
marked His sojourn when on earth.
  His condescension in coming down from heaven, in leaving
His Father's glory and taking flesh, is so far beyond power of
words or thought, that one might consider at first sight that it
mattered little whether He came as a prince or a beggar. And
yet after all, it is much more wonderful that He came in low
estate, for this reason; because it might have been thought

---

[1] Preached on Christmas Day.
[2] Is. liii.2; John xiv.9.

beforehand, that, though He condescended to come on earth, yet He would not submit to be overlooked and despised: now the rich are not despised by the world, and the poor are. If He had come as a great prince or noble, the world without knowing a whit more that He was God, yet would at least have looked up to Him and honoured Him, as being a prince; but when He came in a low estate, He took upon Him one additional humiliation, *contempt*,—being contemned, scorned, rudely passed by, roughly profaned by His creatures.

What were the actual circumstances of His coming? His Mother is a poor woman; she comes to Bethlehem to be taxed, travelling, when her choice would have been to remain at home. She finds there is no room in the inn; she is obliged to betake herself to a stable; she brings forth her firstborn Son, and lays Him in a manger. That little babe, so born, so placed, is none other than the Creator of heaven and earth, the Eternal Son of God.

Well; he was born of a poor woman, laid in a manger, brought up to a lowly trade, that of a carpenter; and when He began to preach the Gospel He had not a place to lay His head: lastly, He was put to death, to an infamous and odious death, the death which criminals then suffered.

For the three last years of His life, He preached the Gospel, I say, as we read in Scripture; but He did not begin to do so till He was thirty years old. For the first thirty years of His life, He seems to have lived, just as a poor man would live now. Day after day, season after season, winter and summer, one year and then another, passed on, as might happen to any of us. He passed from being a babe in arms to being a child, and then He became a boy, and so He grew up "like a tender plant," increasing in wisdom and stature; and then He seems to have followed the trade of Joseph, his reputed father; going on in an ordinary way without any great occurrence, till He was thirty years old. How very wonderful is all this! that He should live here, doing nothing great, so long; living here, as if for the sake of living; not preaching, or collecting disciples, or apparently in any way furthering the cause which brought Him down from heaven. Doubtless there were deep and wise reasons in God's counsels for His going on so long in obscurity; I only mean, that *we* do not know them.

And it is remarkable that those who were about Him, seem to have treated Him as one of their equals. His brethren, that is, His near relations, His cousins, did not believe in Him. And it is very observable, too, that when He began to preach and a multitude collected, we are told, "When His friends heard of it they went out to lay hold on Him; for they said, He is beside Himself."[3] They treated Him as we might be disposed, and rightly, to treat any ordinary person now, who began to preach in the streets. I say "rightly" because such persons generally preach a *new* Gospel, and therefore must be wrong. Also, they preach without being sent, and against authority; all which is wrong too. Accordingly we are often tempted to say that such people are "beside themselves," or mad, and not unjustly. It is often charitable to say so, for it is better to be mad than to be disobedient. Well, what we should say of such persons, this is what our Lord's friends said of Him. They had lived so long with Him, and yet did not know Him; did not understand what He was. They saw nothing to mark a difference between Him and them. He was dressed as others, He ate and drank as others, He came in and went out, and spoke, and walked, and slept, as others. He was in all respects a man; except that He did not sin, and this great difference the many would not detect, because none of us understands those who are much better than himself: so that Christ, the sinless Son of God, might be living close to us, and we not discover it.

2. I say that Christ, the sinless Son of God, might be living now in the world as our next door neighbour, and perhaps we not find it out. And this is a thought that should be dwelt on. I do not mean to say that there are not a number of persons, who we could be sure were not Christ; of course, no persons who lead bad and irreligious lives. But there are a number of persons who are in no sense irreligious or open to serious blame, who are very much like each other at first sight, yet in God's eyes are very different. I mean the great mass of what are called respectable men, who vary very much: some are merely decent and outwardly correct persons, and have no great sense of religion, do not deny themselves, have no ardent love of God, but love the world; and, whereas their interest lies in being regular and orderly, or they have no strong passions, or have early got into the way of being regular, and their habits are formed accordingly, they are what they are, decent and correct, but very little more. But there are others who look just the same to the world, who in their hearts are very different; they make no great show, they go on in the same quiet ordinary way as the others, but really they are training to be saints in Heaven. They do all they can to change themselves, to become like God, to obey God, to

[3] Mark iii.21.

discipline themselves, to renounce the world; but they do it in secret, both because God tells them so to do, and because they do not like it to be known. Moreover, there are a number of others between these two with more or less of worldliness and more or less of faith. Yet they all look about the same, to common eyes, because true religion is a hidden life in the heart; and though it cannot exist without deeds, yet these are for the most part secret deeds, secret charities, secret prayers, secret self-denials, secret struggles, secret victories.

Of course in proportion as persons are brought out into public life, they will be seen and scrutinized, and (in a certain sense) known more; but I am talking of the ordinary condition of people in private life, such as our Saviour was for thirty years; and these look very like each other. And there are so many of them, that unless we get very near them, we cannot see any distinction between one and another; we have no means to do so, and it is no business of ours. And yet, though we have no right to judge others, but must leave this to God, it is very certain that a really holy man, a true saint, though he looks like other men, still has a sort of secret power in him to attract others to him who are like-minded, and to influence all who have any thing in them like him. And thus it often becomes a test, whether we are like-minded with the Saints of God, whether they have influence over us. And though we have seldom means of knowing at the time who are God's own Saints, yet after all is over we have; and then on looking back on what is past, perhaps after they are dead and gone, if we knew them, we may ask ourselves what power they had over us, whether they attracted us, influenced us, humbled us, whether they made our hearts burn within us. Alas! too often we shall find that we were close to them for a long time, had means of knowing them, and knew them not; and that is a heavy condemnation on us, indeed. Now this was singularly exemplified in our Saviour's history, by how much He was so very holy. The holier a man is, the less he is understood by men of the world. All who have any spark of living faith will understand him in a measure, and the holier he is, they will, for the most part, be attracted the more; but those who serve the world will be blind to him, or scorn and dislike him, the holier he is. This, I say, happened to our Lord. He was All-holy, but "the light shined in darkness, and the darkness comprehended it not." His near relations did not believe in Him. And if this was really so, and for the reason I have said, it surely becomes a question whether we should have understood Him better than they: whether though He had been our next

door neighbour, or one of our family, we should have distinguished Him from any one else, who was correct and quiet in
his deportment; or rather, whether we should not, though we
respected Him, (alas, what a word! what language towards the
Most High God!) yet even if we went as far as this, whether we
should not have thought Him strange, eccentric, extravagant,
and fanciful. Much less should we have detected any sparks of
that glory which He had with the Father before the world was,
and which was merely hidden not quenched by His earthly tabernacle. This, truly, is a very awful thought; because if He were
near us for any long time, and we did not see any thing wonderful in Him, we might take it as a clear proof that we were not
His, for "His sheep know His voice, and follow Him;" we
might take it as a clear proof that we should not know Him, or
admire His greatness, or adore His glory, or love His excellency,
if we were admitted to His presence in heaven.

3. And here we are brought to another most serious thought,
which I will touch upon. We are very apt to wish we had been
born in the days of Christ, and in this way we excuse our misconduct, when conscience reproaches us. We say, that had we
had the advantage of being with Christ, we should have had
stronger motives, stronger restraints against sin. I answer, that
so far from our sinful habits being reformed by the presence of
Christ, the chance is, that those same habits would have hindered us from recognizing Him. We should not have known He
was present; and if He had even told us who He was, we should
not have believed Him. Nay, had we seen His miracles (incredible as it may seem), even they would not have made any lasting
impression on us. Without going into this subject, consider
only the possibility of Christ being close to us, even though He
did no miracle, and our not knowing it; yet I believe this literally would have been the case with most men. But enough on
this subject. What I am coming to is this: I wish you to observe
what a fearful light this casts upon our prospects in the next
world. We think heaven must be a place of happiness to us, if
we do but get there; but the great probability is, if we can judge
by what goes on here below, that a bad man, if brought to
heaven, would not know he was in heaven;—I do not go to the
further question, whether, on the contrary, the very fact of his
being in heaven with all his unholiness upon him, would not be
a literal torment to him, and light up the fires of hell within
him. This indeed would be a most dreadful way of finding out
where he was. But let us suppose the lighter case: let us suppose
he could remain in heaven unblasted, yet it would seem that at

least he would not know that he was there. He would see nothing wonderful there. Could men come nearer to God than when they seized Him, struck Him, spit on Him, hurried Him along, stripped Him, stretched out His limbs upon the cross, nailed Him to it, raised it up, stood gazing on Him, jeered Him, gave Him vinegar, looked close whether He was dead, and then pierced Him with a spear? O dreadful thought, that the nearest approaches man has made to God upon earth have been in blasphemy! Whether of the two came closer to Him, St. Thomas, who was allowed to reach forth his hand and reverently touch His wounds, and St. John, who rested on His bosom, or the brutal soldiers who profaned Him limb by limb, and tortured Him nerve by nerve? His Blessed Mother, indeed, came closer still to Him; and we, if we be true believers, still closer, who have Him really, though spiritually, within us; but this is another, an inward sort of approach. Of those who approached Him externally, they came nearest, who knew nothing about it. So it is with sinners: they would walk close to the throne of God; they would stupidly gaze at it; they would touch it; they would meddle with the holiest things; they would go on intruding and prying, not meaning any thing wrong by it, but with a sort of brute curiosity, till the avenging lightnings destroyed them;—all because they have no *senses* to guide them in the matter. Our bodily senses tell us of the approach of good or evil on earth. By sound, by scent, by feeling we know what is happening to us. We know when we are exposing ourselves to the weather, when we are exerting ourselves too much. We have warnings, and feel we must not neglect them. Now, sinners have no spiritual senses; they can presage nothing; they do not know what is going to happen the next moment to them. So they go fearlessly further and further among precipices, till on a sudden they fall, or are smitten and perish. Miserable beings! and this is what sin does for immortal souls; that they should be like the cattle which are slaughtered at the shambles, yet touch and smell the very weapons which are to destroy them!

4. But you may say, how does this concern us? Christ is not here; *we* cannot thus or in any less way insult His Majesty. Are we so sure of this? Certainly we cannot commit such open blasphemy; but it is another matter whether we cannot commit as great. For often sins are greater which are less startling; insults more bitter, which are not so loud; and evils deeper, which are more subtle. Do we not recollect a very awful passage? "Whosoever speaketh a word against the Son of man, it shall be

forgiven him; but whosoever speaketh against the Holy Ghost, it shall not be forgiven him." [4] Now, I am not deciding whether or no this denunciation can be fulfilled in the case of Christians now, though when we recollect that we *are* at present under the ministration of that very Spirit of whom our Saviour speaks, this is a very serious question; but I quote it to show that there may be sins greater even than insult and injury offered to Christ's Person, though we should think that impossible, and though they could not be so flagrant or open. With this thought let it be considered:—

First, that Christ is still on earth. He said expressly that He would come again. The Holy Ghost's coming is so really His coming, that we might as well say that He was not here in the days of His flesh, when He was visibly in this world, as deny that He is here now, when He is here by His Divine Spirit. This indeed is a mystery, how God the Son and God the Holy Ghost, two Persons, can be one, how He can be in the Spirit and the Spirit in Him; but so it is.

Next, if He is still on earth, yet is not visible (which cannot be denied), it is plain that He keeps Himself still in the condition which He chose in the days of His flesh. I mean, He is a hidden Saviour, and may be approached (unless we are careful) without due reverence and fear. I say, wherever He is (for that is a further question), still He is here, and again He is secret; and whatever be the tokens of His Presence, still they must be of a nature to admit of persons doubting where it is; and if they will argue, and be sharpwitted and subtle, they may perplex themselves and others, as the Jews did even in the days of His flesh, till He seems to them nowhere present on earth now. And when they come to think Him far away, of course they *feel* it to be impossible so to insult Him as the Jews did of old; and if nevertheless He is here, they *are* perchance approaching and insulting Him, though they so feel. And this was just the case of the Jews, for they too were ignorant what they were doing. It is probable, then, that we can now commit at least as great blasphemy towards Him as the Jews did first, because we are under the dispensation of that Holy Spirit, against whom even more heinous sins *can* be committed; next, because His presence now as little witnesses of itself, or is impressive to the many, as His bodily presence formerly.

We see a further reason for this apprehension, when we consider what the tokens of His presence now are; for they will be

<hr>

[4] Matt. xii.32.

found to be of a nature easily to lead men into irreverence, unless they be humble and watchful. For instance, the Church is called "His Body:" what His material Body was when He was visible on earth, such is the Church now. It is the instrument of His Divine power; it is that which we must approach, to gain good from Him; it is that which by insulting we awaken His anger. Now, what is the Church but, as it were, a body of humiliation, almost provoking insult and profaneness, when men do not live by faith? an earthen vessel, far more so even than His body of flesh, for that was at least pure from all sin, and the Church is defiled in all her members. We know that her ministers at best are but imperfect and erring, and of like passions with their brethren; yet of them He has said, speaking not to the Apostles merely but to all the seventy disciples (to whom Christian ministers are in office surely equal), "He that heareth you, heareth Me, and He that despiseth you despiseth Me, and he that despiseth Me, despiseth Him that sent Me."

Again: He has made the poor, weak, and afflicted, tokens and instruments of His Presence; and here again, as is plain, the same temptation meets us to neglect or profane it. What He was, such are His chosen followers in this world; and as His obscure and defenceless state led men to insult and ill-treat Him, so the like peculiarities, in the tokens of His Presence, lead men to insult Him now. That such are His tokens is plain from many passages of Scripture: for instance, He says of children, "Whoso shall receive one such little child in My Name, receiveth Me." Again: He said to Saul, who was persecuting His followers, "Why persecutest thou Me?" And He forewarns us, that at the Last Day He will say to the righteous, "I was an hungered, and ye gave Me meat; I was thirsty, and ye gave Me drink; I was a stranger, and ye took Me in; naked, and ye clothed Me; I was sick and ye visited Me; I was in prison, and ye came unto Me." And He adds, "Inasmuch as ye have done it unto the least of these My brethren, ye have done it unto Me." [5] He observes the same connexion between Himself and His followers in His words to the wicked. What makes this passage the more awful and apposite, is this, which has been before now remarked,[6] that neither righteous nor wicked *knew* what they had done; even the righteous are represented as unaware that they had approached Christ. They say, "Lord, *when* saw we Thee an hungered, and fed Thee, or thirsty, and gave Thee drink?" In every

[5] Matt. xviii.5; Acts ix.4; Matt. xxv.35–40.
[6] *Vide* Pascal's *Thoughts*.

age, then, Christ is both in the world, and yet not publicly so more than in the days of His flesh.

And a similar remark applies to His Ordinances, which are at once most simple, yet most intimately connected with Him. St. Paul, in his First Epistle to the Corinthians, shows both how easy and how fearful it is to profane the Lord's Supper, while he states how great the excess of the Corinthians had been, yet also that it was a want of "*discerning* the Lord's Body." When He was born into the world, the world knew it not. He was laid in a rude manger, among the cattle, but "all the Angels of God worshipped Him." Now too He is present upon a table, homely perhaps in make, and dishonoured in its circumstances; and faith adores, but the world passes by.

Let us then pray Him ever to enlighten the eyes of our understanding, that we may belong to the Heavenly Host, not to this world. As the carnal-minded would not perceive Him even in Heaven, so the spiritual heart may approach Him, possess Him, see Him, even upon earth.

CHRIST MANIFESTED IN REMEMBRANCE

"He shall glorify Me."—John xvi. 14.

WHEN our Lord was leaving His Apostles, and they were sorrowful, He consoled them by the promise of another Guide and Teacher, on whom they might rely instead of Him, and who should be more to them even than He had been. He promised them the Third Person in the Ever-blessed Trinity, the Holy Ghost, the Spirit of Himself and of His Father, who should come invisibly, and with the greater power and comfort, inasmuch as He was invisible; so that His presence would be more real and efficacious by how much it was more secret and inscrutable. At the same time this new and most gracious Comforter, while bringing a higher blessedness, would not in any degree obscure or hide what had gone before. Though He did more for the Apostles than Christ had done, He would not throw into the shade and supersede Him whom He succeeded. How could that be? who could come greater or holier than the Son of God? who could obscure the Lord of glory? how could the Holy Ghost, who was one with the Son, and the Spirit proceeding from the Son, do otherwise than manifest the Son, while manifesting Himself? how could He fail to illuminate the mercies and perfections of Him, whose death upon the Cross opened a way for Himself, the Holy Ghost, to be gracious to man also? Accordingly, though it was expedient that the Son should go away, in order that the Comforter might come, we did not lose the sight of the Son in the presence of the Comforter. On the contrary, Christ expressly announced to the Apostles concerning Him in the words of the text, "He shall glorify Me."

Now these words lead us first to consider in what special way the Holy Ghost gives glory to the Son of God; and next to inquire whether there is not in this appointment some trace of a general law of Divine Providence, which is observed, as in Scripture, so in the world's affairs.

The special way in which God the Holy Ghost gave glory to God the Son, seems to have been His revealing Him as the Only-begotten Son of the Father, who had appeared as the Son of man. Our Saviour said most plainly, that He was the Son of God; but it is one thing to declare the whole truth, another to receive it. Our Saviour said all that need be said, but His Apostles understood Him not. Nay, when they made confession, and that in faith, and by the secret grace of God, and therefore acceptably to Christ, still they understood not fully what they said. St. Peter acknowledged Him as the Christ, the Son of God. So did the centurion who was present at His crucifixion. Did that centurion, when he said, "Truly, this was the Son of God," understand his own words? Surely not. Nor did St. Peter, though he spoke, not through flesh and blood, but by the revelation of the Father. Had he understood, could he so soon after, when our Lord spoke of His passion which lay before Him, have presumed to "take Him, and begin to rebuke Him?" Certainly he did not understand that our Lord, as being the Son of God, was not the creature of God, but the Eternal Word, the Only-begotten Son of the Father, one with Him in substance, distinct in Person.

And when we look into our Saviour's conduct in the days of His flesh, we find that He purposely concealed that knowledge, which yet He gave; as if intending it should be enjoyed, but not at once; as if His words were to stand, but to wait awhile for their interpretation; as if reserving them for His coming, who at once was to bring Christ and His words into the light. Thus when the young ruler came to Him, and said, "Good Master," He showed Himself more desirous of correcting him than of revealing Himself, desirous rather to make him weigh his words, than Himself to accept them. At another time, when He had so far disclosed Himself that the Jews accused Him of blasphemy, in that He, being a man, made Himself God, far from repeating and insisting on the sacred Truth which they rejected, He invalidated the terms in which He had conveyed it, by intimating that even the prophets of the Old Testament were called gods as well as He. And when He stood before Pilate, He refused to bear witness to Himself, or say what He was, or whence He came.

Thus He was among them "as he that serveth." Apparently, it was not till after His resurrection, and especially after His ascension, when the Holy Ghost descended, that the Apostles understood who had been with them. When all was over they knew it, not at the time.

Now here we see, I think, the trace of a general principle, which comes before us again and again both in Scripture and in the world, that God's presence is not discerned at the time when it is upon us, but afterwards, when we look back upon what is gone and over.

Our Saviour's history itself will supply instances in evidence of the existence of this remarkable law.

St. Philip, for instance, when he asked to see the Almighty Father, little understood the privilege he had already so long enjoyed; accordingly, our Lord answered, "Have I been so long time with you, and yet hast thou not known Me, Philip?"

Again, on another occasion, He said to St. Peter, "What I do thou knowest not now, but thou shalt know hereafter." [1] Again, "These things understood not His disciples at the first; but when Jesus was glorified, then remembered they that these things were written of Him, and that they had done these things unto Him." [2]

And in like manner while He talked with the two disciples going to Emmaus, their eyes were holden that they did not know Him. When they recognized Him, at once He vanished out of their sight. *Then* "they said one to another, Did not our heart burn within us, while He talked with us by the way?" [3]

Such too are the following, taken from the Old Testament. Jacob, when he fled from his brother, "lighted upon a certain place, and tarried there all night, because the sun was set." In his sleep he saw the vision of Angels, and the Lord above them. Accordingly when he awaked out of his sleep, he said, "Surely the Lord is in this place, and I knew it not. And he was afraid, and said, How dreadful is this place! This is none other but the house of God, and this is the gate of heaven." [4]

Again, after wrestling all night with the Angel, not knowing who it was, and asking after His name, then at length "Jacob called the name of the place Peniel; for I have seen God face to face, and my life is preserved." [5]

So again, after the Angel had departed from Gideon, who had treated Him like a man, then, and not till then, he discovered who had been with him and he said, "Alas, O Lord God; for because I have seen an Angel of the Lord face to face." [6]

And so in like manner, after the Angel had departed from Manoah and his wife, then, and not till then, they discovered Him. Then "they fell on their faces to the ground. . . . . And

---

[1] John xiii.7.   [2] John xii.16.   [3] Luke xxiv.32.
[4] Gen. xxviii.11–17.   [5] Gen. xxxii.30.   [6] Judges vi.22.

Manoah said unto his wife, We shall surely die, because we have seen God."[7]

Such is God's rule in Scripture, to dispense His blessings, silently and secretly; so that we do not discern them at the time, except by faith, afterwards only. Of which, as I have said, we have two special instances in the very outline of the Gospel history; the mission of our Saviour, who was not understood till afterwards to be the Son of God Most High, and the mission of the Holy Ghost, which was still more laden with spiritual benefits, and is still more secret. Flesh and blood could not discern the Son of God, even when He wrought visible miracles; the natural man still less discerns the things of the Spirit of God; yet in the next world all shall be condemned, for not believing here what it was never given them to see. Thus the presence of God is like His glory as it appeared to Moses; He said, "Thou canst not see my face . . . . and live;" but He passed by, and Moses saw that glory, as it retired, which he might not see in front, or in passing; he saw it, and he acknowledged it, and "made haste and bowed his head toward the earth, and worshipped."[8]

Now consider how parallel this is to what takes place in the providences of daily life. Events happen to us pleasant or painful; we do not know at the time the meaning of them, we do not see God's hand in them. If indeed we have faith, we confess what we do not see, and take all that happens as His; but whether we will accept it in faith or not, certainly there is no other way of accepting it. We see nothing. We see not why things come, or whither they tend. Jacob cried out on one occasion, "All these things are against me;"[9] certainly so they seemed to be. One son made away with by the rest, another in prison in a foreign land, a third demanded;—"Me have ye bereaved of my children; Joseph is not, and Simeon is not, and ye will take Benjamin away: all these things are against me." Yet all these things were working for good. Or pursue the fortunes of the favourite and holy youth who was the first taken from him; sold by his brethren to strangers, carried into Egypt, tempted by a very perilous temptation, overcoming it but not rewarded, thrown into prison, the iron entering into his soul, waiting there till the Lord should be gracious, and "look down from heaven;" but waiting—why? and how long? It is said again and again in the sacred narrative, "The Lord was with Joseph;" but do you think he saw at the time any tokens of God? any tokens, except so far as by faith he realized them, in faith he saw them?

---

[7] Judges xiii.20, 22   [8] Exod. xxxiii.20; xxxiv.8.   [9] Gen. xlii.36.

His faith was its own reward; which to the eye of reason was no reward at all, for faith forsooth did but judge of things by that standard which it had originally set up, and pronounce that Joseph was happy because he ought to be so. Thus though the Lord was with him, apparently all things were against him. Yet afterwards he saw, what was so mysterious at the time;—"God did send me before you," he said to his brethren, "to preserve life. . . . . It was not you that sent me hither, but God; and He hath made me a father to Pharaoh, and lord of all his house, and a ruler throughout all the land of Egypt."

Wonderful providence indeed, which is so silent, yet so efficacious, so constant, so unerring! This is what baffles the power of Satan. He cannot discern the Hand of God in what goes on; and though he would fain meet it and encounter it, in his mad and blasphemous rebellion against heaven, he cannot find it. Crafty and penetrating as he is, yet his thousand eyes and his many instruments avail him nothing against the majestic serene silence, the holy imperturbable calm which reigns through the providences of God. Crafty and experienced as he is, he appears like a child or a fool, like one made sport of, whose daily bread is but failure and mockery, before the deep and secret wisdom of the Divine Counsels. He makes a guess here, or does a bold act there, but all in the dark. He knew not of Gabriel's coming, and the miraculous conception of the Virgin,[10] or what was meant by that Holy Thing which was to be born, being called the Son of God. He tried to kill Him, and he made martyrs of the innocent children; he tempted the Lord of all with hunger and with ambitious prospects; he sifted the Apostles, and got none but one who already bore his own name, and had been already given over as a devil. He rose against his God in his full strength, in the hour and power of darkness, and then he seemed to conquer; but with his utmost effort, and as his greatest achievement, he did no more than "whatsoever Thy hand and Thy counsel determined before to be done."[11] He brought into the world the very salvation which He feared and hated. He accomplished the Atonement of that world, whose misery He was plotting. Wonderfully silent, yet resistless course of God's providence! "Verily, Thou art a God that hidest Thyself, O God of Israel, the Saviour;" and if even devils, sagacious as they are, spirits by nature and experienced in evil, cannot detect His hand, while He works, how can we hope to see it except by that way which the devils cannot take, by a loving faith? how can we

---

[10] *Vide* Ignat. ad Eph. 19.   [11] Acts iv.28.

see it except afterwards as a reward to our faith, beholding the cloud of glory in the distance, which when present was too rare and impalpable for mortal sense?

And so, again, in a number of other occurrences, not striking, not grievous, not pleasant, but ordinary, we are able afterwards to discern that He has been with us, and, like Moses, to worship Him. Let a person who trusts he is on the whole serving God acceptably, look back upon his past life, and he will find how critical were moments and acts, which at the time seemed the most indifferent: as for instance, the school he was sent to as a child, the occasion of his falling in with those persons who have most benefited him, the accidents which determined his calling or prospects whatever they were. God's hand is ever over His own, and He leads them forward by a way they know not of. The utmost they can do is to believe, what they cannot see now, what they shall see hereafter; and as believing, to act together with God towards it.

And hence perchance it is, that years that are past bear in retrospect so much of fragrance with them, though at the time perhaps we saw little in them to take pleasure in; or rather we did not, could not realize that we were receiving pleasure, though we received it. We received pleasure, because we were in the presence of God, but we knew it not; we knew not what we received; we did not bring home to ourselves or reflect upon the pleasure we were receiving; but afterwards, when enjoyment is past, reflection comes in. We feel at the time; we recognize and reason afterwards. Such, I say, is the sweetness and softness with which days long passed away fall upon the memory, and strike us. The most ordinary years, when we seemed to be living for nothing, these shine forth to us in their very regularity and orderly course. What was sameness at the time, is now stability; what was dulness, is now a soothing calm; what seemed unprofitable, has now its treasure in itself; what was but monotony, is now harmony; all is pleasing and comfortable, and we regard it all with affection. Nay, even sorrowful times (which at first sight is wonderful) are thus softened and illuminated afterwards: yet why should they not be so, since then, more than at other times, our Lord is present, when He seems leaving His own to desolateness and orphanhood? The planting of Christ's Cross in the heart is sharp and trying; but the stately tree rears itself aloft, and has fair branches and rich fruit, and is good to look upon. And if all this be true, even of sad or of ordinary times, much more does it hold good of seasons of religious obedience and comfort.

Such are the feelings with which men often look back on their childhood, when any accident brings it vividly before them. Some relic or token of that early time, some spot, or some book, or a word, or a scent, or a sound, brings them back in memory to the first years of their discipleship, and they then see, what they could not know at the time, that God's presence went up with them and gave them rest. Nay, even now perhaps they are unable to discern fully what it was which made that time so bright and glorious. They are full of tender, affectionate thoughts towards those first years, but they do not know why. They think it is those very years which they yearn after, whereas it is the presence of God which, as they now see, was then over them, which attracts them. They think that they regret the past, when they are but longing after the future. It is not that they would be children again, but that they would be Angels and would see God; they would be immortal beings, crowned with amaranth, robed in white, and with palms in their hands, before His throne.

What happens in the fortunes of individuals, happens also to the Church. Its pleasant times are pleasant in memory. We cannot know who are great and who are little, what times are serious and what are their effects, till afterwards. Then we make much of the abode, and the goings out and the comings in of those who in their day lived familiarly with us, and seemed like other men. Then we gather up the recollection of what they did here, and what they said there. Then their persecutors, however powerful, are not known or spoken of, except by way of setting off *their* achievements and triumphs in the Gospel. "Kings of the earth, and the great men, and rich men, and the chief captains, and the mighty men," who in their day so magnified themselves, so ravaged and deformed the Church, that it could not be seen except by faith, then are found in nowise to have infringed the continuity of its outlines, which shine out clear and glorious, and even more delicate and tender for the very attempt to obliterate them. It needs very little study of history to prove how really this is the case; how little schism and divisions and disorders and troubles and fears and persecutions and scatterings and threatenings interfere with the glory of Christ Mystical, as looked upon afterwards, though at the time they almost hid it. Great Saints, great events, great privileges, like the everlasting mountains, grow as we recede from them.

And it is a sort of instinct, felt by the multitude, that they really are in possession of that which they neither see nor in faith accept, which (as some have remarked) makes them so unwilling just at the last moment to give up those privileges which they have so long possessed without valuing or using. Sometimes at the last moment, when mercies are about to be withdrawn, when it is too late, or all but too late, a feeling comes over them that something precious is going from them. They seem to hear the sound of arms, and the voices in the Temple saying, "Let us depart hence;" and they attempt to retain what they cannot see;—penitents, when the day of grace is over.

Once more: every one of us surely must have experienced this general feeling most strongly, at one time or other, as regards the Sacraments and Ordinances of the Church. At the time, we cannot realize, we can but believe that Christ is with us; but after an interval a sweetness breathes from them, as from His garments, "of myrrh, aloes, and cassia." Such is the memory of many a Holy Communion in Church, of Holy Communions solemnized at a sick-bed, of Baptisms assisted in, of Confirmation, of Marriage, of Ordination; nay, Services which at the time we could not enjoy, from sickness, from agitation, from restlessness,—Services which at the time, in spite of our belief in their blessedness, yet troubled our wayward hearts,—Services which we were tempted to think long, feared beforehand, nay, and wished over when they were performing (alas! that we should be so blind and dead to our highest good), yet afterwards are full of God. We come, like Jacob, in the dark, and lie down with a stone for our pillow; but when we rise again, and call to mind what has passed, we recollect we have seen a vision of Angels, and the Lord manifested through them, and we are led to cry out, "How dreadful is this place! This is *none other* than the house of God, and this is the gate of heaven."

To conclude. Let us profit by what every day and hour teaches us, as it flies. What is dark while it is meeting us, reflects the Sun of Righteousness when it is past. Let us profit by this in future, so far as this, to have *faith in what* we cannot see. The world seems to go on as usual. There is nothing of heaven in the face of society; in the news of the day there is nothing of heaven; in the faces of the many, or of the great, or of the rich, or of the busy, there is nothing of heaven; in the words of the eloquent, or the deeds of the powerful, or the counsels of the wise, or the resolves of the lordly, or the pomps of the wealthy, there is nothing of heaven. And yet the Ever-blessed Spirit of God is here the Presence of the Eternal Son, ten times more glorious, more powerful than when He trod the earth in our flesh, is with us. Let us ever bear in mind this divine truth,—the more secret God's hand is, the more powerful—the more silent, the more awful. We are under the awful ministration of the Spirit, against whom whoso speaks, hazards more than can be reckoned up; whom whoso grieves, loses more of blessing and glory than can be fathomed. The Lord was with Joseph, and the Lord was with David, and the Lord, in the days of His flesh, was with His Apostles; but now, He is with us in the Spirit. And inasmuch as the Divine Spirit is more than flesh and blood; inasmuch as the risen and glorified Saviour is more powerful than when He was in the form of a servant; inasmuch as the Eternal Word, spiritualizing His own manhood, has more of virtue for us, and grace, and blessing, and life, than when concealed in it, and subject to temptation and pain; inasmuch as faith is more blessed than sight; by so much more are we now more highly privileged, have more title to be called kings and priests unto God, even than the disciples who saw and touched Him. He who glorified Christ, imparts Him thus glorified to us. If He could work miracles in the days of His flesh, how much more can He work miracles now? and if His visible miracles were full of power, how much more His miracles invisible? Let us beg of Him grace wherewith to enter into the depth of our privileges,—to enjoy what we possess,—to believe in, to use, to improve, to glory in our present gifts as "members of Christ, children of God, and inheritors of the kingdom of heaven."

THE GAINSAYING OF KORAH

"Woe unto them; for they have gone in the way of Cain, and ran greedily after the error of Balaam for reward, and perished in the gainsaying of Core."—Jude ii.

THERE are two special sins which trouble the Church, and are denounced in Scripture, ambition and avarice, the sin of Korah and the sin of Balaam; both of which are spoken of in the text. The sin of Balaam is denounced again and again by St. Paul, in his Epistles to Timothy and Titus; as where he says, "A Bishop must be . . . . not greedy of filthy lucre . . . . not covetous;" "the Deacons must be . . . . not greedy of filthy lucre;" noticing the while that some supposed that "gain was godliness," and "taught things which they ought not for filthy lucre's sake."[1] And the sin of Korah, or ambition, is condemned by our Lord, when He commands, Whosoever will be great among you, let him be your minister; by St. James, when he says, "Be not many masters, knowing that we shall receive the greater condemnation;" and by St. Paul, when he directs that a Bishop should not be a "novice, lest being lifted up with pride he fall into the condemnation of the devil."[2] And both sins together are spoken of by St. Peter, in his exhortation to the Elders to "feed the flock of God . . . . not for filthy lucre, but of a ready mind; neither as being lords over God's heritage, but being ensamples to the flock."[3]

Accordingly, these are the two sins brought before us by our Church in the first lessons of the first Sunday after Easter, which is, as it were, the festival in commemoration of the Ministerial Commission. After celebrating the resurrection of Christ, when He became "a Priest for ever after the order of Melchizedek," we proceed to make mention of the means which He has instituted for exercising His Priesthood on earth continually,—for commemorating and applying in the Spirit, among His elect people, again and again, day after day, to the

[1] 1 Tim. iii.8; vi.5; Tit. i.7, 11.
[2] Matt. xx.26; James iii.1; 1 Tim. iii.6.
[3] 1 Pet. v.2, 3.

end of the world, that atoning death and glorious resurrection, which He wrought out once for all in His own person on Calvary. He Himself instituted that means on the very day that He rose from the dead, ordaining man, frail and fallible as he is, to be the vessel of His gifts, and to represent Him. When He was risen, He did not first show Himself to His enemies, nor manifest the Spirit, nor unfold His new law, nor destroy the Temple; but He consecrated His Ministers: "As My Father hath sent Me," He said to His Apostles, "even so send I you." And, as if after His pattern, we too, even at this day, follow up the celebration of His "taking to Himself His great power," with that of His delegating it to His Church, as the Gospel selected for the same Sunday shows.

Of such high importance then, in our Church's judgment, is the subject of the Christian Ministry; so intimately connected with the Divine scheme of mercy, so full of reverence and awe. This will be best seen by proceeding, as I shall now do, to consider the lesson derived from the rebellion of Korah, Dathan, and Abiram, which, though properly belonging to the Old Covenant, our Church certainly considers applicable to us Christians.

The history in question contains an account, not only of the ambition of Korah himself, who was a Levite or minister, but of the rebellion of Dathan and Abiram, who were not ministers, but, as we now speak, laymen.

In considering it, I shall confine myself to this point, viz. to determine the feelings and circumstances under which these wicked men rebelled against Moses and Aaron, and that, with a view of warning those who speak lightly of schism, separation, and dissent, in this day. For I think it will be seen that they are feelings and circumstances which prevail very widely now as well as then, and, if they do prevail, are as evil now as they were then; St. Jude, in the text plainly intimating that such gainsaying as Korah's is a sin in a Christian, as well as formerly in the Jews, and that those who commit it are in the way to perish. This, then, is a very serious thought; considering, as I have said, how men in these days make light of it.

The outline of the history of Korah, Dathan, and Abiram is this: they rebelled against Moses and Aaron, and in consequence Dathan and Abiram were swallowed up by an earthquake, and Korah's company was burnt with fire. Now, then let us proceed to the remarks proposed.

1. First, then, let the number and dignity of the offenders be observed. They seem to have been some of the most eminent

and considerable persons in Israel. Dathan and Abiram's party are said more than once, with some emphasis, to have been "famous in the congregation, men of renown."[4] Moreover there were among them as many as two hundred and fifty *princes*, or as we should now say, noblemen. A very great and formidable opposition to Moses and Aaron was it, when so great a number of eminent persons rebelled against, or (in modern language) became dissenters from the Church. Nor was this all,—a portion of God's appointed ministers joined them. The Levites, as we all know, were the especially holy tribe: a portion of them, viz. the family of Aaron, were priests; but all of them were ministers. Such was Korah; but, dissatisfied with being merely what God had made him, he aspired to be something more, to have the priesthood. And it appears that just as many of his brethren joined him in his rebellion as there were princes who joined Dathan and Abiram. Two hundred and fifty Levites, or ministers, were banded together in this opposition to Moses, forming, from their rank and number a body (to use once more modern language) of very high respectability, to say the least, that is, respectability in the eyes of men.

2. Next, let us observe how confident they were that they were right. They seemed to have entertained no kind of doubt or hesitation. When Moses denounced Dathan and Abiram, and bade all those who wished to escape their curse, to "depart" at once "from the tents of those wicked men," "Dathan and Abiram came out, and stood in the door of their tents, and their wives, and their sons, and their little children." You see they had no misgivings, no fears, no perplexity; they saw their way clear; they were sure they were in the right; and they came out, to stand any test, any sentence of wrath which Moses might attempt, as thinking that nothing could come of it. Nor was Korah's confidence less. Moses challenged him and the rest to appear before God, to perform the priest's office, and so to stand the test whether or not He would accept them; and they promptly accepted the proposal. They were to "take their censers, and put fire therein, and put incense in them before the Lord," "and it shall be, that the man whom the Lord doth choose, he shall be holy." Korah and his company accordingly "stood in the door of the tabernacle of the congregation with Moses and Aaron;" nay, in that sacred and awful place, where was the glory of the Lord visibly displayed, did Korah endure to "gather all *the congregation*" against Moses and Aaron.

[4] Numb. xvi.2; xxvi.9.

Sceptics, were there such standing by, might have made the remark, that both parties were equally sincere, equally confident; and therefore neither was more pleasing to God than the
other.

Such was the confidence of Korah, Dathan, and Abiram, of
the two hundred and fifty princes or nobles, and the two hundred and fifty ministers of God. And we, who believe that in
spite of their confidence Almighty God was against them, are
perhaps at first sight tempted to attribute it to some extraordinary infatuation, judicial blindness, special hard-heartedness,
or the like,—something quite out of the way, peculiar perhaps
to the Jews,—something which cannot happen now. We cannot comprehend how their confidence could possibly be based
on *reason*—I do not say on correct reason, but on even *apparent*
reason. We do not consider that perhaps they *thought* they had
good reasons for what they did, as we often think in our own
case, when we really have not. Rather we attribute their conduct to something irrational, to pride, obstinacy, or hatred of
the truth, as indeed it was in its origin; but I mean, to some such
evil principle operating on the soul *at once*, and not operating on
it *through* the pretence of reason, not so operating as to be hidden whether from themselves or others. And thus we lose the
lesson which this solemn history is calculated to convey to us at
this day; because, since the opposition made to God's Church in
these days is professedly based upon reason, not upon mere
prejudice, passion, or wilfulness, persons think that the confidence with which they oppose themselves to it, is a very different sort of confidence from that of Korah, Dathan, and
Abiram, whereas it is really very much the same.

3. What, then, were the *reasons* or *arguments* which made
Korah, Dathan, and Abiram so confident they were in the
right,—so confident, that they even ventured to appeal to
God, and to rise up against Moses and Aaron as if in the Name
of the Lord? Their ground was this: they accused Moses and
Aaron of what is now called *priestcraft*. Let us pay attention to
this circumstance.

Now, let it be observed, that there were many rebellions of
the people, founded on open and professed *unbelief*. This was
not the character of the particular sin under review: it was not a
disbelief in God, but in Moses. Distrust in Moses, indeed, was
mixed up in all their rebellions; but generally their rebellion
was more strictly directed against Almighty God. Thus, when
the spies returned, and spread about an evil report of the good
land, and the people believed them, this implied a disbelief in

the Divine Arm altogether, as manifested in their deliverance
and protection. Thus they complained of the manna; and thus
they went out on the seventh day to gather it. But it is remarkable, that in the rebellion before us, there is no hint of the promoters of it disbelieving in the power or providence of God over
the chosen people; only they accuse Moses of altering or (as we
should say) corrupting the divine system. Dathan and Abiram
were sons of Reuben, the first-born of the tribes: they might
consider that Moses was interfering with their prerogative by
birth to lead and govern the people. But, any how, they seem to
have relied on their rank and eminence; they and their companions were "famous in the congregation, men of renown;" and
they could not bring themselves to submit to God's appointment, by which the nation was formed into a Church, and Levi
was chosen, at God's inscrutable will, to be the priest instead of
Reuben. Accordingly, far from denying that God was with the
nation, they maintained it; they only said that He was not specially with Moses and Aaron; they only claimed all equality of
honour and power with Moses and Aaron; they only denounced Moses and Aaron as usurpers, tyrants, and hypocrites.
Far from showing any scoffing or lightness of mind, or profaneness, such as Esau's who rejected the blessing, they so esteemed
it as to claim it as their own, in all its fulness; nay, they claimed
it for the whole people. They were only opposed to what is now
called *exclusiveness*; they were champions of the rights of the
people against what they called the encroachments, the arrogant pretensions, the priestcraft of Moses their Lawgiver, and
Aaron the Saint of the Lord. They said, "Ye take too much
upon you, seeing *all* the congregation are holy, *every one of them*;
and the Lord is among them; wherefore then lift ye up yourselves *above* the congregation of the Lord?" Their objection was,
that Moses was interposing himself as a mediator between God
and them,—limiting the mercies of God, restraining the freedom, obscuring the glory of His grace, and robbing them of
their covenanted privileges; that he had instituted an order of
priests, whereas they were *all* priests, every one, and needed no
human assistance, no voice or advice, or direction, or performance, from fallible man, from men of like passions and imperfections with themselves, in order to approach God withal, and
serve Him acceptably. "*All* the congregation are holy," say they,
"every one of them; and the Lord is among them." "The Lord is
not far off; He is not in the clouds only, He is not on Sinai, He is
not on the mercy-seat, He is not with Aaron; but He is among
us, in the congregation, as near one man as another, as near to

all of us as He is to Moses." Their partisans affect the same tone even after God's judgment has fallen on the rebels. The people say to Moses and Aaron, "Ye have killed the people of the Lord." Yes; they call those separatists and schismatists "the Lord's people," and they accuse Moses and Aaron forsooth of having, by some device of juggling priests, some strange and diabolical stratagem, some secret of magic or science, compassed the death of their enemies, while they pretended to refer it to a miraculous judgment; and they seem as if to pride themselves on their discernment, on the clearness of intellectual vision by which they saw through the fraud, and brought it home to the impostors.

Awful guilt indeed in these self-wise men, if this representation be true! yet it is apparently true, as the words show with which the rebels themselves answer the summons of Moses to come to him. "Wilt thou," say they, "put out the eyes of these men? we will not come up." No; we have eyes; we are not mere dull, brutish, superstitious bigots, to crouch before a priest, and submit to his yoke of bondage; we can reason, we can argue, we are resolved to exercise our free unfettered private judgment, and to determine (candidly indeed and dispassionately), but still to determine for ourselves before we act. We will indeed give a fair hearing to what is told us; we will listen with a becoming deference and with all patience, nay with a sort of consideration and prepossession to what you, O Moses and Aaron, say to us; but still we will not have our eyes put out. No, seeing is believing; we will not go by instinctive feeling, by conscience, by mere probabilities; but everything shall be examined in a rational and enlightened way, everything searched, and sifted, and scrutinized, and rigidly tested, before it is admitted. The burden of proof lies with you; till you have proved to us your claims, we will not go up, we will not obey. To tell the truth, we are suspicious of you. We are "jealous with a godly jealousy" (alas! for men do so speak!) of any encroachments on our spiritual liberty, any assumption of superior holiness, superior acceptableness in one of us over another. We are all brethren, we are all equal, all independent. "Wilt thou make thyself altogether a prince over us?" "Moreover," they continue, "thou hast not brought us into a land that floweth with milk and honey, or given us inheritance of fields and vineyards;" or as men now speak, The present system does not work well; there are many abuses, abundant need of reform, much still undone which should be done, much idleness, much inefficiency, many defects in the Church. We see it quite plainly. Do not seek to defend yourselves. "Wilt thou put out the eyes of these men? we will not come up."

Something of the same kind of spirit had already shown itself in the sin of the golden calf, though that sin was open idolatry. Then also the people thought that they had found a better religion than Moses had taught them. They were far from denying God's miraculous providences; but they said that Moses had taken to himself what belonged to the nation; he had taught them in his own way, and they had a right to choose for themselves. "Up," they said, "make us gods, which shall go before us; for as for this Moses, the man that brought us up out of the land of Egypt, we wot not what is become of him." [5] And where was Moses? He was with God in prayer and vision. They did not know, or at least understand this. So they said, "What a time for a ruler to be absent! in what a crisis! how much is there that wants doing!—forty days are gone, and he is still away. Is he lost? has he left us here to ourselves? is he feigning any communication from heaven? any how, what binds us to *him*? We are bound indeed to the God who has brought us out of Egypt, but not to the rule of Moses or the line of Aaron." Moses was away; and where was Aaron?—where? the people could not ask, for they were partakers in his sin, rather, they had forced him into their sin, the sin of the golden calf. Aaron was receiving their gold ornaments, and was moulding them into an idol. Alas! the people could not accuse him, who had seduced him into the sin. But there *were* those who might, who did complain; and who they were, since I have been led to the subject, it will be found to our present purpose to inquire.

They were the Levites. While Aaron sinned, they, the inferior ministers, stood silent, but wondering and distressed. These had no part in the sin; and when Moses came down from the mount and said, "Who is on the Lord's side ?" [6] then they, and they only, answered the call. "All the sons of Levi gathered themselves together unto him;" and when he ordered them, they promptly "put every man his sword by his side, and went in and out from gate to gate throughout the camp, and slew every man his brother, and every man his companion, and every man his neighbour;" and "there fell of the people that day about three thousand men." This is considered in Scripture[7] the act of consecration by which the Levites became the sacred tribe; so that their advancement to the ministerial office is historically coincident with Aaron's temporary defection from his more sacred duties in it. All this had happened, as some suppose shortly before, as others think as much as twenty years before, the occurrence which has been under our immediate review; but whether or not the one occurrence, as has been reasonably conjectured, led to the other, whether or not Korah's stout-hearted rebellion was the result[8] of ambitious views in the Levites, which their advancement to the sacred ministry had occasioned, still certain it is that at this time "it seemed but a small thing unto them" (in Moses' words) "that the God of Israel had separated them from the congregation of Israel, to bring them near to Himself to do the service of the tabernacle of the Lord, and to stand before the congregation to minister unto them;" and "they sought the priesthood also," Aaron's portion, on whom they were appointed to attend.[9] And the circumstance that Aaron had failed on that trying occasion when they were rewarded, might dispose them to contemn him at this time, not recollecting that God's will made the difference between man and man, and that He who gave them His covenanted blessings through bulls and calves, might also vouchsafe them, did it please Him, through frail and erring men; and might dispense with inward perfection, and take up with mere earthen vessels, and be content with faith instead of consistent obedience, as He dispensed with eloquence, or wisdom, or strength. Such then were the circumstances under which the Levites rebelled, being elated by their existing privileges, as the Reubenites were stimulated by jealousy.

The parties then concerned in this formidable conspiracy were not besotted idolaters; they were not infidels; they were not obstinate, prejudiced, unreasoning zealots; they were not the victims of unscrupulous and desperate ambition; but though ambitious, proud, headstrong, obstinate, unbelieving, they veiled all these bad principles, even from their own conscience, under a show of reason, of clear, simple, straightforward, enlightened reason, under a plain argument open to the meanest capacity: "*All* the congregation," they said, "were holy, *every one*." God had signified no exception or exclusion; all had been baptized in the Red Sea, all had been at Sinai. Moses, however thus they might speak, had added to this simple and primitive religion a system of his own, a system of priestcraft. The especial favours which God had shown Moses were done twenty years before, and could be denied without much chance of contradiction; or if the rebellion took place (as others say) shortly

---

[8] V*ide* Patrick on Numb. xvi.2.   [9] Numb. iii.10.

after the Exodus, then it came close upon Aaron's sin in the matter of the golden calf. Any how, an excuse was easily found for explaining away the authority of Moses and Aaron, for denying the priesthood, and accusing it of being a corruption; and for professing to be the champions of a pure and enlightened, and uncorrupt worship,—a worship which would be quite clear of the idolatrous acts of Aaron, because in it Aaron's prerogative would be destroyed altogether.

Such is the history of the Church in the wilderness, in which we see as in a type the history of the Gospel. And how did it end? I stated in the commencement. The earth opened, and swallowed up Dathan, and covered the congregation of Abiram, their houses, their families, their possessions, and all that belonged to them. Fire went out from the Lord, and consumed the two hundred and fifty men who offered incense.

A very few words will suffice to suggest the lesson to be derived from this awful history; it is this:—If the Old Testament is still our rule of duty, except in such details as imply a local religion and a material sanctuary; if it is our rule of duty in its principles, its doctrines, its precepts; if the Gospel is but the fulfilment and development of the Law: if the parts in both are the same, only the circumstances without and the Spirit within new; if though Circumcision is abolished, yet there is Baptism instead of it; the Passover abolished, yet Holy Communion instead; the Sabbath abolished, yet instead of it the Lord's Day; if the two tables of stone which contained the Law are destroyed, yet the Sermon on the Mount takes their place; if though Moses is gone, Christ is come; and if in like manner, though Aaron is gone and his priestly line, another order of priests is come instead; (and unless this is so, the Old Testament is in a great measure but a dead letter to Christians; and if there be but a chance that it is so, and if it has always been taken to be so, it is a most serious matter to act as if it were not so;) how great must be the sin of resisting the ministers of Christ, or of intruding into their office! How great the sin of presuming to administer the rites of the Church, to baptize, to celebrate the Holy Communion, or to ordain, or to bless, without a commission! Korah's sin was kept in remembrance for ever on the covering of the Altar, "to be a memorial," says the inspired writer, "that no stranger which is not of the seed of Aaron, come near to offer incense before the Lord, that he be not as Korah and his company;" in other words (as the warning is to be interpreted now), "that no one, who is not descended from the Apostles by laying on of hands, come near to perform the ministerial office before the Lord, that he be not such as Korah and his company." Many, you will say, intrude into it in this day in ignorance. True, it is so. Therefore, for them let us pray in our Lord's words, "Father, forgive them, for they know not what they do."

THE MYSTERIOUSNESS OF
OUR PRESENT BEING

"I will praise Thee, for I am fearfully and wonderfully made;
marvellous are Thy works, and that my soul knoweth right well."
—Ps. cxxxix.14.

IN the very impressive Psalm from which these words are
taken, this is worth noticing among other things,—that the
inspired writer finds in the mysteries without and within him, a
source of admiration and praise. "I will *praise* Thee, *for* I am
fearfully and wonderfully made; *marvellous* are Thy works."
When Nicodemus heard of God's wonderful working, he said,
"How can these things be?" But holy David glories in what the
natural man stumbles at. It awes his heart and imagination, to
think that God sees him, wherever he is, yet without provoking
or irritating his reason. He has no proud thoughts rising against
what he cannot understand, and calling for his vigilant control.
He does not submit his reason by an effort, but he bursts forth
in exultation, to think that God is so mysterious. "Such knowledge," he says, "is too wonderful for me; it is high, I cannot
attain unto it." Again, "How precious are Thy thoughts unto
me, O God!"

This reflection is suitable on the Festival[1] which we are at
present engaged in celebrating, on which our thoughts are especially turned to the great doctrine of the Trinity in Unity. It
is my intention now to make some remarks upon it; not however explanatory of the doctrine itself, which we have to-day
confessed in the Athanasian Creed as fully and explicitly as it
can be set forth in human words; but I will endeavour from the
text to show, that the difficulty which human words have in
expressing it, is no greater than we meet with when we would
express in human words even those earthly things of which we
actually have experience, and which we cannot deny to exist,
because we witness them: so that our part evidently lies in using

[1] Trinity Sunday.

the mysteries of religion, as David did, simply as a means of impressing on our minds the inscrutableness of Almighty God. Mysteries in religion are measured by the proud according to their own comprehension, by the humble, according to the power of God; the humble glorify God for them, the proud exalt themselves against them.

The text speaks of earthly things,—"I am fearfully and wonderfully made." Now, let us observe some of the mysteries which are involved in our own nature.

1. First, we are made up of soul and body. Now, if we did not know this, so that we cannot deny it, what notion could our minds ever form of such a mixture of natures, and how should we ever succeed in making those who go only by abstract reason take in what we meant? The body is made of matter; this we see; it has a certain extension, make, form, and solidity: by the soul we mean that invisible principle which thinks. We are conscious we are alive, and are rational; each man has his own thoughts, feelings, and desires; each man is one to himself, and he knows himself to be one and indivisible,—one in such sense, that while he exists, it were an absurdity to suppose he can be any other than himself; one in a sense in which no material body which consists of parts can be one. He is sure that he is distinct from the body, though joined to it, because he is one, and the body is not one, but a collection of many things. He feels moreover that he is distinct from it, because he uses it; for what a man can use, to that he is superior. No one can by any possibility mistake his body for himself. It is *his*; it is not he. This principle, then, which thinks and acts in the body, and which each person feels to be himself, we call the soul. We do not know what it is; it cannot be reached by any of the senses; we cannot see it or touch it. It has nothing in common with extension or form; to ask what shape the soul is, would be as absurd as to ask what is the shape of a thought, or a wish, or a regret, or a hope. And hence we call the soul spiritual and immaterial, and say that it has no parts, and is of no size at all. All this seems undeniable. Yet observe, if all this be true, what is meant by saying that it is *in* the body, any more than saying that a thought or a hope is in a stone or a tree? *How* is it joined to the body? what keeps it one with the body? what keeps it in the body? what prevents it any moment from separating from the body? when two things which we see are united, they are united by some connexion which we can understand. A chain or cable keeps a ship in its place; we lay the foundation of a building in the earth, and the building

endures. But what is it which unites soul and body? how do they touch? how do they keep together? how is it we do not wander to the stars or the depths of the sea, or to and fro as chance may carry us, while our body remains where it was on earth? So far from its being wonderful that the body one day dies, how is it that it is made to live and move at all? how is it that it keeps from dying a single hour? Certainly it is as incomprehensible as any thing can be, how soul and body can make up one man; and, unless we had the instance before our eyes, we should seem in saying so to be using words without meaning. For instance, would it not be extravagant and idle to speak of time as deep or high, or of space as quick or slow? Not less idle, surely, it perhaps seems to some races of spirits to say that thought and mind have a body, which in the case of man they have, according to God's marvellous will. It is certain, then, that experience outstrips reason in its capacity of knowledge; why then should reason circumscribe faith, when it cannot compass sight?

2. Again: the soul is not only one, and without parts, but moreover, as if by a great contradiction even in terms, it is in every part of the body. It is no where, yet every where. It may be said, indeed, that it is especially in the brain; but, granting this for argument's sake, yet it is quite certain, since every part of his body belongs to him, that a man's self is in every part of his body. No part of a man's body is like a mere instrument, as a knife, or a crutch might be, which he takes up and may lay down. Every part of it is part of himself; it is connected into one by his soul, which is one. Supposing we take stones and raise a house, the building is not *really* one; it is composed of a number of separate parts, which viewed as collected together, we call one, but which are not one except in our notion of them. But the hands and feet, the head and trunk, form one body under the presence of the soul within them. Unless the soul were in every part, they would not form one body; so that the soul is in every part, uniting it with every other, though it consists of no parts at all. I do not of course mean that there is any real contradiction in these opposite truths; indeed, we know there is not, and cannot be, because they *are* true, because human nature is a fact before us. But the state of the case is a contradiction *when put into words*; we cannot so express it as not to involve an apparent contradiction; and then, if we discriminate our terms, and make distinctions, and balance phrases, and so on, we shall seem to be technical, artificial and speculative, and to use words without meaning.

Now, this is precisely our difficulty, as regards the doctrine of the Ever-blessed Trinity. We have never been in heaven; God, as He is in Himself, is hid from us. We are informed concerning Him by those who were inspired by Him for the purpose, nay by One who "knoweth the Father," His Co-eternal Son Himself, when He came on earth. And, in the message which they brought to us from above, are declarations concerning His nature, which seem to run counter the one to the other. He is revealed to us as One God, the Father, One indivisible Spirit; yet there is said to exist in Him from everlasting His Only-begotten Son, the same as He is, and yet distinct, and from and in Them both, from everlasting and indivisibly, exists the Co-equal Spirit. All this, put into words, seems a contradiction in terms; men have urged it as such; then Christians, lest they should seem to be unduly and harshly insisting upon words which clash with each other, and so should dishonour the truth of God, and cause hearers to stumble, have guarded their words, and explained them; and then for doing this they have been accused of speculating and theorizing. The same result, doubtless, would take place in the parallel case already mentioned. Had we no bodies, and were a revelation made us that there was a race who had bodies as well as souls, what a number of powerful objections should we seem to possess against that revelation! We might plausibly say, that the words used in conveying it were arbitrary and unmeaning. What (we should ask) was the meaning of saying that the soul had no parts, yet was in every part of the body? what was meant by saying it was every where and no where? how could it be one, and yet repeated, as it were, ten thousand times over in every atom and pore of the body, which it was said to exist in? how could it be confined to the body at all? how did it act upon the body? how happened it, as was pretended, that, when the soul did but will, the arm moved or the feet walked? how can a spirit which cannot touch any thing, yet avail to move so large a mass of matter, and so easily as the human body? These are some of the questions which might be asked, partly on the ground that the alleged fact was impossible, partly that the idea was self-contradictory. And these are just the kind of questions with which arrogant and profane minds do assail the revealed doctrine of the Holy Trinity.

3. Further consider what a strange state we are in when we dream, and how difficult it would be to convey to a person who had never dreamed what was meant by dreaming. *His* vocabulary would contain no words to express any middle idea

between perfect possession and entire suspension of the mind's powers. He would understand what it was to be awake, what it was to be insensible; but a state between the two he would neither have words to describe, nor, if he were self-confident and arrogant, inclination to believe, however well it was attested by those who ought to know. I do not say there is no conceivable accumulation of evidence that would subdue such a man's reason, since we see sometimes men's reason subdued by the evidences of the Gospel, whose hearts are imperfectly affected: but I mean, that this earthly mystery *might* be brought before a man with about that degree of evidence in its favour which the Gospel actually has, not ordinarily overpowering, but constituting a *trial* of his heart, a trial, that is, whether the mysteries contained in it do or do not rouse his pride. Dreaming is not a fiction, but a real state of the mind, though only one or two in the whole world ever dreamed; and if these one or two or a dozen men, spoke to the rest of the world, and unanimously witnessed to the existence of that mysterious state, many doubtless would resist their report, as they do the mysteries of the Gospel, on the ground of its being unintelligible: yet in that case they would be resisting a truth, and would be wrong (not indeed blameably so, compared with those who on a like account reject the Gospel, which comes to us as a practical, not a mere abstract matter), yet they would undeniably be considering a thing false which was true.

It is no great harm to be wrong in a matter of opinion; but in matters which influence conduct, which bear upon our eternal interests, such as Revealed Religion, surely it is most hazardous, most unwise, though it is so common to stumble at its mysteries, instead of believing and acting upon its threats and promises. Instead of embracing what they can understand, together with what they cannot, men criticise the wording in which truths are conveyed, which came from heaven. The inspired Apostles taught them to the first Christian converts, and they, according to the capacities of human language, whether their own or the Apostles', partly one and partly the other, preserved them; and we, instead of thanking them for the benefit, instead of rejoicing that they should have handed on to us those secrets concerning God, instead of thanking Him for His condescension in allowing us to hear them, have hearts cold enough to complain of their mysteriousness. Profane minds ask, "Is God one, or three?" They are answered, He is One and He is also Three. They reply "He cannot be One in the same sense in which He is Three." It is in reply allowed to them, "He is Three in one sense, One in another." They ask, "In what sense? what is that sense in which He is Three Persons,—what is that sense of the word Person, such that it neither stands for one separate Being, as it does with men, nor yet comes short of such a real and sufficient sense as the word requires?" We reply that we do *not know* that intermediate sense; we cannot reconcile, we confess, the distinct portions of the doctrine; we can but take what is given us, and be content. They rejoin, that, if this be so, we are using words without meaning. We answer, No, not without meaning in themselves, but without meaning which we fully apprehend. God understands His own words, though human. God, when He gave the doctrine, put it into words, and the doctrine, as we word it, is the doctrine as the Apostles worded it; it is conveyed to us with the same degree of meaning in it, intelligible to us, with which the Apostles received it; so that it is no reason for giving it up that in part it is not intelligible. This we say; and they insist in reply, as if it were a sufficient answer, that the doctrine, as a whole, *is* unintelligible to us (which we grant); that the words which we use have very little meaning (which is not true, though *we* may not see the full meaning); and so they think to excuse their rejection of them.

But surely all this, I say, is much the same as what might take place in any discussion about dreaming, in a company where one or two persons had experienced it, and the multitude not. It might be said to those who told us of it, Do you mean that it is a state of waking or insensibility? is it one or the other? what is that sense in which we are not insensible in dreaming, and yet are not awake and ourselves ? Now if we have mysteries even about ourselves, which we cannot even put into words accurately, much more may we suppose, even were we not told it, that there are mysteries in the nature of Almighty God; and so far from its being improbable that there should be mysteries, the declaration that there are, even adds some probability to the revelation which declares them. On the other hand, still more unreasonable is disbelief, if it be grounded on the mysteriousness of the revelation; because, if we cannot put into consistent human language human things, if the state of dreaming, which we experience commonly, must be described in words either vague or contradictory, much less is there to surprise us if human words are insufficient to describe heavenly things.

These are a few, out of the many remarks which might be made concerning our own mysterious state, that is, concerning things in us which we know to be really and truly, yet which we cannot accurately reflect upon and contemplate, cannot describe, cannot put into words, and cannot convey to another's comprehension who does not experience them. But this is a very large subject. Let a man consider how hardly he is able and how circuitously he is forced to describe the commonest objects of nature, when he attempts to substitute reason for sight, how difficult it is to define things, how impracticable it is to convey to another any complicated, or any deep or refined feeling, how inconsistent and self-contradictory his own feelings seem, when put into words, how he subjects himself in consequence to misunderstanding, or ridicule, or triumphant criticism; and he will not wonder at the impossibility of duly delineating in earthly words the first Cause of all thought, the Father of spirits, the One Eternal Mind, the King of kings and Lord of lords, who only hath immortality, dwelling in light unapproachable, whom no man hath seen nor can see, the incomprehensible infinite God.

To conclude. One objection only, as it seems to me, can be made to these reflections, and that is soon answered. It may be said that, though there be, as there well may be, ten thousand mysteries about the Divine Nature, yet why should they be disclosed in the Gospel? because the very circumstance that they *cannot* be put into words is a reason why this should not be attempted. But this surely is a very bold and presumptuous way of speaking, not to say more about it; as if we had any means of knowing, as if we had any right to ask, why God does what He does in the very way He does it; as if sinners, receiving a great and unmerited favour, were not very unthankful and acting almost madly, in saying, Why was it given us in this way, not in that? Is God obliged to take us into counsel, and explain to us the reason for every thing He does; or is it our plain duty to take what is given us, and feed upon it in faith? And to those who do thus receive the blessed doctrine under consideration, it will be found to produce special and singular practical effects on them, on the very ground of its mysteriousness. There is nothing, according as we are given to see and judge of things, which will make a greater difference in the temper, character, and habits of an individual, than the circumstance of his holding or not holding the Gospel to be mysterious. Even then, if we go by its influence on our minds, we might safely pronounce that the doctrine of the Holy Trinity, and of other like mysteries, cannot be unimportant. If it be true (as we hold it to be), it must be of consequence; for it tends to draw the mind in one particular direction, and to form it on a different mould from theirs who do not believe in it. And thus what we actually are given to see, does go a certain way in confirming to us what Scripture and the Church declare to us, that belief in this doctrine is actually necessary to salvation, by showing us that such belief has a moral effect on us. The temper of true faith is described in the text,—"Marvellous are Thy works; and that my soul knoweth right well." A religious mind is ever marvelling, and irreligious men laugh and scoff at it because it marvels. A religious mind is ever looking out of itself, is ever pondering God's words, is ever "looking into" them with the Angels, is ever realizing to itself Him on whom it depends, and who is the centre of all truth and good. Carnal and proud minds are contented with self; they like to remain at home; when they hear of mysteries, they have no devout curiosity to go and see the great sight, though it be ever so little out of their way; and when it actually falls in their path, they stumble at it. As great then as is the difference between hanging upon the thought of God and resting in ourselves, lifting up the heart to God and bringing all things in heaven and earth down to ourselves, exalting God and exalting reason, measuring things by God's power and measuring them by our own ignorance, so great is the difference between him who believes in the Christian mysteries and him who does not. And were there no other reason for the revelation of them, but this gracious one, of raising us, refining us, making us reverent, making us expectant and devout, surely this would be more than a sufficient one.

Let us then all, learned and unlearned, gain this great benefit from the mystery of the Ever-blessed Trinity. It is calculated to humble the wise in this world with the thought of what is above them, and to encourage and elevate the lowly with the thought of Almighty God, and the glories and marvels which shall one day be revealed to them. In the Beatific Vision of God, should we through His grace be found worthy of it, we shall comprehend clearly what we now dutifully repeat and desire to know, how the Father Almighty is truly and by Himself God, the Eternal Son truly and by Himself God, and the Holy Ghost truly and by Himself God, and yet not three Gods but one God.

THE VENTURES OF FAITH

"They say unto Him, We are able."—Matt. xx.22.

THESE words of the holy Apostles James and John were in reply to a very solemn question addressed to them by their Divine Master. They coveted, with a noble ambition, though as yet unpractised in the highest wisdom, untaught in the holiest truth,—they coveted to sit beside Him on His Throne of Glory. They would be content with nothing short of that special gift which He had come to grant to His elect, which He shortly after died to purchase for them, and which He offers to us. They ask the gift of eternal life; and He in answer told them, not that they should have it (though for them it was really reserved), but He reminded them what they *must venture for it;* "Are ye able to drink of the cup that I shall drink of, and to be baptized with the baptism that I am baptized with? They say unto Him, We are able." Here then a great lesson is impressed upon us, that our duty as Christians lies in this, in making ventures for eternal life without the absolute certainty of success.

Success and reward everlasting they will have, who persevere unto the end. Doubt we cannot, that the ventures of all Christ's servants must be returned to them at the Last Day with abundant increase. This is a true saying,—He returns far more than we lend to Him, and without fail. But I am speaking of individuals, of ourselves one by one. No one among us knows for certain that he himself will persevere; yet every one among us, to give himself even a chance of success at all, must make a venture. As regards individuals, then, it is quite true, that all of us must for certain make ventures for heaven, yet without the certainty of success through them. This, indeed, is the very meaning of the word "venture;" for that is a strange venture which has nothing in it of fear, risk, danger, anxiety, uncertainty. Yes; so it certainly is; and in this consists the excellence and nobleness of *faith*; this is the very reason why *faith* is singled out from other graces, and honoured as the especial means of our justification, because its presence implies that we have the heart to make a venture.

St. Paul sufficiently sets this before us in the eleventh chapter of his Epistle to the Hebrews, which opens with a definition of faith, and after that, gives us examples of it, as if to guard against any possibility of mistake. After quoting the text, "the just shall live by faith," and thereby showing clearly that he is speaking of what he treats in his Epistle to the Romans as *justifying* faith, he continues, "Now faith is the substance," that is, the realizing, "of things hoped for, the evidence," that is, the ground of proof, "of things not seen."[1] It is in its very essence the making present what is unseen; the acting upon the mere prospect of it, as if it really were possessed; the venturing upon it, the staking present ease, happiness, or other good, upon the chance of the future. And hence in another epistle he says pointedly, "If in this life only we have hope in Christ, we are of all men most miserable."[2] If the dead are not raised, we have indeed made a most signal miscalculation in the choice of life, and are altogether at fault. And what is true of the main doctrine itself, is true also of our individual interest in it. This he shows us in his Epistle to the Hebrews, by the instance of the Ancient Saints, who thus risked their present happiness on the chance of future. Abraham "went out, not knowing whither he went." He and the rest died "not having received the promises, but having seen them afar off, and were persuaded of them, and embraced them, and confessed that they were strangers and pilgrims on the earth." Such was the faith of the Patriarchs: and in the text the youthful Apostles, with an untaught but generous simplicity, lay claim to the same. Little as they knew what they said in its fulness, yet their words were any how expressive of their hidden hearts, prophetic of their future conduct. They say unto Him, "We are able." They pledge themselves as if unawares, and are caught by One mightier than they, and, as it were, craftily made captive. But, in truth, their unsuspicious pledge was, after all, heartily made, though they knew not what they promised; and so was accepted. "Are ye able to drink of My cup, and be baptized with My baptism? They say unto Him, We are able." He in answer, without promising them heaven, graciously said, "*Ye shall* drink indeed of My cup, and be baptized with the baptism that I am baptized with."

Our Lord appears to act after the same manner towards St. Peter: He accepted his office of service, yet warned him how little he himself understood it. The zealous Apostle wished to follow his Lord at once: but He answered, "Whither I go thou

---

[1] Heb. xi.1.   [2] 1 Cor. xv.19.

canst not follow Me now, but thou shalt follow me afterwards."[3] At another time, He claimed the promise already
made to Him; He said, "Follow thou Me;" and at the same time
explained it, "Verily, verily, I say unto thee, when thou wast
young, thou girdedst thyself, and walkedst whither thou
wouldest: but when thou shalt be old, thou shalt stretch forth
thy hands, and another shall gird thee, and carry thee whither
thou wouldest not."[4]

Such were the ventures made in faith, and in uncertainty, by
Apostles. Our Saviour, in a passage of St. Luke's Gospel, binds
upon us all the necessity of deliberately doing the like,—
"Which of you, intending to build a tower, sitteth not down
first and counteth the cost, whether he have sufficient to finish
it ? Lest haply, after he hath laid the foundation, and is not able
to finish it, all that behold it, begin to mock him, saying, This
man began to build, and is not able to finish." And then He
presently adds, "So likewise, whosoever he be of you that
forsaketh not all that he hath, he cannot be My disciple:"[5] thus
warning us of the full sacrifice we must make. We give up our
all to Him; and He is to claim this or that, or grant us somewhat
of it for a season, according to His good pleasure. On the other
hand, the case of the rich young man, who went away sorrowful, when our Lord bade him give up his all and follow Him, is
an instance of one who had *not* faith to make the venture of this
world for the next, upon His word.

If then faith be the essence of a Christian life, and if it be what
I have now described, it follows that our duty lies in risking
upon Christ's word what we have, for what we have not; and
doing so in a noble, generous way, not indeed rashly or lightly,
still without knowing accurately what we are doing, not knowing either what we give up, nor again what we shall gain; uncertain about our reward, uncertain about our extent of sacrifice,
in all respects leaning, waiting upon Him, trusting in Him to
fulfil His promise, trusting in Him to enable us to fulfil our own
vows, and so in all respects proceeding without carefulness or
anxiety about the future.

Now I dare say that what I have said as yet seems plain and
unexceptionable to most of those who hear me; yet surely,
when I proceed to draw the practical inference which immediately follows, there are those who in their secret hearts, if not in
open avowal, will draw back. Men allow us Ministers of Christ
to proceed in our preaching, while we confine ourselves to gen-

---

[3] John xiii.36.   [4] John xxi.18–22.   [5] Luke xiv.28–33.

eral truths, until they see that they themselves are implicated in them, and have to act upon them; and then they suddenly come to a stand; they collect themselves and draw back, and say, "They do not see *this*—or do not admit *that*"—and though they are quite unable to say why that should not follow from what they already allow, which we show *must* follow, still they persist in saying, that they do not see that it does follow; and they look about for excuses, and they say we carry things too far, and that we are extravagant, and that we ought to limit and modify what we say, that we do not take into account times, and seasons, and the like. This is what they pretend; and well has it been said, "where there is a will there is a way;" for there is no truth, however overpoweringly clear, but men may escape from it by shutting their eyes; there is no duty, however urgent, but they may find ten thousand good reasons against it, in their own case. And they are sure to say we carry things too far, when we carry them home to themselves.

This sad infirmity of men, called Christians, is exemplified in the subject immediately before us. Who does not at once admit that faith consists in venturing on Christ's word without seeing? Yet in spite of this, may it not be seriously questioned, whether men in general, even those of the better sort, venture any thing upon His truth at all?

Consider for an instant. Let every one who hears me ask himself the question, what stake has *he* in the truth of Christ's promise? How would he be a whit the worse off, supposing (which is impossible), but, supposing it to fail? We know what it is to have a stake in any venture of this world. We venture our property in plans which promise a return; in plans which we trust, which we have faith in. What have we ventured for Christ? What have we given to Him on a belief of His promise? The Apostle said, that he and his brethren would be of all men most miserable, if the dead were not raised. Can we in any degree apply this to ourselves? We think, perhaps, at present, we have some hope of heaven; well, *this* we should lose of course; but after all, how should we be worse off as to our *present* condition? A trader, who has embarked some property in a speculation which fails, not only loses his prospect of gain, but somewhat of His own, which he ventured with the *hope* of the gain. This is the question, What have *we* ventured? I really fear, when we come to examine, it will be found that there is nothing we resolve, nothing we do, nothing we do not do, nothing we avoid, nothing we choose, nothing we give up, nothing we pursue, which we should not resolve, and do, and not do, and avoid, and choose, and give up, and pursue, if Christ had not died, and heaven were not promised us. I really fear that most men called Christians, whatever they may profess, whatever they may think they feel, whatever warmth and illumination and love they may claim as their own, yet would go on almost as they do, neither much better nor much worse, if they believed Christianity to be a fable. When young, they indulge their lusts, or at least pursue the world's vanities; as time goes on, they get into a fair way of business, or other mode of making money; then they marry and settle; and their interest coinciding with their duty, they seem to be, and think themselves, respectable and religious men; they grow attached to things as they are; they begin to have a zeal against vice and error; and they follow after peace with all men. Such conduct indeed, as far as it goes, is right and praiseworthy. Only I say, it has not necessarily any thing to do with religion at all; there is nothing in it which is any proof of the presence of religious principle in those who adopt it; there is nothing they would not do still, though they had nothing to gain from it, except what they gain from it now: they do gain something now, they do gratify their present wishes, they are quiet and orderly, because it is their interest and taste to be so; but they *venture* nothing, they risk, they sacrifice, they abandon nothing on the faith of Christ's word.

For instance: St. Barnabas had a property in Cyprus; he gave it up for the poor of Christ. Here is an intelligible sacrifice. He did something he would not have done, unless the Gospel were true. It is plain, if the Gospel turned out a fable (which God forbid), but if so, he would have taken his line most unskilfully; he would be in a great mistake, and would have suffered a loss. He would be like a merchant whose vessels were wrecked, or whose correspondents had failed. Man has confidence in man, he trusts to the credit of his neighbour; but Christians do not risk largely upon their Saviour's word; and this is the one thing they have to do. Christ tells us Himself, "Make to yourselves friends of the mammon of unrighteousness; that, when ye fail, they may receive you into everlasting habitations;"[6] *i.e.* buy an interest in the next world with that wealth which this world uses unrighteously; feed the hungry, clothe the naked, relieve the sick, and it shall turn to "bags that wax not old, a treasure in the heavens that faileth not."[7] Thus almsdeeds, I say, are an intelligible *venture*, and an evidence of faith.

[6] Luke xvi.9.   [7] Luke xii.33.

So again the man who, when his prospects in the world are good, gives up the promise of wealth or of eminence, in order to be nearer Christ, to have a place in His temple, to have more opportunity for prayer and praise, he makes a sacrifice.

Or he who, from a noble striving after perfection, puts off the desire of worldly comforts, and is, like Daniel or St. Paul, in much labour and business, yet with a solitary heart, he too ventures something upon the certainty of the world to come.

Or he who, after falling into sin, repents in deed as well as in word; puts some yoke upon his shoulder; subjects himself to punishment; is severe upon his flesh; denies himself innocent pleasures; or puts himself to public shame,—he too shows that his faith is the realizing of things hoped for, the warrant of things not seen.

Or again: he who only gets himself to pray against those things which the many seek after, and to embrace what the heart naturally shrinks from; he who, when God's will seems to tend towards worldly ill, while he deprecates it, yet prevails on himself to say heartily, "Thy will be done;" he, even, is not without his sacrifice. Or he who, being in prospect of wealth, honestly prays God that he may never be rich; or he who is in prospect of station, and earnestly prays that he may never have it; or he who has friends or kindred, and acquiesces with an entire heart in their removal while it is yet doubtful, who can say, "Take them away, if it be Thy will, to Thee I give them up, to Thee I commit them," who is willing to be taken at his word; he too risks somewhat, and is accepted.

Such a one is taken at his word, while he understands not, perhaps, what he says; but he is accepted, as meaning somewhat, and risking much. Generous hearts, like James and John, or Peter, often speak largely and confidently beforehand of what they will do for Christ, not insincerely, yet ignorantly; and for their sincerity's sake they are taken at their word as a reward, though they have yet to learn how serious that word is. "They say unto Him, We are able;"—and the vow is recorded in heaven. This is the case of all of us at many seasons. First, at Confirmation; when we promise what was promised for us at Baptism, yet without being able to understand how much we promise, but rather trusting to God gradually to reveal it, and to give us strength according to our day. So again they who enter Holy Orders promise they know not what, engage themselves they know not how deeply, debar themselves of the world's ways they know not how intimately, find perchance they must cut off from them the right hand, sacrifice the desire of their eyes and the stirring of their hearts at the foot of the Cross, while they thought, in their simplicity, they were but choosing the quiet easy life of "plain men dwelling in tents." And so again, in various ways, the circumstances of the times cause men at certain seasons to take this path or that, for religion's sake. They know not whither they are being carried; they see not the end of their course; they know no more than this, that it is right to do what they are now doing; and they hear a whisper within them, which assures them, as it did the two holy brothers, that whatever their present conduct involves in time to come, they shall, through God's grace, be equal to it. Those blessed Apostles said, "We are able;" and in truth they were enabled to do and suffer as they had said. St. James was given strength to be steadfast unto death, the death of martyrdom; being slain with the sword in Jerusalem. St. John, his brother, had still more to bear, dying last of the Apostles, as St. James first. He had to bear bereavement, first, of his brother, then of the other Apostles. He had to bear a length of years in loneliness, exile, and weakness. He had to experience the dreariness of being solitary, when those whom he loved had been summoned away. He had to live in his own thoughts, without familiar friend, with those only about him who belonged to a younger generation. Of him were demanded by his gracious Lord, as pledges of his faith, all his eye loved and his heart held converse with. He was as a man moving his goods into a far country, who at intervals and by portions sends them before him, till his present abode is well-nigh unfurnished. He sent forward his friends on their journey, while he stayed himself behind, that there might be those in heaven to have thoughts of him, to look out for him, and receive him when his Lord should call. He sent before him, also, other still more voluntary pledges and ventures of his faith,—a self-denying walk, a zealous maintenance of the truth, fasting and prayers, labours of love, a virgin life, buffetings from the heathen, persecution, and banishment. Well might so great a Saint say, at the end of his days "Come, Lord Jesus!" as those who are weary of the night, and wait for the morning. All his thoughts, all his contemplations, desires, and hopes, were stored in the invisible world; and death, when it came, brought back to him the sight of what he had worshipped, what he had loved, what he had held intercourse with, in years long past away. Then, when again brought into the presence of what he had lost, how would remembrance revive, and familiar thoughts long buried come to life! Who shall dare to describe the blessedness of those who find all their pledges safe returned to them, all their ventures abundantly and beyond measure satisfied?

Alas! that we, my brethren, have not more of this high and unearthly spirit! How is it that we are so contented with things as they are,—that we are so willing to be let alone, and to enjoy this life,—that we make such excuses, if any one presses on us the necessity of something higher, the duty of bearing the Cross, if we would earn the Crown, of the Lord Jesus Christ?

I repeat it; what are our ventures and risks upon the truth of His word? for He says expressly, "Every one that hath forsaken houses, or brethren, or sisters, or father, or mother, or wife, or children, or lands, for My Name's sake, shall receive an hundred-fold, and shall inherit everlasting life. But many that are first shall be last; and the last shall be first." [8]

[8] Matt. xix.29, 30.

FAITH AND LOVE

"Though I have all Faith, so that I could remove mountains, and have no Charity, I am nothing."—1 Cor. xiii.2.

I SUPPOSE that all thoughtful readers of the chapter from which these words are taken, have before now been struck with surprise at the varied characteristics which are there ascribed to the excellent grace called love, or charity. What *is* charity? St. Paul answers, by giving a great number of properties of it, all distinct and special. It is patient, it is kind, it has no envy, no self-importance, no ostentation, no indecorum, no selfishness, no irritability, no malevolence. Which of all these is it? for if it is all at once, surely it is a name for all virtues at once.

And what makes this conclusion still more plausible, is, that St. Paul elsewhere actually calls charity "the fulfilling of the Law:" and our Saviour, in like manner, makes our whole duty consist in loving God and loving our neighbour. And St. James calls it "the royal law:" and St. John says, "We know that we have passed from death unto life, because we love the brethren." [1] Thus the chapter from which the text is taken seems but an exemplification in detail of what is declared in general terms by the inspired writers.

It is well too, by way of contrast, to consider the description of faith given elsewhere by the same Apostle, who, in the chapter before us, describes charity. In his Epistle to the Hebrews he devotes a much longer chapter to it: but his method in treating it is altogether different. He starts with a definition of it, and then he illustrates his clear and precise account of it in a series of instances. The chapter is made up of a repetition again and again, in Noah, in Abraham, in Moses, in David, and in the Prophets, of one and the same precisely marked excellence, called faith, which is such as no one can mistake. Again mention is made of it in the text; and then, though in a different Epistle, and in the midst of a train of thought altogether different, its description, as far as it goes, accurately agrees with what

[1] Rom. xiii.10; Matt. xxii.40; James ii.8; 1 John iii.14.

is said in the Hebrews; ".... faith, so that I could remove mountains;" which moreover is the very account of it given by our Lord, and expresses surely the same habit of mind as that by which Noah, Abraham, Moses, and David, preached righteousness, obtained promises, renounced the world, waxed valiant in fight. How then is it that faith is of so definite a character, and love so large and comprehensive?

Now the reason seems to be pretty much what at first sight is the difficulty. The difficulty is whether, if love be such as St. Paul describes, it is not all virtues at once; and I answer, that in one sense it is all virtues at once, and therefore St. Paul cannot describe it more definitely, more restrictedly than he does. In other words, it is the root of all holy dispositions, and grows and blossoms into them: they are its parts; and when it is described, they of necessity are mentioned. Love is the material (so to speak) out of which all graces are made, the quality of mind which is the fruit of regeneration, and in which the Spirit dwells; according to St. John's words, "Every one that loveth is born of God;" .... "he that dwelleth in love, dwelleth in God and God in him." [2] Such is love, and, as being such, it will last for ever. "Charity," or love, "never faileth." Faith and hope are graces of an imperfect state, and they cease with that state; but love is greater, because it is perfection. Faith and hope are graces, as far as we belong to this world,—which is for a time; but love is a grace, because we are creatures of God whether here or elsewhere, and partakers in a redemption which is to last for ever. Faith will not be when there is sight, nor hope when there is enjoyment; but love will (as we believe) increase more and more to all eternity. Faith and hope are means by which we express our love: we believe God's word, because we love it; we hope after heaven because we love it. We should not have any hope or concern about it, unless we loved it; we should not trust or confide in the God of heaven, unless we loved Him. Faith, then, and hope are but instruments or expressions of love; but as to love itself, we do not love because we believe, for the devils believe, yet do not love; nor do we love because we hope, for hypocrites hope, who do not love. But we love for no cause beyond itself: we love, because it is our nature to love; and it is our nature, because God the Holy Ghost has made it our nature. Love is the immediate fruit and the evidence of regeneration.

It is expressing the same thing in other words, to say, as we may, that faith and hope are not in themselves necessarily

[2] 1 John iv.7, 16.

graces, but only as grafted on and found in love. Balaam had faith and hope, but not love. "May I die the death of the righteous!" is an act of hope. "The word that the Lord putteth into my mouth, that will I speak," is an act of faith; but his conduct showed that neither his faith nor his hope was loving. The servant in the parable, who fell down at his lord's feet, and begged to be excused his debt, had both faith and hope. He believed his lord able, and he hoped him willing, to forgive him. He went out, and saw a fellow-servant who owed him a small sum, and he behaved at once unmercifully to him, and unthankfully by his lord. He had neither love of God, because he was high-minded, nor love of his brother, because he was hard-hearted. There are then two kinds of faith in God, a good faith and a worthless faith; and two kinds of hope in God, good and worthless: but there are not two kinds of love of God. Love must always be heavenly; it is always the sign of the regenerate. Faith and hope are not in themselves signs, but only that faith "which worketh by love," and that hope which "loves the thing which God commandeth, and desires that which God doth promise." In the text it is said, "Though I had all faith, yet without love I am nothing:" it is nowhere said, "Though I have all love, without faith I am nothing."

Love, then, is the seed of holiness, and grows into all excellences, not indeed destroying their peculiarities, but making them what they are. A weed has stalk, leaves, and flowers; so has a sweet-smelling plant; because the latter is sweet-smelling, it does not cease to have stalk, leaves, and flowers; but they are all pleasant, because they come of it. In like manner, the soul which is quickened with the spirit of love has faith and hope, and a number of faculties and habits, some of which it might have without love, and some not; but any how, in that soul one and all exist *in* love, though distinct from it; as stalk, leaves, and flowers are as distinct and entire in one plant as in another, yet vary in their quality, according to the plant's nature.

But here it may be asked, whether Scripture does not make faith, not love, the root, and all graces its fruits. I think not; on the contrary, it pointedly intimates that something besides faith is the root, not only in the text, but in our Lord's parable of the Sower; in which we read of persons who, "when they hear, receive the word with joy," yet having no "root,"[3] fall away. Now, receiving the word with joy, surely implies faith; faith, then, is certainly distinct from the *root*, for these persons

---

[3] Luke viii.13.

receive with joy, yet have "*no* root." However, it is allowable to call faith the root, because, in a certain sense at least, works *do* proceed from it. And hence Scripture speaks of "faith *working by love*," which would imply in the form of expression that faith was prior to love. And again: in the chapter in which the text occurs, we read of "faith, hope, and charity," an order of words which seems to imply that faith precedes love, or charity. And again, St. Paul says elsewhere, "The *end* of the commandment is *charity*, out of a pure heart, and of a good conscience, and *of faith unfeigned*;" [4] where faith is spoken of as if it were the origin of love.

This must be granted then; and accordingly a question arises, how to adjust these opposite modes of speaking; in *what* sense faith is the beginning of love, and in what sense love is the origin of faith; whether love springs from faith, or faith from love, which comes first, and which last. I observe, then, as follows:—

Faith is the first element of *religion*, and love, of *holiness*; and as holiness and religion are distinct, yet united, so are love and faith. Holiness can exist without religion; religion cannot exist without holiness. Baptized infants, before they come to years of understanding, are holy; they are not religious. Holiness is love of the Divine Law. When God regenerates an infant, He imparts to it the gift of His Holy Spirit; and what is the Spirit thus imparted but the Law written on its heart? Such was the promise, "I will put My laws into their mind, and write them in their hearts." And hence it is said, "This is the love of God, that we keep His *commandments*." [5] God comes to us as a Law, before He comes as a Lawgiver; that is, He sets up His throne within us, and enables us to obey Him, before we have learned to reflect on our own sensations, and to know the voice of God. Such, as if in a type, was Samuel's case; he knew not who it was who called him, till Eli the priest told him. Eli stands for religion, Samuel for holiness; Eli for faith, Samuel for love.

Love then is the motion within us of the new spirit, the holy and renewed heart which God the Holy Ghost gives us; and, as being such, we see how it may exist in infants, who obey the inward law without knowing it, by a sort of natural service, as plants and trees fulfil the functions of their own nature; a service which is most acceptable to God, as being moral and spiritual, though not intellectual. And this, for what we know, may be the state of those little ones who are baptized and taken away before they have learned either to reason or to sin. They may be

---

[4] I Tim. i.5.   [5] Heb. viii.10; I John v.3.

as the stones of the Everlasting Pavement, crying out continually in praise to God; dimly visible, as if absorbed in the glory
which encompasses God's throne; or as the wonderful wheels
described by the Prophet, which were living, yet in a way instrumental; for in heaven, where there is no gross matter, the
very framework of the Temple is composed of spirits.

Love, then, is the life of those who know not an external
world, but who worship God as manifested within them. Such
a life however can last but a little while on earth. The eyes see
and the reason embraces a lower world, sun, moon, stars, and
earth, and men, and all that man does or makes; and this external world does not speak of God upon the face of it. It shows as
if it were itself God, and an object of worship, or at least it becomes the creature of a usurper, who has made himself "the
god of this world." We are at once forced to reflect, reason,
decide, and act; for we are between two, the inward voice
speaking one thing within us, and the world speaking another
without us; the world tempting, and the Spirit whispering
warnings. Hence faith becomes necessary; in other words, God
has most mercifully succoured us in this contest, by speaking
not only in our hearts, but through the sensible world; and this
Voice we call revelation. God has overruled this world of sense,
and put a word in its mouth, and bid it prophesy of Him. And
thus there are two voices even in the external world; the voice
of the tempter calling us to fall down and worship him, and he
will give us all; and the voice of God, speaking in aid of the voice
in our hearts: and as love is that which hears the voice within us,
so faith is that which hears the voice without us; and as love
worships God within the shrine, faith discerns Him in the
world; and as love is the life of God in the solitary soul, faith is
the guardian of love in our intercourse with men; and, while
faith ministers to love, love is that which imparts to faith its
praise and excellence.

And thus it is that faith is to love as religion to holiness; for
religion is the Divine Law as coming to us from without, as holiness is the acquiescence in the same Law as written within.
Love then is meditative, tranquil, pure, gentle, abounding in all
offices of goodness and truth; and faith is strenuous and energetic, formed for this world, combating it, training the mind
towards love, fortifying it in obedience, and overcoming sense
and reason by representations more urgent than their own.

Moreover it is plain, that, while love is the root out of which
faith grows, faith by receiving the wonderful tidings of the
Gospel, and presenting before the soul its sacred Objects, the

mysteries of the faith, the Holy Trinity, and the Incarnate Saviour, expands our love, and raises it to a perfection which otherwise it could never reach.

And thus our duty lies in faith working by love; love is the
sacrifice we offer to God, and faith is the sacrificer. Yet they are
not distinct from each other except in our way of viewing them.
Priest and sacrifice are one; the loving faith and the believing
love.

And thus I answer the question concerning the connexion of
love and faith. Love is the condition of faith; and faith in turn is
the cherisher and maturer of love; it brings love out into works,
and therefore is called the root of *works* of love; the substance of
the works is love, the outline and direction of them is faith.

This being so, surely we need not be surprised at St. Paul's
language, as in the text and verses following. Love is the true
ruling principle of the regenerate soul, and faith ministers to it.
Love is the end, faith the means; and if the means be difficult,
much more is the end. St. Paul says that faith which could remove mountains will not avail without love; and in truth, faith
is only half way (as it were) to heaven. By faith we give up this
world, but by love we reach into the next world; and it often
happens from one cause or another, men are able to get as far as
the one, without going on to the other. Too true is it, that the
mass of men live neither with faith nor love; they live to themselves, they love themselves selfishly, and do not desire any
thing beyond the visible framework of things. This world is
their all in all. But I speak of religious persons; and these, I
think, will confess that distaste for the world is quite a distinct
thing from the spirit of love. As years go on, the disappointments, troubles, and cares of life, wean a religious mind from
attachment to this world. A man sees it is but vanity. He neither
receives, nor looks for enjoyment from it. He does not look to
the future with hope; he has no prospects; he cares not for the
world's smile or frown; for what it can do, what it can withhold. Nay, even his friends are nothing to him; he knows they
cannot help him really in his greatest needs, and he has no dependence that they will be continued to him. And thus in the
course of time, with a very scanty measure of true divine love,
he is enabled, whatever his sphere is, to act above the world, in
his degree; to do his plain straightforward duty, because reason
tells him he should do it, and because he has no great temptation seducing him from it. Observe, *why* he keeps God's commandments; from *reason*, because he knows he ought, and
because he has no strong motives keeping him from doing so.

Alas! not from *love* towards those commandments. He has only just so much of the spirit of love as suffices to hinder his resignation from being despondency, and his faith from being dead. Or again, he has had experience of the misery of a laden conscience, the misery of the pollution involved in the numberless little sins of every day, the odiousness of his pride, vanity, fretfulness, wilfulness, arrogance, irritability, profaneness, hardness of heart, and all the other evils which beset him; and he desires earnestly to be cleansed;—yet rather from dislike of sin than direct love of God and Christ.

This then is that middle state in which some of us may be standing in our progress from earth to heaven, and which the text warns us against. It tells us that faith at most only makes a hero, but that love makes a saint; that faith can but put us above the world, but that love brings us under God's throne; that faith can but make us sober, but love makes us happy. It warns us that it is possible for a man to have the clearest, calmest, exactest view of the realities of heaven; that he may most firmly realize and act upon the truths of the Gospel; that he may understand that all about him is but a veil, not a substance; that he may have that full confidence in God's word as to be able to do miracles; that he may have such simple absolute faith as to give up his property, give up all his goods to feed the poor; that he may so scorn the world, that he may with so royal a heart trample on it, as even to give his body to be burned by a glorious martyrdom; and yet—I do not say, be without love; God forbid! I do not suppose the Apostle means there ever *was* actually such a case, but that it is abstractedly possible; that no one of the proper acts of faith, in itself, and necessarily, implies love; that it is distinct from love. He says this,—that, though a person *be* all that has been said, yet unless he be also something besides, unless he have love, it profiteth him nothing. O fearful lesson, to all those who are tempted to pride themselves in their labours, or sufferings, or sacrifices, or works! We are Christ's, not by faith merely, nor by works merely, but by love; not by hating the world, nor by hating sin, nor by venturing for the world to come, nor by calmness, nor by magnanimity,—though we must do and be all this; and if we *have* love in perfection we *shall*,—but it is love makes faith, not faith love. We are saved, not by any of these things, but by that heavenly flame within us, which, while it consumes what is seen, aspires to what is unseen. Love is the gentle, tranquil, satisfied acquiescence and adherence of the soul in the contemplation of God; not only a preference of God before all things, but a delight in Him because He is God, and because His commandments are good; not any violent emotion or transport, but as St. Paul describes it, long-suffering, kind, modest, unassuming, innocent, simple, orderly, disinterested, meek, pure-hearted, sweet-tempered, patient, enduring. Faith without Charity is dry, harsh, and sapless; it has nothing sweet, engaging, winning, soothing; but it was Charity which brought Christ down. Charity is but another name for the Comforter. It is eternal Charity which is the bond of all things in heaven and earth; it is Charity wherein the Father and the Son are one in the unity of the Spirit; by which the Angels in heaven are one, by which all Saints are one with God, by which the Church is one upon earth.

WATCHING

"Take ye heed, watch and pray; for ye know not when the time is."
—Mark xiii.33.

O UR Saviour gave this warning when He was leaving this world,—leaving it, that is, as far as His visible presence is concerned. He looked forward to the many hundred years which were to pass before He came again. He knew His own purpose and His Father's purpose gradually to leave the world to itself, gradually to withdraw from it the tokens of His gracious presence. He contemplated, as contemplating all things, the neglect of Him which would spread even among his professed followers; the daring disobedience, and the loud words, which would be ventured against Him and His Father by many whom He had regenerated: and the coldness, cowardice, and tolerance of error which would be displayed by others, who did not go so far as to speak or to act against Him. He foresaw the state of the world and the Church, as we see it this day, when His prolonged absence has made it practically thought, that He never will come back in visible presence: and in the text, He mercifully whispers into our ears, not to trust in what we see, not to share in that general unbelief, not to be carried away by the world, but to "take heed, watch,[1] pray," and look out for His coming.

Surely this gracious warning should be ever in our thoughts, being so precise, so solemn, so earnest. He foretold His first coming, yet He took His Church by surprise when He came; much more will He come suddenly the second time, and overtake men, now that He has not measured out the interval before it, as then He did, but left our watchfulness to the keeping of faith and love.

Let us then consider this most serious question, which concerns every one of us so nearly;—What it is to *watch* for Christ? He says, "*Watch* ye therefore, for ye know not when the Master of the house cometh; at even, or at midnight, or at the cock-

[1] ἀγρυπνεῖτε.

crowing, or in the morning; lest coming suddenly He find you sleeping. And what I say unto you, I say unto all, *Watch*."[2] And again, "If the goodman of the house had known what hour the thief would come, he would have *watched*, and not have suffered his house to be broken through."[3] A like warning is given elsewhere both by our Lord and by His Apostles. For instance; we have the parable of the Ten Virgins, five of whom were wise and five foolish; on whom the bridegroom, after tarrying came suddenly, and five were found without oil. On which our Lord says, "*Watch* therefore, for ye know neither the day nor the hour wherein the Son of man cometh."[4] Again He says, "Take heed to yourselves, lest at any time your hearts be overcharged with surfeiting and drunkenness, and cares of this life, and so that day come upon you unawares; for as a snare shall it come on all them that dwell on the face of the whole earth. *Watch* ye therefore, and pray always, that ye may be accounted worthy to escape all these things that shall come to pass, and to stand before the Son of man."[5] In like manner He upbraided Peter thus: "Simon, sleepest thou? couldest not thou *watch* one hour?"[6]

In like manner St. Paul in his Epistle to the Romans. "Now it is high time to awake out of sleep. . . . . The night is far spent, the day is at hand."[7] Again, "*Watch* ye, stand fast in the faith, quit you like men, be strong."[8] "Be strong in the Lord, and in the power of His might; put on the whole armour of God, that ye may be able to stand against the wiles of the devil; . . . . that ye may be able to withstand in the evil day, and having done all to stand."[9] "Let us not sleep as do others, but let us watch and be sober."[10] In like manner St. Peter, "The end of all things is at hand; be ye therefore sober, and *watch* unto prayer." "Be sober, be *vigilant*, because your adversary the devil, as a roaring lion, walketh about seeking whom he may devour."[11] And St. John, "Behold I come as a thief; blessed is he that *watcheth* and keepeth his garments."[12]

Now I consider this word *watching*, first used by our Lord, then by the favoured Disciple, then by the two great Apostles, Peter and Paul, is a remarkable word; remarkable because the idea is not so obvious as might appear at first sight, and next because they all inculcate it. We are not simply to believe, but to watch; not simply to love, but to watch; not simply to obey, but to watch; to watch for what? for that great event, Christ's

[2] Mark xiii.35-37, γρηγορεῖτε.   [3] Luke xii.39.   [4] Matt. xxv.13.
[5] Luke xxi.36.   [6] Mark xiv.37.   [7] Rom. xiii.11, 12.
[8] 1 Cor. xvi.13.   [9] Eph. vi.10-13.   [10] 1 Thess. v.6.
[11] 1 Pet. iv.7, νήψατε, v.8.   [12] Rev. xvi.15.

coming. Whether then we consider what is the obvious meaning of the word, or the Object towards which it directs us, we seem to see a special duty enjoined on us, such as does not naturally come into our minds. Most of us have a general idea what is meant by believing, fearing, loving, and obeying; but perhaps we do not contemplate or apprehend what is meant by watching.

And I conceive it is one of the main points, which, in a practical way, will be found to separate the true and perfect servants of God from the multitude called Christians; from those who are, I do not say false and reprobate, but who are such that we cannot speak much about them, nor can form any notion what will become of them. And in saying this, do not understand me as saying, which I do not, that we can tell for certain who are the perfect, and who the double-minded or incomplete Christians; or that those who discourse and insist upon these subjects are necessarily on the right side of the line. I am but speaking of two *characters*, the true and consistent character, and the inconsistent; and these I say will be found in no slight degree discriminated and distinguished by this one mark,—true Christians, whoever they are, watch, and inconsistent Christians do not. Now what is watching?

I conceive it may be explained as follows:—Do you know the feeling in matters of this life, of expecting a friend, expecting him to come, and he delays? Do you know what it is to be in unpleasant company, and to wish for the time to pass away, and the hour strike when you may be at liberty? Do you know what it is to be in anxiety lest something should happen which may happen or may not, or to be in suspense about some important event, which makes your heart beat when you are reminded of it, and of which you think the first thing in the morning? Do you know what it is to have a friend in a distant country, to expect news of him, and to wonder from day to day what he is now doing, and whether he is well? Do you know what it is so to live upon a person who is present with you, that your eyes follow his, that you read his soul, that you see all its changes in his countenance, that you anticipate his wishes, that you smile in his smile, and are sad in his sadness, and are downcast when he is vexed, and rejoice in his successes? To watch for Christ is a feeling such as all these; as far as feelings of this world are fit to shadow out those of another.

He watches for Christ who has a sensitive, eager, apprehensive mind; who is awake, alive, quick-sighted, zealous in seeking and honouring Him; who looks out for Him in all that happens, and who would not be surprised, who would not be over-agitated or overwhelmed, if he found that He was coming at once.

And he watches *with* Christ, who, while he looks on to the future, looks back on the past, and does not so contemplate what his Saviour has purchased for him, as to forget what He has suffered for him. He watches with Christ, who ever commemorates and renews in his own person Christ's Cross and Agony, and gladly takes up that mantle of affliction which Christ wore here, and left behind Him when he ascended. And hence in the Epistles, often as the inspired writers show their desire for His second coming, as often do they show their memory of His first, and never lose sight of His Crucifixion in His Resurrection. Thus if St. Paul reminds the Romans that they "wait for the redemption of the body" at the Last Day, he also says, "If so be that we *suffer with Him,* that we may be also glorified together." If he speaks to the Corinthians of "waiting for the coming of our Lord Jesus Christ," he also speaks of "always bearing about in the body the *dying* of the Lord Jesus, *that* the life also of Jesus might be made manifest in our body." If to the Philippians of "the power of His resurrection," he adds at once "*and the fellowship of His sufferings,* being made conformable unto His death." If he consoles the Colossians with the hope "when Christ shall appear," of their "appearing with Him in glory," he has already declared that he "*fills up that which remains of the afflictions of Christ* in his flesh for His body's sake, which is the Church." [13] Thus the thought of what Christ is, must not obliterate from the mind the thought of what He was; and faith is always sorrowing with Him while it rejoices. And the same union of opposite thoughts is impressed on us in Holy Communion, in which we see Christ's death and resurrection together, at one and the same time; we commemorate the one, we rejoice in the other; we make an offering, and we gain a blessing.

This then is to watch; to be detached from what is present, and to live in what is unseen; to live in the thought of Christ as He came once, and as He will come again; to desire His second coming, from our affectionate and grateful remembrance of His first. And this it is, in which we shall find that men in general are wanting. They are indeed without faith and love also; but at least they profess to have these graces, nor is it easy to convince them that they have not. For they consider they have

[13] Rom. viii.17–23; 1 Cor. i.7; 2 Cor. iv.10; Phil. iii.10; Col. iii.4; i.24.

faith, if they do but own that the Bible came from God, or that they trust wholly in Christ for salvation; and they consider they have love if they obey some of the most obvious of God's commandments. Love and faith they think they have; but surely they do not even fancy that they watch. What is meant by watching, and how it is a duty, they have no definite idea; and thus it accidentally happens that watching is a suitable test of a Christian, in that it is that particular property of faith and love, which, essential as it is, men of this world do not even profess; that particular property, which is the life or energy of faith and love, the way in which faith and love, if genuine, show themselves.

It is easy to exemplify what I mean, from the experience which we all have of life. Many men indeed are open revilers of religion, or at least openly disobey its laws; but let us consider those who are of a more sober and conscientious cast of mind. They have a number of good qualities, and are in a certain sense and up to a certain point religious; but they do not watch. Their notion of religion is briefly this: loving God indeed, but loving this world too; not only doing their *duty*, but finding their chief and highest *good*, in that state of life to which it has pleased God to call them, resting in it, taking it as their portion. They serve God, and they seek Him; but they look on the present world as if it were the eternal, not a mere temporary, scene of their duties and privileges, and never contemplate the prospect of being separated from it. It is not that they forget God, or do not live by principle, or forget that the goods of this world are His gift; but they love them for their own sake more than for the sake of the Giver, and reckon on their remaining, as if they had that permanence which their duties and religious privileges have. They do not understand that they are called to be strangers and pilgrims upon the earth, and that their worldly lot and worldly goods are a sort of accident of their existence, and that they really have no property, though human law guarantees property to them. Accordingly, they set their heart upon their goods, be they great or little, not without a sense of religion the while, but still idolatrously. *This* is their fault,—an identifying God with this world, and therefore an idolatry towards this world; and so they are rid of the trouble of looking out for their God, for they think they have found Him in the goods of this world. While, then, they are really praiseworthy in many parts of their conduct, benevolent, charitable, kind, neighbourly, and useful in their generation, nay, constant perhaps in the ordinary religious duties which custom has established, and while

they display much right and amiable feeling, and much correctness in opinion, and are even in the way to improve in character
and conduct as time goes on, correct much that is amiss, gain
greater command over themselves, mature in judgment, and
are much looked up to in consequence; yet still it is plain that
they love this world, would be loth to leave it, and wish to have
more of its good things. They like wealth, and distinction, and
credit, and influence. They may improve in conduct, but not in
aims; they advance, but they do not mount; they are moving on
a low level, and were they to move on for centuries, would
never rise above the atmosphere of this world. "I will stand
upon my watch, and set me upon the tower, and will watch to
see what He will say unto me, and what I shall answer when I
am reproved." [14] This is the temper of mind which they have
not; and when we reflect how rarely it *is* found among professing Christians, we shall see why our Lord is so urgent in enforcing it;—as if He said, "I am not warning you, My followers,
against open apostasy; that will not be; but I foresee that very
few will keep awake and watch while I am away. Blessed are the
servants who do so; few will open to me *immediately*, when I
knock. They will have something to do first; they will have to
get ready. They will have to recover from the surprise and confusion which overtake them on the first news of My coming,
and will need time to collect themselves, and summon about
them their better thoughts and affections. They feel themselves
very well off as they are; and wish to serve God as they are. They
are satisfied to remain on earth; they do not wish to move; they
do not wish to change."

Without denying, then, to these persons the praise of many
religious habits and practices, I would say that they want the
tender and sensitive heart which hangs on the thought of
Christ, and lives in His love. The breath of the world has a peculiar power in what may be called rusting the soul. The mirror
within them, instead of reflecting back the Son of God their
Saviour, has become dim and discoloured; and hence, though
(to use a common expression) they have a good deal of good *in*
them, it is only *in* them, it is not through them, around them,
and upon them. An evil crust is *on* them: they think with the
world; they are full of the world's notions and modes of speaking; they appeal to the world, and have a sort of reverence for
what the world will say. There is a want of naturalness, simplicity, and childlike teachableness in them. It is difficult to touch

[14] Hab. ii.1.

them, or (what may be called) get at them, and to persuade
them to a straightforward course in religion. They start off
when you least expect it: they have reservations, make distinctions, take exceptions, indulge in refinements, in questions
where there are really but two sides, a right and a wrong. Their
religious feelings do not flow forth easily, at times when they
ought to flow; either they are diffident, and can say nothing, or
else they are affected and strained in their mode of conversing.
And as a rust preys upon metal and eats into it, so does this
worldly spirit penetrate more and more deeply into the soul
which once admits it. And this is one great end; as it would
appear, of afflictions, viz., to rub away and clear off these outward defilements, and to keep the soul in a measure of its baptismal purity and brightness.

Now, it cannot surely be doubted that multitudes in the
Church are such as I have been describing, and that they would
not, could not, at once welcome our Lord on His coming. We
cannot, indeed, apply what has been said to this or that individual; but on the whole, viewing the multitude, one cannot
be mistaken. There may be exceptions; but after all conceivable deductions, a large body must remain thus double-
minded, thus attempting to unite things incompatible. This we
might be sure of; though Christ had said nothing on the subject; but it is a most affecting and solemn thought, that He has
actually called our attention to this very danger, the danger of
a worldly religiousness, for so it may be called, though it *is* religiousness; this mixture of religion and unbelief, which serves
God indeed, but loves the fashions, the distinctions, the pleasures, the comforts of this life,—which feels a satisfaction in
being prosperous in circumstances, likes pomps and vanities, is
particular about food, raiment, house, furniture, and domestic
matters, courts great people, and aims at having a position in
society. He warns His disciples of the danger of having their
minds drawn off from the thought of Him, by whatever cause;
He warns them against *all* excitements, *all* allurements of this
world; He solemnly warns them that the world will not be prepared for His coming, and tenderly intreats of them not to take
their portion with the world. He warns them by the instance
of the rich man whose soul was required, of the servant who
ate and drank, and of the foolish virgins. When He comes,
they will one and all want time; their head will be confused,
their eyes will swim, their tongue falter, their limbs totter, as
men who are suddenly awakened. They will not all at once collect their senses and faculties. O fearful thought! the bridal

train is sweeping by,—Angels are there,—the just made perfect are there,—little children, and holy teachers, and white-robed saints, and martyrs washed in blood; the marriage of the Lamb is come, and His wife hath made herself ready. She has already attired herself: while we have been sleeping, she has been robing; she has been adding jewel to jewel, and grace to grace; she has been gathering in her chosen ones, one by one, and has been exercising them in holiness, and purifying them for her Lord; and now her marriage hour is come. The holy Jerusalem is descending, and a loud voice proclaims, "Behold, the bridegroom cometh; go ye out to meet Him!" but we, alas! are but dazzled with the blaze of light, and neither welcome the sound, nor obey it,—and all for what? what shall we have gained then? what will this world have then done for us? wretched, deceiving world! which will then be burned up, unable not only to profit us, but to save itself. Miserable hour, indeed, will that be, when the full consciousness breaks on us of what we will not believe now, viz., that we *are* at present serving the world. We trifle with our conscience now; we deceive our better judgment; we repel the hints of those who tell us that we are joining ourselves to this perishing world. We *will* taste a little of its pleasures, and follow its ways, and think it no harm, so that we do not altogether neglect religion. I mean, we allow ourselves to covet what we have not, to boast in what we have, to look down on those who have less; or we allow ourselves to profess what we do not try to practise, to argue for the sake of victory, and to debate when we should be obeying; and we pride ourselves on our reasoning powers, and think ourselves enlightened, and despise those who had less to say for themselves, and set forth and defend our own theories; or we are over-anxious, fretful, and care-worn about worldly matters, spiteful, envious, jealous, discontented, and evil-natured: in one or other way we take our portion with this world, and we will not believe that we do. We obstinately refuse to believe it; we know we are not altogether irreligious, and we persuade ourselves that we are religious. We learn to think it is possible to be too religious; we have taught ourselves that there is nothing high or deep in religion, no great exercise of our affections, no great food for our thoughts, no great work for our exertions. We go on in a self-satisfied or a self-conceited way, not looking out of ourselves, not standing like soldiers on the watch in the dark night; but we kindle our own fire, and delight ourselves in the sparks of it. This is our state, or something like this, and the Day will declare it; the Day is at hand,

and the Day will search our hearts, and bring it home even to
ourselves, that we have been cheating ourselves with words,
and have not served Christ, as the Redeemer of the soul
claims, but with a meagre, partial, worldly service, and without really contemplating Him who is above and apart from this
world.

Year passes after year silently; Christ's coming is ever nearer
than it was. O that, as He comes nearer earth, we may approach
nearer heaven! O, my brethren, pray Him to give you the heart
to seek Him in sincerity. Pray Him to make you in earnest. You
have one work only, to bear your cross after Him. Resolve in
His strength to do so. Resolve to be no longer beguiled by
"shadows of religion," by words, or by disputings, or by notions, or by high professions, or by excuses, or by the world's
promises or threats. Pray Him to give you what Scripture calls
"an honest and good heart," or "a perfect heart," and, without
waiting, begin at once to obey Him with the best heart you
have. Any obedience is better than none,—any profession
which is disjoined from obedience, is a mere pretence and deceit. Any religion which does not bring you nearer to God is of
the world. You have to seek His face; obedience is the only way
of seeking Him. All your duties are obediences. If you are to
believe the truths He has revealed, to regulate yourselves by His
precepts, to be frequent in His ordinances, to adhere to His
Church and people, why is it, except because *He* has bid you?
and to do what He bids is to obey Him, and to obey Him is to
approach Him. Every act of obedience is an approach,—an approach to Him who is not far off though He seems so, but close
behind this visible screen of things which hides Him from us.
He is behind this material framework; earth and sky are but a
veil going between Him and us; the day will come when He will
rend that veil, and show Himself to us. And then, according as
we have waited for Him, will He recompense us. If we have forgotten Him, He will not know us; but "blessed are those servants whom the Lord, when He cometh shall find watching.
. . . . He shall gird Himself, and make them sit down to meat,
and will come forth and serve them. And if He shall come in the
second watch, or come in the third watch, and find them so,
blessed are those servants." [15] May this be the portion of every
one of us! It is hard to attain it; but it is woeful to fail. Life is
short; death is certain and the world to come is everlasting.

[15] Luke xii.37, 38.

KEEPING FAST AND FESTIVAL

*"A time to weep, and a time to laugh: a time to mourn,
and a time to dance."*—Eccles. iii.4.

A T Christmas we joy with the natural, unmixed joy of children, but at Easter our joy is highly wrought and refined
in its character. It is not the spontaneous and unartificial out-
break which the news of Redemption might occasion, but it is
thoughtful; it has a long history before it, and has run through
a long course of feelings before it becomes what it is. It is a last
feeling and not a first. St. Paul describes its nature and its formation, when he says, "Tribulation worketh patience, and patience experience, and experience hope; and hope maketh not
ashamed, because the love of God is shed abroad in our hearts
by the Holy Ghost which is given unto us." [2] And the prophet
Isaiah, when he says, "They joy before Thee according to the
joy in harvest, and as men rejoice when they divide the
spoil." [3] Or as it was fulfilled in the case of our Lord Himself,
who, as being the Captain of our salvation, was made perfect
through sufferings. Accordingly, Christmas Day is ushered in
with a time of awful expectation only, but Easter Day with the
long fast of Lent, and the rigours of the Holy Week just past:
and it springs out and (as it were) is born of Good Friday.

On such a day, then, from the very intensity of joy which
Christians ought to feel, and the trial which they have gone
through, they will often be disposed to say little. Rather, like
sick people convalescent, when the crisis is past, the illness over,
but strength not yet come, they will go forth to the light of day
and the freshness of the air, and silently sit down with great
delight under the shadow of that Tree, whose fruit is sweet to
their taste. They are disposed rather to muse and be at peace,
than to use many words; for their joy has been so much the
child of sorrow, is of so transmuted and complex a nature, so
bound up with painful memories and sad associations, that

---

[1] Preached on Easter-day.

[2] Rom. v.3–5.   [3] Is. ix.3.

though it is a joy only the greater from the contrast, it is not, cannot be, as if it had never been sorrow.

And in this too the feeling at Easter is not unlike the revulsion of mind on a recovery from sickness, that in sickness also there is much happens to us that is strange, much that we must feebly comprehend and vaguely follow after. For in sickness the mind wanders from things that are seen into the unknown world, it turns back into itself; and is in company with mysteries; it is brought into contact with objects which it cannot describe, which it cannot ascertain. It sees the skirts of powers and providences beyond this world, and is at least more alive, if not more exposed to the invisible influences, bad and good, which are its portion in this state of trial. And afterwards it has recollections which are painful, recollections of distress, of which it cannot recall the reasons, of pursuits without an object, and gleams of relief without continuance. And what is all this but a parallel feeling to that, with which the Christian has gone through the contemplations put before his faith in the week just passed, which are to him as a fearful harrowing dream, of which the spell is now broken? The subjects, indeed, which have been brought before him are no dream, but a reality,—his Saviour's sufferings, his own misery and sin. But, alas! to him at best they are but a dream, because, from lack of faith and of spiritual discernment, he understands them so imperfectly. They have been to him a dream, because only at moments his heart has caught a vivid glimpse of what was continually before his reason,—because the impression it made upon him was irregular, shifting, and transitory,—because even when he contemplated steadily his Saviour's sufferings, he did not, could not understand the deep reasons of them, or the meaning of His Saviour's words,—because what most forcibly affected him came through his irrational nature, was not of the mind but of the flesh, not of the scenes of sorrow which the Lessons and Gospels record, but of his own discomfort of body, which he has been bound, as far as health allows, to make sympathize with the history of those sufferings which are his salvation. And thus I say his disquiet during the week has been like that of a bad dream, restless and dreary; he has felt he ought to be very sorry, and could not say why,—could not master his grief; could not realize his fears, but was as children are, who wonder, weep, and are silent, when they see their parents in sorrow, from a feeling that there is something wrong, though they cannot say what.

And therefore now, though it is over, he cannot so shake off at once what has been, as to enter fully into what is. Christ indeed, though He suffered and died, yet rose again vigorously on the third day, having loosed the pains of death: but we cannot accomplish in our contemplation of Him, what He accomplished really; for He was the Holy One, and we are sinners. We have the languor and oppression of our old selves upon us, though we be new; and therefore we must beg Him who is the Prince of Life, the Life itself, to carry us forth into His new world, for we cannot walk thither, and seat us down whence, like Moses, we may see the land, and meditate upon its beauty!

And yet, though the long season of sorrow which ushers in this Blessed Day, in some sense sobers and quells the keenness of our enjoyment, yet without such preparatory season, let us be sure we shall not rejoice at all. None rejoice in Easter-tide less than those who have not grieved in Lent. This is what is seen in the world at large. To them, one season is the same as another, and they take no account of any. Feast-day and fast-day, holy tide and other tide, are one and the same to them. Hence they do not realize the next world at all. To them the Gospels are but like another history; a course of events which took place eighteen hundred years since. They do not make our Saviour's life and death present to them: they do not transport themselves back to the time of His sojourn on earth. They do not act over again, and celebrate His history, in their own observance; and the consequence is, that they feel no interest in it. They have neither faith nor love towards it; it has no hold on them. They do not form their estimate of things upon it; they do not hold it as a sort of practical principle in their heart. This is the case not only with the world at large, but too often with men who have the Name of Christ in their mouths. They think they believe in Him, yet when trial comes, or in the daily conduct of life, they are unable to act upon the principles which they profess: and why? because they have thought to dispense with the religious Ordinances, the course of Service, and the round of Sacred Seasons of the Church, and have considered it a simpler and more spiritual religion, not to act religiously except when called to it by extraordinary trial or temptation; because they have thought that, since it is the Christian's duty to rejoice evermore, they would rejoice better if they never sorrowed and never travailed with righteousness. On the contrary, let us be sure that, as previous humiliation sobers our joy, it alone secures it to us. Our Saviour says, "Blessed are they that mourn, for they shall be comforted;" and what is true hereafter, is true here. Unless we have mourned, in the weeks that are gone, we shall not rejoice in the season now commencing. It is often said, and truly, that providential affliction brings a man nearer to God. What is the observance of Holy Seasons but such a means of grace?

This too must be said concerning the connexion of Fasts and Feasts in our religious service, viz., that that sobriety in feasting which previous fasting causes, is itself much to be prized, and especially worth securing. For in this does Christian mirth differ from worldly, that it is subdued; and how shall it be subdued except that the past keeps its hold upon us, and while it warns and sobers us, actually indisposes and tames our flesh against indulgence? In the world feasting comes first and fasting afterwards; men first glut themselves, and then loathe their excesses; they take their fill of good, and then suffer; they are rich that they may be poor; they laugh that they may weep; they rise that they may fall. But in the Church of God it is reversed; the poor *shall* be rich, the lowly shall be exalted, those that sow in tears shall reap in joy, those that mourn shall be comforted, those that suffer with Christ shall reign with Him; even as Christ (in our Church's words) "went not up to joy, but first He suffered pain. He entered not into His glory before He was crucified. So truly our way to eternal joy is to suffer here with Christ, and our door to enter into eternal life is gladly to die with Christ, that we may rise again from death, and dwell with Him in everlasting life."[4] And what is true of the general course of our redemption is, I say, fulfilled also in the yearly and other commemorations of it. Our Festivals are preceded by humiliation, that we may keep them duly; not boisterously or fanatically, but in a refined, subdued, chastised spirit, which is the true rejoicing in the Lord.

In such a spirit let us endeavour to celebrate this most holy of all Festivals, this continued festal Season, which lasts for fifty days, whereas Lent is forty, as if to show that where sin abounded, there much more has grace abounded. Such indeed seems the tone of mind which took possession of the Apostles when certified of the Resurrection; and while they waited for, or when they had the sight of their risen Lord. If we consider, we shall find the accounts of that season in the Gospels, marked with much of pensiveness and tender and joyful melancholy; the sweet and pleasant frame of those who have gone through pain, and out of pain receive pleasure. Whether we read the account of St. Mary Magdalen weeping at the sepulchre, seeing Jesus and knowing Him not, recognizing His

---

[4] Visitation of the Sick.

voice, attempting to embrace His feet, and then sinking into silent awe and delight, till she rose and hastened to tell the perplexed Apostles;—or turn to that solemn meeting, which was the third, when He stood on the shore and addressed His disciples, and Peter plunged into the water, and then with the rest was awed into silence and durst not speak, but only obeyed His command, and ate of the fish in silence, and so remained in the presence of One in whom they joyed, whom they loved, as He knew, more than all things, till He broke silence by asking Peter if he loved Him:—or lastly, consider the time when He appeared unto a great number of disciples on the mountain in Galilee, and all worshipped Him, but some doubted:—who does not see that their Festival was such as I have been describing it, a holy, tender, reverent, manly joy, not *so* manly as to be rude, not *so* tender as to be effeminate, but (as if) an Angel's mood, the mingled offering of all that is best and highest in man's and woman's nature brought together,—St. Mary Magdalen and St. Peter blended into St. John? And here perhaps we learn a lesson from the deep silence which Scripture observes concerning the Blessed Virgin[5] after the Resurrection; as if she, who was too pure and holy a flower to be more than seen here on earth, even during the season of her Son's humiliation, was altogether drawn by the Angels within the veil on His Resurrection, and had her joy in Paradise with Gabriel who had been the first to honour her, and with those elder Saints who arose after the Resurrection, appeared in the Holy City, and then vanished away.

May we partake in such calm and heavenly joy; and, while we pray for it, recollecting the while that we are still on earth, and our duties in this world, let us never forget that, while our love must be silent, our faith must be vigorous and lively. Let us never forget that in proportion as our love is "rooted and grounded" in the next world, our faith must branch forth like a fruitful tree into this. The calmer our hearts, the more active be our lives; the more tranquil we are, the more busy; the more resigned, the more zealous; the more unruffled, the more fervent. This is one of the many paradoxes in the world's judgment of him, which the Christian realizes in himself. Christ is risen; He is risen from the dead. We may well cry out, "Alleluia, the Lord Omnipotent reigneth." He has crushed all the power of the enemy under His feet. He has gone upon the lion and the adder. He has stopped the lion's mouth for us His

[5] *Vide* Christian year. Fourth Sunday in Lent.

people, and has bruised the serpent's head. There is nothing impossible to us now, if we do but enter into the fulness of our privileges, the wondrous power of our gifts. The thing cannot be named in heaven or earth within the limits of truth and obedience which we cannot do through Christ; the petition cannot be named which may not be accorded to us for His Name's sake. For, we who have risen with Him from the grave, stand in His might, and are allowed to use His weapons. His infinite influence with the Father is ours,—not always to use, for perhaps in this or that effort we make, or petition we prefer, it would not be good for us; but so far ours, so fully ours, that when we ask and do things according to His will, we are really possessed of a power with God, and do prevail:—so that little as we may know when and when not, we are continually possessed of heavenly weapons, we are continually touching the springs of the most wonderful providences in heaven and earth; and by the Name, and the Sign, and the Blood of the Son of God, we are able to make devils tremble and Saints rejoice. Such are the arms which faith uses, small in appearance, yet "not carnal, but mighty through God to the pulling down of strongholds;"[6] despised by the world, what seems a mere word, or a mere symbol, or mere bread and wine; but God has chosen the weak things of the world to confound the mighty, and foolish things of the world to confound the wise; and as all things spring from small beginnings, from seeds and elements invisible or insignificant, so when God would renew the race of man, and reverse the course of human life and earthly affairs, He chose cheap things for the rudiments of His work, and bade us believe that He *could* work through them, and He would do so. As then we Christians discern in Him, when He came on earth, not the carpenter's son, but the Eternal Word Incarnate, as we see beauty in Him in whom the world saw no form or comeliness, as we discern in that death an Atonement for sin in which the world saw nothing but a malefactor's sentence; so let us believe with full persuasion that all that He has bequeathed to us has power from Him. Let us accept His Ordinances, and His Creed, and His precepts; and let us stand upright with an undaunted faith, resolute, with faces like flint, to serve Him in and through them; to inflict them upon the world without misgiving, without wavering, without anxiety; being sure that He who saved us from hell through a Body of flesh which the world insulted, tortured, and triumphed over, much more can now apply the

[6] 2 Cor. x.4.

benefits of His passion through Ordinances which the world has lacerated and now mocks.

This then, my brethren, be our spirit on this day. God rested from His labours on the seventh day, yet He worketh evermore. Christ entered into His rest, yet He too ever works. We too, if it may be said, in adoring and lowly imitation of what is infinite, while we rest in Christ and rejoice in His shadow, let us too beware of sloth and cowardice, but serve Him with steadfast eyes yet active hands; that we may be truly His in our hearts, as we were made His by Baptism,—as we are made His continually, by the recurring celebration of His purifying Fasts and holy Feasts.

v

WORSHIP, A PREPARATION FOR CHRIST'S COMING

(Advent)

"Thine eyes shall see the King in His beauty: they shall behold the land that is very far off."—Is. xxxiii.17.

YEAR after year, as it passes, brings us the same warnings again and again, and none perhaps more impressive than those with which it comes to us at this season. The very frost and cold, rain and gloom, which now befall us, forebode the last dreary days of the world, and in religious hearts raise the thought of them. The year is worn out; spring, summer, autumn, each in turn, have brought their gifts and done their utmost; but they are over, and the end is come. All is past and gone, all has failed, all has sated; we are tired of the past; we would not have the seasons longer; and the austere weather which succeeds, though ungrateful to the body, is in tone with our feelings, and acceptable. Such is the frame of mind which befits the end of the year; and such the frame of mind which comes alike on good and bad at the end of life. The days have come in which they have no pleasure; yet they would hardly be young again, could they be so by wishing it. Life is well enough in its way; but it does not satisfy. Thus the soul is cast forward upon the future, and in proportion as its conscience is clear and its perception keen and true, does it rejoice solemnly that "the night is far spent, the day is at hand," that there are "new heavens and a new earth" to come, though the former are failing; nay, rather that, because they are failing, it will "soon see the King in His beauty," and "behold the land which is very far off." These are feelings for holy men in winter and in age, waiting, in some dejection perhaps, but with comfort on the whole, and calmly though earnestly, for the Advent of Christ.

And such, too, are the feelings with which we now come before Him in prayer day by day. The season is chill and dark, and the breath of the morning is damp, and worshippers are few, but all this befits those who are by profession penitents and mourners, watchers and pilgrims. More dear to them that loneliness, more cheerful that severity, and more bright that gloom, than all those aids and appliances of luxury by which men nowadays attempt to make prayer less disagreeable to them. True faith does not covet comforts. It only complains when it is forbidden to kneel, when it reclines upon cushions, is protected by curtains, and encompassed by warmth. Its only hardship is to be hindered, or to be ridiculed, when it would place itself as a sinner before its Judge. They who realize that awful Day when they shall see Him face to face, whose eyes are as a flame of fire, will as little bargain to pray pleasantly now, as they will think of doing so then.

One year goes and then another, but the same warnings recur. The frost or the rain comes again; the earth is stripped of its brightness; there is nothing to rejoice in. And then, amid this unprofitableness of earth and sky, the well-known words return; the Prophet Isaiah is read; the same Epistle and Gospel, bidding us "awake out of sleep," and welcome Him "that cometh in the Name of the Lord;" the same Collects, beseeching Him to prepare us for judgment. O blessed they who obey these warning voices, and look out for Him whom they have not seen, because they "love His appearing!"

We cannot have fitter reflections at this Season than those which I have entered upon. What may be the destiny of other orders of beings we know not;—but this we know to be our own fearful lot, that before us lies a time when we must have the sight of our Maker and Lord face to face. We know not what is reserved for other beings; there may be some, which, knowing nothing of their Maker, are never to be brought before Him. For what we can tell, this may be the case with the brute creation. It may be the law of their nature that they should live and die, or live on an indefinite period, upon the very outskirts of His government, sustained by Him, but never permitted to know or approach Him. But this is not our case. We are destined to come before Him; nay, and to come before Him in judgment; and that on our first meeting; and that suddenly. We are not merely to be rewarded or punished, we are to be judged. Recompense is to come upon our actions, not by a mere general provision or course of nature, as it does at present, but from the Lawgiver Himself in person. We have to stand before His righteous Presence, and that one by one. One by one we shall have to endure His holy and searching eye. At present we are in a world of shadows. What we see is not substantial. Suddenly it will be rent in twain and vanish away, and our Maker will appear. And then, I say, that first appearance will be nothing less than a personal intercourse between the Creator and every creature. He will look on us, while we look on Him.

I need hardly quote any of the numerous passages of Scripture which tell us this, by way of proof; but it may impress the truth of it upon our hearts to do so. We are told then expressly, that good and bad shall see God. On the one hand holy Job says, "Though after my skin worms destroy this body, yet in my flesh shall I see God: whom I shall see for myself, and mine eyes shall behold, and not another." On the other hand unrighteous Balaam says, "I shall see Him, but not now; I shall behold Him, but not nigh; there shall come a Star out of Jacob, and a Sceptre shall rise out of Israel." Christ says to His disciples, "Look up, and lift up your heads, for your redemption draweth nigh;" and to His enemies, "Hereafter ye shall see the Son of man sitting on the right hand of power, and coming in the clouds of heaven." And it is said generally of all men, on the one hand, "Behold He cometh with clouds; and every eye shall see Him, and they also which pierced Him; and all kindreds of the earth shall wail because of Him." And on the other, "When He shall appear, we shall be like Him; for we shall see Him as He is." Again, "Now we see through a glass, darkly; but then face to face:" and again, "They shall see His face; and His Name shall be in their foreheads."[1]

And, as they see Him, so will He see them, for His coming will be to judge them. "We must all appear before the judgment-seat of Christ," says St. Paul. Again, "We shall all stand before the judgment-seat of Christ. For it is written, As I live, saith the Lord, every knee shall bow to Me, and every tongue shall confess to God. So then every one of us shall give account of himself to God." And again, "When the Son of man shall come in His glory, and all the holy Angels with Him, then shall He sit upon the throne of His glory. And before Him shall be gathered all nations; and He shall separate them one from another, as a shepherd divideth his sheep from the goats."[2]

Such is our first meeting with our God; and, I say, it will be as sudden as it is intimate. "Yourselves know perfectly," says St. Paul, "that the day of the Lord so cometh as a thief in the night. For when they shall say, Peace and safety, then sudden destruc-

[1] Job xix.26, 27; Numb. xxiv.17; Luke xxi.28; Matt. xxvi.64; Rev. i.7; 1 John iii.2; 1 Cor. xiii.12; Rev. xxii.4.
[2] 2 Cor. v.10; Rom. xiv.10–12; Matt. xxv.31, 32.

tion cometh upon them." This is said of the wicked,—elsewhere He is said to surprise good as well as bad. "While the Bridegroom tarried," the wise and foolish virgins "all slumbered and slept. And at midnight there was a cry made, Behold, the Bridegroom cometh; go ye out to meet Him." [3]

Now, when this state of the case, the prospect which lies before us, is brought home to our thoughts, surely it is one which will lead us anxiously to ask, Is this all that we are told, all that is allowed to us, or done for us? Do we know only this, that all is dark now, and all will be light then; that now God is hidden, and one day will be revealed? That we are in a world of sense, and are to be in a world of spirits? For surely it is our plain wisdom, our bounden duty, to prepare for this great change;—and if so, are any directions, hints, or rules given us *how* we are to prepare? "Prepare to meet thy God," "Go ye out to meet Him," is the dictate of natural reason, as well as of inspiration. But *how* is this to be?

Now observe, that it is scarcely a sufficient answer to this question to say that we must strive to obey Him, and so to approve ourselves to Him. This indeed might be enough, were reward and punishment to follow in the mere way of nature, as they do in this world. But, when we come steadily to consider the matter, appearing before God, and dwelling in His presence, is a very different thing from being merely subjected to a system of moral laws, and would seem to require another preparation, a special preparation of thought and affection, such as will enable us to endure His countenance, and to hold communion with Him as we ought. Nay, and, it may be, a preparation of the soul itself for His presence, just as the bodily eye must be exercised in order to bear the full light of day, or the bodily frame in order to bear exposure to the air.

But, whether or not this be safe reasoning, Scripture precludes the necessity of it, by telling us that the Gospel Covenant is intended, among its other purposes, to prepare us for this future glorious and wonderful destiny, the sight of God,—a destiny which, if not most glorious, will be most terrible. And in the worship and service of Almighty God, which Christ and His Apostles have left to us, we are vouchsafed means, both moral and mystical, of approaching God, and gradually learning to bear the sight of Him.

This indeed is the most momentous reason for religious worship as far as we have grounds for considering it a true one. Men

---

[3] 1 Thess. v.2, 3; Matt. xxv.5, 6.

sometimes ask, Why need they *profess* religion? Why need they go to church? Why need they observe certain rites and ceremonies? Why need they watch, pray, fast, and meditate? Why is it not enough to be just, honest, sober, benevolent, and otherwise virtuous? Is not this the true and real worship of God? Is not activity in mind and conduct the most acceptable way of approaching Him? How can they please Him by submitting to certain religious forms, and taking part in certain religious acts? Or if they must do so, why may they not choose their own? Why must they come to church for them? Why must they be partakers in what the Church calls Sacraments? I answer, they must do so, first of all and especially, because God tells them so to do. But besides this, I observe that we see this plain reason why, that they are one day to change their state of being. They are not to be here for ever. Direct intercourse with God on their part now, prayer and the like, may be necessary to their meeting Him suitably hereafter: and direct intercourse on His part with them, or what we call sacramental communion, may be necessary in some incomprehensible way, even for preparing their very nature to bear the sight of Him.

Let us then take this view of religious service; it is "going out to meet the Bridegroom," who, if not seen "in His beauty," will appear in consuming fire. Besides its other momentous reasons, it is a preparation for an awful event, which shall one day be. What it would be to meet Christ at once without preparation, we may learn from what happened even to the Apostles when His glory was suddenly manifested to them. St. Peter said, "Depart from me, for I am a sinful man, O Lord." And St. John, "when he saw Him, fell at His feet as dead." [4]

This being the case, it is certainly most merciful in God to vouchsafe to us the means of preparation, and such means as He has actually appointed. When Moses came down from the Mount, and the people were dazzled at his countenance, he put a veil over it. That veil is so far removed in the Gospel, that we are in a state of preparation for its being altogether removed. We are with Moses in the Mount so far, that we have a sight of God; we are with the people beneath it so far, that Christ does not visibly show Himself. He has put a veil on, and He sits among us silently and secretly. When we approach Him, we know it only by faith; and when He manifests Himself to us, it is without our being able to realize to ourselves that manifestation.

[4] Luke v.8; Rev. i.17.

Such then is the spirit in which we should come to all His ordinances, considering them as anticipations and first-fruits of that sight of Him which one day must be. When we kneel down in prayer in private, let us think to ourselves, Thus shall I one day kneel down before His very footstool, in this flesh and this blood of mine; and He will be seated over against me, in flesh and blood also, though divine. I come, with the thought of that awful hour before me, I come to confess my sin to Him now, that He may pardon it then, and I say, "O Lord, Holy God, Holy and Strong, Holy and Immortal, in the hour of death and in the day of judgment, deliver us, O Lord!"

Again, when we come to church, then let us say:—The day will be when I shall see Christ surrounded by His Holy Angels. I shall be brought into that blessed company, in which all will be pure, all bright. I come then to learn to endure the sight of the Holy One and His Servants; to nerve myself for a vision which is fearful before it is ecstatic, and which they only enjoy whom it does not consume. When men in this world have to undergo any great thing, they prepare themselves beforehand, by thinking often of it, and they call this making up their mind. Any unusual trial they thus make familiar to them. Courage is a necessary step in gaining certain goods, and courage is gained by steady thought. Children are scared, and close their eyes, at the vision of some mighty warrior or glorious king. And when Daniel saw the Angel, like St. John, "his comeliness was turned in him into corruption, and he retained no strength."[5] I come then to church, because I am an heir of heaven. It is my desire and hope one day to take possession of my inheritance: and I come to make myself ready for it, and I would not see heaven yet, for I could not bear to see it. I am allowed to be in it without seeing it, that I may learn to see it. And by psalm and sacred song, by confession and by praise, I learn my part.

And what is true of the ordinary services of religion, public and private, holds in a still higher or rather in a special way, as regards the sacramental ordinances of the Church. In these is manifested in greater or less degree, according to the measure of each, that Incarnate Saviour, who is one day to be our Judge, and who is enabling us to bear His presence then, by imparting it to us in measure now. A thick black veil is spread between this world and the next. We mortal men range up and down it, to and fro, and see nothing. There is no access through it into the next world. In the Gospel this veil is not removed; it remains,

[5] Dan. x.8.

but every now and then marvellous disclosures are made to us of what is behind it. At times we seem to catch a glimpse of a Form which we shall hereafter see face to face. We approach, and in spite of the darkness, our hands, or our head, or our brow, or our lips become, as it were, sensible of the contact of something more than earthly. We know not where we are, but we have been bathing in water, and a voice tells us that it is blood. Or we have a mark signed upon our foreheads, and it spake of Calvary. Or we recollect a hand laid upon our heads, and surely it had the print of nails in it, and resembled His who with a touch gave sight to the blind and raised the dead. Or we have been eating and drinking; and it was not a dream surely, that One fed us from His wounded side, and renewed our nature by the heavenly meat He gave. Thus in many ways He, who is Judge to us, prepares us to be judged,—He, who is to glorify us, prepares us to be glorified, that He may not take us unawares; but that when the voice of the Archangel sounds, and we are called to meet the Bridegroom, we may be ready.

Now consider what light these reflections throw upon some remarkable texts in the Epistle to the Hebrews. If we have in the Gospel this supernatural approach to God and to the next world, no wonder that St. Paul calls it an "enlightening," "a tasting of the heavenly gift," a being "made partaker of the Holy Ghost," a "tasting of the good word of God, and the powers of the world to come." No wonder, too, that utter apostasy after receiving it should be so utterly hopeless; and that in consequence, any profanation of it, any sinning against it, should be so perilous in proportion to its degree. If He, who is to be our Judge, condescend here to manifest Himself to us, surely if that privilege does not fit us for His future glory, it does but prepare us for His wrath.

And what I have said concerning Ordinances, applies still more fully to Holy Seasons, which include in them the celebration of many Ordinances. They are times when we may humbly expect a larger grace, because they invite us especially to the means of grace. This in particular is a time for purification of every kind. When Almighty God was to descend upon Mount Sinai, Moses was told to "sanctify the people," and bid them "wash their clothes," and to "set bounds to them round about:" much more is this a season for "cleansing ourselves from all defilement of the flesh and spirit, perfecting holiness in the fear of God;"[6] a season for chastened hearts and religious eyes; for

---

[6] Exod. xix.10–12; 2 Cor. vii.1.

severe thoughts, and austere resolves, and charitable deeds; a season for remembering what we are and what we shall be. Let us go out to meet Him with contrite and expectant hearts; and though He delays His coming, let us watch for Him in the cold and dreariness which must one day have an end. Attend His summons we must, at any rate, when He strips us of the body; let us anticipate, by a voluntary act, what will one day come on us of necessity. Let us wait for Him solemnly, fearfully, hopefully, patiently, obediently; let us be resigned to His will, while active in good works. Let us pray Him ever, to "remember us when He cometh in His kingdom;" to remember all our friends; to remember our enemies; and to visit us according to His mercy here, that He may reward us according to His righteousness hereafter.

REVERENCE, A BELIEF IN
GOD'S PRESENCE

(Advent)

"Thine eyes shall see the King in His beauty: they shall behold the land that is very far off."—Is. xxxiii.17.

THOUGH Moses was not permitted to enter the land of promise, he was vouchsafed a sight of it from a distance. We too, though as yet we are not admitted to heavenly glory, yet are given to see much, in preparation for seeing more. Christ dwells among us in His Church really though invisibly, and through its Ordinances fulfils towards us, in a true and sufficient sense, the promise of the text. We are even now permitted to "see the King in His beauty," to "behold the land that is very far off." The words of the Prophet relate to our present state as well as to the state of saints hereafter. Of the future glory it is said by St. John, "They shall see His face, and His name shall be in their foreheads."[1] And of the present, Isaiah himself speaks in passages which may be taken in explanation of the text: "The glory of the Lord shall be revealed, and all flesh shall see it together;" and again, "They shall see the glory of the Lord, and the excellency of our God."[2] We do not see God face to face under the Gospel, but still, for all that, it is true that "we know in part;" we see, though it be "through a glass darkly;" which is far more than any but Christians are enabled to do. Baptism, by which we become Christians, is an illumination; and Christ, who is the Object of our worship, is withal a Light to worship by.

Such a view is strange to most men; they do not realize the presence of Christ, nor admit the duty of realizing it. Even those who are not without habits of seriousness, have almost or quite forgotten the duty. This is plain at once: for, unless they had, they would not be so very deficient in reverence as they

[1] Rev. xxii.4. [2] Is. xl.5; xxxv.2.

are. It is scarcely too much to say that awe and fear are at the present day all but discarded from religion. Whole societies called Christian make it almost a first principle to disown the duty of reverence; and we ourselves, to whom as children of the Church reverence is as a special inheritance, have very little of it, and do not feel the want of it. Those who, in spite of themselves, are influenced by God's holy fear, too often are ashamed of it, consider it even as a mark of weakness of mind, hide their feeling as much as they can, and, when ridiculed or censured for it, cannot defend it to themselves on intelligible grounds. They wish indeed to maintain reverence in their mode of speaking and acting, in relation to sacred things, but they are at a loss how to answer objections, or how to resist received customs and fashions; and at length they begin to be suspicious and afraid of their own instinctive feelings. Let us then take occasion from the promise in the text both to describe the religious defect to which I have alluded, and to state the remedy for it.

There are two classes of men who are deficient in awe and fear, and, lamentable to say, taken together, they go far to make up the religious portion of the community. This is lamentable indeed, if so it is: it is not wonderful that sinners should live without the fear of God; but what shall we say of an age or country, in which even the more serious classes, those who live on principle, and claim to have a judgment in religious matters, who look forward to the future, and think that their account stands fair, and that they are in God's favour, when even such persons maintain, or at least act as if they maintained, that "the spirit of God's holy fear" is no part of religion? "If the light that is in us be darkness, how great is that darkness!"

These are the two classes of men who are deficient in this respect: first, those who think that they never were greatly under God's displeasure; next, those who think that, though they once were, they are not at all now, for all sin has been forgiven them;—those on the one hand who consider that sin is no great evil in itself, those on the other who consider that it is no great evil in them, because their persons are accepted in Christ for their faith's sake.

Now it must be observed that the existence of fear in religion does not depend on the circumstance of our being sinners; it is short of that. Were we pure as the Angels, yet in His sight, one should think, we could not but fear, before whom the heavens are not clean, nor the Angels free from folly. The Seraphim themselves veiled their faces while they cried, Glory! Even then were it true that sin was not a great evil, or was no great evil in us, nevertheless the mere circumstance that God is infinite and all-perfect is an overwhelming thought to creatures and mortal men, and ought to lead all persons who profess religion to profess also religious fear, however natural it is for irreligious men to disclaim the feeling.

And next let it be observed, it is no dispute about terms. For at first sight we may be tempted to think that the only question is whether the word "fear" is a good or bad word;—that one man makes it all one with slavish dread, and another with godly awe and reverence;—and that therefore the two seem to oppose each other, when they do not,—as if both parties agreed that reverence is right and selfish terror wrong, and the only point between them were, whether by the word fear was meant terror or reverence. This is not the case: it is a question not of words but of things; for these persons whom I am describing plainly consider that state of mind wrong, which the Church Catholic has ever prescribed and her Saints have ever exemplified.

To show that this is so, I will in a few words state what the two sets of opinion are to which I allude and what that fault is, which, widely as they differ in opinion from each other, they have in common.

The one class of persons consists of those who think the Catholic Creed too strict,—who hold that no certain doctrines need be believed in order to salvation, or at least question the necessity; who say that it matters not what a man believes, so that his conduct is respectable and orderly,—who think that all rites and ceremonies are mere niceties (as they speak) and trifles, and that a man pleases God equally by observing them or not,—who perhaps go on to doubt whether Christ's death is strictly speaking an atonement for the sin of man,—who, when pressed, do not allow that He is strictly speaking and literally God,—and who deny that the punishment of the wicked is eternal. Such are the tenets, more or less clearly apprehended and confessed, which mark the former of the two classes of which I speak.

The other class of men are in their formal doctrines widely different from the former. They consider that, though they were by nature children of wrath, they are now by God's grace so fully in His favour, that, were they to die at once, they would be certain of heaven,—they consider that God so absolutely forgives them day by day their trespasses, that they have nothing to answer for, nothing to be tried upon at the Last Day,—that they have been visited by God's grace in a manner quite distinct from all around them, and are His children in a sense in which others are not, and have an assurance of their saving state peculiar to themselves, and an interest in the promises such as Baptism does not impart;—they profess to be thus beyond the reach of doubt and anxiety, and they say that they should be miserable without such a privilege.

I have alluded to these schools of religion, to show how widely a feeling must be spread which such contrary classes of men have in common. Now, what they agree in is this: in considering God as simply a God of love, not of awe and reverence also,—the one meaning by love *benevolence*, and the other *mercy*; and in consequence neither the one nor the other regard Almighty God with *fear*; and the signs of want of fear in both the one and the other, which I proposed to point out, are such as the following.

For instance:—they have no scruple or misgiving in speaking freely of Almighty God. They will use His Name as familiarly and lightly, as if they were open sinners. The one class adopts a set of words to denote Almighty God, which remove the idea of His personality, speaking of Him as the "Deity," or the "Divine Being;" which, as they use them, are of all others most calculated to remove from the mind the thought of a living and intelligent Governor, their Saviour and their Judge. The other class of men, going into the other extreme, but with the same result, use freely that incommunicable Name by which He has vouchsafed to denote to us His perfections. When He appeared to Moses, He disclosed His Name; and that Name has appeared so sacred to our translators of Scripture, that they have scrupled to use it, though it occurs continually in the Old Testament, substituting the word "Lord" out of reverence. Now, the persons in question delight in a familiar use, in prayers and hymns and conversation, of that Name by which they designate Him before whom Angels tremble. Not even our fellow-men do we freely call by their own names, unless we are at our ease with them; yet sinners can bear to be familiar with the Name by which they know the Most High has distinguished Himself from all creatures.

Another instance of want of fear, is the bold and unscrupulous way in which men speak of the Holy Trinity and the Mystery of the Divine Nature. They use sacred terms and phrases, should occasion occur, in a rude and abrupt way, and discuss points of doctrine concerning the All-holy and Eternal, even (if I may without irreverence state it) over their cups, perhaps arguing against them, as if He were such a one as themselves.

Another instance of this want of fear is found in the peremptory manner in which men lay down what Almighty God must do, what He cannot but do, as if they were masters of the whole scheme of salvation, and might anticipate His high providence and will.

And another is the confidence with which they often speak of their having been converted, pardoned, and sanctified, as if they knew their own state as well as God knows it.

Another is the unwillingness so commonly felt, to bow at the Name of Jesus, nay the impatience exhibited towards those who do; as if there were nothing awful in the idea of the Eternal God being made man, and as if we did not suitably express our wonder and awe at it by practising what St. Paul has in very word prescribed.

Another instance is the careless mode in which men speak of our Lord's earthly doings and sayings, just as if He were a mere man. He was man indeed, but He was more than man: and He did what man does, but then those deeds of His were the deeds of God,—and we can as little separate the deed from the Doer as our arm from our body. But, in spite of this, numbers are apt to use rude, familiar, profane language, concerning their God's childhood, and youth, and ministry, though He is their God.

And another is the familiarity with which many persons address our Lord in prayer, applying epithets to Him and adopting a strain of language which does not beseem creatures, not to say sinners.

And another is their general mode of prayer; I mean, in diffuse and free language, with emphatic and striking words, in a sort of coloured or rich style, with pomp of manner, and an oratorical tone, as if praying were preaching, and as if its object were not to address Almighty God, but to impress and affect those who heard them.

And another instance of this want of reverence is the introduction in speaking or writing, of serious and solemn words, for the sake of effect, to round, or to give dignity to, a sentence.

And another instance is irreverence in church, sitting instead of kneeling in prayer, or pretending to kneel but really sitting, or lounging or indulging in other unseemly attitudes; and, much more, looking about when prayers are going on, and observing what others are doing.

These are some out of a number of peculiarities which mark the religion of the day, and are instanced, some in one class of men, some in another; but all by one or other;—and they are specimens of what I mean when I say that the religion of this day is destitute of *fear*.

Many other instances might be mentioned of very various kinds. For instance, the freedom with which men propose to alter God's ordinances, to suit their own convenience, or to meet the age; their reliance on their private and antecedent notions about sacred subjects; their want of interest and caution in inquiring what God's probable will is; their contempt for any view of the Sacraments which exceeds the evidence of their senses; and their confidence in settling the order of importance in which the distinct articles of Christian faith stand;—all which shows that it is no question of words whether men have fear or not, but that there *is* a something they really have not, whatever name we give it.

So far I consider to be plain:—the only point which can be debated is this, whether the feelings which I have been describing are necessary; for each of the two classes which I have named contends that they are unnecessary; the one decides them inconsistent with reason, the other with the Gospel; the one calls them superstitious, and the other legal or Jewish. Let us then consider, are these feelings of fear and awe Christian feelings or not? A very few words will surely be sufficient to decide the question.

I say this, then, which I think no one can reasonably dispute. They are the class of feelings we *should* have,—yes, have in an intense degree—if we literally had the sight of Almighty God; therefore they are the class of feelings which we shall have, *if* we realize His presence. In proportion as we believe that He is present, we shall have them; and not to have them, is not to realize, not to believe that He is present. If then it is a duty to feel as though we saw Him, or to have faith, it is a duty to have these feelings; and if it is a sin to be destitute of faith, it is a sin to be without them. Let us consider this awhile.

Who then is there to deny, that if we saw God, we should fear? Take the most cold and secular of all those who explain away the Gospel; or take the most heated and fanatic of those who consider it peculiarly their own; take those who think that Christ has brought us nothing great, or those who think He has brought it all to themselves,—I say, would either party keep from fearing greatly if they saw God? Surely it is quite a truism to say that any creature would fear. But why would he fear? would it be merely because he saw God, or because he knew that God was present? If he shut his eyes, he would still fear, for his eyes had conveyed to him this solemn truth; to *have* seen would be enough. But if so, does it not follow at once, that, if men do not fear, it is because they do not act as they would act if they saw Him, that is,—they do not feel that He is present? Is it not quite certain that men would not use Almighty God's Name so freely, if they thought He was really in hearing,—nay, close beside them when they spoke? And so of those other instances of want of godly fear, which I mentioned, they one and all come from deadness to the presence of God. If a man believes Him present, he will shrink from addressing Him familiarly, or using before Him unreal words, or peremptorily and on his own judgment deciding what God's will is, or claiming His confidence, or addressing Him in a familiar posture of body. I say, take the man who is most confident that he has nothing to fear from the presence of God, and that Almighty God is at peace with him, and place him actually before the throne of God; and would he have no misgivings? and will he dare to say that those misgivings are a weakness, a mere irrational perturbation, which he ought not to feel?

This will be seen more clearly, by considering how differently we feel towards and speak of our friends as present or absent. Their presence is a check upon us; it acts as an external law, compelling us to do or not do what we should not do or do otherwise, or should do but for it. This is just what most men lack in their religion at present,—such an external restraint arising from the consciousness of God's presence. Consider, I say, how differently we speak of a friend, however intimate, when present or absent; consider how we feel, should it so happen that we have begun to speak of him as if he were not present, on finding suddenly that he is; and that, though we are conscious of nothing but what is loving and open towards him. There is a tone of voice and a manner of speaking about persons absent, which we should consider disrespectful, or at least inconsiderate, if they were present. When that is the case, we are ever thinking more or less, even though unconsciously to ourselves, how they will take what we say, how it will affect them, what they will say to us or think of us in turn. When a person is absent, we are tempted perhaps confidently to say what his opinion is on certain points;—but should he be present, we qualify our words; we hardly like to speak at all, from the vivid consciousness that we may be wrong, and that he is present to tell us so. We are very cautious of pronouncing what his feelings are on the matter in hand, or how he is disposed towards ourselves; and in all things we observe a deference and delicacy in our conduct towards him. Now, if we feel this towards our fellows, what shall we feel in the presence of an Angel? and if so, what in the presence of the All-knowing, All-searching Judge of men? What is respect and consideration in the case of our fellows, becomes godly fear as regards Almighty God; and they who do not fear Him, in one word, do not believe that He sees and hears them. If they did, they would cease to boast so confidently of His favourable thoughts of them, to foretell His dealings, to pronounce upon His revelations, to make free with His Name, and to address Him familiarly.

Now, in what has been said, no account has been taken, as I have already observed, of our being sinners, a corrupt, polluted race at the best, while He is the All-holy God,—which must surely increase our fear and awe greatly, and not at all the less because we have been so wonderfully redeemed. Nor, again, has account been taken of another point, on which I will add two or three words.

There is a peculiar feeling with which we regard the dead. What does this arise from?—that he is absent? No; for we do not feel the same towards one who is merely distant, though he be at the other end of the earth. Is it because in this life we shall never see him again? No, surely not; because we may be perfectly certain we shall never see him when he goes abroad, we may know he is to die abroad, and perhaps he does die abroad; but will any one say that, when the news of his death comes, our feeling when we think of him is not quite changed? Surely it is the passing into another state which impresses itself upon us, and makes us speak of him as we do,—I mean, with a sort of awe. We cannot tell what he is now,—what his relations to us,—what he knows of us. We do not understand him,—we do not see him. He is passed into the land "that is very far off;" but it is not at all certain that he has not some mysterious hold over us. Thus his not being seen with our bodily eyes, while perchance he is present, makes the thought of him more awful. Apply this to the subject before us, and you will perceive that there is a sense, and a true sense, in which the *invisible* presence of God is more awful and overpowering than if we saw it. And so again, the presence of Christ, now that it is invisible, brings with it a host of high and mysterious feelings, such as nothing else can inspire. The thought of our Saviour, absent yet present, is like that of a friend taken from us, but, as it were, in dream returned to us, though in this case not in dream, but in reality and truth. When He was going away, He said to His disciples, "I will see you again, and your heart shall rejoice." Yet He had at another time said, "The days will come when the Bridegroom shall be taken from them, and then shall they fast in those days." See what an apparent contradiction, such as attends the putting any high feeling into human language! they were to joy because Christ was come, and yet weep because He was away; that is, to have a feeling so refined, so strange and new, that nothing could be said of it, but that it combined in one all that was sweet and soothing in contrary human feelings, as commonly experienced. As some precious fruits of the earth are said to taste like all others at once, not as not being really distinct from all others, but as being thus best described, when we would come as near the truth as we can, so the state of mind which they are in who believe that the Son of God is here, yet away,—is at the right hand of God, yet in His very flesh and blood among us,—is present, though invisible,—is one of both joy and pain, or rather one far above either; a feeling of awe, wonder, and praise, which cannot be more suitably expressed than by the Scripture word *fear*; or by holy Job's words, though he spoke in grief, and not as being possessed of a blessing. "Behold, I go forward, but He is not there; and backward, but I cannot perceive Him: on the left hand, where He doth work, but I cannot behold Him: He hideth Himself on the right hand, that I cannot see Him. Therefore am I troubled at His presence; when I consider I am afraid of Him." [3]

To conclude. Enough has been said now to show that godly fear must be a duty, if to live as in God's sight is a duty,—must be a privilege of the Gospel, if the spiritual sight of "the King in His beauty" be one of its privileges. Fear follows from faith necessarily, as would be plain, even though there were not a text in the Bible saying so. But in fact, as it is scarcely needful to say, Scripture abounds in precepts to fear God. Such are the words of the Wise Man: "The fear of the Lord is the beginning of knowledge." Such again is the third commandment, in which we are solemnly bidden not to take God's Name in vain. Such the declaration of the prophet Habakkuk, who beginning by declaring "The just shall live by his faith," ends by saying, "The Lord is in His Holy Temple; let the whole earth keep silence before Him." Such is St. Paul's, who, in like manner, after having discoursed at length upon faith as "the realizing of things hoped for, the evidence of things not seen;" adds: "Let us have grace, whereby we may serve God acceptably with reverence and godly fear." Such St. Luke's account of the Church militant on earth, that "walking in the fear of the Lord and in the

[3] John xxiii.8, 9, 15.

comfort of the Holy Ghost," it was "multiplied." Such St. John's account of the Church triumphant in heaven, "Who shall not fear Thee," they say, "O Lord, and glorify Thy Name; for Thou only art Holy?" Such the feeling recorded of the three Apostles on the Mount of Transfiguration, who, when they heard God's voice, "fell on their face, and were sore afraid." [4] And now, if this be so, can anything be clearer than that the *want* of fear is nothing else but *want* of faith, and that in consequence we in this age are approaching in religious temper that evil day of which it is said, "When the Son of Man cometh, shall He find faith on the earth?" [5] Is it wonderful that we have no fear in our words and mutual intercourse, when we exercise no *acts* of faith? What, you will ask, are acts of faith? Such as these,—to come often to prayer, is an act of faith; to kneel down instead of sitting, is an act of faith; to strive to attend to your prayers, is an act of faith; to behave in God's House otherwise than you would in a common room, is an act of faith; to come to it on week-days as well as Sundays, is an act of faith; to come often to the most Holy Sacrament, is an act of faith; and to be still and reverent during that sacred service, is an act of faith. These are all acts of faith, because they all are acts such as we should perform, if we saw and heard Him who *is* present, though with our bodily eyes we see and hear Him *not*. But, "blessed are they who have not seen, and yet have believed;" for, be sure, if we thus act, we shall, through God's grace, be gradually endued with the spirit of His holy fear. We shall in time, in our mode of talking and acting, in our religious services and our daily conduct, manifest, not with constraint and effort, but spontaneously and naturally, that we fear Him while we love Him.

---

[4] Prov. i.7; Hab. ii.4, 20; Heb. xii.28; Acts ix.31; Rev. xv.4; Matt. xvii.6.

[5] Luke xviii.8.

UNREAL WORDS

(Advent)

"Thine eyes shall see the King in His beauty: they shall behold the land that is very far off."—Is. xxxiii.17.

THE Prophet tells us, that under the Gospel covenant God's servants will have the privilege of seeing those heavenly sights which were but shadowed out in the Law. Before Christ came was the time of shadows; but when He came, He brought truth as well as grace; and as He who is the Truth has come to us, so does He in return require that we should be true and sincere in our dealings with Him. To be true and sincere is really to see with our minds those great wonders which He has wrought in order that we might see them. When God opened the eyes of the ass on which Balaam rode, she saw the Angel and acted upon the sight. When He opened the eyes of the young man, Elisha's servant, he too saw the chariots and horses of fire, and took comfort. And in like manner, Christians are now under the protection of a Divine Presence, and that more wonderful than any which was vouchsafed of old time. God revealed Himself visibly to Jacob, to Job, to Moses, to Joshua, and to Isaiah; to us He reveals Himself not visibly, but more wonderfully and truly; not without the co-operation of our own will, but upon our faith, and for that very reason more truly; for faith is the special means of gaining spiritual blessings. Hence St. Paul prays for the Ephesians "that Christ may dwell in their hearts by faith," and that "the eyes of their understanding may be enlightened." And St. John declares that "the Son of God hath given us all understanding that we may know Him that is true: and we are in Him that is true, even in His Son Jesus Christ."[1]

We are no longer then in the region of shadows: we have the true Saviour set before us, the true reward, and the true means of spiritual renewal. We know the true state of the soul by nature and by grace, the evil of sin, the consequences of sinning,

[1] Eph. iii.17; i.18; 1 John v.20.

the way of pleasing God, and the motives to act upon. God has revealed Himself clearly to us; He has "destroyed the face of the covering cast over all people, and the veil that is spread over all nations." "The darkness is past, and the True light now shineth."[2] And therefore, I say, He calls upon us in turn to "walk in the light as He is in the light." The Pharisees might have this excuse in their hypocrisy, that the plain truth had not been revealed to them; we have not even this poor reason for insincerity. We have no opportunity of mistaking one thing for another: the promise is expressly made to us that "our teachers shall not be removed into a corner any more, but our eyes shall see our teachers;" that "the eyes of them that see shall not be dim;" that every thing shall be called by its right name; that "the evil person shall be no more called liberal, nor the churl said to be bountiful;"[3] in a word, as the text speaks, that "our eyes shall see the King in His beauty; we shall behold the land that is very far off." Our professions, our creeds, our prayers, our dealings, our conversation, our arguments, our teaching must henceforth be sincere, or, to use an expressive word, must be *real*. What St. Paul says of himself and his fellow-labourers, that they were true because Christ is true, applies to all Christians: "Our rejoicing is this, the testimony of our conscience, that in simplicity and godly sincerity, not with fleshly wisdom, but by the grace of God, we have had our conversation in the world, and more abundantly to you-ward. . . . The things that I purpose, do I purpose according to the flesh, that with me there should be yea yea, and nay nay? But as God is true, our word toward you was not yea and nay. For the Son of God, Jesus Christ, . . . was not yea and nay, but in Him was yea. For all the promises of God in Him are yea, and in Him Amen, unto the glory of God by us."[4]

And yet it need scarcely be said, nothing is so rare as honesty and singleness of mind; so much so, that a person who is really honest, is already perfect. Insincerity was an evil which sprang up within the Church from the first; Ananias and Simon were not open opposers of the Apostles, but false brethren. And, as foreseeing what was to be, our Saviour is remarkable in His ministry for nothing more than the earnestness of the dissuasives which He addressed to those who came to Him, against taking up religion lightly, or making promises which they were likely to break.

[2] Is. xxv.7; 1 John ii.8.   [3] Is. xxx.20; xxii.3, 5.
[4] 2 Cor. i.12–20.

Thus He, "the True Light, which lighteth every man that cometh into the world," "the Amen, the faithful and true Witness, the Beginning of the creation of God," [5] said to the young Ruler, who lightly called Him "Good Master," "Why callest thou Me good?" as bidding him weigh his words; and then abruptly told him, "One thing thou lackest." When a certain man professed that he would follow Him whithersoever He went, He did not respond to him, but said, "The foxes have holes, and the birds of the air have nests, but the Son of Man hath not where to lay His head." When St. Peter said with all his heart in the name of himself and brethren, "To whom shall we go? Thou hast the words of eternal life," He answered pointedly, "Have not I chosen you twelve, and one of you is a devil?" as if He said, "Answer for thyself." When the two Apostles professed their desire to cast their lot with Him, He asked whether they could "drink of His cup, and be baptized with His baptism." And when "there went great multitudes with Him," He turned and said, that unless a man hated relations, friends, and self, he could not be His disciple. And then he proceeded to warn all men to "count the cost" ere they followed Him. Such is the merciful severity with which He repels us that He may gain us more truly. And what He thinks of those who, after coming to Him, relapse into a hollow and hypocritical profession, we learn from His language towards the Laodiceans: "I know thy works, that thou art neither cold nor hot: I would thou wert cold or hot. So then, because thou art lukewarm, and neither cold nor hot, I will cast thee out of My mouth." [6]

We have a striking instance of the same conduct on the part of that ancient Saint who prefigured our Lord in name and office, Joshua, the captain of the chosen people in entering Canaan. When they had at length taken possession of that land which Moses and their fathers had seen "very far off," they said to him, "God forbid that we should forsake the Lord, and serve other gods. We will . . . serve the Lord, for He is our God." He made answer, "Ye cannot serve the Lord; for He is a holy God; He is a jealous God; He will not forgive your transgressions nor your sins." [7] Not as if he would hinder them from obeying, but to sober them in professing. How does his answer remind us of St. Paul's still more awful words, about the impossibility of renewal after utterly falling away!

[5] John i.9; Rev. iii.14.
[6] Mark x.17–21; Matt. viii.20; John vi.68–70; Matt. xx.22; Luke xiv.25–28; Rev. iii.15, 16.
[7] Josh. xxiv.16–19.

And what is said of profession of *discipleship* applies undoubtedly in its degree to *all* profession. To make professions is to play
with edged tools, unless we attend to what we are saying.
Words have a meaning, whether we mean that meaning or not;
and they are imputed to us in their real meaning, when our not
meaning it is our own fault. He who takes God's Name in vain,
is not counted guiltless because he means nothing by it,—he
cannot frame a language for himself; and they who make professions, of whatever kind, are heard in the sense of those professions, and are not excused because they themselves attach no
sense to them. "By thy words thou shalt be justified, and by thy
words thou shalt be condemned." [8]

Now this consideration needs especially to be pressed upon
Christians at this day; for this is especially a day of professions.
You will answer in my own words, that all ages have been ages
of profession. So they have been, in one way or other, but this
day in its own especial sense;—because this is especially a day of
individual profession. This is a day in which there is (rightly or
wrongly) so much of private judgment, so much of separation
and difference, so much of preaching and teaching, so much of
authorship, that it involves individual profession, responsibility, and recompense in a way peculiarly its own. It will not then
be out of place if, in connexion with the text, we consider some
of the many ways in which persons, whether in this age or in
another, make unreal professions, or seeing see not, and hearing hear not, and speak without mastering, or trying to master,
their words. This I will attempt to do at some length, and in
matters of detail, which are not the less important because they
are minute.

Of course it is very common in all matters, not only in religion, to speak in an unreal way; viz., when we speak on a subject with which our minds are not familiar. If you were to hear
a person who knew nothing about military matters, giving directions how soldiers on service should conduct themselves, or
how their food and lodging, or their marching, was to be duly
arranged, you would be sure that his mistakes would be such as
to excite the ridicule and contempt of men experienced in
warfare. If a foreigner were to come to one of our cities, and
without hesitation offer plans for the supply of our markets, or
the management of our police, it is so certain that he would
expose himself, that the very attempt would argue a great
want of good sense and modesty. We should feel that he did

[8] Matt. xii.37.

not understand us, and that when he spoke about us, he would be using words without meaning. If a dim-sighted man were to attempt to decide questions of proportion and colour, or a man without ear to judge of musical compositions, we should feel that he spoke on and from general principles, on fancy, or by deduction and argument, not from a real apprehension of the matters which he discussed. His remarks would be theoretical and unreal.

This unsubstantial way of speaking is instanced in the case of persons who fall into any new company, among strange faces and amid novel occurrences. They sometimes form amiable judgments of men and things, sometimes the reverse,—but whatever their judgments be, they are to those who know the men and the things strangely unreal and distorted. They feel reverence where they should not; they discern slights where none were intended; they discover meaning in events which have none; they fancy motives; they misinterpret manner; they mistake character; and they form generalizations and combinations which exist only in their own minds.

Again, persons who have not attended to the subject of morals, or to politics, or to matters ecclesiastical, or to theology, do not know the relative value of questions which they meet with in these departments of knowledge. They do not understand the difference between one point and another. The one and the other are the same to them. They look at them as infants gaze at the objects which meet their eyes, in a vague unapprehensive way, as if not knowing whether a thing is a hundred miles off or close at hand, whether great or small, hard or soft. They have no means of judging, no standard to measure by,—and they give judgment at random, saying yea or nay on very deep questions, according as their fancy is struck at the moment, or as some clever or specious argument happens to come across them. Consequently they are inconsistent; say one thing one day, another the next;—and if they must act, act in the dark; or if they can help acting, do not act; or if they act freely, act from some other reason not avowed. All this is to be unreal.

Again, there cannot be a more apposite specimen of unreality than the way in which judgments are commonly formed upon important questions by the mass of the community. Opinions are continually given in the world on matters, about which those who offer them are as little qualified to judge as blind men about colours, and that because they have never exercised their minds upon the points in question. This is a day in which all men are obliged to have an opinion on all questions, political, social, and religious, because they have in some way or other an influence upon the decision; yet the multitude are for the most part absolutely without capacity to take their part in it. In saying this, I am far from meaning that this need be so,—I am far from denying that there is such a thing as plain good sense, or (what is better) religious sense, which will see its way through very intricate matters, or that this is in fact sometimes exerted in the community at large on certain great questions; but at the same time this practical sense is so far from existing as regards the vast mass of questions which in this day come before the public, that (as all persons who attempt to gain the influence of the people on their side know well) their opinions must be purchased by interesting their prejudices or fears in their favour;—not by presenting a question in its real and true substance, but by adroitly colouring it, or selecting out of it some particular point which may be exaggerated, and dressed up, and be made the means of working on popular feelings. And thus government and the art of government becomes, as much as popular religion, hollow and unsound.

And hence it is that the popular voice is so changeable. One man or measure is the idol of the people to-day, another to-morrow. They have never got beyond accepting shadows for things.

What is instanced in the mass is instanced also in various ways in individuals, and in points of detail. For instance, some men are set perhaps on being eloquent speakers. They use great words and imitate the sentences of others; and they fancy that those whom they imitate had as little meaning as themselves, or they perhaps contrive to think that they themselves have a meaning adequate to their words.

Another sort of unreality, or voluntary profession of what is above us, is instanced in the conduct of those who suddenly come into power or place. They affect a manner such as they think the office requires, but which is beyond them, and therefore unbecoming. They wish to act with dignity, and they cease to be themselves.

And so again, to take a different case, many men when they come near persons in distress and wish to show sympathy, often condole in a very unreal way. I am not altogether laying this to their fault; for it is very difficult to know what to do, when on the one hand we cannot realize to ourselves the sorrow, yet withal wish to be kind to those who feel it. A tone of grief seems necessary, yet (if so be) cannot under our circumstances be genuine. Yet even here surely there is a true way, if we could find it, by which pretence may be avoided, and yet respect and consideration shown.

And in like manner as regards religious emotions. Persons are aware from the mere force of the doctrines of which the Gospel consists, that they ought to be variously affected, and deeply and intensely too, in consequence of them. The doctrines of original and actual sin, of Christ's Divinity and Atonement, and of Holy Baptism, are so vast, that no one can realize them without very complicated and profound feelings. Natural reason tells a man this, and that if he simply and genuinely believes the doctrines, he must have these feelings; and he professes to believe the doctrines absolutely, and therefore he professes the correspondent feelings. But in truth he perhaps does *not* really believe them absolutely, because such absolute belief is the work of long time, and therefore his profession of feeling outruns the real inward existence of feeling, or he becomes unreal. Let us never lose sight of two truths,—that we ought to have our hearts penetrated with the love of Christ and full of self-renunciation; but that if they be not, professing that they are does not make them so.

Again, to take a more serious instance of the same fault, some persons pray, not as sinners addressing their God, not as the Publican smiting on his breast, and saying, "God be merciful to me a sinner," but in such a way as they conceive to be becoming *under* circumstances of guilt, in a way becoming such a strait. They are self-conscious, and reflect on what they are about, and instead of actually approaching (as it were) the mercy-seat, they are filled with the thought that God is great, and man His creature, God on high and man on earth, and that they are engaged in a high and solemn service, and that they ought to rise up to its sublime and momentous character.

Another still more common form of the same fault, yet without any definite pretence or effort, is the mode in which people speak of the shortness and vanity of life, the certainty of death, and the joys of heaven. They have commonplaces in their mouths, which they bring forth upon occasions for the good of others, or to console them, or as a proper and becoming mark of attention towards them. Thus they speak to clergymen in a professedly serious way, making remarks true and sound, and in themselves deep, yet unmeaning in their mouths; or they give advice to children or young men; or perhaps in low spirits or sickness they are led to speak in a religious strain as if it was spontaneous. Or when they fall into sin, they speak of man being frail, of the deceitfulness of the human heart, of God's

mercy, and so on:—all these great words, heaven, hell, judgment, mercy, repentance, works, the world that now is, the
world to come, being little more than "lifeless sounds, whether
of pipe or harp," in their mouths and ears, as the "very lovely
song of one that hath a pleasant voice and can play well on an
instrument,"—as the proprieties of conversation, or the civilities of good breeding.

I am speaking of the conduct of the world at large, called
Christian; but what has been said applies, and necessarily, to
the case of a number of well-disposed or even religious men. I
mean, that before men come to know the realities of human
life, it is not wonderful that their view of religion should be
unreal. Young people who have never known sorrow or anxiety, or the sacrifices which conscientiousness involves, want
commonly that depth and seriousness of character, which sorrow only and anxiety and self-sacrifice can give. I do not notice
this as a fault, but as a plain fact, which may often be seen, and
which it is well to bear in mind. This is the legitimate use of this
world, to make us seek for another. It does its part when it repels us and disgusts us and drives us elsewhere. Experience of it
gives experience of that which is its antidote, in the case of religious minds; and we become real in our view of what is spiritual
by the contact of things temporal and earthly. And much more
are men unreal when they have some secret motive urging them
a different way from religion, and when their professions therefore are forced into an unnatural course in order to subserve
their secret motive. When men do not like the conclusions to
which their principles lead, or the precepts which Scripture
contains, they are not wanting in ingenuity to blunt their force.
They can frame some theory, or dress up certain objections, to
defend themselves withal; a theory, that is, or objections,
which it is difficult to refute perhaps, but which any rightly-
ordered mind, nay, any common bystander, perceives to be unnatural and insincere.

What has been here noticed of individuals, takes place even
in the case of whole Churches, at times when love has waxed
cold and faith failed. The whole system of the Church, its discipline and ritual, are all in their origin the spontaneous and exuberant fruit of the real principle of spiritual religion in the
hearts of its members. The invisible Church has developed itself into the Church visible, and its outward rites and forms are
nourished and animated by the living power which dwells
within it. Thus every part of it is real, down to the minutest
details. But when the seductions of the world and the lusts of

the flesh have eaten out this divine inward life, what is the outward Church but a hollowness and a mockery, like the whited sepulchres of which our Lord speaks, a memorial of what was and is not? and though we trust that the Church is nowhere thus utterly deserted by the Spirit of truth, at least according to God's ordinary providence, yet may we not say that in proportion as it approaches to this state of deadness, the grace of its ordinances, though not forfeited, at least flows in but a scanty or uncertain stream?

And lastly, if this unreality may steal over the Church itself, which is in its very essence a practical institution, much more is it found in the philosophies and literature of men. Literature is almost in its essence unreal; for it is the exhibition of thought disjoined from practice. Its very home is supposed to be ease and retirement; and when it does more than speak or write, it is accused of transgressing its bounds. This indeed constitutes what is considered its true dignity and honour, viz. its abstraction from the actual affairs of life; its security from the world's currents and vicissitudes; its saying without doing. A man of literature is considered to preserve his dignity by doing nothing; and when he proceeds forward into action, he is thought to lose his position, as if he were degrading his calling by enthusiasm, and becoming a politician or a partisan. Hence mere literary men are able to say strong things against the opinions of their age, whether religious or political, without offence; because no one thinks they mean anything by them. They are not expected to go forward to act upon them, and mere words hurt no one.

Such are some of the more common or more extended specimens of profession without action, or of speaking without really seeing and feeling. In instancing which, let it be observed, I do not mean to say that such profession, as has been described, is always culpable and wrong; indeed I have implied the contrary throughout. It is often a misfortune. It takes a long time really to feel and understand things as they are; we learn to do so only gradually. Profession beyond our feelings is only a fault when we might help it;—when either we speak when we need not speak, or do not feel when we might have felt. Hard insensible hearts, ready and thoughtless talkers, these are they whose unreality, as I have termed it, is a sin; it is the sin of every one of us, in proportion as our hearts are cold, or our tongues excessive.

But the mere fact of our saying more than we feel is not necessarily sinful. St. Peter did not rise up to the full meaning of his

confession, "Thou art the Christ," yet he was pronounced
blessed. St. James and St. John said, "We are able," without
clear apprehension, yet without offence. We ever promise
things greater than we master, and we wait on God to enable us
to perform them. Our promising involves a prayer for light and
strength. And so again we all say the Creed, but who comprehends it fully? All we can hope is, that we are in the way to
understand it; that we partly understand it; that we desire, pray,
and strive to understand it more and more. Our Creed becomes
a sort of prayer. Persons are culpably unreal in their way of
speaking, not when they say more than they feel, but when
they say things different from what they feel. A miser praising
almsgiving, or a coward giving rules for courage, is unreal; but
it is not unreal for the less to discourse about the greater, for the
liberal to descant upon munificence, or the generous to praise
the noble-minded, or the self-denying to use the language of
the austere, or the confessor to exhort to martyrdom.

What I have been saying comes to this:—be in earnest, and
you will speak of religion where, and when, and how you
should; aim at things, and your words will be right without
aiming. There are ten thousand ways of looking at this world,
but only one right way. The man of pleasure has his way, the
man of gain his, and the man of intellect his. Poor men and rich
men, governors and governed, prosperous and discontented,
learned and unlearned, each has his own way of looking at the
things which come before him, and each has a wrong way.
There is but one right way; it is the way in which God looks at
the world. Aim at looking at it in God's way. Aim at seeing
things as God sees them. Aim at forming judgments about persons, events, ranks, fortunes, changes, objects, such as God
forms. Aim at looking at this life as God looks at it. Aim at looking at the life to come, and the world unseen, as God does. Aim
at "seeing the King in His beauty." All things that we see are but
shadows to us and delusions, unless we enter into what they
really mean.

It is not an easy thing to learn that new language which
Christ has brought us. He has interpreted all things for us in a
new way; He has brought us a religion which sheds a new light
on all that happens. Try to learn this language. Do not get it by
rote, or speak it as a thing of course. Try to understand what
you say. Time is short, eternity is long; God is great, man is
weak; he stands between heaven and hell; Christ is his Saviour;
Christ has suffered for him. The Holy Ghost sanctifies him; repentance purifies him, faith justifies, works save. These are sol-

emn truths, which need not be actually spoken, except in the way of creed or of teaching; but which must be laid up in the heart. That a thing is true, is no reason that it should be said, but that it should be done; that it should be acted upon; that it should be made our own inwardly.

Let us avoid talking, of whatever kind; whether mere empty talking, or censorious talking, or idle profession, or descanting upon Gospel doctrines, or the affectation of philosophy, or the pretence of eloquence. Let us guard against frivolity, love of display, love of being talked about, love of singularity, love of seeming original. Let us aim at meaning what we say, and saying what we mean; let us aim at knowing when we understand a truth, and when we do not. When we do not, let us take it on faith, and let us profess to do so. Let us receive the truth in reverence, and pray God to give us a good will, and divine light, and spiritual strength, that it may bear fruit within us.

SHRINKING FROM
CHRIST'S COMING

(Advent)

"Thine eyes shall see the King in His beauty: they shall behold the land that is very far off."—Is. xxxiii.17.

BEFORE Christ came, the faithful remnant of Israel were consoled with the promise that "their eyes should see" Him, who was to be their "salvation." "Unto you that fear My Name shall the Sun of righteousness arise with healing in His wings." Yet it is observable that the prophecy, though cheering and encouraging, had with it something of an awful character too. First, it was said, "The Lord whom ye seek shall suddenly come to His Temple, even the messenger of the Covenant whom ye delight in." Yet it is soon added, "But who may abide the day of His coming? and who shall stand when He appeareth? for He is like a refiner's fire, and like fullers' soap." [1]

The same mixture of fear with comfort is found in the Disciples after His Resurrection. The women departed from the sepulchre "with fear and great joy." They "trembled and were amazed: neither said they any thing to any man, for they were afraid." The Apostles "were terrified and affrighted, and supposed that they had seen a spirit." "They believed not for joy, and wondered." And our Lord said to them, "Why are ye troubled? and why do thoughts arise in your hearts?" On another occasion, "None of the disciples durst ask him, Who art thou? knowing that it was the Lord." [2] It might be from slowness to believe, or from misconception, or from the mere perplexity of amazement, but so it was; they exulted and they were awed.

Still more remarkable is the account of our Lord's appearance to St. John in the Book of Revelation; more remarkable be-

---

[1] Mal. iv.2; iii.1, 2.
[2] Matt. xxviii.8; Mark xvi.8; Luke xxiv.37, 38; John xxi.12.

cause St. John had no doubt or perplexity. Christ had ascended; the Apostle had received the gift of the Holy Ghost; yet he "fell at His feet as dead."

This reflection leads us on to a parallel thought concerning the state and prospects of all Christians in every age. We too are looking out for Christ's coming,—we are bid look out,—we are bid pray for it; and yet it is to be a time of judgment. It is to be the deliverance of all Saints from sin and sorrow for ever; yet they, every one of them, must undergo an awful trial. How then can any look forward to it with joy, not knowing (for no one knows) the certainty of his own salvation? And the difficulty is increased when we come to pray for it,—to pray for its coming soon: how can we pray that Christ would come, that the day of judgment would hasten, that His kingdom would come, that His kingdom may be at once,—may come on us this day or to-morrow,—when by so coming He would be shortening the time of our present life, and cut off those precious years given us for conversion, amendment, repentance and sanctification? Is there not an inconsistency in professing to wish our Judge already come, when we do not feel ourselves ready for Him? In what sense can we really and heartily pray that He would cut short the time, when our conscience tells us that, even were our life longest, we should have much to do in a few years?

I do not deny that there is some difficulty in the question, but surely not more so than there is on every side of us in religious matters. Religion has (as it were) its very life in what are paradoxes and contradictions in the eye of reason. It is a seeming inconsistency how we can pray for Christ's coming, yet wish time to "work out our salvation," and "make our calling and election sure." It was a seeming contradiction, how good men were to desire His first coming, yet be unable to abide it; how the Apostles feared, yet rejoiced after His resurrection. And so it is a paradox how the Christian should in all things be sorrowful yet always rejoicing, and dying yet living, and having nothing yet possessing all things. Such seeming contradictions arise from the want of depth in our minds to master the whole truth. We have not eyes keen enough to follow out the lines of God's providence and will, which meet at length, though at first sight they seem parallel.

I will now try to explain how these opposite duties of fearing yet praying to have the sight of Christ are not necessarily inconsistent with each other. Why we should fear it, is not strange. Surely when a man gets himself steadily to contemplate a state of things beyond this life, he is in the way to be overpowered by the thoughts which throng upon him. How dreadful to the imagination is every scene of that unknown hereafter! This life indeed is full of dangers and pains, but we know what they are like; we do not know what shall be in the world to come. "Lord, whither goest Thou?" said the Apostles; "we know not whither Thou goest." Supposing a man told that he should suddenly be carried off to some unknown globe in the heavens,—this is the kind of trouble in its least fearful shape, which the future presents, when dwelt upon. And still more trying is the peculiar prospect which presents itself of Christ's coming in judgment. What a prospect, to be judged for all our doings by an unerring Judge. Try to trace back the history of your life in memory, and fancy every part of it confessed by you in words, put into words before some intimate friend, how great would be your shame! but how gladly would you in that day resign yourself to a disclosure to a fellow-sinner, how gladly to a disclosure to a world of sinners, compared with the presence of an All-holy, All-seeing Creator with His eyes upon you, "beholding you," as the gospel speaks of Him in the days of His flesh,—and one deed of evil after another told forth, while all your best actions and best qualities fade away and become as discoloured and unsightly as if there were nothing good in them; and you the while uncertain how the decision shall be. I do not presume to say that all this will happen in detail; but this is what is meant by a judgment in the earthly sense of the word, and that awful trial is surely not called a judgment for nothing, but that we may gain some ideas from it. Think of all this, and you will not deny that the thought of standing before Christ is enough to make us tremble. And yet His presence is held out to us by Himself as the greatest of goods; all Christians are bound to pray for it, to pray for its hastening; to pray that we may speedily look on Him whom none can see "without holiness," none but "the pure in heart;"—and now the question is, How can we pray for it with sincerity?

1. Now first, though we could not at all reconcile our feelings about ourselves with the command given us, still it is our duty to obey the latter on faith. If Abraham could lift up his knife to slay his son, we may well so far subdue our fears as to pray for what nevertheless is terrible. Job said, "Though he slay me, yet I will trust in him." Under all circumstances surely, we may calmly resign ourselves into His hands. Can we suppose that He would deceive us? deal unkindly or hardly with us? Can He make use of us, if I may say so, against ourselves? Let us not

so think of the most merciful Lord. Let us do what He bids, and leave the rest to Him. Thus, I say, we might reason with ourselves, if nothing else could be said.

2. But next, I observe, that when we pray for the coming of Christ, we do but pray in the Church's words, that He would "*accomplish the number* of His elect and would hasten His kingdom.*" That is, we do not pray that He would simply cut short the world, but, so to express myself, that He would make time go quicker, and the wheels of His chariot speed on. Before He comes, a certain space must be gone over; all the Saints must be gathered in; and each Saint must be matured. Not a grain must fall to the ground; not an ear of corn must lose its due rain and sunshine. All we pray is, that He would please to crowd all this into a short space of time; that He would "finish the work and cut it short *in righteousness*," and "make a short work upon the earth;" that He would accomplish,—not curtail, but fulfil,— the circle of His Saints, and hasten the age to come without disordering this. Indeed it cannot be otherwise. All God's works are in place and season; they are all complete. As in nature, the structure of its minutest portions is wrought out to perfection, and an insect is as wonderful as Leviathan; so, when in His providence He seems to hurry, He still keeps time, and moves upon the deep harmonies of truth and love. When then we pray that He would come, we pray also that we may be ready; that all things may converge and meet in Him; that He may draw us while He draws near us, and makes us the holier the closer He comes. We pray that we may not fear that which at present we justly do fear; "that when He shall appear, we may have confidence, and not be ashamed before Him at His coming." [3] He can condense into an hour a life of trial. He who frames the worlds in a moment, and creates generations by the breath of His month, and melts, and hardens, and deluges, and dries up the solid rocks in a day, and makes bones to live, grow, and die, and buries them in the earth, and changes them into stone, apart from time and at His mere will, more wondrously can He deal with the world of spirits, who are never subject to the accidents of matter. He can by one keen pang of agony punish the earthly soul, or by one temptation justify it, or by one vision glorify it. Adam fell in a moment; Abraham was justified upon his seizing the knife; Moses lost Canaan for a word; David said, "I have sinned," and was forgiven; Solomon gained wisdom in a dream; Peter made one confession and received the

[3] 1 John ii.28.

keys; our Lord baffled Satan in three sentences; He redeemed us
in the course of a day; He regenerates us by a form of words. We
know not how "fearfully and wonderfully" our souls "are
made." To men in sleep, in drowning, or in excitement, moments are as years. They suddenly become other men, nature or
grace dispensing with time.

3. But again, you say, How can I pray to see Christ, who am
so unclean? You say well that you are unclean. But in what time
do you propose to become otherwise? Do you expect in this life
ever to be clean? Yes, in one sense, by the presence of the Holy
Ghost within you; but that presence we trust you have now. But
if by "clean," you mean free from that infection of nature, the
least drop of which is sufficient to dishonour all your services,
clean you never will be till you have paid the debt of sin, and
lose that body which Adam has begotten. Be sure that the
longer you live, and the holier you become, you will only perceive that misery more clearly. The less of it you have, the more
it will oppress you; its full draught does but confuse and stupify
you; as you come to yourself your misery begins. The more
your soul becomes one with Him who deigns to dwell within it,
the more it sees with His eyes. You dare not pray for His presence now;—would you pray for it had you lived Methuselah's
years? I trow not. You will never be good enough to desire it; no
one in the whole Church prays for it except on conditions implied. To the end of the longest life you are still a beginner.
What Christ asks of you is not sinlessness, but diligence. Had
you lived ten times your present age, ten times more service
would be required of you. Every day you live longer, more will
be required. If He were to come to-day, you would be judged up
to to-day. Did He come to-morrow, you would be judged up to
to-morrow. Were the time put off a year, you would have a year
more to answer for. You cannot elude your destiny, you cannot
get rid of your talent; you are to answer for your opportunities,
whatever they may be, not more nor less. You cannot be profitable to Him even with the longest life; you can show faith and
love in an hour. True it is, if you have turned from Him and
served sin, and in proportion as you have done this, you have a
great work before you,—to undo what you have done. If you
have given years to Satan, you have a double duty, to repent as
well as to work; but even then you may pray without dread; for
in praying for His presence you still are praying, as I have said,
to be ready for it.

4. But once more. You ask, how you can make up your mind
to stand before your Lord and God; I ask in turn, how do you

bring yourself to come before Him now day by day?—for what is this but meeting Him? Consider what it is you mean by praying, and you will see that, at that very time that you are asking for the coming of His kingdom you are anticipating that coming, and accomplishing the thing you fear. When you pray, you come into His presence. Now reflect on yourself, what your feelings are in coming. They are these: you seem to say,—I am in myself nothing but a sinner, a man of unclean lips and earthly heart. I am not worthy to enter into His presence. I am not worthy of the least of all His mercies. I know He is All-holy, yet I come before Him; I place myself under His pure and piercing eyes, which look me through and through, and discern every trace and every notion of evil within me. Why do I do so? First of all, for this reason. To whom should I go? What can I do better? Who is there in the whole world that can help me? Who that will care for me, or pity me, or have any kind thought of me, if I cannot obtain it of Him? I know He is of purer eyes than to behold iniquity; but I know again that He is All-merciful, and that He so sincerely desires my salvation that He has died for me. Therefore, though I am in a great strait, I will rather fall into His hands, than into those of any creature. True it is I could find creatures more like myself, imperfect or sinful; it might seem better to betake myself to some of these who have power with God, and to beseech them to interest themselves for me. But no; somehow I cannot content myself with this;—no, terrible as it is, I had rather go to God alone. I have an instinct within me which leads me to rise and go to my Father, to name the Name of His well-beloved Son, and having named it, to place myself unreservedly in His hands, saying, "If Thou, Lord, wilt be extreme to mark what is done amiss, O Lord, who may abide it? But there is forgiveness with Thee."—This is the feeling in which we come to confess our sins, and to pray to God for pardon and grace day by day; and observe, it is the very feeling in which we must prepare to meet Him when He comes visibly. Why, even children of this world can meet a judicial process and a violent death with firmness. I do not say that we must have aught of their pride or their self-trusting tranquillity. And yet there is a certain composure and dignity which become us who are born of immortal seed, when we come before our Father. If indeed we have habitually lived to the world, then truly it is natural we should attempt to fly from Him whom we have pierced. Then may we well call on the mountains to fall on us, and on the hills to cover us. But if we have lived, however imperfectly, yet habitually, in His fear, if we trust that His Spirit is in us, then we need not be ashamed before Him. We shall then come before Him, as now we come to pray—with profound abasement, with awe, with self-renunciation, still as relying upon the Spirit which He has given us, with our faculties about us, with a collected and determined mind, and with hope. He who cannot pray for Christ's coming, ought not in consistency to pray at all.

I have spoken of coming to God in prayer generally; but if this is awful, much more is coming to Him in the Sacrament of Holy Communion; for this is in very form an anticipation of His coming, a near presence of Him in earnest of it. And a number of men feel it to be so; for, for one reason or another, they never come before Him in that most Holy Ordinance, and so deprive themselves of the highest of blessings here below. Thus their feeling is much the same as theirs would be, who from fear of His coming, did not dare look out for it. They indeed who are in the religious practice of communicating, understand well enough how it is possible to feel afraid and yet to come. Surely it is possible, and the case is the same as regards the future day of Christ. You must tremble, and yet pray for it. We have all of us experienced enough even of this life, to know that the same seasons are often most joyful and also most painful. Instances of this must suggest themselves to all men. Consider the loss of friends, and say whether joy and grief, triumph and humiliation, are not strangely mingled, yet both really preserved. The joy does not change the grief nor the grief the joy, into some third feeling; they are incommunicable with each other, both remain, both affect us. Or consider the mingled feelings with which a son obtains forgiveness of a father,—the soothing thought that all displeasure is at an end, the veneration, the love, and all the undescribable emotions, most pleasurable, which cannot be put into words,—yet his bitterness against himself. Such is the temper in which we desire to come to the Lord's table; such in which we must pray for His coming; such in which His elect will stand before Him when He comes.

5. Lastly, let me say more distinctly what I have already alluded to, that in that solemn hour we shall have, if we be His, the inward support of His Spirit too, carrying us on towards Him, and "witnessing with our spirits that we are the children of God." God is mysteriously threefold; and while He remains in the highest heaven, He comes to judge the world;—and while He judges the world, He is in us also, bearing us up and going forth in us to meet Himself. God the Son is without, but God the Spirit is within,—and when the Son asks, the Spirit

will answer. That Spirit is vouchsafed to us here; and if we yield ourselves to His gracious influences, so that He draws up our thoughts and wills to heavenly things, and becomes one with us, He will assuredly be still in us and give us confidence at the Day of Judgment. He will be with us, and strengthen us; and how great His strength is, what mind of man can conceive? Gifted with that supernatural strength, we may be able to lift up our eyes to our Judge when He looks on us, and look on Him in turn, though with deep awe, yet without confusion of face, as if in the consciousness of innocence.

That hour must come at length upon every one of us. When it comes, may the countenance of the Most Holy quicken, not consume us; may the flame of judgment be to us only what it was to the Three Holy Children, over whom the fire had no power!

EQUANIMITY

(Christmas)

"Rejoice in the Lord alway, and again I say, Rejoice."—Phil. iv.4.

IN other parts of Scripture the prospect of Christ's coming is made a reason for solemn fear and awe and a call for watching and prayer, but in the verses connected with the text a distinct view of the Christian character is set before us, and distinct duties urged on us. "The Lord is at hand," and what then?—why, if so, we must "rejoice in the Lord" we must be conspicuous for "moderation;" we must be "careful for nothing;" we must seek from God's bounty, and not from man, whatever we need; we must abound in "thanksgiving;" and we must cherish, or rather we must pray for, and we shall receive from above, "the peace of God which passeth all understanding," to "keep our hearts and minds through Christ Jesus."

Now this is a view of the Christian character definite and complete enough to admit of commenting on,—and it may be useful to show that the thought of Christ's coming not only leads to fear, but to a calm and cheerful frame of mind.

Nothing perhaps is more remarkable than that an Apostle,—a man of toil and blood, a man combating with powers unseen, and a spectacle for men and Angels, and much more that St. Paul, a man whose natural temper was so zealous, so severe, and so vehement,—I say, nothing is more striking and significant than that St. Paul should have given us this view of what a Christian should be. It would be nothing wonderful, it *is* nothing wonderful, that writers in a day like this should speak of peace, quiet, sobriety, and cheerfulness, as being the tone of mind that becomes a Christian; but considering that St. Paul was by birth a Jew, and by education a Pharisee, that he wrote at a time when, if at any time, Christians were in lively and incessant agitation of mind; when persecution and rumours of persecution abounded; when all things seemed in commotion around them; when there was nothing fixed; when there were no churches to soothe them, no course of worship to sober them, no homes to refresh them; and, again, considering that the Gospel is full of high and noble, and what may be called even romantic, principles and motives, and deep mysteries;—and, further, considering the very topic which the Apostle combines with his admonitions is that awful subject, the coming of Christ;—it is well worthy of notice, that, in such a time, under such a covenant, and with such a prospect, he should draw a picture of the Christian character as free from excitement and effort, as full of repose, as still and as equable, as if the great Apostle wrote in some monastery of the desert or some country parsonage. Here surely is the finger of God; here is the evidence of supernatural influences, making the mind of man independent of circumstances! This is the thought that first suggests itself; and the second is this, how deep and refined is the true Christian spirit!—how difficult to enter into, how vast to embrace, how impossible to exhaust! Who would expect such composure and equanimity from the fervent Apostle of the Gentiles? We know St. Paul could do great things; could suffer and achieve, could preach and confess, could be high and could be low: but we might have thought that all this was the limit and the perfection of the Christian temper, as he viewed it; and that no room was left him for the feelings which the text and following verses lead us to ascribe to him.

And yet he who "laboured more abundantly than all" his brethren, is also a pattern of simplicity, meekness, cheerfulness, thankfulness, and serenity of mind. These tempers were especially characteristic of St. Paul, and are much insisted on in his Epistles. For instance.—"Mind not high things, but condescend to men of low estate. Be not wise in your own conceits. . . . Provide things honest in the sight of all men. If it be possible, as much as lieth in you, live peaceably with all men." He enjoins, that "the aged men be sober, grave, temperate, sound in faith, in charity, in patience." "The aged women likewise . . . not false accusers, not given to much wine, teachers of good things, that they may teach the young women to be sober, to love their husbands, to love their children, to be discreet, chaste, keepers at home, good, obedient to their own husbands." And "young men" to be "sober-minded." And it is remarkable that he ends this exhortation with urging the same reason as is given in the verse after the text: "looking for that blessed hope, and the glorious appearing of our great God and Saviour Jesus Christ." In like manner, he says, that Christ's ministers must show "uncorruptness in doctrine, gravity, sincerity, sound speech that cannot be condemned;" that they must be "blameless, not self-willed, not soon angry . . . . lovers of good men, sober, just, holy, temperate."[1] All this is the description of what seems almost an ordinary character; I mean, it is so staid, so quiet, so unambitious, so homely. It displays so little of what is striking or extraordinary. It is so negligent of this world, so unexcited, so singleminded.

It is observable, too, that it was foretold as the peculiarity of Gospel times by the Prophet Isaiah: "The work of righteousness shall be peace; and the effect of righteousness, quietness and assurance for ever. And My people shall dwell in a peaceable habitation, and in sure dwellings, and in quiet resting-places."[2]

Now then let us consider more particularly what is this state of mind, and what the grounds of it. These seem to be as follows:—The Lord is at hand; this is not your rest; this is not your abiding-place. Act then as persons who are in a dwelling not their own; who are not in their own home; who have not their own goods and furniture about them; who, accordingly, make shift and put up with anything that comes to hand, and do not make a point of things being the best of their kind. "But this I say, brethren, the time is short." What matters it what we eat, what we drink, how we are clothed, where we lodge, what is thought of us, what becomes of us, since we are not at home? It is felt every day, even as regards this world, that when we leave home for a while we are unsettled. This, then, is the kind of feeling which a belief in Christ's coming will create within us. It is not worth while establishing ourselves here; it is not worth while spending time and thought on such an object. We shall hardly have got settled when we shall have to move.

This being apparently the general drift of the passage, let us next enter into the particular portions of it.

1. "Be careful for nothing," he says, or, as St. Peter, "casting all your care upon Him," or, as He Himself, "Take no thought" or care "for the morrow, for the morrow will take thought for the things of itself."[3] This of course is the state of mind which is directly consequent on the belief, that "the Lord is at hand." Who would care for any loss or gain to-day, if he knew for certain that Christ would show Himself to-morrow? no one. Well, then, the true Christian feels as he would feel, did he know for certain that Christ would be here to-morrow. For he knows for certain, that at least Christ will come to him when he dies; and

---

[1] Rom. xii.16–18; Titus ii.2–13; i.7, 8.
[2] Is. xxxii.17, 18.   [3] 1 Pet. v.7; Matt. vi.34.

faith anticipates his death, and makes it just as if that distant day, if it *be* distant, were past and over. One time or another Christ will come, for certain: and when He once *has* come, it matters not what length of time there was before He came;—however long that period may be, it has an end. Judgment is coming, whether it comes sooner or later, and the Christian realizes that it is coming; that is, time does not enter into his calculation, or interfere with his view of things. When men expect to carry out their plans and projects, then they care for them; when they know these will come to nought, they give them over, or become indifferent to them.

So, again, it is with all forebodings, anxieties, mortifications, griefs, resentments of this world. "The time is short." It has sometimes been well suggested, as a mode of calming the mind when set upon an object, or much vexed or angered at some occurrence, what will you feel about all this a year hence? It is very plain that matters which agitate us most extremely now, will then interest us not at all; that objects about which we have intense hope and fear now, will then be to us nothing more than things which happen at the other end of the earth. So will it be with all human hopes, fears, pleasures, pains, jealousies, disappointments, successes, when the last day is come. They will have no life in them; they will be as the faded flowers of a banquet, which do but mock us. Or when we lie on the bed of death, what will it avail us to have been rich, or great, or fortunate, or honoured, or influential? All things will then be vanity. Well, what this world will be understood by all to be then, such is it felt to be by the Christian now. He looks at things as he then will look at them, with an uninterested and dispassionate eye, and is neither pained much nor pleased much at the accidents of life, because they are accidents.

2. Another part of the character under review is, what our translation calls moderation; "Let your moderation be known unto all men," or, as it may be more exactly rendered, your consideration, fairness, or equitableness. St. Paul makes it a part of a Christian character to have a reputation for candour, dispassionateness, tenderness towards others. The truth is, as soon and in proportion as a person believes that Christ is coming, and recognises his own position as a stranger on earth, who has but hired a lodging in it for a season, he will feel indifferent to the course of human affairs. He will be able to look on, instead of taking a part in them. They will be nothing to him. He will be able to criticise them, and pass judgment on them without partiality. This is what is meant by "our moderation" being

acknowledged by all men. Those who have strong interests one way or the other, cannot be dispassionate observers and candid judges. They are partisans; they defend one set of people, and attack another. They are prejudiced against those who differ from them, or who thwart them. They cannot make allowances, or show sympathy for them. But the Christian has no keen expectations, no acute mortifications. He is fair, equitable, considerate towards all men, because he has no temptation to be otherwise. He has no violence, no animosity, no bigotry, no party feeling. He knows that his Lord and Saviour must triumph; he knows that He will one day come from heaven, no one can say how soon. Knowing then the end to which all things tend, he cares less for the road which is to lead to it. When we read a book of fiction, we are much excited with the course of the narrative, till we know how things will turn out; but when we do, the interest ceases. So is it with the Christian. He knows Christ's battle will last till the end; that Christ's cause will triumph in the end; that His Church will last till He comes. He knows what is truth and what is error, where is safety and where is danger; and all this clear knowledge enables him to make concessions, to own difficulties, to do justice to the erring, to acknowledge their good points, to be content with such countenance, greater or less, as he himself receives from others. He does not fear; fear it is that makes men bigots, tyrants, and zealots; but for the Christian, it is his privilege, as he is beyond hopes and fears, suspense and jealousy, so also to be patient, cool, discriminating, and impartial;—so much so, that this very fairness marks his character in the eyes of the world, is "known unto all men."

3. Joy and gladness are also characteristics of him, according to the exhortation in the text, "Rejoice in the Lord alway," and this in spite of the fear and awe which the thought of the Last Day ought to produce in him. It is by means of these strong contrasts that Scripture brings out to us what is the real meaning of its separate portions. If we had been told merely to fear, we should have mistaken a slavish dread, or the gloom of despair, for godly fear; and if we had been told merely to rejoice, we should perhaps have mistaken a rude freedom and familiarity for joy; but when we are told both to fear and to rejoice, we gain thus much at first sight, that our joy is not to be irreverent, nor our fear to be desponding; that though both feelings are to remain, neither is to be what it would be by itself. This is what we gain at once by such contrasts. I do not say that this makes it at all easier to combine the separate duties to which they relate;

that is a further and higher work; but thus much we gain at once, a better knowledge of these separate duties themselves. And now I am speaking about the duty of rejoicing, and I say, that whatever be the duty of fearing greatly and trembling greatly at the thought of the Day of Judgment, and of course it is a great duty, yet the command so to do cannot reverse the command to rejoice; it can only so far interfere with it as to explain what is meant by rejoicing. It is as clear a duty to rejoice in the prospect of Christ's coming, as if we were not told to fear it. The duty of fearing does but perfect our joy; that joy alone is true Christian joy, which is informed and quickened by fear, and made thereby sober and reverent.

How joy and fear can be reconciled, words cannot show. Act and deed alone can show how. Let a man try both to fear and to rejoice, as Christ and His Apostles tell him, and in time he will learn how; but when he has learned, he will be as little able to explain how it is he does both, as he was before. He will seem inconsistent, and may easily be proved to be so, to the satisfaction of irreligious men, as Scripture is called inconsistent. He becomes the paradox which Scripture enjoins. This is variously fulfilled in the case of men of advanced holiness. They are accused of the most opposite faults; of being proud, and of being mean; of being over-simple, and being crafty; of having too strict, and, at the same time, too lax a conscience; of being unsocial, and yet being worldly; of being too literal in explaining Scripture, and yet of adding to Scripture, and superseding Scripture. Men of the world, or men of inferior religiousness, cannot understand them, and are fond of criticising those who, in seeming to be inconsistent, are but like Scripture teaching.

But to return to the case of joy and fear. It may be objected, that at least those who fall into sin, or who have in times past sinned grievously, cannot have this pleasant and cheerful temper which St. Paul enjoins. I grant it. But what is this but saying that St. Paul enjoins us *not* to fall into sin? When St. Paul warns us against sadness and heaviness, of course he warns us against those things which make men sad and heavy; and therefore especially against sin, which is an especial enemy of joyfulness. It is not that sorrowing for sin is wrong when we *have* sinned, but the *sinning* is wrong which causes the sorrowing. When a person has sinned, he cannot do anything better than sorrow. He ought to sorrow; and so far as he does sorrow, he is certainly *not* in the perfect Christian state; but it is his sin that has forfeited it. And yet even here sorrow is not inconsistent with rejoicing. For there are few men, who are really in earnest in their sorrow, but after a time may be conscious that they are so; and, when man knows himself to be in earnest, he knows that God looks mercifully upon him; and this gives him sufficient reason for rejoicing, even though fear remains. St. Peter could appeal to Christ, "Lord, Thou knowest all things; Thou knowest that I love Thee." We of course cannot appeal so unreservedly—still we can timidly appeal—we can say that we humbly trust that, whatever be the measure of our past sins, and whatever of our present self-denial, yet at bottom we do wish and strive to give up the world and to follow Christ; and in proportion as this sense of sincerity is strong upon our minds, in the same degree shall we rejoice in the Lord, even while we fear.

4. Once more, peace is part of this same temper also. "The peace of God," says the Apostle, "which passeth all understanding, shall keep your hearts and minds through Christ Jesus." There are many things in the Gospel to alarm us, many to agitate us, many to transport us, but the end and issue of all these is *peace*. "Glory to God in the highest, and on earth peace." It may be asked indeed whether warfare, perplexity, and uncertainty be not the condition of the Christian here below; whether St. Paul himself does not say that he has "the care," or the anxiety, "of all the Churches," and whether he does not plainly evince and avow in his Epistles to the Galatians and Corinthians much distress of mind? "Without were fightings, within fears." [4] I grant it; he certainly shows at times much agitation of mind; but consider this. Did you ever look at an expanse of water, and observe the ripples on the surface? Do you think that disturbance penetrates below it? Nay; you have seen or heard of fearful tempests on the sea; scenes of horror and distress, which are in no respect a fit type of an Apostle's tears or sighings about his flock. Yet even these violent commotions do not reach into the depths. The foundations of the ocean, the vast realms of water which girdle the earth, are as tranquil and as silent in the storm as in a calm. So is it with the souls of holy men. They have a well of peace springing up within them unfathomable; and though the accidents of the hour may make them seem agitated, yet in their hearts they are not so. Even Angels joy over sinners repentant, and, as we may therefore suppose, grieve over sinners impenitent,—yet who shall say that they have not perfect peace? Even Almighty God Himself deigns to speak of His being grieved, and angry, and rejoicing,—yet is He not the unchangeable? And in like manner, to

[4] 2 Cor. vii.5.

compare human things with divine, St. Paul had perfect peace, as being stayed in soul on God, though the trials of life might vex him.

For, as I have said, the Christian has a deep, silent, hidden peace, which the world sees not,—like some well in a retired and shady place, difficult of access. He is the greater part of his time by himself and when he is in solitude, that is his real state. What he is when left to himself and to his God, that is his true life. He can bear himself; he can (as it were) joy in himself; for it is the grace of God within him, it is the presence of the Eternal Comforter, in which he joys. He can bear, he finds it pleasant, to be with himself at all times,—"never less alone than when alone." He can lay his head on his pillow at night, and own in God's sight, with overflowing heart, that he wants nothing,—that he "is full and abounds,"—that God has been all things to him, and that nothing is not his which God could give him. More thankfulness, more holiness, more of heaven he needs indeed, but the thought that he can have more is not a thought of trouble, but of joy. It does not interfere with his peace to know that he may grow nearer God. Such is the Christian's peace, when, with a single heart and the Cross in his eye, he addresses and commends himself to Him with whom the night is as clear as the day. St. Paul says that "the peace of God shall *keep* our hearts and minds." By "keep" is meant "guard," or "garrison," our hearts; so as to keep out enemies. And he says, our "hearts and minds" in contrast to what the world sees of us. Many hard things may be said of the Christian, and done against him, but he has a secret preservative or charm, and minds them not.

These are some few suggestions on that character of mind which becomes the followers of Him who was once "born of a pure Virgin," and who bids them as "new-born babes desire the sincere milk of the Word, that they may grow thereby." The Christian is cheerful, easy, kind, gentle, courteous, candid, unassuming; has no pretence, no affectation, no ambition, no singularity; because he has neither hope nor fear about this world. He is serious, sober, discreet, grave, moderate, mild, with so little that is unusual or striking in his bearing, that he may easily be taken at first sight for an ordinary man. There are persons who think religion consists in ecstasies, or in set speeches;—he is not of those. And it must be confessed, on the other hand, that there is a common-place state of mind which does show itself calm, composed, and candid, yet is very far from the true

Christian temper. In this day especially it is very easy for men to be benevolent, liberal, and dispassionate. It costs nothing to be dispassionate when you feel nothing, to be cheerful when you have nothing to fear, to be generous or liberal when what you give is not your own, and to be benevolent and considerate when you have no principles and no opinions. Men nowadays are moderate and equitable, not because the Lord is at hand, but because they do not feel that He is coming. Quietness is a grace, not in itself, only when it is grafted on the stem of faith, zeal, self-abasement, and diligence.

May it be our blessedness, as years go on, to add one grace to another, and advance upward, step by step, neither neglecting the lower after attaining the higher, nor aiming at the higher before attaining the lower. The first grace is faith, the last is love; first comes zeal, afterwards comes loving-kindness; first comes humiliation, then comes peace; first comes diligence, then comes resignation. May we learn to mature all graces in us;—fearing and trembling, watching and repenting, because Christ is coming; joyful, thankful, and careless of the future, because He is come.

REMEMBRANCE OF PAST MERCIES

(Christmas)

"I am not worthy of the least of all the mercies, and of all the truth, which Thou hast showed unto Thy servant."—Gen. xxxii.10.

THE spirit of humble thankfulness for past mercies which these words imply, is a grace to which we are especially called in the Gospel. Jacob, who spoke them, knew not of those great and wonderful acts of love with which God has since visited the race of man. But though he might not know the depths of God's counsels, he knew himself so far as to know that he was worthy of no good thing at all, and he knew also that Almighty God had shown him great mercies and great truth: mercies, in that He had done for him good things, whereas he had deserved evil; and truth, in that He had made him promises, and had been faithful to them. In consequence, he overflowed with gratitude when he looked back upon the past; marvelling at the contrast between what he was in himself and what God had been to him.

Such thankfulness, I say, is eminently a Christian grace, and is enjoined on us in the New Testament. For instance, we are exhorted to be "thankful," and to let "the Word of Christ dwell in us richly in all wisdom; teaching and admonishing one another in psalms and hymns and spiritual songs, singing with grace in our hearts to the Lord."

Elsewhere, we are told to "speak to ourselves in psalms and hymns and spiritual songs, singing and making melody in our heart to the Lord: giving thanks always for all things unto God and the Father, in the Name of our Lord Jesus Christ."

Again: "Be careful for nothing: but in every thing by prayer and supplication, with thanksgiving, let your requests be made known unto God."

Again: "In every thing give thanks: for this is the will of God in Christ Jesus concerning you." [1]

---

[1] Col. iii.15, 16; Eph. v.19, 20; Phil. iv.6; 1 Thess. v.18.

The Apostle, who writes all this, was himself an especial pattern of a thankful spirit: "Rejoice in the Lord alway," he says: "and again I say, Rejoice." "I have learned, in whatsoever state I am, therewith to be content. I have all and abound; I am full." Again: "I thank Christ Jesus our Lord, who hath enabled me, for that He counted me faithful, putting me into the ministry; who was before a blasphemer and a persecutor, and injurious. But I obtained mercy, because I did it ignorantly in unbelief. And the grace of our Lord was exceeding abundant, with faith and love which is in Christ Jesus." [2] O great Apostle! how could it be otherwise, considering what he had been and what he was,—transformed from an enemy to a friend, from a blind Pharisee to an inspired preacher? And yet there is another Saint, besides the patriarch Jacob, who is his fellow in this excellent grace,—like them, distinguished by great vicissitudes of life, and by the adoring love and the tenderness of heart with which he looked back upon the past:—I mean, "David, the son of Jesse, the man who was raised up on high, the anointed of the God of Jacob, and the sweet Psalmist of Israel." [3]

The Book of Psalms is full of instances of David's thankful spirit, which I need not cite here, as we are all so well acquainted with them. I will but refer to his thanksgiving, when he set apart the precious materials for the building of the Temple, as it occurs at the end of the First Book of Chronicles; when he rejoiced so greatly, because he and his people had the heart to offer freely to God, and thanked God for his very thankfulness. "David, the king . . rejoiced with great joy; wherefore David blessed the Lord before all the congregation; and David said, Blessed be Thou, Lord God of Israel, our Father, for ever and ever. . . Both riches and honour come of Thee, and Thou reignest over all; and in Thine hand is power and might, and in Thine hand it is to make great, and to give strength unto all. Now, therefore, our God, we thank Thee, and praise Thy glorious Name. But who am I, and what is my people, that we should be able to offer so willingly after this sort? for all things come of Thee, and of Thine own have we given Thee." [4]

Such was the thankful spirit of David, looking back upon the past, wondering and rejoicing at the way in which his Almighty Protector had led him on, and at the works He had enabled him to do; and praising and glorifying Him for His mercy and truth.

[2] Phil. iv.4, 11, 18; 1 Tim. i.12–14.
[3] 2 Sam. xxiii.1.   [4] 1 Chron. xxix.9–14.

David, then, Jacob, and St. Paul, may be considered the three great patterns of thankfulness, which are set before us in Scripture;—saints, all of whom were peculiarly the creation of God's grace, and whose very life and breath it was humbly and adoringly to meditate upon the contrast between what, in different ways, they had been, and what they were. A perishing wanderer had unexpectedly become a patriarch; a shepherd, a king; and a persecutor, an apostle: each had been chosen, at God's inscrutable pleasure, to fulfil a great purpose, and each, while he did his utmost to fulfil it, kept praising God that he was made His instrument. Of the first, it was said, "Jacob have I loved, but Esau have I hated;" of the second, that "He refused the tabernacle of Joseph, and chose not the tribe of Ephraim, but chose the tribe of Judah, even the hill of Sion, which He loved: He chose David also His servant, and took him away from the sheepfolds." And St. Paul says of himself, "Last of all, He was seen of me also, as of one born out of due time." [5]

These thoughts naturally come over the mind at this season, when we are engaged in celebrating God's grace in making us His children, by the incarnation of His Only-begotten Son, the greatest and most wonderful of all His mercies. And to the Patriarch Jacob our minds are now particularly turned, by the First Lessons for this day,[6] taken from the Prophet Isaiah, in which the Church is addressed and comforted under the name of Jacob. Let us then, in this season of thankfulness, and at the beginning of a new year, take a brief view of the character of this Patriarch; and though David and Isaiah be the prophets of grace, and St. Paul its special herald and chief pattern, yet, if we wish to see an actual specimen of a habit of thankfulness occupied in the remembrance of God's mercies, I think we shall not be wrong in betaking ourselves to Jacob.

Jacob's distinguishing grace then, as I think it may be called, was a habit of affectionate musing upon God's providences towards him in times past, and of overflowing thankfulness for them. Not that he had not other graces also, but this seems to have been his distinguishing grace. All good men have in their measure all graces; for He, by whom they have any, does not give one apart from the whole: He gives the root, and the root puts forth branches. But since time, and circumstances, and their own use of the gift, and their own disposition and character, have much influence on the mode of its manifestation, so it

[5] Rom. ix.13; Ps. lxxviii.68–71; 1 Cor.xv.8.
[6] Second Sunday after Christmas.

happens, that each good man has his own distinguishing grace, apart from the rest, his own particular line and fragrance and fashion, as a flower may have. As, then, there are numberless flowers on the earth, all of them flowers, and so far like each other; and all springing from the same earth, and nourished by the same air and dew, and none without beauty; and yet some are more beautiful than others; and of those which are beautiful, some excel in colour, and others in sweetness, and others in form; and then, again, those which are sweet have such perfect sweetness, yet so distinct, that we do not know how to compare them together, or to say which is the sweeter: so is it with souls filled and nurtured by God's secret grace. Abraham, for instance, Jacob's forefather, was the pattern of faith. This is insisted on in Scripture, and it is not here necessary to show that he was so. It will be sufficient to say, that he left his country at God's word; and, at the same word, took up the knife to slay his own son. Abraham seems to have had something very noble and magnanimous about him. He could realize and make present to him things unseen. He followed God in the dark as promptly, as firmly, with as cheerful a heart, and bold a stepping, as if he were in broad daylight. There is something very great in this; and, therefore, St. Paul calls Abraham *our* father, the father of Christians as well as of Jews. For we are especially bound to walk by faith, not by sight; and are blessed in faith, and justified by faith, as was faithful Abraham. Now (if I may say it, with due reverence to the memory of that favoured servant of God, in whose praise I am now speaking) that faith in which Abraham excelled was not Jacob's characteristic excellence. Not that he had not faith, and great faith, else he would not have been so dear to God. His buying the birthright and gaining the blessing from Esau were proofs of faith. Esau saw nothing or little precious in them,—he was profane; easily parted with the one, and had no high ideas of the other. However, Jacob's faith, earnest and vigorous as it was, was not like Abraham's. Abraham kept his affections loose from everything earthly, and was ready, at God's word, to slay his only son. Jacob had many sons, and may we not even say that he indulged them overmuch? Even as regards Joseph, whom he so deservedly loved, beautiful and touching as his love of him is, yet there is a great contrast between his feelings towards the "son of his old age" and those of Abraham towards Isaac, the unexpected offspring of his hundredth year,—nor only such, but his long-promised only son, with whom were the promises. Again: Abraham left his country,—so did Jacob; but Abraham, at God's word,—Jacob, from necessity on the threat of Esau. Abraham, from the first, felt that God was his portion and his inheritance, and, in a great and generous spirit, he freely gave up all he had, being sure that he should find what was more excellent in doing so. But Jacob, in spite of his really living by faith, wished (if we may so say), as one passage of his history shows, to see before he fully believed. When he was escaping from Esau and came to Bethel, and God appeared to him in a dream and gave him promises, but not yet the performance of them,—what did he do? Did he simply accept them? He says, "*If* God will be with me, and will keep me in this way that I go, and will give me bread to eat, and raiment to put on, so that I come again to my father's house in peace, *then* shall the Lord be my God."[7] He makes his obedience, in some sense, depend on a condition; and although we must not, and need not, take the words as if he meant that he would not serve God *till* and *unless* He did for him what He had promised, yet they seem to show a fear and anxiety, gentle indeed, and subdued, and very human (and therefore the more interesting and winning in the eyes of us common men, who read his words), yet an anxiety which Abraham had not. We feel Jacob to be more like ourselves than Abraham was.

What, then, was Jacob's distinguishing grace, as faith was Abraham's? I have already said it: I suppose, thankfulness. Abraham appears ever to have been looking forward in *hope*,— Jacob looking back in *memory*: the one rejoicing in the future, the other in the past; the one setting his affections on the future, the other on the past; the one making his way towards the promises, the other musing over their fulfilment. Not that Abraham did not look back also, and Jacob, as he says on his death-bed, did not "wait for the salvation" of God; but this was the difference between them, Abraham was a hero, Jacob "a plain man, dwelling in tents."

Jacob seems to have had a gentle, tender, affectionate, timid mind—easily frightened, easily agitated, loving God so much that he feared to lose Him, and, like St. Thomas perhaps, anxious for sight and possession from earnest and longing desire of them. Were it not for faith, love would become impatient, and thus Jacob desired to possess, not from cold incredulity or hardness of heart, but from such a loving impatience. Such men are easily downcast, and must be treated kindly; they soon despond, they shrink from the world, for they feel its rudeness, which bolder natures do not. Neither Abraham nor Jacob loved

---

[7] Gen. xxviii.20, 21.

the world. But Abraham did not fear, did not feel it. Jacob felt and winced, as being wounded by it. You recollect his touching complaints, "All these things are against me!"—"Then shall ye bring down my grey hairs with sorrow to the grave."—"If I am bereaved of my children, I am bereaved." Again, elsewhere we are told, "All his sons and all his daughters rose up to comfort him, but he refused to be comforted." At another time, "Jacob's heart fainted, for he believed them not." Again, "The spirit of Jacob their father revived."[8] You see what a child-like, sensitive, sweet mind he had. Accordingly, as I have said, his happiness lay, not in looking forward to the hope, but backwards upon the experience, of God's mercies towards him. He delighted lovingly to trace, and gratefully to acknowledge, what had been given, leaving the future to itself.

For instance, when coming to meet Esau, he brings before God in prayer, in words of which the text is part, what He had already done for him, recounting His past favours with great and humble joy in the midst of his present anxiety. "O God of my father Abraham," he says, "and God of my father Isaac, the Lord which saidst unto me, Return unto thy country, and to thy kindred, and I will deal well with thee: I am not worthy of the least of all the mercies, and of all the truth, *which Thou hast showed unto Thy servant; for with my staff I passed over this Jordan, and now I am become two bands.*" Again, after he had returned to his own land, he proceeded to fulfil the promise he had made to consecrate Bethel as a house of God, "Let us arise, and go up to Bethel; and I will make there an altar unto God, *who answered me in the day of my distress, and was with me in the way which I went.*" Again, to Pharaoh, still dwelling on the past: "The days of the years of my pilgrimage are an hundred and thirty years; few and evil have the days of the years of my life been," he means, in themselves, and as separate from God's favour, "and have not attained unto the days of the years of the life of my fathers, in the days of their pilgrimage." Again, when he was approaching his end, he says to Joseph, "God Almighty *appeared unto me* at Luz," that is, Bethel, "in the land of Canaan, and blessed me." Again, still looking back, "As for me, when I came from Padan, Rachel died by me in the land of Canaan, in the way, when yet there was but a little way to come to Ephrath; and I buried her there in the way of Ephrath." Again, his blessing upon Ephraim and Manasseh: "God, before whom my fathers Abraham and Isaac did walk, *the God which fed me all my life long unto this day*, the

[8] Gen. xlii.36, 38; xliii.14; xxxvii.35; xlv.26, 27.

Angel which redeemed me from all evil, bless the lads." Again he looks back on the land of promise, though in the plentifulness of Egypt: "Behold, I die, but God shall be with you, and bring you again unto the land of your fathers." And when he gives command about his burial, he says: "I am to be gathered unto my people; bury me with my fathers in the cave that is in the field of Ephron the Hittite." He gives orders to be buried with his fathers; this was natural, but observe, he goes on to *enlarge* on the subject, after his special manner: "There they buried Abraham and Sarah his wife; there they buried Isaac and Rebekah his wife; and *there I buried Leah.*" And further on, when he speaks of waiting for God's salvation, which is an act of hope, he so words it as at the same time to dwell upon the past: "I *have* waited," he says, that is, all my life long, "I have waited for Thy salvation, O Lord."[9] Such was Jacob, living in memory rather than in hope, counting times, recording seasons, keeping days; having his history by heart, and his past life in his hand; and as if to carry on his mind into that of his descendants, it was enjoined upon them, that once a year every Israelite should appear before God with a basket of fruit of the earth, and call to mind what God had done for him and his father Jacob, and express his thankfulness for it. "A Syrian ready to perish was my father," he had to say, meaning Jacob; "and he went down into Egypt, and sojourned there, and became a nation, great, mighty, and populous. . . . . And the Lord brought us forth out of Egypt with an outstretched arm, and with great terribleness, and with signs, and with wonders; and hath brought us into this land . . . . that floweth with milk and honey. And now, behold, I have brought the first-fruits of the land, which Thou, O Lord, hast given me."[10]

Well were it for us, if we had the character of mind instanced in Jacob, and enjoined on his descendants; the temper of dependence upon God's providence, and thankfulness under it, and careful memory of all He has done for us. It would be well if we were in the habit of looking at all we have as God's gift, undeservedly given, and day by day continued to us solely by His mercy. He gave; He may take away. He gave us all we have, life, health, strength, reason, enjoyment, the light of conscience; whatever we have good and holy within us; whatever faith we have; whatever of a renewed will; whatever love to-

[9] Gen. xxxii.9, 10; xxxv.3; xlvii.9; xlviii.3, 7, 15, 16, 21; xlix.29–31, 18.
[10] Deut. xxvi.5–10.

wards Him; whatever power over ourselves; whatever prospect of heaven. He gave us relatives, friends, education, training, knowledge, the Bible, the Church. All comes from Him. He gave; He may take away. Did He take away, we should be called on to follow Job's pattern, and be resigned: "The Lord gave, and the Lord hath taken away. Blessed be the Name of the Lord." [11] While He continues His blessings, we should follow David and Jacob, by living in constant praise and thanksgiving, and in offering up to Him of His own.

We are not our own, any more than what we possess is our own. We did not make ourselves; we cannot be supreme over ourselves. We cannot be our own masters. We are God's property by creation, by redemption, by regeneration. He has a triple claim upon us. Is it not our happiness thus to view the matter? Is it any happiness, or any comfort, to consider that we *are* our own? It may be thought so by the young and prosperous. These may think it a great thing to have everything, as they suppose, their own way,—to depend on no one,—to have to think of nothing out of sight,—to be without the irksomeness of continual acknowledgment, continual prayer, continual reference of what they do to the will of another. But as time goes on, they, as all men, will find that independence was not made for man—that it is an unnatural state—may do for a while, but will not carry us on safely to the end. No, we are creatures; and, as being such, we have two duties, to be resigned and to be thankful.

Let us then view God's providences towards us more religiously than we have hitherto done. Let us try to gain a truer view of what we are, and where we are, in His kingdom. Let us humbly and reverently attempt to trace His guiding hand in the years which we have hitherto lived. Let us thankfully commemorate the many mercies He has vouchsafed to us in time past, the many sins He has not remembered, the many dangers He has averted, the many prayers He has answered, the many mistakes He has corrected, the many warnings, the many lessons, the much light, the abounding comfort which He has from time to time given. Let us dwell upon times and seasons, times of trouble, times of joy, times of trial, times of refreshment. How did He cherish us as children! How did He guide us in that dangerous time when the mind began to think for itself, and the heart to open to the world! How did He with His sweet discipline restrain our passions, mortify our hopes, calm our

[11] Job i.21.

fears, enliven our heavinesses, sweeten our desolateness, and strengthen our infirmities! How did He gently guide us towards the strait gate! how did He allure us along His everlasting way, in spite of its strictness, in spite of its loneliness, in spite of the dim twilight in which it lay! He has been all things to us. He has been, as He was to Abraham, Isaac, and Jacob, our God, our shield, and great reward, promising and performing, day by day. "Hitherto hath He helped us." "He hath been mindful of us, and He will bless us." He has not made us for nought; He has brought us thus far, in order to bring us further, in order to bring us on to the end. He will never leave us nor forsake us; so that we may boldly say, "The Lord is my Helper; I will not fear what flesh can do unto me." We may "cast all our care upon Him, who careth for us." What is it to us how our future path lies, if it be but His path? What is it to us whither it leads us, so that in the end it leads to Him? What is it to us what He puts upon us, so that He enables us to undergo it with a pure conscience, a true heart, not desiring anything of this world in comparison of Him? What is it to us what terror befalls us, if He be but at hand to protect and strengthen us? "Thou, Israel," He says, "art My servant Jacob, whom I have chosen, the seed of Abraham My friend." "Fear not, thou worm Jacob, and ye men of Israel; I will help thee, saith the Lord, and thy Redeemer, the Holy One of Israel." "Thus saith the Lord that created thee, O Jacob, and He that formed thee, O Israel, Fear not; for I have redeemed thee, I have called thee by thy name; thou art Mine. When thou passest through the waters, I will be with thee; and through the rivers, they shall not overflow thee; when thou walkest through the fire, thou shalt not be burned; neither shall the flame kindle upon thee. For I am the Lord thy God, the Holy One of Israel, thy Saviour." [12]

---

[12] Is. xli.8, 14; xliii.1–3.

THE MYSTERY OF GODLINESS

(Christmas)

*"Both He that sanctifieth and they who are sanctified are all of one:
for which cause He is not ashamed to call them brethren."*
—Heb. ii.11.

OUR Saviour's birth in the flesh is an earnest, and, as it were,
beginning of our birth in the Spirit. It is a figure, promise, or pledge of our new birth, and it effects what it promises.
As He was born, so are we born also; and since He was born,
therefore we too are born. As He is the Son of God by nature, so
are we sons of God by grace; and it is He who has made us such.
This is what the text says; He is the "Sanctifier," we the
"sanctified." Moreover, He and we, says the text, "are all of
one." God sanctifies the Angels, but there the Creator and the
creature are not of one. But the Son of God and we are of one;
He has become "the firstborn of every creature;" He has taken
our nature, and in and through it He sanctifies us. He is our
brother by virtue of His incarnation, and, as the text says, "He
is not ashamed to call us brethren;" and, having sanctified our
nature in Himself, He communicates it to us.

1. This is the wonderful economy of grace, or mystery of
godliness, which should be before our minds at all times, but
especially at this season, when the Most Holy took upon Him
our flesh of "a pure Virgin," "by the operation of the Holy
Ghost, without spot of sin, to make us clean from all sin." God
"dwelleth in the Light which no man can approach unto;" He
"is Light, and in Him is no darkness at all." "His garment," as
described in the Prophet's Vision, is "white as snow, and the
hair of His head like the pure wool; His throne the fiery flame,
and His wheels burning fire." And in like manner the Son of
God, because He is the Son, is light also. He is "the True Light,
which lighteth every man that cometh into the world." On His
transfiguration "His face did shine as the sun," and "His raiment became shining, exceeding white as snow," "white and
glistering." And when He appeared to St. John, "His head and

His hairs were white like wool, as white as snow; and His eyes were as a flame of fire: and His feet like unto fine brass, as if they burnt in a furnace; and His countenance was as the sun shineth in his strength."[1] Such was our Lord's holiness because He was the Son of God from eternity. There was always the Father, always the Son: always the Father, *therefore* always the Son, for the Name of Father implies the Son, and never was there a time when the Father Almighty was not, and in the Father the Son also. He it is who is spoken of in the beginning of St. John's Gospel, when it is said, "In the beginning was the Word, and the Word was with God, and the Word was God." Soon after, the same Apostle speaks of Him as "in the bosom of the Father." And He speaks Himself of "the glory which He had with the Father before the world was." And St. Paul calls Him "the Brightness of God's glory, and the express Image of His Person." And elsewhere, "the Image of the Invisible God." Thus what our Lord is, that none other can be; He is the Only-begotten Son; He has the Divine nature, and is of one substance with the Father, which cannot be said of any creature. He is one with God, and His nature is secret and incommunicable. Hence St. Paul contrasts His dignity with that of Angels, the highest of all creatures, with a view of showing the infinite superiority of the Son. "Unto which of the Angels said He at any time, Thou art My Son, this day have I begotten Thee?" Again, "When He bringeth in the first-begotten into the world, He saith, And let all the Angels of God worship Him." And again, "To which of the Angels saith He at any time, Sit on My right hand until I make Thine enemies Thy footstool?" Of the Angels we are told, "He putteth no trust in His saints; yea, the heavens are not clean in His sight;" but our Lord is His "beloved Son, in whom He is well pleased."[2]

He it was who created the worlds; He it was who interposed of old time in the affairs of the world, and showed Himself to be a living and observant God, whether men thought of Him or not. Yet this great God condescended to come down on earth from His heavenly throne, and to be born into His own world; showing Himself as the Son of God in a new and second sense, in a created nature as well as in His eternal substance. Such is the first reflection which the birth of Christ suggests.

2. And next, observe, that since He was the All-holy Son of God, though He condescended to be born into the world, He

[1] 1 Tim.vi.16; 1 John i.5; Dan. vii.9; John i.9; Matt. xvii.2; Mark ix.3; Luke xi.29; Rev. i.14–16.

[2] John i.1; xvii.5; Heb. i.3, *et seq.*; Col. i.15; Job xv.15; Matt. iii.17.

necessarily came into it in a way suitable to the All-holy, and different from that of other men. He took our nature upon Him, but not our sin; taking our nature in a way above nature. Did He then come from heaven in the clouds? did He frame a body for Himself out of the dust of the earth? No; He was, as other men, "made of a woman," as St. Paul speaks, that He might take on Him, not another nature, but the nature of man. It had been prophesied from the beginning, that the Seed of the woman should bruise the serpent's head. "I will put enmity," said Almighty God to the serpent at the fall, "between thee and the woman, and between thy seed and her Seed; It shall bruise thy head."[3] In consequence of this promise, pious women, we are told, were in the old time ever looking out in hope that in their own instance peradventure the promise might find its accomplishment. One after another hoped in turn that she herself might be mother of the promised King; and therefore marriage was in repute, and virginity in disesteem, as if then only they had a prospect of being the Mother of Christ, if they waited for the blessing according to the course of nature, and amid the generations of men. Pious women they were, but little comprehending the real condition of mankind. It was ordained, indeed, that the Eternal Word should come into the world by the ministration of a woman; but born in the way of the flesh He could not be. Mankind is a fallen race; ever since the Fall there has been a "fault and corruption of the nature of every man that naturally is engendered of the offspring of Adam; . . . so that the flesh lusteth always contrary to the Spirit, and therefore in every person born into this world it deserveth God's wrath and damnation." And "the Apostle doth confess that concupiscence and lust hath of itself the nature of sin." "That which is born of the flesh, is flesh." "Who can bring a clean thing out of an unclean?" "How can he be clean that is born of a woman?" Or as holy David cries out, "Behold, I was shapen in wickedness, and in sin hath my mother conceived me."[4] No one is born into the world without sin; or can rid himself of the sin of his birth except by a second birth through the Spirit. How then could the Son of God have come as a Holy Saviour, had He come as other men? How could He have atoned for our sins, who Himself had guilt? or cleansed our hearts, who was impure Himself? or raised up our heads, who was Himself the son of shame? Surely any such messenger had

---

[3] Gen. iii.15.
[4] John iii.6; Job xiv.4; xxv.4; Ps. li.5.

needed a Saviour for his own disease, and to such a one would apply the proverb, "Physician, heal thyself." Priests among men are they who have to offer "first for their own sins, and then for the people's;"[5] but He, coming as the immaculate Lamb of God, and the all-prevailing Priest, could not come in the way which those fond persons anticipated. He came by a new and living way, by which He alone has come, and which alone became Him. The Prophet Isaiah had been the first to announce it: "The Lord Himself shall give you a sign," he says, "Behold, a Virgin shall conceive and bear a Son, and shall call His Name Immanuel." And accordingly St. Matthew after quoting this text, declares its fulfilment in the instance of the Blessed Mary. "All this," he says, "was done that it might be fulfilled which was spoken by the prophet." And further, two separate Angels, one to Mary, one to Joseph, declare who the adorable Agent was, by whom this miracle was wrought. "Joseph, thou son of David," an Angel said to him, "fear not to take unto thee Mary thy wife, for that which is conceived in her is of the Holy Ghost;" and what followed from this? He proceeds, "And she shall bring forth a Son, and thou shalt call His Name Jesus, for He shall save His people from their sins." Because He was "incarnate by the Holy Ghost of the Virgin Mary," therefore He was "Jesus," a "Saviour from sin." Again, the Angel Gabriel had already said to Mary, "Hail, thou that art highly favoured, the Lord is with thee: blessed art thou among women." And then he proceeds to declare, that her Son should be called Jesus; that He "should be great, and should be called the Son of the Highest;" and that "of His Kingdom there shall be no end." And he concludes by announcing, "The Holy Ghost shall come upon thee, and the power of the Highest shall overshadow thee; therefore that Holy Thing which shall be born of thee shall be called the Son of God."[6] Because God the Holy Ghost wrought miraculously, therefore was her Son a "Holy Thing," "the Son of God," and "Jesus," and the heir of an everlasting kingdom.

3. This is the great Mystery which we are now celebrating, of which mercy is the beginning, and sanctity the end: according to the Psalm, "Righteousness and peace have kissed each other." He who is all purity came to an impure race to raise them to His purity. He, the brightness of God's glory, came in a body of flesh, which was pure and holy as Himself, "without spot, or wrinkle, or any such thing, but holy and without

[5] Heb. vii.27.   [6] Matt. i.20, 21; Luke i.28-35.

blemish;" and this He did for our sake, "that we might be partakers of His holiness." He needed not a human nature for
Himself,—He was all-perfect in His original Divine nature; but
He took upon Himself what was ours for the sake of us. He who
"hath made of one blood all nations of men," so that in the sin
of one all sinned, and in the death of one all died, He came in
that very nature of Adam, in order to communicate to us that
nature as it is in His Person, that "our sinful bodies might be
made clean by His Body, and our souls washed through His
most precious Blood;" to make us partakers of the Divine nature; to sow the seed of eternal life in our hearts; and to raise us
from "the corruption that is in the world through lust," to that
immaculate purity and that fulness of grace which is in Him.
He who is the first principle and pattern of all things, came to
be the beginning and pattern of human kind, the firstborn of
the whole creation. He, who is the everlasting Light, became
the Light of men; He, who is the Life from eternity, became the
Life of a race dead in sin; He, who is the Word of God, came to
be a spiritual Word, "dwelling richly in our hearts," an "en-
grafted Word, which is able to save our souls;" He, who is the
co-equal Son of the Father, came to be the Son of God in our
flesh, that He might raise us also to the adoption of sons, and
might be first among many brethren. And this is the reason why
the Collect for the season, after speaking of our Lord as the
Only-begotten Son, and born in our nature of a pure Virgin,
proceeds to speak of our new birth and adopted sonship, and
renewal by the grace of the Holy Ghost.

4. And when He came into the world, He was a pattern of
sanctity in the circumstances of His life, as well as in His birth.
He did not implicate and contaminate Himself with sinners. He
came down from heaven, and made a short work in righteousness, and then returned back again where He was before. He
came into the world, and He speedily left the world; as if to
teach us how little He Himself, how little we His followers,
have to do with the world. He, the Eternal Ever-living Word of
God, did not outlive Methuselah's years, nay, did not even exhaust the common age of man; but He came and He went, before men knew that He had come, like the lightning shining
from one side of heaven unto the other, as being the beginning
of a new and invisible creation and having no part in the old
Adam. He was in the world, but not of the world; and while He
was here, He, the Son of man, was still in heaven: and as well
might fire feed upon water, or the wind be subjected to man's
bidding, as the Only-begotten Son really be portion and mem-

ber of that perishable system in which He condescended to move. He could not rest or tarry upon earth; He did but do His work in it; He could but come and go.

And while He was here, since He could not acquiesce or pleasure Himself in the earth, so He would none of its vaunted goods. When He humbled himself unto His own sinful creation, He would not let that creation minister to Him of its best, as if disdaining to receive offering or tribute from a fallen world. It is only nature regenerate which may venture to serve the Holy One. He would not accept lodging or entertainment, acknowledgment, or blandishment, from the kingdom of darkness. He would not be made a king; He would not be called, Good Master; He would not accept where He might lay His head. His life lay not in man's breath, or man's smile; it was hid in Him from whom He came and to whom He returned.

"The Light shineth in darkness, and the darkness comprehended it not." He seemed like other men to the multitude. Though conceived of the Holy Ghost, He was born of a poor woman, who, when guests were numerous, was thrust aside, and gave birth to Him in a place for cattle. O wondrous mystery, early manifested, that even in birth He refused the world's welcome! He grew up as the carpenter's son, without education, so that when He began to teach, His neighbours wondered how one who had not learned letters, and was bred to a humble craft, should become a prophet. He was known as the kinsman and intimate of humble persons; so that the world pointed to them when He declared Himself, as if their insufficiency was the refutation of His claims. He was brought up in a town of low repute, so that even the better sort doubted whether good could come out of it. No; He would not be indebted to this world for comfort, aid, or credit; for "the world was made by Him, and the world knew Him not." He came to it as a benefactor, not as a guest; not to borrow from it, but to impart to it.

And when He grew up, and began to preach the kingdom of heaven, the Holy Jesus took no more from the world then than before. He chose the portion of those Saints who preceded and prefigured Him, Abraham, Moses, David, Elijah, and His forerunner John the Baptist. He lived at large, without the ties of home or peaceful dwelling; He lived as a pilgrim in the land of promise; He lived in the wilderness. Abraham had lived in tents in the country which his descendants were to enjoy. David had wandered for seven years up and down the same during Saul's persecutions. Moses had been a prisoner in the howling wilderness, all the way from Mount Sinai to the borders of Canaan. Elijah wandered back again from Carmel to Sinai. And the Baptist had remained in the deserts from his youth. Such in like manner was our Lord's manner of life, during His ministry: He was now in Galilee, now in Judaea; He is found in the mountain, in the wilderness, and in the city; but He vouchsafed to take no home, not even His Almighty Father's Temple at Jerusalem.

Now all this is quite independent of the special objects of mercy which brought Him upon earth. Though He had still submitted Himself by an incomprehensible condescension to the death on the cross at length, yet why did He from the first so spurn this world, when He was not atoning for its sins? He might at least have had the blessedness of brethren who believed in Him; He might have been happy and revered at home; He might have had honour in His own country; He might have submitted but at last to what he chose from the first; He might have delayed His voluntary sufferings till that hour when His Father's and His own will made Him the sacrifice for sin.

But He did otherwise; and thus He becomes a lesson to us who are His disciples. He, who was so separate from the world, so present with the Father even in the days of His flesh, calls upon us, His brethren, as we are in Him and He in the Father, to show that we really are what we have been made, by renouncing the world while in the world, and living as in the presence of God.

Let them consider this, who think the perfection of our nature still consists, as before the Spirit was given, in the exercise of all its separate functions, animal and mental, not in the subjection and sacrifice of what is inferior in us to what is more excellent. Christ, who is the beginning and pattern of the new creature, lived out of the body while He was in it. His death indeed was required as an expiation; but why was His life so mortified, if such austerity be not man's glory?

Let us at this season approach Him with awe and love, in whom resides all perfection, and from whom we are allowed to gain it. Let us come to the Sanctifier to be sanctified. Let us come to Him to learn our duty, and to receive grace to do it. At other seasons of the year we are reminded of watching, toiling, struggling, and suffering; but at this season we are reminded simply of God's gifts towards us sinners. "Not by works of righteousness which we have done, but according to His mercy He saved us." We are reminded that we can do nothing, and that God does everything. This is especially the season of grace. We come to see and to experience God's mercies. We come before

Him as the helpless beings, during His ministry, who were brought on beds and couches for a cure. We come to be made whole. We come as little children to be fed and taught, "as new-born babes, desiring the sincere milk of the word, that we may grow thereby."[7] This is a time for innocence, and purity, and gentleness, and mildness, and contentment, and peace. It is a time in which the whole Church seems decked in white, in her baptismal robe, in the bright and glistering raiment which she wears upon the Holy Mount. Christ comes at other times with garments dyed in blood; but now He comes to us in all serenity and peace, and He bids us rejoice in Him, and to love one another. This is not a time for gloom, or jealousy, or care, or indulgence, or excess, or licence: not for "rioting and drunken-ness," not for "chambering and wantonness," not for "strife and envying,"[8] as says the Apostle; but for putting on the Lord Jesus Christ, "who knew no sin, neither was guile found in His mouth."

May each Christmas, as it comes, find us more and more like Him, who as at this time became a little child for our sake, more simple-minded, more humble, more holy, more affectionate, more resigned, more happy, more full of God.

---

[7] I Pet. ii.2. [8] Rom. xiii.13.

THE STATE OF INNOCENCE

(Christmas)

*"God hath made man upright, but they have sought out
many inventions."*—Eccles. vii.29.

T HE state of our parents as God made them "upright," and
"very good," in the day that they were created, presents
much to excite our interest and sympathy, though we, their descendants, have passed away into a far different state. Since that
time our nature has gone through many fortunes,—through
much evil to greater good. That primeval state is no longer
ours. It is no longer ours, though it is no longer forfeited. The
penalties are removed; the flaming sword no longer bars the
entrance of Eden; yet have we not returned to it. For so is it
with all that happens to us,—the past *never* returns, not in what
it contained, any more than in itself. Each time has its own peculiar attributes; it is impressed with its own characters. We
recognise them in memory. When from time to time this or
that passage of our lives rises in our minds, it comes to us with
its own savour. We know it as if by taste and scent, and we know
that that peculiar and indescribable token, be it good or bad,
never can attach to anything else. And what is true of indifferent things, is true also when right and wrong come into question, and in the great destinies of man. If we sin and forfeit what
God has given, not God Himself (such seems to be His will), not
God Himself, in the fulness of His mercies, ever brings back
what we were. He may wash out our sin,—He may give us
blessings, greater blessings than we had,—He does not give us
the same. When man was driven out of Paradise, it was for good
and all,—he never has returned,—he never will return,—he
has been born again, but not into possession of the garden of
innocence: he has a rest in store, and a happier one,—a more
glorious paradise, but still another.

This being so, it would seem as if there was little to interest us
now in the first condition of Adam. As lost, it would only raise
remorse and distress; as found again, it is something new. And

yet, though Almighty God does not bring back the past, His dispensations move forward in an equable uniform way, like circles expanding about one centre;—the greater good to come being, not indeed the same as the past good, but nevertheless resembling it, as a substance resembles its type. In the past we see the future as if in miniature and outline. Indeed how can it be otherwise? seeing that all goods are but types and shadows of God Himself the Giver, and are like each other because they are like Him. Hence the garden of Eden, though long past away, is brought again and again to our notice in the progress of God's dealings with us, not only in order to instruct us by the past, but unavoidably, if I may so speak, from the resemblance which one condition of God's favour bears to another;—of Adam's first state to the Law, and of the Law to the Gospel, and of the Gospel to the state of rest after death, and of that to heaven. For instance, the land that flowed with milk and honey, was a sort of visible return of the lost garden; and in a manner reversed the sentence of banishment which God has laid upon our first parents. Again, the reign of Christ too is imaged as a state in which the beasts return to the dominion of man, and are harmless;— when the serpent is no longer venomous, and when "the desert shall rejoice, and blossom as the rose," and "instead of the thorn shall come up the fir-tree, and instead of the brier shall come up the myrtle-tree;" when "the mountains and the hills shall break forth into singing, and all the trees of the field shall clap their hands." [1] And so of the intermediate state; for our Lord says to the penitent thief, "To-day shalt thou be with Me in *paradise*." And lastly, to describe heaven too, in the last words which God has vouchsafed to us, ending His revelations as He began them, He sets before us the vision of a happy garden. "He showed me a pure river of water of life, clear as crystal, proceeding out of the throne of God and of the Lamb. In the midst of the street of it, and on either side of the river, was there the Tree of Life, which had twelve manner of fruits, and yielded her fruit every month; and the leaves of the Tree were for the healing of the nations." [2] Thus God takes away the less to give the greater,—not reversing the past, but remedying and heightening it; preserving the pattern of it, and so keeping us from forgetting it.

Therefore we may well look back on the garden of Eden, as we would on our own childhood. That childhood is a type of the perfect Christian state; our Saviour so made it when He said

[1] Is. xxxv.1; lv.13, 12.   [2] Rev. xxii.1, 2.

that we must become as little children to enter His kingdom. Yet it too is a thing past and over. We are not, we cannot be children; grown men have faculties, passions, aims, principles, views, duties, which children have not; still, however, we must become *as* little children; in them we are bound to see Christian perfection, and to labour for it with them in our eye. Indeed there is a very much closer connexion between the state of Adam in Paradise and our state in childhood, than may at first be thought; so that in surveying Eden, we are in a way looking back on our own childhood; and in aiming to be children again, we are aiming to be as Adam on his creation. Let us then now compare together these two parallel states, and in doing so let us have an eye to that third state, higher than either; I mean our regenerate state in Christ, of which these two are both types.

There is, for what we know, a very mysterious real connexion between the garden of Eden and our childhood, on which, however, I am not going to enlarge. I mean, the doctrine of original sin does connect together, in some unknown and awful way, Adam and each of us. If, as we believe, Adam's sin is imputed to each of us, if we enter into the world with it upon us, in all its consequences, just as if it were ours, certainly we cannot be in Adam's state when he was in Eden (rather what he was when leaving it), but still so much may be said, that our childhood is in some sense a continuation of Adam's state when in Eden, a carrying it on through and after his fall, and not a beginning; though in thus speaking we use words beyond our own meaning.

But dismissing this subject, I would have you observe, that as far as we are given to know it, Adam's state in Eden seems to have been like the state of children now—in being simple, inartificial, inexperienced in evil, unreasoning, uncalculating, ignorant of the future, or (as men now speak) unintellectual. The tree of the knowledge of good and evil was kept from him. Also, I would observe, that whereas we who do know good and evil, are bid to become as simple children; so again we are promised a paradise in which shall be no Tree of Knowledge. St. John describes to us the future paradise, and tells us of the Tree of Life there, but it has no Tree of Knowledge; instead of which "the glory of God doth lighten it, and the Lamb is the light thereof." It would seem then, taking human nature according to what it was on its creation, according to what it is in childhood (which is the type of its perfection), and according to what is implied about its future state, that in all these states the "knowledge of good and evil" is away, whatever be the meaning of that phrase, and that instead of it the Lord is our Light, "and in His light shall we see light." This remarkably corresponds with the words of the text: "God hath made man upright, but they have sought out many *inventions*." But to return to our first parents.

The state in Eden seems, I say, to be very much what is called the life of innocents, of such as are derided and contemned by men, as they now are,—their degenerate descendants.

1. First Adam and Eve were placed in a garden to cultivate it; how much is implied even in this! "The Lord God took the man and put him into the garden of Eden, to dress it and to keep it." If there was a mode of life free from tumult, anxiety, excitement, and fever of mind, it was the care of a garden. You will say it could not be otherwise, while he was but one man in the whole world;—the accumulation of human beings, the mutual action of mind on mind, this it is which creates all the hurry and variety of life. Adam was a hermit, whether he would or no. True; but does not this very circumstance that God made him such, point out to us what is our true happiness, if we were given it, which we are not? At least we see in type what our perfection is, in these first specimens of our nature, which need not, unless God had so willed, have been created in this solitary state, but might have been myriads at once, as the Angels were created. And let it be noted, that, when the Second Adam came, He returned, nay, more than returned to that life which the First had originally been allotted. He too was alone, and lived alone, the immaculate Son of a Virgin Mother; and He chose the mountain summit or the garden as His home. Save always, that in His case sorrow and pain went with His loneliness; not, like Adam, eating freely of all trees but one, but fasting in the wilderness for forty days—not tempted to eat of that one through wantonness, but urged in utter destitution of food to provide Himself with some necessary bread,—not as a king giving names to fawning brutes, but one among the wild beasts, —not granted a help meet for His support, but praying alone in the dark morning,—not dressing the herbs and flowers, but dropping blood upon the ground in agony,—not falling into a deep sleep in His garden, but buried there after His passion;— yet still like the first Adam, solitary,—like the first Adam, living with His God and Holy Angels. And this is the more remarkable, both because He came to do a great work in a short ministry, and because the same characteristic will be found in His servants also; nay, in His most laboriously employed and most successfully active servants, before and after Him. Abraham,

Isaac, and Jacob, were as "plain men dwelling in tents;" Moses
lived for forty years a shepherd's life; and when at length he was
set over the chosen people, still in one of the most critical moments of his government, he had long retirements in the Mount
with God. Samuel was brought up within the Temple: Elijah
lived in the deserts; so did the Baptist, his antitype. Even the
Apostles had their seasons of solitude. We hear of St. Peter at
Joppa; and St. Paul had his labours again and again suspended
by imprisonment; as if such occasional respite from exertion
were as necessary for the spirit as sleep is necessary for the body.
If then the life of Christ and His servants be any guide to us,
certainly it would appear as if the simplicity and the repose of
life, with which human nature began, is an indication of its perfection. And again, does not our infancy teach us the same lesson? which is especially a season when the soul is left to itself,
withdrawn from its fellows as effectually as if it were the only
human being on earth, like Adam in his inclosed garden, fenced
off from the world, and visited by Angels.

2. Fenced off from the world, nay, fenced off even from himself; for so it is, and most strange too, that our infant and childish state is hidden from ourselves. We cannot recollect it. We
know not what it was, what our thoughts in it were, and what
our probation, more than we know Adam's. This is a remarkable analogy for such persons as question and object to the account of our first parents in Eden. To what does their difficulty
amount at the utmost, but to this, that they do not know what
their state was? that there is a depth and a secret about the Word
of God, which they cannot penetrate? And is it greater than
that which hangs over themselves personally, in their own most
mysterious infancy? the history of which, doubtless, if it could
be put into words, and set before us, would be as strange and
foreign to us, would be as little recognised by us as our own, as
the second and third chapters of Genesis. And here again occurs
a parallel in our state of perfection; "we know not what we *shall*
be." We know not what we are tending to, any more than what
we have started from. St. Paul was once caught up to Paradise,
and he witnesses to the incomprehensible nature of that life,
which was begun and broken off in Eden. "I knew such a
man . . . how he was caught up into Paradise, and heard *unspeakable* words, which it is not lawful for a man to utter."[3] And
all this is further paralleled by the state of regeneration in the
present world, as far as this, that those who advance far in the

[3] 2 Cor. xii.3, 4.

divine life, both are themselves hidden, and see things hidden from common men. "The light shineth in darkness, and the darkness comprehended it not." "The world was made by Him, and the world knew Him not." "The world knoweth us not because it knew Him not." And on the other hand, "The secret of the Lord is with them that fear Him." "He that believeth in the Son of God, hath the witness in himself." "To him that overcometh will I give a white stone, and in the stone a new name written, which no man knoweth saving he that receiveth it."[4]

3. Another resemblance between the state of Adam in paradise, and that of children is this, that children are saved, not by their purpose and habits of obedience, not by faith and works, but by the influence of baptismal grace; and into Adam God "breathed the breath of life, and man became a living soul." Far different is our state since the fall:—at present our moral rectitude, such as it is, is acquired by trial, by discipline: but what does this really mean? by sinning, by suffering, by correcting ourselves, by improving. We advance to the truth by experience of error; we succeed through failures. We know not how to do right except by having done wrong. We call virtue a mean,—that is, as considering it to lie between things that are wrong. We know what is right, not positively, but negatively;—we do not see the truth at once and make towards it, but we fall upon and try error, and find it is *not* the truth. We grope about by touch, not by sight, and so by a miserable experience exhaust the possible modes of acting till nought is left, but truth, remaining. Such is the process by which we succeed; we walk to heaven backward; we drive our arrows at a mark, and think him most skilful whose shortcomings are the least.

So it is not with children baptized and taken away. So was it not while Adam was still upright, as God created him. Adam might probably have matured in holiness, had he remained in his first state, without experience of evil, whether pain or error; for he had that within him which was to him more than all the habits which trial and discipline painfully form in us. Unless it be presumptuous to say it, grace was to him instead of a habit; grace was his clothing within and without. Grace dispensed with efforts towards holiness, for holiness lived in him. We do not know what we mean by a habit, except as a state or quality of mind *under* which we act in this or that particular way; it is a permanent power in the mind; and what is grace but this?

[4] John i.5, 10; 1 John iii.1; Ps. xxv.14; 1 John v.10; Rev. i.17.

What then man fallen gains by dint of exercise, working up towards it by religious acts, that Adam already acted *from*. He had that light within him, which he might make brighter by obedience, but which he had not to create. Not till he fell, did he lose that supernatural endowment, which raised him into a state above himself, and made him in a certain sense more than man, and what the Angels are, or Saints hereafter. This robe of innocence and sanctity he lost when he fell; he knew and confessed that he had lost it; but while he possessed it, he was sinless and perfect, and acceptable to God, though he had gone through nothing painful to obtain it. He tired of it; he tired of being upright from the heart only, and not in the way of reason. He desired to obey, not in the way of children, but of those who choose for themselves. He ate of the forbidden fruit, that he might choose with his eyes open between good and evil, and his eyes *were* opened, and he "knew that he was naked;" for the strength of God's inward glory went from him, and he was left henceforth to struggle on towards obedience as he best might in his fallen state by experience of sin and misery. And here again let it be observed, as in former points of the parallel, that this gift which sanctified Adam and saves children, does become the ruling principle of Christians generally when they advance to perfection. According as habits of holiness are matured, principle, reason, and self-discipline are unnecessary; a moral instinct takes their place in the breast, or rather, to speak more reverently, the Spirit is sovereign there. There is no calculation, no struggle, no self-regard, no investigation of motives. We act from love. Hence the Apostles say, "Ye have an unction from the Holy One, and ye know all things;" "Ye are the temple of the living God; as God hath said, I will dwell in them, and walk in them." [5]

Now if the doctrine on which this parallel is founded be true, which one cannot doubt, how miserable that state, which is so often praised and magnified as the perfection of our nature, whereas it is the very curse that has come upon us,—the knowledge of evil. Yet can anything be more certain than that men do glory in it; glory in their shame, and consider they are advancing in moral excellence, when they are but gaining a knowledge of moral evil?

For instance, I suppose great numbers of men think that it is slavish and despicable to go on in that narrow way in which they are brought up as children, without experience of the

[5] 1 John ii.20; 2 Cor. vi.16.

world. It *is* the narrow way, and they call it narrow in contumely. They fret at the restraints of their father's roof, and
wish to judge and act for themselves. They think it manly to
taste the pleasures of sin; they think it manly to know what sin
is before condemning it. They think they are then better
judges, when they are not blindly led by others, but have taken
upon them, by their own act, the yoke of evil. They think it a
fine thing to curse and swear, and to revel, and to ridicule God's
sacred truth, and to profess themselves the devil's scholars.
They look down upon the innocent, upon women and children, and solitaries, and holy and humble men of heart, who,
like the Cherubim, see God and worship, as unfit for the great
business of life, and worthless in the real estimate of things.
They think it no great harm to leave off a correct life for a time,
so that they return to it at length. They consider that it is even
more pleasing to God, a more "reasonable service" to subdue
evil than to follow good. They consider that to bring "the motions of sin" under, and show their power over it, is a higher
thing than not to have them to fight against.[6] They think it
more noble to have an enemy to overcome and rebels to control
than to be in peace. Alas! they commonly do not acknowledge
so much as that there is a rebel power within them; they call sin
but a venial evil, and no wonder that, so thinking, they can bear
to talk of trying it, and cannot understand that it is better to be
ever pure than to have been at one time stained.

This is one kind of knowledge, and most miserable doubtless,
which we have gained by the fall, to know sin by experience;—
not to gaze at it with awe as the Angels do, or as children when
they wonder how there can be wicked men in the world, but to
admit it into our hearts. Alas! ever since the fall this has been
more or less the state of the natural man, to live in sin; and
though here and there, under the secret stirrings of God's
grace, he has sought after God and obeyed Him, it has been in a
grovelling sort, like worms working their way upwards through
the dust of the earth, turning evil against itself, and unlearning
it from having known it. And such too seems to be one chief
way in which Providence carries on His truth even under the
Gospel; not by a direct flood of light upon the Church, but by
setting one mischief upon another, bidding one serpent destroy
another, the less the greater; thus gradually thinning the brood
of sin, and wasting them by their own contrariety. And in this
way doubtless we are to regard sects and heresies, as witnesses

[6] *Vide* Froude's Sermons, XIII.

and confessors of particular truths, as God's means of destroying evil,—mortal themselves, yet greedy of each other.

4. The mention of heresy and error opens upon us a large
subject to which I will but allude. What then is intellect itself as
exercised in the world, but a fruit of the fall, not found in paradise or in heaven, more than in little children, and at the utmost
but tolerated in the Church, and only not incompatible with
the regenerate mind? Children do not go by reason: Adam in
his state of innocence had no opportunity for aught but what
we should call a calm and simple life. To God Most High we
ascribe moral excellences, truth, faithfulness, love, justice, holiness: again we speak of His power, knowledge, and wisdom:
but it would be profane even to utter His great Name in
connexion with those powers of mind which we call ability, and
prize so highly. Christ again displays no eloquence or power of
words, no subtle or excursive reasoning, no brilliancy, ingenuity, or fertility of thought, such as the world admires. Nay, the
same truth holds as regards our own regenerate state; for
though doubtless every power of the intellect has its use in the
Church, yet surely, after all, faith is made supreme, and reason
then only is considered in place when it is subordinate. "Blessed
are they," says our Lord, "that have not seen and yet have believed;" and Paul again, "The Jews require a sign, and the
Greeks seek after wisdom; but we preach Christ crucified, unto
the Jews a stumbling-block, and to the Greeks foolishness but
unto them which are called, both Jews and Greeks, Christ the
power of God and the wisdom of God."[7] What a contrast to
such passages is presented by a mere catalogue of the powers of
mind by which men succeed in life, and by which the structure
of society is kept together! Take the world as it is, with its intelligence, its bustle, its feverish efforts, its works, its results, the
ceaseless ebb and flow of the great tide of mind: view society, I
mean, not in its adventitious evil, but in its essential characters,
and what is all its intellectual energy but a fruit of the tree of
the knowledge of good and evil, and though not sinful, yet, in
fact, the consequence of sin? Consider its professions, trades,
pursuits, or, in the words of the text, "inventions;" trace them
down to their simplest forms and first causes, and what is their
parent, but the loss of original uprightness? What place have its
splendours, triumphs, speculations, or theories in that pure and
happy region which was our cradle, or in that heaven which is
to be our rest? Dexterity, promptness, presence of mind, sagac-

[7] John xx.29; 1 Cor. i.22–24.

ity, shrewdness, powers of persuasion, talent for business, what are these but developments of intellect which our fallen state has occasioned, and probably far from the highest which our mind is capable of? And are not these and others at best only of use in remedying the effects of the fall, and, so far, indeed, demanding of us deep thankfulness towards the Giver, but not having a legitimate employment except in a world of sickness and infirmity?

Now, in thus speaking, let it be observed, I am not using light words of what is a great gift of God, and one distinguishing mark of man over the brutes, our reason; I have but spoken of the *particular exercises and developments*, in which it has its life in the world, as we see them; and these, though in themselves excellent, and often admirable, yet would not have been but for sin, and now that they are, subserve the purposes of sin. Reason, I say, is God's gift; but so are the passions; Adam had the gift of reason, and so had he passions; but he did not *walk* by reason, nor was he led by his passions; he, or at least Eve, was tempted to follow passion and reason, instead of her Maker, and she fell. Since that time passion and reason have abandoned their due place in man's nature, which is one of subordination, and conspired together against the Divine light within him, which is his proper guide. Reason has been as guilty as passion here. God made man upright, and grace was his strength; but he has found out many inventions, and his strength is reason.

To conclude: Let us learn from what has been said, whatever gifts of mind we have, henceforth to keep them under, and to subject them to innocence, simplicity, and truth. Let our characters be formed upon faith, love, contemplativeness, modesty, meekness, humility. I know well that men differ so much here one from another, that it were folly to expect their outward character to appear one and the same. One man carries his gentleness on the surface, or his humbleness, or his simplicity; and his intellectual gifts are hid within him. We look at him, and cannot understand how he should possess those endowments of mind, which we know he has. Another's graces are buried, or nearly so; he overflows with thought, or is powerful in speech, or takes a keen view of the world, and is ever present and ready wherever he is; while he keeps his self-abasement and seriousness to himself. These are accidents; "the Lord seeth not as man seeth; for man looketh on the outward appearance, but the Lord looketh on the heart."[8] Let us labour to approve our-

[8] 1 Sam. xvi.7.

selves to Christ. If we be in a crowd, still be we as hermits in the wilderness; if we be rich as if poor, if married as single, if gifted in mind, still as little children. Let the tumult of error teach us the simplicity of truth; the miseries of guilt the peace of innocence; and "the many inventions" of the reason the stability of faith. Let us, with St. Paul, be "all things to all men," while we "live unto God;" "wise as serpents and harmless as doves," "in malice children, in understanding men."

CHRISTIAN SYMPATHY

(Christmas)

"For verily He took not on Him the nature of Angels, but He took on Him the seed of Abraham."—Heb. ii.16.

WE are all of one nature, because we are sons of Adam; we are all of one nature, because we are brethren of Christ. Our old nature is common to us all, and so is our new nature. And because our old nature is one and the same, therefore is it that our new nature is one and the same. Christ could not have taken the nature of every one of us, unless every one of us had the same nature already. He could not have become our brother, unless we were all brethren already; He could not have made us His brethren, unless by becoming our Brother; so that our brotherhood in the first man is the means towards our brotherhood in the second.

I do not mean to limit the benefits of Christ's atoning death, or to dare to say that it may not effect ends infinite in number and extent beyond those expressly recorded. But still so far is plain, that it is by taking our nature that He has done for us what He has done for none else; that, by taking the nature of Angels, He would not have done for us what He has done; that it is not only the humiliation of the Son of God, but His humiliation in our nature, which is our life. He might have humbled Himself in other natures besides human nature; but it was decreed that "the Word" should be "made flesh." "Forasmuch as the children are partakers of flesh and blood, He also Himself likewise took part of the same." And, as the text says, "He took not hold of Angels, but He took hold of the seed of Abraham."

And since His taking on Him our nature is a necessary condition of His imparting to us those great benefits which have accrued to us from His death, therefore, as I have said, it was necessary that we should, one and all, have the same original nature, in order to be redeemed by Him; for, in order to be redeemed, we must all have that nature which He the Redeemer took. Had our natures been different, He would have redeemed one and not another. Such a common nature we have, as being one and all children of one man, Adam; and thus the history of our fall is connected with the history of our recovery.

Christ then took our nature, when He would redeem it; He redeemed it by making it suffer in His own Person; He purified it, by making it pure in His own Person. He first sanctified it in Himself, made it righteous, made it acceptable to God, submitted it to an expiatory passion, and then He imparted it to us. He took it, consecrated it, broke it, and said, "Take, and divide it among yourselves."

And moreover, He raised the condition of human nature, by submitting it to trial and temptation; that what it failed to do in Adam, it might be able to do in Him. Or, in other words, which it becomes us rather to use, He condescended, by an ineffable mercy, to be tried and tempted in it; so that, whereas He was God from everlasting, as the Only-begotten of the Father, He took on Him the thoughts, affections, and infirmities of man, thereby, through the fulness of His Divine Nature, to raise those thoughts and affections, and destroy those infirmities, that so, by God's becoming man, men, through brotherhood with Him, might in the end become as gods.

There is not a feeling, not a passion, not a wish, not an infirmity, which we have, which did not belong to that manhood which He assumed, except such as is of the nature of sin. There was not a trial or temptation which befalls us, but was, in kind at least, presented before Him, except that He had nothing within Him, sympathizing with that which came to Him from without. He said upon His last and greatest trial, "The Prince of this world cometh and hath nothing in Me;" yet at the same time we are mercifully assured that "we have not a High Priest which cannot be touched with the feeling of our infirmities, but" one, who "was in all points tempted like as we are, yet without sin." And again, "In that He Himself hath suffered being tempted, He is able to succour them that are tempted." [1]

But what I would to-day draw attention to, is the thought with which I began, viz. the comfort vouchsafed to us in being able to contemplate Him whom the Apostle calls "the man Christ Jesus," the Son of God in our flesh. I mean, the thought of Him, "the beginning of the creation of God," "the firstborn of every creature," binds us together by a sympathy with one another, as much greater than that of mere nature, as Christ is greater than Adam. We were brethren, as being of one nature

[1] Heb. iv.15; ii.18.

with him, who was "of the earth, earthy;" we are now brethren, as being of one nature with "the Lord from heaven." All
those common feelings, which we have by birth, are far more
intimately common to us, now that we have obtained the second birth. Our hopes and fears, likes and dislikes, pleasures
and pains, have been moulded upon one model, have been
wrought into one image, blended and combined unto "the
measure of the stature of the fulness of Christ." What they become, who have partaken of "the Living Bread, which came
down from heaven," the first converts showed, of whom it is
said that they "had all things common;" that "the multitude
of them that believed were of one heart and of one soul;" as
having "one body, and one Spirit, one hope, one Lord, one
Faith, one Baptism, one God and Father of all." [2] Yes, and one
thing needful; one narrow way; one business on earth; one and
the same enemy; the same dangers; the same temptations; the
same afflictions; the same course of life; the same death; the
same resurrection; the same judgment. All these things being
the same, and the new nature being the same, and from the
Same, no wonder that Christians can sympathise with each
other, even as by the power of Christ sympathising in and with
each of them.

Nay, and further, they sympathise together in those respects
too, in which Christ has not, could not have, gone before them;
I mean in their common sins. This is the difference between
Christ's temptation and ours. His temptations were without
sin, but ours with sin. Temptation with us almost certainly in-
vokes sin. We sin, almost spontaneously, in spite of His grace. I
do not mean, God forbid, that His grace is not sufficient to
subdue all sin in us; or that, as we come more and more under
its influence, we are not less and less exposed to the involuntary
impression of temptation, and much less exposed to voluntary
sin; but that so it is, our evil nature remains in us in spite of that
new nature which the touch of Christ communicates to us; we
have still earthly principles in our souls, though we have heavenly ones, and these so sympathise with temptation, that, as a
mirror reflects promptly and of necessity what is presented to
it, so the body of death which infects us, when the temptations
of this world assail it,—when honour, pomp, glory, the world's
praise, power, ease, indulgence, sensual pleasure, revenge are
offered to it,—involuntarily responds to them, and sins—sins
because it *is* sin; sins before the better mind can control it,

[2] Acts ii.44; iv.32; Eph. iv.4–6.

because it exists, because its life is sin; sins *till* it is utterly subdued and expelled from the soul by the gradual growth of holiness and the power of the Spirit. Of all this, Christ had nothing.
He was "born of a pure Virgin," the immaculate Lamb of God;
and though He was tempted, yet it was by what was good in the
world's offers, though unseasonable and unsuitable, and not by
what was evil in them. He overcame what it had been unbecoming to yield to, while He felt the temptation. He overcame
also what was sinful, but He felt no temptation to it.

And yet it stands to reason, that though His temptations differed from ours in this main respect, yet His presence in us
makes us sympathise one with another, even in our sins and
faults, in a way which is impossible without it; because, whereas
the grace in us is common to us all, the sins against that grace
are common to us all also. We have the same gifts to sin against,
and therefore the same powers, the same responsibilities, the
same fears, the same struggles, the same guilt, the same repentance, and such as none can have but we. The Christian is one
and the same, wherever found; as in Christ, who is perfect, so in
himself, who is training towards perfection; as in that righteousness which is imputed to him in fulness, so in that righteousness which is imparted to him only in its measure, and not
yet in fulness.

This is a consideration full of comfort, but of which commonly we do not avail ourselves as we might. It is one comfortable thought, and the highest of all, that Christ, who is on the
right hand of God exalted, has felt all that we feel, sin excepted;
but it is very comfortable also, that the new and spiritual man,
which He creates in us, or creates us into,—that is, the Christian, as he is naturally found everywhere,—has everywhere the
same temptations, and the same feelings under them, whether
innocent or sinful; so that, as we are all bound together in our
Head, so are we bound together, as members of one body, in
that body, and believe, obey, sin, and repent, all in common.

I do not wish to state this too strongly. Doubtless there are
very many differences between Christian and Christian.
Though their nature is the same, and their general duties, hindrances, helps, privileges, and rewards the same, yet certainly
there are great differences of character, and peculiarities belonging either to individuals or to classes. High and low, rich
and poor, Jew and Gentile, man and woman, bond and free,
learned and unlearned, though equal in the Gospel, do in
many respects differ, so that descriptions of what passes in the
mind of one will often appear strange and new to the other.

Their temptations differ, and their diseases of mind. And the difference becomes far greater, by the difficulty persons have of expressing exactly what they mean, so that they convey wrong ideas to one another, and offend and repel those who really do feel what they feel, though they would express themselves otherwise.

Again, of course there is this great difference between Christians, that some are penitents, and some have never fallen away since they were brought near to God; some have fallen for a time, and grievously; others for long years, yet perhaps only in lesser matters. These circumstances will make real differences between Christian and Christian, so as sometimes even to remove the possibility of sympathy almost altogether. Sin certainly does contrive this victory in some cases, to hinder us being even fellows in misery; it separates us while it seduces, and, being the broad way, has different lesser tracks marked out upon it.

But still, after all such exceptions, I consider that Christians, certainly those who are in the same outward circumstances, are very much more like each other in their temptations, inward diseases, and methods of cure, than they at all imagine. Persons think themselves isolated in the world; they think no one ever felt as they feel. They do not dare to expose their feelings, lest they should find that no one understands them. And thus they suffer to wither and decay what was destined in God's purpose to adorn the Church's paradise with beauty and sweetness. Their "mouth is not opened," as the Apostle speaks, nor their "heart enlarged;" they are "straitened" in themselves, and deny themselves the means they possess of at once imparting instruction and gaining comfort.

Nay, instead of speaking out their own thoughts, they suffer the world's opinion to hang upon them as a load, or the influence of some system of religion which is in vogue. It very frequently happens that ten thousand people all say what not any one of them feels, but each says it because every one else says it, and each fears not to say it lest he should incur the censure of all the rest. Such are very commonly what are called the opinions of the age. They are bad principles or doctrines, or false notions or views, which live in the mouths of men, and have their strength in their public recognition. Of course by proud men, or blind, or carnal, or worldly, these opinions which I speak of are really felt and entered into; for they are the natural growth of their own evil hearts. But very frequently the same are set forth, and heralded, and circulated, and become current opinions, among vast multitudes of men who do not feel them. These multitudes, however, are obliged to receive them by what is called the force of public opinion; the careless of course, carelessly, but the better sort superstitiously. Thus ways of speech come in, and modes of thought quite alien to the minds of those who give in to them, who feel them to be unreal, unnatural, and uncongenial to themselves, but consider themselves obliged, often from the most religious principles, not to confess their feelings about them. They dare not say, they dare not even realize to themselves their own judgments. Thus it is that the world cuts off the intercourse between soul and soul, and substitutes idols of its own for the one true Image of Christ, in and through which only souls can sympathise. Their best thoughts are stifled, and when by chance they hear them put forth elsewhere, as may sometimes be the case, they feel as it were conscious and guilty, as if some one were revealing something against them, and they shrink from the sound as from a temptation, as something pleasing indeed but forbidden. Such is the power of false creeds to fetter the mind and bring it into captivity; false views of things, of facts, of doctrines, are imposed on it tyrannically, and men live and die in bondage, who were destined to rise to the stature of the fulness of Christ. Such, for example, I consider to be, among many instances, the interpretation which is popularly received among us at present, of the doctrinal portion of St. Paul's Epistles, an interpretation which has troubled large portions of the Church for a long three hundred years.

But, I repeat, we are much more like each other, even in our sins, than we fancy. I do not of course mean to say, that we are one and all at the same point in our Christian course, or have one and all had the same religious history in times past; but that, even taking a man who has never fallen from grace, and one who has fallen most grievously and repented, even they will be found to be very much more like each other in their view of themselves, in their temptations, and feelings upon those temptations, than they might fancy beforehand. This we see most strikingly instanced when holy men set about to describe their real state. Even bad men at once cry out, "This is just our case," and argue from it that there is no difference between bad and good. They impute all their own sins to the holiest of men, as making their own lives a sort of comment upon the text which his words furnish, and appealing to the appositeness of their own interpretation in proof of its correctness. And I suppose it cannot be denied, concerning all of us, that we are generally surprised to hear the strong language which good men use of themselves, as if such confessions showed them to be more like ourselves, and much less holy than we had fancied them to be. And on the other hand, I suppose, any man of tolerably correct life, whatever his positive advancement in grace, will seldom read accounts of notoriously bad men, in which their ways and feelings are described, without being shocked to find that these more or less cast a meaning upon his own heart, and bring out into light and colour lines and shapes of thought within him, which, till then, were almost invisible. Now this does not show that bad and good men are on a level, but it shows this, that they are of the same nature. It shows that the one has within him in tendency, what the other has brought out into actual existence; so that the good has nothing to boast of over the bad, and while what is good in him is from God's grace, there is an abundance left, which marks him as being beyond all doubt of one blood with those sons of Adam who are still far from Christ their Redeemer. And if this is true of bad and good, much more is it true in the case of which I am speaking, that is of good men one with another; of penitents and the upright. They understand each other far more than might at first have been supposed. And whereas their sense of the heinousness of sin rises with their own purity, those who are holiest will speak of themselves in the same terms as impure persons use about themselves; so that Christians, though they really differ much, yet as regards the power of sympathising with each other will be found to be on a level. The one is not too high or the other too low. They have common ground; and as they have one faith and hope, and one Spirit, so also they have one and the same circle of temptations, and one and the same confession.

It were well if we understood all this. Perhaps the reason why the standard of holiness among us is so low, why our attainments are so poor, our view of the truth so dim, our belief so unreal, our general notions so artificial and external is this, that we dare not trust each other with the secret of our hearts. We have each the same secret, and we keep it to ourselves, and we fear that, as a cause of estrangement, which really would be a bond of union. We do not probe the wounds of our nature thoroughly; we do not lay the foundation of our religious profession in the ground of our inner man; we make clean the outside of things; we are amiable and friendly to each other in words and deeds, but our love is not enlarged, our bowels of affection are straitened, and we fear to let the intercourse begin at the root; and, in consequence, our religion, viewed as a social system, is hollow. The presence of Christ is not in it.

To conclude. If it be awful to tell to another in our own way what we are, what will be the awfulness of that Day when the secrets of all hearts shall be disclosed! Let us ever bear this in mind when we fear that others should know what we are really:—whether we are right or wrong in hiding our sins now, it is a vain notion if we suppose they will always be hidden. The Day shall declare it; the Lord will come in Judgment; He "will bring to light the hidden things of darkness, and will make manifest the counsels of the hearts." [3] With this thought before us, surely it is a little thing whether or not man knows us here. *Then* will be knowledge without sympathy: then will be shame with everlasting contempt. Now, though there be shame, there is comfort and a soothing relief; though there be awe, it is greater on the side of him who hears than of him who makes avowal.

[3] 1 Cor. iv. 5.

RIGHTEOUSNESS NOT OF US,
BUT IN US

(Epiphany)

"Of Him are ye in Christ Jesus, who of God is made unto us
wisdom, and righteousness, and sanctification, and redemption; that,
according as it is written, he that glorieth, let him glory in the Lord."
—1 Cor. i.30, 31.

S T. PAUL is engaged, in the chapter from which these words
are taken, in humbling the self-conceit of the Corinthians.
They had had gifts given them; they did not forget they had
them; they used, they abused them; they forgot, not that they
were theirs, but that they were given them. They seem to have
thought that those gifts were theirs by a sort of right, because
they were persons of more cultivation of mind than others, of
more knowledge, more refinement. Corinth was a wealthy
place; it was a place where all nations met, and where men saw
much of the world; and it was a place of science and philosophy.
It had indeed some good thing in it which Athens had not. The
wise men of Athens heard the Apostle and despised him, but of
Corinth it was said to him by Christ Himself, "I have much
people in this city." [1] Yet, though there were elect of God at
Corinth, yet in a place of so much luxury and worldly wisdom,
difficulties so great stood in the way of a simple, humble faith,
as to seduce, if it were possible, even the elect,—as to bring it to
pass that those who were saved were saved "as by fire." In spite
of the clear views which the Apostle had doubtless given them
on their conversion of their utter nothingness in themselves; in
spite too of their confessing it (for we can hardly suppose that
they said in so many words that their gifts were their own), yet
they did not feel that they came from God. They seemed, as it
were, to claim them, or at least to view their possession of them
as a thing of course; they acted as if they were their own, not

---

[1] Acts xviii.10.

with humbleness and gratitude towards their Giver, not with a sense of responsibility, not with fear and trembling, but as if they were lords over them, as if they had sovereign power to do what they would with them, as if they might use them from themselves and for themselves.

Our bodily powers and limbs also come from God, but they are in such sense part of our original formation, or (if I may say so) of our essence, that though we ought ever to lift up our hearts in gratitude to God while we use them, yet we use them as *our* instruments, organs and ministers. They spring from us, and (as I may say) hold of us, and we use them for our own purposes. Well, this seems to have been the way in which the Corinthians used their supernatural gifts, viz. as if they were parts of themselves,—as natural faculties, instead of influences *in* them, but not *of* them, *from* the Giver of all good,—not with awe, not with reverence, not with worship. They considered themselves, not members of the Kingdom of saints, and dependent on an unseen Lord, but mere members of an earthly community, still rich men, still scribes, still philosophers, still disputants, who had the *addition* of certain gifts, who had aggrandized their existing position by the reception of Christianity. They became proud, when they should have been thankful. They had forgotten that to be members of the Church they must become as little children; that they must give up all, that they might win Christ; that they must become poor in spirit to gain the true riches; that they must put off philosophy, if they would speak wisdom among the perfect. And, therefore, St. Paul reminds them that "not many wise men after the flesh, not many mighty, not many noble are called;" and that all true power, all true wisdom flows from Christ, who is "the power of God, and the wisdom of God;" and that all who are Christians indeed, renounce their own power and their own wisdom, and come to Him that He may be the Source and Principle of their power, and of their wisdom; that they may depend on Him, and hold of Him, not of themselves; that they may exist in Him, or have Him in them; that they may be (as it were) His members; that they may glory simply in Him, not in themselves. For, whereas the wisdom of the world is but foolishness in God's sight, and the power of the world but weakness, God had set forth His Only-begotten Son to be the First-born of creation, and the standard and original of true life; to be a wisdom of God and a power of God, and a "righteousness, sanctification, and redemption" of God, to all those who are found in Him. "Of Him," says he, "are ye in Christ Jesus, who is made unto us a wisdom from God, namely, righteousness, and sanctification, and redemption; that according as it is written, He that glorieth, let him glory in the Lord."

In every age of the Church, not in the primitive age only, Christians have been tempted to pride themselves on their gifts, or at least to forget that they were gifts, and to take them for granted. Ever have they been tempted to forget their own responsibilities, their having received what they are bound to improve, and the duty of fear and trembling, while improving it. On the other hand, how they ought to behave under a sense of their own privileges, St. Paul points out when he says to the Philippians, "Work out your own salvation with fear and trembling, *for* it is God which worketh in you both to will and to do of His good pleasure." [2] God is in you for righteousness, for sanctification, for redemption, through the Spirit of His Son, and you must use His influences, His operations, not as your own (God forbid!), not as you would use your own mind or your own limbs, irreverently, but as His presence in you. All your knowledge is from Him; all good thoughts are from Him; all power to pray is from Him; your Baptism is from Him; the consecrated elements are from Him; your growth in holiness is from Him. You are not your own, you have been bought with a price, and a mysterious power is working in you. Oh that we felt all this as well as were convinced of it!

This then is one of the first elements of Christian knowledge and a Christian spirit, to refer all that is good in us, all that we have of spiritual life and righteousness, to Christ our Saviour; to believe that He works in us, or, to put the same thing more pointedly, to believe that saving truth, life, light, and holiness are not *of* us, though they must be *in* us. I shall now enlarge on each of these two points.

1. Whatever we have, is not of us, but of God. This surely it will not take many words to prove. Our unassisted nature is represented in Scripture as the source of much that is evil, but not of anything that is good. We read much in Scripture of *evil* coming out of the natural heart, but nothing of good coming out of it. When did not the multitude of men turn away from Him who is their life? when was it that the holy were not the few, and the unholy the many? and what does this show but that the law of man's nature tends towards evil, not towards good? As is the tree, so is its fruit; if the fruit be evil, therefore the tree must be evil. When was the face of human society,

---

[2] Phil. ii.13.

which is the fruit of human nature, other than evil? When was the power of the world an upholder of God's truth? When was its wisdom an interpreter of it? or its rank an image of it? Shall we look at the early age of the world? What fruit do we find there? "The earth was corrupt before God, and the earth was filled with violence." "God saw that the wickedness of man was great upon the earth, and that every imagination of the thoughts of his heart was only evil continually. And it repented the Lord that He had made man on the earth, and it grieved Him at His heart." Shall we find good in man's nature after the flood more easily than before? "And the Lord said, Behold, the people is one, and they have all one language; and this they begin to do, and now nothing will be restrained from them which they have imagined to do . . . So the Lord scattered them abroad from thence upon the face of all the earth." Shall we pass on to the days of David? "The Lord looked down from heaven upon the children of men, to see if there were any that did understand and seek God. They are all gone aside, they are all together become filthy; there is none that doeth good, no not one." Thus three times did God look down from heaven, and three times was man the same, God's enemy, a rebel against his Maker. Let us see if Solomon will lighten this fearful testimony. He says, "The heart of the sons of men is full of evil, and madness is in their heart while they live, and after that they go to the dead." Shall we ask of the prophet Isaiah? He answers, "We are all as an unclean thing, and all our righteousnesses are as filthy rags; and we all do fade as a leaf; and our iniquities as the wind have taken us away." Or Jeremiah? "The heart is deceitful above all things, and desperately wicked." Or what did our Lord Himself, when He came in the flesh, witness of the fruits of the heart? He said, "Out of the heart proceed evil thoughts, murders, adulteries, fornications, thefts, false witnesses, blasphemies." And will His coming have improved the world? How will it be, when He comes again? "When the Son of Man cometh, shall He find faith on the earth?"[3] What then human nature *tends* to, is very plain, and according to the end, so I say must be the beginning. If the end is evil, so is the beginning; if the termination is astray, the first direction is wrong. "Out of the abundance of the heart the mouth speaketh," and the hand worketh; and such as is the work and the word, such is the heart. Nothing then can be more certain, if we go by Scrip-

[3] Gen. vi.11, 5, 6; xi.6–8; Ps. xiv.2, 3. Eccles. ix.3; Is. lxiv.6; Jer. xvii.9; Matt. xv.19; Luke xviii.8.

ture, not to speak of experience, than that the present nature of man is evil, and not good; that evil things come from it, and not good things. If good things come from it, they are the exception, and therefore not of it, but in it merely; first given to it, and then coming from it; not of it by nature, but in it by grace. Our Lord says expressly, "That which is born of the flesh, is flesh; and that which is born of the Spirit, is spirit. Marvel not that I say unto thee, Ye must be born again."[4] And again, "Without Me ye can do nothing;"[5] and St. Paul, "I can do all things through Christ, that strengtheneth me." And again, in the Epistle before us, "Who maketh thee to differ from another? and what hast thou that thou didst not receive? now if thou didst receive it, why dost thou glory, as if thou hadst not received it?"[6]

This is that great truth which is at the foundation of all true doctrine as to the way of salvation. All teaching about duty and obedience, about attaining heaven, and about the office of Christ towards us, is hollow and unsubstantial, which is not built *here*, in the doctrine of our original corruption and helplessness; and, in consequence, of original guilt and sin. Christ Himself indeed is the foundation, but a broken, self-abased, self-renouncing heart is (as it were) the ground and soil in which the foundation must be laid; and it is but building on the sand to profess to believe in Christ, yet not to acknowledge that without Him we can do nothing. It is what is called the Pelagian heresy, of which many of us perhaps have heard the name. I am not, indeed, formally stating what that heresy consists in, but I mean, that, speaking popularly, I may call it the belief, that "holy desires, good counsels, and just works," can come of *us*, can be *from* us, as well as *in* us: whereas they are from God only; from whom, and not from ourselves, is that righteousness, sanctification, and redemption, which is in us,—from whom is the washing away of our inward guilt, and the implanting in us of a new nature. But when men take it for granted that they are natural objects of God's favour,—when they view their privileges and powers as natural things,—when they look upon their Baptism as an ordinary work, bringing about its results as a matter of course,—when they come to Church without feeling that they are highly favoured in being allowed to come,—when they do not understand the necessity of prayer for God's grace,—when they refer everything to system, and subject the provisions of God's free bounty to the laws of cause and

<hr>

[4] John iii. 7.   [5] John xv. 5.   [6] 1 Cor. iv. 7.

effect,—when they think that education will do everything, and that education is in their own power,—when, in short, they think little of the Church of God, which is the great channel of God's mercies, and look upon the Gospel as a sort of literature or philosophy, contained in certain documents, which they may use as they use the instruction of other books; then, not to mention other instances of the same error, are they practically Pelagians, for they make themselves their own centre, instead of depending on Almighty God and His ordinances.

2. And, secondly, while truth and righteousness are not of us, it is quite as certain that they are also in us if we be Christ's; not merely nominally given to us and imputed to us, but really implanted in us by the operation of the Blessed Spirit. Our Lord and Saviour Jesus Christ, when He came on earth in our flesh, made a perfect atonement, "sacrifice, oblation, and satisfaction for the sins of the whole world." He was born of a woman, He wrought miracles, He fasted and was tempted in the desert, He suffered and was crucified, He was dead and buried; He rose again from the dead, He ascended on high, and "liveth ever" with the Father,—all for our sakes. And as His incarnation and death were in order to our salvation, so also He really accomplished the end which that humiliation had in view. All was done that needed to be done, except what could not be done at a time, when they were not yet in existence on whom it was to be done. All was done for us except the actual grant of mercy made to us one by one. He saved us by anticipation, but we were not yet saved in fact, for as yet we were not. But everything short of this was then finished. Satan was vanquished; sin was atoned for; the penalty was paid; God was propitiated; righteousness, sanctification, redemption, life, all were provided for the sons of Adam, and all that remained to do was to dispense, to impart, these divine gifts to them one by one. This was not done, because it could not be done all at once; it could not be done forthwith to individuals, and salvation was designed in God's counsels to be an individual gift. He did not once for all restore the whole race, and change the condition of the world in His sight immediately on Christ's death. The sun on Easter-day did not rise, nor did He rise from the grave, on a new world, but on the old world, the sinful rebellious outcast world as before. Men were just what they had been, both in themselves and in His sight. They were guilty and corrupt before His crucifixion, and so they were after it; so they remain to this day, except so far as He by His free bounty and at His absolute will, vouchsafes to impart the gift of His passion to this

man or that. He provided, not gave salvation, when He suffered; and there must be a giving or applying in the case of all those who are to be saved. The gift of life is in us, as truly as it is not of us; it is not only *from* Him but it is *unto* us. This must carefully be borne in mind, for as there are those who consider that life, righteousness, and salvation are of us, so there are others who hold that they are not in us; and as there are many who more or less forget that justification is of God, so there are quite as many who more or less forget that justification must be in man if it is to profit him. And it is hard to say which of the two errors is the greater.

But there is another ground for saying that Christ did not finish His gracious economy by His death; viz. because the Holy Spirit came in order to finish it. When He ascended, He did not leave us to ourselves, so far the work was not done. He sent His Spirit. Were all finished as regards individuals, why should the Holy Ghost have condescended to come? But the Spirit came to finish in us, what Christ had finished in Himself, but left unfinished as regards us. To Him it is committed to apply to us severally all that Christ had done for us. As then His mission proves on the one hand that salvation is not from ourselves, so does it on the other that it must be wrought in us. For if all gifts of grace are with the Spirit, and the presence of the Spirit is within us, it follows that these gifts are to be manifested and wrought in us. If Christ is our sole hope, and Christ is given to us by the Spirit, and the Spirit be an inward presence, our sole hope is in an inward change. As a light placed in a room pours out its rays on all sides, so the presence of the Holy Ghost imbues us with life, strength, holiness, love, acceptableness, righteousness. God looks on us in mercy, because He sees in us "the mind of the Spirit," for whoso has this mind has holiness and righteousness within him. Henceforth all his thoughts, words, and works as done in the Spirit, are acceptable, pleasing, just before God; and whatever remaining infirmity there be in him, that the presence of the Spirit hides. That divine influence, which has the fulness of Christ's grace to purify us, has also the power of Christ's blood to justify.

Let us never lose sight of this great and simple view, which the whole of Scripture sets before us. What was actually done by Christ in the flesh eighteen hundred years ago, is in type and resemblance really wrought in us one by one even to the end of time. He was born of the Spirit, and we too are born of the Spirit. He was justified by the Spirit, and so are we. He was pronounced the well-beloved Son, when the Holy Ghost descended on Him; and we too cry Abba, Father, through the Spirit sent into our hearts. He was led into the wilderness by the Spirit; He did great works by the Spirit; He offered Himself to death by the Eternal Spirit; He was raised from the dead by the Spirit; He was declared to be the Son of God by the Spirit of holiness on His resurrection: we too are led by the same Spirit into and through this world's temptations; we, too, do our works of obedience by the Spirit; we die from sin, we rise again unto righteousness through the Spirit; and we are declared to be God's sons,—declared, pronounced, dealt with as righteous,—through our resurrection unto holiness in the Spirit. Or, to express the same great truth in other words; Christ Himself vouchsafes to repeat in each of us in figure and mystery all that He did and suffered in the flesh. He is formed in us, born in us, suffers in us, rises again in us, lives in us; and this not by a succession of events, but all at once: for He comes to us as a Spirit, all dying, all rising again, all living. We are ever receiving our birth, our justification, our renewal, ever dying to sin, ever rising to righteousness. His whole economy in all its parts is ever in us all at once; and this divine presence constitutes the title of each of us to heaven; this is what He will acknowledge and accept at the last day. He will acknowledge Himself,—His image in us,—as though we reflected Him, and He, on looking round about, discerned at once who were His; those, namely, who gave back to Him His image. He impresses us with the seal of the Spirit, in order to avouch that we are His. As the king's image appropriates the coin to him, so the likeness of Christ in us separates us from the world and assigns us over to the kingdom of heaven.

Scripture is full of texts to show that salvation is such an inward gift. For instance: What is it that rescues us from being reprobates? "Know ye not," says St. Paul, "that Jesus Christ is in you, except ye be reprobates?" What is our hope? "Christ in us, the hope of glory." What is it that hallows and justifies? "The Name of the Lord Jesus, and the Spirit of our God." What makes our offerings acceptable? "Being sanctified by the Holy Ghost." What is our life? "The Spirit is life because of righteousness." How are we enabled to fulfil the law? "The righteousness of the law is fulfilled in us who walk not after the flesh, but after the Spirit." Who is it makes us righteous? "The fruit of the *Spirit* is in all goodness, and righteousness, and truth."[7]

[7] 2 Cor. xiii.5; Col. i.27; 1 Cor. vi.11; Rom. xv.16; Rom. viii.10; Eph. v.9.

To conclude.—I have said that there are two opposite errors: one, the holding that salvation is not of God; the other, that it is not in ourselves. Now it is remarkable that the maintainers of both the one and the other error, whatever their differences in other respects, agree in this,—in depriving a Christian life of its mysteriousness. He who believes that he can please God of himself, or that obedience can be performed by his own powers, of course has nothing more of awe, reverence, and wonder in his personal religion, than when he moves his limbs and uses his reason, though he might well feel awe then also. And in like manner he also who considers that Christ's passion once undergone on the Cross absolutely secured his own personal salvation, may see mystery indeed in that Cross (as he ought), but he will see no mystery, and feel little solemnity, in prayer, in ordinances, or in his attempts at obedience. He will be free, familiar, and presuming, in God's presence. Neither will "work out their salvation with fear and trembling;" for neither will realize, though they use the words, that God is in them "to will and to do." Both the one and the other will be content with a low standard of duty: the one, because he does not believe that God requires much; the other, because he thinks that Christ in His own person has done all. Neither will honour and make much of God's Law: the one, because he brings down the Law to his own power of obeying it; the other, because he thinks that Christ has taken away the Law by obeying it in his stead. They only feel awe and true seriousness who think that the Law remains; that it claims to be fulfilled by them; and that it can be fulfilled in them through the power of God's grace. Not that any man alive arises up to that perfect fulfilment, but that such fulfilment is not impossible; that it is begun in all true Christians; that they all are tending to it; are growing into it; and are pleasing to God because they are becoming, and in proportion as they are becoming like Him who, when He came on earth in our flesh, fulfilled the Law perfectly.

THE LAW OF THE SPIRIT

(Epiphany)

*"Christ is the end of the Law for righteousness
to every one that believeth."*—ROM. X.4.

IN the Epistle to the Romans, St. Paul argues against Jews who
rejected the Gospel; in his Epistles to the Corinthians, he rebukes Christians who had abused it. The sin of the fickle and
vain-glorious Corinthians was very different from that of the
hard-hearted Jews; and yet in either case it rose from one and
the same root, pride. Both Jews and Greeks prided themselves
on what they were, on what Moses had left them, or what
Christ's Apostles had brought them; both forgot that whatever
they had was God's gift, and that it was their duty to be dependent and watchful. But in appearance they differed: the Jews
insisted on God's former mercies unseasonably; and the Greeks
of Corinth thought even of His last and best, lightly and unthankfully.

Sinful feelings and passions generally take upon themselves
the semblance of reason, and affect to argue. It was in this way
that the Jews, whom St. Paul is opposing in the text, disguised
from themselves their own unbelief; and this has turned out a
benefit to the Church ever since, as having led St. Paul, in consequence, to set forth views of the Gospel which otherwise
might not have come to us with the authority of inspiration.
The text contains such a view, expressed very concisely, which
I now propose to explain; and after doing so, I will add a few
words on the feelings of the Jews, in contrast with the doctrine
it contains.

St. Paul tells us, that "Christ is the end of the Law for righteousness to every one that believeth." Here are three subjects
which call for remark: the Law, Righteousness, and Faith. I will
speak of them in succession.

1. In the first place, of "the Law." By the Law is meant the
eternal, unchangeable Law of God, which is the revelation of
His will, the standard of perfection, and the mould and fashion

to which all creatures must conform, as they would be happy. God is holy, and His Law is holy. His Law is the image of Himself; it is the word of Life and Truth commanding that, of which He is the perfect pattern. "Be ye holy," He says, "for I am holy." "Be ye perfect, even as your Father which is in heaven is perfect." [1] His Law is the declaration of His infinite and glorious attributes, and thereby becomes the rule by which all beings imitate, approach, and resemble Him. And when He created them, He provided that it should be to them what it ought to be. God loves holiness, and therefore, as became a good and kind Father, He created all His children holy. He created them to be His children, not His enemies; beings in whom He might take pleasure; who might be near Him, not far off from Him; whom He might love and reward. He formed them upon the pattern of the Law; He moulded them into symmetry by means of it. He created man "in His own image, and after His likeness;" that is, upon the type of the Law. He put His Spirit within him, and set up the Law in his heart; so that, what He is in His infinite nature, such was man, such was Adam in a finite nature,—perfect after his kind.

And in this sense, the Law given to the Israelites from Mount Sinai is called in Scripture, and may be considered, the holy and eternal Law of God. Not that any number of commandments, uttered in man's language and written upon tables, could be commensurate with what is of an infinite and of a spiritual nature; not that a code of precepts, addressed to one portion of a fallen race, in one country, and in one particular state of moral and social existence, could rise to the majesty and beauty of what is perfect;—but that the Law of Moses represented the Law of God in its place and age; was the fullest revelation of it, and the nearest approximation to it, then vouchsafed; and was that Law, as far as it went. As Adam, a child of the dust, was also an "image of God," so the Jewish Law, though earthly and temporary, had at the same time a divine character. It was the light of God shining in a gross medium, in order that it might be "comprehended;" and if it did not teach the chosen people all, it taught them much, and in the only way in which they could be taught it. And hence, as in the text, St. Paul, when on the subject of the Jews, speaks of their Law as if it were the eternal Law of God; and so it was, but only as brought down to its hearers, and condescending to their infirmity.

[1] 1 Pet. i.16; Matt. v.48.

2. Such is "the Law," as spoken of in the text; and by "Righteousness" is meant conformity to the Law,—that one state of soul which is pleasing to God. It is a relative word, having reference to a standard set up, and expressing the fulfilment of its requirements. To be righteous is to act up to the Law, whatever the Law be, and thereby to be acceptable to Him who gave it. Such Adam was in Paradise; the Law was his inward life, and Almighty God dealt with him accordingly,—He called, accounted, dealt with him as righteous, because he was righteous.

It was far otherwise with him when he had fallen. He then forfeited the presence of the Holy Spirit; he no longer fulfilled the Law; he lost his righteousness, and he knew he had lost it. He knew it before God told him; he condemned himself, he pronounced himself unrighteous, before God formally rejected him from his state of justification. And in this unrighteous state he has remained, viewed in himself, ever since; knowing the Law, but not doing it; admiring, not loving; assenting, not following; not utterly without the Law, yet not with it; with the Law not within him, but before him,—not any longer in his heart, as the pillar of a cloud, which was a gracious token and a guide to the Israelites, but departing from him, and moving away, and taking up its place, as it were over against him, and confronting him as an enemy, accuser, and avenger. It was a cloud of thick darkness, instead of a pillar of light; and from it the Lord looked out upon him, and troubled him. Or in St. Paul's words, "the commandment, which was ordained to life, he found to be unto death."[2] What had been a law of innocence, became a law of conscience; what was freedom, became bondage: what was peace, became dread and misery.

Let us thank God that dread and misery are left us. Better is it that the Law remain to us externally, and in the way of an upbraiding conscience, than that it should be utterly removed. While, and so far as it so remains, our own judgment upon ourselves is a warning to us, what the judgment of God will be hereafter, what His view of us is at present. For is not the pain of a bad conscience different from any other pain that we know? I do not ask whether it is greater or less than other pain, but whether it is not unlike any other, peculiar and individual. Can that pain be compensated and overcome by the wages of sin, whatever they be,—or rather, does it not, while it lasts, remain distinctly perceptible and entire in the midst of them? In conscience, then, we have the figure of the wrath of God upon

[2] Rom. vii.10.

transgressors of the Law; the pain which it inflicts on us at times, or in certain cases, is a sort of indication how God regards, and will one day visit, all sins, according to the sure word of Scripture. Take an instance, which, though extreme, will serve to explain what I would say. What accounts do we read of the frightful sleepless remorse which murderers have before now shown! so much so that, though no one knew their crime, yet they could not help confessing it,—as if death were a lighter suffering than a bad conscience. Here you see the misery of being unjustified. Or, again, consider the peculiar piercing distress which follows upon the commission of sins of impurity;— here you have a corroboration in a particular instance of what Scripture affirms generally, concerning the misery of sinning. Or, think of those indescribable feelings in our nature, to which our first parent alludes, when he says, "I heard Thy voice in the garden, and I was afraid, because I was naked; and I hid myself." [3] Are not these feelings a type of the horror with which Angels now look, with which we shall look hereafter, upon all transgression of the Law, or unrighteousness?

Unrighteousness then is a state of misery, frightful as the murderer's, acute as theirs who follow Belial, and overpowering as Adam's when he fled from God. And from this state Christ came to save us, by bringing us back again to righteousness. Man was righteous at the first, because the Law of God ruled him; he became unrighteous when this Law ceased to rule him; and he becomes righteous again by the Law of God once more ruling him. He was righteous at the first by the presence of the Holy Spirit, which enabled him to obey the Law; and such too is his second righteousness. And thus the words of the text are fulfilled; "Christ is the end of the Law for" or unto "righteousness." He effects what the Law contemplates and enjoins, but cannot accomplish, our righteousness. And how? St. Paul does not mention it in the text, but in many other places in his Epistles; viz. by that great gift of His passion, the abiding influence of the Holy Ghost, which enables us to offer to God an acceptable obedience, such as by nature we cannot offer.

Now let me show from Scripture some of these points on which I have been insisting.

First, not much need be said to make it plain that by nature we cannot please God, or, in other words, have no principle of righteousness in us. St. Paul says in so many words, "They that

[3] Gen. iii.10.

are in the flesh cannot please God;" and just before, "The carnal mind is enmity against God; for it is not subject to the Law of God, neither indeed can be." In the foregoing chapter he says, "We know that the Law is spiritual; but I am carnal, sold under sin. For that which I do, I allow not; for what I would, that do I not: but what I hate, that do I. I know that in me (that is, in my flesh) dwelleth no good thing." Again, "By the deeds of the Law there shall no flesh be justified in His sight; for by the Law is the knowledge of sin." In like manner the prophet Isaiah says, "We are all as an unclean thing; and all our righteousnesses are as filthy rags." [4] Such is our state by nature: the best things we do are displeasing to God in themselves, as savouring of the Old Adam, and being works of the flesh and not spiritual.

And as this is our natural state, so the desire of religious men, and the one promise of a merciful God has ever been, that we should be made obedient to the Law, or righteous. Thus David says, "Thou requirest truth *in the inward parts*; and shalt make me to understand wisdom secretly. Thou shalt purge me with hyssop, and I shall be clean; Thou shalt wash me and I shall be *whiter than snow*. Make me a *clean heart*, O God, and renew a right spirit within me. O give me the comfort of Thy help again; and stablish me with Thy free Spirit." Again, "I will wash my hands in *innocency*, O Lord, and so will I go to Thine altar." Again, "Give me understanding, and I shall keep Thy Law, yea, *I shall keep it* with my *whole heart*. . . . Behold, my delight is in Thy commandments. O quicken me in Thy righteousness." "Teach me to do the thing that pleaseth Thee; for Thou art my God: let Thy loving Spirit lead me forth into the land of *righteousness*." [5]

And what Psalmists ask, Prophets promise. They make it the one great distinction of Gospel times, that that original righteousness which is so necessary for us and from which we are so far gone, should be vouchsafed again to us, and that through the Spirit. Daniel states the object of Christ's coming to be the "making reconciliation for iniquity, *and* bringing in everlasting *righteousness*." Malachi says that Christ should "purify the sons of Levi," that they may "offer unto the Lord an offering in *righteousness*." In Isaiah, Almighty God speaks to them "that know *righteousness*," viz. "the people in whose heart is My *law*;" and he also speaks of "the *Spirit* being poured upon us from on high," and in consequence of "*righteousness* remaining in the fruitful field, and the work of righteousness being *peace*, and the

---

[4] Rom. viii.7, 8; vii.14, 15, 18; iii.20; Is. lxiv.6.
[5] Ps. li.6, 7, 10, 12; xxvi.6; cxix.30, 40; cxliii.10.

effect of righteousness, *quietness and assurance* for ever." Still more clear is the prophet Jeremiah in declaring what the Gospel gift consists in; "Behold, the days come, saith the Lord, that I will make a new covenant with the house of Israel and with the house of Judah: I will *put My law in their inward parts*, and write it in their hearts." In similar terms does the prophet Ezekiel describe the great gift of the Gospel, "*A new heart* also will I give you, and a new Spirit will I put within you; and I will put *My Spirit* within you, and *cause you* to walk in My statutes, and ye shall keep My judgments and do them." Again elsewhere the prophet Isaiah calls this new nature, or righteousness, or gift of the Spirit, which the Gospel furnishes, a sort of garment or robe of the soul, being that glory which Adam had before sin stripped him of it; "He hath clothed me with the garment of salvation, He hath covered me with *the robe of righteousness*, as a bridegroom decketh himself with ornaments, and as a bride adorneth herself with her jewels." With this passage must be compared St. John's words in the Revelations, "The marriage of the Lamb is come, and His wife hath made herself ready. And to her was granted that she should be arrayed in fine linen, clean and white; *for the fine linen is the righteousness of saints*." Our Lord also speaks of the great gift of the Gospel under the same figure, when he tells us of the man who came to the marriage feast without a wedding-garment, that is, without righteousness or holiness.[6]

Thus, if we listen to the voices of the Prophets, we must believe that the righteousness of the Law really *is* fulfilled in us under the Gospel through the Spirit;—but as this is a truth in this day denied by some persons, it may be well to insist upon it.

Now that it is a plain truth of Scripture, is proved, in addition to what has been said, by those numerous passages which speak of holy men as "righteous *before God*." This is an expression to which we shall do well to attend, as being an additional explanation of the word "righteousness;" for if holy men are righteous *before God*, they come up to God's *standard* of perfection. The phrase "in the sight of" or "before" often occurs in Scripture, and it means "in the *judgment*," "with the *witness*" of him or them to whom it is applied. Thus in the last chapter of St. Luke, where it is said, "Their words seemed to them as idle tales," this stands in the original Greek, "Their words seemed *in their sight*" or "*before them*," that is, "*in their judgment*." And hence

---

[6] Dan. ix.24; Mal. iii.3; Is. li.7; xxxii.15, 16, 17; Jer. xxxi.31; Ezek. xxxvi.26, 27; Is. lxi.10; Rev. xix.7, 8.

when St. Paul speaks with an oath, he uses these words, "Now the things which I write unto you, behold, *before God*, I lie not," that is, "with the *witness* of God." And so Peter and John answer the council, "Whether it be right *in the sight of God* to hearken unto you more than unto God, judge ye," *i.e.* "in the *presence*" and "with the *witness* of God." And hence the Angels are said "to stand in the *presence* of God," or to be "before His throne," for they can bear it. And on the other hand, the prodigal son says, "Father, I have sinned *before thee*," that is, I know that thou art conscious of my sin. When then it is said, as it so often is said in Scripture, that the righteous are righteous "before God," this means that their righteousness is not merely the name or semblance of righteousness, nor righteousness up to an earthly standard, but a real and true righteousness which approves itself to God. They are able to stand before God and yet not be condemned. They are not sinners before God, but they are righteous before God, and bear His scrutiny. By nature no one can stand in His presence. "All the world becomes guilty *before God*." "By the deeds of the Law no flesh shall be justified in *His sight*." *How* then are we able to come before Him? How shall we stand in His sight? The answer is given us in the Old Testament, in the words of Balaam to Balak. Balak asked, "Wherewith shall *I come before the Lord*, and bow myself before the High God?" and the answer was, "He hath showed thee, O man, what is good; and what doth the Lord require of thee, but to do justly, and to love mercy, and to walk humbly with thy God?" Or again, the answer may be given in the words of Zacharias, who blesses the Lord God of Israel for fulfilling His promise, and enabling us to come into His presence to "serve Him, *without fear*, in holiness and righteousness *before Him*." And accordingly, to come to the case of individuals, Noah, even before the Gospel times, is said to have "found grace in the eyes of the Lord." Why? Because, in the words of Almighty God to him, "*Thee* have I seen righteous *before Me*," or, in My sight, "in this generation;" and Daniel escaped the lions, "forasmuch as *before God* innocency was found in him." In like manner Zacharias and Elizabeth "were both righteous *before God*," or in the judgment of God. It was told to Cornelius that "his prayers and alms had come up for a memorial *in the sight*" or judgment, of God. And St. Paul speaks of intercession for governors being "good and acceptable *in the sight* of God our Saviour." And he prays for his brethren that God would "work *in* them that which is well pleasing in *His sight*," or judgment. St. Peter too speaks of a "meek and quiet spirit," being, "in the *sight of God*, of great price." And St. John, that "we receive what we ask of Him, because we do those things that are pleasing *in His sight*." And Christ warns the Church of Sardis to "be watchful, and strengthen the things which remain, which are ready to die;" for He says, "I have not found thy works perfect *before God*," or in the witness of God. And accordingly the word "witness" is itself used elsewhere to express the same thing, as in the instance of Abel, who, St. Paul says, by his "more excellent sacrifice," "*obtained witness* that he was righteous; God testifying of his gifts." [7] If then it is plain from Scripture, as it is, that by nature we are unrighteous in God's sight, and cannot stand before God, the same Scripture also proves that by the gift of grace we *are* righteous, and can stand before Him; and it is as easy, by some evasion, to explain away the Scripture proofs for the doctrine of original sin, as to get rid of those which Scripture furnishes us for the doctrine of implanted righteousness, and that through the Spirit.

St. Paul has a number of other passages concerning the office of the Holy Spirit, which are equally apposite to show that He it is who vouchsafes to give us inward righteousness under the Gospel, or to justify, or make us acceptable to God. For instance, he says, "Ye are washed, ye are sanctified, ye are *justified* in the Name of the Lord Jesus, and by the *Spirit* of our God." Elsewhere he first calls the Gospel "the ministration of the *Spirit*," and in the next verse, "the ministration of righteousness." Elsewhere he speaks of the Holy Ghost as "the Spirit of *adoption*." And he intimates that "the *righteousness* of the law" is "*fulfilled*" in those "who walk after the *Spirit*." Again he says that the presence of the Spirit in us pleads, as it were, for us with the Father, "making intercession for us with plaints unutterable;" and that God, "who searcheth the hearts," "*knoweth* what is the mind of the Spirit, because He maketh intercession for the saints, according," or, in a way acceptable, "to God." And elsewhere he contrasts the state of nature and the state of grace in this plain way, clearly implying that that inward gift of righteousness which we lost in Adam we have recovered in Christ; "As by the offence of one, judgment came upon all men to condemnation, even so by the righteousness of One the free gift came upon all men unto justification *of life*. For *as* by one man's disobedience many were made sinners, so by the obedi-

[7] Luke xxiv.11; Gal. i.20; Acts iv.19; Luke i.19; Rev. viii.2; i.5; Rom. iii.19; Micah vi.8; Luke i.74, 75; Gen. vii.1; Dan. vi.22; Luke i.6; Acts x.4; 1 Tim. ii.3; Heb. xiii.21; 1 Pet. iii.4; 1 John iii.22; Rev. iii.2; Heb. xi.4

ence of One shall many be *made righteous* . . . that, as sin hath reigned unto death, even so might grace reign through righteousness unto eternal life by Jesus Christ our Lord."[8] Sin, which we derive through Adam, is not a name merely, but a dreadful reality; and so our new righteousness also is a real and not a merely imputed righteousness. It is real righteousness, because it comes from the Holy and Divine Spirit, who vouchsafes, in our Church's language, to pour His gift into our hearts, and who thus makes us acceptable to God, whereas by nature, on account of original sin, we are displeasing to Him. We are "not in the flesh, but in the Spirit," and therefore in a state of *grace*. Again, St. Paul speaks of the "offering of the Gentiles being *acceptable*." How acceptable? He proceeds, "being sanctified by the Holy Ghost." He speaks of presenting our "bodies as a living sacrifice, holy, acceptable unto God." He says that Christ has "saved us, according to His mercy, by the washing of regeneration, and the renewing of the Holy Ghost," and that we are able thereby to "walk worthy of the Lord unto all *pleasing*."[9]

Such then is the meaning of the words of the text, "Christ is the end of the Law for righteousness." As if the Apostle said, Would you fulfil the righteousness of the Law? You cannot in your own strength. You cannot without that divine gift which His passion has purchased, the gift of the Spirit; with it "the righteousness of the Law *may* be fulfilled in you." Christ then is the end of the Law for righteousness, because He effects the purpose of the Law. He brings that about which "the Law cannot do, because it is weak through the flesh," through our unregenerate, unrenewed, carnal nature.

3. But here this question may be asked,—"How can we be said to *fulfil* the Law, and to offer an *acceptable* obedience, since we do not obey *perfectly*? At best we only obey in part; the best obedience of ours is sullied with imperfection. Even with the gift of the Spirit, we do nothing which will bear the strict inspection of a holy and just Judge. Adam, on the other hand, had no sinful nature at all, before his fall; there was nothing in him to counteract or to defile the influences of grace. He then might be justified by his inward righteousness, but we cannot."

I answer as follows:—We can only be justified, certainly, by what is perfect; no work of ours, as far as it is ours, is perfect: and therefore by no work of ours, viewed in its human imperfections, are we justified. But when I speak of our righteousness

[8] 1 Cor. vi.11; 2 Cor. iii.8, 9; Gal. iv.5, 6; Rom. viii, 26, 27; v.18–21.
[9] Rom. xv.16; xii.1; Titus iii.5; Col. i.10.

I speak of the work of the Spirit, and this work, though imperfect, considered as ours, is perfect as far as it comes from Him. Our works, done in the Spirit of Christ, have a justifying *principle* in them, and that is the presence of the All-holy Spirit. His influences are infinitely pleasing to God, and able to overcome in His sight all our own infirmities and demerits. This we are expressly told by St. Paul, in reference to one work of the Holy Ghost, the exercise of prayer, as I just now quoted his words. "He that searcheth the hearts, knoweth what is the mind of the Spirit, because He maketh intercession for the saints," that is, in their hearts, "according to God." [10] Not then for anything of our own are we acceptable to God, but for the work of grace in us; and as having this work of grace in us we *are* acceptable. And this Divine Presence in us, makes us altogether pleasing to God. It makes those works pleasing to God, which it produces, though human infirmity be mixed with them: it hallows those acts, that life, that obedience of which it is the original cause, and which it orders and fashions; so that our new obedience or righteousness is justifying, though imperfect, not for its own sake, but for this new and heavenly principle of grace infused into it.

But again, there is another reason why, for Christ's sake, we are dealt with as perfectly righteous, though we be not so. Not only for the Spirit's presence in us, but for what is ours;—not indeed what is now ours, but for what we shall be. We are not unreprovable, and unblemished in holiness yet, but we shall be at length through God's mercy. They who persevere to the end, will be perfect in soul and body, when they stand before God in heaven; and now that perfection is beginning in them, now they have a gift in them which will in due time, through God's mercy, leaven the whole mass within them. They will one day be presented blameless before the Throne, and they are now to labour towards, and begin that perfect state. And in consideration that it is begun in them, God of His great mercy imputes it to them as if it were already completed. He anticipates what will be, and treats them as that which they are labouring to become. This is what is meant by faith being imputed for righteousness, which St. Paul often insists on, and which is implied in the last words of the text, which I have not yet explained. "Christ is the end of the Law for righteousness *to every one that believeth.*" Faith is the element of all perfection; he who begins with faith, will end in unspotted and entire holiness. It is the

[10] Rom. viii.27.

earnest of a great deal more than itself, and therefore is allowed, in God's consideration, to stand for, to be a pledge of, to be taken in advance for that, which it for certain will end in. He who believes has not yet perfect righteousness and unblame-ableness, but he has the first fruits of it. And all through a man's life, whether his righteous deeds be more or less, or his righ-teousness of heart more or less, his faith is something quite dis-tinct from anything he had in a state of nature, and though it does not satisfy the requirements of God's law, yet since it tends to perfection, it is mercifully taken as perfection. "Abraham believed God, and it was counted to him for righteousness," because God, who sees the end from the beginning, knew it would end in perfect and unblemished righteousness. And in like manner to us "it shall be imputed, if we believe on Him that raised up Jesus our Lord from the dead, who was delivered for our offences, and raised again for our justification." [11]

4. Lastly, such being the Law, such our righteousness, such the work of Christ in us through the Spirit, and such the office of faith, we see what the mistake of the Jews was, of which so much is said in St. Paul's Epistle to the Romans, and which seems to be the reason why the text itself was written. They were in a path which never would lead to holiness and heaven. They were in a state which was destitute of grace and help. They were under the threatening and condemning Law. Many good men doubtless there had been and were under the Law, but their spiritual excellence was not from the Law, but from the Gospel, the blessings of which were anticipated under it, and which the Apostle was at that time preaching throughout the world. But the Pharisees and others, not understanding the real nature and office of their Law, and the reason why God had given it through Moses, thought to be saved by it,—thought it led to heaven. Whereupon St. Paul attempted to show them that they were, as I may say, in the wrong road. They aimed at eternal life; that was the object towards which they professed to be travelling. Now St. Paul told them that the Jewish Law did not lead to it. He said that if they desired to reach the eternal rest of heaven, they must betake themselves to another road. And that they could not as it were, cross over into it, but that they must go back and enter in at the gate, and that this gate was faith. He said that the further they went on in their present course, the less they would really advance, towards their object; and, though it seemed lost time to go back, it was not so. They

[11] Rom. iv.24, 25.

might do as many works and services as they would in their present state, but these would not advance them at all, and why?—not that works were not necessary, God forbid! but that such works were not good works; that no works were good works but those done in the Spirit, and that nothing could gain them the gift of the Spirit but faith in Christ. They desired to be righteous; it was well; but Christ alone was "the end of the Law for righteousness to every one that believed." They desired to fulfil the Law; well then, let them seek "the Law of the Spirit of life," whereby "the righteousness of the Law might be fulfilled in them." They desired the reward of righteousness: be it so; let them then "wait through the Spirit for the hope of righteousness by faith." [12] But they were too proud to confess that they had anything to learn, that they had to begin again, to submit to be taught, to believe in Him they had crucified, to come suppliantly for the gift of the Spirit. They refused the true righteousness which God had provided, thinking they were righteous as they were, and that they could be saved in the flesh. Hence St. Paul says, "They, being ignorant of God's righteousness, and going about to establish their own righteousness, have not submitted themselves unto the righteousness of God." [13] They thought that faith was something mean and weak,—so it was; and, therefore, that it was unable to do great things,—so it was not; for Christ's strength is made perfect in weakness, and He has chosen the despicable things of this world to put to shame such as are highly esteemed. They considered that they were God's people by a sort of right, that they did not need grace, and that their outward ceremonies and their dead works would profit them. Therefore the Apostle warned them, that Abraham himself was justified, not by circumcision, but by faith; that circumcision was not taken for righteousness in his case, for it never would arrive at righteousness, but that faith would arrive, and therefore it was taken; that "to him that worketh not, but believeth on him that justifieth the ungodly, his faith is counted for righteousness;" [14] that "by grace are we saved through faith, not of works, for we are *God's* workmanship, *created in* Christ Jesus *unto* good works;" [15] that "if by grace, then is it no more of works, otherwise grace is no more grace; but if it be of works, then is it no more grace, otherwise work is no more work." [16] However, the Jews still preferred their old works to good works; they refused to go the way by which alone

[12] Gal. v.5.   [13] Rom. x.3.   [14] Rom. iv.5.
[15] Eph. ii.8–10.   [16] Rom. xi.6.

their persons, thoughts, words, actions, services could be made acceptable to God; they would not exercise that loving faith which alone could gain for them the gift of the Spirit, and was fruitful in true righteousness; they refused to be justified in God's way, and determined to use the Law of Moses for a purpose for which it was never given, for their justification in His sight, and for attaining eternal life.

And in consequence God turned from them, and gave to others what was first offered to them. He manifested Himself to the Gentiles. Those who had hitherto been without any tokens of God's favour, outstripped in the race those who had long enjoyed it. The first became last, and the last first. "The Gentiles, which followed not after righteousness, have attained to righteousness, even the righteousness which is of faith; but Israel, which followed after the law of righteousness, hath not attained to the law of righteousness. Wherefore? Because they sought it, not by faith, but, as it were, by the works of the Law; for they stumbled at that stumbling-stone." [17]

Let us see to it, lest in any way we too stumble at God's commands or promises; let us beg of Him to lead us on in His perfect and narrow way, and to be "a lantern to our feet, and a light to our path," while we walk in it.

[17] Rom. xi.30–32.

THE NEW WORKS OF
THE GOSPEL

*"If any man be in Christ, he is a new creature: old things are passed
away; behold, all things are become new."*—2 Cor. v.17.

Nothing, is more clearly stated, or more strongly insisted
on, by St. Paul, than the new creation, or second beginning, or regeneration, of the world, which has been vouchsafed
in Christ. It had been announced in prophecy. "Behold, I create
new heavens and a *new* earth; and the former shall not be remembered, nor, come into mind." Again: "Behold, the days
come, saith the Lord, that I will make a *new* covenant with the
house of Israel and with the house of Judah. . . . I will put My
law in their inward parts, and write it in their hearts; and will be
their God, and they shall be My people." And again: "A *new*
heart will I give you, and a *new* spirit will I put within you; and
I will take away the stony heart out of your flesh, and I will give
you an heart of flesh. And I will put My Spirit within you, and
cause you to walk in My statutes, and ye shall keep My judgments and do them."[1] In the text, St. Paul declares the fulfilment of these promises in the Gospel. "If any man be in
Christ, he is a *new* creature; *old things are passed away*," as the
heavens and earth shall pass away, at the end of the world; "behold, all things are become *new*." And hence he calls Christ, not
only "the Image of the Invisible God," but also "the *first-born* of
every creature;" or, as He calls Himself in the book of Revelation, "the *beginning* of the creation of God."[2] St. Paul also
speaks of "the *new* and living way which He hath consecrated
for us through His flesh;" of Christians having "put off the old
man with his deeds," and having "put on the *new* man, which is
renewed in knowledge, after the Image of Him that created
him;" of "*newness* of life," and "*newness* of spirit;" of "ministers
of the *New* Testament, not of the letter, but of the Spirit;" and

[1] Is. lxv.17; Jer. xxxi.31, 33; Ezek. xxxvi.26, 27.
[2] Col. i.15; Rev. iii.14.

of our being God's "workmanship, *created* in Christ Jesus unto good works."[3] Elsewhere he says, that true and availing "circumcision is that of the heart, in the Spirit and not in the letter, whose praise is not of men, but of God;" and that "circumcision is nothing, and uncircumcision is nothing, but the keeping the commandments of God."[4]

Now it may be asked, Is there not some contrariety in these statements? The Gospel is said to be a *new* covenant, and yet, after all, it is to consist in "walking in God's statutes" and "doing His judgments," and "keeping His commandments," and being "created unto good works." Now these were but the terms of the old covenant: "Fear God and keep His commandments;" "If thou wilt enter into life, keep the commandments;" "The man that doeth those things shall live by them."[5] If the new Covenant be of works too, how is the Gospel other than the Law? how can it justly be called new? If the way of salvation be now what it ever has been, how are we gainers? What privilege is there in being brought under the Gospel? what has Christ done for us? Hence some persons have concluded that salvation under the Gospel is *not* of works; and in confirmation of this they urge, that St. Paul elsewhere speaks expressly of salvation as being not of works but of faith; and they allege that faith is a new way of salvation, though works of obedience are not and cannot be.

Now there can be no doubt at all that salvation is by faith, and that its being by faith is one of those special circumstances which make the Gospel a new covenant; but still it may be by works also; for, to use a familiar illustration, obedience is the *road* to heaven, and faith the *gate*. Those who attempt to be saved simply without works, are like persons who should attempt to travel to a place, not along the road, but across the fields. If we wish to get to our journey's end, we shall keep to the road; but even then we may go the *wrong* road. This was the case with the Jews. They professed to go along the road of works,—they did not wander into the fields,—so far well: but they took the wrong road. That particular road of which faith is the gate, that particular obedience, those particular works, which commence in faith, these are the only right and sure road to heaven. It is wrong to leave the road for the open country; again, it is wrong to go along the wrong road;—but it is not wrong to go along the right road. And in like manner it is sinful to attempt no obedi-

[3] Heb. x.20; Col. iii.9, 10; Rom. vi.4; vii.6; 2 Cor. iii.6; Eph. ii.10.
[4] Rom. ii.29; 1 Cor. vii.19.   [5] Eccles. xii.13; Rom. x.5.

ence whatever; it is blind perversity to attempt obedience by the Jewish law or the law of nature; but it is not sinful, it is not perverse, it is nothing else than wisdom, nothing else than true godliness, to follow after that obedience which is of faith.

The illustration may be pursued further. A road may want repairing,—it may get worse and worse as we go on, till it ceases to be a road: it may fall off from a road into a lane, from a lane to a path, or a wild heath, or a marsh; or it may be cut off by high impassable mountains; so that a person who attempts that way will never arrive at his journey's end. This was the case with the works of the Law by which the Jews thought to gain heaven,—this is the case with all works done in our natural strength: they are like a road over fens or precipices, which is sure to fail us. At first we might seem to go on well, but we should find at length that we made no progress. We should never get to our journey's end. Our best obedience in our own strength is worth nothing; it is altogether unsound, it is ever failing, it never grows firmer, it never can be reckoned on, it does nothing well, it has nothing in it pleasing or acceptable to God:—and not only so, it is the obedience of souls born and living under God's wrath, for a state of nature is a state of wrath. On the other hand, obedience which is done in faith is done with the aid of the Holy Spirit; it is holy and acceptable in God's sight; it grows habitual and consistent; it tends to possess the soul wholly; and it leads straight onward to heaven. This was the very promise of the Gospel as the prophet Isaiah announces it. "An highway shall be there and a way, and it shall be called the *way of holiness*: the unclean shall not pass over it . . . the wayfaring men, though fools, shall not err therein."[6] This being understood, we shall have no difficulty in understanding St. Paul's language. The way of salvation is by works, as under the Law, but it is by "works which spring out of faith," and which come of "the inspiration of the Spirit." It is because works are living and spiritual, from the heart, and by faith, that the Gospel is a new covenant. Hence in the passages above quoted we are told again and again of "the law *in our inward parts*;" "a new *heart*;" "a new *spirit*;" the Holy "*Spirit within us*;" "newness of *life*;" and "circumcision of the *heart* in the Spirit." And hence St. Paul says, that though we have not been "saved by works," yet we are "*created* unto *good* works;" and that "the blood of Christ purges the conscience from *dead* works to *serve* the *living* God."[7] Salvation then is not by dead works, but by living works. The Jews could but do dead works; but Christians can do good and spiritual works. The Gospel Covenant, then, is both a new way and not a new way. It is not a new way, seeing it is *in* works: it is a new way, in that it is *by* faith. It is, as St. Paul words it, the "obedience of faith;"— "new because of faith, old because of obedience."

And thus there is no opposition between St. Paul and St. James. St. James says, that justification is by works, and St. Paul that it is by faith: but, observe, St. James does not say that it is by dead or Jewish works; he mentions expressly *both* faith *and* works; he only says, "not faith *only* but works also:"—and St. Paul is far from denying it is by works, he only says that it is by faith and denies that it is by *dead* works. And what proves this, among other circumstances, is, that he never calls those works, which he condemns and puts aside, *good* works, but simply works: whenever he speaks of good works in his Epistles, he speaks of Christian works; not of Jewish. On the whole, then, salvation is both by faith and by works. St. James says, not *dead* faith, and St. Paul, not *dead* works. St. James, "not by faith *only*," for that *would* be dead faith: St. Paul, "not by works only," for such *would* be dead works. Faith alone can make works living; works alone can make faith living. Take away either, and you take away both;—he alone has faith who has works,—he alone has works who has faith.

It is not at all wonderful, then, that though the way of salvation under the Gospel is new, still in certain respects it is still what the Jews, nay, and what the heathen thought it to be. The way of justification has in all religions been by means of works; so it is under the Gospel; but in the Gospel alone it is by the means of good works.

However, this statement, simple and obvious as it is, is a hard saying to many persons, who think that the way of salvation should be altogether new under the Gospel, altogether different from what is prescribed under other religions; whereas they think little has been gained for us by Christ, if after all He has left us, as before, to be saved by obedience. This is a difficulty with them. They think Christianity is made Jewish, or almost heathen, if salvation is attained by what is the old way; and this being the case, I shall make some remarks, with the hope of reconciling the mind to it.

I observe, then, that whether it came from Noah after the flood or not, so it is, that all religions, the various heathen religions as well as the Mosaic religion, have many things in them which are very much the same. They seem to come from one common origin, and so far have the traces of truth upon them.

They are all branches, though they are corruptions and perversions, of that patriarchal religion which came from God. And of course the Jewish religion came entirely and immediately from God. Now God's works are like each other, not different; if, then, the Gospel is from God, and the Jewish religion was from God, and the various heathen religions in their first origin were from God, it is not wonderful, rather it is natural, that they should have in many ways a resemblance one with another. And, accordingly, that the Gospel is in certain points like the religions which preceded it, is but an argument that "God is One, and that there is none other but He;"—the difference between them being that the heathen religions are a true religion corrupted; the Jewish, a true religion dead; and Christianity, the true religion living and perfect. The heathen thought to be saved by works, so did the Jews, so do Christians; but the heathen took the works of darkness for good works, the Jews thought cold, formal and scanty works to be good works, and Christians believe that works done in the Spirit of grace, the fruit of faith, and offered up under the meritorious intercession of Christ, that these only are good works, but that these really *are* good:—so that while the heathen thinks to be saved by sin, and the Jew by self, the Christian relies on the Spirit of Him who died on the Cross for him. Thus they differ; but they all agree in thinking that works are the means of salvation; they differ in respect to the quality of these works.

Let us take some parallel instances in religious doctrine and worship, for they abound.

1. For example: Religion, considered in itself, cannot but have much which is the same in all systems, true and false. It is the worship of God. This involves saying prayers, postures of devotion, and the like, whatever the particular worship be; nor is the Gospel less a new covenant, because it retains these old usages, unless it ceases to be new, because it retains religion. While man is man, it could not be otherwise. These observances are right when performed well, evil when performed ill; evil as performed by the heathen, right as performed by Christians. The heathen worship devils, as St. Paul tells us. As is their god, such is their service. The Gospel came to destroy the worship of devils, not to destroy worship; we do not cease to have a new worship, because we worship, not devils, but Almighty God.

2. Again, meetings for worship have been in all religions from the first. But it does not follow from this that "old things" have not been made to pass away, till coming to church is denounced as a sin. On the contrary, St. Paul expressly tells us *not*

to forsake the assembling of ourselves together, though "all things have become new." What had been done of old time for bad purposes or in a bad way, is to be done for a holy purpose and in a heavenly way under the Gospel. A new life is infused into what once was evil, or at least profitless; so that, whereas of old time men came together to worship as "dry bones," in consequence of the creative power of Christ, "the dead bones live."

3. Again, religion has ever existed in a large organized body, with orders and officers, with ministers and people. It has always exercised an influence over the State, and it has ever been what is called established, or had rank and property. Now there is abundant evidence that this was intended to be the condition of religion under the Gospel, in spite of its being a new religion. Ranks existed from the first,—Apostles, Evangelists, Prophets, Bishops, and Deacons, as we read in Scripture. And property was held by the Church, for the rich gave up their wealth, and laid it at the Apostles' feet. And St. Paul used his privilege as a citizen of Rome. Here again, then, though salvation be of faith, and religion be spiritual, and old things be passed away, and all things have become new, yet the old framework remains as far as this, that there are men set apart to preach the Gospel, and that they "live by the Gospel."

4. Again, all religions, before the Gospel came, had their mysteries; I mean alleged disclosures of Truth, which could not be fully understood all at once, if at all, and which were open to some more than to others. The Gospel, though it be light and liberty, has not materially altered things here. It has mysteries as we all know; such as the doctrines of the Holy Trinity, and the Incarnation. And these mysteries cannot be equally entered into by all, but in proportion as men are humble and holy, and intellectually gifted, and blessed with leisure. St. Paul speaks of "the hidden wisdom;" and declares that "the natural man receiveth not the things of the Spirit of God, for they are foolishness unto him; neither can he know them, because they are spiritually discerned." And elsewhere he declines to speak to the Hebrews about Melchizedec, "of whom," he had "many things to say, and hard to be uttered, seeing" they were "dull of hearing."[8]

5. Again, religions before Christ came ever had holy days and festivals, both among heathen and Jews. The Gospel has not done away with holy days, only it has changed them, and made them more truly holy. For instance, it has not destroyed

[8] 1 Cor. ii.14; Heb. v.11.

the Feast of one day in seven, or the Lord's day; not to mention other instances. This is the more remarkable, because St. Paul's words are at first sight very strong against the observance, under the Gospel, of any days above others, as a matter of religion. He finds fault with the Galatians, because they observe "days, and months, and times, and years." And he bids the Colossians not to let any man "judge them in meat or in drink, or in respect of an holy day, or of the new moon, or of the Sabbath days, which are a shadow of things to come, but the body is of Christ."[9] Who would not, at first sight, suppose from these words, that all holy days, all holy seasons, were to be done away, under the Gospel, as mere shadows,—Sunday, Christmas-day, Easter-tide, Lent, and all the rest? Yet it is not so. The Apostles in the Acts, and St. John in the Revelation, observe and recognise the Lord's day as a Gospel festival. Jewish days *are* shadows, but Christian are not; just as Jewish works, or works of the Law, avail not, but Christian works avail. The weekly festival is not one of the "old things" which have "passed away" in Christ, neither have righteous works. The Sabbath has "become new" by becoming the Lord's day; works become new, by becoming spiritual.

6. Again, washing with water was a heathen rite of purification, and also a Jewish rite. Yet it remains under the Gospel; and with the same change. The "divers washings" of the Jews were "carnal ordinances;"[10] but Baptism, our washing, is a washing of the Spirit; and because the former are annulled, it does not follow that the latter should be. On the contrary, our Lord distinctly commanded His Apostles, "Go ye and teach all nations, baptizing them."[11]

7. Once more. The heathen had temples; the Jews had a temple; and our Lord said to the Samaritan woman, that the hour was coming when the true worshippers should worship, not in the temple at Jerusalem, but "in spirit and in truth." But this did not mean that there were to be no Christian temples, or churches, as we call them; at least it has never been taken so to mean. All it would seem to mean is, that the Jewish temple is not like a Christian temple, but differs in some essential points.

I have said enough to explain St. Paul's statement in the text, that "old things are passed away," and "all things new" under the Gospel. By all things being *"new"* is meant that they are *renewed*; by "old things *passing away*" is meant that they are

---

[9] Gal. iv.10; Col. ii.16, 17.   [10] Heb. ix.10.
[11] Matt. xxviii.19.

changed. The substance remains; the form, mode, quality, and circumstances are different and more excellent. Religion has still forms, ordinances, precepts, mysteries, duties, assemblies, festivals, and temples as of old time; but, whereas all these were dead and carnal before, now, since Christ came, they have a life in them. He has brought life to the world; He has given life to religion; He has made everything spiritual and true by His touch, full of virtue, full of grace, full of power so that ordinances, works, forms, which before were unprofitable, now, by the inward meritorious influence of His blood imparted to them, avail for our salvation.

This one point, in addition, is clear from what has been said; that if all Christian worship is "in spirit and in truth," nothing has a place under the Gospel which is *not* spiritual. It is very inconsistent then, to say, as some people do say, that Baptism should be observed, and yet that it does not convey Divine grace, and is a mere outward ordinance; for if so, it is nothing better than a Jewish rite, and instead of being observed, it ought to be abolished altogether. And again, unless the Church itself and the ministerial order attached to it, be a means of grace and the instrument of the Holy Ghost, they are no better than the Jewish temple and the Jewish priests, which have come to nought, and have no part in the spiritual system of the Gospel. And so, in like manner, works of obedience also, if they are no better than "the works of the Law," which cannot justify; if they are not pleasing to God, if they be filthy rags, as some persons say, and as the works of nature *are*; if so, then I do not see that they need be attempted at all; for all works of the Law are done away. Everything is done away in the Gospel but what is spirit and truth; and our works, our ordinances, our discipline, are spirit and truth, or they are done away.

And, lastly, hereby we see why justification must be of faith: because, as Christ, by means of His Spirit, makes a new beginning in us, so faith, on our part, receives that new beginning, and co-operates with Him. And it is the only principle which can do this: for as things spiritual are unseen, so faith is in its very nature that which apprehends and uses things unseen. We renounce our old unprofitable righteousness, which is from Adam, and accept, through faith, that new righteousness which is imparted by the Spirit; or, in St. Paul's words, "we, through the Spirit, wait for the hope of righteousness by faith."

To conclude. Let us think much, and make much, of the grace of God; let us beware of receiving it in vain; let us pray God to prosper it in our hearts, that we may bring forth much fruit. We see how grace wrought in St. Paul: it made him labour, suffer, and work righteousness almost above man's nature. This was not his own doing; it was not through his own power. He says himself, "Yet not I, but the grace of God which was in me." God's grace was "sufficient for him." It was its triumph in him, that it made him quite another man from what he was before. May God's grace be efficacious in us also. Let us aim at doing nothing in a dead way; let us beware of dead works, dead forms, dead professions. Let us pray to be filled with the spirit of love. Let us come to Church joyfully; let us partake the Holy Communion adoringly; let us pray sincerely; let us work cheerfully; let us suffer thankfully; let us throw our heart into all we think, say, and do; and may it be a spiritual heart! This is to be a new creature in Christ; this is to walk by faith.

THE STATE OF SALVATION

"That ye put on the new man, which after God is created in
righteousness and true holiness."
—Eph. iv.24.

THESE words express very strongly a doctrine which is to be found in every part of the New Testament, that the Gospel covenant is the means of introducing us into a state of life so different from that in which we were born, and should otherwise continue, that it may not unfitly be called a new creation. As that which is created differs from what is not yet created, so the Christian differs from the natural man. He is brought into a new world, and, as being in that new world, is invested with powers and privileges which he absolutely had not in the way of nature. By nature his will is enslaved to sin, his soul is full of darkness, his conscience is under the wroth of God; peace, hope, love, faith, purity, he has not; nothing of heaven is in him; nothing spiritual; nothing of light and life. But in Christ all these blessings are given: the will and the power; the heart and the knowledge; the light of faith, and the obedience of faith. As far as a being can be changed without losing his identity, as far as it is sense to say that an existing being can be new created, so far has man this gift when the grace of the Gospel has its perfect work and its maturity of fruit in him. A brute differs less from a man, than does man, left to himself with his natural corruption allowed to run its course, differ from man fully formed and perfected by the habitual indwelling of the Holy Spirit.

Hence, in the text, the Apostle speaks of the spiritual state which Christ has bought for us, as being a "new creature in righteousness and true holiness." Elsewhere he says, "If any man be in Christ he is a new creature; old things are passed away; behold all things are become new." Elsewhere, "Be ye transformed by the renewing of your mind." Elsewhere, "Ye are dead, and your life is hid with Christ in God." Elsewhere, "Ye are buried with Him by baptism into death; that, like as

Christ was raised up from the dead by the glory of the Father, even so we also should walk in newness of life."[1]

What then is this new state in which a Christian finds himself compared with the state of nature? It is worth the inquiry.

Now, first, there ought to be no difficulty in our views about it so far as this:—that there *is* a certain new state, and that a state of salvation; and that Christ came to bring into it all whom He had chosen out of the world. Christ "gave Himself for our sins (says St. Paul), that He might deliver us from the present evil world." He "hath delivered us from the power of darkness, and hath translated us into the kingdom of His dear Son." He came "to gather together in one the children of God, which are scattered abroad." "As many as received Him, to them gave He power to become the sons of God."[2] This is most clear. There can be no doubt at all that there is a certain state of grace now vouchsafed to us, who are born in sin and the children of wrath, such that those who are to be saved hereafter are (to speak generally) those, and those only, who are placed in that saving state here. I am not going on to the question, whether or not there is a visible Church; but I insist only on this, that it has not seemed fit to Almighty God to transplant His elect at once from this world and from a state of nature to the eternal happiness of heaven. He does not suffer them to die as they were born, and then, on death, change them outwardly and inwardly; but He brings them into a saving state here, preparatory to heaven;—a state which the Catechism calls a "state of salvation;" and which St. Luke denotes, when he says, "The Lord added daily to the Church such as should be saved;"[3] that is, persons called to salvation, placed in a saving state.

No one ought to deny this; though in this day, when all kinds of error abound, some persons seem to have taken up a notion that the world was fully reconciled all at once by Christ's death at the very time of it, and wholly transferred into a state of acceptance so that there is no new state necessary now for those who shall ultimately be benefited by it; that they have but to do their duty, and they will be rewarded accordingly; whereas it does certainly appear, from such texts of Scripture as have been quoted, that there is a certain state, or kingdom of Christ, into which all must enter here who shall be saved hereafter. We cannot attain to heaven hereafter, without being in this new kingdom here; we cannot escape from the miseries and horrors of

[1] 2 Cor. v.17; Rom. xii.2; Col. iii.3; Rom. vi.4.
[2] Gal. i.4; Col. i.13; John xi.52; i.12.
[3] Acts ii.47.

the Old Adam, except by being brought into this Kingdom, as into an asylum, and there remaining.

And further, this new state is one of "righteousness and true holiness," as the text speaks. Christ brings us into it by coming to us through His Spirit; and, as His Spirit is holy, we are holy, if we are in the state of grace. Christ is present in that heart which He visits with His grace. So that to be in His kingdom is to be in righteousness, to live in obedience, to breathe, as it were, an atmosphere of truth and love.

Now it is necessary to insist upon this also: for here again some men go wrong; and while they go so far as to acknowledge that there is a new state, or kingdom, into which souls must be brought, in order to salvation, yet they consider it as a state, not of holiness and righteousness, but merely or mainly of acceptance with God. It has been maintained by some persons, that human nature, even when regenerate, is not, and cannot be, really holy; nay, that it is idle to suppose that, even with the aid of the Holy Spirit, it can do any thing really good in any degree; that our best actions are sins; and that we are always sinning, not only in slighter matters, but so as to need pardon in all we do, in the same sense in which we needed it when we were as yet unregenerate; and, consequently, that it is vain to try to be holy and righteous, or, rather, that it is presumptuous.

Now, of course it is plain, that even the best of men are full of imperfections and failings; so far is undeniable. But, consider, by nature we are in a state of death. Now, is this the state of our hearts under the Gospel? Surely not; for, while "to be carnally minded is death," "to be spiritually minded is life and peace." I mean, that the state of salvation in which we stand is not one in which "our righteousnesses are" what the prophet calls "filthy rags," but one in which we can help sinning unto death,—can help sinning in the way men do sin when left in a state of nature. If we do so sin, we *cease* to be in that state of salvation; we fall back into a state resembling our original state of wrath, and must pass back again from wrath to grace (if it be so), as we best may, in such ways as God has appointed: whereas it is not an uncommon notion at this time, that a man may be an habitual sinner, and yet be in a state of salvation, and in the kingdom of grace. And this doctrine many more persons hold than think they do; not in words, but in heart. They think that faith is all in all; that faith, if they have it, blots out their sins as fast as they commit them. They sin in distinct acts in the morning,—their faith wipes all out; at noon,—their faith still avails; and in the evening,—still the same. Or they remain contentedly in sinful habits or practices, under the dominion of sin, not warring against it, in ignorance what is sin and what is not; and they think that the only business of a Christian is, not to be holy, but to have faith, and to think and speak of Christ; and thus, perhaps, they are really living, whether by habit or by act, in extortion, avarice, envy, rebellious pride, self-indulgence, or worldliness, and neither know nor care to know it. If they sin in habits, they are not aware of these at all; if by acts, instead of viewing them one and all together, they take them one by one, and set their faith against each separate act. So far has this been carried, that some men of name in the world have, before now, laid it down as a great and high principle, that there is no mortal sin but one, and that is want of faith; and have hereby meant, not that he who commits mortal sin cannot be said to have faith, but that he who has faith cannot be said to commit mortal sin; or, to speak more clearly, they have, in fact, defined a state of salvation to be nothing more or less than a state *in which* our sins are forgiven; a state of mere acceptance, not of substantial holiness. Persons who hold these opinions, consider that the great difference between a state of nature and a state of salvation is, that in a state of nature when we sin, we are not forgiven (which is true); but that, in a state of salvation, when we sin, our sins are forgiven us, because we *are* in that state. On the other hand, I would maintain from Scripture, that a state of salvation is so far from being a state in which sins of every kind are forgiven, that it is a state in which there are not sins of every kind to forgive and that, if a man commit them, so far from being forgiven *by* his state, he falls at once *from* his state by committing them; so far from being justified by faith, he, for that very reason, has not faith whereby to justify him. I say, our state of grace is a state of holiness; not one in which we may be *pardoned*, but in which we are *obedient*. He who acts unworthily of it, is not sheltered by it, but forfeits it. It is a state in which power is given us to act rightly, and therefore punishment falls on us if we act wrongly.

This is plain, from Scripture, on many reasons; of which I will here confine myself to one or two.

1. Let us first consider such Parables of our Lord as speak of the Christian state, to see what its characteristics are. These will be found not to recognise at all the case of instable, variable minds, falling repeatedly into gross sins, and saved by that state of grace in which they have been placed. The Christian state does not shelter a man who sins, but it lets him drop. Just as we cannot hold in our hands a thing in flames, but however dear it

be to us, though it be a child, we are forced at length to let it go; so wilful sin burns like fire, and the Church drops us, however unwillingly, when we sin wilfully. Not our faith, not our past services, not God's past mercies, avail to keep us in a state of grace, if "we sin wilfully after receiving the knowledge of the truth." [4] Now I say, agreeably with this, we shall find our Saviour's parables divide Christians into two states, those who continue in God's favour, and those who lose it; and those who continue in it are said to be, not those who merely have repentance and faith, who sin, but ever wash out their sins by coming for pardon, but those who do not sin;—not those whose one great aim is to obtain *forgiveness*, but those who (though they abound in infirmities, and so far have much to be forgiven) yet are best *described* by saying that they aim at *increasing* their talents, aim at "laying up for themselves a good foundation for the time to come, that they may lay hold of eternal life." [5]

For example, in our Saviour's first parable, who is he who builds his house upon a rock? not he who has faith merely, but he, who having doubtless faith to begin the work, has faith also strong enough to perfect it; who "heareth *and doeth*."

Again, in the parable of the Sower, the simple question considered is, who they are who profit by what they have received; what a Christian has to do is represented as a *work*, a process which has a beginning, middle, and end; a consistent course of obedience, not a state in which we have done nothing more at the end of our lives than at the beginning, except sin the oftener, according to its length. In that parable one man is said not to admit the good seed; a second admits it, but its root withers; a third goes further, the seed strikes root, and shoots upwards, but its leaves and blossoms get entangled and overlaid with thorns. The fourth takes root, shoots upwards, and does more, bears fruit to perfection. This then is the Christian's great aim, viz. not to come short after grace given him. This forms his peculiar danger, and his special dread. Of course he is not secure from peril of gross sin; of course he is continually defiled with sins of infirmity; but whereas, how to be forgiven is the main inquiry for the natural man, so, how to fulfil his calling, how to answer to grace given, how to increase his Lord's money, how to attain, this is the great problem of man regenerate. Faith gained him pardon; but works gain him a reward.

Again, the Net had two kinds of fish, good and bad, just and wicked; they differ in character and conduct; whereas men

[4] Heb. x.26.   [5] I Tim. vi.19.

allow themselves to speak as if, in point of moral condition, the saved and the reprobate were pretty much on a level; the real difference being, that the one have faith appropriating Christ's merits, and a spiritual conviction of their own perishing state, and the other have not. And so I might go on to the parables of the Ten Virgins, the Talents, and others, and show in like manner that the state of a Christian, as our Lord contemplates it, is one in which he is, not lamenting the victories of sin, but working out salvation; beginning, continuing, and at last perfecting, a course of obedience.

2. This being the doctrine of the Gospels, we shall understand why it is that so little is said in the Epistles of the sins of Christians. Indeed, no one can be sufficiently aware, till he inquires into the subject, how very few texts can be produced from the Apostles' writings containing a promise of forgiveness when Christians sin.[6] And yet this apparent omission is not difficult to explain. They had sins before they were Christians; they were forgiven that they might not sin again. St. Paul and his brethren never pray that Christians' sins may be pardoned, but that they may fulfil their calling. Their description of the state of the Church is almost like an account of Angels and the spirits of the just. "Our conversation is in heaven," says St. Paul, thus summing up in few words what almost all his Epistles testify to us. We hear of their "glorying in tribulations," their being "alive from the dead," their "joy and peace in believing," their being "fruitful in every good work," their "increasing in the knowledge of God," their "work of faith, and labour of love, and patience of hope." This is a picture of those whom the Apostle acknowledges as true Christians; as if in the case of true Christians gross transgression were impossible. They were far beyond that; what they had to avoid was shortcoming in the end. They were day by day to lessen the distance between themselves and their goal. They were to produce something positive, and they were gifted with the grace of the Holy Spirit for this purpose. There was nothing generous, nothing grateful, nothing of the high temper of faith, in sitting at home and merely praying for pardon. This might be well enough, it was all that they could do, while they were in a state of unassisted nature, in the house of bondage, with fetters upon them, and the iron entering into them. But their chains had been struck off; they could work, they could run; and they had a work to do, a road to journey. If they wilfully transgressed, they *left* the road, they

[6] *Vide* of these Sermons, Vol. iv. Serm. vii.

abandoned the work. Then they were like Demas, who went back, and they had to be restored; to be pardoned, not *in* the state of grace, but, if I may so say, *into* it.

3. Let us now turn our thoughts to St. John's description of the Christian state. For instance, in his first Epistle he expressly tells us, "Whosoever is born of God *sinneth not*, but he that is begotten of God keepeth himself, and that wicked one toucheth him not."[7] Such is the state of the true Christian; he is not only born again, but is born of God. All who are baptized, indeed, are born of God, as well as born again; but those who fall into sin, though they cannot undo what once has been, and are still born again, yet they are born again to their greater condemnation, and, therefore, not born again of God any longer, but, till they repent, born again unto judgment. But he in whom the divine birth is realized, "sinneth not, but keepeth himself," and what is the consequence? "that wicked one toucheth him not:" why? because he is in the kingdom of God. Satan cannot touch any one who keeps within that kingdom. God has "translated us from the power of darkness into the kingdom of His dear Son." It is by seducing us out of that kingdom that Satan destroys us; but while we continue within the sheepfold, the wolf cannot harm us. And hence the prophecy, which belongs to all Christ's followers in their degree as well as to our Lord Himself, "He shall give His Angels charge over thee to keep thee *in all thy ways*." "He shall deliver thee from the snare of the hunter, and from the noisome pestilence. He shall defend thee under His wings, and thou shalt be safe under His feathers. There shall no evil happen unto thee, neither shall any plague come nigh thy dwelling. Thou shalt go upon the lion and adder: the young lion and the dragon shalt thou tread under thy feet."[8] The serpent can but tempt, he cannot harm us, while we are in the paradise of God. This, I repeat, is the state of salvation, of which the Catechism speaks, and St. John assures us that they only are thus kept from the touch of that wicked one, who are so born of God as not to sin.

Again, "Whosoever is born of God, doth not commit sin, for His *seed remaineth* in him; and he cannot sin, because he is born of God." Again He says, "He that saith he abideth in Him, ought himself also so to walk even as He walked." Again, "If that which ye have heard from the beginning shall abide in you, ye also shall abide in the Son and in the Father." What is this but to say, that if it did not, they were no longer in grace?

[7] 1 John v. 18.   [8] Ps. xci. 11, 3, 10, 13.

"Whosoever abideth in Him, sinneth not." Again, "We know that we have passed from death unto life, because we love the brethren." [9]

And on the other hand the same Apostle plainly declares, that they who do sin are *not* in a state of grace. For instance, "If we say that we have fellowship with Him, and walk in darkness, we lie, and do not the truth." "He that saith he is in the light, and hateth his brother, is in darkness even until now." Again, "Whosoever committeth sin, transgresseth also the law, for sin is the transgression of the law. . . . Whosoever sinneth, hath not seen Him, neither known Him." "He that committeth sin is of the devil." "Whosoever transgresseth, and abideth not in the doctrine of Christ, hath not God." [10]

You see here are two states distinctly mentioned, and two states only; a state of grace, and a state of wrath; and he who sins in the state of grace, falls at once into the state of wrath. There is no such person under the Gospel as a "justified sinner," to use a phrase which is sometimes to be heard. If he is justified and accepted, he has ceased to be a sinner. The Gospel only knows of justified saints; if a saint sins, he ceases to be justified, and becomes a *condemned* sinner. Some persons, I repeat, speak as if men might go on sinning, and sinning ever so grossly, yet without falling from grace, without the necessity of taking direct and formal means to get back again. They *can* get back, praised be God, but still they *have* to get back, and the error I am speaking of is forgetfulness that they *have* fallen, and *have* to return.

4. That they who sin fall into a hopeless state,—that is hopeless *while* they continue in it, so that they can only gain hope *by leaving* it,—is shown more forcibly still in St. Paul's Epistle to the Hebrews. For instance, the inspired writer says, "If we sin wilfully, after that we have received the knowledge of the truth, there remaineth no more sacrifice for sins, but a certain fearful looking for of judgment and fiery indignation, which shall devour" or eat "the adversaries." [11] Here it is expressly said that wilful sin against knowledge does not leave us as it found us. We cannot receive pardon as we received it at the first, freely and instantly, merely on faith, we are thrown out of grace; and though our prospects are not at once hopeless, yet our *state* is hopeless, tends to perdition, nay, in itself, is perdition, one in which, *while* we are in it, we are lost. Hence all through this Epistle St. Paul, equally with St. John, speaks of but two states,

[9] 1 John iii.9; ii.6, 24; iii.6, 14.   [10] 1 John i.6; ii.9; iii.4, 6, 8; 2 John 9.
[11] Heb. x.27.

a state of grace and glory in the heavenly Jerusalem, a communion with God, Christ, Angels, saints departed, saints on earth;
and, on the other hand, a state of wrath; and he warns his brethren that they cannot sin without falling into the state of wrath.
"We are not of them that draw back unto perdition, but of
them that believe to the saving of the soul." [12] He does not speak
of sin and sinners tenderly; he does not merely say, "If you sin,
you are an evidence of human frailty; you are *inconsistent*; you
ought to keep from sin from *gratitude*; you should be deeply
humbled at your sins; you should betake yourselves to the atonement of Christ if you sin." All this is true, but it would be short
of the real state of the case; and St. Paul, therefore, says much
more: "If you sin wilfully, you throw yourselves out of God's
kingdom; you by the very act disinherit yourselves, you bring
yourselves into a dreadful region;" and he leaves it to them to
draw the inference what they ought to do to get back again. He
urges against them "the terrors of the Lord." He bids them not
deceive themselves, for sinners have no inheritance in the kingdom. Accordingly he warns them "to look diligently, lest any
man come short of the grace of God;" and to "fear, lest a promise being left us of entering into His rest, any of them should
seem to *come short* of it." [13]

Such is the new state of "righteousness and true holiness," in
which Christians are created, and such is the state of those who
draw back from it; and if any one asks whether St. Paul does not
say that "by *faith* we stand?" I answer, as I have already answered, that doubtless faith does keep us in a state of grace, and
is the means of blotting out for us those sins which we commit
in it. But *what* are those sins which we do commit? Sins of infirmity;—all other sins faith itself excludes. If we do commit
greater sins, we have not faith. Faith we cannot use to blot out
the greater sins, for faith we have not at all, if we commit such.
That faith which has not power over our hearts to keep us
from transgressing, has not power with God to keep Him from
punishing.

To conclude. This is our state:—Christ has healed each of us,
and has said to us, "See thou sin no more, lest a worse thing
come unto thee." [14] If we commit sin, we fall,—not at once back
again into the unredeemed and lost world; no, but at least we
fall out of the kingdom, though for a while we may linger on
the skirts of the kingdom. We fall into what will in the event
lead us back *into* the lost world, or rather into what is worse,

[12] Heb. x.39.   [13] Heb. xii.15; iv.1.   [14] John v.14.

unless we turn heavenward, and extricate ourselves from our fearful state as speedily as we can. We come into what may be called the passage or vestibule of hell; a place full of those unclean spirits who "seek rest and find none," and rejoice in getting possession of souls, from which they were once cast out. We are no longer in the light of God's countenance, and though (blessed be His Name) doubtless we can through His help get back into it, yet we have to get back into it;—and then the whole subject becomes an anxious and serious one. Yes, it is indeed very serious, considering how the common run of Christians go on. If wilful sin throws us out of a state of grace, and if men do sin wilfully, and then forget that they have done so, and years pass away, and they merely smooth over what has happened by forgetting it, and assume that they are still in a state of grace, making no efforts by true repentance to be put into it again, only assuming that they are in it; and then go about their duties as Christians, just as if they were still God's children in the sense in which Baptism made them, and were not presumptuously intruding without leave, and not by the door, into a house whence they have been sent out; and if they so live and so die, what are we to say about them? Alas! what a dreadful thought it is, that there may be numbers outwardly in the Christian Church, nay, who at present are in a certain sense religious men, who, nevertheless, have no principle of *growth* in them, because they have sinned, and never duly repented. They may be under a disability for past sins, which they have never been at the pains to remove, or to attempt to remove. Alas! to think that they do not know their state at all and esteem themselves in the unreserved enjoyment of God's favour, when, after all, their religion is for the most part but the reflection from without upon their surface, not a light within them, or at least but the remains of grace once given. O dreadful thought, if we are in the number! O most dreadful thought, if an account lies against us in God's books, which we have never manfully encountered, never inquired into, never even prayed against, only and simply *forgotten*; which we leave to itself to be settled as it may; and if at any time some sudden memory of it comes across us, we think of it without fear, as if what has gone out of our minds had been forgotten of God also!—or even, as the way of some is, if, when we recollect any former sins of whatever kind, we palliate them, give them soft names, make excuses, saying they were done in youth or under great temptation, or cannot be helped now, or have been forsaken. May God give us all grace ever to think of these things; to reflect on the brightness of that state in which God once placed us, its purity, its sweetness, its radiance, its beauty, its majesty, its glory: and to think, in contrast of the wretchedness and filthiness of that load of sin, with which our own wilfulness has burdened us: and to pray Him to show us how to unburden ourselves,—how to secure to ourselves again those gifts which, for what we know, we have forfeited.

TRANSGRESSIONS AND INFIRMITIES

*"Now the just shall live by faith; but if any man draw back, My
soul shall have no pleasure in him."*—Heb. x.38.

WARNINGS such as this would not be contained in Scripture, were there no danger of our drawing back, and
thereby losing that "life" in God's presence which faith secures
to us. The blessedness of a creature is to "live before God,"[1] to
have an "access"[2] into the court of the King of kings, that state
of grace and glory which Christ has purchased for us. Faith is
the tenure upon which this divine life is continued to us: by
faith the Christian lives, but if he draws back he dies; his faith
profits him nothing; or rather, his drawing back to sin is a reversing of his faith; after which, God has no pleasure in him.
And yet, clearly as this is stated in Scripture, men in all ages
have fancied that they might sin grievously, yet maintain
their Christian hope. They have comforted themselves with
thoughts of the infinite mercy of God, as if He could not punish the sinner; or they have laid the blame of their sins on their
circumstances; or they have hoped that zeal for the truth, or
that almsgiving, would make up for a bad life; or they have relied upon repenting in time to come. And not the least subtle
of such excuses is that which results from a doctrine popularly
received at this day, that faith in Christ is compatible with a
very imperfect state of holiness, or with unrighteousness, and
avails for the pardon of an unrighteous life. So that a man may,
if so be, go on pretty much like other men, with this only difference, that he has what he considers faith,—a certain spiritual insight into the Gospel scheme, a renunciation of his own
merit, and a power of effectually pleading and applying to his
soul Christ's atoning sacrifice, such as others have not;—that
he sins indeed much as others, but then is deeply grieved that
he sins; that he *would* be under the wrath of God as others are,
had he not faith to remove it withal. And thus the necessity of a
holy life is in fact put out of sight quite as fully as if he said in so

[1] Gen. xvii.18.   [2] Rom. v.2.

many words, that it was not required; and a man may, if it so happen, be low-minded, sordid, worldly, arrogant, imperious, self-confident, impure, self-indulgent, ambitious or covetous, nay, may allow himself from time to time in wilful acts of sin which he himself condemns, and yet, by a great abuse of words, may be called spiritual.

Now I quite grant that there are sins which faith is the means of blotting out continually, so that the "just" still "lives" in God's sight in spite of them. There is no one but sins continually so far as this, that all that he does might be more perfect, entire, blameless than it is. We are all encompassed by infirmities, weaknesses, ignorances; and all these besetting sins are certainly, as Scripture assures us, pardoned on our faith; but it is another thing to assert this of greater and more grievous sins, or what may be called transgressions. For faith keeps us from transgressions, and they who transgress, for that very reason, have not true and lively faith; and, therefore, it avails them nothing that faith, as Scripture says, is imputed to Christians for righteousness, for they have not faith. Instead of faith blotting out transgressions, transgressions blot out faith. Faith, if it be true and lively, both precludes transgressions and gradually triumphs over infirmities; and while infirmities continue, it regards them with so perfect an hatred, as avails for their forgiveness, and is taken for that righteousness which it is gradually becoming. And such *is* a holy doctrine; for it provides for our pardon without dispensing with our obedience.

This distinction in the character of sins, viz. that some argue absence of faith and involve the loss of God's favour, and that others do not, is a very important one to insist upon, even though we cannot in all cases draw the line and say what sins imply the want of faith, and what do not; because, if we know that there *are* sins which do throw us out of grace, though we do not know *which* they are, this knowledge, limited as it is, will, through God's mercy, put us on our guard against acts of sin of any kind; both from the dread we shall feel lest these in particular, whatever they are, may be of that fearful nature, and next, from knowing that at least they tend that way. The common mode of reasoning adopted by the religion of the day is this: some sins are compatible with true faith, viz. sins of infirmity; therefore, wilful transgression, or what the text calls "departing" from God, is compatible with it also. Men do not, and say they cannot, draw the line; and thus, from putting up with small sins, they go on to a sufferance of greater sins. Well, I would take the reverse way, and begin at the other end. I would force upon men's notice that there are sins which do forfeit grace; and then if, as is objected, that we cannot draw the line between one kind of sin and another, this very circumstance will make us shrink not only from transgressions, but also from infirmities. From hatred and abhorrence of large sins, we shall, please God, go on to hate and abhor the small.

Now then let us betake ourselves to Scripture, in proof of this distinction between sin and sin. I say then this: first, that there are sins which forfeit a state of grace; next, that there are sins which do not forfeit it; and, lastly, that sins which do not forfeit it, nevertheless tend to forfeit it.

1. No one surely can doubt that there are sins which exclude a man, while he is under their power, from salvation. This is brought home to us by all that meets us on the very surface of the inspired text. "He that committeth sin, is of the devil," says St. John; "whosoever doeth not righteousness, is not of God." And, again, St. Paul, "Many walk, of whom I have told you often, and now tell you even weeping, that they are the enemies of the Cross of Christ; whose end is destruction." Again, "Christ is of no effect unto you, whosoever of you are justified by the Law; ye are fallen from grace."[3] Again, in the text, "The just shall live by faith, but if he draw back, My soul shall have no pleasure in him." Here are instances, at first sight, of sins which forfeit our hope of salvation; but let me be more particular.

(1.) All habits of vice are such. For instance, St. Paul says, "Know ye not that the unrighteous shall not inherit the Kingdom of God? Be not deceived: neither fornicators, nor idolaters, nor adulterers, nor effeminate, nor drunkards," and so he proceeds, "shall inherit the kingdom of God."[4] As, then, Baptism made us "inheritors of the kingdom of heaven," so sins such as these forfeit that kingdom. Accordingly, the Apostle goes on, by way of contrast, to speak of what they had become in Christ,—"And such were some of you; but ye are washed, but ye are sanctified, but ye are justified."

(2.) Next, it is fearful to think (fearful, because, among ourselves at this day, men are almost blind to the sin), that covetousness is mentioned in connexion with sins of the flesh, as incurring forfeiture of grace equally with them. St. Paul says, "neither adulterers, nor effeminate, nor *covetous*." Again, to the Ephesians, "This ye know, that no whoremonger, nor unclean person, nor *covetous man*, who is an idolater, hath any inheritance in the kingdom of Christ and of God." This accords with

[3] 1 John iii.8, 10; Phil. iii.18, 19; Gal. v.4.   [4] 1 Cor. vi.9, 10.

our Lord's warning, "ye cannot serve God and mammon;"[5] as much as to say, If you serve mammon, you forthwith quit God's service; you cannot serve two masters at once; you have passed into the kingdom of mammon, that is, of Satan.

(3.) All violent breaches of the law of charity are inconsistent with a state of grace; for the Apostle, in the places just cited, speaks of "thieves, revilers, and extortioners." In like manner St. John says in the Book of Revelations, "Without are dogs, and sorcerers and *murderers*."[6]

(4.) And in like manner all profaneness, heresy, and false worship; thus St. John speaks of "idolaters," with murderers; and St. Paul says that Esau, as being "a profane person," lost the blessing; and declares of all who "preach any other Gospel" than the true one, "Let him be accursed."[7]

(5.) And further, "hardness of heart," or going against light; according to the text, "Let us labour to enter into that rest, lest any man fall after the same example of unbelief;" and "To-day, if ye will hear his voice, harden not your hearts."[8]

Such are greater sins or transgressions. They are here specified, not as forming a complete list of such sins, which indeed cannot be given, but in proof of what ought not to be doubted, that there are sins which are not found in persons in a state of grace.

2. In the next place, that there are sins of infirmity, or such as do not throw the soul out of a state of salvation, is evident directly it is granted that there are sins which do; for no one will pretend to say that all sins exclude from grace, else no one can be saved, for there is no one who is sinless. However, Scripture expressly recognises sins of infirmity as distinct from transgressions, as shall now be shown.

For instance: St. Paul says to the Galatians, "The flesh lusteth against the Spirit, and the Spirit against the flesh; and these are contrary the one to the other, so that ye cannot do the things that ye would."[9] In these words he allows that it is possible for the power of the flesh and the grace of the Spirit to co-exist in the soul; neither the flesh quenching the Spirit, nor the Spirit all at once subduing the flesh. Here then is a sinfulness which is compatible with a state of salvation.

Again, the same Apostle says, that we have a High Priest who is "touched with the feeling of our *infirmities*," in that He had them Himself, *all but* their sin:—this implies that we have sinful

---

[5] Eph. v.5; Matt. vi.24.   [6] Rev. xxii.15.   [7] Heb. xii.16; Gal. i.8.
[8] Heb. iv.7, 11.   [9] Gal. v.17.

infirmities, yet of that light nature that they can be said to be in substance partaken by One who was pure from all sin. Accordingly, in the next verse St. Paul bids us "come boldly to the throne of grace, that we may obtain mercy." Such words do not imply a return *into* a state of salvation, but pardon *in* that state, and they correspond to what he afterwards says, "Let us draw near with a true heart in full assurance of faith, having boldness to enter into the holiest by the blood of Jesus," that is, by a continual approach; or, as he says to the Romans, By Christ "we have access," or admission, "by faith into this grace wherein we *stand*." [10]

In like manner he says, that "the Spirit helpeth our infirmities," [11] whereas transgression on the contrary quenches the Spirit.

And somewhat parallel to this is his language about himself, when, after speaking of a trial to which he was subjected, he says that Christ said to him, "My grace is sufficient for thee, for My strength is made perfect in weakness;" and he adds, "Most gladly therefore will I rather glory in my infirmities, that the power of Christ may rest upon me." [12]

And so in an earlier part of the same Epistle he says, apparently with the same meaning, "We have this treasure," the knowledge of the Gospel, "in earthen vessels, that the excellency of the power may be of God, and not of us." [13]

Sins of infirmity seem also intended in his exhortation to the Corinthians in another part of the same Epistle. After showing that righteousness has no fellowship with unrighteousness, and bidding them "be separate, and touch not the unclean thing," he adds, "Having therefore these promises, let us cleanse ourselves from all defilement of the flesh and spirit, *perfecting holiness* in the fear of God." [14]

In like manner St. John says, "If we walk in the light, as He is in the light, we have fellowship one with another; and the blood of Jesus Christ His Son cleanseth us from all sin." It seems then that there is sin which is consistent with "walking in the light," and that from this sin "the blood of Christ cleanseth us." [15]

Again, the same Apostle says soon after, "My little children, these things write I unto you, that ye sin not; and if any man sin, we have an Advocate with the Father, Jesus Christ the Righteous, and He is the Propitiation for our sins." Here sins are contemplated as attaching to a Christian, and as passed over

[10] Heb. iv.15, 16; x.19–22; Rom. v.2.

[11] Rom. viii.26.   [12] 2 Cor. xii.9.   [13] 2 Cor. iv.7.

[14] 2 Cor. vii.1.   [15] 1 John i.7.

in the view of Christ's righteousness; yet presently St. John says, "Whosoever is born of God, doth not commit sin," [16] that is, infirmities he may admit, transgressions he cannot.

And St. James says, "In many things we all offend," that is, we all stumble. We are ever stumbling along our course, while we walk; but if we actually fall in it, we fall from it.

And St. Jude: "Of some have compassion, making a difference; and others save with fear, pulling them out of the fire." [17] Distinct kinds of sins are evidently implied here.

And lastly, our Lord Himself had already implied that there are sins which are not inconsistent with a state of grace, when He said of His Apostles, "The spirit is willing, but the flesh is weak." [18]

3. It remains to show that these sins of infirmity tend to those which are greater, and forfeit grace; which is not the least important point which comes under consideration.

An illustration will explain what I mean, and may throw light on the whole subject. You know it continually happens that some indisposition overtakes a man, such that persons skilled in medicine, when asked if it is dangerous, answer, "Not at present, but they do not know what will come of it; it may turn out something very serious; but there is nothing much amiss yet; at the same time, if it be not checked, and, much more, if it be neglected, it will be serious." This, I conceive, is the state of Christians day by day, as regards their souls; they are always ailing, always on the point of sickness; they are sickly, easily disarranged, obliged to take great care of themselves against air, sun, and weather; they are full of tendencies to all sorts of grievous diseases, and are continually showing these tendencies, in slight symptoms; but they are not yet in a dangerous way. On the other hand, if a Christian falls into any serious sin, then he is at once cast out of grace, as a man who falls into a pestilential fever is quite in a distinct state from one who is merely in delicate health.

Now with respect to this progress of sin from infirmity to transgression, here, as before, we have no need to go to Scripture in proof of a truth which every day teaches us, that men begin with little sins and go on to great sins, that the course of sin is a continuous declivity, with nothing to startle those who walk along it, and that the worst transgressions seem trifles to the sinner, and that the lightest infirmities are grievous to the holy. "He that despiseth small things," says the wise man,

[16] 1 John ii.1; iii.9.   [17] Jude 22, 23.   [18] Matt. xxvi.41.

"shall fall by little and little;" this surely is the doctrine of inspired Scripture throughout; and here I will do no more than cite two passages from two Apostles in behalf of it. St. James says expressly, "When lust hath conceived, it bringeth forth sin; and sin, *when it is finished*, bringeth forth *death*."[19] You see that from the first it tends to death; for it ends in death, but not *till* it ends, till it is *finished*. Again, St. Paul says, "Make straight paths for your feet, *lest* that which is *lame* be *turned out of the way*; but let it rather be healed."[20] We are ever in a degree lame in this world, even in our best estate. All Christians are such; but when in consequence of their lameness they proceed to turn aside, or, as the text says, to "draw back," then they differ from those who are merely lame, as widely as those who halt along a road differ from those who fall out of it. Those who have turned aside, have to return, they have fallen into a different state: those who are lame must be "healed" *in* the state of grace in which they are, and while they are in it; and that, *lest* they "turn out" of it. Thus lameness is at once distinct from backsliding, yet leads to it.

And here an observation may be made concerning that sin against the Holy Ghost, which shall never be forgiven. I am very far from denying that there is a certain special sin to which that awful title belongs, though I will not undertake to say what it is; but I observe thus much:—that, whereas it is the unpardonable sin, there is not a sin which we do but may be considered to tend towards it, and to be the beginning of that which *ends* in death, which ends in impenitence, ends in quenching those gracious influences, by which alone we are able to do any good. And this is a very serious thought to all who sin wilfully; that, though their sin be slight, they are beginning a course, which, if let run on freely, ends in apostasy and reprobation. Hence the force of the following passage, which describes the ultimate result of a course of wilful sin, or what every wilful sin tends to become: "It is impossible for those who were once enlightened, and have tasted of the heavenly gift, and were made partakers of the Holy Ghost, and have tasted of the good word of God, and the powers of the world to come, *if they shall fall away*," so as utterly to quench the grace given them, "to renew them again to repentance."[21]

On the whole, then, this may be considered a Christian's state, ever about to fall, yet by God's mercy never falling; ever dying, yet always alive; full of infirmities, yet free from trans

---

[19] James i.15.   [20] Heb. xii.13.   [21] Heb. vi.6.

gressions: and, as time goes on, more and more free from infirmities also, as tending to that perfect righteousness which is the fulfilling of the Law;—on the other hand, should he fall, recoverable, but not without much pain, with fear and trembling.

I conclude with advising you, my brethren, one thing, which is obviously suggested by what I have said. Never suffer sin to remain upon you; let it not grow old in you; wipe it off while it is fresh, else it will stain; let it not get ingrained; let it not eat its way in, and rust in you. It is of a consuming nature; it is like a canker; it will eat your flesh. I say, beware, my brethren, of suffering sin in yourselves, and this for a great many reasons. First, if for no other than this, you will forget you have committed it, and never repent of it at all. Repent of it while you know it; let it not be wiped from your memory without being first wiped away from your soul. What may be the state of our souls from the accumulating arrears of the past! Alas! what difficulties we have involved ourselves in, without knowing it. Many a man doubtless in this way lives in a languid state, has a veil intercepting God from him, derives little or no benefit from the ordinances of grace, and cannot get a clear sight of the truth. Why? His past sins weigh upon him like a load, and he knows it not. And then again, sin neglected not only stains and infects the soul, but it becomes habitual. It perverts and deforms the soul; it permanently enfeebles, cripples, or mutilates us. Let us then rid ourselves of it at once day by day, as of dust on our hands and faces. We wash our hands continually. Ah! is not this like the Pharisees, unless we wash our soiled souls also? Let not then this odious state continue in you; in the words of the prophet, "Wash you, make you clean, put away the evil of your doings" from before the eyes of your Lord and Saviour. Make a clean breast of it. You sin day by day; let not the sun go down upon your guilt. You sin continually, at least so far as to make you most miserable, most offensive, most unfit for the Angels who are your companions. Come then continually to the Fount of cleansing for cleansing. St. John says that the Blood of Jesus Christ cleanseth from all sin. Use the means appointed,—confession, prayer, fasting, making amends, good resolves, and the ordinances of grace. Do not stop to ask the degree of your guilt,—whether you have actually drawn back from God or not. Let your ordinary repentance be as though you had. You cannot repent too much. Come to God day by day, intreating Him for all the sins of your whole life up to the very hour present. This is the way to keep your baptismal robe bright. Let it be washed as your garments of this world are, again and again;

washed in the most holy, most precious, most awfully salutary of all streams, His blood, who is without blemish and without spot. It is thus that the Church of God, it is thus that each individual member of it, becomes all glorious within, and filled with grace.

Thus it is that we return in spirit to the state of Adam on his creation, when as yet the grace and glory of God were to him for a robe, and rendered earthly garments needless. Thus we prepare ourselves for that new world yet to come, for the new heavens and the new earth, and all the hosts of them, in the day when they shall be created;—when the marriage of the Lamb shall come, and His wife shall make herself ready, and to her shall be granted to be arrayed in fine linen clean and white; for the fine linen is the righteousness of Saints.

SINS OF INFIRMITY

"The flesh lusteth against the Spirit, and the Spirit against the flesh; and these are contrary the one to the other, so that ye cannot do the things that ye would."—Gal. v.17.

I<small>T</small> is not uncommonly said of the Church Catholic, and we may humbly and thankfully receive it, that though there is error, variance, and sin in an extreme degree in its separate members, yet what they do all in common, what they do in combination, what they do gathered together in one, or what they universally receive or allow, is divine and holy; that the sins of individuals are overruled, and their wanderings guided and brought round, so that they end in truth, in spite, or even in one sense, by means of error. Not as if error had any power of arriving at truth, or were a necessary previous condition of it, but that it pleases Almighty God to work out His great purposes in and through human infirmity and sin. Thus Balaam had a word put in his mouth in the midst of his enchantments, and Caiaphas prophesied in the act of persuading our Lord's death.

What is true of the Church as a body, is true also of each member of it who fulfils his calling: the continual results, as I may call them, of his faith, are righteous and holy, but the process through which they are obtained is one of imperfection; so that could we see his soul as Angels see it, he would, when seen at a distance, appear youthful in countenance, and bright in apparel; but approach him, and his face has lines of care upon it, and his dress is tattered. His righteousness then seems, I do not mean superficial, this would be to give a very wrong idea of it, but though reaching deep within him, yet not whole and entire in the depth of it; but, as it were, wrought out of sin, the result of a continual struggle,—not spontaneous nature, but habitual self-command.

True faith is not shown here below in peace, but rather in conflict; and it is no proof that a man is not in a state of grace that he continually sins, provided such sins do not remain on him as what I may call ultimate results, but are ever passing on into something beyond and unlike themselves, into truth and righteousness. As we gain happiness through suffering, so do we arrive at holiness through infirmity, because man's very condition is a fallen one, and in passing out of the country of sin, he necessarily passes through it. And hence it is that holy men are kept from regarding themselves with satisfaction, or resting in any thing short of our Lord's death, as their ground of confidence; for, though that death has already in a measure wrought life in them, and effected the purpose for which it took place, yet to themselves they seem but sinners, their renewal being hidden from them by the circumstances attending it. The utmost they can say of themselves is, that they are not in the commission of any such sins as would plainly exclude them from grace; but how little of firm hope can be placed on such negative evidence is plain from St. Paul's own words on the subject, who, speaking of the censures passed upon him by the Corinthians, says, "I know nothing by myself," that is, I am conscious of nothing, "yet am I not hereby justified; but He that judgeth me is the Lord." As men in a battle cannot see how it is going, so Christians have no certain signs of God's presence in their hearts, and can but look up towards their Lord and Saviour, and timidly hope. Hence they will readily adopt the well-known words, not as expressing a matter of doctrine, but as their own experience about themselves. "The little fruit which we have in holiness, it is, God knoweth, corrupt and unsound; we put no confidence at all in it; . . . our continual suit to Him is, and must be, to bear with our infirmities and pardon our offences."[1]

Let us then now enumerate some of the infirmities which I speak of; infirmities which, while they certainly beset those who are outcasts from God's grace, and that with grievous additions and fatal aggravations, yet are also possible in a state of acceptance, and do not in themselves imply the absence of true and lively faith. The review will serve to humble all of us, and perhaps may encourage those who are depressed by a sense of their high calling, by reminding them that they are not reprobate, though they be not all they should be.

1. Now of the sins which stain us, though without such a consent of the will as to forfeit grace, I must mention first original sin. How it is that we are born under a curse which we did not bring upon us, we do not know; it is a mystery; but when we become Christians, that curse is removed. We are no longer under God's wrath; our guilt is forgiven us, but still the

---

[1] Hooker on Justification, § 9.

infection of it remains. I mean, we still have an evil principle within us, dishonouring our best services. How far, by God's grace, we are able in time to chastise, restrain, and destroy this infection, is another question; but still it is not removed at once by Baptism, and if not, surely it is a most grievous humiliation to those who are striving to "walk worthy of the Lord unto all pleasing."[2] It is involuntary, and therefore does not cast us out of grace; yet in itself it is very miserable and very humbling: and every one will discover it in himself, if he watches himself narrowly. I mean, what is called the old Adam, pride, profaneness, deceit, unbelief, selfishness, greediness, the inheritance of the Tree of the knowledge of good and evil; sins which the words of the serpent sowed in the hearts of our first parents, which sprang up and bore fruit, some thirty-fold, some sixty, some an hundred, and which have been by carnal descent transmitted to us.

2. Another class of involuntary sins, which often are not such as to throw us out of grace, any more than the infection of nature, but are still more humbling and distressing, consists of those which arise from our former habits of sin, though now long abandoned. We cannot rid ourselves of sin when we would; though we repent, though God forgives us, yet it remains in its power over our souls, in our habits, and in our memories. It has given a colour to our thoughts, words, and works; and though, with many efforts, we would wash it out from us, yet this is not possible except gradually. Men have been slothful, or self-conceited, or self-willed, or impure, or worldly-minded in their youth, and afterwards they turn to God, and would fain be other than they have been, but their former self clings to them, as a poisoned garment, and eats into them. They cannot do the things that they would, and from time to time they seem almost reduced back again to that heathen state, which the Apostle describes, when he cries out, "O wretched man that I am! who shall deliver me from the body of this death?"[3]

3. Another class of involuntary sins are such as arise from want of self-command; that is, from the mind being possessed of more light than strength, the conscience being informed, but the governing principle weak. The soul of man is intended to be a well-ordered polity, in which there are many powers and faculties, and each has its due place; and for these to exceed their limits is sin; yet they cannot be kept within those limits except

[2] Col. i.10.   [3] Rom. vii.24.

by being governed, and we are unequal to this task of governing ourselves except after long habit. While we are learning to govern ourselves, we are constantly exposed to the risk, or rather to the occurrence, of numberless failures. We have failures by the way, though we triumph in the end; and thus, as I just now implied, the process of learning to obey God is, in one sense, a process of sinning, from the nature of the case. We have much to be forgiven; nay, we have the more to be forgiven the more we attempt. The higher our aims, the greater our risks. They who venture much with their talents, gain much, and in the end they hear the words, "Well done, good and faithful servant;" but they have so many losses in trading by the way, that to themselves they seem to do nothing but fail. They cannot believe that they are making any progress; and though they do, yet surely they have much to be forgiven in all their services. They are like David, men of blood; they fight the good fight of faith, but they are polluted with the contest.

I am not speaking of cases of extraordinary devotion, but of what every one must know in his own case, how difficult it is to command himself, and do that he wishes to do;—how weak the governing principle of his mind is, and how poorly and imperfectly he comes up to his own notions of right and truth; how difficult it is to command his feelings, grief, anger, impatience, joy, fear; how difficult to govern his tongue, to say just what he would; how difficult to rouse himself to do what he would, at this time or that; how difficult to rise in the morning; how difficult to go about his duties and not be idle; how difficult to eat and drink just what he should, how difficult to fix his mind on his prayers; how difficult to regulate his thoughts through the day; how difficult to keep out of his mind what should be kept out of it.

We are feeble-minded, excitable, effeminate, wayward, irritable, changeable, miserable. We have no lord over us, because we are but partially subject to the dominion of the true King of Saints. Let us try to do right as much as we will, let us pray as earnestly, yet we do not, in a time of trial, come up even to our own notions of perfection, or rather we fall quite short of them, and do perhaps just the reverse of what we had hoped to do. While there is no external temptation present, our passions sleep, and we think all is well. Then we think, and reflect, and resolve what we will do; and we anticipate no difficulty in doing it. But when the temptation is come, where are we then? We are like Daniel in the lions' den; and our passions are the lions; except that we have not Daniel's grace to prevail with God for the shutting of the lions' mouths lest they devour us. Then our reason is but like the miserable keeper of wild beasts, who in ordinary seasons is equal to them, but not when they are excited. Alas! Whatever the affection of mind may be, how miserable it is! It may be a dull, heavy sloth, or cowardice, which throws its huge limbs around us, binds us close, oppresses our breath, and makes us despise ourselves, while we are impotent to resist it; or it may be anger, or other baser passion, which, for the moment, escapes from our control after its prey, to our horror and our disgrace; but anyhow, what a miserable den of brute creatures does the soul then become, and we at the moment (I say) literally unable to help it! I am not, of course speaking of *deeds* of evil, the fruits of wilfulness,—malice, or revenge, or uncleanness, or intemperance, or violence, or robbery, or fraud;—alas! the sinful heart often goes on to commit sins which hide from it at once the light of God's countenance; but I am supposing what was Eve's case, when she looked at the tree and saw that the fruit was good, but before she plucked it, when lust had conceived and was bringing forth sin, but ere sin was finished and had brought forth death. I am supposing that we do not exceed so far as to estrange God from us, that He mercifully chains the lions at our cry, before they do more than frighten us by their moanings or their roar,—before they fall on us to destroy us: yet, at best, what misery, what pollution, what sacrilege, what a chaos is there then in that consecrated spot, which is the temple of the Holy Ghost! How is it that the lamp of God does not go out in it at once, when the whole soul seems tending to hell, and hope is almost gone? Wonderful mercy indeed it is, which bears so much! Incomprehensible patience in the Holy One, so to dwell, in such a wilderness, with the wild beasts! Exceeding and divine virtue in the grace given us, that it is not stifled! Yet such is the promise, not to those who sin contentedly after they have received grace; there is no hope while they so sin; but where sin is not part of a course, though it is still sin, whether sin of our birth, or of habits formed long ago, or of want of self-command which we are trying to gain, God mercifully allows and pardons it, and "the blood of Jesus Christ cleanseth us from" it all.

4. Further, I might dwell upon sins which we fall into from being taken unawares,—when the temptation is sudden,—as St. Peter, when he first denied Christ; though whether it became of a different character, when he denied twice and thrice, is a further question.

5. And again, those sins which rise from the devil's temptations, inflaming the wounds and scars of past sins healed, or nearly so; exciting the memory, and hurrying us away; and thus making use of our former selves against our present selves contrary to our will.

6. And again, I might speak of those which rise from a deficiency of practical experience, or from ignorance how to perform duties which we set about. Men attempt to be munificent, and their acts are prodigal; they wish to be firm and zealous, and their acts are cruel; they wish to be benevolent, and they are indulgent and weak; they do harm when they mean to do good; they engage in undertakings, or they promote designs, or they put forth opinions, or they set a pattern, of which evil comes; they countenance evil; they mistake falsehood for truth; they are zealous for false doctrines; they oppose the cause of God. One can hardly say all this is without sin, and yet in them it may be involuntary sin and pardonable on the prayer of faith.

7. Or I might speak of those unworthy motives, low views, mistakes in principle, false maxims, which abound on all sides of us, and which we catch (as it were) from each other;—that spirit of the world which we breathe, and which defiles all we do, yet which can hardly be said to be a wilful pollution; but rather it is such sin as is consistent with the presence of the grace of God in us, which that grace will blot out and put away.

8. And, lastly, much might be said on the subject of what the Litany calls "negligences and ignorances," on forgetfulnesses, heedlessnesses, want of seriousness, frivolities, and a variety of weaknesses, which we may be conscious of in ourselves, or see in others.

Such are some of the classes of sins which may be found, if it so happen, where the will is right, and faith lively; and which in such cases are not inconsistent with the state of grace, or may be called infirmities. Of course it must be ever recollected, that infirmities are not always to be regarded *as* infirmities; they attach also to those who live in the commission of wilful sins, and who have no warrant whatever for considering themselves in a saving state. Men do not cease to be under the influence of original sin, or sins of past years, they do not gain self-command, or unlearn negligences and ignorances, by adding to these offences others of a more grievous character. Those who are out of grace, have infirmities and much more. And there will always be a tendency in such persons to explain away their wilful sins into infirmities. This is ever to be borne in mind. I am not attempting to draw the line between infirmities and transgressions; I only say, that to whomsoever besides such infirmities do attach, they may happen to attach to those who are free from transgressions, and who need not despond, or be miserable on account of failings which in them are not destructive of faith or incompatible with grace. Who these are He only knows for certain, who "tries the reins and the heart," who "knoweth the mind of the Spirit," and "discerns between the righteous and the wicked." He is able, amid the maze of contending motives and principles within us, to trace out the perfect work of righteousness steadily going on there, and the rudiments of a new world rising from out the chaos. He can discriminate between what is habitual and what is accidental; what is on the growth and what is in decay; what is a result and what is indeterminate; what is of us and what is in us. He estimates the difference between a will that is honestly devoted to Him, and one that is insincere. And where there is a willing mind, He accepts it "according to that a man hath, and not according to that he hath not." [4] In those whose wills are holy, He is present for sanctification and acceptance; and, like the sun's beams in some cave of the earth, His grace sheds light on every side, and consumes all mists and vapours as they rise.

We indeed have not knowledge such as His; were we ever so high in God's favour, a certainty of our justification would not belong to us. Yet, even to know only thus much, that infirmities are no necessary mark of reprobation, that God's elect have infirmities, and that our own sins may possibly be no more than infirmities, this surely, by itself, is a consolation. And to reflect that at least God continues us visibly in His Church; that He does not withdraw from us the ordinances of grace; that He gives us means of instruction, patterns of holiness, religious guidance, good books; that He allows us to frequent His house, and to present ourselves before Him in prayer and Holy Communion; that He gives us opportunities of private prayer; that He has given us a care for our souls; an anxiety to secure our salvation; a desire to be more strict and conscientious, more simple in faith, more full of love than we are; all this will tend to soothe and encourage us, when the sense of our infirmities makes us afraid. And if further, God seems to be making us His instruments for any purpose of His, for teaching, warning, guiding, or comforting others, resisting error, spreading the knowledge of the truth, or edifying His Church, this too will

---

[4] 2 Cor. viii. 12.

create in us the belief, not that God is certainly pleased with us, for knowledge of mysteries may be separated from love, but that He has not utterly forsaken us in spite of our sins, that He still remembers us, and knows us by name, and desires our salvation. And further, if, for all our infirmities, we can point to some occasions on which we have sacrificed anything for God's service, or to any habit of sin or evil tendency of nature which we have more or less overcome, or to any habitual self-denial which we practise, or to any work which we have accomplished to God's honour and glory; this perchance may fill us with the humble hope that God is working in us, and therefore is at peace with us. And, lastly, if we have, through God's mercy, an inward sense of our own sincerity and integrity, if we feel that we can appeal to God with St. Peter, that we love Him only, and desire to please Him in all things,—in proportion as we feel this, or at such times as we feel it, we have an assurance shed abroad on our hearts, that we are at present in His favour, and are in training for the inheritance of His eternal kingdom.

SINCERITY AND HYPOCRISY

*"If there be first a willing mind, it is accepted according to that a
man hath, and not according to that he hath not."*
—2 Cor. viii.12.

M EN may be divided into two great classes, those who profess religious obedience, and those who do not; and of
those who do profess to be religious, there are again those who
perform as well as profess, and those who do not. And thus on
the whole there are three classes of men in the world, open sinners, consistent Christians, and between the two, (as speaking
with the one, and more or less acting with the other,) professing Christians, or, as they are sometimes called, nominal
Christians. Now the distinction between open sinners and
consistent Christians is so clear, that there is no mistaking it;
for they agree in nothing; they neither profess the same things
nor practise the same. But the difference between professing
Christians and true Christians is not so clear, for this reason,
that true Christians, however consistent they are, yet do sin, as
being not yet perfect; and so far as they sin, are inconsistent,
and this is all that professing Christians are. What then, it may
be asked, is the real difference between true and professing
Christians, since both the one and the other profess more than
they practise? Again, if you put the question to one of the latter class, however inconsistent his life may be, yet he will be
sure to say that he wishes he was better; that he is sorry for his
sins; that the flesh is weak; that he cannot overcome it; that
God alone can overcome it; that he trusts God will, and that he
prays to Him to enable him to do it. There is no form of words
conceivable which a mere professing Christian cannot use,—
nay, more, there appears to be no sentiment which he cannot
feel,—as well as the true Christian, and at first sight apparently
with the same justice. He *seems* just in the very position of the
true Christian, only perhaps behind him; not *so* consistent, not
advanced so much; still, on the same line. Both confess to a
struggle within them; both sin, both are sorry; what then is the
difference between them?

There are many differences; but, before going on to mention that one to which I shall confine my attention, I would have you observe that I am speaking of differences in God's sight. Of course, we men may after all be unable altogether, and often are unable, to see differences between those who, nevertheless, are on different sides of the line of life. Nor may we judge anything absolutely before the time, whereas God "searcheth the hearts." He alone, "who searcheth the hearts," "knoweth what is the mind of the Spirit." We do not even know ourselves absolutely. "Yea, I judge not mine own self," says St. Paul, "but He that judgeth me is the Lord." God alone can unerringly discern between sincerity and insincerity, between the hypocrite and the man of perfect heart. I do not, of course, mean that we can form no judgment at all upon ourselves, or that it is not useful to do so; but here I will chiefly insist upon the point of *doctrine*, viz., how does the true Christian differ in God's sight from the insincere and double-minded?—leaving any practical application which it admits, to be incidentally brought out in the course of my remarks.

Now the real difference between the true and the professing Christian seems to be given us in the text, "If there be a willing mind, it is accepted." St. Paul is speaking of almsgiving; but what he says seems to apply generally. He is laying down a principle, which applies of course in many distinct cases, though he uses it with reference to one in particular. An honest, unaffected *desire* of doing right is the test of God's true servants. On the other hand, a double mind, a pursuing other ends besides the truth, and in consequence an inconsistency in conduct, and a half-consciousness (to say the least) of inconsistency, and a feeling of the necessity of defending oneself to oneself, and to God, and to the world; in a word, hypocrisy; these are the signs of the merely professed Christian. Now I am going to give some instances of this distinction, in Scripture and in fact.

For instance. The two great Christian graces are faith and love. Now, how are these characterised in Scripture?—By their being honest or single-minded. Thus St. Paul, in one place, speaks of "the end of the commandment being love;" what love?—"love *out of a pure heart*," he proceeds, "and of a *good conscience*;" and still further, "and of faith,"—what kind of faith?—"faith *unfeigned*;" or, as it may be more literally translated, "unhypocritical faith;" for so the word means in Greek. Again, elsewhere he speaks of his "calling to remembrance the *unfeigned* faith" which dwelt in Timothy, and in his mother and grandmother before him; that is, literally, "unhypocritical faith." Again, he speaks of the Apostles approving themselves as the ministers of God, "by kindness, by the Holy Ghost, by love *unfeigned*," or, more literally, "unhypocritical love." Again, as to love towards man. "Let love be *without dissimulation*," or, more literally, as in the other cases, "let love be unhypocritical." In like manner, St. Peter speaks of Christians "having purified their souls in obeying the truth through the Spirit unto unhypocritical love of the brethren." And in like manner, St. James speaks of "the wisdom that is from above, being first *pure* . . ." and, presently, "without partiality, and *without hypocrisy*." [1] Surely it is very remarkable that three Apostles, writing on different subjects and occasions, should each of them thus speak about whether faith or love as without hypocrisy.

A true Christian, then, may almost be defined as one who has a ruling sense of God's presence within him. As none but justified persons have that privilege, so none but the justified have that practical perception of it. A true Christian, or one who is in a state of acceptance with God, is he, who, in such sense, has faith in Him, as to live in the thought that He is present with him,—present not externally, not in nature merely, or in providence, but in his innermost heart, or in his *conscience*. A man is justified whose conscience is illuminated by God, so that he habitually realizes that all his thoughts, all the first springs of his moral life, all his motives and his wishes, are open to Almighty God. Not as if he was not aware that there is very much in him impure and corrupt, but he wishes that all that is in him should be bare to God. He believes that it is so, and he even joys to think that it is so, in spite of his fear and shame at its being so. He alone admits Christ into the shrine of his heart; whereas others wish in some way or other, to be by themselves, to have a home, a chamber, a tribunal, a throne, a self where God is not,—a home within them which is not a temple, a chamber which is not a confessional, a tribunal without a judge, a throne without a king;—that self may be king and judge; and that the Creator may rather be dealt with and approached as though a second party, instead of His being that true and better self, of which self itself should be but an instrument and minister.

Scripture tells us that God the Word, who died for us and rose again, and now lives for us, and saves us, is "quick and powerful, and sharper than any two-edged sword, piercing even to the dividing asunder of soul and spirit, and of the joints and

[1] 2 Cor. vi.6; Rom. xii.9; 1 Pet. i.22; James iii.17.

marrow, and a discerner of the thought and intents of the heart. Neither is there any creature that is not manifest in His sight; but all things are naked and opened unto the eyes of Him with whom we have to do." [2] Now the true Christian realizes this; and what is the consequence?—Why, that he enthrones the Son of God in his conscience, refers to Him as a sovereign authority, and uses no reasoning with Him. He does not reason, but he says, "Thou, God, seest me." He feels that God is too near him to allow of argument, self-defence, excuse, or objection. He appeals in matters of duty, not to his own reason, but to God Himself, whom with the eyes of faith he sees, and whom he makes the Judge; not to any fancied fitness, or any preconceived notion, or any abstract principle, or any tangible experience.

The Book of Psalms continually instances this temper of profound, simple, open-hearted confidence in God. "O Lord, Thou hast searched me out and known me. Thou knowest my downsitting and mine uprising. Thou understandest my thoughts long before . . . There is not a word in my tongue but Thou knowest it altogether." "My soul hangeth upon Thee. Thy right hand hath upholden me." "When I wake up, I am present with Thee." "Into Thy hands I commend my spirit, for Thou hast redeemed me, O Lord, Thou God of Truth." "Commit thy way unto the Lord, and put thy trust in Him, and He shall bring it to pass. He shall make thy righteousness as clear as the light, and thy just dealing as the noonday." "Against Thee only have I sinned, and done this evil in Thy sight." "Hear the right, O Lord, consider my complaint, and hearken unto my prayer that goeth not out of feigned lips. Let my sentence come forth from Thy presence, and let Thine eyes look upon the thing that is equal. Thou hast proved and visited mine heart in the night season. Thou hast tried me, and shalt find no wickedness in me; for I am utterly purposed that my mouth shall not offend." Once more, "Thou shalt guide me with Thy counsel, and after that receive me with glory. Whom have I in heaven but Thee? and there is none upon earth that I desire in comparison of Thee. My flesh and my heart faileth, but God is the strength of mine heart and my portion for ever." [3]

Or, again, consider the following passage in St. John's First Epistle. "If our heart condemn us, God is greater than our heart and knoweth all things. Beloved, if our heart condemn us not,

[2] Heb. iv.12, 13.
[3] Ps. cxxxix.1, 2, 4; lxiii.8; xxxi.5; xxxvii.5, 6; li.4; xvii.1–3; lxxiii.24–26.

then have we confidence towards God." And in connexion with this, the following from the same Epistle: "God is Light, and in Him is no darkness at all. If we say that we have fellowship with Him, and walk in darkness, we lie, and do not the truth. . . . If we confess our sins, He is faithful and just to forgive us our sins, and to cleanse us from all unrighteousness." Again, "the darkness is past, and the true light now shineth." Again, "Hereby we know that He abideth in us, by the Spirit which He hath given us." And again, "He that believeth on the Son of God, hath the witness in himself." And, in the same connexion, consider St. Paul's statement, that "the Spirit itself beareth witness with our spirit, that we are the children of God."[4]

And, now, on the other hand, let us contrast such a temper of mind, which loves to walk in the light, with that of the merely professing Christian, or, in Scripture language, of the *hypocrite*. Such are they who have two ends which they pursue, religion *and* the world; and hence St. James calls them "double-minded." Hence, too, our Lord, speaking of the Pharisees who were hypocrites, says, "Ye cannot serve God *and* mammon."[5] A double-minded man, then, as having two ends in view, dare not come to God, lest he should be discovered; for "all things that are reproved are made manifest by the light."[6] Thus, whereas the Prodigal Son "rose and came to his father," on the contrary, Adam hid himself among the trees of the garden. It was not simple dread of God, but dread joined to an unwillingness to be restored to God. He had a secret in his heart which he kept from God. He felt towards God,—as it would seem, or at least his descendants so feel,—as one man often feels towards another in the intercourse of life. You sometimes say of a man, "he is friendly, or courteous, or respectful, or considerate, or communicative; but, after all, there is something, perhaps without his knowing it, in the background. He professes to be agreed with me; he almost displays his agreement; he says he pursues the same objects as I; but still I do not know him, I do not make progress with him, I have no confidence in him, I do not know him better than the first time I saw him." Such is the way in which the double-minded approach the Most High,—they have a something private, a hidden self at bottom. They look on themselves, as it were, as independent parties, treating with Almighty God as one of their fellows. Hence, so far from seeking God, they hardly like to be sought by Him. They would

---

[4] 1 John iii.20, 21; i.5–9; ii.8; iii.24; v.10; Rom. viii.16.
[5] Luke xvi.13.   [6] Eph. v.13.

rather keep their position and stand where they are,—on earth, and so make terms with God in heaven; whereas, "he that doeth truth, cometh to the light, that his deeds may be made manifest that they are wrought in God."[7]

This being the case, there being in the estimation of the double-minded man two parties, God and self, it follows (as I have said), that reasoning and argument is the mode in which he approaches his Saviour and Judge; and that for two reasons,—first, because he will not *give* himself up to God, but stands upon his rights and appeals to his notions of fitness: and next, because he has some secret misgiving after all that he is dishonest, or some consciousness that he may appear so to others; and therefore, he goes about to fortify his position, to explain his conduct, or to excuse himself.

Some such argument or excuse had the unprofitable servant, when called before his Lord. The other servants said, "Lord, Thy pound hath gained ten," or "five pounds." They said no more; nothing more was necessary; the case spoke for itself. But the unprofitable servant did not dare leave his conduct to tell its own tale at God's judgment-seat; he said not merely, "Lord, I have kept Thy pound laid up in a napkin;" he appealed, as it were, to the reasonableness of his conduct against his Maker: he felt he must make out a case, and he went on to attempt it. He trusted not his interests to the Eternal and All-perfect Reason of God, before whom he stood, but entrenched himself in his own.

Again:—When our Lord said to the scribe, who had answered Him that eternal life was to be gained by loving God and his neighbour, "Thou hast answered right," this ought to have been enough. But his object was not to please God, but to exalt himself. And, therefore, he went on to make an objection. "But he, willing to *justify himself,* said unto Jesus, And who is my neighbour?" whereas they only are justified in God's judgment, who give up the notion of justifying themselves by word or deed, who start with the confession that they are unjust, and who come to God, not upon their own merits, but for His mercy.

Again: we have the same arguing and insincere spirit exposed in the conduct of the Pharisees, when they asked Christ for the authority on which He acted. They said, "By what authority doest thou these things?" This might be the question of sincere inquirers or mere objectors, of faith or of hypocrisy. Observe

[7] John iii.21.

how our Lord detects it. He asked them about St. John's baptism; meaning to say, that if they acknowledged St. John, they
must acknowledge Himself of whom St. John spake. They, unwilling to submit to Christ as a teacher and Lord, preferred to
deny John to going on to acknowledge Him. Yet, on the other
hand, they dare not openly deny the Baptist, because of the
people; so, between hatred of our Lord and dread of the people,
they would give no answer at all. "They *reasoned* among themselves," we are told. In consequence, our Lord left them to their
reasonings; He refused to tell them what, had they reasoned
sincerely, they might learn for themselves.

What is seen in the Gospels, had taken place from the beginning. Our first parents were as ready with excuses, as their posterity when Christ came. First, Adam says, "I hid myself, for I
was afraid;" though fear and shame were not the sole or chief
reasons why he fled, but an incipient hatred, if it may be said,
of his Maker. Again, he says, "The woman, whom Thou gavest
me . . . she gave me of the tree." And the woman says, "The
serpent beguiled me." They did not honestly surrender themselves to their offended God, but had something to say in their
behalf. Again, Cain says, when asked where his brother was,
whom he had murdered, "Am I my brother's keeper?"

Balaam, again, is a most conspicuous instance of a double
mind, or of hypocrisy. He has a plausible reason for whatever he
does; he can so skilfully defend himself, that to this day he looks
like a good man, and his conduct and fortunes are a perplexity
to many minds. But it is one thing to have good excuses, another to have good motives. He had not the love of the truth,
the love of God, in his heart; he was covetous of worldly goods;
and, therefore, all his excuses only avail to mark him as double-
minded.

Again:—Saul is another very remarkable instance of a man
acting for his own ends, and yet having plausible *reasons* for
what he did. He offered sacrifice on one occasion, not having a
commission; this was a sin; yet what was his excuse?—a very
fair one. Samuel had promised to come to offer the sacrifice,
and did not. Saul waited some days, the people grew discouraged, his army fell off and the enemy was at hand,—so, as he
says, he "*forced* himself." [8]

Such is the conduct of insincere men in difficulty. Perhaps
their difficulty may be a real one; but in this they differ from the
sincere:—the latter seek God *in* their difficulty, feeling that He

[8] 1 Sam. xiii. 12.

only who imposes it can remove it; but insincere men do not like to go to God; and to them the difficulty is only so much gain, for it gives them an apparent reason, a sort of excuse, for not going by God's rule, but for deciding in their own way. Thus Saul took his own course; thus Jeroboam, when in a difficulty, put up calves of gold and instituted a new worship without Divine command. Whereas, when Hezekiah was in trouble, he took the letter of Sennacherib, "and went up into the house of the Lord, and spread it before the Lord."[9] And when St. Peter was sinking in the water, he cried out to Christ, "Lord, save me."[10] And in like manner holy David, after he had sinned in numbering the people, and was told to choose between three punishments offered him, showed the same honest and simple-hearted devotion in choosing that of the three which might be the most exactly called falling into the Lord's hands. If he must suffer, let the Lord chastise him.—"I am in a great strait," he says; "let us fall now into the hands of the Lord; for His mercies are great; and let me not fall into the hand of man."[11]

Great, then, is the difference between sincere and insincere Christians, however like their words may be to each other; and it is needless to say, that what I have shown in a few examples, might be instanced again and again from every part of Scripture, particularly from the history of the Jews, as contained in the Prophets. All men, even after the gift of God's grace, sin: God's true servants profess and sin,—sin, and are sorry; and hypocrites profess and sin,—sin and are sorry. Thus the two parties look like each other. But the word of God discriminates one from the other by this test,—that Christ dwells in the conscience of one, not of the other; that the one opens his heart to God, the other does not; the one views Almighty God only as an accidental guest, the other as Lord, and owner of all that he is; the one admits Him as if for a night, or some stated season, the other gives himself over to God, and considers himself God's servant and instrument now and for ever. Not more different is the intimacy of friends from mere acquaintance; not more different is it to know a person in society, to be courteous and obliging to him, to interchange civilities, from opening one's heart to another, admitting him into it, seeing into his, loving him, and living in him;—than the external worship of the hypocrite, from the inward devotion of true faith; approaching God with the lips, from believing on Him with the heart; so opening to the Spirit that He opens to us,

[9] Is. xxxvii.14.   [10] Matt. xiv.30.   [11] 2 Sam. xxiv.14.

from so living to self as to exclude the light of heaven.

Now, as to applying what I have been showing from Scripture to ourselves, this shall here be left, my brethren, to the consciences of each of us, and a few words will suffice to do this. Do you, then, habitually thus unlock your hearts and subject your thoughts to Almighty God? Are you living in this conviction of His Presence, and have you this special witness that that Presence is really set up within you unto your salvation, viz. that you live in the sense of it? Do you believe, and act on the belief, that His light penetrates and shines through your heart, as the sun's beams through a room? You know how things look when the sun's beams are on it,—the very air then appears full of impurities, which, before it came out, were not seen. So is it with our souls. We are full of stains and corruptions, we see them not, they are like the air before the sun shines; but though we see them not, God sees them: He pervades us as the sun-beam. Our souls, in His view, are full of things which offend, things which must be repented of, forgiven, and put away. He, in the words of the Psalmist, "has set our misdeeds before Him, our secret sins in the light of His countenance." [12] This is most true, though it be not at all welcome doctrine to many. We cannot hide ourselves from Him; and our wisdom, as our duty, lies in embracing this truth, acquiescing in it, and acting upon it. Let us then beg Him to teach us the Mystery of His Presence in us, that, by acknowledging it, we may thereby possess it fruitfully. Let us confess it in faith, that we may possess it unto justification. Let us so own it, as to set Him before us in everything. "I have set God always before me," says the Psalmist, "for He is on my right hand, therefore I shall not fall." [13] Let us, in all circumstances, thus regard Him. Whether we have sinned, let us not dare keep from Him, but with the prodigal son, rise and go to Him. Or, if we are conscious of nothing, still let us not boast in ourselves or justify ourselves, but feel that "He who judgeth us is the Lord." In all circumstances, of joy or sorrow, hope or fear, let us aim at having Him in our inmost heart; let us have no secret apart from Him. Let us acknowledge Him as enthroned within us at the very springs of thought and affection. Let us submit ourselves to His guidance and sovereign direction; let us come to Him that He may forgive us, cleanse us, change us, guide us, and save us.

This is the true life of saints. This is to have the Spirit witnessing with our spirits that we are sons of God. Such a faith

[12] Ps. xc.8.   [13] Ps. xvi.8.

alone will sustain the terrors of the Last Day; such a faith alone will be proof against those fierce flames which are to surround the Judge, when He comes with His holy Angels to separate between "those who serve God, and those who serve Him not."[14]

[14] Mal. iii.18.

THE TESTIMONY OF CONSCIENCE

"Our rejoicing is this, the testimony of our conscience, that in simplicity and godly sincerity, not with fleshly wisdom, but by the grace of God, we have had our conversation in the world, and more abundantly to you-ward."—2 Cor. i.12.

IN these words the great Apostle appeals to his conscience that he had lived in simplicity and sincerity, with a single aim and an innocent heart, as one who was illuminated and guided by God's grace. The like appeal he makes on other occasions; when brought before the Jewish council he says, "Men and brethren, I have lived in all good conscience before God until this day." [1] And in his Second Epistle to Timothy he speaks of having served God from his forefathers "with pure conscience." [2]

And in the text he expressly says, what he implies, of course, whenever he appeals to his conscience at all, that he is able to rejoice in this appeal. He was given to know his own sincerity in such measure, that he could humbly take pleasure in it, and be comforted by it. "Our *rejoicing* is this," he says, "the testimony of our conscience." In like manner he says to the Galatians, "Let every man prove his own work, and then shall he have *rejoicing* in himself alone, and not in another." [3] And so also speaks St. John: "If our heart condemn us not, then have we *confidence* towards God." [4] Such was the confidence, such the rejoicing of St. Paul and St. John; not that they could do anything acceptable to God by their unaided powers, but that by His grace they could so live as to enjoy a cheerful hope of His favour, both now and evermore.

The same feeling is frequently expressed in the Psalms: a consciousness of innocence and integrity, a satisfaction in it, an appeal to God concerning it, and a confidence of God's favour in consequence. For instance, "Be thou my judge, O Lord," says David; he appeals to the heart-searching God, "for I have

[1] Acts xxiii.1.
[3] Gal. vi.4.
[2] 2 Tim. i.2, 3.
[4] 1 John iii.21.

walked innocently; my trust hath been also in the Lord, there-fore shall I not fall." He proceeds to beg of God to aid him in this self-knowledge: "Examine me, O Lord, and prove me; try out my reins and my heart," that is, lest he should be deceived in thinking himself what he was not. He next enumerates the special points in which God had enabled him to obey: "I have not dwelt with vain persons; neither will I have fellowship with the deceitful; I have hated the congregation of the wicked, and will not sit among the ungodly. . . . As for me, I have walked innocently; O deliver me, and be merciful unto me. My foot standeth right; I will praise the Lord in the congregations."[5] In this and other passages of the Psalms two points are brought before us: that it is possible to be innocent, and to have that sense of our innocence which makes us happy in the thought of God's eye being upon us. Let us then dwell on a truth, of which Apostles and Prophets unite in assuring us.

What the text means by "simplicity and sincerity," I consider for all practical purposes to be the same as what Scripture else-where calls "a perfect heart;" at least this latter phrase will give us some insight into the meaning of the former. You know that it is a frequent account of the kings of Judah in the Sacred his-tory, that they walked or did not walk with God, *with a perfect heart*. In contrast with this phrase, consider what our Saviour says of the attempt made by the Pharisees to serve God *and* mammon, and St. James's account of a *double-minded* man. A man serves with a perfect heart, who serves God in all parts of his duty; and, not here and there, but here and there and every-where; not perfectly indeed as regards the quality of his obedi-ence, but perfectly as regards its extent; not completely, but consistently. So that he may appeal to God with the Psalmist, and say, "Examine me, O Lord, and prove me: and seek the ground of my heart," with the humble trust that there is no department of his duty on which Almighty God can put His hand, and say, "Here thou art not with Me:" no part in which he does not set God before him, and desire to please Him, and to be governed by Him. And something like this seems to be St. James's meaning, when he says, on the other hand, that "Who-soever shall keep the whole law, and yet offend in one point, he is guilty of all;"[6] for such a one is of imperfect heart, or double-minded.

Again, such seems to be our Saviour's meaning when He uses the word *hypocrite*. A hypocrite is one who professes to be

---

[5] Ps. xxvi.1, 2, etc.   [6] James ii.10.

serving God faithfully, while he serves Him in only some one part of his duty, not in all parts. The word is now commonly taken to mean one who uses a profession of religion as a mere instrument of gaining his worldly ends, or who wishes to deceive men into thinking that he is what he is not. This is not exactly its Scripture sense, which seems rather to denote a person who would (if I may use the words) deceive God; one who, though his heart would tell him, were he honest with it, that he is *not* serving God perfectly, yet will not *ask* his heart, will not listen to it, trifles with his conscience, is *determined* to believe that he *is* religious, and (as if to strengthen himself in his own false persuasion, and from a variety of mixed motives difficult to analyse) protests his sincerity and innocence before God, appeals to God, and thus claims as his own the reward of innocence.

Now then to attempt to describe that state of heart, which Scripture calls simple and sincere, or perfect, or innocent; and which is such, that a man may know he has it, and humbly rejoice in it.

We are by nature what we are; very sinful and corrupt, we know; however, we like to be what we are, and for many reasons it is very unpleasant to us to change. We cannot change ourselves; this too we know full well, or, at least, a very little experience will teach us. God alone can change us; God alone can give us the desires, affections, principles, views, and tastes which a change implies: this too we know; for I am all along speaking of men who have a sense of religion. What then is it that we who profess religion lack? I repeat it, this: a willingness to *be* changed, a willingness to suffer (if I may use such a word), to suffer Almighty God to change us. We do not like to let go our old selves; and in whole or part, though all is offered to us freely, we cling hold to our old selves. Though we were promised no trouble at all in the change, though there were no self-denial, no exertion in changing, the case would not be altered. We do not like to be new-made; we are afraid of it; it is throwing us out of all our natural ways, of all that is familiar to us. We feel as if we should not *be* ourselves any longer, if we do not keep some portion of what we have been hitherto; and much as we profess in general terms to wish to be changed, when it comes to the point, when particular instances of change are presented to us, we shrink from them, and are content to remain unchanged.

It is this principle of self-seeking, so to express myself, this influence of self upon us, which is our ruin. I repeat, I am speaking of those who make a *profession* of religion. Others, of course, avowedly follow self altogether; they indulge the flesh, or pursue the world. But when a man comes to God to be saved, then, I say, the essence of true conversion is a *surrender* of himself, an unreserved, unconditional surrender; and this is a saying which most men who come to God cannot receive. They wish to be saved, but in their own way; they wish (as it were) to capitulate upon terms, to carry off their goods with them; whereas the true spirit of faith leads a man to look off from self to God, to think nothing of his own wishes, his present habits, his importance or dignity, his rights, his opinions, but to say, "I put myself into Thy hands, O Lord; make Thou me what Thou wilt; I forget myself; I divorce myself from myself; I am dead to myself; I will follow Thee." Samuel, Isaiah, and St. Paul, three Saints in very different circumstances, all instance this. The child Samuel, under Eli's instruction, says, "Speak, Lord; for Thy servant heareth."[7] The prophet Isaiah says, "Here am I: send me."[8] And still more exactly to the point are St. Paul's words, when arrested by the miraculous vision, "Lord, what wilt Thou have me to do?"[9] Here is the very voice of self-surrender, "What wilt thou have me to do? Take Thy own way with me; whatever it be, pleasant or painful, I will do it." These are words worthy of one who was to be to after-ages the pattern of simplicity, sincerity, and a pure conscience: and as he spake, so he acted; for in his own narrative of what happened, he goes on to say, "I was not disobedient unto the heavenly vision."

Now to give some instances in illustration.

1. One very common case, though it is not one in which men have any pretensions to be considered as sincere, is when they determine to repent more fully by and by, or to be more strict in their mode of living by and by. However, it will serve to explain what I would say. Alas! so common is it, that I should not wonder if some persons here present, were they but honest, would confess it of themselves, that they dare not put themselves into God's hands, lest He should make them what they love not. Here then is the absence of a perfect heart, a shrinking from the absolute surrender and sacrifice of self to God.

2. Again, in a number of cases want of perfectness is shown in their keeping away, as they obstinately do, from the Lord's Supper. I am not speaking of the case of open sinners. Of course, it is well that they should feel reluctant; it would be dreadful indeed if they did not. Nor do I mean to say that many

---

[7] 1 Sam. iii.9.   [8] Is. vi.8.   [9] Acts ix.6.

are not kept away by fears, which they ought not to have, which are mistaken. But still there are a great number, who have good words in their mouth, who profess all reverence, all service towards God, acknowledge His power and love, believe in what Christ has done for them, and say they desire to be ruled by Him, and to die the death of the righteous, who yet are quite unmovable on this particular point. Why is this? I fear, for this reason. They dare not profess in God's sight that they will serve Him. They dare not promise; they dare not pray to Him. They dare not beg Him to make them wholly His. They dare not ask Him to disclose to them their secret faults. They dare not come to an Ordinance, in which God meets them face to face. As many a man will tell an untruth who dare not swear it, so there are many men who make random professions of obedience, who dare not put themselves in circumstances when perhaps they may be taken at their word. And as cowards disguise from themselves their own cowardice, till brought into danger, so do these their hypocrisy, till obliged to take a side. They profess vaguely; but they dare not definitely and solemnly say, "And here we offer and present unto Thee, O Lord, our souls and bodies, to be a reasonable, holy, and lively sacrifice unto Thee."

3. Another instance of insincerity is set before us in the conduct of the young man in the Gospel, who came running to Christ, and saying, "Good Master." He did not justly know himself, and he flattered himself that he was perfect in heart when he had a reserve in his obedience. You will observe he was even forward and rude in his manner; and here we seem to gain a lesson. When young persons address themselves to religious subjects without due reverence and godly fear, when they rush towards them impetuously, engage in them hotly, talk about them vehemently, and profess them conspicuously, they should be very suspicious of themselves, lest there be something or other wrong about them. Men who are quite honest, who really wish to surrender themselves to Christ, have counted the cost. They feel it is no slight sacrifice which they are making; they feel its difficulty and its pain; and therefore they cannot make an impetuous offer of their services. They cannot say, "Lord, I will follow Thee whithersoever Thou goest;" it is too great a profession. They dare not say, "All these have I kept from my youth up;" lest, after all, they discover something in themselves lacking. They have no heart to say, "Good Master," in a familiar, light manner, before him who stands to them instead of God, and whose words involve duties. The young ruler came running, not waiting till Christ should look on him or call—

not fearing, but intruding himself. Christ exposed what was in his heart, and he who ran to accost Him, stole away sorrowing.

4 And here perhaps we shall understand something of the contrast between St. Peter's first and second profession of service to Christ. He made the first of his own accord. Christ had said, "Whither I go, thou canst not follow Me now." [10] He answered, "Lord, why cannot I follow Thee now? I will lay down my life for Thy sake." Now, we may indeed say that his fall was merely an instance of weakness;—so it may have been;—yet it does seem likely too, that, at the time he said it, he had not that perfect devotion to Christ which he had afterwards. Let it not be imagined that on that former occasion, when "he forsook all and followed" Christ, or again, when he went to meet Him on the sea, the holy Apostle did not act out of the fulness of a perfect heart; but may we not reverently suppose that till Pentecost his state of mind was variable, and sometimes had more of heaven in it than at other times? We may surmise that he, who first said, "Thou art the Christ," and next, "Be it far from Thee, Lord," earning blessing and rebuke almost in one breath, on this occasion came short of the sincerity which he showed before and afterwards. We may surmise that his fault was not merely self-deception, but, in a measure, a reserved devotion; that there was one corner (as it were) of his heart, which at that moment was not Christ's; for the more that is the case, the louder men commonly talk, in order to beat down the risings of conscience. When a man half suspects his own honesty, he makes loud professions of it. Contrast, with this, St. Peter's words after our Lord's resurrection. First, he waits for Christ to say, "Follow Me;" next, observe his answer to Christ, "Lord, Thou knowest all things; Thou knowest that I love Thee." [11] Then he felt that he dare appeal to his heart-searching Judge, in witness that he was making an unreserved surrender of himself. He did not thus speak before.

5. Another illustration may be drawn from the state of mind which not unfrequently is found in a person who has been injured or insulted, and is bound in duty to forgive the offenders. I am supposing a well-meaning and religious man; and he often lies under the temptation to forgive them up to a certain point, but at the same time to make a reserve in favour of his own dignity, or to satisfy his sense of justice, and thus to take the matter in part into his own hands. He cannot get himself honestly to surrender every portion of resentment, and to leave his

[10] John xiii.33.   [11] John xxi.15.

cause simply to God, as remembering the words, "Vengeance is Mine; I will repay." [12] This reluctance is sometimes seen very clearly under other circumstances, in the instance of children, who, whether they be out of temper, or obstinate, or otherwise what they should not be, cannot bring themselves to do that very thing which they ought to do, which is enough, which comes up to the mark. They are quite conscious that they are wrong, and they wish to be right; and they will do a number of good things short of what is required of them; they will show their wish to be at one again with the parties who are displeased with them; they will go round about their duty,—but from pride, or other wrong feeling, they shrink from going close to it, and, as it were, embracing it. And so again, if they have been in fault, they will make excuses, or half confess; they will do much, but they cannot bring themselves to do a whole deed, and make a clean breast of it.

6. Lastly may be mentioned, the case of persons seeking the truth. How often are they afraid or loth to throw themselves on God's guidance, and beg Him to teach them! how loth to promise in His sight that they will follow the truth wherever it leads them! but whether from fear of what the world will say, fear of displeasure of friends, or of ridicule of strangers, or of triumph of enemies, or from entertaining some fancy or conceit of their own, which they are loth to give up, they hang back, and think to gain the truth, not by rising and coming for it, but, as it were, by a mere careless extension and grasp of the hand, while they sit at ease, or proceed with other work that employs them. Much might be said on what is a very fertile part of the subject.

In all these ways, then, to which many more might be added, men serve God, but do not serve Him with a *perfect* heart, or "in simplicity and sincerity." And in explaining what I consider Scripture to mean by perfectness of purpose, I have explained also in a measure how it is that a person must know if he has it. For it is a state of mind which will not commonly lie hid from those who are blest with it. Not more different is ice from the flowing stream, than a half purpose from a whole one. "He bloweth with His wind, and the waters flow." So is it when God prevails on a heart to open itself to Him, and admit Him wholly. There is a perceptible difference of feeling in a man, compared with what he was, which, in common circumstances, he cannot mistake. He may have made resolves before, he may have argued himself into a belief of his own sincerity, he may have (as

[12] Rom. xii. 19.

it were) convinced himself that nothing can be required of him more than he has done, he may have asked himself what more *is* there to do, and yet have felt a something in him still which *needed* quieting, which was ever rising up and troubling him, and had to be put down again. But when he really gives himself up to God, when he gets himself honestly to say, "I sacrifice to Thee this cherished wish, this lust, this weakness, this scheme, this opinion: make me what *Thou* wouldest have me; I bargain for nothing; I make no terms; I seek for no previous information whither Thou art taking me; I will be what Thou wilt make me, and all that Thou wilt make me. I say not, I will follow Thee whithersoever Thou goest, for I am weak; but I give myself to Thee, to lead me anywhither. I will follow Thee in the dark, only begging Thee to give me strength according to my day. Try me, O Lord, and seek the ground of my heart; prove me, and examine my thoughts; look well if there be any way of wickedness in me;" search each dark recess with Thy own bright light, "and lead me in the way everlasting,"—what a difference is this! what a plain perceptible change, which cannot be mistaken! what a feeling of satisfaction is poured over the mind! what a sense that at length we are doing what we should do, and approving ourselves to God our Saviour! Such is the blessedness and reward of confession. "I said I will confess my sins unto the Lord, and so Thou forgavest the wickedness of my sin." It matters little whether it is a resolve for the future or a confession of the past; the same temper is involved in both. If a person does not confess with a desire of amendment, it is not a real confession; but he who comes to God to tell before Him sorrowfully all that he knows wrong in himself, is thereby desiring and beginning what is right and holy; and he who comes to beg Him to work in him all that is right and holy, does thereby implicitly condemn and repent of all that is wrong in him. And thus he is altogether innocent; for all his life is made up either of honest endeavour or of honest confession, exactness in doing or sorrow for not doing, of simplicity and sincerity, repentance being on the one side and obedience on the other. Such is the power divinely vouchsafed in the Gospel to an honest purpose. It either *does*, or blots out what is *not* done; or rather by one act, and in itself which is one, it both performs part, and blots out the rest.

And here it is obvious to point out the bearing of what has been said on the subject of Justification. We know that faith justifies us; but what is the test of true faith? Works are its evidence; but they are so on the whole, after a sufficient period of time, to others, and at the judgment of the last day. They scarcely can be considered an evidence definite and available for a man's own comfort at any moment when he seeks for one. He does some things well, some ill; and he is more clear-sighted and more sensitive in the instance of his failings than of his successful endeavours. If what he does well be an evidence of faith, what he does ill will be to him a more convincing proof that he has not faith; and thus he cannot conclusively appeal to his works. Now, I suppose, absolute certainty about our state cannot be attained at all in this life; but the nearest approach to such certainty which is possible, would seem to be afforded by this consciousness of openness and singleness of mind, this good understanding (if I may use such an expression) between the soul and its conscience, to which St. Paul so often alludes. "Our rejoicing is this," he says, "the testimony of our conscience, that in simplicity and godly sincerity we have had our conversation in the world." He did not rejoice in his faith, but he was justified by faith, because he could rejoice in his sincerity. Perfectness of heart, simple desire to please God, "a spirit without guile," a true and loyal will, where these are present, faith is justifying; and whereas those who have this integrity will more or less be conscious of it, therefore, after all exceptions duly made on the score of depression of spirits, perplexity of mind, horror at past sins, and the like, still, on the whole, really religious persons will commonly enjoy a subdued but comfortable hope and trust that they are in a state of justification. They may have this hope more or less; they may deserve to have it more or less; at times they may even be unconscious of it, and yet it may secretly support them; they may fancy themselves in perfect darkness, yet it may be a light cheering them forward; they may vary in their feelings about their state from day to day, and yet, whether or not they can collect evidence to satisfy their reason, still if they be really perfect in heart, there will be this secret sense of their sincerity, with their reason or against reason, to whisper to them peace. And on the other hand, it never will rise above a sober trust, even in the most calm, peaceful, and holy minds. They to the end will still but say, "Lord, I believe; help Thou mine unbelief." They still will say, in St. Paul's words, "I am conscious to myself of nothing, yet am I not hereby justified, but he that judgeth me is the Lord." "Judge me, O Lord; examine me; search the ground of my heart; judge *Thou* me, who art the sole Judge; I judge not myself. I do but say, *Thou* knowest me; I say not, I know." It was but the Pharisee that said, "Lord, I thank Thee I am not as other men are." We can but "gird up the loins of our minds, be sober, and hope to the end, and pass the time of our sojourning here in fear,"[13] though "the day has dawned, and the day star has arisen in our hearts."[14]

One more remark must be made. It may be objected, that, if the feeling of a good conscience be the evidence to us of our justification, then are persons in a justified state who are external to the Church, provided they have this feeling. I reply briefly,—for to say much here would be out of place,—that every one will be judged according to his light and his privileges; and any man who has really the testimony of a good conscience is acting up to his light, whatever that is. This does not, however, show that he has always so acted; nor determine what his light is; nor what degree of favour he is in; nor whether he might have been in greater, had his past actions been other than they have been. It but shows that he is accepted *in* that state in which he is, be it one of greater favour or less, heathenism,[15] schism, superstition, or heresy; and that, because his faults and errors *at present* are not wilful. And in like manner, in the case of members of the Church, a good conscience evidences God's acceptance, according to that measure of acceptance which He gives in His Church,—that is, it evidences their justification; whereas what privileges attach to bodies or creeds external to the Church we do not know. No inward feeling can do more than what is here assigned to it, unless an inward feeling can be the evidence of an external revelation.

But here I am speaking to members of the Church; to those who, if they serve God with a perfect heart, are justified. Let us then, since this is our privilege, attempt to share in St. Paul's sincerity, that we may share in his rejoicing. Let us endeavour to become friends of God and fellow-citizens with the saints; not by sinless purity, for we have it not; not in our deeds of price, for we have none to show; not in our privileges, for they are God's acts, not ours; not in our Baptism, for it is outward; but in that which is the fruit of Baptism within us, not a word but a power, not a name but a reality, which, though it can claim nothing, can beg everything;—an honest purpose, an unreserved, entire submission of ourselves to our Maker, Redeemer, and Judge. Let us beg Him to aid us in our endeavour, and, as He has begun a good work in us, to perform it until the day of the Lord Jesus.

---

[13] 1 Pet. i.13–17.   [14] 2 Pet. i.19.   [15] Acts x.35.

MANY CALLED, FEW CHOSEN

(Septuagesima)

"Know ye not that they which run in a race run all, but one receiveth the prize? So run, that ye may obtain."—1 Cor. ix.24.

NOTHING is more clearly brought out in Scripture, or more remarkable in itself than this, that in every age, out of the whole number of persons blessed with the means of grace, few only have duly availed them of this great benefit. So certain, so uniform is the fact, that it is almost stated as a doctrine. "Many are called, few are chosen." Again, "Strive to enter in at the strait gate; for many, I say unto you, shall seek to enter in, and shall not be able." And again, "Wide is the gate, and broad is the way, that leadeth to destruction, and many there be which go in thereat. . . . Strait is the gate, and narrow is the way that leadeth unto life, and few there be that find it." And St. Paul seems expressly to turn the historical fact into a doctrine, when he says, by way of remark upon his own day as compared with former ages of the Church, "Even so then, at this present time also," that is, as formerly, "there is a *remnant*, according to the election of grace." [1]

The word "remnant" is frequent with the prophets, from whom St. Paul takes it. Isaiah, for instance, says, "Though the number of the children of Israel be as the sand of the sea, a *remnant* shall be saved." Jeremiah speaks of "the *remnant* of Judah," and the "small number," to which a return was promised. Ezekiel, too, declares that God "will leave a *remnant*," "that ye may have some," continues the divine oracle, "that shall escape the sword among the nations, when ye shall be scattered through the countries. And they that escape of you shall remember Me among the nations, whither they shall be carried captives." And so well understood was this, that the hope of good men never reached beyond it. Neither the promise, on the one hand, nor the hope, on the other, ever goes beyond the

[1] Matt. xx.16; Luke xiii.24; Matt. vii.13, 14; Rom. xi.5.

prospect of a remnant being saved. Thus the consolation given to the Church in the Book of Jeremiah is, that God "will not make a *full* end;" and Ezra, confessing the sins of his people, expresses his dread lest there should be "*no* remnant."[2] Thus Christ, His Apostles, and His Prophets, all teach the same doctrine, that the chosen are few, though many are called: that one gains the prize, though many run the race.

This rule in God's dispensations is most abundantly and awfully illustrated in their history. At the time of the Flood, out of a whole world, in spite of Adam's punishment, in spite of Enoch's preaching, in spite of Noah's setting about the ark, eight only found acceptance with God, and even one of these afterwards incurred a curse. When the Israelites were brought out of Egypt by miracle, two only of the whole generation entered the land of promise. Two tribes alone out of twelve remained faithful at the time of the great schism, and continued in possession of God's covenanted mercies. And when Christ came, the bulk of His own people rejected Him, and His Church came but of the scanty remnant, "as a root out of a dry ground."

Moreover, it is observable that Almighty God seems as if to rejoice, and deigns to delight Himself in this small company who adhere to Him, as if their fewness had in it something of excellence and preciousness. "Fear not," he says, "little flock, for it is your Father's good pleasure to give you the kingdom." "Behold, I send you forth as sheep in the midst of wolves." "I pray not for the world, but for those whom Thou hast given Me." In a like spirit, St. Paul says, "Whom He did foreknow, He also did predestinate." And in the time of Elijah, "I have reserved to myself seven thousand men, who have not bowed the knee to the image of Baal." And in the time of Moses, "The Lord did not set His love upon you, nor choose you, because ye were more in number than any people, for ye were the fewest of all people."[3]

And it need scarcely be added, that the same bountifulness on God's part, the same ingratitude on the part of man, the same scarcity of faith, sanctity, truth, and conscientiousness, have marked the course of the Christian Dispensation, as well as of those former ones of which the inspired volume is the record.

So clear is this, that persons who, from unwillingness to take the narrow way, or from other like cause, have disputed it, have

---

[2] Rom. ix.27; Jer. xliv.28; Ezek. vi.8, 9; Jer. xlvi.28; Ezra ix.14.
[3] Luke xii.32; Matt. x.16; John xvii.9; Rom. viii.29; xi.4; Deut. vii.7.

scarcely anything left them to urge but certain false views or consequences, which have been, or may be, entertained concerning the doctrine. And as these misconceptions tend at once to prejudice the mind against it, and to pervert its reception of it, I shall now examine one or two of the objections to which it is exposed.

1. Now, first, it has often happened that, because the elect are few, serious men have considered that this took place in consequence of some fixed decree of God. They have thought that they were few, because it was God's will that they should not be many. Now it is doubtless a great mystery, why this man receives the truth and practises it, and that man does not. We do not know how it comes to pass; but surely we do not tend to solve it, by saying God has so decreed it. If you say that God does absolutely choose the one and reject the other, then *that* becomes the mystery. You do but throw it back a step. It is as difficult to explain this absolute willing or not willing, on the part of Almighty God, as to account for the existence of free will in man. It is as inexplicable why God should act differently towards this man and that, as it is why this man or that should act differently towards God. On the other hand, we are solemnly assured in Scripture that God "hath no pleasure in the death of the wicked;" that He is "not willing that any should perish, but that all should come to repentance."[4]

The doctrine, then, which is implied in the text, does not lead us to any hard notions of God. He is a most loving Father still, though few are chosen. His mercy is over all His works, and to no one does the word of life come but with the intent that he may live. If the many remain in unbelief, they "are not straitened" in God's love, but they "are straitened in their own bowels." Man will not be what by God's renewing and co-operating grace he might be. It is man's doing, not God's will, that, while the visible Church is large, the Church invisible is small.

2. But it may be said that this doctrine lies open to another objection: that to believe that few only find the gate of life, necessarily makes a man self-confident and uncharitable towards others, whether he considers himself predestined to life or not. Every one, it is said, will place himself on the safe side of the line, and, of course, will place his friends with him; and all others he will give over, as if they were to be classed among the many. Now the text, and the verses which follow it, supply the

---

[4] Ezek. xxxiii.11; 2 Pet. iii.9.

readiest answer to this objection. St. Paul speaks as if the Christian course were a race, in which one only out of many could succeed. And what is the conclusion he arrives at? "I keep under my body, and bring it into subjection, lest that by any means when I have preached to others, I myself should be a castaway." You see how far the holy Apostle was from security and self-satisfaction, though he, if any one, would have had a right to feel easy about his state. And the exhortation he gives his brethren is, "So run, that ye may obtain." Are candidates for a prize confident, because only one can gain it? What is the meaning then of asserting that "they which run in a race" take it for granted that they are on the winning side?

And yet it is quite true that there are men who, in consequence of holding the doctrine that the chosen are few, instead of exerting themselves, become proud and careless. But then, let it be observed, these persons hold another doctrine besides, which is the real cause of their carnal security. They not merely think that Christ's flock is small, but that every man can tell whether or no he belongs to it, and that they do know that they themselves belong to it. Now, if a man thinks he knows for certain that he shall be saved, of course he will be much tempted to indulge in a carnal security, and to look down upon others, and that, whether the true flock of Christ is large or small. It is not the knowledge that the chosen are *few* which occasions these bad feelings, but a man's private assurance that *he* is chosen.

St. Paul tells us, that whom God "did foreknow He also did predestinate," and "whom he did predestinate, them He also called; and whom He called them He also justified; and whom He justified, them He also glorified;" but he does not say that God discloses this to the persons who are subjects of it. He has deep and eternal counsels, but they are secret ones; He has a decree, founded on righteousness and truth, but it is not revealed. We know not, we cannot know, whom God has chosen for salvation; and while we understand this, and keep it before us, we shall not be puffed up about ourselves, nor harsh and censorious towards others, though we bear in mind ever so much that the gate of heaven is narrow, and few there be that find it.

This, I think, is very plain; yet it may be useful to enlarge upon it. Let us take an illustration, not exact, but sufficient for the purpose. Supposing we had to cast lots for some worldly benefit, a sum of money, or some desirable post, or the like, and only three or four out of a great number could succeed, how should we be affected beforehand? Should we be at all led to speculate or judge who were to be successful, who unsuccessful? And why not? Because it would be idle to employ our thoughts about an event which nothing we saw before us, nothing we could see, tended to discover to us; idle to attempt to decide in a case where there were no means of deciding. For what any of us could know, one man had as good a prospect as another. We should feel as much as this, that a certain prize was destined for some out of all of us; we should feel anxious and expectant, and that would be the end of the matter. Now, as regards our heavenly prospects, the decision indeed is not a matter of chance; God forbid!—but yet it is as much hid from us as if it were. Nothing that we see, or think we see, can enable us to decide about the future. We do not know but those who are the greatest sinners now, may repent, reform, and in severity and austereness of life surpass ourselves; the last oftentimes become the first. Nor do we know about ourselves, however fair we seem, but we may fall away. We cannot compare ourselves with others at all. All we know is, and a most awful thought it is, that out of the whole number of those who have received the Christian calling, out of ourselves and our friends, and all whom we see and hear of in the intercourse of life, but a few are chosen; but a few act up to their privileges. Now, considering the inscrutable darkness in which the event lies, hid almost like the time of judgment in the prescience of Almighty God, is this a thought to fill us with confidence and pride, or is it not rather an exceedingly solemn and dreadful thought? Should a prophet declare that out of a given number of persons but a few would be alive this time next year, that the greater part would die, should we, under any circumstances, feel altogether easy, were our health ever so good in appearance, or were there ever so many older persons than ourselves in the number addressed? Should we not be made very anxious at every little indisposition, or at every symptom of illness, or at every chance of accident from without? Should we have much heart for speculating about others?

And this surely is the real state of the case. Our means of judging ourselves or others are so very insufficient, that they are practically nothing; and it is our wisdom to let the attempt alone. We may know about ourselves, that at present we are sincere and earnest, and so far in God's favour; we may be able to say that such and such words or deeds are right or wrong in another; but how different is this from having the capacity to decide absolutely about our or his eternal doom! How different this from being able to take in the whole compass of our lives, the whole range and complication of our thoughts, words, deeds, habits, principles, and motives! How different from being able to argue from what we see to what God knows, or from discerning whether the divine seed has taken root in particular minds! St. Paul himself, though conscious of nothing, says to the Corinthians, "Yet am I not hereby justified, but He that judgeth me is the Lord; therefore judge nothing before the time, until the Lord come, who both will bring to light the hidden things of darkness, and will make manifest the counsels of the hearts."[5] We cannot estimate the real value of anything which we or others do; or how it stands in making up their or our final account in God's sight. What is a sign of faith in one man, is not in another; what is a great deed in one man, is not in another. The differences of disposition, education, and guidance are so great, and make the problem so intricate, that it would seem to be the height of madness (were it not sometimes attempted by persons not mad) to attempt to solve it. St. Paul says in one place that he has not "attained." On the contrary, at the end of his life, after fighting a good fight, then he says that "henceforth there *was* laid up for him a crown of righteousness."[6] Thus there was a point at which, and not before, his salvation was, practically speaking, secured. What happened in his case, may, for what we know to the contrary, happen in ours also; and the point at which victory is certain may vary in the case of every one of us.

Or, again, let us recur to the Apostle's words in the text: "Know ye not," he says, "that they which run in a race run all, but one receiveth the prize? So run, that ye may obtain." When a number of persons are contending for a prize, since one alone can obtain it, it is plain that no one, from what he knows about himself, can conclude anything concerning his own success; because, even be he ever so likely in himself, yet another may be more likely. The event is utterly and totally hid from him, unless he be very well acquainted with his rivals. Now here, again, the illustration used is not altogether parallel. In the prize which we run for, praised be God, there is no such rivalry of one against another; there is no restriction; and if all did their duty, all would succeed. Yet the effect is the same as regards our knowledge, as if only one could succeed; I mean, we do not know the *standard* by which God will judge us. Nothing that we are can assure us that we shall answer to what He expects of us; for we do not know what that is; what we are can

[5] 1 Cor. iv.5.   [6] Phil. iii.12; 2 Tim. iv.8.

but cheer us and give us hopes and good spirits. In contending for the prize, it is of no use to be second best. He who comes second, as little gains it as he who comes last. And so in striving to enter in at the strait gate, unless we rise to that which God requires of us, unless we attain, no matter how near we once were to attaining;—after all, it has come to this, that we have not attained. This thought will surely ever keep us from dwelling on our own proficiency, whatever it is; rather it will lead us, with the great Apostle, to "follow after, if that we may apprehend that for which we are apprehended of Christ Jesus." It is not till life is over, when we have lived in the fear of God consistently, when death has put its seal upon us, and cut us off from the chance of falling, that others, surveying us, and observing our consistency and perseverance in well-doing, will humbly trust that we are in St. Paul's case, to whom, after "finishing his course," it was revealed that "a crown of righteousness was laid up for him."

The doctrine, then, that few are chosen though many be called, properly understood, has no tendency whatever to make us fancy ourselves secure and others reprobate. We cannot see the heart, we can but judge from externals, from words and deeds, professions and habits. But these will not save us, unless we persevere in them to the end; and they are no evidence that we shall be saved, except so far as they suggest hope that we shall persevere. They are but a beginning; they tell for nothing till they are completed. Till we have done all, we have done nothing; we have but a prospect, not possession. If we ultimately do attain, every good thing we shall have done will have tended to that attainment, as a race tends to a goal; but, unless we attain, it will not have so tended; and, therefore, from no good thing which we do can we argue that we are sure to attain.

3. One other misconception of this doctrine shall be mentioned, and then I will conclude. It may be said, then, that the belief that true Christians are few leads men to isolate themselves in their own opinions, to withdraw from the multitude, to adopt new and extravagant views, and to be singular in their conduct, as if what the many held and did could not be right. This may sometimes be the case; but I would have it remarked, that if true Christians are few, they must in a certain sense be singular. Singularity indeed is no proof that we are right in our opinions, or are Christ's chosen, because there are a great many ways of being singular, and all cannot be right. And persons are often, as is objected, singular, from love of being so, from conceit, or desire to excite remark; and therefore it does not follow

that even those who profess the views of Christ's true servants, are themselves in their number. But, on the other hand, neither does it follow, because men are singular in their opinions, that they are wrong, nor, because other opinions are generally received in their day, that therefore these are right. If the multitude of men are ever in the broad way "that leadeth to destruction," there is no ground for maintaining that, in order to be right in our religious views, we must agree with the many; rather, if such as persons are, their opinions are also, it would seem to be certain that those opinions which are popular will ever be mistaken and dangerous as being popular opinions. Those who serve God faithfully must ever look to be accounted, in their generation, singular, intemperate, and extreme. They are not so; they must guard against becoming so; if they are so, they are equally wrong as the many, however they may in other respects, differ from them; but still it is no proof that they are so, because the many call them so. It is no proof that they are so, because others take it for granted that they are, pass their doctrines over, put their arguments aside without a word,—treat them gravely, or are vexed about them, or impatient with them, or ridicule them, or fiercely oppose them. No; there are numberless clouds which flit over the sky, there are numberless gusts which agitate the air to and fro: as many, as violent, as far-spreading, as fleeting, as uncertain, as changing, are the clouds and the gales of human opinion; as suddenly, as impetuously, as fruitlessly, do they assail those whose mind is stayed on God. They come and they go; they have no life in them, nor abidance. They agree together in nothing but in this, in threatening like clouds, and sweeping like gusts of wind. They are the voice of the many; they have the strength of the world, and they are directed against the few. Their argument, the sole argument in their behalf, is their prevalence at the moment; not that they existed yesterday, not that they will exist to-morrow; not that they base themselves on reason, or ancient belief, but that they are merely what every one now takes for granted, or, perhaps, supposes to be in Scripture, and therefore not to be disputed:—not that they have most voices through long periods, but that they happen to be most numerously professed in the passing hour. On the other hand, divine truth is ever one and the same; it changes not, any more than its Author: it stands to reason, then, that those who uphold it must ever be exposed to the charge of singularity, either for this or for that portion of it, in a world which is ever varying.

What a most awful view does human society present to those who would survey it religiously! Go where you will, you find persons with their own standards of right and wrong, yet each different from each. Thus everywhere you find both a witness that there is a standard, and yet an evidence everywhere that that standard is lost. Go where you will, you find in each separate circle certain persons held in esteem as patterns of what men should be; each sect and party has its Doctors, its Confessors, and its Saints. And in all parties you will find so many men possessed of good points of character, if not exemplary in their lives, that to judge by appearances, you do not know why the chosen should not be many instead of few. Your very perplexity in reconciling the surface of things with our Lord's announcements, the very temptation you lie under to explain away the plain words of Scripture, shows you that your standard of good and evil, and the standard of all around you, must be very different from God's standard. It shows you, that if the chosen are few, there must be some particular belief necessary, or some particular line of conduct, or something else different from what the world supposes, in order to account for this solemn declaration. It suggests to you that perchance there must be a certain perfection, completeness, consistency, entireness of obedience, for a man to be chosen, which most men miss in one point or another. It suggests to you that there is a great difference between being a hearer of the word and a doer; a well-wisher of the truth, or an approver of good men or good actions, and a faithful servant of the truth. It suggests to you that it is one thing to be in earnest, another and higher to be "rooted and grounded in love." It suggests to you the exceeding dangerousness of single sins, or particular bad habits. It suggests to you the peril of riches, cares of this life, station, and credit.

Of course we must not press the words of Scripture; we do not know the exact meaning of the word "chosen;" we do not know what is meant by being saved "so as by fire;" we do not know what is meant by "few." But still the few can never mean the many and to be called without being chosen cannot but be a misery. We know that the man, in the parable, who came to the feast without a wedding garment, was "cast into outer darkness."[7] Let us then set at nought the judgment of the many, whether about truth and falsehood, or about ourselves, and let us go by the judgment of that line of Saints, from the Apostles' times downwards, who were ever spoken against in their gen-

---

[7] Matt. xxii.13.

eration, ever honoured afterwards,—singular in each point of time as it came, but continuous and the same in the line of their history,—ever protesting against the many, ever agreeing with each other. And, in proportion as we attain to their judgment of things, let us pray God to make it live in us; so that at the Last Day, when all veils are removed, we may be found among those who are inwardly what they seem outwardly,—who with Enoch, and Noah, and Abraham, and Moses, and Joshua, and Caleb, and Phineas, and Samuel, and Elijah, and Jeremiah, and Ezekiel, and the Baptist, and St. Paul, have "borne and had patience, and for His Name-sake laboured and not fainted," watched in all things, done the work of an Evangelist, fought a good fight, finished their course, kept the faith.

PRESENT BLESSINGS

(Septuagesima)

"I have all, and abound: I am full."—Phil. iv.18.

S UCH is St. Paul's confession concerning his temporal condition, even in the midst of his trials. Those trials brought
with them spiritual benefits; but, even as regarded this world,
he felt he had cause for joy and thankfulness, in spite of sorrows, pains, labours, and self-denials. He did not look on this
life with bitterness, complain of it morosely, or refuse to enjoy
it; he was not soured, as the children of men often are, by his
trials; but he felt, that if he had troubles in this world, he had
blessings also; and he did not reject these, but made much of
them. "I have all, and abound: I am full," he says. And, elsewhere, he tells us, that "every creature of God is good," and
that "godliness is profitable unto all things, having the promise
of the life that now is, and of that which is to come." [1]

Gloom is no Christian temper; that repentance is not real,
which has not love in it; that self-chastisement is not acceptable, which is not sweetened by faith and cheerfulness. We
must live in sunshine, even when we sorrow; we must live in
God's presence, we must not shut ourselves up in our own
hearts, even when we are reckoning up our past sins.

These thoughts are suitable on this day, when we first catch a
sight, as it were, of the Forty Days of Lent. If God then gives us
grace to repent, it is well; if He enables us to chasten heart and
body, to Him be praise; and for that very reason, while we do
so, we must not cease rejoicing in Him. All through Lent we
must rejoice, while we afflict ourselves. Though "many be
called, but few chosen;" though all run in the race, but "one
receiveth the prize;" though we must "so run that we may obtain;" though we must be "temperate in all things," and "keep
under our body and bring it into subjection, lest we be castaways;" yet through God alone we can do this; and while He is

[1] i Tim. iv.4, 8.

with us, we cannot but be joyful; for His absence only is a cause
for sorrow. The Three Holy Children are said to have stood up
in the midst of the fire, and to have called on all the works of
God to rejoice with them; on sun and moon, stars of heaven,
nights and days, showers and dew, frost and cold, lightnings
and clouds, mountains and hills, green things upon the earth,
seas and floods, fowls of the air, beasts and cattle, and children
of men,—to praise and bless the Lord, and magnify Him for
ever. We have no such trial as theirs; we have no such awful
suspense as theirs, when they entered the burning fiery furnace; we attempt for the most part what we know; we begin
what we think we can go through. We can neither instance
their faith nor equal their rejoicing; yet we can imitate them so
far, as to look abroad into this fair world, which God made
"very good," while we mourn over the evil which Adam
brought into it; to hold communion with what we see there,
while we seek Him who is invisible; to admire it, while we abstain from it; to acknowledge God's love, while we deprecate
His wrath; to confess that, many as are our sins, His grace is
greater. Our sins are more in number than the hairs of our head;
yet even the hairs of our head are all numbered by Him. He
counts our sins, and, as He counts, so can He forgive; for that
reckoning, great though it be, comes to an end; but His mercies
fail not, and His Son's merits are infinite.

Let us, then, on this day, dwell upon a thought, which it will
be a duty to carry with us through Lent, the thought of the
blessings and mercies of which our present life is made up. St.
Paul said that he had all, and abounded, and was full; and this,
in a day of persecution. Surely, if we have but religious hearts
and eyes, we too must confess that our daily and hourly blessings in this life are not less than his. Let us recount some of
them.

1. First, then, we ought to bless and praise God that we have
the gift of life. By this I mean, not merely that we live, but for
those blessings which are included in the notion of our living.
He has made life in its very nature to imply the existence of
certain blessings which are themselves a happiness, and which
bring it to pass that, in spite of all evils, life in itself, except in
rare cases, cannot be otherwise than desirable. We cannot live
without the means of life; without the means of life we should
die; and the means of life are means of pleasure. It might have so
been ordered that life could not have been sustained without
the use of such means as were indifferent, neither pleasurable
nor painful,—or of means which were even painful; as in the

case of illness or disease, when we actually find that we cannot preserve it without painful remedies. Now, supposing the ordinary ways of preserving it had been what are now but extraordinary: supposing food were medicine; supposing wounds or blows imparted health and strength. But it is not so. On the contrary, life consists in things pleasant; it is sustained by blessings. And, moreover, the Gospel, by a solemn grant, guarantees these things to us. After the Flood, God Almighty condescended to promise that there never should be such a flood again; that seed-time and harvest should not fail. He ratified the stability of nature by His own Word, and by that Word it is upheld. And in like manner He has, in a special way, guaranteed to us in the Gospel that law of nature whereby good and pleasant gifts are included in our idea of life, and life becomes a blessing. Did He so will, He might sustain us Christians, not by bread only, but by every word that proceedeth out of His mouth. But He has not done so. He has pledged to us those ordinary means of sustenance which we naturally like: "bread shall be given us; our water shall be sure;" "all these things shall be added unto us." He has not indeed promised us what the world calls its great prizes; He has not promised us those goods, so called, of which the goodness depends on the imagination; He has not promised us large estates, magnificent domains, houses like palaces, sumptuous furniture, retainers and servants, chariots and horses, rank, name, credit, popularity, power, the deference of others, the indulgence of our wills, luxuries, sensual enjoyments. These, on the contrary, He denies us; and, withal, He declares, that, specious and inviting as they are, really they are evil. But still He has promised that this shall be His rule,—that thus shall it be fulfilled to us as His ordinary providence, viz.—that life shall not be a burden to us, but a blessing, and shall contain more to comfort than to afflict. And giving us as much as this, He bids us be satisfied with it; He bids us confess that we "have all" when we have so much: that we "abound" when we have enough; He promises us food, raiment, and lodging; and He bids us, "having food and raiment, therewith to be content." [2] He bids us be content with those gifts, and withal unsolicitous about them; tranquil, secure, and confident, because He has promised them; He bids us be sure that we shall have so much, and not be disappointed that it is no more. Such is His merciful consideration of us; He does not separate us from this world, though He calls us out of it; He

[2] 1 Tim. vi.8.

does not reject our old nature when He gives us a new one; He does but redeem it from the curse, and purify it from the infection which came through Adam, and is none of His. He especially blesses the creation to our use, though we be regenerate. "Every creature of God," says the Apostle, "is good, and nothing to be refused, if it be received with thanksgiving, for it is sanctified by the word of God and prayer."[3] He does not bid us renounce the creation, but associates us with the most beautiful portions of it. He likens us to the flowers with which He has ornamented the earth, and to the birds that live solitary under heaven, and makes them the type of a Christian. He denies us Solomon's regal magnificence, to unite us to the lilies of the field and the fowls of the air. "Take no thought for your life, what ye shall eat or what ye shall drink: nor yet for your body, what ye shall put on. Is not the life more than meat, and the body than raiment? Behold the fowls of the air, for they sow not, neither do they reap, nor gather into barns; yet your heavenly Father feedeth them. Are ye not much better than they? .... And why take ye thought for raiment? Consider the lilies of the field, how they grow; they toil not, neither do they spin; and yet I say unto you, that even Solomon in all his glory was not arrayed like one of these."[4]

Here then, surely, is a matter for joy and thankfulness at all seasons, and not the least at times when, with a religious forbearance, and according to the will of the Giver, not from thanklessness but from prudence, we, for a while, more or less withhold from ourselves His good gifts. Then, of all times, when we think it right to suspend our use of the means of life, so far as may not hurt that life, His gift, and to prove how pleasant is the using them by the pain of abstaining from them,— now especially, my brethren, in the weeks in prospect, when we shall be called on to try ourselves, as far as may be, by hunger, or cold, or watching, or seclusion, that we may be brought nearer to God,—let us now thank God that He has not put us into an evil world, or subjected us to a cruel master, but has given us a continual record of His own perfections in all that lies around us. Alas! it will be otherwise hereafter with those whom God puts out of His sight for ever. Their world will be evil; their life will be death; their rulers will be the devil and his angels; flames of fire and the lake of brimstone will be their meat and drink; the heaven above them will be brass; their earth will be dust and ashes; the blood in their veins will be as molten lead. Fearful

---

[3] 1 Tim. iv.4, 5.   [4] Matt. vi.25–29.

thought! which it is not right to do more than glance at. Let us utter it, and pass by. Rather it is for us to rejoice that we are still in the light of His countenance, on His good earth, and under His warm sun. Let us thank Him that He gives us the fruits of the earth in their season; that He gives us "food out of the earth, and wine that maketh glad the heart of man, and oil to make him a cheerful countenance, and bread to strengthen man's heart." [5] Thus was it with our fathers of old time; thus is it with us now. After Abraham had fought with the kings, Melchizedek brought forth bread and wine to refresh him. The Angels who visited him made themselves men, and ate of the calf which he dressed for them. Isaac blessed Jacob after the savoury meat. Joseph's brethren ate and drank, and were merry with him. The seventy elders went up Mount Sinai with Moses, Aaron, Nadab, and Abihu, and they saw God, and moreover "did eat and drink." David, after his repentance, had "bread set before him, and he did eat." When Elijah went for his life, and requested that he might die, "an Angel touched him, and said unto him, Arise and eat;" and he did eat and drink, once and twice, and lay down to sleep between his meals; and when he arose, he "went in the strength of that meat forty days and forty nights unto Horeb the mount of God." St. Paul also, after his conversion and baptism, "received meat and was strengthened." [6]

2. Again, what a great blessing is that gift, of which I have just spoken in Elijah's case, the gift of sleep. Almighty God does not suffer us to be miserable for a long while together, even when He afflicts us; but He breaks our trial into portions; takes us out of this world ever and anon, and gives us a holy-day time, like children at school, in an unknown and mysterious country.

All this then must be borne in mind, in reflecting on those solemn and sobering truths concerning the Christian's calling, which it is necessary often to insist upon. It is often said, and truly, that the Christian is born to trouble,—that sorrow is the rule with him, and pleasure the exception. But when this is said, it is with reference to seasons, circumstances, events, such things as are adventitious and additional to the gift of life itself. The Christian's *lot* is one of sorrow, but, as the regenerate *life* with him is happiness, so is the gift of natural life also. We live, therefore we are happy; *upon* this life of ours come joys and sorrows; and in proportion as we are favourites of God, it is sorrow

[5] Ps. civ.14, 15.

[6] Gen. xiv.18; xviii.8; xxvii.25; xliii.34; Exod. xxiv.11; 2 Sam. xii.20; 1 Kings xix.5–8; Acts ix.19.

that comes, not joy. Still after all considered in ourselves, that we live; that God breathes in us; that we exist in Him; that we think and act; that we have the means of life; that we have food, and sleep, and raiment, and lodging; and that we are not lonely, but in God's Church, and are sure of brethren by the very token of our having a Father which is in heaven; so far, rejoicing is the very condition of our being, and all pain is little more than external, not reaching to our inmost heart. So far all men almost are on a level, seasons of sickness excepted. Even delicate health and feebleness of life does not preclude these pleasures. And as to seasons of sickness, or even long and habitual pain or disease, the good Lord can compensate for them in His own way by extraordinary supplies of grace, as in early times He made even the torments of Christians in persecution literally pleasant to them. He who so ordered it, that even the red-hot iron did feel pleasant to the Martyrs after a while, cannot fail of means to support His servants when life becomes a burden. But, generally speaking, it is a happiness, and that to all ranks. High and low, rich and poor, have the same refreshment in their pilgrimage. Hunger is as pleasantly appeased by the low as by the high, on coarse fare as on delicate. Sleep is equally the comfort and recruiting of rich and poor. We eat, drink, and sleep, whether we are in sorrow or in joy, in anxiety or in hope. Our natural life is the type of our spiritual life, and thus, in a literal as well as higher sense, we may bless Him "who saveth our life from destruction, and crowneth us with mercy and loving-kindness; who satisfieth our mouth with good things, making us young and lusty as an eagle." [7]

3. Now, again, consider the blessings which we have in Christian brotherhood. In the beginning, woman was made, that man might not be alone, but might have a help meet for him; and our Lord promised that all who gave up this world and this world's kindred for Him, should "receive manifold more in this present time, houses, and brethren, and sisters, and mothers, and children, and lands, with persecutions." [8] You see He mentions the troubles of Christians, which were their lot *as* Christians; but still these did not interfere with the prior law of their very nature, that they should not be friendless. As food and raiment are necessary conditions of life, society is an inseparable adjunct of it. God does not take away food and raiment when He gives grace, nor does He take away brotherhood. He removes from the world to put into the Church.

[7] Ps. ciii.4, 5.   [8] Mark x.30.

Religion without a Church is as unnatural as life without food and raiment. He began our life anew, but He built it up upon the same foundations; and as He did not strip us of our body, when He made us Christians, neither did He of social ties. Christ finds us in the double tabernacle, of a house of flesh and a house of brethren, and He sanctifies both, not pulls them down. Our first life is in ourselves; our second in our friends. They whom God forces to part with their near of kin, for His sake, find brethren in the spirit at their side. They who remain solitary, for His sake, have children in the spirit raised up to them. How should we thank God for this great benefit! Now especially, when we are soon to retire, more or less, into ourselves, and to refrain from our ordinary intercourse with one another, let us acknowledge the blessing, whether of the holy marriage bond, or of family affection, or of the love of friends, which He so bounteously bestows. He gives, He takes away; blessed be His Name. But He takes away to give again, and He withdraws one blessing, to restore fourfold. Abraham offered his only son, and received Him back again at the Angel's voice. Isaac "took Rebekah, and she became his wife, and he loved her; and Isaac was comforted after his mother's death." Jacob lost Joseph, and found him governor of Egypt. Job lost all his children, yet his end was more blessed than his beginning. We too, through God's mercy, whether we be young or old, whether we have many friends or few, if we be Christ's, shall all along our pilgrimage find those in whom we may live, who will love us and whom we may love, who will aid us and help us forward, and comfort us, and close our eyes. For His love is a secret gift, which, unseen by the world, binds together those in whom it lives, and makes them live and sympathise in one another.

4. Again, let us bless and praise God for the present peace of the Church, and the freedom of speech and action which He has vouchsafed to us. There have been times when, to be a Christian, was to be an outcast and a criminal, when to profess the faith of the Saints would have subjected us to bonds and imprisonment. Let us thank God that at present we have nothing to fear, but may serve Him zealously, "no man forbidding" us. No thanks indeed to the world, which has given us this peace, not from any love to the Church or the Truth, but from selfish and ungodly principles of its own; but great thanks to God, who has made use of the world, and has overruled its course of opinion to our benefit. We have large and noble Churches to worship in; we may go freely to worship when we

will; we may enjoy the advice of those who know better than ourselves; we may speak our mind one to another; we may move about freely; we may hold intercourse with whom we will; we may write what we will, explaining, defending, recommending, spreading the truth, without suffering or inconvenience. This is the blessing which we pray for in our Collects; and wonderfully has God granted it for very many years past. We pray daily that God would "give peace in our time." We pray three times a week that "those evils, which the craft and subtilty of the devil or man worketh against us, be brought to nought;" and "that, being hurt by no persecutions, we may evermore give thanks unto God in His Holy Church." We pray yearly that "the course of this world may be so peaceably ordered by His governance, that His Church may joyfully serve Him in all godly quietness;" and that He may "keep His household, the Church, in continual godliness, that through His protection it may be free from all adversities, and devoutly given to serve Him, in good works, to the glory of His Name." Now all this is most wonderfully fulfilled to us at this day,—praised be His great mercy! You will ask, perhaps, whether too much prosperity is not undesirable for the Church?—It is so; but I am speaking, not of the Church, but of ourselves as individuals: what is dangerous to the body, may be a blessing to the separate members. As to ourselves, one by one, God has His own secret chastisements for us, which, if He loves us, He will apply when we need them; but, if we know how to use the blessing duly, it is, I say, a great gift, that we are allowed to serve God with such freedom and in such peace as are now vouchsafed us. Great mercy indeed, which we forget because we are used to it; which many prophets and righteous men in the first ages of the Gospel had not, yet which we have had from our youth up. We from our youth up have lived in peace; with no persecution, no terror, no hindrance in serving God. The utmost we have had to endure, is what is almost too trifling for a Christian to mention,—cold looks, or contempt, or ridicule, from those who have not the heart themselves to attempt the narrow way.

5. Lastly, and very briefly, my brethren, let us remind ourselves of our own privileges here in this place. How great is our privilege, my brethren!—every one of us enjoys the great privilege of daily Worship and weekly Communion. This great privilege God has given to me and to you,—let us enjoy it while we have it. Not any one of us knows how long it may be his own. Perhaps there is no one among us all who can reckon upon it for a continuance. Perhaps, or rather probably, it is a bright

spot in our lives. Perhaps we shall look upon these days or years, time hence; and then reflect, when all is over, how pleasant they were; how pleasant to come, day after day, quietly and calmly, to kneel before our Maker,—week after week, to meet our Lord and Saviour. How soothing will then be the remembrance of His past gifts! we shall remember how we got up early in the morning, and how all things, light or darkness, sun or air, cold or freshness, breathed of Him,—of Him, the Lord of glory, who stood over us, and came down upon us, and gave Himself to us, and poured forth milk and honey for our sustenance, though we saw Him not. Surely we have all, and abound: we are full.

ENDURANCE,
THE CHRISTIAN'S PORTION

(Sexagesima)

"All these things are against me."—Gen. xlii.36.

So spoke the Patriarch Jacob, when Joseph had been made away with, Simeon was detained in Egypt, Benjamin threatened, and his remaining sons suspected by him and distrusted; when out of doors, nay, at his door, was a grievous famine, enemies or strangers round about, evil in prospect, and in the past a number of sad remembrances to pain, not to cheer him,—the dreadful misconduct of his own family and its consequences, and, further back, the wrath of Esau, his separation from his father's house, his wanderings, and his ill-usage by Laban. From his youth upwards he had been full of sorrows, and he bore them with a troubled mind. His first words are, "If God will be with me . . . then shall the Lord be my God." His next, "Deliver me, I pray Thee." His next, "Ye have troubled me." His next, "I will go down into the grave unto my son mourning." His next, "All these things are against me." And his next, "Few and evil have the days of the years of my life been." [1] Blow after blow, stroke after stroke, trouble came like hail. That one hailstone falls is a proof, not that no more will come, but that others are coming surely; when we feel the first, we say, "It *begins* to hail,"—we do not argue that it is over, but that it is to come. Thus was it with Jacob: the storm muttered around him, and heavy drops fell while he was in his father's house; it drove him abroad. It did not therefore cease because he was out in it: it did not end because it had begun. Rather, it continued, because it had begun; its beginning marked its presence; it began upon a law, which was extended over him in manhood also and old age, as in early youth. It was his calling to be in the storm: it was his very life to be a

[1] Gen. xxviii.20, 21; xxxii.11; xxiv.30; xxxvii.35; xlii.36; xlvii.9.

pilgrimage; it was the very thread of the days of his years to be few and evil.

And what Jacob was all his life, that was his son Joseph at least in the early part of it; for thirteen years, from seventeen to thirty, he was in trouble far greater than Jacob's;—in captivity, in slavery, in prison, in bonds so tight that the iron is said to have entered into his soul. And what Joseph was in the beginning of life, such was Abraham, his forefather, in the latter half of it. For seventy-five years he lived in his "father's house;" but henceforward he was a wanderer. Thus did Almighty God, by the instance of the patriarchs of His ancient people, remind that people themselves that this world was not their rest; thus did He foreshadow that condition of life, which is not only a lesson, but a pattern to us of our very state of life, "if we live godly in Christ Jesus." [2] He Himself, the Lord Incarnate, chose only to sojourn on earth; He had not where to lay His head. "Let us go forth, therefore, unto Him without the camp, bearing His reproach, for here we have no continuing city, but we seek one to come." [3] In Jacob is prefigured the Christian. He said, "All these things are against me;" and what he said in a sort of dejection of mind that must the Christian say, not in dejection, not sorrowfully, or passionately, or in complaint, or in impatience, but calmly, as if confessing a doctrine. "All these things are against me;" but it is my portion they are against me, that I may fight against them and overcome them. If there were no enemy, there could be no conflict; were there no trouble, there could be no faith; were there no trial, there could be no love; were there no fear, there could be no hope. Hope, faith, and love are weapons, and weapons imply foes and encounters; and, relying on my weapons, I will glory in my suffering, being "persuaded that neither death, nor life, nor Angels, nor principalities, nor powers, nor things present, nor things to come, nor height, nor depth, nor any other creature, shall be able to separate us from the love of God which is in Christ Jesus our Lord." [4]

That trouble and sorrow are in some especial sense the lot of the Christian, is plain from such passages of Scripture as the following:—For instance, St. Paul and St. Barnabas remind the disciples "that we must through much tribulation enter into the kingdom of God." Again, St. Paul says, "If so be that we suffer with Him, that we may be also glorified together." Again, "If we suffer, we shall also reign with Him." Again, "Yea, and all that will live godly in Christ Jesus, shall suffer persecution."

---

[2] 2 Tim. iii.12.   [3] Heb. xiii.13, 14.   [4] Rom. viii.38, 39.

Again, St. Peter, "If, when ye do well, and suffer for it, ye take it patiently, this is acceptable with God; for even hereunto were ye called." And our Saviour declares, that those who have given up the relations of this world "for His sake and the Gospel's" shall receive "an hundredfold" now, "with persecutions." And St. Paul speaks in his own case of his "perils," by sea and land, from friend and foe, without and within him, of the body and of the soul. Yet he adds, "I will glory of the things which concern mine infirmities." [5]

To passages, however, like these, it is natural to object that they do not apply to the present time; that they apply to a time of persecution, which is past and over; and that men enter the kingdom now, without the afflictions which it once involved. What we see, it may be said, is a disproof of so sad and severe a doctrine. In this age, and in this country, the Church surely is in peace; rights are secured to it, and privileges added. Christians now, to say the very least, have liberty of person and property; they live without disquietude, and they die happily. Nay, they have much more than mere toleration, they have possession of the whole country; there are none but Christians in it; and if they suffer persecution, it must be (as it were) self-inflicted from the hands of each other. Christianity is the law of the land; its ministry is a profession, its offices are honours, its name a recommendation. So far from Christians being in trial because they are Christians, those who are not Christians, infidels and profligates, it is they who are under persecution. Under disabilities indeed these are, and justly; but it would be as true to say that Christians are justly in trouble, as to say that they are in trouble at all. What confessorship is there in a man's putting himself in the front of the Christian fight, when that front is a benefice or a dignity? Rulers of the Church were aforetime marks for the persecutor; now they are but forced into temporal rank and power. Aforetime, the cross was in the inventory of holy treasures, handed down from Bishop to Bishop; but now what self-denial is there in the Apostolate, what bitterness in Christ's cup, what marks of the Lord Jesus in the touch of His Hand, what searching keenness in His sacred Breath? Of old time, indeed, as the Spirit forthwith drave Him into the wilderness to be tempted of the devil, so they, also, who received the Almighty Comforter, in any of His high gifts, were at once among the wild beasts of Ephesus, or amid the

[5] Acts xiv.22; Rom. viii.17; 2 Tim. ii.12; iii.12; 1 Pet. ii.20; Matt. xix.29; Mark x.30; 2 Cor. xi.30.

surges of the sea; but there are no such visible proofs now of the triumphs of God's grace, humbling the individual, while using him for heavenly purposes.

This is what objectors may say; and, in corroboration, they may tell us to look at the feelings of the world towards the Church and its sacred offices, and to judge for ourselves whether they have not the common sense of mankind with them. For is not the ministry of the Church what is called an easy profession? Do we not see it undertaken by those who love quiet, or who are unfit for business; by those who are less keen, less active-minded, less venturous than others? Does it not lead rather to a land of Canaan as of old time, than to the narrow rugged way and the thorny couch of the Gospel? Has it not fair pastures, and pleasant resting-places, and calm refreshing streams, and milk and honey flowing, according to the promise of the Old Covenant, rather than that baptism and that draught which is the glory of the New? Facts then, it will be said, refute such notions of the suffering character of the Christian Church. It suffered at first,—suffering was the price of its triumphing; and since that, it has ceased to suffer. It is as truly in peace now, as it was truly in suffering then;—one might as well deny that it did suffer, as that it is in peace; and to apply texts which speak of what it was then to what it is now, is unreal, offends some hearers, and excites ridicule in others. This is what may be said.

Yet is it so indeed? Let us look into the Bible again. Are we to go by faith or by sight?—for surely, whatever conclusions follow from what we see, these cannot undo what is written. What is written remains; and if sight is against it, we must suppose that there is some way of solving the difficulty, though we may not see how; and we will try, as well as we can, to solve it in the case before us.

Let us, I say, consider the words of Scripture again. Surely, if endurance be not in some sense or other the portion of Christians, the whole New Testament itself has but a temporary meaning; for it is all built upon this doctrine as a groundwork. If "the present distress,"[6] of which St. Paul speaks, does not denote the ordinary state of the Christian Church, the New Testament is scarcely written for us, but must be remodelled before it can be made apply. There are men of the world in this day who are attempting to supersede the precepts of Christ about almsgiving and the maintenance of the poor. We are

[6] 1 Cor. vii.26.

accustomed to object, that they contravene Scripture. Again, we hear of men drawing up a Church government for themselves, or omitting Sacraments, or modifying doctrines. We say they do not read Scripture rightly. They answer, perhaps, that Scripture commands or countenances many things which are not binding on us eighteen hundred years after. They consider that the management of the poor, the form of the Church, the power of the State over it, the nature of its faith, or the choice of its ordinances, are not points on which we need rigidly keep to Scripture; that times have changed. This is what they say; and can we find fault with them if we ourselves allow that the New Testament is a dead letter in another most essential part of it? Is it strange that they should think that the world may now tyrannize over the Church, when we allow that the Church may now indulge in the world? Surely they do but make a fair bargain with us; both they and we put aside Scripture, and then agree together, we to live in ease, and they to rule. We have taken the world's pay, and must not grudge its yoke. Independence surely is not the Church's privilege, unless hardship is her portion.

Well, and perhaps affliction, hardship, distress, ill-usage, evil report, are her portion, both promised and bestowed, though at first sight they may seem not to be. What proof is there that temporal happiness was the gift of the Law, which will not avail for temporal adversity being that of the Gospel? You say the Jews had the promise of this world. True. But look at their history. Is that promise fulfilled on its surface? Had they not long periods of captivity, war, famine, pestilence, weakness, internal division? Look at their history as a whole. Is it not very like other histories? Had not their power a beginning, a progress, and an end? Did they not pass through those successive stages which other states pass through? What prosperity had they, to go by appearances, which other states had not? What trouble had other states which they were spared? If, then, the face of things be taken to prove that the Christian Church is not born to trouble, would it not also prove that the Jewish Church was not allotted prosperity? And if in spite of appearances, we yet say that the Israelites had special temporal blessings, why may we not, in spite of the appearance, say that Christians have special temporal trials?

You will say, perhaps, that the Jewish promise was suspended on a condition, the condition of obedience, and that the Jews forfeited the reward, because they did not merit it. True; let it be so. And what hinders, in like manner, if Christians are in

prosperity, not in adversity, that it is because they too have forfeited the promise and privilege of affliction by disobedience?
And what hinders that, as in spite of the sins of the people, the
Jewish Church still in some sufficient sense did obtain the temporal promise; so, in like manner, in spite of the sins of the
multitude of Christians, the Christian Church as a whole, and
her true children in particular, may partake in the promise of
distress?

It is very difficult then to argue from what we see, and there
are many ways in which what is written may be fulfilled in
spite, or by means, of it. All that clearly can be pointed out is
the word of promise. It was said of Israel, "He loved the people;
all His saints are in Thy hand; and they sat down at Thy feet;
every one shall receive of Thy words. . . . Let Reuben live and
not die; and let not his men be few. . . . Hear, Lord, the voice of
Judah, and bring him unto his people. Let his hands be sufficient for him, and be Thou an help to him from his enemies."
And of Levi; "Let Thy Thummim and Thy Urim be upon Thy
Holy One. . . . Bless, Lord, his substance, and accept the work
of his hands: smite through the loins of them that rise against
him, and of them that hate him, that they rise not again." And
of Benjamin: "The Beloved of the Lord shall dwell in safety by
Him." And of Joseph: "Blessed of the Lord be his land, for the
precious things of heaven, for the dew, and for the deep that
coucheth beneath, and for the precious things brought forth by
the sun, and for the precious things brought forth by the moon,
and for the chief things of the ancient mountains, and for the
precious things of the lasting hills, and for the precious things
of the earth, and the fulness thereof." And of Zebulun: "Rejoice, Zebulun; in thy going out; and, Issachar, in thy tents . . . .
they shall suck of the abundance of the seas, and of treasures hid
in the sand." And, "Blessed be he that enlargeth Gad; he dwelleth as a lion, and teareth the arm with the crown of the head."
And, "O Naphtali, satisfied with favour, and full of the blessing
of the Lord, possess thou the west and the south." And, "Let
Asher be blessed with children; thy shoes shall be iron and
brass; and as thy days, so shall thy strength be." And of all of
them together it was said, "Israel shall dwell in safety alone; the
fountain of Jacob shall be upon a land of corn and wine; and his
heavens shall drop down dew."[7] These were the bright and
pleasant things promised to the first people of God, in the plains
of Moab, on their entering into the land. And now in turn,

---

[7] Deut. xxxiii.

what did the second and greater Prophet of the Church declare, when He was set upon the mount, with the people around Him, and published His covenant of grace. "He opened His mouth and said, Blessed are the poor in spirit, for theirs is the kingdom of heaven. Blessed are they that mourn, for they shall be comforted. Blessed are the meek. . . . Blessed are they which do hunger and thirst after righteousness. . . . Blessed are the merciful. . . . Blessed are the pure in heart. . . . Blessed are the peacemakers." And lastly, "Blessed are ye when men shall revile you and persecute you, and shall say all manner of evil against you falsely for my sake. Rejoice, and be exceeding glad; for great is your reward in heaven; for so persecuted they the Prophets which were before you." And by contrast, He added, "But woe unto you that are rich, for ye have received your consolation. Woe unto you that are full, for ye shall hunger. Woe unto you that laugh now, for ye shall mourn and weep. Woe unto you when all men shall speak well of you, for so did their fathers unto the false prophets."[8]

At another time He spoke thus: "Sell that ye have, and give alms." "If thou wilt be perfect, go and sell that thou hast, and give to the poor." "It is easier for a camel to go through the eye of a needle, than for a rich man to enter into the kingdom of God." "Whosoever will be chief among you, let him be your servant." "If any man will come after Me, let him deny himself, and take up his cross, and follow Me." And, in a word, the doctrine of the Gospel, and the principle of it, is thus briefly stated by the Apostle, in the words of the Wise Man. "Whom the Lord loveth He chasteneth, and scourgeth every son whom He receiveth. If ye endure chastening, God dealeth with you as with sons. . . . If ye be without chastisement, *whereof all are partakers*, then are ye bastards, and not sons."[9] Can words speak it plainer, that, as certainly as temporal prosperity is the gift of the Law, so also are hardship and distress the gift of the Gospel?

Take up thy portion, then, Christian soul, and weigh it well, and learn to love it. Thou wilt find, if thou art Christ's, in spite of what the world fancies, that after all, even at this day, endurance, in a special sense, is the lot of those who offer themselves to be servants of the King of sorrows. There is an inward world, which none see but those who belong to it; and though the outside robe be many-coloured, like Joseph's coat, inside it is lined with camel's hair, or sackcloth, fitting those who desire to be

[8] Matt. v.2–12; Luke vi.24–26.
[9] Luke xii.33; Matt. xix.21, 24; xx.27; xvi.24; Heb. xii.6–8.

one with Him who fared hardly in the wilderness, in the mountain, and on the sea. There is an inward world into which they enter who come near to Christ, though to men in general they seem the same as before. They hold the same place as before in the world's society; their employments are the same, their ways, their comings in and goings out. If they were high in rank, they are still high; if they were in active life, they are still active; if they were wealthy, they still have wealth. They have still great friends, powerful connexions, ample resources, fair name in the world's eye; but, if they have drunk of Christ's cup, and tasted the bread of His Table in sincerity, it is not with them as in time past. A change has come over them, unknown indeed to themselves, except in its effects, but they have a portion in destinies to which other men are strangers, and, as having destinies, they have conflicts also. They drank what looked like a draught of this world, but it associated them in hopes and fears, trials and purposes, above this world. They came as for a blessing, and they have found a work. They are soldiers in Christ's army; they fight against "things that are seen," and they have "all these things against them." To their surprise, as time goes on, they find that their lot is changed. They find that in one shape or other adversity happens to them. If they refuse to afflict themselves, God afflicts them. One blow falls, they are startled; it passes over, it is well; they expect nothing more. Another comes; they wonder; "Why is this?" they ask; they think that the first should be their security against the second; they bear it, however; and it passes too. Then a third comes; they almost murmur; they have not yet mastered the great doctrine that endurance is their portion. O simple soul, is it not the law of thy being to endure since thou camest to Christ? Why camest thou but to endure? Why didst thou taste His heavenly feast, but that it might work in thee? Why didst thou kneel beneath His hand, but that He might leave on thee the print of His wounds? Why wonder then that one sorrow does not buy off the next? Does one drop of rain absorb the second? Does the storm cease because it has begun? Understand thy place in God's kingdom, and rejoice, not complain, that in thy day thou hast thy lot with Prophets and Apostles. Envy not the gay and thriving world. Religious persons ask, "Why are we so marked out for crosses? Others get on in the world; others are prosperous; their schemes turn out well, and their families settle happily; there is no anxiety, no bereavement among them, while the world fights against us." This is what they sometimes say, though with some exaggeration certainly, for almost all men, sooner or later, have their troubles, and Christians, as well as others, have their continual comforts. But what then, be it ever so true? If so, it is but what was foretold long ago, and even under the Law fulfilled in its degree. "They have children at their desire, and leave the rest of their substance for their babes." "They are in no peril of death, but are lusty and strong. They come in no misfortune like other folk, neither are they plagued like other men. . . . Their eyes swell with fatness, they do even what they lust. . . . Lo, these are the ungodly, these prosper in the world, and these have riches in possession." Such is the portion, such the punishment of those who forsake their God. "Verily, I say unto you, They have their reward." [10]

When, then, my brethren, it is objected that times are changed since the Gospel was first preached, and that what Scripture says of the lot of Christians does not apply to us, make answer, that the Church of Christ doubtless is in high estate everywhere, and so must be, for it is written, "I will give Thee the heathen for Thine inheritance, and the uttermost parts of the earth for Thy possession." Yet that while she maintains her ground, she ever suffers *in* maintaining it; she has to fight the good fight, in order to maintain it: she fights and she suffers, in proportion as she plays her part well; and if she is without suffering, it is because she is slumbering. Her doctrines and precepts never can be palatable to the world; and if the world does not persecute, it is because she does not preach. And so of her individual members: they in their own way suffer; not after her manner, perhaps, nor for the same reason, nor in the same degree, but more or less, as being under the law of suffering which Christ began. Judge not then by outward appearance; think not that His servants are in ease and security because things look smooth, else you will be startled, perhaps, and offended, when suffering falls upon you. Temporal blessings, indeed, He gives to you and to all men in abundance; "He maketh His sun to rise upon the just and unjust;" but in your case it will be "houses and brethren and lands, with persecutions." Judge not by appearance, but be sure that, even when things seem to brighten and smile upon God's true servants, there is much within to try them, though you see it not. Of old time they wore clothing of hair and sackcloth under rich robes. Men do not observe this custom now-a-days; but be quite sure still, that there are as many sharp distresses, underneath the visible garb of things, as if they did. Many a secret ailment or

----

[10] Ps. xvii.15; lxxiii.4–12; Matt. vi.5.

scarcely-observed infirmity exercises him who has it, better than thorns or knotted cord. Many a silent grief, lying like lead within the breast, or like cold ice upon the heart. Many a sad secret, which a man dare not tell lest he should find no sympathy. Many a laden conscience laden because the owner of it has turned to Christ, and which he would not have felt, had he kept from Him. Many an apprehension for the future which cannot be spoken; many a bereavement which has robbed the world's gifts of their pleasant savour, and leads the heart but to sigh at the sight of them. No; never while the Church lasts, will the words of old Jacob be reversed,—all things here are against us but God; but if God be for us, who can really be against us? If He is in the midst of us, how shall we be moved? If Christ has died and risen again, what death can come upon us, though we be made to die daily? what sorrow, pain, humiliation, trial, but must end as His has ended, in a continual resurrection into His new world, and in a nearer and nearer approach to Him? He pronounced a blessing over His Apostles, and they have scattered it far and wide all over the earth unto this day. It runs as follows: "Peace I leave with you, My peace I give unto you; not as the world giveth, give I unto you." "These things I have spoken unto you, that in Me ye might have peace. In the world ye shall have tribulation; but be of good cheer, I have overcome the world." [11]

[11] John xiv.27; xvi.38.

AFFLICTION, A SCHOOL
OF COMFORT

(Sexagesima)

"Who comforteth us in all our tribulation, that we may be able to comfort them which are in any trouble, by the comfort wherewith we ourselves are comforted of God."—2 Cor. i.4.

IF there is one point of character more than another which belonged to St. Paul, and discovers itself in all he said and did, it was his power of sympathising with his brethren, nay, with all classes of men. He went through trials of every kind, and this was their issue, to let him into the feelings, and thereby to introduce him to the hearts, of high and low, Jew and Gentile. He knew how to persuade, for he knew where lay the perplexity; he knew how to console, for he knew the sorrow. His spirit within him was as some delicate instrument, which, as the weather changed about him, as the atmosphere was moist or dry, hot or cold, accurately marked all its variations, and guided him what to do. "To the Jews he became as a Jew, that he might gain the Jews; to them that were under the Law, as under the Law, that he might gain them that were under the Law: to them that were without Law, as without Law, that he might gain them that were without Law." "To the weak," he says, "became I as weak, that I might gain the weak. I am made all things to all men, that I might by all means save some." And so again, in another place, after having recounted his various trials by sea and land, in the bleak wilderness and the stifling prison, from friends and strangers, he adds, "Who is weak and I am not weak? who is offended, and I burn not? If I must needs glory, I will glory of the things which concern mine infirmities." Hence, in the Acts of the Apostles, when he saw his brethren weeping, though they could not divert him from his purpose, which came from God, yet he could not keep from crying out, "What mean ye to weep, and to break my heart? for I am ready, not to be bound only, but also to die at Jerusalem, for the Name of the Lord Jesus." And even of his own countrymen who persecuted him, he speaks in the most tender and affectionate terms, as understanding well where they stood, and what their view of the Gospel was. "I have great heaviness and continual sorrow in my heart; for I could wish that myself were accursed from Christ for my brethren, my kinsmen according to the flesh." And again, "Brethren, my heart's desire and prayer to God for Israel is, that they might be saved. For I *bear them record* that they have a zeal of God, but not according to knowledge." And hence so powerful was he in speech with them, wherever they were not reprobate, that even King Agrippa, after hearing a few words of St. Paul's own history, exclaimed, "Almost thou persuadest me to be a Christian!" [1] And what he was in persuasion, such he was in consolation. He himself gives this reason for his trials in the text, speaking of Almighty God's comforting him in all his tribulation, in order that he might be able to comfort them which were in any trouble, by the comfort wherewith he himself was comforted of God.

Such was the great Apostle St. Paul, the Apostle of grace, whom we hold in especial honour in the early part of the year. At this season we commemorate his conversion; and at this season we give attention, more than ordinary, to his Epistles. And on Sexagesima Sunday we almost keep another Festival in his memory, the Epistle for the day being expressly on the subject of his trials. He was beaten, he was scourged, he was chased to and fro, he was imprisoned, he was shipwrecked, he was in this life of all men most miserable, that he might understand how poor a thing mortal life is, and might learn to contemplate and describe fitly the glories of the life immortal.

"Experience," he tells us elsewhere, "worketh hope,"—that grace which of all others most tends to comfort and assuage sorrow. In somewhat a similar way our Lord says to St. Peter, "Simon, Simon, behold, Satan hath desired to have you, that he may sift you as wheat: but I have prayed for thee, that thy faith fail not; and when thou art converted, strengthen thy brethren." [2] Nay, the same law was fulfilled, not only in the case of Christ's servants, but even He Himself, "who knoweth the hearts," condescended, by an ineffable mystery, to learn to strengthen man, by the experiencing of man's infirmities. "In all things it behoved Him to be made like unto His brethren, that He might be a merciful and faithful High Priest in things

[1] 1 Cor. ix.20–22; 2 Cor. xi.29, 30; Acts xxi.13; Rom. ix.3; x.1, 2; Acts xxvi.28.

[2] Luke xxii.31, 32.

pertaining to God, to make reconciliation for the sins of the people; for in that He Himself suffered being tempted, He is able to succour them that are tempted." "We have not a High Priest who cannot be touched with the feeling of our infirmities, but was in all points tempted like as we are, yet without sin." [3]

Such is one chief benefit of painful trial, of whatever kind, which it may not be unsuitable to enlarge on. Man is born to trouble, "as the sparks fly upward." More or less, we all have our severe trials of pain and sorrow. If we go on for some years in the world's sunshine, it is only that troubles, when they come, should fall heavier. Such at least is the general rule. Sooner or later we fare as other men; happier than they only if we learn to bear our portion more religiously; and more favoured if we fall in with those who themselves have suffered, and can aid us with their sympathy and their experience. And then, while we profit from what they can give us, we may learn from them freely to give what we have freely received, comforting in turn others with the comfort which our brethren have given us from God.

Now, in speaking of the benefits of trial and suffering, we should of course never forget that these things by themselves have no power to make us holier or more heavenly. They make many men morose, selfish, and envious. The only sympathy they create in many minds, is the wish that others should suffer with them, not they with others. Affliction, when love is away, leads a man to wish others to be as he is; it leads to repining, malevolence, hatred, rejoicing in evil. "Art thou also become weak as we? art thou become like unto us?" said the princes of the nations to the fallen king of Babylon. The devils are not incited by their own torments to any endeavour but that of making others devils also. Such is the effect of pain and sorrow, when unsanctified by God's saving grace. And this is instanced very widely and in a variety of cases. All afflictions of the flesh, such as the Gospel enjoins and St. Paul practised, watchings and fastings, and subjecting of the body, have no tendency whatever in themselves to make men better; they often have made men worse; they often (to appearance) have left them just as they were before. They are no sure test of holiness and true faith, taken by themselves. A man may be most austere in his life, and, by that very austerity, learn to be cruel to others, not tender. And, on the other hand (what seems strange), he may

[3] Heb. ii.17; iv.15.

be austere in his personal habits, and yet be a waverer and a coward in his conduct. Such things have been,—I do not say they
are likely in this state of society,—but I mean, it should ever be
borne in mind, that the severest and most mortified life is as
little a passport to heaven, or a criterion of saintliness, as benevolence is, or usefulness, or amiableness. Self-discipline is a
necessary condition, but not a sure sign of holiness. It may leave
a man worldly, or it may make him a tyrant. It is only in the
hands of God that it is God's instrument. It only ministers to
God's purposes when God uses it. It is only when grace is in the
heart, when power from above dwells in a man, that anything
outward or inward turns to his salvation. Whether persecution,
or famine, or the sword, they as little bring the soul to Christ, as
they separate it from Him. He alone can work, and He can
work through all things. He can make the stones bread. He can
feed us with "every word which proceedeth from His mouth."
He could, did He so will, make us calm, resigned, tender-
hearted, and sympathising, without trial; but it is His will ordinarily to do so by means of trial. Even He Himself, when He
came on earth, condescended to gain knowledge by experience;
and what He did Himself, that He makes His brethren do.

And while affliction does not necessarily make us gentle and
kind, nay, it may be, even makes us stern and cruel, the want of
affliction does not mend matters. Sometimes we look with
pleasure upon those who never have been afflicted. We look
with a smile of interest upon the smooth brow and open countenance, and our hearts thrill within us at the ready laugh or the
piercing glance. There is a buoyancy and freshness of mind in
those who have never suffered, which, beautiful as it is, is perhaps scarcely suitable and safe in sinful man. It befits an Angel;
it befits very young persons and children, who have never been
delivered over to their three great enemies. I will not dare to
deny that there are those whom white garments and unfading
chaplets show that they have a right thus to rejoice always, even
till God takes them. But this is not the case of the many, whom
earth soils, and who lose their right to be merry-hearted. In
them lightness of spirits degenerates into rudeness, want of
feeling, and wantonness; such is the change, as time goes on,
and their hearts become less pure and childlike. Pain and sorrow are the almost necessary medicines of the impetuosity of
nature. Without these, men, though men, are like spoilt children; they act as if they considered everything must give way to
their own wishes and conveniences. They rejoice in their
youth. They become selfish; and it is difficult to say which

selfishness is the more distressing and disagreeable, self in high
spirits, or self in low spirits; self in joy, or self in sorrow; in the
rude health of nature, or in the languor and fretfulness of trial.
It is difficult to say which will comfort the worse, hearts hard
from suffering, or hard from having never suffered; cruel despair, which rejoices in misery, or cruel pride, which is impatient at the sight of it. The cruelty, indeed, of the despairing is
the more hateful, for it is more after Satan's pattern, who feels
the less for others, the more he suffers himself; yet the cruelty
of the prosperous and wanton is like the excesses of the elements, or of brute animals, not designed, more at random, yet
perhaps even more keen and trying to those who incur it.

Such is worldly happiness and worldly trial; but Almighty
God, while He chose the latter as the portion of His Saints,
sanctified it by His heavenly grace, to be their great benefit. He
rescues them from the selfishness of worldly comfort without
surrendering them to the selfishness of worldly pain. He brings
them into pain, that they may be like what Christ was, and may
be led to think of Him, not of themselves. He brings them into
trouble, that they may be near Him. When they mourn, they
are more intimately in His presence than they are at any other
time. Bodily pain, anxiety, bereavement, distress, are to them
His forerunners. It is a solemn thing, while it is a privilege, to
look upon those whom He thus visits. Why is it that men
would look with fear and silence at the sight of the spirit of
some friend departed, coming to them from the grave? Why
would they abase themselves and listen awfully to any message
he brought them? Because he would seem to come from the
very presence of God. And in like manner, when a man, in
whom dwells His grace, is lying on the bed of suffering, or
when he has been stripped of his friends and is solitary, he has,
in a peculiar way, tasted of the powers of the world to come, and
exhorts and consoles with authority. He who has been long
under the rod of God, becomes God's possession. He bears in
his body marks, and is sprinkled with drops, which nature
could not provide for him. He comes "from Edom, with dyed
garments from Bozrah," and it is easy to see with whom he has
been conversing. He seems to say to us in the words of the
Prophet, "I am the man that hath seen affliction by the rod of
His wrath. He hath led me and brought me into darkness, but
not into light . . . . He hath bent His bow, and set me as a mark
for the arrow."[4] And they who see him, gather around like Job's

4 Lam. iii.1, 2, 12.

acquaintance, speaking no word to him, yet more reverently than if they did; looking at him with fear, yet with confidence, with fellow-feeling, yet with resignation, as one who is under God's teaching and training for the work of consolation towards his brethren. Him they will seek when trouble comes on themselves; turning from all such as delighted them in their prosperity, the great or the wealthy, or the man of mirth and song, or of wit, or of resource, or of dexterity, or of knowledge; by a natural instinct turning to those for consolation whom the Lord has heretofore tried by similar troubles. Surely this is a great blessing and cause of glorying, to be thus consecrated by affliction as a minister of God's mercies to the afflicted.

Some such thoughts as these may be humbly entertained by every one of us, when brought even into any ordinary pain or trouble. Doubtless if we are properly minded, we shall be very loth to take to ourselves titles of honour. We shall be slow to believe that we are specially beloved by Christ. But at least we may have the blessed certainty that we are made instruments for the consolation of others. Without impatiently settling anything absolutely about our own real state in God's sight, and how it will fare with us at the last day, at least we may allow ourselves to believe that we are at present evidently blessed by being made subservient to His purposes of mercy to others; as washing the disciples' feet, and pouring into their wounds oil and wine. So we shall say to ourselves, Thus far, merciful Saviour, we have attained; not to be assured of our salvation, but of our usefulness. So far we know, and enough surely for sinful man, that we are allowed to promote His glory who died for us. Taught by our own pain, our own sorrow, nay, by our own sin, we shall have hearts and minds exercised for every service of love towards those who need it. We shall in our measure be comforters after the image of the Almighty Paraclete, and that in all senses of the word,—advocates, assistants, soothing aids. Our words and advice, our very manner, voice, and look, will be gentle and tranquillizing, as of those who have borne their cross after Christ. We shall not pass by His little ones rudely, as the world does. The voice of the widow and the orphan, the poor and destitute, will at once reach our ears, however low they speak. Our hearts will open towards them; our word and deed befriend them. The ruder passions of man's nature, pride and anger, envy and strife, which so disorder the Church, these will be quelled and brought under in others by the earnestness and kindness of our admonitions.

Thus, instead of being the selfish creatures which we were by nature, grace, acting through suffering, tends to make us ready teachers and witnesses of Truth to all men. Time was when, even at the most necessary times, we found it difficult to speak of heaven to another; our mouth seemed closed, even when our heart was full; but now our affection is eloquent, and "out of the abundance of the heart our mouth speaketh." Blessed portion indeed, thus to be tutored in the sweetest, softest strains of Gospel truth, and to range over the face of the earth pilgrims and sojourners, with winning voices, singing, as far as in the flesh it is possible to sing, the song of Moses the servant of God, and the song of the Lamb;[5] severed from ties of earth by the trials we have endured, without father, without mother, without abiding place, as that patriarch whom St. Paul speaks of, and, like him, allowed to bring forth bread and wine to refresh the weary soldiers of the most High God. Such too was our Lord's forerunner, the holy Baptist, an austere man, cut off from among his brethren, living in the wilderness, feeding on harsh fare, yet so far removed from sternness towards those who sincerely sought the Lord, that his preaching was almost described in prophecy as the very language of consolation, "Comfort ye, comfort ye My people . . . speak ye comfortably to Jerusalem."

Such was the high temper of mind instanced in our Lord and His Apostles, and thereby impressed upon the Church of Christ. And for this we may thank God, that much as the Church has erred in various ways since her setting up, this great truth she never has forgotten, that we must all "take up our cross daily," and "through much tribulation enter into the kingdom of God." She has never forgotten that she was set apart for a comforter of the afflicted, and that to comfort well we must first be afflicted ourselves. St. Paul was consecrated by suffering to be an Apostle of Christ; by fastings, by chastisements, by self-denials for his brethren's sake, by his forlorn, solitary life, thus did he fill up day by day those intervals of respite which the fury of his persecutors permitted. And so the Church Catholic after him has never forgotten that ease was a sin, favoured as she might be with peace from external enemies. Even when riches and honours flowed in upon her, still has she always proclaimed that affliction was her proper portion. She has felt she could not perform the office of a comforter, if she enjoyed this world; and, though doubtless her

[5] Rev. xv.3.

separate branches have at times forgotten this truth, yet it remains, and is transmitted from age to age; and though she has
had many false sons, yet even they have often been obliged to
profess what they did not practise. This indeed is strange news
to men of the world, who are bent on gratifying themselves,
and who think they have gained a point, and have just cause for
congratulation, when they have found out a way of saving
themselves trouble, and of adding to their luxuries and conveniences. But those who are set on their own ease, most certainly are bad comforters of others; thus the rich man, who
fared sumptuously every day, let Lazarus lie at his gate, and left
him to be "comforted" after this life by Angels. As to comfort
the poor and afflicted is the way to heaven, so to have affliction
ourselves is the way to comfort them.

And, lastly, let us ever anxiously remember that affliction is
sent for our own personal good also. Let us fear, lest, after we
have ministered to others, we ourselves should be castaways;
lest our gentleness, consideration, and patience, which are so
soothing to them, yet should be separated from that inward
faith and strict conscientiousness which alone unites us to
Christ;—lest, in spite of all the good we do to others, yet we
should have some secret sin, some unresisted evil within us,
which separates us from Him. Let us pray Him who sends us
trial, to send us a pure heart and honesty of mind wherewith to
bear it.

THE THOUGHT OF GOD, THE STAY
OF THE SOUL

(Quinquagesima)

*"Ye have not received the spirit of bondage again to fear, but ye have
received the Spirit of adoption, whereby we cry, Abba, Father."*
—Rom. viii.15.

WHEN Adam fell, his soul lost its true strength; he forfeited the inward light of God's presence, and became
the wayward, fretful, excitable, and miserable being which his
history has shown him to be ever since; with alternate strength
and feebleness, nobleness and meanness, energy in the beginning and failure in the end. Such was the state of his soul in
itself, not to speak of the Divine wrath upon it, which followed,
or was involved in the Divine withdrawal. It lost its spiritual life
and health, which was necessary to complete its nature, and to
enable it to fulfil the ends for which it was created,—which was
necessary both for its moral integrity and its happiness; and as if
faint, hungry, or sick, it could no longer stand upright, but
sank on the ground. Such is the state in which every one of us
lies as born into the world; and Christ has come to reverse this
state, and restore us the great gift which Adam lost in the beginning. Adam fell from his Creator's favour to be a bond-servant;
and Christ has come to set us free again, to impart to us the
Spirit of adoption, whereby we become God's children, and
again approach Him as our Father.

I say, by birth we are in a state of defect and want; we have not
all that is necessary for the perfection of our nature. As the
body is not complete in itself, but requires the soul to give it a
meaning, so again the soul till God is present with it and manifested in it, has faculties and affections without a ruling principle, object, or purpose. Such it is by birth, and this Scripture
signifies to us by many figures; sometimes calling human nature
blind, sometimes hungry, sometimes unclothed, and calling the
gift of the Spirit light, health, food, warmth, and raiment; all

by way of teaching us what our first state is, and what our gratitude should be to Him who has brought us into a new state. For
instance, "Because thou sayest, I am rich, and increased in
goods, and have need of nothing; and knowest not that thou art
wretched, and miserable, and poor, and blind, and naked: I
counsel thee to buy of Me gold tried in the fire, that thou
mayest be rich; and white raiment, that thou mayest be clothed,
. . . and anoint thine eyes with eye-salve, that thou mayest see."
Again, "God, who commanded the light to shine out of darkness, hath shined in our hearts, to give the light of the knowledge of the glory of God, in the face of Jesus Christ." Again,
"Awake, thou that sleepest, and arise from the dead, and Christ
shall give thee light." Again, "Whosoever drinketh of the water that I shall give him, shall never thirst; but the water that I
shall give him shall be in him a well of water springing up into
everlasting life." And in the Book of Psalms, "They shall be
satisfied with the plenteousness of Thy house; and Thou shalt
give them drink of Thy pleasures as out of the river. For with
Thee is the well of life, and in Thy Light shall we see light." And
in another Psalm, "My soul shall be satisfied, even as it were
with marrow and fatness, when my mouth praiseth Thee with
joyful lips." And so again, in the Prophet Jeremiah, "I will satiate the souls of the priests with fatness; and My people shall be
satisfied with My goodness. . . . I have satiated the weary soul,
and I have replenished every sorrowful soul." [1]

Now the doctrine which these passages contain is often truly
expressed thus: that the soul of man is made for the contemplation of its Maker; and that nothing short of that high contemplation is its happiness; that, whatever it may possess besides, it
is unsatisfied till it is vouchsafed God's presence, and lives in the
light of it. There are many aspects in which the same solemn
truth may be viewed; there are many ways in which it may be
signified. I will now dwell upon it as I have been stating it.

I say, then, that the happiness of the soul consists in the exercise of the affections; not in sensual pleasures, not in activity,
not in excitement, not in self-esteem, not in the consciousness
of power, not in knowledge; in none of these things lies our
happiness, but in our affections being elicited, employed, supplied. As hunger and thirst, as taste, sound, and smell, are the
channels through which this bodily frame receives pleasure,
so the affections are the instruments by which the soul has

[1] Rev. iii.17, 18; 2 Cor. iv.6; Eph. v.14; John iv.14; Ps. xxxvi.8, 9;
lxiii.5; Jer. xxxi.14, 25.

pleasure. When they are exercised duly, it is happy; when they are undeveloped, restrained, or thwarted, it is not happy. This is our real and true bliss, not to know, or to affect, or to pursue; but to love, to hope, to joy, to admire, to revere, to adore. Our real and true bliss lies in the possession of those objects on which our hearts may rest and be satisfied.

Now, if this be so, here is at once a reason for saying that the thought of God, and nothing short of it, is the happiness of man; for though there is much besides to serve as subject of knowledge, or motive for action, or means of excitement, yet the affections require a something more vast and more endur-ing than anything created. What is novel and sudden excites, but does not influence; what is pleasurable or useful raises no awe; self moves no reverence, and mere knowledge kindles no love. He alone is sufficient for the heart who made it. I do not say, of course, that nothing short of the Almighty Creator can awaken and answer to our love, reverence, and trust; man can do this for man. Man doubtless is an object to rouse his brother's love, and repays it in his measure. Nay, it is a great duty, one of the two chief duties of religion, thus to be minded towards our neighbour. But I am not speaking here of what we can do, or ought to do, but what it is our happiness to do; and surely it may be said that though the love of the brethren, the love of all men, be one half of our obedience, yet exercised by itself, were that possible, which it is not, it would be no part of our reward. And for this reason, if for no other, that our hearts require something more permanent and uniform than man can be. We gain much for a time from fellowship with each other. It is a relief to us, as fresh air to the fainting, or meat and drink to the hungry, or a flood of tears to the heavy in mind. It is a sooth-ing comfort to have those whom we may make our confidants; a comfort to have those to whom we may confess our faults; a comfort to have those to whom we may look for sympathy. Love of home and family in these and other ways is sufficient to make this life tolerable to the multitude of men, which other-wise it would not be; but still, after all, our affections exceed such exercise of them, and demand what is more stable. Do not all men die? are they not taken from us? are they not as uncer-tain as the grass of the field? We do not give our hearts to things irrational, because these have no permanence in them. We do not place our affections in sun, moon, and stars, or this rich and fair earth, because all things material come to nought, and van-ish like day and night. Man, too, though he has an intelligence within him, yet in his best estate he is altogether vanity. If our

happiness consists in our affections being employed and recompensed, "man that is born of a woman" cannot be our happiness; for how can he stay another, who "continueth not in one
stay" himself?

But there is another reason why God alone is the happiness of
our souls, to which I wish rather to direct attention:—the contemplation of Him, and nothing but it, is able fully to open and
relieve the mind, to unlock, occupy, and fix our affections. We
may indeed love things created with great intenseness, but such
affection, when disjoined from the love of the Creator, is like a
stream running in a narrow channel, impetuous, vehement,
turbid. The heart runs out, as it were, only at one door; it is not
an expanding of the whole man. Created natures cannot open
us, or elicit the ten thousand mental senses which belong to us,
and through which we really live. None but the presence of our
Maker can enter us; for to none besides can the whole heart in
all its thoughts and feelings be unlocked and subjected. "Behold," He says, "I stand at the door and knock; if any man hear
My voice and open the door, I will come in to him, and will sup
with him, and he with Me." "My Father will love him, and We
will come unto him, and make Our abode with him." "God
hath sent forth the Spirit of His Son into your hearts." "God is
greater than our heart, and knoweth all things."[2] It is this feeling of simple and absolute confidence and communion, which
soothes and satisfies those to whom it is vouchsafed. We know
that even our nearest friends enter into us but partially, and
hold intercourse with us only at times; whereas the consciousness of a perfect and enduring Presence, and it alone, keeps the
heart open. Withdraw the Object on which it rests, and it will
relapse again into its state of confinement and constraint; and in
proportion as it is limited, either to certain seasons or to certain
affections, the heart is straitened and distressed. If it be not over
bold to say it, He who is infinite can alone be its measure; He
alone can answer to the mysterious assemblage of feelings and
thoughts which it has within it. "There is no creature that is not
manifest in His sight, but all things are naked and opened unto
the eyes of Him with whom we have to do."[3]

This is what is meant by the peace of a good conscience; it is
the habitual consciousness that our hearts are open to God,
with a desire that they should be open. It is a confidence in God,
from a feeling that there is nothing in us which we need be

[2] Rev. iii.20; John xiv.23; Gal. iv.6; 1 John iii.20.
[3] Heb. iv.13.

ashamed or afraid of. You will say that no man on earth is in such a state; for we are all sinners, and that daily. It is so; certainly we are quite unfitted to endure God's all-searching Eye, to come into direct contact (if I may so speak) with His glorious Presence, without any medium of intercourse between Him and us. But, first, there may be degrees of this confidence in different men, though the perfection of it be in none. And again, God in His great mercy, as we all well know, has revealed to us that there is a Mediator between the sinful soul and Himself. And as His merits most wonderfully intervene between our sins and God's judgment, so the thought of those merits, when present with the Christian, enables him, in spite of his sins, to lift up his heart to God; and believing, as he does, that he is (to use Scripture language) in Christ, or, in other words, that he addresses Almighty God, not simply face to face, but in and through Christ, he can bear to submit and open his heart to God, and to wish it open. For while he is very conscious both of original and actual sin, yet still a feeling of his own sincerity and earnestness is possible; and in proportion as he gains as much as this, he will be able to walk unreservedly with Christ his God and Saviour, and desire His continual presence with him, though he be a sinner, and will wish to be allowed to make Him the one Object of his heart. Perhaps, under somewhat of this feeling, Hagar said, "Thou, God, seest me." It is under this feeling that holy David may be supposed to say, "Examine me, O Lord, and prove me; try out my reins and my heart." "Try me, O God, and seek the ground of my heart; prove me, and examine my thoughts. Look well, if there be any way of wickedness in me; and lead me in the way everlasting." [4] And especially is it instanced in St. Paul, who seems to delight in the continual laying open of his heart to God, and submitting it to His scrutiny, and waiting for His Presence upon it; or, in other words, in the joy of a good conscience. For instance, "I have lived in all good conscience before God until this day." "Herein do I exercise myself, to have always a conscience void of offence toward God, and toward men." "I say the truth in Christ, I lie not; my conscience also bearing me witness in the Holy Ghost." "Our rejoicing is this, the testimony of our conscience, that in simplicity and godly sincerity, not with fleshly wisdom, but by the grace of God, we have had our conversation in the world, and more abundantly to you-ward." [5] It is, I say, the characteristic of

[4] Ps. xxvi.2; cxxxix.23, 24.
[5] Acts xxii.1; xxiv.16; Rom. ix.1; 2 Cor. i.12.

St. Paul, as manifested to us in his Epistles, to live in the sight of Him who "searcheth the reins and the heart," to love to place himself before Him, and, while contemplating God, to dwell on the thought of God's contemplating him.

And, it may be, this is something of the Apostle's meaning, when he speaks of the witness of the Spirit. Perhaps he is speaking of that satisfaction and rest which the soul experiences in proportion as it is able to surrender itself wholly to God, and to have no desire, no aim, but to please Him. When we are awake, we are conscious we are awake, in a sense in which we cannot fancy we are, when we are asleep. When we have discovered the solution of some difficult problem in science, we have a conviction about it which is distinct from that which accompanies fancied discoveries or guesses. When we realize a truth we have a feeling which they have not, who take words for things. And so, in like manner, if we are allowed to find that real and most sacred Object on which our heart may fix itself, a fulness of peace will follow, which nothing but it can give. In proportion as we have given up the love of the world, and are dead to the creature, and, on the other hand, are born of the Spirit unto love of our Maker and Lord, this love carries with it its own evidence whence it comes. Hence the Apostle says, "The Spirit itself beareth witness with our spirit, that we are the children of God." Again, he speaks of Him "who hath sealed us, and given the earnest of the Spirit in our hearts." [6]

I have been saying that our happiness consists in the contemplation of God;—(such a contemplation is alone capable of accompanying the mind always and everywhere, for God alone can be always and everywhere present;)—and that what is commonly said about the happiness of a good conscience, confirms this; for what is it to have a good conscience, when we examine the force of our words, but to be ever reminded of God by our own hearts, to have our hearts in such a state as to be led thereby to look up to Him, and to desire His eye to be upon us through the day? It is in the case of holy men the feeling attendant on the contemplation of Almighty God.

But, again, this sense of God's presence is not only the ground of the peace of a good conscience, but of the peace of repentance also. At first sight it might seem strange how repentance can have in it anything of comfort and peace. The Gospel, indeed, promises to turn all sorrow into joy. It makes us take pleasure in desolateness, weakness, and contempt. "We glory

[6] Rom. viii.16; 2 Cor. i.22.

in tribulations also," says the Apostle, "because the love of God is shed abroad in our hearts by the Holy Ghost which is given unto us." It destroys anxiety: "Take no thought for the morrow, for the morrow shall take thought for the things of itself." It bids us take comfort under bereavement: "I would not have you ignorant, brethren, concerning them which are asleep, that ye sorrow not, even as others which have no hope." [7] But if there be one sorrow, which might seem to be unmixed misery, if there be one misery left under the Gospel, the awakened sense of having abused the Gospel might have been considered that one. And, again, if there be a time when the presence of the Most High would at first sight seem to be intolerable, it would be then, when first the consciousness vividly bursts upon us that we have ungratefully rebelled against Him. Yet so it is that true repentance cannot be without the thought of God; it has the thought of God, for it seeks Him; and it seeks Him, because it is quickened with love; and even sorrow must have a sweetness, if love be in it. For what is to repent but to surrender ourselves to God for pardon or punishment; as loving His presence for its own sake, and accounting chastisement from Him better than rest and peace from the world? While the prodigal son remained among the swine, he had sorrow enough, but no repentance; remorse only; but repentance led him to rise and go to his Father, and to confess his sins. Thus he relieved his heart of its misery, which before was like some hard and fretful tumour weighing upon it. Or, again, consider St. Paul's account of the repentance of the Corinthians; there is sorrow in abundance, nay, anguish, but no gloom, no dryness of spirit, no sternness. The penitents afflict themselves, but it is from the fulness of their hearts, from love, gratitude, devotion, horror of the past, desire to escape from their present selves into some state holier and more heavenly. St. Paul speaks of their "earnest desire, their mourning, their fervent mind towards him." He rejoices, "not that they were made sorry, but that they sorrowed to repentance." "For ye were made sorry," he proceeds, "after a godly manner, that ye might receive damage by us in nothing." And he describes this "sorrowing after a godly sort," to consist in "carefulness, which it wrought in them," "clearing of themselves,"—"indignation,"—"fear,"—"vehement desire,"—"zeal,"—"revenge," [8]—feelings, all of them,

[7] Rom. v.3, 5; Matt. vi.23; 1 Thess. iv.13.
[8] 2 Cor. vii.7, 9, 11.

which open the heart, yet, without relaxing it, in that they terminate in acts or works.

On the other hand, remorse, or what the Apostle calls "the sorrow of the world," worketh death. Instead of coming to the Fount of Life, to the God of all consolation, remorseful men feed on their own thoughts, without any confidant of their sorrow. They disburden themselves to no one: to God they will not, to the world they cannot confess. The world will not attend to their confession; it is a good associate, but it cannot be an intimate. It cannot approach us or stand by us in trouble; it is no Paraclete; it leaves all our feelings buried within us, either tumultuous, or, at best, dead: it leaves us gloomy or obdurate. Such is our state, while we live to the world, whether we be in sorrow or in joy. We are pent up within ourselves, and are therefore miserable. Perhaps we may not be able to analyse our misery, or even to realize it, as persons oftentimes who are in bodily sicknesses. We do not know, perhaps, what or where our pain is; we are so used to it that we do not call it pain. Still so it is; we need a relief to our hearts, that they may be dark and sullen no longer, or that they may not go on feeding upon themselves; we need to escape from ourselves to something beyond; and much as we may wish it otherwise, and may try to make idols to ourselves, nothing short of God's presence is our true refuge; everything else is either a mockery, or but an expedient useful for its season or in its measure.

How miserable then is he, who does not practically know this great truth! Year after year he will be a more unhappy man, or, at least, he will emerge into a maturity of misery at once, when he passes out of this world of shadows into that kingdom where all is real. He is at present attempting to satisfy his soul with that which is not bread; or he thinks the soul can thrive without nourishment. He fancies he can live without an object. He fancies that he is sufficient for himself; or he supposes that knowledge is sufficient for his happiness; or that exertion, or that the good opinion of others, or (what is called) fame, or that the comforts and luxuries of wealth, are sufficient for him. What a truly wretched state is that coldness and dryness of soul, in which so many live and die, high and low, learned and unlearned. Many a great man, many a peasant, many a busy man, lives and dies with closed heart, with affections undeveloped, unexercised. You see the poor man, passing day after day, Sunday after Sunday, year after year, without a thought in his mind, to appearance almost like a stone. You see the educated man, full of thought, full of intelligence, full of action, but still with a stone heart, as cold and dead as regards his affections, as if he were the poor ignorant countryman. You see others, with warm affections, perhaps, for their families, with benevolent feelings towards their fellow-men, yet stopping there; centring their hearts on what is sure to fail them, as being perishable. Life passes, riches fly away, popularity is fickle, the senses decay, the world changes, friends die. One alone is constant; One alone is true to us; One alone can be true; One alone can be all things to us; One alone can supply our needs; One alone can train us up to our full perfection; One alone can give a meaning to our complex and intricate nature; One alone can give us tune and harmony; One alone can form and possess us. Are we allowed to put ourselves under His guidance? this surely is the only question. Has He really made us His children, and taken possession of us by His Holy Spirit? Are we still in His kingdom of grace, in spite of our sins? The question is not whether we should go, but whether He will receive. And we trust, that, in spite of our sins, He will receive us still, every one of us, if we seek His face in love unfeigned, and holy fear. Let us then do our part, as He has done His, and much more. Let us say with the Psalmist, "Whom have I in heaven but Thee? and there is none upon earth I desire in comparison of Thee. My flesh and my heart faileth; but God is the strength of my heart, and my portion for ever." [9]

[9] Ps. lxxiii.25, 26.

LOVE, THE ONE THING NEEDFUL

(Quinquagesima)

*"Though I speak with the tongues of men and of angels,
and have not charity, I am become as sounding brass,
or a tinkling cymbal."*—1 Cor. xiii.1.

I SUPPOSE the greater number of persons who try to live Christian lives, and who observe themselves with any care, are dissatisfied with their own state on this point, viz. that, whatever their religious attainments may be, yet they feel that their motive is not the highest;—that the love of God, and of man for His sake, is not their ruling principle. They may do much, nay, if it so happen, they may suffer much; but they have little reason to think that they love much, that they do and suffer for love's sake. I do not mean that they thus express themselves exactly, but that they are dissatisfied with themselves, and that when this dissatisfaction is examined into, it will be found ultimately to come to this, though they will give different accounts of it. They may call themselves cold, or hard-hearted, or fickle, or double-minded, or doubting, or dim-sighted, or weak in resolve, but they mean pretty much the same thing, that their affections do not rest on Almighty God as their great Object. And this will be found to be the complaint of religious men among ourselves, not less than others; their reason and their heart not going together; their reason tending heavenwards, and their heart earthwards.

I will now make some remarks on the defect I have described, as thinking that the careful consideration of it may serve as one step towards its removal.

Love, and love only, is the fulfilling of the Law, and they only are in God's favour in whom the righteousness of the Law is fulfilled. This we know full well; yet, alas! at the same time, we cannot deny that whatever good thing we have to show, whether activity, or patience, or faith, or fruitfulness in good works, love to God and man is not ours, or, at least, in very scanty measure; not at all proportionately to our apparent attainments. Now, to enlarge upon this.

In the first place, love clearly does not consist merely in great sacrifices. We can take no comfort to ourselves that we are God's own, merely on the ground of great deeds or great sufferings. The greatest sacrifices without love would be nothing worth, and that they are great does not necessarily prove they are done with love. St. Paul emphatically assures us that his acceptance with God did not stand in any of those high endowments, which strike us in him at first sight, and which, did we actually see him, doubtless would so much draw us to him. One of his highest gifts, for instance, was his spiritual knowledge. He shared, and felt the sinfulness and infirmities of human nature; he had a deep insight into the glories of God's grace, such as no natural man can have. He had an awful sense of the realities of heaven, and of the mysteries revealed. He could have answered ten thousand questions on theological subjects, on all those points about which the Church has disputed since his time, and which we now long to ask him. He was a man whom one could not come near, without going away from him wiser than one came; a fount of knowledge and wisdom ever full, ever approachable, ever flowing, from which all who came in faith, gained a measure of the gifts which God had lodged in him. His presence inspired resolution, confidence, and zeal, as one who was the keeper of secrets, and the revealer of the whole counsel of God; and who, by look, and word, and deed encompassed, as it were, his brethren with God's mercies and judgments, spread abroad and reared aloft the divine system of doctrine and precept, and seated himself and them securely in the midst of it. Such was this great servant of Christ and Teacher of the Gentiles; yet he says, "Though I speak with the tongues of men and of Angels, though I have the gift of prophecy, and understand all mysteries, and all knowledge, and have not charity, I am become as sounding brass, or a tinkling cymbal. . . . I am nothing." Spiritual discernment, an insight into the Gospel covenant, is no evidence of love.

Another distinguishing mark of his character, as viewed in Scripture, is his faith, a prompt, decisive, simple assent to God's word, a deadness to motives of earth, a firm hold of the truths of the unseen world, and keenness in following them out; yet he says of his faith also, "Though I have all faith, so that I could remove mountains, and have not charity, I am nothing." Faith is no necessary evidence of love.

A tender consideration of the temporal wants of his brethren is another striking feature of his character, as it is a special characteristic of every true Christian; yet he says, "Though I bestow all my goods to feed the poor, and have not charity, it profiteth me nothing." Self-denying alms-giving is no necessary evidence of love.

Once more. He, if any man, had the spirit of a martyr; yet he implies that even martyrdom, viewed in itself, is no passport into the heavenly kingdom. "Though I give my body to be burned, and have not charity, it profiteth me nothing." Martyrdom is no necessary evidence of love.

I do not say that at this day we have many specimens or much opportunity of such high deeds and attainments; but in our degree we certainly may follow St. Paul in them,—in spiritual discernment, in faith, in works of mercy, and in confessorship. We may, we ought to follow him. Yet though we do, still, it may be, we are not possessed of the one thing needful, of the spirit of love, or in a very poor measure; and this is what serious men feel in their own case.

Let us leave these sublimer matters, and proceed to the humbler and continual duties of daily life; and let us see whether these too may not be performed with considerable exactness, yet with deficient love. Surely they may; and serious men complain of themselves here, even more than when they are exercised on greater subjects. Our Lord says, "If ye love Me, keep My commandments;" but they feel that though they are, to a certain point, keeping God's commandments, yet love is not proportionate, does not keep pace, with their obedience; that obedience springs from some source short of love. This they perceive; they feel themselves to be hollow; a fair outside, without a spirit within it.

I mean as follows:—It is possible to obey, not from love towards God and man, but from a sort of conscientiousness short of love; from some notion of acting up to a *law*; that is, more from the fear of God than from love of Him. Surely this is what, in one shape or other, we see daily on all sides of us; the case of men living to the world, yet not without a certain sense of religion, which acts as a restraint on them. They pursue ends of this world, but not to the full; they are checked, and go a certain way only, because they dare not go further. This external restraint acts with various degrees of strength on various persons. They all live to this world, and act from the love of it; they all allow their love of the world a certain range; but, at some particular point, which is often quite arbitrary, this man stops, and that man stops. Each stops at a different point in the course of the world, and thinks every one else profane who goes further, and superstitious who does not go so far,—laughs at the latter, is shocked at the former. And hence those few who are miserable enough to have rid themselves of all scruples, look with great contempt on such of their companions as have any, be those scruples more or less, as being inconsistent and absurd. They scoff at the principle of mere fear, as a capricious and fanciful principle; proceeding on no rule, and having no evidence of its authority, no claim on our respect; as a weakness in our nature, rather than an essential portion of that nature, viewed in its perfection and entireness. And this being all the notion which their experience gives them of religion, as not knowing really religious men, they think of religion, only as a principle which interferes with our enjoyments unintelligibly and irrationally. Man is made to love. So far is plain. They see that clearly and truly; but religion, as far as they conceive of it, is a system destitute of objects of love; a system of fear. It repels and forbids, and thus seems to destroy the proper function of man, or, in other words, to be unnatural. And it is true that this sort of fear of God, or rather slavish dread, as it may more truly be called, is unnatural; but then it is not religion, which really consists, not in the mere fear of God, but in His love; or if it be religion, it is but the religion of devils, who believe and tremble; or of idolaters, whom devils have seduced, and whose worship is superstition,—the attempt to appease beings whom they love not; and, in a word, the religion of the children of this world, who would, if possible, serve God and Mammon, and, whereas religion consists of love *and* fear, give to God their fear, and to Mammon their love.

And what takes place so generally in the world at large, this, I say, serious men will feel as happening, in its degree, in their own case. They will understand that even strict obedience is no evidence of fervent love, and they will lament to perceive that they obey God far more than they love Him. They will recollect the instance of Balaam, who was even exemplary in his obedience, yet had not love; and the thought will come over them as a perplexity, what proof they have that they are not, after all, deceiving themselves, and thinking themselves religious when they are not. They will indeed be conscious to themselves of the sacrifice they make of their own wishes and pursuits to the will of God; but they are conscious also that they sacrifice them because they know they *ought* to do so, not simply from love of God. And they ask, almost in a kind of despair, How are we to learn, not merely to obey, but to love?

They say, How are we to fulfil St. Paul's words, "The life which I now live in the flesh I live by the faith of the Son of God, who loved me, and gave Himself for me"? And this would seem an especial difficulty in the case of those who live among men, whose duties lie amid the engagements of this world's business, whose thoughts, affections, exertions, are directed towards things which they see, things present and temporal. In their case it seems to be a great thing, even if their *rule* of life is a heavenly one, if they *act* according to God's will; but how can they hope that heavenly Objects should fill their heart, when there is no room left for them? how shall things absent displace things present, things unseen the things that are visible? Thus they seem to be reduced, as if by a sort of necessity, to that state, which I just now described as the state of men of the world, that of having their hearts set on the world, and being only re-strained outwardly by religious rules.

To proceed. Generally speaking, men will be able to bring against themselves positive charges of want of love, more unsat-isfactory still. I suppose most men, or at least a great number of men, have to lament over their hardness of heart, which, when analysed, will be found to be nothing else but the absence of love. I mean that hardness which, for instance, makes us unable to repent as we wish. No repentance is truly such without love; it is love which gives it its efficacy in God's sight. Without love there may be remorse, regret, self-reproach, self-condemna-tion, but there is not saving penitence. There may be convic-tion of the reason, but not conversion of the heart. Now, I say, a great many men lament in themselves this want of love in re-penting; they are hard-hearted; they are deeply conscious of their sins; they abhor them; and yet they can take as lively inter-est in what goes on around them, as if they had no such con-sciousness; or they mourn this minute, and the next are quite impenetrable. Or, though, as they think and believe, they fear God's anger, and are full of confusion at themselves, yet they find (to their surprise, I may say) that they cannot abstain from any indulgence ever so trivial, which would be (as their reason tells them) a natural way of showing sorrow. They eat and drink with as good a heart, as if they had no distress upon their minds; they find no difficulty in entering into any of the recre-ations or secular employments which come in their way. They sleep as soundly; and, in spite of their grief, perhaps find it most difficult to persuade themselves to rise early to pray for pardon. These are signs of want of love.

Or, again, without reference to the case of penitence, they

have a general indisposition towards prayer and other exercises of devotion. They find it most difficult to get themselves to pray; most difficult, too, to rouse their minds to attend to their prayers. At very best they do but feel satisfaction in devotion *while* they are engaged in it. Then perhaps they find a real pleasure in it, and wonder they can ever find it irksome; yet if any chance throws them out of their habitual exercises, they find it most difficult to return to them. They do not like them well enough to seek them *from* liking them. They are kept in them by habit, by regularity in observing them; not by love. When the regular course is broken, there is no inward principle to act at once in repairing the mischief. In wounds of the body, nature works towards a recovery, and, left to itself, would recover; but we have no spiritual principle strong and healthy enough to set religious matters right in us when they have got disordered, and to supply for us the absence of rule and custom. Here, again, is obedience, more or less mechanical, or without love.

Again:—a like absence of love is shown in our proneness to be taken up and engrossed with trifles. Why is it that we are so open to the power of excitement? why is it that we are looking out for novelties? why is it that we complain of want of variety in a religious life? why that we cannot bear to go on in an ordinary round of duties year after year? why is it that lowly duties, such as condescending to men of low estate, are distasteful and irksome? why is it that we need powerful preaching, or interesting and touching books, in order to keep our thoughts and feelings on God? why is it that our faith is so dispirited and weakened by hearing casual objections urged against the doctrine of Christ? why is it that we are so impatient that objections should be answered? why are we so afraid of worldly events, or the opinions of men? why do we so dread their censure or ridicule?—Clearly because we are deficient in love. He who loves, cares little for any thing else. The world may go as it will; he sees and hears it not, for his thoughts are drawn another way; he is solicitous mainly to walk with God, and to be found with God; and is in perfect peace because he is stayed in Him.

And here we have an additional proof how weak our love is; viz. when we consider how little adequate our professed principles are found to be, to support us in affliction. I suppose it often happens to men to feel this, when some reverse or unexpected distress comes upon them. They indeed most especially will feel it, of course, who have let their words, nay their thoughts, much outrun their hearts; but numbers will feel it too, who have tried to make their reason and affections keep pace with each other. We are told of the righteous man, that "he will not be afraid of any evil tidings, for his heart standeth fast, and believeth in the Lord. His heart is established, and will not shrink."[1] Such must be the case of every one who realizes his own words, when he talks of the shortness of life, the wearisomeness of the world, and the security of heaven. Yet how cold and dreary do all such topics prove, when a man comes into trouble? and why, except that he has been after all set upon things visible, not on God? while he has been speaking of things invisible? There has been much profession and little love.

These are some of the proofs which are continually brought home to us, if we attend to ourselves, of our want of love to God; and they will readily suggest others to us. If I must, before concluding, remark upon the mode of overcoming the evil, I must say plainly this, that, fanciful though it may appear at first sight to say so, the comforts of life are the main cause of it; and, much as we may lament and struggle against it, till we learn to dispense with them in good measure, we shall not overcome it. Till we, in a certain sense, detach ourselves from our bodies, our minds will not be in a state to receive divine impressions, and to exert heavenly aspirations. A smooth and easy life, an uninterrupted enjoyment of the goods of Providence, full meals, soft raiment, well-furnished homes, the pleasures of sense, the feeling of security, the consciousness of wealth,—these, and the like, if we are not careful, choke up all the avenues of the soul, through which the light and breath of heaven might come to us. A hard life is, alas! no certain method of becoming spiritually minded, but it is one out of the means by which Almighty God makes us so. We must, at least at seasons, defraud ourselves of nature, if we would not be defrauded of grace. If we attempt to force our minds into a loving and devotional temper, without this preparation, it is too plain what will follow,—the grossness and coarseness, the affectation, the effeminacy, the unreality, the presumption, the hollowness, (suffer me, my brethren, while I say plainly, but seriously, what I mean,) in a word, what Scripture calls the Hypocrisy, which we see around us; that state of mind in which the reason, seeing what we should be, and the conscience enjoining it, and the heart being unequal to it, some or other pretence is set up, by way of compromise, that men may say, "Peace, peace, when there is no peace."

[1] Ps. cxii.7, 8.

And next, after enjoining this habitual preparation of heart, let me bid you cherish, what otherwise it were shocking to attempt, a constant sense of the love of your Lord and Saviour in dying on the cross for you. "The love of Christ," says the Apostle, "constraineth us;" not that gratitude leads to love, where there is no sympathy, (for, as all know, we often reproach ourselves with not loving persons who yet have loved us,) but where hearts are in their degree renewed after Christ's image, there, under His grace, gratitude to Him will increase our love of Him, and we shall rejoice in that goodness which has been so good to us. Here, again, self-discipline will be necessary. It makes the heart tender as well as reverent. Christ showed His love in deed, not in word, and you will be touched by the thought of His cross far more by bearing it after Him, than by glowing accounts of it. All the modes by which you bring it before you must be simple and severe; "excellency of speech," or "enticing words," to use St. Paul's language, is the worst way of any. Think of the Cross when you rise and when you lie down, when you go out and when you come in, when you eat and when you walk and when you converse, when you buy and when you sell, when you labour and when you rest, consecrating and sealing all your doings with this one mental action, the thought of the Crucified. Do not talk of it to others; be silent, like the penitent woman, who showed her love in deep subdued acts. She "stood at His feet behind Him weeping, and began to wash His feet with tears, and did wipe them with the hairs of her head, and kissed His feet, and anointed them with the Ointment." And Christ said of her, "Her sins, which are many, are forgiven her, for she loved much; but to whom little is forgiven, the same loveth little." [2]

And, further, let us dwell often upon those His manifold mercies to us and to our brethren, which are the consequence of His coming upon earth; His adorable counsels, as manifested in our personal election,—how it is that we are called and others not; the wonders of His grace towards us, from our infancy until now; the gifts He has given us; the aid He has vouchsafed; the answers He has accorded to our prayers. And, further, let us, as far as we have the opportunity, meditate upon His dealings with His Church from age to age; on His faithfulness to His promises, and the mysterious mode of their fulfilment; how He has ever led His people forward safely and prosperously on the whole amid so many enemies; what unexpected events have

[2] Luke vii.38, 47.

worked His purposes; how evil has been changed into good; how His sacred truth has ever been preserved unimpaired; how Saints have been brought on to their perfection in the darkest times. And, further, let us muse over the deep gifts and powers lodged in the Church: what thoughts do His ordinances raise in the believing mind!—what wonder, what awe, what transport, when duly dwelt upon!

It is by such deeds and such thoughts that our services, our repentings, our prayers, our intercourse with men, will become instinct with the spirit of love. Then we do everything thankfully and joyfully, when we are temples of Christ, with His Image set up in us. Then it is that we mix with the world without loving it, for our affections are given to another. We can bear to look on the world's beauty, for we have no heart for it. We are not disturbed at its frowns, for we live not in its smiles. We rejoice in the House of Prayer, because He is there "whom our soul loveth." We can condescend to the poor and lowly, for they are the presence of Him who is Invisible. We are patient in bereavement, adversity, or pain, for they are Christ's tokens.

Thus let us enter the Forty Days of Lent now approaching. For Forty Days we seek after love by means of fasting. May we find it more and more, the older we grow, till death comes and gives us the sight of Him who is at once its Object and its Author.

THE POWER OF THE WILL

(Quinquagesima)

*"Finally, my brethren, be strong in the Lord,
and in the power of His might."*—Eph. vi.10.

WE know that there are great multitudes of professed Christians, who, alas! have actually turned from God with a deliberate will and purpose, and, in consequence, are at present strangers to the grace of God; though they do not know, or do not care about this. But a vast number of Christians, half of the whole number at least, are in other circumstances. They have not thrown themselves out of a state of grace, nor have they to repent and turn to God, in the sense in which those must, who have allowed themselves in wilful transgression, after the knowledge of the truth has been imparted to them. Numbers there are in all ranks of life, who, having good parents and advisers, or safe homes, or religious pursuits, or being without strong feelings and passions, or for whatever reason, cannot be supposed to have put off from them the garment of divine grace, and deserted to the ranks of the enemy. Yet are they not safe, nevertheless. It is plain,—for surely it is not enough to avoid evil in order to attain to heaven,—we must follow after good. What, then, is their danger?—That of the unprofitable servant who hid his lord's money. As far removed as that slothful servant was from those who traded with their talents, in his state and in his destiny, so far separate from one another are two classes of Christians who live together here as brethren,—the one class is using grace, the other neglecting it; one is making progress, the other sitting still; one is working for a reward, the other is idle and worthless.

This view of things should ever be borne in mind when we speak of the state of grace. There are different degrees in which we may stand in God's favour; we may be rising or sinking in His favour; we may not have forfeited it, yet we may not be securing it; we may be safe for the present, but have a dangerous prospect before us. We may be more or less "hypocrites," "slothful," "unprofitable," and yet our day of grace not be passed. We may still have the remains of our new nature lingering on us, the influences of grace present with us, and the power of amendment and conversion within us. We may still have talents which we may put to account, and gifts which we may stir up. We may not be cast out of our state of justification, and yet may be destitute of that love of God, love of God's truth, love of holiness, love of active and generous obedience, that honest surrender of self, which alone will secure to us hereafter the blessed words, "Well done, good and faithful servant; enter thou into the joy of thy Lord." [1]

The only qualification which will avail us for heaven is the love of God. We may keep from gross sinning, and yet not have this divine gift, "without which we are dead" in God's sight. This changes our whole being; this makes us live; this makes us grow in grace and abound in good works; this makes us fit for God's presence hereafter.

Now, here I have said a number of things, each of which will bear drawing out by itself, and insisting on.

No one can doubt that we are again and again exhorted in Scripture to be holy and perfect, to be holy and blameless in the sight of God, to be holy as He is holy, to keep the commandments, to fulfil the Law, to be filled with the fruit of righteousness. Why do we not obey as we ought? Many people will answer that we have a fallen nature, which hinders us; that we cannot help it, though we ought to be very sorry for it; that this is the reason of our shortcomings. Not so: we can help it; we are not hindered; what we want is the will; and it is our own fault that we have it not. We have all things granted to us; God has abounded in His mercies to us; we have a depth of power and strength lodged in us; but we have not the heart, we have not the will, we have not the love to use it. We lack this one thing, a desire to be new made; and I think any one who examines himself carefully, will own that he does, and that this is the reason why he cannot and does not obey or make progress in holiness.

That we have this great gift within us, or are in a state of grace, for the two statements mean nearly the same thing, is very plain of course from Scripture. We all know what Scripture says on the subject, and yet even here it may be as well to dwell on one or two passages by way of reminding and impressing ourselves.

[1] Matt. xxv.21.

Consider then our Saviour's words: "The water that I shall give him, shall be in him a *well of water* springing up into everlasting life."[2] Exhaust the sea, it will not fill the infinite spaces of the heavens, but the gift within us may be drawn out till it fills eternity.

Again, consider St. Paul's most wonderful words in the Epistle from which the text is taken, when he gives glory to "Him who is able to do exceeding abundantly above all that we ask or think, according to the power that worketh in us."[3] You observe here, that there is a power given to us Christians, which "worketh in us," a special hidden mysterious power, which makes us its instruments. Even that we have souls, is strange and mysterious. We do not see our souls; but we see in others and we are conscious in ourselves of a principle which rules our bodies, and makes them what the brutes are not. We have that in us which informs our bodies, and changes them from mere animal bodies into human. Brutes cannot talk; brutes have little expression of countenance; they cannot form into societies; they cannot progress. Why? Because they have not that hidden gift which we have?—reason. Well, in like manner St. Paul speaks of Christians too as having a special power within them, which they gain because they are, and when they become Christians; and he calls it, in the text to which I am referring, "the power that worketh in us." In a former chapter of the Epistle, he speaks of "the exceeding greatness of His power to us-ward who believe, according to the working of His mighty power;"[4] and he says that our eyes must be enlightened in order to recognise it; and he compares it to that divine power in Christ our Saviour, by which, working in due season, He was raised from the dead, so that the bonds of death had no dominion over Him. As seeds have life in them, which seem lifeless, so the Body of Christ had life in itself, when it was dead; and so also, though not in a similar way, we too, sinners as we are, have a spiritual principle in us, if we did but exert it, so great, so wondrous, that all the powers in the visible world, all the conceivable forces and appetites of matter, all the physical miracles which are at this day in process of discovery, almost superseding time and space, dispensing with numbers, and rivalling mind, all these powers of nature are nothing to this gift within us. Why do I say this? because the Apostle tells us that God is able thereby "to do *exceeding abundantly above all* that we ask or think." You see he labours for words to express the exuberant,

[2] John iv. 14.   [3] Eph. iii. 20.   [4] Eph. i. 19.

overflowing fulness, the vast and unfathomable depth, or what he has just called "the breadth, and length, and depth, and height" of the gift given us. And hence he elsewhere says, "I can do all things through Christ, which *strengtheneth* me;"[5] where he uses the same word which occurs also in the text,—"My brethren, be *strong* in the Lord, and in the power of His might." See, what an accumulation of words! First, be *strong*, or be ye made strong. Strong in what? strong in power. In the power of what? in the power of His might, the might of God. Three words are used one on another, to express the manifold gift which God has given us. He to might has added power, and power He has made grow into strength. We have the power of His might; nor only so, but the strength of the power of His might who is Almighty.

And this is the very account which St. Luke gives us of St. Paul's own state in the Acts, after his conversion. The Jews wondered, but "Saul increased the more in *strength*, and confounded the Jews who dwelt at Damascus."[6] He became more and more strong. And, at the end of his course, when brought before the Romans, "The Lord," as he says, "stood with him, and *strengthened* him;" and in turn he too exhorts Timothy, "Thou, therefore, my son, be *strong* in the grace that is in Christ Jesus; and the things that thou hast heard of me among many witnesses, the same commit thou to faithful men, who shall be able to teach others also. Thou therefore endure hardness, as a good soldier of Jesus Christ."[7]

I said just now that we did not need Scripture to tell us of our divinely imparted power; that our own consciousness was sufficient. I do not mean to say that our consciousness will enable us to rise to the fulness of the Apostle's expressions; for trial, of course, cannot ascertain an inexhaustible gift. All we can know of it by experience is, that it goes beyond *us*, that *we* have never fathomed it, that we have drawn from it, and never emptied it; that we have evidence that there is a power with us, how great we know not, which does for us what we cannot do for ourselves, and is always equal to all our needs. And of as much as this, I think, we have abundant evidence.

Let us ask ourselves, why is it that we so often wish to do right and cannot? why is it that we are so frail, feeble, languid, wayward, dim-sighted, fluctuating, perverse? why is it that we cannot "do the things that we would?" why is it that, day after day, we remain irresolute, that we serve God so poorly, that we

---

[5] Phil. iv.13.　　　[6] Acts ix.22.　　　[7] 2 Tim. ii.1–3; iv.17.

govern ourselves so weakly and so variably, that we cannot command our thoughts, that we are so slothful, so cowardly, so discontented, so sensual, so ignorant? Why is it that we, who trust that we are not by wilful sin thrown out of grace (for of such I am all along speaking), why is it that we, who are ruled by no evil masters and bent upon no earthly ends, who are not covetous, or profligate livers, or worldly-minded, or ambitious, or envious, or proud, or unforgiving, or desirous of name,—why is it that we, in the very kingdom of grace, surrounded by Angels, and preceded by Saints, nevertheless can do so little, and instead of mounting with wings like eagles, grovel in the dust, and do but sin, and confess sin, alternately? Is it that the *power* of God is not within us? Is it literally that we are *not able* to perform God's commandments? God forbid! We are able. We have that given us which makes us able. We are not in a state of nature. We have had the gift of grace implanted in us. We have a power within us to do what we are commanded to do. What is it we lack? The power? No; the will. What we lack is the real, simple, earnest, sincere inclination and aim to use what God has given us, and what we have in us. I say, our experience tells us this. It is no matter of mere doctrine, much less a matter of words, but of things; a very practical plain matter.

To take an instance of the simple kind. Is not the power to use our limbs our own, nay, even by nature? What then is sloth but a want of will? When we are not set on an object so greatly as to overcome the inconvenience of an effort, we remain as we are; —when we ought to exert ourselves we are slothful. But is the effort any effort at all, when we desire that which needs the effort?

In like manner, to take a greater thing. Are not the feelings as distinct as well can be, between remorse and repentance? In both a man is very sorry and ashamed of what he has done; in both he has a painful foreboding that he may perchance sin again in spite of his present grief. You will hear a man perhaps lament that he is so weak, so that he quite dreads what is to come another time, after all his good resolutions. There are cases, doubtless, in which a man is thus weak in power, though earnest in will; and, of course, it continually happens that he has ungovernable feelings and passions in spite of his better nature. But in a very great multitude of cases this pretence of want of power is really but a want of will. When a man complains that he is under the dominion of any bad habit, let him seriously ask himself whether he has ever *willed* to get rid of it.

Can he, with a simple mind, say in God's sight, "I wish it removed?"

A man, for instance, cannot attend to his prayers; his mind wanders; other thoughts intrude; time after time passes, and it is the same. Shall we say, this arises from want of power? Of course it may be so; but before he says so, let him consider whether he has ever roused himself, shaken himself, awakened himself, got himself to will, if I may so say, attention. We know the feeling in unpleasant dreams, when we say to ourselves, "This is a dream," and yet cannot exert ourselves to will to be free from it; and how at length by an effort we will to move, and the spell at once is broken; we wake. So it is with sloth and indolence; the Evil One lies heavy on us, but he has no power over us except in our unwillingness to get rid of him. He cannot battle with us; he flies; he can do no more, as soon as we propose to fight with him.

There is a famous instance of a holy man of old time, who, before his conversion, felt indeed the excellence of purity, but could not get himself to say more in prayer than "Give me chastity, but not yet." I will not be inconsiderate enough to make light of the power of temptation of any kind, nor will I presume to say that Almighty God will certainly shield a man from temptation for his wishing it; but whenever men complain, as they often do, of the arduousness of a high virtue, at least it were well that they should first ask themselves the question, whether they desire to have it. We hear much in this day of the impossibility of heavenly purity;—far be it from me to say that every one has not his proper gift from God, one after this manner, another after that;—but, O ye men of the world, when ye talk, as ye do, so much of the impossibility of this or that supernatural grace, when you disbelieve in the existence of severe self-rule, when you scoff at holy resolutions, and affix a slur on those who make them, are you sure that the impossibility which you insist upon does not lie, not in nature, but in the will? Let us but will, and our nature is changed, "according to the power that worketh in us." Say not, in excuse for others or for yourselves, that you cannot be other than Adam made you; you have never brought yourselves to will it,—you cannot bear to will it. You cannot bear to be other than you are. Life would seem a blank to you, were you other; yet what you are from not desiring a gift, this you make an excuse for not possessing it.

Let us take what trial we please,—the world's ridicule or censure, loss of prospects, loss of admirers or friends, loss of ease, endurance of bodily pain,—and recollect how easy our course has been, directly we had once made up our mind to submit to it; how simple all that remained became, how wonderfully difficulties were removed from without, and how the soul was strengthened inwardly to do what was to be done. But it is seldom we have heart to throw ourselves, if I may so speak, on the Divine Arm; we dare not trust ourselves on the waters, though Christ bids us. We have not St. Peter's love to ask leave to come to Him upon the sea. When we once are filled with that heavenly charity, we can do all things, because we attempt all things,—for to attempt is to do.

I would have every one carefully consider whether he has ever found God fail him in trial, when his own heart had not failed him; and whether he has not found strength greater and greater given him according to his day; whether he has not gained clear proof on trial that he *has* a divine power lodged within him, and a certain conviction withal that he has not made the extreme trial of it, or reached its limits. Grace ever outstrips prayer. Abraham ceased interceding ere God stayed from granting. Joash smote upon the ground but thrice, when he might have gained five victories or six. All have the gift, many do not use it at all, none expend it. One wraps it in a napkin, another gains five pounds, another ten. It will bear thirty-fold, or sixty, or a hundred. We know not what we are, or might be. As the seed has a tree within it, so men have within them Angels.

Hence the great stress laid in Scripture on growing in grace. Seeds are intended to grow into trees. We are regenerated in order that we may be renewed daily after the Image of Him who has regenerated us. In the text and verses following, we have our calling set forth, in order to "stir up our pure minds, by way of remembrance,"[8] to the pursuit of it. "Be strong in the Lord," says the Apostle, "and in the power of His might. Put on the whole armour of God," with your loins girt about with truth, the breastplate of righteousness, your feet shod with the preparation of the gospel of peace, the shield of faith, the helmet of salvation, the sword of the Spirit. One grace and then another is to be perfected in us. Each day is to bring forth its own treasure, till we stand, like blessed spirits, able and waiting to do the will of God.

Still more apposite are St. Peter's words, which go through the whole doctrine which I have been insisting on, point by point. First, he tells us that "divine power hath given unto us all

[8] 2 Pet. iii.1.

things that pertain unto life and godliness;"[9] that is, we have the *gift*. Then he speaks of the *object* which the gift is to effect,— "exceeding great and precious promises are given unto us, that by these we may be *partakers of the divine nature*;" that we who, by birth, are children of wrath, should become inwardly and really sons of God; putting off our former selves, or, as he says, "having escaped the corruption that is in the world through lust;" that is, cleansing ourselves from all that remains in us of original sin, the infection of concupiscence. With which closely agree St. Paul's words to the Corinthians, "Having these promises," he says, "dearly beloved, let us cleanse ourselves from all defilement of the flesh and spirit, perfecting holiness in the fear of God."[10] But to continue with St. Peter,—"Giving all diligence," he says, "add to your faith virtue, and to virtue knowledge, and to knowledge temperance, and to temperance patience, and to patience godliness, and to godliness brotherly kindness, and to brotherly kindness charity." Next he speaks of those who, though they cannot be said to have forfeited God's grace, yet by a sluggish will and a lukewarm love have become but unprofitable, and "cumber the ground" in the Lord's vineyard. "He that lacketh these things is blind, and cannot see afar off, and hath forgotten that he was purged from his old sins,"— has forgotten that cleansing which he once received, when he was brought into the kingdom of grace. "Wherefore the rather, brethren, give diligence to make your calling and election sure; for if ye do these things, ye shall never fall; for so an entrance shall be ministered unto you abundantly, into the everlasting kingdom of our Lord and Saviour Jesus Christ." Day by day shall ye enter deeper and deeper into the fulness of the riches of that kingdom, of which ye are made members.

Or, lastly, consider St. Paul's account of the same growth, and of the course of it, in his Epistle to the Romans. "Tribulation worketh patience, and patience experience, and experience hope, and hope maketh not ashamed." Such is the series of gifts, patience, experience, hope, a soul without shame,— and whence all this? He continues, "because the *love* of God is shed abroad in our hearts, by the Holy Ghost which is given unto us."[11]

Love can do all things; "charity never faileth;" he that has the will, has the power. You will say, "But is not the will itself from God? and, therefore, is it not after all *His* doing, not ours, if we have *not* the will?" Doubtless, by nature, our will is in bondage;

[9] 2 Pet. i.3.　　　　　　[10] 2 Cor. vii.1.　　　　　　[11] Rom. v.3–5.

we cannot will good; but by the grace of God our will has been set free; we obtain again, to a certain extent, the gift of free-will; henceforth, we can will, or not will. If we will, it is doubt-less from God's grace, who gave us the power to will, and to Him be the praise; but it is from ourselves too, because we have used that power which God gave. God enables us to will and to do; by nature we cannot will, but by grace we can; and now if we do not will, we are the cause of the defect. What can Al-mighty Mercy do for us which He hath not done? "He has given *all* things which pertain to life and godliness;" and we, in conse-quence, can "make our calling and election sure," as the holy men of God did of old time. Ah, how do those ancient Saints put us to shame! how were they "out of weakness made strong," how "waxed" they "valiant in fight," and became as Angels upon earth instead of men! And why?—because they had a heart to contemplate, to design, to *will* great things. Doubtless, in many respects, we all are but men to the end; we hunger, we thirst, we need sustenance, we need sleep, we need society, we need instruction, we need encouragement, we need example; yet who can say the heights to which in time men can proceed in all things, who beginning by little and little, yet in the distance shadow forth great things? "Enlarge the place of thy tent, and let them stretch forth the curtains of thine habita-tions; spare not, lengthen thy cords, and strengthen thy stakes; for thou shalt break forth on the right hand and on the left. . . . Fear not; for thou shalt not be ashamed; neither shalt thou be confounded, for thou shalt not be put to shame. . . . In righ-teousness shalt thou be established; thou shalt be far from op-pression, for thou shalt not fear; and from terror, for it shall not come near thee. . . . This is the heritage of the servants of the Lord, and their righteousness is of Me, saith the Lord." [12]

High words like these relate in the first place to the Church, but doubtless they are also fulfilled in their measure in each of her true children. But we sit coldly and sluggishly at home; we fold our hands and cry "a little more slumber;" we shut our eyes, we cannot see things afar off, we cannot "see the land which is very far off;" we do not understand that Christ calls us after Him; we do not hear the voice of His heralds in the wilder-ness; we have not the heart to go forth to Him who multiplies the loaves and feeds us by every word of His mouth. Other chil-dren of Adam have before now done in His strength what we put aside. We fear to be too holy. Others put us to shame; all

[12] Is. liv.2–4, 14, 17.

around us, others are doing what we will not. Others are entering deeper into the kingdom of heaven than we. Others are fighting against their enemies more truly and bravely. The unlettered, the ungifted, the young, the weak and simple, with sling and stones from the brook, are encountering Goliath, as having on divine armour. The Church is rising up around us day by day towards heaven, and we do nothing but object, or explain away, or criticise, or make excuses, or wonder. We fear to cast in our lot with the Saints, lest we become a party; we fear to seek the strait gate, lest we be of the few not the many. Oh may we be loyal and affectionate before our race is run! Before our sun goes down in the grave, oh may we learn somewhat more of what the Apostle calls the love of Christ which passeth knowledge, and catch some of the rays of love which come from Him! Especially at the season of the year now approaching, when Christ calls us into the wilderness, let us gird up our loins and fearlessly obey the summons. Let us take up our cross and follow Him. Let us take to us "the whole armour of God, that we may be able to stand against the wiles of the devil; for we wrestle not against flesh and blood, but against principalities, against powers, against the rulers of the darkness of this world, against spiritual wickedness in high places; wherefore, take unto you the whole armour of God, that ye may be able to withstand in the evil day, and having done all, to stand."

VI

FASTING A SOURCE OF TRIAL

(First Sunday in Lent)

"And when He had fasted forty days and forty nights, He was afterward an hungered."—Matt. iv.2.

THE season of humiliation, which precedes Easter, lasts for forty days, in memory of our Lord's long fast in the wilderness. Accordingly on this day, the first Sunday in Lent, we read the Gospel which gives an account of it; and in the Collect we pray Him, who for our sakes fasted forty days and forty nights, to bless our abstinence to the good of our souls and bodies.

We fast by way of penitence, and in order to subdue the flesh. Our Saviour had no need of fasting for either purpose. His fasting was unlike ours, as in its intensity, so in its object. And yet when we begin to fast, His pattern is set before us; and we continue the time of fasting till, in number of days, we have equalled His.

There is a reason for this;—in truth, we must do nothing except with Him in our eye. As He it is, through whom alone we have the power to do any good thing, so unless we do it for Him it is not good. From Him our obedience comes, towards Him it must look. He says, "Without Me ye can do nothing."[1] No work is good without grace and without love.

St. Paul gave up all things "to be found in Christ, not having his own righteousness which is of the law, but the righteousness which is from God upon faith."[2] Then only are our righteousnesses acceptable when they are done, not in a legal way, but in Christ through faith. Vain were all the deeds of the Law, because they were not attended by the power of the Spirit. They were the mere attempts of unaided nature to fulfil what it ought indeed, but was not able to fulfil. None but the blind and carnal, or those who were in utter ignorance, could find aught in them to rejoice in. What were all the righteousnesses of the Law, what its deeds, even when more than ordinary, its alms

---

[1] John xv.5. [2] Phil. iii.9.

and fastings, its disfiguring of faces and afflicting of souls; what was all this but dust and dross, a pitiful earthly service, a miserable hopeless penance, so far as the grace and the presence of Christ were absent? The Jews might humble themselves, but they did not rise in the spirit, while they fell down in the flesh; they might afflict themselves, but it did not turn to their salvation; they might sorrow, but not as always rejoicing; the outward man might perish, but the inward man was not renewed day by day. They had the burden and heat of the day, and the yoke of the Law, but it did not "work out for them a far more exceeding and eternal weight of glory." But God hath reserved some better thing for us. This is what it is to be one of Christ's little ones,—to be able to do what the Jews thought they could do, and could not; to have that within us through which we can do all things; to be possessed by His presence as our life, our strength, our merit, our hope, our crown; to become in a wonderful way His members, the instruments, or visible form, or sacramental sign, of the One Invisible Ever-Present Son of God, mystically reiterating in each of us all the acts of His earthly life, His birth, consecration, fasting, temptation, conflicts, victories, sufferings, agony, passion, death, resurrection, and ascension;—He being all in all,—we, with as little power in ourselves, as little excellence or merit, as the water in Baptism, or the bread and wine in Holy Communion; yet strong in the Lord and in the power of His might. These are the thoughts with which we celebrated Christmas and Epiphany, these are the thoughts which must accompany us through Lent.

Yes, even in our penitential exercises, when we could least have hoped to find a pattern in Him, Christ has gone before us to sanctify them to us. He has blessed fasting as a means of grace, in that He has fasted; and fasting is only acceptable when it is done for His sake. Penitence is mere formality, or mere remorse, unless done in love. If we fast, without uniting ourselves in heart to Christ, imitating Him, and praying that He would make our fasting His own, would associate it with His own, and communicate to it the virtue of His own, so that we may be in Him, and He in us; we fast as Jews, not as Christians. Well then, in the Services of this first Sunday, do we place the thought of Him before us, whose grace must be within us, lest in our chastisements we beat the air and humble ourselves in vain.

Now in many ways the example of Christ may be made a comfort and encouragement to us at this season of the year.

And, first of all, it will be well to insist on the circumstance, that our Lord did thus retire from the world, as confirming to us the like duty, as far as we can observe it. This He did specially in the instance before us, before His entering upon His own ministry; but it is not the only instance recorded. Before He chose His Apostles, He observed the same preparation. "It came to pass in those days that He went out into a mountain to pray, and continued all night in prayer to God."[3] Prayer through the night was a self-chastisement of the same kind as fasting. On another occasion, after sending away the multitudes, "He went up into a mountain apart to pray;"[4] and on this occasion also, He seems to have remained there through great part of the night. Again, amid the excitement caused by His miracles, "In the morning, rising up a great while before day, He went out and departed into a solitary place, and there prayed."[5] Considering that our Lord is the pattern of human nature in its perfection, surely we cannot doubt that such instances of strict devotion are intended for our imitation, if we would be perfect. But the duty is placed beyond doubt by finding similar instances in the case of the most eminent of His servants. St. Paul, in the Epistle for this day, mentions among other sufferings, that he and his brethren were "in watchings, in fastings," and in a later chapter, that he was "in fastings often." St. Peter retired to Joppa, to the house of one Simon, a tanner, on the sea-shore, and there fasted and prayed. Moses and Elijah both were supported through miraculous fasts, of the same length as our Lord's. Moses, indeed, at two separate times; as he tells us himself, "Thus I fell down before the Lord, as at the first, forty days and forty nights; I did neither eat bread, nor drink water."[6] Elijah, having been fed by an Angel, "went in the strength of that meat forty days and forty nights."[7] Daniel, again, "set his face unto the Lord his God, to seek by prayer and supplications, with fasting, and sackcloth, and ashes." Again, at another time, he says, "In those days, I Daniel was mourning three full weeks. I ate no pleasant bread, neither came flesh nor wine in my mouth, neither did I anoint myself at all, till three whole weeks were fulfilled."[8] These are instances of fastings after the similitude of Christ.

Next I observe, that our Saviour's fast was but introductory to His temptation. He went into the wilderness to be tempted of the devil, but before He was tempted He fasted. Nor, as is worth notice, was this a mere preparation for the conflict, but it was the cause of the conflict in good measure. Instead of its

[3] Luke vi.12.   [4] Matt. xiv.23.   [5] Mark i.35.
[6] Deut. ix.18.   [7] 1 Kings xix.8.   [8] Dan. ix.3; x.2, 3.

simply arming Him against temptation, it is plain, that in the first instance, His retirement and abstinence exposed Him to it. Fasting was the primary occasion of it. "When He had fasted forty days and forty nights, He was afterwards an hungered;" and then the tempter came, bidding Him turn the stones into bread. Satan made use of His fast against Himself.

And this is singularly the case with Christians now, who endeavour to imitate Him; and it is well they should know it, for else they will be discouraged when they practise abstinences. It is commonly said, that fasting is intended to make us better Christians, to sober us, and to bring us more entirely at Christ's feet in faith and humility. This is true, viewing matters on the whole. On the whole, and at last, this effect will be produced, but it is not at all certain that it will follow at once. On the contrary, such mortifications have at the time very various effects on different persons, and are to be observed, not from their visible benefits, but from faith in the Word of God. Some men, indeed, are subdued by fasting and brought at once nearer to God; but others find it, however slight, scarcely more than an occasion of temptation. For instance, it is sometimes even made an objection to fasting, as if it were a reason for not practising it, that it makes a man irritable and ill-tempered. I confess it often may do this. Again, what very often follows from it is, a feebleness which deprives him of his command over his bodily acts, feelings, and expressions. Thus it makes him seem, for instance, to be out of temper when he is not; I mean, because his tongue, his lips, nay his brain, are not in his power. He does not use the words he wishes to use, nor the accent and tone. He seems sharp when he is not; and the consciousness of this, and the reaction of that consciousness upon his mind, is a temptation, and actually makes him irritable, particularly if people misunderstand him, and think him what he is not. Again, weakness of body may deprive him of self-command in other ways; perhaps, he cannot help smiling or laughing, when he ought to be serious, which is evidently a most distressing and humbling trial; or when wrong thoughts present themselves, his mind cannot throw them off; any more than if it were some dead thing, and not spirit; but they then make an impression on him which he is not able to resist. Or again, weakness of body often hinders him from fixing his mind on his prayers, instead of making him pray more fervently; or again, weakness of body is often attended with languor and listlessness, and strongly tempts a man to sloth. Yet, I have not mentioned the most distressing of the effects which may follow from even the moderate exercise of this great Christian duty. It is undeniably a means of temptation, and I say so, lest persons should be surprised, and despond when they find it so. And the merciful Lord knows that so it is from experience; and that He has experienced and thus knows it, as Scripture records, is to us a thought full of comfort. I do not mean to say, God forbid, that aught of sinful infirmity sullied His immaculate soul; but it is plain from the sacred history, that in His case, as in ours, fasting opened the way to temptation. And, perhaps, this is the truest view of such exercises, that in some wonderful unknown way they open the next world for good and evil upon us, and are an introduction to somewhat of an extraordinary conflict with the powers of evil. Stories are afloat (whether themselves true or not matters not, they show what the voice of mankind thinks *likely* to be true), of hermits in deserts being assaulted by Satan in strange ways, yet resisting the evil one, and chasing him away, after our Lord's pattern, and in His strength; and, I suppose, if we knew the secret history of men's minds in any age, we should find *this* (at least, I think I am not theorizing),—viz. a remarkable union in the case of those who by God's grace have made advances in holy things (whatever be the case where men have not), a union on the one hand of temptations offered to the mind, and on the other, of the mind's not being affected by them, not consenting to them, even in momentary acts of the will, but simply hating them, and receiving no harm from them. At least, I can conceive this—and so far persons are evidently brought into fellowship and conformity with Christ's temptation, who was tempted, yet without sin.

Let it not then distress Christians, even if they find themselves exposed to thoughts from which they turn with abhorrence and terror. Rather let such a trial bring before their thoughts, with something of vividness and distinctness, the condescension of the Son of God. For if it be a trial to us creatures and sinners to have thoughts alien from our hearts presented to us, what must have been the suffering to the Eternal Word, God of God, and Light of Light, Holy and True, to have been so subjected to Satan, that he could inflict every misery on Him short of sinning? Certainly it is a trial to us to have motives and feelings imputed to us before men, by the accuser of the brethren, which we never entertained; it is a trial to have ideas secretly suggested within, from which we shrink; it is a trial to us for Satan to be allowed so to mix his own thoughts with ours, that we feel guilty even when we are not; nay, to be able to set on fire our irrational nature, till in some sense we really sin against our will: but has not One gone before us more awful in His trial, more glorious in His victory? He was tempted in all points "like as we are, yet without sin." Surely here too, Christ's temptation speaks comfort and encouragement to us.

This then is, perhaps, a truer view of the consequences of fasting, than is commonly taken. Of course, it *is* always, under God's grace, a spiritual benefit to our hearts eventually, and improves them,—through Him who worketh all in all; and it often is a sensible benefit to us at the time. Still it is often otherwise; often it but increases the excitability and susceptibility of our hearts; in all cases it is therefore to be viewed, chiefly as an *approach to God*—an approach to the powers of heaven—yes, and to the powers of hell. And in this point of view there is something very awful in it. For what we know, Christ's temptation is but the fulness of that which, in its degree, and according to our infirmities and corruptions, takes place in all His servants who seek Him. And if so, this surely was a strong reason for the Church's associating our season of humiliation with Christ's sojourn in the wilderness, that we might not be left to our own thoughts, and, as it were, "with the wild beasts," and thereupon despond when we afflict ourselves; but might feel that we are what we really are, not bondmen of Satan, and children of wrath, hopelessly groaning under our burden, confessing it, and crying out, "O wretched man!" but sinners indeed, and sinners afflicting themselves, and doing penance for sin; but withal God's children, in whom repentance is fruitful, and who, while they abase themselves are exalted, and at the very time that they are throwing themselves at the foot of the Cross, are still Christ's soldiers, sword in hand, fighting a generous warfare, and knowing that they have that in them, and upon them, which devils tremble at, and flee.

And this is another point which calls for distinct notice in the history of our Saviour's fasting and temptation, viz. the *victory* which attended it. He had three temptations, and thrice He conquered,—at the last He said, "Get thee behind Me, Satan;" on which "the devil leaveth Him." This conflict and victory in the world unseen, is intimated in other passages of Scripture. The most remarkable of these is what our Lord says with reference to the demoniac, whom His Apostles could not cure. He had just descended from the Mount of Transfiguration, where, let it be observed, He seems to have gone up with His favoured Apostles to pass the night in prayer. He came down after that communion with the unseen world, and cast out the unclean spirit, and then He said, "This kind can come forth by nothing but by prayer and fasting," [9] which is nothing less than a plain declaration that such exercises give the soul power over the unseen world; nor can any sufficient reason be assigned for confining it to the first ages of the Gospel. And I think there is enough evidence, even in what may be known afterwards of the effects of such exercises upon persons now (not to have recourse to history), to show that these exercises are God's instruments for giving the Christian a high and royal power above and over his fellows.

And since prayer is not only the weapon, ever necessary and sure, in our conflict with the powers of evil, but a deliverance from evil is ever implied as the object of prayer, it follows that all texts whatever which speak of our addressing and prevailing on Almighty God, with prayer and fasting, do, in fact, declare this conflict and promise this victory over the evil one. Thus in the parable, the importunate widow, who represents the Church in prayer, is not only earnest *with* God, but *against* her adversary. "Avenge me of mine adversary," she says; and our "adversary" is "the devil, who, like a roaring lion, walketh about seeking whom he may devour; whom resist," adds St. Peter, "stedfast in the faith." Let it be observed that, in this parable, *perseverance* in prayer is especially recommended to us. And this is part of the lesson taught us by the long continuance of the Lent fast,—that we are not to gain our wishes by one day set apart for humiliation, or by one prayer, however fervent, but by "continuing instant in prayer." This too is signified to us in the account of Jacob's conflict. He, like our Saviour, was occupied in it *through* the night. Who it was whom he was permitted to meet in that solitary season, we are not told; but He with whom he wrestled, gave him strength to wrestle, and at last left a token on him, as if to show that he had prevailed only by the condescension of Him over whom he prevailed. So strengthened, he persevered till the morning broke, and asked a blessing; and He whom he asked did bless him, giving him a new name, in memory of his success. "Thy name shall be called no more Jacob, but Israel; for as a prince hast thou power with God and with men, and hast prevailed." [10] In like manner, Moses passed one of his forty days' fast in confession and intercession for the people, who had raised the golden calf. "Thus I fell down before the Lord forty days and forty nights, as I fell down at the first; because the Lord had said He would destroy you. I prayed therefore unto the Lord, and said, O Lord God, destroy not Thy

[9] Mark ix.29.   [10] Gen. xxxii.28.

people and Thine inheritance, which Thou hast redeemed through Thy greatness, which Thou hast brought forth out of Egypt with a mighty hand." [11] Again, both of Daniel's recorded fasts ended in a blessing. His first was intercessory for his people, and the prophecy of the seventy weeks was given him. The second was also rewarded with prophetical disclosures; and what is remarkable, it seems to have had an influence (if I may use such a word) upon the unseen world, from the time he began it.—"The Angel said, Fear not, Daniel, for *from the first day* that thou didst set thine heart to understand, and to chasten thyself before thy God, thy words were heard, and *I am come* for thy words." [12] He came at the end, but he prepared to go at the beginning. But more than this, the Angel proceeds, "But the prince of the kingdom of Persia withstood me one and twenty days;" just the time during which Daniel had been praying— "but lo, Michael, one of the chief princes, came to help me, and I remained there with the kings of Persia."

An Angel came to Daniel upon his fast; so too in our Lord's instance, Angels came and ministered unto Him; and so we too may well believe, and take comfort in the thought, that even now, Angels are especially sent to those who thus seek God. Not Daniel only, but Elijah too was, during his fast, strengthened by an Angel; an Angel appeared to Cornelius, while he was fasting, and in prayer; and I do really think, that there is enough in what religious persons may see around them, to serve to confirm this hope thus gathered from the word of God.

"He shall give His Angels charge over Thee, to keep Thee in all Thy ways;" [13] and the devil knows of this promise, for he used it in that very hour of temptation. He knows full well what our power is, and what is his own weakness. So we have nothing to fear while we remain within the shadow of the throne of the Almighty. "A thousand shall fall beside Thee, and ten thousand at Thy right hand, but it shall not come nigh Thee." While we are found in Christ, we are partakers of His security. He has broken the power of Satan; He has gone "upon the lion and adder, the young lion and the dragon hath He trod under His feet;" and henceforth evil spirits, instead of having power over us, tremble and are affrighted at every true Christian. They know he has that in him which makes him their master; that he may, if he will, laugh them to scorn, and put them to flight. They know this well, and bear it in mind, in all their assaults upon him; sin alone gives them power over him; and

---

[11] Deut. ix.25, 26.   [12] Dan. x.12.   [13] Ps. xci.11.

their great object is, to make him sin, and therefore to surprise him into sin, knowing they have no other way of overcoming him. They try to scare him by the appearance of danger, and *so* to surprise him; or they approach stealthily and covertly to seduce him, and *so* to surprise him. But except by taking him at unawares, they can do nothing. Therefore let us be, my brethren, "not ignorant of their devices;" and as knowing them, let us watch, fast, and pray, let us keep close under the wings of the Almighty, that He may be our shield and buckler. Let us pray Him to make known to us His will,—to teach us our faults,—to take from us whatever may offend Him,—and to lead us in the way everlasting. And during this sacred season, let us look upon ourselves as on the Mount with Him—within the veil—hid with Him—not out of Him, or apart from Him, in whose presence alone is life, but with and in Him—learning of His Law with Moses, of His attributes with Elijah, of His counsels with Daniel—learning to repent, learning to confess and to amend—learning His love and His fear—unlearning ourselves, and growing up unto Him who is our Head.

LIFE THE SEASON OF REPENTANCE

(Second Sunday in Lent)

"And when Esau heard the words of his father, he cried with a great
and exceeding bitter cry, and said unto his father, Bless me,
even me also, O my father."—Gen. xxvii.34.

I SUPPOSE no one can read this chapter without feeling some
pity for Esau. He had expected that his father would give
him his blessing, but his brother was beforehand with him and
got the blessing instead. He did not know what had happened,
and he came in to his father to be blessed, without any suspicion
that he was not to be blessed. His father, full of amazement and
distress, told him, that without knowing it, for he was blind and
could not see, he had already given the blessing to his brother
Jacob, and he could not recall it. On hearing this, Esau burst
out into "a great and exceeding bitter cry," as the text expresses
it. All his hopes were disappointed in a moment. He had built
much upon this blessing. For Esau, when he was young, had
committed a very great sin against God. He was his father's
first-born, and in those times, as now among the rich and
noble, it was a great thing to be the eldest in a family. In Esau's
case these privileges were the greater, for they were the direct
gift of God. Esau, as being the eldest born of his father Isaac,
inherited certain rights and privileges which Isaac, the long-
expected heir of Abraham, had received from Abraham. Now
Esau's sin, when he was a young man, had been this—he parted
with his birthright to his younger brother Jacob. He thought
lightly of God's great gift. How little he thought of it is plain by
the price he took for it. Esau had been hunting, and he came
home tired and faint. Jacob, who had remained at home, had
some pottage; and Esau begged for some of it. Jacob knew the
worth of the birthright, though Esau did not; he had faith to
discern it. So, when Esau asked for pottage, he said he would
give it to Esau in exchange for his birthright; and Esau, caring
nothing for the birthright, sold it to Jacob for the mess of food.
This was a great sin, as being a contempt of a special gift of God,

a gift, which, after his father Isaac, no one in the whole world had but he.

Time went on. Esau got older; and understood more than before the value of the gift which he had thus profanely surrendered. Doubtless he would fain have got it back again if he could; but that was impossible. Under these circumstances, as we find in the chapter which has been read in the course of to-day's Service, his father proposed to give him his solemn blessing before he died. Now this blessing in those times carried great weight with it, as being of the nature of a prophecy, and it had been from the first divinely intended for Jacob; Esau had no right to it, but he thought that in this way he should in a certain sense get back his birthright, or what would stand in its place. He had parted with it easily, and he expected to regain it easily. Observe, he showed no repentance for what he had done, no self-reproach; he had no fear that God would punish him. He only regretted his loss, without humbling himself; and he determined to retrace his steps as quickly and quietly as he could. He went to hunt for venison, and dress it as savoury meat for his father, as his father bade him. And having got all ready, he came with it and stood before his father. Then was it that he learned, to his misery, that God's gifts are not thus lightly to be treated; he had sold, he could not recover. He had hoped to have had his father's blessing, but Jacob had received it instead. He had thought to regain God's favour, not by fasting and prayer, but by savoury meat, by feasting and making merry.

Such seems, on the whole, St. Paul's account of the matter, in his Epistle to the Hebrews. After having given examples of faith, he bids his Christian brethren beware lest there should be any one among them like Esau, whom he calls a "profane person;" as having thought and acted with so little of real perception of things unseen; "looking diligently," he says, "lest any man fail of the grace of God; lest there be any fornicator, or profane person, as Esau, who for one morsel of meat sold his birthright. For ye know how that afterwards, when he would have inherited the blessing, he was rejected; for he found no place of repentance, though he sought it carefully with tears." [1]

This then is the meaning of Esau's great and bitter cry, which at first sight we are disposed to pity. It is the cry of one who has rejected God, and God in turn has rejected him. It is the cry of one who has trifled with God's mercies, and then sought to regain them when it was all too late. It is the cry of one who has

---

[1] Heb. xii. 15–17.

not heeded the warning, "See that ye receive not the grace of God in vain," and who has "come short of the grace of God."[2] It is the cry predicted by the wise man, "Then shall they call upon Me, but I will not answer; they shall seek Me early, but they shall not find Me."[3] That subtilty and keenness of his brother Jacob, by which he got before him, and took the kingdom of heaven by violence, was God's act; it was God's providence punishing Esau for former sin. Esau had sinned; he had forfeited his birthright, and he could not get it back. That cry of his, what was it like? it was like the entreaty of the five foolish Virgins when the door was shut, "Lord, Lord, open to us; but He answered and said, Verily, I say unto you, I know you not."[4] It was like "the weeping and gnashing of teeth" of lost souls. Yes, surely, a great and bitter cry it well might be. Well may they weep and cry, as they will most largely, who have received God's grace and done despite to it.

The mournful history then which I have been reviewing, is a description of one who was first profane and then presumptuous. Esau was profane in selling his birthright, he was presumptuous in claiming the blessing. Afterwards, indeed, he did repent, but when it was too late. And I fear such as Esau was of old time, such are too many Christians now. They despise God's blessings when they are young, and strong, and healthy; then, when they get old, or weak, or sick, they do not think of repenting, but they think they may take and enjoy the privileges of the Gospel as a matter of course, as if the sins of former years went for nothing. And then, perhaps, death comes upon them; and then after death, when it is too late, they would fain repent. Then they utter a great, bitter, and piercing cry to God; and when they see happy souls ascending towards heaven in the fulness of Gospel blessings, they say to their offended God, "Bless me, even me also, O my Father."

Is it not, I say, quite a common case for men and for women to neglect religion in their best days? They have been baptized, they have been taught their duty, they have been taught to pray, they know their Creed, their conscience has been enlightened, they have opportunity to come to Church. This is their birthright, the privileges of their birth of water and of the Spirit; but they sell it, as Esau did. They are tempted by Satan with some bribe of this world, and they give up their birthright in exchange for what is sure to perish, and to make them perish with it. Esau was tempted by the mess of pottage which he saw in

Jacob's hands. Satan arrested the eyes of his lust, and he gazed on the pottage, as Eve gazed on the fruit of the tree of knowledge of good and evil. Adam and Eve sold their birthright for the fruit of a tree—that was their bargain. Esau sold his for a mess of lentils—that was his. And men now-a-days often sell theirs, not indeed for any thing so simple as fruit or herbs, but for some evil gain or other, which at the time they think worth purchasing at any price; perhaps for the enjoyment of some particular sin, or more commonly for the indulgence of general carelessness and spiritual sloth, because they do not like a strict life, and have no heart for God's service. And thus they are profane persons, for they despise the great gift of God.

And then, when all is done and over, and their souls sold to Satan, they never seem to understand that they *have* parted with their birthright. They think that they stand just where they did, before they followed the world, the flesh, and the devil; they take for granted that when they choose to become more decent, or more religious, they have all their privileges just as before. Like Samson, they propose to go out as at other times before, and shake themselves. And like Esau, instead of repenting for the loss of the birthright, they come, as a matter of course, for the blessing. Esau went out to hunt for venison gaily, and promptly brought it to his father. His spirits were high, his voice was cheerful. It did not strike him that God was angry with him for what had passed years ago. He thought he was as sure of the blessing as if he had *not* sold the birthright.

And then, alas! the truth flashed upon him; he uttered a great and bitter cry, when it was too late. It would have been well, had he uttered it before he came for the blessing, not after it. He repented when it was too late—it had been well if he had repented in time. So I say of persons who have in any way sinned. It is good for them not to forget that they have sinned. It is good that they should lament and deplore their past sins. Depend upon it, they will wail over them in the next world, if they wail not here. Which is better, to utter a bitter cry now or then?—then, when the blessing of eternal life is refused them by the just Judge at the last day, or now, in order that they may gain it? Let us be wise enough to have our agony in this world, not in the next. If we humble ourselves now, God will pardon us then. Ye cannot escape punishment, here or hereafter; we must take our choice, whether to suffer and mourn a little now, or much then.

Would you see how a penitent should come to God? turn to the parable of the Prodigal Son. He, too, had squandered away his birthright, as Esau did. He, too, came for the blessing, like Esau. Yes; but how differently he came! he came with deep confession and self-abasement. He said, "Father, I have sinned against heaven and before thee, and am no more worthy to be called thy son: make me as one of thy hired servants:" but Esau said, "Let my father arise, and eat of his son's venison, that thy soul may bless me." The one came for a son's privileges, the other for a servant's drudgery. The one killed and dressed his venison with his own hand, and enjoyed it not; for the other the fatted calf was prepared, and the ring for his hand, and shoes for his feet, and the best robe, and there was music and dancing.

These are thoughts, I need hardly say, especially suited to this season. From the earliest times down to this day, these weeks before Easter have been set apart every year, for the particular remembrance and confession of our sins. From the first age downward, not a year has passed but Christians have been exhorted to reflect how far they have let go their birthright, as a preparation for their claiming the blessing. At Christmas we are born again with Christ; at Easter we keep the Eucharistic Feast. In Lent, by penance, we join the two great sacraments together. Are you, my brethren, prepared to say,—is there any single Christian alive who will dare to profess,—that he has not in greater or less degree sinned against God's free mercies as bestowed on him in Baptism without, or rather against his deserts? Who will say that he has so improved his birthright that the blessing is his fit reward, without either sin to confess, or wrath to deprecate? See, then, the Church offers you this season for the purpose. "Now is the accepted time, now the day of salvation." Now it is that, God being your helper, you are to attempt to throw off from you the heavy burden of past transgression, to reconcile yourselves to Him who has once already imparted to you His atoning merits, and you have profaned them.

And be sure of this: that if He has any love for you, if He sees aught of good in your soul, *He* will afflict you, if you will not afflict yourselves. He will not let you escape. He has ten thousand ways of purging those whom He has chosen, from the dross and alloy with which the fine gold is defaced. He can bring diseases on you, or can visit you with misfortunes, or take away your friends, or oppress your minds with darkness, or refuse you strength to bear up against pain when it comes upon you. He can inflict on you a lingering and painful death. He can make "the bitterness of death pass" not. We, indeed, cannot decide in the case of others, when trouble is a punishment, and when not; yet this we know, that all sin brings affliction. We have no means of judging others, but we may judge ourselves. Let us judge ourselves, that we be not judged. Let us afflict ourselves, that God may not afflict us. Let us come before Him with our best offerings, that He may forgive us.

Such advice is especially suitable to an age like this, when there is an effort on all hands to multiply comforts, and to get rid of the daily inconveniences and distresses of life. Alas! my brethren, how do you know, if you avail yourselves of the luxuries of this world without restraint, but that you are only postponing, and increasing by postponing, an inevitable chastisement? How do you know, but that, if you will not satisfy the debt of daily sin now, it will hereafter come upon you with interest? See whether this is not a thought which would spoil that enjoyment which even religious persons are apt to take in this world's goods, if they would but admit it. It is said that we ought to enjoy this life as the gift of God. Easy circumstances are generally thought a special happiness; it is thought a great point to get rid of annoyance or discomfort of mind and body; it is thought allowable and suitable to make use of all means available for making life pleasant. We desire, and confess we desire, to make time pass agreeably, and to live in the sunshine. All things harsh and austere are carefully put aside. We shrink from the rude lap of earth, and the embrace of the elements, and we build ourselves houses in which the flesh may enjoy its lust, and the eye its pride. We aim at having all things at our will. Cold, and hunger, and hard lodging, and ill usage, and humble offices, and mean appearance, are all considered serious evils. And thus year follows year, to-morrow as to-day, till we think that this, our artificial life, is our natural state, and must and ever will be. But, O ye sons and daughters of men, what if this fair weather but ensure the storm afterwards? what if it be, that the nearer you attain to making yourselves as gods on earth now, the greater pain lies before you in time to come, or even (if it must be said), the more certain becomes your ruin when time is at an end? Come down, then, from your high chambers at this season to avert what else may be. Sinners as ye are, act at least like the prosperous heathen, who threw his choicest trinket into the water, that he might propitiate fortune. Let not the year go round and round, without a break and interruption in its circle of pleasures. Give back some of God's gifts to God, that you may safely enjoy the rest. Fast, or watch, or abound in alms, or be instant in prayer, or deny yourselves society, or pleasant books, or easy clothing, or take on you some irksome task or employment; do one or other, or some, or all of these, unless you say that you have never sinned, and may go like Esau with a light heart to take your crown. Ever bear in mind that Day which will reveal all things, and will test all things "so as by fire," and which will bring us into judgment ere it lodges us in heaven.

And for those who have in any grievous way sinned or neglected God, I recommend such persons never to forget they *have* sinned; if they forget it not, God in mercy *will* forget it. I recommend them every day, morning and evening, to fall on their knees, and say, "Lord, forgive me my past sins." I recommend them to pray God to visit their sins in this world rather than in the next. I recommend them to go over their dreadful sins in their minds (unless, alas! it makes them sin afresh to do so), and to confess them to God again and again with great shame, and to entreat His pardon. I recommend them to look on all pain and sorrow which comes on them as a *punishment* for what they once were; and to take it patiently on that account, nay, joyfully, as giving them a hope that God *is* punishing them here instead of hereafter. If they have committed sins of uncleanness, and are now in narrow circumstances, or have undutiful children, let them take their present distress as God's merciful punishment. If they have lived to the world, and now have worldly anxieties, these anxieties arc God's punishment. If they have led intemperate lives, and now are afflicted by any malady, this is God's punishment. Let them not cease to pray, under all circumstances, that God will pardon them, and give them back what they have lost. And thus, by God's grace, it shall be restored to them, and Esau's great and bitter cry never shall be theirs.

APOSTOLIC ABSTINENCE
A PATTERN FOR CHRISTIANS

(Lent)

"Drink no longer water, but use a little wine for thy stomach's sake, and thine often infirmities."—1 Tim. v.23.

THIS is a remarkable verse, because it accidentally tells us so much. It is addressed to Timothy, St. Paul's companion, the first Bishop of Ephesus. Of Timothy we know very little, except that he did minister to St. Paul, and hence we might have *inferred* that he was a man of very saintly character; but we know little or nothing of him, except that he had been from a child a careful reader of Scripture. This indeed, by itself, in that Apostolic age, would have led us to infer, that he had risen to some great height in spiritual excellence; though it must be confessed that instances are frequent at this day, of persons knowing the Bible well, and yet being little stricter than others in their lives for all their knowledge. Timothy, however, had so read the Old Testament, and had so heard from St. Paul the New, that he was a true follower of the Apostle, as the Apostle was of Christ: St. Paul accordingly calls him "my own son," or "my true son in the faith." And elsewhere he says to the Philippians, that he has "no man like-minded to Timothy, who would naturally" or truly "care for their state." [1] But still, after all, this is but a general account of him, and we seem to desire something more definite in the way of description, beyond merely knowing that he was a great saint, which conveys no clear impression to the mind. Now, in the text we have accidentally a glimpse given us of his mode of life. St. Paul does not expressly tell us that he was a man of mortified habits; but he reveals the fact indirectly by cautioning him against an excess of mortification. "Drink no longer water," he says, "but use a little wine." It should be observed, that wine, in the southern

[1] Phil. ii.20.

countries, is the same ordinary beverage that beer is here; it is nothing strong or costly. Yet even from such as this, Timothy was in the habit of abstaining, and restricting himself to water; and, as the Apostle thought, imprudently, to the increase of his "often infirmities."

There is something very striking in this accidental mention of the private ways of this Apostolical Bishop. We know indeed from history the doctrine and the life of the great saints, who lived some time after the Apostles' age; but we are naturally anxious to know something more of the Apostles themselves, and their associates. We say, "Oh that we could speak to St. Paul,—that we could see him in his daily walk, and hear his oral and familiar teaching!—that we could ask him what he meant by this expression in his Epistles, or what he thought of this or the other doctrine." This is not given to us. God might give us greater light than He does; but it is His gracious will to give us the less. Yet perhaps much more is given us in Scripture, as it has come to us, than we think, if our eyes were enlightened to discern it there. Such, for instance, is the text; it is a sudden revelation, a glimpse of the personal character of Apostolic Christians; it is a hint which we may follow out. For no one will deny that a very great deal of doctrine, and a very great deal of precept, goes with such a fact as this; viz. that this holy man, without impiously disparaging God's creation, and thanklessly rejecting God's gifts, yet, on the whole, lived a life of abstinence.

I cannot at all understand why such a life is not excellent in a Christian now, if it was the characteristic of Apostles, and friends of Apostles, then. I really do not see why the trials and persecutions, which environed them from Jews and Gentiles, their forlorn despised state, and their necessary discomforts, should not even have exempted them from voluntary sufferings in addition, unless such self-imposed hardships were pleasing to Christ. Yet we find that St. Paul, like Timothy, who (as the Apostle says) had known "his doctrine and manner of life,"[2] I say, St. Paul also, in addition to his "weariness and painfulness," "hunger and thirst," "cold and nakedness," was "in watchings often," "in fastings often." Such were holy men of old time. How far are we below them! Alas for our easy sensual life, our cowardice, our sloth! is this the way by which the kingdom of heaven is won? is this the way that St. Paul fought a good fight, and finished his course? or was it by putting behind

[2] 2 Tim. iii.10.

his back all things on earth, and looking stedfastly towards Him who is invisible?

Now at first sight it may not be clear why this moderation, and at least occasional abstinence, in the use of God's gifts, should be so great a duty, as our Lord, for instance, seems to imply, when He places fasting in so prominent a place in the Sermon on the Mount, with almsgiving and prayer. But thus much we are able to see, that the great duty of the Gospel is love to God and man; and that this love is quenched and extinguished by self-indulgence, and cherished by self-denial. They who enjoy this life freely, make it or self their idol; they are gross-hearted, and have no eyes to see God withal. Hence it is said, "Blessed are the pure in heart, for they shall see God." [3] And again, it was the rich man who fared sumptuously every day, who neglected Lazarus; for sensual living hardens the heart, while abstinence softens and refines it. Now, observe, I do not mean that abstinence produces this effect as a matter of course in any given person,—else all the poor ought to be patterns of Christian love,—but that where men are religiously-minded, there those out of the number will make greater attainments in love and devotional feeling, who do exercise themselves in self-denial of the body. I should really be disposed to say,—You must make your choice, you must in some way or another deny the flesh, or you cannot possess Christian love. Love is no common grace in its higher degrees. It is true, indeed, that, as being the necessary token of every true Christian, it must be possessed in some degree even by the weakest and humblest of Christ's servants—but in any of its higher and maturer stages, it is rare and difficult. It is easy to be amiable or upright; it is easy to live in regular habits;—it is easy to live conscientiously, in the common sense of the word. I say, all this is comparatively easy; but one thing is needful, and one thing is often lacking,—love. We may act rightly, yet without doing our right actions from the love of God. Other motives, short of love, are good in themselves; these we may have, and not have love. Now I do not think that this defect arises from any one cause, or can be removed by any one remedy; and yet still, it does seem as if abstinence and fasting availed much towards its removal; so much so, that, granting love *is* necessary, then these are necessary; assuming love to be the characteristic of a Christian, so is abstinence. You may think to dispense with fasting; true; and you may neglect also to cultivate love.

[3] Matt. v.8.

And here a connexion may be traced between the truth I have been insisting on, and our Lord's words, when asked why His disciples did not fast. He said, that they could not fast while the Bridegroom was with them; but that when He was taken from them, then they would fast. The one thing, which is all in all to us, is to live in Christ's presence; to hear His voice, to see His countenance. His first disciples had Him in bodily presence among them; and He spoke to them, warned them, was a pattern to them, and guided them with His eye. But when He withdrew Himself from the world of sense, how should they see Him still? When their fleshly eyes and ears saw Him no more, when He had ascended whither flesh and blood cannot enter, and the barrier of the flesh was interposed between Him and them, how should they any longer see and hear Him? "Lord, whither goest Thou?" they said; and He answered to Peter, "Whither I go thou canst not follow Me now, but thou shalt follow Me afterwards." They were to follow Him through the veil, and to break the barrier of the flesh after His pattern. They must, as far as they could, weaken and attenuate what stood between them and Him; they must anticipate that world where flesh and blood are not; they must discern truths which flesh and blood could not reveal; they must live a life, not of sense, but of spirit; they must practise those mortifications which former religions had enjoined, which the Pharisees and John's disciples observed, with better fruit, for a higher end, in a more heavenly way, in order to see Him who is invisible. By fasting, Moses saw God's glory; by fasting, Elijah heard the "still small voice;" by fasting, Christ's disciples were to express their mourning over the Crucified and Dead, over the Bridegroom taken away: but that mourning would bring Him back, that mourning would be turned to joy; in that mourning they would see Him, they would hear of Him, again; they would see Him, as they mourned and wept. And while they mourned, so long would they see Him and rejoice—for "blessed are they that mourn, for they shall be comforted;" they are "sorrowful, yet always rejoicing;" hungering and thirsting after and unto righteousness,—fasting in body, that their soul may hunger and thirst after its true good; fasting in body, that they may be satisfied in spirit; in a "barren and dry land, where no water is," [4] that they may look for Him in holiness, and behold His power and glory. "My heart is smitten down, and withered like grass (says the Psalmist), so that I forget to eat my bread. For the

[4] Ps. lxiii.2.

voice of my groaning, my bones will scarce cleave to my flesh. I am become like a pelican in the wilderness, and like an owl that is in the desert. I have watched, and am even as a sparrow that sitteth alone upon the house-top." "All day long have I been punished, and chastened every morning." And what was the consequence? "Nevertheless, I am alway by Thee: for Thou hast holden me by my right hand. Thou shalt guide me with Thy counsel, and after that receive me with glory. Whom have I in heaven but Thee? and there is none upon earth that I desire in comparison of Thee? My flesh and my heart faileth, but God is the strength of my heart, and my portion for ever." [5]

Such was the portion which St. Paul and St. Timothy received, when they gave up this world and its blessings; not that they might not have enjoyed them had they chosen; but because they might, and yet gave them up, therefore they received blessings out of sight instead. And in like manner, applying this to ourselves, it is our duty also to be ever moderate, and at times to abstain, in the use of God's earthly gifts; nay, happy is it for us, if God's secret grace call us on, as it called St. Paul and Timothy, to a more divine and tranquil life than that of the multitude. It is our duty to war against the flesh as they warred against it, that we may inherit the gifts of the Spirit as they inherited them. If Saints are our patterns, this surely means that we must copy them.

Here, however, it may be objected, that there is presumption in wishing to be what Apostles and their associates were. That they had high spiritual gifts which we have not, and that to attempt their life without these, is all one with attempting to work such miracles as they did, which any one would grant to *be* presumptuous. There is much truth in such a remark so far as this, that to attempt *at once* all they did would be presumptuous; we can but put ourselves in the way. God gives second and third gifts to those who improve the first; let us improve the first, and then we know not how high may be the spiritual faculties which at length He will give us. Who is there, who, on setting out on a journey, sees before him his destination? How often, when a person is making for a place which he has never seen, he says to himself, that he cannot believe that at a certain time he really will be there? There is nothing in what he at present sees, which conveys to him the assurance of the future; and yet, in time, that future will be present. So is it as regards our spiritual course: we know not what we shall be; but begin it, and, at

[5] Ps. cii.4–7; lxxiii.13.22–25.

length, by God's grace, you will end it; not, indeed, with the grace He now has given, but by fresh and fresh grace, fuller and fuller, increased according to your need. Thus you will *end*, if you do but begin; but begin not *with* the end; begin with the beginning; mount up the heavenly ladder step by step. Fasting is a duty; but we ought to fast according to our strength. God requires nothing of us beyond our strength; but the utmost according to our strength. "She has done what she could," was His word of commendation to Mary. Now, to forget or to miss this truth, is very common with beginners, even through mere ignorance or inadvertence. They know not what they can do, and what they cannot, as not having yet tried themselves. And then, when what they hoped was easy, proves a great deal too much for them, they fail, and then are dispirited. They wound their conscience, as being unable to fulfil their own resolves, and they are reduced to a kind of despair; or they are tempted to be reckless, and to give up all endeavours whatever to obey God, because they are not strong enough for every thing. And thus it often happens, that men rush from one extreme to another; and even profess themselves free to live without any rule of self-government at all, after having professed great strictness, or even extravagance, in their mode of living.

This applies of course to all duties whatever. We should be very much on our guard, when we are engaged in contemplating the lives of holy men, against attempting just what they did; which might be right indeed in them, and yet may be wrong in us. Holy men may say and do things which we have no right to say and do. Profession by word of mouth, religious language, rebuking others, and the like, may be natural and proper in them, and forced and out of place in us. We ought to attempt nothing but what we can do. There is a kind of inward feeling which often tells us what we have a right to do, and what we have not. We have often a kind of misgiving, as if what we are tempted to do does not really belong to us. Let us carefully attend to this inward voice. This applies especially to our devotions: common men have no right to use the prayers which advanced Christians use without offending; and if they attempt it, they become *unreal*; an offence which all persons, who have any faith and reverence, will endeavour earnestly to avoid. But if we will thus commence our religious course, it is certain we shall soon get tired of it; we shall give it up; and our devotional feelings will thus be shown, by the event, to have been but a fashion or an impulse, which has no true excellence in it.

And here I will observe, what may be of use even to those who are most cautious and prudent in their mode of conducting their self-denials, supposing they have seasons in which they practise them, such as Lent ought to be to all of us. Be very much on your guard against a reaction to a careless way of life after Lent is over. It is a caution commonly and usefully given, that after a *day* of fasting we should not, when we break our fast, eat unduly; now I am giving a similar warning concerning a *season* of abstinence, and not only as regards eating largely, but against all laxity and self-indulgence. In Lent, serious thoughts are brought more regularly before the mind. The rule of abstinence which we adopt, however slight it may be in itself, acts as a continual restraint and memento upon us in other things. We cannot range at will through the field of thinking and wishing. We are more frequent also in prayer. And especially, if we feel ourselves able to be strict in our fast, the weakness of body consequent on it is an additional check upon us. Let us beware, then, lest, when this time is over, and Easter comes, we fall back into a lawless state of mind, and a random life, as if God's paradise were some Judaical heaven, where we might indulge ourselves the more freely in this world's goods, for having renounced them for a while. This grievous consequence is said actually to happen in some foreign countries, in the case of the multitude, who never will have a deep and consistent devotion while the world lasts; and we should be much on our guard, lest it happens to us in our degree. It will be a sad thought for remembrance hereafter, if we shall find after all, that we have undone what was right and profitable in our Lent exercises by a relapse in Easter-tide.

This, however, may be added for our encouragement, that to abstain for any length of time is the beginning of a habit; and we may trust, that what we have begun will continue, or tend to continue. And even though, through our frailty, we fall back (which God forbid!), yet we shall find our self-denials easier next Lent. Nay, as I just now said, we shall be able to do more. Self-denial will become natural to us. We shall feel no desire for those indulgences, whether animal or mental, which savour of this world; and our tastes and likings will begin to be formed upon a heavenly rule. To those who are accustomed to self-denials, it is more painful to indulge than to abstain, as every one of common self-control must know, from ordinary matters of his own experience. Persons in the humbler ranks, of unrefined minds, look up to the rich, and wonder they do not do this or that, which *they* would do for certain, had they the like means. The reason is, that these rich persons, having a more perfect education, have too much taste and sense of propriety, even though religion should be absent, to use their wealth in what may be called a barbarian way. Now the same dislike of self-indulgence, in all its shapes, is matured, under God's grace, in the souls of those who seek Him in the way of austerity. Timothy had to be reminded by St. Paul to use a little wine; for to drink wine was a trouble to Timothy, as putting him (to use a common phrase) out of his way. He was happy in his own way. All men have each his own way, and they wonder at one another. Each looks down upon his neighbour, because his neighbour does not like the very things he likes himself. We look down on foreigners, because their way is not ours. Happy he whose way is God's way; when he is used to it, it is as easy as any other way—nay, much easier, for God's service is perfect freedom, whereas Satan is a cruel taskmaster.

To conclude, let those who attempt to make this Lent profitable to their souls, by such observances as have ever been in use at this season since Christianity was, beware lest they lose this world without gaining the next;—for instance, as I said just now, by relapsing. Or again, by observing what is in itself right in a cold and formal manner. We can use the means, but it is God alone who blesses them. He alone turns the stones into bread, and brings water from the hard rock. He can turn all things into nourishment, but He alone can do so. Let us pray Him to bless what we venture for Him, that we may not only labour, but may receive our wages, and gather fruit unto life eternal. This world is a very little thing to give up for the next. Yet, if we give it up in heart and conversation, we shall gain the next. Let us aim at the consistent habit of mind, of looking towards God, and rejoicing in the glory which shall be revealed. In that case, whether we eat or drink, or abstain, or whatever we do, we shall do all unto Him. Let us aim at being true heirs of the promise; let us humbly aspire to be His elect, in whom He delighteth, holy and undefiled, "blameless and harmless, the sons of God, without rebuke, in the midst of a crooked and perverse nation," among whom we may shine "as lights in the world, holding forth the word of life."

CHRIST'S PRIVATIONS
A MEDITATION FOR CHRISTIANS

(Fifth Sunday in Lent)

"Ye know the grace of our Lord Jesus Christ, that, though He was rich, yet for your sakes He became poor, that ye through His poverty might be rich."—2 Cor. viii.9.

As time goes on, and Easter draws nearer, we are called upon not only to mourn over our sins, but especially over the various sufferings which Christ our Lord and Saviour underwent on account of them. Why is it, my brethren, that we have so little feeling on the matter as we commonly have? Why is it that we are used to let the season come and go just like any other season, not thinking more of Christ than at other times, or, at least, not feeling more? Am I not right in saying that this is the case? and if so, have I not cause for asking why it is the case? We are not moved when we hear of the bitter passion of Jesus Christ, the Son of God, for us. We neither bewail our sins which caused it, nor have any sympathy with it. We do not suffer *with* Him. If we come to Church, we hear, and then we go away again; not distressed at all; or if distressed, only for the moment. And many do not come to Church at all; and to them, of course, this holy and solemn time is like other times. They eat, and drink, and sleep, and rise up, and go about their business and their pleasure, just as usual. They do not carry the thought of Him who died for them, along with them,—with them wherever they are,—with them "whether they eat, or drink, or whatever they do." They in no sense "live," to use St. Paul's words, "by the faith of the Son of God, who loved them and gave Himself for them."

This, alas! cannot be denied. Yet, if it be so, that the Son of God came down from heaven, put aside His glory, and submitted to be despised, cruelly treated, and put to death by His own creatures,—by those whom He had made, and whom He had preserved up to that day, and was then upholding in life and being,—is it reasonable that so great an event should not move us? Does it not stand to reason that we must be in a very irreligious state of mind, unless we have some little gratitude, some little sympathy, some little love, some little awe, some little self-reproach, some little self-abasement, some little repentance, some little desire of amendment, in consequence of what He has done and suffered for us? Or, rather, may not so great a Benefactor demand of us some overflowing gratitude, keen sympathy, fervent love, profound awe, bitter self-reproach, earnest repentance, eager desire and longing after a new heart? Who can deny all this? Why then, O my brethren is it not so? why are things with us as they are? Alas! I sorrowfully foretell that time will go on, and Passion-tide, Good Friday, and Easter-Day will pass by, and the weeks after it, and many of you will be just what you were—not at all nearer heaven, not at all nearer Christ in your hearts and lives, not impressed lastingly or savingly with the thought of His mercies and your own sins and demerits.

But why is this? why do you so little understand the Gospel of your salvation? why are your eyes so dim, and your ears so hard of hearing? why have you so little faith? so little of heaven in your hearts? For this one reason, my brethren, if I must express my meaning in one word, because you so little *meditate*. You do not meditate, and therefore you are not impressed.

What is meditating on Christ? it is simply this, thinking habitually and constantly of Him and of His deeds and sufferings. It is to have Him before our minds as One whom we may contemplate, worship, and address when we rise up, when we lie down, when we eat and drink, when we are at home and abroad, when we are working, or walking, or at rest, when we are alone, and again when we are in company; this is meditating. And by this, and nothing short of this, will our hearts come to feel as they ought. We have stony hearts, hearts as hard as the highways; the history of Christ makes no impression on them. And yet, if we would be saved, we must have tender, sensitive, living hearts; our hearts must be broken, must be broken up like ground, and dug, and watered, and tended, and cultivated, till they become as gardens, gardens of Eden, acceptable to our God, gardens in which the Lord God may walk and dwell; filled, not with briars and thorns, but with all sweet-smelling and useful plants, with heavenly trees and flowers. The dry and barren waste must burst forth into springs of living water. This change must take place in our hearts if we would be saved; in a word, we must have what we have not by nature, faith and love;

and how is this to be effected, under God's grace, but by godly and practical meditation through the day?

St. Peter describes what I mean, when he says, speaking of Christ, "Whom having not seen ye love: in whom, though now ye see Him not, yet believing, ye rejoice with joy unspeakable and full of glory." [1]

Christ is gone away; He is not seen; we never saw Him, we only read and hear of Him. It is an old saying, "Out of sight, out of mind." Be sure, so it *will* be, so it *must* be with us, as regards our blessed Saviour, unless we make continual efforts all through the day to think of Him, His love, His precepts, His gifts, and His promises. We must recall to mind what we read in the Gospels and in holy books about Him; we must bring before us what we have heard in Church; we must pray God to enable us to do so, to bless the doing so, and to make us do so in a simple-minded, sincere, and reverential spirit. In a word, we must meditate, for all this is meditation; and this even the most unlearned person can do, and will do, if he has a will to do it.

Now of such meditation, or thinking over Christ's deeds and sufferings, I will say two things; the first of which would be too plain to mention, except that, did I not mention it, I might seem to forget it, whereas I grant it. It is this: that such meditation is not at all pleasant at first. I know it; people will find it at first very irksome, and their minds will gladly slip away to other subjects. True: but consider, if Christ thought your salvation worth the great sacrifice of voluntary sufferings for you, should not you think (what is your own concern) your own salvation worth the slight sacrifice of learning to meditate upon those sufferings? Can a less thing be asked of you, than, when He has done the work, that you should only have to believe in it and accept it?

And my second remark is this: that it is only by slow degrees that meditation is able to soften our hard hearts, and that the history of Christ's trials and sorrows really moves us. It is not once thinking of Christ or twice thinking of Christ that will do it. It is by going on quietly and steadily, with the thought of Him in our mind's eye, that by little and little we shall gain something of warmth, light, life, and love. We shall not perceive ourselves changing. It will be like the unfolding of the leaves in spring. You do not see them grow; you cannot, by watching, detect it. But every day, as it passes, has done

[1] 1 Pet. i.8.

something for them; and you are able, perhaps, every morning to say that they are more advanced than yesterday. So is it with our souls; not indeed every morning, but at certain periods, we are able to see that we are more alive and religious than we were, though during the interval we were not conscious that we were advancing.

Now, then, as if by way of specimen, I will say a few words upon the voluntary self-abasement of Christ, to suggest to you thoughts, which you ought, indeed, to bear about you at all times, but especially at this most holy season of the year; thoughts which will in their poor measure (please God) prepare you for seeing Christ in heaven, and, in the meanwhile, will prepare you for seeing Him in His Easter Festival. Easter-Day comes but once a year; it is short, like other days. O that we may make much of it, that we may make the most of it, that we may enjoy it! O that it may not pass over like other days, and leave us no fragrance after it to remind us of it!

Come then, my brethren, at this time, before the solemn days are present, and let us review some of the privations of the Son of God made man, which should be your meditation through these holy weeks.

And, chiefly, He seems to speak to the poor. He came in *poverty*. St. Paul says, in the text, "Ye know the grace of our Lord Jesus Christ, that though He was rich, yet for your sakes He became poor, that ye through His poverty might be rich." Let not the poor suppose that their hardships are their own only, and that no one else ever felt them. The Most High God, God the Son, who had reigned with the Father from everlasting, supremely blessed, He, even He, became a poor man, and suffered the hardships of the poor. What are their hardships? I suppose such as these:—that they have bad lodging, bad clothing, not enough to eat, or of a poor kind, that they have few pleasures or amusements, that they are despised, that they are dependent upon others for their living, and that they have no prospects for the future. Now how was it with Christ, the Son of the Living God? Where was He born? In a stable. I suppose not many men suffer an indignity so great; born, not in quiet and comfort, but amid the brute cattle; and what was His first cradle, if I may so call it? a manger. Such were the beginnings of His earthly life; nor did His condition mend as life went on. He says on one occasion, "Foxes have holes, and birds of the air have nests, but the Son of Man hath not where to lay His head." [2] He

---

[2] Luke ix.58.

had no home. He was, when He began to preach, what would now be called with contempt a vagrant. There are persons who are obliged to sleep where they can; such, in good measure, seems to have been our blessed Lord. We hear of Martha who was hospitable to Him, and of others; but, though little is told us, He seems, from what is told, to have lived a rougher life than any village peasant. He was forty days in the wilderness: where do you think He slept then? in caves of the rock. And who were His companions then? worse companions even than those He was born among. He was born in a cave; He passed forty nights in a cave; but on His birth, at least, they were tame beasts whom He was among, the ox and the ass. But during His forty days' temptation He "was with the wild beasts." Those caverns in the wilderness are filled with fierce and poisonous creatures. There Christ slept; and doubtless, but for His Father's unseen arm and His own sanctity, they would have fallen upon Him.

Again, cold is another hardship which sensibly afflicts us. This, too, Christ endured. He remained whole nights in prayer upon the mountains. He rose before day and went into solitary places to pray. He was on the sea at night.

Heat is a suffering which does not afflict us much in our country, but is very formidable in the eastern parts, where our Saviour lived. Men keep at home when the sun is high, lest it should harm them; yet we read of His sitting down on Jacob's well at mid-day, being wearied with His journey.

Observe this also, to which I have already referred. He was constantly journeying during His ministry, and journeying on foot. Once He rode into Jerusalem, to fulfil a prophecy.

Again, He endured hunger and thirst. He was athirst at the well, and asked the Samaritan woman to give Him water to drink. He was hungry in the wilderness, when He fasted forty days. At another time, when actively engaged in His works of mercy, He and His disciples had no time to eat bread.[3] And, indeed, wandering about as He did, He seldom could have been certain of a meal. And what was the kind of food He lived on? He was much in the neighbourhood of an inland sea or lake, called the sea of Gennesaret, or Tiberias, and He and His Apostles lived on bread and fish; as spare a diet as poor men have now, or sparer. We hear, on one well-known occasion, of five barley loaves and two small fishes. After His resurrection He provided for His Apostles—"a fire, and fish laid thereon, and bread;"[4] as it would seem, their usual fare.

[3] Mark vi.31. [4] John xxi.9.

Yet it deserves notice that, in spite of this penury, He and His were in the custom of giving something to the poor notwithstanding. They did not allow themselves to make the most even of the little they had. When the traitor Judas rose up and went out to betray Him, and Jesus spoke to him, some of the Apostles thought that He was giving directions about alms to the poor; this shows His practice.

And He was, as need scarcely be added, quite dependent on others. Sometimes rich men entertained Him. Sometimes, as I have said, pious persons ministered to Him of their substance.[5] He lived, in His own blessed words, like the ravens, whom God feeds, or like the grass of the field, which God clothes.

Need I add that He had few pleasures, few recreations? it is hardly in place to speak on such a topic in the case of One who came from God, and who had other thoughts and ways than we have. Yet there are innocent enjoyments which God gives us here to counterbalance the troubles of life; our Lord was exposed to the trouble, and might have taken also its compensation. But He refrained. It has been observed, that He is never spoken of as mirthful; we often read of His sighing, groaning, and weeping. He was "a man of sorrows and acquainted with grief."

Now let us proceed to other greater sufferings, which He took on Himself when He became poor. Contempt, hatred, and persecution from the world was one of these. Even in His infancy Mary had to flee with Him into Egypt to hinder Herod from killing Him. When He returned, it was not safe to dwell in Judea, and He was brought up at Nazareth, a place of evil name, where the holy Virgin had been when Gabriel the Angel came to her. I need not say how He was set at nought and persecuted by the Pharisees and priests when He began to preach, and had again and again to flee for His life, which they were bent on taking.

Another great suffering from which our Lord did not withdraw Himself, was what in our case we call bereavement, the loss of relations or friends by death. This, indeed, it was not easy for Him to sustain, who had but one earthly near relation, and so few friends; but even this affliction He tasted for our sakes. Lazarus was His friend, and He lost him. He knew, indeed, that He could restore him, and He did. Yet still He bitterly lamented him, for whatever reason, so that the Jews said, "Behold how He loved him." But a greater and truer bereave-

[5] Luke viii.3.

ment, as far as we dare speak of it, was His original act of humiliation itself in leaving His heavenly glory and coming down on earth. This, of course, is a great mystery to us from beginning to end; still, He certainly vouchsafes to speak, through His Apostle, of His "emptying Himself" of His glory; so that we may fairly and reverently consider it as an unspeakable and wondrous bereavement, which He underwent, in being for the time, as it were, disinherited, and made in the likeness of sinful flesh.

But all these were but the beginning of sorrows with Him; to see their fulness we must look on to His passion. In the anguish which He then endured, we see all His other sorrows concentrated and exceeded; though I shall say little of it now, when His "time is not yet come."

But I will observe thus much; first, what is very wonderful and awful, the overwhelming fear He had of His sufferings before they came. This shows how great they were; but it would seem besides this, as if He had decreed to go through all trials for us, and, among them, the trial of fear. He says, "Now is My soul troubled, and what shall I say? Father, save Me from this hour; but for this cause came I unto this hour." And when the hour came, this terror formed the beginning of His sufferings, and caused His agony and bloody sweat. He prayed, "O My Father, if it be possible, let this cup pass from Me; nevertheless, not My will, but Thine, be done." St. Luke adds; "And being in an agony, He prayed more earnestly, and His sweat was as it were great drops of blood falling down to the ground." [6]

Next, He was betrayed to death by one of His own friends. What a bitter stroke was this! He was lonely enough without this: but in this last trial, one of the twelve Apostles, His own familiar friend, betrayed Him, and the others forsook Him and fled; though St. Peter and St. John afterwards recovered heart a little, and followed Him. Yet soon St. Peter himself incurred a worse sin, by denying Him thrice. How affectionately He felt towards them, and how He drew towards them with a natural movement of heart upon the approach of His trial, though they disappointed Him, is plain from the words He used towards them at His Last Supper; "He said unto them, With desire I have desired to eat this passover with you before I suffer." [7]

Soon after this His sufferings began; and both in soul and in body was this Holy and Blessed Saviour, the Son of God, and

[6] John xii.27; Matt. xxvi.39; Luke xxii.44.
[7] Luke xxii.15.

Lord of life, given over to the malice of the great enemy of God
and man. Job was given over to Satan in the Old Testament, but
within prescribed limits; first, the Evil One was not allowed to
touch his person, and afterwards, though his person, yet not his
life. But Satan had power to triumph, or what he thought was
triumphing, over the life of Christ, who confesses to His persecutors, "This is your hour, and the power of darkness."[8] His
head was crowned and torn with thorns, and bruised with
staves; His face was defiled with spitting; His shoulders were
weighed down with the heavy cross; His back was rent and
gashed with scourges; His hands and feet gored through with
nails; His side, by way of contumely, wounded with the spear;
His mouth parched with intolerable thirst; and His soul so
bedarkened, that He cried out, "My God, My God, why hast
Thou forsaken Me?"[9] And thus He hung upon the Cross for six
hours, His whole body one wound, exposed almost naked
to the eyes of men, "despising the shame,"[10] and railed at,
taunted, and cursed by all who saw Him. Surely to Him alone,
in their fulness, apply the Prophet's words; "Is it nothing to
you, all ye that pass by? behold, and see if there be any sorrow
like unto My sorrow which is done unto Me, wherewith the
Lord hath afflicted Me in the day of His fierce anger."[11]

How little are our sorrows to these! how little is our pain, our
hardships, our persecutions, compared with those which Christ
voluntarily undertook for us! If He, the sinless, underwent
these, what wonder is it that we sinners should endure, if it so
be, the hundredth part of them? How base and miserable are
we, for understanding them so little, for being so little impressed by them! Alas! if we felt them as we ought, of course
they would be to us, at seasons such as that now coming, far
worse than what the death of a friend is, or his painful illness.
We should not be able at such times to take pleasure in this
world; we should lose our enjoyment of things of earth; we
should lose our appetite, and be sick at heart, and only as a matter of duty eat, and drink, and go about our work. The Holy
Season on which we shall soon enter would be a week of
mourning, as when a dead body is in a house. We cannot, indeed, thus feel, merely because we wish and ought so to feel.
We cannot force ourselves into so feeling. I do not exhort this
man or that so to feel, since it is not in his power. We cannot
work ourselves up into such feelings; or, if we can, it is better we

[8] Luke xxii.53.   [9] Matt. xxvii.46.
[10] Heb. xii.2.   [11] Lam. i.12.

should not, because it *is* a working up, which is bad. Deep feeling is but the natural or necessary attendant on a holy heart. But though we cannot at our will thus feel, and at once, we can go the way thus to feel. We can grow in grace till we thus feel. And, meanwhile, we can observe such an outward abstinence from the innocent pleasures and comforts of life, as may prepare us for thus feeling; such an abstinence as we should spontaneously observe if we did thus feel. We may meditate upon Christ's sufferings; and by this meditation we *shall* gradually, as time goes on, be brought to these deep feelings. We may pray God to do for us what we cannot do for ourselves, to *make* us feel; to give us the spirit of gratitude, love, reverence, self-abasement, godly fear, repentance, holiness, and lively faith.

CHRIST, THE SON OF GOD MADE MAN

(Fifth Sunday in Lent)

"Christ being come, an High Priest of good things to come, by a greater and more perfect tabernacle, not made with hands, that is to say, not of this building."—Heb. ix.11.

BEFORE the Passover the Jews numbered fourteen days, and then the Feast came. It was to be the fourteenth day of the month, at even; and to mark the beginning of that period more distinctly, it was made the beginning of months, that is, the first month of the year. We then, if our Easter answers to the Passover, as substance answers to shadow, may well account that from this day, which is fourteen days before Easter, a more sacred season begins. And so our Church seems to have determined it, since from this day, the character of the Services changes. Henceforth they have more immediate reference to Him, whose death and resurrection we are soon to commemorate. The first weeks in Lent are spent in repentance, though with the thought of Him withal, who alone can give grace and power to our penitential exercises; the last, without precluding repentance, are more especially consecrated to the thought of those sufferings, whereby grace and power were purchased for us.

The history of the destruction of Sodom and Gomorrah; of Dinah, Jacob's daughter; and of Joseph in Potiphar's house; the account of our Lord's temptation; and the parable of the man out of whom the evil spirit went and returned sevenfold, which have been read on Sundays at this season, may fitly be called penitential subjects; and of the same character have been the Epistles. On the other hand, to-day's Epistle,[1] from which the text is taken, speaks of Christ's Incarnation and Atonement; while the Gospel tells us of His Divinity, He being that

---

[1] Heb. ix.11–15.

same God who, as the first Morning Lesson relates, called Himself in the bush "I am that I am." And so again, next Sunday's Epistle is also upon our Lord's Divinity and voluntary humiliation, and one of the Lessons and the Gospel contain the sacred narrative of His passion and death. The other second Lesson is also on the subject of His humiliation, from St. Paul. And further: all four first Lessons of to-day and next Sunday relate to the deliverance of the Israelites from Egypt, which is the type of our redemption.

Let us then to-day, in accordance with the apparent disposition of our Services, remind ourselves of one or two of the great truths which the Epistle contains;—of course we cannot do so with any great exactness or completeness;—but still, sufficiently to serve, through God's mercy, as a sort of preparation for the solemn days which lie before us in the course of the next fortnight. It will be a fitting preparation, please God, for Good Friday, to bear in mind who our Lord is, and what He has done for us. And, at present, let us confine ourselves to this one subject, who our Lord is,—God and man in one Person. On this most sacred and awful subject, I shall speak as simply and plainly as I can; merely stating what has to be stated, after the pattern of the Creeds, and leaving those who hear me, as the Creeds leave them, to receive it into their hearts fruitfully, and to improve it, under God's grace, for themselves.

Let us, I say, consider who Christ is, as the Epistle for the day sets forth in the words of the text.

1. First, Christ is God: from eternity He was the Living and True God. This is not mentioned expressly in the Epistle for this day, though it is significantly implied there in various ways; but it is all but expressly stated, and that by Himself, in the Gospel. He says there, "Before Abraham was, I am:" [2] by which words He declares that He did not begin to exist from the Virgin's womb, but had been in existence before. And by using the words *I am*, He seems to allude, as I have already said, to the Name of God, which was revealed to Moses in the burning bush, when he was commanded to say to the children of Israel, "*I am* hath sent me unto you." [3] Again: St. Paul says of Christ, that He was "in the form of God," and "thought it not robbery to be equal with God," yet "made Himself of no reputation." In like manner St. John says; "In the beginning was the Word, and the Word was with God, and the Word was God." And St. Thomas addressed Him as his Lord and his God; and St. Paul

[2] John viii.58.   [3] Exod. iii.14.

declares that He is "God over all, blessed for ever;" and the prophet Isaiah, that He is "the mighty God, the Everlasting Father;" and St. Paul again, that He is "our great God and Saviour;" and St. Jude, that He is "our only Sovereign God and Lord."[4] It is not necessary, surely, to enlarge on this point, which is constantly brought before us in Scripture and in our Services. "Day by day we magnify Him, and we worship His Name ever world without end;" which would be idolatry were He not the Very and Eternal God, our Maker and Lord. We know, indeed, that the Father is God also, and so is the Holy Ghost; but still Christ is God and Lord, most fully, completely, and entirely, in all attributes as perfect and as adorable, as if nothing had been told us of Father or of Holy Ghost; as much to be adored, as, before He came in the flesh, the Father was adored by the Jews, and is now to be adored by us "in spirit and in truth." For He tells us expressly Himself, "He that hath seen Me, hath seen the Father;" and "all men" are to "honour the Son, even as they honour the Father;" and "He that honoureth not the Son, honoureth not the Father which hath sent Him."[5]

2. And here we are brought to the second point of doctrine which it is necessary to insist upon, that while our Lord is God He is also the Son of God, or rather, that He is God because He is the Son of God. We are apt, at first hearing, to say that He is God though He is the Son of God, marvelling at the mystery. But what to man is a mystery, to God is a cause. He is God, not *though*, but *because* He is the Son of God. "That which is born of the flesh is flesh, that which is born of the Spirit is spirit," and That which is begotten of God is God. I do not say that we could presume thus to reason for ourselves, but Scripture draws the conclusion for us. Christ tells us Himself, "as the Father hath life in Himself, so hath He given to the Son to have life in Himself." And St. Paul says, that He is "the brightness of God's glory, and the express Image of His Person."[6] And thus, though we could not presume to reason of ourselves that He that is begotten of God is God, as if it became us to reason at all about such ineffable things, yet, by the light of Scripture, we may. And after all, if the truth must be said, it is surely not so marvellous and mysterious that the Son of God should be God, as that there should be a Son of God at all. It is as little level to natural reason that God should have a Son, as that, if there be a Son, He must be God because He is the Son. Both are mysteries; and if

---

[4] Phil. ii.6, 7; John i.1; xx.28; Rom. ix.5; Is. ix.6; Titus ii.13; Jude 4.
[5] John xiv.9; v.23.   [6] John v.26; Heb. i.3.

we admit with Scripture that there be an Only-begotten Son, it is even less to admit, what Scripture also teaches, that that Only-begotten Son is God because He is Only-begotten. And this is what makes the doctrine of our Lord's Eternal Sonship of such supreme importance, viz. that He is God because He is begotten of God; and they who give up the latter truth, are in the way to give up, or will be found already to have given up, the former. The great safeguard to the doctrine of our Lord's Divinity is the doctrine of His Sonship; we realize that He is God only when we acknowledge Him to be by nature and from eternity Son.

Nay, our Lord's Sonship is not only the guarantee to us of His Godhead, but also the condition of His incarnation. As the Son was God, so on the other hand was the Son suitably made man; it belonged to Him to have the Father's perfections, it became Him to assume a servant's form. We must beware of supposing that the Persons of the Ever-blessed and All-holy Trinity differ from each other only in this, that the Father is not the Son, and the Son is not the Father. They differ in this besides, that the Father *is* the Father, and the Son *is* the Son. While They are one in substance, Each has distinct characteristics which the Other has not. Surely those sacred Names have a meaning in them, and must not lightly be passed over. And they will be found, if we reverently study them, to supply a very merciful use towards our understanding Scripture; for we shall see a fitness, I say, now that that sacred truth is revealed, in the *Son* of God taking flesh, and we shall thereby understand better what He says of Himself in the Gospels. The Son of God became the Son a second time, though not a second Son, by becoming man. He was a Son both before His incarnation, and, by a second mystery, after it. From eternity He had been the Only-begotten in the bosom of the Father; and when He came on earth, this essential relation to the Father remained unaltered; still, He was a Son, when in the form of a servant,—still performing the will of the Father, as His Father's Word and Wisdom, manifesting His Father's glory and accomplishing His Father's purposes.

For instance, take the following passages of Scripture: "I do nothing of Myself;" "He that sent Me is with Me;" "the Father hath not left Me alone;" "My Father worketh hitherto, and I work;" "Whatsoever I speak, even as the Father said unto Me, so I speak;" "I am in the Father, and the Father in Me."[7] Now, it is true, these passages may be understood of our Lord's

[7] John viii.28, 29; v.17; xii.50; xiv.10.

human nature; but, surely, if we confine them to this interpretation, we run the risk of viewing Christ as two separate beings,
not as one Person; or, again, of gradually forgetting or explaining away the doctrine of His Divinity altogether. If we speak as
if our Lord had a human personality, then, if He has another
personality as God, He is not one Person; and if He has not, He
is not God. Such passages, then, as the foregoing, would seem
to speak neither of Christ's human nature simply, nor of His
divine, but of both together; that is, of Him who being the Son
of God is also man. He who spoke was one really existing Person, and He, that one Living and Almighty Son, both God
and man, was the brightness of God's glory and His Power, and
wrought what His Father willed, and was in the Father and the
Father in Him, not only in heaven but on earth. In heaven He
was this, and did this, as God; and on earth He was this, and
did this, in that manhood which He assumed, but whether in
heaven, or on earth, still as the Son. It was therefore true of
Him *altogether*, when He spoke, that He was not alone, nor
spoke or wrought of Himself, but where He was, there was the
Father, and whoso had seen Him had seen the Father, whether
we think of Him as God or as man.

Again, we read in Scripture of His being sent by the Father,
addressing the Father, interceding to Him for His disciples,
and declaring to them that His Father is greater than He; in
what sense says and does He all this? Some will be apt to say
that He speaks only in His human nature; words which are
perplexing to the mind that tries really to contemplate Him as
Scripture describes Him, as if He were speaking only under a
representation, and not in His Person. No; it is truer to say
that He, that One All-gracious Son of God, who had been
with the Father from the beginning, equal in all divine perfections and one in substance, but subordinate as being the Son,
—as He had ever been His Word, and Wisdom, and Counsel,
and Will, and Power in Heaven,—so after His incarnation,
and upon the earth, still spoke and acted after, yet with, the
Father as before, though in a new nature, which He had put
on, and in humiliation.

This, then, is the second point of doctrine which I had to
mention, that our Lord was not only God, but the Son of God.
We know more than that God took on Him our flesh; though
all is mysterious, we have a point of knowledge further and
more distinct, viz. that it was neither the Father nor the Holy
Ghost, but the Son of the Father, God the Son, God from God,
and Light from Light, who came down upon earth, and who

thus, though graciously taking on Him a new nature, remained in Person as He had been from everlasting, the *Son* of the Father, and spoke and acted towards the Father as a Son.

3. Now, thirdly, let us proceed to consider His mercy in taking on Him our nature, and what that act of mercy implies. The text speaks of "a greater and more perfect tabernacle," that is, greater than any thing earthly. This means His pure and sinless flesh, which was miraculously formed of the substance of the Blessed Virgin, and therefore called "not of this building," or more literally, "not of this creation," for it was a new creation by which He was formed, even by the descent of the Holy Ghost. This was the new and perfect tabernacle into which He entered; entered, but not to be confined, not to be circumscribed by it. The Most High dwelleth not in temples made with hands; though His own hands "made it and fashioned it," still He did not cease to be what He was, because He became man, but was still the Infinite God, manifested in, not altered by the flesh. He took upon Him our nature, as an instrument of His purposes, not as an agent in the work. What is one thing cannot become another; His manhood remained human, and His Godhead remained divine. God became man, yet was still God, having His manhood as an adjunct, perfect in its kind, but dependent upon His Godhead. So much so, that unless Scripture had expressly called Him man, we might well have scrupled to do so. Left to ourselves, we might have felt it more reverential to have spoken of Him, as *incarnate* indeed, come in human flesh, human and the like, but not simply as man. But St. Paul speaks in plain terms of our one Mediator as "the man Christ Jesus," not to speak of our Lord's own words on the subject. Still, we must ever remember, that though He was in nature perfect man, He was not man in exactly the same sense in which any one of us is a man. Though man, He was not, strictly speaking, in the English sense of the word, *a* man; He was not such as one of us, and one out of a number. He was man because He had our human nature wholly and perfectly, but His Person is not human like ours, but divine. He who was from eternity, continued one and the same, but with an addition. His incarnation was a "taking of the manhood into God." As He had no earthly father, so has He no human personality. We may not speak of Him as we speak of any individual man, acting from and governed by a human intelligence within Him, but He was God, acting not only as God, but now through the flesh also, when He would. He was not a man made God, but God made man.

(1.) Thus, when He prayed to His Father, it was not the prayer of a man supplicating God, but of the Eternal Son of God who had ever shared the glory of the Father, addressing Him, as before, but under far other circumstances, and in a new way, not according to those most intimate and ineffable relations which belonged to Him who was in the bosom of the Father, but in the economy of redemption, and in a lower world, viz. through the feelings and thoughts of human nature. When He wept at the grave of Lazarus, or sighed at the Jews' hardness of heart, or looked round about in anger, or had compassion on the multitudes, He manifested the tender mercy, the compassion, the long-suffering, the fearful wrath of Almighty God, yet not in Himself, as from eternity, but as if indirectly through the outlets of that manhood with which He had clothed Himself.

(2.) When "He spat on the ground, and made clay of the spittle, and He anointed the eyes of the blind man with the clay,"[8] He exerted the virtue of His Divine Essence through the properties and circumstances of the flesh. When He breathed on His disciples and said, "Receive ye the Holy Ghost,"[9] He vouchsafed to give His Holy Spirit through the breath of His human nature. When virtue went out of Him, so that whoso touched Him was made whole, here too, in like manner, He shows us that He was not an individual man, like any of us, but God acting through human nature as His assumed instrument.

(3.) When He poured out His precious blood upon the Cross, it was not a man's blood, though it belonged to His manhood, but blood full of power and virtue, instinct with life and grace, as issuing most mysteriously from Him who was the Creator of the world. And the case is the same in every successive communication of Himself to individual Christians. As He became the Atoning Sacrifice by means of His human nature, so is He our High Priest in heaven by means of the same. He is now in heaven, entered into the Holy place, interceding for us, and dispensing blessings to us. He gives us abundantly of His Spirit; but still He gives It not at once from His Divine nature, though from eternity the Holy Ghost proceeds from the Son as well as from the Father, but by means of that incorruptible flesh which He has taken on Him. For Christ is come a High Priest through the perfect tabernacle which He assumed, a tabernacle not of this creation, or in the ordinary course of nature, but framed miraculously of the substance of the Virgin by the Holy Ghost;

[8] John ix.6.   [9] John xx.22.

and therefore the streams of life flow to us from Him, as God indeed, but still as God incarnate. "That which quickeneth us is the Spirit of the Second Adam, and His flesh is that wherewith He quickeneth."

(4.) I shall mention a fourth and last point in this great mystery. I have said that our High Priest and Saviour, the Son of God, when He took our nature upon Him, acted through it, without ceasing to be what He was before, making it but the instrument of His gracious purposes. But it must not be supposed, because it was an instrument, or because in the text it is called a tabernacle, that therefore it was not intimately one with Him, or that it was merely like what is commonly meant by a tabernacle, which a man dwells in, and may come in and out of; or like an instrument, which a man takes up and lays down. Far from it; though His Divine Nature was sovereign and supreme when He became incarnate, yet the manhood which He assumed was not kept at a distance from Him (if I may so speak) as a mere instrument, or put on as a mere garment, or entered as a mere tabernacle, but it was really taken into the closest and most ineffable union with Him. He received it into His Divine Essence (if we may dare so to speak) almost as a new attribute of His Person; of course I speak by way of analogy, but I mean as simply and indissolubly. Let us consider what is meant by God's justice, or mercy, or wisdom, and we shall perhaps have some glimpse of the meaning of the inspired writers, when they speak of the Son's incarnation. If we said that the Son of God is just or merciful, we should mean that these are attributes which attach to all He is or was. Whatever He says, whatever He designs, whatever He works, He is just and loving when He thus says, designs, or works. There never was a moment, there never was an act or providence, in which God wrought, without His being just and loving, even though both attributes may not be exercised at once in the same act. In somewhat the same way the Son of God is man; all that is necessary to constitute a perfect manhood is attached to His eternal Person absolutely and entirely, belonging to Him as really and fully as His justice, truth, or power; so that it would be as unmeaning to speak of dividing one of His attributes from Him as to separate from Him His manhood.

This throws light upon the Catholic tenet, that the Godhead and Manhood were "joined together in One Person, never to be divided;" words which also serve too often to bring home to us how faintly we master the true doctrine: for we are sometimes tempted to ask, where is it said in Scripture that the manhood shall never be divided from the Godhead? which is as incongruous a question as if we were to ask whether God's justice, mercy, or holiness can be divided from Him; or whether Scripture ever declares that this or that attribute may not disappear: for as these have no real existence except as *in* God, neither has our Lord's manhood except as in His Divine nature; it never subsisted except as belonging to His divinity; it has no subsistence in itself.

Thus all that He did and said on earth was but the immediate deed and word of God the Son acting by means of His human tabernacle. He surrounded Himself with it; He lodged it within Him; and thenceforth the Eternal Word, the Son of God, the Second Person in the Blessed Trinity, had two natures, the one His own as really as the other, Divine and human; and He acted through both of them, sometimes through both at once, sometimes through One and not through the other, as Almighty God acts sometimes by the attribute of justice, sometimes by that of love, sometimes through both together. He was as entirely man as if He had ceased to be God, as fully God as if He had never become man, as fully both at once as He was in being at all.

The Athanasian Creed expresses all this as follows: "The right faith is, that we believe and confess that our Lord Jesus Christ the Son of God is God and Man; God of the substance of His Father, begotten before the worlds; and Man of the substance of His Mother, born in the world. Perfect God; and perfect Man, of a reasonable soul and human flesh subsisting: who, although He be God and Man, yet is not two but one Christ; one, not by conversion of the Godhead into flesh," as if He could cease to be God, "but by taking of the Manhood into God," taking it into His Divine Person as His own: "one altogether, not by confusion of substance," not by the Divine Nature and the human becoming some one new nature, as if He ceased to be God, and did not become a man, "but by unity of *Person*." This is what His unity consists in,—not unity of nature, but in this, that He who came on earth, was the very Same who had been from everlasting.

In conclusion, let me observe, that we ought not to speak, we ought not to hear, such high truths, without great reverence and awe, and preparation of mind. And this is a reason, perhaps, why this is a proper season for dwelling on them; when we have been engaged, not in mirth and festivity, but in chastening and sobering ourselves. The Psalmist says, "Lord, I am not high minded; I have no proud looks. I do not exercise myself in great matters which are too high for me. But I refrain my soul and keep it low, like as a child that is weaned from his mother." When we are engaged in weaning ourselves from this world, when we are denying ourselves even lawful things, when we have a subdued tone of thought and feeling, then is an allowable time surely to speak of the high mysteries of the faith. And then, too, are they especially a comfort to us; but those who neglect fasting, make light of orthodoxy too. But to those who through God's grace are otherwise minded, the Creed of the Church brings relief; when, amid the gloom of their own hearts, Christ rises like the Sun of righteousness, giving them peace for disquiet, "beauty for ashes, the oil of joy for mourning, the garment of praise for the spirit of heaviness, that they may be called trees of righteousness, the planting of the Lord that He may be glorified."

THE INCARNATE SON,
A SUFFERER AND SACRIFICE

(Sixth Sunday in Lent)

"Being found in fashion as a man, He humbled Himself,
and became obedient unto death, even the death of the Cross."
—Phil. ii.8.

HE who thus humbled Himself—being first made man, then dying, and that upon the shameful and agonizing Cross—was the same who from eternity had been "in the form of God," and was "equal with God," as the Apostle declares in a preceding verse. "In the beginning was the Word, and the Word was with God; and the Word was God; the same was in the beginning with God;" thus speaks St. John, a second witness to the same great and awful truth. And he, too, goes on to say, "And the Word was made flesh, and dwelt among us." And at the close of his Gospel, as we know, he gives an account of our Lord's death upon the Cross.

We are now approaching that most sacred day when we commemorate Christ's passion and death. Let us try to fix our minds upon this great thought. Let us try, what is so very difficult, to put off other thoughts, to clear our minds of things transitory, temporal, and earthly, and to occupy them with the contemplation of the Eternal Priest and His one ever-enduring Sacrifice;—that Sacrifice which, though completed once for all on Calvary, yet ever abideth, and, in its power and its grace, is ever present among us, and is at all times gratefully and awfully to be commemorated, but now especially, when the time of year is come at which it was made. Let us look upon Him who was lifted up that He might draw us to Him; and, by being drawn one and all to Him, let us be drawn to each other, so that we may understand and feel that He has redeemed us one and all, and that, unless we love one another, we cannot really have love to Him who laid down His life for us.

With the hope, then, of suggesting to you some serious

thoughts for the week which begins with this day, I will make a few remarks, such as the text suggests, upon that dreadful yet most joyful event, the passion and death of our Lord.

And, first, it ought not to be necessary to say, though it may be necessary even because it is so obvious,—(for, what is very plain is sometimes taken for granted by those who know it, and hence is never heard by others at all,)—this, I say, in the first place, must be ever remembered, that Christ's death was not a mere martyrdom. A martyr is one who dies for the Church, who is put to death for preaching and maintaining the truth. Christ, indeed, was put to death for preaching the Gospel; yet He was not a Martyr, but He was much more than a Martyr. Had He been a mere man, He would have been rightly called a Martyr, but as He was not a mere man, so He was not a mere Martyr. Man dies as a Martyr, but the Son of God dies as an Atoning Sacrifice.

Here then, as you see, we are at once introduced into a very mysterious subject, though one which concerns us most nearly. There was a virtue in His death, which there could be in no other, for He was God. *We*, indeed, could not have told beforehand what would follow from so high an event as God becoming incarnate and dying on the Cross; but that something extraordinary and high would issue from it, we might have been quite sure, though nothing had been told us. He would not have so humbled Himself for nought; He could not so humble Himself (if I may use the expression) without momentous consequences.

It would be well if we opened our minds to what is meant by the doctrine of the Son of God dying on the Cross for us. I do not say we shall ever be able to solve the mystery of it, but we may understand in what the Mystery consists; and that is what many men are deficient in. They have no clear views what the truth of the matter is; if they had, it would make them more serious than they are. Let it be understood, then, that the Almighty Son of God, who had been in the bosom of the Father from everlasting, became man; became man as truly as He was always God. He was God from God, as the Creed says; that is, as being the Son of the Father, He had all those infinite perfections from the Father which the Father had. He was of one substance with the Father, and was God, because the Father was God. He was truly God, but He became as truly man. He became man, yet so as not to cease in any respect being what He was before. He added a new nature to Himself, yet so intimately, that it was *as if* He had actually left His former self, which He did not. "The Word became flesh:" even this would seem mystery and marvel enough, but even this was not all; not only was He "made man," but, as the Creed goes on to state, He "was crucified also for us under Pontius Pilate, He suffered and was buried."

Now here, I say, is a fresh mystery in the history of His humiliation, and the thought of it will cast a new and solemn light on the chapters we shall read during the week. I have said that, after His incarnation, man's nature was as much and as truly Christ's as His Divine attributes; St. Paul even speaks of God "purchasing us with His own blood," and of the "Lord of glory" being "killed,"—expressions which, more than any other, show how absolutely and simply He had put on Him the nature of man. As the soul acts through the body as its instrument,—in a more perfect way, but as intimately, did the Eternal Word of God act through the manhood which He had taken. When He spoke, it was literally God speaking; when He suffered, it was God suffering. Not that the Divine Nature itself could suffer, any more than our soul can see or hear; but, as the soul sees and hears through the organs of the body, so God the Son suffered *in* that human nature which He had taken to Himself and made His own. And in that nature He did truly suffer; as truly as He framed the worlds through His Almighty power, so through His human nature did He suffer; for when He came on earth, His manhood became as truly and personally His, as His Almighty power had been from everlasting.

Think of this, all ye light-hearted, and consider whether with this thought you can read the last chapters of the four Gospels without fear and trembling.

For instance; "When He had thus spoken, one of the officers which stood by struck Jesus with the palm of his hand, saying, Answerest Thou the high priest so?" The words must be said, though I hardly dare say them,—that officer lifted up his hand against God the Son. This is not a figurative way of speaking, or a rhetorical form of words, or a harsh, extreme, and unadvisable statement; it is a literal and simple truth, it is a great Catholic doctrine.

Again: "Then they did spit in His face, and buffeted Him, and others smote Him with the palms of their hands."

"The men that held Jesus mocked Him, and smote Him, and when they had blindfolded Him, they struck Him on the face, and asked Him, saying, Prophesy, who is it that smote Thee? and many other things blasphemously spake they against Him."

"And Herod with his men of war set Him at nought, and mocked Him, and arrayed Him in a gorgeous robe, and sent Him again to Pilate."

"Pilate therefore took Jesus and scourged Him; and the soldiers platted a crown of thorns, and put it on His head, and a reed in His right hand, and they put on Him a purple robe, and said, Hail, King of the Jews! and they smote Him on the head with a reed, and did spit upon Him, and, bowing their knees, worshipped Him. Then came Jesus forth, wearing the crown of thorns and the purple robe."

Lastly: "When they were come to the place which is called Calvary, there they crucified Him"[1]—between two malefactors, and even there they did not cease insulting and mocking Him; but all of them, chief priests and people, stood beholding, and bidding Him come down from the Cross.

Now I bid you consider that that Face, so ruthlessly smitten, was the Face of God Himself; the Brows bloody with the thorns, the sacred Body exposed to view and lacerated with the scourge, the Hands nailed to the Cross, and, afterwards, the Side pierced with the spear; it was the Blood, and the sacred Flesh, and the Hands, and the Temples, and the Side, and the Feet of God Himself, which the frenzied multitude then gazed upon. This is so fearful a thought, that when the mind first masters it, surely it will be difficult to think of any thing else; so that, while we think of it, we must pray God to temper it to us, and to give us strength to think of it rightly, lest it be too much for us.

Taking into account, then, that Almighty God Himself, God the Son, was the Sufferer, we shalt understand better than we have hitherto the description given of Him by the Evangelists; we shall see the meaning of His general demeanour, His silence, and the words He used when He spoke, and Pilate's awe at Him.

"And the high priest arose and said unto Him, Answerest Thou nothing? What is it which these witness against Thee? But Jesus held His peace."[2]

"When He was accused of the chief priests and elders, He answered nothing. Then said Pilate unto Him, Hearest Thou not how many things they witness against Thee? and He answered him to never a word, insomuch that the governor marvelled greatly."[3]

---

[1] John xviii.22; Matt. xxvi.67; Luke xxii.63–65; xxiii.11; John xix.1,2; Matt. xxvii.29; Mark xv.19; Luke xxiii.33.

[2] Matt.xxvi.62, 63.   [3] Matt. xxvii.12–14.

"The Jews answered Him, We have a law, and by our law He ought to die, because He made Himself the Son of God. When Pilate therefore heard that saying, he was the more afraid, and went again into the judgment hall, and saith unto Jesus, Whence art Thou? But Jesus gave him no answer."[4]

"And when Herod saw Jesus, he was exceeding glad: for he was desirous to see Him of a long season, because he had heard many things of Him; and he hoped to have seen some miracle done by Him. Then he questioned with Him in many words, but He answered him nothing."[5]

Lastly, His words to the women who followed Him, "Daughters of Jerusalem, weep not for Me, but weep for yourselves and for your children. For behold the days are coming, in the which they shall say, Blessed are the barren, and the wombs that never bare, and the paps which never gave suck. Then shall they begin to say to the mountains, Fall on us; and to the hills, Cover us."[6]

After these passages, consider the words of the beloved disciple, in anticipation of His coming at the end of the world. "Behold He cometh with clouds, and every eye shall see Him, they also which pierced Him: and all the kindreds of the earth shall wail because of Him. Even so, Amen."[7]

Yes, we shall all of us, for weal or for woe, one day see that holy Countenance which wicked men struck and dishonoured; we shall see those Hands that were nailed to the cross; that Side which was pierced. We shall see all this; and it will be the sight of the Living God.

This being the great mystery of Christ's Cross and Passion, we might with reason suppose, as I have said, that some great thing would result from it. The sufferings and death of the Word Incarnate could not pass away like a dream; they could not be a mere martyrdom, or a mere display or figure of something else, they must have a virtue in them. This we might be sure of, though nothing had been told us about the result. But that result is also revealed: it is this—our reconciliation to God, the expiation of our sins, and our new creation in holiness.

We had need of a reconciliation, for by nature we are outcasts. From the time that Adam fell, all his children have been under a curse. "In Adam all die,"[8] as St. Paul says. So that every one of us is born into this world in a state of *death*; such is our natural life from our very first breath; we are children of wrath; conceived in sin; shapen in iniquity. We are under the bondage

---

[4] John xix.7–9.　　　　[5] Luke xxiii.8, 9.　　　　[6] Luke xxiii.28–30.
[7] Rev. i.7.　　　　[8] 1 Cor. xv.22.

of an inborn element of evil, which thwarts and stifles whatever principles remain of truth and goodness in us, directly we attempt to act according to them. This is that "body of death" under which St. Paul describes the natural man as groaning, and saying, "O wretched man, who shall deliver me?" Now for ourselves, my brethren, we know (praised be God) that all of us have from our infancy been taken out of this miserable heathen state by holy baptism, which is God's appointed means of regeneration. Still it is not less our natural state; it is the state in which every one of us was born; it is the state in which every little child is, when brought to the font. Dear as he is to those who bring him thither, and innocent as he may look, there is, till he is baptized, an evil spirit in his heart, a spirit of evil lying hid, seen of God, unseen by man (as the serpent among the trees of Eden), an evil spirit which from the first is hateful to God, and at length will be his eternal ruin. That evil spirit is cast out by Holy Baptism, without the privilege of which his birth would but be a misery to him. But whence did Baptism gain its power? From that great event we are so soon to commemorate; the death of the Son of God incarnate. Almost all religions have their outward cleansings; they feel the need of man, though they cannot supply it. Even the Jewish system, though Divine, effected nothing here; its washings were but carnal; the blood of bulls and goats was but earthly and unprofitable. Even St. John's baptism, our Lord's forerunner, had no inward propitiatory power. Christ was not yet crucified. But when that long-expected season came, when the Son of God had solemnly set Himself apart as a Victim in the presence of His twelve Apostles, and had gone into the garden, and before three of them had undergone His agony and bloody sweat, and then had been betrayed, buffeted, spit upon, scourged, and nailed to the cross, till He died, then He with His last breath said, "It is finished;" and from that time the virtue of the Highest went forth through His wounds and with His blood, for the pardon and regeneration of man; and hence it is that baptism has its power.

This is why He "humbled Himself and became obedient unto death, even the death of the cross." "Christ hath redeemed us," says the Apostle elsewhere, "from the curse of the Law, being made a curse for us." Again, he says that Christ has "made peace by the blood of His cross." He has "reconciled" us "in the body of His flesh through death, to present us holy and unblameable, and unreproveable in His sight." Or, as St. John says, the saints "have washed their robes, and made them white in the blood of the Lamb." And no one speaks more explicitly on this great mystery than the prophet Isaiah, many hundred years before it was accomplished. "Surely He hath borne our griefs and carried our sorrows. He was wounded for our transgressions, He was bruised for our iniquities; the chastisement of our peace was upon Him, and with His stripes we are healed. All we like sheep have gone astray, we have turned every one to his own way, and the Lord hath laid on Him the iniquity of us all." [9]

We believe, then, that when Christ suffered on the cross, our nature suffered in Him. Human nature, fallen and corrupt, was under the wrath of God, and it was impossible that it should be restored to His favour till it had expiated its sin by suffering. Why this was necessary, we know not; but we are told expressly, that we are "all by nature children of wrath," that "by the deeds of the law there shall no flesh be justified," and that "the wicked shall be turned into hell, and all the people that forget God." The Son of God then took our nature on Him, that in Him it might do and suffer what in itself was impossible to it. What it could not effect of itself, it could effect in Him. He carried it about Him through a life of penance. He carried it forward to agony and death. In Him our sinful nature died and rose again. When it died in Him on the cross, that death was its new creation. In Him it satisfied its old and heavy debt; for the presence of His Divinity gave it transcendent merit. His presence had kept it pure from sin from the first. His Hand had carefully selected the choicest specimen of our nature from the Virgin's substance; and, separating from it all defilement, His personal indwelling hallowed it and gave it power. And thus, when it had been offered up upon the Cross, and was made perfect by suffering, it became the first-fruits of a new man; it became a Divine leaven of holiness for the new birth and spiritual life of as many as should receive it. And thus, as the Apostle says, "If one died for all, then did *all* die;" "our old man is crucified *in Him*, that the *body* of sin might be destroyed;" and "together" with Christ "when we were dead in sins, hath He quickened us, and raised us up together, and made us sit together in heavenly places in Christ Jesus." Thus "we are members of His body, from His flesh, and from His bones: for whosoever eateth His flesh and drinketh His blood, hath eternal life," for His flesh is meat indeed, and His blood is drink indeed; and "he that eateth His flesh and drinketh His blood dwelleth in Him, and He in him." [10]

---

[9] Gal. iii.13; Col. i.20–22; Rev. vii.14; Is. liii.4–6.
[10] 2 Cor. v.14; Rom. vi.6; Eph. ii.5, 6; v.30; John vi.54.

What a very different view of life do these doctrines present to us from that which the world takes. Only think of this one thing—of the eagerness of the great mass of men after matters of time, after engagements of this world, after gain, after national aggrandizement, after speculations which promise public or private advantage; and having thought of this, turn back to the contemplation of Christ's Cross, and then say, as candid men, whether the world, and all that is in the world, is not as unbelieving now as when Christ came. Does there not seem too great cause to fear that this nation, in spite of its having been baptized into the Cross of Christ, is in so unholy a state, that, did Christ come among us as He came among the Jews, we should, except a small remnant, reject Him as well as they? May we not be sure that men now-a-days, had they been alive when He came, would have disbelieved and derided the holy and mysterious doctrines which He brought? Alas! is there any doubt at all, that they would have fulfilled St. John's words,— "the darkness comprehended it not?" Their hearts are set on schemes of this world: there would have been no *sympathy* between them and the calm and heavenly mind of the Lord Jesus Christ. They would have said that His Gospel was strange, extravagant, incredible. The only reason they do not say so now is, that they are used to it, and do not really dwell on what they profess to believe. What! (it would have been said,) the Son of God taking human flesh, impossible! the Son of God, separate from God yet one with Him! "how can these things be?" God Himself suffering on the Cross, the Almighty Everlasting God in the form of a servant, with human flesh and blood, wounded, insulted, dying? and all this as an Expiation for human sin? Why (they would ask) was an Expiation necessary? why could not the All-merciful Father pardon without one? why is human sin to be accounted so great an evil? We see no necessity for so marvellous a remedy; we refuse to admit a course of doctrine so utterly unlike any thing which the face of this world tells us of. These are events without parallels; they belong to a new and distinct order of things; and, while our heart has no sympathy with them, our reason utterly rejects them.—And as for Christ's miracles, if they had not seen them, they would not have believed the report; if they had, they would have been ready enough to refer them to juggling craft,—if not, as the Jews did, to Beelzebub.

Such will the holy truths of the Gospel ever appear to those who live to this world, whether they love its pleasures, its comforts, its prizes, or its struggles; their eyes are waxen gross, they cannot see Christ spiritually. When they see Him, there is no beauty in Him that they should desire Him. Thus they become unbelieving. In our Lord's words, "No servant can serve two masters: for either he will hate the one and love the other, or else he will hold to the one and despise the other. *Ye cannot serve God and mammon.*"[11] When He said this, the Pharisees *derided Him.* And He said unto them, "Ye are they which justify yourselves before men; but God knoweth your hearts, for that which is highly esteemed among men is abomination in the sight of God." God grant that we may not be of those who "justify themselves before men," and "deride" those who preach the severe doctrine of the Cross! God grant that, if we have any misgivings about the corruptions and defects of the religion now so popular among us, we may have the grace forthwith to desire honestly to know God's will! God grant that we may not attempt to deceive our consciences, and to reconcile together, by some artifice or other, the service of this world and of God! God grant that we may not pervert and dilute His holy Word, put upon it the false interpretations of men, reason ourselves out of its strictness, and reduce religion to an ordinary common-place matter—instead of thinking it what it *is*, a mysterious and supernatural subject, as distinct from any thing that lies on the surface of this world, as day is from night and heaven from earth!

[11] Luke xvi.13–15.

THE CROSS OF CHRIST
THE MEASURE OF THE WORLD

(Sixth Sunday in Lent)

"And I, if I be lifted up from the earth, will draw all men unto Me."
—John xii.32.

A GREAT number of men live and die without reflecting at all
upon the state of things in which they find themselves.
They take things as they come, and follow their inclinations as
far as they have the opportunity. They are guided mainly by
pleasure and pain, not by reason, principle, or conscience; and
they do not attempt to *interpret* this world, to determine what it
means, or to reduce what they see and feel to system. But when
persons, either from thoughtfulness of mind, or from intellectual activity, begin to contemplate the visible state of things
into which they are born, then forthwith they find it a maze
and a perplexity. It is a riddle which they cannot solve. It seems
full of contradictions and without a drift. Why it is, and what it
is to issue in, and how it is what it is, and how we come to be
introduced into it, and what is our destiny, are all mysteries.

In this difficulty, some have formed one philosophy of life,
and others another. Men have thought they had found the key,
by means of which they might read what is so obscure. Ten
thousand things come before us one after another in the course
of life, and what are we to think of them? what colour are we
to give them? Are we to look at all things in a gay and mirthful
way? or in a melancholy way? in a desponding or a hopeful
way? Are we to make light of life altogether, or to treat the
whole subject seriously? Are we to make greatest things of
little consequence, or least things of great consequence? Are
we to keep in mind what is past and gone, or are we look on to
the future, or are we to be absorbed in what is present? *How* are
we to look at things? this is the question which all persons of
observation ask themselves, and answer each in his own way.
They wish to think by rule; by something within them, which

may harmonise and adjust what is without them. Such is the need felt by reflective minds. Now, let me ask, what *is* the real key, what is the Christian interpretation of this world? What is given us by revelation to estimate and measure this world by? The event of this season,—the Crucifixion of the Son of God.

It is the death of the Eternal Word of God made flesh, which is our great lesson how to think and how to speak of this world. His Cross has put its due value upon every thing which we see, upon all fortunes, all advantages, all ranks, all dignities, all pleasures; upon the lust of the flesh, and the lust of the eyes, and the pride of life. It has set a price upon the excitements, the rivalries, the hopes, the fears, the desires, the efforts, the triumphs of mortal man. It has given a meaning to the various, shifting course, the trials, the temptations, the sufferings, of his earthly state. It has brought together and made consistent all that seemed discordant and aimless. It has taught us how to live, how to use this world, what to expect, what to desire, what to hope. It is the tone into which all the strains of this world's music are ultimately to be resolved.

Look around, and see what the world presents of high and low. Go to the court of princes. See the treasure and skill of all nations brought together to honour a child of man. Observe the prostration of the many before the few. Consider the form and ceremonial, the pomp, the state, the circumstance; and the vain-glory. Do you wish to know the worth of it all? look at the Cross of Christ.

Go to the political world: see nation jealous of nation, trade rivalling trade, armies and fleets matched against each other. Survey the various ranks of the community, its parties and their contests, the strivings of the ambitious, the intrigues of the crafty. What is the end of all this turmoil? the grave. What is the measure? the Cross.

Go, again, to the world of intellect and science: consider the wonderful discoveries which the human mind is making, the variety of arts to which its discoveries give rise, the all but miracles by which it shows its power; and next, the pride and confidence of reason, and the absorbing devotion of thought to transitory objects, which is the consequence. Would you form a right judgment of all this? look at the Cross.

Again: look at misery, look at poverty and destitution, look at oppression and captivity; go where food is scanty, and lodging unhealthy. Consider pain and suffering, diseases long or violent, all that is frightful and revolting. Would you know how to rate all these? gaze upon the Cross.

Thus in the Cross, and Him who hung upon it, all things meet; all things subserve it, all things need it. It is their centre and their interpretation. For He was lifted up upon it, that He might draw all men and all things unto Him.

But it will be said, that the view which the Cross of Christ imparts to us of human life and of the world, is not that which we should take, if left to ourselves; that it is not an obvious view; that if we look at things on their surface, they are far more bright and sunny than they appear when viewed in the light which this season casts upon them. The world seems made for the enjoyment of just such a being as man, and man is put into it. He has the *capacity* of enjoyment, and the world supplies the *means*. How natural this, what a simple as well as pleasant philosophy, yet how different from that of the Cross! The doctrine of the Cross, it may be said, disarranges two parts of a system which seem made for each other; it severs the fruit from the eater, the enjoyment from the enjoyer. How does this solve a problem? does it not rather itself create one?

I answer, first, that whatever force this objection may have, surely it is merely a repetition of that which Eve felt and Satan urged in Eden; for did not the woman see that the forbidden tree was "good for food," and "a tree to be *desired?*" Well, then, is it wonderful that we too, the descendants of the first pair, should still be in a world where there is a forbidden fruit, and that our trials should lie in being within reach of it, and our happiness in abstaining from it? The world, at first sight, appears *made* for pleasure, and the vision of Christ's Cross is a solemn and sorrowful sight interfering with this appearance. Be it so; but why may it not be our duty to abstain from enjoyment notwithstanding, if it was a duty even in Eden?

But again; it is but a superficial view of things to say that this life is made for pleasure and happiness. To those who look under the surface, it tells a very different tale. The doctrine of the Cross does but teach, though infinitely more forcibly, still after all it does but teach the very same lesson which this world teaches to those who live long in it, who have much experience in it, who know it. The world is sweet to the lips, but bitter to the taste. It pleases at first, but not at last. It looks gay on the outside, but evil and misery lie concealed within. When a man has passed a certain number of years in it, he cries out with the Preacher, "Vanity of vanities, all is vanity." Nay, if he has not religion for his guide, he will be forced to go further, and say, "All is vanity and vexation of spirit;" all is disappointment; all is sorrow; all is pain. The sore judgments of God upon sin are concealed within it, and force a man to grieve whether he will or no. Therefore the doctrine of the Cross of Christ does but anticipate for us our experience of the world. It is true, it bids us grieve for our sins in the midst of all that smiles and glitters around us; but if we will not heed it, we shall at length be forced to grieve for them from undergoing their fearful punishment. If we will not acknowledge that this world has been made miserable by sin, from the sight of Him on whom our sins were laid, we shall experience it to be miserable by the recoil of those sins upon ourselves.

It may be granted, then, that the doctrine of the Cross is not on the surface of the world. The surface of things is bright only, and the Cross is sorrowful; it is a hidden doctrine; it lies under a veil; it at first sight startles us, and we are tempted to revolt from it. Like St. Peter, we cry out, "Be it far from Thee, Lord; this shall not be unto Thee."[1] And yet it is a true doctrine; for truth is not on the surface of things, but in the depths.

And as the doctrine of the Cross, though it be the true interpretation of this world, is not prominently manifested in it, upon its surface, but is concealed; so again, when received into the faithful heart, there it abides as a living principle, but deep, and hidden from observation. Religious men, in the words of Scripture, "live by the faith of the Son of God, who loved them and gave Himself for them:"[2] but they do not tell this to all men; they leave others to find it out as they may. Our Lord's own command to His disciples was, that when they fast, they should "anoint their head and wash their face."[3] Thus they are bound not to make a display, but ever to be content to look outwardly different from what they are really inwardly. They are to carry a cheerful countenance with them, and to control and regulate their feelings, that those feelings, by not being expended on the surface, may retire deep into their hearts and there live. And thus "Jesus Christ and He crucified" is, as the Apostle tells us, "a hidden wisdom;"—hidden in the world, which seems at first sight to speak a far other doctrine,—and hidden in the faithful soul, which to persons at a distance, or to chance beholders, seems to be living but an ordinary life, while really it is in secret holding communion with Him who was "manifested in the flesh," "crucified through weakness," "justified in the Spirit, seen of Angels, and received up into glory."

This being the case, the great and awful doctrine of the Cross of Christ, which we now commemorate, may fitly be called, in

[1] Matt. xvi.22.   [2] Gal. ii.20.   [3] Matt. vi.17.

the language of figure, the *heart* of religion. The heart may be considered as the seat of life; it is the principle of motion, heat, and activity; from it the blood goes to and fro to the extreme parts of the body. It sustains the man in his powers and faculties; it enables the brain to think; and when it is touched, man dies. And in like manner the sacred doctrine of Christ's Atoning Sacrifice is the vital principle on which the Christian lives, and without which Christianity is not. Without it no other doctrine is held profitably; to believe in Christ's Divinity, or in His manhood, or in the Holy Trinity, or in a judgment to come, or in the resurrection of the dead, is an untrue belief, not Christian faith, unless we receive also the doctrine of Christ's sacrifice. On the other hand, to receive it presupposes the reception of other high truths of the Gospel besides; it involves the belief in Christ's true divinity, in His true incarnation, and in man's sinful state by nature; and it prepares the way to belief in the sacred Eucharistic feast, in which He who was once crucified is ever given to our souls and bodies, verily and indeed, in His Body and in His Blood. But again, the heart is hidden from view; it is carefully and securely guarded; it is not like the eye set in the forehead, commanding all, and seen of all: and so in like manner the sacred doctrine of the Atoning Sacrifice is not one to be talked of, but to be lived upon; not to be put forth irreverently, but to be adored secretly; not to be used as a necessary instrument in the conversion of the ungodly, or for the satisfaction of reasoners of this world, but to be unfolded to the docile and obedient; to young children, whom the world has not corrupted; to the sorrowful, who need comfort; to the sincere and earnest, who need a rule of life; to the innocent, who need warning; and to the established, who have earned the knowledge of it.

One more remark I shall make, and then conclude. It must not be supposed, because the doctrine of the Cross makes us sad, that therefore the Gospel is a sad religion. The Psalmist says, "They that sow in tears shall reap in joy;" and our Lord says, "They that mourn shall be comforted." Let no one go away with the impression that the Gospel makes us take a gloomy view of the world and of life. It hinders us indeed from taking a superficial view, and finding a vain transitory joy in what we see; but it forbids our immediate enjoyment, only to grant enjoyment in truth and fulness afterwards. It only forbids us to *begin* with enjoyment. It only says, If you begin with pleasure, you will end with pain. It bids us begin with the Cross of Christ, and in that Cross we shall at first find sorrow, but in a while peace and comfort will rise out of that sorrow. That Cross will lead us to mourning, repentance, humiliation, prayer, fasting; we shall sorrow for our sins, we shall sorrow with Christ's sufferings; but all this sorrow will only issue, nay, will be undergone in a happiness far greater than the enjoyment which the world gives,—though careless worldly minds indeed will not believe this, ridicule the notion of it, because they never have tasted it, and consider it a mere matter of words, which religious persons think it decent and proper to use, and try to believe themselves, and to get others to believe, but which no one really feels. This is what they think; but our Saviour said to His disciples, "Ye now therefore have sorrow, but I will see you again, and your heart shall rejoice, and your joy no man taketh from you." . . . "Peace I leave with you; My peace I give unto you; not as the world giveth, give I unto you." And St. Paul says, "The natural man receiveth not the things of the Spirit of God; for they are foolishness unto him; neither can he know them, because they are spiritually discerned." "Eye hath not seen, nor ear heard, neither have entered into the heart of man, the things which God hath prepared for them that love Him."[4] And thus the Cross of Christ, as telling us of our redemption as well as of His sufferings, wounds us indeed, but so wounds as to heal also.

And thus, too, all that is bright and beautiful, even on the surface of this world, though it has no substance, and may not suitably be enjoyed for its own sake, yet is a figure and promise of that true joy which issues out of the Atonement. It is a promise beforehand of what is to be: it is a shadow, raising hope because the substance is to follow, but not to be rashly taken instead of the substance. And it is God's usual mode of dealing with us, in mercy to send the shadow before the substance, that we may take comfort in what is to be, before it comes. Thus our Lord before His Passion rode into Jerusalem in triumph, with the multitudes crying Hosanna, and strewing His road with palm branches and their garments. This was but a vain and hollow pageant, nor did our Lord take pleasure in it. It was a shadow which stayed not, but flitted away. It could not be more than a shadow, for the Passion had not been undergone by which His true triumph was wrought out. He could not enter into His glory before He had first suffered. He could not take pleasure in this semblance of it, knowing that it was unreal. Yet that first shadowy triumph was the omen and presage of the

---

[4] John xvi.22; xiv.27; 1 Cor. ii.9, 14.

true victory to come, when He had overcome the sharpness of death. And we commemorate this figurative triumph on the last Sunday in Lent, to cheer us in the sorrow of the week that follows, and to remind us of the true joy which comes with Easter-Day.

And so, too, as regards this world, with all its enjoyments, yet disappointments. Let us not trust it; let us not give our hearts to it; let us not begin with it. Let us begin with faith; let us begin with Christ; let us begin with His Cross and the humiliation to which it leads. Let us first be drawn to Him who is lifted up, that so He may, with Himself, freely give us all things. Let us "seek first the Kingdom of God and His righteousness," and then all those things of this world "will be added to us." They alone are able truly to enjoy this world, who begin with the world unseen. They alone enjoy it, who have first abstained from it. They alone can truly feast, who have first fasted; they alone are able to use the world, who have learned not to abuse it; they alone inherit it, who take it as a shadow of the world to come, and who for that world to come relinquish it.

DIFFICULTY OF REALIZING
SACRED PRIVILEGES

(Easter)

*"This is the Day which the Lord hath made; we will rejoice
and be glad in it."*—Ps. cxviii.24.

IT is always very difficult to realize any great joy or great
sorrow. We cannot realize it by wishing to do so. What
brings joys and sorrows of this world home to us, is their circumstances and accompaniments. When a friend dies, we cannot believe him taken from us at first;—we cannot believe
ourselves to be in any new place when we are just come to it.
When we are told a thing, we assent to it, we do not doubt it,
but we do not feel it to be true, we do not understand it as a fact
which must take up a position or station in our thoughts, and
must be acted from and acted towards, must be dealt with *as*
existing: that is, we do not realize it. This seems partly the reason why, when Almighty God reveals Himself in Scripture to
this man or that, he, on the other hand, asks for some sign
whereby he shall know that God has spoken. Doubtless sinful
infirmity sometimes mixed itself up in such questions, as in the
case of Zacharias, who being a Priest in the Temple, the very
dwelling-place of the Living God, where, if any where, Angels
were present, where, if any where, God would speak, ought to
have needed nothing whereby to realize to himself God's
power, God's superintending eye, God's faithfulness towards
the house of Israel and its priests. Under the same feeling,
though blamelessly, Gideon asked for the miracle upon the
fleece. He could not bring himself to believe that *he* was to be
what God's Angel had declared. What? *he*, the least of his
father's house, and his family poor in Manasseh, how could he
understand that *he* was to be the greatest champion of Israel
against the Midianites? Not that he doubted it, for God had said
it; but he could not feel, think, speak, act as if it were true. If he
attempted to do so, it was in an unreal way, and he spoke and

acted unnaturally and on a theory, on a view of things which he had mastered one minute and which was gone the next. The special favour of God towards him, according to the words, "The Lord is with thee, thou mighty man of valour!"[1] seemed like a dream, and confused him. So he said "If now so it be, certain consequences flow from it; if God is with me, it is the God of miracles who is with me, who can change the creature as He will; may He then vouchsafe to do so! that I may have the full impression on my soul, heart, and mind, of what my reason receives; that I may be familiarized to this strange and overpowering Providence, that *I* should be raised above my brethren, and made God's minister to them for good." And therefore he asked, first, that the fleece might be wet, then that it might be dry; not as evidence whereon to build his faith, but as a manifestation impressing his imagination and heart.

In somewhat the same way we are told of Jacob also; "when he saw the waggons which Joseph had sent to carry him, the spirit of Jacob their father revived."[2] Jacob, to be sure, did doubt what his sons reported, from distrust of them; yet the mere sight of the waggons did not serve to prove their veracity nearly so much, as to quiet his perplexed imagination, and to reconcile it to the sudden news. That news was more startling, than the reporters were untrustworthy.

And thus we Christians, though born in our very infancy into the kingdom of God, and chosen above all other men to be heirs of heaven and witnesses to the world, and though knowing and believing this truth entirely, yet have very great difficulty and pass many years in learning our privilege. Not any one, of course, fully understands it;—doubtless; but we have not even a fair, practical hold of it. And here we are, even on this great Day, this Day of days, on which Christ arose from the dead,—here are we, on this very Day as infants, lying helpless and senseless on the ground, without eyes to see or heart to comprehend who we are.

Surely so it is: and it cannot be denied that we have much to do, very much, before we rise to the understanding of our new nature and its privileges, and learn to rejoice and be glad in the Day which the Lord hath made; "the eyes of our understanding being enlightened, that we may know what is the hope of His calling, and what the riches of the glory of His inheritance in the Saints, and what is the exceeding greatness of His power to us-ward who believe, according to the working of His mighty

---

[1] Judges vi.12.   [2] Gen. xlv.27.

power, which He wrought in Christ, when He raised Him from the dead, and set Him at His own right hand in the heavenly places."[3] Such high words as these are, alas! scarcely more than mere words when spoken to us; at best, we but believe them, we do not in any good measure realize them.

Now this insensibility or want of apprehension rises in great measure, it is scarcely necessary to say, from our exceeding frailness and sinfulness. Our old nature is continually exerting itself against the new; "the flesh lusteth against the Spirit."[4] Its desire is towards this world. This world is its food; its eyes apprehend this world. Because it is what it is, it allies itself to this world. The world and the flesh form a compact with each other; the one asks, and the other supplies. Therefore, in proportion as it seduces us into the world's company, of course, in an equal degree, it blunts our perception of that world which we do not see; it prevents our realizing it. And thus one special cause of our difficulty in realizing our election into the kingdom of heaven is our evil nature, which familiarizes us with this world, Satan's kingdom, and weighs on us and pulls us down when we would lift up our hearts, lift them up unto the Lord. This is certain: yet, besides this, there are certainly other reasons too which make it difficult for us to apprehend our state, and cause us to do so but gradually; and which are not our fault, but which arise out of our position and circumstances.

We are born almost into the fulness of Christian blessings, long before we have reason. We could not apprehend them at all, and that without our own fault, when we were baptized; for we were infants. As, then, we acquire reason itself but gradually, so we acquire the knowledge of what we are but gradually also; and as it is no fault in us, but a blessing to us, that we were baptized so early, so, from the nature of the case, and not from any fault of ours, do we but slowly enter into the privileges of our baptism. So it is as regards all our knowledge of ourselves and of our position in the world; we but gradually gain it. At first children do not know that they are responsible beings; but by degrees they not only feel that they are, but reflect on the great truth, and on what it implies. Some persons recollect a time as children when it fell on them to reflect what they were, whence they came, whither they tended, why they lived, what was required of them. The thought fell upon them long after they had heard and spoken of God; but at length they began to realize what they had heard, and they began to muse about

[3] Eph. i.18–20.   [4] Gal. v.17.

themselves. So, too, it is in matters of this world. As our minds open, we gradually understand where we are in human society. We have a notion of ranks and classes, of nations, of countries. We begin to see how we stand relatively to others. Thus a man differs from a boy; he has a general view of things; he sees their bearings on each other; he sees his own position, sees what is becoming, what is expected of him, what his duty is in the community, what his rights. He understands his place in the world, and, in a word, he is at home in it.

Alas, that while we thus grow in knowledge in matters of time and sense, yet we remain children in knowledge of our heavenly privileges! St. Paul says, that whereas Christ is risen, He "hath raised us up together, and made us sit together in heavenly places in Christ Jesus."[5] This is what we have still to learn; to know our place, position, situation as "children of God, members of Christ, and inheritors of the kingdom of heaven." We are risen again, and we know it not. We begin our Catechism by confessing that we are risen, but it takes a long life to apprehend what we confess. We are like people waking from sleep, who cannot collect their thoughts at once, or understand where they are. By little and little the truth breaks upon us. Such are we in the present world; sons of light, gradually waking to a knowledge of themselves. For this let us meditate, let us pray, let us work,—gradually to attain to a real apprehension of what we are. Thus, as time goes on, we shall gain first one thing, then another. By little and little we shall give up shadows and find the substance. Waiting on God day by day, we shall make progress day by day, and approach to the true and clear view of what He has made us to be in Christ. Year by year we shall gain something, and each Easter, as it comes, will enable us more to rejoice with heart and understanding in that great salvation which Christ then accomplished.

This we shall find to be one great providential benefit arising from those duties which He exacts of us. Our duties to God and man are not only duties done to Him, but they are means of enlightening our eyes and making our faith apprehensive. Every act of obedience has a tendency to strengthen our convictions about heaven. Every sacrifice makes us more zealous; every self-denial makes us more devoted. This is a use, too, of the observance of sacred seasons; they wean us from this world, they impress upon us the reality of the world which we see not. We trust, if we thus proceed, we shall understand more and

[5] Eph. ii.6.

more where we are. We humbly trust that, as we cleanse ourselves from this world, our eyes will be enlightened to see the
things which are only spiritually discerned. We hope that to
us will be fulfilled in due measure the words of the beatitude,
"Blessed are the pure in heart, for they shall see God." [6] We
have good hope, which cannot deceive us, that if we wait upon
God, as the Saints have ever waited, with fastings and prayers,
—if we seek Him as Anna sought Him, or St. Peter at Joppa, or
holy Daniel before them, Christ will be manifested to us; the
day will dawn, and the day-star arise in our hearts. We shall see
the sign of the Son of man in heaven; we shall eat of the hidden
manna, and possess that secret of the Lord which is with those
that fear Him; and, like St. Paul, we shall "know whom we have
believed, and be persuaded that He is able to keep that which
we have committed unto Him against that day." [7]

While then we feel keenly, as we ought, that we do not
honour this Blessed Day with that lively and earnest joy which
is its due, yet let us not be discouraged, let us not despond at
this. We *do* feel joy; we feel more joy than we know we do. We
see more of the next world than we know we see. If we have
duly improved the sacred season which is now past; if we have in
good earnest, and without trifling with ourselves, denied ourselves in meat and drink, and other indulgences, according to
our strength; if we have been frequent in prayers according
to our opportunities; it cannot be but that a blessing has come
upon us, and is upon us now. We may not be sensible of it, but
by and by we shall know it, when we look back upon it. What
has already happened in our past experience surely is enough to
assure us of this. We know in what way we have been hitherto
brought to recognize so much as we do recognize of our Christian blessedness; how very gradually, how silently. We may recollect, perhaps, one or other striking occurrence. Perhaps, as I
have said, we can put our hand, as it were, on a time in our
childhood, when the thought first came on us that we had relations towards other beings, and they towards us, and we marvelled what we were and why we existed. Perhaps, in after life,
we recollect seasons when the force of Divine truth came on us
more sensibly and distinctly; but for the most part it is not
so. For the most part we have gained truth, and made progress
from truth to truth, without knowing it. We cannot tell when
we first held this, or first held that doctrine, which is now our
joy and treasure. It is "as if a man should cast seed into the

[6] Matt. v.8.   [7] 2 Tim. i.12.

ground, and should sleep and rise night and day, and the seed should spring and grow up he knoweth not how . . . first the blade, then the ear, after that the full corn in the ear."[8] One may see this on all sides; one may see it especially at this time. God Almighty seems at this time to be mercifully leading numbers on to the full truth, as it is in Jesus (if it be not presumptuous thus to speak); He is leading them on, and they do not know it themselves. They are gradually modifying and changing their opinions, while they think they remain stationary. Others, perhaps, see how it is with them: they do not; in due time they will. Such is God's wonderful way. Jacob was at Bethel before he knew it. We, too, are in the kingdom of grace without knowing it, and it is manifested in us before we are sensible of the manifestation. As infants gaze around them, and yet seem to look at nothing, we too see our privileges, yet do not master them. Let us pray ever, that we may know more and more what we are, and that we may duly apprehend our own knowledge; in a word, that we may have right feelings, and a corresponding creed.

And now, to conclude, for it is hardly befitting on this Day to speak much, when God has done His greatest work. Let us think of it and of Him. Let us rejoice in the Day which He has made, and let us be "willing in the Day of His Power." This is Easter Day. Let us say this again and again to ourselves with fear and great joy. As children say to themselves, "This is the spring," or "This is the sea," trying to grasp the thought, and not let it go; as travellers in a foreign land say, "This is that great city," or "This is that famous building," knowing it has a long history through centuries, and vexed with themselves that they know so little about it; so let us say, This is the Day of Days, the Royal Day, the Lord's Day. This is the Day on which Christ arose from the dead; the Day which brought us salvation. It is a Day which has made us greater than we know. It is our Day of rest, the true Sabbath. Christ entered into His rest, and so do we. It brings us, in figure, through the grave and gate of death to our season of refreshment in Abraham's bosom. We have had enough of weariness, and dreariness, and listlessness, and sorrow, and remorse. We have had enough of this troublesome world. We have had enough of its noise and din. Noise is its best music. But now there is stillness; and it is a stillness that speaks. We know how strange the feeling is of perfect silence after continued sound. Such is our blessedness now. Calm and serene

---

[8] Mark iv.26–28.

days have begun; and Christ is heard in them, and His still small voice, because the world speaks not. Let us only put off the world, and we put on Christ. The receding from one is an approach to the other. We have now for some weeks been trying, through His grace, to unclothe ourselves of earthly wants and desires. May that unclothing be unto us a clothing upon of things invisible and imperishable! May we grow in grace, and in the knowledge of our Lord and Saviour, season after season, year after year, till He takes to Himself, first one, then another, in the order He thinks fit, to be separated from each other for a little while, to be united together for ever, in the kingdom of His Father and our Father, His God and our God.

THE GOSPEL SIGN
ADDRESSED TO FAITH

(Easter)

"Then certain of the Scribes and of the Pharisees answered, saying,
Master, we would see a Sign from Thee."—Matt. xii.38.

THESE Scribes and Pharisees, though Christ had wrought among them "works which none other man did," and, as one of their own company confessed, no man could do miracles such as His "except God were with him," persisted in asking for some decisive Sign, which would prove His Divinity beyond all question. In His reply, our Lord denied and yet promised such a sign. He says, "An evil and adulterous generation seeketh after a sign; there shall no sign be given to it, but the Sign of the Prophet Jonas." In this sentence it is implied, both that their wishes were not to be granted, yet that a great miracle was to be wrought.

On a second occasion they asked again, Sadducees as well as Pharisees: they "came, and tempting, desired Him that He would show them a sign from heaven." Joshua had stopped the sun and moon "in the sight of Israel;" Samuel had brought thunder at harvest time; they asked for a similar miracle. They asked for a sign from heaven; He answered still by promising a Sign from the earth,—a Sign like his, who was "three days and three nights in the whale's belly." A Sign was to be wrought and was to disappoint them: it was to be a Sign, but not to them; hence our Lord says in the parallel passage in St. Mark, "Verily I say unto you, There shall no sign be given to this generation." [1]

In an earlier part of His ministry, the same question had been asked, and the same answer given under a different image. The Jews "said unto Him, What sign showest Thou unto us, seeing that Thou doest these things?" He in like manner answers; "Destroy this temple, and in three days I will raise it up." [2] They

---

[1] Matt. xvi.1; Mark viii.12.   [2] John ii.19.

misunderstood Him, and He did not set them right. For they
were to see, and see not; they were not to witness the Sign then,
nor were they allowed to apprehend His language now. He
spoke of the resurrection of His body, and they were not at that
season to see Him whom they had pierced.

Now what is remarkable in this passage is this, that our Lord
promised a great sign parallel to those wrought by the old
prophets; yet instead of being public as theirs was, it was in the
event, like Jonah's, a secret sign. Few saw it; it was to be received
by all, but on faith; it was addressed to the humble and lowly.
When it took place, and St. Thomas refused to believe without
sight, our Lord said to him, "Thomas, because thou hast seen
Me, thou hast believed; blessed are they that have not seen, and
yet have believed." The Apostle, perhaps, might have been arguing, "If this be the Lord's great Sign, surely it is to be seen.
What is meant by the resurrection but an evidence which is to
be addressed to my senses? I have to believe, and this is to assure
my belief." Yet St. Thomas would have been more blessed, had
he believed Christ's miraculous Presence without seeing it; and
our Lord implied that such persons there would be.

Now what makes this a subject of interest to us is, that our
Lord does expressly promise all Christians a certain gracious
manifestation of Himself, which it is natural, at first sight, to
suppose a sensible one: and many persons understand it to be
such, as if it were not more blessed to believe than to see. Our
Lord says; "He that hath My commandments and keepeth
them, he it is that loveth Me; and he that loveth Me, shall be
loved of My Father, and I will love him, and will manifest Myself to him." When Jude asked Him, "Lord, how is it that Thou
wilt manifest Thyself unto us, and not unto the world?" our
Lord answered, "If a man love Me, he will keep My words; and
My Father will love him, and We will come unto him, and
make our abode with him." [3] In accordance with this promise,
St. Paul says, "The Spirit Itself beareth witness with our spirit,
that we are the children of God;" and St. John, "He that
believeth on the Son of God hath the witness in himself."

Now, that this great gift, whatever it be, is of a nature to impart illumination, sanctity, and peace, to the soul to which it
comes, far from disputing, I would earnestly maintain. And, in
this indirect way, doubtless, it is in a certain sense apprehended
and perceived; perceived in its effects, with a consciousness that
those effects cannot come of themselves, but imply a gift from

[3] John xiv.21–23.

which they come, and a presence of which they are, as it were, the shadow, a voice of which they are the echo. But there are persons who desire the inward manifestation of Christ to be much more sensible than this. They will not be contented without some sensible sign and direct evidence that God loves them; some assurance, in which faith has no part, that God has chosen them; and which may answer to their anticipations of what Scripture calls "the secret of the Lord," and "that hidden manna" which Christ invites us to partake. Some men, for instance, hold that their conscience would have no peace, unless they recollected the time when they were converted from darkness to light, from a state of wrath to the kingdom of God. Others consider, that in order to possess the seal of election, they must be able to discern in themselves certain feelings or frames of mind, a renunciation of their own merit, and an apprehension of gospel salvation; as if it were not enough to renounce ourselves and follow Christ, without the lively consciousness that we are doing so; and that in this lies "the secret of the Lord." Others go further; and think that without a distinct inward assurance of his salvation, a man is not in a saving state. This is what men often conceive; not considering that whatever be the manifestation promised to Christians by our Lord, it is not likely to be more sensible and more intelligible than the great sign of His own Resurrection. Yet even that, like the miracle wrought upon Jonah, was in secret, and they who believed without seeing it were more blessed than those who saw.

All this accords with what is told us about particular Divine manifestations in other parts of Scripture. The Saints reflected on them afterwards, and mastered them, but can hardly be considered as sensible of them at the very time. Thus Jacob, after the vision, says; "Surely the Lord is in this place, and I knew it not." Manoah said to his wife, after the Angel had departed, "We shall surely die, because we have seen God." Gideon in like circumstances said, "Alas, O Lord God! for because I have seen an Angel of the Lord face to face." And St. Peter, while the Angel was delivering him out of prison, though he obeyed him, yet "wist not that it was true which was done by the Angel, but thought he saw a vision;" but "when he was come to himself, he said, Now I know of a surety that the Lord hath sent His Angel." [4]

Let no one think it strange to say, that God may be holding communion with us without our knowing it. Do not all good

---

[4] Gen. xxviii.16; Judges xiii.22; vi.22; Acts xii.9, 11.

thoughts come from Him? Yet are we sensible that they so
come? Can we tell how they come? We commonly speak of being influenced by God's grace, and resisting His grace; this implies a certain awful intercourse between the soul and God; yet
who will say that he himself can tell in particular instances
when God moves him, and when he is responding this way or
that? It is one thing, then, to receive impressions, another to
reflect upon them and to be conscious of them. God may manifest Himself to us, and that to the increase of our comfort, and
yet we not realize that He does so.

But now to proceed; for there is more information given us
on the subject. There was another occasion on which the Jews
asked for a sign, and on which our Lord answered by promising
one, not to His Apostles only, but in continuance, like the
manifestation He speaks of, to all His faithful followers. And it
was a sign not more sensible or palpable, not less the object of
faith as regards the many, than that sign of His resurrection
which He gave once for all. He had just before been feeding five
thousand men with five barley loaves and two small fishes;
when, not contented with this, the Jews said, "What sign
showest Thou, that we may see and believe Thee? What dost
Thou *work*?" and they proceeded to refer to the "sign from
heaven," which Moses had given them. "Our Fathers did eat
manna in the desert, as it is written, He gave them bread from
heaven to eat." It was a little thing, they seemed to say, to multiply bread, but it was a great thing to send down bread from
heaven,—a great thing, when the nature of the creature was
changed, and men were made to live by the word of the Lord.
Was the Son of man able to give them bread such as this? Yes,
surely, He had a Sign,—a Sign from heaven, more wonderful, a
fearful Sign, surpassing thought and surpassing sight too, addressed to faith only, but not the less true because it was hidden.
Moses gave their fathers bread from heaven; they saw it, ate it,
and were dead; His sign was greater. He was Himself the Bread
from heaven under the Gospel, and the Bread of life. He took
not of the creature to satisfy their need, but He gave Himself
for the life of the world. "Moses gave you not that bread from
heaven; but My Father giveth you the True Bread from heaven,
for the Bread of God is He which cometh down from heaven
and giveth life unto the world. I am the Bread of Life. This is the
Bread which cometh down from heaven, that a man may eat
thereof and not die." Now I am not led to speak here of that
special ordinance in which His Divine announcement is fulfilled; this would be foreign to my present purpose. I do but

wish to consider the gift in itself, and the sign in itself, as these words describe it. It is a sign greater than manna, yet beyond dispute, as the passage itself shows, a sign not addressed to sight, but to faith. For our Lord speaks of our "coming to Him," and "believing on Him;" and He says that "it is the Spirit that quickeneth, the flesh profiteth nothing;" and He warns us, "No one can come unto Me, except the Father which hath sent Me draw him." His coming up from the heart of the earth was a sign for faith, not for sight; and such is His coming down from heaven as Bread.

I have been speaking of the signs which He Himself promised; but others were announced concerning Him by His servants, and these, let it be observed, are secret also, and addressed to faith. The Prophet Isaiah was commissioned to promise Ahaz a sign; "Ask thee a sign of the Lord thy God," he says, "ask it either in the depth or in the height above." When Ahaz would not speak, the Prophet proceeded: "The Lord Himself shall give you a Sign; behold, a Virgin shall conceive, and bear a Son, and shall call His name Immanuel." [5] Yet could there be a Sign more secret, less exposed to the senses, less addressed to the reason, than the Conception of Christ? It was a miracle, yet not an evidence.

And so again, when our Lord was born, the Angel gave the Shepherds a Sign; but which was the greater evidence, the Angel himself, and the multitude of the heavenly host, or the Sign itself which he sent them to see? "This shall be a Sign unto you," he said, "Ye shall see the Babe wrapped in swaddling clothes, lying in a manger." Was this an evidence of greatness or of meanness? Did it prove Him to be God, or was it a trial of faith?

And so again, though it is not called a sign, yet it had been published in the manner of a sign, that the Lord should suddenly come to His Temple, even the "Messenger of the Covenant," that "the glory of the latter house should be greater than that of the former," and that God would "glorify the house of His glory." But how did He come to fulfil these prophecies? As an infant in arms, recognized by one or two holy persons, and that by means of faith, without pomp, or display of greatness. Simeon held in his hands the immaculate form of the Saviour of men, the Light and Life of the world, the all-holy and incorruptible Presence which the Angels of God worship; yet in what an outward appearance! Yet still he said

[5] Is. vii.11, 14.

undoubtingly, "Mine eyes have seen Thy salvation; a light to lighten the Gentiles, and the glory of Thy people Israel."

What is true in these instances, is true of all the parts of our Lord's gracious economy. He was "manifested in the flesh; justified in the Spirit; seen of Angels; preached unto the Gentiles; believed on in the world; received up into glory;" yet what was the nature of the manifestation? The Annunciation was secret; the Nativity was secret; the miraculous Fasting in the wilderness was secret; the Resurrection secret; the Ascension not far from secret; the abiding Presence secret. One thing alone was public, and in the eyes of the world,—His Death; the only event which did not speak of His Divinity, the only event in which He seemed a sign, not of power, but of weakness. He was crucified in weakness, but He was not crucified in secret. His humiliation was proclaimed and manifested all over the earth. When lifted up indeed from the earth, He displayed His power; He drew all men to Him, but not from what was seen, but from what was hidden, from what was not known, from what was matter of faith, from His atoning virtue. As far as seen, He was, in holy Simeon's words, "a Sign which should be spoken against." It is not by reason or by sight that we accept and glory in the sign of the Cross; it is by "laying aside all malice, and all guile, and hypocrisies, and envies, and all evil speakings," and "as new-born babes desiring the sincere milk of the word, that we may grow thereby." "If so be," as St. Peter proceeds, "ye have tasted that the Lord is gracious; to whom coming, as unto a living stone, disallowed indeed of men, but chosen of God, and precious, ye also as lively stones are built up a spiritual house, a holy priesthood, to offer up spiritual sacrifice, acceptable to God by Jesus Christ. Unto you, therefore, *that believe*, He is precious; but unto them which be disobedient, the Stone which the builders disallowed, the same is made the head of the corner."[6]

Let us not seek then for signs and wonders, or ask for sensible inward tokens of God's favour; let us not indulge enthusiasm, or become the slaves of superstition, who are children of God by faith. Faith only can introduce us to the unseen Presence of God; let us venture to believe, let us make trial before we see, and the evidence which others demand before believing, we shall gain more abundantly by believing. Almighty God is hidden from us; the world does not discover Him to us; we may go to the right hand and the left, but we find Him not. The utmost

[6] 1 Pet. ii.1–7.

we can do in the way of nature is to feel after Him, who, though we see Him not, yet is not far from every one of us. "Lo He goeth by me," says Job, "and I see Him not; He passeth on also, and I perceive Him not." "O that I knew where I might find Him! that I might come even to His seat. . . . Behold, I go forward, and He is not there; and backward, but I cannot perceive Him. On the left hand where He doth work, but I cannot behold Him; He hideth Himself on the right hand, that I cannot see Him." [7] This is the veil that is cast over all nations; the want of intercourse or communion between the soul and Him who made it. We can speak to His creatures, we cannot speak to Him. Once it was not so; man was created upright, and then He saw God; he fell, and lost God's image and God's presence. How must he regain his privilege, but by becoming what he once was? He lost it by sinning, he must regain it by pureness. And till this recovery he must accept it on faith; he is allowed to apprehend and enjoy it by faith. He begins with faith, that he may end with holiness; he is allowed to begin with faith, because faith is itself of a holy nature, and the first fruits and earnest of holiness to come. Faith is the religion of sinners beginning to purify themselves for God, and in every age, and under every dispensation, the just have lived by faith. "By faith" Moses "endured, as seeing Him who is invisible;" for lack of faith Balaam met an Angel in the way and discerned him not. Thus "we walk by faith, not by sight;" we "look not at the things which are seen, but at the things which are not seen." We set Him on our right hand, "whom having not seen, we love: in whom, though now we see Him not, yet believing, we rejoice with joy unspeakable and full of glory, receiving the end of our faith, even the salvation of our souls."

Opposed to this generous and vigorous faith are carnal blindness and grossness of heart, of which Scripture speaks so often. Whatever there is of spiritual light within us, is quenched by indulging our natural tastes and appetites. Our Lord says, "Ye cannot serve God and mammon;" He bids us watch and pray, and beware of eating and drinking, buying and selling, marrying and being given in marriage. We cannot have our eyes at once on this world and on the other. Those who live in the sun's glare, can see nothing in twilight; but those whose eyes are used to the shade, see many things which the others will not believe they can see. So is it with our souls; the minding of the flesh, aiming at this world's goods, seeking to rise or succeed in life,

[7] Job ix.11; xxiii.3, 8, 9.

gazing on greatness, rank, distinction, abundance, pomp and show, coveting wealth, measuring things by wealth, eating and drinking without restraint, placing no curb upon the passions, exercising no self-command, living without rule, indolently and weakly following the first idea which presents itself, the first impulse, the first temptation, all this makes the heart irreligious. Then it is that men ask for clearer evidence, and reject the truth; then they say, "How can these things be?" or "This is a hard saying:" or "What sign showest Thou?" for "the heart of this people," in the prophet's words, "is waxed gross, and their ears are dull of hearing, and their eyes have they closed; lest they should see with their eyes, and hear with their ears, and understand with their hearts, and should be converted, and I should heal them." When He healed men in the days of His flesh, it was indeed by means of His own sacred Person, His touch, or His breath, or His voice; but still faith was the condition on the part of the suppliants; and now too, though He is with us ever so really and fully according to His promise, yet He requires faith, as before, in order to our restoration to His favour and to His image.

What a contrast to such thoughts as these is the conduct of the mass of men! Truly they are "without God in the world,"— that is, they do not keep before their minds, in any sense, that He is present, though unseen; they do not even admit that they ought to do so, or try to do so, or approach even to the idea that there are persons who do live as in the sight of the Invisible. Go into the general concourse of men, and what notion is there entertained of such a dependence upon, such an intercourse with, things unseen, as Scripture prescribes? They are engaged in their several trades and professions; they are active, companionable, and friendly; they are unexceptionable as far as the civilities and kindnesses of mutual intercourse are concerned; but what are they more? Have they seriousness? Are they under the habitual influence of religion? Do they sacrifice this life to the next? Is there any thing which they do or do not, which they would not do, or would not omit to do, were religion a mere idle tale? Is God in any one of their thoughts? Do they fear Him? Do they recollect that they are to be judged? What "marks" have they "of the Lord Jesus?" How show they that they are waiting for Him who has gone away only to come back again? What an awful sight does the baptized world present to any one who retires some few steps out of it! O fearful thought, a Day will come when every eye shall see Him bodily, whom they will not learn now to see spiritually! O fearful thought indeed, when all these indolent and careless men, to say nothing of open scoffers and profligates, will be gathered together before His Judgment-seat, to receive their doom once for all! At present they look upon religion as a dream, and religious men as dreamers; they only think of them as narrow-minded men, or superstitiously strict, or weak, or fanciful, or hypocrites, or fanatical, or party-spirited; as persons who profess much, but are, after all, much the same as other men, governed by the same weaknesses, passions, and inducements.

O miserable and most dreadful Day of His coming, and who shall abide it? when those who will not acknowledge the secret glory, shall at length feel the manifested power of the Lamb; when those who will not discern His tokens now, but think His ordinances, His Church, His servants, to be but things of this world, will then see "the Sign of the Son of man in heaven," and against their will must believe and tremble. For "then shall all the tribes of the earth mourn, and they shall see the Son of man coming in the clouds of heaven with power and great glory." Let us be wise in time; let us seek Him "while it is called to-day;" let us "seek the Lord and His strength, seek His face evermore." Let us seek Him in His Temple, and in its ordinances; especially in that most sacred Ordinance in which He all but reveals to us His heavenly countenance, all but gives us to touch His hands and feet, and put our hand into His side, that we may see that it is He Himself, and that we are following no deceitful vision. He said to Mary, "Touch Me not, for I am not yet ascended to My Father." He is now ascended, therefore we may touch Him. Let us, as far as is permitted us, approach Him, who walked upon the sea, and rebuked the wind, and multiplied the loaves, and turned the water into wine, and made the clay give sight, and entered through the closed doors, and came and vanished at His will. Let us see Him by faith, though our eyes are holden, that we know it not. Evermore may He so be with us, a gracious Lord, whose "garments smell of myrrh, aloes, and cassia," of "spikenard and saffron, calamus and cinnamon, and all trees of frankincense, myrrh, and aloes, with all the chief spices."[8] So may He be with us evermore, moving our hearts within us, "until the day break and the shadows flee away."

[8] Ps. xlv.8; Cant. iv.14.

THE SPIRITUAL PRESENCE
OF CHRIST IN THE CHURCH

(Easter)

"A little while, and ye shall not see Me: and again, a little while, and ye shall see Me, because I go to the Father."—John xvi.16.

VERY opposite lessons are drawn in different parts of Scripture from the doctrine of Christ's leaving the world and returning to His Father; lessons so opposite the one to the other, that at first sight a reader might even find a difficulty in reconciling them together. In an earlier season of His ministry, our Lord intimates that when He was removed, His disciples should sorrow,—that then was to be the special time for humiliation. "Can the children of the Bride-chamber mourn," He asks, "as long as the Bridegroom is with them? but the days will come, when the Bridegroom shall be taken from them, and *then* shall they fast."[1] Yet in the words following the text, spoken by Him when He was going away, He says; "I will see you again, and your heart shall rejoice, and your joy no man taketh from you." And He says shortly before it, "It is expedient for you that I go away." And again: "I will not leave you comfortless, I will come to you. Yet a little while, and the world seeth Me no more: but ye see Me." Thus Christ's going to the Father is at once a source of sorrow, because it involves His absence; and of joy, because it involves His presence. And out of the doctrine of His resurrection and ascension, spring those Christian paradoxes, often spoken of in Scripture, that we are sorrowing, yet always rejoicing; as having nothing, yet possessing all things.

This, indeed, is our state at present; we have lost Christ and we have found Him; we see Him not, yet we discern Him. We embrace His feet, yet He says, "Touch Me not." How is this? it is thus: we have lost the sensible and conscious perception of Him; we cannot look on Him, hear Him, converse with Him,

[1] Matt. ix.15.

follow Him from place to place; but we enjoy the spiritual, immaterial, inward, mental, real sight and possession of Him; a possession more real and more present than that which the Apostles had in the days of His flesh, *because* it is spiritual, *because* it is invisible. We know that the closer any object of this world comes to us, the less we can contemplate it and comprehend it. Christ has come so close to us in the Christian Church (if I may so speak), that we cannot gaze on Him or discern Him. He enters into us, He claims and takes possession of His purchased inheritance; He does not present Himself to us, but He takes us to Him. He makes us His members. Our faces are, as it were, turned from Him; we see Him not, and know not of His presence, except by faith, because He is over us and within us. And thus we may at the same time lament because we are not conscious of His presence, as the Apostles enjoyed it before His death; and may rejoice because we know we do possess it even more than they, according to the text, "whom having not seen (that is, with the bodily eyes) ye love; in whom, though now ye see Him not, yet believing, ye rejoice with joy unspeakable and full of glory: receiving the end of your faith, even the salvation of your souls." [2]

Concerning this great and mysterious gift, the presence of Christ, invisible to sense, apprehended by faith, which seems to be spoken of in the text, and is suggested by this season of the year, I purpose now to say some few words.

Now observe what the promise is, in the text and the verses following—a new era was to commence, or what is called in Scripture "a day of the Lord." We know how much is said in Scripture about the awfulness and graciousness of a *day* of the Lord, which seems to be some special time of visitation, grace, judgment, restoration, righteousness, and glory. Much is said concerning days of the Lord in the Old Testament. In the beginning we read of those august days, seven in number, each perfect, perfect all together, in which all things were created, finished, blessed, acknowledged, approved by Almighty God. And all things will end with a day greater still, which will open with the coming of Christ from heaven, and the judgment; this is especially the Day of the Lord, and will introduce an eternity of blessedness in God's presence for all believers. And another special day predicted and fulfilled, is that long season which precedes and prepares for the day of heaven, viz. the Day of the Christian Church, the Day of the gospel, the Day of grace. This

[2] 1 Pet. i.8, 9.

is a day much spoken of in the Prophets, and it is the day of which our Saviour speaks in the passage before us. Observe how solemn, how high a day it is: this is His account of it, "I will see you again, and your heart shall rejoice; your joy no man taketh from you. And in that Day ye shall ask Me nothing. Verily, verily, I say unto you, Whatsoever ye shall ask the Father in My Name, He will give it you. Hitherto have ye asked nothing in My name; ask, and ye shall receive, that your joy may be full. . . . At that Day ye shall ask in my Name, and I say not unto you, that I will pray the Father for you, for the Father Himself loveth you, because ye have loved Me, and have believed that I came out from God. I came forth from the Father, and am come into the world; again I leave the world, and go to the Father." The Day, then, that dawned upon the Church at the Resurrection, and beamed forth in full splendour at the Ascension, that Day which has no setting, which will be, not ended, but absorbed in Christ's glorious appearance from heaven to destroy sin and death; that Day in which we now are, is described in these words of Christ as a state of special Divine manifestation, of special introduction into the presence of God. By Christ, says the Apostle, "we have the access by faith into this grace wherein we stand." He "hath raised us up together, and made us sit together in heavenly places in Christ Jesus." "Your life is hid with Christ in God." "Our conversation is in heaven, from whence also we look for the Saviour, the Lord Jesus Christ." "God, who commanded the light to shine out of darkness, hath shined in our hearts, to give the light of the knowledge of the glory of God in the face of Jesus Christ." "As many as have been baptized into Christ have put on Christ." And our Lord says; "I will love him, and will manifest Myself to him. . . . We will come unto him, and make Our abode with him." Thus we Christians stand in the courts of God Most High, and, in one sense, see His face; for He who once was on earth, has now departed from this visible scene of things in a mysterious, twofold way, both to His Father and into our hearts, thus making the Creator and His creatures one; according to His own words, "I will not leave you comfortless: I will come to you. Yet a little while, and the world seeth Me no more; but ye see Me: because I live, ye shall live also. At that Day ye shall know that I am in the Father, and ye in Me, and I in you."[3]

Now, in behalf of this mystery, I observe:—

[3] Rom. v.2; Eph. ii.6; Col. iii.3; Phil. iii.20; 2 Cor. iv.6; Gal. iii.27; John xiv.21–23; 18–20.

First, that Christ really is with us now, whatever be the mode of it. This He says expressly Himself; "Lo, I *am with you* always, even unto the end of the world." He even says, "Where two or three are gathered together in My Name, there am I in the midst of them." [4] And in a passage already quoted more than once, "I will not leave you comfortless: I will come to you." Christ's presence, then, is promised to us still, though He is on the right hand of the Father. You will say, "Yes; He is present as God." Nay, I answer; more than this, He is the Christ, and the Christ is promised, and Christ is man as well as God. This surely is plain even from the words of the text. He said He was going away. Did He go away as God or as man? "A little while, and ye shall not see Me;" this was on His death. He went away as man, He died as man; if then, He promises to come again, surely He must mean that He would return as man, in the only sense, that is, in which He could return. As God He is ever present, never was otherwise than present, never went away; when His body died on the Cross and was buried, when His soul departed to the place of spirits, still He was with His disciples in His Divine ubiquity. The separation of soul and body could not touch His impassible everlasting Godhead. When then He says He should go away, and come again and abide for ever, He is speaking, not merely of His omnipresent Divine nature, but of His human nature. As being Christ, He says that He, the Incarnate Mediator, shall be with His Church for ever.

But again: you may be led to explain His declaration thus; "He *has* come again, but in His Spirit; that is, His Spirit has come instead of Him and when it is said that He is with us, this only means that His Spirit is with us." No one, doubtless, can deny this most gracious and consolatory truth, that the Holy Ghost is come; but why has He come? to supply Christ's absence, or to accomplish His presence? Surely to make Him present. Let us not for a moment suppose that God the Holy Ghost comes in such sense that God the Son remains away. No; He has not so come that Christ does not come, but rather He comes that Christ may come in His coming. Through the Holy Ghost we have communion with Father and Son. "In Christ we are builded together," says St. Paul, "for an habitation of God through the Spirit." "Ye are the temple of God, and the Spirit of God dwelleth in you." "Strengthened with might by His Spirit in the inner man, that Christ may dwell in your hearts by faith." The Holy Spirit causes, faith welcomes, the indwelling

[4] Matt. xxviii.20; xviii.20.

of Christ in the heart. Thus the Spirit does not take the place of Christ in the soul, but secures that place to Christ. St. Paul insists much on this presence of Christ in those who have His Spirit. "Know ye not," he says, "that your bodies are the members of Christ?" "By one Spirit are we all baptized into one Body . . . ye are the body of Christ, and members in particular." "Know ye not your own selves, how that Jesus Christ is in you, except ye be reprobates?" "Christ in you, the hope of glory." And St. John: "He that hath the Son, hath Life; and he that hath not the Son of God, hath not Life." And our Lord Himself, "Abide in Me and I in you: I am the Vine, ye are the branches. He that abideth in Me, and I in Him, the same bringeth forth much fruit." The Holy Spirit, then, vouchsafes to come to us, that by His coming Christ may come to us, not carnally or visibly, but may enter into us. And thus He is both present and absent; absent in that He has left the earth, present in that He has not left the faithful soul; or, as He says Himself, "The *world* seeth Me no more, but *ye* see Me." [5]

You will say, How can He be present to the Christian and in the Church, yet not be on earth but on the right hand of God? I answer, that the Christian Church is made up of faithful *souls*, and how can any of us say where the soul is, simply and really? The soul indeed acts through the body, and perceives through the body; but where is it? or what has it to do with place? or why should it be a thing incredible that the power of the Spirit should so visit the soul as to open upon it a Divine manifestation, which yet it perceives not, because its present perceptions are only through the body? Who shall limit the power of the gracious Spirit of God? How know we, for instance, but that He makes Christ present with us, by making us present with Christ? As the earth goes round the sun, yet the sun is said to move, so our souls, in fact, may be taken up to Christ, when He is said to come to us. But no need to insist on one mode in which the mystery may be conceived, when ten thousand ways are possible with God, of which we know nothing. Scripture says enough to show us that influences may be exerted upon the soul so marvellous, that we cannot decide whether the soul remains in the body or not, while subjected to them. St. Paul, speaking of himself, says, "Whether in the body, I cannot tell, or whether out of the body, I cannot tell; God knoweth: . . . caught up to the third heaven." And he repeats his statement: "I

[5] Eph. ii.22; 1 Cor. iii.16; Eph. iii.17; 1 Cor. vi.15; xii.13, 27; 2 Cor. xiii.5; Col. i.27; 1 John v.12; John xv.4, 5; xiv.19.

knew such a man," meaning himself, "whether in the body I cannot tell, or out of the body I cannot tell, God knoweth: how that he was caught up into Paradise, and heard unspeakable words which it is not lawful for a man to utter." St. Paul was brought into Paradise, yet his body remained where it was; and whether his soul was separated from it, was a question which he could not decide. How can we pretend to decide what the Holy Spirit may or may not do towards faithful souls now, and whether He does not manifest Christ to and in them, by bringing them to Christ? Again; consider Satan's power in showing our Lord all the kingdoms of the world *"in a moment of time;"* may not the Almighty Spirit much more do with us, what the evil one did with our Lord? May He not in less than a moment bring our souls into God's presence, while our bodies are on earth?

And again; while we know so little about our own souls, on the other hand, we are utterly ignorant of the state in which our Blessed Lord exists at present, and the relation of this visible world to Him; or whether it may not be possible for Him, in some mysterious way, to come to us, though He is set down on the right hand of God. Did He not, after His resurrection, come into a room, of which the doors were shut, yet suffer Himself to be handled, to prove that He was not a spirit? Certainly then, though He is clothed in our nature, and is perfect man, yet His glorified body is not confined by those laws under which our mortal bodies lie.

But further; whether it is difficult to conceive or no, Scripture actually gives us at least one instance of His appearing after His ascension, as if to satisfy us that His presence is possible, though it be mysterious. We all know that He has often vouchsafed to appear to His saints in *visions*. Thus He appeared to St. John, as related in the Book of Revelation; and to St. Paul, when he was at Corinth, at Jerusalem several times, and in the ship. *These* appearances were not an actual presence of Christ, as we may conjecture, but impressions divinely made, and shadows cast upon the mind. And in the same way we may explain His appearing to St. Stephen. When that blessed Martyr said, "Behold I see the heavens open, and the Son of Man standing on the right hand of God," we may suppose he did not see this great sight really, but only had a vision of it. These, I repeat, may be *visions*; but what shall we say to Christ's appearance to St. Paul on his conversion, while he was on the way to Damascus? For then the Lord Jesus plainly was seen and heard by him close at hand. "He fell to the earth, and heard a voice saying unto him, Saul, Saul, why persecutest thou Me? And he said, Who art Thou, Lord? And the Lord said, I am Jesus, whom thou persecutest."[6] How was this? We do not know. Can a body be in two places at once? I do not say so; I only say, Here is a mystery. By way of contrast with this *real sight* of the Lord, we are presently told that to Ananias the Lord appeared "in a *vision*." And hence, moreover, when Ananias came to Saul, he said that God had chosen him that *he* should "*see* that Just One, and *hear* the voice of His mouth."[7] And hence, too, he says himself in his Epistle to the Corinthians, "Am I not an Apostle? am I not free? have I not *seen* Jesus Christ our Lord?"[8] Would he have said this, if he had had but a vision of Him? Had he not many more visions of Him, not one only? And again, after mentioning our Lord's appearance to St. Peter, the Eleven, and five hundred brethren at once, and St. James, he adds, "last of all, He was seen of me also, as of one born out of due time."[9] That is, he speaks of his having been favoured with a sight of Christ in as real, true, and literal a sense, as that in which the other Apostles had seen Him. St. Paul then saw Him, and heard Him speak, who was on the right hand of God. And this literal sight seems to have been, for some unknown reason, necessary for the office of an Apostle; for, in accordance with St. Paul's words, just now cited, St. Peter says, when an Apostle was to be chosen in the place of Judas, "Of these men which have companied with us . . . from the baptism of John unto that same day when He was taken up from us, must one be ordained to be a witness with us of His resurrection." And again, to Cornelius, "Him God raised up the third day, and showed Him openly, not to all the people, but unto witnesses chosen before of God, even to us."[10] If St. Paul saw only a vision of Christ, and not Christ "verily and indeed," in that case he was not a witness of His resurrection. But if he *did* see Him, it is possible for Christ to be present with *us* also, as with him.

Once more: it may be said that "St. Paul was *conscious* of the presence of Christ on his conversion, and that he actually *saw* the sights and *heard* the sounds of Paradise, but that we see and hear nothing. We, then, are not in Christ's presence, else we should be conscious of it." Now, with a view of meeting this objection, let us turn to the account of His appearances to His disciples after the Resurrection, which are most important, first, as showing that such an unconscious communion with

---

[6] Acts ix.4, 5. [7] Acts xxii.14. [8] 1 Cor. ix.1.
[9] 1 Cor. xv.8. [10] Acts i.21, 22; x.40, 41.

Christ is possible; next, that it is likely to be the sort of communion now granted to us, from the circumstance that in that period of forty days after the Resurrection, He began to be in that relation towards His Church, in which He is still, and probably intended to intimate to us thereby what His presence with us is now.

Now observe what was the nature of His presence in the Church after His Resurrection. It was this, that He came and went as He pleased; that material substances, such as the fastened doors, were no impediments to His coming; and that when He was present His disciples did not, as a matter of course, know Him. St. Mark says He appeared to the two disciples who were going into the country, to Emmaus, "*in another form.*" St. Luke, who gives the account more at length, says, that while He talked with them their heart burned within them. And it is worth remarking, that the two disciples do not seem to have been conscious of this at the time, but on looking back, they recollected that as *having* been, which did not strike them while it *was*. "*Did* not," they say, "*did* not our heart burn within us, while He talked with us by the way, and while He opened to us the Scriptures?" But at the time, their hearts seem to have been holden (if we may use the expression) as well as their eyes. They were receiving impressions, but could not *realize* to themselves that they were receiving them; afterwards, however, they became aware of what had been. Let us observe, too, *when* it was that their eyes were opened; here we are suddenly introduced to the highest and most solemn Ordinance of the Gospel, for it was when He consecrated and brake the Bread that their eyes were opened. There is evidently a stress laid on this, for presently St. Luke sums up his account of the gracious occurrence with an allusion to it in particular; "They told what things were done in the way, and how He was known of them in breaking of bread." For so it was ordained, that Christ should not be both seen and known at once; first He was seen, then He was known. Only by faith is He known to be present; He is not recognized by sight. When He opened His disciples' eyes, He at once vanished. He removed His visible presence, and left but a memorial of Himself. He vanished from sight that He might be present in a sacrament; and in order to connect His visible presence with His presence invisible, He for one instant manifested Himself to their open eyes; manifested Himself, if I may so speak, while He passed from His hiding-place of sight without knowledge, to that of knowledge without sight.

Or again: consider the account of His appearing to St. Mary Magdalene. While she stood at the sepulchre weeping He appeared, but she knew Him not. When He revealed Himself, He did not, indeed, at once vanish away, but He would not let her touch Him; as if, in another way, to show that His presence in His new kingdom was not to be one of sense. The two disciples were not allowed to *see* Him after recognizing Him, St. Mary Magdalene was not allowed to *touch* Him. But afterwards, St. Thomas *was* allowed both to see and touch; he had the full evidence of sense: but observe what our Lord says to him, "Thomas, because thou hast seen Me, thou hast believed; blessed are they that have not seen, and yet have believed." Faith is better than sight or touch.

Let so much suffice, by way of suggesting thoughts upon this most solemn and elevating subject. Christ has promised He will be with us to the end,—be with us, not only as He is in the unity of the Father and the Son, not in the Omnipresence of the Divine Nature, but personally, as the Christ, as God and man; not present with us locally and sensibly, but still really, in our hearts and to our faith. And it is by the Holy Ghost that this gracious communion is effected. How He effects it we know not; in what precisely it consists we know not. We see Him not; but we are to believe that we possess Him,—that we have been brought under the virtue of His healing hand, of His life-giving breath, of the manna flowing from His lips, and of the blood issuing from His side. And hereafter, on looking back, we shall be conscious that we have been thus favoured. Such is the Day of the Lord in which we find ourselves, as if in fulfilment of the words of the prophet, "The Lord my God shall come, and all the saints with Thee. And it shall come to pass in that Day, that the light shall not be clear, nor dark: but it shall be one day which shall be known to the Lord, not day, nor night: but it shall come to pass, that at evening time it shall be light." [11] Nay, even before the end comes, Christians, on looking back on years past, will feel, at least in a degree, that Christ has been with them, though they knew it not, only believed it, at the time. They will even recollect then the burning of their hearts. Nay, though they seemed not even to believe any thing at the time, yet afterwards, if they have come to Him in sincerity, they will experience a sort of heavenly fragrance and savour of immortality, when they least expect it, rising upon their minds, as if in token that God has been with them, and investing all that has taken place, which

[11] Zech. xiv. 5–7.

before seemed to them but earthly, with beams of glory. And this is true, in one sense, of all the rites and ordinances of the Church, of all providences that happen to us; that, on looking back on them, though they seemed without meaning at the time, elicited no strong feeling, or were even painful and distasteful, yet if we come to them and submit to them in faith, they are afterwards transfigured, and we feel that it has been good for us to be there; and we have a testimony, as a reward of our obedience, that Christ has fulfilled His promise, and, as He said, is here through the Spirit, though He be with the Father.

May He enable us to make full trial of His bounty, and to obtain a full measure of blessing. "There is a river, the streams whereof shall make glad the city of God, the holy place of the tabernacles of the Most High. God is in the midst of her; she shall not be moved: God shall help her and that right early. . . . Be still, and know that I am God; I will be exalted among the heathen, I will be exalted in the earth. The Lord of hosts is with us; the God of Jacob is our refuge." [12]

[12] Ps. xlvi.4, 5, 10, 11.

THE EUCHARISTIC PRESENCE

(Easter)

"This is the Bread which cometh down from heaven, that a man may eat thereof and not die."—John vi.50.

THE quarter of the year from Ash-Wednesday to Trinity Sunday may fittingly be called the Sacramental Season, as the Season preceding it is the Season of grace; and as we are specially called in the Christmas Season to sincerity of purpose, so now we are called to faith. God does good to those who are good and true of heart; and He reveals His mysteries to the believing. The earnest heart is the good ground in which faith takes root, and the truths of the Gospel are like the dew, the sunshine, and the soft rain, which make that heavenly seed to grow.

The text speaks of the greatest and highest of all the Sacramental mysteries, which faith has been vouchsafed, that of Holy Communion. Christ, who died and rose again for us, is in it spiritually present, in the fulness of His death and of His resurrection. We call His presence in this Holy Sacrament a spiritual presence, not as if "spiritual" were but a name or mode of speech, and He were really absent, but by way of expressing that He who is present there can neither be seen nor heard; that He cannot be approached or ascertained by any of the senses; that He is not present in place, that He is not present carnally, though He is really present. And how this is, of course is a mystery. All that we know or need know is that He *is* given to us, and that in the Sacrament of Holy Communion.

Now, with reference to the text and the chapter from which it is taken, I begin by observing, what at first sight one would think no one could doubt, that this chapter of St. John does treat of the Lord's Supper, and is, in fact, a comment upon the account of it, given by the other three Evangelists. We know it is St. John's way to supply what his brethren omit, and that especially in matters of doctrine; and in like manner to omit what they record. Hence, while all three give an account of the institution of Holy Communion at the last Supper, St. John omits it; and, because they omit to enlarge upon the great gift contained in it, he enters upon it. This, I say, is his rule: thus, for instance, St. Matthew and St. Mark give an account of the accusation brought against our Lord at His trial, that He had said He could destroy and build again the Temple of God in three days. They do not inform us when He so said; accordingly, St. John supplies the omission; and, while he passes over the charge at the time of His trial, he relates in his second chapter the circumstances some years before out of which it was framed. The Jews had come to Him and asked Him for a sign; then said He, referring in His mind to His resurrection which was to be, "Destroy this Temple, and in three days I will raise it up;" meaning by Temple His own body, and by His raising it up His resurrection, after He had been put to death.

Again; St. Matthew and St. Mark also give an account of His instituting the Sacrament of Baptism. Christ instituted it on His ascending on high, but He did not explain the meaning and value of Baptism, at least there is no record of His doing so in St. Matthew and St. Mark. But St. John, while He omits mention of the institution of that Sacrament after the Resurrection, does teach us its doctrinal meaning, by means of a previous discourse of our Lord's with Nicodemus on the subject, a discourse which he alone of the Evangelists introduces. And in like manner, I say, in the chapter before us he explains as a doctrine, what the other Evangelists deliver as an ordinance. And, further, it is remarkable that in our Lord's discourse with Nicodemus, no express mention is made of Baptism, though Baptism is evidently the subject of that discourse. Our Lord speaks of being born "of *water* and the Spirit;" He does not say, "of Baptism and the Spirit," yet none of us can doubt that Baptism is meant. In like manner, in the passage before us, He does not say definitely that bread and wine are His Body and Blood; but He speaks only of bread, and, again, of His flesh and blood; words, however, which as evidently refer to the Sacrament of His Supper, as His discourse to Nicodemus refers to Baptism, in spite of His not naming Baptism in express words. Of course it would be very unreasonable to say that when He spoke of "water and the Spirit," He did not allude to Baptism; and it is as unreasonable, surely, to say that in the chapter before us He does not refer to His Holy Supper.

The bearing, then, of our Lord's sacred words would seem to be as follows, if one may venture to investigate it. At Capernaum, in the chapter now before us, He solemnly declares to

His Apostles that none shall live for ever, but such as eat and drink His flesh and blood; and then afterwards, just before He was crucified, as related in the other three Gospels, He points out to them the way in which this mystery of grace was to be fulfilled in them. He assigns the consecrated Bread as that Body of which He had spoken, and the consecrated Wine as His Blood; and in partaking of the Bread and the Cup, they were partakers of His Body and Blood.

It is remarkable, too, considering that our Lord's institution of His Supper took place just before His betrayal by Judas, and that Judas had just partaken of it, that in the discourse before us He alludes to Judas. "Have I not chosen you twelve, and one of you is a devil?" as if He had before His mind, in His divine pre-science, what was to take place when He instituted the Sacra-ment formally. Observe, too, at the time of that last Supper, He recurs to the idea of *choosing* them. "I speak not of you all; I know whom I have chosen." [1]

When, then, Christ used the words of the text and of other parts of the chapter containing it, He was describing prospec-tively that gift, which, in due season, the consecrated bread and wine were to convey to His Church for ever. Speaking with ref-erence to what was to be, He says, "I am that Bread of Life. Your fathers did eat manna in the wilderness, and are dead. This is the Bread which cometh down from heaven, that a man may eat thereof and not die. I am the Living Bread which came down from heaven: if any man eat of this Bread he shall live for ever: and the Bread that I will give is My flesh, which I will give for the life of the world."

In corroboration I would observe, that our Lord had been just then working the miracle of the loaves, in which He had actually blessed and broken the Bread; *upon this*, He goes on to say as follows, "I have wrought a miracle on the bread and fed you, but the time shall come when I will give you the true Eu-charistic Bread, which is not like these perishable barley loaves, but such, that by it you shall live for ever, for it is My flesh." When, then, before He was taken away, He *did* take bread, and blessed, and brake, using just the same action as He had used in the instance of the miracle of the loaves, and even *called it* His body, how could the Apostles doubt that by that significant ac-tion He intended to recall to their minds His discourse recorded in the sixth chapter of St. John, and that they were to recognize in that action the interpretation of His discourse? He had said

[1] John xiii.18.

He would give them a bread which should be His flesh and should have life, and surely they recollected this well. Who among us, had he been present, would not under such circumstances, have recognized in His institution of His Supper the fulfilment of that previous promise? Surely, then, we cannot doubt that this announcement in St. John does look on towards, and is accomplished in, the consecrated Bread and Wine of Holy Communion.

If this be so, it requires no proof at all how great is the gift in that Sacrament. If this chapter does allude to it, then the very words "Flesh and Blood" show it. Nor do they show it at all the less, if we do not know what they precisely mean; for on the face of the matter they evidently mean something very high, so high that *therefore* we cannot comprehend it.

Nothing can show more clearly how high the blessing is, than to observe that the Church's tendency has been, not to detract from its marvellousness, but to increase it. The Church has never thought little of the gift; so far from it, we know that one very large portion of Christendom holds more than we hold. That belief, which goes beyond ours, shows how great the gift is really. I allude to the doctrine of what is called Transubstantiation, which we do not admit; or that the bread and wine cease to be, and that Christ's sacred Body and Blood are directly seen, touched, and handled, under the *appearances* of Bread and Wine. This our Church considers there is no ground for saying, and our Lord's own words contain marvel enough, even without adding any thing to them by way of explanation. Let us, then, now consider them in themselves, apart from additions which came afterwards.

He says, then, "Except ye eat the flesh of the Son of Man and drink His blood, ye have no life in you. Whoso eateth My Flesh and drinketh My Blood, hath eternal life, and I will raise him up at the last day. For My Flesh is meat indeed, and My Blood is drink indeed."

1. About these words I observe, first, that they evidently declare on the face of them some very great mystery. How can they be otherwise taken? If they do not, they must be a figurative way of declaring something which is not mysterious, but plain and intelligible. But is it conceivable that He who is the Truth and Love itself, should have used difficult words when plain words would do? Why should He have used words, the sole effect of which, in that case, would be to perplex, to startle us needlessly? Does His mercy delight in creating difficulties? Does He put stumbling blocks in our way without cause? Does

He excite hopes, and then disappoint them? It is possible; He may have some deep purpose in so doing: but which is more likely, that His meaning is beyond us, or His words beyond His meaning? All who read such awful words as those in question will be led by the first impression of them, either with the disciples to go back, as at a hard saying, or with St. Peter to welcome what is promised: they will be excited in one way or the other, with incredulous surprise or with believing hope? And are the feelings of these opposite witnesses, discordant indeed, yet all of them deep, after all unfounded? Are they to go for nothing? Are they no token of our Saviour's real meaning? This desire, and again this aversion, so naturally raised, are they without a real object, and the mere consequence of a general mistake on all hands, of what Christ meant as imagery, for literal truth? Surely this is very improbable.

2. Next, consider our Lord's allusion to the Manna. Persons there are who explain our eating Christ's flesh and blood, as merely meaning our receiving a *pledge* of the *effects* of the *passion* of His Body and Blood; that is, in other words, of the *favour* of Almighty God: but how can Christ's giving us His Body and Blood mean merely His giving us a pledge of His favour? Surely these awful words are far too clear and precise to be thus carelessly treated. Christ, as I have said, surely would not use such definite terms, did He intend to convey an idea so far removed from their meaning and so easy of expression in simple language. Now it increases the force of this consideration to observe that the manna, to which He compares His gift, was not a figure of speech, but a something definite and particular, really given, really received. The manna was not simply health, or life, or God's favour, but a certain something which caused health, continued life, and betokened God's favour. The manna was a gift external to the Israelites, and external also to God's own judgment of them and resolve concerning them, a gift created by Him and partaken by His people. And Christ, in like manner, says, that He Himself is to us the *true* Manna, the *true* Bread that came down from heaven; not like that manna which could not save its partakers from death, but a life-imparting manna. What therefore the manna was in the wilderness, that surely is the spiritual manna in the Christian Church; the manna in the wilderness was a real gift, taken and eaten; so is the manna in the Church. It is not God's mercy, or favour, or imputation; it is not a state of grace, or the promise of eternal life, or the privileges of the Gospel, or the new covenant; it is not, much less, the doctrine of the Gospel, or faith in that doctrine; but it is

what our Lord says it is, the gift of His own precious Body and Blood, really given, taken, and eaten as the manna might be (though in a way unknown), at a certain particular time, and a certain particular spot; namely, as I have already made it evident, at the time and spot when and where the Holy Communion is celebrated.

3. Next, I observe, that our Lord reproves the multitude, for not dwelling on the miracle of the loaves *as* a miracle, but only as a means of gaining food for the body. Now observe, this is *contrary* to what He elsewhere says, with a view of discountenancing the Jews' desire after signs and wonders. It would seem then as if there must be something peculiar and singular in what He is here setting before them. He generally represses their desire for signs, but here He stimulates it. He finds fault here, because they did not dwell upon the *miracle*. "Ye seek Me," He says, "not because ye saw the miracles, but because ye did eat of the loaves and were filled." Now supposing the Eucharistic Gift is a special Sign, the Sign which He meant to give them for ever of His Divine power, this will account for the difference between His conduct on this occasion and on others, it being as unbelieving to overlook signs when given, as to ask for them when withheld. It will account for His bidding them marvel, when about to promise them Bread from heaven. They were but imitating their ancestors in the wilderness. Their ancestors, on the seventh day, went out to gather manna in spite of Moses' telling them they would not find it. What was this but to look for mere food, and to forget that it was miraculously given, and as such immediately dependent on the Giver? Let me ask, is their conduct in this age very different, who come to the Lord's Table without awe, admiration, hope; without that assemblage of feelings which the expectation of so transcendent a marvel should raise in us? Let us fear, lest a real, though invisible work of power being vouchsafed to us, greater far than that of the loaves, which related only to this life's sustenance, we lose the benefit of it by disbelieving it. This reflection is strengthened by finding that St. Paul expressly warns the Corinthians of the great peril of "not *discerning* the Lord's Body."

4. In what has been said, it has been implied that the miracle of the Loaves was a type of Holy Communion; this it is all but declared to be in the chapter before us, and much follows from it. For let it be considered, if the type be a miracle, which it is, how great must the fulfilment be, unless the shadow be greater than the reality? unless indeed we are willing to argue in the spirit of those who deny the Atonement, on the ground that

though the Jewish Priests were types of Christ, the Antitype need not be a Priest Himself. Moreover, the incomprehensible nature of the miracle of the loaves is a kind of protection of the mystery of the Eucharist against objections with which men are wont to assail it; as, for instance, that it is impossible. For to speak of five thousand persons being fed with five loaves, may be speciously represented to be almost a contradiction in terms. How could it be? did the substance of the bread grow? or was it the same bread here and there and every where, for this man and for that, at one and the same time? Or was it created in the shape of bread, in that ultimate condition into which the grain is reduced by the labour of man, and this created again and again out of nothing, till the whole five thousand were satisfied. What, in short, is *meant* by multiplying the loaves? As to Christ's other miracles, they are, it may be said, intelligible though supernatural. We do not know *how* a blind man's eyes are opened, or the dead raised; but we know what *is meant* by saying that the blind saw, or the dead arose: but what *is meant* by saying that the loaves fed five thousand persons? Such then is the objection which may be brought against the miracle of the loaves; and let it be observed, it is just such as this which is urged against the mystery of Christ's Presence in Holy Communion. If the marvellousness of the miracle of the loaves is no real objection to its truth, neither is the marvellousness of the Eucharistic presence any real difficulty in our believing that gift.

And as if still more closely to connect this Holy Sacrament with the miracle of the Loaves, and to make the latter interpret the former, our Lord, as I have observed, wrought the miracle of the loaves by means of the same outward acts, which He observed in the mystery of His Supper, and which His Apostles have carefully recorded as the appointed means of consecrating it. St. John says, "He *took* the loaves, and when *He had given thanks*, He *distributed* to the disciples." Compare this with St. Luke's account of the institution of the Lord's Supper. "He *took* bread, and *gave thanks*, and brake it, and *gave* unto them." Again, a fuller account of the consecration of the loaves is given by the other Evangelists thus:—"He . . . *took* the five loaves and the two fishes," says St. Matthew, "and looking up to heaven, He *blessed*, and *brake*, and *gave* the loaves to His disciples." And what, on the other hand, is told us by the same Evangelist, in his account of the institution of the Holy Communion? "Jesus *took* bread and *blessed* it, and *brake* it, and *gave* it to the disciples." Again, in the second miracle of the seven loaves, He observed the same form:—"He *took* the seven loaves and the fishes, and *gave thanks*, and *brake* them, and *gave* to His disciples." And the form is the same in the account of our Lord's celebration of the Sacrament after His resurrection:—"As He sat at meat with them, He *took* bread and *blessed* it, and *brake*, and *gave* to them." And of St. Paul we read, "he *took* bread and *gave thanks* to God in the presence of them all, and when he had *broken* it, he began to eat."[2]

One cannot doubt, then, that the taking bread, blessing or giving thanks, and breaking is a necessary form in the Lord's Supper, since it is so much insisted on in these narratives; and it evidently betokens something extraordinary,—else why *should* it be insisted on?—and what that is, the miracle of the Loaves tells us. For there the same form is observed, and there it was Christ's outward instrument in working a great "work of God." The feeding then of the multitude with the loaves, interprets the Lord's Supper; and as the one is a supernatural work, so is the other also.

5. One more observation I will make besides. At first sight, an objection may be brought against what has been said from a circumstance, which, when examined, will be found rather to tell the other way. The Jews objected to our Lord, that He had said what was incredible, when He spoke of giving us His flesh. They "strove among themselves, saying, How can this man give us His flesh to eat?" Our Saviour in answer, instead of retracting what He had said, spoke still more strongly—"Except ye eat the flesh of the Son of man, and drink His blood, ye have no life in you." But when they still murmured at it, and said, "This is a hard saying, who can hear it?"—then He did in appearance withdraw His words. He said, "It is the Spirit that quickeneth, the flesh profiteth nothing." It would take us too long to enter now into the meaning of this declaration; but let us, for argument's sake, allow that He seems in them to qualify the wonderful words He had used at first; what follows from such an admission? This:—that our Lord acted according to His usual course on other occasions when persons refused His gracious announcements, not urging and insisting on them, but as if withdrawing them, and thus in one sense aiding those persons even in rejecting what they ought to have accepted without hesitation. This rule of God's dealings with unbelief, we find most fully exemplified in the instance of Pharaoh, whose heart God hardened because he himself hardened it. And so in this

[2] John vi.11; Luke xxii.19; Matt. xiv.19; xxvi.26; xv.36; Luke xxiv.30; Acts xxvii.35.

very chapter, as if in allusion to some such great law, He says, "Murmur not among yourselves; No man can come to Me, except the Father which hath sent Me draw him;" as if He said, "It is by a Divine gift that ye believe; beware, lest by objections you provoke God to take from you His aid, His preventing and enlightening grace." And then, after they *had* complained, He did in consequence withdraw from them that gracious light which He had given, and spoke the words in question about the flesh and spirit, which would seem to carnal minds to unsay, or explain away, what He had said. But observe, He adds, "There are some of you that believe not. . . . *Therefore* said I unto you, that no man can come unto Me, except it were given unto Him of My Father."

All this is parallel, let it be observed, to His dealings with the Jews in the tenth chapter of the same Gospel. He there declares, "I and My Father are One." The Jews, instead of embracing, stumble at the truth, and accuse Him of blasphemy, as if He being a man made Himself God. This was their inference from His words, and a correct inference, just as in the other case they rightly understood Him to promise that He would give us His flesh to eat. But when they, instead of embracing the truth which they had correctly inferred, instead of humbling themselves before the Mystery, repel it from them, He does not force it upon them. He does not tell them, that it *is* a correct conclusion which they had drawn, but He recedes (as it were) and explains away His words. He asks them whether the rulers and prophets spoken of in the Old Testament were not called gods figuratively; if so, much more might He call Himself God, and the Son of God, being the Christ. He does not tell them that He *is* God, though He is; but He argues with them as if He admitted as true the ground of their objection. In judgment, He reduces His creed to names and figures. As then He is really God, though He seemed on one occasion to say that He was but called so figuratively, so He gives us verily and indeed His Body and Blood in Holy Communion, though, on another occasion, after saying so, He seemingly went on to explain those words merely into a strong saying; and as none but heretics take advantage of His apparent denial that He is God, so none but they ought to make use of His apparent denial that He vouchsafes to us His flesh, and that the Holy Communion is a high and heavenly means of giving it.

Such reflections as the foregoing lead us to this conclusion,—to understand that it is our duty to make much of Christ's miracles of love; and instead of denying or feeling cold towards them, to desire to possess our hearts with them. There is indeed a mere carnal curiosity,—a high-minded, irreverent prying into things sacred; but there is also a holy and devout curiosity which all who love God will in their measure feel. The former is exemplified in the instance of the men of Bethshemesh, when they looked into the ark; the latter in the case of the Holy Angels, who (as St. Peter tells us) "desire to look into" the grace of God in the Gospel. Under the Gospel surely there are wonders performed, such as "eye hath not seen, nor ear heard, neither have entered into the heart of man." Let us feel interest and awful expectation at the news of them; let us put ourselves in the way of them; let us wait upon God day by day for the treasures of grace, which are hid in Christ, which are great beyond words or thought.

Above all, let us pray Him to draw us to Him, and to give us faith. When we feel that His mysteries are too severe for us, and occasion us to doubt, let us earnestly wait on Him for the gift of humility and love. Those who love and who are humble will apprehend them;—carnal minds do not seek them, and proud minds are offended at them;—but while love desires them, humility sustains them. Let us pray Him then to give us such a real and living insight into the blessed doctrine of the Incarnation of the Son of God, of His birth of a Virgin, His atoning death, and resurrection, that we may desire that the Holy Communion may be the effectual type of that gracious Economy. No one realizes the Mystery of the Incarnation but must feel disposed towards that of Holy Communion. Let us pray Him to give us an earnest longing after Him—a thirst for His presence—an anxiety to find Him—a joy on hearing that He is to be found, even now, under the veil of sensible things,—and a good hope that *we* shall find Him there. Blessed indeed are they who have not seen, and yet have believed. They have their reward *in* believing; they enjoy the contemplation of a mysterious blessing, which does not even enter into the thoughts of other men; and while they are more blessed than others, in the gift vouchsafed to them, they have the additional privilege of knowing that they are vouchsafed it.

FAITH THE TITLE FOR JUSTIFICATION

(Easter)

"Many shall come from the east and west, and shall sit down with Abraham, and Isaac, and Jacob, in the kingdom of heaven."
—Matt. viii.11.

O UR Lord here says, what He frequently says elsewhere, that the Gentiles, who were heretofore thought reprobate, should inherit the favour of God with Abraham and the other patriarchs. Moreover, He says, that they would gain that great privilege *through faith*; for the words immediately preceding the text are, "Verily I say unto you, I have not found so great faith," that is, as that of the Centurion, "no, not in Israel;" then He adds, "and I say unto you, That many shall come from the east and west, and shall sit down with Abraham, and Isaac, and Jacob, in the kingdom of heaven." St. Paul, it is scarcely necessary to observe, declares the same thing most emphatically; so that he may be called the Apostle, as of the Gentiles, so of faith: —as for instance, "the Scripture, foreseeing that God would justify the heathen *through faith*, preached before the Gospel unto Abraham, saying, In thee shall *all* nations be blessed. So then they which be of faith are blessed with faithful Abraham."[1] In the history of Cornelius's baptism, the same great truth is declared by St. Peter, with some accidental variety of expression. "In every nation he that feareth Him, and worketh righteousness, is accepted with Him."[2]

Now here the question may be asked, and has been asked,—If all that is necessary for acceptance with God be faith in Christ, how is Church Communion, how are Sacraments, necessary? It is taught in Church, that the grace of Christ is not a mere favourable regard with which He views us, a mere state of acceptance and external imputation of His merits given to

[1] Gal. iii.8, 9. [2] Acts x.35.

faith, but that it is a real and spiritual principle residing in the Church, and communicated from the Church into the heart of individuals, and extended far and wide, according as they come for it to the Church, and diffused all over the earth by their joining the Church. This is what is taught by the Church itself of its own gift; and the question is, How is this consistent with the impression legitimately produced on the mind by such passages of Scripture as the text and others such as I have cited? *They* seem to speak as if the great gift of Christ were His favourable account of us, and the means of it were faith; whereas *we* seem to speak of it as being an inward renewal in us, and of the means of it being an union with the Church. They seem to speak of it as what any one may gain for himself, and have by himself; we speak of it as a certain benefit, one and the same for all, gained by coming to it and for it. They seem to speak of the way of life as being something individual and solitary; we speak of it as a social and united enterprise, and a journey in company.

To this it may be replied, that it is unfair and dangerous to insist on certain texts to the exclusion of others; that true though it be, that some texts speak of faith and nothing else, still others speak of Church communion and nothing else, as being the way of salvation; and if so, *both*, both faith and Church communion, are necessary, and that one will not save without the other; that our duty is to come to Christ *in* faith, *through* the Church,—and if we do this, we shall observe the rule given us both in the one set of texts, and in the other,—and that they deal with Scripture as violently, who think to be saved by faith without Church fellowship, as those who think to be saved by Church fellowship without faith. For instance, if our Lord says, "All things are possible to him that believeth," yet He elsewhere says, "If he neglect to hear the Church, let him be unto thee as a heathen man and a publican." If He says, "Believe, and ye shall have," yet elsewhere, "Except a man be born of water and of the Spirit, he cannot enter into the kingdom of God." If St. Paul says, that we are justified by faith without the works of the Law, still he expressly assures us, that Christ saves us "by the laver of regeneration," "that as many as have been baptized into Christ have put on Christ," and there is "one baptism, one body, one spirit," as well as "one faith," and that the Church is "the pillar and ground of the truth." Further, if St. Peter says, that every one is accepted with God who fears Him and works righteousness, yet he elsewhere says that "baptism saves us," and exhorts his hearers to be baptized, in order to the remission of their sins, and the gift of the Holy Ghost.

And further, it may be shown, that nothing can be more natural than this union of *various* distinct means, in order to gain some particular benefit, and that there is nothing forced in thus interpreting the one set of expressions in harmony with the other; and nothing in the impression conveyed by the one inconsistent with the impression conveyed by the other. We have cases of this kind every day, and we use similar forms of speech every day. For instance, were a person to say that he would give some benefit, food or clothing, to any poor person who wanted it, would any one say that he broke his promise, if he appointed some particular place where the food or the clothing was to be got, and where those who desired it must go for it? And would it be thought reasonable, if a poor person accosted him abruptly in the public way, and insisted on his giving it directly from himself, without his having to go to the place appointed? and why, forsooth?—on the ground that the other had said that he would give to any one who asked of him. As then a charitable person might say, "Ask, and ye shall have," and yet might not mean to excuse those who asked from the necessity of going to some place, and at some hour, when and where he dispensed his charity; so in like manner Christ may say by Himself or His Apostles, "Ask, and ye shall receive." "Believe, and ye shall be saved," and yet may mean to enjoin upon us certain rules, and to appoint a certain treasure-house, for our gaining that gift to which our asking and our faith are sufficient to entitle us.

This is so plain, that it is hardly necessary to say so much about it; but it may be objected, that it is more true in itself, than to the present purpose: for there are passages of Scripture, it may be said, which speak so largely and absolutely, that to suppose any conditions implied in them which are not specified, any other means of gaining God's favour besides simple faith, is doing violence to their language. For instance, suppose a rich man promised an alms to his poor neighbour, and then, when the latter came for it, said, "I promised you indeed an alms, and as a free gift—and I mean to give it you—nevertheless, I shall exact *one* condition, which I did not then mention, but which I meant nevertheless, and which is not inconsistent in set terms with what I said, and this one condition is, that you should walk some five hundred miles for my bounty, to some place where I have stored it, or that you should first learn a foreign language, and petition me in it;"—every one would feel that such conduct was a mockery in the rich man, and a cruelty to the poor one. Now, it is contended by the persons I speak of, that faith is so prominently spoken of in certain passages of

Scripture, as *the* means of gaining the benefits of Christ's death, that it *must* be meant to be the *only* means; the silence observed in such passages concerning other means being equivalent to a denial of any other; and therefore, that in very truth we must be justified by faith only in a full and absolute and real sense (if the word of Scripture be sure), not in a certain sense merely, or in a certain point of view, but in a sense peculiar and proper, by a prerogative which no other means possesses, whether rite, or work, or temper of mind.

For example, it is said by St. Paul without restriction, "There is no difference between the Jew and the Greek: for the same Lord over all is rich unto all that *call* upon Him. For *whosoever* shall call upon the Name of the Lord shall be saved. How then shall they call on Him in whom they have not believed? and how shall they believe in Him of whom they have not heard? and how shall they hear without a preacher?" And then the Apostle concludes; "So then faith cometh by hearing, and hearing by the word of God." Surely, it may be said, these words plainly do imply that the *knowledge* of the truth is all that is necessary for any person's application of it to himself. Give him a book, the Bible; give him the revealed doctrine, or what St. Paul calls the word of God; give him a preacher;—he requires nothing more. He may at will seize, claim, appropriate, use the promise. He has but to call, and he will be answered; he has but to believe, and he is justified. "For with the heart man believeth unto righteousness, and with the mouth confession is made unto salvation."[3]

Again; how wide, it may be said, how comprehensive, how simple are the words, "Ask, and it shall be given you; seek, and ye shall find; knock, and it shall be opened unto you; for every one that asketh receiveth, and he that seeketh findeth, and to him that knocketh it shall be opened."[4] Is Scripture, it may be said, for plain men or not?—Does it speak to the artless, guileless, and simple-minded, or does it require a refined and cultivated intellect to understand it? If to the poor the Gospel is preached, can we doubt that it is meant to convey that meaning which at first sight it has?—that all to whom the sound of the Gospel comes have but to call on God, to ask, to pray, to believe, and according to their faith so shall it be done unto them?

And such, too, it may be added, was St. Paul's language to the jailor at Philippi; he said, "Believe on the Lord Jesus Christ, and thou shalt be saved, and thy house."[5]

---

[3] Rom. x.10–17.   [4] Matt. vii.7, 8.   [5] Acts xvi.31.

There is certainly much in such considerations, and they are by no means lightly to be put aside. They do seem, with some explanation, to be true. I mean, it does seem as if every one to whom the message of life came, had an *offer* of it; had, if he chose to avail himself of it, an interest in it, a right to take it to himself; that his hearing is his warrant, his knowledge is his evidence, that his believing is his power. This would seem to be a broad truth, whatever else is true; and in the present most miserable state of Christendom there is comfort in believing it. I proceed, then, to explain in what sense it is true, what it implies, and what it does not involve, and what follows from it.

I say, then, that hearing and believing,—that is, knowing, confessing, and asking,—give us under the covenant of grace a title, nay, are the sole necessary right and title to receive the gifts purchased for us by our Lord Jesus on the Cross. And now observe, first, what this does *not* imply.

1. It does not imply any thing about the time or mode of our justification. Faith is our right and title to be justified, the sole right and title necessary; but has a person forthwith that, to which he has a right? is nothing more necessary for the possession and enjoyment of things than a just title to them? Is it so in human matters? is not a right the first thing indeed, but is it all that is necessary for having, holding, and using? Are there no forms to be gone through, no necessary instruments of possession? Or, take again the case of the children of Christian parents. The infant children of Christians have a right to be made Christians; but are they made Christians merely *by* the right to be so made? if so, why do we baptize them? Faith, then, in the general scheme of the Gospel, is what their very birth and origin is in the particular case of the children of Christians. It constitutes a claim in our case that we should be made Christians; it is an evidence, an inward spiritual token from God that He means us to be made Christians; it is a promise from Him who is the Author and Finisher of our faith, that He means us, that He wills us, to be Christians. To him that hath, more shall be given. Him whom God gifts with faith, will He also in due time gift with evangelical, justifying grace: but the first gift does not give the second gift, it does not involve it; it does but prepare for it, it does but constitute a title to it. Again: good works form our title for heaven; but does a person who is fruitful in good works and prepared for the next world at once die? or rather, I should ask, is he without death translated at once both soul and body into heaven? is there nothing to wait for? nothing to go through, even in the case of those who are ready for death? are

there no persons detained in the flesh, who, if they died yesterday or a year since, would go to heaven? are there no saints upon
earth? Surely, then, to have a title is not the same thing as to be
in possession; and all the texts which can be brought to prove
that faith is our title *to be* justified, fail to prove of themselves
that it involves in it our justification, unless indeed children are
Christians without baptism because their parents were Christians, and Saints are in heaven before death because they are fit
for heaven. If, I say, the texts in question do but show that faith
is our sole title to be justified, they prove nothing about any
thing else. A title to a certain benefit is still a title, whether the
benefit has been conferred or not. It does not cease to be the
title because we have the benefit, nor is it less of a title because
we have not yet received it. It is not at all bound to past, present,
or future. It is that *on* which we once received, or *by* which we
now hold, or *for* which we are still claiming the benefit, as the
case may be. If, then, the texts in question merely say that he
who has faith has a right to the benefit of redemption, they
merely say (which is indeed much, but is all they do say) that he
who believes *shall* to a certainty at some time and by some
means be justified. And that they say this, and no more, is plain
from those texts to which reference has already been made. For
instance, "Whosoever shall call upon the Name of the Lord
shall be saved;" a promise is given, but the how, the when, the
where, the by what, these particulars are by the very form of
the proposition left uncertain. Time is not mentioned, nor
mode;—but a *promise* given, that it *shall* be.

But, on the other hand, if we say that faith is the mode or the
time as well as the title, we may as well say, too, that it is the
Author of our justification. We may as well say it supersedes
Christ's Atonement as a meritorious cause, as Baptism as an instrument. And so again of the text; it says, that many shall *come*
from the East and West, and *sit* down in the kingdom of
heaven. Is coming the same as sitting down? coming stands for
faith, sitting down for baptism; coming is our title, sitting
down is possession. Coming goes before, leads to, sitting down;
but it is not sitting down. A title is one thing, and possession is
another. And the same might be shown of the other texts which
are commonly cited in the question.

2. This becomes still more clear, on considering that whereas
faith is in some passages made the means of gaining acceptance,
prayer is, in other places, spoken of as the means; and, moreover,
prayer is evidently the *expression* of faith, so that whatever is
true of prayer is true of faith also. Now it is too plain to insist

upon, that, though success is certainly promised to prayer in the *event*, yet the *time* of succeeding is *not* promised, and so far from it being immediate, we are expressly told to pray again and again, to continue instant in prayer, *in order to succeed*. For instance, "Ask, and it shall be given you; seek, and ye shall find; knock, and it shall be opened unto you." Here salvation is, as it were, put in our own power: to *hear* the invitation is our sufficient title for coming; to *pray* for the gift is the sure and certain means of receiving it. Most true; but does the word *seek* imply one act, and one only? does it imply that we gain at once what we ask for? The contrary: we are elsewhere told to "*strive* to enter in at the strait gate, for many will *seek* to enter in," that is, seek *without* striving, "and shall not be able."[6] Again; "He spake a parable unto them to this end, that men ought always to pray, and not to faint."[7] It is not one act of prayer, then, or two, but a course and continuance of prayer, which entitle us to God's mercy; and therefore, in like manner, it is not one act of faith which justifies us, or two acts, but to live in faith and to walk in faith is our title; and to *begin* to have faith is to enter the road leading, infallibly leading, to justification, by a series of events or conditions, of which faith is the first and sole on our part. I say that the message "Believe, and thou shalt have," "Call, and thou shalt be saved," as little imply that one act of faith, one call, is all that is requisite, as "Ask, and it shall be given you," implies that we can gain answers to prayer at the mere willing. Sometimes, doubtless, God mercifully answers upon one prayer, and sometimes He justifies on one act of faith; but I am speaking of what we have a right to gather from such passages; and I say, that all they can prove is this, that he who has faith has a *promise* from God that he *shall*, shall in God's own way, in God's own time, shall certainly and surely in the event, be justified; that, as he who begins to pray will sooner or later obtain, so he who believes shall, unless he "draw back," be justified.

3. But this is made a matter of certainty by the *instances* which we find given us in the New Testament of justification by faith. We find that faith was not thought enough, but was made to lead on to other conditions. A man was not thought to have all, to have obtained, on believing, but to have a title whereby to find and obtain. For instance, even in a case which admits of being otherwise interpreted in some respects, so much as this is certain. Cornelius was a special instance of *faith*; but did this

[6] Luke xiii.24.   [7] Luke xviii.1.

faith suffice to make him a justified Christian? No; it did but give him a *title* to it. It moved the God of mercy to work miracles for him. There was this circumstance, special and remarkable in his case, that the first spiritual gift was not given through baptism, but still it was not given at once upon his faith. So far from it, he had to send to an Apostle *before* it was given.

Take again the instance of St. Paul himself. By faith he obeyed the heavenly vision, and went into Damascus, and waited. But he *had* to wait, he was not justified. He waited three days—he prayed; then Ananias was sent; and *he* said, "Arise, and be baptized, and *wash away thy sins*, calling on the Name of the Lord."[8] To believe, to confess, to pray, to call, were the sufficient *title* for the gift; but baptism was the instrument of receiving it. St. Paul having faith, was sure, in God's great mercy, eventually of receiving baptism, but not at once.

Again, consider the case of the Ethiopian Eunuch. "Faith cometh by hearing; and hearing by the word of God." This was fulfilled in his case. He read the Prophet Isaiah concerning Christ's atoning sufferings. He heard Philip preaching on the sacred text. He had faith in Christ. He had a *title* to justification; but he was baptized in order to *receive* it. Hear his own words declaring it. "See, here is water; what doth hinder me to be baptized?"[9] You see, baptism was the great end which he was seeking; why, except that it conveyed the gift of life? Would it have been rational to have been so earnest for a dead ordinance, for a mere outward rite? especially since now he had heard, and had believed. Would he have asked about "*hindrances*" to a mere outward rite, when he had already obtained the inward gift? No, he sought baptism because it was worth seeking. And Philip treats it as such: he says, "Thou mayest, *if*." He puts a condition. Men do not put conditions before worthless things. A condition is a price;—men do not buy nothing with something. The Eunuch was going to *receive a gift*, else there had been no delay, no scrutiny, no engagement. Now what *was* the condition? "If thou *believest* with all thine heart, thou mayest." If thou believest. "And he answered and said, I believe that Jesus Christ is the Son of God." Faith, then, was the *title*, the sole *title*. "And he commanded the chariot to stand still: and they went down both into the water, both Philip and the Eunuch; and he baptized him." At length it was finished. The deed was done— the gift was given—justification was accomplished—and therefore, "when they were come up out of the water the Spirit of

<hr>

[8] Acts xxii.16.   [9] Acts viii.36.

the Lord caught away Philip." He did not take him away before; He did not think it enough for Philip to preach. Philip preached *and* baptized; and then he was caught away. Had he but preached, and not baptized, and the Eunuch still had had faith, then doubtless, in God's great mercy and good providence, another messenger from Him would have baptized him; the Eunuch would not have gone without baptism; he would not have been frustrated of the fruit of his faith; only he would not have had it so soon. He would still have had the title, the claim to baptism. But God "finished the work, and cut it short in righteousness."[10] He justified the believing soul through water; and then Philip, his instrument, was caught away, and the Christian "went on his way rejoicing."

One more instance: St. Paul said to the jailor, "Believe on the Lord Jesus Christ, and thou shalt be saved,"—and then he and Silas "spake unto him the word of the Lord, and to all that were in his house."[11] Here, then, "faith came by hearing, and hearing by the word of God." Accordingly, the *promise* was unto him and his; and what next? Let St. Peter tell us what, on the day of Pentecost. "The *promise*," he says, "is unto you, and to your children, and to all that are afar off, even as many as the Lord our God shall call;" and therefore, "be *baptized*." This was the issue—be baptized—why? "for the remission of sins, and ye shall receive the gift of the Holy Ghost." What St. Peter said to the Jews, that St. Paul did to the jailor, or rather St. Silas did it; for St. Paul says of himself, that he was not sent to baptize, but to preach the Gospel. *He* did not baptize, because so great a gift was baptism, that the Apostles wished to avoid the chance of seeming to baptize in their own name, and of seeming to be setting up *themselves* for the meritorious means through which men are saved. St. Paul says, then, "I thank my God that I baptized *none* of you," except one or two whom he mentions, "lest any should say that I had baptized in mine own name."[12] As water is a feeble element, so the minister chosen was the feeblest vessel in the Church, to show that all was of God. Accordingly, the Apostle generally had with him some friend, who, while a companion and comfort to him, administered those offices which he did not take upon himself. Philip was a deacon, and baptized; St. Paul was an Apostle, and did not baptize; and, therefore, I say, it is more likely, in the case before us, that Silas baptized the jailor, and not St. Paul. However, baptized he was and all his; and then, and not before, took place in him the same

[10] Rom. ix.28.   [11] Acts xvi.30–34.   [12] 1 Cor. i.14, 15.

inward change which happened to the Eunuch, "he *rejoiced*, believing in God with all his house." He had *believed* before baptism, but he did not *rejoice* before baptism—he rejoiced after baptism. Men rejoice when they have *found* what they seek. Both the noble Ethiopian and the humble jailor rejoiced on their being *baptized*. Faith gave a title: baptism gave possession. Faith procured them what nothing else would procure, and baptism conveyed it.

Enough has been said to explain in what sense faith is what nothing else is, and does what nothing else can do. He who has the means of hearing the Gospel, and believes in it heartily, has not a means of gaining, but a title to receive justification; he has within him a warrant, not that God has justified him, but that He will justify him. And this was so fully understood and received by the early Church of Christ, that, supposing a person, who was candidate and under preparation for baptism, happened to die before its administration, it was believed that that person on his death was put by God's mercy into that state of salvation, into which he would have entered by baptism. Or, again, suppose a person was martyred for his faith and not baptized, then, too, his salvation was considered to be secured in like manner without baptism. For where a man has true faith, Christ, we humbly trust, would rather work a miracle for his justification, than deprive him of that which He graciously considers as his right. He that hath begun a good work in us, will perform it in some way or other and bring it to perfection. He will, by His providence, create Churches and Ministers of Baptism round about the souls whom He visits; or He will lead them from Ethiopia to Jerusalem, and send Philip to meet them; or He will speak in dreams by His Angel, and send unto Joppa for Peter; or in a prison He will even make a spring of water gush forth miraculously from the rock at an Apostle's voice; or He will, if all other means are suspended, reconcile the soul to Him without the appointed ordinance at the moment of dissolution. In some way or other, where He gives faith, He will open a way for saving grace. For whom He foreknows, them He predestinates; and whom He predestinates, them He calls; and whom He calls, them He justifies; and whom He justifies, them He glorifies.

And now it is plain what a consolatory light these considerations throw upon the present disordered state of Christendom. I trust there is no presumption in thus interpreting Scripture and in thus judging of the state of things which we see; and if not, we may be thankful in being able to do so. It is most true, then, and never to be explained away, that the grace of the Gospel is lodged in a divinely appointed body, and spreads from *it*. It diffuses itself like leaven over the world, according to the parable, by a continuity and progression; not found here, and found there, in a detached isolated way, but here, and there, and wherever it is, as portions of one whole. As well may the branches of a tree be strewed on the earth, and the trunk be in the ground, and the leaves be whirled in the air, and the fruit be at the bottom of the stream, and yet all be one whole living tree, as the Church be divided. It is impossible. None who are external to it are included in it; it is quite a truism to say this. Neither faith nor any thing else can make that to be, which is not. Wishing will not serve instead of coming, and faith cannot serve in the place of baptism. None are justified but those who are grafted into the justified body; and faith is not an instrument of grafting, but a title to be grafted. It is baptism, "whereby, as an instrument, they that receive it rightly," that is, by faith, "are grafted into the Church." And *with* the Church go all its privileges; and on *communion* with it depends the *inflowing into* the soul of its privileges. He who never has entered into the Church has not the privileges; he who has seceded from it, or sinned grievously in it, or is born in a schismatical branch or heretical sect, to him the privileges are suspended. There are great numbers, then, all about us, vast multitudes, who, for one reason or other, through their own fault or the fault of their fathers, are in a position which fails of the enjoyment of the privileges of regeneration. The power of the Spirit, the cleanness and lustre of the new creature, the intercourse with heaven, the light of God's countenance, the fulness of justification, are not participated by these masses of men, at least according to the provisions of the Gospel covenant. But in spite of this, we may humbly, yet confidently say, that where there is true faith, there justification shall be; there it is promised, it is due, it is coming, somehow, somewhile. Whether, as the Saints of the Old Testament waited, and were not gifted with Gospel justification till Christ's first coming, these faithful souls will be received into the glory and grace of the Church at His second coming; or whether they enter into the kingdom upon death; or whether, by an extraordinary dispensation unknown to us and to themselves, they receive the gift here; or whether in this world their eyes shall at length be opened, and the Church revealed to them, as the true treasure-house of grace and home of refuge to all believers, and they be led to seek it, and renounce the sect of their birth or of their choice,—any how, they have a title; if they call, they shall be answered,—if they knock, it shall be opened to them. *Who* have this true faith we cannot tell, any more than *when* God rewards it; no, nor what measure of assistance, what power of spiritual influence He gives to those who nevertheless, like the Jews, have not the peculiar gifts and endowments of the Covenant of the Gospel. Yet it is a great comfort to believe that God's favour is not limited to the bounds of His heritage, but that, in the Church or out of the Church, every one that calleth on the Name of the Lord with a pure and perfect heart shall be saved.

And thus the possession of the Holy Scriptures is an inestimable gift in a country, to those who use it rightly, whether they belong to the Church or not, and so far we may well rejoice in their circulation; not that possession justifies, or reading, or knowing; not that the Bible is our *religion*, according to the strange phrase, which however has, alas, too true a meaning in fact; but the Bible is the means, through God's secret help, towards faith, and faith is the means towards justification. And as reading does not involve faith, yet is the way to it, so faith, though it does not involve justification, yet is a sure title to it. And thus by reading Scripture, thousands, we may trust, who are not baptized, yet are virtually catechumens, and in heart and spirit *candidates* for the cleansing Sacrament. Thousands who are in unconscious heresy or unwilling schism, still are, through faith, in the state of Cornelius, when his prayers and alms went up before God. Thousands who are obliged to partake of the elements of Holy Communion unconsecrated, or administered with doubtful rites, yet have that within them which the fault or ignorance of the minister cannot take away,—a preparation of heart. Thousands who are in branches of the Church which profane men have stripped of holy ordinances, though the two Sacraments themselves remain to it, may through their faith receive *in* the Sacraments those graces besides, which were wont to be given through those lost ordinances. And thousands, who have been born and trained in separation, become, through their faith, divinely enlightened to seek and to join that One Holy and Catholic Body, in which God's presence abides. Such is the power of faith, not to disparage ordinances, but to secure graces.

Lastly, at the same time it is plain, and the face of Christendom shows it, how mournful is that spiritual state, even though happy in the end, in which, contrary to Christ's will, faith is disjoined from justification. Christ willed that justification should come at once upon faith through the Sacrament of

Baptism. Satan has so disordered Christendom, that numbers perhaps have faith without as yet having justification; an interval, not of days, as in Cornelius's case, but of years, nay, perhaps of a life, lying between the two. We see the consequence of such an anomalous state all around us. How miserable is the inconsistency of even our good men! how excellent in some points, how very faulty in others! How clear and edifying seems the faith of many who yet are very poorly advanced in sanctification! how is faith (strange to say) combined with profaneness, or with pride, or with despondency, or with headstrong blindness to the truth! What does all this show but that God's Spirit indeed is striving among us, but that the Church of the living God is hardly here; that beams of His favour are shed on us, but that the Sun of Righteousness is hid; that He has hid His face; that we have aids, but not Gospel graces; signs and evidences of mercy, but not justification; faith producing such fruits as it best may in the wide world, in a wild uncertain way, just as sweet plants might flower, and rich trees bear, on the outside of Eden.

But let *us* bless and praise God, my brethren, if He has placed *us*, as we trust, *within* the bounds of His kingdom; let us pray Him that we may avail ourselves of this inestimable privilege; let us pray Him to bring all others into it, to give light where He gives faith, and to join to the city of the Living God all those whose faces are turned thitherward.

JUDAISM OF THE PRESENT DAY

(Easter)

"These all died in faith, not having received the promises, but having seen them afar off, and were persuaded of them, and embraced them, and confessed that they were strangers and pilgrims on the earth."
—Heb. xi.13.

W HAT St. Paul here plainly states is a paradox to many persons of this day, viz. that any should have faith, and yet should not have the promise. Yet the whole of this chapter is about the faith of the old fathers; and again and again in the course of it does the Apostle deny them the object of their faith. "They died in *faith*," yet "not having received the promises," being "persuaded of them, and embracing them," yet only "seeing them afar off," and "confessing that they were strangers and pilgrims on the earth." "By faith Isaac blessed Jacob and Esau:" concerning what? "about things to come." Again he says, "These all, having obtained a good report through faith, received not the promise." And observe in the text the strong words, "persuaded of them, and *embraced them*;" in modern language, their faith *apprehended* the promise, yet they had it not. It is one thing, then, to have faith, another thing to receive the promise through faith. Faith does not involve in itself the receipt of the promise.

It is equally clear *what* the promise is which is spoken of,—regeneration. "This is the covenant that I will make with the house of Israel,"—thus was it announced in the prophets,—"After those days, saith the Lord, I will put My *law* in their inward parts, and write it in their hearts." Again, "I will pour My *Spirit* upon thy seed, and My blessing upon thine offspring." And again, "A *new heart* also will I give you, and a *new spirit* will I put within you . . . And I will put My *Spirit* within you." Accordingly, when our Lord was going away, He said to His Apostles, "Behold, I send the *promise* of My Father upon you." Again, "Wait for the *promise* of the Father, which, saith He, ye have heard of Me." And hence, when the multitude asked St.

Peter what to do, he said, "Repent, and be *baptized* . . . for the remission of sins, and ye shall receive the gift of the *Holy Ghost*; for the *promise* is unto you, and to your children." And St. Paul, in like manner, says that we receive "the *promise* of the *Spirit* through *faith.*" Soon after he speaks of "the *promise* by *faith* of Jesus Christ."[1] Elsewhere he speaks of our being "sealed with that Holy *Spirit* of *promise.*"

It appears, then, that faith gains the promise, and that the promise is the great gift of the Spirit; and moreover (from the instance of the old Fathers, spoken of in the chapter from which the text is taken), that it is not the same thing to have faith, so as to embrace and apprehend the promise, and to enjoy it; that faith is a condition of Christ's grace, and yet not a token. A man may have true faith, and still not yet be justified; he may have a faith for justification, he may be ordained unto justification, yet the time of justification not yet have arrived; or, rather, though justification is not yet his, still in God's secret counsels he may be ordained unto it.

This doctrine seems to me a very consolatory one at this time, when so many persons have not, or have not certainly, the grant of justifying grace. When we consider that baptism of water is solemnly connected with regeneration by our Lord, and that such numbers among us either are not baptized at all, or in such a way, or by such persons, or under such circumstances, as to make it very doubtful whether it is real efficacious baptism or no, it is a great consolation to believe, that though they are *not* new-born and justified, yet they may have faith, as the old saints had, who were not justified in the Spirit; and that if they have faith, even though they have not Christian justification to the day of their death, they are but in the condition of the old believers; and He who allowed the latter to die without receiving the promise, He who justified martyrs of old time, not through baptism, but in their streaming blood, may at the moment of death, or before death, should it so please Him, justify them too, even though unbaptized, in His own secret way. This, of course, allows no one to slight baptism when he can obtain it, nor to quench the whispers of grace within him, suggesting to him the necessity of baptism; nor does it warrant us rashly to assert that this or that unbaptized person has true faith, much less that he is justified; nor to suppose that such persons as are in a measure accepted without baptism, would

[1] Jer. xxxi.33; Is. xliv.3; Ezek. xxxvi.26, 27; Luke xxiv.49; Acts i.4; ii.38, 39; Gal. iii.14, 22; Eph. i.13.

not have a much higher acceptance with it; but it comforts us with the thought, that *if* a man has faith, he has or will have justification. Sooner would an Angel descend from heaven, or an Apostle be provided, than one, whose prayers and alms had gone up before God, should not, at one time or another, receive the gift. Almighty God has declared the immutability of His counsel to the heirs of promise; that whom He calls, them He justifies; whom He justifies, them He glorifies. The when and the where are with Him. He will do it in His time;—as, according to His will, sooner or later, He takes from earth and brings into paradise those whom He has justified, so, sooner and later, does He translate from the world into the Church, through His Spirit, those whom He has called by faith. But it is not for us "to know the times or the seasons which the Father hath put in His own power." [2]

Now there can be no doubt that Christ meant no length of time to interfere between faith and the cleansing and justifying new birth. A long and dreary interval had intervened in past ages, but that was over. St. Peter's words are sufficient to show this, "Repent *and* be baptized," or our Lord's, "He that believeth *and* is baptized shall be saved." [3] Sufficient too is the history of Cornelius, to whom regeneration was conveyed by a series of miracles; and still, nevertheless, in Cornelius's instance, some interval there was; and thus in the case of Cornelius and of the Jews we have specimens given us, at least in kind, of that long and miserable delay which so often occurs now, when the times of the Law seem to have returned, and men believe and embrace what they die without possessing.

Now if we have in various ways gone back unwittingly to the state of the Law; if without our fault, being falsely educated, or for other reasons, we have rested on faith solely, in an unscriptural way, and neglected God's ordinances; if we have remained without baptism or have not been confirmed, or have not been frequent at the Lord's Table, or have fallen away to religious bodies where that sacred rite cannot be administered, or in any way have been deprived of that full circle of privileges which Holy Church dispenses; if we have thus been at disadvantage in one or other way, and yet are not without faith; if, I say, we have fallen into a Jewish *state*, it might be expected that we should display also a Jewish *character of mind*, and *course of conduct*, and should exemplify in ourselves that paradox, which we so wonder at when recorded of the Jews in the

[2] Acts i.7.   [3] Acts ii.38; Matt. xvi.16.

text, of embracing promises which we do not or do but partially enjoy;—and we are, I think, in such circumstances, as I
now proceed to show.

If the Jews had not received the promised Spirit, it is not
wonderful that they did not show forth the special fruits of
that Spirit which was promised. Now the office of the promised Spirit was to mortify the flesh, to write the law in our
hearts, to enable us to fulfil the righteousness of the law, to
pour into our hearts "that most excellent gift of love," to enable us to do works acceptable to God, and to be conformed in
body, soul, and spirit to Him. The Jews were aided by God's
grace (else they could not have had faith), but they were not
inhabited by it; they did good actions, they had holy desires
and tempers, but they had not that regenerate life within them
which Christians are promised. I am not speaking of this or
that highly-favoured saint, but of the people; they were at best
great now, and little again; in some points high, and in others
low; with one grace, and not another. Some graces they had,
because they had faith; all they had not, because they had not
the Indwelling Spirit. This is seen in some of the instances of
faith given by St. Paul in the chapter immediately before us.
For instance, he says, "By faith the harlot Rahab perished not
with them that believed not;" and what is still more to the
purpose, he refers to Samson and Jephthah as examples of true
and acceptable faith; yet is the history of these men, particularly of Samson, *consistent* with their faith? Nay, did we possess
merely the Old Testament, and knew not of St. Paul's inspired
comment upon it, should we say that Samson had faith at all?
See what it is to be in that middle state between faith and
justification of the Spirit, between title and possession. And
hence it has been the belief of many, that the old Fathers did
not, after departing this life, at once enjoy the blessed rest of a
justified people, till Christ came, and, having overcome death
and risen again, gave them to be justified by that faith, with
which they had so long waited for Him, and to become members of His spiritual kingdom.

Again, the Apostle says, "By faith they passed through the
Red Sea as by dry land." Now this is said of that people "whose
carcases fell in the wilderness," and who could not enter into
the promised land:—why? "because of *unbelief*," as St. Paul tells
us in the same Epistle. Here, you see, even their faith failed
them. How different is it with the faith of Christ's disciples!
"Simon, Simon," said our Lord to St. Peter, "behold Satan
hath desired to have you, that he might sift you as wheat; but I

have prayed for thee that thy faith *fail not*."[4] Peter had before this been commended for his faith, and now it was in jeopardy; but in truth that faith was not from flesh and blood, it was attended with the beginnings of those Gospel gifts which the Jews had not; and which are "without repentance," for they are as inward habits, and He who begins a good work in us, in His mercy carries it forward to an end.

Again; St. Paul, in his own history, gives us an account of the state of the Jews, whose faith was not supported, strengthened, spiritualized by the gift of inward justification. "The law is spiritual, but I am carnal, sold under sin; for that which I do, I allow not; for what I would, that do I not; but what I hate, that do I. O wretched man that I am, who shall deliver me from the body of this death!" How different this from St. John's description of the true regeneration; "Whosoever is born of God doth not commit sin, for His *seed* remaineth in him"—what is that seed but the Spirit?—"His seed remaineth in him, and he cannot sin, because he is born of God."[5]

Such is the case of those who have faith, yet are not yet justified with the grace of the Gospel; and may we not, with all reverence to so great and holy a prophet, say this in a measure even of David? Surely it is no irreverence to speak of what he seems to have been in the flesh, if we think that now he is with Christ in the spirit, in the lot of the blessed, and the light of the justified, though in his earthly life the fulness of that gift had not yet been accorded to him. Surely it is no irreverence to speak of what he was before he had received the promise, now that he has received it, more than to speak of what St. Paul was when he was Saul. Nay, far less, if we may talk of less where there is none. For St. Paul was even under God's displeasure before he was Christian; but David was the man after God's own heart, and an inspired prophet. His Psalms are our portion even to this day. We reverence him as one who was favoured on earth, and destined to be more favoured in heaven. We see in him much actually secured, though we allow that much was but in rudiment. And therefore even we, without blame may notice, and profitably consider, the imperfections of holy David's life in this point of view, viz. as showing the state in which men are found when they have faith, but have not yet received the promise. Consider, then, the high excellences of his character; view him leading the worshippers to the house of God; think of

[4] Luke xxii.31, 32.
[5] Rom. vii.14, 15, 24; 1 John iii.9.

his zeal for God's service; his lofty devotional spirit; the tenderness and the piety of his thoughts; his dutifulness to God's commands; his humility, simplicity, generosity, nobleness, and
affectionateness; and then, on the other hand, view him in
those particular passages of his history which inspiration
records for our instruction, and you will, I think, see by the
instance even of so great a light, what the case was with the
multitude, who, however inferior to him in gifts and graces,
had faith, yet had not yet Gospel justification.

And now, after these remarks on the state of the Jews, let me
ask you to turn to the present state of this country, and to say
whether numbers are not, by their own confession, in that
same Jewish state; and therefore whether it is not true of
them, as of the Jews, in a certain sense, that, granting they
have faith (and it is a consolation to believe they have), yet
they are at best, in matter of fact, in that intermediate, provi-
sional, unspiritual state in which *we* view them, who hold that
the Sacraments of the Church are, over and above faith, necessary for justification.

If, I say, justification is conveyed through Baptism and the
other sacred rites, those who reject the latter, either have not
received, or have lost the former. But on the other hand, if true
faith gives men a title to be justified, then they will be justified
in God's own time, provided their faith endure. Such, then,
being the state of good men who, from involuntary ignorance
are in dissent, or in other grievous ecclesiastical error, do they
not, I say, stand exactly in the state of the Jews? Certainly; for
the Jews had faith, yet had not yet received the promise of the
Spirit, which is Christian justification. Well then, I repeat, if
this be so, we should expect that their *opinions and lives* would
actually *show* that they *were* in a Jewish state. This is what I am
now insisting on. I have said what the state of the Jews was,
moral and spiritual, and now I am going to show that just in
that state, and in no other, according to their own confession,
are Christians now, who neglect the justifying ordinances of
the Church. And,

1. Great numbers absolutely confess and believe, that the
Christian ordinances are just the same as the Jewish. They *own*
themselves to be in the state in which the Church lay before
Christ suffered and rose again. They distinctly assert that Baptism is no more than circumcision. Thus they bear witness
against themselves. They do not look for any high mysterious
gift in Holy Communion, but they think it the same as the Jewish Passover; each, as they think, figures our Lord's passion; the

difference being that, in the one case, it was yet to come, in the other it is past. The Passover prefigured, the Lord's Supper commemorates it; the Jews looked forward, Christians look back. This is what they hold. They *claim* to be in the state of the Jews, in the state of those who had faith without Gospel justification.

2. Next, let it be observed, that they consider justification to be nothing more than God's *accounting* them righteous, which is just what justification was to the Jews. Justification *is* God's accounting a man righteous; yes, but it is, in the case of the Christian, something more; it is God's *making* him righteous too. As beasts live, and men live, and life is life, and yet life is not the same in man and beast; but in man consists in the presence of a soul; so in somewhat the same way Jews were justified, and Christians are justified, and in the case of both justification means God's accounting men righteous; but in Christians it means not only an accounting, but it involves a making; so that as the presence of a soul is the mode in which God gives man life, so the presence of the Holy Spirit is the mode in which God gives him righteousness. This is that promise of the Spirit of life, because of which the Gospel is called "a ministration of righteousness." But the multitude of religious professors at this day whom I speak of, do not admit this; they even protest against the notion. They think justification to be something, not inward, but merely outward; that is, they acknowledge themselves, they claim to be, in the state of the Jews, and though of course they contend that they *are* justified, yet they own that their own justification is not more than an outward or imputative justification. There is no room here for difference in the use of words, and mutual misunderstandings. If we maintain that they have not inward justification, it is not as if they maintained that they had, as if they aspired to it; it is no more than they allow as well as we. They only contend they are justified in *their* sense, that is, in such sense as we allow they may be, if they have true faith; I mean in that sense in which the Jews were justified, who died, not having received the promise.

3. Again. They lay an especial stress upon *faith* for salvation, and comparatively neglect love; they put faith *before* love. Now, is not this in so many words to assent to us when we place them with the Jews? For, whereas faith is the essence of *all* religion, and of the Jewish inclusive, love is the great grace of Christianity; Christianity is religion, and something more; and the spirit of love is faith, and something more. *Christian* faith is faith developed into love, it lives in love, and love is greater than faith,

because it is its Gospel perfection, according to the Apostle's declaration, "Now abideth faith, hope, charity, these three; but the greatest of these is charity." "The just shall live by faith," is a Jewish truth as well as a Christian; "Love is the fulfilling of the Law," is Christian only. When these persons say that faith is all in all, what do they but allow that they are on a level with the Jews,—with those who had indeed faith, but had not yet attained the Christian promise?

4. Again. The Jews, as I have said, had the will without the power; whereas Christ has unfettered the will, and enabled it to obey. "Awake, thou that sleepest, and arise from the dead," He says. "The Law of the Spirit of Life hath made me free from the law of sin and death." [6] Christ, by fulfilling the Law for us, has given us also power to fulfil it after our measure, "who walk not after the flesh, but after the Spirit." The very test of a mature Christian, of a true saint, is consistency in all things. Now, is it not a very remarkable fact, that the bodies of men I speak of unhesitatingly appropriate that melancholy seventh chapter to the Romans, to which I have been referring, and claim it as being accurately descriptive of their own state? Nay, so strongly and earnestly, that sometimes they will even say that no one is, in their sense, a true Christian, who does not claim it also;— and why? because they say that if a man does not find *his own experience* bear witness to the truth of the Apostle's statement in that chapter, he cannot possess that state of mind which they consider essential to all believers. O true confession to the misery of having faith without inward justification! They make the test of a true Christian to be, not spiritual perfection, but confession of sin. Thus they glory, I will not say in their shame, but in their misfortune. They are in bondage; they are carnal, sold under sin; they confess it; they are like the Jews, and they call this a spiritual mind, and say that none are true Christians but those who are in a similar state. Do I mean to promise men that they shall be at once and altogether free from their natural bondage if they follow Christ in His Church? Do I mean to say that we do not, as well as the Jews, in a certain sense recognize those miserable cries of human nature as our own? No, but I mean to say, that *so far* as we feel them, we too are in an inferior Jewish state; that there *is* a higher state, that we are bound to seek after it, and that we can attain to it. But the multitudes I speak of, *own* that their peculiar and intended condition, that state to which they give the name of spiritual, is one in which

[6] Eph. v.14; Rom. viii.2.

the Spirit has no power. Such is the consequence of starting with faith rightly, but stopping short of the Sacraments wrongly.

5. Once more. There is one virtue which of old time good men especially had not. Indulgences were allowed the Jews on account of the hardness of their hearts. Divorce of marriage was allowed them. More wives than one at once were not denied them. If there is one grace in which Christianity stands in especial contrast to the old religion, it is that of purity. Christ was born of a Virgin; He remained a virgin; His beloved disciple was a virgin; He abolished polygamy and divorce; and He said that there were those who for the kingdom of heaven's sake would be even as He. Now, as the Apostle says, "Every man hath his proper gift of God." I accept the word; I do not outstep it; but as surely as each has his gift, so, according to the Apostle, some have *this* gift. But now, my brethren, who will question that the way of the world at present is to deny that there is such a gift? I am not objecting here, I am not wondering, that all men have it not; but what I wonder at is, that *none* have it; and I ask, does not this, if there were no other reason, show, that we have fallen back into a Jewish state? It is now a recognized principle with the world, that there can be no certainty of holiness except in married life; and that celibacy is all but a state of sin. Nay, so far has this gone, that some of the greatest masters of the doctrine of faith without love and sacraments, have actually sanctioned bigamy in particular cases, and advocated polygamy in writing. Too well then does that religion, which they promulgated, bear witness against itself, that, though faith still be among its followers, which I am far from denying, and have comfort in thinking, yet it is but the faith of Jews, who had a law in their members warring against the law of their mind, and who died indeed in faith, but without having received the promise.

To conclude, though it is our Church's blessedness to have withstood the torrent of that error to which I have been referring, yet it could not be expected that her individual members should have kept themselves free from it. And in proportion as the acts of individuals can counteract her own intentions, so far doubtless we have suffered as others have, and in no slight degree. It is our business, instead of exalting ourselves over others, to repent of our own sins, and to try to escape from the disadvantages under which we find ourselves after all. Especially should we turn our thoughts to the consideration of Holy Communion, which in ancient times was used in many or most places to be celebrated daily, but now is celebrated commonly but three or four times a year. If that holy ordinance be the continual life of the Church, if the Jews "did eat manna in the wilderness, and are dead," but if any man "eat of this bread he shall live for ever,"[7] is it wonderful that those of us who relinquish this Gospel gift, and rest in our faith for salvation, should fall back into a state like the Jews? Is it wonderful that we who are the children of promise should not enjoy the promise, seeing we will not accept it; seeing we think it enough to believe that we already have it, or though God offers it, will not put out our hand to take it? Is it wonderful that we have no command over ourselves, when we do not come to Christ, "that our sinful bodies may be made clean by His body, and our souls washed through His most precious blood?" Is it wonderful that we are so inconsistent and variable, when we will not seek of Him such daily sustenances of grace as He offers to us?—when we do not pray to Him daily, or seek His house daily,—that day by day we may walk with Him, and not after our own hearts? Is it wonderful that we have no love, when we neglect altogether that great ordinance whereby love is nurtured, abstinence and fasting?

We cannot hinder others thus acting; we cannot change the course of things, nor heal what is sick, nor bind up what is broken, at our will. But we can act for ourselves, whether men will hear, or whether they will forbear; and, while we so act, they may oppose us, but, through God's grace, they will at length be moved to follow us, till at length He will fulfil in them "all the good pleasure of His goodness, and the work of faith with power."

[7] John vi.51.

THE FELLOWSHIP OF
THE APOSTLES

(Easter)

*"And John answered Him, saying, Master, we saw one casting out
devils in Thy Name, and he followeth not us; and we forbad him,
because he followeth not us. But Jesus said, Forbid him not; for there
is no man which shall do a miracle in My Name, that can lightly
speak evil of Me."*—Mark ix.38, 39.

PERSONS who choose their religion for themselves, or who
wander about from one communion of Christians to another at their will, often urge upon us who wish to be disciples
of the One Faith, which was once delivered to the saints, this
passage of Scripture. They say that Christians may follow
strange teachers, who come in their way, because our Saviour
did not allow St. John to hinder the stranger mentioned in the
text from casting out devils in our Saviour's Name. St. John
came to Christ, and told Him that he and the other Apostles
had fallen in with a man who, though he wrought miracles, yet
did not follow the Apostles, and that they in consequence had
forbidden him. To which our Lord answered, "Forbid him
not." Therefore they argue, as the Apostles were not allowed to
forbid this stranger, neither may the Church forbid strange
teachers and preachers; that all have a right to preach, whether
they follow the Church or no, so that they do but preach in the
Name of Jesus, without any molestation. Such is the objection,
and I propose now to consider it.

Now I deny that the case in the text is at all parallel to that
which it is brought to justify, as a few remarks will show.

1. First, then, this man was not preaching; he was casting out
devils. This is a great difference—he was doing a miracle. Our
Saviour says so expressly; "There is no man which shall do a
miracle in My Name, that can lightly speak evil of Me." Now any
one can preach; not every one can cast out devils. Very few can
cast out devils; nay, at first sight, it would seem that none but a

servant of God can cast out devils. *Man* cannot overcome the devil, Christ only overcomes him. If a man cast out a devil, he has power from Christ; and if he has power from Christ, he must have a commission from Christ; and who shall forbid one, to whom God gives commission to do miracles, from doing them? That would be fighting against God. But, on the other hand, many a man may preach without being sent from God and having power from Him; for Christ expressly warns us against false prophets, and He says that "many shall come in His Name, saying, I am Christ, and shall deceive many." It does not follow, then, because we must not prohibit those who come with a Divine commission from working miracles, that therefore we may not prohibit those who do not come with a commission from preaching.

2. But it may be said, "The effects of preaching *are* a miracle. A good preacher converts persons, that is, he casts out devils from the hearts of those whom he changes from sin to holiness; and this is a miracle. This he could not do without power from God. Therefore he is sent from God, and therefore he ought not to be forbidden. The question turns on this, whether his preaching is with power or not, whether he *is* influential, whether he touches the hearts of his hearers. If he does, no matter whether he follows the Apostles or not. For the Apostles were but messengers from God, and he is a messenger from God because he is able to do God's work, and one messenger need not follow another messenger? What is Paul? or what is Apollos? He is as little bound to follow the Apostles, as the Apostles to follow him: he has just as much right to forbid the Church to preach, as the Church to forbid him. And since we may not forbid him, we may follow him." This is what is said.

I answer, that though such a person's preaching *were* all that it is said to be, though it did work what looks like a miracle, this would not prove that he came from God; for the false prophets against whom our Saviour warns us, are to do "signs and wonders, to seduce, if it were possible, even the elect."[1] I do not suppose that they will work miracles such as God's servants work, but what seem to be such, what are sufficiently like miracles to perplex those who see them; yet these prophets, of course, are not to be listened to. And, therefore, if a preacher, who kept apart from the Church, were said to do much good to the souls of others, I should very much rejoice to hear the report of it, but I should pause and require many things to be

[1] Mark xiii.22.

decided first, before I could be sure that good really was done; or, if so, that it was his doing. What seems good, is often not good. Persons who hear preaching often take up a serious life for a time, and then get tired of it. Or they profess a great deal more than they feel, and think themselves more in earnest than they are; or they take that to be true religion which is not; or they change one bad state of mind for another, and account certain feelings, or tempers, or opinions, or doings to be pleasing to God, which are not so. For all these reasons it is not at all an easy matter to determine that the self-appointed preachers in question do really convert the hearts of men, that is, *do* cast out devils, do work miracles, as they say they do.

3. But again; even if sinners *are* converted upon such a one's preaching, this would not show that *he* did the work, or, at least, that he had more than a share in it. The miracle after all might belong to the Church, not to him. If sinners are converted, it is partly in consequence of their having been baptized, and perhaps not owing to the preacher in question more than to any other accident. Men are touched, and roused to think of religion continually, by a variety of striking accidents, which God uses indeed, which He overrules for good, but which do not therefore necessarily come *from* Him. Supposing a man falls into sin, and that rouses his conscience, fills him with remorse, makes him fly to God for pardon, leads him to repentance and newness of life; all this comes from his having committed this particular sin, whatever it is; but who would say that the *sin* came from God? God forbid; the sin came from the man's own self-will, and God mercifully overruled it to him for good; and, in like manner, God may condescend to overrule the preaching of those who preach at their own will, and not from Him, without countenancing them thereby in so preaching. They are but the *occasion* of the miracle, not the *instrument* of it.

And let it be observed, that persons who take up with new religions, and leave the Church to follow preachers, often grant that they gained their *first* impression *in* the Church. Well, if so, the Church, as they themselves say, has a share in the work wrought in them. The Church did part of the miracle. How many a man, who thinks he is converted by this or that preacher, gains the benefit after all from the parents or the clergymen who have taught him when young, and trained him up in holiness, though he did not profit by their instructions at the time, and who, now that he lives more religiously, ungratefully forgets *them*, and refers it all to some strange preacher, who, at the very farthest, did but put the finishing stroke to the

1308 THE FELLOWSHIP OF THE APOSTLES

work,—who led him to profit by what he had been already taught, who rekindled what once before was lighted, and who, perhaps, *in* rekindling hurts the flame, so that instead of being pure, serene, and heavenly, it smoulders, and is full of smoke, or blazes and sinks by fits and starts, or flares wildly and lights a conflagration!

For all these reasons, then, it would seem as if the instance in the text did not apply to persons who teach new religions now: we may forbid them, first, because they do not work miracles, as the man in the text did; and next, even though they seemed in particular cases to convert the souls of their hearers, which *would* be a miracle, it would be very difficult to prove that they really have done this, both because what seems conversion often is not real conversion in spirit and truth; and, again, because though it be real conversion, yet, perhaps, *they* are not the doers of it, but the Church itself before them. To proceed:—

1. It should be observed, then, that if our Saviour says on this occasion, "He that is not against us is on our part," yet elsewhere He says, "He that is not with Me is against Me."[2] The truth is, while a system is making way against an existing state of things, help of any kind advances it; but when it is established, the same kind of professed help tells against it. Before the Gospel was received, those who did not oppose the Apostles actually aided them; when it was received, the very same parties interfered with them. Let us consider when it was that our Saviour spoke the words in the text. It was at a time when there was *no* Church, when He had not yet set up His Church; we have no warrant, then, for saying, that because men might work in Christ's name, without following the Apostles, before He had built up His Church, and had made them the foundations of it, therefore such persons may do so lawfully since. He did not set up His Church, and the Apostles in it, till after His resurrection. When He spoke to St. John in the text, He had not given to St. John and the rest their commission; even though the man who cast out devils had no commission, still the Apostles had none either. In this respect he was not inferior to St. John, who, though nearer to Christ, was not as yet His representative. Our Lord had said to St. Peter, "Thou art Peter, and upon this rock I *will* build My Church,"[3] it was still future; but after His resurrection He founded it. Then He said to him, "Simon, son of Jonas, lovest thou Me? feed My lambs, feed My sheep."[4] In like manner He had said to all the Apostles before His resurrection,

[2] Matt. xii.30.   [3] Matt. xvi.18.   [4] John xxi.15–17.

"Whatsoever ye *shall* bind on earth, shall be bound in heaven;" the time was not yet come; but after it, He said, "As My Father hath sent Me, even so send I you." [5] Then He *did*, what before He promised; henceforth all men must join themselves to the Apostles, which they were not told to do before. Accordingly, we read in the second chapter of the Acts, that those who were converted and baptized, "continued stedfastly in the Apostles' doctrine,"—but not only doctrine, it was not enough to preach and hold the same doctrine as they, but it is added, in the Apostles' "fellowship,"—they "continued stedfastly in the Apostles' doctrine and fellowship." [6] That is, they *followed* the Apostles; and if they had wished to depart from that fellowship, the Apostles would have *forbidden* it, nor would our Lord have said to them then, "Forbid them not."

Accordingly, when the Christians of Corinth went into parties, and set up forms of doctrine of their own, and neglected St. Paul their Apostle, what did he say? did he *forbear* to forbid them? no, he forbade them. And he gave this reason; "What?" he said, "came the word of God out from you?" [7] that is, did the word of God originate with you? And in like manner we may say to those who set up a distinct sect or communion for themselves, Where did you get your knowledge of the truth? You may think the word of God came out from you, but really it came to you *from us*; nor have you received what you teach, as far as it is true, except through that Church which you oppose. That Church made you what you are, as far as you are Christian; and the Church that made you has a right to rule you, and to protest against you when you will not be ruled; she has a right to bid you follow her, and to claim jurisdiction over you, for you are hers; whereas the man in the text who cast out devils had not received the power through the Apostles, and therefore the Apostles had no claim on him to submit to them.

Afterwards, however, the Apostles were the sole channels of grace; and as they were the sole grace-givers under Christ, so they were the sole governors, under Him, of all Christian people; and as they transmitted life, so they claimed obedience. For instance, St. John the Baptist's disciples were believers, religious men, and in God's favour; but, when once the Church was set up, they were obliged to submit to the Church, and to leave the sect, though divinely founded, to which they belonged. We read, in the Acts of the Apostles, of Apollos, "an eloquent man, and mighty in the Scriptures," who was

[5] Matt. xviii.18; John xx.21.   [6] Acts ii.42.   [7] 1 Cor. xiv.36.

"instructed in the way of the Lord, and being fervent in the spirit, spake and taught diligently the things of the Lord, knowing only the baptism of John."[8] All this availed, and was accepted with God, till He had set up His Church; but when once it was set up, it availed Apollos nothing, though eloquent, though scriptural, nay, mighty in the Scriptures, though instructed in the Lord's way, though fervent in spirit, though diligent in speaking and teaching, and that boldly, though belonging to the sect and baptized with the baptism of him than whom, among those born of women, no prophet was greater. The Baptist had taught him true doctrine, had taught him that Christ was the Son of God, the Lamb of God, our Atoning Sacrifice; and this Apollos doubtless taught in turn. What did he not teach which persons now teach who call themselves especially Gospel preachers? But as the Baptist submitted to Christ, so must the Baptist's followers submit to Christ's followers, Apollos to the Church. Apollos must not stand apart and so preach Him who taketh away the sin of the world; but he must come to those servants of His, who alone could convey the Spirit; he must come for Christian Baptism, in spite of his knowledge of the Gospel. So Aquila and Priscilla "took him unto them, and expounded unto him the way of God more perfectly."

Another instance is given us directly after, in the beginning of the nineteenth chapter. St. Paul found certain disciples who had been baptized into John's baptism. He told them this was not enough, and accordingly they were baptized in the *Name* of the Lord Jesus; and were next confirmed, and received the Holy Ghost, even His miraculous gifts. And here I would observe that, for what we know, the very man in the text was one of St. John's disciples, or, if not, one who had received his religious impressions from John; who might lawfully remain as he was, and cast out devils in the Name of Jesus, without joining the Apostles, *till* the Apostles received the gift of the Holy Ghost, and then he was bound to join *them*.

2. And here too we have light thrown upon an expression in the text which I have just used, and which at first sight may seem to need no explanation: "In My Name." Our Lord speaks of those who do miracles "in His Name." Now what is implied in this? At first sight we might think that every one who uses the Name of Jesus, and professes to work in and by it, *does* do what he does *in* His Name. But this is not so; as is plain from

[8] Acts xviii.24, 25.

another part of the chapter already quoted, where we read of certain vagabond Jews, "who took upon them to call over them which had evil spirits the Name of the Lord Jesus." Here, then, were persons who did not follow the Apostles, using the Lord's Name; but could they in consequence be said really to *speak* in His Name? No; for what happened? The evil spirit whom they were attempting to expel, cast it in their teeth, that *they* did *not* follow the Apostles. He answered, "Jesus I know, and *Paul* I know" (I know the Apostle Paul); "but who are ye?" And now, in like manner, the hosts of evil may say to those who preach without being sent, "Jesus I know, and the Church I know; but who are ye?"

Merely, then, to use the Name of Jesus is not enough to constitute what Scripture means by speaking in the Name of the Lord; we must look for that sacred Name, and use that sacred Name, *where* He has lodged it. His Name is a Name of power; we must seek *where* He has lodged His power, if we would speak with power. He has not left His Name at large in the world, but He has lodged His Name in a secure dwelling-place; and we have that Name engraven on us only when we *are in* that dwelling-place. For instance, you recollect the account of the Angel who led the Israelites out of Egypt into the land of promise, how God Almighty speaks of him. "Behold, I send an Angel before thee, to keep thee in the way, and to bring thee into the place which I have prepared. Beware of him, and obey his voice, and provoke him not, for he will not pardon your transgressions, for *My Name is in him*." [9] The Israelites were to go forward in the Name of the Lord; but it was not enough to use His Name, it was necessary to seek it *where* He had put that awful Name. He had lodged it with the Angel; and to be under the Name's protection, it was necessary to follow the Angel, and obey him. Again, when they came into the promised land, we find still that they might not take up any religion they chose, and use it in God's Name, but that they must seek and use the Name of God where He placed it; for Moses speaks thus to them, "Unto the place which the Lord your God shall *choose* out of all your tribes to put His Name there, even unto *His habitation* shall ye seek, and *thither* thou shalt come. . . . Ye shall *not* do after all the things that we do here this day," that is, in the wilderness; "every man whatsoever is right in his own eyes. For ye are not as yet come to the rest and to the inheritance which the Lord your God giveth you." [10] The Israelites in the wilderness

[9] Exod. xxiii.20, 21.   [10] Deut. xii.5, 8, 9.

were somewhat in the condition of Christ's followers before Christ had set up His Church, and put His Name there. Men might use His Name without following His Apostles then; but when once He had put His Name in the Church, then they were bound "unto His habitation to seek, and thither to come." And, that His Name, which was once placed in Shiloh and in Jerusalem, is now named upon the Church, is plain from the prophet Jeremiah, who first says, speaking of Christ, "This is His Name, whereby He shall be called," that is, under the Gospel, "The Lord our Righteousness;" [11] and next applies this special title to the Church, thus,—in his thirty-third chapter, "This is the Name whereby *she* shall be called, The Lord our Righteousness." His Name is upon her; His Name is her Name. And hence the prophet Malachi, speaking of the Church Catholic, and its perpetual feast of bread and wine in Holy Communion, says, "From the rising of the sun unto the going down of the same, *My Name* shall be great among the Gentiles; and in every place incense shall be offered unto *My Name*, and a pure offering, for *My Name* shall be great among the heathen, saith the Lord of Hosts." [12] His Name is there, where is the predicted "pure offering."

On the whole, then, it would appear that the stranger in the text might use the Name of Jesus without following the Apostles, because they, though Christ's Apostles, had not yet had the Name of Christ named upon them, in order to their forming together His Church; but that ever since His resurrection that Church has existed, and has borne His Name; and to use His Name except in and under the Church, is to treat His sacred Name irreverently, which whoso does, God will not hold him guiltless, unless he does it in ignorance; and then, though his work will perish, he will be saved, yet so as by fire.

And hence such earnest exhortations are given us by St. Paul against division and disobedience; for instance, "Mark them who cause divisions and offences contrary to the doctrine which ye have learned, and avoid them;" [13] "Whereas there is among you envying and strife and divisions; are ye not carnal?" [14] "We command you that ye withdraw yourselves from every brother that walketh disorderly, and not after the tradition which he received of us;" "Obey them that have the rule over you, and submit yourselves." [15]

---

[11] Jer. xxiii.6; xxxiii.16.
[12] Mal. i.11.
[13] Rom. xvi.17.
[14] 1 Cor. iii.3.
[15] 2 Thess. iii.6; Heb. xiii.17.

I have but one point more to dwell upon before I conclude. I have been showing what the text must *not* be taken to mean at this day. I have shown that it must not and cannot rightly be applied to countenance those who now set up against the Church; but the question arises, to what *does* it now apply? Every word of Christ has a meaning for all times; it is not enough to expose the wrong meaning, unless we expound the right also. This is just the reason why so much of Scripture is taken in a wrong sense, because orthodox men have been satisfied merely with refuting the wrong, instead of giving the right sense. The way to refute error is to preach truth: till we apply this text rightly, it will continue, in spite of all our refutations, to be applied wrongly. I proceed, then, to say a few words by way of showing the right explanation; and, in doing so, you will see, I shall be enforcing from the text this very principle.

Let it be observed, then, *who* it was who was not to be forbidden to use the Name of Jesus, though he did not follow the Apostles. Not one who preached *false* doctrine, not one who opposed the Apostles, or interfered with them, or had separated from them. Nothing then can be inferred from the text,—though we take it ever so literally, or apply it ever so exactly to the present times,—nothing, I repeat it, can be inferred in favour of those who *separate* from the Church, who *set up against* the Church, or who *interfere* with it, and *trouble* it. But there are a number of persons to whom the text does more or less apply, and whom we ought to treat according to its spirit. There are a number of persons not members of the Church, who neither have themselves separated from it, nor oppose it, nor usurp its place, but who are more or less in the condition of the man in the text, "not following us," yet using the Name of Jesus. Many sects and parties in this country are of long standing; many men are born in them; many men have had no opportunities of knowing the truth. Again, it may so happen they are exerting themselves for the cause of Christ in places where the Church is unknown, or where it does not extend itself. And, moreover, it may so be that they have upon them many consolatory proofs of seriousness and earnestness, of a true love for Christ, and desire to obey Him and not to magnify themselves. Here, then, our Lord seems to say, "Forbid them not in their preaching."

The greater part of the world is in heathen darkness; sectaries of various descriptions will be found sending out missions for the conversion of souls to Christ, into places whither the Church has not sent missionaries. Now we are not bound to support them, for this reason, because they do not hold the *whole* truth of the Gospel. But we are not to behave towards them in a hostile way; rather we ought to bless God for whatever they mean well in doing, and pray Him that they may mean and act still better.

Or, again, even in a country into which the Church *is* sending missions, it seems the duty of those whom she sends thither to be kind and tolerant towards all Christian bodies who are labouring there in the same cause, *as far* as these latter do not actively interfere with her, or oppose her doctrine, which, alas! will too often be the case. We are not bound to join them, were their doctrine ever so like ours, any more than the Apostles were bound to follow the stranger who did not follow *them*, which no one will say; but we are to suffer them to go their way, while we go ours.

And again; even at home there are many parts of the country into which the Church has not duly come, and which perhaps owe what they have of the Gospel to the labours of sectaries. *Here*, too, as is evident, we are bound to act very differently from what would be our duty in places where they had established themselves in the face of the Church, and against the Church; and, without going into details, it is evident that there is a sense in which our Lord's words in the text apply to *them*.

On the whole, then, I would say this; when strangers to the Church preach great Christian truths, and do not oppose the Church, then, though we may not *follow* them, though we may not join them, yet we are not allowed to *forbid* them; but in proportion as they preach what is in itself untrue, and do actively oppose God's great Ordinance, so far they are not like the man whom our Lord told His Apostles not to forbid.

But in all cases, whether they preach true doctrine or not, or whether they oppose us or not, so much we may learn, viz. that we must overcome them, not so much by refuting them, as by preaching *the truth*. As we are told to overcome evil with good, so must we overcome falsehood with truth; and as in baptism the curse of Adam is removed by the in-coming of Divine grace, so in like manner the reign of heresy is put to flight, not by merely attacking *it*, but by the manifestation of the pure Gospel instead. Let us be far more bent on preaching our own doctrine than on refuting another's. Let us be far more set upon alluring souls into the right way than on forbidding them the wrong. Let us be like racers in a course, who do not impede, but try to outstrip each other. Let us outstrip others in our lives and conversation, "by pureness, by knowledge, by long-suffering, by kindness, by the Holy Ghost, by love unfeigned, by the word of truth, by the power of God, by the armour of righteousness on the right hand and on the left, by honour and dishonour, by evil report and good report." Let us conquer by meekness, gentleness, forbearance, and perseverance. When the voice of error and strife is loud, let us keep silence; let us not be unwilling to be triumphed over as blind and prejudiced persons, as bigots, or as fanatics, or as zealots, or to be called any other hard names by the world. Let us forbid them not. God will avenge us in His own way and at His own time. The weak shall be strong, and the despised shall become honourable. "He shall make our righteousness as clear as the light, and our just dealing as the noon-day. Leave off wrath and let go displeasure; fret not thyself, else shalt thou be moved to do evil. Hope thou in the Lord and keep His way, and He shall promote thee, that thou shalt possess the land. Keep innocency, and take heed unto the thing that is right, for that shall bring a man peace at the last." [16]

[16] Ps. xxxvii.6, 8, 35, 38.

RISING WITH CHRIST

(Ascension)

"If ye then be risen with Christ, seek those things which are above, where Christ sitteth on the right hand of God. Set your affection on things above, not on things on the earth. For ye are dead, and your life is hid with Christ in God."—Col. iii.1–3.

IN the Communion Service we are exhorted to "lift up our hearts;" we answer, "We lift them up unto the Lord,"— unto the Lord, that is, who is ascended on high; to Him who is not here, but has risen, appeared to His Apostles, and retired out of sight. To that ascended and unseen Saviour, who has overcome death, and opened the kingdom of heaven to all believers, this day and all days, but especially at this season, when we commemorate His Resurrection and Ascension, are we bound to rise in spirit after His pattern. Far otherwise, alas! is it with the many: they are hindered, nay, possessed and absorbed by this world, and they cannot rise because they have no wings. Prayer and fasting have been called the wings of the soul, and they who neither fast nor pray, cannot follow Christ. They cannot lift up their hearts to Him. They have no treasure above, but their treasure, and their heart, and their faculties are all upon the earth; the earth is their portion, and not heaven.

Great, then, is the contrast between the many, and those holy and blessed souls (and may we be in their company!) who rise with Christ, and set their affection on things above, not on things on the earth. The one are in light and peace, the others form the crowd who are thronging and hurrying along the broad way "which leadeth to destruction;" who are in tumult, warfare, anxiety, and bitterness, or, at least, in coldness and barrenness of mind; or, at best, in but a short-lived merriment, hollow and restless; or altogether blind to the future. This is the case of the many; they walk without aim or object, they live irreligiously, or in lukewarmness, yet have nothing to say in their defence. They follow whatever strikes them and pleases them; they indulge their natural tastes. They do not think of forming their tastes and principles, and of rising higher than they are, but they sink and debase themselves to their most earthly feelings and most sensual inclinations, because these happen to be the most powerful. On the contrary, holy souls take a separate course; they have risen with Christ, and they are like persons who have climbed a mountain and are reposing at the top. All is noise and tumult, mist and darkness at its foot; but on the mountain's top it is so very still, so very calm and serene, so pure, so clear, so bright, so heavenly, that to their sensations it is as if the din of earth did not sound below, and shadows and gloom were no where to be found.

And, indeed, the mountain's top is a frequent image in Scripture, under which the Almighty Spirit speaks to us of our calling in Christ. Thus, for instance, it was prophesied of the Christian Church, "that the mountain of the Lord's House should be established in the top of the mountains . . . and many people should go and say, Come ye, and let us go up to the mountain of the Lord." And, in like manner, the Temple built by Solomon was upon a high place; doubtless, among other reasons, which at first sight seem of an opposite nature, by way of showing us that religion consists in retiring from the world, and rising towards heaven. "He chose the tribe of Judah," says the Psalmist, "even the hill of Sion which He loved. And there He built His Temple on high."[1] I do not mean, of course, that a man can be religious who neglects his duties of this world; but that there is an inner and truer life in religious men, beyond the life and conversation which others see, or, in the words of the text, their "life is hid with Christ in God." Christ, indeed, Himself worketh hitherto, as His Father worketh, and He bids us also "work while it is day;" yet, for all this, it is true that the Father and the Son are invisible, that They have an ineffable union with each other, and are not in any dependence upon the mortal concerns of this world; and so we, in our finite measure, must live after Their Divine pattern, holding communion with Them, as if we were at the top of the Mount, while we perform our duties towards that sinful and irreligious world which lies at the foot of it.

The history of Moses affords us another instance of this lifting up of the heart to God, and that, too, represented to us under the same image. He went up to the Mount for forty days, and there he saw visions. And observe, he remained all this time without eating bread or drinking water. That miraculous fast

---

[1] Is. ii.2, 3; Ps. lxxviii.69, 70.

was a lesson to us, how it is that we Christians are to draw near to God. But observe, again, while he was on the Mount, what was going on in the plain. *There* was the turbulence, the ungodliness, the sin of the world. His servant Joshua said, as they heard the noise of the shouting, "There is a noise of war in the camp:" but Moses said, "It is not the voice of them that shout for mastery, neither is it the voice of them that cry for being overcome: but the noise of them that sing do I hear."[2]

Our Saviour's own history gives us another striking instance of this Divine communion, and the troublesome world in contrast. When He ascended the Mount of Transfiguration with His three Apostles, on the summit all was still and calm as heaven. He appeared in glory; Moses and Elias with Him; the Father's voice was heard: St. Peter said, "Master, it is good for us to be here." Then he and his brother Apostles felt that their life was hid with Christ in God. But when they came down the mountain, how the scene was changed! It was descending from heaven to the world. "When He came to His disciples," says the Evangelist, "He saw a great multitude about them, and the scribes questioning with them. And straightway all the people, when they beheld Him, were greatly amazed, and running to Him, saluted Him." And He found that the Apostles were trying to cast out a devil, and could not. And then He spoke the word, conformable with Moses' deed, "This kind can come forth by nothing, but by prayer and fasting."[3]

And again; we may even say that, when our Lord was lifted up on the Cross, then, too, He presented to us the same example of a soul raised heavenwards and hid in God, with the tumultuous world at its feet. The unbelieving multitude swarmed about the Cross, they that passed by reviled Him, and the scribes mocked Him. Meanwhile, He Himself was, amid His agony, in Divine contemplations. He said, "Father, forgive them;" "Why hast Thou forsaken Me?" "It is finished;" "Into Thy hands I commend My Spirit." And as He was hid in God, so too, even at that awful moment, one was at His side gazing on Him, and hid in God with Him. The penitent thief said, "Lord, remember me when Thou comest into Thy kingdom; and Jesus said unto him, Verily, I say unto thee, To-day shalt thou be with Me in paradise."[4]

And much more on His resurrection was He withdrawn from this troublesome world, and at peace, as the Psalmist foretold it. "I have set My King upon My holy *hill* of Sion." "Ever since the

[2] Exod. xxxii.17, 18.   [3] Mark ix.5, 14, 15, 29.   [4] Luke xxiii.42, 43.

world began hath Thy seat been prepared; Thou art from ever-lasting. The floods are risen, O Lord, the floods have lift up their voice; the floods lift up their waves. The waves of the sea are mighty and rage horribly; but yet the Lord, who dwelleth on high, is mightier."[5]

These passages may be taken as types, if not as instances, of the doctrine and precept which the text contains. Christ is risen on high, we must rise with Him. He is gone away out of sight, and we must follow Him. He is gone to the Father, we, too, must take care that our new life is hid with Christ in God. This was the gracious promise, which is signified in the prayer He offered before His passion for all His disciples, even to the end of the world. "Holy Father," He said, "keep through Thine own Name, those whom Thou hast given Me, that they may be one, as We are. . . . I pray not that Thou shouldest take them out of the world, but that Thou shouldest keep them from the evil. They are not of the world, even as I am not of the world. . . . Neither pray I for these alone, but for them also which shall believe on Me through their word; that they all may be one, as Thou, Father, art in Me, and I in Thee; that they may be one in Us. . . . I in them, and Thou in Me, that they may be made perfect in one . . . that the love wherewith Thou hast loved Me, may be in them, and I in them."[6] Agreeably to this sacred and awful announcement, St. Paul speaks in the text and following verses; "If ye, then, be risen with Christ," he says, "seek those things which are above, where Christ sitteth at the right hand of God. Set your affection on things above, not on things on the earth. For ye are dead, and your life is hid with Christ in God. Mortify, therefore, your members which are upon the earth."

It is then the duty and the privilege of all disciples of our glorified Saviour, to be exalted and transfigured with Him; to live in heaven in their thoughts, motives, aims, desires, likings, prayers, praises, intercessions, even while they are in the flesh; to look like other men, to be busy like other men, to be passed over in the crowd of men, or even to be scorned or oppressed, as other men may be, but the while to have a secret channel of communication with the Most High, a gift the world knows not of; to have their life *hid* with Christ in God. Men of this world live in this world, and depend upon it; they place their happiness in this world; they look out for its honours or comforts. *Their* life is not hid. And every one they meet they suppose to be like-minded. They think they can be as sure that

----

[5] Ps. ii.6; xciii.3–5.   [6] John xvii.11, 15, 16, 20, 21, 23, 26.

every other man looks out for the things which they covet, as they can be sure he has the same outward appearance, the same make, a soul and body, eyes and tongue, hands and feet. They look up and down the world, and, as far as they see, one man is just like another. They know that a great many, nay, far the greater part, are like themselves, lovers of this world, and they infer, in consequence, that all are such. They discredit the possibility of any other motives and views being paramount in a man but those of this world. They admit, indeed, that a man may be *influenced* by religious motives, but to be *governed* by them, *to live* by them, to own them as turning points, and primary and ultimate laws of his conduct, this is what they do not credit. They have devised proverbs and sayings to the effect that every man has his price; that all of us have our weak side; that religion is a beautiful theory; and that the most religious man is only he who hides most skilfully from himself, as well as from others, his own love of the world; and that men would not be men if they did not love and desire wealth and honour. And, in accordance with these views, they imputed all base and evil things to our Lord Himself, rather than believe Him to be what He said He was. They said He was a deceiver; that He wished to make Himself a king; that His miracles were wrought through Beelzebub. But He all the while, the Son of Man, was but in outward act sojourning here, and was in spirit in heaven. Follow Him into the wilderness during His forty days' fast, when He did neither eat nor drink; or after the devil's temptation, when Angels came and ministered unto Him; or go with Him up that mountain to pray, where, as I have already said, He was transfigured, and talked with Moses and Elias; and you will see where He really was, and with whom, while He sojourned upon earth,—with Saints and Angels, with His Father, who announced Him as His beloved Son, and with the Holy Ghost, who descended upon Him. He was "the Son of Man which is in heaven," and "had meat to eat" which others "knew not of."

And such in our measure shall we be, both in the appearance and in the reality, if we be His. "Truly our fellowship is with the Father, and with His Son Jesus Christ;" but, as far as this world goes, we shall be of little account. "The world knoweth us not, because it knew Him not."[7] Or, more than this, we may be perhaps ridiculed for our religion, despised, or punished; "If they have called the Master of the house Beelzebub, how much more them of His household?"[8] Such is the condition of those who

[7] 1 John i.3; iii.1.   [8] Matt. x.25.

rise with Christ. He rose in the night, when no one saw Him; and we, too, rise we know not when nor how. Nor does any one know any thing of our religious history, of our turnings to God, of our growings in grace, of our successes, but God Himself, who secretly is the cause of them.

In this way let us enjoy and profit by this holy season; Christ hath "died, yea, rather hath risen again, who is even at the right hand of God, who also maketh intercession for us." Wonderful things had taken place, while the world seemed to go on as usual. Pontius Pilate thought himself like other governors. The Jewish rulers went on with the aims and the prejudices which had heretofore governed them. Herod went on in his career of sin, and having seen and put to death one prophet, hoped to see miracles from a second. They all viewed all things as of this world; they said, "tomorrow shall be as to-day, and much more abundant." They heard the news and saw the sights and provided for the needs of the moment, and forgot the thought of God. Thus men went on at the foot of the mount, and they cared not for what was on the summit. They did not understand that another and marvellous system, contrary to this world, was proceeding forward under the veil of this world. So it was then: so it is now. The world witnesses not the secret communion of the Saints of God, their prayers, praises, and intercessions. But *they* have the present privileges of saints, not-withstanding,—a knowledge, and a joy, and a strength, which they cannot compass or describe, and would not if they could. "O how plentiful is Thy goodness, which Thou hast laid up for them that fear Thee; and that Thou hast prepared for them that put their trust in Thee, even before the sons of men." Are they in anxiety? "Thou shalt hide them privily by Thine own presence from the provoking of all men; Thou shalt keep them secretly in Thy tabernacle from the strife of tongues." Are they in disappointment? "Thou hast put gladness in their heart, since the time that their enemies' corn, and wine, and oil increased." Are they despised by the prosperous? "*They* have children at their desire," says another Psalm, "and leave the rest of their substance for their babes; but as for me, I will behold Thy presence in righteousness, and when I awake up after Thy likeness, I shall be satisfied with it." Are they in despondency? The Psalmist has provided them with a consolation: "Nevertheless, I am alway by Thee, For Thou hast holden me by my right hand; Thou shalt guide me with Thy counsel, and after that receive me with glory. Whom have I in heaven but Thee? and there is none upon earth that I desire in comparison of Thee.

My flesh and my heart faileth, but God is the strength of my heart, and my portion for ever." Are they in peril? "Whoso dwelleth under the defence of the Most High, shall abide under the shadow of the Almighty . . . a thousand shall fall beside thee, and ten thousand at thy right hand, but it shall not come nigh thee." Thus there is fulness without measure for every need, to be found in Him with whom our life is lodged; there is what will "satisfy us with the plenteousness of His house, who gives us to drink of His pleasures, as out of the river. For with Him is the well of life, and in His light shall we see light." So that they may fittingly cry out, "Praise the Lord, O my soul, and all that is within me praise His holy name . . . who forgiveth all thy sin, and healeth all thine infirmities; who saveth thy life from destruction, and crowneth thee with mercy and lovingkindness; who satisfieth thy mouth with good things, making thee young and lusty as an eagle."[9]

All this, my brethren, I say is our portion, if we choose but to accept it. "Who shall ascend into the hill of the Lord, or who shall rise up in His holy place? Who shall dwell in Thy tabernacle, or who shall rest upon Thy holy hill? Even he that leadeth an uncorrupt life, and doeth the thing that is right, and speaketh the truth from his heart. He shall receive the blessing from the Lord, and righteousness from the God of his salvation. This is the generation of them that seek Him, even of them that seek thy face, O Jacob." Aspire, then, to be "fellow-citizens of the Saints and of the household of God." Follow their steps as they have followed Christ. Though the hill be steep, yet faint not, for the reward is great; and till you have made the trial, you can form no idea how great that reward is, or how high its nature. The invitation runs, "O taste, and see how gracious the Lord is." If you have hitherto thought too little of these things, if you have thought religion lies *merely* in what it certainly does consist in also, in filling your worldly station well, in being amiable, and well-behaved, and considerate, and orderly,—but if you have thought it was nothing more than this, if you have neglected to stir up the great gift of God which is lodged deep within you, the gift of election and regeneration, if you have been scanty in your devotions, in intercession, prayer, and praise, and if, in consequence, you have little or nothing of the sweetness, the winning grace, the innocence, the freshness, the tenderness, the cheerfulness, the composure of the elect of

[9] Ps. xxxi.21, 22; iv.8; xvii.15, 16; lxxiii.22–25; xci.1–7; xxxvi.8, 9; ciii.1, 3–5.

God, if you are at present really deficient in praying, and other divine exercises, make a new beginning henceforth. Start, now, with this holy season, and rise with Christ. See, He offers you His hand; He is rising; rise with Him. Mount up from the grave of the old Adam; from grovelling cares, and jealousies, and fretfulness, and worldly aims; from the thraldom of habit, from the tumult of passion, from the fascinations of the flesh, from a cold, worldly, calculating spirit, from frivolity, from selfishness, from effeminacy, from self-conceit and highmindedness. Henceforth set about doing what it is so difficult to do, but what should not, must not be left undone; watch, and pray, and meditate, that is, according to the leisure which God has given you. Give freely of your time to your Lord and Saviour, if you have it. If you have little, show your sense of the privilege by giving that little. But any how, show that your heart and your desires, show that your life is with your God. Set aside every day times for seeking Him. Humble yourself that you have been hitherto so languid and uncertain. Live more strictly to Him; take His yoke upon your shoulder; live by rule. I am not calling on you to go out of the world, or to abandon your duties in the world, but to redeem the time; not to give hours to mere amusement or society, while you give minutes to Christ; not to pray to Him only when you are tired, and fit for nothing but sleep; not altogether to omit to praise Him, or to intercede for the world and the Church; but in good measure to realize honestly the words of the text, to "set your affection on things above;" and to prove that you are His, in that your heart is risen with Him, and your life hid in Him.

WARFARE THE CONDITION
OF VICTORY

(Ascension)

*"And they worshipped Him, and returned to Jerusalem
with great joy: and were continually in the Temple, praising and
blessing God. Amen."*—Luke xxiv.52, 53.

For forty days after His resurrection did our Saviour Christ
endure to remain below, at a distance from the glory which
He had purchased. The glory was now His, He might have entered into it. Had He not had enough of earth? what should
detain Him here, instead of returning to the Father, and taking
possession of His throne? He delayed in order to comfort and
instruct those who had forsaken Him in the hour of trial. A
time had just passed when their faith had all but failed, even
while they had His pattern before their eyes; and a time, or
rather a long period was in prospect, when heavier trials far
were to come upon them, yet He was to be withdrawn. They
hitherto understood not that suffering is the path to glory, and
that none sit down upon Christ's throne, who do not first overcome, as He overcame. He stayed to impress upon them this
lesson, lest they should still misunderstand the Gospel, and fail
a second time. "Ought not Christ," He said, "to suffer these
things, and to enter into His glory?" And having taught them
fully, after forty days, at length He rose above the troubles of
this world. He rose above the atmosphere of sin, sorrow, and
remorse, which broods over it. He entered into the region of
peace and joy, into the pure light, the dwelling-place of Angels,
the courts of the Most High, through which resound continually the chants of blessed spirits and the praises of the Seraphim.
There He entered, leaving His brethren in due season to come
after Him, by the light of His example, and the grace of His
Spirit.

Yet, though forty days was a long season for Him to stay, it
was but a short while for the Apostles to have Him among

them. What feeling must have been theirs, when He parted from them? So late found, so early lost again. Hardly recognized, and then snatched away. The history of the two disciples at Emmaus was a figure or picture of the condition of the eleven. Their eyes were holden that they should not know Him, while He talked with them for three years; then suddenly they were opened, and He forthwith vanished away. So had it been, I say, with all of them. "Have I been so long time with you, and yet hast thou not known Me, Philip?"[1] had already been His expostulation with one of them. They had not known Him all through His ministry. Peter, indeed, had confessed Him to be the Christ, the Son of the Living God; but even he showed inconsistency and change of mind in his comprehension of this great truth. They did not understand at that time who and what He was. But after His resurrection it was otherwise: Thomas touched His hands and His side, and said, "My Lord and my God;" in like manner, they all began to know Him; at length they recognized Him as the Living Bread which came down from heaven, and was the Life of the world. But hardly had they recognized Him, when He withdrew Himself once for all from their sight, never to see them again, or to be seen by them on earth; never to visit earth again, till He comes at the last day to receive all Saints unto Himself, and to take them to their rest. "So, then, after the Lord had spoken unto them, He was received up into heaven, and sat on the right hand of God."[2] Late found, early lost. This, perhaps, was the Apostles' first feeling on His parting from them. And the like often happens here below. We understand our blessings just when about to forfeit them; prospects are most hopeful, just when they are to be hopelessly clouded. Years upon years we have had great privileges, the light of truth, the presence of holy men, opportunities of religious improvement, kind and tender parents. Yet we knew not, or thought not of our happiness; we valued not our gift; and then it is taken away, just when we have begun to value it.

What a time must that forty days have been, during which, while He taught them, all His past teaching must have risen in their minds, and their thoughts then must have recurred in overpowering contrast to their thoughts now. His manner of life, His ministry, His discourses, His parables, His miracles, His meekness, gravity, incomprehensible majesty, the mystery of His grief and joy; the agony, the scourge, the cross, the

---

[1] John xiv.9.   [2] Mark xvi.19.

crown of thorns, the spear, the tomb; their despair, their unbelief, their perplexity, their amazement, their sudden transport,
their triumph,—all this was in their minds; and surely not the
least at that awful hour, when He led His breathless followers
out to Bethany, on the fortieth day. "He led them out as far as to
Bethany, and He lifted up His hands, and blessed them. And it
came to pass, while He blessed them, He was parted from them
and carried up into heaven." [3] Surely all His history, all His
dealings with them, came before them, gathered up in that moment. Then, as they gazed upon that dread Divine countenance
and that heavenly form, every thought and feeling which they
ever had had about Him came upon them at once. He had gone
through His work; theirs was to come, their work and their sufferings. He was leaving them just at the most critical time.
When Elijah went up, Elisha said: "My father, my father, the
chariot of Israel and the horsemen thereof." With a like feeling,
might the Apostles now gaze up into heaven, as if with the hope
of arresting His ascent. Their Lord and their God, the light of
their eyes, the stay of their hearts, the guide of their feet, was
taken away. "My beloved had withdrawn Himself and was
gone. My soul failed when He spake; I sought Him, but I could
not find Him; I called Him, but He gave me no answer." [4] Well
might they use the Church's words as now; "We beseech Thee,
leave us not comfortless." O Thou who wast so gentle and familiar with us, who didst converse with us by the way, and sit at
meat with us, and didst enter the vessel with us, and teach us on
the Mount, and bear the malice of the Pharisees, and feast with
Martha, and raise Lazarus, art Thou gone, and shall we see
Thee no more? Yet so it was determined: privileges they were to
have, but not the same; and their thoughts henceforth were to
be of another kind than heretofore. It was in vain wishing back
what was past and over. They were but told, as they gazed,
"This same Jesus, which is taken up from you into heaven, shall
so come in like manner as ye have seen Him go into heaven."

Such are some of the feelings which the Apostles may have
experienced on our Lord's ascension; but these are after all but
human and ordinary, and of a kind which all of us can enter
into; but other than these were sovereign with them at that solemn time, for upon the glorious Ascension of their Lord, "they
worshipped Him," says the text, "and returned to Jerusalem
with *great joy*, and were continually in the Temple praising and
blessing God." Now how was it, that when nature would have

[3] Luke xxiv. 50, 51.   [4] Cant. v. 6.

wept, the Apostles rejoiced? When Mary came to the sepulchre and found not our Lord's body, she stood without at the sepulchre weeping, and the Angels said unto her, as Christ said after them, "Woman, why weepest thou?" [5] Yet, on our Saviour's departure forty days afterwards, when the Angels would reprove the Apostles, they did but say, "Why stand ye gazing up into heaven?" There was no sorrow in the Apostles, in spite of their loss, in spite of the prospect before them, but "great joy," and "continual praise and blessing." May we venture to surmise that this rejoicing was the high temper of the brave and noble-minded, who have faced danger in idea and are prepared for it? Moses brought out of Egypt a timid nation, and in the space of forty years trained it to be full of valour for the task of conquering the promised land; Christ in forty days trains His Apostles to be bold and patient instead of cowards. "They mourned and wept" at the beginning of the season, but at the end they are full of courage for the good fight; their spirits mount high with their Lord, and when He is received out of their sight, and their own trial begins, "they return to Jerusalem with great joy, and are continually in the Temple, praising and blessing God."

For Christ surely had taught them what it was to have their treasure in heaven; and they rejoiced, not that their Lord was gone, but that their hearts had gone with Him. Their hearts were no longer on earth, they were risen aloft. When He died on the Cross, they knew not whither He was gone. Before He was seized, they had said to Him, "Lord, whither goest Thou? Lord, we know not whither Thou goest?" They could but follow Him to the grave and there mourn, for they knew no better; but now they saw Him ascend on high, and in spirit they ascended with Him. Mary wept at the grave because she thought enemies had taken Him away, and she knew not where they had laid Him. "Where your treasure is, there will your heart be also." [6] Mary had no heart left to her, for her treasure was lost; but the Apostles were continually in the Temple, praising and blessing God, for their hearts were in heaven, or, in St. Paul's words, they "were dead, and their life was hid with Christ in God."

Strengthened, then, with this knowledge, they were able to face those trials which Christ had first undergone Himself, and had foretold as their portion. "Whither I go," He had said to St. Peter, "thou canst not follow Me now, but thou shalt follow Me afterwards." And He told them, "They shall put you out of the

[5] John xx.15.   [6] Matt. vi.21.

synagogues, yea, the time cometh, that whosoever killeth you will think that he doeth God service."[7] That time was now coming, and they were able to rejoice in what so troubled them forty days before. For they understood the promise, "To him that overcometh, will I grant to sit with Me in My throne, even as I also overcame, and am set down with My Father in His Throne."[8]

It will be well if we take this lesson to ourselves, and learn that great truth which the Apostles shrank from at first, but at length rejoiced in. Christ suffered, and entered into joy; so did they, in their measure, after Him. And in our measure, so do we. It is written, that "through much tribulation we must enter into the kingdom of God." God has all things in His own hands. He can spare, He can inflict: He often spares (may He spare us still!) but He often tries us,—in one way or another He tries every one. At some time or other of the life of every one there is pain, and sorrow, and trouble. So it is; and the sooner perhaps we can look upon it as a law of our Christian condition, the better. One generation comes, and then another. They issue forth and succeed like leaves in spring; and in all, this law is observable. They are tried, and then they triumph; they are humbled, and then are exalted; they overcome the world, and then they sit down on Christ's throne.

Hence St. Peter, who at first was in such amazement and trouble at his Lord's afflictions, bids us not look on suffering as a strange thing, "as though some strange thing happened to us, but *rejoice*, inasmuch as we are *partakers* of Christ's sufferings; that when His glory shall be revealed, we may be glad also with exceeding joy." Again, St. Paul says, "We glory in tribulations, knowing that tribulation worketh patience." And again, "If so be we suffer with Him, that we may be also glorified together." And again, "If we suffer, we shall also reign with Him." And St. John, "The world knoweth us not, because it knew Him not." "We know that when He shall appear, we shall be like Him, for we shall see Him as He is."[9] What is here said of persecution will apply of course to all trials, and much more to those lesser trials which are the utmost which Christians have commonly to endure now. Yet I suppose it is a long time before any one of us recognizes and understands that his own state on earth is in one shape or other a state of trial and sorrow; and that if he has intervals of external peace, this is all gain, and more than he has

[7] John xvi.2.   [8] Rev. iii.21.
[9] 1 Pet. iv.12, 13; Rom. v.3; 2 Tim. ii.12; 1 John iii.1, 2.

a right to expect. Yet how different must the state of the Church appear to beings who can contemplate it as a whole, who have contemplated it for ages,—as the Angels! We know what experience does for us in this world. Men get to see and understand the course of things, and by what rules it proceeds; and they can foretell what will happen, and they are not surprised at what does happen. They take the history of things as a matter of course. They are not startled that things happen in one way, not in another; it is the rule. Night comes after day; winter after summer; cold, frost, and snow, in their season. Certain illnesses have their times of recurrence, or visit at certain ages. All things go through a process,—they have a beginning and an end. Grown men know this, but it is otherwise with children. To them every thing that they see is strange and surprising. They by turns feel wonder, admiration, or fear at every thing that happens; they do not know whether it will happen again or not; and they know nothing of the regular operation of causes, or the connexion of those effects which result from one and the same cause. And so too as regards the state of our souls under the Covenant of mercy; the heavenly hosts, who see what is going on upon earth, well understand, even from having seen it often, what is the course of a soul travelling from hell to heaven. They have seen, again and again, in numberless instances, that suffering is the path to peace; that they that sow in tears shall reap in joy; and that what was true of Christ is fulfilled in a measure in His followers.

Let us try to accustom ourselves to this view of the subject. The whole Church, all elect souls, each in its turn, is called to this necessary work. Once it was the turn of others, and now it is our turn. Once it was the Apostles' turn. It was St. Paul's turn once. He had all cares on him all at once; covered from head to foot with cares, as Job with sores. And, as if all this were not enough, he had a thorn in the flesh added,—some personal discomfort ever with him. Yet he did his part well,— he was as a strong and bold wrestler in his day, and at the close of it was able to say, "I have fought a good fight, I have finished my course, I have kept the faith." [10] And after him, the excellent of the earth, the white-robed army of Martyrs, and the cheerful company of Confessors, each in his turn, each in his day, have likewise played the man. And so down to this very time, when faith has well-nigh failed, first one and then another have been called out to exhibit before the Great King. It

[10] 2 Tim. iv.7.

is as though all of us were allowed to stand around His Throne at once, and He called on first this man, and then that, to take up the chant by himself, each in his turn having to repeat the melody which his brethren have before gone through. Or as if we held a solemn dance to His honour in the courts of heaven, and each had by himself to perform some one and the same solemn and graceful movement at a signal given. Or as if it were some trial of strength, or of agility, and, while the ring of by-standers beheld and applauded, we in succession, one by one, were actors in the pageant. Such is our state;—Angels are looking on,—Christ has gone before,—Christ has given us an example, that we may follow His steps. He went through far more, infinitely more, than we can be called to suffer. Our brethren have gone through much more; and they seem to encourage us by their success, and to sympathize in our essay. Now it is our turn; and all ministering spirits keep silence and look on. O let not your foot slip, or your eye be false, or your ear dull, or your attention flagging! Be not dispirited; be not afraid; keep a good heart; be bold; draw not back;—you will be carried through. Whatever troubles come on you, of mind, body, or estate; from within or from without; from chance or from intent; from friends or foes;—whatever your trouble be, though you be lonely, O children of a heavenly Father, be not afraid! quit you like men in your day; and when it is over, Christ will receive you to Himself, and your heart shall rejoice, and your joy no man taketh from you.

Christ is already in that place of peace, which is all in all. He is on the right hand of God. He is hidden in the brightness of the radiance which issues from the everlasting Throne. He is in the very abyss of peace, where there is no voice of tumult or distress, but a deep stillness,—stillness, that greatest and most awful of all goods which we can fancy,—that most perfect of joys, the utter, profound, ineffable tranquillity of the Divine Essence. He has entered into His rest.

O how great a good will it be, if, when this troublesome life is over, we in our turn also enter into that same rest,—if the time shall one day come, when we shall enter into His tabernacle above, and hide ourselves under the shadow of His wings; if we shall be in the number of those blessed dead who die in the Lord, and rest from their labour. Here we are tossing upon the sea, and the wind is contrary. All through the day we are tried and tempted in various ways. We cannot think, speak, or act, but infirmity and sin are at hand. But in the unseen world, where Christ has entered, all is peace. There is the eternal

Throne, and a rainbow round about it, like unto an emerald; and in the midst of the throne the Lamb that has been slain, and has redeemed many people by His blood: and round about the throne four and twenty seats for as many elders, all clothed in white raiment, and crowns of gold upon their heads. And four living beings full of eyes before and behind. And seven Angels standing before God, and doing His pleasure unto the ends of the earth. And the Seraphim above. And withal, a great multitude which no man can number, of all nations, and kindreds, and people, and tongues, clothed with white robes, and palms in their hands. "These are they which came out of great tribulation, and have washed their robes and made them white in the blood of the Lamb." [11] "They shall hunger no more, neither thirst any more; neither shall the sun light on them, nor any heat." "There is no more death, neither sorrow nor crying, neither any more pain; for the former things are passed away." [12] Nor any more sin; nor any more guilt; no more remorse; no more punishment; no more penitence; no more trial; no infirmity to depress us; no affection to mislead us; no passion to transport us; no prejudice to blind us; no sloth, no pride, no envy, no strife; but the light of God's countenance, and a pure river of water of life, clear as crystal, proceeding out of the Throne. That is our *home*; here we are but on pilgrimage, and Christ is calling us home. He calls us to His many mansions, which He has prepared. And the Spirit and the Bride call us too, and all things will be ready for us by the time of our coming. "Seeing then that we have a great High Priest that has passed into the heavens, Jesus the Son of God, let us hold fast our profession;" seeing we have "so great a cloud of witnesses, let us lay aside every weight;" "let us labour to enter into our rest;" "let us come boldly unto the Throne of Grace, that we may obtain mercy, and find grace to help in time of need." [13]

---

[11] Rev. vii.14.   [12] Rev. xxi.4.
[13] Heb. iv.11, 14, 16; xii.1.

WAITING FOR CHRIST

(Ascension)

*"He who testifieth these things, saith, Surely I come quickly. Amen.
Even so, come, Lord Jesus."*—Rev. xxii.20.

WHEN our Lord was going away, He said He would quickly come again; yet knowing that by "quickly" He did not mean what would be at first sight understood by the word, He added, "suddenly," or "as a thief." "Behold I come as a thief; blessed is he that watcheth, and keepeth his garments."[1] Had His coming been soon, in our sense of the word, it could not well have been sudden. Servants who are bid to wait for their master's return from an entertainment, could not, one should think, be overtaken by that return. It was because to us His coming would not *seem* soon, that it *was* sudden. What you expect to come, you wait for; what fails to come, you give up; while, then, Christ said that His coming would be soon, yet by saying it would be sudden, He said that to us it would seem long.

Yet though to us He seems to delay, yet He has declared that His coming is speedy, He has bid us ever look out for His coming; and His first followers, as the Epistles show us, *were* ever looking out for it. Surely it is our duty to look out for it, as likely to come immediately, though hitherto for near two thousand years the Church has been looking out in vain.

Is it not something significant that, in the last book of Scripture, which more than any other implies a long continuance to the Christian Church,—that there we should have such express and repeated assurances that Christ's coming would be speedy? Even in the last chapter we are told it three times. "Behold I come quickly; blessed is he that keepeth the sayings of the prophecy of this book." "Behold I come quickly, and My reward is with Me." And again, in the text, "He that testifieth these things, saith, Surely I come quickly." Such is

[1] Rev. xvi.15.

the announcement; and, in consequence, we are commanded to be ever looking out for the great Day, to "wait for His Son from heaven;"[2] to "look and haste unto the coming of the day of God."[3]

It is true, indeed, that in one place St. Paul cautions his brethren against expecting the immediate coming of Christ; but he does not say more than that Christ will send a sign immediately before His coming,—a certain dreadful enemy of the truth— which is to be followed by Himself at once, and therefore does not stand in our way, or prevent eager eyes from looking out for Him. And, in truth, St. Paul seems rather to be warning his brethren against being disappointed if Christ did not come, than hindering them from expecting Him.

Now it may be objected that this is a kind of paradox; how is it possible, it may be asked, ever to be expecting what has so long been delayed? What has been so long coming, may be longer still. It was possible, indeed, for the early Christians, who had no experience of the long period which the Church was to remain on earth, to look out for Christ; but we cannot help using our reason: there are no more grounds to expect Christ now than at those many former times, when, as the event showed, He did not come. Christians have ever been expecting the last day, and ever meeting with disappointment. They have seen what they thought symptoms of His coming, and peculiarities in their own times, which a little more knowledge of the world, a more enlarged experience, would have shown them to be common to all times. They have ever been frightened without good reason, fretting in their narrow minds, and building on their superstitious fancies. What age of the world has there been in which people did not think the Day of Judgment coming? Such expectation has but evidenced and fostered indolence and superstition; it is to be considered as a mere weakness.

Now I shall attempt to say something in answer to this objection.

1. And first, considered as an objection to a habit of continual waiting (to use the common phrase), it proves too much. If it is consistently followed up, no age ought ever to expect the day of Christ; the age in which He shall come (whenever it is) ought not to expect Him;—which is the very thing He has warned us against. He no where warns us against what is contemptuously called superstition; but He expressly warns us

---

[2] 1 Thess. i.10.   [3] 2 Pet. iii.12.

against high-minded security. If it be true that Christians have expected Him when He did not come, it is quite as true that when He does come, the world will not expect Him. If it be true that Christians have fancied signs of His coming, when there were none, it is equally true that the world will not see the signs of His coming when they are present. His signs are not so plain but you have to search for them; not so plain but you may be mistaken *in* your search; and your choice lies between the risk of thinking you see what is not, and of not seeing what is. True it is, that many times, many ages, have Christians been mistaken in thinking they discerned Christ's coming; but better a thousand times think Him coming when He is not, than once think Him not coming when He is. Such is the difference between Scripture and the world; judging by Scripture, you would ever be expecting Christ; judging by the world, you would never expect Him. Now He must come one day, sooner or later. Worldly men have their scoff at our failure of discernment now; but whose will be the want of discernment, whose the triumph then? And what does Christ think of their present scoff? He expressly warns us, by His Apostle, of scoffers, who shall say, "Where is the promise of His coming? for since the fathers fell asleep, all things continue as they were from the beginning of the creation. . . . But, beloved (continues St. Peter), be not ignorant of this one thing, that one day is with the Lord as a thousand years, and a thousand years as one day." [4]

It should be recollected, too, that the enemies of Christ have ever been expecting the downfall of His religion, age after age; and I do not see why the one expectation is more unreasonable than the other; indeed they illustrate each other. So it is, undeterred by the failure of former anticipations, unbelievers are ever expecting that the Church and the religion of the Church are coming to an end. They thought so in the last century. They think so now. They ever think the light of truth is going out, and that their hour of victory is come. Now, I repeat, I do not see why it is reasonable to expect the overthrow of religion still, after so many failures; and yet unreasonable, because of previous disappointments, to expect the coming of Christ. Nay, Christians at least, over and above the aspect of things, can point to an express promise of Christ, that He will one day come; whereas unbelievers, I suppose, do not profess any grounds at all for expecting their own triumph, except the signs of the times. They are sanguine, because they seem so strong,

[4] 2 Pet. iii.4, 8.

and the Church of God seems so weak; yet they have not enlarged their minds enough by the contemplation of past history
to know that such apparent strength on the one side, and such
apparent weakness on the other, has ever been the state of the
world and the Church; and that this has ever been one chief or
rather the main reason, why Christians have expected the immediate end of all things, because the prospects of religion *were*
so gloomy. So that, in fact, Christians and unbelievers have
taken precisely the same view of the facts of the case; only they
have drawn distinct conclusions from them, according to their
creed. The Christian has said, "All looks so full of tumult, that
the world is coming to an end;" and the unbeliever has said,
"All is so full of tumult, that the Church is coming to an end;"
and there is nothing, surely, more superstitious in the one opinion than in the other.

Now when Christians and unbelievers thus unite in expecting substantially the same thing, though they view it differently, according to their respective modes of thought, there
cannot be any thing very extravagant in the expectation itself;
there must be something ever present in the world which warrants it. And I hold this to be the case. Ever since Christianity
came into the world, it has been, in one sense, going out of it. It
is so uncongenial to the human mind, it is so spiritual, and man
is so earthly, it is apparently so defenceless, and has so many
strong enemies, so many false friends, that every age, as it
comes, may be called "the last time." It has made great conquests, and done great works; but still it has done all, as the
Apostle says of himself "in weakness, and in fear, and in much
trembling."[5] *How* it is that it is always failing, yet always continuing, God only knows who wills it,—but so it is; and it is no
paradox to say, on the one hand, that it has lasted eighteen hundred years, that it may last many years more, and yet that it
draws to an end, nay, is likely to end any day. And God would
have us give our minds and hearts to the latter side of the alternative, to open them to impressions *from* this side, viz. that the
end is coming;—it being a wholesome thing to live as if *that* will
come in our day, which may come any day.

It was different during the ages before Christ came. The Saviour was to come. He was to bring perfection, and religion was
to grow *towards* that perfection. There was a system of successive revelations going on, first one and then another; each
prophet in his turn adding to the store of Divine truth, and

[5] 1 Cor. ii.3.

gradually tending towards the full Gospel. Time was measured out for believing minds before Christ came, by the word of prophecy; so that He never could be expected in any age before the "fulness of time" in which He came. The chosen people were not bidden to expect Him at once; but after a sojourning in Canaan, and a captivity in Egypt, and a wandering in the wilderness, and judges, and kings, and prophets, at length seventy long weeks were determined to introduce Him into the world. Thus His delay was, as I may say, *recognized* then; and, *during* His delay, other doctrines, other rules, were given to fill the interval. But when once the Christ had come, as the Son over His own house, and with His perfect Gospel, nothing remained but to gather in His saints. No higher Priest could come,—no truer doctrine. The Light and Life of men had appeared, and had suffered, and had risen again; and nothing more was left to do. Earth had had its most solemn event and seen its most august sight; and therefore it was the last time. And hence, though time intervene between Christ's first and second coming, it is not *recognized* (as I may say) in the Gospel scheme, but is, as it were, an accident. For so it was, that up to Christ's coming in the flesh, the course of things ran straight towards that end, nearing it by every step; but now, under the Gospel, that course has (if I may so speak) altered its direction, as regards His second coming, and runs, not towards the end, but along it, and on the brink of it; and is at all times equally near that great event, which, did it run towards, it would at once run into. Christ, then, is ever at our doors; as near eighteen hundred years ago as now, and not nearer now than then; and not nearer when He comes than now. When He says that He will come soon, "soon" is not a word of time, but of natural order. This present state of things, "the present distress" as St. Paul calls it, is ever *close upon* the next world, and resolves itself into it. As when a man is given over, he may die any moment, yet lingers; as an implement of war may any moment explode, and must at some time; as we listen for a clock to strike, and at length it surprises us; as a crumbling arch hangs, we know not how, and is not safe to pass under; so creeps on this feeble weary world, and one day, before we know where we are, it will end.

And here I may observe in passing, on the light thus thrown upon the doctrine, that Christ is the sole Priest under the Gospel, or that the Apostles ever sit on twelve thrones, judging the twelve tribes of Israel, or that Christ is with them always, even unto the end of the world. Do you not see the force of these expressions? The Jewish Covenant, indeed, had "sundry times," which were ordered "in divers manners;" it had a long array of priests and a various history; one part of the series holier than another, and nearer heaven. But when Christ had come, suffered, and ascended, He was henceforth ever near us, ever at hand, even though He was not actually returned, ever scarcely gone, ever all but come back. He is the only Ruler and Priest in His Church, dispensing gifts, and has appointed none to supersede Him, because He is departed only for a brief season. Aaron took the place of Christ, and had a priesthood of His own; but Christ's priests have no priesthood but His. They are merely His shadows and organs, they are His outward signs; and what they do, He does; when they baptize, He is baptizing; when they bless, He is blessing. He is in all acts of His Church, and one of its acts is not more truly His act than another, for all are His. Thus we are, in all times of the Gospel, brought close to His Cross. We stand, as it were, under it, and receive its blessings fresh from it; only that since, historically speaking, time has gone on, and the Holy One is away, certain outward forms are necessary, by way of bringing us again under His shadow; and we enjoy those blessings through a mystery, or sacramentally, in order to enjoy them really. All this witnesses to the duty both of remembering and of looking out for Christ, teaching us to neglect the present, to rely on no plans, to form no expectations, for the future, but so to live in faith, as if He had not left us, so in hope, as if He had returned to us. We must try to live as if the Apostles were living, and we must try to muse upon our Lord's life in the Gospels, not as a history, but as if a recollection.

2. This leads me to remark upon a second aspect under which the objection in question may be urged; viz. that this waiting for Christ is not only extravagant in its very idea, but becomes a superstition and weakness whenever carried into effect. The mind, intent upon the thought of an awful visitation close at hand, begins to fancy signs of it in the natural and moral world, and mistakes the ordinary events of God's providence for miracles. Thus Christians are brought into bondage, and substitute for the Gospel a fond religion, in which imagination takes the place of faith, and things visible and earthly take the place of Scripture. This is the objection; yet the text, on the other hand, while it sanctions the expectation, in the words "Surely I come quickly," surely sanctions the temper of waiting also, by adding, "Amen, even so, come, Lord Jesus."

I observe, then, that though Christians might be mistaken in what they took to be signs of Christ's coming, yet they were not wrong in their state of mind, they were not mistaken in looking out, and that for Christ. Whether credulous or not, they only acted as one acts towards some person beloved, or revered, or admired on earth. Consider the mode in which loyal persons look up to a good prince; you will find stories current, up and down the country, in his favour; people delight in believing that they have fallen in with tokens of his beneficence, nobleness, and paternal kindness. Many of these reports are false, yet others are true, and, on the whole, we should not think highly of that man who, instead of being touched at this mutual sympathy between sovereign and people, occupied himself merely in carping at what he called their credulity, and sifting the accuracy of this or that particular story. A great thing, truly, after all, to be able to detect a few mis-statements, and to expose a few fictions, and to be without a heart! And forsooth, on the other hand, a sad deficiency in that people, I suppose, merely to be right on the whole, not in every particular, and to have the heart right! Who would envy such a man's knowledge? who would not rather have that people's ignorance? And, in like manner, I had rather be he, who, from love of Christ and want of science, thinks some strange sight in the sky, comet or meteor, to be the sign of His coming, than the man, who, from more knowledge and from lack of love, laughs at the mistake.

Before now, religious persons have taken appearances in the heaven for signs of Christ's coming, which do not now frighten us at all. Granted, but what then? let us consider the state of the case. Of old time it was not *known* generally that certain heavenly bodies moved and appeared at *fixed* times and by a rule; now it is known; that is, now men are *accustomed* to see them, then they were not accustomed. We know as little now as then *how* they come, or why; but then men were startled when they saw them, because they were strange, and now they are not strange, and therefore men are not startled. But how was it therefore absurd and ridiculous (for so it is that persons now-a-days talk), why was it a foolish fond thing in a man to be impressed by what was rare and strange? Take a parallel case: travelling is common now, it was not common formerly. In consequence, we now travel without any serious emotion at parting from our friends; but then, because it was uncommon, even when risks were the same and the absence as long, persons did not go from home without much preparation, many prayers, and much leave-taking. I do not see any thing very censurable in being more impressed at uncommon things than at common.

And you will observe, that in the case of which I am speaking, persons who are looking out for Christ are not only, *in that* they look out, acting in obedience to Him, but are looking out,—in their very *way* of looking out, through the very signs through which they look out,—in obedience to Him. Always since the first, Christians have been looking out for Christ *in* the signs of the natural and moral world. If they have been poor and unedu-cated, strange sights in the sky, or tremblings of the ground, storms, failure of harvest, or disease, or any thing monstrous and unnatural, has made them think that He was at hand. If they were in a way to take a view of the social and political world, then the troubles of states—wars, revolutions, and the like,—have been additional circumstances which served to im-press them, and kept their hearts awake for Christ. Now all these are nothing else but those very things which He Himself has told us to dwell upon and has given us as signs of His com-ing. "There shall be signs," He says, "in the sun, and in the moon, and in the stars; and upon the earth distress of nations, with perplexity, the sea and the waves roaring; men's hearts failing them for fear, and for looking after those things which are coming on the earth; for the powers of heaven shall be shaken. . . . . And when these things begin to come to pass, then look up and lift up your heads, for your redemption draweth nigh." [6] One day the lights of heaven *will* be signs; one day the affairs of nations also *will* be signs; why, then, is it super-stitious to *look* towards them? It is not. We may be wrong in the particulars we rest upon, and may show our ignorance in doing so; but there is nothing ridiculous or contemptible in our igno-rance, and there is much that is religious in our watching. It is better to be wrong in our watching, than not to watch at all.

Nor does it follow that Christians were wrong, even in their particular anticipations, though Christ did not come, whereas they said, they saw His signs. Perhaps they *were* His signs, and He withdrew them again. Is there no such thing as counter-manding? Do not skilful men in matters of this world some-times form anticipations which turn out wrong, and yet we say that they *ought* to have been right? The sky threatens and then clears again. Or some military leader orders his men forward, and then for some reason recalls them; shall we say that infor-mants were wrong who brought the news that he was moving? Well, in one sense Christ is ever moving forward, ever check-ing, the armies of heaven. Signs of the white horses are ever

[6] Luke xxi.25, 26, 28.

appearing, ever vanishing. "Clouds return after the rain;" and His servants are not wrong in pointing to them, and saying that the weather is breaking, though it does not break, for it is ever unsettled.

And another thing should be observed, that though Christians have ever been expecting Christ, ever pointing to His signs, they have never said that He was come. They have but said that He was just coming, *all but* come. And so He was and is. Enthusiasts, sectaries, wild presumptuous men, *they* have said that He was *actually* come, or they have pointed out the exact year and day in which He would come. Not so His humble followers. They have neither announced nor sought Him, either in the desert or in the secret chambers, nor have they attempted to determine "the times and seasons, which the Father has put in His own power." They have but waited; when He actually comes, they will not mistake Him; and before then, they pronounce nothing. They do but see His forerunners.

Surely there can be no great harm, and nothing very ridiculous, where men are religious, in thus thinking the events of their day more than ordinary, in fancying that the world's matters are winding up, and that events are thickening for a final visitation; for, let it be observed, Scripture sanctions us in interpreting *all* that we see in the world in a religious sense, and as if all things were tokens and revelations of Christ, His Providence, and will. I mean that if this lower world, which seems to go on in its own way, independently of Him, governed by fixed laws or swayed by lawless hearts, will, nevertheless, one day in an awful way, herald His coming to judge it, surely it is not impossible that the same world, both in its physical order and its temporal course, speaks of Him also in other manners. At first, indeed, one might argue that this world did but speak a language contrary to Him; that in Scripture it is described as opposed to God, to truth, to faith, to heaven; that it is said to be a deceitful veil, misrepresenting things, and keeping the soul from God. How then, it may be asked, can this world have upon it tokens of His presence, or bring us near to Him? Yet certainly so it is, that in spite of the world's evil, after all, He is in it and speaks through it, though not loudly. When He came in the flesh "He was in the world, and the world was made by Him, and the world knew Him not." Nor did He strive nor cry, nor lift up His voice in the streets. So it is now. He still is here; He still whispers to us, He still makes signs to us. But His voice is so low, and the world's din is so loud, and His signs are so covert, and the world is so restless, that it is difficult to determine when

He addresses us, and what He says. Religious men cannot but feel, in various ways, that His providence is guiding them and blessing them personally, on the whole; yet when they attempt to put their finger upon the times and places, the traces of His presence disappear. Who is there, for instance, but has been favoured with answers to prayer, such that, at the time, he has felt he never could again be unbelieving? Who has not had strange coincidences in his course of life which brought before him, in an overpowering way, the hand of God? Who has not had thoughts come upon him with a sort of mysterious force, for his warning or his direction? And some persons, perhaps, experience stranger things still. Wonderful providences have before now been brought about by means of dreams; or in other still more unusual ways Almighty God has at times interposed. And then, again, things which come before our eyes, in such wise take the form of types and omens of things moral or future, that the spirit within us cannot but reach forward and presage what it is not told from what it sees. And sometimes these presages are remarkably fulfilled in the event. And then, again, the fortunes of men are so singularly various, as if a law of success and prosperity embraced a certain number, and a contrary law others. All this being so, and the vastness and mystery of the world being borne in upon us, we may well begin to think that there is nothing here below, but, for what we know has a connexion with every thing else; the most distant events may yet be united, the meanest and highest may be parts of one; and God may be teaching us and offering us knowledge of His ways, if we will but open our eyes, in all the ordinary matters of the day. This is what thoughtful persons come to believe, and they begin to have a sort of faith in the Divine meaning of the accidents (as they are called) of life, and a readiness to take impressions from them, which may easily become excessive, and which, whether excessive or not, is sure to be ridiculed by the world at large as superstition. Yet, considering Scripture tells us that the very hairs of our head are all numbered by God, that all things are ours, and that all things work together for our good, it does certainly encourage us in thus looking out for His presence in every thing that happens, however trivial, and in holding that to religious ears even the bad world prophesies of Him.

Yet, I say, this religious waiting upon God through the day, which is so like that spirit of watching which is under consideration, is just as open to objection and scoffing from the world. God does not so speak to us through the occurrences of life, that you can persuade others that He speaks. He does not act upon such explicit laws, that you can speak of them with certainty. He gives us sufficient tokens of Himself to raise our minds in awe towards Him; but He seems so frequently to undo what He has done, and to suffer counterfeits of His tokens, that a conviction of His wonder-working presence can but exist in the individual himself. It is not a truth that can be taught and recognized in the face of men; it is not of a nature to be urged upon the world at large, nay, even on religious persons, as a principle. God gives us enough to make us inquire and hope; not enough to make us insist and argue.

I have all along been speaking of thoughtful and conscientious persons; those who do their duty, and who study Scripture. It is quite certain that this regard to outward occurrences does become superstition, when it is found in men of irreligious lives, or of slender knowledge of Scripture. The great and chief revelation which God has made us of His will is through Christ and His Apostles. They have given us a knowledge of the truth; they have sent forth heavenly principles and doctrines into the world; they have accompanied that revealed truth by Divine sacraments, which convey to the heart what otherwise would be a mere outward and barren knowledge; and they have told us to practise what we know, and obey what we are taught, that the Word of Christ may be formed and dwell in us. They have been inspired, moreover, to write Holy Scriptures for our learning and comfort; and in those Scriptures we find the history of this world interpreted for us by a heavenly rule. When, then, a man, thus formed and fortified within, with these living principles in his heart, with this firm hold and sight of things invisible, with likings, opinions, views, aims, moulded upon God's revealed law, looks abroad into the world, he does not come to the world for a revelation,—he has one already. He does not take his religion from the world, nor does he set an over-value upon the tokens and presages which he sees there. But far different is the case when a man is not thus enlightened and informed by revealed truth. Then he is but a prey, he becomes the slave, of the occurrences and events, the sights and sounds, the omens and prodigies, which meet him in the world, natural and moral. His religion is a bondage to things perishable, an idolatry of the creature, and is, in the worst sense of the word, superstition. Hence it is a common remark, that irreligious men are most open to superstition. For they have a misgiving that there is something great and Divine somewhere: and since they have it not within them, they have no difficulty in believing that it is anywhere else, wherever men pretend to the possession of it. Thus you find in history men in high place practising unlawful arts, consulting professed wizards or giving heed to astrology. Others have had their lucky and unlucky days; others have been the sport of dreams, or of other idle fancies. And you have had others bowing themselves down to idols. For they have had no principle, no root in themselves. They have been ignorant, too, of Scripture, in which God has most mercifully removed the veil off a portion of this world's history, in order that we may see *how* He works. Scripture is the key by which we are given to interpret the world; but they who have it not, roam amid the shadows of the world, and interpret things at random.

The same want of inward religious principle is shown in the light, senseless way in which so many adopt wrong forms of religious profession. He who has the light of Christ within him, hears the voice of enthusiastic, mistaken, self-willed, or hypocritical men, calling him to follow them, without being moved. But when a man is conscious he is a wilful sinner, and not at peace with God, when his own heart is against him, and he has no principle, no stay within him, then he is the prey of the first person who comes to him with strong language, and bids him believe in him. Hence you find numbers running eagerly after men who profess to work miracles, or who denounce the Church as apostate, or who maintain that none are saved but those who agree with themselves, or any one who, without any warrant of his being right, speaks confidently. Hence the multitude is so open to sudden alarms. You hear of their rushing out of a city in numbers at some idle prediction that the Day of Judgment is coming. Hence so many, in the private and lower ranks of life, are so full of small superstitions, which are too minute to mention; all because they have not the light of truth burning in their heart.

But the true Christian is not of these. To him apply St. Paul's words, "All things are lawful unto me, but all things are not expedient; all things are lawful for me, but I will not be brought under the power of any."[7] He knows how to "use this world as not abusing it." He *depends* on nothing in this world. He trusts not *its* sights against the revealed Word. "Thou wilt keep him in perfect peace whose mind is stayed on Thee, because he trusteth in Thee." Such is the promise made to him. And if he looks out into the world to seek, it is not to seek what he does not know, but what he does. He does not seek a Lord and

[7] 1 Cor. vi.12.

Saviour. He has "found the Messias" long since; and he is looking out for *Him*. His Lord Himself has *bid* him look for Him in
the signs of the world, and therefore he looks out. His Lord
Himself has shown him, in the Old Testament, how He, the
Lord of Glory, condescends to humble Himself to the things of
heaven and earth. He knows that God's Angels are about the
earth. He knows that once they were even used to come in human shape. He knows that the Son of God, ere now, has come
on earth. He knows that He promised to His Church the presence of a miraculous agency, and has never recalled His promise. Again, he reads, in the Book of the Revelation, quite
enough, not to show him what is coming, but to show him that
now, as heretofore, a secret supernatural system is going on *under* this visible scene. And therefore he looks out for Christ, for
His present providences, and for His coming; and though often
deceived in his expectation, and fancying wonderful things are
coming on the earth, when they still delay, he uses, and comforts him with the Prophet's words, "I will stand upon my
watch, and set me upon the tower, and will watch to see what
He will say unto me, and what I shall answer when I am reproved. And the Lord answered me. . . . The vision is yet for an
appointed time, but at the end it shall speak and not lie; though
it tarry, wait for it, because it will surely come, it will not tarry.
Behold, his soul, which is lifted up, is not upright in him; but
the just shall live by his faith." [8]

[8] Hab. ii. 1–4.

SUBJECTION OF THE REASON AND FEELINGS TO THE REVEALED WORD

(Ascension)

"Bringing into captivity every thought to the obedience of Christ."
—2 Cor. x.5.

THE question may be asked, How is it possible to live as if the coming of Christ were not far off, when our reason tells us that it probably is distant? It may be objected that there are no grounds for expecting it now, more than for the last eighteen hundred years; that if His long absence is a reason for expecting it now, yet His promise of a speedy return was a reason for expecting it in earlier times; and if the one reason has turned out insufficient, so may the other; that if, in spite of His promise to be speedy, He has tarried so long, He may tarry longer still; that no signs of His coming can be greater than were abroad soon after His departure; that, certainly, there are no such signs now; nay, that during the first seven hundred years, and again about the year 1000, and later, there were many more signs of Christ's coming than there are now,—more trouble of nations, more distress, more sickness, more terror. It may be said, that we cannot hope, and fear, and expect, and wait, as we will,—but that we must have *reasons* for so doing; and that if we are persuaded, in our deliberate judgment, that Christ's coming is not probable, we cannot make ourselves feel as if it were probable.

Now in considering this objection, which I shall do, I may have an opportunity of stating a great principle which obtains in Christian duty, the subjection of the whole mind to the law of God.

1. I deny, then, that our feelings and likings are only moved according to the dictates of what we commonly mean by reason; so far from it, that nothing is more common, on the other hand, than to say, that reason goes one way, and our wishes go another. There is nothing impossible, then, in learning to look out for the day of Christ's coming more earnestly than accord-

ing to its probability in the judgment of reason. As reason may be a right guide for our feelings and likings to go by up to a certain point, so there may be cases in which it is unable to guide us, from its weakness; and as it is not impossible for sinful and irreligious men to like what their reason tells them they should not like; therefore it is not impossible for religious men also to desire, expect, and hope, what their reason is unequal to approve and accept. What is more common than to hear it said, "I love a person more than I respect him"? or, "I admire him more than I love him"? Or, again, we know how easy it is to open the mind to the influence of some feeling or emotion, and how difficult it is to avoid such influence; how difficult it is to get a thought out of the mind, which reason says ought to be kept out, and which will intrude itself again and again; how difficult to restrain anger, fear, or other passion, which yet reason tells us should be restrained. It is, then, quite possible to have feelings and thoughts present with us in a way which is disproportionate, according to the judgment of reason. Or, take another instance. We know how the mind sometimes dwells upon the chance of what is barely possible, quite unreasonably, and often wrongly and dangerously. A number of things may happen, one perhaps as likely as another; and yet, from weakness of health, or excitement, it often happens that we cannot help thinking overmuch of some one of these possible events, and getting unduly anxious lest it should happen. Thus, if some dreadful occurrence has taken place, a fire, or a murder, or some horrible accident, persons become frightened, lest the same should happen to them, in a measure far exceeding what a mere calculation of probabilities warrants. Their imagination magnifies the danger; they cannot persuade themselves to look at things calmly, and according to their general course. They fix their thoughts upon one particular chance, in a way quite contrary to what reason suggests. Thus, so far from our feelings being moved according to the strict probabilities of things, the contrary is rather the rule. What Almighty God then requires of us is, to do that in one instance for His sake, which we do so commonly in indulgence of our own waywardness and weakness; to hope, fear, expect our Lord's coming, more than reason warrants, and in a way which His word alone warrants; that is, to trust Him above our reason. You say, that it is not probable Christ will come at this time, and therefore you cannot expect it. Now, I say, you can expect it. You must feel there is a chance that He will come. Well, then, dwell on that chance; open your mind to it; treat that chance just as you so often treat the chance of fire, or peril by sea, or peril by land, or thieves. Our Lord says, that He shall come as a thief in the night. Now you know that if there has been some remarkable robbery, people are frightened far more than according to the chance of their being themselves robbed. They are haunted by the idea; it may be that the probability of their own houses being attempted is but small, yet the thing itself is an object of great apprehension to them, and they think more of the grievousness of the event apprehended, should it happen, than of the small chance of its happening. They are moved by the risk. And in like manner, as regards the coming of Christ; I do not say we must be excited, or unsettled, or engrossed with the thought, but still we must not let the long delay persuade us not to watch for it. "Though it tarry, wait for it." If He bids us, as a matter of duty, impress the prospect of His coming upon our imagination, He asks no hard thing; no hard thing, that is, to the willing mind; and what we can do we are bound to do.

2. This is what first suggests itself, but it opens the way to further thoughts. For only reflect, what is faith itself but an acceptance of things unseen, from the love of them, *beyond* the determinations of calculation and experience? Faith outstrips argument. If there is only a fair chance that the Bible is true, that heaven is the reward of obedience, and hell of wilful sin, it is worth while, it is safe, to sacrifice this world to the next. It were worth while, though Christ told us to sell all that we have and follow Him, and to pass our time here in poverty and contempt, it were worth while on that chance to do it. This, then, is what is meant by faith going against reason, that it cares not for the measure of probabilities; it does not ask whether a thing is more or less likely; but if there is a fair and clear likelihood what God's will is, it acts upon it. If Scripture were not true, we should in the next world be left where we were; we should, in the event, be no worse off than before; but if it be true, then we shall be infinitely worse off for not believing it than if we had believed it. We all know the retort which the aged saint made in the story, when a licentious youth reminded him, how he would have wasted life if there were *no* future state of recompense: "True, my son," he answered, "but how *much* worse a waste is yours if there *is*."

Faith, then, does not regard *degrees* of evidence. You might lay it down as a rule, speaking in the way of reason, that we ought to have faith according to the evidence; that the more evidence there is, the more firm it should be; and the less evidence, the weaker will it be required of us. But this is not the case as regards religious faith,—which accepts the Word of God as firmly on the evidence which it is vouchsafed, as if that evidence were doubled. This, indeed, we see to be the case as regards things of earth; and surely what we do towards men, we may bear to do towards God. If any one whom we trust and revere told us any news, which he had perfect means of knowing, we should believe him; we should not believe it more thoroughly because presently another told it to us also. And in like manner, though it is quite certain that Almighty God might have given us greater evidence than we possess, that He speaks to us in the Bible; yet since He has given us enough, faith does not ask for more, but is satisfied, and acts upon what *is* enough; whereas unbelief is ever asking for signs, more and greater, before it will yield to the Divine Word.

Returning to my main subject, I observe, in like manner, what is true of faith is true of hope. We may be commanded, if so be, to hope against hope, or to expect Christ's coming, in a certain sense, against reason. It is not inconsistent with God's general dealings towards us, that He should bid us feel and act as if that were at hand, which yet, if we went by what experience tells us, we should say was not likely to be at hand. If He bids us to believe in Him with our whole heart, whether the evidence of His speaking to us be greater or less, why may He not bid us wait for Him perseveringly, though the signs of His coming disappoint us, and reason desponds? We cannot tell in such a matter what is more probable and what is not; we can but attempt what we are told to do. And *that* we can do: we can direct and fashion our feelings according to His word, and leave the rest to Him.

3. Here, then, I am led to make a further remark; that as it is our duty to bring some things before our minds, and contemplate them much more vividly than reason by itself would bid us, so, again, there are other things which it is a duty to put away from us, not to dwell upon, and not to realize, though they be brought before us. And yet it is evident, too, that persons might here also object, and say that it is impossible to help being moved and influenced by what we know for certain, just as they say that it is impossible to believe and expect what we know to be not certain.

For instance; we know that it is a duty not to be vain and conceited about any personal advantage we may happen to possess. Yet a man might ask, How is it possible to help it? He might say, "If persons excel in any respect, they must know it; it is quite absurd to suppose, as a rule, that they should not; but if they know it, how is it possible they should not take pleasure in their own excellence, and admire themselves for it? Admiration is the natural consequence of the sight of excellence: if persons know they excel, they cannot help admiring themselves; and if they excel, generally speaking, they cannot but know it; and this, whatever it be they excel in, whether in personal appearance, or in power of speech, or in gifts of mind, or in character, or in any other way."

But now, on the other hand, I suppose that it is quite certain that Scripture tells us *not* to pride ourselves on any thing we are, any thing we do; that is, not to indulge those feelings which, it seems, are the natural and legitimate result of our knowing what we do know. Now what is to be said to this? how are these opposites to be reconciled?

One answer would of course be this; that religious men know how defective, after all, their best deeds are, or their best points of character; or they know how much more others do; or they know their own great deficiencies in other respects; or they know how trifling some of those points are on which they may happen to be superior to others. But this is not a sufficient answer; because the points in question *are* excellences, whether great excellences or not, or whether or not there be others greater, or however wanting the parties may be in other respects. And herein lies, I think, the temptation which all persons have to self-esteem, that in a certain sense their judgment about themselves is not wrong; not that they are not very deficient in many things, not as if they did not know this, but that they *have* certain excellences, which really *are* excellences, and they *feel* them; and the question is, how can they help feeling them?

It may be suggested, perhaps, to account for the humility of religious men, that, whatever personal gifts they may have, they are *used* to them; and this it is which keeps them from thinking much of them. There is truth in this remark, of course, but it does not explain why they *once* have not thought much of them, viz. when the sight of what they were, was not so familiar to them as it is; and if they did, we may be sure that the effects of their former self-conceit will remain upon them now, having become habitual.

Another and far better reason why religious persons are not self-conceited is, that they dislike to think of whatever is good in them, and turn away from the thought of it, whether their superiority to others be in mind or body, in intellectual powers or in moral attainments. But there is, I think, another more direct reason, and more connected with my present subject.

It is this: though religious men have gifts, and though they know it, yet they do not *realize* them. It is not necessary here to explain exactly what is meant by the word "realizing;" we all understand the word enough for my present purpose, and shall all confess that, at least, there is an abundance of matters which men do *not* realize, though they ought to do so. For instance; how loudly men talk of the shortness of this life, of its vanity and unprofitableness, and of the claims which the world to come has upon us! This is what we hear said daily, yet few act upon the truths they utter; and why? because they do not *realize* what they are so ready to proclaim. They do not see Him who is invisible, and His eternal kingdom.

Well, then, what men omit to do when the doing is a duty, that they can surely also omit to do in cases when omission is a duty. Serious men may know indeed, if it so be, what their excellences are, whether religious, or moral, or any other, but they do not feel them in that vivid way which we call realizing. They do not open their hearts to the knowledge, so that it be- comes fruitful. Barren knowledge is a wretched thing, when knowledge ought to bear fruit; but it is a good thing, when it would otherwise act merely as a temptation. When men realize a truth, it becomes an influential principle within them, and leads to a number of consequences both in opinion and in con- duct. The case is the same as regards realizing our own gifts. But men of superior minds know them without realizing. They may know that they have certain excellences, if they have them, they may know that they have good points of character, or abilities, or attainments; but it is in the way of an unproductive knowledge, which leaves the mind just as it found it. And this seems to be what gives such a remarkable simplicity to the char- acter of holy men, and amazes others so much that they think it a paradox or inconsistency, or even a mark of insincerity, that the same persons should profess to know so much about them- selves, and yet so little,—that they can hear so much said about themselves, that they can bear so much praise, so much popu- larity, so much deference, and yet without being puffed up, or arrogating aught, or despising others; that they can speak about themselves, yet in so unaffected a tone, with so much nature, with such childlike innocence, and such graceful frankness.

Another instance of this great gift of knowing without real- izing, is afforded us in relation to subjects to which I will but allude. Men who indulge their passions have a knowledge, dif- ferent in kind from those who have abstained from such indul- gence; and when they speak on subjects connected with it, realize them in a way in which others cannot realize them. The very ideas which are full of temptation to the former, the words which are painful to them to utter, all that causes them shame and confusion of face, can be said and thought of by the innocent without any distress at all. Angels can look upon sin with simple abhorrence and wonder, without humiliation or secret emotion; and a like simplicity is the reward of the chaste and holy; and that to the great amazement of the unclean, who cannot understand the state of mind of such a one, or how he can utter or endure thoughts which to themselves are full of misery and guilt. And hence sometimes you find men in these days, in which the will of the natural man is indulged to the full, taking up the writings of holy men who have lived in deserts or in cloisters, or with an Angel's heart have ruled Christ's flock, and broken with holy hands the bread of life, and viewing their words in their own murky atmosphere, and imputing to them their own grossness; nay, carping at the words of Holy Scripture, which are God's, and at the words of the Church, as if the sacred mystery of the Incarnation had not introduced a thousand new and heavenly associations into this world of sin.

And hence, again, you will find self-indulgent men unable to comprehend the real existence of sanctity and severity of mind in any one. They think that all persons must be full of the same wretched thoughts and feelings which torment themselves. They think that none can avoid it, from the nature of the case; only that certain persons contrive to hide what goes on in their hearts, and, in consequence, they call them pretenders and hypocrites.

This, too, is what they also say as regards the instance which I took first,—a man's knowledge of his gifts. They think that men who appear to think little of themselves are conceited within, and that what is called modesty is affectation.

I might make the same remark also as regards the absence of resentment upon injury or insult, which characterizes a really religious man. Often, indeed, such a one feels keenly what is done against him, though he represses the feeling as a matter of duty; but the higher state of mind is when he does not feel, that is, when he does not realize, that any injustice has been done him; so that if he attempts to speak of it, it will be in the same sort of strange, unreal, and (as I may say) forced and unnatural way in which pretenders to religion speak of religious joy and spiritual comfort, for he is as little at home with anger and re-venge as hypocrites are with thoughts of heaven.

Again; we may so unduly realize that a life of virtue is for our interest, as to act on prudential motives, not from a sense of duty. And again; though it be our duty to inquire and search out for ourselves the truth in religious matters, yet we may so vaunt in our private judgment, and make a merit of the exercise of it, that our search becomes almost a sin.

Here then are a number of cases, all in point, to illustrate one and the same truth, that the Christian's character is formed by a rule higher than that of calculation and reason, consisting in a Divine principle or life, which transcends the anticipations and criticisms of ordinary men. Judging by mere worldly reason, the Christian ought to be self-conceited, for he is gifted; he ought to understand evil, because he sees and speaks of it; he ought to feel resentment, because he is conscious of being injured; he ought to act from self-interest, because he knows that what is right is also expedient; he ought to be conscious and fond of the exercises of private judgment, because he engages in them; he ought to be doubting and hesitating in his faith, because his evidence for it might be greater than it is; he ought to have no expectation of Christ's coming, because Christ has delayed so long; but not so: his mind and heart are formed on a different mould. In these, and ten thousand other ways, he is open to the misapprehensions of the world, which neither has his feelings nor can enter into them. Nor can he explain and defend them on considerations which all men, good and bad, can understand. He goes by a law which others know not; not his own wisdom or judgment, but by Christ's wisdom and the judgment of the Spirit, which is imparted to him,—by that inward incommunicable perception of truth and duty, which is the rule of his reason, affections, wishes, tastes, and all that is in him, and which is the result of persevering obedience. This it is which gives so unearthly a character to his whole life and conversation, which is "hid with Christ in God;" he has ascended with Christ on high, and there "in heart and mind continually dwells;" and he is obliged, in consequence, to put a veil upon his face, and is mysterious in the world's judgment, and "becomes as it were a monster unto many," though he be "wiser than the aged," and have "more understanding than his teachers, because he keeps God's commandments." Thus "he that is spiritual judgeth all things, yet he himself is judged of no man;" and with him "it is a very small thing to be judged of man's judgment," for "He that judgeth him is the Lord." [1]

[1] 1 Cor. ii.15; iv.3, 4.

One additional remark is necessary in conclusion, with reference to the subject with which I began, the duty of waiting for our Lord's coming. It must not be supposed, then, that this implies a neglect of our duties in this world. As it is possible to watch for Christ in spite of earthly reasonings to the contrary, so is it possible to engage in earthly duties, in spite of our watching. Christ has told us, that when He comes two men shall be in the field, two women at the mill, "the one shall be taken, and the other left." You see that good and bad are engaged in the same way; nor need it hinder any one from having his heart firmly fixed on God, that he is engaged in worldly business with those whose hearts are upon the world. Nay, we may form large plans, we may busy ourselves in new undertakings, we may begin great works which we cannot do more than begin; we may make provision for the future, and anticipate in our acts the certainty of centuries to come, yet be looking out for Christ. Thus indeed we are bound to proceed, and to leave "times and seasons in His Father's power." Whenever He comes, He will cut things short; and, for what we know, our efforts and beginnings, though they be nothing more, are just as necessary in the course of His Providence, as could be the most successful accomplishment. Surely, He will end the world abruptly, whenever He comes; He will break off the designs and labours of His elect, whatever they are, and give them what their dutiful anxiety aims at, though not through it. And, as He will end, so did He begin the world abruptly; He began the world which we see, not from its first seeds and elements, but He created at once the herb and the fruit-tree perfect "whose seed is in itself," not a gradual formation, but a complete work. And with even a greater abruptness did He display His miracles when He came and new made all things, creating bread, not corn, for the supply of the five thousand, and changing water, not into any simpler, though precious liquid, but into wine. And as He began without beginning, so will He end without an ending; or rather, all that we do,—whatever we are doing,—whether we have time for more or time for less,—yet our work, finished or unfinished, will be acceptable, if done for Him. There is no inconsistency, then, in watching yet working, for we may work without setting our hearts on our work. Our sin will be if we idolize the work of our hands; if we love it so well as not to bear to part with it. The test of our faith lies in our being able to fail without disappointment.

Let us pray God to rule our hearts in this respect as well as in others; that "when He shall appear, we may have confidence, and not be ashamed before Him at His coming."

THE GOSPEL PALACES

(Whitsuntide)

"He built His sanctuary like high palaces, like the earth which He hath established for ever."—Ps. lxxviii.69.

THERE was one occasion when our Saviour said, "The hour cometh, when ye shall neither in this mountain, nor yet at Jerusalem, worship the Father. The hour cometh, when the true worshippers shall worship the Father in spirit and in truth."[1] Did we take these words by themselves, we might consider they implied, that, under the Gospel, there would be no outward tokens of religion, no rites and ordinances at all, no public services, no assemblings of ourselves together, and, especially, no sacred buildings. Such an inference, however, would be a great error, if it were only for this reason, that it has never been received, never acted on in any age of the Church; so far from it, that I suppose there are few indeed but would shrink from the very mention of it, and none at all who could be found to testify that they had adopted it in their own case, yet had not suffered from it in point of inward devotion to God's service. That cannot be the true sense of Scripture, which never has been fulfilled, which ever has been contradicted and disobeyed; for God's word shall not return unto Him void, but shall accomplish His pleasure and prosper in His purpose. Our Saviour did *not* say to the Samaritan woman that there should be no places and buildings for worship under the Gospel, *because* He has *not* brought it to pass, *because* such ever have been, at all times and in all countries, and amid all differences of faith. And the same reasons which lead us to believe that religious edifices are a Christian ordinance, though so very little is said about them in Scripture, will also show that it is right and pious to make them enduring, and stately, and magnificent, and ornamental; so that our Saviour's declaration, when He foretold the destruction of the Temple at Jerusalem, was not that there

[1] John iv.21, 23.

should never be any other house built to His honour, but rather that there should be many houses; that they should be built, not merely at Jerusalem, or at Gerizim, but every where; what was under the Law a local ordinance, being henceforth a Catholic privilege, allowed not here and there, but wherever was the Spirit and the Truth. The glory of the Gospel is not the *abolition* of rites, but their *dissemination*; not their absence, but their living and efficacious presence through the grace of Christ. Accordingly, such passages as the text, though spoken in the times of the Law, are fulfilled even at this day, and, as we trust, among ourselves. The Jewish Temple, indeed, of which the Psalmist spoke in the first instance, has come to nought; but he has a meaning still, and a noble one, as signifying the Christian institution of Churches.

"He built His sanctuary like high palaces, like the earth which He hath established for ever." How much more strikingly and fully is this accomplished in our times than in those of the Law! Rich and "exceeding magnifical" as was Solomon's Temple, and built at the immediate command of God, it is not presumptuous surely to say that Christian Temples have as far surpassed it in size, beauty, and costliness, as in divine gifts and privileges, as in spirit and in truth. "He built His sanctuary like high palaces;" look through this very country,—compare its palaces with its Cathedrals and Churches, even in their present state of disadvantage, and say whether these words are not more than accomplished; so that the palaces of England should rather, by way of honour, be compared to the Cathedrals, than the Cathedrals to the palaces. And rightly so; for our first duty is towards our Lord and His Church, and our second towards our earthly Sovereign. And still more strikingly has the promise of permanence been fulfilled to us. For what were the years of Solomon's Temple? Four hundred. What of the second Temple? Six hundred. These were long periods, certainly; yet is it plain that the Church of Christ can more than equal them, and that in a great number of cases. Nay, there are Christian Temples in some parts of the world, which have lasted as much as fourteen hundred years. Surely, then, when Christ multiplied His sacred palaces, He also gave them an extended age, bringing back under the Gospel the days of the Antediluvian patriarchs. The times are reversed, and a more vigorous life has been infused among us than at the first, and the reign of Christ and His saints has begun long since, and the Apostles fill their thrones in His Temples. "He hath built His sanctuary like high palaces, like the earth which He hath established for ever."

Stability and permanence are, perhaps, the especial ideas which a Church brings before the mind. It represents, indeed, the beauty, the loftiness, the calmness, the mystery, and the sanctity of religion also, and that in many ways; still, I will say, more than all these, it represents to us its eternity. It is the witness of Him who is the beginning and the ending, the first and the last; it is the token and emblem of "Jesus Christ, the same yesterday, to-day, and for ever;" it is the pledge of One, who has said, "I will never leave thee nor forsake thee," but "even to your old age I am He, and even to hoar hairs I will carry you." All ye who take part in the building of a Church, know that you have been admitted to the truest symbol of God's eternity. You have built what may be destined to have no end but in Christ's coming. Cast your thoughts back on the time when our ancient buildings were first reared. Consider the Churches all around us; how many generations have past since stone was put upon stone till the whole edifice was finished! The first movers and instruments of its erection, the minds that planned it, and the limbs that wrought at it, the pious hands that contributed to it, and the holy lips that consecrated it, have long, long ago, been taken away; yet we benefit by their good deed. Does it not seem a very strange thing that *we* should be fed, and lodged, and clothed in spiritual things, by persons we never saw or heard of, and who never saw us, or could think of us, hundreds of years ago? Does it not seem strange that men should be able, not merely by acting on others, not by a continued influence carried on through many minds in a long succession, but by one simple and direct act, to come into contact with us, and as if with their own hand to benefit us, who live centuries later? What a visible, palpable specimen this, of the communion of saints! What a privilege thus to be immediately interested in the deeds of our forefathers! and what a call on us, in like manner, to reach out our own hands towards our posterity! Freely we have received; let us freely give. Let us not be slack to do what our fathers have done; to do a work, the fruits of which we cannot see, because they are too vast to be seen. If it were told us, that a word of ours, uttered by the mouth, should take, as it were, consistence, and float and continue in the air, and impart advice or comfort to men who were to live five hundred years to come, it would be an inspiring thought; and what but this is our very privilege, in the leave granted us to multiply the One Temple of God all over the earth, unto all time? It is to make our deeds live; it is to hold fellowship with the future.

See what a noble principle faith is. Faith alone lengthens a man's existence, and makes him, in his own feelings, live in the future and in the past. Men of this world are full of plans of the day. Even in religion they are ever coveting immediate results, and will do nothing at all, unless they can do every thing,—can have their own way, choose their methods, and see the end. But the Christian throws himself fearlessly upon the future, because he believes in Him which is, and which was, and which is to come. He can endure to be one of an everlasting company while in this world, as well as in the next. He is content to begin, and break off; to do his part, and no more; to set about what others must accomplish; to sow where others must reap. None has finished his work, and cut it short in righteousness but He who is One. We, His members, who have but a portion of His fulness, execute but a part of His purpose. One lays the foundation, and another builds thereupon; one levels the mountain, and another "brings forth the headstone with shoutings." Thus were our Churches raised. One age would build a Chancel, and another a Nave, and a third would add a Chapel, and a fourth a Shrine, and a fifth a Spire. By little and little the work of grace went forward; and they could afford to take time about it, and be at pains to do it best, who had a promise that the gates of hell should not prevail against it. Powers of the earth rise and fall; revolutions come in course; great families appear, and are swept away; wise men are in high places, and walk amid the sparks which they have kindled. They *feel* that they are short-lived, and they determine to make the most of their time. They grasp and push forwards, they are busy and feverish, not only from the feebleness and waywardness of their nature but from the conviction of their reason, that they have but a short time. "Our time is short," say they; "let us buy and sell, and plant and build, and marry wives, and give in marriage, and eat and drink, for to-morrow we die." Poor worms of the earth, it is too true of them! Their aims and desires, their instruments, their goods, their bodies, their souls, are all perishable. In the words of the wise man, "as soon as they are born, they *begin* to draw to an end," [2] they begin to die. Their growth and progress, their successes, are but the first stages of corruption and dissolution. Poor children of time, what are they? They triumph over religion in their day; they insult its ordinances and its ministers; they tyrannize in its Temples, showing themselves that they are gods. They carry away its massive

[2] Wisd. v.13.

stones to their own houses, and trick themselves out with its jewels. They build up their families by rapine and sacrilege; they are wanton when they are not covetous; and, when satiated with pillage, they mutilate and defile what they do not destroy. But, after all, how speaks the Psalmist? "I have said, Ye are gods, and ye are all the children of the Most Highest. But ye shall die like men, and fall like one of the princes." "The proud have robbed, they have slept their sleep, and all the men whose hands were mighty have found nothing." "Fret not thyself because of the ungodly; neither be thou envious against the evildoers; for they shall soon be cut down like the grass, and be withered even as the green herb. I myself have seen the ungodly in great power, and flourishing like a green bay tree; I went by, and lo, he was gone; I sought him, but his place could no where be found."[3] We rise in the morning, and, behold, they are all dead corpses. The storm has passed, the morning has broken, the Egyptians are cast on the sea-shore, God's Tabernacle is still standing. As though no violence had been in the night, no assaults of Satan and Antichrist, no arm of force, no envious or covetous eye, they remain, those holy places, where they were; for the Church abides for evermore, and her Temples, in their deep foundations, and their arching heights, are her image and manifestation.

I have said that the sacred edifices which we see around us, and in which we worship, remind us of their builders, though they lived so long ago; but in truth they remind us of a time far earlier even than theirs. Do we suppose that the very builders of these shrines were all in all in their building? Could any men whatever, did they but will it, at any time, build what they have built? is a Cathedral the offspring of a random thought, a thing to will and to accomplish at our pleasure? or rather, were not those builders merely the successors and the children of others long before them, who made them what they were, and enabled them, under God, to do works, which it was not given to every one to do, but only to the sons of such fathers? Surely the Churches which we inherit are not the purchase of wealth nor the creation of genius, they are the fruits of martyrdom. They come of high deeds and sufferings, as long before their very building as we are after it. Their foundations are laid very deep, even in the preaching of Apostles, and the confession of Saints, and the first victories of the Gospel in our land. All that is so noble in their architecture, all that captivates the eye and

[3] Ps. lxxii.6, 7; lxxvi.5; xxxvii.1, 2, 36, 37.

makes its way to the heart, is not a human imagination, but a divine gift, a moral result, a spiritual work. The Cross is ever planted in hazard and suffering, and is watered with tears and blood. No where does it take root and bear fruit, except its preaching be with self-denial. It is easy, indeed, for the ruling powers to make a decree, and set religion on high, and extend its range, and herald its name; but they cannot plant it, they can but impose it. The Church alone can plant the Church. The Church alone can found her sees, and inclose herself within walls. None but saintly men, mortified men, preachers of righteousness, and confessors for the truth, can create a home for the truth in any land. Thus the Temples of God are withal the monuments of His Saints, and we call them by their names while we consecrate them to His glory. Their simplicity, grandeur, solidity, elevation, grace, and exuberance of ornament, do but bring to remembrance the patience and purity, the courage, meekness, and great charity, the heavenly affections, the activity in well-doing, the faith and resignation, of men who themselves did but worship in mountains, and in deserts, and in caves and dens of the earth. They laboured, but not in vain, for other men entered into their labours; and, as if by natural consequence, at length their word prospered after them, and made itself a home, even these sacred palaces in which it has so long dwelt, and which are still vouchsafed to us, in token, as we trust, that they too are still with us who spoke that word, and, with them, His Presence, who gave them grace to speak it.

O happy they, who, in a sorrowful time, avail themselves of this bond of communion with the Saints of old and with the Universal Church! O wise and dutiful, who, when the world has robbed them of so much, set the more account upon what remains! We have not lost all, while we have the dwelling-places of our forefathers; while we can repair those which are broken down, and build upon the old foundations, and propagate them upon new sites! Happy they, who, when they enter within their holy limits, enter in heart into the court of heaven! And most unhappy, who, while they have eyes to admire, admire them only for their beauty's sake, and the skill they exhibit; who regard them as works of art, not fruits of grace; bow down before their material forms, instead of worshipping "in spirit and in truth;" count their stones, and measure their spaces, but discern in them no tokens of the invisible, no canons of truth, no lessons of wisdom, to guide them forward in the way heavenward!

In heaven is the substance, of which here below we are vouchsafed the image; and thither, if we be worthy, we shall at length attain. There is the holy Jerusalem, whose light is like unto a stone most precious, even like a jasper stone, clear as crystal; and whose wall is great and high, with twelve gates, and an Angel at each;—whose glory is the Lord God Almighty, and the Lamb is the light thereof.

THE VISIBLE TEMPLE

(Whitsuntide)

"Whether is greater, the gold, or the Temple that
sanctifieth the gold?"—Matt. xxiii.17.

A Temple there has been upon earth, a spiritual Temple, made up of living stones, a Temple, as I may say, composed of souls; a Temple with God for its Light, and Christ for the High Priest, with wings of Angels for its arches, with Saints and Teachers for its pillars, and with worshippers for its pavement; such a Temple has been on earth ever since the Gospel was first preached. This unseen, secret, mysterious, spiritual Temple exists every where, throughout the kingdom of Christ, in all places, as perfect in one place as if it were not in another. Wherever there is faith and love, this Temple is; faith and love, with the Name of Christ, are as heavenly charms and spells, to make present to us this Divine Temple, in every part of Christ's kingdom. This Temple is invisible, but it is perfect and real because it is invisible, and gains nothing in perfection by possessing visible tokens. There needs no outward building to meet the eye, in order to make it more of a Temple than it already is in itself. God, and Christ, and Angels, and souls, are not these a heavenly court, all perfect, to which this world can add nothing? Though faithful Christians worship without splendour, without show, in a homely and rude way, still their worship is as acceptable to God, as excellent, as holy, as though they worshipped in the public view of men, and with all the glory and riches of the world.

Such was the Church in its beginnings; "built upon the foundation of Apostles and Prophets, Jesus Christ Himself being the chief corner-stone," "builded together for an habitation of God through the Spirit." In the Apostles' lifetime it was poor and persecuted, and the holy Temple was all but invisible. There were no edifying rites, no various ceremonies, no rich music, no high Cathedrals, no mystic vestments, no solemn altars, no stone, or marble, or metals, or jewels, or woods of cost, or fine linen, to signify outwardly, and to honour duly, the heavenly Temple in which we stand and serve. The place where our Lord and Saviour first celebrated the holy Sacrament of the Eucharist, was the upper room of a house, hired too or used for the occasion;[1] that in which the Apostles and the holy women waited for the promised coming of the Comforter, was also "an upper room;"[2] and that also in which St. Paul preached at Troas, was an "upper chamber, where they were gathered together."[3] What other places of worship do we hear of? The water side, out in the open air; as at Philippi, where, we are told, "on the Sabbath," St. Paul and his companions "went out of the city by a river side, where prayer was wont to be made."[4] And the sea shore; "They all brought us on our way with wives and children, till we were out of the city; and we kneeled down on the shore and prayed."[5] And St. Peter was in prayer on the house-top; and St. Paul and St. Silas sang their hymns and psalms in prison with their feet in the stocks; and St. Philip baptized the Ethiopian eunuch in the desert. Yet, wherever they were, whether in prison, or on the house-top, or in the wilderness, or by the river side, or on the sea shore, or in a private room, God and Christ were with them. The Spirit of Grace was there, the Temple of God was around them. They were come unto the mystical Sion, and to the heavenly Jerusalem, and to an innumerable company of Angels, and to the spirits of the Just. There needed not gold, nor jewels, nor costly array for those, who had, what according to the text was greater, who had the Temple. It might be right and fitting, if possible, to have these precious things also, but it was not necessary; for which was the greater? Such things did not make the temple more holy, but became themselves holy by being used for the Temple; the gold did not sanctify the Temple, but the Temple was greater, and sanctified the gold. Gold is a thing of nought without Christ's presence; and with His Presence, as in the days of His earthly ministry, it might be dispensed with.

The case is the same as regards the immediate successors of the Apostles, who were in still more forlorn circumstances, as regards worship, than the Apostles themselves. The Christians who came after them, were obliged to worship in graves and tombs to save their lives from the persecutor. In the eastern and southern parts, where the Apostles and the first converts lived, before the glad sound of the Gospel had reached these northern

---

[1] Mark xiv.15.   [2] Acts i.13.   [3] Acts xx.8.
[4] Acts xvi.13.   [5] Acts xxi.5.

and distant countries, they were accustomed to bury in caves dug out of the rock. Long galleries there are still remaining, in some places for miles underground, on each side of which the dead were placed. There the poor persecuted Christians met for worship, and that by night. Or the great people of the time built for themselves high and stately tombs above ground, as large as houses for the living; here too, in the darkness and solitude of night, did the Saints worship. Or in the depth of some wood, perhaps, where no one was likely to discover them. Such were the places in which the Invisible Temple manifested itself in times of heathenism; and who shall say that it wanted aught of outward show to make it perfect?

This is true and ever to be borne in mind; and yet no one can deny, on the other hand, that a great object of Christ's coming was to subdue this world, to claim it as His own, to assert His rights as its Master, to destroy the usurped dominion of the enemy, to show Himself to all men, and to take possession. He is that Mustard-tree which was destined silently to spread and overshadow all lands; He is that Leaven which was secretly to make its way through the mass of human opinion and institutions till the whole was leavened. Heaven and earth had hitherto been separate. His gracious purpose was to make them one, and that by making earth like heaven. He was in the world from the beginning, and man worshipped other gods; He came into the world in the flesh, and the world knew Him not; He came unto His own, and His own received Him not. But He came in order to *make* them receive Him, know Him, worship Him. He came to absorb this world into Himself; that, as He was light, so it might be light also. When He came, He had not a place to lay His head; but He came to make Himself a place, to make Himself a home, to make Himself houses, to fashion for Himself a glorious dwelling out of this whole world, which the powers of evil had taken captive. He came in the dark, in the dark night was He born, in a cave underground; in a cave where cattle were stabled, there was He housed; in a rude manger was He laid. There first He laid His head; but He meant not, blessed be His Name! He meant not there to remain for ever. He did not resign Himself to that obscurity; He came into that cave to leave it. The King of the Jews was born to claim the kingdom;—yea, rather, the Hope of all nations and the King of the whole earth, the King of kings and Lord of lords; and He gave not "sleep to His eyes or slumber to His eyelids," till He had changed His manger for a royal throne, and His grot for high palaces. Lift up your eyes, my brethren, and look around, for it is fulfilled at this day; yea, long ago, for many ages, and in many countries. "Wisdom hath builded her house, she hath hewn out her seven pillars." Where is the grot? where the stall for cattle? where the manger? where the grass and straw? where the unseemly furniture of that despised place? Is it possible that the Eternal Son should have been born in a hole of the earth? was the great miracle there wrought, whereby a pure and spotless Virgin brought forth God? Strange condescension undergone to secure a strange triumph! He purposed to change the earth, and He began "in the lowest pit, in a place of darkness, and in the deep." All was to be by Him renewed, and He availed Himself of nothing that was, that out of nothing He might make all things. He was not born in the Temple of Jerusalem; He abhorred the palace of David; He laid Himself on the damp earth in the cold night, a light shining in a dark place, till by the virtue that went out of Him, He should create a Temple worthy of His Name.

And lo, in omen of the future, even in His cradle, the rich and wise of the earth seek Him with gold, and frankincense, and myrrh, as an offering. And He puts aside the swaddling clothes, and takes instead "a coat without seam, woven from the top throughout." And He changes water into wine; and Levi feasts Him; and Zacchæus receives Him; and Mary anoints His head. Pass a few generations, and the whole face of things is changed; the earth is covered with His Temples; as it has been for ages. Go where you will, you find the eternal mountains hewn and fashioned into shrines where He may dwell, who was an outcast in the days of His flesh. Rivers and mines pay tribute of their richest jewels; forests are searched for their choicest woods; the skill of man is put to task to use what nature furnishes. Go through the countries where His name is known, and you will find all that is rarest and most wonderful in nature or art has been consecrated to Him. Kings' palaces are poor, whether in architecture or in decoration, compared with the shrines which have been reared to Him. The Invisible Temple has become visible. As on a misty day, the gloom gradually melts and the sun brightens, so have the glories of the spiritual world lit up this world below. The dull and cold earth is penetrated by the rays. All around we see glimpses or reflections of those heavenly things, which the elect of God shall one day see face to face. The kingdoms of this world are become the kingdoms of our Lord and of His Christ; "the Temple has sanctified the gold," and the prophecies made to the Church have been fulfilled to the letter. "The glory of Lebanon" has been "given unto it, the excellency of Carmel and Sharon." "The glory of Lebanon, the fir-tree, the pine-tree, and the box together, to beautify the place of His sanctuary, and to make the place of His feet glorious. The multitude of camels have covered it, the dromedaries of Midian and Ephah; all they from Sheba have come; they have brought gold and incense and shown forth the praises of the Lord." "The labour of Egypt, and merchandize of Ethiopia, and of the Sabeans, men of stature, have come over to it, in chains have they come over; they have fallen down, they have made supplication."[6]

And He has made Him a Temple, not only out of inanimate things, but of men also as parts of it. Not gold and silver, jewels and fine linen, and skill of man to use them, make the House of God, but worshippers, the souls and bodies of men, whom He has redeemed. Not souls alone, He takes possession of the whole man, body as well as soul; for St. Paul says, "I beseech you, therefore, brethren, by the mercies of God, that ye present your *bodies* a living sacrifice, holy, acceptable unto God, which is your reasonable service."[7] And He claims us as His own, not one by one, but altogether, as one great company; for St. Peter says, that we "as living stones, are built up a spiritual house, an holy priesthood, to offer up spiritual sacrifices, acceptable to God by Jesus Christ."[8] All of us, and every one, and every part of every one, must go to make up His mystical body; for the Psalmist says, "O God, my heart is ready; I will sing and give praise with the best member that I have. Awake thou, lute and harp, I myself will awake right early. I will give thanks unto Thee, O Lord, among the people; I will sing praises unto Thee among the nations."[9] Our tongues must preach Him, and our voices sing of Him, and our knees adore Him, and our hands supplicate Him, and our heads bow before Him, and our countenances beam of Him, and our gait herald Him. And hence arise joint worship, forms of prayer, ceremonies of devotion, the course of services, orders of ministers, holy vestments, solemn music, and other things of a like nature; all which are, as it were, the incoming into this world of the Invisible Kingdom of Christ, the fruit of its influence, the sample of its power, the earnest of its victories, the means of its manifestation.

Things temporal have their visible establishment. Kings' courts and palaces, councils and armies, have dazzled the multitude, and blinded them, till they worshipped them as idols.

---

[6] Is. xxxv.2; lx.6, 13; xlv.14.

[7] Rom. xii.1.

[8] 1 Pet. ii.5.

[9] Ps. cviii.1–3.

Such is our nature, we must have something to look up to. We cannot help admiring *something*; and if there is nothing good to admire, we admire what is bad. When then men see proud Babel set up on high with all her show and pomp, when they see or hear of great cities, with their stately mansions, the streets swarming with chariots and horses innumerable, and the shops filled with splendid wares, and great men and women richly dressed, with many attendants, and men crying, Bow the knee, and soldiers in bright array, with the sound of the trumpet, and other military music, and other things which one could mention, were it reverent to be particular,—simple men are tempted to look up to all this as the summit of perfection and blessedness, nay, as I have said, to worship what seems to them, though they do not so express it, the presence of the Unseen. Hence come in servility, coveting, jealousy, ambition; men wish to be great in this world, and try to be great; they aim at riches, or they lie in wait for promotion. Christ, then, in order to counteract this evil, has mercifully set up His own court and His own polity, that men might have something to fix their eyes upon of a more Divine and holy character than the world can supply; that poverty might at least divide men's admiration with riches; that meekness might be set up on high as well as pride, and sanctity become our ambition as well as luxury. Saintly bishops with their clergy, officials of all kinds, religious bodies, austere Nazarites, prayer and praise without ceasing,— all this hath Christ mercifully set up, to outshine the fascinations of the world. So ran the promise: "I have set watchmen upon thy walls, O Jerusalem, which shall never hold their peace day nor night." "Sing unto the Lord a new song, and His praise from the end of the earth; ye that go down to the sea, and all that is therein. . . . Let the wilderness and the cities thereof lift up their voice, the villages that Kedar doth inhabit; let the inhabitants of the rock sing; let them shout from the top of the mountains. Let them give glory unto the Lord, and declare His praise in the islands."[10] And these words began to have their fulfilment even from the time that Christ came; for, as I said when I began, St. Paul and St. Silas *sang* in the prison; and when he and his party left Tyre, the men, women, and children, who accompanied them out, *kneeled down* on the shore with them, and prayed. Such were the forms of worship in the beginning; till, as time went on, the Church, like some fair tree, put out her branches and foliage, and stood complete in all manner of

[10] Is. lxii.6; xlii.10–12.

holy symbols and spiritual ordinances, an outward sign of that unseen Temple in which Christ had dwelt from the first.

And now, in conclusion, let me observe, that such a view as has been taken of the connexion of the ritual of religion with its spiritual and invisible power will enable us to form a right estimate of things external, and keep us both from a curious and superstitious use, and an arrogant neglect of them. The Temple is greater than the gold; therefore care not though the gold be away:—it sanctifies it; therefore cherish the gold while it is present. Christ is with us, though there be no outward show; suppose all the comely appendages of our worship stripped off, yet where two or three are gathered together in His Name, He is in the midst of them. Be it a cottage, or the open fields, or even a prison or a dungeon, Christ can be there, and will be there, if His servants are there. You will ask whether this does not countenance persons who hold meetings apart from the Church, or who preach in the streets? No, it does not; because, in such cases, men do not meet together "in the Name of Christ." He says, "Where two or three are gathered together in My Name." Now, it does not follow that men *are* met in His Name because they say or think they are; for He warns us, "Many shall come in My Name, saying, I am Christ, and shall deceive many." Many a man *thinks* he is speaking in Christ's Name, when he is preaching his own doctrine. Christ did not send such men, yet they have run; and He owns them not, though they even worship in Church. In Church, or in the fields, would be the same in this matter. Stone walls do not make a Church. Though they were in the vastest, noblest, richest building on earth, still Christ would not be with those who preach another gospel than that which He delivered once for all. This is the very point I am insisting on. It is the Temple which sanctifieth the gold; it is nothing but the invisible and heavenly Presence which sanctifieth any place or any thing. Magnificent or mean, costly or common, it alone sanctifies either worshippers or building. As it avails not to have sumptuous Churches without the Spirit of Christ, so it is but a mockery to have large congregations, eloquent preachers, and much excitement, if that gracious Spirit is away. But where He really places His *Name*, there, be the spot a palace or a cottage, it is sacred and glorious. He who once lay in a manger, will still condescend to manifest Himself any where, as He did in primitive times. No indignities can be done to Him who inhabiteth eternity. "Heaven is His throne, and earth His footstool;" "the very heaven of heavens cannot contain Him;" much less any house which we can build. High or low is alike to Him.

This is an obvious and very comfortable reflection, when we think of the great irreverences and profanations which sometimes take place in Church. Men come in lightly and thoughtlessly; they care not to uncover their heads; they talk, and laugh, and even sing, as if they were in a common building; or, when there is any needful work to be done in it, and tools and other implements are brought in, they seem to think as if, all of a sudden, it were turned into an unconsecrated place, because it is necessary to exercise a trade in it. Or, perhaps, if it so happen, they turn aside into it at other times, and think that God is not there, because man is not there to see them. And so again, when we go into certain Churches, and see the neglected state in which they are left, the font cast aside, or, if not, used as a place to keep any sort of litter in; and the Holy Table mean and unsightly, with a miserable covering, and the pavement defiled and broken, and the whole building in a state of neglect, of which any neat person would be ashamed even in his own cottage (to say nothing what wealthy people would feel, if their rooms were left in such a condition); I say, when these and such like sights meet us, perhaps, for an instant, we are tempted to say, Can Christ be here? Can the Holy Spirit deign to sanctify water for the washing away of sins, brought in, as it is, with such irreverence of manner, and in so mean a vessel? Or, can the life-giving Presence and the sacrificial power of Christ be upon that Altar? nay, can it *be* an Altar, which is so wretched to look upon? But, I ask, or rather, any one will ask himself, on second thoughts, Could Christ be in a manger? Doubtless then He, whom the Angels of God worshipped as the Only-begotten, when brought into the world in a place for cattle, can be manifested, can be worshipped, in the most neglected Church. No; our distress must not be at all for *Him*; such would be superstitious and carnal; our distress must be for the insult offered Him, and so far as there is insult. If the state of neglect I am speaking of is no one's fault, then distress there must be none. But if there be blame, then we may and must feel distress, that our Lord should be insulted by His own servants; and yet more on their account, that they should insult Him. They who profane His Presence, who treat its resting-place as a common house, and make free with it, these men do not hurt Christ, but they hurt themselves. The Temple is greater than the gold.

And, while He is displeased with the profane, He accepts such offerings as are made in faith, whether they be greater or less. He accepts our gold and our silver, not to honour Himself thereby, but in mercy to us. When Mary poured the ointment upon His head, it was her advantage, not His: He praised her, and said, "She hath done what she could." Every one must do his best; he must pray his best, he must sing his best, he must attend his best. If we did all, it would be little, not worthy of Him; if we do little, it may suffice to show our faith, and He in His mercy will accept whatever we can offer. He will accept, what we prefer giving to Him to giving to ourselves. When, instead of spending money on our own homes, we spend it on His house, when we prefer that He should have the gold and silver to our having it, we do not make our worship more spiritual, but we bring Christ nearer to us; we show that we are in earnest, we evidence our faith. It requires very little of true faith and love, to feel an unwillingness to spend money on one's self. Fine dresses, fine houses, fine furniture, fine establishments, are painful to a true Christian; they create misgivings in his mind whether his portion is with the Saints or with the world. Rather he will feel it suitable to lay out his money in God's service, to feed the hungry, to clothe the naked, to educate the young, to spread the knowledge of the truth; and, among other pious objects, to build and to decorate the visible House of God.

"Remember me, O my God, concerning this, and wipe not out my good deeds that I have done for the house of my God, and for the offices thereof." [11] Such was Nehemiah's prayer, when he had been stirred up to cleanse the sanctuary. May God remember us also, if in any measure His grace has moved us to similar acts of zeal for His glory! And, O may He in His mercy grant that our outward show does not outstrip our inward progress; that whatever gift, rare or beautiful, we introduce here, may be but a figure of inward beauty and unseen sanctity ornamenting our hearts! Hearts are the true shrine wherein Christ must dwell. "The King's daughter is all-glorious within;" and when we are repenting of past sin, and cleansing ourselves from all defilement of flesh and spirit, and perfecting holiness in the fear of the Lord, then, and then only, may we safely employ ourselves in brightening, embellishing, and making glorious the dwelling-place of His invisible Presence, doing it with that severity, gravity, and awe, which a chastened heart and sober thoughts will teach us.

[11] Neh. xiii.14.

OFFERINGS FOR THE SANCTUARY

(Whitsuntide)

"The glory of Lebanon shall come unto thee, the fir-tree, the pine-tree, and the box together, to beautify the place of My Sanctuary; and I will make the place of My feet glorious."—Is. lx.13.

E VERY attentive reader of Scripture must be aware what stress is there laid upon the duty of costliness and magnificence in the public service of God. Even in the first rudiments of the Church, Jacob, an outcast and wanderer, after the vision of the Ladder of Angels, thought it not enough to bow down before the Unseen Presence, but parted with, or, as the world would say, wasted a portion of the provisions he had with him for the way, in an act of worship. Like David, he did not "offer unto the Lord of that which cost him nothing;" but like that religious woman at the opening of a more gracious Covenant, though he had not "an alabaster box of ointment of spikenard very precious," yet he did "what he could;" making a sacrifice less than hers in its costliness, greater in his own destitute condition, for he "took the stone that he had put for his pillows, and set it up for a pillar, and poured oil upon the top of it."[1]

What Jacob did as a solitary pilgrim, David as a wealthy king, Mary as a private woman, is pressed upon us both in sacred history and in prophecy, as fulfilled under the Law, as foretold of the Gospel. The Book of Exodus shows what cost was lavished upon the Tabernacle even in the wilderness; the Books of Kings and Chronicles set before us the devotion of heart, the sedulous zeal, the carelessness of expense or toil, with which the first Temple was reared upon Mount Sion, in the commencement of the monarchy of Israel. "Now have I prepared," says David, "*with all my might* for the house of my God, the gold . . . and the silver . . . and the brass . . . the iron . . . and wood . . . onyx stones, and stones to be set, glis-

[1] Gen. xxviii.18.

tering stones, and of divers colours, and all manner of precious stones, and marble stones in abundance. Moreover, because I *have set my affection* to the house of my God, I have *of my own proper good*, of gold and silver, which I have given to the house of my God, over and above all that I have prepared for the Holy House." And he "rejoiced with great joy," and "blessed the Lord," because the people also "*offered willingly*, because *with perfect heart* they offered willingly to the Lord." And Solomon, when he came to use these costly offerings, sent to another country for "a cunning man," "skilful to work in gold, and in silver, in brass, in iron, in stone, and in timber, in purple, in blue, and in fine linen and in crimson; also to grave any manner of graving, and to find out every device which should be put to him, with the cunning men in Judah and in Jerusalem." [2] Such was the outward splendour of the Jewish Sanctuary; nor were the glories of the Christian to be less outward and visible, though they were to he more spiritual also. The words of the Prophet in the text are but one instance out of several, of the promise of temporal magnificence made to that Covenant which was to be eternal. "The glory of Lebanon," says Isaiah, addressing the Gospel Church, "shall come unto thee, the fir-tree, the pine-tree, and the box together, to beautify the place of My Sanctuary; and I will make the place of My feet glorious." Again; "For brass I will bring gold, and for iron I will bring silver, and for wood brass, and for stones iron; thou shalt call thy walls Salvation, and thy gates Praise." And again; "O thou afflicted, tossed with tempest, and not comforted, behold, I will lay thy stones with fair colours, and lay thy foundations with sapphires. And I will make thy windows of agates, and thy gates of carbuncles, and all thy borders of pleasant stones." [3] Now if it be said that some of these expressions are figurative, this may be true; but still the very fact that such figures are used in the prophecy, would seem to show that the materials literally denoted may be suitably used in its fulfilment, unless, indeed, such use is actually forbidden. They do not cease to be figures because they are actually present as well as spoken of. Real gold is as much a figure in the Church, as the mention of it is such in Scripture; and it is surely in itself dutiful and pleasant thus to make much of the words of inspired truth; and moreover, the mere circumstance that, when the Gospel came, Christians did thus proceed, and sanctified

---

[2] 1 Chron. xxix.2, 3, 9, 10; 2 Chron. ii.7, 14.
[3] Is. lx.17, 18; liv.11, 12.

the precious things of this world to religious uses, looks like the fulfilment of the prophecy, and is of the nature of an authoritative command.

However, it may be objected that every attentive reader of Scripture will be familiar with this circumstance also, that such outward splendour in the worship of God is spoken of in terms of censure or jealousy by our Lord and Saviour. Thus He says, when enumerating the offences of the Pharisees, "Woe unto you, Scribes and Pharisees, hypocrites! for ye make clean the *outside* of the cup and of the platter, but within they are full of extortion and excess." And again, "Ye are like unto whited sepulchres, which indeed appear beautiful outward, but are within full of dead men's bones, and of all uncleanness." And when His disciples pointed out to our Lord the great size of the stones of which the Temple was built—a Temple, let it be noted, thus ornamented by the impious Herod,—He answered abruptly, "There shall not be left here one stone upon another, that shall not be thrown down." [4]

These passages certainly should be taken into account; but what do they mean? did our Saviour say that magnificence in worshipping God, magnificence in His house, in its furniture, and in its decorations, is wrong, wrong since He has come into the world? Does He discourage us from building handsome Churches, or beautifying the ceremonial of religion? Did He exhort us to niggardness? did He put a slight on architectural skill? did He imply we should please Him the more, the less study and trouble we gave to the externals of worship? In rejecting the offering of Herod, did He forbid the devotion of Christians?

This is what many persons think. I do not exaggerate when I say, that they think the more homely and familiar their worship is, the more spiritual it becomes. And they argue, that to aim at external beauty in the service of the Sanctuary, is to be like the Pharisees, to be fair without and hollow within; that whereas the Pharisees pretended a sanctity and religiousness outside which they had not inside, therefore, every one who aims at outward religion sacrifices to it inward.

This is a consideration worth dwelling on; not indeed for its own weight, but because it weighs with so many people. The objection is this; because the hollow Pharisees were outwardly holy, therefore every one who shows any outward holiness is, or is in danger of becoming, a Pharisee.

---

[4] Matt. xxiii.25, 27; xxiv.2.

Now, to take a parallel instance, most of us perhaps have heard a proverb, that "cleanliness is next to godliness;" which means, that the habit spoken of is of a moral nature, at least accidentally, and is a moral excellence, and that those who are deficient in it are commonly deficient also in other and more religious excellences also. Who among us will not admit that nothing is more unwelcome, nay, under circumstances, nothing raises more serious and anxious thoughts, than the absence of neatness and what is called tidiness, in appearance and dress? We can often tell at once how young persons are conducting themselves by the first glance at them. Alas! we read what is painful in their history; we read of a change in their religious state in the disorder of their look and the negligence of their gait. Or enter a village school: are we not at once pleased with a neat and bright-faced child? and do we not at once take a dislike to such as are not so?

But, now, suppose any one were to come to us and say, "This is all outside; what God requires is a clean heart, not a neat appearance:" would this seem a pertinent objection? We should answer surely, that what our duty requires of us is cleanness of heart *and* decency of attire also; that the one point of duty does not interfere with the other; nay, on the contrary, that inward exactness and sanctity are likely to *show* themselves in this very way,—in propriety of appearance; and that if persons who are exact in their lives are, notwithstanding, negligent in their persons, this ought not to be so, and we wish it were otherwise.

But supposing the objector went on to say that those who were neat and respectable in their persons and homes had often very bad tempers, were ever making a *point* of being neat, and what is called "particular," and quarrelled with every one who interfered with their own habits and ways. We should answer, that if so, it was to be lamented; but still, in spite of this, it was a right thing to be neat, and a wrong thing to be slovenly; that exactness within best showed itself in exactness without; and that cleanliness was the natural and most appropriate attendant on godliness.

And again; supposing the objector in question said that propriety in dress became love of finery; that those who attended to their persons became vain; that it was impossible to be neat and respectable without going on to dress gaily, and making a show to attract the attention of others. We should answer that all this ought not to be, and was very wrong; that vanity was a great sin; that those who studied their dress disobeyed our Lord's command not to think about raiment, and were exposing themselves to temptations, and were going forth they knew not whither, going the way of death, going the way to become reckless, as about greater matters, so about dress itself. This we should say; but we should add, that such considerations did not prove that neatness and decency were not praiseworthy, but that love of finery was perilous, and vanity sinful.

But supposing the objector supported what he said by Scripture: supposing he said, for instance, that our Lord blamed persons who washed their hands before eating bread, and that this proves that washing the hands before a meal is wrong. I am taking no fictitious case; such objections really have been made before now: yet the answer surely is easy, namely, that our Saviour objected, not to the mere washing of the hands, but to the making too much of such an observance; to our thinking it religion, thinking that it would stand in the stead of inward religion, and would make up for sins of the heart. This is what He condemned, the show of great attention to outward things, *while* inward things, which were more important, were neglected. This, He says Himself, in His denunciation of the Pharisees, "These ought ye to have done," He says, "*and not* to leave the other," the inward, "*undone.*" He says expressly they ought to do the outward, but they ought to do more. They did the one and not the other; they ought to have done both the one and the other.

Now, apply this to the case of beautifying Churches:—as is neatness and decency in an individual, such is decoration in a Church; and as we should be offended at slovenliness in an individual, so ought we to be offended at disorder and neglect in our Churches. It is quite true, men *are* so perverse (as the Pharisees were) that they sometimes attend only to the outward forms, and neglect the inward spirit; they may offer to Him costly furniture and goodly stones, while they are cruel or bigoted;—just as persons may be neat in their own persons and houses, and yet be ill-tempered and quarrelsome. Or, again, they may carry their attention to the outward forms of religion too far, and become superstitious; just as persons may carry on a love of neatness into love of finery. And, moreover, Scripture speaks against the hypocrisy of those who are religious outwardly, while they live in sin,—just as it speaks against those who wash their hands, while their heart is defiled. But still, in spite of all this, propriety in appearance and dress is a virtue,— is next to godliness; and, in like manner, decency and reverence are to be observed in the worship of God, and are next to devotion, in spite of its being true that not all are holy who are grave and severe, not all devout who are munificent.

What Scripture reproves is the *inconsistency*, or what it more solemnly called the *hypocrisy* of being fair without and foul within; of being religious in appearance, not in truth. It was one offence not to be religious, it was a second offence to pretend to be religious. "Ye fools," says our Lord, "did not He that made that which is without, make that which is within also?" Such as a man is outwardly, such should he be inwardly. "How can ye, being evil, speak good things? for out of the abundance of the heart the mouth speaketh. A good man, out of the good treasure of the heart, bringeth forth good things; and an evil man, out of the evil treasure, bringeth forth evil things."[5] The light of Divine truth, when in the heart, ought to beam forth outwardly; and when a man is dark within, well were it that he should show himself outwardly what he is. Such as a man is inside, such should be his outside. Well; but do you not see that such a view of doctrine condemns not only those who affect outward religion without inward, but those also who affect inward without outward? For, if it is an inconsistency to pretend to religion outwardly, while we neglect it inwardly, it is also an inconsistency, surely, to neglect it outwardly while we pretend to it inwardly. It is wrong, surely, to believe and not to profess; wrong to put our light under a bushel. St. Paul says expressly, "If thou shalt *confess with thy mouth* the Lord Jesus, and shalt believe in thine heart that God had raised Him from the dead, thou shalt be saved."[6] Belief is not enough; we must confess. Nor must we confess with our mouth only; but by word and by deed, by speech and by silence, by doing and by not doing, by walk and conversation, when in company and when alone, in time and in place, when we labour and when we rest, when we lie down and when we rise up, in youth and in age, in life and in death,—and, in like manner, in the world and in Church. Now, to adorn the worship of God our Saviour, to make the beauty of holiness visible, to bring offerings to the Sanctuary, to be curious in architecture, and reverent in ceremonies,—all this external religion is a sort of profession and confession; it is nothing but what is natural, nothing but what is consistent, in those who are cultivating the life of religion within. It is most unbecoming, most offensive, in those who are not religious; but most becoming, most necessary, in those who are so.

[5] Luke xi.40; Matt. xii.34, 35.   [6] Rom. x.9.

Persons who put aside gravity and comeliness in the worship of God, that they may pray more spiritually, forget that God is a Maker of *all* things, *visible* as well as invisible; that He is the Lord of our bodies as well as of our souls; that He is to be worshipped in public as well as in secret. The Creator of this world is none other than the Father of our Lord Jesus Christ; there are not two Gods, one of matter, one of spirit; one of the Law, and one of the Gospel. There is one God, and He is Lord of all we are, and all we have; and, therefore, all we do must be stamped with His seal and signature. We must begin, indeed, with the heart; for out of the heart proceed all good and evil; but while we begin with the heart, we must not end with the heart. We must not give up this visible world, as if it came of the evil one. It is our duty to change it into the kingdom of heaven. We must manifest the kingdom of heaven upon earth. The light of Divine truth must proceed *from* our hearts, and shine out *upon* every thing we are, and every thing we do. It must bring the *whole* man, soul and body, into captivity to Christ. They who are holy in spirit, are holy in body. They who submit their wills to Christ, bow their bodies; they who offer the heart, bow the knee; they who have faith in His Name, bow the head; they who honour His cross inwardly, are not ashamed of it before men. They who rejoice *with* their brethren in their common salvation, and desire to worship together, *build a place* to worship in, and they build it as the *expression* of their feelings, of their mutual love, of their common reverence. They build a building which will, as it were, speak; which will profess and confess Christ their Saviour; which will herald forth His death and passion at first sight; which will remind all who enter that we are saved by His cross, and must bear our cross after Him. They will build what may tell out their deepest and most sacred thoughts, which they dare not utter in word: not a misshapen building, not a sordid building, but a noble dwelling, a palace all-glorious within; unfit, indeed, for God's high Majesty, whom even the heaven of heavens cannot contain, but fit to express the feelings of the builders,—a monument which may stand and (as it were) preach to all the world while the world lasts; which may show how they desire to praise, bless, and glorify their eternal Benefactor; how they desire to get others to praise Him also; a Temple which may cry out to all passers by, "Oh, magnify the Lord our God, and fall down before His footstool, for He is Holy! Oh, magnify the Lord our God, and worship Him upon His holy hill, for the Lord our God is Holy!" [7]

[7] Ps. xcix.5, 9.

This, then, is the real state of the case; and when our Lord blamed the Pharisees as hypocrites, it was not for attending to the outside of the cup, but for not attending to the inside also.

Now, in answer to the parallel I have been drawing out, it may be objected, that "if the decoration of God's public service be like the personal duty of propriety in dress and demeanour, then decoration is wrong when it is intentional and studied. Those who are anxious how they look, and what others think of them, are in the way to be vain, if they are not so already; decorum should be the *spontaneous* result of inward exactness; grace in manner and apparel should be the mere outward image of harmony and purity of soul. Therefore, holy persons attire themselves with simplicity, speak with modesty, behave with gravity. Their ease, and their amiableness, and their gentleness, and their composure, and their majesty, are as little known to themselves as the features of their countenance. If, then, the parallel holds, external religion becomes excessive as soon as it is made an object; and this, of course, becomes practically an argument against all consecration of wealth and of art to the worship of God." One single remark, however, is sufficient to invalidate this objection; for, let it be observed, in making much of our own appearance, we are contemplating ourselves; but in making much of the ceremonial of religion, we are contemplating another, and Him our Maker and Redeemer. This is so obvious and decisive a distinction, that I should not care to notice the objection to which it is an answer, except that it will open upon us a further consideration connected with our subject. For it so happens that, at present, far from acknowledging its force, it is the way of the world to be most sensitively jealous of over-embellishment in the worship of God, while it has no scruples or misgivings whatever at an excess of splendour and magnificence in its own apparel, houses, furniture, equipages, and establishments.

I say it is the way with us Englishmen, who are the richest people upon earth, to lay out our wealth upon ourselves; and when the thought crosses our minds, if it ever does, that such an application of God's bounties is unworthy those who are named after Him who was born in a stable, and died upon the Cross, we quiet them by asking, "What is the use of all the precious things which God has given us, if we may not enjoy them? The earth overflows with beauty and richness, and man is gifted with skill to improve and perfect what he finds in it. What delicate and costly things do the streets of any rich town present to our eyes! what bales of merchandize! what fine linen! what silks from afar! what precious metals! what jewels! what choice marbles! and what exquisite workmanship, making what is in itself excellent, of double worth! What," it is inquired, "*can* be done with all this bounty of Providence? has He not poured it all lavishly into our hands? was it given, except to be used? And what is true of the more precious things, is true of the less precious; it is true of such things as come in the way of ordinary persons; the luxuries of opulence are, in their degree, offered to all of us, as if we were opulent, for we partake in the common opulence of our country; why, then, may we not enjoy the gifts of nature and art, which God has given?"

I have already suggested the true answer to this difficulty. The earth is full of God's wonderful works, do you say, and what are we to do with them? what to do with marbles and precious stones, gold and silver, and fine linen? Give them to God. Render them to Him from whom, and through whom, and to whom are all things. This is their proper destination. Is it a better thing to dress up our sinful bodies in silk and jewels, or to ornament therewith God's House and God's ritual? Does any one doubt what all these excellent things are meant for? or, at least, can he doubt what they are *not* meant for? not meant, surely, for sinners to make themselves fine withal. What presumption would that be, what senselessness! Does not the whole world speak in praise of God? Does not every star in the sky, every tree and flower upon earth, all that grows, all that endures, the leafy woods, the everlasting mountains, speak of God? Do not the pearls in the sea, and the jewels in the rocks, and the metals in the mine, and the marbles in the quarry,—do not all rich and beautiful substances every where witness of Him who made them? Are they not His work, His token, His glory? Are they not a portion of a vast natural Temple, the heavens, earth, and sea,—a vast Cathedral for the Bishop of our souls, the All-sufficient Priest, who first created all things, and then again, became, by purchase, their Possessor? Does it not strike you, then, as extreme presumption, and a sort of sacrilege, to consecrate them to any one's glory but God's? If we saw things aright, could there be a more frightful spectacle, an instance of more complete self-worship, a more detestable idolatry, than men and women making themselves fine that others might admire them? keeping all these things for self, denying them to the rightful Owner? viewing them as if mere works of "nature," as they are sometimes called, and incapable of any religious purpose? Recollect Herod; he was smitten by the Angel and eaten of worms, because he gave not God the glory; and *how* did he withhold it? By arraying himself in royal apparel, making an oration, and being patient of the cry, "It is the voice of a god and not of a man." The royal apparel was imputed to him as a sin, because he used it, not to remind himself that he was God's minister, but to impress upon the people that he was a god. And every one, high and low, who is in the practice of dressing ostentatiously, whether in silk or in cotton, that is, every one who dresses to be looked at and admired, is using God's gifts for an idol's service, and offering them up to self.

No; let us master this great and simple truth, that all rich materials and productions of this world, being God's property, are intended for God's service; and sin only, nothing but sin, turns them to a different purpose. All things are His; He in His bounty has allowed us to take freely of all that is in the world, for food, clothing, and lodging; He allows us a large range, He afflicts us not by harsh restrictions; He gives us a discretionary use, for which we are answerable to Him alone. Still, after all permission, on the whole we must not take what we do not need. We may take for life, for comfort, for enjoyment; not for luxury, not for pride. Let us give Him of His own, as David speaks; let us honour Him, and not ourselves. Let the house of God be richly adorned, for it is His dwelling-place; priests, for they represent Him; kings, magistrates, judges, heads of families, for they are His ministers. These are called gods in Scripture, and "all that is called God or that is worshipped," may receive of His gifts whose Name they bear. Nothing, however rich, is sinful, which has a religious meaning; which reminds us of God,—or of the absent, whom we revere or love,—or of relations or friends departed; or which is a gift, and not a purchase. In proportion as we disengage it from the thought of self, and associate it with piety towards others, do we succeed in sanctifying it.

Hence it is that while Abraham sent jewels to Rebekah, and Jacob made Joseph a coat of many colours, St. Paul gives his judgment "that women adorn themselves with shamefacedness and sobriety, *not* with broidered hair, or gold, or pearls, or costly array;" and St. Peter, that their "adorning" should not be "that outward adorning of plaiting the hair, and of wearing of gold, or of putting on of apparel, but the hidden man of the heart." [8] Or again; compare the Book of Ezekiel with the Apocalypse, and you will see the right and the wrong use of earthly magnificence instanced in the city of Antichrist and Holy

---

[8] I Tim. ii.9; I Pet. iii.3, 4.

Jerusalem. God's judgments are denounced upon Tyre by the Prophet, for being proud of her wealth and spending it on herself. "Thou hast been in Eden, the garden of God; every precious stone was thy covering; the sardius, topaz, and the diamond, the beryl, the onyx, and the jasper, the sapphire, the carbuncle, and gold." And what followed or was involved in this? "Thine heart was lifted up because of thy beauty; thou hast corrupted thy wisdom by reason of thy brightness; I will cast thee to the ground." On the other hand, of new Jerusalem we read also, that the foundations of her wall "were garnished with all manner of precious stones. The first foundation was jasper, the second sapphire, the third a chalcedony, the fourth an emerald, the fifth sardonyx, the sixth sardius, the seventh chrysolite, the eighth beryl, the ninth a topaz, the tenth a chrysoprasus, the eleventh a jacinth, the twelfth an amethyst. And the twelve gates were twelve pearls; every several gate was of one pearl, and the street of the city was pure gold as it were transparent glass." And all this suitably; for it was God's city, "and the glory of God did lighten it, and the Lamb was the light thereof." [9]

Let us then, from what has been said, on the whole, learn this lesson:—to be at least as exact and as decent in the service of God, as we are in our own persons and our own homes; and if we are in possession of precious things besides, let us rather devote them to God than keep them for ourselves. And let us never forget that all we can give, though of His creation, is worthless in comparison of the more precious gifts which He bestows on us in the Gospel. Though our Font and Altar were of costly marbles, though our communion vessels were of gold and jewels, though our walls were covered with rich tapestries, what is all this compared to Christ, the Son of God and Son of man, present here, but unseen! Let us use visible things not to hide, but to remind us of things invisible; and let us pray Him, that while we cleanse the outside of the cup and of the platter, He will give us the Living Bread from heaven, and the Wine, which is His Blood.

[9] Ezek. xxviii.13, 17; Rev. xxi.19–23.

THE WEAPONS OF SAINTS

(Whitsuntide)

"Many that are first shall be last, and the last shall be first."—
Matt. xix.30.

THESE words are fulfilled under the Gospel in many ways. Our Saviour in one place applies them to the rejection of the Jews and the calling of the Gentiles; but in the context, in which they stand as I have cited them, they seem to have a further meaning, and to embody a great principle, which we all indeed acknowledge, but are deficient in mastering. Under the dispensation of the Spirit all things were to become new and to be reversed. Strength, numbers, wealth, philosophy, eloquence, craft, experience of life, knowledge of human nature, these are the means by which worldly men have ever gained the world. But in that kingdom which Christ has set up, all is contrariwise. "The weapons of our warfare are not carnal, but mighty through God to the pulling down of strongholds." What was before in honour, has been dishonoured; what before was in dishonour, has come to honour; what before was successful, fails; what before failed, succeeds. What before was great, has become little; what before was little, has become great. Weakness has conquered strength, for the hidden strength of God "is made perfect in weakness." Death has conquered life, for in that death is a more glorious resurrection. Spirit has conquered flesh; for that spirit is an inspiration from above. A new kingdom has been established, not merely different from all kingdoms before it, but contrary to them; a paradox in the eyes of man,—the visible rule of the invisible Saviour.

This great change in the history of the world is foretold or described in very many passages of Scripture. Take, for instance, St. Mary's Hymn, which we read every evening; she was no woman of high estate, the nursling of palaces and the pride of a people, yet she was chosen to an illustrious place in the Kingdom of heaven. What God began in her was a sort of type of His dealings with His Church. So she spoke of His "scattering the proud," "putting down the mighty," "exalting the humble and meek," "filling the hungry with good things," and "sending the rich empty away." This was a shadow or outline of that Kingdom of the Spirit, which was then coming on the earth.

Again; when our Lord, in the beginning of His ministry, would declare the great principles and laws of His Kingdom, after what manner did He express Himself? Turn to the Sermon on the Mount. "He opened His mouth and said, Blessed are the poor in spirit, blessed are they that mourn, blessed are the meek, blessed are they which are persecuted for righteousness' sake." [1] Poverty was to bring into the Church the riches of the Gentiles; meekness was to conquer the earth; suffering was "to bind their kings in chains, and their nobles with links of iron."

On another occasion He added the counterpart; "Woe unto you that are rich! for ye have received your consolation; woe unto you that are full! for ye shall hunger; woe unto you that laugh now! for ye shall mourn and weep; woe unto you when all men shall speak well of you! for so did their fathers to the false prophets." [2]

St. Paul addresses the Corinthians in the same tone: "Ye see your calling, brethren, how that not many wise men after the flesh, not many mighty, not many noble, are called: but God hath chosen the foolish things of the world to confound the wise; and God hath chosen the weak things of the world to confound the things which are mighty; and base things of the world, and things which are despised, hath God chosen, yea, and things which are not, to bring to nought things that are: that no flesh should glory in His presence." [3]

Once more; consider the Book of Psalms, which, if any part of the Old Testament, belongs immediately to Gospel times, and is the voice of the Christian Church; what is the one idea in that sacred book of devotion from beginning to end? This: that the weak, the oppressed, the defenceless shall be raised to rule the world in spite of its array of might, its threats, and its terrors; that "the first shall be last, and the last first."

Such is the kingdom of the sons of God; and while it endures, there is ever a supernatural work going on by which all that man thinks great is overcome, and what he despises prevails.

Yes, so it is; since Christ sent down gifts from on high, the Saints are ever taking possession of the kingdom, and with the

[1] Matt. v.2–10.   [2] Luke vi.24–26.   [3] 1 Cor. i.26–29.

weapons of Saints. The invisible powers of the heavens, truth, meekness, and righteousness, are ever coming in upon the earth, ever pouring in, gathering, thronging, warring, triumphing, under the guidance of Him who "is alive and was dead, and is alive for evermore." The beloved disciple saw Him mounted on a white horse, and going forth "conquering and to conquer." "And the armies which were in heaven followed Him upon white horses, clothed in fine linen, white and clean. And out of His mouth goeth a sharp sword, that with it He should smite the nations, and He shall rule them with a rod of iron."[4]

Now let us apply this great truth to ourselves; for be it ever recollected, *we* are the sons of God, *we* are the soldiers of Christ. The kingdom is within us, and among us, and around us. We are apt to speak of it as a matter of history; we speak of it as at a distance; but really we are a part of it, or ought to be; and, as we wish to be a living portion of it, which is our only hope of salvation, we must learn what its characters are in order to imitate them. It is the characteristic of Christ's Church, that the first should be last, and the last first; are we realizing in ourselves and taking part in this wonderful appointment of God?

Let me explain what I mean:—We have most of us by nature longings more or less, and aspirations, after something greater than this world can give. Youth, especially, has a natural love of what is noble and heroic. We like to hear marvellous tales, which throw us out of things as they are, and introduce us to things that are not. We so love the idea of the invisible, that we even build fabrics in the air for ourselves, if heavenly truth be not vouchsafed us. We love to fancy ourselves involved in circumstances of danger or trial, and acquitting ourselves well under them. Or we imagine some perfection, such as earth has not, which we follow, and render it our homage and our heart. Such is the state more or less of young persons before the world alters them, before the world comes upon them, as it often does very soon, with its polluting, withering, debasing, deadening influence, before it breathes on them, and blights and parches, and strips off their green foliage, and leaves them, as dry and wintry trees without sap or sweetness. But in early youth we stand with our leaves and blossoms on which promise fruit; we stand by the side of the still waters, with our hearts beating high, with longings after our unknown good, and with a sort of contempt for the fashions of the world; with a contempt for the world, even though we engage in it. Even though we allow

[4] Rev. xix.14, 15.

ourselves in our degree to listen to it, and to take part in its mere gaieties and amusements, yet we feel the while that our happiness is not there; and we have not yet come to think, though we are in the way to think, that all that is beyond this world is after all an idle dream. We are on our way to think it, for no one stands where he was; his desires after what he has not, his earnest thoughts after things unseen, if not fixed on their true objects, catch at something which he does see, something earthly and perishable, and seduce him from God. But I am speaking of men *before* that time, before they have given their hearts to the world, which promises them true good, then cheats them, and then makes them believe that there is no truth any where, and that they were fools for thinking it. But before that time, they have desires after things above this world, which they embody in some form of this world, because they have no other way at all of realizing them. If they are in humble life, they dream of becoming their own masters, rising in the world, and securing an independence; if in a higher rank, they have ambitious thoughts of gaining a name and exercising power. While their hearts are thus unsettled, Christ comes to them, if they will receive Him, and promises to satisfy their great need, this hunger and thirst which wearies them. He does not wait till they have learned to ridicule high feeling as mere romantic dreams: He comes to the young; He has them baptized betimes, and then promises them, and in a higher way, those unknown blessings which they yearn after. He seems to say, in the words of the Apostle, "What ye ignorantly worship, that declare I unto you." You are seeking what you see not, I give it you: you desire to be great, I will make you so; but observe how,—Just in the reverse way to what you expect; the way to real glory is to become unknown and despised.

He says, for instance, to the aspiring, as to His two Apostles, "Whosoever will be great among you, let him be your minister: and whosoever will be chief among you, let him be your servant; even as the Son of man came not to be ministered unto, but to minister." [5] Here is our rule. The way to mount up is to go down. Every step we take downward, makes us higher in the kingdom of heaven. Do you desire to be great? make yourselves little. There is a mysterious connexion between real advancement and self-abasement. If you minister to the humble and despised, if you feed the hungry, tend the sick, succour the distressed; if you bear with the froward, submit to insult, endure

[5] Matt. xx.26–28.

ingratitude, render good for evil, you are, as by a divine charm, getting power over the world and rising among the creatures. God has established this law. Thus He does His wonderful works. His instruments are poor and despised; the world hardly knows their names, or not at all. They are busied about what the world thinks petty actions, and no one minds them. They are apparently set on no great works; nothing is seen to come of what they do: they seem to fail. Nay, even as regards religious objects which they themselves profess to desire, there is no natural and visible connexion between their doings and sufferings and these desirable ends; but there is an unseen connexion in the kingdom of God. They rise by falling. Plainly so, for no condescension *can* be so great as that of our Lord *Himself*. Now the more they abase themselves the more *like* they are to Him; and the more like they are to Him, the greater must be their power with Him.

When we once recognize this law of God's providence we shall understand better, and be more desirous to imitate, our Lord's precepts, such as the following:—

"Ye call Me Master and Lord: and ye say well; for so I am. If I then, your Lord and Master, have washed your feet; ye also ought to wash one another's feet. For I have given you an example, that ye should do as I have done to you. Verily, verily, I say unto you, The servant is not greater than his lord; neither he that is sent greater than he that sent him." And then our Lord adds, "If ye know these things, happy are ye if ye do them." [6] As if He should say to us of this day, You know well that the Gospel was at the first preached and propagated by the poor and lowly against the world's power; you know that fishermen and publicans overcame the world. You know it; you are fond of bringing it forward as an evidence of the truth of the Gospel, and of enlarging on it as something striking, and a topic for many words; happy are ye if ye yourselves fulfil it; happy are ye if *ye* carry on the work of those fishermen; if ye in your generation follow them as they followed Me, and triumph over the world and ascend above it by a like self-abasement.

Again, "When thou art bidden of any man to a wedding, sit not down in the highest room; . . . but when thou art bidden, go and sit down in the lowest room, that when he that bade thee cometh, he may say unto thee, Friend, go up higher: then shalt thou have Worship in the presence of them that sit at meat with thee; for whosoever exalteth himself shall be abased, and he

[6] John xiii. 13–17.

that humbleth himself shall be exalted."[7] Here is a rule which extends to whatever we do. It is plain that the spirit of this command leads us, as a condition of being exalted hereafter, to cultivate here all kinds of little humiliations; instead of loving display, putting ourselves forward, seeking to be noticed, being loud or eager in speech, and bent on having our own way, to be content, nay, to rejoice in being made little of, to perform what to the flesh are servile offices, to think it enough to be barely suffered among men, to be patient under calumny; not to argue, not to judge, not to pronounce censures, unless a plain duty comes in; and all this because our Lord has said that such conduct is the very way to be exalted in His presence.

Again, "I say unto you, That ye resist not evil; but whosoever shall smite thee on thy right cheek, turn to him the other also."[8] What a precept is this? why is this voluntary degradation? what good can come to it? is it not an extravagance? Not to *resist* evil is going far; but to court it, to turn the left cheek to the aggressor and to offer to be insulted! what a wonderful command! What? must we take pleasure in indignities? Surely we must; however difficult it be to understand it, however arduous and trying to practise it. Hear St. Paul's words, which are a comment on Christ's: "Therefore I *take pleasure* in infirmities, in reproaches, in necessities, in persecutions, in distresses for Christ's sake;" he adds the reason: "*for when I am weak, then* am I strong."[9] As health and exercise and regular diet are necessary to strength of the body, so an enfeebling and afflicting of the natural man, a chastising and afflicting of soul and body, are necessary to the exaltation of the soul.

Again, St. Paul says, "Avenge not yourselves, but rather give place unto wrath: for it is written, Vengeance is Mine; I will repay, saith the Lord. Therefore if thine enemy hunger, feed him; if he thirst, give him drink: for in so doing thou shalt heap coals of fire on his head."[10] As if he said, *This* is a *Christian's* revenge; *this* is how a *Christian* heaps punishment and suffering on the head of his enemy; viz. by returning good for evil. Is there pleasure in seeing an injurer and oppressor at your feet? has a man wronged you, slandered you, tyrannized over you, abused your confidence, been ungrateful to you? or to take what is more common, has a man been insolent to you, shown contempt of you, thwarted you, outwitted you, been cruel to you, and you feel resentment,—and your feeling is this, "I wish

[7] Luke xiv.8, 10, 11.
[9] 2 Cor. xii.10.
[8] Matt. v.39.
[10] Rom. xii.19, 20.

him no ill, but I should like him just to be brought down for this, and to make amends to me;" rather say, hard though it be, "I will overcome him with love; except severity be a duty, I will say nothing, do nothing; I will keep quiet, I will seek to do him a service; I owe him a service, not a grudge; and I will be kind, and sweet, and gentle, and composed; and while I cannot disguise from him that I know well where he stands, and where I, still this shall be with all peaceableness and purity of affection." O hard duty, but most blessed! for even to take into account the *pleasure* of revenge, such as it is, is there not greater gratification in thus melting the proud and injurious heart, than in triumphing over it outwardly, without subduing it within? Is there not more of true enjoyment, in looking up to God, and calling Him (so to speak) as a witness of what is done, and having His Angels as conscious spectators of your triumph, though not a soul on earth knows any thing of it, than to have your mere carnal retaliation of evil for evil known and talked of, in the presence of all, and more than all, who saw the insult or heard of the wrong?

The case is the same as regards poverty, which it is the fashion of the world to regard not only as the greatest of evils, but as the greatest *disgrace*. Men count it a disgrace, because it certainly does often arise from carelessness, sloth, imprudence, and other faults. But, in many cases, it is nothing else but the very state of life in which God has placed a man; but still, even then, it is equally despised by the world. Now if there is one thing clearly set forth in the Bible it is this, that "Blessed are the poor." Our Saviour was the great example of poverty; He was a poor man. St. Paul says, "Ye know the grace of our Lord Jesus Christ, that, though He was rich, yet for your sakes He became poor, that ye through His poverty might be rich." [11] Or consider St. Paul's very solemn language about the danger of wealth: "The love of money is the root of all evil, which while some coveted after, they have erred from the faith, and pierced themselves through with many sorrows." [12] Can we doubt that poverty is under the Gospel *better* than riches? I say *under* the Gospel, and *in* the regenerate, and *in* the true servants of God. Of course out of the Gospel, among the unregenerate, among the lovers of this world, it matters not whether one is rich or poor; a man is any how unjustified, and there is no better or worse in his outward circumstances. But, I say, *in Christ* the poor is in a more blessed lot than the wealthy. Ever since the Eternal Son of God

---

[11] 2 Cor. viii.9.   [12] 1 Tim. vi.10.

was born in a stable, and had not a place to lay His head, and died an outcast and as a malefactor, heaven has been won by poverty, by disgrace, and by suffering. Not by these things in themselves, but by faith working in and through them.

These are a few out of many things which might be said on this most deep and serious subject. It is strange to say, but it is a truth which our own observation and experience will confirm, that when a man discerns in himself most sin and humbles himself most, when his comeliness seems to him to vanish away and all his graces to wither, when he feels disgust at himself, and revolts at the thought of himself,—seems to himself all dust and ashes, all foulness and odiousness, then it is that he is really rising in the kingdom of God: as it is said of Daniel, "From the first day that thou didst set thine heart to understand and to chasten thyself before thy God, thy words were heard, and I am come for thy words." [13]

Let us then, my brethren, understand our place, as the redeemed children of God. Some *must* be great in this world, but woe to those who make themselves great; woe to any who take one step out of their way with this object before them. Of course no one is safe from the intrusion of corrupt motives; but I speak of persons *allowing* themselves in such a motive, and acting mainly from such a motive. Let this be the settled view of all who would promote Christ's cause upon earth. If we are true to ourselves, nothing can really thwart us. Our warfare is not with carnal weapons, but with heavenly. The world does not understand what our real power is, and where it lies. And until we put ourselves into its hands of our own act, it can do nothing against us. Till we leave off patience, meekness, purity, resignation, and peace, it can do nothing against that Truth which is our birthright, that Cause which is ours, as it has been the cause of all saints before us. But let all who would labour for God in a dark time beware of any thing which ruffles, excites, and in any way withdraws them from the love of God and Christ, and simple obedience to Him.

This be our duty in the dark night, while we wait for the day; while we wait for Him who is our Day, while we wait for His coming, who is gone, who will return, and before whom all the tribes of the earth will mourn, but the sons of God will rejoice. "It doth not yet appear what we shall be: but we know that, when He shall appear, we shall be like Him; for we shall see Him as He is. And every man that hath this hope in Him

[13] Dan. x.12.

purifieth himself, even as He is pure." [14] It is our blessedness to be made like the all-holy, all-gracious, long-suffering, and merciful God; who made and who redeemed us; in whose presence is perfect rest, and perfect peace; whom the Seraphim are harmoniously praising, and the Cherubim tranquilly contemplating, and Angels silently serving, and the Church thankfully worshipping. All is order, repose, love, and holiness in heaven. There is no anxiety, no ambition, no resentment, no discontent, no bitterness, no remorse, no tumult. "Thou wilt keep him in perfect peace, whose mind is stayed on Thee: because He trusteth in Thee. Trust ye in the Lord for ever: for in the Lord Jehovah is everlasting strength." [15]

---

[14] 1 John iii.2, 3.   [15] Is. xxvi.3, 4.

FAITH WITHOUT DEMONSTRATION

(Trinity Sunday)

"Except ye see signs and wonders, ye will not believe."
—John iv.48.

W E are now celebrating the last great Festival in the course of Holy services which began in Advent; the Feast of the Ever-blessed Trinity, Father, Son, and Holy Ghost, whose mercy has planned, accomplished, and wrought in us "life and immortality." And the present Festival has this peculiarity in it,—that it is the commemoration of a mystery. Other Festivals celebrate mysteries also, but not because they are mysteries. The Annunciation, the birth of Christ, His death on the Cross, His Resurrection, the descent of the Holy Ghost, are all mysteries; but we celebrate them, not on this account, but for the blessings which we gain from them. But to-day we celebrate, not an act of God's mercy towards us, but, forgetting ourselves, and looking only upon Him, we reverently and awfully, yet joyfully, extol the wonders, not of His works, but of His own Nature. We lift up heart and eyes towards Him, and speak of what He is in Himself. We dare to speak of His everlasting and infinite Essence; we directly contemplate a mystery, the deep unfathomable mystery of the Trinity in Unity.

Doubtless, from that deep mystery proceeds all that is to benefit and bless us. Without an Almighty Son we are not redeemed,—without an Ever-present Spirit we are not justified and sanctified. Yet, on this day, we celebrate the mystery for its own sake, not for our sake.

On this day, then, we should forget ourselves, and fix our thoughts upon God. Yet men are not willing to forget themselves; they do not like to become, as it were, nothing, and to have no work but faith. They like argument and proof better; they like to be convinced of a truth to their own satisfaction before they receive it, when, perhaps, such satisfaction is impossible. This happens in the sacred subject before us. The solemn mystery of the Trinity in Unity is contained in Scripture.

We all know this; there is no doubt about it. Yet, though it be in Scripture, it does not follow that every one of us should be a fit judge whether and where it *is* in Scripture. It may be contained there fully, and yet we may be unable to see it fully, for various reasons. Now this is the great mistake which some persons fall into: they think, because the doctrine is maintained as being in Scripture by those who maintain it as true, that therefore they have a right to say that *they* will not believe it till it is proved to *them* from Scripture. It is nothing to them that the great multitude of good and holy men in all ages have held it. They act like Thomas, who would not believe his brother Apostles that our Lord was risen, till he had as much proof as they, and who said, "Except I see and touch for myself, I will not believe." And they are like the Jews whom our Lord reproves in the text, saying, "Except ye see signs and wonders, ye will not believe." They call it an enlightened, rational belief, to demand for themselves proof from Scripture before they believe; and they think that any other admission of the doctrine is blind and superstitious, and unacceptable to Almighty God.

And when, perhaps, we have gone so far as to indulge them, and to profess that we *are* willing to prove the doctrine from Scripture to their satisfaction, and that, as a previous step to their believing and worshipping, then they meet us with such shallow and light-minded questions as the following:— "Where in Scripture do you find the word Trinity?" "Why do you insist upon it, if it is not in Scripture?" Again, "Where is the Holy Ghost expressly and plainly called God, in Scripture?" Again, "Where does Scripture speak of One Substance, Three Persons, as the Athanasian Creed speaks? Where does Scripture say that the Son and the Holy Ghost are uncreate? where, that 'the Godhead of the Father, of the Son, and of the Holy Ghost, is all one, the glory equal, the majesty co-eternal?'" And so they go through the whole of our Divine faith, carping, objecting, and traducing, even though they do not mean it; and all for this—because they *will* be judges themselves what is in Scripture and what is not; what necessary to salvation, and what not; what words are important, and what not; what sources of instruction God has given besides Scripture, and what not.

Now, on such conduct, I observe as follows:—that they who think it unreasonable to believe without proof, are surely unreasonable themselves in so thinking. What warrant in reason, what right have they, to say that they will not believe the Creed unless it is proved to *them* to be in Scripture? They profess to act by reason. Well, then, I ask them, Is it according to reason to say, that they will not believe the Creed without reasons drawn out to their satisfaction from Scripture? I think not; I think I can prove that it is not. I think a very few words will make it evident, that they are unreasonable and inconsistent in refusing to believe before they see the Scripture proof.

1. I would ask, in the first place, whether we reason and prove before we act, in the affairs of this life? For instance, we are bound to obey the laws; we know that we shall get into great trouble if we do not; that if we break them, loss of property or imprisonment will be the consequence; so that it is of great importance that we should obey them; and we know that these laws are not always obvious to common sense; so that at times, a person may break them with the best intentions possible, if he act upon his own private notions of right and wrong. Accordingly, every now and then you find persons, under particular circumstances, alarmed lest they should be unawares breaking the law; and what do they then do? they consult some one skilled in the law, who has made the law his study and profession. It never occurs to a man so circumstanced to buy law books, and to make out the truth of any important matter for himself, though it is really contained in law books. No; neither in ordinary nor in extraordinary matters does he trust his own judgment how the law stands. In ordinary matters he thinks it safe to go by the opinion of men in general; in extraordinary, he consults men learned in the law;—feeling too vividly how much is at stake to trust *himself*. It is not that he doubts, for an instant, that the laws of the land *are* put into writing, and are to be found in law books, and might be drawn out of them; but he distrusts *himself*. He distrusts, not the law books, but his own ability. There is too great a risk,—too much at stake,—his property, his character, his person, are at stake. He cannot afford, in such a case, to indulge his love of argument, disputation, and criticism. No; this love of argument can only be indulged in a case in which we have no fears. It is reserved for religious subjects. Such subjects differ from all other practical subjects, as being those on which the world feels free to speculate, because it does not *fear*. It has no fears about religious doctrine, no keen sensibilities; it does not feel, though it may confess, that its eternal interests are at stake. It suspends its judgment; for what matters it to the world whether it makes up its mind on a point of religion, or no? It can *afford* to say, "I will not believe till I see proof in Scripture for believing," though it does not say, "I will not believe lawyers till I understand the law," because it sees clearly and feels deeply that the law of the

land is a real power, and that to come into collision with it is a real disaster; but it does not see and feel that "the Word of God is quick and powerful, and sharper than any two-edged sword, piercing even to the dividing asunder of soul and spirit, and of the joints and marrow, and is a discerner of the thoughts and intents of the heart." Men well understand that they will be sure to suffer from human law, for all they cannot judge of it by themselves, on the ground that they can, if they choose, get other competent men to judge for them; but they cannot be made to feel that they will hereafter have to answer for having been told the truth, however, or from whatever quarter they were told it,—at Church, or from teachers, or from religious books. They act as if it were no matter what they knew, unless they came to know it in one particular way, through Scripture.

Now, surely, this parallel holds most exactly, unless one or other of two things could be shown,—unless we have reason for thinking, first, that it matters not *what* we believe; or, secondly, that no faith is acceptable in the case of individuals which does not arise from their own *personal inferences* from Scripture. Let, then, grounds be produced for either of these two positions,— that correct faith is unimportant, or that personal faith must be built upon argument and proof. Till then, surely the general opinion of all men around us, and that from the first,—the belief of our teachers, friends, and superiors, and of all Christians in all times and places,—that the doctrine of the Holy Trinity must be held in order to salvation, is as good a reason for our believing it ourselves, even without being able to prove it in all its parts from Scripture; I say, this general reception of it by others, is as good a reason for accepting it without hesitation, considering the fearful consequences which may follow from not accepting it, as the general belief how the law stands and the opinion of skilful lawyers about the law is a reason for following their view of the law, though we cannot verify that view from law books.

2. But it may here be said, that the cases are different in this respect,—that the commonly-received notions about what the law of the land is, do not impose upon our belief any thing improbable or difficult to accept, but that the Catholic doctrine of the Trinity is mysterious and unlikely; and, therefore, though it is reasonable to go by what others say in legal matters, it is not reasonable to go by others in respect to this doctrine.

Now, on the contrary, I consider that this mysteriousness is, as far as it proves any thing, a recommendation of the doctrine. I do not say that it *is* true, *because* it is mysterious; but that if it *be*

true, it cannot help being mysterious. It would be strange, indeed, as has often been urged in argument, if any doctrine concerning God's infinite and eternal Nature were not mysterious.
It would even be an objection to any professed doctrine concerning His Nature, if it were not mysterious. That the sacred
doctrine, then, of the Trinity in Unity is mysterious, is no objection to it, but rather the contrary; the only objection that
can plausibly he urged is, why, if so, should it be revealed? Why
should we be told *any thing* about God's Adorable Nature, if incomprehensible He is, and mysterious the doctrine about Him
must be? This, it is true, we *may* ask; though can we ask it piously and reverently? how can *we* be judges what He will do on
such a point? how can *we*, worms of the earth, and creatures of
a day, pretend to determine what is most suitable to Him to tell,
what is best for us to know, when He condescends to reveal
Himself to us? Is it not enough for us that He speaks to us at all?
and cannot we consent to leave Him (if I may so express myself)
to speak to us in His own way? Whether, then, He will reveal to
us any thing about His own Nature or no, our reason cannot
determine; but this it can determine, that *if* He does, it will
be mysterious. It is no *objection*, then, I repeat, to the doctrine,
that it is mysterious; and it is no reason, therefore, against receiving it on the general belief of others, that it is mysterious. It
is not more improbable that that doctrine should be what it is,
than that the law of the land should be what it is; and as we
believe the testimony of others about the law, without having
studied the law, so we may well receive the doctrine of the Trinity on the testimony of our friends and superiors, our Church,
all good men, learned men, and men in general, though *we* have
not learning, attainments, or leisure sufficient to draw it for
ourselves from Scripture. It is not stranger that the testimony
of others should be our guide as to the next world, than that it is
our guide in this.

This is the first answer that I should make to this objection;
but now I will give another, which will open the state of the case
more fully.

I suppose, then, there is no one who has not heard of, and no
one but would be shocked at seeing, what is called an Atheist,
that is, a person who denies that there is any God at all. We
should be shocked, not from any unchristian feeling towards
the unhappy man who blasphemed his Maker and Saviour, but,
without thinking of *him*, we should feel that Satan alone could
be the author of such an impiety, and we should be sure that we
had close beside us a very special manifestation of Satan. We

should be shocked to think how very low human nature could fall, when it so yielded to the temptations of Satan. Such would be our feelings, and surely very right ones; yet, perhaps, the unhappy man in question, quite unconscious himself of his great misery, as unconscious as persons who deny the doctrine of the Trinity are of theirs (for this is the property of Satan's delusions, that the men seized by them do not suspect that they are delusions), I say, this man, altogether unconscious what a mournful object he was to all believers, might begin to argue and dispute in his defence, and his argument might be such as the following:

"You tell me that I must believe in a God, but I want this doctrine *proved* to my satisfaction before I believe it. It is very unreasonable in you to deal with me in any other way. Nay, you have gone against reason in your own case, in that you believe. For which of you has ever set about proving that God exists? which of you has not believed it before proving it? You believe it because you have been taught it. But prove to me the truth of this doctrine from the world which we see and touch, from the course of nature and of human affairs, and then I will believe it."

Now is it not a very happy thing that men are not accustomed to speak in this way? Why, if so, all our life would be spent in proving things; our whole being would be one continued disputation; we should have no time for action; we should never get so far as action. Some things, nay, the greatest things, must be taken for granted, unless we make up our minds to fritter away life, doing nothing. But to return to the particular case before us;—should we think ourselves weak and dull in not seeking proof that God exists before believing in God, or the man in question miserable in needing it? Yet, if he persisted, and was of an acute and subtle mind, is it not plain, that abundant as is the evidence of God's existence, providence, power, wisdom, and love, on the face of nature and in human affairs, yet it would not at all be easy to prove it to *him*, not merely to *his* satisfaction, but to *our* satisfaction either. Clearly as we should feel the evidence, we should not be able to bring out the proof so as to come up to our own notions what a proof *ought* to be, and we should be disappointed with our own attempt.

For, let us see how this man would argue,—(after all, I scarcely like to say what he would urge, lest I should speak in a way unsuitable to this sacred place; and yet it may be useful to hint at one or two things, by way of showing *how much* we should be bound in consistency to admit, if we grant a man need believe nothing for which he cannot be given a clear and convenient proof,)—he will say then thus:

"You tell me that there is but one God; and you tell me to look abroad into the world, and I shall see proofs of it. I do look abroad, and I see good *and* evil. I see the proof, then, of two gods, a good God, and another, evil. I see two principles struggling with each other." This shocking doctrine has before now been held by those who were determined to prove to themselves every thing before they believed; and when it is a question of argument and disputation, blasphemous as it is, much that is plausible can be said for it. For evil certainly has a kingdom of its own in the world; it seems to have a place here, and to act on system. Even Scripture calls Satan the god of this world; not meaning that he is really god of it (God forbid!), but that he has usurped the power of it, and seems to be god of it. If, then, every one is bound to prove his faith for himself before believing, then he is bound, not only to prove for himself the doctrine of the Blessed Trinity from Scripture, but he must first prove from the face of the world the doctrine of the Unity; and, as in the first case, he will, unless properly qualified, be in great risk of perplexing himself and denying that God is Three, so will he, in the latter, run great risk of denying that God is One. And it is to be feared that it is only because men have the doctrine of the Holy Trinity to speak against, that they do not speak against the doctrine of the Unity; they *will* doubt and cavil about something or other; and were revealed religion not before them, then they would speak against natural religion, as in other times and places they have already done.

Again; the deluded man I am supposing will continue his bad arguments as follows: "You tell me that God is almighty; now you may prove Him to be mighty, but how do you prove Him to be almighty? You cannot prove more than you see, and you must be *all-seeing* to judge of what is *almighty*." Again, "You say that God is infinite; but all you can know on the subject is, that the Intelligence that created the world surpasses your comprehension; but by how much, whether infinitely, you cannot know, you cannot prove." Again, "You tell me to believe that God had no beginning; this is incomprehensible; I do not know what you mean; I cannot take in the sense of your words. It is as easy to believe the doctrine of the Trinity in Unity, as that God had no beginning. And there is less proof for it than for the doctrine of the Trinity; for, at least, there *is* proof in Scripture for that doctrine, but what possible proof can you pretend to bring from the face of the world that God was from everlasting?"

Now I do not see how such an objector can be answered satisfactorily, if he is pertinacious. You meet, indeed, with books written to prove to us (as they profess) the being of an Almighty, Infinite, Everlasting God, from what is seen in the natural world, but they do *not* strictly prove it; they do but recommend, evidence, and confirm the doctrine to those who believe it already. They do not make an approach to a complete argumentative proof of it. They are obliged to pass over, or take for granted, many of the most important points in the doctrine. They are, doubtless, useful to Christians, as far as they tend to enliven their devotion, to strengthen their faith, to excite their gratitude, and to enlarge their minds; but they are little or no evidence to unbelievers. And, in saying all this, I must not be understood to say, that the course of the world does not justly impress upon us the doctrine of One True, Infinite, and Almighty God;—it does so,—but that the proof is too deep, subtle, complex, indirect, delicate, and spiritual to be analyzed and brought out into formal argument, level to the comprehension of the multitude of men. And I say the same of the proof of the doctrine of the Holy Trinity in Scripture. A humble, teachable, simple, believing mind, will imbibe the doctrine from Scripture, how it knows not, as we drink in the air without seeing it; but when a man wants formal grounds for his belief laid before him in a definite shape, and has little time for reflection and study, and little learning or cultivation of mind, then, I say, he can do little better than to fall back upon his impressions instead of proof, on the belief of all around him, and on the testimony of all ages.

Let us, then, learn from this Festival to walk *by faith*; that is, not to ask jealously and coldly for strict arguments, but to follow generously what has fair evidence for it, even though it might have fuller or more systematic evidence. It is in this way that we all believe that there is a God. A subtle infidel might soon perplex any one of us. Of course he might. Our very state and warfare is one of faith. Let us aim at, let us reach after and (as it were) catch at the things of the next world. There is a voice within us, which assures us that there is something higher than earth. We cannot analyze, define, contemplate what it is that thus whispers to us. It has no shape or material form. There is that in our hearts which prompts us to religion, and which condemns and chastises sin. And this yearning of our nature is met and sustained, it finds an object to rest upon, when it hears of the existence of an All-powerful, All-gracious Creator. It incites us to a noble faith in what we cannot see.

Let us exercise a similar faith, as regards the Mysteries of Revelation also. Here is the true use of Scripture in leading us to the truth. If we read it humbly and inquire teachably, we shall find; we shall have a deep impression on our minds that the doctrines of the Creed are there, though we may not be able to put our hands upon particular texts, and say how much of it is contained here and how much there. But, on the other hand, if we read in order to *prove* those doctrines, in a critical, argumentative way, then all traces of them will disappear from Scripture as if they were not there. They will fade away insensibly like hues at sunset, and we shall be left in darkness. We shall come to the conclusion that they are not in Scripture, and shall, perhaps, boldly call them unscriptural. Religious convictions cannot be forced; nor is Divine truth ours to summon at will. If we *determine* that we will find it out, we shall find nothing. Faith and humility are the only spells which conjure up the image of heavenly things into the letter of inspiration; and faith and humility consist, not in going about to prove, but in the outset confiding on the testimony of others. Thus afterwards on looking back, we shall find we have proved what we did not set out to prove. We cannot control our reasoning powers, nor exert them at our will or at any moment. It is so with other faculties of the mind also. Who can command his memory? The more you try to recall what you have forgotten, the less is your chance of success. Leave thinking about it, and perhaps memory returns. And in like manner, the more you set yourself to argue and prove, in order to discover truth, the less likely you are to reason correctly and to infer profitably. You will be caught by sophisms, and think them splendid discoveries. Be sure, the highest reason is not to reason on system, or by rules of argument, but in a natural way; not with formal intent to draw out proofs, but trusting to God's blessing that you may gain a right impression from what you read. If your reasoning powers are weak, using argumentative forms will not make them stronger. They will enable you to dispute acutely and to hit objections, but not to discover truth. There is nothing creative, nothing progressive in exhibitions of argument. The utmost they do is to enable us to state well what we have already discovered by the tranquil exercise of our reason. Faith and obedience are the main things; believe and do, and pray to God for light, and you will reason well without knowing it.

Let us not then seek for signs and wonders; for clear, or strong, or compact, or original arguments; but let us *believe*; evidence will come after faith as its reward, better than before it as its groundwork. Faith soars aloft; it listens for the notes of heaven, the faint voices or echoes which scarcely reach the earth, and it thinks them worth all the louder sounds of cities or of schools of men. It is foolishness in the eyes of the world; but it is a foolishness of God wiser than the world's wisdom. Let us embrace the sacred Mystery of the Trinity in Unity, which, as the Creed tells us, is the ground of the Catholic religion. Let us think it enough, let us think it far too great a privilege, for sinners such as we are, for a fallen people in a degenerate age, to inherit the faith once delivered to the Saints; let us accept it thankfully; let us guard it watchfully; let us transmit it faithfully to those who come after us.

THE MYSTERY
OF THE HOLY TRINITY

(Trinity Sunday)

*"Go ye, therefore, and teach all nations; baptizing them in the Name
of the Father, and of the Son, and of the Holy Ghost."*
—Matt. xxviii.19.

THAT in some real sense the Father, and the Son, and the
Holy Ghost are They whom we are bound to serve and
worship, from whom comes the Gospel of grace, and in whom
the profession of Christianity centres, surely is shown, most
satisfactorily and indisputably, by the words of this text. When
Christ was departing, He gave commission to His Apostles, and
taught them what to teach and preach; and first of all they were
to introduce their converts into His profession, or into His
Church, and that by a solemn rite, which, as He had told
Nicodemus at an earlier time, was to convey a high spiritual
grace. This solemn and supernatural ordinance of discipleship
was to be administered in the Name—of whom? in the Name
(can we doubt it?) of Him whose disciples the converts forthwith became; of that God whom, from that day forward, they
confessed and adored; whom they promised to obey; in whose
word they trusted; by whose bounty they were to be rewarded.
Yet when Christ would name the Name of God, He does but
say, "in the Name of the Father, and of the Son, and of the Holy
Ghost." I consider, then, that on the very face of His sacred
words there is a difficulty, *till* the doctrine of the Holy Trinity is
made known to us. What can be meant by saying, in the Name,
not of God, but of Three? It is an unexpected manner of speech.

Now even if it were merely said, "of the Father and the Son,"
there would surely be a difficulty in the terms of His command.
We might indeed suppose that He meant thereby to denote the
Supreme Lord of all, and the instrument and mediator of His
mercies in the Dispensation then commencing (as we read of
the Israelites "believing God and His servant Moses," and

"worshipping the Lord and the king," David); but surely even then it would be strange and inexplicable that Christ should say, "the Father and Son," and not "God and the Son," or "God and Christ," or the like; whereas the Name of God does not occur at all, and the two words used instead are what are called *correlatives*, one implies the other, they look from the one to the other. There is no mention of a Fount of mercies and a channel, and that, towards man the recipient; but it is like the statement of some sacred doctrine which has its meaning in itself, independently of man or of any economy of mercy towards him. And the force of this remark is increased by our Lord's making mention, in addition, of the Holy Ghost, which much confirms this impression that the Three Sacred Names introduced have a meaning relatively to each other, and not to any temporal dispensation. Did the text run, "in the Name of God, Jesus Christ, and the Comforter," I do not say that this would have overcome the difficulty, or that it would be satisfactory to interpret it of an Author of grace and His instruments; but at all events there is far more difficulty, or rather an insuperable difficulty in such an interpretation of the text, taken as Christ actually spoke it. And then, considering that if there was one boon above another which a convert might naturally claim of an Apostle, it was to know *whom* he was to worship, *whose* servant he was to become, *who* was to be his God, now that he had abandoned idols—(as, for instance, Moses said, "When I come unto the children of Israel, and shall say unto them, The God of your fathers hath sent me unto you, and they shall say to me, *What is His Name?* what shall I say unto them?" and Almighty God acknowledged that the request was right by granting it; and as Jacob said, "Tell me, I pray thee, Thy *Name?*" and as Manoah said, "What is Thy *Name?*" and as, in accordance with these instances, St. Paul said to the Athenians, "Whom ye *ignorantly worship*, Him *declare* I unto you");—I say, with these considerations before us, we might have expected that there would have been in the Baptismal form a clear and simple announcement of the Christian's God, such as this, "In the Name of the God and Father of our Lord Jesus Christ," that is, *unless* the Catholic doctrine of the Holy Trinity be true. If indeed so it be, as the Church has ever taught, that the Father, Son, and Holy Ghost are the One God into whose service Christians are enrolled, then good reason that They should be named upon the convert on his initiation. In that case there is no difficulty; the sacred form of words precisely answers to the worshipper's question, "What is Thy Name?" to the Apostle's promise, "Him declare I unto you:"

but on the supposition, which impugners of the doctrine maintain, that by "Son" is meant a man, and that the Holy Spirit is not God and not an intelligent person at all, certainly a great and unexpected, and (I may say, humanly speaking) unnecessary obscurity hangs over the first act of the Gospel teaching.

Nor let it be objected to Catholic believers, that there can be no greater obscurity than a mystery; and that the Sacred Truth which they confess is a greater perplexity to the convert than any which can arise from considerations such as I have been insisting on. For the point I have been urging, is the improbability that our Lord should introduce an obscurity of *mere words*, with none existing in fact, which is the case in the heretical interpretation; and that He should prefer to speak so darkly when He might have spoken simply and intelligibly; whereas, if there be an eternal mystery in the Godhead, such as we aver, then, from the nature of the case, there could not but be a difficulty in the words in which He revealed it. Christ, in that case, makes no mystery for the occasion; He uses the plainest and most exact form of speech which human language admits of. And this deserves notice; for it may be extended to the details of this great Catholic doctrine, of which I propose presently to give some brief account. I mean that, much as is idly and profanely said against the Creed of St. Athanasius as being unintelligible, yet the real objection which misbelievers feel, if they spoke correctly, is, that it is too plain. No sentences can be more simple, nor statements more precise, than those of which it consists. The difficulty is not in any one singly; but in their combination. And herein lies a remarkable difference between the doctrine of the Holy Trinity, and some modern dogmatic statements on other points, some true, and some not true, which have been at times put forward as necessary to salvation. Much controversy, for instance, has taken place in late centuries about the doctrine of justification, and about faith; but here endless perplexities and hopeless disputes arise, as we all know, as to what is meant by "faith," and what by "justification;" whereas most of the *words* used in the Creed to which I have referred are only common words used in their common sense, as "Lord" and "God," "eternal" and "almighty," "one" and "three;" nor again are the statements difficult. There is no difficulty, except such as is in the nature of things, in the Adorable Mystery spoken of, which no wording can remove or explain.

And now I propose to state the doctrine, as far as it can be done, in a few words, in the mode in which it is disclosed to us in the text of Scripture; in doing which, if I shall be led on to mention one or two points of detail, it must not be supposed, as some persons strangely mistake, as if such additional statements were intended for *explanation*; whereas they leave the great Mystery just as it was before, and are only useful as impressing on our mind *what* it is that the Catholic Church means to assert, and as making it a matter of real faith and apprehension, and not a mere assemblage of words.

And first, I need scarcely say, considering how often it is told us in Scripture, that God is One. "Hear, O Israel," says Moses, "the Lord our God is one Lord." "To us there is but one God, the Father," says St. Paul. Again, "One Lord, one Faith, one Baptism, one God and Father of all." Again, "One God, and one Mediator between God and men." [1] Now, it may be asked, in what sense "one"? for we speak of things being one which really are many; as Scripture speaks of all Christians being made *one* body; of God being made at *one* with sinners; of God and man being *one* Christ; and of *one* Baptism, though administered to multitudes. I answer, that God is one in the simplest and strictest sense, as all Scripture shows; this is true, whatever else is true: not in any nominal or secondary sense; but one, as being individual; as truly one as any individual soul or spirit is one; nay, infinitely more truly so, because all creatures are imperfect, and He has all perfection. In Him there are no parts or passions, nothing inchoate or incomplete, nothing by communication, nothing of quality, nothing which admits of increase, nothing common to others. He is separate from all things, and whole, and perfect, and simple, and like Himself and none else; and one, not in name, or by figure, or by accommodation, or by abstraction, but one in Himself, or, as the Creed speaks, one in substance or essence. All that He is, is Himself, and nothing short of Himself; His attributes are He. Has He wisdom? this does but mean that He is wisdom. Has He love? that is, "God is love," as St. John speaks. Has He omnipresence? that is, He is omnipresent. Has He omniscience? He is all-knowing. Has He power? He is almighty. He is holy, and just, and true, and good, not in the way of qualities of His essence, but holiness, justice, truth, and goodness, are all one and the self-same He, according as He is contemplated by His creatures in various aspects and relations. We men are incapable of conceiving of Him as He is; we cannot attain to more than glimpses, accidental or partial views, of His Infinite Majesty, and these we call by different names, as if He had attributes, and

[1] Deut. vi.4; 1 Cor. viii.6; Eph. iv.5, 6; 1 Tim. ii.5.

were of a compound nature; and thus He deigns in mercy to us to speak of Himself, using even human, sensible, and material terms; as if He could be angry, who is not touched by evil; or could repent, in whom is no variableness; or had eyes, or arms, or breath, who is a Spirit; whereas He is at once and absolutely all perfection, and whatever is He, is all He is, and He is Himself always and altogether.

Thus we must ever commence in all our teaching concerning the Holy Trinity; we must not begin by saying that there are Three, and then afterwards go on to say that there is One, lest we give false notions of the nature of that One; but we must begin by laying down the great Truth that there is One God in a simple and strict sense, and then go on to speak of Three, which is the way in which the mystery was progressively revealed in Scripture. In the Old Testament we read of the Unity; in the New, we are enlightened in the knowledge of the Trinity.

And here, let it be observed, that we have a sort of figure or intimation of the sacred Mystery of the Trinity in Unity even in what has been now said concerning the Divine Attributes. For as the Attributes of God are many in one mode of speaking, yet all One in God; so, too, there are Three Divine Persons, yet these Three are One. Let it not be for an instant supposed that I am *paralleling* the two cases, which is the Sabellian heresy; but I use the one in *illustration* of the other; and, in way of illustration, I observe as follows: When we speak of God as Wisdom, or as Love, we mean to say that He is Wisdom, and that He is Love; that He is each separately and wholly, yet not that Wisdom is the same as Love, though He is both at once. Wisdom and Love stand for ideas quite distinct from each other, and not to be confused, though they are united in Him. In all He is and all He does, He is Wisdom and He is Love; yet it is both true that He is but One, and without qualities, and withal true again that Love is not Wisdom. Again, as God is Wisdom or Love, so is Wisdom or Love in and with God, and whatever God is. Is God eternal? so is His wisdom. Is He unchangeable? so is His wisdom. Is He uncreate, infinite, almighty, all-holy? His wisdom has these characteristics also. Since God has no parts or passions, whatever is really of or from God, is all that He is. If there is confusion of language here, and an apparent play upon words, this arises from our incapacity in comprehension and expression. We see that all these separate statements must be true, and if they result in an apparent contrariety with each other, this we cannot avoid; nor need we be perplexed about them, nor shrink from declaring any one of them. That simple accuracy of statement which would harmonize all of them is beyond us, because the power of contemplating the Eternal, as He is, is beyond us. We must be content with what we can see, and use it for our practical guidance, without caring for the apparent contradiction of terms involved in our profession of it.

A second illustration may be taken from the material images which Scripture condescends to employ. We read of the eye of God, and the arm of God. Now we know that man has an eye and an arm as really parts of him, and not as figures; but let us suppose for a moment that his body were made spiritual, what would be the consequence? What really would follow we cannot say, for it is beyond us; but, since a spirit has no parts, we may *conceive* that all those separate organs of man's body which at present exist, instead of having a local disposition in it any longer, and of springing out of it by extension, would be all one, though all distinct still. A spiritual body might possibly be all eye, all ear, all arm, all heart; yet not as if all these were confused together, and names only; not as if henceforth there were no seeing, no hearing, no working, and no feeling, but because a spirit has no parts in extension, and is what it is all at once. And I notice this, because it shows us that things may really exist in a subject which we are contemplating, though they look like ideas only or notions created by our own minds. As a body need not be supposed to lose eye and hand by becoming spiritual, but its organs might exist in it as truly as before, because it was a body, but in a new manner, because it was spiritual, so as to seem like mere abstractions or unreal qualities; so may we suppose that though God is a Spirit and One, yet He may be also a Trinity: not as if that Trinity were a name only, or stood for three manifestations, or qualities, or attributes, or relations,—such mere ideas or conceptions as we may come to form when contemplating God;—but that, as in that body which had become spiritual, eye and hand would not be abstractions after the change, since they were not so before it, nor would eye necessarily be the same as the hand, though the body was all eye and all hand; so (if we may dare to use human illustrations on this most sacred subject), the Eternal Three (I do not say *in the same way*, for I am not attempting to explain *how* the mystery is, but to bring out distinctly *what* we mean by it), in like manner I say, the Eternal Three are worshipped by the Catholic Church as distinct, yet One;—the Most High God being wholly the Father, and wholly the Son, and wholly the Holy Ghost; yet the Three Persons being distinct from each other, not merely in name, or by human abstraction, but in very truth, as truly as a fountain is distinct from the stream which flows from it, or the root of a tree from its branches.

Now should any one be tempted to say that this is dark language, and difficult speculation to set before a Christian people, I answer that it is not more dark and difficult than the sacred mystery which is our great subject to-day; that it is in fact but the *exposition* of the sacred mystery as the Church has received it; that I am not engaged in defending the Creed of St. Athanasius, but am stating its meaning; and, My Brethren, that you may well bear once in the year to be reminded that Christianity gives exercise to the whole mind of man, to our highest and most subtle reason, as well as to our feelings, affections, imagination, and conscience. If we find it tries us, and is too severe, whether for our reason, or our imagination, or our feelings, let us bow down in silent adoration, and submit to it each of our faculties by turn, not complain of its sublimity or its range. And now to proceed:—

We hear much in the Old Testament of those attributes of God of which I have already spoken. His omnipotence: "I am the Almighty God; walk before Me, and be thou perfect." Self-existence: "And God said unto Moses, I Am that I Am: thus shalt thou say unto the children of Israel, I Am hath sent me unto you." Holiness: "Who is like Thee, glorious in holiness, fearful in praises, doing wonders!" His mercy, and justice, and faithfulness: "The Lord, the Lord God, merciful and gracious, long-suffering, and abundant in goodness and truth, keeping mercy for thousands, forgiving iniquity, and transgression, and sin, and that will by no means clear the guilty." Awful majesty: "That thou mayest fear this glorious and fearful Name, the Lord thy God." Truth: "His truth endureth from generation to generation." Omnipresence: "If I climb up into heaven, Thou art there; if I go down to hell, Thou art there also." Omniscience: "The eyes of the Lord are in every place, beholding the evil and the good." Knowledge of the heart: "Thou only knowest the hearts of the children of men." Mysteriousness: "Verily Thou art a God that hidest Thyself, O God of Israel the Saviour." Eternity: "Thus saith the High and Lofty One that inhabiteth eternity, whose Name is Holy." [2] These are some out of numberless announcements in the Old Testament of the Divine Attributes; and though every thing concerning the Supreme Being is mysterious, yet we do not commonly feel any

---

[2] Gen. xvii.1; Exod. iii.14; xv.11; xxxiv.6, 7; Deut. xxviii.58; Ps. c.4; cxxxix.7; Prov. xv.3; 2 Chron. vi.30; Is. xlv.15; lvii.15.

mystery here, because we see a sort of parallel to these attributes in what we call the qualities, properties, powers, and habits of our own minds. We are endowed by nature and through grace with a portion of certain excellences which belong in perfection to the Most High,—as benevolence, wisdom, justice, truth, and holiness; and though we do not know how these attributes exist in God, nay how they exist in ourselves, yet since we are ourselves used to them, and cannot deny their existence, we are not startled when we are told they exist in God. But there are certain other disclosures made to us concerning the Divine Nature, even from the first page of Scripture, and growing in definiteness as Revelation proceeds, of which we have no image or parallel in ourselves, and which in consequence we feel to be strange and startling, and call unintelligible because we are not used to them, and mysterious because we cannot account for them. Thus in the history of the creation we read: "The Spirit of God moved upon the face of the waters;" who shall say how this awful intimation is to be interpreted? who but will "desire to look into" such deep things, yet be silent from conscious weakness, till he hears the Catholic doctrine of the Trinity, which explains to him the inspired text by revealing the mystery? Again we read, that, when Jacob had wrestled with the Angel, "he called the name of the place Peniel," for he had seen God's Face or Countenance, "and," he adds, "my life is preserved." And Almighty God promised Moses, "My Presence shall go with thee, and I will give thee rest." And again Moses asks, "I beseech Thee, shew me Thy Glory. And He said, I will make all My Goodness pass before thee . . . thou canst not see My face, for there shall no man see Me and live." And we are told that "the Lord revealed Himself to Samuel in Shiloh by the Word of the Lord." And the Psalmist says, "By the Word of the Lord were the heavens made, and all the hosts of them by the Breath of His mouth." And Wisdom says in the Proverbs, "The Lord possessed Me in the beginning of His way; before His works of old. I was set up from everlasting, from the beginning, or ever the earth was. . . . I was by Him, as one brought up with Him; and I was daily His delight, rejoicing always before Him." And in the prophet Isaiah we read, "Awake, awake, put on strength, O Arm of the Lord;" and again, "I have covered thee in the shadow of My Hand."[3] Now any one such expression once or twice used

---

[3] Gen. i.2; xxxii.30; Exod. xxxiii.14–20; 1 Sam. iii.21; Ps. xxxiii.6; Prov. viii.22, 23, 30; Is. li.9, 16.

might not have excited attention; but this mention of the Word, and Wisdom, and Presence, and Glory, and Spirit, and Breath, and Countenance, and Arm, and Hand of the Almighty is too frequent, and with too much of personal characteristic, to be dutifully passed over by the careful reader of Scripture; and in matter of fact it did, before Christ came, attract the attention of Jewish believers, as is proved to us most clearly by some remarkable passages in the books of Wisdom and Ecclesiasticus, to which I need not do more than allude.[4]

It would appear, then, from the revelations of the Old Testament, that while God is in His essence most simply and absolutely one, yet there is a real sense in which He is not one, though created natures do not, cannot, furnish such representations of Him as to enable us easily to acquiesce in the conclusions to which the Scripture announcements inevitably lead. We understand things unknown, by the pattern of things seen and experienced; we are able to contemplate Almighty God so far as earthly things are partial reflexions of Him; when they fail us, we are lost. And as of course nothing earthly or created is His exact and perfect image, we have at best but dim glimpses of His infinite glory; and if Scripture reveal to us aught concerning Him, we must be content to take it on faith, without comprehending how it is, or having any clear understanding of our own words. When it declares to us that God is wise and good, we form some idea of what is meant from the properties and habits which attach to the human soul; when we read of His arm or eye, we have some faint, though unworthy shadow of the truth in the members and organs of the human body; but when we read of His Spirit, or Word, or Presence, as at once very distinct from Him, yet most intimately one with Him,— more intimately one than our properties are one with our souls, more real and distinct than the members and organs of our bodies,—we feel the weight of that Mystery, which exists also when mention is made of the Divine Wisdom, or the Divine Arm, though we feel it not.

And this Mystery, which the Old Testament obscurely signifies, is in the New clearly declared; and it is this,—that the God of all, who is revealed in the Old Testament, is the Father of a Son from everlasting, called also His Word and Image, of His substance and partaker of all His perfections, and equal to Himself, yet without being separate from Him, but one with Him; and that from the Father and the Son proceeds eternally

[4] Wisd. vii.14, et seq; Ecclus. xxiv.3, et seq.

the Holy Spirit, who also is of one substance, Divinity, and majesty with Father and Son. Moreover we learn that the Son or Word is a Person,—that is, is to be spoken of as "He," not "it," and can be addressed; and that the Holy Ghost also is a Person. Thus God subsists in Three Persons, from everlasting to everlasting; first, God is the Father, next God is the Son, next God is the Holy Ghost; and the Father is not the Son, nor the Son the Holy Ghost, nor the Holy Ghost the Father. And God is Each of these Three, and nothing else; that is, He is either the Father, or the Son, or the Holy Ghost. Moreover, God is as wholly and entirely God in the Person of the Father, as though there were no Son and Spirit; as entirely in that of the Son, as though there were no Spirit and Father; as entirely in that of the Spirit, as though there were no Father and Son. And the Father is God, the Son God, and the Holy Ghost God, while there is but one God; and that without any inequality, because there is but One God, and He is without parts or degrees; though how it is that that same Adorable Essence, indivisible, and numerically One, should subsist perfectly and wholly in Each of Three Persons, no words of man can explain, nor earthly illustration typify.

Now the passages in the New Testament in which this Sacred Mystery is intimated to us, are such as these. First, we read, as I have said already, that God is One; next, that He has an Onlybegotten Son; further, that this Only-begotten Son is "in the bosom of the Father;" and that "He and the Father are One." Further, that He is also the Word; that "the Word is God, and is with God;" moreover, that the Son is in Himself a distinct Person, in a real sense, for He has taken on Him our nature, and become man, though the Father has not. What is all this but the doctrine, that that God who is in the strictest sense One, is both entirely the Father, and is entirely the Son? or that the Father is God, and the Son God, yet but One God? Moreover the Son is the express "Image" of God, and He is "in the form of God," and "equal with God;" and "he that hath seen Him, hath seen the Father," and "He is in the Father and the Father in Him." Moreover the Son has all the attributes of the Father: He is "Alpha and Omega, the beginning and the ending, which is, and which was, and which is to come, the Almighty;" "by Him were all things created, visible and invisible;" "by Him do all things consist;" none but He "knoweth the Father," and none but the Father "knoweth the Son." He "knoweth all things;" He "searcheth the hearts and the reins;" He is "the Truth and the Life;" and He is the Judge of all men.

And again, what is true of the Son is true of the Holy Ghost; for He is "the Spirit of God;" He "proceedeth from the Father;" He is in God as "the spirit of a man that is in him;" He "searcheth all things, even the deep things of God;" He is "the Spirit of Truth;" the "Holy Spirit;" at the creation, He "moved upon the face of the waters;" "Whither shall I go," says the Psalmist, "from Thy Spirit?" He is the Giver of all gifts, "dividing to every man severally as He will;" we are born again "of the Spirit." To resist Divine grace is to grieve, to tempt, to resist, to quench, to do despite to the Spirit. He is the Comforter, Ruler, and Guide of the Church; He reveals things to come; and blasphemy against Him has never forgiveness. In all such passages, it is surely implied both that the Holy Ghost has a Personality of His own, and that He is God.

And thus, on the whole, the words of the Creed hold good, that "there is one Person of the Father, another of the Son, and another of the Holy Ghost; but the Godhead of the Father, of the Son, and of the Holy Ghost is all one,—the glory equal, the majesty co-eternal. Such as the Father is, such is the Son, and such is the Holy Ghost. And in this Trinity, none is afore or after other, none is greater or less than another; but the whole Three Persons are co-eternal together and co-equal; so that in all things, as is aforesaid, the Unity in Trinity, and the Trinity in Unity, is to be worshipped."

Lastly, it is added, "He therefore that will be saved, must thus think of the Trinity:" on which I make two remarks, and so conclude. First, what is very obvious, that such a declaration supposes that a person has the opportunity of believing. We are not speaking of heathens, but of Christians; of those who are taught the truth, who have the offer of it, and who reject it. Accordingly, we do not contemplate in this Creed cases of imperfect or erroneous teaching;—or of what may be called misinformation of the reason; or any case of invincible ignorance; but of a man's wilful rejection of what has been fairly set before him. Secondly, when the Creed says that we "must think *thus* of the Trinity," it would seem to imply, that it had been drawing out a certain clear, substantive, consistent, and distinctive view of the doctrine, which is the Catholic view; and that, in opposition to other views of it, whether Sabellian, or Arian, or Tritheistic, or others that might be mentioned; all of which, without denying in words the Holy Three, do deny Him in fact and in the event, and involve their wilful maintainers in the anathema which is here proclaimed, not in harshness, but as a faithful warning, and a solemn protest.

May we never speak on subjects like this without awe; may we never dispute without charity; may we never inquire without a careful endeavour, with God's aid, to sanctify our knowledge, and to impress it on our hearts, as well as to store it in our understandings!

PEACE IN BELIEVING

(Trinity Sunday)

"And one cried unto another, and said, Holy, Holy, Holy, is the Lord of Hosts."—Is. vi.3.

EVERY Lord's day is a day of rest, but this, perhaps, more than any. It commemorates, not an act of God, however gracious and glorious, but His own unspeakable perfections and adorable mysteriousness. It is a day especially sacred to peace. Our Lord left His peace with us when He went away; "Peace I leave with you; My peace I give unto you: not as the world giveth, give I unto you;" [1] and He said He would send them a Comforter, who should give them peace. Last week we commemorated that Comforter's coming; and to-day, we commemorate in an especial way the gift He brought with Him, in that great doctrine which is its emblem and its means. "These things have I spoken unto you, that in Me ye might have peace: in the world ye shall have tribulation." [2] Christ here says, that instead of this world's troubles, He gives His disciples peace; and, accordingly, in to-day's Collect, we pray that we may be kept in the faith of the Eternal Trinity in Unity, *and* be "defended from all adversities," for in keeping that faith we are kept from trouble.

Hence, too, in the blessing which Moses told the priests to pronounce over the children of Israel, God's Name is put upon them, and that three times, in order to bless and keep them, to make His face shine on them, and to give them peace. And hence again, in our own solemn form of blessing, with which we end our public service, we impart to the people "the peace of God, which passeth all understanding," and "the blessing of the Father, the Son, and the Holy Ghost."

God is the God of peace, and in giving us peace He does but give Himself, He does but manifest Himself to us; for His presence is peace. Hence our Lord, in the same discourse in which He promised His disciples peace, promised also, that "He

---

[1] John xiv.27.   [2] John xvi.33.

would come and manifest Himself unto them," that "He and His Father would come to them, and make Their abode with them."[3] Peace is His everlasting state; in this world of space and time He has wrought and acted; but from everlasting it was not so. For six days He wrought, and then He rested according to that rest which was His eternal state; yet not so rested, as not in one sense to "work hitherto," in mercy and in judgment, towards that world which He had created. And more especially, when He sent His Only-begotten Son into the world, and that most Gracious and All-pitiful Son, our Lord, condescended to come to us, both He and His Father wrought with a mighty hand; and They vouchsafed the Holy Ghost, the Comforter, and He also wrought wonderfully, and works hitherto. Certainly the whole economy of redemption is a series of great and continued works; but still they all tend to rest and peace, as at the first. They began out of rest, and they end in rest. They end in that eternal state out of which they began. The Son was from eternity in the bosom of the Father, as His dearly-beloved and Only-begotten. He loved Him before the foundation of the world. He had glory with Him before the world was. He was in the Father, and the Father in Him. None knew the Son but the Father, nor the Father but the Son. "In the beginning was the Word, and the Word was with God, and the Word was God." He was "the Brightness of God's glory and the express Image of His Person;" and in this unspeakable Unity of Father and Son, was the Spirit also, as being the Spirit of the Father, and the Spirit of the Son; the Spirit of Both at once, not separate from them, yet distinct, so that they were Three Persons, One God, from everlasting.

Thus was it, we are told, from everlasting;—before the heavens and the earth were made, before man fell or Angels rebelled, before the sons of God were formed in the morning of creation, yea, before there were Seraphim to veil their faces before Him and cry "Holy," He existed without ministers, without attendants, without court and kingdom, without manifested glory, without any thing but Himself; He His own Temple, His own infinite rest, His own supreme bliss, from eternity. O wonderful mystery! O the depth of His majesty! O deep things which the Spirit only knoweth! Wonderful and strange to creatures who grovel on this earth, as we, that He, the All-powerful, the All-wise, the All-good, the All-glorious, should for an eternity, for years without end, or rather, apart

[3] John xiv.21, 23.

from time, which is but one of His creatures, that He should have dwelt without those through whom He might be powerful, in whom He might be wise, towards whom He might be good, by whom He might be glorified. O wonderful, that all His deep and infinite attributes should have been without manifestation! O wonderful thought! and withal, O thought comfortable to us worms of the earth, as often as we feel in ourselves and see in others gifts which have no exercise, and powers which are quiescent! He, the All-powerful God, rested from eternity, and did not work; and yet, why *not* rest, wonderful though it be, seeing He was so blessed in Himself? why should *He* seek external objects to know, to love, and to commune with, who was all-sufficient in Himself? How could He need fellows, as though He were a man, when He was not solitary, but had ever with Him His Only-begotten Word in whom He delighted, whom He loved ineffably, and the Eternal Spirit, the very bond of love and peace, dwelling in and dwelt in by Father and Son? Rather how was it that He ever began to create, who had a Son without beginning and without imperfection, whom He could love with a perfect love? What exceeding exuberance of goodness was it that *He* should deign at length to surround Himself with creation, who had need of nothing, and to change His everlasting silence for the course of Providence and the conflict of good and evil! I say nothing of the apostasies against Him, the rebellions and blasphemies which men and devils have committed. I say nothing of that unutterable region of woe, the prison of the impenitent, which is to last for eternity, coeval with Himself henceforth, as if in rivalry of His blissful heaven. I say nothing of this, for God cannot be touched with evil; and all the sins of those reprobate souls cannot impair His everlasting felicity. But, I ask, how was it that He who needed nothing, who was all in all, who had infinite Equals in the Son and the Spirit, who were One with Him, how was it that He created His Saints, but from simple love of them from eternity? Why should He make man in the Image of God, whose Image already was the Son, All-perfect, All-exact, without variableness, without defect, by a natural propriety and unity of substance? And when man fell, why did He not abandon or annihilate the whole race, and create others? why did He go so far as to begin a fresh and more wonderful dispensation towards us, and, as He had wrought marvellously in Providence, work marvellously also in grace, even sending His Eternal Son to take on Him our fallen nature, and to purify and renew it by His union with it, but that, infinite as was His own blessedness, and the Son's perfection, and man's unprofitableness, yet, in His loving-kindness, He determined that unprofitable man should be a partaker of the Son's perfection and His own blessedness?

And thus it was that, as He had made man in the beginning, so also He redeemed him; and the history of this redemption we have been tracing for the last six months in our sacred Services. We have gone through in our memory the whole course of that Dispensation of active providences, which God, in order to our redemption, has superinduced upon His eternal and infinite repose. First, we commemorated the approach of Christ, in the weeks of Advent; then His birth, of the Blessed Mary, after a miraculous conception, at Christmas; then His circumcision; His manifestation to the wise men; His baptism and beginning of miracles; His presentation in the Temple; His fasting and temptation in the wilderness, in Lent; His agony in the garden; His betrayal; His mocking and scourging; His cross and passion; His burial; His resurrection; His forty days, converse with His disciples after it; then His Ascension; and, lastly, the coming of the Holy Ghost in His stead to remain with the Church unto the end,—unto the end of the world; for so long is the Almighty Comforter to remain with us. And thus, in commemorating the Spirit's gracious office during the past week, we were brought, in our series of representations, to the end of all things; and now what is left but to commemorate what will follow after the end?—the return of the everlasting reign of God, the infinite peace and blissful perfection of the Father, the Son, and the Holy Ghost, differing indeed from what it once was by the fruits of creation and redemption, but not differing in the supreme blessedness, the ineffable mutual love, the abyss of holiness in which the Three Persons of the Eternal Trinity dwell. He, then, is the subject of this day's celebration,—the God of love, of holiness, of blessedness; in whose presence is fulness of joy and pleasures for evermore; who is what He ever was, and has brought us sinners to that which He ever was. He did not bring into being peace and love as part of His creation, but He was Himself peace and love from eternity, and He blesses us by making us partakers of Himself, through the Son, by the Spirit, and He so works in His temporal dispensations that He may bring us to that which is eternal.

And hence, in Scripture, the promises of eternity and security go together; for where time is not, there vicissitude also is away. "The Eternal God is thy refuge," says Moses, before his death, "and underneath are the everlasting arms: and He shall thrust out the enemy from before thee, and shall say, Destroy them; Israel then shall dwell in safety alone." And again, "Thou wilt keep him in perfect peace, whose mind is stayed on Thee, because he trusteth in Thee. Trust ye in the Lord for ever; for in the Lord Jehovah is everlasting strength." And again, "Thus saith the High and Lofty One that inhabiteth eternity. . . . I dwell in the high and holy place, with him also that is of a contrite and humble spirit, to revive the spirit of the humble, and to revive the heart of the contrite ones. . . . I create the fruit of the lips; peace, peace to him that is afar off, and to him that is near." And, in like manner, our Lord and Saviour is prophesied of as being "the *Everlasting* Father, the Prince of *peace*." And again, speaking more especially of what He has done for us, "The work of righteousness shall be *peace*; and the effect of righteousness, quietness and *assurance for ever*."[4]

As then we have for many weeks commemorated the economy by which righteousness was restored to us, which took place in time, so from this day forth do we bring before our minds the infinite perfections of Almighty God, and our hope hereafter of seeing and enjoying them. Hitherto we have celebrated His great works; henceforth we magnify Himself. Now, for twenty-five weeks we represent in figure what is to be hereafter. We enter into our rest, by entering in with Him who, having wrought and suffered, has opened the kingdom of heaven to all believers. For half a year we stand still, as if occupied solely in adoring Him, and, with the Seraphim in the text, crying, "Holy, Holy, Holy," continually. All God's providences, all God's dealings with us, all His judgments, mercies, warnings, deliverances, tend to peace and repose as their ultimate issue. All our troubles and pleasures here, all our anxieties, fears, doubts, difficulties, hopes, encouragements, afflictions, losses, attainments, tend this one way. After Christmas, Easter, and Whitsuntide, comes Trinity Sunday, and the weeks that follow; and in like manner, after our soul's anxious travail; after the birth of the Spirit; after trial and temptation; after sorrow and pain; after daily dyings to the world; after daily risings unto holiness; at length comes that "rest which remaineth unto the people of God." After the fever of life; after wearinesses and sicknesses; fightings and despondings; languor and fretfulness; struggling and failing, struggling and succeeding; after all the changes and chances of this troubled unhealthy state, at length comes death, at length the White Throne of God, at length the Beatific Vision. After restlessness comes

[4] Deut. xxxiii.27, 28; Is. xxvi.3, 4; lvii.15, 19; ix.6; xxxii.17.

rest, peace, joy;—our eternal portion, if we be worthy;—the sight of the Blessed Three, the Holy One; the Three that bear witness in heaven; in light unapproachable; in glory without spot or blemish; in power without "variableness, or shadow of turning." The Father God, the Son God, and the Holy Ghost God; the Father Lord, the Son Lord, and the Holy Ghost Lord; the Father uncreate, the Son uncreate, and the Holy Ghost uncreate; the Father incomprehensible, the Son incomprehensible, and the Holy Ghost incomprehensible. For there is one Person of the Father, another of the Son, and another of the Holy Ghost; and such as the Father is, such is the Son, and such is the Holy Ghost; and yet there are not three Gods, nor three Lords, nor three incomprehensibles, nor three uncreated; but one God, one Lord, one uncreated, and one incomprehensible.

Let us, then, use with thankfulness the subject of this day's Festival, and the Creed of St. Athanasius, as a means of peace, till it is given us, if we attain thereto, to see the face of God in heaven. What the Beatific Vision will then impart, the contemplation of revealed mysteries gives us as in a figure. The doctrine of the Blessed Trinity has been made the subject of especial contention among the professed followers of Christ. It has brought a sword upon earth, but it was intended to bring peace. And it does bring peace to those who humbly receive it in faith. Let us beg of God to bless it to us to its right uses, that it may not be an occasion of strife, but of worship; not of division, but of unity; not of jealousy, but of love. Let us devoutly approach Him of whom it speaks, with the confession of our lips and of our hearts. Let us look forward to the time when this world will have passed away and all its delusions; and when we, when every one born of woman, must either be in heaven or in hell. Let us desire to hide ourselves under the shadow of His wings. Let us beg Him to give us an understanding heart, and that love of Him which is the instinct of the new creature, and the breath of spiritual life. Let us pray Him to give us the spirit of obedience, of true dutifulness; an honest spirit, earnestly set to do His will, with no secret ends, no selfish designs of our own, no preferences of the creature to the Creator, but open, clear, conscientious, and loyal. So will He vouchsafe, as time goes on, to take up His abode in us; the Spirit of Truth, whom the world cannot receive, will dwell in us, and be in us, and Christ "will love us, and will manifest Himself to us," and "the Father will love us, and They will come unto us, and make Their abode with us." And when at length the inevitable hour comes, we shall be able meekly to surrender our souls, our sinful yet redeemed souls, in much weakness and trembling, with much self-reproach and deep confession, yet in firm faith, and in cheerful hope, and in calm love, to God the Father, God the Son, God the Holy Ghost; the Blessed Three, the Holy One; Three Persons, One God; our Creator, our Redeemer, our Sanctifier, our Judge.

VII

THE LAPSE OF TIME

"Whatsoever thy hand findeth to do, do it with thy might; for there is no work, nor device, nor knowledge, nor wisdom, in the grave, whither thou goest."—Eccles. ix. 10.

S OLOMON'S advice that we should do whatever our hand findeth to do with our might, naturally directs our thoughts to that great work in which all others are included, which will outlive all other works, and for which alone we really are placed here below—the salvation of our souls. And the consideration of this great work, which must be done with all our might, and completed before the grave, whither we go, presents itself to our minds with especial force at the commencement of a new year. We are now entering on a fresh stage of our life's journey; we know well how it will end, and we see where we shall stop in the evening, though we do not see the road. And we know in what our business lies while we travel, and that it is important for us to do it with our "might; for there is no work, nor device, nor knowledge, nor wisdom, in the grave." This is so plain, that nothing need be said in order to convince us that it is true. We know it well; the very complaint which numbers commonly make when told of it, is that they know it already, that it is nothing new, that they have no need to be told, and that it is tiresome to hear the same thing said over and over again, and impertinent in the person who repeats it. Yes; thus it is that sinners silence their conscience, by quarrelling with those who appeal to it; they defend themselves, if it may be called a defence, by pleading that they already know what they should do and do not; that they know perfectly well that they are living at a distance from God, and are in peril of eternal ruin; that they know they are making themselves children of Satan, and denying the Lord that bought them, and want no one to tell them so. Thus they witness against themselves.

However, though we already know well enough that we have much to do before we die, yet (if we will but attend) it may be of use to hear the fact dwelt upon; because by thinking over it steadily and seriously, we may possibly, through God's grace, gain some deep conviction of it; whereas while we keep to general terms, and confess that this life is important and is short, in the mere summary way in which men commonly confess it, we have, properly speaking, no knowledge of that great truth at all.

Consider, then, what it is to die; "there is no work, device, knowledge, or wisdom, in the grave." Death puts an end absolutely and irrevocably to all our plans and works, and it is inevitable. The Psalmist speaks to "high and low, rich and poor, one with another." "No man can deliver his brother, nor make agreement unto God for him." Even "wise men die, as well as the ignorant and foolish, and leave their riches for other."[1] Difficult as we may find it to bring it home to ourselves, to realize it, yet as surely as we are here assembled together, so surely will every one of us, sooner or later, one by one, be stretched on the bed of death. We naturally shrink from the thought of death, and of its attendant circumstances; but all that is hateful and fearful about it will be fulfilled in our case, one by one. But all this is nothing compared with the consequences implied in it. Death stops us; it stops our race. Men are engaged about their work, or about their pleasure; they are in the city, or the field; any how they are stopped; their deeds are suddenly gathered in —a reckoning is made—all is sealed up till the great day. What a change is this! In the words used familiarly in speaking of the dead, they are no more. They were full of schemes and projects; whether in a greater or humbler rank, they had their hopes and fears, their prospects, their pursuits, their rivalries; all these are now come to an end. One builds a house, and its roof is not finished; another buys merchandise, and it is not yet sold. And all their virtues and pleasing qualities which endeared them to their friends are, as far as this world is concerned, vanished. Where are they who were so active, so sanguine, so generous? the amiable, the modest, and the kind? We were told that they were dead; they suddenly disappeared; that is all we know about it. They were silently taken from us; they are not met in the seat of the elders, nor in the assemblies of the people; in the mixed concourse of men, nor in the domestic retirement which they prized. As Scripture describes it, "the wind has passed over them, and they are gone, and their place shall know them no more." And they have burst the many ties which held them; they were parents, brothers, sisters, children, and friends; but the bond of kindred is broken, and the silver cord of love is loosed. They have been followed by the vehement grief of tears,

[1] Ps. xlix.2–10.

and the long sorrow of aching hearts; but they make no return, they answer not; they do not even satisfy our wish to know that they sorrow for us as we for them. We talk about them thenceforth as if they were persons we do not know; we talk about them as third persons; whereas they used to be always with us, and every other thought which was within us was shared by them. Or perhaps, if our grief is too deep, we do not mention their names at all. And their possessions, too, all fall to others. The world goes on without them; it forgets them. Yes, so it is; the world contrives to forget that men have souls, it looks upon them all as mere parts of some great visible system. This continues to move on; to this the world ascribes a sort of life and personality. When one or other of its members die, it considers them only as falling out of the system, and as come to nought. For a minute, perhaps, it thinks of them in sorrow, then leaves them—leaves them for ever. It keeps its eye on things seen and temporal. Truly whenever a man dies, rich or poor, an immortal soul passes to judgment; but somehow we read of the deaths of persons we have seen or heard of, and this reflection never comes across us. Thus does the world really cast off men's souls, and recognizing only their bodies, it makes it appear as if "that which befalleth the sons of men befalleth beasts, even one thing befalleth them, as the one dieth so dieth the other; yea, they have all one breath, so that a man hath no pre-eminence over a beast, for all is vanity." [2]

But let us follow the course of a soul thus casting off the world, and cast off by it. It goes forth as a stranger on a journey. Man seems to die and to be no more, when he is but quitting us, and is really beginning to live. Then he sees sights which before it did not even enter into his mind to conceive, and the world is even less to him than he to the world. Just now he was lying on the bed of sickness, but in that moment of death what an awful change has come over him! What a crisis for him! There is stillness in the room that lately held him; nothing is doing there, for he is gone, he now belongs to others; he now belongs entirely to the Lord who bought him; to Him he returns; but whether to be lodged safely in His place of hope, or to be imprisoned against the great Day, that is another matter, that depends on the deeds done in the body, whether good or evil. And now what are his thoughts? How infinitely important now appears the value of time, now when it is nothing to him! Nothing; for though he spend centuries waiting for Christ, he cannot now

<hr>

[2] Eccles. iii. 19.

alter his state from bad to good, or from good to bad. What he dieth that he must be for ever; as the tree falleth so must it lie. This is the comfort of the true servant of God, and the misery of the transgressor. His lot is cast once and for all, and he can but wait in hope or in dread. Men on their death-beds have declared, that no one could form a right idea of the value of time till he came to die; but if this has truth in it, how much more truly can it be said after death! What an estimate shall we form of time while we are waiting for judgment! Yes, it is we—all this, I repeat, belongs to us most intimately. It is not to be looked at as a picture, as a man might read a light book in a leisure hour. *We* must die, the youngest, the healthiest, the most thoughtless; *we* must be thus unnaturally torn in two, soul from body; and only united again to be made more thoroughly happy or to be miserable for ever.

Such is death considered in its inevitable necessity, and its unspeakable importance—nor can we ensure to ourselves any certain interval before its coming. The time may be long; but it may also be short. It is plain, a man may die any day; all we can say is, that it is unlikely that he will die. But of this, at least, we are certain, that, come it sooner or later, death is continually on the move towards us. We are ever nearer and nearer to it. Every morning we rise we are nearer that grave in which there is no work, nor device, than we were. We are now nearer the grave, than when we entered this Church. Thus life is ever crumbling away under us. What should we say to a man, who was placed on some precipitous ground, which was ever crumbling under his feet, and affording less and less secure footing, yet was careless about it? Or what should we say to one who suffered some precious liquor to run from its receptacle into the thoroughfare of men, without a thought to stop it? who carelessly looked on and saw the waste of it, becoming greater and greater every minute? But what treasure can equal time? It is the seed of eternity: yet we suffer ourselves to go on, year after year, hardly using it at all in God's service, or thinking it enough to give Him at most a tithe or a seventh of it, while we strenuously and heartily sow to the flesh, that from the flesh we may reap corruption. We try how little we can safely give to religion, instead of having the grace to give abundantly. "Rivers of water run down mine eyes, because men keep not Thy law;" so says the holy Psalmist. Doubtless an inspired prophet saw far more clearly than we can see, the madness of men in squandering that treasure upon sin, which is meant to buy their chief good;—but if so, what must this madness appear in God's sight! What an inveterate malignant evil is it in the hearts of the sons of men, that thus leads them to sit down to eat, and drink, and rise up to play, when time is hurrying on and judgment coming? We have been told what He thinks of man's unbelief, though we cannot enter into the depths of His thoughts. He showed it to us in act and deed, as far as we could receive it, when He even sent His Only-begotten Son into the world as at this time, to redeem us from the world,—which, most surely, was not lightly done; and we also learn His thoughts about it from the words of that most merciful Son,—which most surely were not lightly spoken, "The wicked," He says, "shall go into everlasting punishment."

Oh that there were such a heart in us that we would fear God and keep His commandments always! But it is of no use to speak; men know their duty—they will not do it. They say they do not need or wish to be told it, that it is an intrusion, and a rudeness, to tell them of death and judgment. So must it be,—and we, who have to speak to them, must submit to this. Speak we must, as an act of duty to God, whether they will hear, or not, and then must leave our words as a witness. Other means for rousing them we have none. We speak from Christ our gracious Lord, their Redeemer, who has already pardoned them freely, yet they will not follow Him with a true heart; and what can be done more?

Another year is now opening upon us; it speaks to the thoughtful, and is heard by those, who have expectant ears, and watch for Christ's coming. The former year is gone, it is dead, there it lies in the grave of past time, not to decay however, and be forgotten, but kept in the view of God's omniscience, with all its sins and errors irrevocably written, till, at length, it will be raised again to testify about us at the last day; and who among us can bear the thought of his own doings, in the course of it?—all that he has said and done, all that has been conceived within his mind, or been acted on, and all that he has not said and done, which it was a duty to say or do. What a dreary prospect seems to be before us, when we reflect that we have the solemn word of truth pledged to us, in the last and most awful revelation, which God has made to us about the future, that in that day, the books will be opened, "and another book opened, which is the book of life, and the dead judged out of those things which were written in the books according to their works!"[3] What would a man give, any one of us, who has any real insight into his polluted and miserable state, what would he

[3] Rev. xx.12.

give to tear away some of the leaves there preserved! For how heinous are the sins therein written! Think of the multitude of sins done by us since we first knew the difference between right and wrong. We have forgotten them, but there we might read them clearly recorded. Well may holy David exclaim, "Remember not the sins of my youth nor my transgressions, according to Thy mercy remember Thou me." Conceive, too, the multitude of sins which have so grown into us as to become part of us, and in which we now live, not knowing, or but partially knowing, that they are sins; habits of pride, self-reliance, self-conceit, sullenness, impurity, sloth, selfishness, worldliness. The history of all these, their beginnings, and their growth, is recorded in those dreadful books; and when we look forward to the future, how many sins shall we have committed by this time next year,—though we try ever so much to know our duty, and overcome ourselves! Nay, or rather shall we have the opportunity of obeying or disobeying God for a year longer? Who knows whether by that time our account may not be closed for ever?

"Remember me, O Lord, when Thou comest into Thy kingdom."[4] Such was the prayer of the penitent thief on the cross, such must be our prayer. Who can do us any good, but He, who shall also be our Judge? When shocking thoughts about ourselves come across us and afflict us, "Remember me," this is all we have to say. We have "no work, nor device, nor knowledge, nor wisdom" of our own, to better ourselves withal. We can say nothing to God in defence of ourselves,—we can but acknowledge that we are grievous sinners, and addressing Him as suppliants, merely beg Him to bear us in mind in mercy, for His Son's sake to do us some favour, not according to our deserts, but for the love of Christ. The more we try to serve Him here, the better; but after all, so far do we fall short of what we should be, that if we had but what we are in ourselves to rely upon, wretched are we,—and we are forced out of ourselves by the very necessity of our condition. To whom should we go? Who can do us any good, but He who was born into this world for our regeneration, was bruised for our iniquities, and rose again for our justification? Even though we have served Him from our youth up, though after His pattern we have grown, as far as mere man can grow, in wisdom as we grew in stature, though we ever have had tender hearts, and a mortified will, and a conscientious temper, and an obedient spirit; yet, at the very best,

[4] Luke xxiii.42.

how much have we left undone, how much done, which ought to be otherwise! What He can do for our nature, in the way of sanctifying it, we know indeed in a measure; we know, in the case of His saints; and we certainly do not know the limit of His carrying forward in those objects of His special favour the work of purification, and renewal through His Spirit. But for ourselves, we know full well that much as we may have attempted, we have done very little, that our very best service is nothing worth,—and the more we attempt, the more clearly we shall see how little we have hitherto attempted.

Those whom Christ saves are they who at once attempt to save themselves, yet despair of saving themselves; who aim to do all, and confess they do nought; who are all love, and all fear; who are the most holy, and yet confess themselves the most sinful; who ever seek to please Him, yet feel they never can; who are full of good works, yet of works of penance. All this seems a contradiction to the natural man, but it is not so to those whom Christ enlightens. They understand in proportion to their illumination, that it is possible to work out their salvation, yet to have it wrought out for them, to fear and tremble at the thought of judgment, yet to rejoice always in the Lord, and hope and pray for His coming.

RELIGION A WEARINESS TO
THE NATURAL MAN

*"He hath no form nor comeliness; and when we shall see Him, there
is no beauty that we should desire Him."*—Is. liii.2.

RELIGION is a weariness;" such is the judgment commonly
passed, often avowed, concerning the greatest of blessings
which Almighty God has bestowed upon us. And when God
gave the blessing, He at the same time foretold that such would
be the judgment of the world upon it, even as manifested in the
gracious Person of Him whom He sent to give it to us. "He hath
no form nor comeliness," says the Prophet, speaking of our
Lord and Saviour, "and when we shall see Him, there is no
beauty that we should desire Him." He declared beforehand,
that to man His religion would be uninteresting and distasteful.
Not that this prediction excuses our deadness to it; this dislike
of the religion given us by God Himself, seen as it is on all sides
of us,—of religion in all its parts, whether its doctrines, its precepts, its polity, its worship, its social influence,—this distaste
for its very name, must obviously be an insult to the Giver. But
the text speaks of it as a fact, without commenting on the guilt
involved in it; and as such I wish you to consider it, as far as this
may be done in reverence and seriousness. Putting aside for an
instant the thought of the ingratitude and the sin which indifference to Christianity implies, let us, as far as we dare, view it
merely as a matter of fact, after the manner of the text, and
form a judgment on the probable consequences of it. Let us
take the state of the case as it is found, and survey it dispassionately, as even an unbeliever might survey it, without at the
moment considering whether it is sinful or not; as a misfortune,
if we will, or a strange accident, or a necessary condition of our
nature,—one of the phenomena, as it may be called, of the
present world.

Let me then review human life in some of its stages and conditions, in order to impress upon you the fact of this contrariety
between ourselves and our Maker: He having one will, we an-

other; He declaring one thing to be good for us, and we fancying other objects to be our good.

1. "Religion is a weariness;" alas! so feel even children before they can well express their meaning. Exceptions of course now and then occur; and of course children are always more open to religious impressions and visitations than grown persons. They have many good thoughts and good desires, of which, in after life, the multitude of men seem incapable. Yet who, after all, can have a doubt that, in spite of the more intimate presence of God's grace with those who have not yet learned to resist it, still, on the whole, religion is a weariness to children? Consider their amusements, their enjoyments,—what they hope, what they devise, what they scheme, and what they dream about themselves in time future, when they grow up; and say what place religion holds in their hearts. Watch the reluctance with which they turn to religious duties, to saying their prayers, or reading the Bible; and then judge. Observe, as they get older, the influence which the fear of the ridicule of their companions has in deterring them even from speaking of religion, or seeming to be religious. Now the dread of ridicule, indeed, is natural enough; but why should religion inspire ridicule? What is there absurd in thinking of God? Why should we be ashamed of worshipping Him? It is unaccountable, but it is natural. We may call it an accident, or what we will; still it is an undeniable fact, and that is what I insist upon. I am not forgetful of the peculiar character of children's minds: sensible objects first meet their observation; it is not wonderful that they should at first be inclined to limit their thoughts to things of sense. A distinct profession of faith, and a conscious maintenance of principle, may imply a strength and consistency of thought to which they are as yet unequal. Again, childhood is capricious, ardent, lighthearted; it cannot think deeply or long on any subject. Yet all this is not enough to account for the fact in question—why they should feel this distaste for the very subject of religion. Why should they be ashamed of paying reverence to an unseen, all-powerful God, whose existence they do not disbelieve? Yet they do feel ashamed of it. Is it that they are ashamed of themselves, not of their religion; feeling the inconsistency of professing what they cannot fully practise? This refinement does not materially alter the view of the case; for it is merely their own acknowledgment that they do not love religion as much as they ought. No; we seem compelled to the conclusion, that there is by nature some strange discordance between what we love and what God loves. So much, then, on the state of boyhood.

2. "Religion is a weariness." I will next take the case of young persons when they first enter into life. Here I may appeal to some perhaps who now hear me. Alas! my brethren, is it not so? Is not religion associated in your minds with gloom, melancholy, and weariness? I am not at present going so far as to reprove you for it, though I might well do so; if I did, perhaps you might at once turn away, and I wish you calmly to think the matter over, and bear me witness that I state the fact correctly. It is so; you cannot deny it. The very terms "religion," "devotion," "piety," "conscientiousness," "mortification," and the like, you find to be inexpressibly dull and cheerless: you cannot find fault with them, indeed, you would if you could; and whenever the words are explained in particulars and realized, then you do find occasion for exception and objection. But though you cannot deny the claims of religion used as a vague and general term, yet how irksome, cold, uninteresting, uninviting, does it at best appear to you! how severe its voice! how forbidding its aspect! With what animation, on the contrary, do you enter into the mere pursuits of time and the world! What bright anticipations of joy and happiness flit before your eyes! How you are struck and dazzled at the view of the prizes of this life, as they are called! How you admire the elegancies of art, the brilliance of wealth, or the force of intellect! According to your opportunities you mix in the world, you meet and converse with persons of various conditions and pursuits, and are engaged in the numberless occurrences of daily life. You are full of news; you know what this or that person is doing, and what has befallen him; what has not happened, which was near happening, what may happen. You are full of ideas and feelings upon all that goes on around you. But, from some cause or other, religion has no part, no sensible influence, in your judgment of men and things. It is out of your way. Perhaps you have your pleasure parties; you readily take your share in them time after time; you pass continuous hours in society where you know that it is quite impossible even to mention the name of religion. Your heart is in scenes and places when conversation on serious subjects is strictly forbidden by the rules of the world's propriety. I do not say we should discourse on religious subjects, wherever we go; I do not say we should make an effort to discourse on them at any time, nor that we are to refrain from social meetings in which religion does not lie on the surface of the conversation: but I do say, that when men find their pleasure and satisfaction to lie in society which proscribes religion, and when they deliberately and habitually prefer those

amusements which have necessarily nothing to do with religion, such persons cannot view religion as God views it. And this is the point: that the feelings of our hearts on the subject of religion are different from the declared judgment of God; that we have a natural distaste for that which He has said is our chief good.

3. Now let us pass to the more active occupations of life. Here, too, religion is confessedly felt to be wearisome, it is out of place. The transactions of worldly business, speculations in trade, ambitious hopes, the pursuit of knowledge, the public occurrences of the day, these find a way directly to the heart; they rouse, they influence. It is superfluous to go about to prove this innate power over us of things of time and sense, to make us think and act. The name of religion, on the other hand, is weak and impotent; it contains no spell to kindle the feelings of man, to make the heart beat with anxiety, and to produce activity and perseverance. The reason is not merely that men are in want of leisure, and are sustained in a distressing continuance of exertion, by their duties towards those dependent on them. They have their seasons of relaxation, they turn for a time from their ordinary pursuits; still religion does not attract them, they find nothing of comfort or satisfaction in it. For a time they allow themselves to be idle. They want an object to employ their minds upon; they pace to and fro in very want of an object; yet their duties to God, their future hopes in another state of being, the revelation of God's mercy and will, as contained in Scripture, the news of redemption, the gift of regeneration, the sanctities, the devotional heights, the nobleness and perfection which Christ works in His elect, do not suggest themselves as fit subjects to dispel their weariness. Why? Because religion makes them melancholy, say they, and they wish to relax. Religion is a labour, it is a weariness, a greater weariness than the doing nothing at all. "Wherefore," says Solomon, "is there a price in the hand of a fool to get wisdom, seeing he hath no heart to it?" [1]

4. But this natural contrariety between man and his Maker is still more strikingly shown by the confessions of men of the world who have given some thought to the subject, and have viewed society with somewhat of a philosophical spirit. Such men treat the demands of religion with disrespect and negligence, on the ground of their being unnatural. They say, "It is natural for men to love the world for its own sake; to be

---

[1] Prov. xvii.16.

engrossed in its pursuits, and to set their hearts on the rewards of industry, on the comforts, luxuries, and pleasures of this life. Man would not be man if he could be made otherwise; he would not be what he was evidently intended for by his Maker." Let us pass by the obvious *answer* that might be given to this objection; it is enough for my purpose that it is *commonly urged*, recognizing as it does the fact of the disagreement existing between the claims of God's word, and the inclinations and natural capacities of man. Many, indeed, of those unhappy men who have denied the Christian faith, treat the religious principle altogether as a mere unnatural, eccentric state of mind, a peculiar untoward condition of the affections to which weakness will reduce a man, whether it has been brought on by anxiety, oppressive sorrow, bodily disease, excess of imagination or the like, and temporary or permanent, according to the circumstances of the disposing cause; a state to which we all are liable, as we are liable to any other mental injury, but unmanly and unworthy of our dignity as rational beings. Here again it is enough for our purpose, that it is allowed by these persons that the love of religion is unnatural and inconsistent with the original condition of our minds.

The same remark may be made upon the notions which secretly prevail in certain quarters at the present day, concerning the unsuitableness of Christianity to an enlightened age. Men there are who look upon the inspired word of God with a sort of indulgence, as if it had its use, and had done service in its day; that in times of ignorance it awed and controlled fierce barbarians, whom nothing else could have subdued; but that from its very claim to be divine and infallible, and its consequent unalterableness, it is an obstacle to the improvement of the human race beyond a certain point, and must ultimately fall before the gradual advancement of mankind in knowledge and virtue. In other words, the literature of the day is weary of Revealed Religion.

5. Once more; that religion is in itself a weariness is seen even in the conduct of the better sort of persons, who really on the whole are under the influence of its spirit. So dull and uninviting is calm and practical religion, that religious persons are ever exposed to the temptation of looking out for excitements of one sort or other, to make it pleasurable to them. The spirit of the Gospel is a meek, humble, gentle, unobtrusive spirit. It doth not cry nor lift up its voice in the streets, unless called upon by duty so to do, and then it does it with pain. Display, pretension, conflict, are unpleasant to it. What then is to be

thought of persons who are ever on the search after novelties to make religion interesting to them; who seem to find that Christian activity cannot be kept up without unchristian party-spirit, or Christian conversation without unchristian censoriousness? Why, this; that religion is to them as to others, taken by itself, a weariness, and requires something foreign to its own nature to make it palatable. Truly it is a weariness to the natural man to serve God humbly and in obscurity; it is very wearisome, and very monotonous, to go on day after day watching all we do and think, detecting our secret failings, denying ourselves, creating within us, under God's grace, those parts of the Christian character in which we are deficient; wearisome to learn modesty, love of insignificance, willingness to be thought little of, backwardness to clear ourselves when slandered, and readiness to confess when we are wrong; to learn to have no cares for this world, neither to hope nor to fear, but to be resigned and contented!

I may close these remarks, by appealing to the consciences of all who have ever set about the work of religion in good earnest, whoever they may be, whether they have made less, or greater progress in their noble toil, whether they are matured saints, or feeble strugglers against the world and the flesh. They have ever confessed how great efforts were necessary to keep close to the commandments of God; in spite of their knowledge of the truth, and their faith, in spite of the aids and consolations they receive from above, still how often do their corrupt hearts betray them! Even their privileges are often burdensome to them, even to pray for the grace which in Christ is pledged to them is an irksome task. They know that God's service is perfect freedom, and they are convinced, both in their reason and from their own experience of it, that it is true happiness; still they confess withal the strange reluctance of their nature to love their Maker and His Service. And this is the point in question; not only the mass of mankind, but even the confirmed servants of Christ, witness to the opposition which exists between their own nature and the demands of religion.

This then is the remarkable fact which I proposed to show. Can we doubt that man's will runs contrary to God's will—that the view which the inspired word takes of our present life, and of our destiny, does not satisfy us, as it rightly ought to do? that Christ hath no form nor comeliness in our eyes; and though we see Him, we see no desirable beauty in Him? That holy, merciful, and meek Saviour, the Eternal, the Only-begotten Son of God, our friend and infinite benefactor—He who left the glory

of His Father and died for us, who has promised us the overflowing riches of His grace both here and hereafter, He is a light shining in a dark place, and "the darkness comprehendeth it not."
"Light is come into the world and men love darkness rather than
light." The nature of man is flesh, and that which is born of the
flesh is flesh, and ever must so remain; it never can discern, love,
accept, the holy doctrines of the Gospel. It will occupy itself in
various ways, it will take interest in things of sense and time, but
it can never be religious. It is at enmity with God.

And now we see what must at once follow from what has
been said. If our hearts are by nature set on the world for its own
sake, and the world is one day to pass away, what are they to be
set on, what to delight in, then? Say, how will the soul feel
when, stripped of its present attire, which the world bestows, it
stands naked and shuddering before the pure, tranquil, and severe majesty of the Lord its God, its most merciful, yet dishonoured Maker and Saviour? What are to be the pleasures of
the soul in another life? Can they be the same as they are here?
They cannot; Scripture tells us they cannot; the world passeth
away—now what is there left to love and enjoy through a long
eternity? What a dark, forlorn, miserable eternity that will be!

It is then plain enough, though Scripture said not a word on
the subject, that if we would be happy in the world to come, we
must make us new hearts, and begin to love the things we naturally do not love. Viewing it as a practical point, the end of the
whole matter is this, we must be changed; for we cannot, we
cannot expect the system of the universe to come over to us;
the inhabitants of heaven, the numberless creations of Angels,
the glorious company of the Apostles, the goodly fellowship of
the Prophets, the noble army of Martyrs, the holy Church universal, the Will and Attributes of God, these are fixed. We
must go over to them. In our Saviour's own authoritative
words: "Verily, verily, except a man be born again, he cannot
see the kingdom of God."[2] It is a plain matter of self-interest,
to turn our thoughts to the means of changing our hearts, putting out of the question our duty towards God and Christ, our
Saviour and Redeemer.

"He hath no form nor comeliness, and when we see Him,
there is no beauty that we should desire Him." It is not His loss
that we love Him not, it is our loss. He is All-blessed, whatever
becomes of us. He is not less blessed because we are far from
Him. It is we who are not blessed, except as we approach Him,

[2] John iii.3.

except as we are like Him, except as we love Him. Woe unto us, if in the day in which He comes from Heaven we see nothing desirable or gracious in His wounds; but instead, have made for ourselves an ideal blessedness, different from that which will be manifested to us in Him. Woe unto us, if we have made pride, or selfishness, or the carnal mind, our standard of perfection and truth; if our eyes have grown dim, and our hearts gross, as regards the true light of men, and the glory of the Eternal Father. May He Himself save us from our self-delusions, whatever they are, and enable us to give up this world, that we may gain the next;—and to rejoice in Him, who had no home of His own, no place to lay His head, who was poor and lowly, and despised and rejected, and tormented and slain!

THE WORLD OUR ENEMY

*"We know that we are of God, and the whole world
lieth in wickedness."*—1 John v.19.

FEW words are of more frequent occurrence in the language
of religion than "the world;" Holy Scripture makes continual mention of it, in the way of censure and caution; in the
Service for Baptism it is described as one of three great enemies
of our souls; and in the ordinary writings and conversation of
Christians, I need hardly say, mention is made of it continually.
Yet most of us, it would appear, have very indistinct notions
what the world means. We know that the world is a something
dangerous to our spiritual interests, and that it is in some way
connected with human society—with men as a mixed multitude, contrasted with men one by one, in private and domestic
life; but what it is, how it is our enemy, how it attacks, and how
it is to be avoided, is not so clear. Or if we conceive some
distinct notion concerning it, still probably it is a wrong notion,—which leads us, in consequence, to misapply the Scripture precepts relating to the world; and this is even worse than
overlooking them. I shall now, then, attempt to show what is
meant by the world, and how, in consequence, we are to understand the information and warnings of the sacred writers
concerning it.

1. Now, first, by the world is very commonly meant the present visible system of things, without taking into consideration
whether it is good or bad. Thus St. John contrasts the world
with the things that are in it, which are evil, "Love not the
world, *neither* the things that are in the world." [1] Again, he presently says, "The world passeth away, *and* the lust thereof."
Here, as in many other parts of Scripture, the world is not spoken of as actually sinful in itself (though its lusts are so, of
course), but merely as some present visible system which is
likely to attract us, and is not to be trusted, because it cannot
last. Let us first consider it in this point of view.

[1] 1 John ii.15.

There is, as a matter of necessity, a great variety of stations and fortunes among mankind; hardly two persons are in the same outward circumstances, and possessed of the same mental resources. Men differ from each other, and are bound together into one body or system by the very points in which they differ; they depend on each other; such is the will of God. This system is the world, to which it is plain belong our various modes of supporting ourselves and families by exertion of mind and body, our intercourse with others, our duty towards others, the social virtues,—industry, honesty, prudence, justice, benevolence, and the like. These spring all from our present lot in life, and tend to our present happiness. This life holds out prizes to merit and exertion. Men rise above their fellows; they gain fame and honours, wealth and power, which we therefore call worldly goods. The affairs of nations, the dealings of people with people, the interchange of productions between country and country, are of this world. We are educated in boyhood for this world; we play our part on a stage more or less conspicuous, as the case may be; we die, we are no more, we are forgotten, as far as the present state of things is concerned; all this is of the world.

By the world, then, is meant this course of things which we see carried on by means of human agency, with all its duties and pursuits. It is not necessarily a sinful system; rather it is framed, as I have said, by God Himself, and therefore cannot be otherwise than good. And yet even thus considering it, we are bid not to love the world: even in this sense the world is an enemy of our souls; and for this reason, because the love of it is dangerous to beings circumstanced as we are,—things in themselves good being not good to us sinners. And this state of things which we see, fair and excellent in itself, is very likely (for the very reason that it is seen, and because the spiritual and future world is not seen) to seduce our wayward hearts from our true and eternal good. As the traveller on serious business may be tempted to linger, while he gazes on the beauty of the prospect which opens on his way, so this well-ordered and divinely-governed world, with all its blessings of sense and knowledge, may lead us to neglect those interests which will endure when itself has passed away. In truth it promises more than it can fulfil. The goods of life and the applause of men have their excellence, and, as far as they go, are really good; but they are short-lived. And hence it is that many pursuits in themselves honest and right, are nevertheless to be engaged in with caution, lest they seduce us; and those perhaps with especial caution, which tend to the well-being of men in this life. The sciences, for instance, of good government, of acquiring wealth, of preventing and relieving want, and the like, are for this reason especially dangerous; for fixing, as they do, our exertions on this world as an end, they go far to persuade us that they have no other end; they accustom us to think too much of success in life and temporal prosperity; nay, they may even teach us to be jealous of religion and its institutions, as if these stood in our way, preventing us from doing so much for the worldly interests of mankind as we might wish.

In this sense it is that St. Paul contrasts sight and faith. We see this world; we only believe that there is a world of spirits, we do not see it: and inasmuch as sight has more power over us than belief, and the present than the future, so are the occupations and pleasures of this life injurious to our faith. Yet not, I say, in themselves sinful; as the Jewish system was a temporal system, yet divine, so is the system of nature—this world—divine, though temporal. And as the Jews became carnal-minded even by the influence of their divinely-appointed system, and thereby rejected the Saviour of their souls; in like manner, men of the world are hardened by God's own good world, into a rejection of Christ. In neither case through the fault of the things which are seen, whether miraculous or providential, but accidentally, through the fault of the human heart.

2. But now, secondly, let us proceed to consider the world, not only as dangerous, but as positively sinful, according to the text—"the whole world lieth in wickedness." It was created well in all respects, but even before it as yet had fully grown out into its parts, while as yet the elements of human society did but lie hid in the nature and condition of the first man, Adam fell; and thus the world, with all its social ranks, and aims, and pursuits, and pleasures, and prizes, has ever from its birth been sinful. The infection of sin spread through the whole system, so that although the frame-work is good and divine, the spirit and life within it are evil. Thus, for instance, to be in a high station is the gift of God; but the pride and injustice to which it has given scope is from the Devil. To be poor and obscure is also the ordinance of God; but the dishonesty and discontent which are often seen in the poor is from Satan. To cherish and protect wife and family is God's appointment; but the love of gain, and the low ambition, which lead many a man to exert himself, are sinful. Accordingly, it is said in the text, "The world lieth in wickedness,"—it is plunged and steeped, as it were, in a flood of sin, not a part of it remaining as God origi-

nally created it, not a part pure from the corruptions with which Satan has disfigured it.

Look into the history of the world, and what do you read there? Revolutions and changes without number, kingdoms rising and falling; and when without crime? States are established by God's ordinance, they have their existence in the necessity of man's nature; but when was one ever established, nay, or maintained, without war and bloodshed? Of all natural instincts, what is more powerful than that which forbids us to shed our fellows' blood? We shrink with natural horror from the thought of a murderer; yet not a government has ever been settled, or a state acknowledged by its neighbours, without war and the loss of life; nay, more than this, not content with unjustifiable bloodshed, the guilt of which must lie somewhere, instead of lamenting it as a grievous and humiliating evil, the world has chosen to honour the conqueror with its amplest share of admiration. To become a hero, in the eyes of the world, it is almost necessary to break the laws of God and man. Thus the deeds of the world are matched by the opinions and principles of the world: it adopts bad doctrine to defend bad practice; it loves darkness because its deeds are evil.

And as the affairs of nations are thus depraved by our corrupt nature, so are all the appointments and gifts of Providence perverted in like manner. What can be more excellent than the vigorous and patient employment of the intellect; yet in the hands of Satan it gives birth to a proud philosophy. When St. Paul preached, the wise men of the world, in God's eyes, were but fools, for they had used their powers of mind in the cause of error; their reasonings even led them to be irreligious and immoral; and they despised the doctrine of a resurrection which they neither loved nor believed. And again, all the more refined arts of life have been disgraced by the vicious tastes of those who excelled in them; often they have been consecrated to the service of idolatry; often they have been made the instruments of sensuality and riot. But it would be endless to recount the manifold and complex corruption which man has introduced into the world which God made good; evil has preoccupied the whole of it, and holds fast its conquest. We know, indeed, that the gracious God revealed Himself to His sinful creatures very soon after Adam's fall. He showed His will to mankind again and again, and pleaded with them through many ages; till at length His Son was born into this sinful world in the form of man, and taught us how to please Him. Still, hitherto the good work has proceeded slowly: such is His pleasure. Evil had the start of good by many days; it filled the world, it holds it: it has the strength of possession, and it has its strength in the human heart; for though we cannot keep from approving what is right in our conscience, yet we love and encourage what is wrong; so that when evil was once set up in the world, it was secured in its seat by the unwillingness with which our hearts relinquish it.

And now I have described what is meant by the sinful world; that is, the world as corrupted by man, the course of human affairs viewed in its connexion with the principles, opinions, and practices which actually direct it. There is no mistaking these; they are evil; and of these it is that St. John says, "If any man love the world, the love of the Father is not in him. For all that is in the world, the lust of the flesh, and the lust of the eyes, and the pride of life, is not of the Father, but is of the world." [2]

The world then is the enemy of our souls; first, because, however innocent its pleasures, and praiseworthy its pursuits may be, they are likely to engross us, unless we are on our guard: and secondly, because in all its best pleasures, and noblest pursuits, the seeds of sin have been sown; an enemy hath done this; so that it is most difficult to enjoy the good without partaking of the evil also. As an orderly system of various ranks, with various pursuits and their several rewards, it is to be considered not sinful indeed, but dangerous to us. On the other hand, considered in reference to its principles and actual practices, it is really a sinful world. Accordingly, when we are bid in Scripture to shun the world, it is meant that we must be cautious, lest we love what is good in it too well, and lest we love the bad at all.— However, there is a mistaken notion sometimes entertained, that the world is some particular set of persons, and that to shun the world is to shun them; as if we could point out, as it were, with the finger, what is the world, and thus could easily rid ourselves of one of our three great enemies. Men, who are beset with this notion, are often great lovers of the world notwithstanding, while they think themselves at a distance from it altogether. They love its pleasures, and they yield to its principles, yet they speak strongly against men of the world, and avoid them. They act the part of superstitious people, who are afraid of seeing evil spirits in what are considered haunted places, while these spirits are busy at their hearts instead, and they do not suspect it.

3. Here then is a question, which it will be well to consider, viz. how far the world is a separate body from the Church of

[2] 1 John ii.15, 16.

God. The two are certainly contrasted in the text, as elsewhere in Scripture. "We know that *we* are of God, and *the whole world lieth in wickedness.*" Now the true account of this is, that the Church so far from being literally, and in fact, separate from the wicked world, is within it. The Church is a body, gathered together in the world, and in a process of separation from it. The world's power, alas! is over the Church, because the Church has gone forth into the world to save the world. All Christians are in the world, and of the world, so far as sin still has dominion over them; and not even the best of us is clean every whit from sin. Though then, in our idea of the two, and in their principles, and in their future prospects, the Church is one thing, and the world is another, yet in present matter of fact, the Church is of the world, not separate from it; for the grace of God has but partial possession even of religious men, and the best that can be said of us is, that we have two sides, a light side and a dark, and that the dark happens to be the outermost. Thus we form part of the world to each other, though we be not of the world. Even supposing there were a society of men influenced individually by Christian motives, still this society, viewed as a whole, would be a worldly one; I mean a society holding and maintaining many errors, and countenancing many bad practices. Evil ever floats at the top. And if we inquire why it is that the good in Christians is seen less than the bad? I answer, first, because there is less of it; and secondly, because evil forces itself upon general notice, and good does not. So that in a large body of men, each contributing his portion, evil displays itself on the whole conspicuously, and in all its diversified shapes. And thirdly, from the nature of things, the soul cannot be understood by any but God, and a religious spirit is in St. Peter's words, "the hidden man of the heart." It is only the actions of others which we see for the most part, and since there are numberless ways of doing wrong, and but one of doing right, and numberless ways too of regarding and judging the conduct of others, no wonder that even the better sort of men, much more the generality, are, and seem to be, so sinful. God only sees the circumstances under which a man acts, and why he acts in this way and not in that. God only sees perfectly the train of thought which preceded his action, the motive, and the reasons. And God alone (if aught is ill done, or sinfully) sees the deep contrition afterwards,—the habitual lowliness, then bursting forth into special self-reproach,—and the meek faith casting itself wholly upon God's mercy. Think for a moment, how many hours in the day every man is left wholly to himself

and his God, or rather how few minutes he is in intercourse
with others—consider this, and you will perceive how it is that
the life of the Church is hid with God, and how it is that the
outward conduct of the Church must necessarily look like the
world, even far more than it really is like it, and how vain, in
consequence, the attempt is (which some make) of separating
the world distinctly from the Church. Consider, moreover,
how much there is, while we are in the body, to stand in the way
of one mind communicating with another. We are imprisoned
in the body, and our intercourse is by means of words, which
feebly represent our real feelings. Hence the best motives and
truest opinions are misunderstood, and the most sound rules of
conduct misapplied by others. And Christians are necessarily
more or less strange to each other; nay, and as far as the appearance of things is concerned, almost mislead each other, and are,
as I have said, the world one to another. It is long, indeed, before we become at all acquainted with each other, and we appear the one to the other cold, or harsh, or capricious, or
self-willed, when we are not so. So that it unhappily comes to
pass, that even good men retire from each other into themselves, and to their God, as if retreating from the rude world.

And if all this takes place in the case of the better sort of men,
how much more will it happen in the case of those multitudes
who are still unstable in faith and obedience, half Christians,
not having yet wrought themselves into any consistent shape of
opinion and practice! These, so far from showing the better
part of themselves, often affect to be worse even than they are.
Though they have secret fears and misgivings, and God's grace
pleads with their conscience, and seasons of seriousness follow,
yet they are ashamed to confess to each other their own seriousness, and they ridicule religious men lest they should be themselves ridiculed.

And thus, on the whole, the state of the case is as follows: that
if we look through mankind in order to find out who make up
the world, and who do not, we shall find none who are not of
the world; inasmuch as there are none who are not exposed to
infirmity. So that if to shun the world is to shun some body of
men so called, we must shun all men, nay, ourselves too—
which is a conclusion which means nothing at all.

But let us, avoiding all refinements which lead to a display of
words only, not to the improvement of our hearts and conduct,
let us set to work practically; and instead of attempting to judge
of mankind on a large scale, and to settle deep questions, let us
take what is close at hand and concerns ourselves, and make use

of such knowledge as we can obtain. Are we tempted to neglect the worship of God for some temporal object? this is of the world, and not to be admitted. Are we ridiculed for our conscientious conduct? this again is a trial of the world, and to be withstood. Are we tempted to give too much time to our recreations; to be idling when we should be working; reading or talking when we should be busy in our temporal calling; hoping for impossibilities, or fancying ourselves in some different state of life from our own; over anxious of the good opinion of others; bent upon getting the credit of industry, honesty, and prudence? all these are temptations of this world. Are we discontented with our lot, or are we over attached to it, and fretful and desponding when God recalls the good He has given? this is to be worldly-minded.

Look not about for the world as some vast and gigantic evil far off—its temptations are close to you, apt and ready, suddenly offered and subtle in their address. Try to bring down the words of Scripture to common life, and to recognize the evil in which this world lies, in your own hearts.

When our Saviour comes, He will destroy this world, even His own work, and much more the lusts of the world, which are of the evil one; then at length we must lose the world, even if we cannot bring ourselves to part with it now. And we shall perish with the world, if on that day its lusts are found within us. "The world passeth away, and the lust thereof, but he that doeth the will of God abideth for ever."

THE PRAISE OF MEN

"They loved the praise of men more than the praise of God."
—John xii.43.

THIS is spoken of the chief rulers of the Jews, who, though they believed in Christ's Divine mission, were afraid to confess Him, lest they should incur temporal loss and shame from the Pharisees. The censure passed by St. John on these persons is too often applicable to Christians at the present day; perhaps, indeed, there is no one among us who has not at some time or other fallen under it. We love the good opinion of the world more than the approbation of Him who created us, redeemed us, has regenerated us, and who still preserves to us the opportunity of preparing ourselves for His future presence. Such is too often the case with us. It is well we should be aware that it is so; it is well we should dwell upon it, and that we should understand and feel that it is wrong, which many men do not.

Now it is an obvious question, Why is it wrong to love the praise of men? For it may be objected, that we are accustomed to educate the young by means of praise and blame; that we encourage them by kind words *from us*, that is, from man; and punish them for disobedience. If, then, it may be argued, it is right to regard the opinions of others concerning us in our youth, it cannot be in itself wrong to pay attention to it at any other period of life. This is true; but I do not say that the mere love of praise and fear of shame are evil: regard to the corrupt world's praise or blame, this is what is sinful and dangerous. St. John, in the text, implies that the praise of men was, at the time spoken of, in opposition to the praise of God. It *must* be wrong to prefer any thing to the will of God. To seek praise is in itself as little wrong, as it is wrong to hope, and to fear, and to love, and to trust; all depends upon the object hoped, or feared, or loved, or trusted; to seek the praise of good men is not wrong, any more than to love or to reverence good men; only wrong when it is in excess, when it interferes with the exercise of love and reverence towards God. Not wrong while we look on good men singly as instruments and servants of God; or, in the words of Scripture, while "we glorify God in them." [1] But to seek the praise of bad men, is in itself as wrong as to love the company of bad men, or to admire them. It is not, I say, merely the love of praise that is a sin, but love of the corrupt world's praise. This is the case with all our natural feelings and affections; they are all in themselves good, and implanted by God; they are sinful, because we have in us by nature a something more than them, viz. an evil principle which perverts them to a bad end. Adam, before his fall, felt, we may suppose, love, fear, hope, joy, dislike, as we do now; but then he felt them only when he ought, and as he ought; all was harmoniously attempered and rightly adjusted in his soul, which was at unity with itself. But, at the fall, this beautiful order and peace was broken up; the same passions remained, but their use and action were changed; they rushed into extremes, sometimes excessive, sometimes the reverse. Indignation was corrupted into wrath, self-love became selfishness, self-respect became pride, and emulation envy and jealousy. They were at variance with each other; pride struggled with self-interest, fear with desire. Thus his soul became a chaos, and needed a new creation. Moreover, as I have said, his affections were set upon unsuitable objects. The natural man looks to this world, the world is his god; faith, love, hope, joy, are not excited in his mind by things spiritual and divine, but by things seen and temporal.

Considering, then, that love of praise is not a bad principle in itself, it is plain that a parent may very properly teach his child to love his praise, and fear his blame, when that praise and blame are given in accordance with God's praise and blame, and made subservient to them. And, in like manner, if the world at large took a correct and religious view of things, then its praise and blame would in its place be valuable too. Did the world admire what God admires; did it account humility, for instance, a great virtue, and pride a great sin; did it condemn that spirit of self-importance and sensitiveness of disgrace, which calls itself a love of honour; did it think little of temporal prosperity, wealth, rank, grandeur, and power; did it condemn arrogant and irreverent disputing, the noisy, turbulent spirit of ambition, the love of war and conquest, and the perverse temper which leads to jealousy and hatred; did it prefer goodness and truth to gifts of the intellect; did it think little of quickness, wit, shrewdness, power of speech and general acquirements, and

[1] Gal. i.24.

much of patience, meekness, gentleness, firmness, faith, conscientiousness, purity, forgiveness of injuries,—then there
would be no sin in our seeking the world's praise; and though
we still ought to love God's praise above all, yet we might love
the praise of the world in its degree, for it would be nothing
more nor less than the praise of good men. But since, alas! the
contrary is the case, since the world (as Scripture tells us) "lieth
in wickedness," and the principles and practices which prevail
on all sides of us are not those which the All-holy God sanctions, we cannot lawfully seek the world's praise. We cannot
serve two masters who are enemies the one to the other. We are
forbidden to love the world or any thing that is of the world, for
it is not of the Father, but passeth away.

This is the reason why it is wrong to pursue the world's
praise; viz. because we cannot have it and God's praise too. And
yet, as the pursuit of it is wrong, so is it common,—for this
reason: because God is unseen, and the world is seen; because
God's praise and blame are future, the world's are present; because God's praise and blame are inward, and come quietly and
without keenness, whereas the world's are very plain and intelligible, and make themselves felt.

Take, for instance, the case of the young, on (what is called)
entering into life. Very many, indeed, there are, whether in a
higher or lower station, who enter into the mixed society of
others early; so early, that it might be thought they had hardly
had time to acquire any previous knowledge of right and
wrong, any standard of right and wrong, other than the world
gives, any principles by which to fight against the world. And
yet it cannot quite be so. Whatever is the first time persons hear
evil, it is quite certain that good has been beforehand with
them, and they have a something within them which tells them
it is evil. And much more, if they have been blessed, as most
men are, with the protection of parents, or the kind offices of
teachers or of God's ministers, they generally have principles of
duty more or less strongly imprinted on their minds; and on
their first intercourse with strangers they are shocked or
frighted at seeing the improprieties and sins, which are openly
countenanced. Alas! there are persons, doubtless (though God
forbid it should be the case with any here present!), whose consciences have been so early trained into forgetfulness of religious duties, that they can hardly, or cannot at all, recollect the
time I speak of; the time when they acted with the secret feeling
that God saw them, saw all they did and thought. I will not
fancy this to be the case with any who hear me. Rather, there

are many of you, in different ranks and circumstances, who have, and ever have had, general impressions on your minds of the claims which religion has on you, but, at the same time, have been afraid of acting upon them, afraid of the opinion of the world, of what others would say if you set about obeying your conscience. Ridicule is a most powerful instrument in the hands of Satan, and it is most vividly felt by the young. If any one wishes to do his duty, it is most easy for the cold, the heartless, and the thoughtless, to find out harsh, or provoking, or ridiculous names to fix upon him. My brethren, so many of you as are sensitive of the laughter or contempt of the world, this is your cross; you must wear it, you must endure it patiently; it is the mark of your conformity to Christ; He despised the shame: you must learn to endure it, from the example and by the aid of your Saviour. You must love the praise of God more than the praise of men. It is the very trial suited to you, appointed for you, to establish you in the faith. You are not tempted with gain or ambition, but with ridicule. And be sure, that unless you withstand it, you cannot endure hardships as good soldiers of Jesus Christ, you will not endure other temptations which are to follow. How can you advance a step in your after and more extended course till the first difficulty is overcome? You need faith, and "a double-minded man," says St. James, "is unstable in all his ways." Moreover, be not too sure that all who show an inclination to ridicule you, feel exactly as they say. They speak with the loudest speaker; speak you boldly, and they will speak with you. They have very little of definite opinion themselves, or probably they even feel with you, though they speak against you. Very likely they have uneasy, unsatisfied consciences, though they seem to sin so boldly; and are as afraid of the world as you can be, nay, more so; they join in ridiculing you, lest others should ridicule them; or they do so in a sort of self-defence against the reproaches of their own consciences. Numbers in this bad world talk loudly against religion in order to encourage each other in sin, because they need encouragement. They are cowards, and rely on each other for support against their fears. They know they ought to be other than they are, but are glad to avail themselves of any thing that looks like argument, to overcome their consciences withal. And ridicule is a kind of argument—such as it is; and numbers ridiculing together are a still stronger one—of the same kind. Any how, there are few indeed who will not feel afterwards, in times of depression or alarm, that you are right, and they themselves are wrong. Those who serve God faithfully have a friend of their own, in each man's bosom, witnessing for them; even in those who treat them ill. And I suppose no young person has been able, through God's mercy, to withstand the world's displeasure, but has felt at this time or that, that this is so, and in a little time will, with all humility, have the comfort of feeling it while he is withstanding the world.

But now supposing he has not had strength of mind to withstand the world; but has gone the way of the world. Suppose he has joined the multitude in saying and doing what he should not. We know the careless, thoughtless, profane habits which most men live in, making light of serious subjects, and being ashamed of godliness and virtue; ashamed of going to church regularly, ashamed of faith, ashamed of chastity, ashamed of innocence, ashamed of obedience to persons in authority. Supposing a person has been one of these, and then through God's grace repents. It often pleases God, in the course of His Providence, to rouse men to reflection by the occurrences of life. In such circumstances they certainly will have a severe trial to stand against the world. Nothing is more painful in the case of such persons, than the necessity often imposed upon them of acting contrary to the opinion and wishes of those with whom they have till now been intimate,—whom they have admired and followed. Intimacies have already been formed, and ties drawn tight, which it is difficult to sever. What is the person in question to do? rudely to break them at once? no. But is he to share in sins in which he formerly took part? no; whatever censure, contempt, or ridicule attaches to him in consequence. But what, then, is he to do? His task, I say, is painful and difficult, but he must not complain, for it is his own making; it is the natural consequence of his past neglect of God. So much is plain,—he must abstain from all sinful actions; not converse lightly or irreverently where formerly he was not unwilling so to do; not spend his time, as heretofore, in idleness or riot; avoid places whither he is not called by actual duty, which offer temptation to sin; observe diligently attendance on church; not idle away the Lord's Day in vanity, or worse; not add to the number of his acquaintance any thoughtless persons. All this is quite plain, and in doing this I know he will incur the ridicule of his companions. He will have much to bear. He must bear to be called names, to be thought a hypocrite, to be thought to be affecting something out of the way, to be thought desirous of recommending himself to this or that person. He must be prepared for malicious and untrue reports about himself; many other trials must he look for. They are his portion. He must pray God to enable him to bear them meekly. He must pray for himself, he must pray for those who ridicule him. He has deserved ridicule. He has nothing to boast of, if he bears it well. He has nothing to boast of that he incurs it. He has nothing to boast of, as if he were so much better than those who ridicule him; he was once as they are now. He is now just a little better than they are. He has just begun a new life. He has got a very little way in it, or rather no way, nothing beyond professing it; and he has the reproach of the world in consequence of his profession. Well, let him see to it that this reproach is not in vain, that he has a right to the reproach. Let him see to it that he acts as well as professes. It will be miserable indeed if he incurs the reproach, and yet does not gain the reward. Let him pray God to perfect in him what He has begun in him, and to begin and perfect it also in all those that reproach him. Let him pray for Christ's grace to bear hardships in Christ's spirit; to be able to look calmly in the world's face, and bear its frown; to trust in the Lord, and be doing good; to obey God, and so to be reproached, not for professing only, but for performing, not for doing nothing, but for doing something, and in God's cause. If we *are* under reproach, let us have something to show for it. At present, such a one is but a child in the Gospel; but in time, St. Peter's words will belong to him, and he may appropriate them. "This is thankworthy, if a man for conscience towards God endure grief, suffering wrongfully. For what glory is it, if when ye be buffeted for your faults ye shall take it patiently? but if, when ye do well and suffer for it, ye take it patiently, this is acceptable with God."

What happens to the young in one way, and to penitent sinners in another, happens in one way or other to all of us. In the case of all of us occasions arise, when practices countenanced by others do not approve themselves to our consciences. If after serious thought we find we cannot acquiesce in them, we must follow our consciences, and stand prepared for the censure of others. We must submit (should it be unavoidable) to appear to those who have no means of understanding us, self-willed, or self-conceited, or obstinate, or eccentric, or headstrong, praying the while that God's mercy may vouchsafe to us, that we be not really what we seem to the world.

Some are exposed to a temptation of a different kind, that of making themselves seem more religious than they really are. It may happen, that to advocate right opinions may be profitable to our worldly interests, and be attended by the praise of men. You may ask, since in such cases God and man approve the same thing, why should the applause of the world be accounted dangerous then? I answer, it is dangerous because God requires of us a modest silence in our religion; but we cannot be religious in the eyes of men without displaying religion. I am now speaking of display. God sees our thoughts without our help, and praises *them*; but we cannot be praised by men without being seen by men: whereas often the very excellence of a religious action, according to our Saviour's precept, consists in the not being seen by others. This is a frequent cause of hypocrisy in religion. Men begin by feeling as they should feel, then they think it a very hard thing that men should not know how well they feel, and in course of time they learn to speak without feeling. Thus they have learned to "love the praise of men more than the praise of God."—We have to guard against another danger, against the mistake of supposing that the world's despising us is a proof that we are particularly religious; for this, too, is often supposed. Frequently it happens that we encumber our religion with extravagances, perversions, or mistakes, with which religion itself has no necessary connexion, and these, and not religion, excite the contempt of the world. So much is this the case, that the censure of numbers, or of the sober-minded, or of various and distinct classes of men, or censure consistently urged, or continued consistently, ought always to lead a man to be very watchful as to what he considers right to say or do in the line of duty, to lead him to examine his principles; to lead him, however thoroughly he adheres to these after all, to be unaffectedly humble about himself, and to convince him in matter of fact (what he might be quite sure of beforehand, from the nature of the case), that, however good his principles are in themselves, he is mixing up with them the alloy of his own frail and corrupt nature.

In conclusion, I would say to those who fear the world's censure, this:—

1. Recollect you cannot please all parties, you must disagree with some or other: you have only to choose (if you are determined to look to man) with which you will disagree. And, further, you may be sure that those who attempt to please all parties, please fewest; and that the best way to gain the world's good opinion (even if you were set upon this, which you must not be) is to show that you prefer the praise of God. Make up your mind to be occasionally misunderstood, and undeservedly condemned. You must, in the Apostle's words, go through evil report, and good report, whether on a contracted or a wider field of action. And you must not be anxious even for the praise

of good men. To have, indeed, the approbation of those whose hearts are guided by God's Holy Spirit, is indeed much to be coveted. Still this is a world of discipline, not of enjoyment; and just as we are sometimes bound in duty to abstain from indulgences of sense in themselves innocent, so are we sometimes bound to deny ourselves the satisfaction derived from the praise even of the religious and conscientious. Only let us beware in all this, lest we act from pride and self-conceit.

2. In the next place, think of the multitude of beings, who, unseen themselves, may yet be surveying our conduct. St. Paul charges Timothy by the elect Angels;[2] and elsewhere he declares that the Apostles were made "a spectacle unto the world, and to Angels, and to men."[3] Are we then afraid to follow what is right, lest the world should scoff? rather let us be afraid not to follow it, because God sees us, and Christ, and the holy Angels. They rejoice over one sinner that repenteth; how must they mourn over those who fall away! What interest, surely, is excited among them, by the sight of the Christian's trial, when faith and the desire of the world's esteem are struggling in his heart for victory! what rejoicing if, through the grace of God, he overcomes! what sorrow and pity if he is overcome by the world! Accustom yourselves, then, to feel that you are on a public stage, whatever your station of life may be; that there are other witnesses to your conduct besides the world around you; and, if you feel shame of men, you should much more feel shame in the presence of God, and those servants of His that do His pleasure.

3. Still further: you fear the judgment of men upon you. What will you think of it on your death-bed? The hour must come, sooner or later, when your soul is to return to Him who gave it. Perhaps you will be sensible of your awful state. What will you then think of the esteem of the world? will not all below seem to pass away, and be rolled up as a scroll, and the extended regions of the future solemnly set themselves before you? Then how vain will appear the applause or blame of creatures, such as we are, all sinners and blind judges, and feeble aids, and themselves destined to be judged for their deeds. When, then, you are tempted to dread the ridicule of man, throw your mind forward to the hour of death. You know what you will then think of it, if you are then able to think at all.

4. The subject is not exhausted. You fear shame; well, and will you not shrink from shame at the judgment-seat of Christ?

[2] 1 Tim. v.21.   [3] 1 Cor. iv.9.

There will be assembled all the myriads of men who ever lived, a vast multitude! There will be Apostles, prophets, martyrs, and all saints from the beginning of time. There will be all the good men you ever heard of or knew. There will be your own kindest and best friends, your pious parents, or brothers, or children. Now what think you of being put to shame before all these? You fear the contempt of one small circle of men; what think you of the Saints of God, of St. Mary, of St. Peter and St. Paul, of the ten thousand generations of mankind, being witnesses of your disgrace? You dread the opinion of those whom you do not love; but what if a father then shrink from a dear son, or the wife, or husband, your earthly companion, then tremble at the sight of you, and feel ashamed of you? Nay, there is One greater than parents, husbands, or brothers; One of whom you have been ashamed on earth; and what will He, that merciful, but neglected Saviour, think of you then? Hear His own words:—"Whosoever shall be ashamed of Me and of My words, of him shall the Son of Man be ashamed, when He shall come in His own glory, and in His Father's, and of the holy Angels." Then such unhappy men, how will they feel shame at themselves! they will despise and loathe themselves; they will hate and abominate their own folly; they will account themselves brutish and mad, so to have been beguiled by the devil, and to have trifled with the season of mercy. "Many of them that sleep in the dust of the earth," says Daniel, "shall awake, some to everlasting life, and some to shame and everlasting contempt."

Let us, then, rouse ourselves, and turn from man to God; what have we to do with the world, who from our infancy have been put on our journey heavenward? Take up your cross and follow Christ. He went through shame far greater than can be yours. Do you think He felt nothing when He was lifted up on the Cross to public gaze, amid the contempt and barbarous triumphings of His enemies, the Pharisees, Pilate and his Roman guard, Herod and his men of war, and the vast multitude collected from all parts of the world? They all looked on Him with hatred and insult; yet He endured (we are told), "despising the shame."[4] It is a high privilege to be allowed to be conformed to Christ; St. Paul thought it so, so have all good men. The whole Church of God, from the days of Christ to the present, has been ever held in shame and contempt by men of this world. Proud men have reasoned against its Divine origin;

---

[4] Heb. xii.2.

crafty men have attempted to degrade it to political purposes: still it has lasted for many centuries; it will last still, through the promised help of God the Holy Ghost; and that same promise which is made to it first as a body, is assuredly made also to every one of us who seeks grace from God through it. The grace of our Lord and Saviour is pledged to every one of us without measure, to give us all necessary strength and holiness when we pray for it; and Almighty God tells us Himself, "Fear ye not the reproach of men, neither be ye afraid of their revilings. For the moth shall eat them up like a garment, and the worm shall eat them like wool; but My righteousness shall be for ever, and My salvation from generation to generation."

TEMPORAL ADVANTAGES

*"We brought nothing into this world, and it is certain
we can carry nothing out. And having food and raiment
let us be therewith content."*—1 Tim. vi.7, 8.

E VERY age has its own special sins and temptations. Impatience with their lot, murmuring, grudging, unthank-
fulness, discontent, are sins common to men at all times; but I
suppose one of those sins which belongs to our age more than to
another, is desire of a greater portion of worldly goods than
God has given us,—ambition and covetousness in one shape or
another. This is an age and country in which, more than in any
other, men have the opportunity of what is called rising in life,
—of changing from a lower to a higher class of society, of gaining wealth; and upon wealth all things follow,—consideration,
credit, influence, power, enjoyment, the lust of the flesh, and
the lust of the eyes, and the pride of life. Since, then, men now-
a-days have so often the opportunity of gaining worldly goods
which formerly they had not, it is not wonderful they should be
tempted to gain them; nor wonderful that when they have
gained them, they should set their heart upon them.

And it will often happen, that from coveting them before
they are gained, and from making much of them when they are
gained, men will be led to take unlawful means, whether to increase them, or not to lose them. But I am not going so far as to
suppose the case of dishonesty, fraud, double-dealing, injustice, or the like: to these St. Paul seems to allude when he goes
on to say, "They that will be rich fall into temptation and a
snare;" again, "The love of money is the root of all evil." But let
us confine ourselves to the consideration of the nature itself,
and the natural effects, of these worldly things, without extending our view to those further evils to which they may give
occasion. St. Paul says in the text, that we ought to be content
with food and raiment; and the wise man says, "Give me neither poverty nor riches; feed me with food convenient for me." [1]

[1] Prov. xxx.8.

And our Lord would have us "take no thought for the morrow;" which surely is a dissuasion from aggrandizing ourselves, accumulating wealth, or aiming at distinction. And He has taught us when we pray to say, "Give us this day our *daily* bread." Yet a great number of persons, I may say, nearly all men, are not content with enough, they are not satisfied with sufficiency; they wish for something more than simplicity, and plainness, and gravity, and modesty, in their mode of living; they like show and splendour, and admiration from the many, and obsequiousness on the part of those who have to do with them, and the ability to do as they will; they like to attract the eye, to be received with consideration and respect, to be heard with deference, to be obeyed with promptitude; they love greetings in the markets, and the highest seats; they like to be well dressed, and to have titles of honour. Now, then, I will attempt to show that these gifts of the world which men seek are not to be reckoned good things; that they are ill suited to our nature and our present state, and are dangerous to us; that it is on the whole best for our prospects of happiness even here, not to say hereafter, that we should be without them.

Now, first, that these worldly advantages, as they are called, are not productive of any great enjoyment even now to the persons possessing them, it does not require many words to prove. I might indeed maintain, with no slight show of reason, that these things, so far from increasing happiness, are generally the source of much disquietude; that as a person has more wealth, or more power, or more distinction, his cares generally increase, and his time is less his own: thus, in the words of the preacher, "the abundance of the rich will not suffer him to sleep," and, "in much wisdom is much grief, and he that increaseth knowledge increaseth sorrow." [2] But however this may be, at least these outward advantages do not increase our happiness. Let me ask any one who has succeeded in any object of his desire, has he experienced in his success that full, that lasting satisfaction which he anticipated? Did not some feeling of disappointment, of weariness, of satiety, of disquietude, after a short time, steal over his mind? I think it did; and if so, what reason has he to suppose that that greater share of reputation, opulence, and influence which he has not, and which he desires, would, if granted him, suffice to make him happy? No; the fact is certain, however slow and unwilling we may be to believe it, none of these things bring the pleasure which we

[2] Eccles. i.18.

beforehand suppose they will bring. Watch narrowly the persons who possess them, and you will at length discover the same uneasiness and occasional restlessness which others have; you will find that there is just a something beyond, which they are striving after, or just some one thing which annoys and distresses them. The good things you admire please for the most part only while they are new; now those who have them are accustomed to them, so they care little for them, and find no alleviation in them of the anxieties and cares which still remain. It is fine, in prospect and imagination, to be looked up to, admired, applauded, courted, feared, to have a name among men, to rule their opinions or their actions by our word, to create a stir by our movements, while men cry, "Bow the knee," before us; but none knows so well how vain is the world's praise, as he who has it. And why is this? It is, in a word, because the soul was made for religious employments and pleasures; and hence, that no temporal blessings, however exalted or refined, can satisfy it. As well might we attempt to sustain the body on chaff, as to feed and nourish the immortal soul with the pleasures and occupations of the world.

Only thus much, then, shall I say on the point of worldly advantages not bringing present happiness. But next, let us consider that, on the other hand, they are positively dangerous to our eternal interests.

Many of these things, if they did no other harm, at least are injurious to our souls, by taking up the time which might else be given to religion. Much intercourse with the world, which eminence and station render a duty, has a tendency to draw off the mind from God, and deaden it to the force of religious motives and considerations. There is a want of sympathy between much business and calm devotion, great splendour and a simple faith, which will be to no one more painful than to the Christian, to whom God has assigned some post of especial responsibility or distinction. To maintain a religious spirit in the midst of engagements and excitements of this world is possible only to a saint; nay, the case is the same though our business be one of a charitable and religious nature, and though our chief intercourse is with those whom we believe to have their minds set upon religion, and whose principles and conduct are not likely to withdraw our feet from the narrow way of life. For here we are likely to be deceived from the very circumstance that our employments are religious; and our end, as being a right one, will engross us, and continually tempt us to be inattentive to the means, and to the spirit in which we pursue it. Our Lord alludes to the danger of multiplied occupations in the Parable of the Sower: "He that received seed among thorns, is he that heareth the word, and the cares of this world and the deceitfulness of riches choke the word, and he becometh unfruitful."

Again, these worldly advantages, as they are called, will seduce us into an excessive love of them. We are too well inclined by nature to live by sight, rather than by faith; and besides the immediate enjoyment, there is something so agreeable to our natural tastes in the honours and emoluments of the world, that it requires an especially strong mind, and a large measure of grace, not to be gradually corrupted by them. We are led to set our hearts upon them, and in the same degree to withdraw them from God. We become unwilling to leave this visible state of things, and to be reduced to a level with those multitudes who are at present inferior to ourselves. Prosperity is sufficient to seduce, although not to satisfy. Hence death and judgment are unwelcome subjects of reflection to the rich and powerful; for death takes from them those comforts which habit has made necessary to them, and throws them adrift on a new order of things, of which they know nothing, save that in it there is no respect of persons.

And as these goods lead us to love the world, so again do they lead us to trust in the world: we not only become worldly-minded, but unbelieving; our wills becoming corrupt, our understandings also become dark, and disliking the truth, we gradually learn to maintain and defend error. St. Paul speaks of those who "having put away a good conscience, concerning faith made shipwreck."[3] Familiarity with this world makes men discontented with the doctrine of the narrow way; they fall into heresies, and attempt to attain salvation on easier terms than those which Christ holds out to us. In a variety of ways this love of the world operates. Men's opinions are imperceptibly formed by their wishes. If, for instance, we see our worldly prospects depend, humanly speaking, upon a certain person, we are led to court him, to honour him, and adopt his views, and trust in an arm of flesh, till we forget the overruling power of God's providence, and the necessity of His blessing, for the building of the house and the keeping of the city.

And moreover, these temporal advantages, as they are considered, have a strong tendency to render us self-confident. When a man has been advanced in the world by means of his own industry and skill, when he began poor and ends rich, how

[3] 1 Tim. i. 19.

apt will he be to pride himself, and confide, in his own contrivances and his own resources! Or when a man feels himself possessed of good abilities; of quickness in entering into a subject, or of powers of argument to discourse readily upon it, or of acuteness to detect fallacies in dispute with little effort, or of a delicate and cultivated taste, so as to separate with precision the correct and beautiful in thought and feeling from the faulty and irregular, how will such an one be tempted to self-complacency and self-approbation! how apt will he be to rely upon himself, to rest contented with himself; to be harsh and impetuous; or supercilious; or to be fastidious, indolent, unpractical; and to despise the pure, self-denying, humble temper of religion, as something irrational, dull, enthusiastic, or needlessly rigorous!

These considerations on the extreme danger of possessing temporal advantages, will be greatly strengthened by considering the conduct of holy men when gifted with them. Take, for instance, Hezekiah, one of the best of the Jewish kings. He, too, had been schooled by occurrences which one might have thought would have beaten down all pride and self-esteem. The king of Assyria had come against him, and seemed prepared to overwhelm him with his hosts; and he had found his God a mighty Deliverer, cutting off in one night of the enemy an hundred fourscore and five thousand men. And again, he had been miraculously recovered from sickness, when the sun's shadow turned ten degrees back, to convince him of the certainty of the promised recovery. Yet when the king of Babylon sent ambassadors to congratulate him on this recovery, we find this holy man ostentatiously displaying to them his silver, and gold, and armour. Truly the heart is "deceitful above all things;" and it was, indeed, to manifest this more fully that God permitted him thus to act. God "left him," says the inspired writer, "to try him, that he might know all that was in his heart."[4] Let us take David as another instance of the great danger of prosperity; he, too, will exemplify the unsatisfactory nature of temporal goods; for which, think you, was the happier, the lowly shepherd or the king of Israel? Observe his simple reliance on God and his composure, when advancing against Goliath: "The Lord," he says, "that delivered me out of the paw of the lion and out of the paw of the bear, He will deliver me out of the hand of this Philistine."[5] And compare this with his grievous sins, his continual errors, his weaknesses, inconsistencies, and then his

---

[4] 2 Chron. xxxii.31.   [5] 1 Sam. xvii.37.

troubles and mortifications after coming to the throne of Israel; and who will not say that his advancement was the occasion of both sorrow and sin, which, humanly speaking, he would have escaped, had he died amid the sheepfolds of Jesse? He was indeed most wonderfully sustained by Divine grace, and died in the fear of God; yet what rightminded and consistent Christian but must shrink from the bare notion of possessing a worldly greatness so corrupting and seducing as David's kingly power was shown to be in the instance of so great a Saint? The case of Solomon is still more striking; his falling away even surpasses our anticipation of what our Saviour calls "the deceitfulness of riches." He may indeed, for what we know, have repented; but at least the history tells us nothing of it. All we are told is, that "King Solomon loved many strange women . . . and it came to pass when Solomon was old, that his wives turned away his heart after other gods; and his heart was not perfect with the Lord his God, as was the heart of David his father. For Solomon went after Ashtaroth, the goddess of the Sidonians, and after Milcom, the abomination of the Ammonites." [6] Yet this was he who had offered up that most sublime and affecting prayer at the Dedication of the Temple, and who, on a former occasion, when the Almighty gave him the choice of any blessing he should ask, had preferred an understanding heart to long life, and honour, and riches.

So dangerous, indeed, is the possession of the goods of this world, that, to judge from the Scripture history, seldom has God given unmixed prosperity to any one whom He loves. "Blessed is the man," says the Psalmist, "whom Thou chastenest, and teachest him out of Thy law." [7] Even the best men require some pain or grief to sober them and keep their hearts right. Thus, to take the example of St. Paul himself, even his labours, sufferings, and anxieties, he tells us, would not have been sufficient to keep him from being exalted above measure, through the abundance of the revelations, unless there had been added some further cross, some "thorn in the flesh" [8] as he terms it, some secret affliction, of which we are not particularly informed, to humble him, and to keep him in a sense of his weak and dependent condition.

The history of the Church after him affords us an additional lesson of the same serious truth. For three centuries it was exposed to heathen persecution; during that long period God's Hand was upon His people: what did they do when that Hand

[6] 1 Kings xi. 1, 4, 5.   [7] Ps. xciv. 12.   [8] 2 Cor. xii. 7.

was taken off? How did they act when the world was thrown open to them, and the saints possessed the high places of the earth? did they enjoy it? far from it, they shrank from that which they might, had they chosen, have made much of; they denied themselves what was set before them; when God's Hand was removed, their own hand was heavy upon them. Wealth, honour, and power, they put away from them. They recollected our Lord's words, "How hardly shall they that have riches enter into the kingdom of God!"[9] And St. James's, "Hath not God chosen the poor of this world, rich in faith, and heirs of the kingdom?"[10] For three centuries they had no need to think of those words, for Christ remembered them, and kept them humble; but when He left them to themselves, then they did voluntarily what they had hitherto suffered patiently. They were resolved that the Gospel character of a Christian should be theirs. Still, as before, Christ spoke of His followers as poor and weak, and lowly and simple-minded; men of plain lives, men of prayer, not "faring sumptuously," or clad in "soft raiment," or "taking thought for the morrow." They recollected what He said to the young Ruler, "If thou wilt be perfect, go and sell that thou hast, and give to the poor, and thou shalt have treasure in heaven, and come and follow Me." And so they put off their "gay clothing," their "gold, and pearls, and costly array;" they "sold that they had, and gave alms;" they "washed one another's feet;" they "had all things common." They formed themselves into communities for prayer and praise, for labour and study, for the care of the poor, for mutual edification, and preparation for Christ; and thus, as soon as the world professed to be Christian, Christians at once set up among them a witness against the world, and kings and monks came into the Church together. And from that time to this, never has the union of the Church with the State prospered, but when the Church was in union also with the hermitage and the cell.

Moreover, in those religious ages, Christians avoided greatness in the Church as well as in the world. They would not accept rank and station on account of their spiritual peril, when they were no longer encompassed by temporal trials. When they were elected to the episcopate, when they were appointed to the priesthood, they fled away and hid themselves. They recollected our Lord's words, "Whosoever will be chief among you, let him be your servant;" and again, "Be not ye called Rabbi; for one is your Master, even Christ, and all ye are

[9] Mark x.23.   [10] James ii.5.

brethren."[11] And when discovered and forced to the eminence which they shunned, they made much lament, and were in many tears. And they felt that their higher consideration in the world demanded of them some greater strictness and self-denial in their course of life, lest it should turn to a curse, lest the penance of which it would defraud them here, should be visited on them in manifold measure hereafter. They feared to have "their good things" and "their consolation" on earth, lest they should not have Lazarus' portion in heaven. That state of things indeed is now long passed away, but let us not miss the doctrinal lesson which it conveys, if we will not take it for our pattern.

Before I conclude, however, I must take notice of an objection which may be made to what I have been saying. It may be asked, "Are not these dangerous things the gifts of God? Are they not even called blessings? Did not God bestow riches and honour upon Solomon as a reward? And did He not praise him for praying for wisdom? And does not St. Paul say, 'Covet earnestly the best gifts?'"[12] It is true; nor did I ever mean to say that these things were bad in themselves, but bad, for us, if we seek them as ends; and dangerous to us from their fascination. "Every creature of God is good," as St. Paul says, "and nothing to be refused;"[13] but circumstances may make good gifts injurious in our particular case. Wine is good in itself, but not for a man in a fever. If our souls were in perfect health, riches and authority, and strong powers of mind, would be very suitable to us: but they are weak and diseased, and require so great a grace of God to bear these advantages well, that we may be well content to be without them.

Still it may be urged, Are we then absolutely to give them up if we have them, and not accept them when offered? It may be a duty to keep them, it is sometimes a duty to accept them; for in certain cases God calls upon us not so much to put them away, as to put away our old natures, and make us new hearts and new spirits, wherewith to receive them. At the same time, it is merely for our safety to know their perilous nature, and to beware of them, and in no case to take them simply for their own sake, but with a view to God's glory. They must be instruments in our hands to promote the cause of Gospel truth. And, in this light, they have their value, and impart their real pleasure; but be it remembered, that value and that happiness are imparted by the end to which they are dedicated; It is "the altar that

[11] Matt. xx.27; xxiii.8.   [12] 1 Cor. xii.31.   [13] 1 Tim. iv.4.

sanctifieth the gift:"[14] but, compared with the end to which they must be directed, their real and intrinsic excellence is little indeed.

In this point of view it is that we are to covet earnestly the best gifts: for it is a great privilege to be allowed to serve the Church. Have we wealth? let it be the means of extending the knowledge of the truth—abilities? of recommending it— power? of defending it.

From what I have said concerning the danger of possessing the things which the world admires, we may draw the following rule: use them, as far as given, with gratitude for what is really good in them, and with a desire to promote God's glory by means of them; but do not go out of the way to seek them. They will not on the whole make you happier, and they may make you less religious.

For us, indeed, who are all the adopted children of God our Saviour, what addition is wanting to complete our happiness? What can increase their peace who believe and trust in the Son of God? Shall we add a drop to the ocean, or grains to the sand of the sea? Shall we ask for an earthly inheritance, who have the fulness of an heavenly one; power, when in prayer we can use the power of Christ; or wisdom, guided as we may be by the true Wisdom and Light of men? It is in this sense that the Gospel of Christ is a leveller of ranks: we pay, indeed, our superiors full reverence, and with cheerfulness as unto the Lord; and we honour eminent talents as deserving admiration and reward; and the more readily act we thus, because these are little things to pay. The time is short; year follows year, and the world is passing away. It is of small consequence to those who are beloved of God, and walk in the Spirit of truth, whether they pay or receive honour, which is but transitory and profitless. To the true Christian the world assumes another and more interesting appearance; it is no longer a stage for the great and noble, for the ambitious to fret in, and the wealthy to revel in; but it is a scene of probation. Every soul is a candidate for immortality. And the more we realize this view of things, the more will the accidental distinctions of nature or fortune die away from our view, and we shall be led habitually to pray, that upon every Christian may descend, in rich abundance, not merely worldly goods, but that heavenly grace which alone can turn this world to good account for us, and make it the path of peace and of life everlasting.

[14] Matt. xxiii.19.

THE SEASON OF EPIPHANY

"This beginning of miracles did Jesus in Cana of Galilee, and manifested forth His glory; and His disciples believed on Him."
—John ii.11.

THE Epiphany is a season especially set apart for adoring the glory of Christ. The word may be taken to mean the manifestation of His glory, and leads us to the contemplation of Him as a King upon His throne in the midst of His court, with His servants around Him, and His guards in attendance. At Christmas we commemorate His grace; and in Lent His temptation; and on Good Friday His sufferings and death; and on Easter Day His victory; and on Holy Thursday His return to the Father; and in Advent we anticipate His second coming. And in all of these seasons He does something, or suffers something: but in the Epiphany and the weeks after it, we celebrate Him, not as on His field of battle, or in His solitary retreat, but as an august and glorious King; we view Him as the Object of our worship. Then only, during His whole earthly history, did He fulfil the type of Solomon, and held (as I may say) a court, and received the homage of His subjects; viz. when He was an infant. His throne was His undefiled Mother's arms; His chamber of state was a cottage or a cave; the worshippers were the wise men of the East, and they brought presents, gold, frankincense, and myrrh. All around and about Him seemed of earth, except to the eye of faith; one note alone had He of Divinity. As great men of this world are often plainly dressed, and look like other men, all but as having some one costly ornament on their breast or on their brow; so the Son of Mary in His lowly dwelling, and in an infant's form, was declared to be the Son of God Most High, the Father of Ages, and the Prince of Peace, by His star; a wonderful appearance which had guided the wise men all the way from the East, even unto Bethlehem.

This being the character of this Sacred Season, our services throughout it, as far as they are proper to it, are full of the image of a king in his royal court, of a sovereign surrounded by subjects, of a glorious prince upon a throne. There is no thought of war, or of strife, or of suffering, or of triumph, or of vengeance connected with the Epiphany, but of august majesty, of power, of prosperity, of splendour, of serenity, of benignity. Now, if at any time, it is fit to say, "The Lord is in His holy temple, let all the earth keep silence before Him."[1] "The Lord sitteth above the waterflood, and the Lord remaineth a king for ever." "The Lord of Hosts is with us; the God of Jacob is our refuge." "O come, let us worship, and fall down, and kneel before the Lord our Maker." "O magnify the Lord our God, and fall down before His footstool, for He is Holy." "O worship the Lord in the beauty of holiness; bring presents, and come into His courts."

I said that at this time of year the portions of our services which are proper to the season are of a character to remind us of a king on his throne, receiving the devotion of his subjects. Such is the narrative itself, already referred to, of the coming of the wise men, who sought Him with their gifts from a place afar off, and fell down and worshipped Him. Such too, is the account of His baptism, which forms the Second Lesson of the feast of the Epiphany, when the Holy Ghost descended on Him, and a Voice from heaven acknowledged Him to be the Son of God. And if we look at the Gospels read throughout the season, we shall find them all containing some kingly action of Christ, the Mediator between God and man. Thus in the Gospel for the First Sunday, He manifests His glory in the temple at the age of twelve years, sitting among the doctors, and astonishing them with His wisdom. In the Gospel for the Second Sunday He manifests His glory at the wedding feast, when He turned the water into wine, a miracle not of necessity or urgency, but especially an august and bountiful act—the act of a King, who out of His abundance gave a gift to His own, therewith to make merry with their friends. In the Third Sunday, the leper worships Christ, who thereupon heals him; the centurion, again, reminds Him of His Angels and ministers, and He speaks the word, and his servant is restored forthwith. In the Fourth, a storm arises on the lake, while He is peacefully sleeping, without care or sorrow, on a pillow; then He rises and rebukes the winds and the sea, and a calm follows, deep as that of His own soul, and the beholders worship Him. And next He casts out Legion, after the man possessed with it had also "run and worshipped Him."[2] In the Fifth, we hear of His kingdom on earth, and of the enemy sowing tares amid the good seed. And in the Sixth, of His second Epiphany from heaven, "with power and great glory."

[1] Hab. ii.20.   [2] Mark v.6.

Such is the series of manifestations which the Sundays after the Epiphany bring before us. When He is with the doctors in the temple, He is manifested as a prophet—in turning the water into wine, as a priest—in His miracles of healing, as a bounteous Lord, giving out of His abundance—in His rebuking the sea, as a Sovereign, whose word is law—in the parable of the wheat and tares, as a guardian and ruler—in His second coming, as a lawgiver and judge.

And as in these Gospels we hear of our Saviour's greatness, so in the Epistles and First Lessons we hear of the privileges and the duties of the new people, whom He has formed to show forth His praise. Christians are at once the temple of Christ, and His worshippers and ministers *in* the temple; they are the Bride of the Lamb taken collectively, and taken individually, they are the friends of the Bridegroom and the guests at the marriage feast. In these various points of view are they presented to us in the Services during these weeks. In the Lessons from the prophet Isaiah we read of the gifts and privileges, the characteristics, the power, the fortunes of the Church—how widely spreading, even throughout all the Gentiles; how awful and high, how miraculously endowed, how revered, how powerful upon earth, how rich in temporal goods, how holy, how pure in doctrine, how full of the Spirit. And in the Epistles for the successive Sundays, we hear of the duties and distinguishing marks of her true members, principally as laid down in the twelfth and thirteenth chapters of St. Paul to the Romans; then as the same Apostle enjoins them upon the Colossians; and then in St. John's exhortations in his General Epistle.

The Collects are of the same character, as befit the supplications of subjects coming before their King. The first is for knowledge and power, the second is for peace, the third is for strength in our infirmities, the fourth is for help in temptation, the fifth is for protection, and the sixth is for preparation and purification against Christ's second coming. There is none which would suit a season of trial, or of repentance, or of waiting, or of exultation—they befit a season of peace, thanksgiving, and adoration, when Christ is not manifested in pain, conflict, or victory, but in the tranquil possession of His kingdom.

It will be sufficient to make one reflection, which suggests itself from what I have been saying.

You will observe, then, that the only display of royal greatness, the only season of majesty, homage, and glory, which our Lord had on earth, was in His infancy and youth. Gabriel's message to Mary was in its style and manner such as befitted an

Angel speaking to Christ's Mother. Elisabeth, too, saluted Mary, and the future Baptist his hidden Lord, in the same honourable way. Angels announced His birth, and the shepherds worshipped. A star appeared, and the wise men rose from the East and made Him offerings. He was brought to the temple, and Simeon took Him in His arms, and returned thanks for Him. He grew to twelve years old, and again He appeared in the temple, and took His seat in the midst of the doctors. But here His earthly majesty had its end, or if seen afterwards, it was but now and then, by glimpses and by sudden gleams, but with no steady sustained light, and no diffused radiance. We are told at the close of the last-mentioned narrative, "And He went down with His parents, and came to Nazareth, *and was subjected unto them.*" [3] His subjection and servitude now began in fact. He had come in the form of a servant, and now He took on Him a servant's office. How much is contained in the idea of His subjection! and it began, and His time of glory ended, when He was twelve years old.

Solomon, the great type of the Prince of Peace, reigned forty years, and his name and greatness was known far and wide through the East. Joseph, the much-loved son of Jacob, who in an earlier age of the Church, was a type of Christ in His kingdom, was in power and favour eighty years, twice as long as Solomon. But Christ, the true Revealer of secrets, and the Dispenser of the bread of life, the true wisdom and majesty of the Father, manifested His glory but in His early years, and then the Sun of Righteousness was clouded. For He was not to reign really, till He left the world. He has reigned ever since; nay, reigned *in* the world, though He is not in sensible presence in it—the invisible King of a visible kingdom—for He came on earth but to show what His reign would be, after He had left it, and to submit to suffering and dishonour, that He *might* reign.

It often happens, that when persons are in serious illnesses, and in delirium in consequence, or other disturbance of mind, they have some few minutes of respite in the midst of it, when they are even more than themselves, as if to show us what they really are, and to interpret for us what else would be dreary. And again, some have thought that the minds of children have on them traces of something more than earthly, which fade away as life goes on, but are the promise of what is intended for them hereafter. And somewhat in this way, if we may dare

[3] Luke ii.51.

compare ourselves with our gracious Lord, in a parallel though higher way, Christ descends to the shadows of this world, with the transitory tokens on Him of that future glory into which He could not enter till He had suffered. The star burned brightly over Him for awhile, though it then faded away.

We see the same law, as it may be called, of Divine Providence in other cases also. Consider, for instance, how the prospect of our Lord's passion opens upon the Apostles in the sacred history. Where did they hear of it? "Moses and Elias on the mountain appeared with Him in glory, and spake of His decease, which He should accomplish at Jerusalem."[4] That is, the season of His bitter trial was preceded by a short gleam of the glory which was to be, when He was suddenly transfigured, "and the fashion of His countenance was altered, and His raiment was white and glistering."[5] And with this glory in prospect, our Lord abhorred not to die: as it is written, "Who for the joy that was set before Him, endured the Cross, despising the shame."

Again, He forewarned His Apostles that they in like manner should be persecuted for righteousness' sake, and be afflicted and delivered up, and hated and killed. Such was to be their life in this world, "that if in this world only they had had hope in Christ, they had been of all men most miserable."[6] Well then, observe, their trial too was preceded by a season of peace and pleasantness, in anticipation of their future reward; for before the day of Pentecost, for forty days Christ was with them, soothing, comforting, confirming them, "and speaking of the things pertaining unto the kingdom of God."[7] As Moses stood on the mount and saw the promised land and all its riches, and yet Joshua had to fight many battles before he got possession, so did the Apostles, before descending into the valley of the shadow of death, whence nought of heaven was to be seen, stand upon the heights, and look over that valley, which they had to cross, to the city of the living God beyond it.

And so again, St. Paul, after many years of toil, refers back to a time when he had a celestial vision, anticipatory of what was to be his blessedness in the end. "I knew a man in Christ," he says, meaning himself, "about fourteen years ago, caught up to the third heaven. . . . And I knew such a man . . . how that he was caught up into Paradise, and heard unspeakable words, which it is not lawful for a man to utter."[8] St. Paul then, as the

---

[4] Luke ix.30, 31. [5] Luke ix.29. [6] 1 Cor. xv.19.
[7] Acts i.3. [8] 2 Cor. xii.3, 4.

twelve Apostles, and as our Lord before him, had his brief season of repose and consolation before the battle.

And lastly: the whole Church also may be said to have had a similar mercy vouchsafed to it at first, in anticipation of what is to be in the end. We know, alas, too well, that, according to our Lord's account of it, tares are to be with the wheat, fish of every kind in the net, all through its sojourning on earth. But in the end, "the saints shall stand before the throne of God, and serve Him day and night in His temple: and the Lamb shall feed them, and shall lead them unto living fountains of waters," and there shall be no more "sorrow nor pain, nor any thing that defileth or worketh abomination," "for without are dogs, and sorcerers, and whore-mongers, and murderers, and idolaters, and whosoever loveth and maketh a lie." Now was not this future glory shadowed forth in that infancy of the Church, when before the seal of the new dispensation was opened and trial began, "there was silence in heaven for half an hour;" and "the disciples continued daily with one accord in the temple, and in prayers, breaking bread from house to house, being of one heart, and of one soul, eating their meat with gladness and singleness of heart, praising God, and having favour with all the people;"[9] while hypocrites and "liars," like Ananias and Sapphira, were struck dead, and "sorcerers," like Simon, were detected and denounced?

To conclude; let us thankfully cherish all seasons of peace and joy which are vouchsafed us here below. Let us beware of abusing them, and of resting in them, of forgetting that they *are* special privileges, of neglecting to look out for trouble and trial, as our due and our portion. Trial is our portion here—we must not think it strange when trial comes after peace. Still God mercifully does grant a respite now and then; and perhaps He grants it to us the more, the more careful we are not to abuse it. For all seasons we must thank Him, for time of sorrow and time of joy, time of warfare and time of peace. And the more we thank Him for the one, the more we shall be drawn to thank Him for the other. Each has its own proper fruit, and its own peculiar blessedness. Yet our mortal flesh shrinks from the one, and of itself prefers the other;—it prefers rest to toil, peace to war, joy to sorrow, health to pain and sickness. When then Christ gives us what is pleasant, let us take it as a refreshment by the way, that we may, when God calls, go in the strength of that meat forty days and forty nights unto Horeb, the mount of

[9] Acts ii.46, 47.

God. Let us rejoice in Epiphany with trembling, that at Septuagesima we may go into the vineyard with the labourers with cheerfulness, and may sorrow in Lent with thankfulness; let us rejoice now, not as if we have attained, but in hope of attaining. Let us take our present happiness, not as our true rest, but, as what the land of Canaan was to the Israelites,—a type and shadow of it. If we now enjoy God's ordinances, let us not cease to pray that they may prepare us for His presence hereafter. If we enjoy the presence of friends, let them remind us of the communion of saints before His throne. Let us trust in nothing here, yet draw hope from every thing—that at length the Lord may be our everlasting light, and the days of our mourning may be ended.

THE DUTY OF SELF-DENIAL

"Surely I have behaved and quieted myself, as a child that is weaned of his mother: my soul is even as a weaned child."
—Ps. cxxxi.2.

SELF-DENIAL of some kind or other is involved, as is evident, in the very notion of renewal and holy obedience. To change our hearts is to learn to love things which we do not naturally love—to unlearn the love of this world; but this involves, of course, a thwarting of our natural wishes and tastes. To be righteous and obedient implies self-command; but to possess power we must have gained it; nor can we gain it without a vigorous struggle, a persevering warfare against ourselves. The very notion of being religious implies self-denial, because by nature we do not love religion.

Self-denial, then, is a subject never out of place in Christian teaching; still more appropriate is it at a time like this, when we have entered upon the forty days of Lent, the season of the year set apart for fasting and humiliation.

This indeed is not all that is meant by self-denial; but before proceeding with the subject, I would ask whether the generality of mankind go as far as this: it is plain that they do not. They do not go so far as to realize to themselves that religious obedience involves a thwarting of those wishes and inclinations which are natural to them. They do not like to be convinced, much less will they act upon the notion, that religion is difficult. You may hear men of the world say plainly, and as if in the way of argument, "that God will not punish us for indulging the passions with which we are born; that it is no praise to be unnatural; and no crime to be a man." This, however, may seem an extreme case; yet are there not a great many decent and respectable men, as far as outward character goes, who at least fix their thoughts on worldly comfort, as the greatest of goods, and who labour to place themselves in easy circumstances, under the notion that, when they can retire from the business of their temporal calling, then they may (in a quiet, unexceptionable way of course) consult their own tastes and likings, take their pleasure, and indulge themselves in self-importance and self-satisfaction, in the enjoyment of wealth, power, distinction, popularity, and credit? I am not at this moment asking whether such indulgences are in themselves allowable or not, but whether the life which centres in them does not imply the absence of any very deep views of sanctification as a process, a change, a painful toil, of working out our own salvation with fear and trembling, of preparing to meet our God, and waiting for the judgment? You may go into mixed society; you will hear men conversing on their friend's prospects, openings in trade, or realized wealth, on his advantageous situation, the pleasant connexions he has formed, the land he has purchased, the house he has built; then they amuse themselves with conjecturing what this or that man's property may be, where he lost, where he gained, his shrewdness, or his rashness, or his good fortune in this or that speculation. Observe, I do not say that such conversation is wrong; I do not say that we must always have on our lips the very thoughts which are deepest in our hearts, or that it is safe to judge of individuals by such speeches; but when this sort of conversation is the customary standard conversation of the world, and when a line of conduct answering to it is the prevalent conduct of the world (and this is the case), is it not a grave question for each of us, as living in the world, to ask himself what abiding notion we have of the necessity of self-denial, and how far we are clear of the danger of resembling that evil generation which "ate and drank, which married wives, and were given in marriage, which bought and sold, planted, and builded, till it rained fire and brimstone from heaven, and destroyed them all?"[1]

It is strange, indeed, how far this same forgetfulness and transgression of the duty of self-denial at present spreads. Take another class of persons, very different from those just mentioned, men who profess much love for religion—I mean such as maintain, that if a man has faith he will have works without his trouble, so that he need be at no pains about performing them. Such persons at best seem to say, that religious obedience is to follow as a matter of course, an easy work, or rather a necessary consequence, from having some strong urgent motive, or from some bright vision of the Truth acting on the mind; and thus they dismiss from their religion the notion of self-denial, or the effort and warfare of faith against our corrupt natural will, whether they actually own that they dismiss it or not. I

[1] Luke xvii.27–29.

say that they do this at best; for it often happens, as I just now intimated, that they actually avow their belief that faith is all-sufficient, and do not let their minds dwell at all on the necessity of works of righteousness. All this being considered, surely I am not wrong in saying that the notion of self-denial as a distinct religious duty, and, much more (as it may well be called), the essence of religious obedience, is not admitted into the minds of the generality of men.

But let it be observed, I have hitherto spoken of self-denial not as a distinct duty actually commanded in Scripture, but merely as it is involved in the very notion of sanctification, as necessarily attendant on that change of nature which God the Holy Spirit vouchsafes to work within us. But now let us consider it in the light of the Scripture precepts concerning it, and we shall come to a still more serious view of it, serious (I mean) to those who are living to the world; it is this,—that it is our duty, not only to deny ourselves in what is sinful, but even, in a certain measure, in lawful things, to keep a restraint over ourselves even in innocent pleasures and enjoyments.

Now the first proof I shall give of this will at the same time explain what I mean.

Fasting is clearly a Christian duty, as our Saviour implies in His Sermon on the Mount. Now what is fasting but a refraining from what is lawful; not merely from what is sinful, but what is innocent?—from that bread which we might lawfully take and eat with thanksgiving, but which at certain times we do not take, in order to deny ourselves. Such is Christian self-denial,—not merely a mortification of what is sinful, but an abstinence even from God's blessings.

Again: consider the following declaration of our Saviour: He first tells us, "Strait is the gate, and narrow is the way which leadeth unto life, and few there be that find it." And again: "Strive to enter in, for many, I say unto you, will seek (only seek) to enter in, and shall not be able." Then He explains to us what this peculiar difficulty of a Christian's life consists in: "If any man come to Me, and hate not his father, and mother, and wife, and children, and brethren, and sisters, yea, and his own life also, he cannot be My disciple." [2] Now whatever is precisely meant by this (which I will not here stop to inquire), so far is evident, that our Lord enjoins a certain refraining, not merely from sin, but from innocent comforts and enjoyments of this life, or a self-denial in things lawful.

---

[2] Matt. vii.14; Luke xiii.24; xiv.26.

Again, He says, "If any man will come after Me, let him deny himself and take up his cross daily, and follow Me."[3] Here He shows us from His own example what Christian self-denial is. It is taking on us a cross after His pattern, not a mere refraining from sin, for He had no sin, but a giving up what we might lawfully use. This was the peculiar character in which Christ came on earth. It was this spontaneous and exuberant self-denial which brought Him down. He who was one with God, took upon Him our nature, and suffered death—and why? to save us whom He needed not save. Thus He denied Himself and took up His cross. This is the very aspect, in which God, as revealed in Scripture, is distinguished from that exhibition of His glory, which nature gives us: power, wisdom, love, mercy, long-suffering—these attributes, though far more fully and clearly displayed in Scripture than in nature, still are in their degree seen on the face of the visible creation; but self-denial, if it may be said, this incomprehensible attribute of Divine Providence, is disclosed to us only in Scripture. "God so loved the world that He gave His Son."[4] Here is self-denial. And the Son of God so loved us, that "though He was rich yet for our sakes He became poor."[5] Here is our Saviour's self-denial. "He pleased not Himself."

And what Christ did when He came on earth, that have all His saints done both before and since His coming. Even the saints of the Old Testament so conducted themselves, to whom a temporal promise was made, and who, if any, might have surrendered themselves to the enjoyment of it. They had a temporal promise, they had a present reward; yet, with a noble faith, and a largeness of soul (how they put us to shame who have so much higher privileges!) the Jewish believers grudged themselves the milk and honey of Canaan, as seeking a better country, that is a heavenly. Elijah, how unlike is he to one who had a temporal promise! Or take again the instance of Daniel, which is still more striking,—"They that wear soft clothing are in kings' houses." Daniel was first in power in the palace of the greatest monarchs of his time. Yet what do we read of him? First of his living upon pulse and water, afterwards of his fasting in sackcloth and ashes, at another time of his mourning three full weeks, eating no pleasant bread, neither flesh nor wine coming in his mouth, nor anointing himself at all, till those three weeks were fulfilled. Can any thing more clearly show the duty of self-denial, even in lawful things, in the case of Christians,

[3] Luke ix.23.   [4] John iii.16.   [5] 2 Cor. viii.9.

when even God's servants, before Christ came and commanded it, in proportion as they had evangelical gifts, observed it?

Or again, consider the words of the text spoken by David, who, if any, had riches and power poured upon him by the hand of God. He says, he has "behaved and quieted" himself lest he should be proud, and made himself "as a weaned child." What an impressive word is "weaned!" David had put away the unreserved love and the use of this world. We naturally love the world, and innocently; it is before us, and meets our eyes and hands first; its pleasures are dear to us, and many of them not in themselves sinful, only in their excess, and some of them not sinful at all;—those, for instance, which we derive from our home, our friends, and our prospects, are the first and natural food of our mind. But as children are weaned from their first nourishment, so must our souls put away childish things, and be turned from the pleasures of earth to those of heaven; we must learn to compose and quiet ourselves as a weaned child, to put up with the loss of what is dear to us, nay, voluntarily to give it up for Christ's sake.

Much more after Christ came does St. Paul give us this same lesson in the ninth chapter of his first Epistle to the Corinthians: "Every one that striveth for the mastery is temperate in all things," i.e. has power over himself and keeps himself in subjection, as he presently says. Again in the seventh chapter, "The time is short; it remaineth that both they that have wives be as though they had none, and they that weep as though they wept not, and they that rejoice as though they rejoiced not, and they that buy as though they possessed not, and they that use this world as not abusing it." Here the same doctrine of moderation or temperance in lawful indulgences is strongly enforced; to weep, to rejoice, to buy, to possess, to marry, to use this world, are not unlawful, yet we must not use God's earthly gifts to the full, but in all things we must be self-denying.

Such is Christian self-denial, and it is incumbent upon us for many reasons. The Christian denies himself in things lawful because he is aware of his own weakness and liability to sin; he dares not walk on the edge of a precipice; instead of going to the extreme of what is allowable, he keeps at a distance from evil, that he may be safe. He abstains lest he should not be temperate; he fasts lest he should eat and drink with the drunken. As is evident, many things are in themselves right and unexceptionable which are inexpedient in the case of a weak and sinful creature: his case is like that of a sick person; many kinds of food, good for a man in health, are hurtful when he is ill—wine is poison to a man in a fierce fever. And just so, many acts, thoughts, and feelings, which would have been allowable in Adam before his fall, are prejudicial or dangerous in man fallen. For instance, anger is not sinful in itself. St. Paul implies this, when he says, "Be ye angry and sin not." [6] And our Saviour on one occasion is said to have been angry, and He was sinless. Almighty God, too, is angry with the wicked. Anger, then, is not in itself a sinful feeling; but in man, constituted as he is, it is so highly dangerous to indulge it, that self-denial here is a duty from mere prudence. It is almost impossible for a man to be angry only so far as he ought to be; he will exceed the right limit; his anger will degenerate into pride, sullenness, malice, cruelty, revenge, and hatred. It will inflame his diseased soul, and poison it. Therefore, he must abstain from it, as if it were *in itself* a sin (though it is not), for it is practically such to him.

Again, the love of praise is in itself an innocent passion, and might be indulged, were the world's opinion right and our hearts sound; but, as things are, human applause, if listened to, will soon make us forget how weak and sinful we are; so we must deny ourselves, and accept the praise even of good men, and those we love, cautiously and with reserve.

So, again, love of power is commonly attendant on a great mind; but he is the greatest of a sinful race who refrains himself, and turns from the temptation of it; for it is at once unbecoming and dangerous in a son of Adam. "Whosoever will be great among you, let him be your minister," says our Lord; "and whosoever will be chief among you, let him be your servant." [7] His reward will be hereafter; to reign with Christ, to sit down with Him on His throne, to judge angels,—yet without pride.

Again, even in affection towards our relations and friends, we must be watchful over ourselves, lest it seduce us from the path of duty. Many a father, from a kind wish to provide well for his family, neglects his own soul. Here, then, is a fault; not that we can love our relations too well, but that that strong and most praiseworthy affection for them may, accidentally, ensnare and corrupt our weak nature.

These considerations will show us the meaning of our Saviour's words already cited, about the duty of hating our friends. To hate is to feel that perfect distaste for an object, that you wish it put away and got rid of; it is to turn away from it, and to blot out the thought of it from your mind. Now this is just the feeling we must cherish towards all earthly blessings, so

[6] Eph. iv.26.   [7] Matt. xx.26, 27.

far as Christ does not cast His light upon them. He (blessed be His name) has sanctioned and enjoined love and care for our relations and friends. Such love is a great duty; but should at any time His guidance lead us by a strange way, and the light of His providence pass on, and cast these objects of our earthly affection into the shade, then they must be at once in the shade to *us*,—they must, for the time, disappear from our hearts. "He that loveth father or mother more than Me, is not worthy of Me." So He says; and at such times, though still loving them, we shall seem to hate them; for we shall put aside the thought of them, and act as if they did not exist. And in this sense an ancient and harsh proverb is true: we must always so love our friends as feeling that one day or other we may perchance be called upon to hate them,—that is, forget them in the pursuit of higher duties.

Here, again, then, is an instance of self-denial in lawful things; and if a person says it is painful thus to feel, and that it checks the spontaneous and continual flow of love towards our friends to have this memento sounding in our ears, we must boldly acknowledge that it *is* painful. It is a sad thought, not that we can ever be called upon actually to put away the love of them, but to have to act as if we did not love them,—as Abraham when called on to slay his son. And this thought of the uncertainty of the future, doubtless, does tinge all our brightest affections (as far as this world is concerned) with a grave and melancholy hue. We need not shrink from this confession, remembering that this life is not our rest or happiness;—"*that* remaineth" to come. This sober chastised feeling is the very temper of David, when he speaks of having composed and quieted his soul, and weaned it from the babe's nourishment which this world supplies.

I hope I have made it clear, by these instances, what is meant by Christian self-denial. If we have good health, and are in easy circumstances, let us beware of high-mindedness, self-sufficiency, self-conceit, arrogance; of delicacy of living, indulgences, luxuries, comforts. Nothing is so likely to corrupt our hearts, and to seduce us from God, as to surround ourselves with comforts,—to have things our own way,—to be the centre of a sort of world, whether of things animate or inanimate, which minister to us. For then, in turn, we shall depend on them; they will become necessary to us; their very service and adulation will lead us to trust ourselves to them, and to idolize them. What examples are there in Scripture of soft luxurious men! Was it Abraham before the Law, who wandered through his days, without a home? or Moses, who gave the Law, and died in the wilderness? or David under the Law, who "had no proud looks," and was "as a weaned child?" or the Prophets, in the latter days of the Law, who wandered in sheep-skins and goat-skins? or the Baptist, when the Gospel was superseding it, who was clad in raiment of camel's hair, and ate the food of the wilderness? or the Apostles, who were "the offscouring of all things"? or our blessed Saviour, who "had not a place to lay His head"? Who are the soft luxurious men in Scripture? There was the rich man, who "fared sumptuously every day," and then "lifted up his eyes in hell, being in torments." There was that other, whose "ground brought forth plentifully," and who said, "Soul, thou hast much goods laid up for many years;" and his soul was required of him that night. There was Demas, who forsook St. Paul, "having loved this present world." And, alas! there was that highly-favoured, that divinely-inspired king, rich and wise Solomon, whom it availed nothing to have measured the earth, and numbered its inhabitants, when in his old age he "loved many strange women," and worshipped their gods.

Far be it from us, soldiers of Christ, thus to perplex ourselves with this world, who are making our way towards the world to come. "No man that warreth, entangleth himself with the affairs of this life, that he may please Him who hath chosen him to be a soldier. If a man also strive for masteries, yet is he not crowned, except he strive lawfully." This is St. Paul's rule, as has already been referred to: accordingly, in another place, he bears witness of himself that he "died daily." Day by day he got more and more dead to this world; he had fewer ties to earth, a larger treasure in heaven. Nor let us think that it is over-difficult to imitate him, though we be not Apostles, nor are called to any extraordinary work, nor are enriched with any miraculous gifts: he would have all men like himself, and all may be like him, according to their place and measure of grace. If we would be followers of the great Apostle, first let us with him fix our eyes upon Christ our Saviour; consider the splendour and glory of His holiness, and try to love it. Let us strive and pray that the love of holiness may be created within our hearts; and then acts will follow, such as befit us and our circumstances, in due time, without our distressing ourselves to find what they should be. You need not attempt to draw any precise line between what is sinful and what is only allowable: look up to Christ, and deny yourselves every thing, whatever its character, which you think He would have you relinquish. You need not calculate and measure, if you love much: you need not perplex yourselves with points of curiosity, if you have a heart to venture after Him. True, difficulties will sometimes arise, but they will be seldom. He bids you take up your cross; therefore accept the daily opportunities which occur of yielding to others, when you need not yield, and of doing unpleasant services, which you might avoid. He bids those who would be highest, live as the lowest: therefore, turn from ambitious thoughts, and (as far as you religiously may) make resolves against taking on you authority and rule. He bids you sell and give alms; therefore, hate to spend money on yourself. Shut your ears to praise, when it grows loud: set your face like a flint, when the world ridicules, and smile at its threats. Learn to master your heart, when it would burst forth into vehemence, or prolong a barren sorrow, or dissolve into unseasonable tenderness. Curb your tongue, and turn away your eye, lest you fall into temptation. Avoid the dangerous air which relaxes you, and brace yourself upon the heights. Be up at prayer "a great while before day," and seek the true, your only Bridegroom, "by night on your bed." So shall self-denial become natural to you, and a change come over you, gently and imperceptibly; and, like Jacob, you will lie down in the waste, and will soon see Angels, and a way opened for you into heaven.

THE YOKE OF CHRIST

"Take my yoke upon you, and learn of Me, for I am meek and lowly in heart, and ye shall find rest unto your souls; for My yoke is easy, and My burden is light."—Matt. xi.29, 30.

THESE words, which are brought before us in the Gospel of to-day's festival,[1] are also found in the address made to us upon Ash Wednesday, in which we are told that if we "return unto Him who is the merciful Receiver of all true penitent sinners, if we will take His easy yoke and light burden upon us, to follow Him in lowliness, patience, and charity; this, if we do, Christ will deliver us from the curse of the law, and from the extreme malediction which shall light upon them that shall be set on the left hand." A few days since we were upon a Fast-day called to take on us Christ's yoke, and now on a Festival of an Apostle the call is repeated.

And with a particular fitness it occurs, now as often, that we celebrate the feast of St. Matthias, during Lent; for if there be an Apostle who above the rest may be taken to remind us of the duty of mortification, it is he. Our Lord, when asked why His disciples did not fast, said, they could not fast while He was with them, but that the time would come, when the Bridegroom should be taken away from them, and then should they fast in those days. That time was now come, when St. Matthias was chosen to be an Apostle. Christ *had* gone away. Peace and joy the Apostles had abundantly, more so than when He was with them; but for that very reason, it was not such a joy "as the world giveth." It was His own joy which arose out of pain and chastisement. This was the joy which St. Matthias received when he was made an Apostle. He never had been an Apostle under age. He had indeed been with our Lord, but not as an Apostle. The rest had been chosen (as it were) as children; they had been heirs of the kingdom, while under tutors and governors, and, though Apostles, had not understood their calling, had had ambitious thoughts or desires after riches, and were

[1] Preached on St. Matthias's day during Lent.

indulged for a while, ere new made, with the old wine, lest the bottles should burst. But St. Matthias came into his inheritance at once. He took upon him at once, upon his election, the power and the penalty of the Apostolate. No dreams of earthly prosperity could flit around that throne, which was reared over the grave of one who had been tried and had fallen, and under the immediate shadow of the cross of Him whom he had betrayed.

Well, then, does St. Matthias repeat to us on this day our Lord's words, "Take My yoke upon you, and learn of Me," for he had taken it on him from the first. His Pastoral Staff had ever been a crosier. He had had no youth. He had borne the yoke in his youth. He entered at once upon his long Lent, and he rejoiced in it.

The exhortation, then, which our Saviour gives in today's Gospel, and of which St. Matthias's history reminds us, is at the present season most suitable. Our Saviour says, "Come unto Me," and then He adds, "Take My yoke upon you, and learn of Me." Thus He first calls us to Him, and next shows us the way. "Come unto Me," He says, "and I will give you rest;" and then adds, "Take My yoke upon you, and ye shall find rest for your souls." He told the Apostles that they must come to Him, but did not at once tell them the way; He told them they must bear a yoke, but did not at once tell them what it was. St. Peter, in consequence, inquired about it on one occasion, and was bid to wait awhile, and he should know of it more plainly. Our Lord had said, "Whither I go, thou canst not follow Me now, but thou shalt follow Me afterwards." "Ye shall seek Me," He said, "and whither I go ye cannot come." [2] He spoke of His yoke, the way of His cross, as St. Peter found when at length, after His resurrection, he was told plainly what should befall him. "When thou wast young," said our Lord to him, by the lake of Tiberias, when thou wast a child in the faith, and hadst thine own way, "thou girdedst thyself, and walkedst whither thou wouldest," as just before St. Peter had girt his fisher's coat unto him, and cast himself into the sea; "but when thou shalt be old, thou shalt stretch forth thy hands, and another shall gird thee, and carry thee whither thou wouldest not." [3] And then He added, "Follow Me." St. Peter, indeed, was called upon literally to take Christ's yoke upon him, to learn of Him and walk in His ways; but what he underwent in fulness, all Christ's disciples must share in their measure, in some way or other. Again, in

[2] John xiii.36, 33.   [3] John xxi.18.

another place, our Lord speaks more expressly; "If any man will come after Me, let him deny himself, and take up his cross, and follow Me." [4] Here we have the words of the text emphatically repeated. To come to Christ, is to come after Him; to take up our cross, is to take upon us His yoke; and though He calls this an easy yoke, yet it is easy because it is His yoke, and He makes it easy; still it does not cease to be a yoke, and it is troublesome and distressing, because it is a yoke.

Let us set it down then, as a first principle in religion, that all of us must come to Christ, in some sense or other, through things naturally unpleasant to us; it may be even through bodily suffering, such as the Apostles endured, or it may be nothing more than the subduing of our natural infirmities and the sacrifice of our natural wishes; it may be pain greater or pain less, on a public stage or a private one; but, till the words "yoke" and "cross" can stand for something pleasant, the bearing of our yoke and cross is something not pleasant; and though rest is promised as our reward, yet the way to rest must lie through discomfort and distress of heart.

This I say must be taken as a first principle in religion; it concerns us all, it concerns young and old, rich and poor, all of whom are apt to consider it a valid reason for disregarding and speaking against a religious life, that it is so strict and distasteful. They shrink from religion as something gloomy, or frightful, or dull, or intrusive, or exorbitant. And, alas, sometimes it is attempted to lead them to religion by making it appear not difficult and severe. Severe truths are put aside; religion is made to consist in a worldly security, or again in a heated enthusiastic state of mind. But this is a deceit. I do not of course mean, far from it, that religion is not full of joy and peace also; "My yoke," says Christ, "is easy, and My burden is light:" but grace makes it so; in itself it is severe, and any form of doctrine which teaches otherwise forgets that Christ calls us to His yoke, and that that yoke is a cross.

If you call to mind some of the traits of that special religious character to which we are called, you will readily understand how both it, and the discipline by which it is formed in us, are not naturally pleasant to us. That character is described in the text as meekness and lowliness; for we are told to "learn" of Him who was "meek and lowly in heart." The same character is presented to us at greater length in our Saviour's sermon on the Mount, in which seven notes of a Christian are given to us, in

[4] Matt. xvi. 24.

themselves of a painful and humbling character, but joyful, because they are blessed by Him. He mentions, first, "the poor in spirit;" this is denoted in the text, under the word "lowly in heart;"—secondly, those "that mourn;" and this surely is their peculiarity who are bearing on their shoulders the yoke of Christ;—thirdly, "the meek;" and these too are spoken of in the text, when He bids us to be like Himself who "is meek;"—fourthly, those which do "hunger and thirst after righteousness;" and what righteousness, but that which Christ's Cross wrought out, and which becomes our righteousness when we take on us the yoke of the Cross? Fifthly, "the merciful;" and as the Cross is in itself the work of infinite mercy, so when we bear it, it makes us merciful. Sixthly, "the pure in heart;" and this is the very benefit which the Cross first does to us when marked on our forehead when infants, to sever us from the world, the flesh, and the devil, to circumcise us from the first Adam, and to make us pure as He is pure. Seventhly, "the peace-makers," and as He "made peace by the blood of His Cross," so do we become peace-makers after His pattern. And, lastly, after all seven, He adds, those "which are persecuted for righteousness' sake;" which is nothing but the Cross itself, and the truest form of His yoke, spoken of last of all, after mention has been made of its fruits.

Such is the character of which the text speaks. A man who is poor in spirit, meek, pure in heart, merciful, peace-making, penitent, and eager after righteousness, is truly (according to a term in current use) a mortified man. He is of a character which does not please us by nature even to see, and much less to imitate. We do not even approve or love the character itself, till we have some portion of the grace of God. We do not like the look of mortification till we are used to it, and associate pleasant thoughts with it. "And when we shall see Him, there is no beauty, that we should desire Him," says the Prophet. To whom has some picture of saint or doctor of the Church any charm at first sight? Who does not prefer the ruddy glow of health and brightness of the eyes? "He hath no form nor comeliness," as his Lord and Master before him. And as we do not like the look of saintliness, neither do we like the life. When Christ first announced His destined sufferings, Peter took Him and began to rebuke Him, saying, "Be it far from Thee, Lord, this shall not be unto Thee." Here was the feeling of one who was as yet a mere child in grace; "When he was a child, he spake as a child, he understood as a child, he thought as a child," before he had "become a man and had put away childish things."

This is St. Paul's language, writing to the Corinthians, and he there furnishes us with another description, under the name of charity, of that same heavenly temper of mind in which Christian manhood consists, and which our Lord had already described in the sermon on the Mount; he says, "Though I speak with the tongues of men and of angels, and have not charity, I am become as sounding brass, or a tinkling cymbal." And then he describes it as suffering long, kind, envying not, vaunting not, behaving seemly, unselfish, rejoicing in the truth, slow to be provoked, bearing all things and hoping all. And with this agrees St. James's account of wisdom, that it is "pure, peaceable, gentle, easy to be entreated, full of mercy and good fruits, without partiality and without hypocrisy." [5]

In all these passages, one and the same character is described acceptable to God, unacceptable to man; unacceptable to man both in itself, and because it involves a change, and that a painful one, in one shape or other. Nothing short of suffering, except in rare cases, makes us what we should be; gentle instead of harsh, meek instead of violent, conceding instead of arrogant, lowly instead of proud, pure-hearted instead of sensual, sensitive of sin instead of carnal. This is the especial object which is set before us, to become holy as He who has called us is holy, and to discipline and chasten ourselves in order that we may become so; and we may be quite sure, that unless we chasten ourselves, God will chasten us. If we judge ourselves, through His mercy we shall not be judged of Him; if we do not afflict ourselves in light things, He will afflict us in heavy things; if we do not set about changing ourselves by gentle measures, He will change us by severe remedies. "I refrain my soul," says David, "and keep it low, like as a child that is weaned from his mother." "I keep under my body, and bring it into subjection," says St. Paul. Of course Satan will try to turn all our attempts to his own purposes. He will try to make us think too much of ourselves for what we do; he would fain make us despise others; he will try to ensnare us in other ways. Of course he turns all things to evil, as far as he can; all our crosses may become temptations: illness, affliction, bereavement, pain, loss of worldly prospects, anxiety, all may be instruments of evil; so likewise may all methods of self-chastisement, but they ought not to be, and need not. And their legitimate effect, through the grace of the Holy Spirit, is to make us like Him who suffered all pain, physical and moral, sin excepted, in its fulness. We know what

[5] James iii.17.

His character was; how grave and subdued His speech, His manner, His acts; what calmness, self-possession, tenderness, and endurance; how He resisted evil; how He turned His cheek to the smiter; how He blessed when persecuted; how He resigned Himself to His God and Father, how He suffered silently, and opened not His mouth, when accused maliciously.

Alas! so it is; not only does the world not imitate such a temper of mind as this; but, if the truth must be spoken, it despises it. As regards, indeed, our Lord's instance itself, the force of education, habit, custom, fear of each other, and some remaining awe, keep the world from reflecting upon the notes of character which the Gospels ascribe to Him, but in His followers, it does discern them, it understands and it condemns them. We are bidden lend and give, asking for nothing again; revenge not ourselves; give our cloak when our coat is taken; offer the left cheek when the right is smitten; suffer without complaint; account persons better than they are; keep from bitter words; pray only when others would be impatient to act; deny ourselves for the sake of others; live contented with what we are; preserve an ignorance of sin and of the world: what is all this, but a character of mind which the world scorns and ridicules even more than it hates? a character which seems to court insult, because it endures it? Is not this what men of the world would say of such a one? "Such a man is unfit for life; he has no eye for any thing; he does not know the difference between good and evil; he is tame and spiritless, he is simple and dull, and a fit prey for the spoiler or defrauder; he is cowardly and narrow-minded, unmanly, feeble, superstitious, and a dreamer," with many other words more contemptuous and more familiar than would be becoming to use in Church. Yet such is the character of which Christ gave us the pattern; such was the character of Apostles; such the character which has ever conquered the world. "In much patience, in afflictions, in necessities, in distresses, in stripes, in imprisonments, in watchings, in fastings, by pureness, by knowledge, by long-suffering, by kindness, by the Holy Ghost, by love unfeigned, by the word of truth, by the power of God, by the armour of righteousness on the right hand and on the left, by honour and dishonour, by evil report and good report, as deceivers and yet true, as chastened and not killed, as sorrowful yet alway rejoicing;"—these are the weapons of our warfare, "which are not carnal, but mighty through God to the pulling down of strong holds."[6] These are

---

[6] 2 Cor. vi.4–10; x.4.

despised by the world, but they have subdued the world. Nay, though they seem most unmanly, they in the event have proved most heroic. For the heroical character springs out of them. He who has thrown himself out of this world, alone can overcome it; he who has cut himself loose of it, alone cannot be touched by it; he alone can be courageous, who does not fear it; he alone firm, who is not moved by it; he alone severe with it, who does not love it. Despair makes men bold, and so it is that he who has nothing to hope from the world, has nothing to fear from it. He who has really tasted of the true Cross, can taste no bitterer pain, no keener joy.

I have been trying to urge on you, my brethren, that the taking of Christ's yoke, and learning of Him, is something very distinct and special, and very unlike any other service and character. It is the result of a change from a state of nature, a change so great as to be called a death or even a crucifixion of our natural state. Never allow yourselves, my brethren, to fancy that the true Christian character can coalesce with this world's character, or is the world's character improved—merely a superior kind of worldly character. No, it is a new character; or, as St. Paul words it, "a new creation." Speaking of the Cross of Christ, he says, "God forbid that I should glory, save in the Cross of our Lord Jesus Christ, by whom the world is crucified unto me, and I unto the world. For in Christ Jesus neither circumcision availeth any thing, nor uncircumcision, but a new creature."[7] It is a new character, and it is one; it is ever one and the same. It is not one in Apostles, and another in the Christian of this day; not one in the high, another in the low; one in rich, another in poor; one in Englishman, another in foreigner; one in man, another in woman. Where Christ is put on, St. Paul tells us, there is neither Jew nor Greek, bond nor free, male nor female, but all are one in Christ Jesus.[8] What Lazarus is, that must Dives become; what Apostles were, that must each of us be. The high in this world think it suitable in them to show a certain pride and self-confidence; the wealthy claim deference on account of their wealth; kings and princes think themselves above instruction from any; men in the middle ranks consider it enough to be decent and respectable, and deem sanctity superfluous in them; the poor think to be saved by their poverty;— but to one and all Christ speaks, "Come unto Me," "Learn of Me." There is but one Cross and one character of mind formed by it; and nothing can be further from it than those tempers and

[7] Gal. vi. 14, 15.   [8] Gal. iii. 28.

dispositions in which the greater part of men called Christians live. To have one's own way, to follow one's own tastes, to please one's self, to have things to one's mind, not to be thwarted, to indulge in the comforts of life, to do little for God, to think of Him now and then indeed, but to live to this world; to aim at things of this world; to judge of things by our own accidental judgment, be it better or worse; to measure religious men, to decide upon right or wrong in religion, by our favourite fancy; to take a pride in forming and maintaining our own opinion; to stand upon our rights; to fear the hard words and cold looks of men, to be afraid of being too religious, to dread singularity; to leave our hearts and minds, our thoughts, words, and actions, to take care of themselves:—this, on one side or the other, in this measure or that, is the sort of character which the multitude, even of what are called respectable men, exemplify; and no wonder, this being the case, that they speak against those who have, or strive to have, a more serious view of religion, and whose mode of living condemns them. If there be but one character of heart that can please God, both of these contrary characters cannot please Him, one or the other does not; if the easy religion is right, the strict religion is wrong; if strict religion is right, easy religion is wrong. Let us not deceive ourselves; there are not two ways of salvation—a broad and a narrow. The world, which chooses the broad way, in consequence hates and spurns the narrow way; and in turn our Blessed Lord, who has chosen for us the narrow way, hates, scorns, spurns, denounces, the broad way. Surely He does so; He hates the broad way as entirely as the world hates the narrow way; and if we are persuaded to take part with the world, we take part against Him. When St. Peter said, "Be it far from Thee, Lord," being shocked at the notice that his Lord should suffer, what was His answer? Did He thank him for his zeal? Did He, at least, let it pass in silence? He answered, "Get thee behind Me, Satan, for thou art an offence unto Me; for thou savourest not the things that be of God, but those that be of men." [9] And in like manner to the corrupt church of Laodicea He says, "Because thou art lukewarm, and neither cold nor hot, I will cast thee out of My mouth. Because thou sayest, I am rich, and increased with goods, and have need of nothing; and knowest not, that thou art wretched and miserable, and poor, and blind, and naked; I counsel thee to buy of Me gold tried in the fire, that thou mayest be rich, and white raiment, that thou

[9] Matt. xvi.23.

mayest be clothed; and anoint thine eyes with eye-salve, that thou mayest see." And then He adds: "As many as I love, I rebuke and chasten;" that is, He puts on them His yoke; "Be zealous therefore and repent." [10]

To conclude. If Almighty God moves any of us, so that we have high thoughts; if from reading Scripture or holy books we find that we can embrace views above the world; if it is given us to recognize the glory of Christ's kingdom, to discern its spiritual nature, to admire the life of saints, and to desire to imitate it; if we feel and understand that it is good to bear the yoke in our youth, good to be in trouble, good to be poor, good to be in low estate, good to be despised; if in imagination we put ourselves at the feet of those mortified men of old time, who, after St. Paul's pattern, died daily, and knew no one after the flesh; if we feel all this, and are conscious we feel it; let us not boast—why? because of a surety such feelings are a pledge to us that God will in some way or other give them exercise. He gives them to us that He may use them. He gives us the opportunity of using them. Dare not to indulge in high thoughts; be cautious of them, and refrain; they are the shadows of coming trials; they are not given for nothing; they are given for an end; that end is coming. My brethren, count the cost; never does God give faith but He tries it; never does He implant the wish to sit on His right hand and on His left, but He fulfils it by making us wash our brethren's feet. O fearful imaginations, which are sure to be realized! O dangerous wishes, which are heard and forthwith answered! Only may God temper things to us, that nothing may be beyond our strength!

[10] Rev. iii.16–19.

MOSES THE TYPE OF CHRIST

"The Lord thy God will raise up unto thee a Prophet from the midst of thee, of thy brethren, like unto me; unto Him ye shall hearken."
—Deut. xviii.15.

THE history of Moses is valuable to Christians, not only as giving us a pattern of fidelity towards God, of great firmness, and great meekness, but also as affording us a type or figure of our Saviour Christ. No prophet arose in Israel like Moses, till Christ came, when the promise in the text was fulfilled—"The Lord thy God," says Moses, "shall raise up unto thee a Prophet like unto me:" that was Christ. Now let us consider in what respects Moses resembled Christ; we shall find that this inquiry is very suitable at this time of year.[1]

1. First, if we survey the general history of the Israelites, we shall find that it is a picture of man's history, as the dispensation of the Gospel displays it to us, and that in it Moses takes the place of Christ. The Israelites were in the land of strangers, viz. the Egyptians; they were slaves, hardly tasked, and wretched, and God broke their bonds, led them out of Egypt, after many perils, to the promised land, Canaan, a land flowing with milk and honey. How clearly this prefigures to us the condition of the Christian Church! We are by nature in a strange country; God was our first Father, and His Presence our dwelling-place: but we were cast out of paradise for sinning, and are in a dreary land, a valley of darkness and the shadow of death. We are born in this spiritual Egypt, the land of strangers. Still we have old recollections about us, and broken traditions, of our original happiness and dignity as freemen. Thoughts come across us from time to time which show that we were born for better things than to be slaves; yet by nature slaves we are, slaves to the Devil. He is our hard task-master, as Pharaoh oppressed the Israelites; so much the worse than he, in that his chains, though we do not see them, become more and more heavy every year. They cling about us and grow; they multiply themselves, they

[1] Lent.

1488

shoot out and spread forth, and encircle us, those chains of sin, with many links, minute but heavy, weighing us down to the earth, till at last we are mere slaves of the soil, with an evil husbandry, slaves of that fearful harvest which is eternal death. Satan is a tyrant over us, and it seems to us useless to rebel. If we attempt it, we are but overpowered by his huge might, and his oppressive rule, and are made twice the children of hell that we were before: we may groan and look about, but we cannot fly from his country. Such is our state by nature.

But Moses conducted the Israelites from the house of bondage to their own land, from which their fathers had descended into Egypt. He came to them from God, and, armed with God's power, he smote their cruel enemies, led them out of Pharaoh's territory, divided the Red Sea, carried them through it, and at length brought them to the borders of Canaan. And who is it that has done this for us Christians? Who but the Eternal Son of God, our Lord and Saviour, whose name in consequence we bear? He has rescued us from the arm of him who was stronger than we; and therefore I say in this respect first of all, Christ is a second Moses, and a greater. Christ has broken the power of the Devil. He leads us forth on our way, and makes a path through all difficulties, that we may go forward towards heaven. Most men, who have deliberately turned their hearts to seek God, must recollect times when the view of the difficulties which lay before them, and of their own weakness, nearly made them sink through fear. Then they were like the children of Israel on the shore of the Red Sea. How boisterous did the waves look! and they could not see beyond them; they seemed taken by their enemies as in a net. Pharaoh with his horsemen hurried on to reclaim his runaway slaves; the Israelites sank down in terror on the sand of the sea-shore; every moment brought death or captivity nearer to them. Then it was that Moses said, "Stand still, and see the salvation of God." And in like manner has Christ spoken to us. When our hearts fainted within us, when we said to ourselves, "How is it possible that we should attain heaven?" When we felt how desirable it was to serve God, but felt keenly the power of temptation; when we acknowledged in our hearts that God was holy and most adorable, and obedience to His will most lovely and admirable, and yet recollected instances of our past disobedience, and feared lest all our renewed resolutions to serve Him would be broken and swept away by the old Adam as mercilessly as heretofore, and that Satan would regain us, and yet prayed earnestly to God for His saving help; then He saved us against our fear, surprising us by the strangeness of our salvation. This, I say, many a one must recollect in his own case. It happens to Christians not once, but again and again through life. Troubles are lightened, trials are surmounted, fears disappear. We are enabled to do things above our strength by trusting to Christ; we overcome our most urgent sins, we surrender our most innocent wishes; we conquer ourselves; we make a way through the powers of the world, the flesh, and the devil; the waves divide, and our Lord, the great Captain of our salvation, leads us over. Christ, then, is a second Moses, and greater than he, inasmuch as Christ leads from hell to heaven, as Moses led the Israelites from Egypt to Canaan.

2. Next, Christ reveals to us the will of God, as Moses to the Israelites. He is our Prophet, as well as our Redeemer. None was so favoured as Moses in this respect: before Christ came, Moses alone saw God face to face; all prophets after him but heard His voice or saw Him in vision. Samuel was called by name, but he knew not who called him in the dark night till Eli told him. Isaiah saw the vision of the Seraphim, and heard them cry "Holy" before the Lord; but it was not heaven that he saw, but the mere semblance of the earthly temple in which God dwelt among the Jews, and clouds filled it. But Moses in some sense saw God and lived; thus God honoured him. "If there be a prophet among you," said Almighty God, "I the Lord will make Myself known unto him in a vision, and will speak unto him in a dream. My servant Moses is not so, who is faithful in all Mine house. With him will I speak mouth to mouth, even apparently, and not in dark speeches, and the similitude of the Lord shall he behold:" [2] and on his death we are told, "there arose not a prophet since in Israel like unto Moses, whom the Lord knew face to face." [3] When he was in the Mount Sinai it is said of him still more expressly, "The Lord spake unto Moses face to face, as a man speaketh unto his friend." [4] In the Mount he received from God the revelation of the Law, and the patterns of the holy services which the Jews were to offer to God; and so, being favoured with the intimate knowledge of God's counsels, when he came down, his face shone with glory. The Divine majesty was reflected from it, and the people dared not look upon him. "The skin of his face shone while he talked with Him. And when Aaron and the children of Israel saw Moses, they were afraid to come nigh

---

[2] Numb. xii.6–8.   [3] Deut. xxxiv.10.   [4] Exod. xxxiii.11.

him." "And till he had done speaking with them, he put a veil on his face."[5]

Yet, after all, favoured as he was, Moses saw not the true presence of God. Flesh and blood cannot see it. Even when Moses was in the Mount, he was aware that the very fulness of God's glory then revealed to him, was after all but the surface of His infinitude. The more he saw, the deeper and wider did he know that to be which he saw not. He prayed, "If I have found grace in Thy sight, show me now Thy way, that I may know Thee, that I may find grace in Thy sight; and God said, My Presence shall go with thee, and I will give thee rest."[6] Moses was encouraged to ask for further blessings; he said, "I beseech Thee, show me Thy glory." This could not be granted; "Thou canst not see My face; for there shall no man see Me, and live." So, as the greatest privilege which he might attain, Moses was permitted to see the skirts of God's greatness—"The Lord passed by in a cloud, and proclaimed the Name of the Lord; and Moses made haste, and bowed his head toward the earth, and worshipped."[7] And it was this sight of the mere apparel in which God Almighty was arrayed, which made his face to shine.

But Christ really saw, and ever saw, the face of God, for He was no creature of God, but the Only-begotten Son, who is in the bosom of the Father. From eternity He was with Him in glory, as He says Himself, dwelling in the abyss of the infinite greatness of the Most High. Not for forty days, as Moses on the mount in figure, but for ever and ever was He present as the Counsellor of God, as His Word, in whom He delighted. Such was He of old; but at the time appointed He came forth from the Father, and showed Himself in this external world, first as its Creator, then as its Teacher, the Revealer of secrets, the Mediator, the Off-streaming of God's glory, and the Express Image of His Person. Cloud nor image, emblem nor words, are interposed between the Son and His Eternal Father. No language is needed between the Father and Him, who is the very Word of the Father; no knowledge is imparted to Him, who by His very Nature and from eternity knows the Father, and all that the Father knows. Such are His own words, "No man knoweth the Son but the Father, neither knoweth any man the Father save the Son, and he to whomsoever the Son will reveal Him."[8] Again He says, "He that hath seen Me hath seen the Father;"[9] and He accounts for this when He tells us, that He

[5] Exod. xxxiv.29, 30, 33.   [6] Exod. xxxiii.13, 14.
[7] Exod. xxxiv.6, 8.   [8] Matt. xi.27.   [9] John xiv.9.

and the Father are one;[10] and that He is in the bosom of the Father, and so can disclose Him to mankind, being still in heaven, even while He was on earth.

Accordingly, the Blessed Apostle draws a contrast between Moses and Christ to our comfort; "the Law," he says, "was given by Moses, but grace and truth came by Jesus Christ."[11] In Him God is fully and truly seen, so that He is absolutely the Way, and the Truth, and the Life. All our duties are summed up for us in the message He brings us. Those who look towards Him for teaching, who worship and obey Him, will by degrees see "the light of the knowledge of the glory of God in His face," and will be "changed into the same image from glory to glory." And thus it happens that men of the lowest class and the humblest education may know fully the ways and works of God; fully, that is, as man can know them; far better and more truly than the most sagacious man of this world, to whom the Gospel is hid. Religion has a store of wonderful secrets which no one can communicate to another, and which are most pleasant and delightful to know. "Call on Me," says God by the prophet, "and I will answer thee, and show thee great and mighty things which thou knowest not of." This is no mere idle boast, but a fact which all who seek God will find to be true, though they cannot perhaps clearly express their meaning. Strange truths about ourselves, about God, about our duty, about the world, about heaven and hell, new modes of viewing things, discoveries which cannot be put into words, marvellous prospects and thoughts half understood, deep convictions inspiring joy and peace, these are a part of the revelation which Christ, the Son of God, brings to those who obey Him. Moses had much toil to gain from the great God some scattered rays of the truth, and that for his personal comfort, not for all Israel; but Christ has brought from His Father for all of us the full and perfect way of life. Thus He brings grace as well as truth, a most surprising miracle of mercy from the freeness of the gift, as will as a true wisdom from its fulness.

And yet, alas! in spite of all this bounty, men called Christians, and how many! live heartlessly, not caring for the gracious benefit. Look at the world. Men begin life with sinning; they quench the early promise of grace, and defile their souls; they block up the entrances of the spiritual senses by acts of sin, lying and deceit, intemperance, profaneness, or uncleanness,—by a foolish and trifling turn of mind,—by neglect of prayer

[10] John x.30.   [11] John i.17.

when there is no actual vice,—or by an obstinate selfishness. How many are the ways in which men begin to lose sight of God!—how many are the fallings away of those who once began well! And then they soon forget that they have really left God; they still think they see His face, though their sins have begun to blind them. Like men who fall asleep, the real prospect still flits before them in their dreams, but out of shape and proportion, discoloured, crowded with all manner of fancies and untruths; and so they proceed in that dream of sin, more or less profound,—sometimes rousing, then turning back again for a little more slumber, till death awakens them. Death alone gives lively perceptions to the generality of men, who then see the very truth, such as they saw it before they began to sin, but more clear and more fearful: but they who are the pure in heart, like Joseph; or the meek among men, like Moses; or faithful found among the faithless, as Daniel; these men see God all through life in the face of His Eternal Son; and, while the world mocks them, or tries to reason them out of their own real knowledge, they are like Moses on the mount, blessed and hidden,—"hid with Christ in God," beyond the tumult and idols of the world, and interceding for it.

3. This leads me to mention a third point of resemblance between Moses and Christ. Moses was the great intercessor when the Israelites sinned: while he was in the mount, his people corrupted themselves; they set up an idol, and honoured it with feasting and dancing. Then God would have cut them off from the land of promise, had not Moses interposed. He said, "Lord, why doth Thy wrath wax hot against Thy people? Turn from Thy fierce wrath, and repent of this evil against Thy people." [12] In this way he gained a respite, and then he renewed his supplications. He said to the people, "Ye have sinned a great sin; but now I will go up unto the Lord: peradventure I shall make an atonement for your sin." Then he said to their offended Creator, "Oh, this people have sinned a great sin, and have made them gods of gold. Yet now, if Thou wilt, forgive their sin."

Here Moses, as is obvious, shadows out the true Mediator between God and man, who is ever at the right hand of God making intercession for us; but the parallel is closer still than appears at first sight. After Moses had said, "If Thou wilt, forgive their sin," he added, "and if not, blot me, I pray Thee, out of Thy book, which Thou hast written." He was taken at his word. Observe, rather than Israel should forfeit the promised

---

[12] Exod. xxxii. 11.

land, he here offered to give up his own portion in it, and the exchange was accepted. He was excluded, dying in sight, not in enjoyment of Canaan, while the people went in under Joshua. This was a figure of Him that was to come. Our Saviour Christ died, that we might live: He consented to lose the light of God's countenance, that we might gain it. By His cross and passion, He made atonement for our sins, and bought for us the forgiveness of God. Yet, on the other hand, observe how this history instructs us, at the same time, in the unspeakable distance between Christ and Moses. When Moses said, "Blot me, I pray Thee, out of Thy book," God did not promise to accept the exchange, but He answered, "Whosoever hath sinned against Me, him will I blot out of My book." Moses was not taken instead of Israel, except in figure. In spite of Moses, the sinful people were plagued and died,[13] though their children entered the promised land. And again, Moses, after all, suffered for his own sin. True, he was shut out from Canaan. But why? Not in spite of his having "done nothing amiss," as the Divine Sufferer on the cross, but because he spake unadvisedly with his lips, when the people provoked him with their murmurings. The meek Moses was provoked to call them rebels, and seemed to arrogate to himself the power and authority which he received from God; and therefore he was punished by dying in the wilderness. But Christ was the spotless Lamb of God, "who, when He was reviled, reviled not again; when He suffered, He threatened not, but committed Himself to Him that judgeth righteously." And His death is meritorious; it has really gained our pardon.

Moreover, it is well to observe how apparently slight a fault it was for which Moses suffered; for this shows us the infinite difference between the best of a sinful race and Him who was sinless,—the least taint of human corruption having in it an unspeakable evil. Moses was the meekest of men, yet it was for one sudden transgression of the rule of meekness that he suffered; all his former gentleness, all his habitual humbleness of mind, availed him nothing. It was unprofitable, and without merit, because it was merely his duty. It could not make up for a single sin, however slight. Thus we see how it would be with us if God were extreme to mark what is done amiss: and thus, on the other hand, we see how supremely holy and pure that Saviour must be whose intercession is meritorious, who has removed from us God's anger. None can bring us to Him but He

[13] *Vide* Exod. xxxii.34.

who came from Him. He reveals God, and He cleanses man. The same is our Prophet and our Priest.

We are now approaching the season when we commemorate His death upon the cross: we are entering upon the most holy season of the whole year. May we approach it with holy hearts! May we renew our resolutions of leading a life of obedience to His commandments, and may we have the grace to seal our good resolutions at His most sacred Supper, in which "Jesus Christ is evidently set forth crucified among us." It is useless to make resolves without coming to Him for aid to keep them: and it is useless coming to His table without earnest and hearty resolves; it is provoking God "to plague us with divers diseases, and sundry kinds of death." But what shall be said of those who do neither the one nor the other,—who neither vow obedience, nor come to Him for grace?—who sin deliberately after they have known the truth—who review their sins in time past in a reckless hard-hearted way, or put them aside out of their thoughts—who can bear to jest about them, to speak of them to others unblushingly, or even to boast of them, and to determine on sinning again,—who think of repenting at some future day, and resolve on going their own way now, trusting to chance for reconciliation with God, as if it were not a matter to be very anxious about? This state of mind brings upon man a judgment heavier than all the plagues of Egypt,—a judgment compared with which that darkness which could be felt is as the sun's brightness, and the thunders and hail are as the serene sky,— the wrath to come.

Awake, then, my brethren, with this season, to meet your God, who now summons you from His cross and tomb. Put aside the sin that doth so easily beset you, and be ye holy even as He is holy. Stand ready to suffer with Him, should it be needful, that you may rise together with Him. He can make bitter things sweet to you, and hard ways easy, if you have but the heart to desire Him to do so. He can change the Law into the Gospel. He can, for Moses, give you Himself. He can write the Law on your hearts, and thereby take away the hand-writing that is against you, even the old curse which by nature you inherit. He has done this for many in time past. He does it for many at all times. Why should He not do it for you? Why should you be left out? Why should you not enter into His rest? Why should you not see His glory? O, why should you be blotted out from His book?

THE CRUCIFIXION

"He was oppressed, and He was afflicted, yet He opened not His mouth; He is brought as a lamb to the slaughter, and as a sheep before her shearers is dumb, so He openeth not His mouth."
—Is. liii.7.

S T. PETER makes it almost a description of a Christian, that he loves Him whom he has not seen; speaking of Christ, he says, "whom having not seen, ye love; in whom, though now ye see Him not, yet believing, ye rejoice with joy unspeakable and full of glory." Again he speaks of "tasting that the Lord is gracious."[1] Unless we have a true love of Christ, we are not His true disciples; and we cannot love Him unless we have heartfelt gratitude to Him; and we cannot duly feel gratitude, unless we feel keenly what He suffered for us. I say it seems to us impossible, under the circumstances of the case, that any one can have attained to the love of Christ, who feels no distress, no misery, at the thought of His bitter pains, and no self-reproach at having through his own sins had a share in causing them.

I know quite well, and wish you, my brethren, never to forget, that feeling is not enough; that it is not enough merely to feel and nothing more; that to feel grief for Christ's sufferings, and yet not to go on to obey Him, is not true love, but a mockery. True love both feels right, and acts right; but at the same time as warm feelings without religious conduct are a kind of hypocrisy, so, on the other hand, right conduct, when unattended with deep feelings, is at best a very imperfect sort of religion. And at this time of year[2] especially are we called upon to raise our hearts to Christ, and to have keen feelings and piercing thoughts of sorrow and shame, of compunction and of gratitude, of love and tender affection and horror and anguish, at the review of those awful sufferings whereby our salvation has been purchased.

Let us pray God to give us *all* graces; and while, in the first place, we pray that He would make us holy, really holy, let us

---

[1] 1 Pet. i.8; ii.3.   [2] Passion-tide.

also pray Him to give us the *beauty* of holiness, which consists in tender and eager affection towards our Lord and Saviour: which is, in the case of the Christian, what beauty of person is to the outward man, so that through God's mercy our souls may have, not strength and health only, but a sort of bloom and comeliness; and that as we grow older in body, we may, year by year, grow more youthful in spirit.

You will ask, *how* are we to learn to feel pain and anguish at the thought of Christ's sufferings? I answer, *by* thinking of them, that is, by *dwelling* on the thought. This, through God's mercy, is in the power of every one. No one who will but solemnly think over the history of those sufferings, as drawn out for us in the Gospels, but will gradually gain, through God's grace, a sense of them, will in a measure realize them, will in a measure be as if he saw them, will feel towards them as being not merely a tale written in a book, but as a true history, as a series of events which took place. It is indeed a great mercy that this duty which I speak of, though so high, is notwithstanding so level with the powers of all classes of persons, learned and unlearned, if they wish to perform it. Any one can think of Christ's sufferings, if he will; and knows well what to think about. "It is not in heaven that thou shouldst say, Who shall go up for us to heaven and bring it to us, that we may hear it and do it? Neither is it beyond the sea that thou shouldst say, Who shall go over the sea for us? . . . but the word is very nigh unto thee;" very nigh, for it is in the four Gospels, which, at this day at least, are open to all men. All men may read or hear the Gospels, and in knowing them, they will know all that is necessary to be known in order to feel aright; they will know all that any one knows, all that has been told us, all that the greatest saints have ever had to make them full of love and sacred fear.

Now, then, let me make one or two reflections by way of stirring up your hearts and making you mourn over Christ's sufferings, as you are called to do at this season.

1. First, as to these sufferings you will observe that our Lord is called a lamb in the text; that is, He was as defenceless, and as innocent, as a lamb is. Since then Scripture compares Him to this inoffensive and unprotected animal, we may without presumption or irreverence take the image as a means of conveying to our minds those feelings which our Lord's sufferings should excite in us. I mean, consider how very horrible it is to read the accounts which sometimes meet us of cruelties exercised on brute animals. Does it not sometimes make us shudder to hear tell of them, or to read them in some chance publication which

we take up? At one time it is the wanton deed of barbarous and angry owners who ill-treat their cattle, or beasts of burden; and at another, it is the cold-blooded and calculating act of men of science, who make experiments on brute animals, perhaps merely from a sort of curiosity. I do not like to go into particulars, for many reasons; but one of those instances which we read of as happening in this day, and which seems more shocking than the rest, is, when the poor dumb victim is fastened against a wall, pierced, gashed, and so left to linger out its life. Now do you not see that I have a reason for saying this, and am not using these distressing words for nothing? For what was this but the very cruelty inflicted upon our Lord? He was gashed with the scourge, pierced through hands and feet, and so fastened to the Cross, and there left, and that as a spectacle. Now what is it moves our very hearts, and sickens us so much at cruelty shown to poor brutes? I suppose this first, that they have done no harm; next, that they have no power whatever of resistance; it is the cowardice and tyranny of which they are the victims which makes their sufferings so especially touching. For instance, if they were dangerous animals, take the case of wild beasts at large, able not only to defend themselves, but even to attack us; much as we might dislike to hear of their wounds and agony, yet our feelings would be of a very different kind; but there is something so very dreadful, so satanic in tormenting those who never have harmed us, and who cannot defend themselves, who are utterly in our power, who have weapons neither of offence nor defence, that none but very hardened persons can endure the thought of it. Now this was just our Saviour's case: He had laid aside His glory, He had (as it were) disbanded His legions of Angels, He came on earth without arms, except the arms of truth, meekness, and righteousness, and committed Himself to the world in perfect innocence and sinlessness, and in utter helplessness, as the Lamb of God. In the words of St. Peter, "Who did no sin, neither was guile found in His mouth; who, when He was reviled, reviled not again; when He suffered, He threatened not; but committed Himself to Him that judgeth righteously."[3] Think then, my brethren, of your feelings at cruelty practised upon brute animals, and you will gain one sort of feeling which the history of Christ's Cross and Passion ought to excite within you. And let me add, this is in all cases one good use to which you may turn any accounts you read of wanton and unfeeling acts shown towards the inferior animals; let them

[3] 1 Pet. ii.22, 23.

remind you, as a picture, of Christ's sufferings. He who is higher than the Angels, deigned to humble Himself even to the state of the brute creation, as the Psalm says, "I am a worm, and no man; a very scorn of men, and the outcast of the people." [4]

2. Take another example, and you will see the same thing still more strikingly. How overpowered should we be, nay not at the sight only, but at the very hearing of cruelties shown to a little child, and why so? for the same two reasons, because it was so innocent, and because it was so unable to defend itself. I do not like to go into the details of such cruelty, they would be so heart-rending. What if wicked men took and crucified a young child? What if they deliberately seized its poor little frame, and stretched out its arms, nailed them to a cross bar of wood, drove a stake through its two feet, and fastened them to a beam, and so left it to die? It is almost too shocking to say; perhaps, you will actually say it *is* too shocking, and ought not to be said. O, my brethren, you feel the horror of this, and yet you can bear to read of Christ's sufferings without horror; for what is that little child's agony to His? and which deserved it more? which is the more innocent? which the holier? was He not gentler, sweeter, meeker, more tender, more loving, than any little child? Why are you shocked at the one, why are you not shocked at the other?

Or take another instance, not so shocking in its circumstances, yet introducing us to another distinction, in which Christ's passion exceeds that of any innocent sufferers, such as I have supposed. When Joseph was sent by his father to his brethren on a message of love, they, when they saw him, said, "Behold, this dreamer cometh; come now, therefore, and let us slay him." [5] They did not kill him, however, but they put him in a pit in spite of the anguish of his soul, and sold him as a slave to the Ishmaelites, and he was taken down into a foreign country, where he had no friends. Now this was most cruel and most cowardly in the sons of Jacob; and what is so especially shocking in it is, that Joseph was not only innocent and defenceless, their younger brother whom they ought to have protected, but besides that, he was so confiding and loving, that he need not have come to them, that he would not at all have been in their power, *except* for his desire to do them service. Now, whom does this history remind us of but of Him concerning whom the Master of the vineyard said, on sending Him to the husbandmen, "They will reverence My Son?" [6] "But when the husbandmen

---

[4] Ps. xxii.6.   [5] Gen. xxxvii.19, 20.   [6] Matt. xxi.37–39.

saw the Son, they said among themselves, This is the Heir, come, let us kill Him, and let us seize on His inheritance. And they caught Him, and cast Him out of the vineyard, and slew Him." Here, then, is an additional circumstance of cruelty to affect us in Christ's history, such as is suggested in Joseph's, but which no instance of a brute animal's or of a child's sufferings can have; our Lord was not only guiltless and defenceless, but He had come among His persecutors in love.

3. And now, instead of taking the case of the young, innocent, and confiding, let us take another instance which will present to us our Lord's passion under another aspect. Let us suppose that some aged and venerable person whom we have known as long as we could recollect any thing, and loved and reverenced, suppose such a one, who had often done us kindnesses, who had taught us, who had given us good advice, who had encouraged us, smiled on us, comforted us in trouble, whom we knew to be very good and religious, very holy, full of wisdom, full of heaven, with grey hairs and awful countenance, waiting for Almighty God's summons to leave this world for a better place; suppose, I say, such a one whom we have ourselves known, and whose memory is dear to us, rudely seized by fierce men, stripped naked in public, insulted, driven about here and there, made a laughing-stock, struck, spit on, dressed up in other clothes in ridicule, then severely scourged on the back, then laden with some heavy load till he could carry it no longer, pulled and dragged about, and at last exposed with all his wounds to the gaze of a rude multitude who came and jeered him, what would be our feelings? Let us in our mind think of this person or that, and consider how we should be overwhelmed and pierced through and through by such a hideous occurrence.

But what is all this to the suffering of the holy Jesus, which we bear to read of as a matter of course! Only think of Him, when in His wounded state, and without garment on, He had to creep up the ladder, as He could, which led Him up the cross high enough for His murderers to nail Him to it; and consider *who* it was that was in that misery. Or again, view Him dying, hour after hour bleeding to death; and how? in peace? no; with His arms stretched out, and His face exposed to view, and any one who pleased coming and staring at Him, mocking Him, and watching the gradual ebbing of His strength, and the approach of death. These are some of the appalling details which the Gospels contain, and surely they were not recorded for nothing; but that we might dwell on them.

Do you think that those who saw these things had much heart for eating or drinking or enjoying themselves? On the contrary, we are told that even "the people who came together to that sight, smote their breasts and returned." [7] If these were the feelings of the people, what were St. John's feelings, or St. Mary Magdalene's, or St. Mary's, our Lord's blessed mother? Do we desire to be of this company? do we desire, according to His own promise, to be rather blessed than the womb that bare Him, and the paps that He sucked? do we desire to be as His brother, and sister, and mother? [8] Then, surely, ought we to have some portion of that mother's sorrow! When He was on the cross and she stood by, then, according to Simeon's prophecy, "a sword pierced through her soul." [9] What is the use of our keeping the memory of His cross and passion, unless we lament and are in sorrow with her? I can understand people who do not keep Good Friday at all; they are indeed very ungrateful, but I know what they mean; I understand them. But I do not understand at all, I do not at all see what men mean who *do* profess to keep it, yet do not sorrow, or at least try to sorrow. Such a spirit of grief and lamentation is expressly mentioned in Scripture as a characteristic of those who turn to Christ. If then *we* do not sorrow, have *we* turned to Him? "I will pour upon the house of David," says the merciful Saviour Himself, before He came on earth, speaking of what was to come, "upon the inhabitants of Jerusalem, the spirit of grace and of supplications; and they shall look upon Me whom they have pierced, and they shall *mourn* for Him, as one mourneth for his only son, and shall be in bitterness for Him, as one that is in bitterness for his firstborn." [10]

One thing I will add:—if there be persons here present who are conscious to themselves that they do not feel the grief which this season should cause them, who feel now as they do at other times, let them consider with themselves whether perhaps this defect does not arise from their having neglected to come to church, whether during this season or at other times, as often as they might. Our feelings are not in our own power; God alone can rule our feelings; God alone can make us sorrow, when we would but cannot sorrow; but *will* He, if we have not diligently sought Him according to our opportunities in this house of grace? I speak of those who might come to prayers more frequently, and do not. I know well that many cannot come. I speak of those who can, if they will. Even if they come as often as they are able, I know well they will not be *satisfied* with their own feelings; they will be conscious even then that they ought to grieve more than they do; of course none of us feels the great event of this day as he ought, and therefore we all *ought* to be dissatisfied with ourselves. However, if this is not our own fault, we need not be out of heart, for God will mercifully lead us forward in His own time; but if it arises from our not coming to prayers here as often as we might, then our coldness and deadness *are* our own fault, and I beg you all to consider that that fault is not a slight one. It is said in the Book of Revelation, "Behold He cometh with clouds; and every eye shall see Him, and they also which pierced Him: and all kindreds of the earth shall wail because of Him." [11] We, my brethren, every one of us, shall one day rise from our graves, and see Jesus Christ; we shall see Him who hung on the cross, we shall see His wounds, we shall see the marks in His hands, and in His feet, and in His side. Do we wish to be of those, then, who wail and lament, or of those who rejoice? If we would not lament at the sight of Him then, we must lament at the thought of Him now. Let us prepare to meet our God; let us come into His Presence whenever we can; let us try to fancy as if we saw the Cross and Him upon it; let us draw near to it; let us beg Him to look on us as He did on the penitent thief, and let us say to Him, "Lord remember me when Thou comest in Thy kingdom." [12]

Let this be added to the prayer, my brethren, with which you are about to leave this church. After I have given the blessing, you will say to yourselves a short prayer. Well; fancy you see Jesus Christ on the cross, and say to Him with the penitent thief, "Lord, remember me when Thou comest in Thy kingdom;" that is, "Remember me, Lord, in mercy, remember not my sins, but Thine own cross; remember Thine own sufferings, remember that Thou sufferedst for me, a sinner; remember in the last day that I, during my lifetime, felt Thy sufferings, that I suffered on my cross by Thy side. Remember me then, and make me remember Thee now."

[11] Rev. i.7.   [12] Luke xxiii.42.

ATTENDANCE ON
HOLY COMMUNION

"Ye will not come to Me, that ye might have life."
—John v.40.

S T. JOHN tells us in to-day's Epistle[1] that "God hath given unto us eternal life, and this life is in His Son. He that hath the Son hath life, and he that hath not the Son hath not life." Yet in the text the Son Himself, our Saviour, sorrowfully and solemnly expostulates with His own brethren, "Ye will not come to Me, that ye might have life." "He came unto His own, and His own received Him not." We know from history, as a matter of fact, that they did not receive Him, that they did not come to Him when He came to them; but He says in the text that they would not come, that they did not wish to come, implying that they, and none else but they, were the cause of their not coming.

Does it not seem a plain natural instinct that every one should seek his own good? What then is meant by this unwillingness to come for the greatest of goods, life; an unwillingness, which, guided by the light of Scripture and by experience, we can confidently affirm to prevail at this day as widely and as fully as in the age in which Christ said it?

Here is no question of a comparison of good with good. We cannot account for this unconcern about Christ's gift, by alleging that we have a sufficient treasure in our hands already, and therefore are not interested by the news of a greater. Far from it; for is not the world continually taking away its own gifts, whatever they are? and does it not thereby bring home to us, does it not importunately press upon us, and weary us with the lesson of its own nothingness? Do we not confess that eternal life is the best of all conceivable gifts, before which none other deserve to be mentioned? yet we live to the world.

Nay, and sin also warns us not to trust to its allurements; like

[1] First Sunday after Easter.

the old prophet of Bethel, sin is forced to bear witness against itself, and in the name of the Lord to denounce the Lord's judgments upon us. While it seduces us, it stings us with remorse; and even when the sense of guilt is overcome, still the misery of sinning is inflicted on us in the inward disappointments and the temporal punishments which commonly follow upon transgression. Yet we will not come unto Christ that we may have life.

Further, it is not that God treats us as servants or slaves; He does not put a burden on us above our strength: He does not repel us from His Presence till we have prepared some offering to bring before Him, or have made some good progress in the way of life. No; He has begun His dealings with us with special, spontaneous acts of mercy. He has, by an inconceivable goodness, sent His Son to be our life. Far from asking any gift at our hands in the first instance, He has from our infancy taken us in charge, and freely given us "all things that pertain unto life and godliness." He has been urgent with us in the very morning of our days, and by the fulness of His grace has anticipated the first stirrings of pride and lust, while as yet sin slept within us. Is it not so? What more could have been done for us? Yet, in spite of all this, men will not come unto Him that they may have life.

So strange is this, that thoughtful persons are sometimes tempted to suppose that the mass of mankind do not sufficiently know what their duty is; that they need teaching, else they would be obedient. And others fancy that if the doctrines of the Gospel were set before them in a forcible or persuasive manner, this would serve as a means of rousing them to an habitual sense of their true state. But ignorance is not the true cause why men will not come to Christ.

Who are these willing outcasts from Christ's favour, of whom I speak? Do not think I say a strong thing, my brethren, when I tell you that I am speaking of some of those who now hear me. Not that I dare draw the line any where, or imagine that I can give any rule for knowing for certain, just who come to Him in heart and spirit, and who do not; but I am quite sure that many, who would shrink from giving up their interest in the Gospel, and who profess to cast their lot with Christ, and to trust in His death for their salvation, nevertheless do not really seek Him that they may have life, in spite of their fair speeches. This I say I am too well enabled to know, because in fact so it is, that He has shown us *how* to come to Him, and I see that men do *not* come to Him in that way which He has pointed out. He has shown us, that to come to Him for life is a literal bodily action;

not a mere figure, not a mere movement of the heart towards Him, but an action of the visible limbs; not a mere secret faith, but a coming to church, a passing on along the aisle to His holy table, a kneeling down there before Him, and a receiving of the gift of eternal life in the form of bread and wine. There can be no mistaking His own appointment. He said indeed, "He that cometh to Me shall never hunger;" but then He explained what this coming was, by adding, "He that eateth Me, even he shall live by Me." If then a man does not seek Him where He is, there is no profit in seeking Him where He is not. What is the good of sitting at home seeking Him, when His Presence is in the holy Eucharist? Such perverseness is like the sin of the Israelites who went to seek for the manna at a time when it was not given. May not He who gives the gift, prescribe the place and mode of giving it?

Observe how plain and cogent is the proof of what I have been saying. Our Lord declares, "Except ye eat the flesh of the Son of Man, and drink His blood, ye have no life in you:" no life, life being the gift He offers in the text; also He says of the bread which He had broken, "*This* is My Body;" and of the cup, "*This* is My Blood;" is it not very plain, then, that if we refuse to eat that Bread, and drink that Cup, we are refusing to come unto Him that we may have life?

The true reason why people will not come to this Holy Communion is this,—they do not wish to lead religious lives; they do not like to promise to lead religious lives; and they think that that blessed Sacrament does bind them to do so, bind them to live very much more strictly and thoughtfully than they do at present. Allow as much as we will for proper distrust of themselves, reasonable awe, the burden of past sin, imperfect knowledge, and other causes, still after all there is in most cases a reluctance to bear, or at least to pledge themselves to bear, Christ's yoke; a reluctance to give up the service of sin once for all; a lingering love of their own ease, of their own will, of indolence, of carnal habits, of the good opinion of men whom they do not respect; a distrust of their perseverance in holy resolves, grounded on a misgiving about their present sincerity. This is why men will not come to Christ for life; they know that He will not impart Himself to them, unless they consent to devote themselves to Him.

In what way does He offer Himself to them in Holy Communion? through the commands and sanctions of the Law. First, we are warned against secret sin, and called to self-examination; a week's preparation follows; then, when the time of celebration is come, we hear the Commandments read, we are solemnly exhorted to put off every thing which may offend God; we confess our sins and our deep sorrow for them; lastly, after being admitted to the Sacrament, we expressly bind ourselves to the service of our Lord and Saviour. Doubtless *this* it is which the unrenewed heart cannot bear, the very notion of giving up sin altogether and once for all. And thus, though a gracious voice cry ever so distinctly from the altar, "Come unto Me, and I will refresh you;" and though it be ever so true that this refreshment is nothing short of life, eternal life, yet we recollect the words which follow, "Take My yoke upon you, and learn of Me," and we forthwith murmur and complain, as if the gift were most ungracious, laden with conditions, and hardly purchased, merely because it is offered in that way in which alone a righteous Lord could offer it,—the way of righteousness.

Men had rather give up the promise than implicate themselves in the threats which surround it. Bright and attractive as is the treasure presented to us in the Gospel, still the pearl of great price lies in its native depths, at the bottom of the ocean. We see it indeed, and know its worth; but not many dare plunge in to bring it thence. What reward offered to the diver shall overcome the imminent peril of a frightful death? and those who love sin, and whose very life consists in habits and practices short of religious, what promised prize can reconcile them to the certain destruction of what they delight in, the necessary annihilation of all their most favourite indulgences and enjoyments which are contrary to the rule of the Gospel? Let us not suppose that any exhortations will induce such men to change their conduct; they confess the worth of the soul, their obligation to obey, and their peril if they do not; yet, for all this, the present sacrifice required of them is too much for them. They may be told of their Lord's love for them, His self-denying mercy when on earth, His free gifts, and His long-suffering since; they will not be influenced; and why? because the fault is in their heart; they do not like God's service. *They* know full well what they would have, if they might choose. Christ is said to have done all things for us; "Far from it," say they, "He is not a Mediator suited to our case. Give life, give holiness, give truth, give a Saviour to deliver from sin; this is not enough: no, *we* want a Saviour to deliver *in* sin. This is our need. It is a small thing to offer us life, if it be in the way of God's commandments; it is a mockery of our hopes to call that a free gift, which is, in fact, a heavy yoke. We want to do nothing at all, and then the gift will be free indeed. If our hearts *must* be changed to fit us for heaven, let them be changed, only let us have no trouble in the work ourselves. Let the change be part of the work done for us; let us literally be clay in the hands of the potter; let us sleep, and dream, and wake in the morning new men; let us have no fear and trembling, no working out salvation, no self-denial. Let Christ suffer, but be it ours to rejoice only. What we wish is, to be at ease; we wish to have every thing our own way; we wish to enjoy both this world and the next; we wish to be happy all at once. If the Gospel promises this, we accept it; but if not, it is but a bondage, it has no persuasiveness, it will receive no acceptance from us." Such is the language of men's hearts, though their tongues do not utter it; language most unthankful, most profane, most sinful.

These reflections I recommend to the serious attention of those who live in neglect of Holy Communion; but, alas! I must not quit the subject without addressing some cautions to those who are in the observance of it. I would that none of us had need of cautions; but the best of us is in warfare, and on his trial, and none of us can be the worse for them. I need not remind you, my brethren, that there is a peril attached to the unworthy reception; for this is the very excuse which many plead for not receiving; but it often happens, as in other matters also, that men have fears when they should not fear, and do not fear when they should fear. A slight consideration will show this; for what is the danger in communicating? that of coming to it, as St. Paul implies, *without* fear. It is evident then, that, in spite of what was just now said, when persons are in danger of receiving it unworthily, they commonly do not really feel their danger; for their very danger consists in their not fearing. If they did truly and religiously fear the blessed Sacrament, so far they would not be in danger of an unworthy reception.

Now it is plain when it is that persons are in danger of receiving it fearlessly and thoughtlessly; not when they receive it for the first time, but when they have often received it, when they are in the habit of receiving it. This is the dangerous time.

When a Christian first comes to Holy Communion, he comes with awe and anxiety. At least, I will not suppose the case of a person so little in earnest about his soul, and so profane, as to despise the ordinance when he first attends it. Perhaps he has no clear doctrinal notion of the sacred rite, but the very title of it, as the Sacrament of his Lord's Body and Blood, suffices to make him serious. Let us believe that he examines himself, and prays for grace to receive the gift worthily; and he feels at the time of celebration and afterwards, that, having bound himself more strictly to a religious life, and received Divine influences, he has more to answer for. But after he has repeated his attendance several times, this fear and reverence wear away with the novelty. As he begins to be familiar with the words of the prayers, and the order of the Service, so does he both hear and receive with less emotion and solemnity. It is not that he is a worse man than he was at first, but he is exposed to a greater temptation to be profane. He had no deeper religious principle when he first communicated than he has now (probably not so deep), but his want of acquaintance with the Service kept him from irreverence, indifference, and wandering thoughts: but now this accidental safeguard is removed, and as he has not succeeded in acquiring any habitual reverence from former seasons of communicating, and has no clear knowledge of the nature of the Sacrament to warn and check him, he is exposed to his own ordinary hardness of heart and unbelief, in circumstances much more perilous than those in which they are ordinarily displayed. If it is a sin to neglect God in the world, it is a greater sin to neglect Him in church. Now is the time when he is in danger of not discerning the Lord's Body, of receiving the gift of life as a thing of course, without awe, gratitude, and self-abasement. And the more constant he is in his attendance at the sacred rite, the greater will be his risk; his *risk*, I say; that is, if he neglects to be jealous over himself, to watch himself narrowly, and to condemn and hate in himself the faintest risings of coldness and irreverence; for, of course, if he so acts, the less will be his risk, and the greater will be his security that his heart will not betray him. But I speak of those who are not sufficiently aware of their danger, and these are many.

Here, too, let me mention another sin of a similar character into which communicants are apt to fall; *viz.* a forgetfulness, after communicating, that they have communicated. Even when we resist the coldness which frequent communion may occasion, and strive to possess our minds in as profound a seriousness as we felt when the rite was new to us, even then there is often a painful difference between our feelings before we have attended it, and after. We are diligent in preparation, we are careless in retrospect; we dismiss from our memory what we cherished in our expectations; we forget that we ever hoped and feared. But consider; when we have solemn thoughts about Holy Communion only till we have come to it, what does this imply, but that we imagine that we have received the benefit of it once for all, as a thing done and over, and that there is nothing

more to seek? This is but a formal way of worshipping; as if we
had wiped off a writing which was against us, and there was an
end of the matter. But blessed are those servants who are ever
expecting Him, who is ever coming to them; whether He come
"at even, or at midnight, or at cock-crowing, or in the morning;" whereas those who first come to Him for the gift of grace,
and then neglect to wait for its progressive accomplishment in
their hearts, how profanely they act! it is as if to receive the
blessing in mockery, and then to cast it away. Surely, after so
great a privilege, we ought to behave ourselves as if we had partaken some Divine food and medicine (if great things may be
compared to ordinary), which, in its own inscrutable way, and
in its own good time, will "prosper in the thing whereunto God
sends it"—the fruit of the tree of life which Adam forfeited,
which had that virtue in it, that it was put out of his reach in
haste, lest he should take and eat, and live for ever. How earnest, then, should be our care lest this gracious treasure which
we carry within us should be lost by our own fault, by the unhealthy excitements, or the listless indolence, to which our nature invites us! "Quench not the Spirit," says the Apostle;
surely our privilege is a burden heavy to bear, before it turn to a
principle of life and strength, till Christ be formed in us perfectly; and we the while, what cause have we to watch, and
pray, and fulfil all righteousness, till the day dawn, and the day-
star arise in our hearts!

Nor let us suppose that by once or twice seeking God in this
gracious ordinance, we can secure the gift for ever: "Seek the
Lord and His strength, seek His face evermore." The bread
which comes down from heaven is like the manna, "*daily*
bread," and that "till He come," till His "kingdom come." In
His coming at the end of the world, all our wishes and prayers
rest and are accomplished; and in His present communion we
have a stay and consolation meanwhile, joining together the
past and future, reminding us that He has come once, and
promising us that He will come again. Who can live any time in
the world, pleasant as it may seem on first entering it, without
discovering that it is a weariness, and that if this life is worth
any thing, it is because it is the passage to another? It needs no
great religion to feel this; it is a self-evident truth to those who
have much experience of the world. The only reason why all do
not feel it is, that they have not lived long enough to feel it; and
those who feel it more than others, have but been thrown into
circumstances to feel it more. But while the times wax old, and
the colours of earth fade, and the voice of song is brought low,

and all kindreds of the earth can but wail and lament, the sons of God lift up their heads, for their salvation draweth nigh. Nature fails, the sun shines not, and the moon is dim, the stars fall from heaven, and the foundations of the round world shake; but the Altar's light burns ever brighter; there are sights there which the many cannot see, and all above the tumults of earth the command is heard to show forth the Lord's death, and the promise that the Lord is coming.

"Happy are the people that are in such a case!" who, when wearied of the things seen, can turn with good hope to the things unseen; yea, "blessed are the people who have the Lord for their God!" "Come unto Me," He says, "all ye that labour and are heavy laden, and I will give you rest." Rest is better than toil; peace satisfies, and quietness disappoints not. These are sure goods. Such is the calm of the heavenly Jerusalem, which is the mother of us all; and such is their calm worship, the fore-taste of heaven, who for a season shut themselves out from the world, and seek Him in invisible Presence, whom they shall hereafter see face to face.

THE GOSPEL FEAST

"When Jesus then lifted up His eyes, and saw a great company come unto Him, He saith unto Philip, Whence shall we buy bread that these may eat?"—John vi.5.

AFTER these words the Evangelist adds, "And this He said to prove him, for He Himself knew what He would do." Thus, you see, our Lord had secret meanings when He spoke, and did not bring forth openly all His divine sense at once. He knew what He was about to do from the first, but He wished to lead forward His disciples, and to arrest and open their minds, before He instructed them: for all cannot receive His words, and on the blind and deaf the most sacred truths fall without profit.

And thus, throughout the course of His gracious dispensations from the beginning, it may be said that the Author and Finisher of our faith has hid things from us in mercy, and listened to our questionings, while He Himself knew what He was about to do. He has hid, in order afterwards to reveal, that then, on looking back on what He said and did before, we may see in it what at the time we did not see, and thereby see it to more profit. Thus He hid Himself from the disciples as He walked with them to Emmaus: thus Joseph, too, under different and yet similar circumstances, hid himself from his brethren.

With this thought in our minds, surely we seem to see a new and further meaning still, in the narrative before us. Christ spoke of buying bread, when He intended to create or make bread; but did He not, in that bread which He made, intend further that Heavenly bread which is the salvation of our souls?—for He goes on to say, "Labour not for the meat" or food "which perisheth, but for that food which endureth unto everlasting life, which the Son of man shall give unto you." Yes, surely the wilderness is the world, and the Apostles are His priests, and the multitudes are His people; and that feast, so suddenly, so unexpectedly provided, is the Holy Communion. He alone is the same, He the provider of the loaves then, of the heavenly manna now. All other things change, but He remaineth.

And what is that Heavenly Feast which we now are vouch-safed, but in its own turn the earnest and pledge of that future feast in His Father's kingdom, when "the marriage of the Lamb shall come, and His wife hath made herself ready," and "holy Jerusalem cometh down from God out of heaven," and "blessed shall they be who shall eat bread in the kingdom of God"?

And further, since to that Feast above we do lift up our eyes, though it will not come till the end; and as we do not make remembrance of it once only, but continually, in the sacred rite which foreshadows it; therefore, in like manner, not in the miracle of the loaves only, though in that especially, but in all parts of Scripture, in history, and in precept, and in promise, and in prophecy, is it given us to see the Gospel Feast typified and prefigured, and that immortal and never-failing Supper in the visible presence of the Lamb which will follow upon it at the end. And if they are blessed who shall eat and drink of that table in the kingdom, so too blessed are they who meditate upon it, and hope for it now,—who read Scripture with it in their thoughts, and endeavour to look beneath the veil of the literal text, and to catch a sight of the gleams of heavenly light which are behind it. "Blessed are your eyes, for they see; and your ears, for they hear; for verily I say unto you, that many prophets and righteous men have desired to see those things which ye see, but have not seen them; and to hear those things which ye hear, and have not heard them." "Blessed are they which have not seen, and yet have believed." Blessed they who see in and by believing, and who have, because they doubt not.

Let us, then, at this time of year[1] as is fitting, follow the train of thought thus opened upon us, and, looking back into the Sacred Volume, trace the intimations and promises there given of that sacred and blessed Feast of Christ's Body and Blood which it is our privilege now to enjoy till the end come.

Now the Old Testament, as we know, is full of figures and types of the Gospel; types various, and, in their literal wording, contrary to each other, but all meeting and harmoniously ful-filled in Christ and His Church. Thus the histories of the Israel-ites in the wilderness, and of the Israelites when settled in Canaan, alike are ours, representing our present state as Chris-tians. Our Christian life is a state of faith and trial; it is also a state of enjoyment. It has the richness of the promised land; it

---

[1] Easter.

has the marvellousness of the desert. It is a "good land, a land of brooks of water, of fountains and depths that spring out of vallies and hills; a land of wheat and barley, and vines, and fig-trees, and pomegranates; a land of oil olive, and honey; a land wherein thou shalt eat bread without scarceness; thou shalt not lack any thing in it; a land whose stones are iron, and out of whose hills thou mayest dig brass." And, on the other hand, it is still a land which to the natural man seems a wilderness, a "great and terrible wilderness, wherein are fiery serpents, and scorpions, and drought, where there is no water;" where faith is still necessary, and where, still more forcibly than in the case of Israel, the maxim holds, that "man doth not live by bread only, but by every word that proceedeth out of the mouth of the Lord doth man live."

This is the state in which we are,—a state of faith and of pos-session. In the desert the Israelites lived by the signs of things, without the realities: manna was to stand for the corn, oil, and honey, of the good land promised; water, for the wine and milk. It was a time for faith to exercise itself; and when they came into the promised land, then was the time of possession. That was the land of milk and honey; they needed not any divinely provided compensations or expedients. Manna was not needed, nor the pillar of the cloud, nor the water from the rock. But we Christians, on the contrary, are at once in the wilderness and in the promised land. In the wilderness, because we live amid wonders; in the promised land, because we are in a state of en-joyment. That we are in the state of enjoyment is surely certain, unless all the prophecies have failed; and that we are in a state in which faith alone has that enjoyment, is plain from the fact that God's great blessings are not seen, and in that the Apostle says, "We walk by faith, not by sight." In a word we are in a super-natural state,—a word which implies both its greatness and its secretness: for what is above nature, is at once not seen, and is more precious than what is seen; "the things which are seen are temporal, the things which are not seen are eternal."

And if our state altogether is parallel to that of the Israelites, as an antitype to its type, it is natural to think that so great a gift as Holy Communion would not be without its appropriate fig-ures and symbols in the Old Testament. All that our Saviour has done is again and again shadowed out in the Old Testament; and this, therefore, it is natural to think, as well as other things: His miraculous birth, His life, His teaching, His death, His priesthood, His sacrifice, His resurrection, His glorification, His kingdom, are again and again prefigured: it is not reasonable to suppose that if this so great gift is really given us, it should be omitted. He who died for us, is He who feeds us; and as His death is mentioned, so we may beforehand expect will be mentioned the feast He gives us. Not openly indeed, for neither is His death nor His priesthood taught openly, but covertly, under the types of David or Aaron, or other favoured servants of God; and in like manner we might expect, and we shall find, the like reverent allusions to His most gracious Feast,—allusions which we should not know to *be* allusions but for the event; just as we should not know that Solomon, Aaron, or Samuel, stood for Christ at all, except that the event explains the figure. When Abraham said to Isaac, "God will provide Himself a lamb for a burnt offering," who can doubt this is a prophecy concerning Christ?—yet we are nowhere told it in Scripture. The case is the same as regards the Sacrament of Baptism. Now that it is given, we cannot doubt that the purifications of the Jews, Naaman's bathing, and the prophecy of a fountain being opened for sin and all uncleanness, have reference to it, as being the visible fulfilment of the great spiritual cleansing: and St. Peter expressly affirms this of the Deluge, and St. Paul of the passage of the Red Sea. And in like manner passages in the Bible, which speak prophetically of the Gospel Feast, cannot but refer (if I may so speak) to the Holy Sacrament of the Lord's Supper, as being, in fact, the Feast given us under the Gospel.

And let it be observed, directly we know that we have this great gift, and that the Old Testament history prefigures it, we have a light thrown upon what otherwise is a difficulty; for, it may be asked with some speciousness, whether the Jews were not in a higher state of privilege than we Christians, until we take this gift into account. It may be objected that our blessings are all future or distant,—the hope of eternal life, which is to be fulfilled hereafter, God's forgiveness, who is in heaven: what do we gain now and here above the Jews? God loved the Jews, and He *gave* them something; He gave them present gifts; the Old Testament is full of the description of them; He gave them "the precious things of heaven, and the dew, and the deep that coucheth beneath, and precious things brought forth by the sun, and by the moon, and the chief things of the ancient mountains, and the precious things of the lasting hills, and the precious things of the earth, and the fulness thereof," "honey out of the rock, and oil out of the flinty rock, butter of kine, and milk of sheep, with fat of lambs, and rams of the breed of Bashan, and goats, with the fat of kidneys of wheat, and the pure blood of the grape."[2] These were present real blessings. What has He given *us*?—*nothing* in possession? *all* in promise? This, I say, is in itself not likely; it is not likely that He should so reverse His system, and make the Gospel inferior to the Law. But the knowledge of the great gift under consideration clears up this perplexity; for every passage in the Old Testament which speaks of the temporal blessings given by God to His ancient people, instead of conveying to us a painful sense of destitution, and exciting our jealousy, reminds us of our greater blessedness; for every passage which belongs to them is fulfilled now in a higher sense to us. We have no need to envy them. God did not take away their blessings, without giving us greater. The Law was not so much taken away, as the Gospel given. The Gospel supplanted the Law. The Law went out by the Gospel's coming in. Only our blessings are not seen; *therefore* they are higher, *because* they are unseen. Higher blessings could not be visible. How could spiritual blessings be visible ones? If Christ now feeds us, not with milk and honey, but "with the spiritual food of His most precious Body and Blood;" if "our sinful bodies are made clean by His Body, and our souls washed through His most precious Blood," truly we are not without our precious things, any more than Israel was: but they are unseen, because so much greater, so spiritual; they are given only under the veil of what is seen: and thus we Christians are both with the Church in the wilderness as regards faith, and in the Church in Canaan as regards enjoyment; having the fulfilment of the words spoken by Moses, repeated by our Lord, to which I just now referred, "Man shall not live by bread only, but by every word which proceedeth out of the mouth of God."

Now, then, I will refer to some passages of both the Old Testament and the New, which both illustrate and are illustrated by this great doctrine of the Gospel.

1. And, first, let it be observed, from the beginning, the greatest rite of religion has been a feast; the partaking of God's bounties, in the way of nature, has been consecrated to a more immediate communion with God Himself. For instance, when Isaac was weaned, Abraham "made a great feast,"[3] and then it was that Sarah prophesied; "Cast out this bondwoman and her son," she said, prophesying the introduction of the spirit, grace, and truth, which the Gospel contains, instead of the bondage of the outward forms of the Law. Again, it was at a feast of savoury meat that the spirit of prophecy came upon

[2] Deut. xxxii.13; xxxiii.13–15.   [3] Gen. xxi.10.

Isaac, and he blessed Jacob. In like manner the first beginning of our Lord's miracles was at a marriage feast, when He changed water into wine; and when St. Matthew was converted he entertained our Lord at a feast. At a feast, too, our Lord allowed the penitent woman to wash with tears and anoint His feet, and pronounced her forgiveness; and at a feast, before His passion, He allowed Mary to anoint them with costly ointment, and to wipe them with her hair. Thus with our Lord, and with the Patriarchs, a feast was a time of grace; so much so, that He was said by the Pharisees to come eating and drinking, to be "a winebibber and gluttonous, a friend of publicans and sinners."[4]

2. And next, in order to make this feasting still more solemn, it had been usual at all times to precede it by a direct act of religion,—by a prayer, or blessing, or sacrifice, or by the presence of a priest, which implied it. Thus, when Melchizedek came out to meet Abraham, and *bless* him, "he brought forth bread and wine;"[5] to which it is added, "and he was the priest of the Most High God." Such, too, was the lamb of the Passover, which was eaten roast with fire, and with unleavened bread, and bitter herbs, with girded loins and shoes on, and staff in hand; as the Lord's Passover, being a solemn religious feast, even if not a sacrifice. And such seems to have been the common notion of communion with God all the world over, however it was gained; viz. that we arrived at the possession of His invisible gifts by participation in His visible; that there was some mysterious connexion between the seen and the unseen; and that, by setting aside the choicest of His earthly bounties, as a specimen and representative of the whole, presenting it to Him for His blessing, and then taking, eating, and appropriating it, we had the best hope of gaining those unknown and indefinite gifts which human nature needs. This the heathen practised towards their idols also; and St. Paul seems to acknowledge that in that way they did communicate, though most miserably and fearfully, with those idols, and with the evil spirits which they represented. "The things which the Gentiles sacrifice, they sacrifice to devils, and not to God; and I would not that ye should hold communion with devils."[6] Here, as before, a feast is spoken of as the means of communicating with the unseen world, though, when the feast was idolatrous, it was the fellowship of evil spirits.

3. And next let this be observed, that the descriptions in the Old Testament of the perfect state of religious privilege, viz.

[4] Matt. xi.19; Luke vii.34.　　[5] Gen. xiv.18.　　[6] 1 Cor. x.20.

that under the Gospel which was then to come, are continually made under the image of a feast, a feast of some special and choice goods of this world, corn, wine, and the like; goods of this world chosen from the mass as a specimen of all, as types and means of seeking, and means of obtaining, the unknown spiritual blessings, which "eye hath not seen nor ear heard." And these special goods of nature, so set apart, are more frequently than any thing else, corn or bread, and wine, as the figures of what was greater, though others are mentioned also. Now the first of these of which we read is the fruit of the tree of life, the leaves of which are also mentioned in the prophets. The tree of life was that tree in the garden of Eden, the eating of which would have made Adam immortal; a divine gift lay hid in an outward form. The prophet Ezekiel speaks of it afterwards in the following words, showing that a similar blessing was in store for the redeemed:—"By the river, upon the bank thereof, on this side, and on that side, shall grow all trees for meat, whose leaf shall not fade, neither shall the fruit thereof be consumed. It shall bring forth new fruits according to his months, because their waters they issued out of the sanctuary; and the fruit thereof shall be for meat, and the leaf thereof for medicine."[7] Like to which is St. John's account of the tree of life, "which bare twelve manner of fruits, and yielded her fruit every month; and the leaves of the tree were for the healing of the nations."[8] And hence we read in the Canticles of the appletree, and of sitting down under its shadow, and its fruit being sweet to the taste. Here then in type is signified the sacred gift of which I am speaking; and yet it has not seemed good to the gracious Giver literally to select fruit or leaves as the means of His invisible blessings. He might have spiritually fed us with such, had He pleased—for man liveth not by bread only, but by the word of His mouth. His Word might have made the fruit of the tree His Sacrament, but He has willed otherwise.

The next selection of gifts of the earth which we find in Scripture, is the very one which He at length fixed on, bread and wine, as in the history of Melchizedek; and there the record stands as a prophecy of what was to be: for who is Melchizedek but our Lord and Saviour, and what is the Bread and Wine but the very feast which He has ordained?

Next the great gift was shadowed out in the description of the promised land, which was said to flow with milk and honey, and in all those other precious things of nature which I have

[7] Ezek. xlvii.12.   [8] Rev. xxii.2.

already recounted as belonging to the promised land, oil, butter, corn, wine, and the like. These all may be considered to
refer to the Gospel feast typically, because they were the rarest
and most exquisite of the blessings given to the Jews, as the
Gospel Feast is the most choice and most sacred of all the
blessings given to us Christians; and what is most precious under the one Dispensation is signified by what is most precious
under the other.

Now let us proceed to the Prophets, and we shall find the like
anticipation of the Gospel Feast.

For instance, you recollect, the prophet Hosea says: "It shall
come to pass in that day, I will hear, saith the Lord, I will hear
the heavens, and they shall hear the earth, and the earth shall
hear the corn, and the wine, and the oil, and they shall hear
Jezreel. And I will sow her unto Me in the earth."[9] By Jezreel is
meant the Christian Church; and the Prophet declares in God's
name, that the time was to come when the Church would call
upon the corn, wine, and oil, and they would call on the earth,
and the earth on the heavens, and the heavens on God; and God
should answer the heavens, and the heavens should answer the
earth, and the earth should answer the corn, wine, and oil, and
they should answer to the wants of the Church. Now, doubtless, this may be fulfilled only in a general way; but considering
Almighty God has appointed corn or bread, and wine, to be the
special instruments of His ineffable grace,—He, who sees the
end from the beginning, and who views all things in all their
relations at once,—He, when He spoke of corn and wine, knew
that the word would be fulfilled, not generally only, but even
literally in the Gospel.

Again: the prophet Joel says, "It shall come to pass in that day
that the mountains shall drop down new wine, and the hills
shall flow with milk, and all the rivers of Judah shall flow with
waters, and a fountain shall come forth of the house of the
Lord, and shall water the valley of Shittim."[10] How strikingly is
this fulfilled, if we take it to apply to what God has given us in
the Gospel, in the feast of the Holy Communion!

Again: the prophet Amos says: "Behold, the days come, saith
the Lord, when the plowman shall overtake the reaper, and the
treader of grapes him that soweth seed; and the mountains shall
drop sweet wine, and all the hills shall melt;"[11] that is, with
God's marvellous grace, whereby He gives us gifts new and
wonderful.

---

[9] Hos. ii.21–23.   [10] Joel iii.18.   [11] Amos ix.13.

And the prophet Isaiah: "In this mountain shall the Lord of Hosts make unto all people a feast of fat things, a feast of wines on the lees; of fat things full of marrow, of wines on the lees well refined." And again: "Surely I will no more give thy corn to be meat for thine enemies, and the sons of the stranger shall not drink thy wine, for the which thou hast laboured; but they that have gathered it shall eat it, and praise the Lord, and they that have brought it together shall drink it in the courts of My holiness." And again: "Behold My servants shall eat, but ye shall be hungry; behold My servants shall drink, but ye shall be thirsty." [12]

Again: the prophet Jeremiah says: "They shall come and sing in the height of Zion, and shall flow together to the goodness of the Lord, for wheat, and for wine, and for oil, and for the young of the flock and of the herd; and their soul shall be as a watered garden, and they shalt not sorrow any more at all . . . And I will satiate the soul of the priests with fatness, and My people shall be satisfied with My goodness, saith the Lord." [13]

And the prophet Zechariah: "How great is His goodness, and how great is His beauty! corn shall make the young men cheerful, and new wine the maids." [14]

And under a different image, but with the same general sense, the prophet Malachi: "From the rising of the sun even unto the going down of the same, My Name shall be great among the Gentiles; and in every place incense shall be offered unto My Name, and a pure offering, for My Name shall be great among the heathen, saith the Lord of Hosts." [15]

Further, if the Psalms are intended for Christian worship, as surely they are, the Prophetic Spirit, who inspired them, saw that they too would in various places describe that sacred Christian feast, which we feel they do describe; and surely we may rightly call this coincidence between the ordinance in the Christian Church and the form of words in the Psalms, a mark of design. For instance: "Thou shalt prepare a Table before me against them that trouble me. Thou hast anointed my head with oil, and my Cup shall be full." "I will wash my hands in innocency, O Lord, and so will I go to Thine Altar." "O send out Thy light and Thy truth, that they may lead me, and bring me unto Thy holy hill, and to Thy dwelling; and that I may go unto the Altar of God, even unto the God of my joy and gladness." "The children of men shall put their trust under the

---

[12] Is. xxv.6; lxii.8, 9; lxv.13.

[13] Jer. xxxi.12–14.

[14] Zech. ix.17.

[15] Mal. i.11.

shadow of Thy wings. They shall be satisfied with the plenteousness of Thy house, and Thou shalt give them drink of Thy
pleasures as out of the river. For with Thee is the well of life,
and in Thy light shall we see light." "Blessed is the man whom
Thou choosest and receivest unto Thee; he shall dwell in Thy
court, and shall be satisfied with the pleasures of Thy house,
even of Thy Holy Temple." "My soul shall be satisfied, even as
it were with marrow and fatness, when my mouth praiseth
Thee with joyful lips . . . because Thou hast been my helper,
therefore under the shadow of Thy wings will I rejoice." [16]

The same wonderful feast is put before us in the book of
Proverbs, where Wisdom stands for Christ. "Wisdom hath
builded her house," that is, Christ has built His Church; "she
hath hewn out her seven pillars, she hath killed her beasts, she
hath mingled her wine (that is, Christ has prepared His Supper), she hath also furnished her table (that is, the Lord's
Table), she hath sent forth her maidens (that is, the priests of
the Lord), she crieth upon the highest places of the city, Whoso
is simple, let him turn in hither; as for him that wanteth understanding, she saith to him, Come, eat of My Bread and drink of
the Wine which I have mingled," [17]—which is like saying,
"Come unto Me all ye that labour and are heavy laden and I will
refresh you." Like which are the prophet Isaiah's words: "Ho,
every one that thirsteth, come ye to the waters, and he that hath
no money, come ye buy and eat; yea, come, buy wine and milk
without money and without price." [18] And such too is the description in the book of Canticles: "The fig tree putteth forth
her green figs, and the vines with the tender grapes give a good
smell" . . . . "Until the day break and the shadows flee away, I
will get me to the mountain of myrrh, and to the hill of frankincense" . . . "I have gathered My myrrh with My spice, I have
eaten My honeycomb with My honey, I have drunk My wine
with My milk; eat, O friends, drink, yea drink abundantly, O
beloved!" [19] In connexion with such passages as these should be
observed St. Paul's words, which seem from the antithesis to be
an allusion to the same most sacred Ordinance: "Be not drunk
with wine, wherein is excess, but be filled with the Spirit," with
that new wine which God the Holy Spirit ministers in the Supper of the Great King.

God grant that we may be able ever to come to this Blessed
Sacrament with feelings suitable to the passages which I have

---

[16] Ps. xxiii.5; xxvi.6; xxxvi.7–9; xliii.3, 4; lxv.4; lxiii.6–8.
[17] Prov. ix.1–5.   [18] Is. lv.1.   [19] Cant. ii.13; iv.6; v.1.

read concerning it! May we not regard it in a cold, heartless way, and keep at a distance from fear, when we should rejoice! May the spirit of the unprofitable servant never be ours, who looked at his lord as a hard master instead of a gracious benefactor! May we not be in the number of those who go on year after year, and never approach Him at all! May we not be of those who went, one to his farm, another to his merchandise, when they were called to the wedding! Nor let us be of those, who come in a formal, mechanical way, as a mere matter of obligation, without reverence, without awe, without wonder, without love. Nor let us fall into the sin of those who complained that they have nothing to gather but the manna, wearying of God's gifts.

But let us come in faith and hope, and let us say to ourselves, May this be the beginning to us of everlasting bliss! May these be the first-fruits of that banquet which is to last for ever and ever; ever new, ever transporting, inexhaustible, in the city of our God!

LOVE OF RELIGION,
A NEW NATURE

*"If we be dead with Christ, we believe
that we shall also live with Him."*—Rom. vi.8.

To be dead with Christ, is to hate and turn from sin; and to live with Him, is to have our hearts and minds turned towards God and Heaven. To be dead to sin, is to feel a disgust at it. We know what is meant by disgust. Take, for instance, the case of a sick man, when food of a certain kind is presented to him,—and there is no doubt what is meant by disgust. Consider how certain scents, which are too sweet or too strong, or certain tastes, affect certain persons under certain circumstances, or always,—and you will be at no loss to determine what is meant by disgust at sin, or deadness to sin. On the other hand, consider how pleasant a meal is to the hungry, or some enlivening odour to the faint; how refreshing the air is to the languid, or the brook to the weary and thirsty;—and you will understand the sort of feeling which is implied in being alive with Christ, alive to religion, alive to the thought of heaven. Our animal powers cannot exist in all atmospheres; certain airs are poisonous, others life-giving. So is it with spirits and souls: an unrenewed spirit could not live in heaven, he would die; an Angel could not live in hell. The natural man cannot live in heavenly company, and the angelic soul would pine and waste away in the company of sinners, unless God's sacred presence were continued to it. To be dead to sin, is to be so minded, that the atmosphere of sin (if I may so speak) oppresses, distresses, and stifles us,—that it is painful and unnatural to us to remain in it. To be alive with Christ, is to be so minded, that the atmosphere of heaven refreshes, enlivens, stimulates, invigorates us. To be alive, is not merely to bear the thought of religion, to assent to the truth of religion, to wish to be religious; but to be drawn towards it, to love it, to delight in it, to obey it. Now I suppose most persons called Christians do not go farther than this,—to wish to be religious, and to think it right to be religious, and to feel a respect for religious men; they do not get so far as to have any sort of love for religion.

So far, however, they do go; not, indeed, to do their duty and to love it, but to have a sort of wish that they did. I suppose there are few persons but, at the very least, now and then feel the wish to be holy and religious. They bear witness to the excellence of virtuous and holy living, they consent to all that their teachers tell them, what they hear in church, and read in religious books; but all this is a very different thing from acting according to their knowledge. They confess one thing, they do another.

Nay, they confess one thing *while* they do another. Even sinners,—wilful, abandoned sinners,—if they would be honest enough to speak as they really in their hearts feel, would own, while they are indulging in the pleasures of sin, while they idle away the Lord's Day, or while they keep bad company, or while they lie or cheat, or while they drink to excess, or do any other bad thing,—they would confess, I say, did they speak their minds, that it is a far happier thing, even at present, to live in obedience to God, than in obedience to Satan. Not that sin has not its pleasures, such as they are; I do not mean, of course, to deny that,—I do not deny that Satan is able to give us something in exchange for future and eternal happiness; I do not say that irreligious men do not gain pleasures, which religious men are obliged to lose. I know they do; if they did not, there would be nothing to tempt and try us. But, after all, the pleasures which the servants of Satan enjoy, though pleasant, are always attended with pain too; with a bitterness, which, though it does not destroy the pleasure, yet is by itself sufficient to make it far less pleasant, even while it lasts, than such pleasures as are without such bitterness, viz. the pleasures of religion. This, then, alas! is the state of multitudes; not to be dead to sin and alive to God, but, while they are alive to sin and the world, to have just so much sense of heaven, as not to be able to enjoy either.

I say, when any one, man or woman, young or old, is conscious that he or she is going wrong, whether in greater matter or less, whether in not coming to church when there is no good excuse, neglecting private prayer, living carelessly, or indulging in known sin,—this bad conscience is from time to time a torment to such persons. For a little while, perhaps, they do not feel it, but then the pain comes on again. It is a keen, harassing, disquieting, hateful pain, which hinders sinners from being happy. They *may* have pleasures, but they cannot be *happy*. They know that God is angry with them; and they know that, at

some time or other, He will visit, He will judge, He will punish.
They try to get this out of their minds, but the arrow sticks fast
there; it keeps its hold. They try to laugh it off or to be bold and
daring, or to be angry and violent. They are loud or unkind in
their answers to those, who remind them of it either in set
words, or by their example. But it keeps its hold. And so it is,
that all men who are not very abandoned, bad men as well as
good, wish that they were holy as God is holy, pure as Christ
was pure, even though they do not try to be, or pray to God to
make them, holy and pure; not that they *like* religion, but that
they know, they are convinced in their reason, they feel sure,
that religion alone is happiness.

Oh, what a dreadful state, to have our desires one way, and
our knowledge and conscience another; to have our life, our
breath and food, upon the earth, and our eyes upon Him who
died once and now liveth; to look upon Him who once was
pierced, yet not to rise with Him and live with Him; to feel that
a holy life is our only happiness, yet to have no heart to pursue
it; to be certain that the wages of sin is death, yet to practise sin;
to confess that the Angels alone are perfectly happy, for they do
God's will perfectly, yet to prepare ourselves for nothing else
but the company of devils; to acknowledge that Christ is our
only hope, yet deliberately to let that hope go! O miserable
state! miserable they, if any there are who now hear me, who
are thus circumstanced!

At first sight, it might seem impossible that any such persons
could be found in church. At first sight, one might be tempted
to say, "All who come to church, at least, are in earnest, and
have given up sin; they are imperfect indeed, as all Christians
are at best, but they do not fall into wilful sin." I should be very
glad, my Brethren, to believe this were the case, but I cannot
indulge so pleasant a hope. No; I think it quite certain that
some persons at least, I do not say how many, to whom I am
speaking, have not made up their minds fully to lead a religious
life. They come to church because they think it right, or from
other cause. It is very right that they should come; I am glad
they do. This is good, as far as it goes; but it is not all. They are
not so far advanced in the kingdom of God, as to resist the devil,
or to flee from him. They cannot command themselves. They
act rightly one day, and wrongly the next. They are afraid of
being laughed at. They are attracted by bad company. They put
off religion to a future day. They think a religious life dull and
unpleasant. Yet they have a certain sense of religion; and they
come to church in order to satisfy this sense. Now, I say it is

right to come to church; but, O that they could be persuaded of the simple truth of St. Paul's words, "He is not a Jew which is one outwardly; but he is a Jew which is one inwardly; and circumcision is that of the heart in the spirit, and not in the letter, whose praise is not of men, but of God;"[1] which may be taken to mean:—He is not a Christian who is one outwardly, who merely comes to church, and professes to desire to be saved by Christ. It is very right that he should do so, but it is not enough. He is not a Christian who merely has not cast off religion; but he is the true Christian, who, while he is a Christian outwardly, is one inwardly also; who lives to God; whose secret life is hid with Christ in God; whose heart is religious; who not only knows and feels that a religious life is true happiness, but loves religion, wishes, tries, prays to be religious, begs God Almighty to give him the will and the power to be religious; and as time goes on, grows more and more religious, more fit for heaven.

We can do nothing right, unless God gives us the will and the power; we cannot please Him without the aid of His Holy Spirit. If any one does not deeply feel this as a first truth in religion, he is preparing for himself a dreadful fall. He will attempt, and he will fail signally, utterly. His own miserable experience will make him sure of it, if he will not believe it, as Scripture declares it. But it is not unlikely that some persons, perhaps some who now hear me, may fall into an opposite mistake. They may attempt to excuse their lukewarmness and sinfulness, on the plea that God does not inwardly move them; and they may argue that those holy men whom they so much admire, those saints who are to sit on Christ's right and left, are of different nature from themselves, sanctified from their mother's womb, visited, guarded, renewed, strengthened, enlightened in a peculiar way, so as to make it no wonder that they *are* saints, and no fault that they themselves are not. But this is not so; let us not thus miserably deceive ourselves. St. Paul says expressly of himself and the other Apostles, that they were "men of like passions" with the poor ignorant heathen to whom they preached. And does not his history show this? Do you not recollect what he was before his conversion? Did he not rage like a beast of prey against the disciples of Christ? and how was he converted? by the vision of our Lord? Yes, in one sense, but not by it alone; hear his own words, "Whereupon, O King Agrippa, I was not *disobedient* unto the heavenly vision." His obedience was necessary for his conversion; he could not obey

[1] Rom. ii.28, 29.

without grace; but he would have received grace in vain, had he not obeyed. And, afterwards, was he at once perfect? No; for he says expressly, "not as though I had already attained, either were already perfect;" and elsewhere he tells us that he had a "thorn in the flesh, the messenger of Satan to buffet him;" and he was obliged to "bruise his body and bring it into subjection, lest, after he had preached to others, he should be himself a castaway." St. Paul conquered, as any one of us must conquer, by "striving," struggling, "to enter in at the strait gate;" he "wrought out his salvation with fear and trembling," as we must do.

This is a point which must be insisted on for the encouragement of the fearful, the confutation of the hypocritical, and the abasement of the holy. In this world, even the best of men, though they are dead to sin, and have put sin to death, yet have that dead and corrupt thing within them, though they live to God; they have still an enemy of God remaining in their hearts, though they keep it in subjection. This, indeed, is what all men now have in common, a root of evil in them, a principle of sin, or what may become such;—what they differ in is this, not that one man has it, another not; but that one lives in and to it, another not; one subdues it, another not. A holy man is by nature subject to sin equally with others; but he is holy because he subdues, tramples on, chains up, imprisons, puts out of the way this law of sin, and is ruled by religious and spiritual motives. Of Christ alone can it be said that He "did no sin, neither was guile found in His mouth." The prince of this world came and found nothing in Him. He had no root of sin in His heart; He was not born in Adam's sin. Far different are we. He was thus pure, because He was the Son of God, and born of a Virgin. But we are conceived in sin and shapen in iniquity. And since that which is born of the flesh, is flesh, we are sinful and corrupt because we are sinfully begotten of sinners. Even those then who in the end turn out to be saints and attain to life eternal, yet are not born saints, but have with God's regenerating and renewing grace to make themselves saints. It is nothing but the Cross of Christ, without us and within us, which changes any one of us from being (as I may say) a devil, into an Angel. We are all by birth children of wrath. We are at best like good olive trees, which have become good by being grafted on a good tree. By nature we are like wild trees, bearing sour and bitter fruit, and so we should remain, were we not grafted upon Christ, the good olive tree, made members of Christ, the righteous and holy and well-beloved Son of God. Hence it is that there is such a change in a saint of God from what he was at the first. Consider what a different man St. Paul was after his conversion and before,—raging, as I just now said, like some wild beast, with persecuting fury against the Church, before Christ appeared to him, and meekly suffering persecution and glorying in it afterwards. Think of St. Peter denying Christ before the resurrection, and confessing, suffering, and dying for Him afterwards. And so now many an aged saint, who has good hope of heaven, may recollect things of himself when young, which fill him with dismay. I do not speak as if God's saints led vicious and immoral lives when young; but I mean that their lower and evil nature was not subdued, and perhaps from time to time broke out and betrayed them into deeds and words so very different from what is seen in them at present, that did their friends know of them what they themselves know, they would not think them the same persons, and would be quite overpowered with astonishment. We never can guess what a man is by nature, by seeing what self-discipline has made him. Yet if we do become thereby changed and prepared for heaven, it is no praise or merit to us. It is God's doing—glory be to Him, who has wrought so wonderfully with us! Yet in this life, even to the end, there will be enough evil in us to humble us; even to the end, the holiest men have remains and stains of sin which they would fain get rid of, if they could, and which keep this life from being to them, for all God's grace, a heaven upon earth. No, the Christian life is but a shadow of heaven. Its festal and holy days are but shadows of eternity. But hereafter it will be otherwise. In heaven, sin will be utterly destroyed in every elect soul. We shall have no earthly wishes, no tendencies to disobedience or irreligion, no love of the world or the flesh, to draw us off from supreme devotion to God. We shall have our Saviour's holiness fulfilled in us, and be able to love God without drawback or infirmity.

That indeed will be a full reward of all our longings here, to praise and serve God eternally with a single and perfect heart in the midst of His Temple. What a time will that be, when all will be perfected in us which at present is but feebly begun! Then we shall see how the Angels worship God. We shall see the calmness, the intenseness, the purity, of their worship. We shall see that awful sight, the Throne of God, and the Seraphim before and around it, crying, "Holy!" We attempt now to imitate in church what there is performed, as in the beginning, and ever shall be. In the Te Deum, day by day we say, "Holy, Holy, Holy, Lord God of Sabaoth." In the Creed, we recount God's mercies to us sinners. And we say and sing Psalms and Hymns, to come as near heaven as we can. May these attempts of ours be blest by Almighty God, to prepare us for Him! may they be, not dead forms, but living services, living with life from God the Holy Ghost, in those who are dead to sin and who live with Christ! I dare say some of you have heard persons, who dissent from the Church, say (at any rate, they do say), that our Prayers and Services, and Holy days, are only forms, dead forms, which can do us no good. Yes, they are dead forms to those who are dead, but they are living forms to those who are living. If you come here in a dead way, not in faith, not coming for a blessing, without your hearts being in the service, you will get no benefit from it. But if you come in a living way, in faith, and hope, and reverence, and with holy expectant hearts, then all that takes place will be a living service and full of heaven.

Make use, then, of this Holy Easter Season, which lasts forty to fifty days, to become more like Him who died for you, and who now liveth for evermore. He promises us, "Because I live, ye shall live also." He, by dying on the Cross, opened the Kingdom of Heaven to all believers. He first died, and then He opened heaven. We, therefore, first commemorate His death, and then, for some weeks in succession, we commemorate and show forth the joys of heaven. They who do not rejoice in the weeks after Easter, would not rejoice in heaven itself. These weeks are a sort of beginning of heaven. Pray God to enable you to rejoice; to enable you to keep the Feast duly. Pray God to make you better Christians. This world is a dream,—you will get no good from it. Perhaps you find this difficult to believe; but be sure so it is. Depend upon it, at the last, you will confess it. Young people expect good from the world, and people of middle age devote themselves to it, and even old people do not like to give it up. But the world is your enemy, and the flesh is your enemy. Come to God, and beg of Him grace to devote yourselves to Him. Beg of Him the will to follow Him; beg of Him the power to obey Him. O how comfortable, pleasant, sweet, soothing, and satisfying is it to lead a holy life,—the life of Angels! It is difficult at first; but with God's grace, all things are possible. O how pleasant to have done with sin! how good and joyful to flee temptation and to resist evil! how meet and worthy, and fitting, and right, to die unto sin, and to live unto righteousness!

RELIGION PLEASANT
TO THE RELIGIOUS

*"O taste and see how gracious the Lord is: blessed is the man
that trusteth in Him."*—Ps. xxxiv.8.

YOU see by these words what love Almighty God has towards
us, and what claims He has upon our love. He is the Most
High, and All-Holy. He inhabiteth eternity: we are but worms
compared with Him. He would not be less happy though He
had never created us; He would not be less happy though we
were all blotted out again from creation. But He is the God of
love; He brought us all into existence, because He found satisfaction in surrounding Himself with happy creatures: He made
us innocent, holy, upright, and happy. And when Adam fell
into sin and his descendants after him, then ever since He has
been imploring us to return to Him, the Source of all good, by
true repentance. "Turn ye, turn ye," He says, "why will ye die?
As I live I have no pleasure in the death of the wicked." "What
could have been done more to My vineyard that I have not done
to it?"[1] And in the text He condescends to invite us to Him: "O
taste and see how gracious the Lord is: blessed is the man that
trusteth in Him." As if He said, "If you would but make trial,
one trial, if you would but be persuaded to taste and judge for
yourself, so excellent is His graciousness, that you would never
cease to desire, never cease to approach Him:" according to the
saying of the wise man, "They that eat Me shall yet be hungry,
and they that drink Me shall yet be thirsty."[2]

This excellence and desirableness of God's gifts is a subject
again and again set before us in Holy Scripture. Thus the
Prophet Isaiah speaks of the "feast of fat things, a feast of wines
on the lees; of fat things full of marrow, of wines on the lees
well refined."[3] And again, under images of another kind: "He
hath sent Me . . . to give . . . beauty for ashes, the oil of joy for
mourning, the garment of praise for the spirit of heaviness, that

---

[1] Ezek. xxxiii.11; Is. v.4.　　[2] Ecclus. xxiv.21.　　[3] Is. xxv.6.

they may be called Trees of Righteousness."[4] Or again, the
Prophet Hosea: "I will be as the dew unto Israel: he shall grow
as the lily, and cast forth his roots as Lebanon. His branches
shall spread, and his beauty shall be as the olive-tree, and his
smell as Lebanon. They that dwell under his shadow shall return; they shall revive as the corn, and grow as the vine: the
scent thereof shall be as the wine of Lebanon."[5] And the Psalmist: "O that My people would have hearkened unto Me . . . . the
haters of the Lord should have been found liars, but their time
should have endured for ever. He should have fed them also
with the finest wheat flour, and with honey out of the stony
rock should I have satisfied thee."[6] You see all images of what is
pleasant and sweet in nature are brought together to describe
the pleasantness and sweetness of the gifts which God gives us
in grace. As wine enlivens, and bread strengthens, and oil is
rich, and honey is sweet, and flowers are fragrant, and dew is
refreshing, and foliage is beautiful; so, and much more, are
God's gifts in the Gospel enlivening, and strengthening, and
rich, and sweet, and fragrant, and refreshing, and excellent.
And as it is natural to feel satisfaction and comfort in these gifts
of the visible world, so it is but natural and necessary to be delighted and transported with the gifts of the world invisible;
and as the visible gifts are objects of desire and search, so much
more is it, I do not merely say a duty, but a privilege and blessedness to "taste and see how gracious the Lord is."

Other passages in the Psalms speak of this blessedness, besides
the text. "Thou hast put gladness in my heart," says the Psalmist, "since the time that their corn and wine and oil increased."[7]
"The lot is fallen unto me in a fair ground, yea, I have a goodly
heritage."[8] Again, "The statutes of the Lord are right, and rejoice the heart, . . . more to be desired are they than gold, yea,
than much fine gold, sweeter also than honey and the honeycomb."[9] "My heart trusted in Him, and I am helped; therefore
my heart danceth for joy, and in my song will I praise Him."[10]
Once more: "Blessed is the man whom Thou choosest and
receivest unto Thee: he shall dwell in Thy courts, and shall be
satisfied with the pleasures of Thy house, even of Thy holy
temple."[11]

I wish it were possible, my brethren, to lead men to greater
holiness and more faithful obedience by setting before them the
high and abundant joys which they have who serve God: "In

[4] Is. lxi.1–3. [5] Hos. xiv.5–7. [6] Ps. lxxxi.13–16.
[7] Ps. iv.7. [8] Ps. xvi.6. [9] Ps. xix.10.
[10] Ps. xxviii.7. [11] Ps. lxv.4.

His presence is fulness of joy," "the well of life;" and they are satisfied with "the plenteousness of His house," and "drink of His pleasures as out of a river;" but this is, I know, just what most persons will not believe. They think that it is very right and proper to be religious; they think that it would be better for themselves in the world to come if they were religious now. They do not at all deny either the duty or the expedience of leading a new and holy life; but they cannot understand how it can be pleasant: they cannot believe or admit that it is more pleasant than a life of liberty, laxity, and enjoyment. They, as it were, say, "Keep within bounds, speak within probability, and we will believe you; but do not shock our reason. We will admit that we *ought* to be religious, and that, when we come to die, we shall be very glad to have led religious lives: but to tell us that it is a *pleasant* thing to be religious, this is too much: it is not true; we feel that it is not true; all the world knows and feels it is not true; religion is something unpleasant, gloomy, sad, and troublesome. It imposes a number of restraints on us; it keeps us from doing what we would; it will not let us have our own way; it abridges our liberty; it interferes with our enjoyments; it has fewer, far fewer, joys at present than a worldly life, though it gains for us more joys hereafter." This is what men say, or would say, if they understood what they feel, and spoke their minds freely.

Alas! I cannot deny that this *is* true in the case of most men. Most men do not like the service of God, though it be perfect freedom; they like to follow their own ways, and they are only religious so far as their conscience obliges them; they are like Balaam, desirous of "the death of the righteous," not of his life. Indeed, this is the very thing I am lamenting and deploring. I lament, my brethren, that so many men, nay, I may say, that so many of you, do *not* like religious service. I do not deny it; but I lament it. I do not deny it: far from it. I know quite well how many there are who do not like coming to Church, and who make excuses for keeping away at times when they might come. I know how many there are who do not come to the Most Holy Sacrament. I know that there are numbers who do not say their prayers in private morning and evening. I know how many there are who are ashamed to be thought religious, who take God's name in vain, and live like the world. Alas! this is the very thing I lament,—that God's service is not pleasant to you. It is not pleasant to those who do not like it: true; but it *is* pleasant to those who *do*. Observe, this is what I say; not that it is pleasant to those who like it not, but that it is pleasant to those who like it. Nay, what I say is, that it is much *more* pleasant to those who like it, than any thing of this world is pleasant to those who do not like it. This is the point. I do not say that it is pleasant to most men; but I say that it is in itself the most pleasant thing in the world. Nothing is so pleasant as God's service to those *to whom* it is pleasant. The pleasures of sin are not to be compared in fulness and intensity to the pleasures of holy living. The pleasures of holiness are far more pleasant to the holy, than the pleasures of sin to the sinner. O that I could get you to believe this! O that you had a heart to feel it and know it! O that you had a heart to taste God's pleasures and to make proof of them; to taste and see how gracious the Lord is!

None can know, however, the joys of being holy and pure but the holy. If an Angel were to come down from heaven, even he could not explain them to you; nor could he in turn understand what the pleasures of sin are. Do you think that an Angel could be made to understand what are the pleasures of sin? I trow not. You might as well attempt to persuade him that there was pleasure in feasting on dust and ashes. There are brute animals who wallow in the mire and eat corruption. This seems strange to us: much stranger to an Angel is it how any one can take pleasure in any thing so filthy, so odious, so loathsome as sin. Many men, as I have been saying, wonder what possible pleasure there can be in any thing so melancholy as religion. Well: be sure of this,—it is *more* wonderful to an Angel, what possible pleasure there can be in sinning. It is *more* wonderful, I say. He would turn away with horror and disgust, both because sin is so base a thing in itself and because it is so hateful in God's sight.

Let no persons then be surprised that religious obedience should really be so pleasant in itself, when it seems to them so distasteful. Let them not be surprised that *what* the pleasure is cannot be explained to *them*. It is a secret till they try to be religious. Men know what sin is, by experience. They do not know what holiness is; and they cannot obtain the knowledge of its secret pleasure, till they join themselves truly and heartily to Christ, and devote themselves to His service,—till they "taste," and thereby try. This pleasure is as hidden from them, as the pleasures of sin are hidden from the Angels. The Angels have never eaten the forbidden fruit, and their eyes are not open to know good and evil. And we *have* eaten the forbidden fruit,—at least Adam did, and we are his descendants,—and our eyes *are* open to know evil. And, alas! on the other hand, they have become blinded to good; they require opening to see, to know, to understand good. And till our eyes *are* opened spiritually, we *shall* ever think religion distasteful and unpleasant, and shall wonder how any one can like it. Such is our miserable state,—we are blind to the highest and truest glories, and dead to the most lively and wonderful of all pleasures;—and no one can describe them to us. None other than God the Holy Spirit can help us in this matter, by enlightening and changing our hearts. So it is; and yet I will say one thing, by way of suggesting to you how great and piercing the joys of religion are. Think of this. Is there any one who does not know how very painful the feeling of a bad conscience is? Do not you recollect, my Brethren, some time or other, having done something you knew to be wrong? and do you not remember afterwards what a piercing bitter feeling came on you? Is not the feeling of a bad conscience different from any other feeling, and more distressing than any other, till we have accustomed ourselves to it? Persons do accustom themselves and lose this feeling; but till we blunt our conscience, it is very painful. And why? It is the feeling of God's displeasure, and therefore it is so painful. Consider then: if God's displeasure is so distressing to us, must not God's approval and favour be just the reverse; like life from the dead, most exceedingly joyful and transporting? And this is what it is to be holy and religious. It is to have God's favour. And, as it is a great misery to be under God's wrath, so it is a great and wonderful joy to be in God's favour; and those who know what a misery the former is, may fancy, though they do not know, how high a blessing the latter is. From what you know, then, judge of what you do not know. From the miseries of guilt, which, alas! you have experienced, conjecture the blessedness of holiness and purity which you have not experienced. From the pain of a bad conscience, believe in the unspeakable joy and gladness of a good conscience.

I have been addressing those who do not know what religious peace and Divine pleasures are; but there are those present, I hope, who in a measure are not strangers to them. I know that none of us gain all the pleasure from God's service which it might afford us; still some of us, I hope, gain some pleasure. I hope there are some of those who hear me, who take a pleasure in coming to Church, in saying their prayers, in thinking of God, in singing Psalms, in blessing Him for the mercies of the Gospel, and in celebrating Christ's death and resurrection, as at this season of the year.[12] These persons have "tasted" and tried. I trust they find the taste so heavenly, that *they* will not need any

---

[12] Easter.

proof that religion is a pleasant thing; nay, more pleasant than any thing else, worth the following above all other things, and unpleasant only to those who are not religious.

Let such persons then think of this, that if a religious life is pleasant here, in spite of the old Adam interrupting the pleasure and defiling them, what a glorious day it will be, if it is granted to us hereafter to enter into the Kingdom of Heaven! None of us, even the holiest, can guess *how* happy we shall be; for St. John says, "We know not what we shall be;"[13] and St. Paul, "Now we see in a glass darkly, but then face to face." Yet in proportion to our present holiness and virtue, we have some faint ideas of what will then be our blessedness. And in Scripture various descriptions of heaven are given us, in order to arrest, encourage, and humble us. We are told that the Angels of God are very bright, and clad in white robes. The Saints and Martyrs too are clad in white robes, with palms in their hands; and they sing praises unto Him that sitteth upon the Throne, and to the Lamb. When our Lord was transfigured, He showed us what Heaven is. His raiment became white as snow, white and glistening. Again, at one time He appeared to St. John, and then, "His head and His hairs were white like wool, as white as snow; and His eyes were as a flame of fire; and His feet like unto fine brass, as if they burned in a furnace; and His countenance was as the sun shineth in his strength."[14] And what Christ is, such do His Saints become hereafter. Here below they are clad in a garment of sinful flesh; but when the end comes, and they rise from the grave, they shall inherit glory, and shall be ever young and ever shining. In that day, all men will see and be convinced, even bad men, that God's servants are really happy, and only they. In that day, even lost souls, though they will not be able to understand the blessedness of religion, will have no doubt at all of what they now doubt, or pretend to doubt, that religion *is* blessed. They laugh at religion, think strictness to be narrowness of mind, and regularity to be dulness; and give bad names to religious men. They will not be able to do so then. They think themselves the great men of the earth now, and look down upon the religious; but then, who would not have been a religious man, to have so great a reward? who will then have any heart to speak against religion, even though he has not "a heart to fear God and keep all His commandments always?" In that day, they will look upon the righteous man, and "be amazed at the strangeness of his salvation, so far beyond all that

[13] 1 John iii.2.　　　　[14] Rev. i.14–16.

they looked for. And they, repenting and groaning for anguish of spirit, shall say within themselves, This was he, whom we had sometimes in derision, and a proverb of reproach. We fools accounted his life madness, and his end to be without honour; how is he numbered among the children of God, and his lot is among the saints!" [15]

Think of all this, my Brethren, and rouse yourselves, and run forward with a good courage on your way towards heaven. Be not weary in well-doing, for in due season we shall reap, if we faint not. Strive to enter in at the strait gate. Strive to get holier and holier every day, that you may be worthy to stand before the Son of Man. Pray God to teach you His will, and to lead you forth in the right way, because of your enemies. Submit yourselves to His guidance, and you will have comfort given you, according to your day, and peace at the last.

[15] Wisd. v.2–5.

MENTAL PRAYER

"Pray without ceasing."—1 Thess. v. 17.

THERE are two modes of praying mentioned in Scripture; the one is prayer at set times and places, and in set forms; the other is what the text speaks of,—continual or habitual prayer. The former of these is what is commonly called prayer, whether it be public or private. The other kind of praying may also be called holding communion with God, or living in God's sight, and this may be done all through the day, wherever we are, and is commanded us as the duty, or rather the characteristic, of those who are really servants and friends of Jesus Christ.

These two kinds of praying are also natural duties. I mean, we should in a way be bound to attend to them, even if we were born in a heathen country and had never heard of the Bible. For our conscience and reason would lead us to practise them, if we did but attend to these divinely-given informants. I shall here confine myself to the consideration of the latter of the two, habitual or inward prayer, which is enjoined in the text, with the view of showing what it is, and how we are to practise it; and I shall speak of it, first, as a natural duty, and then as the characteristic of a Christian.

1. At first sight, it may be difficult to some persons to understand what is meant by praying always. Now consider it as a natural duty, that is, a duty taught us by natural reason and religious feeling, and you will soon see what it consists in.

What does nature teach us about ourselves, even before opening the Bible?—that we are creatures of the Great God, the Maker of heaven and earth; and that, as His creatures, we are bound to serve Him and give Him our hearts; in a word, to be religious beings. And next, what is religion but a habit? and what is a habit but a state of mind which is always upon us, as a sort of ordinary dress or inseparable garment of the soul? A man cannot really be religious one hour, and not religious the next. We might as well say he could be in a state of good health one hour, and in bad health the next. A man who is religious, is religious morning, noon, and night; his religion is a certain character, a mould in which his thoughts, words, and actions are cast, all forming parts of one and the same whole. He sees God in all things; every course of action he directs towards those spiritual objects which God has revealed to him; every occurrence of the day, every event, every person met with, all news which he hears, he measures by the standard of God's will. And a person who does this may be said almost literally to pray without ceasing; for, knowing himself to be in God's presence, he is continually led to address Him reverently, whom he sets always before him, in the inward language of prayer and praise, of humble confession and joyful trust.

All this, I say, any thoughtful man acknowledges from mere natural reason. To be religious is, in other words, to have the habit of prayer, or to pray always. This is what Scripture means by doing all things to God's glory; that is, so placing God's presence and will before us, and so consistently acting with a reference to Him, that all we do becomes one body and course of obedience, witnessing without ceasing to Him who made us, and whose servants we are; and in its separate parts promoting more or less directly His glory, according as each particular thing we happen to be doing admits more or less of a religious character. Thus religious obedience is, as it were, a spirit dwelling in us, extending its influence to every motion of the soul; and just as healthy men and strong men show their health and strength in all they do (not indeed equally in all things, but in some things more than in others, because all ac- tions do not require or betoken the presence of that health and strength, and yet even in their step, and their voice, and their gestures, and their countenance, showing in due measure their vigour of body), so they who have the true health and strength of the soul, a clear, sober, and deep faith in Him in whom they have their being, will in all they do, nay (as St. Paul says), even whether they "eat or drink,"[1] be living in God's sight, or, in the words of the same Apostle in the text, live in ceaseless prayer.

If it be said that no man on earth does thus continually and perfectly glorify and worship God, this we all know too well; this is only saying that none of us has reached perfection. We know, alas! that in many things all of us offend. But I am speak- ing not of what we *do*, but of what we *ought to do*, and must aim at doing,—of *our duty*; and, for the sake of impressing our duty on our hearts, it is of use to draw the picture of a man perfectly

[1] I Cor. x.31.

obedient, as a pattern for us to aim at. In proportion as we grow in grace and in the knowledge of our Saviour, so shall we approximate to Him in obedience, who is our great example, and who alone of all the sons of Adam lived in the perfection of unceasing prayer.

Thus the meaning and reasonableness of the command in the text is shown by considering it as a natural duty, religion being no accident which comes and goes by fits and starts, but a certain spirit or life.

2. Now, secondly, I will state all this in the language of Scripture; that is, I will confirm this view of our duty, which natural reason might suggest, by that other and far clearer voice of God, His inspired word.

How is religious obedience described in Scripture? Surely as a certain kind of life. We know what life of the body is; it is a state of the body: the pulse beats; all things are in motion. The hidden principle of life, though we know not how or what it is, is seen in these outward signs of it. And so of the life of the soul. The soul, indeed, was not possessed of this life of God when first born into the world. We are born with dead souls; that is, dead as regards religious obedience. If left to ourselves we should grow up haters of God, and tend nearer and nearer, the longer we had existence, to utter spiritual death, that inward fire of hell torments, maturing in evil through a long eternity. Such is the course we are beginning to run when born into the world; and were it not for the gospel promise, what a miserable event would the birth of children be! Who could take pleasure at the sight of such poor beings, unconscious as yet of their wretchedness, but containing in their hearts that fearful root of sin which is sure in the event of reigning and triumphing unto everlasting woe? But God has given us all, even the little children, a good promise through Christ; and our prospects are changed. And He has given not only a promise of future happiness, but through His Holy Spirit He implants here and at once a new principle within us, a new spiritual life, a life of the soul, as it is called. St. Paul tells us, that "God hath quickened us," made us *live*, "together with Christ, . . . and hath raised us up together" from the death of sin, "and made us sit together in heavenly places in Christ Jesus."[2] Now how God quickens our souls we do not know; as little as how He quickens our bodies. Our spiritual "life" (as St. Paul says) "is *hid* with Christ in God."[3] But as our bodily life discovers itself by its activity, so is

---

[2] Eph. ii. 5, 6.   [3] Col. iii. 3.

the presence of the Holy Spirit in us discovered by a spiritual activity; and this activity is the spirit of continual prayer. Prayer is to spiritual life what the beating of the pulse and the drawing of the breath are to the life of the body. It would be as absurd to suppose that life could last when the body was cold and motionless and senseless, as to call a soul alive which does not pray. The state or habit of spiritual life exerts itself, consists, in the continual activity of prayer.

Do you ask, where does Scripture say this? Where? In all it tells us of the connexion between the new birth and faith; for what is prayer but the expression, the voice, of faith? For instance, St. Paul says to the Galatians, "The *life* which I now live in the flesh" (i.e. the new and spiritual life), "I live by the *faith* of the Son of God, who loved me." [4] For what, I say, is faith, but the looking to God and thinking of Him continually, holding habitual fellowship with Him, that is, speaking to Him in our hearts all through the day, praying without ceasing? Afterwards, in the same Epistle, he tells us first that nothing avails but faith working by love; but soon after, he calls this same availing principle a new creature: so that the new birth and a living faith are inseparable. Never, indeed, must it be supposed, as we are indolently apt to suppose, that the gift of grace which we receive at baptism is a mere outward privilege, a mere outward pardon, in which the heart is not concerned; or as if it were some mere mark put on the soul, distinguishing it indeed from souls unregenerate, as if by a colour or seal, but not connected with the thoughts, mind, and heart of a Christian. This would be a gross and false view of the nature of God's mercy given us in Christ. For the new birth of the Holy Spirit sets the soul in motion in a heavenly way: it gives us good thoughts and desires, enlightens and purifies us, and prompts us to seek God. In a word (as I have said), it gives a spiritual *life*; it opens the eyes of our mind, so that we begin to see God in all things by faith, and hold continual intercourse with Him by prayer; and if we cherish these gracious influences, we shall become holier and wiser and more heavenly, year by year, our hearts being ever in a course of change from darkness to light, from the ways and works of Satan to the perfection of Divine obedience.

These considerations may serve to impress upon our minds the meaning of the precept in the text, and others like it which are found in St. Paul's Epistles. For instance, he enjoins the Ephesians to "pray always with all prayer and supplication in

[4] Gal. ii.20.

the Spirit." To the Philippians he says, "Be careful for nothing; but in every thing by prayer and supplication let your requests be made known unto God." [5] To the Colossians, "Continue in prayer, and watch in the same with thanksgiving." To the Romans, "Continue instant in prayer." [6]

Thus the true Christian pierces through the veil of this world and sees the next. He holds intercourse with it; he addresses God, as a child might address his parent, with as clear a view of Him, and with as unmixed a confidence in Him; with deep reverence indeed, and godly fear and awe, but still with certainty and exactness: as St. Paul says, "I know whom I have believed," [7] with the prospect of judgment to come to sober him, and the assurance of present grace to cheer him.

If what I have said is true, surely it is well worth thinking about. Most men indeed, I fear, neither pray at fixed times, nor do they cultivate an habitual communion with Almighty God. Indeed, it is too plain how most men pray. They pray now and then, when they feel particular need of God's assistance; when they are in trouble or in apprehension of danger; or when their feelings are unusually excited. They do not know what it is either to be habitually religious, or to devote a certain number of minutes at fixed times to the thought of God. Nay, the very best Christian, how lamentably deficient is he in the spirit of prayer! Let any man compare in his mind how many times he has prayed when in trouble, with how seldom he has returned thanks when his prayers have been granted; or the earnestness with which he prays against expected suffering, with the languor and unconcern of his thanksgivings afterwards, and he will soon see how little he has of the real habit of prayer, and how much his religion depends on accidental excitement, which is no test of a religious heart. Or supposing he has to repeat the same prayer for a month or two, the cause of using it continuing, let him compare the earnestness with which he first said it, and tried to enter into it, with the coldness with which he at length uses it. Why is this, except that his perception of the unseen world is not the true view which faith gives (else it would last as that world itself lasts), but a mere dream, which endures for a night, and is succeeded by a hard worldly joy in the morning? Is God habitually in our thoughts? Do we think of Him, and of His Son our Saviour, through the day? When we eat and drink, do we thank Him, not as a mere matter of form, but in spirit? When we do things in themselves right, do

[5] Eph. vi.18; Phil. iv.6.   [6] Col. iv.2; Rom. xii.12.   [7] 2 Tim. i.12.

we lift up our minds to Him, and desire to promote His glory? When we are in the exercise of our callings, do we still think of Him, acting ever conscientiously, desiring to know His will more exactly than we do at present, and aiming at fulfilling it more completely and abundantly? Do we wait on His grace to enlighten, renew, strengthen us?

I do not ask whether we use many words about religion. There is no need to do this: nay, we should avoid a boastful display of our better feelings and practices, silently serving God without human praise, and hiding our conscientiousness except when it would dishonour God to do so. There are times, indeed, when, in the presence of a holy man, to confess is a benefit, and there are times when, in the presence of worldly men, to confess becomes a duty; but these seasons, whether of privilege or of duty, are comparatively rare. But we are always with ourselves and our God; and that silent inward confession in His presence may be sustained and continual, and will end in durable fruit.

But if those persons come short of their duty who make religion a matter of impulse and mere feeling, what shall be said to those who have no feeling or thought of religion at all? What shall be said of the multitude of young people who ridicule seriousness, and deliberately give themselves up to vain thoughts? Alas! my brethren, you do not even observe or recognize the foolish empty thoughts which pass through your minds; you are not distressed even at those of them you recollect; but what will you say at the last day, when, instead of the true and holy visions in which consists Divine communion, you find recorded against you in God's book an innumerable multitude of the idlest, silliest imaginings, nay, of the wickedest, which ever disgraced an immortal being? What will you say, when heaven and hell are before you, and the books are opened, and therein you find the sum total of your youthful desires and dreams, your passionate wishes for things of this world, your low-minded, grovelling tastes, your secret contempt and aversion for serious subjects and persons, your efforts to attract the looks of sinners and to please those who displease God; your hankerings after worldly gaieties and luxuries, your admiration of the rich or titled, your indulgence of impure thoughts, your self-conceit and pitiful vanity? Ah, I may seem to you to use harsh words; but be sure I do not use terms near so severe as you will use against yourselves in that day. Then those men, whom you now think gloomy and over-strict, will seem to you truly wise; and the advice to pray without ceasing, which once you laughed at as fit only for the dull, the formal, the sour, the poor-spirited, or the aged, will be approved by your own experience, as it is even now by your reason and conscience. Oh, that you could be brought to give one serious hour to religion, in anticipation of that long eternity where you *must* be serious! True, you may laugh now, but there is no vain merriment on the other side of the grave. The devils, though they repent not, tremble. *You* will be among those unwilling serious ones then, if you are mad enough to be gay and careless now; if you are mad enough to laugh, jest, and scoff your poor moment now on earth, which is short enough to prepare for eternity in, without your making it shorter by wasting your youth in sin. Could you but see who it is that suggests to you all your lighter thoughts, which you put instead of Divine communion, the shock would make you serious, even if it did not make you religious. Could you see, what God sees, those snares and pitfalls which the devil is placing about your path; could you see that all your idle thoughts which you cherish, which seem so bright and pleasant, so much pleasanter than religious thoughts, are inspired by that Ancient Seducer of Mankind, the Author of Evil, who stands at your side while you deride religion, serious indeed himself while he makes you laugh, not able to laugh at his own jests, while he carries you dancing forward to perdition,—doubtless you would tremble, even as he does while he tempts you. But this you cannot possibly see, you cannot break your delusion, except by first taking God's word in this matter on trust. You cannot see the unseen world at once. They who ever speak with God in their hearts, are in turn taught by Him in all knowledge; but they who refuse to act upon the light, which God gave them by nature, at length come to lose it altogether, and are given up to a reprobate mind.

May God save us all from such wilful sin, old as well as young, and enlighten us one and all in His saving knowledge, and give us the will and the power to serve Him!

INFANT BAPTISM

*"Except a man be born of water and of the Spirit, he cannot enter
into the Kingdom of God."*—John iii.5.

NONE can be saved, unless the blood of Christ, the Immaculate Lamb of God, be imputed to him; and it is His gracious will that it should be imputed to us, one by one, by means of outward and visible signs, or what are called Sacraments. These visible rites represent to us the heavenly truth, and convey what they represent. The baptismal washing betokens the cleansing of the soul from sin; the elements of bread and wine are figures of what is present but not seen, "the body and blood of Christ, which are verily and indeed taken and received by the faithful in the Lord's Supper." So far the two Sacraments agree; yet there is this important difference in their use,—that Baptism is but *once* administered, but the Lord's Supper is to be received *continually*. Our Lord Christ told the Apostles to baptize *at the time* that they made men His disciples. Baptism *admitted* them to His favour once for all; but the Lord's Supper *keeps* us and secures us in His favour day by day. He said, "This do, *as often as* ye drink it, in *remembrance* of Me."

Here, then, a question at once arises, which it is important to consider:—*At what time* in our life are we to be baptized, or made disciples of Christ? The first Christians of course were baptized when they were come to a full age, because then the Gospel was for the first time preached to them; they had no means of being baptized when young. But the case is different with those who are born of Christian parents; so the question now is, at what age are the sons of Christians to be baptized?

Now, for fifteen hundred years there was no dispute or difficulty in answering this question all over the Christian world; none who acknowledged the duty of baptizing at all, but administered the rite to infants, as we do at present. But about three hundred years ago strange opinions were set afloat, and sects arose, doing every thing which had not been done before, and undoing every thing that had been done before, and all this (as they professed) on the principle that it was every one's duty to judge and act for himself; and among these new sects there was one which maintained that Infant Baptism was a mistake, and that, mainly upon this short argument,—that it was nowhere commanded in Scripture.

Let us, then, consider this subject: and first, it is but fair and right to acknowledge at once that Scripture does *not* bid us baptize children. This, however, is no very serious admission; for Scripture does not name *any* time at all for Baptism; yet it orders us to be baptized at some age or other. It is plain, then, whatever age we fix upon, we shall be going beyond the letter of Scripture. This may or may not be a difficulty, but it cannot be avoided: it is not a difficulty of *our* making. God has so willed it. He has kept silence, and doubtless with good reason; and surely we must try to do our part and to find out what He would have us do, according to the light, be it greater or less, which He has vouchsafed to us.

Is it any new thing that it should take time and thought to find out accurately what our duty is? Is it a new thing that the full and perfect truth should not lie on the very surface of things, in the bare letter of Scripture? Far from it. Those who *strive* to enter into life, these alone find the strait gate which leads thereto. It is no proof even that it is a matter of indifference what age is proper for Baptism, that Scripture is not clear about it, but hides its real meaning; not commanding but hinting what we should do. For consider how many things in this life are difficult to attain, yet, far from being matters of indifference, are necessary for our comfort or even well-being. Nay, it often happens that the more valuable any gift is, the more difficult it is to gain it. Take, for instance, the art of medicine. Is there an art more important for our life and comfort? Yet how difficult and uncertain is the science of it! what time it takes to be well versed and practised in it! What would be thought of a person who considered that it mattered little whether a sick man took this course or that, on the ground that men were not physicians by nature, and that if the Creator had meant medicine to be for our good, He would have told us at once, and every one of us, the science and the practice of it? In the same way it does not at all follow, even if it *were* difficult to find out at what age Baptism should be administered, that therefore one time is as good as another. Difficulty is the very attendant upon great blessings, not on things indifferent.

But a man may say that Scripture is given us for the very purpose of making the knowledge of our duty easy to us;—what is meant by a revelation, if it does not reveal?—and that we have no revelation to tell us what medicines are good or bad for the body, but that a revelation *has* been made in order to tell us what is good or bad for the soul:—if, then, a thing *were* important for our soul's benefit, Scripture would have plainly declared it. I answer, who told us all this? Doubtless, Scripture *was* given to make our duty *easier than before*; but how do we know that it was intended to take away *all* difficulty of every kind? So says not Christ, when He bids us seek and strive and so find; to knock, to watch, and to pray. No; Scripture has not undertaken to *tell* us every thing, but merely to give us the means of *finding* every thing; and thus much we can conclude on the subject before us, that if it is important, there are *means* of determining it; but we cannot infer, either that it must actually be *commanded* in the letter of Scripture, or that it can be found out by every individual *for and by himself*.

But it may be said, Scripture says that the times of the Gospel shall be times of great light: "All thy children shall be taught of the Lord, and great shall be the peace of thy children."[1] This is true: but whose children? The Church's. Surely it *is* a time of light, if we come to the Church for information; for she has ever spoken most clearly on the subject. She has ever baptized infants and enjoined the practice; she has ever answered to the prophecy as being "a word behind us, saying, This is the way; walk ye in it." Her teachers surely (according to the prophecy) have never been removed into a corner. But if we will not accept this supernatural mercy, then I say it is not unnatural that we should find ourselves in the same kind of doubt in which we commonly are involved in matters of this world. God has promised us light and knowledge in the Gospel, but in His way, not in *our* way.

But after all, in the present instance, surely there is no great difficulty in finding out what God would have us to do, though He has not told us in Scripture in the plainest way. I say it is not difficult to see, as the Church has ever been led to see, that God would have us baptize young children, and that to delay Baptism is to delay a great benefit, and is hazarding a child's salvation. There is no difficulty, if men are not resolved to make one.

1. Let us consider, first, what is Baptism? It is a means and pledge of God's mercy, pardon, acceptance of us for Christ's sake; it gives us grace to change our natures. Now, surely infants, as being born in sin, have most abundant *need* of God's mercy and grace: this cannot be doubted. Even at first sight, then, it appears *desirable* (to say the least) that they should be

[1] Is. liv.13.

baptized. Baptism is just suited to their need: it contains a promise of the very blessings which they want, and which without God's free bounty they cannot have. If, indeed, Baptism were merely or principally *our* act, then perhaps the case would be altered. But it is not an act of ours so much as of God's; a pledge from Him. And, I repeat, infants, as being by nature under God's wrath, having no elements of spiritual life in them, being corrupt and sinful, are surely, in a singular manner, objects of Baptism as far as the question of desirableness is concerned.

Let us refer to our Saviour's words to Nicodemus in the text. Our Lord tells him none can enter into the kingdom of God who is not born of water and the Spirit. And why? *Because* (He goes on to say) "that which is born of the flesh is flesh." [2] We need a new birth, because our first birth is a birth unto sin. Who does not see that this reason is equally cogent for *infant* Baptism as for Baptism at all? Baptism by water and the Spirit is necessary for salvation (He says), *because* man's *nature* is corrupt; therefore infants must need this regeneration too. If, indeed, sin were not planted deep in man's very heart,—if it were merely an accidental evil into which some fell while others escaped it,—nay, even if, though (as a fact) all men actually fall into sin, yet this general depravity arose merely from bad example, not from natural bias, then indeed Baptism of water and the Spirit would not be necessary except for those who, having come to years of understanding, had actual sin to answer for: but if, as our Saviour implies, even a child's heart, before he begins to think and act, is under Divine wrath, and contains the sure and miserable promise of future sin as the child grows up, can we do otherwise than thankfully accept the pledge and means which He has given us of a new birth unto holiness; and since, by not telling us the time for Baptism, He has in a way left it to ourselves to decide upon it, shall we not apply the medicine given us when we are sure of the disease? "Can any man *forbid* water," to use St. Peter's words under different circumstances, "that" children "should not be baptized?" The burden of proof, as it is called, is with those who withhold the Sacrament.

Will it be said that infants are not properly *qualified* for Baptism? How is this an objection? Consider the text.—"Except one be born of water and the Spirit," says our Lord, "he cannot enter into the kingdom of God." There is nothing said about qualifications or conditions here which might exclude infants from Baptism,—nothing about the necessity of previous faith,

[2] John iii.6.

or previous good works, in order to fit us for the mercy of God. Nor indeed could any thing be said. Christ knew that, without His grace, man's nature could not bear any good fruit, for from above is every good gift. Far from it. Any such notion of man's unassisted strength is wholly detestable, contrary to the very first principles of all true religion, whether Jewish, Christian, or even Pagan. We are miserably fallen creatures, we are by nature corrupt,—we dare not talk even of children being naturally pleasing in God's sight. And if we wait till children are in a condition to bring something to God, in payment (so to say) of His mercy to them, till they have faith and repentance, they never will be baptized; for they will never attain to that condition. To defer Baptism till persons actually have repentance and faith, is refusing to give medicine till a patient begins to get well. It would be hard indeed, if Satan be allowed to have access to the soul from infancy, as soon as it begins to think, and we refuse to do what we can, or what promises well, towards gaining for it the protection of God against the Tempter.

On this first view of the case then, from the original corruption of our nature, from the need which all men are under from their birth of pardon and help from God, from Baptism being a promise of mercy just suited to our need, and from the impossibility of any one (let him be allowed to live unbaptized ever so long) bringing any self-provided recommendation of himself to God's favour; on all these accounts, I say, since God has given us no particular directions in the matter, but has left it to ourselves, it seems, on the first view of the case, most fitting and right to give children the privilege of Baptism.

2. But, in fact, we are not, strictly speaking, left without positive encouragement to bring infants near to Him. We are not merely left to infer generally the propriety of Infant Baptism; Christ has shown us His *willingness* to receive children. Some men have said (indeed most of us perhaps in seasons of unbelief have been tempted in our hearts to ask), "What good can Baptism do senseless children? you might as well baptize things without life; they sleep or even struggle during the ceremony, and interrupt it; it is a mere superstition." This, my brethren, is the language of the world, whoever uses it. It is putting sight against faith. If we are assured that Baptism has been blessed by Christ, as the rite of admittance into His Church, we have nothing to do with those outward appearances, which, though they might prove something perhaps, had He not spoken, now that He has spoken lose all force. To such objections, I would reply by citing our Saviour's "own word

and deed." We find that infants *were* brought to Christ; and His disciples seem to have doubted, in the same spirit of unbelief, what *could* be the good of bringing helpless and senseless children to the Saviour of men. They doubtless thought that His time would be better employed in teaching *them*, than in attending to children; that it was interfering with His usefulness. "But when Jesus saw it, He was much displeased." [3] These are remarkable words: "much displeased,"—that is, He was uneasy, indignant, angry (as the Greek word may be more literally translated) and we are told, "He took them up in His arms, put His hands upon them, and *blessed them*." Christ, then, *can* bless infants, in spite of their being to all appearance as yet incapable of thought or feeling. He can, and did, bless them; and, in the very sense in which they then were blessed, we believe they are capable of a blessing in Baptism.

3. And we may add this consideration. It is certain that children ought to be instructed in religious truth, as they can bear it, from the very first dawn of reason; clearly, they are not to be left without a Christian training till they arrive at years of maturity. Now, let it be observed, Christ seems distinctly to connect teaching with Baptism, as if He intended to convey through it a blessing upon teaching,—"Go ye and teach all the nations, baptizing them." If children, then, are to be considered as under teaching, as learners in the school of Christ, surely they should be admitted into that school by Baptism.

These are the reasons for Infant Baptism which strike the mind, even on the first consideration of the subject; and in the absence of express information from Scripture, they are (as far as they go) satisfactory. At *what age* should we be baptized? I answer, in childhood; because all children *require* Divine pardon and grace (as our Saviour Himself implies), all are *capable* of His blessing (as His action shows), all are *invited* to His blessing, and Baptism is a pledge from Him of His favour, as His Apostles frequently declare. Since infants are to be brought to Christ, we must have invented a rite, if Baptism did not answer the purpose of a dedication. Again, I say, in childhood; because all children need Christian instruction, and Baptism is a badge and mark of a scholar in Christ's school. And moreover, I will add, because St. Paul speaks of the children of Christian parents as being "holy," in a favoured state, a state of unmerited blessing; and because he seems to have baptized at once whole families, where the head of the family was converted to the faith of the Gospel. [4]

---

[3] Mark x.14.   [4] 1 Cor. vii.14; Acts xvi.15, 33.

To conclude. Let me beg of all who hear me, and who wish to serve God, to remember, in their ordinary prayers, their habitual thoughts, the daily business of life, that they were once baptized. If Baptism be merely a ceremony, to be observed indeed, but then at once forgotten,—a decent form, which it would neither be creditable, nor for temporal reasons expedient to neglect,—it is most surely no subject for a Christian minister to speak of; Christ's religion has no fellowship with bare forms, and nowhere encourages mere outward observances. If, indeed, there be any who degrade Baptism into a mere ceremony, which has in it no spiritual promise, let such men look to it for themselves, and defend their practice of baptizing infants as they can. But for me, my brethren, I would put it before you as a true and plain pledge, without reserve, of God's grace given to the souls of those who receive it; not a mere form, but a real means and instrument of blessing verily and indeed received; and, as being such, I warn you to remember what a talent has been committed to you. There are very many persons who do not think of Baptism in this religious point of view; who are in no sense in the habit of blessing God for it, and praying Him for His further grace to profit by the privileges given them in it; who, when even they pray for grace, do not ground their hope of being heard and answered, on the promise of blessing in Baptism made to them; above all, who do not fear to sin after Baptism. This is of course an omission: in many cases it is a *sin*. Let us set ourselves right in this respect. Nothing will remind us more forcibly both of our advantages and of our duties; for from the very nature of our minds outward signs are especially calculated (if rightly used) to strike, to affect, to subdue, to change them.

Blessed is he who makes the most of the privileges given him, who takes them for a light to his feet and a lanthorn to his path. We have had the Sign of the Cross set on us in infancy,—shall we ever forget it? It is our profession. We had the water poured on us,—it was like the blood on the door-posts, when the destroying Angel passed over. Let us fear to sin after grace given, lest a worse thing come upon us. Let us aim at learning these two great truths:—that we can do nothing good without God's grace, yet that we can sin against that grace; and thus that the great gift may be made the cause, on the one hand, of our gaining eternal life, and the occasion to us, on the other, of eternal misery.

THE UNITY OF THE CHURCH

*"And I say also unto thee, That thou art Peter, and upon this rock
I will build My Church; and the gates of hell shall not prevail
against it."*—Matt. xvi.18.

Too many persons at this day,—in spite of what they see
before them, in spite of what they read in history,—too
many persons forget, or deny, or do not know, that Christ has
set up a kingdom in the world. In spite of the prophecies, in
spite of the Gospels and Epistles, in spite of their eyes and their
ears,—whether it be their sin or their misfortune, so it is,—
they do not obey Him in that way in which it is His will that He
should be obeyed. They do not obey Him in His Kingdom; they
think to be His people, without being His subjects. They determine to serve Him in their own way; and though He has formed
His chosen into one body, they think to separate from that
body, yet to remain in the number of the chosen.

Far different is the doctrine suggested to us by the text. In St.
Peter, who is there made the rock on which the Church is
founded, we see, as in a type, its unity, stability, and permanence. It is set up in one name, not in many, to show that it is
one; and that name is Peter, to show that it will last, or, as the
Divine Speaker proceeds, that "the gates of hell shall not prevail against it." In like manner, St. Paul calls it "the pillar and
ground of the truth." [1]

This is a subject especially brought before us at this time of
year,[2] and it may be well now to enlarge upon it.

Now that all Christians are, in some sense or other, one, in
our Lord's eyes, is plain, from various parts of the New Testament. In His mediatorial prayer for them to the Almighty Father, before His passion, He expressed His purpose that they
should be *one*. St. Paul, in like manner, writing to the Corinthians, says, "As the body is one, and hath many members, and
all the members of that one body, being many, are one body, *so
also* is Christ. . . . . . Now ye are *the Body* of Christ, and mem-

---

[1] 1 Tim. iii.15.   [2] Easter and Whitsuntide.

bers in particular." To the Ephesians, he says, "There is *one Body*, and one Spirit, even as ye are called in one hope of your calling: one Lord, one faith, one baptism, one God and Father of all." [3]

And, further, it is to this one Body, regarded as one, that the special privileges of the Gospel are given. It is not that this man receives the blessing, and that man, but one and all, the whole body, as one man, one new spiritual man, with one accord, seeks and gains it. The Holy Church throughout the world, "the Bride, the Lamb's wife," is one, not many, and the elect souls are all elected in her, not in isolation. For instance; "He is our peace who hath made both [Jews and Gentiles] one, . . . to make in Himself of twain *one new man*." In the same Epistle, it is said, that all nations are "*fellow*-heirs, and of *the same body*, and *fellow-partakers* of His promise in Christ;" and that we must "one and all come," or converge, "in the unity of the faith and of the knowledge of the Son of God, unto a perfect man, unto the measure of the stature of the fulness of Christ;" that as "the husband is the head of the wife," *so* "Christ is the Head of the Church," having "loved it and given Himself for it, that He might sanctify and cleanse it with the washing of water by the Word." [4] These are a few out of many passages which connect Gospel privileges with the circumstance or condition of unity in those who receive them; the image of Christ and token of their acceptance being stamped upon them *then*, at that moment, when they are considered as *one*; so that henceforth the whole multitude, no longer viewed as mere individual men, become portions or members of the indivisible Body of Christ Mystical, so knit together in Him by Divine Grace, that all have what He has, and each has what all have.

The same great truth is taught us in such texts as speak of all Christians forming one spiritual building, of which the Jewish Temple was the type. They are temples one by one, simply as being portions of that one Temple which is the Church. "Ye are *built up*," says St. Peter, "a spiritual house, a holy priesthood, to offer spiritual sacrifices acceptable to God by Jesus Christ." Hence the word "edification," which properly means this building up of all Christians in one, has come to stand for individual improvement; for it is by being incorporated into the one Body, that we have the promise of life; by becoming members of Christ, we have the gift of His Spirit.

---

[3] John xvii.23; 1 Cor. xii.12; Eph. iv.4–6.
[4] Eph. ii.14; iii.6; iv.13; v.23–26.

Further, that unity is the condition of our receiving the privileges of the Gospel is confirmed by the mode in which the Prophets describe the Christian Church; that is, instead of addressing individuals as independent and separate from each other, they view the whole as of one body; viz. that one elect, holy, and highly-favoured Mother, of which individuals are but the children favoured through her as a channel. "Lift up thine eyes, and behold," says the inspired announcement; "all these gather themselves together, and come to thee." "O thou afflicted, tossed with tempest, and not comforted, behold, I will lay thy stones with fair colours, and lay thy foundations with sapphires. . . . . All thy children shall be taught of the Lord, and great shall be the peace of thy children."

But here it may be asked, How is this a doctrine to affect our practice? That Christians may be considered in our minds as one, is evident; it is evident, too, that they must be one in spirit; and that hereafter they will be one blessed company in heaven; but what follows now from believing that all saints are one in Christ? *This* will be found to follow: that, as far as may be, Christians should live together in a visible society here on earth, not as a confused unconnected multitude, but united and organized one with another, by an established order, so as evidently to appear and to act as one. And this, you will at once see, *is* a doctrine nearly affecting our practice, yet neglected far and wide at this day.

Any complete and accurate proof indeed of this doctrine shall not here be attempted; nay, I shall not even bring together, as is often done,[5] the more obvious texts on which it rests; let it suffice, on this occasion, to make one or two general remarks bearing upon it, and strongly recommending it to us.

1. When, then, I am asked, why we Christians must unite into a visible body or society, I answer, first, that the very earnestness with which Scripture insists upon a spiritual unseen unity at present, and a future unity in heaven, of itself directs a pious mind to the imitation of that unity visible on earth; for why should it be so continually mentioned in Scripture, unless the thought of it were intended to sink deep into our minds, and direct our conduct here?

2. But again, our Saviour prays that we may be one in affection and in action; yet what possible way is there of many men acting *together*, except that of forming themselves into a visible body or society, regulated by certain laws and officers? and how

---

[5] *Vide* Tracts for the Times, no. 11.

can they act on a large scale, and consistently, unless it be a permanent body?

3. But, again, I might rest the necessity of Christian unity upon one single institution of our Lord's, the Sacrament of Baptism. Baptism is a visible rite confessedly; and St. Paul tells us that, by it, individuals are incorporated into an already existing body. He is speaking of the visible body of Christians, when he says, "By one Spirit are we all baptized *into one body*." [6] But if every one who wishes to become a Christian must come to an existing visible body for the gift, as these words imply, it is plain that no number of men can ever, consistently with Christ's intention, set up a Church for themselves. All must receive their Baptism from Christians already baptized, and they in their turn must have received the Sacrament from former Christians, themselves already incorporated in a body then previously existing. And thus we trace back a visible body or society even to the very time of the Apostles themselves; and it becomes plain that there can be no Christian in the whole world who has not received his title to the Christian privileges from the original apostolical society. So that the very Sacrament of Baptism, as prescribed by our Lord and His Apostles, implies the existence of one visible association of Christians, and only one; and that permanent, carried on by the succession of Christians from the time of the Apostles to the very end of the world.

This is the *design* of Christ, I say, implied in the institution of the baptismal rite. Whether He will be merciful, over and above His promise, to those who through ignorance do not comply with this design, or are in other respects irregular in their obedience, is a further question, foreign to our purpose. Still it remains the revealed design of Christ to connect all His followers in one by a visible ordinance of incorporation. The Gospel faith has not been left to the world at large, recorded indeed in the Bible, but there left, like other important truths, to be taken up by men or rejected, as it may happen. Truths, indeed, in science and the arts *have* been thus left to the chance adoption or neglect of mankind; they are no one's property; cast at random upon the waves of human opinion. In any country soever, men may appropriate them at once, and form themselves at their will into a society for their extension. But for the more momentous truths of revealed religion, the God, who wrought by human means in their first introduction, still

---

[6] 1 Cor. xii.13.

preserves them by the same. Christ formed a body; He secured that body from dissolution by the bond of a Sacrament. He committed the privileges of His spiritual kingdom and the maintenance of His faith as a legacy to this baptized society; and into it, as a matter of historical fact, all the nations *have* flowed. Christianity has not been spread, as other systems, in an isolated manner, or by books; but from a centre, by regularly formed bodies, descendants of the three thousand, who, after St. Peter's preaching on the day of Pentecost, joined themselves to the Apostles' doctrine and fellowship.

And to this apostolical body we must still look for the elementary gift of grace. Grace will not baptize us while we sit at home, slighting the means which God has appointed; but we must "*come* unto Mount Sion, and unto the city of the living God, the heavenly Jerusalem, and to an innumerable company of angels, to the general assembly and Church of the first-born which are written in heaven, and to God the Judge of all, and to the spirits of just men made perfect, and to Jesus the mediator of the new covenant, and to the blood of sprinkling that speaketh better things than that of Abel."

4. And now I will mention one other guarantee, which is especially suggested by our Lord's words in the text, for the visible unity and permanence of His Church; and that is the appointment of rulers and ministers, entrusted with the gifts of grace, and these in succession. The ministerial orders are the ties which bind together the whole body of Christians in one; they are its organs, and they are moreover its moving principle.

Such an institution necessarily implies a succession, unless the appointment was always to be miraculous; for if men cannot administer to themselves the rite of regeneration, it is surely as little or much less reasonable to suppose that they could become Bishops or Priests on their own ordination. And St. Paul expressly shows his solicitude to secure such a continuity of clergy for his brethren: "I left thee in Crete," he says to Titus, "that thou shouldest set in order the things that are wanting, and *ordain elders* in every city, as I had appointed thee." [7] And to Timothy: "The things that thou hast heard of me among many witnesses, the same *commit thou to faithful men*, who shall be able to teach others also." [8]

Now, we know that in civil matters nothing tends more powerfully to strengthen and perpetuate the body politic than hereditary rulers and nobles. The father's life, his prin-

[7] Titus i.5.   [8] 2 Tim. ii.2; *vide* also 1 Tim. v.22.

ciples and interests, are continued in the son; or rather, one life, one character, one idea, is carried on from age to age. Thus a dynasty or a nation is consolidated and secured; whereas where there is no regular succession and inheritance of this kind, there is no safeguard of stability and tranquillity; or rather, there is every risk of revolution. For what is to make a succeeding age think and act in the spirit of the foregoing, but that tradition of opinion and usage from mind to mind which a succession involves? In like manner the Christian ministry affects the unity, inward and without, of the Church to which it is attached. It is a continuous office, a standing ordinance; not, indeed, transmitted from father to son, as under the Mosaic covenant, for the vessels of the Christian election need to be more special, as the treasure committed to them is more heavenly: but still the Apostles have not left it to the mere good pleasure and piety of the Christian body whether they will have a ministry or not. Each preceding generation of clergy have it in charge to ordain the next following to their sacred office. Consider what would be sure to happen, were there no such regular transmission of the Divine gift, but each congregation were left to choose and create for itself its own minister. This would follow, among other evil consequences, that what is every one's duty would prove, as the proverb runs, to be no one's. When their minister or teacher died or left them, there would be first a delay in choosing a fresh one, then a reluctance, then a forgetfulness. At last congregations would be left without teachers; and the bond of union being gone, the Church would be broken up. If a ministry be a necessary part of the Gospel Dispensation, so must also a ministerial succession be. But the gift of grace has not thus dropped out of the hands of its All-merciful Giver. He has committed to certain of His servants to provide for the continuance of its presence and its administration after their own time. Each generation provides for the next; "the parents" lay up "for the children." And we know as a fact, that to this day the ministers of the Church universal are descended from the very Apostles. Amid all the changes of this world, the Church built upon St. Peter and the rest has continued until now in the unbroken line of the ministry. And to put other considerations out of sight, the mere fact in itself, that there has been this perpetual succession, this unforfeited inheritance, is sufficiently remarkable to attract our attention and excite our reverence. It approves itself to us as providential, and enlivens our hope and trust, that an ordinance, thus graciously protected for so many hundred years, will continue unto the end, and that "the gates of hell shall not prevail against it."

I shall now bring these remarks to an end. And in ending, let me remind you, my brethren, how nearly the whole doctrine of ecclesiastical order is connected with personal obedience to God's will. Obedience to the rule of order is every where enjoined in Scripture; obedience to it is an act of faith. Were there ten thousand objections to it, yet, supposing unity were clearly and expressly enjoined by Christ, faith would obey in spite of them. But in matter of fact there are no such objections, nor any difficulty of any moment in the way of observing it. What, then, is to be said to the very serious circumstance, that, in spite of the absence of such impediments, vast numbers of men conceive that they may dispense with it at their good pleasure. In all the controversies of fifteen hundred years, the duty of continuing in order and in quietness was professed on all sides, as one of the first principles of the Gospel of Christ. But now multitudes, both in and without the Church, have set it up on high as a great discovery, and glory in it as a great principle, that forms are worth nothing. They allow themselves to wander about from one communion to another, or from church to meeting-house, and make it a boast that they belong to no party and are above all parties; and argue, that provided men agree in some principal doctrines of the Gospel, it matters little whether they agree in any thing besides.

But those who boast of belonging to no party, and think themselves enlightened in this same confident boasting, I would, in all charity, remind that our Saviour Himself constituted what they must, on their principles, admit to be a party; that the Christian Church is simply and literally a party or society instituted by Christ. He bade us keep together. Fellowship with each other, mutual sympathy, and what spectators from without call party-spirit, all this is a prescribed duty; and the sin and the mischief arise, not from having a party, but in having many parties, in separating from that one body or party which He has appointed; for when men split the one Church of Christ into fragments, they are doing their part to destroy it altogether.

But while the Church of Christ is literally what the world calls a party, it is something far higher also. It is not an institution of man, not a mere political establishment, not a creature of the state, depending on the state's breath, made and unmade at its will, but it is a Divine society, a great work of God, a true relic of Christ and His Apostles, as Elijah's mantle upon Elisha, a bequest which He has left us, and which we must keep for His sake; a holy treasure which, like the ark of Israel, looks like a thing of earth, and is exposed to the ill-usage and contempt of the world, but which in its own time, and according to the decree of Him who gave it, displays to-day, and to-morrow, and the third day, its miracles, as of mercy so of judgment, "lightnings, and voices, and thunderings, and an earthquake, and great hail."

SERMON 18

STEDFASTNESS IN THE OLD PATHS

"Thus saith the Lord, Stand ye in the ways, and see,
and ask for the old paths, where is the good way, and walk therein,
and ye shall find rest for your souls."—Jer. vi.16.

REVERENCE for the old paths is a chief Christian duty. We look to the future indeed with hope; yet this need not stand in the way of our dwelling on the past days of the Church with affection and deference. This is the feeling of our own Church, as continually expressed in the Prayer Book;—not to slight what has gone before, not to seek after some new thing, not to attempt discoveries in religion, but to keep what has once for all been committed to her keeping, and to be at rest.

Now it may be asked, "Why should we for ever be looking back at past times? were men perfect then? is it not possible to improve on the knowledge then possessed?" Let us examine this question.

In what respect should we follow old times? Now here there is this obvious maxim—what God has given us from heaven cannot be improved, what man discovers for himself does admit of improvement: we follow old times then *so far* as God has spoken in them; but in those respects in which God has not spoken in them, we are not bound to follow them. Now what is the knowledge which God has *not* thought fit to reveal to us? *knowledge connected merely with this present world.* All this we have been left to acquire for ourselves. Whatever may have been told to Adam in paradise, or to Noah, about which we know nothing, still at least since that time no divinely authenticated directions (it would appear) have been given to the world at large, on subjects relating merely to this our temporal state of being. How we may till our lands and increase our crops; how we may build our houses, and buy and sell and get gain; how we may cross the sea in ships; how we may make "fine linen for the merchant," or, like Tubal-Cain, be artificers in brass and iron: as to these objects of this world, necessary indeed for the time, not everlastingly important, God has given us no clear instruction. He has not set His sanction here upon any rules of art, and told us what is best. They have been found out by man (as far as we know), and improved by man; and the first essays, as might be expected, were the rudest and least successful. Here then we have no need to follow the old ways. Besides, in many of these arts and pursuits, there is really neither right nor wrong at all; but the good varies with times and places. Each country has its own way, which is best for itself, and bad for others.

Again, God has given us no authority in questions of science. The heavens above, and the earth under our feet, are full of wonders, and have within them their own vast history. But the knowledge of the secrets they contain, the tale of their past revolutions, is not given us from Divine revelation; but left to man to attain by himself. And here again, since discovery is difficult, the old knowledge is generally less sure and complete than the modern knowledge. If we wish to boast about little matters, *we* know more about the motions of the heavenly bodies than Abraham, whose seed was in number as the stars; we can measure the earth, and fathom the sea, and weigh the air, more accurately than Moses, the inspired historian of the creation; and we can discuss the varied inhabitants of this globe better than Solomon, though "he spake of trees, from the cedar that is in Lebanon, even unto the hyssop that springeth out of the wall . . . . and of beasts, and of fowl, and of creeping things, and of fishes." [1] The world is more learned in these things than of old, probably will learn more still; a vast prospect is open to it, and an intoxicating one. Like the children of Cain, before the flood came and destroyed them all, men may increase and abound in such curious or merely useful knowledge; nay, there is no limit to the progress of the human mind here; we may build us a city and a tower, whose top may reach almost to the very heavens.

Such is the knowledge which time has perfected, and in which the old paths are commonly the least direct and safe. But let us turn to that knowledge which God has given, and which therefore does not admit of improvement by lapse of time; this is *religious knowledge*. Here, whether a man might or might not have found out the truth for himself, or how far he was able without Divine assistance, waiving this question, which is nothing to the purpose, as a fact it has been from the beginning given him by revelation. God taught Adam how to please Him, and Noah, and Abraham, and Job. He has taught every nation all over the earth sufficiently for the moral training of every

[1] 1 Kings iv.33.

individual. In all these cases, the world's part of the work has been to pervert the truth, not to disengage it from obscurity. The new ways are the crooked ones. The nearer we mount up to the time of Adam, or Noah, or Abraham, or Job, the purer light of truth we gain; as we recede from it we meet with superstitions, fanatical excesses, idolatries, and immoralities. So again in the case of the Jewish Church, since God expressly gave the Jews a precise law, it is clear man could not improve upon it; he could but add the "traditions of men." Nothing was to be looked for from the cultivation of the human mind. "To the law and to the testimony" was the appeal; and any deviation from it was, not a sign of increasing illumination, but "because there was no light" in the authors of innovation. Lastly, in the Christian Church, we cannot add or take away, as regards the doctrines that are contained in the inspired volume, as regards the faith once delivered to the saints. "Other foundation can no man lay than that is laid, which is Jesus Christ."[2]

But it may be said that, though the word of God is an infallible rule of faith, yet it requires interpreting, and why, as time goes on, should we not discover in it more than we at present know on the subject of religion and morals?

But this is hardly a question of practical importance to us as individuals; for in truth a very little knowledge is enough for teaching a man his duty: and, since Scripture is intended to teach us our duty, surely it was never intended as a storehouse of mere knowledge. Discoveries then in the details of morals and religion, by means of the inspired volume, whether possible or not, must not be looked out for, as the expectation may unsettle the mind, and take it off from matters of duty. Certainly all curious questions at least are forbidden us by Scripture, even though Scripture may be found adequate to answer them.

This should be insisted on. Do we think to become better men by knowing more? Little knowledge is required for religious obedience. The poor and rich, the learned and unlearned, are here on a level. We have all of us the means of doing our duty; we have not the *will*, and this no knowledge can give. We have need to subdue our own minds, and this no other person *can* do for us. The case is different in matters of learning and science. There others can and do labour for us; *we* can make use of *their* labours; we begin where they ended; thus things progress, and each successive age knows more than the preced-

[2] 1 Cor. iii. 11.

ing. But in religion each must begin, go on, and end, for himself. The religious history of each individual is as solitary and
complete as the history of the world. Each man will, of course,
gain more knowledge as he studies Scripture more, and prays
and meditates more; but he cannot make another man wise or
holy by his own advance in wisdom or holiness. When children
cease to be born children, because they are born late in the
world's history, when we can reckon the world's past centuries
for the age of this generation, then only can the world increase
in real excellence and truth as it grows older. The character will
always require forming, evil will ever need rooting out of each
heart; the grace to go before and to aid us in our moral discipline must ever come fresh and immediate from the Holy
Spirit. So the world ever remains in its infancy, as regards the
cultivation of moral truth; for the knowledge required for practice is little, and admits of little increase, except in the case of
individuals, and then to them alone; and it cannot be handed on
to another. "As it was in the beginning, is now, and ever shall
be," such is the general history of man's moral discipline, running parallel to the unchanging glory of that All-Perfect God,
who is its Author and Finisher.

Practical religious knowledge, then, is a personal gift, and,
further, a gift from God; and, therefore, as experience has hitherto shown, more likely to be obscured than advanced by the
lapse of time. But further, we know of the existence of an evil
principle in the world, corrupting and resisting the truth in
its measure, according to the truth's clearness and purity.
Whether it be from the sinfulness of our nature, or from the
malignity of Satan, striving with peculiar enmity against Divine truth, certain it is that the best gifts of God have been the
most woefully corrupted. It was prophesied from the beginning, that the serpent should bruise the heel of Him who was
ultimately to triumph over him; and so it has ever been. Our
Saviour, who was the Truth itself, was the most spitefully entreated of all by the world. It has been the case with His followers too. He was crucified with thieves; *they* have been united
and blended against their will with the worst and basest of mankind. The purer and more precious the gift which God bestows
on us, far from this being a security for its abiding and increasing, rather the more grievously has that gift been abused. St.
John even seems to make the greater wickedness in the world
the clear consequence and evidence of our Lord's having made
His appearing. "Little children, it is the last time" (i.e. the time
of the Christian Dispensation): "and as ye have heard that

Antichrist shall come, even now are there many Antichrists, *whereby we know* that it is the last time."[3] St. Paul drew the same picture. So far from anticipating brighter times in store for the Church before the end, he portends evil only. "This know" (he says to Timothy), "that in the last days perilous times will come. . . . . Evil men and seducers shall wax worse and worse, deceiving and being deceived."[4] In these and other passages surely there is no encouragement to look out for a more enlightened, peaceful, and pure state of the Church than it enjoys at present: rather, there is a call on us to consider the old and original way as the best, and all deviations from it, though they seem to promise an easier, safer, and shorter road, yet as really either tending another way, or leading to the right object with much hazard and many obstacles.

Such is the case as regards the knowledge of our duty,—that kind of knowledge which alone is really worth earnest seeking. And there is an important reason why we should acquiesce in it;—because the conviction that things are so has no slight influence in forming our minds into that perfection of the religious character, at which it is our duty ever to be aiming. While we think it possible to make some great and important improvements in the subject of religion, we shall be unsettled, restless, impatient; we shall be drawn from the consideration of improving ourselves, and from using the day while it is given us, by the visions of a deceitful hope, which promises to make rich but tendeth to penury. On the other hand, if we feel that the way is altogether closed against discoveries in religion, as being neither practicable nor desirable, it is likely we shall be drawn more entirely and seriously to our own personal advancement in holiness; our eyes, being withdrawn from external prospects, will look more at home. We shall think less of circumstances, and more of our duties under them, whatever they are. In proportion as we cease to be theorists we shall become practical men; we shall have less of self-confidence and arrogance, more of inward humility and diffidence; we shall be less likely to despise others, and shall think of our own intellectual powers with less complacency.

It is one great peculiarity of the Christian character to be dependent. Men of the world, indeed, in proportion as they are active and enterprising, boast of their independence, and are proud of having obligations to no one. But it is the Christian's excellence to be diligent and watchful, to work and persevere,

---

[3] 1 John ii.18.   [4] 2 Tim. iii.13.

and yet to be in spirit *dependent*; to be willing to serve, and to rejoice in the permission to do so; to be content to view himself in a subordinate place; to love to sit in the dust. Though in the Church a son of God, he takes pleasure in considering himself Christ's "servant" and "slave;" he feels glad whenever he can put himself to shame. So it is the natural bent of his mind freely and affectionately to visit and trace the footsteps of the saints, to sound the praises of the great men of old who have wrought wonders in the Church and whose words still live; being jealous of their honour, and feeling it to be even too great a privilege for such as he is to be put in trust with the faith once delivered to them, and following them strictly in the narrow way, even as they have followed Christ. To the ears of such persons the words of the text are as sweet music: "Thus saith the Lord, Stand ye in the ways, and see, and ask for the old paths, where is the good way, and walk therein, and ye shall find rest for your souls."

The history of the Old Dispensation affords us a remarkable confirmation of what I have been arguing from these words; for in the time of the Law there was an increase of religious knowledge by fresh revelations. From the time of Samuel especially to the time of Malachi, the Church was bid look forward for a growing illumination, which, though not necessary for religious obedience, subserved the establishment of religious comfort. Now, I wish you to observe how careful the inspired prophets of Israel are to prevent any kind of disrespect being shown to the memory of former times, on account of that increase of religious knowledge with which the later ages were favoured; and if such reverence for the past were a duty among the Jews when the Saviour was still to come, much more is it the duty of Christians, who expect no new revelation, and who, though they look forward in hope, yet see the future only in the mirror of times and persons past, who (in the Angel's words) "wait for that same Jesus: . . . . so to come in like manner as they saw Him go into heaven."

Now, as to the reverence enjoined and taught the Jews towards persons and times past, we may notice first the commandment given them to honour and obey their parents and elders. This, indeed, is a natural law. But that very circumstance surely gives force to the express and repeated injunctions given them to observe it, sanctioned too (as it was) with a special promise. Natural affection might have taught it; but it was rested by the Law on a higher sanction. Next, this duty of reverently regarding past times was taught by such general injunctions (more or less express) as the text. It is remarkable, too, when Micah would tell the Jews that the legal sacrifices appointed in time past were inferior to the moral duties, he states it not as a new truth, but refers to its announcement by a prophet in Moses' age,—to the answer of Balaam to Balak, king of Moab.

But, further, to bind them to the observance of this duty, the past was made the pledge of the future, hope was grounded upon memory; all prayer for favour sent them back to the old mercies of God. "The Lord *hath been* mindful of us, He *will* bless us;"[5] this was the form of their humble expectation. The favour vouchsafed to Abraham and Israel, and the deliverance from Egypt, were the objects on which hope dwelt, and were made the types of blessings in prospect. For instance, out of the many passages which might be cited, Isaiah says, "Awake . . . O arm of the Lord, *as in the ancient days, in the generations of old*."[6] Micah, "Feed thy people with thy rod, the flock of thine heritage, which dwell solitary in the wood, in the midst of Carmel; let them feed in Bashan and Gilead, *as in the days of old*; according to the days of thy coming out of Egypt will I show unto him marvellous things."[7] The Psalms abound with like references to past mercies, as pledges and types of future. Prophesying of the reign of Christ, David says, "The Lord said, I will bring again from Bashan, I will bring My people again from the depths of the sea," and Moses too, speaking to the Israelites—"*Remember the days of old*, consider the years of many generations; ask thy father and he will show thee; thy elders, and they will tell thee."[8] Accordingly, while a coming Saviour was predicted, still the claims of past times on Jewish piety were maintained, by His being represented by the prophets under the name and character of David, or in the dress and office of Aaron; so that, the clearer the revelation of the glory in prospect, in the same degree greater honour was put upon the former Jewish saints who typified it. In like manner the blessings promised to the Christian Church are granted to it in the character of Israel, or of Jerusalem, or of Sion.

Lastly, as Moses directed the eyes of his people towards the line of prophets which the Lord their God was to raise up from among them, ending in the Messiah, they in turn dutifully exalt Moses, whose system they were superseding. Samuel, David, Isaiah, Micah, Jeremiah, Daniel, Ezra, Nehemiah, each

[5] Ps. cxv.12.
[6] Is. li.9.
[7] Micah vii.14, 15.
[8] Deut. xxxii.7.

in succession, bear testimony to Moses. Malachi, the last of the prophets, while predicting the coming of John the Baptist, still gives this charge, "*Remember ye the law of Moses*, My servant, which I commanded unto him in Horeb for all Israel, with the statutes and judgments."[9] In like manner in the New Testament the last of the prophets and apostles describes the saints as singing "the song of Moses, the servant of God" (this is his honourable title, as elsewhere), "*and* the song of the Lamb."[10] Above all, our blessed Lord Himself sums up the whole subject we have been reviewing, both the doctrine and Jewish illustration of it, in His own authoritative words,—"If they hear not Moses and the prophets, neither will they be persuaded, though one rose from the dead."[11] After this sanction, it is needless to refer to the reverence with which St. Paul regards the law of Moses, and to the commemoration he has made of the Old Testament saints in the eleventh chapter of his Epistle to the Hebrews.

Oh that we had duly drunk into this spirit of reverence and godly fear! Doubtless we are far above the Jews in our privileges; we are favoured with the news of redemption; we know doctrines, which righteous men of old time earnestly desired to be told, and were not. To us is revealed the Eternal Son, the Only-begotten of the Father, full of grace and truth. We are branches of the True Vine, which is sprung out of the earth and spread abroad. We have been granted Apostles, Prophets, Evangelists, pastors, and teachers. We celebrate those true Festivals which the Jews possessed only in shadow. For us Christ has died; on us the Spirit has descended. In these respects we are honoured and privileged, oh how far above all ages before He came! Yet our honours are our shame, when we contrast the glory given us with our love of the world, our fear of men, our lightness of mind, our sensuality, our gloomy tempers. What need have we to look with wonder and reverence at those saints of the Old Covenant, who with less advantages yet so far surpassed us; and still more at those of the Christian Church, who both had higher gifts of grace and profited by them! What need have we to humble ourselves; to pray God not to leave us, though we have left Him; to pray Him to give us back what we have lost, to receive a repentant people, to renew in us a right heart and give us a religious will, and to enable us to follow Him perseveringly in His narrow and humbling way.

---

[9] Mal. iv.4.   [10] Rev. xv.3.   [11] Luke xvi.31.

VIII

REVERENCE IN WORSHIP

"Samuel ministered before the Lord, being a child,
girded with a linen ephod."—1 Sam. ii.18.

SAMUEL, viewed in his place in sacred history, that is, in the course of events which connect Moses with Christ, appears as a great ruler and teacher of his people; this is his prominent character. He was the first of the prophets; yet, when we read the sacred narrative itself, in which his life is set before us, I suppose those passages are the more striking and impressive which represent him, in the office which belonged to him by birth, as a Levite, or minister of God. He was taken into God's special service from the first; he lived in His Temple; nay, while yet a child, he was honoured with the apparel of a sacred function, as the text tells us, "he ministered before the Lord, being a child, girded with a linen ephod."

His mother had "given him unto the Lord all the days of his life,"[1] by a solemn vow before his birth; and in him, if in any one, were fulfilled the words of the Psalmist, "Blessed are they that dwell in Thy house, they will be always praising Thee."[2]

Such a constant abode in God's house would make common minds only familiar with holy things, and irreverent; but where God's grace is present in the heart, the effect is the reverse; which we might be sure would happen in the case of Samuel. "The Lord was with him," we are told; and therefore the more the outward signs of that Lord met his eye, the more reverent he became, not the more presuming. The more he acquainted himself with God, the greater would be his awe and holy fear.

Thus the first notice we have of his ministering before the Lord, reminds us of the decency and gravity necessary at all times, and in all persons, in approaching Him. "He ministered before the Lord, being a child, girded with a linen ephod." His mother had made him yearly a little coat for his common use, but in Divine Service he wore, not this, but a garment which would both express, and impress upon him, reverence.

---

[1] 1 Sam. i.11.   [2] Ps. lxxxiv.4.

And, in like manner, in his old age, when Saul sent to seek David at Naioth, where Samuel was, his messengers found Samuel and the prophets under him all in decent order. "They saw the company of prophets prophesying, and Samuel over them." And this was so impressive a sight, that it became an instrument of God's supernatural power towards them, and they prophesied also.

On the other hand, if we would have an example of the want of this reverence, we have it in Saul himself, the reprobate king, who, when he was on his way to Naioth, and was visited by God's Holy Spirit, did not thereupon receive the garment of salvation, nor was clothed in righteousness, but behaved himself in an unseemly wild way, as one whose destitution and shame were but detected by the visitation. He stript off his clothes and prophesied before Samuel, and lay down in that state all that day and all that night.

This difference we see even at this day:—of persons professing religion, some are like Samuel, some like Saul; some (as it were) cast off their garments and prophesy in disorder and extravagance; others minister before the Lord, "girded with a linen ephod," with "their loins girt and their lamps burning," like men awfully expecting the coming of their great and glorious Judge. By the latter, I mean the true children of the Holy Catholic Church; by the former, I mean heretics and schismatics.

There have ever been from the first these two kinds of Christians—those who belonged to the Church, and those who did not. There never was a time since the Apostles' day, when the Church was not; and there never was a time but men were to be found who preferred some other way of worship to the Church's way. These two kinds of professed Christians ever have been—Church Christians, and Christians not of the Church; and it is remarkable, I say, that while, on the one hand, reverence for sacred things has been a characteristic of Church Christians on the whole, so, want of reverence has been the characteristic on the whole of Christians not of the Church. The one have prophesied after the figure of Samuel, the other after the figure of Saul.

Of course there are many exceptions to this remark in the case of individuals. Of course I am not speaking of inconsistent persons and exceptional cases, in the Church, or out of it; but of those who act up to what they profess. I mean that zealous, earnest, and faithful members of the Church have generally been reverent; and zealous, earnest, and faithful members of other religious bodies have generally been irreverent. Again, after all, there will be real exceptions in the case of individuals which we cannot account for; but I mean that, *on the whole*, it will be found that reverence is one of the marks or notes of the Church; true though it may be that some particular individuals, who have kept apart from it, have not been without a reverential spirit notwithstanding.

Indeed so natural is the connexion between a reverential spirit in worshipping God, and faith in God, that the wonder only is, how any one can for a moment imagine he has faith in God, and yet allow himself to be irreverent towards Him. To believe in God, is to believe the being and presence of One who is All-holy, and All-powerful, and All-gracious; how can a man really believe thus of Him, and yet make free with Him? it is almost a contradiction in terms. Hence even heathen religions have ever considered faith and reverence identical. To believe, and not to revere, to worship familiarly, and at one's ease, is an anomaly and a prodigy unknown even to false religions, to say nothing of the true one. Not only the Jewish and Christian religions, which are directly from God, inculcate the spirit of "reverence and godly fear," but those other religions which have existed, or exist, whether in the East or the South, inculcate the same. Worship, forms of worship—such as bowing the knee, taking off the shoes, keeping silence, a prescribed dress, and the like—are considered as necessary for a due approach to God. The whole world, differing about so many things, differing in creed and rule of life, yet agree in this—that God being our Creator, a certain self-abasement of the whole man is the duty of the creature; that He is in heaven, we upon earth; that He is All-glorious, and we worms of the earth and insects of a day.

But those who have separated from the Church of Christ have in this respect fallen into greater than pagan error. They may be said to form an exception to the concordant voice of a whole world, always and every where; they break in upon the unanimous suffrage of mankind, and determine, at least by their conduct, that reverence and awe are not primary religious duties. They have considered that in some way or other, either by God's favour or by their own illumination, they are brought so near to God that they have no need to fear at all, or to put any restraint upon their words or thoughts when addressing Him. They have considered awe to be superstition, and reverence to be slavery. They have learnt to be familiar and free with sacred things, as it were, on principle. I think this is really borne out by facts, and will approve itself to inquirers as true in substance, however one man will differ from another in the words in which he would express the fact itself.

Samuel was a little child who had never fallen away from God, but by His grace had ever served Him. Let us take a very different instance, the instance of a penitent sinner as set before us in the parable of the Publican and Pharisee. I need hardly say which of the two was the most pleasing to God—the Publican; whereas the Pharisee was not accepted by Him. Now what did the Pharisee do? He did not even go so far as to behave in an unseemly, extravagant way: he was grave and solemn, and yet what he did was enough to displease God, because he took too much upon himself, and made too much of himself. Though grave and solemn, he was not reverent; he spoke in a haughty, proud way, and made a long sentence, thanking God that he was not as other men are, and despising the Publican. Such was the behaviour of the Pharisee; but the Publican behaved very differently. Observe how he came to worship God; "he stood afar off; he lift not up so much as his eyes unto heaven, but smote upon his breast, saying, God be merciful to me a sin-ner."[3] You see his words were few, and almost broken, and his whole conduct humble and reverent; he felt that God was in heaven, he upon earth, God All-holy and Almighty, and he a poor sinner.

Now all of us are sinners, all of us have need to come to God as the Publican did; every one, if he does but search his heart, and watch his conduct, and try to do his duty, will find himself to be full of sins which provoke God's wrath. I do not mean to say that all men are equally sinners; some are wilful sinners, and of them there is no hope, till they repent; others sin, but they try to avoid sinning, pray to God to make them better, and come to Church to be made better; but all men are quite sinners enough to make it their duty to behave as the Publican. Every one ought to come into Church as the Publican did, to say in his heart, "Lord, I am not worthy to enter this sacred place; my only plea for coming is the merits of Jesus Christ my Saviour." When, then, a man enters Church, as many do, carelessly and familiarly, thinking of himself, not of God, sits down coldly and at his ease, either does not say a prayer at all, or merely hides his face for form's sake, sitting all the while, not standing or kneeling; then looks about to see who is in the Church, and who is not, and makes himself easy and comfortable in his seat,

[3] Luke xviii.13.

and uses the kneeler for no other purpose than to put his feet upon; in short, comes to Church as a place, not of meeting God and His holy Angels, but of seeing what is to be seen with the bodily eyes, and hearing what is to be heard with the bodily ears, and then goes and gives his judgment about the sermon freely, and says, "I do not like this or that," or "This is a good argument, but that is a bad one," or "I do not like this person so much as that," and so on; I mean when a man acts in all respects as if he was at home, and not in God's House,—all I can say is, that he ventures to do in God's presence what neither Cherubim nor Seraphim venture to do, for they veil their faces, and, as if not daring to address God, praise Him to each other, in few words, and those continually repeated, saying, Holy, holy, holy, Lord God of Sabaoth.

What I have said has been enough to suggest what it is to serve God acceptably, viz. "with reverence and godly fear," as St. Paul says. We must not aim at forms for their own sake, but we must keep in mind where we are, and then forms will come into our service naturally. We must in all respects act as if we saw God; that is, if we believe that God is here, we shall keep silence; we shall not laugh, or talk, or whisper during the Service, as many young persons do; we shall not gaze about us. We shall follow the example set us by the Church itself. I mean, as the words in which we pray in Church are not our own, neither will our looks, or our postures, or our thoughts, be our own. We shall, in the prophet's words, not "do our own ways" there, nor "find our own pleasure," nor "speak our own words;" in imitation of all Saints before us, including the Holy Apostles, who never spoke their own words in solemn worship, but either those which Christ taught them, or which the Holy Ghost taught them, or which the Old Testament taught them. This is the reason why we always pray from a book in Church; the Apostles said to Christ, "Lord, teach us to pray," and our Lord graciously gave them the prayer called the Lord's Prayer. For the same reason we too use the Lord's Prayer, and we use the Psalms of David and of other holy men, and hymns which are given us in Scripture, thinking it better to use the words of inspired Prophets than our own. And for the same reason we use a number of short petitions, such as "Lord, have mercy upon us," "O Lord, save the Queen," "O Lord, open Thou our lips," and the like, not using many words, or rounding our sentences, or allowing ourselves to enlarge in prayer.

Thus all we do in Church is done on a principle of *reverence*; it is done with the thought that we are in God's presence. But irreverent persons, not understanding this, when they come into Church, and find nothing there of a striking kind, when they find every thing is read from a book, and in a calm, quiet way, and still more, when they come a second and a third time, and find every thing just the same, over and over again, they are offended and tired. "There is nothing," they say, "to rouse or interest them." They think God's service dull and tiresome, if I may use such words; for they do not come to Church to honour God, but to please themselves. They want something new. They think the prayers are long, and wish that there was more preaching, and that in a striking oratorical way, with loud voice and florid style. And when they observe that the worshippers in Church are serious and subdued in their manner, and will not look, and speak, and move as much at their ease as out of doors, or in their own houses, then (if they are very profane) they ridicule them, as weak and superstitious. Now is it not plain that those who are thus tired, and wearied, and made impatient by our sacred services below, would most certainly get tired and wearied with heaven above? because there the Cherubim and Seraphim "rest not day and night," saying, "Holy, holy, holy, Lord God Almighty." Such as this, too, will be the way of the Saints in glory, for we are told that there will be a great voice of much people saying, Alleluia; and again they said Alleluia; and the four-and-twenty elders said Alleluia; and a voice of many waters and of mighty thunderings said Alleluia. Such, too, was our Lord's way, when in His agony He three times repeated the same words, "Thy will, not Mine, be done." It is the delight of all holy beings, who stand around the Throne, to use one and the same form of worship; they are not tired, it is ever new pleasure to them to say the words anew. They are never tired; but surely all those persons would be soon tired of hearing them, instead of taking part in their glorious chant, who are wearied of Church now, and seek for something more attractive and rousing.

Let all persons, then, know for certain, and be assured beforehand, that if they come to Church to have their hearts put into strange and new forms, and their feelings moved and agitated, they come for what they will not find. We wish them to join Saints and Angels in worshipping God; to say with the Seraphim, "Holy Lord God of Sabaoth;" to say with the Angels, "Glory to God in the highest, and in earth peace, good-will towards men;" to say after our Lord and Saviour, "Our Father, which art in heaven," and what follows; to say with St. Mary, "My soul doth magnify the Lord;" with St. Simeon,

"Lord, now lettest Thou Thy servant depart in peace;" with the Three Children who were cast into the fiery furnace, "O all ye works of the Lord, bless ye the Lord, praise Him, and magnify Him for ever;" with the Apostles, "I believe in God the Father Almighty, Maker of heaven and earth; and in Jesus Christ His only Son our Lord; and in the Holy Ghost." We wish to read to them words of inspired Scripture, and to explain its doctrine to them soberly after its pattern. This is what we wish them to say, again and again: "Lord, have mercy;" "We beseech Thee to hear us, O Lord;" "Good Lord, deliver us;" "Glory be to the Father, and to the Son, and to the Holy Ghost." All holy creatures are praising God continually—we hear them not, still they are praising Him and praying to Him. All the Angels, the glorious company of the Apostles, the goodly fellowship of the Prophets, the noble army of Martyrs, the Holy Church universal, all good men all over the earth, all the spirits and souls of the righteous, all our friends who have died in God's faith and fear, all are praising and praying to God: we come to Church to join them; our voices are very feeble, our hearts are very earthly, our faith is very weak. We do not deserve to come, surely not;—consider what a great favour it is to be allowed to join in the praises and prayers of the City of the Living God, we being such sinners;—we should not be allowed to come at all but for the merits of our Lord and Saviour. Let us firmly look at the Cross, that is the token of our salvation. Let us ever remember the sacred Name of Jesus, in which devils were cast out of old time. These are the thoughts with which we should come to Church; and if we come a little before the Service begins, and want something to think about, we may look, not at who are coming in and when, but at the building itself, which will remind us of many good things; or we may look into the Prayer Book for such passages as the 84th Psalm, which runs thus: "O how amiable are Thy dwellings, Thou Lord of hosts! my soul hath a desire and longing to enter into the Courts of the Lord: my heart and my flesh rejoice in the Living God."

Such will be our conduct and our thoughts in Church, if we be true Christians; and I have been giving this description of them, not only for the sake of those who are not reverent, but for the sake of those who try to be so,—for the sake of all of us who try to come to Church soberly and quietly, that we may know why we do so, and may have an answer if any one asks us. Such will be our conduct even when we are out of Church. I mean, those who come to Church again and again, in this humble and heavenly way, will find the effect of it, through

God's mercy, in their daily walk. When Moses came down from Mount Sinai, where he had been forty days and forty nights, his face quite shone and dazzled the people, so that he was obliged to put a veil over it. Such is the effect of God's grace on those who come to Church in faith and love; their mode of acting and talking, their very manner and behaviour, show they have been in God's presence. They are ever sober, cheerful, modest, serious, and earnest. They do not disgrace their profession, they do not take God's Name in vain, they do not use passionate language, they do not lie, they do not jest in an unseemly way, they do not use shameful words, they keep their mouth; they have kept their mouth in Church, and avoided rashness, so they are enabled to keep it at home. They have bright, smiling, pleasant faces. They do not wear a mock gravity, and, like the hypocrites whom Christ speaks of, make themselves sad countenances, but they are easy and natural, and without meaning it cannot help showing in their look, and voice, and manner, that they are God's dear children, and have His grace within them. They are civil and obliging, kind and friendly; not envious or jealous, not quarrelsome, not spiteful or resentful, not selfish, not covetous, not niggardly, not lovers of the world, not afraid of the world, not afraid of what man can do against them.

Such are they who worship God in spirit and in truth in Church; they love Him and they fear Him. And, besides those who profess to love without fearing, there are two sorts of persons who fall short; first, and worst, those who neither fear nor love God; and, secondly, those who fear Him, but do not love Him. There are, every where, alas! some bold, proud, discontented persons, who, as far as they dare, speak against religion altogether; they do not come to Church, or if they come, come to see about what is going on, not to worship. These are those who neither love nor fear; but the more common sort of persons are they who have a sort of fear of God without the love of Him, who feel and know that some things are right, and others wrong, yet do not adhere to the right; who are conscious they sin from time to time, and that wilfully, who have an uneasy conscience, who fear to die; who have, indeed, a sort of serious feeling about sacred things, who reverence the Church and its Ordinances, who would be shocked at open impiety, who do not make a mock at Baptism, much less at the Holy Communion, but, still, who have not the heart to love and obey God. This, I fear, my brethren, may be the state of some of you. See to it, that you are clear from the sin of knowing and confessing what is your duty, and yet not doing it. If you be such, and make no effort to become better; if you do not come to Church honestly, for God's grace to make you better, and seriously strive to be better and to do your duty more thoroughly, it will profit you nothing to be ever so reverent in your manner, and ever so regular in coming to Church. God hates the worship of the mere lips; He requires the worship of the heart. A person may bow, and kneel, and look religious, but he is not at all the nearer heaven, unless he tries to obey God in all things, and to do his duty. But if he does honestly strive to obey God, then his outward manner will be reverent also; decent forms will become natural to him; holy ordinances, though coming to him from the Church, will at the same time come (as it were) from his heart; they will be part of himself, and he will as little think of dispensing with them as he would dispense with his ordinary apparel, nay, as he could dispense with tongue or hand in speaking or doing. This is the true way of doing devotional service; not to have feelings without acts, or acts without feelings; but both to do and to feel;—to see that our hearts and bodies are both sanctified together, and become one; the heart ruling our limbs, and making the whole man serve Him, who has redeemed the whole man, body as well as soul.

DIVINE CALLS

*"And the Lord came, and stood, and called as at other times,
Samuel, Samuel. Then Samuel answered,
Speak; for Thy servant heareth."*—1 Sam. iii.10.

In the narrative of which these words form part, we have a remarkable instance of a Divine call, and the manner in which it is our duty to meet it. Samuel was from a child brought to the house of the Lord; and in due time he was called to a sacred office, and made a prophet. He was called, and he forthwith answered the call. God said, "Samuel, Samuel." He did not understand at first who called, and what was meant; but on going to Eli he learned who spoke, and what his answer should be. So when God called again, he said, "Speak, Lord, for Thy servant heareth." Here is prompt obedience.

Very different in its circumstances was St. Paul's call, but resembling Samuel's in this respect, that, when God called, he, too, promptly obeyed. When St. Paul heard the voice from heaven, he said at once, trembling and astonished, "Lord, what wilt Thou have me to do?"[1] This same obedient temper of his is stated or implied in the two accounts which he himself gives of his miraculous conversion. In the 22nd chapter he says, "And I said, What shall I do, Lord?" And in the 26th, after telling King Agrippa what the Divine Speaker said to him, he adds what comes to the same thing, "Whereupon, O King Agrippa, *I was not disobedient* unto the heavenly vision." Such is the account given us in St. Paul's case of that first step in God's gracious dealings with him, which ended in his eternal salvation. "Whom He did foreknow, He also did predestinate;"[2]— "whom He did predestinate, them He also called"—here was the first act which took place in time—"and whom He called, them He also justified; and whom He justified, them He also glorified." Such is the Divine series of mercies; and you see that it was prompt obedience on St. Paul's part which carried on the first act of Divine grace into the second, which knit together

[1] Acts ix.6.   [2] Rom. viii.29.

the first mercy to the second. "Whom He called, them He also justified." St. Paul was called when Christ appeared to him in the way; he was justified when Ananias came to baptize him: and it was prompt obedience which led him from his call to his baptism. "Lord, what wilt Thou have me to do?" The answer was, "Arise, and go into Damascus; and there it shall be told thee of all things which are appointed for thee to do."[3] And when he came to Damascus, Ananias was sent to him by the same Lord who had appeared to him; and he reminded St. Paul of this when he came to him. The Lord had appeared for his call; the Lord appeared for his justification.

This, then, is the lesson taught us by St. Paul's conversion, promptly to obey the call. If we do obey it, to God be the glory, for He it is works in us. If we do not obey, to ourselves be all the shame, for sin and unbelief work in us. Such being the state of the case, let us take care to act accordingly,—being exceedingly alarmed lest we should *not* obey God's voice when He calls us, yet not taking praise or credit to ourselves if we *do* obey it. This has been the temper of all saints from the beginning—working out their salvation with fear and trembling, yet ascribing the work to Him who wrought in them to will and do of His good pleasure; obeying the call, and giving thanks to Him who calls, to Him who fulfils in them their calling. So much on the pattern afforded us by St. Paul.

Very different in its circumstances was Samuel's call, when a child in the temple, yet resembling St. Paul's in this particular,—that for our instruction the circumstance of his obedience to it is brought out prominently even in the words put into his mouth by Eli in the text. Eli taught him what to say, when called by the Divine voice. Accordingly, when "the Lord came, and stood, and called as at other times, Samuel, Samuel. Then Samuel answered, Speak, Lord, for Thy servant heareth."

Such, again, is the temper of mind expressed by holy David in the 27th Psalm, "When Thou saidst, Seek ye My face, my heart said unto Thee, Thy face, Lord, will I seek."

And this temper, which in the above instances is illustrated in words spoken, is in the case of many other Saints in Scripture shown in word and deed; and, on the other hand, is illustrated negatively by being neglected in the case of others therein mentioned, who might have entered into life, and did not.

For instance, we read of the Apostles, that "Jesus, walking by the sea of Galilee, saw two brethren, Simon called Peter, and

[3] Acts xxii.10.

Andrew his brother, casting a net into the sea; for they were fishers. And He saith unto them, Follow Me, and I will make you fishers of men. *And* they *straightway* left their nets and followed Him." [4] Again; when He saw James and John with their father Zebedee, "He *called* them; and they *immediately left the ship, and their father,* and *followed* Him." And so of St. Matthew at the receipt of custom, "He said unto him, Follow Me; and he left all, rose up, and followed Him."

Again, we are told in St. John's Gospel, "Jesus would go forth into Galilee, and findeth Philip, and saith unto Him, *Follow* Me." Again, "Philip findeth Nathanael," and in like manner says to him, "Come and see." "Jesus saw Nathanael coming unto Him, and saith of him, Behold an Israelite indeed, in whom is no guile."

On the other hand, the young ruler shrunk from the call, and found it a hard saying, "If thou wilt be perfect, go and sell that thou hast, and give to the poor, and thou shalt have treasure in heaven; and come, and follow Me. But when the young man heard that saying, he went away sorrowful, for he had great possessions." [5] Others who seemed to waver, or rather who asked for some little delay from human feeling, were rebuked for want of promptitude in their obedience;—for time stays for no one; the word of call is spoken and is gone; if we do not seize the moment, it is lost. Christ was on His road heavenward. He walked by the sea of Galilee; [6] He "passed forth;" [7] He "passed by;" [8] He did not stop; all men must join Him, or He would be calling on others beyond them. [9] "He said to another, Follow Me. But he said, Lord, suffer me first to go and bury my father. Jesus said unto him, Let the dead bury their dead: but go thou and preach the kingdom of God. And another also said, Lord, I will follow Thee: but let me first go bid them farewell, which are at home at my house. And Jesus said unto him, No man, having put his hand to the plough, and looking back, is fit for the kingdom of God." [10]

Not unlike these last instances are the circumstances of the call of the great prophet Elisha, though he does not seem to have incurred blame from Elijah for his lingering on the thoughts of what he was leaving. "He found Elisha, the son of Shaphat, who was ploughing . . . Elijah passed by him, and cast his mantle over him." He did not stay; he passed on, and Elisha was obliged to run after him. "And he left the oxen, and ran

---

[4] Matt. iv.18–20.   [5] Matt. xix.21, 22.   [6] Matt. iv.18.
[7] Matt. ix.9.   [8] Mark ii.14.   [9] Matt. xx.6, 7.
[10] Luke ix.59–62.

after Elijah, and said, Let me, I pray thee, kiss my father and my mother, and then I will follow thee." This the prophet allowed him to do, and after that "he arose and followed Elijah, and ministered unto him."

Or once more consider the circumstances of the call of Abraham, the father of all who believe. He was called from his father's house, but was not told whither. St. Paul was bid go to Damascus, and there he was to receive further directions. In like manner Abraham left his home for a land "that I *will* show thee,"[11] says Almighty God. Accordingly he went out, "not knowing whither he went." "Abram departed as the Lord had spoken unto him."

Such are the instances of Divine calls in Scripture, and their characteristic is this; to require instant obedience, and next to call us we know not to what; to call us on in the darkness. Faith alone can obey them.

But it may be urged, How does this concern us now? We were all called to serve God in infancy, before we could obey or disobey; we found ourselves called when reason began to dawn; we have been called to a state of salvation, we have been living as God's servants and children, all through our time of trial, having been brought into it in infancy through Holy Baptism, by the act of our parents. Calling is not a thing future with us, but a thing past.

This is true in a very sufficient sense; and yet it is true also that the passages of Scripture which I have been quoting do apply to us still,—do concern us, and may warn and guide us in many important ways; as a few words will show.

For in truth we are not called once only, but many times; all through our life Christ is calling us. He called us first in Baptism; but afterwards also; whether we obey His voice or not, He graciously calls us still. If we fall from our Baptism, He calls us to repent; if we are striving to fulfil our calling, He calls us on from grace to grace, and from holiness to holiness, while life is given us. Abraham was called from his home, Peter from his nets, Matthew from his office, Elisha from his farm, Nathanael from his retreat; we are all in course of calling, on and on, from one thing to another, having no resting-place, but mounting towards our eternal rest, and obeying one command only to have another put upon us. He calls us again and again, in order to justify us again and again,—and again and again, and more and more, to sanctify and glorify us.

[11] Gen. xii.1.

It were well if we understood this; but we are slow to master the great truth, that Christ is, as it were, walking among us, and by His hand, or eye, or voice, bidding us follow Him. We do not understand that His call is a thing which takes place now. We think it took place in the Apostles' days; but we do not believe in it, we do not look out for it in our own case. We have not eyes to see the Lord; far different from the beloved Apostle, who knew Christ even when the rest of the disciples knew Him not. When He stood on the shore after His resurrection, and bade them cast the net into the sea, "that disciple whom Jesus loved saith unto Peter, It is the Lord." [12]

Now what I mean is this: that they who are living religiously, have from time to time truths they did not know before, or had no need to consider, brought before them forcibly; truths which involve duties, which are in fact precepts, and claim obedience. In this and such-like ways Christ calls us now. There is nothing miraculous or extraordinary in His dealings with us. He works through our natural faculties and circumstances of life. Still what happens to us in providence is in all essential respects what His voice was to those whom He addressed when on earth: whether He commands by a visible presence, or by a voice, or by our consciences, it matters not, so that we feel it to be a command. If it is a command, it may be obeyed or disobeyed; it may be accepted as Samuel or St. Paul accepted it, or put aside after the manner of the young man who had great possessions.

And these Divine calls are commonly, from the nature of the case, sudden now, and as indefinite and obscure in their consequences as in former times. The accidents and events of life are, as is obvious, one special way in which the calls I speak of come to us; and they, as we all know, are in their very nature, and as the word accident implies, sudden and unexpected. A man is going on as usual; he comes home one day, and finds a letter, or a message, or a person, whereby a sudden trial comes on him, which, if met religiously, will be the means of advancing him to a higher state of religious excellence, which at present he as little comprehends as the unspeakable words heard by St. Paul in paradise. By a trial we commonly mean, a something which if encountered well, will confirm a man in his present way; but I am speaking of something more than this; of what will not only confirm him, but raise him into a high state of knowledge and holiness. Many persons will find it very striking on looking

[12] John xxi. 7.

back on their past lives, to observe what different notions they
entertained at different periods, of what Divine truth was,
what was the way of pleasing God, and what things were allowable or not, what excellence was, and what happiness. I do not
scruple to say, that these differences may be as great as that
which may be supposed to have existed between St. Peter's state
of mind when quietly fishing on the lake, or Elisha's when driving his oxen, and that new state of mind of each of them when
called to be Apostle or Prophet. Elisha and St. Peter indeed
were also called to a new mode of life; that I am not speaking of.
I am not speaking of cases when persons change their condition, their place in society, their pursuit, and the like; I am supposing them to remain pretty much the same as before in
outward circumstances; but I say that many a man is conscious
to himself of having undergone inwardly great changes of view
as to what truth is and what happiness. Nor, again, am I speaking of changes so great, that a man reverses his former opinions
and conduct. He may be able to see that there is a connexion
between the two; that his former has led to his latter; and yet he
may feel that after all they differ in kind; that he has got into a
new world of thought, and measures things and persons by a
different rule.

Nothing, indeed, is more wonderful and strange than the
different views which different persons take of the same subject. Take any single fact, event, or existing thing which meets
us in the world; what various remarks will be made on it by
different persons! For instance, consider the different lights in
which any single action, of a striking nature, is viewed by different persons; or consider the view of wealth or a wealthy
man, taken by this or that class in the community; what different feelings does it excite—envy, or respect, or ridicule, or angry opposition, or indifference, or fear and compassion; here
are states of mind in which different parties may regard it.
These are broad differences; others are quite as real, though
more subtle. Religion, for instance, may be reverenced by the
soldier, the man of literature, the trader, the statesman, and
the theologian; yet how very distinct their modes of reverencing it, and how separate the standard which each sets up in his
mind! Well, all these various modes of viewing things cannot
one and all be the best mode, even were they all good modes;
but this even is not the case. Some are contrary to others; some
are bad. But even of those that are on the whole good, some
are but in part good, some are imperfect, some have much bad
mixed with them; and only one is best. Only one is the truth

and the perfect truth; and which that is, none know but those who are in possession of it, if even they. But God knows which it is; and towards that one and only Truth He is leading us forward. He is leading forward His redeemed, He is training His elect, one and all, to the one perfect knowledge and obedience of Christ; not, however, without their co-operation, but by means of calls which they are to obey, and which if they do not obey, they lose place, and fall behind in their heavenly course. He leads them forward from strength to strength, and from glory to glory, up the steps of the ladder whose top reacheth to heaven. We pass from one state of knowledge to another; we are introduced into a higher region from a lower, by listening to Christ's call and obeying it.

Perhaps it may be the loss of some dear friend or relative through which the call comes to us; which shows us the vanity of things below, and prompts us to make God our sole stay. We through grace do so in a way we never did before; and in the course of years, when we look back on our life, we find that that sad event has brought us into a new state of faith and judgment, and that we are as though other men from what we were. We thought, before it took place, that we were serving God, and so we were in a measure; but we find that, whatever our present infirmities may be, and however far we be still from the highest state of illumination, then at least we were serving the world under the show and the belief of serving God.

Or again, perhaps something occurs to force us to take a part for God or against Him. The world requires of us some sacrifice which we see we ought not to grant to it. Some tempting offer is made us; or some reproach or discredit threatened us; or we have to determine and avow what is truth and what is error. We are enabled to act as God would have us act; and we do so in much fear and perplexity. We do not see our way clearly; we do not see what is to follow from what we have done, and how it bears upon our general conduct and opinions: yet perhaps it has the most important bearings. That little deed, suddenly exacted of us, almost suddenly resolved on and executed, may be as though a gate into the second or third heaven—an entrance into a higher state of holiness, and into a truer view of things than we have hitherto taken.

Or again, we get acquainted with some one whom God employs to bring before us a number of truths which were closed on us before; and we but half understand them, and but half approve of them; and yet God seems to speak in them, and Scripture to confirm them. This is a case which not unfrequently occurs, and it involves a call "to follow on to know the Lord." [13]

Or again, we may be in the practice of reading Scripture carefully, and trying to serve God, and its sense may, as if suddenly, break upon us, in a way it never did before. Some thought may suggest itself to us, which is a key to a great deal in Scripture, or which suggests a great many other thoughts. A new light may be thrown on the precepts of our Lord and His Apostles. We may be able to enter into the manner of life of the early Christians, as recorded in Scripture, which before was hidden from us, and into the simple maxims on which Scripture bases it. We may be led to understand that it is very different from the life which men live now. Now knowledge is a call to action: an insight into the way of perfection is a call to perfection.

Once more, it may so happen that we find ourselves, how or why we cannot tell, much more able to obey God in certain respects than heretofore. Our minds are so strangely constituted, it is impossible to say whether it is from the growth of habit suddenly showing itself, or from an unusual gift of Divine grace poured into our hearts, but so it is; let our temptation be to sloth, or irresolution, or worldly anxiety, or pride, or to other more base and miserable sins, we may suddenly find ourselves possessed of a power of self-command which we had not before. Or again, we may have a resolution grow on us to serve God more strictly in His house and in private than heretofore. This is a call to higher things; let us beware lest we receive the grace of God in vain. Let us beware of lapsing back; let us avoid temptation. Let us strive by quietness and caution to cherish the feeble flame, and shelter it from the storms of this world. God may be bringing us into a higher world of religious truth; let us work with Him.

To conclude. Nothing is more certain in matter of fact, than that some men do feel themselves called to high duties and works, to which others are not called. Why this is we do not know; whether it be that those who are not called, forfeit the call from having failed in former trials, or have been called and have not followed; or that though God gives baptismal grace to all, yet He really does call some men by His free grace to higher things than others; but so it is; this man sees sights which that man does not see, has a larger faith, a more ardent love, and a more spiritual understanding. No one has any leave to take another's lower standard of holiness for his own. It is nothing to

[13] Hosea vi.3.

us what others are. If God calls us to greater renunciation of the world, and exacts a sacrifice of our hopes and fears, this is our gain, this is a mark of His love for us, this is a thing to be rejoiced in. Such thoughts, when properly entertained, have no tendency to puff us up; for if the prospect is noble, yet the risk is more fearful. While we pursue high excellence, we walk among precipices, and a fall is easy. Hence the Apostle says, "Work out your own salvation with fear and trembling, for it is God that worketh in you." [14] Again, the more men aim at high things, the more sensitive perception they have of their own shortcomings; and this again is adapted to humble them especially. We need not fear spiritual pride then, in following Christ's call, if we follow it as men in earnest. Earnestness has no time to compare itself with the state of other men; earnestness has too vivid a feeling of its own infirmities to be elated at itself. Earnestness is simply set on doing God's will. It simply says, "Speak, Lord, for Thy servant heareth," "Lord, what wilt Thou have me to do?" Oh that we had more of this spirit! Oh that we could take that simple view of things, as to feel that the one thing which lies before us is to please God! What gain is it to please the world, to please the great, nay, even to please those whom we love, compared with this? What gain is it to be applauded, admired, courted, followed, compared with this one aim, of not being disobedient to a heavenly vision? What can this world offer comparable with that insight into spiritual things, that keen faith, that heavenly peace, that high sanctity, that everlasting righteousness, that hope of glory, which they have who in sincerity love and follow our Lord Jesus Christ?

Let us beg and pray Him day by day to reveal Himself to our souls more fully; to quicken our senses; to give us sight and hearing, taste and touch of the world to come; so to work within us that we may sincerely say, "Thou shalt guide me with Thy counsel, and after that receive me to glory. Whom have I in heaven but Thee? and there is none upon earth that I desire in comparison of Thee: my flesh and my heart faileth; but God is the strength of my heart, and my portion for ever."

[14] Phil. ii.12, 13.

THE TRIAL OF SAUL

"And Saul said, Bring hither a burnt offering to me, and peace offerings. And he offered the burnt offering."—1 Sam. xiii.9.

WE are all on our trial. Every one who lives is on his trial, whether he will serve God or not. And we read in Scripture of many instances of the trials upon which Almighty God puts us His creatures. In the beginning, Adam, when he was first created, was put upon his trial. He was placed in a beautiful garden, he had every thing given him for his pleasure and comfort; he was created innocent and upright, and he had the great gift of the Holy Spirit given him to enable him to please God, and to attain to heaven. One thing alone he was forbidden—to eat of the tree of the knowledge of good and evil; this was his trial. If he did not eat of the fruit, he was to live; if he did, he was die. Alas, he did eat of the fruit, and he did die. He was tried and found wanting; he fell; such was the end of *his* trial.

Many other trials, besides Adam's, are recorded in Scripture, and that for our warning and instruction; that we may be reminded that we too are on trial, that we may be encouraged by the examples of those who have stood their trial well and not fallen, and may be sobered and put on our guard by the instances of others who have fallen under their trial. Of these latter cases, Saul is one. Saul, of whom we have been reading in the course of this service,[1] is an instance of a man whom God blessed and proved, as Adam before him, whom He put on his trial, and who, like Adam, was found wanting.

Now the history, I say, of this melancholy and awful fall is contained in the chapter which we have been reading, and from which the text is taken; and I will now attempt to explain to you its circumstances.

Saul was not born a king, or the son of a great family; he was a man of humble birth and circumstances, and he was raised by God's free grace to be the ruler and king of His people Israel. Samuel, God's prophet, revealed this to him, anointed him

---

[1] Fourth Sunday after Trinity.

with oil, and after he became king, instructed him in his duty: and, moreover, put him on his trial. Now his trial was this. God's people, the Israelites, over whom Saul was appointed to reign, had been very much oppressed and harassed by their enemies round about; heathen nations, who hated the true God and His worship, rose and fought against them; and of these nations the Philistines were the chief at that time. They overran the country, and brought the Israelites into captivity. They tyrannized over them, and to make sure that they should never be free, they even took away from them the means of forging weapons to fight with. "There was no smith found through all the land of Israel," says the chapter, "for the Philistines said, Lest the Hebrews (i.e. the Israelites) make them swords or spears. But all the Israelites went down to the Philistines, to sharpen every man his share, and his coulter, and his ax, and his mattock." Saul was raised up to throw off this heavy yoke, and to destroy the cruel oppressors of his people. He "chose him three thousand men, and with a third of them Jonathan, his son, smote the garrison of the Philistines which was in Geba."

Upon this, as was naturally to be supposed, these powerful enemies the Philistines became highly incensed, and assembled together a great army to chastise the insurgent people, their subjects as they would call them, who were making head against them. They had "thirty thousand chariots, and six thousand horsemen, and people as the sand which is on the sea-shore in multitude." On the other hand, Saul on his part, "blew the trumpet through all the land," and summoned all Israelites to him. They came together to him at Gilgal. And the Philistines came with their great host, and pitched over against him. Thus the two armies remained in sight of each other, and then it was that Saul's trial began.

Before Saul went to battle, it was necessary to offer a burnt sacrifice to the Lord, and to beg of Him a blessing on the arms of Israel. He could have no hope of victory, unless this act of religious worship was performed. Now priests only and prophets were God's ministers, and they alone could offer sacrifice. Kings could not, unless they were specially commanded to do so by Almighty God. Saul had no leave to offer sacrifice; yet a sacrifice must be offered before he could fight; what must he do? He must wait for Samuel, who had said that he would come to him for that purpose. "Thou shalt go down before me to Gilgal," says Samuel to him, "and behold, I will come down unto thee, to offer burnt offerings, and to sacrifice sacrifices of peace offerings; seven days shalt thou tarry till I come unto thee, and show thee what thou shalt do." [2] Saul, you see, was told to wait seven days till Samuel came; but meanwhile this great trial came upon him. The people he had gathered together to fight against the Philistines were far inferior to them in military qualities. They were not even soldiers; they were country-people brought together, rising against a powerful enemy, who was used to rule, as they were used to subjection. And, as I have already observed, they had no regular arms: "It came to pass," says Scripture, "in the day of battle, that there was neither sword nor spear found in the hand of any of the people that were with Saul and Jonathan." No wonder, under these circumstances, that many did not come to Saul's army at all; many hid themselves; many fled out of the country; and of those who joined him, all were in a state of alarm, and numbers began to desert. "When the men of Israel," says Scripture, "saw that they were in a strait, then the people did hide themselves in caves, and in thickets, and in rocks, and in high places, and in pits. And some of the Hebrews went over Jordan to the land of Gad and Gilead; as for Saul, he was yet in Gilgal, and all the people followed him trembling. And he tarried seven days, according to the set time that Samuel had appointed; but Samuel came not to Gilgal, and the people were scattered from him."

What a great trial this must have been! Here was a king who had been made king for the express purpose of destroying the Philistines; he is in presence of his powerful enemy; he is anxious to fulfil his commission; he fears to fail; his reputation is at stake; he has at best a most difficult task, as his soldiers are very bad ones, and are all afraid of the enemy. His only chance, humanly speaking, is to strike a blow; if he delays, he can expect nothing but total defeat; the longer he delays, the more frightened his men will become. Yet he is told to wait seven days; seven long days must he wait; he does wait through them; and to his great mortification and despair, his soldiers begin to desert; day after day more and more leave him: what will be the end of this? Yet does he govern his feelings so far, as to wait all through the seven days. So far he acquits himself well in the trial; he was told simply to wait seven days, and in spite of the risk, he does wait. Though he sees his army crumbling away, and the enemy ready to attack him, he obeys God; he obeys His prophet; he does nothing; he looks out for Samuel's coming.

At length the seven days are gone and over; those weary wearing days, that long trial of a week, through every hour of which he was tempted to advance against the enemy, yet every hour had to restrain his fierce and impatient spirit. Now then is the time for Samuel to come; he said he would come at the end of seven days, and the days are ended. Now at length is the time for Saul to be relieved. For seven days the Philistines, for some cause or other, have not attacked him; a wonderful chance it is; he may breathe freely; every hour, every minute he expects to hear that Samuel has joined the camp. But now, when his trial seemed over, behold a second trial—Samuel comes not. The prophet of God said he would come; the prophet of God does not come as he said.

Why Samuel did not come, we are not informed; except that we see it was God's will to try Saul still further; however, he did not come, and now let us observe what was Saul's conduct.

Hitherto he had acquitted himself well; he had obeyed to the letter the command of God by His prophet. He had waited in faith though in fear; he feared the Philistines, but had faith in God. Oh that he had continued in his faith! but his faith gave way when his trial was prolonged.

When Samuel did not come, there was no one of course to offer sacrifice; what was to be done? Saul ought to have waited still longer, till Samuel did come. He had had faith in God hitherto, he should have had faith still. He had hitherto trusted that God would save him from the enemy, though his army was scattered, in God's own way. God fights not with sword and bow; He can give victory to whom He will, and when He will; "with His own right hand, and His holy arm," can He accomplish His purposes. Saul was God's servant, and therefore he might securely trust in God. He had trusted for seven days; he might go on trusting for eight, nine, or ten. And let it be observed, that this fresh trial was hardly a greater trial than before, for this reason—that his faith hitherto had met with its reward. Though the Philistines were in his front, and his own men were deserting, yet, strange to say, the Philistines had not attacked him. Thus he had had proof that God could defend him from them. He who had kept him so safely for seven days, why should He not also on the eighth? however, he did not feel this, and so he took a very rash and fatal step.

That step was as follows: since Samuel had not come, he determined to offer the burnt sacrifice instead of him; he determined to do what he could not do without a great sin; viz. intrude into a sacred office to which he was not called; nay, to do what he really could not do at all; for he might call it a sacrifice, but it would not be really such, unless a priest or prophet offered it. You know how great a crime it is for persons now to become teachers and preachers, or to baptize or administer the Lord's Supper without authority; this was Saul's crime, he determined on sacrificing, without being an appointed minister of God. This is a crime often denounced in Scripture, as in the case of Korah, and Jeroboam, and Uzziah. Korah was swallowed up by the earth on account of it; Jeroboam had his hand withered, and was punished in his family; and Uzziah was smitten with leprosy. Yet this was Saul's sin. "And Saul said," in the words of the text, "Bring hither a burnt offering to me, and peace offerings; and he offered the burnt offering." Now observe what happened immediately afterwards. "And it came to pass, that as soon as he had made an end of offering the burnt offering, behold, Samuel came, and Saul went out to meet him, that he might salute him." You see, if he had waited but one hour more, he would have been saved this sin; in other words, he would have succeeded in his trial instead of failing. But he failed, and the consequence was, he lost God's favour, and forfeited his kingdom.

Let us observe what Samuel said to him, and what he answered; "And Samuel said, What hast thou done? And Saul said, Because I saw that the people were scattered from me, and that thou camest not within the days appointed, and that the Philistines gathered themselves together to Michmash; therefore, said I, The Philistines will come down now upon me to Gilgal, and I have not made supplication unto the Lord: I forced myself, therefore, and offered a burnt offering." Such was his excuse; and now hear what Samuel thought of it: "And Samuel said to Saul, Thou hast done foolishly: thou hast not kept the commandment of the Lord thy God, which He commanded thee: for now would the Lord have established thy kingdom upon Israel for ever. But now thy kingdom shall not continue: the Lord hath sought Him a man after His own heart, and the Lord hath commanded him to be captain over His people, because thou hast not kept that which the Lord commanded thee." Such was the end of Saul's trial: he fell; he was not obedient; and in consequence he forfeited God's favour.

How much is there in this melancholy history which applies to us, my brethren, at this day, though it happened some thousand years ago! Man is the same in every age, and God Almighty is the same; and thus what happened to Saul, the king of Israel, is, alas! daily fulfilled in us, to our great shame. We all, as Saul, have been raised by God to great honour and glory; not, indeed, glory of this world, but unseen spiritual glory. We were born in sin, and the children of wrath; and He has caused us to be baptized with water and the Spirit in the Name of Father, Son, and Holy Ghost; and as Saul, by being anointed with oil by Samuel, was made king of Israel, so we, by baptism, are made kings, not kings of this world, but kings and princes in the heavenly kingdom of Christ. He is our head, and we are His brethren; He has sat down on His throne on high, and has been crowned by His Eternal Father as Lord and Christ; and we, too, by being made His brethren, partake His unseen, His heavenly glory. Though we be poor in this world, yet, when we were baptized, we, like Saul, were made strong in the Lord, powerful princes, with Angels to wait upon us, and with a place on Christ's throne in prospect. Hence, I say, we are, like Saul, favoured by God's free grace; and in consequence we are put on our trial like Saul—we are all tried in one way or another; and now consider how many there are who fall like Saul.

1. How many are there who, when in distress of any kind, in want of means, or of necessaries, forget, like Saul, that their distress, whatever it is, comes from God; that God brings it on them, and that God will remove it in His own way, if they trust in Him: but who, instead of waiting for His time, take their own way, their own bad way, and impatiently hasten the time, and thus bring on themselves judgment! Sometimes, telling an untruth will bring them out of their difficulties, and they are tempted to do so. They make light of the sin; they say they cannot help themselves, that they are forced to it, as Saul said to Samuel; they make excuses to quiet their conscience; and instead of bearing the trial well, enduring their poverty, or whatever the trouble may be, they do not shrink from a deliberate lie, which God hears. Or, again, in like circumstances, they are tempted to steal; and they argue that they are in greater want than the person they injure, or that he will never miss what they take; and that they would not take it, were not their distress so great. Thus they act like Saul, and thus they tempt God in turn to deprive them of their heavenly inheritance. Or further, perhaps, they both steal and lie also; first steal, and then lie in order to hide their theft.

2. Again, how many are there who, when in unpleasant situations, are tempted to do what is wrong in order to get out of them, instead of patiently waiting God's time! They have, perhaps, unkind parents, and they are so uncomfortable at home, that they take the first opportunity which presents itself of getting away. They marry irreligious persons, not asking themselves the question whether they are irreligious, merely from

impatience to get out of their present discomfort; "Any thing but this," they say. What is this but to act like Saul? *he* had very little peace or quiet all the time he remained in presence of the enemy, with his own people falling away from him; and he, too, took an unlawful means to get out of his difficulty. And so, again, when persons have harsh masters and employers, or troublesome neighbours, or are engaged in employments which they do not like, they often forget that all this is from God's providence, that to Him they must look up, that He who imposed it can take it away, can take it away in His good time, and without their sin. But they, like Saul, are impatient, and will not wait. And, again, are not some of us tempted to be impatient at the religious disadvantages we lie under; and instead of waiting for God's time, and God's prophet, take the matter into our own hand, leave the place where God has put us, and join some other communion, in order (as we hope) to have clearer light and fuller privileges?

3. Again, how many are there who, though their hearts are not right before God, yet have some sort of religiousness, and by it deceive themselves into an idea that they are religious! Observe, Saul in his way was a religious man; I say, in *his* way, but not in God's way; yet his very disobedience *he* might consider an act of religion. He offered sacrifice *rather* than go to battle without a sacrifice. An openly irreligious man would have drawn up his army and fallen upon the Philistines without any religious service at all. Saul did not do this; no, he wished that an act of worship and prayer should precede the battle; he desired to have God's blessing upon him; and perversely, while he felt that blessing to be necessary, he did not feel that the only way of gaining it was seeking it *in the way* which God had appointed; that, whereas God had not made him His minister, he could not possibly offer the burnt offering acceptably. Thus he deceived himself; and thus many men deceive themselves now; not casting off religion altogether, but choosing their religion for themselves, as Saul did, and fancying they can be religious without being obedient.

4. Again, how many are there, who bear half the trial God puts on them, but not the whole of it; who go on well for a time, and then fall away! Saul bore on for seven days, and fainted not; on the eighth day his faith failed him. Oh may we persevere to the end! Many fall away. Let us watch and pray. Let us not get secure. Let us not think it enough to have got through one temptation well; through our whole life we are on trial. When one temptation is over, another comes; and, perhaps,

our having got through one well, will be the occasion of our falling under the next, if we be not on our guard; because it may make us secure and confident, as if we had already conquered, and were safe.

5. Once more, how many are there, who, in a narrow grudging cold-hearted way, go by the letter of God's commandments, while they neglect the spirit! Instead of considering what Christ wishes them to do, they take His words one by one, and will only accept them in their bare necessary meaning. They do not throw their hearts upon Scripture, and try to consider it as the voice of a Living and Kind Lord and Master speaking to them, but they take it to mean as little as it can. They are wanting in love. Saul was told to wait seven days—he *did* wait seven days; and then he thought he might do what he chose. He, in effect, said to Samuel, "I have done just what you told me." Yes, he fulfilled Samuel's directions literally and rigidly, but not in the spirit of love. Had he loved the Word of God, he would not have been so precise and exact in his reckoning, but would have waited still longer. And, in like manner, persons now-a-days, imitating him, too often say, when taxed with any offence, "Why is it wrong? Where is it so said in Scripture? Show us the text:" all which only shows that they obey carnally, in the letter, and not in the spirit.

How will all excuses, which sinners now make to blind and deaden their consciences, fail them in the Last Day! Saul had his excuses for disobedience. He did not confess he was wrong, but he argued; but Samuel with a word reproved, and convicted, and silenced, and sentenced him. And so in the Day of Judgment all our actions will be tried as by fire. The All-knowing, All-holy Judge, our Saviour Jesus Christ, will sit on His throne, and with the breath of His mouth He will scatter away all idle excuses on which men now depend; and the secrets of men's hearts will be revealed. Then shall be seen who it is that serveth God, and who serveth Him not; who serve Him with the lips, who with the heart; who are hypocrites, and who are true.

God give us grace to be in the number of those whose faith and whose love is without hypocrisy or pretence; who obey out of a pure heart and a good conscience; who sincerely wish to know God's will and who do it as far as they know it!

THE CALL OF DAVID

*"So David prevailed over the Philistine with a sling
and with a stone."*—1 Sam. xvii.50.

THESE words, which are taken from the chapter which you
heard read just now in the course of the Service,[1] declare
the victory which David, the man after God's own heart,
gained over Goliath, who came out of the army of the Philistines to defy the Living God; and they declare the manner of his
gaining it. He gained it with a sling and with a stone; that is, by
means, which to man might seem weak and hopeless, but which
God Almighty blessed and prospered. Let no one think the history of David's calling, and his victory over Goliath, of little
importance to himself; it is indeed interesting to read for its
own sake; it raises the mind of the Christian to God, shows us
His power, and reminds us of the wonderful deliverances with
which He visits His Church in every age; but besides all this,
this history is useful to us Christians, as setting before us our
own calling, and our conflict with the world, the flesh, and the
devil; as such I shall now briefly consider it.

David, the son of a man in humble life, and the youngest of
his brethren, was chosen by Almighty God to be His special servant,—to be a prophet, a king, a psalmist; he was anointed by
Samuel to be all this; and in due time he was brought forward
by Almighty God, and as a first act of might, slew the heathen
giant Goliath, as described in the text. Now let us apply all this
to ourselves.

1. David was the son of a Bethlehemite, one among the families of Israel, with nothing apparently to recommend him to
God; the youngest of his brethren, and despised by them. He
was sent to feed the sheep; and his father, though doubtless he
loved him dearly, yet seems to have thought little of him. For
when Samuel came to Jesse at God's command, in order to
choose one of his sons from the rest as God might direct him,
Jesse did not bring David before him, though he did bring all his

---

[1] Fifth Sunday after Trinity.

other children. Thus David seemed born to live and die among
his sheep. His brothers were allowed to engage in occupations
which the world thinks higher and more noble. Three of them
served as soldiers in the king's army, and in consequence looked
down upon David; on his asking about Goliath, one of them
said to him in contempt, "With whom hast thou left those few
sheep in the wilderness?" Yet God took him from the sheepfolds to make him His servant and His friend. Now this is
fulfilled in the case of all Christians. They are by nature poor,
and mean, and nothing worth; but God chooses them, and
brings them near unto Himself. He looks not at outward
things; He chooses and decrees according to His will, and why
He chooses these men, and passes over those, we know not. In
this country many are chosen, many are not; and why some are
chosen, others not, we cannot tell. Some men are born within
the bounds of holy Church, and are baptized with her baptism;
others are not even baptized at all. Some are born of bad parents, irreligious parents, and have no education, or a bad one.
We, on the contrary, my brethren, are born in the Church; we
have been baptized by the Church's ministers; and why this is
our blessedness, and not the blessedness of others, we cannot
tell. Here we differ from David. He was chosen above his brethren, because he was better than they. It is expressly said, that
when Samuel was going to choose one of his elder brethren,
God said to him, "I have refused him; for the Lord seeth not as
man seeth; for man looketh on the outward appearance, but the
Lord looketh on the heart;"[2] implying, that David's heart was
in a better state than his brother's whom Samuel would have
chosen. But this is not our case; we are in nowise better by nature than they whom God does not choose. You will find good
and worthy men, benevolent, charitable, upright men, among
those who have never been baptized. God hath chosen all of us
to salvation, not for our righteousness, but for His great mercies. He has brought us to worship Him in sacred places where
His saints have worshipped for many hundred years. He has
given us the aid of His ministers, and His Sacraments, and His
Holy Scriptures, and the Ancient Creed. To others, Scripture is
a sealed book, though they hold it in their hands; but to us it is
in good measure an open book, through God's mercy, if we but
use our advantages, if we have but spiritual eyes and ears, to
read and hear it faithfully. To others, the Sacraments and other
rites are but dead ordinances, carnal ceremonies, which profit

[2] 1 Sam. xvi.7.

not, like those of the Jewish Law, outward forms, beggarly elements, as they themselves often confess; but to us, if we have faith, they are full of grace and power. Thus all we have been chosen by God's grace unto salvation, in a special way, in which many others around us have not been chosen, as God passed over David's seven brethren, and chose him.

2. Observe, too, God chose him, whose occupation was that of a shepherd; for He chooses not the great men of the world. He passes by the rich and noble; He chooses "the poor, rich in faith, and heirs of the kingdom which He hath promised to them that love Him," [3] as St. James says. David was a shepherd. The Angel appeared to the shepherds as they kept watch over their sheep at night. The most solitary, the most unlearned, God hears, God looks upon, God visits, God blesses, God brings to glory, if he is but "rich in faith." Many of you are not great in this world, my brethren, many of you are poor; but the greatest king upon earth, even Solomon in all his glory, might well exchange places with you, if you are God's children; for then you are greater than the greatest of kings. Our Saviour said, that even the lilies of the field were more gloriously arrayed than Solomon; for the lily is a living thing, the work of God; and all the glories of a king, his purple robe, and his jewelled crown, all this is but the dead work of man; and the lowest and humblest work of God is far better and more glorious than the highest work of man. But if this be true, even of God's lower works, what shall be said of His higher? If even the lilies of the field, which are cut down and cast into the oven, are more glorious than this world's greatest glory, what shall be said of God's nobler works in the soul of man? what shall be said of the dispensation of the Spirit which "exceeds in glory?" of that new creation of the soul, whereby He makes us His children, who by birth were children of Adam, and slaves of the devil, gives us a new and heavenly nature, implants His Holy Spirit within us, and washes away all our sins? This is the portion of the Christian, high or low; and all glories of this world fade away before it; king and subject, man of war and keeper of sheep, are all on a level in the kingdom of Christ; for they one and all receive those far exceeding and eternal blessings, which make this world's distinctions, though they remain distinctions just as before, yet so little, so unimportant, in comparison of the "glory that excelleth," that it is not worth while thinking about them. One person is a king and rules, another is a subject and

[3] James ii.5.

obeys; but if both are Christians, both have in common a gift so great, that in the sight of it, the difference between ruling and obeying is as nothing. All Christians are kings in God's sight; they are kings in His unseen kingdom, in His spiritual world, in the Communion of Saints. They seem like other men, but they have crowns on their heads, and glorious robes around them, and Angels to wait on them, though our bodily eyes see it not. Such are all Christians, high and low; all Christians who remain in that state in which Holy Baptism placed them. Baptism placed you in this blessed state. God did not wait till you should do some good thing before He blessed you. No! He knew you could do no good thing of yourselves. So He came to you first; He loved you before you loved Him; He gave you a work which He first made you able to do. He placed you in a new and heavenly state, in which, while you remain, you are safe. He said not to you, "Obey Me, and I will give you a kingdom;" but "Lo I give you a kingdom freely and first of all; now obey Me henceforth, for you can, and you shall remain in it;" not "Obey Me, and I will then give you the Holy Spirit as a reward;" but "I give you that great gift in order that you may obey Me." He first gives, and then commands; He tells us to obey Him, not to gain His favour, but in order not to lose it. We are by nature diseased and helpless. We cannot please Him; we cannot move hand or foot; He says not to us, "Get well first, and I will receive you;" but He begins a cure in us, and receives us, and then says, "Take care not to go back; take care of yourselves; beware of a relapse; keep out of danger." Such then is your state, my brethren, unless you have fallen from Christ. If you are living in His faith and fear, you are kings—kings in God's unseen and spiritual kingdom; and that, though like David, you are but keeping sheep, or driving cattle, or, again, working with your hands, or serving in a family, or at any other lowly labour. God seeth not as man seeth, He hath chosen you.

3. Next, observe God chose David by means of the Prophet Samuel. He did not think it enough to choose him silently, but He called him by a voice. And, in like manner, when God calls us, He does so openly; He sent His minister, the Prophet Samuel, to David, and He sends His ministers to us. He said to Samuel, "Fill thy horn with oil, and go, and I will send thee to Jesse the Bethlehemite; for I have provided Me a king among his sons." God was looking out for a king, and sent Samuel to David. And so, in like manner, God is looking out now for kings to fill thrones in His Son's eternal kingdom, and to sit at His right hand and His left; and He sends His ministers to those

whom He hath from eternity chosen. He does not say to them, "Fill thy horn with oil," but "Fill thy font with water;" for as He chose David by pouring oil upon his head, so does He choose us by Baptism. So far, then, God chooses now as He did then, by an outward sign. Samuel was told to do then, what Christ's ministers are told to do now. The one chose David by means of oil, and the other choose Christians by means of water. In this, however, there is a difference. Samuel could choose but one. He was not allowed to choose more than one; him, namely, whom God pointed out; but now Christ's ministers (blessed be His name!) may choose and baptize all whom they meet with; there is no restriction, no narrowness; they need not wait to be told whom to choose. Christ says, "Compel them to come in." Again, the Prophet says, "Ho, every one that thirsteth, come ye to the waters." Now every one by nature thirsteth; every soul born into the world is in a spiritual sickness, in a wasting fever of mind; he has no rest, no ease, no peace, no true happiness. Till he is made partaker of Christ he is hopeless and miserable. Christ then, in His mercy, having died for all, gives His ministers leave to apply His saving death to all whom they can find. Not one or two, but thousands upon thousands are gifted with His high blessings. "Samuel took the horn of oil, and anointed" David "in the midst of his brethren." And so Christ's ministers take water, and baptize; yet not merely one out of a family, but all; for God's mercies are poured as wide as the sun's light in the heavens, they enlighten all they fall upon.

4. When Samuel had anointed David, observe what followed. "Samuel took the horn of oil, and anointed him in the midst of his brethren; and the Spirit of the Lord came upon David from that day forward." And so, also, when Christ's ministers baptize, the Spirit of the Lord comes upon the child baptized henceforth; nay, dwells in him, for the Christian's gift is far greater even than David's. God's Spirit did but come upon David, and visit him from time to time; but He vouchsafes to dwell within the Christian, so as to make his heart and body His temple. Now what was there in the oil, which Samuel used, to produce so great an effect? nothing at all. Oil has no power in itself; but God gave it a power. In like manner the Prophet Elisha told Naaman the Syrian to bathe in Jordan, and so he was healed of his leprosy. Naaman said, What is Jordan more than other rivers? how can Jordan heal? It could not heal, except that God's power made it heal. Did not our Saviour feed five thousand persons with a few loaves and fishes? how could that be? by His power. How could water become wine? by His power. And

so now, that same Divine power, which made water wine, multiplied the bread, gave water power to heal an incurable disease,
and made oil the means of gifting David with the Holy Spirit,
that power now also makes the water of Baptism a means of
grace and glory. The water is like other water; we see no difference by the eye; we use it, we throw it away; but God is with it.
God is with it, as with the oil which Samuel took with him.
Water is something more than water in its effects in the hand of
Christ's Minister, with the words of grace; it does, what by nature it cannot do; it is heavenly water, not earthly.

5. Further, I would have you observe this. Though David received the gift of God's Holy Spirit, yet nothing came of it all at
once. He still seemed like any other man. He went back to the
sheep. Then Saul sent for him to play to him on the harp; and
then he went back to the sheep again. Except that he had
strength given him to kill a lion and a bear which came against
his flock, he did no great thing. The Spirit of the Lord had come
upon him, yet it did not at once make him a prophet or a king.
All was to come in good time, not at once. So it is with Christian Baptism. Nothing shows, for some time, that the Spirit of
God is come into, and dwells in the child baptized; it looks like
any other child, it is pained, it frets, is weak, is wayward, like
any other child; for "the Lord seeth not as man seeth; for man
looketh at the outward appearance, but the Lord looketh on the
heart." And "He who seeth the heart," seeth in the child the
presence of the Spirit, "the mind of the Spirit" "which maketh
intercession for the Saints." God the Holy Ghost leads on the
heirs of grace marvellously. You recollect when our Saviour
was baptized, "immediately the Spirit of God led Him into the
wilderness." What happened one way in our Saviour's course,
happens in ours also. Sooner or later that work of God is manifested, which was at first secret. David went up to see his brothers, who were in the battle; he had no idea that he was going to
fight the giant Goliath; and so it is now, children are baptized
before they know what is to happen to them. They sport and
play as if there was no sorrow in the world, and no high destinies upon themselves; they are heirs of the kingdom without
knowing it; but God is with those whom He has chosen, and in
His own time and way He fashions His Saints for His everlasting kingdom: in His own perfect and adorable counsels He
brings them forward to fight with Goliath.

6. And now, let us inquire who is our Goliath? who is it we
have to contend with? The answer is plain; the devil is our
Goliath: we have to fight Satan, who is far more fearful and

powerful than ten thousand giants, and who would to a certainty destroy us were not God with us; but praised be His
Name, He is with us. "Greater is He that is with us, than he that
is in the world." David was first anointed with God's Holy
Spirit, and then, after a while, brought forward to fight Goliath. We too are first baptized, and then brought forward to
fight the devil. We are not brought to fight him at once; for
some years we are almost without a fight, when we are infants.
By degrees our work comes upon us; as children we have to
fight with him a little; as time goes on, the fight opens; and at
length we have our great enemy marching against us with
sword and spear, as Goliath came against David. And when this
war has once begun, it lasts through life.

7. What then ought you to do, my brethren, when thus assailed? How must you behave when the devil comes against
you? he has many ways of attack; sometimes he comes openly,
sometimes craftily, sometimes he tempts you, sometimes he
frightens you, but whether he comes in a pleasing or a frightful
form, be sure, if you saw him himself with your eyes, he would
always be hateful, monstrous, and abominable. Therefore he
keeps himself out of sight. But be sure he is all this; and, as believing it, take the whole armour of God, that you may be able
to stand in the evil day, and having done all, to stand. Quit you
like men, be strong. Be like David, very courageous to do God's
will. Think what would have happened had David played the
coward, and refused to obey God's inward voice stirring him up
to fight Goliath. He would have lost his calling, he would have
been tried, and have failed. The Prophet's oil would have
profited him nothing, or rather would have increased his condemnation. The Spirit of God would have departed from him
as He departed from Saul, who also had been anointed. So,
also, our privileges will but increase our future punishment,
unless we use them. *He* is truly and really born of God in whom
the Divine seed takes root; others are regenerated to their condemnation. Despise not the gift that is in you: despise not the
blessing which by God's free grace you have, and others have
not. There is nothing to boast in, that you are God's people;
rather the thought is an anxious one; you have much more to
answer for.

When, then, Satan comes against you, recollect you are already dedicated, made over, to God; you are God's property,
you have no part with Satan and his works, you are servants to
another, you are espoused to Christ. When Satan comes against
you, fear not, waver not; but pray to God, and He will help you.

Say to Satan with David, "Thou comest against me with a sword, and with a spear, and with a shield; but I come to thee in the name of the Lord of Hosts." Thou comest to me with temptation; thou wouldest allure me with the pleasures of sin for a season; thou wouldest kill me, nay, thou wouldest make me kill myself with sinful thoughts, words, and deeds; thou wouldest make me a self-murderer, tempting me by evil companions, and light conversation, and pleasant sights, and strong stirrings of heart; thou wouldest make me profane the Lord's day by riot; thou wouldest keep me from Church; thou wouldest make my thoughts rove when they should not; thou wouldest tempt me to drink, and to curse, and to swear, and to jest, and to lie, and to steal: but I know thee; thou art Satan, and I come unto thee in the name of the Living God, in the Name of Jesus Christ my Saviour. That is a powerful name, which can put to flight many foes: Jesus is a name at which devils tremble. To speak it, is to scare away many a bad thought. I come against thee in His All-powerful, All-conquering Name. David came on with a staff; my staff is the Cross—the Holy Cross on which Christ suffered, in which I glory, which is my salvation. David chose five smooth stones out of the brook, and with them he smote the giant. We, too, have armour, not of this world, but of God; weapons which the world despises, but which are powerful in God. David took not sword, spear, or shield; but he slew Goliath with a sling and a stone. Our weapons are as simple, as powerful. The Lord's Prayer is one such weapon; when we are tempted to sin, let us turn away, kneel down seriously and solemnly, and say to God that prayer which the Lord taught us. The Creed is another weapon, equally powerful, through God's grace, equally contemptible in the eyes of the world. One or two holy texts, such as our Saviour used when He was tempted by the devil, is another weapon for our need. The Sacrament of the Lord's Supper is another such, and greater; holy, mysterious, life-giving, but equally simple. What is so simple as a little bread and a little wine? but, in the hands of the Spirit of God, it is the power of God unto salvation. God grant us grace to use the arms which He gives us; not to neglect them, not to take arms of our own! God grant us to use His arms, and to conquer!

CURIOSITY A TEMPTATION TO SIN

"Enter not into the path of the wicked, and go not in the way of evil men. Avoid it, pass not by it, turn from it, and pass away."
—Prov. iv.14, 15.

ONE chief cause of the wickedness which is every where seen in the world, and in which, alas! each of us has more or less his share, is our curiosity to have some fellowship with darkness, some experience of sin, to know what the pleasures of sin are like. I believe it is even thought unmanly by many persons (though they may not like to say so in plain words), unmanly and a thing to be ashamed of, to have no knowledge of sin by experience, as if it argued a strange seclusion from the world, a childish ignorance of life, a simpleness and narrowness of mind, and a superstitious, slavish fear. Not to know sin by experience brings upon a man the laughter and jests of his companions: nor is it wonderful this should be the case in the descendants of that guilty pair to whom Satan in the beginning held out admittance into a strange world of knowledge and enjoyment, as the reward of disobedience to God's commandment. "When the woman saw that the tree was good for food, and that it was pleasant to the eyes, and a tree to be desired to make one wise, she took of the fruit thereof, and did eat, and gave also unto her husband with her, and he did eat;"[1] A discontent with the abundance of blessings which were given, because something was withheld, was the sin of our first parents: in like manner, a wanton roving after things forbidden, a curiosity to know what it was to be as the heathen, was one chief source of the idolatries of the Jews; and we at this day inherit with them a like nature from Adam.

I say, curiosity strangely moves us to disobedience, in order that we may have experience of the pleasure of disobedience. Thus we "rejoice in our youth, and let our heart cheer us in the days of our youth, and walk in the ways of our heart, and in the sight of our eyes."[2] And we thus intrude into things for-

---

[1] Gen. iii.6.   [2] Eccles. xi.9.

bidden, in various ways; in reading what we should not read, in hearing what we should not hear, in seeing what we should not see, in going into company whither we should not go, in presumptuous reasonings and arguings when we should have faith, in acting as if we were our own masters where we should obey. We indulge our reason, we indulge our passions, we indulge our ambition, our vanity, our love of power; we throw ourselves into the society of bad, worldly, or careless men; and all the while we think that, after having acquired this miserable knowledge of good and evil, we can return to our duty, and continue where we left off; merely going aside a moment to shake ourselves, as Samson did, and with an ignorance like his, that our true heavenly strength is departed from us.

Now this delusion arises from Satan's craft, the father of lies, who knows well that if he can get us once to sin, he can easily make us sin twice and thrice, till at length we are taken captive at his will.[3] He sees that curiosity is man's great and first snare, as it was in paradise; and he knows that, if he can but force a way into his heart by this chief and exciting temptation, those temptations of other kinds, which follow in life, will easily prevail over us; and, on the other hand, that if we resist the beginnings of sin, there is every prospect through God's grace that we shall continue in a religious way. His plan of action then lies plain before him—to tempt us violently, while the world is new to us, and our hopes and feelings are eager and restless. Hence is seen the Divine wisdom, as well as the merciful consideration, of the advice contained in so many parts of Scripture, as in the text, "Enter not into the path of the wicked, and go not into the way of evil men. Avoid it, pass not by it, turn from it, and pass away."

Let us, then, now for a few moments give our minds to the consideration of this plain truth, which we have heard so often that for that very reason we are not unlikely to forget it—that the great thing in religion is to set off well; to resist the beginnings of sin, to flee temptation, to avoid the company of the wicked. "Enter not into the path of the wicked . . . . avoid it, pass not by it, turn from it, pass away."

1. And for this reason, first of all, because it is hardly possible to delay our flight without rendering flight impossible. When I say, resist the beginnings of evil, I do not mean the first act merely, but the rising thought of evil. Whatever the temptation may be, there may be no time to wait and gaze, without being

---

[3] 2 Tim. ii.26.

caught. Woe to us if Satan (so to say) sees us first; for, as in the case of some beast of prey, for him to see us is to master us. Directly we are made aware of the temptation, we shall, if we are wise, turn our backs upon it, without waiting to think and reason about it; we shall engage our mind in other thoughts. There are temptations when this advice is especially necessary; but under all it is highly seasonable.

2. For consider, in the next place, what must in all cases be the consequence of allowing evil thoughts to be present to us, though we do not actually admit them into our hearts. This, namely,—we shall make ourselves familiar with them. Now our great security against sin lies in being shocked at it. Eve gazed and reflected when she should have fled. It is sometimes said, "Second thoughts are best:" this is true in many cases; but there are times when it is very false, and when, on the contrary, first thoughts are best. For sin is like the serpent, which seduced our first parents. We know that some serpents have the power of what is called "fascinating." Their eye has the power of sub-duing—nay, in a strange way, of alluring—their victim, who is reduced to utter helplessness, cannot flee away, nay, rather is obliged to approach, and (as it were) deliver himself up to them; till in their own time they seize and devour him. What a dreadful figure this is of the power of sin and the devil over our hearts! At first our conscience tells us, in a plain straightforward way, what is right and what is wrong; but when we trifle with this warning, our reason becomes perverted, and comes in aid of our wishes, and deceives us to our ruin. Then we begin to find, that there are arguments available in behalf of bad deeds, and we listen to these till we come to think them true; and then, if perchance better thoughts return, and we make some feeble effort to get at the truth really and sincerely, we find our minds by that time so bewildered that we do not know right from wrong.

Thus, for instance, every one is shocked at cursing and swear-ing when he first hears it; and at first he cannot help even show-ing that he is shocked; that is, he looks grave and downcast, and feels uncomfortable. But, when he has once got accustomed to such profane talking, and been laughed out of his strictness, and has begun to think it manly, and has been persuaded to join in it, then he soon learns to defend it. He says he means no harm by it; that it does no one any harm; that it is only so many words, and that every body uses them. Here is an instance in which disobedience to what we know to be right makes us blind.

Again, this same confusion frequently happens in the case of temptations from the world. We fear worldly loss or discredit; or we hope some advantage; and we feel tempted to act so as to secure, at any rate, the worldly good, or to avoid the evil. Now in all such cases of conduct there is no end of arguing about right or wrong, if we once begin; there are numberless ways of acting, each of which may be speciously defended by argument, but plain, pure-hearted common sense, generally speaking, at the very first sight decides the question for us without argument; but if we do not listen promptly to this secret monitor, its light goes out at once, and we are left to the mercy of mere conjecture, and grope about with but second-best guides. Then seeming arguments in favour of deceit and evil compliance with the world's wishes, or of disgraceful indolence, urge us, and either prevail, or at least so confuse us, that we do not know how to act. Alas! in ancient days it happened in this way, that Christians who were brought before their heathen persecutors for punishment, because they were Christians, sometimes came short of the crown of martyrdom, "having loved this present world,"[4] and so lost their way in the mazes of Satan's crafty arguments.

Temptations to unbelief may also be mentioned here. Speculating wantonly on sacred subjects, and jesting about them, offend us at first; and we turn away: but if in an evil hour we are seduced by the cleverness or wit of a writer or speaker, to listen to his impieties, who can say where we shall stop? Can we save ourselves from the infection of his profaneness? we cannot hope to do so. And when we come to a better mind (if by God's grace this be afterwards granted to us), what will be our state? like the state of men who have undergone some dreadful illness, which changes the constitution of the body. That ready and clear perception of right and wrong, which before directed us, will have disappeared, as beauty of person, or keenness of eye-sight in bodily disorders; and when we begin to try to make up our minds which way lies the course of duty on particular trials, we shall bring enfeebled, unsteady powers to the examination; and when we move to act, our limbs (as it were) will move the contrary way, and we shall do wrong when we wish to do right.

3. But there is another wretched effect of sinning once, which sometimes takes place;—not only the sinning that once itself, but being so seduced by it, as forthwith to continue in the commission of it ever afterwards, without seeking for argu-

[4] 2 Tim. iv.10.

Temple; had made his son pass through the fire; had dealt with familiar spirits and wizards; had "shed innocent blood very much, till he had filled Jerusalem from one end to another;" in a word, had "done wickedly above all that the Amorites did which were before him."[4] On his return from captivity in Babylon, whither he was taken captive, Manasseh attempted a reformation; but, alas! he found it easier to seduce than to reclaim his people.[5] Amon, who succeeded him, followed the first ways of his father during his short reign. Instead of repenting, as his father had done, he "trespassed more and more."[6] After a while, his subjects conspired and slew him. Josiah was the son of this wicked king.

Here, then, we have sufficient explanation of Josiah's ignorance of the law of Moses. He was brought up among very wicked men—in a corrupt court—after an apostasy of more than half a century; far from God's Prophets, and in the midst of idols.

In such times was Josiah born; and, like Manasseh, he came to the throne in his boyhood. As if to show us that religion depends on a man's self (under God, who gives grace), on the state of his heart, not on outward circumstances, Manasseh was the son of the pious Hezekiah, and Josiah was the son of wicked Amon. Josiah was but eight years old when his father was slain. We hear nothing of his boyhood; but scarcely was he of age to think for himself, and to profess himself a servant of the true God, but he chose that "good part which could not be taken away from him."[7] "In the eighth year of his reign" (i.e. when he was sixteen years of age), "while he was yet young, he began to seek after the God of David his father."[8] Blessed are they who so seek, for they shall find. Josiah had not the aid of a revealed volume, at least not of the Law; he was surrounded by the diversities of idol-worship, the sophistries of unbelief, the seductions of sinful pleasure. He had every temptation to go wrong; and had he done so, we might have made allowances, and said that he was not so bad as the other kings, for he knew no better; he had not sinned against light. Yes, he would have sinned against light—the event shows it; for if he had light enough to go right (which he had, for he did go right), it follows, that if he had gone wrong, it would have been against light. Not, indeed, so strong and clear a light as Solomon disobeyed, or Joash; still against his better knowledge. This is very

---

[4] 2 Kings xxi.11.   [5] 2 Chron. xxxiii.15–25.
[6] 2 Chron. xxxiii.23.   [7] Luke x.42.   [8] 2 Chron. xxxiv.3.

ments to meet our conscience withal; from a mere brutish, headstrong, infatuate greediness after its bad pleasures. There are beasts of prey which are said to abstain from blood till they taste it, but once tasting it, ever seek it: and, in like manner, there is a sort of thirst for sin which is born with us, but which grace quenches, and which is thus kept under *till* we, by our own act, rouse it again; and which, when once aroused, never can be allayed. We sin, while we confess the wages of sin to be death.

4. Sometimes, I say, this is the immediate effect of a first transgression; and if not the immediate effect, yet it is always the tendency and the end of sinning at length, viz. to enslave us to it. Temptation is very powerful, it is true, when it comes first; but, then, its power lies in its own novelty; and, on the other hand, there is power in the heart itself, divinely given, to resist it; but when we have long indulged sin, the mind has become sinful in its habit and character, and the Spirit of God having departed, it has no principle within it of strength sufficient to save it from spiritual death. What being can change its own nature? that would be almost ceasing to be itself: fire cannot cease to burn; the leopard changes not its spots, and ceases not to rend and devour; and the soul which has often sinned, cannot help sinning; but in this respect awfully differing from the condition of the senseless elements or brute animals,—that its present state is all its own fault; that it might have hindered it, and will have one day to answer for not having hindered it.

Thus, easy as it is to avoid sin first of all, at length it is (humanly speaking) impossible. "Enter not into its path," saith the wise man; the two paths of right and wrong start from the same point, and at first are separated by a very small difference, so easy (comparatively) is it to choose the right instead of the wrong way: but wait awhile, and pursue the road leading to destruction, and you will find the distance between the two has widened beyond measurement, and that between them a great gulf has been sunk, so that you cannot pass from the one to the other, though you desire it ever so earnestly.[5]

Now to what do considerations such as these lead us, but to our Lord's simple and comprehensive precept, which is the same as Solomon's, but more impressively and solemnly urged on us by the manner and time of His giving it? "Watch and pray, lest ye enter into temptation." To enter not the path of the wicked, to avoid it, and pass by it, what is this but the exercise of

[5] Luke xvi.26.

CURIOSITY A TEMPTATION TO SIN

watching? Therefore He insists upon it so much, knowing that in it our safety lies. But now, on the other hand, consider *how* many are there among us who can be said to watch and pray? Is not the utmost we do to offer on Sunday some kind of prayer in Church to God; or sometimes some short prayer morning and evening in the week; and then go into the world with the same incaution and forgetfulness as if we had never entertained a serious thought? We go through the business of the day, quite forgetting, to any practical purpose, that all business has snares in it, and therefore needs caution. Let us ask ourselves this question, "How often do we think of Satan in the course of the day as our great tempter?" Yet surely he does not cease to be active because we do not think of him; and surely, too, his powers and devices were revealed to us by Almighty God for the very purpose, that being not ignorant of them, we might watch against them. Who among us will not confess, that many is the time that he has mixed with the world, forgetting who the god of this world is? or rather, are not a great many of us living in habitual forgetfulness that this world is a scene of trial; that is, that this is its *chief* character, that all its employments, its pleasures, its occurrences, even the most innocent, the most acceptable to God, and the most truly profitable in themselves, are all the while so handled by Satan as may be the most conducive to our ruin, if he can possibly contrive it? There is nothing gloomy or superstitious in this, as the plain words of Scripture will abundantly prove to every inquirer. We are told "that the devil, our adversary, as a roaring lion walketh about, seeking whom he may devour;"[6] and therefore are warned to "be sober, be vigilant." And assuredly our true comfort lies, not in disguising the truth from ourselves, but in knowing something more than this;—that though Satan is against us, God is for us; that greater is He that is in us, than he that is in the world;[7] and that He in every temptation will make a way for us to escape, that we may be able to bear it.[8]

God does His part most surely; and Satan too does his part: we alone are unconcerned. Heaven and hell are at war for us and against us, yet we trifle, and let life go on at random. Heaven and hell are before us as our own future abode, one or other of them; yet our own interest moves us no more than God's mercy. We treat sin, not as an enemy to be feared, abhorred, and shunned, but as a misfortune and a weakness; we do not pity and shun sinful men, but we enter into their path so far as to

---

[6] 1 Pet. v.8.　　　[7] 1 John iv.4.　　　[8] 1 Cor. x.13.

keep company with them; and next, being tempted to copy them, we fall almost without an effort.

Be not you thus deceived and overcome, my brethren, by an evil heart of unbelief. Make up your minds to take God for your portion, and pray to Him for grace to enable you so to do. Avoid the great evils of leisure, avoid the snare of having time on your hands. Avoid all bad thoughts, all corrupt or irreligious books, avoid all bad company: let nothing seduce you into it. Though you may be laughed at for your strictness; though you may lose thereby amusements which you would like to partake of; though you may thereby be ignorant of much which others know, and may appear to disadvantage when they are talking together; though you appear behind the rest of the world; though you be called a coward, or a child, or narrow-minded, or superstitious; whatever insulting words be applied to you, fear not, falter not, fail not; stand firm, quit you like men; be strong. They think that in the devil's service there are secrets worthy our inquiry, which you share not: yes, there are secrets, and such that it is a shame even to speak of them; and in like manner you have a secret which they have not, and which far surpasses theirs. "The secret of the Lord is with them that fear Him." Those who obey God and follow Christ have secret gains, so great, that, as well might we say heaven were like hell, as that these are like the gain which sinners have. They have a secret gift given them by their Lord and Saviour in proportion to their faith and love. They cannot describe it to others; they have not possession of it all at once; they cannot have the enjoyment of it at this or that time when they will. It comes and goes according to the will of the Giver. It is given but in small measure to those who begin God's service. It is not given at all to those who follow Him with a divided heart. To those who love the world, and yet are in a certain sense religious, and are well contented with such a religious state, to them it is not given. But those who give themselves up to their Lord and Saviour, those who surrender themselves soul and body, those who honestly say, "I am Thine, new-make me, do with me what Thou wilt," who say so not once or twice merely, or in a transport, but calmly and habitually; these are they who gain the Lord's secret gift, even the "white stone, and in the stone a new name written which no man knoweth, saving he that receiveth it." [9] Sinners think that they know all that religion has to give, and over and above that, they know the pleasures of sin too. No,

[9] Rev. ii.17.

they do not, cannot, never will know the secret gift of God, till
they repent and amend. They never will know what it is to see
God, till they obey; nay, though they are to see Him at the last
day, even that will be no true sight of Him, for the sight of that
Holy One will then impart no comfort, no joy to them. They
never will know the blessedness which He has to give. They do
know the satisfaction of sinning, such as it is; and, alas! if they
go on as they are going, they will know not only what sin is, but
what hell is. But they never will know that great secret which is
hid in the Father and in the Son.

Let us not then be seduced by the Tempter and his promises.
He can show us no good. He has no good to give us. Rather let
us listen to the gracious words of our Maker and Redeemer,
"Call unto Me, and I will answer thee, and show thee great and
mighty things, which thou knowest not." [10]

---

[10] Jer. xxxiii.3.

MIRACLES NO REMEDY
FOR UNBELIEF

"And the Lord said unto Moses, How long will this people provoke
Me? and how long will it be ere they believe Me, for all the signs
which I have showed among them?"—Numb. xiv.11.

NOTHING, I suppose, is more surprising to us at first reading,
than the history of God's chosen people; nay, on second
and third reading, and on every reading, till we learn to view it
as God views it. It seems strange, indeed, to most persons, that
the Israelites should have acted as they did, age after age, in
spite of the miracles which were vouchsafed to them. The laws
of nature were suspended again and again before their eyes; the
most marvellous signs were wrought at the word of God's
prophets, and for their deliverance; yet they did not obey their
great Benefactor at all better than men now-a-days who have
not these advantages, as we commonly consider them. Age after age God visited them by Angels, by inspired messengers; age
after age they sinned. At last He sent His well-beloved Son; and
He wrought miracles before them still more abundant, wonderful, and beneficent than any before Him. What was the effect upon them of His coming? St. John tells us, "Then
gathered the Chief Priests and the Pharisees a council, and said,
What do we? for this Man doeth many miracles. . . . . Then
from that day forth they took counsel together for to put Him
to death."[1]

In matter of fact, then, whatever be the reason, nothing is
gained by miracles, nothing comes of miracles, as regards our
religious views, principles, and habits. Hard as it is to believe,
miracles certainly do not make men better; the history of Israel
proves it. And the only mode of escaping this conclusion, to
which some persons feel a great repugnance, is to fancy that the
Israelites were much worse than other nations, which accordingly has been maintained. It has often been said, that they

---

[1] John xi.47, 53.

were stiff-necked and hard-hearted beyond the rest of the world. Now, even supposing, for argument's sake, I should grant that they were so, this would not sufficiently account for the strange circumstance under consideration; for this people was not moved at all. It is not a question of more or less: surely they must have been altogether distinct from other men, destitute of the feelings and opinions of other men, nay, hardly partakers of human nature, if other men would, as a matter of course, have been moved by those miracles which had no influence whatever upon them. That there *are*, indeed, men in the world who would have been moved, and would have obeyed in consequence, I do not deny; such were to be found among the Israelites also; but I am speaking of men in general; and I say, that if the Israelites had a common nature with us, surely that insensibility which they exhibited on the whole, must be just what we should exhibit on the whole under the same circumstances.

It confirms this view of the subject to observe, that the children of Israel *are* like other men in all points of their conduct, save this insensibility, which other men have not had the opportunity to show as they had. There is no difference between their conduct and ours in point of *fact*; the difference is entirely in the external discipline to which God subjected them. Whether or not miracles ought to have influenced them in a way in which God's dealings in Providence do not influence us, so far is clear, that looking into their modes of living and of thought, we find a nature just like our own, not better indeed, but in no respect worse. Those evil tempers which the people displayed in the desert, their greediness, selfishness, murmuring, caprice, waywardness, fickleness, ingratitude, jealousy, suspiciousness, obstinacy, unbelief, all these are seen in the uneducated multitude now-a-days, according to its opportunity of displaying them.

The pride of Dathan and the presumption of Korah are still instanced in our higher ranks and among educated persons. Saul, Ahithophel, Joab, and Absalom, have had their parallels all over the world. I say there is nothing unlike the rest of mankind in the character or conduct of the chosen people; the difference solely is in God's dealings with them. They *act* as other men; it is their religion which is not as other men; it is miraculous; and the question is, how it comes to pass, their religion being different, their conduct is the same? and there are two ways of answering it; either by saying that they were worse than other men, and were not influenced by miracles when others would have been influenced (as many persons are apt to think), or (what I conceive to be the true reason) that, after all, the difference between miracle and no miracle is not so great in any case, in the case of any people, as to secure the success or account for the failure of religious truth. It was not that the Israelites were much more hard-hearted than other people, but that a miraculous religion is not much more influential than other religions.

For I repeat, though it be granted that the Israelites were much worse than others, still that will not account for the fact that miracles made no impression whatever upon them. However sensual and obstinate they may be supposed to have been in natural character, yet if it be true that a miracle has a necessary effect upon the human mind, it must be considered to have had some effect on their conduct for good or bad; if it had not a good effect, at least it must have had a bad; whereas their miracles left them very much the same in outward appearance as men are now-a-days, who neglect such warnings as are now sent them, neither much more lawless and corrupt than they, nor the reverse. The point is, that while they were so hardened, as it appears to us, in their conduct towards their Lord and Governor, they were not much worse than other men in social life and personal behaviour. It is a rule that if men are extravagantly irreligious, profane, blasphemous, infidel, they are equally excessive and monstrous in other respects; whereas the Jews were like the Eastern nations around them, with this one peculiarity, that they had rejected direct and clear miraculous evidence, and the others had not. It seems, then, I say, to follow, that, guilty as were the Jews in disobeying Almighty God, and blind as they became from shutting their eyes to the light, they were not much more guilty than others may be in disobeying Him; that it is almost as great a sin to reject His service in the case of those who do not see miracles, as in the case of those who do; that the sight of miracles is not the way in which men come to believe and obey, nor the absence of them an excuse for not believing and obeying.

Now let me say something in explanation of this, at first sight, startling truth, that miracles on the whole would not make men in general more obedient or holy than they are, though they were generally displayed. It has sometimes been said by unbelievers, "If the Gospel were written on the Sun, I would believe it." Unbelievers have said so by way of excusing themselves for not believing it, as it actually comes to them; and I dare say some of us, my brethren, have before now uttered the same sentiment in our hearts, either in moments of temptation,

or when under the upbraidings of conscience for sin committed. Now let us consider, why do we think so?

I ask, why should the sight of a miracle make you better than
you are? Do you doubt at all the being and power of God? No.
Do you doubt what you ought to *do*? No. Do you doubt at all
that the rain, for instance, and sunshine, come from Him? or
that the fresh life of each year, as it comes, is His work, and that
all nature bursts into beauty and richness at His bidding? You
do not doubt it at all. Nor do you doubt, on the other hand, that
it is your duty to obey Him who made the world and who made
you. And yet, with the knowledge of all this, you find you cannot prevail upon yourselves to do what you know you should
do. Knowledge is not what you want to make you obedient.
You have knowledge enough already. Now what truth would a
miracle convey to you which you do not learn from the works
of God around you? What would it teach you concerning God
which you do not already believe without having seen it?

But, you will say, a miracle would startle you; true: but
would not the startling pass away? could you be startled for
ever? And what sort of a religion is that which consists in a state
of fright and disturbance? Are you not continually startled by
the accidents of life? You see, you hear things suddenly, which
bring before your minds the thoughts of God and judgment;
calamities befall you which for the time sober you. Startling is
not conversion, any more than knowledge is practice.

But you urge, that perhaps that startling might issue in amendment of life; that it might be the beginning of a new course,
though it passed away itself; that a miracle would not indeed
convert you, but it would be the first step towards thorough
conversion; that it would be the turning point in your life, and
would suddenly force your path into the right direction, and
that in this way shocks and startlings, and all the agitation of the
passions and affections, are really the means of conversion,
though conversion be something more than they. This is very
true: sudden emotions—fear, hope, gratitude, and the like, all
do produce such effects sometimes; but why is a miracle necessary to produce such effects? Other things startle us besides
miracles: we have a number of accidents sent us by God to
startle us. He has not left us without warnings, though He has
not given us miracles; and if we are not moved and converted by
those which come upon us, the probability is, that, like the
Jews, we should not be converted by miracles.

Yes, you say; but if one came from the dead, if you saw the
spirit of some departed friend you knew on earth: what then?

What would it tell you that you do not know now? Do you now in your sober reason doubt the reality of the unseen world? not at all; only you cannot get yourself to act as if it *were* real. Would such a sight produce this effect? you think it would. Now I will grant this on one supposition. Do the startling accidents which happen to you now, produce *any* lasting effect upon you? Do they lead you to *any habits* of religion? If they do produce some effect, then I will grant to you that such a strange visitation, as you have supposed, would produce a greater effect; but if the events of life which now happen to you produce *no* lasting effect on you, and this I fear is the case, then too sure I am, that a miracle too would produce no lasting effect on you, though of course it would startle you more at the time. I say, I fear that what happens to you, as it is, produces no lasting effect on you. I mean, that the warnings which you really have, do not bring you to any habitual and regular religiousness; they may make you a little more afraid of this or that sin, or of this or that particular indulgence of it; but they do not tend at all to make you break with the world, and convert you to God. If they did make you take up religion in earnest, though in ever so poor a way, then I will grant that miracles would make you *more* in earnest. If God's *ordinary* warnings moved you, His extraordinary would move you more. It is quite true, that a serious mind would be made more serious by seeing a miracle, but this gives no ground for saying, that minds which are *not* serious, careless, worldly, self-indulgent persons, who are made not at all better by the warnings which *are* given them, would be made serious by those miraculous warnings which are not given.

Of course it might so happen in this or that particular case,— just as the same person is moved by one warning, not by another; not moved by a warning to-day, moved by a warning to-morrow; but I am sure, taking men as we find them, miracles would leave them, as far as their conduct is concerned, very much as they are. They would be very much startled and impressed at first, but the impression would wear away. And thus our Saviour's words would come true of all those multitudes who have the Bible to read, and know what they ought to do, but do it not:—"If they hear not Moses and the Prophets," He says, "neither will they be persuaded though one rose from the dead." Do we never recollect times when we have said, "We shall never forget this; it will be a warning all through our lives"? have we never implored God's forgiveness with the most eager promises of amendment? have we never felt as if we were brought quite into a new world, in gratitude and joy? Yet was the result what we had expected? We cannot anticipate more from miracles, than before now we have anticipated from warnings, which came to nought.

And now, what *is* the real reason why we do not seek God with all our hearts, and devote ourselves to His service, if the absence of miracles be not the reason, as most assuredly it is not? What was it that made the Israelites disobedient, who *had* miracles? St. Paul informs us, and exhorts *us* in consequence. "Harden not your hearts, *as* in the provocation, in the day of temptation in the wilderness . . . take heed . . . lest there be in any of *you*" (as there was among the Jews) "an evil heart of unbelief in departing from the Living God." Moses had been commissioned to say the same thing at the very time; "Oh that there were such a heart in them, that they would fear Me, and keep My Commandments always!" We cannot serve God, because we want the will and the heart to serve Him. We like any thing better than religion, as the Jews before us. The Jews liked this world; they liked mirth and feasting. "The people sat down to eat and to drink, and rose up to play;" so do we. They liked glitter and show, and the world's fashions. "Give us a king like the nations," they said to Samuel; so do we. They wished to be let alone; they liked ease; they liked their own way; they disliked to make war against the natural impulses and leanings of their own minds; they disliked to attend to the state of their souls, to have to treat themselves as spiritually sick and infirm, to watch, and rule, and chasten, and refrain, and change themselves; and so do we. They disliked to think of God, and to observe and attend His ordinances, and to reverence Him; they called it a weariness to frequent His courts; and they found this or that false worship more pleasant, satisfactory, congenial to their feelings, than the service of the Judge of quick and dead; and so do we: and therefore we disobey God as they did,—not that we have not miracles; for they actually had them, and it made no difference. We act as they did, though they had miracles, and we have not; because there is one cause of it *common* both to them and us—heartlessness in religious matters, an evil heart of unbelief; both they and we disobey and disbelieve, because we do not love.

But this is not all; in another respect we are really far more favoured than they were; they had outward miracles; we too have miracles, but they are not outward but inward. Ours are not miracles of evidence, but of power and influence. They are secret, and more wonderful and efficacious because secret. Their miracles were wrought upon external nature; the sun stood still, and the sea parted. Ours are invisible, and are exercised upon the soul. They consist in the sacraments, and they just do that very thing which the Jewish miracles did not. They really touch the heart, though we so often resist their influence. If then we sin, as, alas! we do, if we do not love God more than the Jews did, if we have no heart for those "good things which pass men's understanding," we are not more excusable than they, but less so. For the supernatural works which God showed to them were wrought outwardly, not inwardly, and did not influence the will; they did but convey warnings; but the supernatural works which He does towards us are in the heart, and impart grace; and if we disobey, we are not disobeying His command only, but resisting His presence.

This is our state; and perhaps so it is that, as the Israelites for forty years hardened their hearts in the wilderness, in spite of the manna and the quails, and the water from the rock, so we for a course of years have been hardening ours in spite of the spiritual gifts which are the portion of Christians. Instead of listening to the voice of conscience, instead of availing ourselves of the aid of heavenly grace, we have gone on year after year with the vain dream of turning to God some future day. Childhood and boyhood are past; youth, perhaps middle age, perhaps old age is come; and now we find that we cannot "love the thing which God commandeth, and desire that which He doth promise;" and then, instead of laying the blame where it is due, on ourselves, for having hardened ourselves against the influences of grace, we complain that enough has not been done for us; we complain we have not enough light, enough help, enough inducements; we complain we have not seen miracles. Alas! how exactly are God's words fulfilled in us, which He deigned to speak to His former people. "O inhabitants of Jerusalem, and men of Judah, judge, I pray you, betwixt Me and My vineyard. What could have been done more to My vineyard that I have not done in it? wherefore, when I looked that it should bring forth grapes, brought it forth wild grapes?" [2]

Let us then put aside vain excuses; and, instead of looking for outward events to change our course of life, be sure of this, that if our course of life is to be changed, it must be from within. God's grace moves us from within, so does our own will. External circumstances have no real power over us. If we do not love God, it is because we have not wished to love Him, tried to love Him, prayed to love Him. We have not borne the idea and the

[2] Is. v.3, 4.

wish in our mind day by day, we have not had it before us in the little matters of the day, we have not lamented that we loved Him not, we have been too indolent, sluggish, carnal, to attempt to love Him in little things, and begin at the beginning; we have shrunk from the effort of moving from within; we have been like persons who cannot get themselves to rise in the morning; and we have desired and waited for a thing impossible,—to be changed once and for all, all at once, by some great excitement from without, or some great event, or some special season; something or other we go on expecting, which is to change us without our having the trouble to change ourselves. We covet some miraculous warning, or we complain that we are not in happier circumstances, that we have so many cares, or so few religious privileges; or we look forward for a time when religion will come easy to us as a matter of course. This we used to look out for as boys; we used to think there was time enough yet to think of religion, and that it was a natural thing, that it came without trouble or effort, for men to be religious as life went on; we fancied that all old persons must be religious; and now even, as grown men, we have not put off this deceit; but, instead of giving our hearts to God, we are waiting, with Felix, for a convenient season.

Let us rouse ourselves, and act as reasonable men, before it is too late; let us understand, as a first truth in religion, that *love* of heaven is the only *way* to heaven. Sight will not move us; else why did Judas persist in covetousness in the very presence of Christ? why did Balaam, whose "eyes were opened," remain with a closed heart? why did Satan fall, when he was a bright Archangel? Nor will reason subdue us; else why was the Gospel, in the beginning, "to the Greeks foolishness"? Nor will excited feelings convert us; for there is one who "heareth the word, and anon with joy receiveth it;" yet "hath no root in himself," and "dureth" only "for a while." Nor will self-interest prevail with us; or the rich man would have been more prudent, whose "ground brought forth plentifully," and would have recollected that "that night his soul" might be "required of him." Let us understand that nothing but the love of God can make us believe in Him or obey Him; and let us pray Him, who has "prepared for them that love Him, such good things as pass man's understanding, to pour into our hearts such love towards Him, that we, loving Him above all things, may obtain His promises, which exceed all that we can desire."

JOSIAH, A PATTERN FOR
THE IGNORANT

"Because thine heart was tender, and thou hast humbled thyself
before the Lord, when thou heardest what I spake against this place,
and against the inhabitants thereof, that they should become a
desolation and a curse, and hast rent thy clothes, and wept before
Me; I also have heard thee, saith the Lord. Behold therefore, I will
gather thee unto thy fathers, and thou shalt be gathered into thy grave
in peace; and thine eyes shall not see all the evil which I will bring
upon this place."—2 Kings xxii. 19, 20.

K ING JOSIAH, to whom these words are addressed, was one
of the most pious of the Jewish kings, and the most eminent reformer of them all. On him, the last sovereign of David's
house (for his sons had not an independent rule), descended the
zeal and prompt obedience which raised the son of Jesse from
the sheepfold to the throne, as a man after God's own heart.
Thus, as an honour to David, the blessing upon his posterity
remained in its fulness even to the end; its light not waxing
"dim," nor "its natural force abating."

Both the character and the fortunes of Josiah are described in
the text; his character, in its saying that his "heart was tender,"
and that he feared God; and his fortunes, viz. an untimely
death, designed as a reward for his obedience: and the text is a
part of the answer which the Prophetess Huldah was instructed
to make to him, when he applied for encouragement and guidance after accidentally finding the book of Moses' Law in the
Temple. This discovery is the most remarkable occurrence of
his reign, and will fitly serve to introduce and connect together
what I wish now to set before you concerning Josiah.

The discovery of Moses' Law in the Temple is a very important occurrence in the history, because it shows us that Holy
Scripture had been for a long while neglected, and to all practical purposes lost. By the book of the law is meant, I need
scarcely say, the five books of Moses, which stand first in the
Bible. These made up one book or volume, and were to a Jew

the most important part of the Old Testament, as containing the original covenant between God and His people, and explaining to them what their place was in the scheme of God's providence, what were their duties, and what their privileges. Moses had been directed to enforce the study of this law on the Israelites in various ways. He exhorts them to "lay up his words in their heart and in their soul, and to bind them for a sign upon their hand, that they might be as frontlets between their eyes." "And ye shall teach them your children," he proceeds, "speaking of them when thou sittest in thine house, and when thou walkest by the way, when thou liest down, and when thou risest up. And thou shalt write them upon the door-posts of thine house, and upon thy gates." [1] Besides this general provision, it was ordered that once in seven years the law should be read to the whole people assembled at the feast of tabernacles. [2] And further still, it was provided, that in case they ever had kings, each king was to write out the whole of it from the original copy which was kept in the ark. "And it shall be with him, and he shall read therein all the days of his life . . . that his heart be not lifted up above his brethren, and that he turn not aside from the commandment, to the right hand or to the left; to the end that he may prolong his days in his kingdom, he, and his children, in the midst of Israel." [3]

However, considering how soon the nation fell into a general disregard of the law and worship which God gave them, it is not wonderful that these wholesome precepts were neglected, which could not be performed without testifying against their multiplied transgressions. And much more when they took to themselves idols, did they neglect, of course, to read the law which condemned them. And when they had set a king over them against the will of God, it is not strange that their kings, in turn, should neglect the direction given them to copy out the law for themselves; such kings especially as fell into idolatry.

All this applies particularly to the age in which Josiah succeeded to the throne, so that it is in no way surprising that he knew nothing of the law till it was by chance found in the Temple some years after his accession. The last good king of Judah before him was Hezekiah, who had been dead sixty or seventy years. That religious king had been succeeded by his son Manasseh, the most profane of all the line of David. He it was who committed those inexpiable sins which sealed the sentence of Judah's destruction. He had set up an idol in the

---

[1] Deut. xi.18–20.   [2] Deut. xxxi.9–13.   [3] Deut. xvii.19, 20.

important. Every one, even the poorest and most ignorant, has knowledge enough to be religious. Education does not make a man religious: nor, again, is it an excuse for a man's disobedience, that he has not been educated in his duty. It only makes him less guilty than those who have been educated; that is all: he is still guilty. Here, I say, the poorest and most un-learned among us, may take a lesson from a Jewish king. Scarcely can any one in a Christian land be in more disadvantageous circumstances than Josiah—nay, scarcely in a heathen: he had idolatry around him, and at the age he began to seek God, his mind was unformed. What, then, was it that guided him? whence his knowledge? He had that, which all men have, heathen as well as Christians, till they pervert or blunt it—a natural sense of right and wrong; and he did not blunt it. In the words of the text, "his heart was *tender*;" he acknowledged a constraining force in the Divine voice within him—he heard and obeyed. Though all the world had told him otherwise, he could not believe and would not, that he might sin without offence—with impunity; that he might be sensual, or cruel, after the manner of idolaters, and nothing would come of it. And further, amid all the various worships offered to his acceptance, this same inward sense of his, strengthened by practice, unhesitatingly chose out the true one, the worship of the God of Israel. It chose between the better and the worse, though it could not have discovered the better of itself. Thus he was led right. In his case was fulfilled the promise, "Who is among you that feareth the Lord, that obeyeth the voice of His servant, that walketh in darkness, and hath no light? Let him trust in the name of the Lord, and stay upon his God." [9] Or, in the Psalmist's words, "The fear of the Lord is the beginning of wisdom: a good understanding have all they that do His commandments." [10] Or (as he elsewhere expresses it), "I understand more than the ancients, because I keep Thy precepts." [11]

Such was the beginning of Josiah's life. At sixteen he began to seek after the God of his fathers; at twenty he commenced his reformation, with a resolute faith and true-hearted generous devotion. From the language of Scripture, it would seem, he began of *himself*; thus he is left a pattern to all ages of prompt obedience for conscience' sake. Jeremiah did not begin to prophesy till *after* the king entered on his reformation, as if the great prophet's call were delayed on purpose to try the strength of Josiah's loyalty to his God, while his hands were

[9] Is. l.10.   [10] Ps. cxi.10.   [11] Ps. cxix.100.

yet unaided by the exertions of others, or by the guidance of inspired men.

What knowledge of God's dealings with his nation and of His revealed purposes Josiah had at this time, we can only conjecture; from the priests he might learn much generally, and from the popular belief. The miraculous destruction of Sennacherib's army was not so long since, and it proved to him God's especial protection of the Jewish people. Manasseh's repentance was more recent still; and the Temple itself, and its service, contained much doctrine to a religious mind, even apart from the law or the prophets. But he had no accurate knowledge.

At twenty, then, he commenced his reformation. At first, not having the Book of the Law to guide him, he took such measures as natural conscience suggested; he put away idolatry generally. Thus he set out, not knowing whither he went. But it is the rule of God's providence, that those who act up to their light, shall be rewarded with clearer light. To him that hath, more shall be given. Accordingly, while he was thus engaged, after a few years, he found the Book of the Law in the *course* of his reformations. He was seeking God in the way of His commandments, and God met him there. He set about repairing the Temple; and it was in the course of this pious work that the high priest found a copy of the Law of Moses in the Temple, probably the original copy which was placed in the ark. Josiah's conduct on this discovery marks his character. Many men, certainly many young men, who had been so zealous as he had already shown himself for six years, would have prided themselves on what they had done, and though they began humbly, by this time would have become self-willed, self-confident, and hard-hearted. He had already been engaged in repressing and punishing God's enemies—this had a tendency to infect him with spiritual pride: and he had a work of destruction to do—this, too, might have made him cruel. Far from it: his peculiar praise is singleness of mind, a pure conscience. Even after years of activity against idolatry, in the words of the text, "his heart was tender," and he still "humbled himself before God." He felt full well the immeasurable distance between himself and his Maker; he felt his own blindness and weakness; and he still earnestly sought to know his duty better than he did, and to practise it more entirely. His was not that stern enthusiasm which has displayed itself in some so-called reformations, fancying itself God's peculiar choice, and "despising others." Here we have the pattern of reformers; singleness of heart, gentleness of temper, in the midst of zeal, resoluteness, and decision in action. All God's Saints have this union of opposite graces; Joseph, Moses, Samuel, David, Nehemiah, St. Paul: but in which of them all is the wonder-working power of grace shown more attractively than in Josiah? "Out of the strong came forth sweetness;" [12] or perhaps, as we may say more truly, Out of the sweet came forth strength.

Observe, then, his conduct when the Law was read to him: "When the king had heard the words of the book of the law, *he rent his clothes*." [13] He thought far more of what he had not done, than of what he had done. He felt how incomplete his reformation had been; and he felt how far more guilty his whole people were than he had supposed, receiving, as they had, such precise guidance in Scripture what to do, and such solemn command to do it; and he learned, moreover, the fearful punishment which was hanging over them; for in that Book of the Law were contained the threats of vengeance to be fulfilled in case of transgression. The passages read to him by the high priest seem to have been some of those contained in the Book of Deuteronomy, in which Moses sets good and evil before the people, to choose their portion. "See, I have set before thee this day life and good, and death and evil. . . . . I call heaven and earth to record this day against you, that I have set before you life and death, blessing and cursing." [14] "A blessing and a curse; a blessing if ye obey the commandments of the Lord your God: . . . a curse if ye will not obey." [15] And there was more than the mere words to terrify him; there had been a fulfilment of them. Samaria, the ten revolting tribes, the kingdom of Israel, had been led away captive. Doubtless he already knew that their sins had caused it; but he found in the Book of the Law that it had been even threatened them beforehand as the punishment; and he discovered that the same punishment awaited his own people, should they persist in sin. Nay, a judgment had already taken place in Judah; for Manasseh, his grandfather, had been carried away into Babylon, and only restored upon his repentance.

In the twenty-eighth chapter of Deuteronomy, you will see what was to be the curse of disobedience: or again, consider the words of the twenty-ninth chapter: "Ye stand this day all of you before the Lord your God . . . that thou shouldest enter into covenant with Him, and into His oath; . . . neither with you

[12] Judges xiv.14.
[13] 2 Kings xxii.11.
[14] Deut. xxx.15, 19.
[15] Deut. xi.26–28.

only do I make this covenant and this oath; but with him that standeth here with us this day before the Lord our God, and *also* with him that is not here with us this day: . . . lest there should be among you man, or woman, or family, or tribe, whose heart turneth away this day from the Lord our God" (alas! as it had happened in the event, even all *ten* tribes, and then the whole twelve had fallen away) "to go and serve the gods of these nations; lest there should be among you a root that beareth gall and wormwood; and it come to pass, when he heareth the words of this curse, that he bless himself in his heart, saying, I shall have peace, though I walk in the imagination of mine heart, to add drunkenness to thirst: the Lord will not spare him, but then the anger of the Lord and His jealousy shall smoke against that man, and all the curses that are written in this book shall lie upon him, . . . so that . . . the strangers that shall come from a far land . . . when they see the plagues of that land, and the sicknesses which the Lord hath laid upon it . . . that it is not sown, nor beareth, nor any grass groweth therein, . . . even all nations shall say, Wherefore hath the Lord done thus unto this land? what meaneth the heat of this great anger? Then men shall say, Because they have forsaken the covenant of the Lord God of their fathers, . . . for they went and served other gods, . . . and the Lord rooted them out of their land in anger, and cast them into another land." These words, or such as these, either about the people or relating to his own duties,[16] Josiah read in the Book of the Law; and thinking of the captivity which had overtaken Israel already, and the sins of his own people Judah, he rent his clothes. Then he bade the priests inquire of God for him what he ought to do to avert His anger. "Go," he said, "inquire of the Lord for me, and for them that are left in Israel and in Judah, concerning the words of the book that is found: for great is the wrath of the Lord that is poured out upon us, because our fathers have not kept the word of the Lord, to do after all that is written in this book."[17]

It is observable, that not even yet does he seem to have known the prophets Jeremiah or Zephaniah, though the former had been called to his office some years. Such was God's pleasure. And the priests and scribes about him, though they seconded his pious designs, were in no sense his guides: they were unacquainted with the Law of Moses, and with the prophets, who were interpreters of that Law. But prophets were, through God's mercy, in every city: and though Jeremiah might be silent

---

[16] *Vide* Deut. xvii. [17] 2 Chron. xxxiv.21.

or might be away, still there were revelations from God even in Jerusalem. To one of these prophets the priests applied. Shallum was keeper of the king's wardrobe—his wife Huldah was known to be gifted with the spirit of prophecy. To her they went. She answered in the words of which the text forms a part: "Thus saith the Lord God of Israel, Tell ye the man that sent you to Me, Thus saith the Lord, Behold, I will bring evil upon this place, and upon the inhabitants thereof, even all the words of the book which the king of Judah hath read: because they have forsaken Me, and have burnt incense unto other gods . . . My wrath shall be kindled against this place, and shall not be quenched. But to the king of Judah, which sent you to inquire of the Lord, thus shall ye say to him, Thus saith the Lord God of Israel, as touching the words which thou hast heard; because thine heart was tender, and thou hast humbled thyself before the Lord, when thou heardest what I spake against this place, and against the inhabitants thereof, that they should become a desolation and a curse, and hast rent thy clothes, and wept before Me; I also have heard thee, saith the Lord. Behold therefore, I will gather thee unto thy fathers, and thou shalt be gathered into thy grave in peace: and thine eyes shall not see all the evil which I will bring upon this place. And they brought the king word again."

How King Josiah conducted himself after this message I need not describe at any length. We have heard it in the First Lesson of this Service.[18] He assembled all Judah at Jerusalem, and publicly read the words of the Book of the Law; then he made all the people renew the covenant with the God of their fathers; then he proceeded more exactly in the work of reformation in Judah and Israel, keeping closely to the directions of the Law; and after that he held his celebrated passover. Thus his greater knowledge was followed by stricter obedience: his accurate attention to the whole ritual is the very praise bestowed on his passover; "Surely there was not holden such a passover from the days of the judges."[19] Whatever he did, he did it with all his heart: "Like unto him was there no king before him, that turned to the Lord with all his heart, and with all his soul, and with all his might, according to all the Law of Moses."[20]

Passing by the particulars of his reformation, let us come to the fulfilment of the promise made to him by Huldah, as the reward of his obedience. "Behold therefore, I will gather thee

[18] Thirteenth Sunday after Trinity.
[19] 2 Kings xxiii.22.   [20] 2 Kings xxiii.25.

to thy fathers, and thou shalt be gathered into thy grave in peace; and thine eyes shall not see all the evil which I will bring upon this place." His reward was an early death; the event proved that it was a violent one also. The king of Egypt came up against the king of Assyria through the land of Judah; Josiah, bound perhaps by an alliance to the king of Assyria, or for some strong reason unknown, opposed him; a battle followed; Josiah disguised himself that he might not be marked out for death; but his hour was come—the promise of release was to be accomplished. "And the archers shot at king Josiah; and the king said to his servants, Have me away; for I am sore wounded. His servants, therefore . . . brought him to Jerusalem; and he died, and was buried in one of the sepulchres of his fathers." [21] Thus the best king of Judah died like Ahab, the worst king of Israel; so little may we judge of God's love or displeasure by outward appearances. "The righteous perisheth, and no man layeth it to heart: and merciful men are taken away, none considering that the righteous is taken away from the evil to come. He shall enter into peace: they shall rest in their beds, each one walking in his uprightness." [22]

The sacred narrative continues: "And all Judah and Jerusalem mourned for Josiah. And Jeremiah lamented for Josiah; and all the singing men and the singing women spake of Josiah in their lamentations to this day, and made them an ordinance in Israel:" probably there was a yearly commemoration of his death; and so great was the mourning at the time, that we find it referred to in the Prophet Zechariah [23] almost as a proverb. So fell the last sovereign of the house of David. God continued His promised mercies to His people through David's line till they were too corrupt to receive them; the last king of the favoured family was forcibly and prematurely cut off, in order to make way for the display of God's vengeance in the captivity of the whole nation. He was taken out of the way; they were carried off to Babylon. "Weep ye not for the dead," says the prophet, "neither bemoan him: but weep sore for him that goeth away: for he shall return no more, nor see his native country." [24] As for Josiah, as it is elsewhere written of him, "His remembrance . . . is sweet as honey in all mouths, and as music at a banquet of wine. He behaved himself uprightly in the conversion of the people, and took away the abominations of iniquity. He directed his heart unto the Lord, and in the time of the ungodly

[21] 2 Chron. xxv.23–25. [22] Is. lvii.1.
[23] Zech. xii.11. [24] Jer. xxii.10.

he established the worship of God. All, except David, and Ezekias, and Josias, were defective; for they forsook the law of the Most High, even the kings of Juda failed." [25]

In conclusion, my brethren, I would have you observe in what Josiah's chief excellence lay. This is the character given him when his name is first mentioned; "He did . . . right in the sight of the Lord, and walked in all the ways of David his father, and turned not aside to the right hand or to the left." [26] He kept the narrow middle way. Now what is this strict virtue called? it is called *faith*. It is no matter whether we call it faith or conscientiousness, they are in substance one and the same: where there is faith, there is conscientiousness—where there is conscientiousness, there is faith; they may be distinguished from each other in words, but they are not divided in fact. They belong to one, and but one, habit of mind—dutifulness; they show themselves in obedience, in the careful, anxious observance of God's will, however we learn it. Hence it is that St. Paul tells us that "the just shall live by faith" under *every* dispensation of God's mercy. And this is called *faith*, because it implies a reliance on the mere word of the unseen God overpowering the temptations of sight. Whether it be we read and accept His word in Scripture (as Christians do), or His word in our conscience, the law written on the heart (as is the case with heathens); in either case, it is by following it, in spite of the seductions of the world around us, that we please God. St. Paul calls it faith; saying after the prophet, "The just shall live by faith:" and St. Peter, in the tenth chapter of the Acts, calls it "fearing and *working righteousness*," where he says, that "in every nation he that feareth God and worketh righteousness is accepted with Him." It is all one: both Apostles say that God loves those who prefer Him to the world; whose *character and frame* of mind is such. Elsewhere St. Paul also speaks like St. Peter, when he declares that God will render eternal life to them, who by "patient *continuance in* well-doing seek for glory." [27] St. John adds his testimony: "Little children, let no man deceive you. He that doeth righteousness is righteous, even as He is righteous." [28] And our Saviour's last words at the end of the whole Scripture, long after the coming of the Spirit, after the death of all the Apostles but St. John, are the same: "Blessed are they that *do His* commandments, that they may *have right* to the tree of life." [29]

And if such is God's mercy, as we trust, to all men, wherever

---

[25] Ecclus. xlix.1–4.   [26] 2 Kings xxii.2.   [27] Rom. ii.7.
[28] 1 John iii.7.   [29] Rev. xxii.14.

any one with a perfect heart seeks Him, what think you is His mercy upon Christians? Something far greater, and more wonderful; for we are elected out of the world, in Jesus Christ our Saviour, to a glory incomprehensible and eternal. We are the heirs of promise; God has loved us before we were born. He had us taken into His Church in our infancy. He by Baptism made us new creatures, giving us powers which we by nature had not, and raising us to the unseen society of Saints and Angels. And all this we enjoy on our faith; that is, on our believing that we have them, and seriously trying to profit by them. May God grant, that we, like Josiah, may improve our gifts, and trade and make merchandise with them, so that, when He cometh to reckon with us, we may be accepted!

INWARD WITNESS TO
THE TRUTH OF THE GOSPEL

"I have more understanding than my teachers, for Thy testimonies are my study; I am wiser than the aged, because I keep Thy commandments."—Ps. cxix.99, 100.

I N these words the Psalmist declares, that in consequence of having obeyed God's commandments he had obtained more wisdom and understanding than those who had first enlightened his ignorance, and were once more enlightened than he. As if he said, "When I was a child, I was instructed in religious knowledge by kind and pious friends, who told me who my Maker was, what great things He had done for me, how much I owed to Him, and how I was to serve Him. All this I learned from them, and I rejoice that they taught it me: yet they did more; they set me in the way to gain a knowledge of religious truth in another and higher manner. They not only taught me, but trained me; they were careful that I should not only know my duty, but do it. They obliged me to obey; they obliged me to begin a religious course of life, which (praised be God!) I have ever pursued; and this obedience to His commandments has brought me to a clearer knowledge of His truth, than any mere instruction could convey. I have been taught, not from without merely, but from within. I have been taught by means of a purified heart, by a changed will, by chastened reins, by a mortified appetite, by a bridled tongue, by eyes corrected and subdued. 'I have more understanding than my teachers, for Thy testimonies,' O Lord, 'are my study; I am wiser than the aged, because I keep Thy commandments.'"

We may sometimes hear men say, "How do you know that the Bible is true? You are told so in Church; your parents believed it; but might they not be mistaken? and if so, you are mistaken also." Now to this objection it may be answered, and very satisfactorily, "Is it then nothing toward convincing us of the truth of the Gospel, that those whom we love best and reverence most believe it? Is it against reason to think that they are right, who have considered the matter most deeply? Do we not receive what they tell us in other matters, though we cannot prove the truth of their information; for instance, in matters of art and science; why then is it irrational to believe them in religion also? Have not the wisest and holiest of men been Christians? and have not unbelievers, on the contrary, been very generally signal instances of pride, discontent, and profligacy? Again, are not the principles of unbelief certain to dissolve human society? and is not this plain fact, candidly considered, enough to show that unbelief cannot be a right condition of our nature? for who can believe that we were intended to live in anarchy? If we have no good reason for believing, at least we have no good reason for disbelieving. If you ask why we are Christians, we ask in turn, Why should we not be Christians? it will be enough to remain where we are, till you do what you never can do—prove to us for certain, that the Gospel is not Divine; it is enough for us to be on the side of good men, to be under the feet of the Saints, to 'go our way forth by the footsteps of the flock, and to feed our kids beside the shepherds' tents.'" [1]

This would be quite a sufficient answer, had we nothing else to say; but I will give another, and that in connexion with the text; I will show you that the most unlearned Christian may have a very real and substantial argument, an intimate token, of the truth of the Gospel, quite independent of the authority of his parents and teachers; nay, that were all the world, even were his teachers, to tell him that religion was a dream, still he would have a good reason for believing it true.

This reason, I say, is contained in the text—"I have more understanding than the aged, *because* I keep Thy commandments." By obeying the commands of Scripture, we learn that these commands really come from God; by trying we make proof; by doing we come to know. Now how comes this to pass? It happens in several ways.

1. Consider the Bible tells us to be meek, humble, single-hearted, and teachable. Now, it is plain that humility and teachableness are qualities of mind necessary for arriving at the truth in any subject, and in religious matters as well as others. By obeying Scripture, then, in practising humility and teachableness, it is evident we are at least *in the way* to arrive at the knowledge of God. On the other hand, impatient, proud, self-confident, obstinate men, are generally wrong in the

---

[1] Cant. i.8.

opinions they form of persons and things. Prejudice and self-conceit blind the eyes and mislead the judgment, whatever be the subject inquired into. For instance, how often do men mistake the characters and misconstrue the actions of others! how often are they deceived in them! how often do the young form acquaintances injurious to their comfort and good! how often do men embark in foolish and ruinous schemes! how often do they squander their money, and destroy their worldly prospects! And what, I ask, is so frequent a cause of these many errors as wilfulness and presumption? The same thing happens also in religious inquiries. When I see a person hasty and violent, harsh and high-minded, careless of what others feel, and disdainful of what they think;—when I see such a one proceeding to inquire into religious subjects, I am sure beforehand he cannot go right—he will not be led into all the truth—it is contrary to the nature of things and the experience of the world, that he should find what he is seeking. I should say the same were he seeking to find out what to believe or do in any other matter not religious,—but especially in any such important and solemn inquiry; for the *fear* of the Lord (humbleness, teachableness, reverence towards Him) is the very *beginning* of wisdom, as Solomon tells us; it leads us to think over things modestly and honestly, to examine patiently, to bear doubt and uncertainty, to wait perseveringly for an increase of light, to be slow to speak, and to be deliberate in deciding.

2. Consider, in the next place, that those who are trained carefully according to the precepts of Scripture, gain an elevation, a delicacy, refinement, and sanctity of mind, which is most necessary for judging fairly of the truth of Scripture.

A man who loves sin does not wish the Gospel to be true, and therefore is not a fair judge of it; a mere man of the world, a selfish and covetous man, or a drunkard, or an extortioner, is, from a sense of interest, against that Bible which condemns him, and would account that man indeed a messenger of good tidings of peace who could prove to him that Christ's doctrine was not from God. "Every one that doeth evil hateth the light, neither cometh to the light, lest his deeds should be reproved."[2] I do not mean to say that such men necessarily reject the word of God, as if we could dare to conclude that all who do not reject it are therefore sure to be not covetous, drunkards, extortioners, and the like; for it is often a man's interest not openly to reject it, though it be against him; and the bulk of men are

[2] John iii.20.

inconsistent, and have some good feelings left, even amid their sins and vices, which keep them from going all lengths. But, while they still profess to honour, at least they try to pervert and misinterpret Scripture, and that comes to the same thing. They try to persuade themselves that Christ will save them, though they continue in sin; or they wish to believe that future punishment will not last for ever; or they conceive that their good deeds or habits, few and miserable as they are at best, will make up for the sins of which they are too conscious. Whereas such men as have been taught betimes to work with God their Saviour—in ruling their hearts, and curbing their sinful passions, and changing their wills—though they are still sinners, have not within them that treacherous enemy of the truth which misleads the judgments of irreligious men.

Here, then, are two very good reasons at first sight, why men who obey the Scripture precepts are more likely to arrive at religious truth, than those who neglect them; first, because such men are teachable men; secondly, because they are pure in heart; such shall see God, whereas the proud provoke His anger, and the carnal are His abhorrence.

But to proceed. Consider, moreover, that those who try to obey God evidently gain a knowledge of themselves at least; and this may be shown to be the first and principal step towards knowing God. For let us suppose a child, under God's blessing, profiting by his teacher's guidance, and trying to do his duty and please God. He will perceive that there is much in him which ought not to be in him. His own natural sense of right and wrong tells him that peevishness, sullenness, deceit, and self-will, are tempers and principles of which he has cause to be ashamed, and he feels that these bad tempers and principles are in his heart. As he grows older, he will understand this more and more. Wishing, then, and striving to act up to the law of conscience, he will yet find that, with his utmost efforts, and after his most earnest prayers, he still falls short of what he knows to be right, and what he aims at. Conscience, however, being respected, will become a more powerful and enlightened guide than before; it will become more refined and hard to please; and he will understand and perceive more clearly the distance that exists between his own conduct and thoughts, and perfection. He will admire and take pleasure in the holy law of God, of which he reads in Scripture; but he will be humbled withal, as understanding himself to be a continual transgressor against it. Thus he will learn from experience the doctrine of original sin, before he knows the actual name of it. He will, in fact, say to himself, what St. Paul describes all beginners in religion as saying, "What I would, that do I not; but what I hate, that do I. I delight in the law of God after the inward man, but I see another law in my members, warring against the law of my mind, and bringing me into captivity. I know that in my flesh dwelleth no good thing." [3] The effect of this experience will be to make him take it for granted, as an elementary truth, that he cannot gain heaven for himself; to make him feel himself guilty before God; and to feel, moreover, that even were he admitted into the Divine presence, yet, till his heart be (so to say) made over again, he cannot perfectly enjoy God. This, surely, is the state of self-knowledge; these are the convictions to which every one is brought on, who attempts honestly to obey the precepts of God. I do not mean that all that I have been saying will necessarily pass through his mind, and in the same order, or that he will be conscious of it, or be able to speak of it, but that on the whole thus he will feel.

When, then, even an unlearned person thus trained—from his own heart, from the action of his mind upon itself, from struggles with self, from an attempt to follow those impulses of his own nature which he feels to be highest and noblest, from a vivid natural perception (natural, though cherished and strengthened by prayer; natural, though unfolded and diversified by practice; natural, though of that new and second nature which God the Holy Ghost gives), from an innate, though supernatural perception of the great vision of Truth which is external to him (a perception of it, not indeed in its fulness, but in glimpses, and by fits and seasons, and in its persuasive influences, and through a courageous following on after it, as a man in the dark might follow after some dim and distant light)—I say, when a person thus trained from his own heart, reads the declarations and promises of the Gospel, are we to be told that he believes in them merely because he has been bid believe in them? Do we not see he has besides this a something in his own breast which bears a confirming testimony to their truth? He reads that the heart is "deceitful above all things and desperately wicked," [4] and that he inherits an evil nature from Adam, and that he is still under its power, except so far as he has been renewed. Here is a mystery; but his own actual and too bitter experience bears witness to the truth of the declaration; he feels the mystery of iniquity within him. He reads, that "without holiness no man shall see the Lord;" [5] and his own love of what

[3] Rom. vii.15, 18, 22, 23.   [4] Jer. xvii.9.   [5] Heb. xii.14.

is true and lovely and pure, approves and embraces the doctrine as coming from God. He reads, that God is angry at sin, and will punish the sinner, and that it is a hard matter, nay, an impossibility, for us to appease His wrath. Here, again, is a mystery: but here, too, his conscience anticipates the mystery, and convicts him; his mouth is stopped. And when he goes on to read that the Son of God has Himself come into the world in our flesh, and died upon the Cross for us, does he not, amid the awful mysteriousness of the doctrine, find those words fulfilled in him which that gracious Saviour uttered, "And I, if I be lifted up from the earth, will draw all men unto Me"? He cannot choose but believe in Him. He says, "O Lord, Thou art stronger than I, and hast prevailed."

Here then, I say, he surely possesses an evidence perfectly distinct from the authority of superiors and teachers; like St. Paul, he is in one way not taught of men, "but by the revelation of Jesus Christ." [6] Others have but bid him look within, and pray for God's grace to be enabled to know himself; and the more he understands his own heart, the more are the Gospel doctrines recommended to his reason. He is assured that Christ does not speak of Himself, but that His word is from God. He is ready, with the Samaritan woman, to say to all around him, "Come, see a man, which told me all things that ever I did: is not this the Christ?" [7] Or, again, in the words which the Samaritans of the same city used to the woman after conversing with Christ; "Now we believe, *not* because of thy saying" (not merely on the authority of friends and relatives); "for *we* have heard Him ourselves, and know that this is indeed the Christ, the Saviour of the world."

The Bible, then, seems to say,—God is not a hard master to require belief, without affording grounds for believing; only follow your own sense of right, and you will gain from that very obedience to your Maker, which natural conscience enjoins, a conviction of the truth and power of that Redeemer whom a supernatural message has revealed; do but examine your thoughts and doings; do but attempt what you know to be God's will, and you will most assuredly be led on into all the truth: you will recognize the force, meaning, and awful graciousness of the Gospel Creed; you will bear witness to the truth of one doctrine, by your own past experience of yourselves; of another, by seeing that it is suited to your necessity; of a third, by finding it fulfilled upon your obeying it. As the

[6] Gal. i.12.   [7] John iv.29.

prophet says, "Bring ye" your offering "into Mine house," saith the Lord, "and prove Me now herewith, if I will not open you the windows of heaven, and pour you out a blessing that there shall not be room enough to receive it."[8]

My brethren, it is always reasonable to insist upon these subjects; but it is peculiarly so in times when a spirit of presumptuous doubting is in many places abroad. As many of us as live in the world must expect to hear our faith despised, and our conscientious obedience ridiculed; we must expect to be taunted and scorned by those who find it much easier to attack another's creed than to state their own. A little learning is a dangerous thing. When men think they know more than others, they often talk for the sake of talking, or to show their ability (as they think), their shrewdness and depth; and they speak lightly of the All-Holy God, to gratify their empty self-conceit and vanity. And often it answers no purpose to dispute with such persons; for not having been trained up to obey their conscience, to restrain their passions, and examine their hearts, they will assent to nothing you can say; they will be questioning and arguing about every thing; they have no common ground with you, and when they talk of religion they are like blind persons talking of colours. If you urge how great a gift it is to be at peace with God, or of the arduousness and yet desirableness of perfection, or the beauty of saintliness, or the dangerousness of the world, or the blessedness of self-control, or the glory of virginity, or the answers which God gives to prayer, or the marvellousness and almost miraculousness of His providences, or the comfort of religion in affliction, or the strength given you over your passions in the Most Holy Sacrament, such persons understand you not at all. They will laugh, they will scoff, at best they will wonder: any how what you say is no evidence to *them*. You cannot convince them, because you differ from them in first principles; it is not that they start from the same point as you, and afterwards strike off in some wayward direction; but their course is altogether distinct, they have no point in common with you. For such persons then you can only pray; God alone can bring down pride, self-conceit, an arrogant spirit, a presumptuous temper; God alone can dissipate prejudice; God alone can overcome flesh and blood. Useful as argument may be for converting a man, in such cases God seldom condescends to employ it. Yet, let not such vain or ignorant reasoners convert you to unbelief in great matters or little; let them not persuade

8 Mal. iii.10.

you, that your faith is built on the mere teaching of fallible men; do not you be ridiculed out of your confidence and hope in Christ. You may, if you will, have an inward witness arising from obedience: and though you cannot make them see it, you can see it yourselves, which is the great thing; and it will be quite sufficient, with God's blessing, to keep you stedfast in the way of life.

Lastly, let me remark how dangerous their state is who are content to take the truths of the Gospel on trust, without caring whether or not those truths are realized in their own heart and conduct. Such men, when assailed by ridicule and sophistry, are likely to fall; they have no root in themselves; and let them be quite sure, that should they fall away from the faith, it will be a slight thing at the last day to plead that subtle arguments were used against them, that they were altogether unprepared and ignorant, and that their seducers prevailed over them by the display of some little cleverness and human knowledge. The inward witness to the truth lodged in our hearts is a match for the most learned infidel or sceptic that ever lived: though, to tell the truth, such men are generally very shallow and weak, as well as wicked; generally know only a little, pervert what they know, assume false principles, and distort or suppress facts: but were they as accomplished as the very author of evil, the humblest Christian, armed with sling and stone, and supported by God's unseen might, is, as far as his own faith is concerned, a match for them. And, on the other hand, the most acute of reasoners and most profound of thinkers, the most instructed in earthly knowledge, is nothing, except he has also within him the presence of the Spirit of truth. Human knowledge, though of great power when joined to a pure and humble faith, is of no power when opposed to it, and, after all, for the comfort of the individual Christian, it is of little value.

May we, then, all grow in heavenly knowledge, and, with that end, labour to improve what is already given us, be it more or be it less, knowing that "he that is faithful in little is faithful also in much," and that "to him that hath, more shall be given."

JEREMIAH, A LESSON FOR
THE DISAPPOINTED

*"Be not afraid of their faces: for I am with thee to deliver thee,
saith the Lord."*—Jer. i.8.

THE Prophets were ever ungratefully treated by the Israelites; they were resisted, their warnings neglected, their
good services forgotten. But there was this difference between
the earlier and the later Prophets; the earlier lived and died in
honour among their people,—in outward honour; though
hated and thwarted by the wicked, they were exalted to high
places, and ruled in the congregation. Moses, for instance, was
in trouble from his people all his life long, but to the end he was
their lawgiver and judge. Samuel, too, even though rejected,
was still held in reverence; and when he died, "all the Israelites
were gathered together and lamented him, and buried him in
his house at Ramah." [1] David died on a royal throne. But in the
latter times, the prophets were not only feared and hated by the
enemies of God, but cast out of the vineyard. As the time approached for the coming of the true Prophet of the Church, the
Son of God, they resembled Him in their earthly fortunes more
and more; and as He was to suffer, so did they. Moses was a
ruler, Jeremiah was an outcast: Samuel was buried in peace,
John the Baptist was beheaded. In St. Paul's words, they "had
trial of cruel mockings and scourgings, yea, moreover, of bonds
and imprisonment. They were stoned; they were sawn asunder,
were tempted, were slain with the sword; they wandered about
in sheepskins and goatskins, being destitute, afflicted, tormented; of whom the world was not worthy; they wandered in
deserts, and in mountains, and in dens and caves of the earth." [2]
Of these, Elijah, who lived in the wilderness, and the hundred prophets whom Obadiah fed by fifty in a cave, are examples of the wanderers. And Micaiah, who was appointed the
bread of affliction and the water of affliction by an idolatrous

[1] 1 Sam. xxv.1.   [2] Heb. xi.36–38.

king, is the specimen of those who "had trial of bonds and imprisonment." Of those who were sawn asunder and slain with the sword, Isaiah is the chief, who, as tradition goes, was by order of Manasseh, the son of Hezekiah, sawn asunder with a wooden saw. And of those who were stoned, none is more famous than Zechariah, the son of Jehoiada, "who was slain between the temple and the altar."[3] But of all the persecuted prophets Jeremiah is the most eminent; i. e. we know more of his history, of his imprisonments, his wanderings, and his afflictions. He may be taken as a representative of the Prophets; and hence it is that he is an especial type of our Lord and Saviour. All the Prophets were types of the Great Prophet whose way they were preparing; they tended towards and spoke of Christ. In their sufferings they foreshadowed His priesthood, and in their teaching His prophetical office, and in their miracles His royal power. The history of Jeremiah, then, as being drawn out in Scripture more circumstantially than that of the other Prophets, is the most exact type of Christ among them; that is, next to David, who, of course, was the nearest resemblance to Him of all, as a sufferer, an inspired teacher, and a king. Jeremiah comes next to David; I do not say in dignity and privilege, for it was Elijah who was taken up to heaven, and appeared at the Transfiguration; nor in inspiration, for to Isaiah one should assign the higher evangelical gifts; but in typifying Him who came and wept over Jerusalem, and then was tortured and put to death by those He wept over. And hence, when our Lord came, while some thought Him Elijah, and others John the Baptist, risen from the dead, there were others who thought Him Jeremiah. Of Jeremiah, then, I will now speak, as a specimen of all those Prophets whom St. Paul sets before us as examples of faith, and St. James as examples of patience.

Jeremiah's ministry may be summed up in three words, good hope, labour, disappointment.

It was his privilege to be called to his sacred office from his earliest years. Like Samuel, the first prophet, he was of the tribe of Levi, dedicated from his birth to religious services, and favoured with the constant presence and grace of God. "Before I formed thee . . . . I knew thee,"[4] says the word of the Lord to him when He gave him his commission, "and before thou camest out of the womb I sanctified thee, and I ordained thee a prophet unto the nations." This commission was given the year after Josiah began his reformation. Jeremiah returned for

---

[3] Matt. xxiii.35. [4] Jer. i.5.

answer, "Ah! Lord God! behold, I cannot speak; for I am a child." He felt the arduousness of a prophet's office; the firmness and intrepidity which were required to speak the words of God. "But the Lord said unto him, Say not I am a child; for thou shalt go to all that I shall send thee, and whatsoever I command thee thou shalt speak. Be not afraid of their faces, for I am with thee to deliver thee, saith the Lord. Then the Lord put forth His hand and touched my mouth, and said unto me, Behold I have put My words in thy mouth."

No prophet commenced his labours with greater encouragement than Jeremiah. A king had succeeded to the throne who was bringing back the times of the man after God's own heart. There had not been a son of David so zealous as Josiah since David himself. The king, too, was young, at most twenty years of age, in the beginning of his reformation. What might not be effected in a course of years, however corrupt and degraded was the existing state of his people? So Jeremiah might think. It must be recollected, too, that religious obedience was under the Jewish covenant awarded with temporal prosperity. There seemed, then, every reason for Jeremiah at first to suppose that bright fortunes were in store for the Church. Josiah was the very king whose birth was foretold by name above three hundred years before, when Jeroboam established idolatry; who was the promised avenger of God's covenant, "the repairer of the breach, the restorer of paths to dwell in." [5] Israel (the ten tribes) having gone into captivity, schism had come to its end; the kings of the house of David again ruled over the whole extent of the promised land; idolatry was destroyed by Josiah in all the cities. Such were the present blessings which the Jewish remnant enjoyed. At first sight, then, it seemed reasonable to anticipate further and permanent improvement. Every one begins with being sanguine; doubtless then, as now, many labourers in God's husbandry entered on their office with more lively hopes than their after fortunes warranted. Whether or not, however, such hope of success encouraged Jeremiah's first exertions, very soon, in his case, this cheerful prospect was overcast, and he was left to labour in the dark. Huldah's message to the king, on his finding the Book of the Law in the temple, fixed the coming fortunes of Judah. Huldah foretold a woe,—an early removal of the good Josiah to his rest as a mercy to him, and to the nation, who were unworthy of him, a fierce destruction. This prophecy was delivered five

[5] Is. lviii.12.

years after Jeremiah entered upon his office; he ministered in all forty years before the captivity; so early in his course were his hopes cut away.

But even though Huldah's message be supposed not to reach him, still he was doubtless soon undeceived as to any hopes he might entertain, whether, by the express Word of God informing him, or by the actual hardened state of sin in which the nation lay. Soon, surely, were his hopes destroyed, and his mind sobered into a more blessed and noble temper,—resignation.

I call resignation a more blessed frame of mind than sanguine hope of present success, because it is the truer, and the more consistent with our fallen state of being, and the more improving to our hearts; and because it is that for which the most eminent servants of God have been conspicuous. To expect great effects from our exertions for religious objects is natural indeed, and innocent, but it arises from inexperience of the kind of work we have to do,—to change the heart and will of man. It is a far nobler frame of mind, to labour, not with the hope of seeing the fruit of our labour, but for conscience' sake, as a matter of duty; and again, in faith, trusting good *will* be done, though we see it not. Look through the Bible, and you will find God's servants, even though they began with success, end with disappointment; not that God's purposes or His instruments fail, but that the time for reaping what we have sown is hereafter, not here; that here there is no great visible fruit in any one man's lifetime. Moses, for instance, began with leading the Israelites out of Egypt in triumph; he ended at the age of an hundred and twenty years, before his journey was finished and Canaan gained, one among the offending multitudes who were overthrown in the wilderness.[6] Samuel's reformations ended in the people's wilfully choosing a king like the nations around them. Elijah, after his successes, fled from Jezebel into the wilderness to mourn over his disappointments. Isaiah, after Hezekiah's religious reign, and the miraculous destruction of Sennacherib's army, fell upon the evil days of his son Manasseh. Even in the successes of the first Christian teachers, the Apostles, the same rule is observed. After all the great works God enabled them to accomplish, they confessed before their death that what they experienced, and what they saw before them, was reverse and calamity, and that the fruit of their labour would not be seen, till Christ came to open the books and collect His saints from the four corners of the earth. "Evil men and

[6] 1 Cor. x. 5.

seducers shall wax worse and worse, deceiving and being deceived,"[7] is the testimony of St. Peter, St. Paul, St. John, and St.
Jude.

Now, in the instance of Jeremiah, we have on record that variety and vicissitude of feelings, which this transition from
hope to disappointment produces, at least in a sensitive mind.
His trials were very great, even in Josiah's reign; but when that
pious king's countenance was withdrawn on his early death, he
was exposed to persecution from every class of men. At one
time we read of the people conspiring against him;[8] at another,
of the men of his own city, Anathoth, "seeking his life,"[9] on
account of his prophesying in the Lord's name. At another time
he was seized by the priests and the prophets in order to be put
to death, from which he was only saved by certain of the princes
and elders who were still faithful to the memory of Josiah.[10]
Then, again, Pashur, the chief governor of the temple, smote
him and tortured him.[11] At another time, the king, Zedekiah,
put him in prison.[12] Afterwards, when the army of the Chaldeans had besieged Jerusalem, the Jews accused him of falling
away to the enemy,[13] and smote him, and imprisoned him; then
they cast him into a dungeon, where he "sunk in the mire," and
almost perished from hunger.[14] When Jerusalem had been
taken by the enemy, Jeremiah was forcibly carried down to
Egypt by men who at first pretended to reverence and consult
him,[15] and there he came to his end—it is believed, a violent
end. Nebuchadnezzar, the heathen king of Babylon and conqueror of Jerusalem, was one of the few persons who showed
him kindness. This great king, who afterwards honoured Daniel, and was at length brought to acknowledge the God of
heaven by a severe chastisement, on the taking of the city delivered Jeremiah from prison,[16] and gave charge to the captain of
his guard concerning him, to "look well to him, and to do him
no harm; but to do unto him even as he should say . . . ." An
Ethiopian, another heathen, is also mentioned as delivering
him from the dungeon.

Such were his trials: his affliction, fear, despondency, and
sometimes even restlessness under them are variously expressed; that succession and tide of feelings which most persons
undergo before their minds settle into the calm of resignation.
At one time he speaks as astonished at his failure: "O Lord, art

[7] 2 Tim. iii.13.   [8] Jer. xviii.18.   [9] Jer. xi.21.
[10] Jer. xxvi.16, etc.   [11] Jer. xx.2.   [12] Jer. xxxii.3.
[13] Jer. xxxvii.14.   [14] Jer. xxxviii.6, 9.   [15] Jer. xlii, xliii.
[16] Jer. xxxix.14.

not Thine eyes upon the truth? Thou hast stricken them, but they have not grieved; Thou hast consumed them, but they have refused to receive correction." [17] Again, "A wonderful and horrible thing is committed in the land; the prophets prophesy falsely, and the priests bear rule by their means; and My people love to have it so." [18] At another time, he expresses his perplexity at the disorder of the world, and the successes of the wicked: "Righteous art Thou, O Lord, when I plead with Thee; yet let me talk with Thee of Thy judgments: wherefore doth the way of the wicked prosper? wherefore are all they happy that deal very treacherously? . . . . but Thou, O Lord, knowest me; Thou hast seen me, and tried mine heart towards Thee." [19] Then, in turn, his mind frets at the thought of its own anxious labours and perplexities: "Woe is me, my mother, that thou hast borne me a man of strife and a man of contention to the whole earth! I have neither lent on usury, nor men have lent to me on usury; yet every one of them doth curse me. . . . . Why is my pain perpetual, and my wound incurable? . . . wilt Thou be altogether unto me as a deceiver, and as waters that fail?" [20] These are the sorrows of a gentle and peaceable mind, forced against its will into the troubles of life, and incurring the hatred of those whom it opposes against its nature. This he elsewhere expresses thus: "As for me, I have not . . . desired the woeful day" (which he foretold); "Thou knowest: that which came out of my lips was right before Thee. Be not a terror unto me: Thou art my hope in the day of evil." [21] When Pashur put him to torture he was still more agitated, and said, "O Lord, Thou hast deceived me, and I was deceived. Thou art stronger than I, and hast prevailed. I am in derision daily, every one mocketh me. . . . Cursed be the day wherein I was born" (here certainly is the language even of impatience), "let not the day wherein my mother bare me be blessed." [22]

However, of such changes of feelings what was the end?—resignation. He elsewhere uses language which expresses that chastened spirit and weaned heart, which is the termination of all agitation and anxiety in the case of religious minds. He, who at one time could not comfort himself, at another was sent to comfort a brother; and, in comforting Baruch, he speaks in that nobler temper of resignation which takes the place of sanguine hope and harassing fear, and betokens calm and clear-sighted faith and inward peace. "Thus saith the Lord the God of Israel

[17] Jer. v.3.   [18] Jer. v.30, 31.   [19] Jer. xii.1–3.
[20] Jer. xv.10–18.   [21] Jer. xvii.16, 17.   [22] Jer. xx.7–14.

unto thee, O Baruch. Thou didst say, Woe is me now, for the Lord hath added grief to my sorrow; I fainted in my sighing, and I find no rest. Behold, that which I have built will I break down, and that which I have planted I will pluck up, even this whole land. And seekest thou great things for thyself? seek them not: for, behold, I will bring evil upon all flesh; . . . but thy life will I give unto thee for a prey in all places whither thou goest;" that is, seek not success, be not impatient, fret not thyself—be content, if, after all thy labours, thou dost but save thyself, without seeing other fruit of them.

And now, my brethren, does what I have been saying apply to all of us, or only to Prophets? It applies to all of us. For all of us live in a world which promises well, but does not fulfil; and all of us (taking our lives altogether apart from religious prospects) begin with hope, and end with disappointment. Doubtless, there is much difference in our respective trials here, arising from difference of tempers and fortunes. Still it is in our nature to begin life thoughtlessly and joyously; to seek great things in one way or other; to have vague notions of good to come; to love the world, and to believe its promises, and seek satisfaction and happiness from it. And, as it is our nature to hope, so it is our lot, as life proceeds, to encounter disappointment. I know that there are multitudes, in the retired ranks of society, who pass their days without any great varieties of fortune; though, even in such cases, thinking persons will have much more to say of themselves than at first sight might appear. Still, that disappointment in some shape or other is the lot of man (that is, looking at our prospects apart from the next world) is plain, from the mere fact, if nothing else could be said, that we begin life with health and end it with sickness; or in other words, that it *comes* to an *end*, for an end is a failure. And even in the quietest walks of life, do not the old feel regret, more or less vividly, that they are not young? Do not they lament the days gone by, and even with the pleasure of remembrance feel the pain? And why, except that they think that they have lost something which they once had, whereas in the beginning of life, they thought of gaining something they had not? A double disappointment.

Now is it religion that suggests this sad view of things? No, it is experience; it is the *world's* doing; it is fact, from which we cannot escape, though the Bible said not a word about the perishing nature of all earthly pleasures.

Here then it is, that God Himself offers us His aid by His Word, and in His Church. Left to ourselves, we seek good from the world, but cannot find it; in youth we look forward, and in age we look back. It is well we should be persuaded of these things betimes, to gain wisdom and to provide for the evil day. Seek we great things? We must seek them where they really are to be found, and in the way in which they are to be found; we must seek them as He has set them before us, who came into the world to enable us to gain them. We must be willing to give up present hope for future enjoyment, this world for the unseen. The truth is (though it is so difficult for us to admit it heartily), our nature is not at first in a state to enjoy happiness, even if we had it offered to us. We seek for it, and we feel we need it; but (strange though it is to say, still so it is) we are not fitted to be happy. If then at once we rush forward to seek enjoyment, it will be like a child's attempting to walk before his strength is come. If we would gain true bliss, we must cease to seek it as an end; we must postpone the prospect of enjoying it. For we are by nature in an unnatural state; we must be changed from what we are when born, before we can receive our greatest good. And as in sickness sharp remedies are often used, or irksome treatment, so it is with our souls; we must go through pain, we must practise self-denial, we must curb our wills, and purify our hearts, before we are capable of any lasting solid peace. To attempt to gain happiness, except in this apparently tedious and circuitous way, is a labour lost; it is building on the sand; the foundation will soon give way, though the house looks fair for a time. To be gay and thoughtless, to be self-indulgent and self-willed, is quite out of character with our real state. We must learn to know ourselves, and to have thoughts and feelings becoming ourselves. Impetuous hope and undisciplined mirth ill-suit a sinner. Should *he* shrink from low notions of himself, and sharp pain, and mortification of natural wishes, whose guilt called down the Son of God from heaven to die upon the cross for him? May he live in pleasure here, and call this world his home, while he reads in the Gospel of his Saviour's lifelong affliction and disappointment?

It cannot be; let us prepare for suffering and disappointment, which befit us as sinners, and which are necessary for us as saints. Let us not turn away from trial when God brings it on us, or play the coward in the fight of faith. "Watch ye, stand fast in the faith, quit you like men, be strong;"[23] such is St. Paul's exhortation. When affliction overtakes you, remember to accept it as a means of improving your hearts, and pray God

[23] 1 Cor. xvi.13.

for His grace that it may do so. Look disappointment in the face. "Take . . . . the Prophets . . . . for an example of suffering affliction, and of patience. Behold, we count them happy who endure." Give not over your attempts to serve God, though you see nothing come of them. Watch and pray, and obey your conscience, though you cannot perceive your own progress in holiness. Go on, and you cannot but go forward; believe it, though you do not see it. Do the duties of your calling, though they are distasteful to you. Educate your children carefully in the good way, though you cannot tell how far God's grace has touched their hearts. Let your light shine before men, and praise God by a consistent life, even though others do not seem to glorify their Father on account of it, or to be benefited by your example. "Cast your bread upon the waters, for you shall find it after many days. . . . . In the morning sow your seed, in the evening withhold not your hand; for you know not whether shall prosper, either this or that; or whether they both shall be alike good." [24] Persevere in the narrow way. The Prophets went through sufferings to which ours are mere trifles; violence and craft combined to turn them aside, but they kept right on, and are at rest.

Now, I know full well, that this whole subject is distasteful to many men, who say we ought to be cheerful. "We are bid rejoice, why then do you bid us mourn?" I bid you mourn in order that you may rejoice more perfectly. "Blessed are they that mourn, for they shall be comforted." [25] "They that sow in tears, shall reap in joy." I bid you take up the cross of Christ, that you may wear His crown. Give your hearts to Him, and you will for yourselves solve the difficulty, how Christians can be sorrowful, yet alway rejoicing. [26] You will find that lightness of heart and cheerfulness are quite consistent with that new and heavenly character which He gives us, though to gain it in any good measure, we must for a time be sorrowful, and ever after thoughtful. But I give you fair warning, you must at first take His word on trust; and if you do not, there is no help for it. He says, "Come unto Me, . . . and I will give you rest." You must begin on faith: you cannot see at first whither He is leading you, and how light will rise out of the darkness. You must begin by denying yourselves your natural wishes,—a painful work; by refraining from sin, by rousing from sloth, by preserving your tongue from insincere words, and your hands from deceitful dealings, and your eyes from beholding vanity; by watching

[24] Eccles. xi.1, 6. [25] Matt. v.4. [26] 2 Cor. vi.10.

against the first rising of anger, pride, impurity, obstinacy, jealousy; by learning to endure the laugh of irreligious men for Christ's sake; by forcing your minds to follow seriously the words of prayer, though it be difficult to you, and by keeping before you the thought of God all through the day. These things you will be able to do if you do but seek the mighty help of God the Holy Spirit which is given you; and while you follow after them, then, in the Prophet's language, "your light shall rise in obscurity, and your darkness shall be as the noonday. And the Lord shall guide you continually, and satisfy your soul in drought: and you shall be like a watered garden, and like a spring of water, whose waters fail not." [27]

[27] Is. lviii.10, 11.

SERMON 10

ENDURANCE OF
THE WORLD'S CENSURE

*"And thou, son of man, be not afraid of them; neither be afraid of
their words, though briars and thorns be with thee, and thou dost
dwell among scorpions; be not afraid of their words, nor be dismayed
at their looks, though they be a rebellious house."*—Ezek. ii.6.

WHAT is here implied, as the trial of the Prophet Ezekiel,
was fulfilled more or less in the case of all the Prophets.
They were not Teachers merely, but Confessors. They came not
merely to unfold the Law, or to foretell the Gospel, but to warn
and rebuke; nor to rebuke only, but to suffer. This world is a
scene of conflict between good and evil. The evil not only
avoids, but persecutes the good; the good cannot conquer, except by suffering. Good men seem to fail; their cause triumphs,
but their own overthrow is the price paid for the success of their
cause. When was it that this conflict, and this character and
issue of it, have not been fulfilled? So it was in the beginning.
Cain, for instance, was envious of his brother Abel, and slew
him. Enoch walked with God, and was a preacher of righteousness, and God took him. Ishmael mocked at Isaac; Esau was full
of wrath with Jacob, and resolved to kill him. Joseph's brethren
were filled with bitter hatred of him, debated about killing
him, cast him into a pit, and at last sold him into Egypt. Afterwards, in like manner, Korah, Dathan, and Abiram rose up
against Moses. And, later still, Saul persecuted David; and
Ahab and Jezebel, Elijah; and the priests and the prophets the
Prophet Jeremiah. Lastly, not to dwell on other instances, the
chief priests and Pharisees, full of envy, rose up against our
Lord Jesus Christ, and delivered Him to the heathen governor,
Pontius Pilate, to be crucified. So the Apostles, after Him, and
especially St. Paul, were persecuted by their fierce and revenge-
ful countrymen: and from the way in which St. Paul speaks on
the subject we may infer that it is ever so to be: "All that will live
godly in Christ Jesus shall suffer persecution:" or, as he says,
after referring to the history of Isaac and Ishmael, "As then he

that was born after the flesh persecuted him that was born after the Spirit, even so it is now:" and indeed we see this fulfilled in its measure before our eyes even at this day. Hence our Saviour, to console all who suffer for His sake, graciously says, "Blessed are they which are persecuted for righteousness' sake, for theirs is the kingdom of heaven." [1]

The case seems to be this:—those who do not serve God with a single heart, know they ought to do so, and they do not like to be reminded that they ought. And when they fall in with any one who does live to God, he serves to remind them of it, and that is unpleasant to them, and that is the first reason why they are angry with a religious man; the sight of him disturbs them and makes them uneasy.

And, in the next place, they feel in their hearts that he is in much better case than they are. They cannot help wishing—though they are hardly conscious of their own wish—they cannot help wishing that they were like him; yet they have no intention of imitating him, and this makes them jealous and envious. Instead of being angry with themselves they are angry with him.

These are their first feelings: what follows? next they are very much tempted to deny that he *is* religious. They wish to get the thought of him out of their minds. Nothing would so relieve their minds as to find that there were no religious persons in the world, none better than themselves. Accordingly, they do all they can to believe that he is making a pretence of religion; they do their utmost to find out what looks like inconsistency in him. They call him a hypocrite and other names. And all this, if the truth must be spoken, because they hate the things of God, and therefore they hate His servants.

Accordingly, as far as they have power to do it, they persecute him, either, as the text implies, with cruel untrue words, or with cold, or fierce, or jealous looks, or in some worse ways. A good man is an offence to a bad man. The sight of him is a sort of insult; and he is irritated at him, and does him what harm he can. Thus Christians, in former times, were put to death by the heathen. As righteous Abel by Cain, as our Lord Jesus Christ, the Son of God, by the Jews, as St. Paul too by the heathen; so, many after him were put to death also, and that by the most cruel torments. It would not be right to describe the horrible inflictions which the children of God once endured at the hands of the children of the flesh; but we have some allusion to what

[1] 2 Tim. iii.12; Gal. iv.29; Matt. v.10.

had taken place in an earlier age, in a passage from St. Paul's Epistle to the Hebrews, from which you may judge of the more cruel trials which Christians afterwards endured. They "had trial of cruel mockings and scourgings, yea, moreover of bonds and imprisonment: they were stoned, they were sawn asunder, were tempted, were slain with the sword: they wandered about in sheep-skins and goat-skins; being destitute, afflicted, tormented; (of whom the world was not worthy:) they wandered in deserts, and in mountains, and in dens and caves of the earth."[2]

Praised be God, we live in times when this cannot take place! Hitherto, at least, He has guarded us in a wonderful way. If any bad man did any serious harm to a religious man, he knows he would incur some punishment from the law of the land. Religious persons are protected in this day from all great persecutions, and they cannot sufficiently be thankful for it. The utmost they can suffer from the world is light indeed compared with what men suffered of old time. Yet St. Paul calls even his and their sufferings "our light affliction;" and if their suffering was but light, compared with the glory which was to follow after death, much more is ours light, who cannot undergo persecution, if we would, and at best can only suffer very slight inconveniences from serving God faithfully.

And yet, nevertheless, most true is it, that even now, no one can give his mind to God, and show by his actions that he fears God, but he will incur the dislike and opposition of the world; and it is important he should be aware of this, and be prepared for it. He must not mind it, he must bear it, and in time (if God so will) he will overcome it.

There are a number of lesser ways in which careless ungodly persons may annoy and inconvenience those who desire to do their duty humbly and fully. Such, especially, are those, which seem intended in the text, unkind censure, carping, slander, ridicule, cold looks, rude language, insult, and, in some cases, oppression and tyranny. Whoever, therefore, sets about a religious life, must be prepared for these,—must be thankful if they do not befall him; but must not be put out, must not think it a strange thing, if they do.

Now, my brethren, observe this; in bidding you endure reproach for Christ's sake, I am bidding you nothing which, as a minister of Christ, I do not wish to practise myself. Nay, it is what all ministers of Christ are obliged to practise; for, in all

[2] Heb. xi.36–38.

ages, *who* do you think it is that the world will first attack and oppose? Christ's ministers, of course. Who is there who can possibly so offend this bad world, as they whose very office is to remind the world of God and heaven? If all serious persons are disliked by the world, because they bring before it unpleasant truths, which it would fain forget if it could, this trial surely applies still more to those whose very profession and business it is to remind men of the truths of religion. A religious man does not intend to remind his neighbours; he goes on his own way; but they see him and cannot help being reminded. They see that he is well-conducted, and sober-minded, and reverent, and conscientious; that he never runs into any excess; that he never uses bad language; that he is regular at his prayers, regular at Church, regular at the most Holy Sacrament; they see all this, and, whether he will or no, they *are* reminded of their duty, and, as disliking to be reminded, they dislike him who reminds them. But if this be so in the case of common men, who wish to go on in a religious way without making any profession, how do you think it will fare with us, Christ's ministers, whose very duty it is to make a profession? Every thing about a clergyman is a warning to men, or ought to be, of the next world, of death and judgment, heaven and hell. His very dress is a memento. He does not dress like other men. His habits are a memento. His mode of speech is graver than that of others. His duties too are a memento. He is seen in Church reading prayers, baptizing, preaching; or he is seen teaching children; he is seen in works of charity; or he is seen studying. His life is given to objects out of sight. All that he does is intended to remind men that time is short, death is certain, and eternity long. And, this being so, do you think that men, being as they mostly are, careless and irre-ligious, do you think they like this? No; and still less, when he goes on to tell men of their errors and faults, and, as far as he can, to restrain them. And so in all ages you will find that the world has resisted and done its utmost to get rid of the preachers of repentance and holiness. It would stone Moses, it cast Daniel into the den of lions, and the three Children into the fiery furnace: St. Paul it beheaded, St. Peter it crucified, others it burnt, others it tortured even to death. And so it went on for many generations. But at last, as I said just now, religious persons have by degrees been sheltered by the law of the land from persecu-tion, and Christ's ministers among them. And the world has got more humane and generous, if not more religious; and God is sovereign over all. But though the devil cannot persecute us, he does what he can to oppose us. Surely this is so; for no one can look into the many publications of the day, without having proof of it; no one can go into places where persons meet together for refreshment, or for recreation, without hearing it; no one can travel on the road, without at times being witness to it. Christ's ministers are called names, untruths are told of them, they are ridiculed; and men encourage each other to oppose them, and to deceive them. And why? for this simple short reason, because they are God's messengers; and men in general do not like to be told of God. They say that they could do well enough without ministers of Christ; which really means, that they wish to do without God in the world.

Such is the portion to which all we, ministers of Christ, are called by our profession; and therefore, when we bid you prepare for the opposition of the world, we are calling you to nothing which we do not bear ourselves. It were well, could we, in all things, do first what we bid *you* do. There is no temptation or trial which you have, which in its kind we may not have to endure, or at least would not wish to endure, so far as it is lawful to wish it. St. Paul said to certain heathens, "We also are men of like passions with you."[3] St. Paul, and the Apostles, and all Christ's ministers after them, are of one nature with other men. They have to go through what other men go through. They suffer pain, sorrow, bereavement, anxiety, desolateness, privations; and they have need, as other men, of patience, cheerfulness, faith, hope, contentment, resignation, firmness, to bear all that comes on them well. But even more than other men are they called on to bear the opposition of the world. They have to bear being ridiculed, slandered, ill-treated, overreached, disliked. All this is not pleasant to them naturally, any more than to other people. But they find it must be so; they cannot alter it; and they learn resignation and patience. This patience and resignation then I exhort you to cherish, my brethren, when the world scorns you for your religion; and withal cheerfulness and meekness, that you may bear your cross lightly, and not gloomily, or sadly, or complainingly.

For instance, persons may press you to do something which you know to be wrong—to tell an untruth, or to do what is not quite honest, or to go to companies whither you should not go; and they may show that they are vexed at the notion of your not complying. Still you must not comply. You must not do what you feel to be wrong, though you should thereby displease even those whom you would most wish to please.

[3] Acts xiv.15.

Again: you must not be surprised, should you find that you are called a hypocrite, and other hard names; you must not mind it.

Again: you may be jeered at and mocked by your acquaintance, for being strict and religious, for carefully coming to Church, keeping from bad language, and the like: you must not care for it.

Again, you may, perhaps, discover to your great vexation, that untruths are told of you by careless persons behind your backs, that what you do has been misrepresented, and that in consequence a number of evil things are believed about you by the world at large. Hard though it be, you must not care for it; remembering that more untruths were told of our Saviour and His Apostles than can possibly be told of you.

Again: you may find that not only the common run of men believe what is said against you, but even those with whom you wish to stand well. But if this happens through your conscientiousness you must not mind it, but must be cheerful, leaving your case in the hand of God, and knowing that He will bring it out into the light one day or another, in His own good time.

Again: persons may try to threaten or frighten you into doing something wrong, but you must not mind that; you must be firm.

In many, very many ways you may be called upon to bear the ill-usage of the world, or to withstand its attempts to draw you from God; but you must be firm, and you must not be surprised that they should be made. You must consider that it is your very calling to bear and to withstand. This is what you offer to God as a sort of return for His great mercies to you. Did not Christ go through much more for you than you can possibly be called upon to undergo for Him? Did He bear the bitter cross who was sinless, and do you, who are at best so sinful, scruple to bear such poor trials and petty inconveniences?

In conclusion, I will but call your attention to two points, to which what I have said leads me.

First; Do not be too eager to suppose you are ill-treated for your religion's sake. Make as light of matters as you can. And beware of being severe on those who lead careless lives, or whom you think or know to be ill-treating you. Do not dwell on such matters. Turn your mind away from them. Avoid all gloominess. Be kind and gentle to those who are perverse, and you will very often, please God, gain them over. You should pray for those who lead careless lives, and especially if they are unkind to you. Who knows but God may hear your prayers, and turn their hearts, and bring them over to you? Do every thing for them but imitate them and yield to them. This is the true Christian spirit, to be meek and gentle under ill-usage, cheerful under slander, forgiving towards enemies, and silent in the midst of angry tongues.

Secondly, I would say, recollect you cannot do any one thing of all the duties I have been speaking of, without God's help. Any one who attempts to resist the world, or to do other good things by his own strength, will be sure to fall. We *can* do good things, but it is when God gives us power to do them. Therefore we must pray to Him for the power. When we are brought into temptation of any kind, we should lift up our hearts to God. We should say to Him, "Good Lord, deliver us." Our Lord, when He was going away, promised to His disciples a Comforter instead of Himself; that was God the Holy Ghost, who is still among us (though we see Him not), as Christ was with the Apostles. He has come in order to enlighten us, to guide us in the right way, and in the end to bring us to Christ in heaven. And He came down, as His name "Comforter" shows, especially to stand by, and comfort, and strengthen those who are in any trouble, particularly trouble from irreligious men. The disciples, when Christ went, had to go through much trouble, and therefore He comforted them by the coming of the Holy and Eternal Spirit, the Third Person in the Blessed Trinity. "These things I have spoken unto you," He says, "that in Me ye might have peace; in the world ye shall have tribulation, but be of good cheer, I have overcome the world." [4] When, then, religious persons are in low spirits, or are any way grieved at the difficulties which the world puts in their way, when they earnestly desire to do their duty, yet feel how weak they are, let them recollect that they are "not their own," but "bought with a price," and the dwelling-places and temples of the All-gracious Spirit.

Lastly; I am quite sure that none of us, even the best, have resisted the world as we ought to have done. Our faces have not been like flints; we have been afraid of men's words, and dismayed at their looks, and we have yielded to them at times against our better judgment. We have fancied, forsooth, the world could do us some harm while we kept to the commandments of God. Let us search our consciences; let us look back on our past lives. Let us try to purify and cleanse our hearts in God's sight. Let us try to live more like Christians, more like

[4] John xvi.33.

children of God. Let us earnestly beg of God to teach us more simply and clearly what our duty is. Let us beg of Him to give us the heart to love Him, and true repentance for what is past. Let us beg Him to teach us *how* to confess Him before men; lest if we deny Him now, He may deny us before the Angels of God hereafter.

DOING GLORY TO GOD
IN PURSUITS OF THE WORLD

*"Whether, therefore, ye eat or drink, or whatsoever ye do,
do all to the glory of God."*—1 Cor. x.31.

WHEN persons are convinced that life is short, that it is unequal to any great purpose, that it does not display adequately, or bring to perfection the true Christian, when they feel that the next life is all in all, and that eternity is the only subject that really can claim or can fill their thoughts, then they are apt to undervalue this life altogether, and to forget its real importance. They are apt to wish to spend the time of their sojourning here in a positive separation from active and social duties: yet it should be recollected that the employments of this world, though not themselves heavenly, are, after all, the way to heaven—though not the fruit, are the seed of immortality—and are valuable, though not in themselves, yet for that to which they lead: but it is difficult to realize this. It is difficult to realize both truths at once, and to connect both truths together; steadily to contemplate the life to come, yet to act in this. Those who meditate, are likely to neglect those active duties which are, in fact, incumbent on them, and to dwell upon the thought of God's glory, till they forget to act to His glory. This state of mind is chided in figure in the words of the holy Angels to the Apostles, when they say, "Ye men of Galilee, why stand ye gazing up into heaven?" [1]

In various ways does the thought of the next world lead men to neglect their duty in this; and whenever it does so we may be sure that there is something wrong and unchristian, not in their thinking of the next world, but in their manner of thinking of it. For though the contemplation of God's glory may in certain times and persons allowably interfere with the active employments of life, as in the case of the Apostles when our Saviour ascended, and though such contemplation is even freely al-

[1] Acts i.11.

lowed or commanded us at certain times of each day; yet that is not a real and true meditation on Christ, but some counterfeit, which makes us dream away our time, or become habitually indolent, or which withdraws us from our existing duties, or unsettles us.

Yet the thought of the world unseen is apt to do so in various ways, and the worst way of all is when we have taken up a notion that it *ought* to do so. And indeed this is a temptation to which persons who desire to be religious are exposed in one shape or another in every age, and in this age as well as in times past. Men come to fancy that to lose taste and patience for the businesses of this life is renouncing the world and becoming spiritually-minded. We will say a person has been thoughtless and irreligious; perhaps openly so; or at least careless about religion, and though innocent of any flagrant sin, yet a follower of his own will and fancy, and unpractised in any regular and consistent course of religion. He has, perhaps, been outwardly respectful to sacred things and persons, but has had no serious thoughts about the next world. He has taken good and evil— religion and the world—as they came, first one and then the other, without much consideration. He has been fond of gaiety and amusements, or he has been deeply interested in some pursuit or other of time and sense,—whether it be his own trade or profession, or some of the studies and employments now popular. He has fallen in with the ways of the company in which he has found himself; has been profane with the profane; then, again, has had for a season religious impressions, which in turn have worn away. Thus he has lived, and something has then occurred really to rouse him and give him what is called a serious turn. Such a person, man or woman, young or old, certainly does need to take a serious turn, does require a change; and no one but must be very glad to hear that a change has taken place, though at the same time there may be changes not much better than the change which happened to him, whose soul, in our Lord's language, was but "swept and garnished;" not really changed in a heavenly way, and having but the semblance of faith and holiness upon it.

Now the cases I am speaking of are somewhat like that which our Saviour seems to speak of in the passage referred to. When a man has been roused to serious resolutions, the chances are, that he fails to take up with the one and only narrow way which leads to life. The chances are that "then cometh the wicked one," and persuades him to choose some path short of the true one—easier and pleasanter than it. And *this* is the kind of course to which he is often seduced, as we frequently witness it; viz. to feel a sort of dislike and contempt for his ordinary worldly business as something beneath him. He knows he must have what Scripture calls a spiritual mind, and he fancies that to have a spiritual mind it is absolutely necessary to renounce all earnestness or activity in his worldly employments, to profess to take no interest in them, to despise the natural and ordinary pleasures of life, violating the customs of society, adopting a melancholy air and a sad tone of voice, and remaining silent and absent when among his natural friends and relatives, as if saying to himself, "I have much higher thoughts than to engage in all these perishing miserable things;" acting with constraint and difficulty in the things about him; making efforts to turn things which occur to the purpose of what he considers spiritual reflection; using certain Scripture phrases and expressions; delighting to exchange Scripture sentiments with persons whom he meets of his own way of thinking; nay, making visible and audible signs of deep feeling when Scripture or other religious subjects are mentioned, and the like. He thinks he lives out of the world, and out of its engagements, if he shuts (as it were) his eyes, and sits down doing nothing. Altogether he looks upon his worldly occupation simply as a burden and a cross, and considers it all gain to be able to throw it off; and the sooner he can release himself from it, and the oftener, so much the better.

Now I am far from denying that a man's worldly occupation *may* be his cross. Again, I am far from denying that under circumstances it may be right even to retire from the world. But I am speaking of cases when it is a person's duty to remain in his worldly calling, and when he does remain in it, but when he cherishes dissatisfaction with it: whereas what he ought to feel is this,—that *while* in it he is to glorify God, not *out* of it, but *in* it, and *by means* of it, according to the Apostle's direction, "not slothful in business, fervent in spirit, serving the Lord." The Lord Jesus Christ our Saviour is best served, and with the most fervent spirit, when men are not slothful in business, but do their duty in that state of life in which it has pleased God to call them.

Now what leads such a person into this mistake is, that he sees that most men who engage cheerfully and diligently in worldly business, do so from a worldly spirit, from a low carnal love of the world; and so he thinks it is *his* duty, on the contrary, *not* to take a cheerful part in the world's business at all. And it cannot be denied that the greater part of the world is *absorbed* in the world; so much so that I am almost afraid to speak of the duty of being active in our worldly business, lest I should seem to give countenance to that miserable devotion to the things of time and sense, that love of bustle and management, that desire of gain, and that aiming at influence and importance, which abound on all sides. Bad as it is to be languid and indifferent in our secular duties, and to account this religion, yet it is far worse to be the slaves of this world, and to have our hearts in the concerns of this world. I do not know any thing more dreadful than a state of mind which is, perhaps, the characteristic of this country, and which the prosperity of this country so miserably fosters. I mean that ambitious spirit, to use a great word, but I know no other word to express my meaning—that low ambition which sets every one on the look-out to succeed and to rise in life, to amass money, to gain power, to depress his rivals, to triumph over his hitherto superiors, to affect a consequence and a gentility which he had not before, to affect to have an opinion on high subjects, to pretend to form a judgment upon sacred things, to choose his religion, to approve and condemn according to his taste, to become a partizan in extensive measures for the supposed temporal benefit of the community, to indulge the vision of great things which are to come, great improvements, great wonders: all things vast, all things new,—this most fearfully earthly and grovelling spirit is likely, alas! to extend itself more and more among our countrymen,—an intense, sleepless, restless, never-wearied, never-satisfied, pursuit of Mammon in one shape or other, to the exclusion of all deep, all holy, all calm, all reverent thoughts. *This* is the spirit in which, more or less (according to their different tempers), men do commonly engage in concerns of this world; and I repeat it, better, far better, were it to retire from the world altogether than thus to engage in it—better with Elijah to fly to the desert, than to serve Baal and Ashtoreth in Jerusalem.

But the persons I speak of, as despising this world, are far removed from the spirit of Elijah. To flee from the world, or strenuously to resist it, implies an energy and strength of mind which they have not. They do neither one thing nor the other; they neither flee it, nor engage zealously in its concerns; but they remain in the midst of them, doing them in an indolent and negligent way, and think this is to be spiritually minded; or, as in other cases, they really take an interest in them, and yet speak as if they despised them.

But surely it is possible to "serve the Lord," yet not to be "slothful in business;" not over devoted to it, but not to retire from it. We may do *all things* whatever we are about to God's glory; we may do all things *heartily*, as to the Lord, and not to man, being both active yet meditative; and now let me give some instances to show what I mean.

1. "Do all to the glory of God," says St. Paul, in the text; nay, "whether we eat or drink;" so that it appears nothing is too slight or trivial to glorify Him in. We will suppose then, to take the case mentioned just now; we will suppose a man who has lately had more serious thoughts than he had before, and determines to live more religiously. In consequence of the turn his mind has taken he feels a distaste for his worldly occupation, whether he is in trade, or in any mechanical employment which allows little exercise of mind. He now feels he would rather be in some other business, though in itself his present occupation is quite lawful and pleasing to God. The ill-instructed man will at once get impatient and quit it; or if he does not quit it, at least he will be negligent and indolent in it. But the true penitent will say to himself, "No; if it be an irksome employment, so much the more does it suit *me*. I deserve no better. I do not deserve to be fed even with husks. I am bound to afflict my soul for my past sins. If I were to go in sackcloth and ashes, if I were to live on bread and water, if I were to wash the feet of the poor day by day, it would not be too great an humiliation; and the only reason I do not, is, that I have no call that way, it would look ostentatious. Gladly then will I hail an inconvenience which will try me without any one's knowing it. Far from repining, I will, through God's grace, go cheerfully about what I do not like. I will deny myself. I know that with His help what is in itself painful, will thus be pleasant as done towards Him. I know well that there is no pain but may be borne comfortably, by the thought of Him, and by His grace, and the strong determination of the will; nay, none but may soothe and solace me. Even the natural taste and smell may be made to like what they naturally dislike; even bitter medicine, which is nauseous to the palate, may by a resolute will become tolerable. Nay, even sufferings and torture, such as martyrs have borne, have before now been rejoiced in and embraced heartily from love to Christ. I then, a sinner, will take this light inconvenience in a generous way, pleased at the opportunity of disciplining myself, and with self-abasement, as needing a severe penitence. If there be parts in my occupation which I especially dislike, if it requires a good deal of moving about and I wish to be at home, or if it be sedentary and I wish to be in motion, or if it requires rising early and I like to rise late, or if it makes me solitary and I like to be with friends, all this unpleasant part, as far as is

consistent with my health, and so that it is not likely to be a snare to me, I will choose by preference. Again, I see my religious views are a hindrance to me. I see persons are suspicious of me. I see that I offend people by my scrupulousness. I see that to get on in life requires far more devotion to my worldly business than I can give consistently with my duty to God, or without its becoming a temptation to me. I know that I ought not, and (please God) I will not, sacrifice my religion to it. My religious seasons and hours shall be my own. I will not countenance any of the worldly dealings and practices, the over-reaching ways, the sordid actions in which others indulge. And if I am thrown back in life thereby, if I make less gains or lose friends, and so come to be despised, and find others rise in the world while I remain where I was, hard though this be to bear, it is an humiliation which becomes me in requital for my sins, and in obedience to God; and a very slight one it is, merely to be deprived of worldly successes, or rather it is a gain. And this may be the manner in which Almighty God will make an opening for me, if it is His blessed will, to leave my present occupation. But leave it without a call from God, I certainly must not. On the contrary, I will work in it the more diligently, as far as higher duties allow me."

2. A second reason which will animate the Christian will be a desire of letting his light shine before men. He will aim at winning others by his own diligence and activity. He will say to himself, "My parents" or "my master" or "employer shall never say of me, Religion has spoiled him. They shall see me more active and alive than before. I will be punctual and attentive, and adorn the Gospel of God our Saviour. My companions shall never have occasion to laugh at any affectation of religious feeling in me. No; I will affect nothing. In a manly way I will, with God's blessing, do my duty. I will not, as far as I can help, dishonour His service by any strangeness or extravagance of conduct, any unreality of words, any over-softness or constraint of manner; but they shall see that the fear of God only makes those who cherish it more respectable in the world's eyes as well as more heavenly-minded. What a blessed return it will be for God's mercies to me, if I, who am like a brand plucked out of the burning, be allowed, through His great mercy, to recommend that Gospel to others which He has revealed to me, and to recommend it, as on the one hand by my strictness in attending God's ordinances, in discountenancing vice and folly, and by a conscientious walk; so, on the other hand, by all that is of good report in social life, by uprightness, honesty, prudence,

and straightforwardness, by good temper, good-nature, and brotherly love!"

3. Thankfulness to Almighty God, nay, and the inward life of the Spirit itself, will be additional principles causing the Christian to labour diligently in his calling. He will see God in all things. He will recollect our Saviour's life. Christ was brought up to a humble trade. When he labours in his own, he will think of his Lord and Master in His. He will recollect that Christ went down to Nazareth and was subject to His parents, that He walked long journeys, that He bore the sun's heat and the storm, and had not where to lay His head. Again, he knows that the Apostles had various employments of this world before their calling; St. Andrew and St. Peter fishers, St. Matthew a tax-gatherer, and St. Paul, even after his calling, still a tent-maker. Accordingly, in whatever comes upon him, he will endeavour to discern and gaze (as it were) on the countenance of his Saviour. He will feel that the true contemplation of that Saviour lies *in* his worldly business; that as Christ is seen in the poor, and in the persecuted, and in children, so is He seen in the employments which He puts upon His chosen, whatever they be; that in attending to his own calling he will be meeting Christ; that if he neglect it, he will not on that account enjoy His presence at all the more, but that while performing it, he will see Christ revealed to his soul amid the ordinary actions of the day, as by a sort of sacrament. Thus he will take his worldly business as a gift from Him, and will love it as such.

4. True humility is another principle which will lead us to desire to glorify God in our worldly employments if possible, instead of resigning them. Christ evidently puts His greater blessings on those whom the world despises. He has bid His followers take the lowest seat. He says that he who would be great must be as the servant of all, that he who humbleth himself shall be exalted; and He Himself washed His disciples' feet. Nay, He tells us, that He will gird Himself, and serve them who have watched for Him; an astonishing condescension, which makes us almost dumb with fear and rejoicing. All this has its effect upon the Christian, and he sets about his business with alacrity, and without a moment's delay, delighting to humble himself, and to have the opportunity of putting himself in that condition of life which our Lord especially blest.

5. Still further, he will use his worldly business as a means of keeping him from vain and unprofitable thoughts. One cause of the heart's devising evil is, that time is given it to do so. The man who has his daily duties, who lays out his time for them

hour by hour, is saved a multitude of sins which have not time to get hold upon him. The brooding over insults received, or the longing after some good not granted, or regret at losses which have befallen us, or at the loss of friends by death, or the attacks of impure and shameful thoughts, these are kept off from him who takes care to be diligent and well employed. Leisure is the occasion of all evil. Idleness is the first step in the downward path which leads to hell. If we do not find employment to engage our minds with, Satan will be sure to find his own employment for them. Here we see the difference of motive with which a religious and a worldly-minded man may do the same thing. Suppose a person has had some sad affliction, say a bereavement: men of this world, having no pleasure in religion, not liking to dwell on a loss to them irreparable, in order to drown reflection, betake themselves to worldly pursuits to divert their thoughts and banish gloom. The Christian under the same circumstances does the same thing; but it is from a fear lest he should relax and enfeeble his mind by barren sorrow; from a dread of becoming discontented; from a belief that he is pleasing God better, and is likely to secure his peace more fully, by not losing time; from a feeling that, far from forgetting those whom he has lost by thus acting, he shall only enjoy the thought of them the more really and the more religiously.

6. Lastly, we see what judgment to give in a question sometimes agitated, whether one should retire from our worldly business at the close of life, to give our thoughts more entirely to God. To wish to do so is so natural, that I suppose there is no one who would not wish it. A great many persons are not allowed the privilege, a great many are allowed it through increasing infirmities or extreme old age; but every one, I conceive, if allowed to choose, would think it a privilege to be allowed it, though a great many would find it difficult to determine *when* was the fit time. But let us consider what is the reason of this so natural a wish. I fear that it is often not a religious wish, often only partially religious. I fear a great number of persons who aim at retiring from the world's business, do so under the notion of their then enjoying themselves somewhat after the manner of the rich man in the Gospel, who said, "Soul, thou hast much goods laid up for many years." If this is the predominant aim of any one, of course I need not say that it is a fatal sin, for Christ Himself has said so. Others there are who are actuated by a mixed feeling; they are aware that they do not give so much time to religion as they ought; they do not

live by rule; nay, they are not satisfied with the correctness or uprightness of some of the practices or customs which their way of life requires of them, and they get tired of active business as life goes on, and wish to be at ease. So they look to their last years as a time of retirement, in which they may *both* enjoy themselves *and* prepare for heaven. And thus they satisfy both their conscience and their love of the world. At present religion is irksome to them; but then, as they hope, duty and pleasure will go together. Now, putting aside all other mistakes which such a frame of mind evidences, let it be observed, that if they are at present *not* serving God with all their hearts, but look forward to a time when they shall do so, then it is plain that, when at length they *do* put aside worldly cares and turn to God, if ever they do, that time must necessarily be a time of deep humiliation, if it is to be acceptable to Him, not a comfortable retirement. Who ever heard of a pleasurable, easy, joyous repentance? It is a contradiction in terms. These men, if they do but reflect a moment, must confess that their present mode of life, supposing it be not so strict as it should be, is heaping up tears and groans for their last years, not enjoyment. The longer they live as they do at present, not only the more unlikely is it that they will repent at all; but even if they do, the more bitter, the more painful must their repentance be. The only way to escape suffering for sin hereafter is to suffer for it here. Sorrow here or misery hereafter; they cannot escape one or the other.

Not for any worldly reason, then, not on any presumptuous or unbelieving motive, does the Christian desire leisure and retirement for his last years. Nay, he will be content to do without these blessings, and the highest Christian of all is he whose heart is so stayed on God, that he does not wish or need it; whose heart is so set on things above, that things below as little excite, agitate, unsettle, distress, and seduce him, as they stop the course of nature, as they stop the sun and moon, or change summer and winter. Such were the Apostles, who, as the heavenly bodies, went out "to all lands," full of business, and yet full too of sweet harmony, even to the ends of the earth. Their calling was heavenly, but their work was earthly; they were in labour and trouble till the last; yet consider how calmly St. Paul and St. Peter write in their last days. St. John, on the other hand, was allowed in a great measure, to retire from the cares of his pastoral charge, and such, I say, will be the natural wish of every religious man, whether his ministry be spiritual or secular; but, not in order to *begin* to fix his mind on God, but merely because, though he may contemplate God as truly and be as holy in heart in active business as in quiet, still it is more becoming and suitable to meet the stroke of death (if it be allowed us) silently, collectedly, solemnly, than in a crowd and a tumult. And hence it is, among other reasons, that we pray in the Litany to be delivered "from *sudden* death."

On the whole, then, what I have said comes to this, that whereas Adam was sentenced to labour as a punishment, Christ has by His coming sanctified it as a means of grace and a sacrifice of thanksgiving, a sacrifice cheerfully to be offered up to the Father in His name.

It is very easy to speak and teach this, difficult to do it; very difficult to steer between the two evils,—to use this world as not abusing it, to be active and diligent in this world's affairs, yet not for this world's sake, but for God's sake. It requires the greater effort for a minister of Christ to speak of it, for this reason; because he is not called upon in the same sense in which others are to practise the duty. He is not called, as his people are, to the professions, the pursuits, and cares of this world; his work is heavenly, and to it he gives himself wholly. It is a work which, we trust, is not likely to carry him off from God; not only because it is His work, but, what is a more sure reason, because commonly it gains no great thanks from men. However, for this reason it is difficult for Christian ministers to speak about your trial in this matter, my brethren, because it is not theirs. We are tried by the command to live out of the world, and you by the command to live in it.

May God give us grace in our several spheres and stations to do His will and adorn His doctrine; that whether we eat and drink, or fast and pray, labour with our hands or with our minds, journey about or remain at rest, we may glorify Him who has purchased us with His own blood!

VANITY OF HUMAN GLORY

"The world knoweth us not, because it knew Him not."
—1 John iii.1.

OF St. Simon and St. Jude, the Saints whom we this day commemorate, little is known.[1] St. Jude, indeed, still lives in the Church in his Catholic epistle; but of his history we only know that he was brother to St. James the Less, and nearly related to our Lord; and that, like St. Peter, he had been a married man. Besides his name of Jude or Judas, he is also called Thaddæus and Lebbæus in the Gospels. Of St. Simon we only know that he was called the Canaanite, or Zealot, for the words have the same meaning, belonging, before his conversion, to a certain fierce sect, who, under the idea they were doing God service, took upon themselves to execute the law upon offenders without legal authority, and without formal accusation or trial. It is said that both Apostles were at length martyred in the course of their efforts to gather together God's elect into His fold.

Little is known of St. Simon and St. Jude; they laboured and they taught in their generation; they were gifted with miraculous powers, and by their preaching founded churches and saved souls; they travelled into the East and West, till at last they were taken away from the earth. Yet we know little of their history now. Although "honoured in their generation, and the glory of their times," yet they "have no memorial, but are perished as though they had never been."[2] St. Jude's Epistle, indeed, is a standing monument, yet not of his doings, but of his gifts. What he wrote leads us to conjecture indeed what he was; but of his history, we know no more than of that of St. Simon.

And hence we draw an important lesson for ourselves, which, however obvious, is continually forgotten by us in the actual business of life; viz. to do our duty without aiming at the

[1] Preached on the Festival of St. Simon and St. Jude.
[2] Ecclus. xliv.7, 9.

world's praise. Mankind knows nothing of St. Simon's and St. Jude's deeds and sufferings, though these were great; yet there is One who "knows their works, and labour, and patience, . . . and how they bore . . . and for His Name's sake laboured, and fainted not."[3] Their deeds are blotted out from history, but not from the Lamb's book of life; for "blessed are they who die in Him, . . . that they may rest from their labours; and their works do follow them."[4]

On this great practical rule, viz. to do what we do heartily, as unto the Lord, and not unto men, I shall now make some remarks; and in doing so, I shall be pointing out a mode in which we may follow these blessed Saints, whose lives at first sight seem to have left no pattern behind them for our imitation.

In heathen times, when men understood that they had souls, yet did not know what was the soul's true happiness, or how it was to be gained, much was thought, and more talked, of what they called *glory, fame, honour.* This was natural, as a little consideration will show. For before men begin to exercise their minds, while they remain ignorant and dull, the common pleasures of sense satisfy them—eating, drinking, and making merry. They do not think of the morrow. They have no end in view, and act on no plan. But when intelligence is awakened, and they learn to feel, reflect, hope, plan, and exert themselves; then mere animal indulgences are not enough for them, and they look about for some higher pleasures, more lasting and more refined. This is the real effect of that civilization which is so much extolled; it gives men refined wishes, and sets them on gratifying them. An enlightened age is one which feels the wants of human nature. Knowledge and mental cultivation render men alive to the things around them, busy, and restless; but they do no more than make men sensible of their wants; they find no remedy for them; they bring no appropriate food to the hunger they create: for it is religion alone can do this.

Now the ancient heathen whom I speak of were just in this state; having minds cultivated and refined intellectually, they felt the capabilities of man for acting on a large field, and the need of some stimulus to make him act thus. They saw that human nature was capable of great things, and they perceived that some great goods must be attainable in some way or other, though they did not well know what they were. Feelings such as these, acting upon men in the tumult of life, with their passions awake, keenly set on (what are called) political objects, and

³ Rev. ii.2, 3.   ⁴ Rev. xiv.13.

averse to those self-denying habits which conscience (if listened to) would have suggested to be the way to that unknown happiness which their heart was imagining, led them to think of what they called glory and popularity as the greatest of goods, and that to which they ought especially to aspire.

Now what exactly they wished to signify by the word "glory," is difficult to say, for they were apt to speak of it as if it were some real thing, and that, too, which one could possess and make one's own; yet, if we come to consider its real meaning, it plainly stands for nothing else than the praise of other men, the being admired, honoured, and feared; or, more commonly, having a celebrated *name*; that is, for a something external to ourselves. But whatever precise notions they wished to attach to the word, they used to talk in glowing language of the necessity of going through dangers and sufferings for glory's sake,—labouring to benefit the world for glory,—and dying for glory.

Now when we read of poor heathens using this language, it is our duty to pity them, for it is plain enough to any sober reasoner, that nothing is so vain as to talk of this glory being a real and substantial good; for there is no better reason for my being happy because my name is celebrated, than because any thing else is celebrated which, accidentally, and for a time, is connected with myself, and called mine. My name is my own only in the case of those who use it in speaking of me; i. e. of those who happen to see and know me. But when those who never saw me talk much of my name, they do me no more good or harm than if they celebrated any thing else which *I* may know to be mine. They may praise a house that was once mine—that is not praising me; nor, in like manner, is it doing me any good, or honouring me, when those who never saw me use my name respectfully. It is a mere imagination, which can give no solid or lasting pleasure. There is some meaning and sense (though great wickedness) in coveting our neighbour's house or garden, horse or ass; the unjust steward, though a bad man, at least acted wisely, i. e. according to a worldly wisdom; but those who covet honour, I mean a great name, really covet no substantial thing at all, and are not only "the most offending men alive," inasmuch as this passion for fame may carry them on to the most atrocious crimes, but also the most foolish of men.

Now, in the ancient heathen we may blame, but we must pity this sin, because it at least evidenced in them a knowledge of a great want of human nature, and was so far the sign of a higher state of mind than that of others who did not feel any wants at all, who had no notion of any but selfish enjoyments, and were content to live and die like the brutes that perish. Their sin lay, not in being anxious for some good or other, which was not before their eyes, but in not consulting their own hearts on the subject, and going the way which their conscience told them. But, I say, they were heathens,—they had no Bible, no Church; and therefore we pity them; and by their errors are reminded to look to ourselves, and see how far we are clean from their sin.

Now it is a most melancholy fact, that Christians are chargeable, for all their light, with the same foolish irrational sin. This was not at first sight to be expected. This is a peculiar case. Observe; I do not say it is wonderful that we should seek the praise of persons we know. This I can understand. We all naturally love to be respected and admired, and in due limits perhaps we may be allowed to do so; the love of praise is capable of receiving a religious discipline and character. But the surprising thing is, that we should leave the thought of present goods, whether sensual enjoyments, or the more refined pleasure which the praise of our friends brings us, yet without going on to seek the good of the next world; that we should deny ourselves, yet not deny ourselves for a reality, but for a shadow. It is natural, I say, to love to have deference and respect paid us by our acquaintance; but I am speaking of the desire of glory, that is, the praise of a vast multitude of persons we never saw, or shall see, or care about; and this, I say, is a depraved appetite, the artificial produce of a falsely enlightened intellect; as unmeaning as it is sinful, or rather more sinful, because it is so very unmeaning; excusable indeed in heathen, not only because they knew no better, but because they had no better good clearly proposed to them; but in Christians, who have the favour of God and eternal life set before them, deeply criminal, turning away, as they do, from the bread of heaven, to feed upon ashes, with a deceived and corrupted imagination.

This love of indiscriminate praise, then, is an odious, superfluous, wanton sin, and we should put it away with a manly hatred, as something irrational and degrading. Shall man, born for high ends, the servant and son of God, the redeemed of Christ, the heir of immortality, go out of his way to have his mere name praised by a vast populace, or by various people, of whom he knows nothing, and most of whom (if he saw them) he would himself be the first to condemn? It is odious; yet young persons of high minds and vigorous powers, are especially liable to be led captive by this snare of the devil. If reasoning does not convince them, let facts,—the love of glory has its peculiar condemnation in its consequences. No sin has been so productive of widespread enduring ruin among mankind: wars and conquests are the means by which men have most reckoned on securing it. A tree is known by its fruit.

These remarks apply to the love of indiscriminate praise in all its shapes. Few persons, indeed, are in a condition to be tempted by the love of glory; but all persons may be tempted to indulge in vanity, which is nothing else but the love of general admiration. A vain person is one who likes to be praised, whoever is the praiser, whether good or bad. Now consider, how few men are not in their measure vain, till they reach that period of life when by the course of nature vanity disappears? Let all Christians carefully ask themselves, whether they are not very fond, not merely of the praise of their superiors and friends—this is right,—but of that of any person, any chance-comer, about whom they know nothing. Who is not open to flattery? and if he seems not to be exposed to it, is it not that he is too shrewd or too refined to be beguiled by any but what is delicate and unostentatious? A man never considers who it is who praises him. But the most dangerous, perhaps, of all kinds of vanity is to be vain of our personal appearance; most dangerous, for such persons are ever under temptation—I may say, ever sinning. Wherever they go they carry their snare with them; and their idle love of admiration is gratified without effort by the very looks of those who gaze upon them.

Now I shall say something upon the natural and rational love of praise, and how far it may be safely indulged. As I have already said, it is *natural* to desire the esteem of all those with whom we have intercourse, all whom we love. Indeed, Almighty God intends us to do so. When we love a person, we cannot but wish he should love us; but he cannot love us, without also feeling respect and esteem towards us. And as to the question, from whom we should desire praise, and how far, we have this simple rule—from all who stand to us in Christ's place. Christ Himself is our great Judge; from Him we must supremely seek praise; and as far as men are in His place, so far may we seek it from men. We may desire the praise of our parents and superiors, and the praise of good men—in a word, all whom we have a value for; but the desire of indiscriminate praise, the praise of those for whom we have no respect or regard, this is the mischief. We *may* desire the praise of those we have never seen, if we believe them to be good men. St. Paul not only speaks of the mutual rejoicing between himself and the

Corinthians,[5] who knew each other, but likewise returns thanks that the fame of the faith of the Romans was spread all over the Christian world.[6] And in this way we may desire the praise of good persons yet unborn—I mean the Church of God, to the end of time. St. Mary, in the hymn we daily use, returns thanks that "from henceforth all generations shall call her blessed."[7] But this feeling of hers is very different from the desire of what is called glory, posthumous fame, fame after death; as if, forsooth, it were a great thing to have one's name familiar to the mouths of the mixed multitude of this world, of swearers, and jesters, and liars, and railers, and blasphemers, and of all those men, who even if they do not sin grossly in deed, yet use their tongues for evil, speak the words of the world, slander the Church, speak evil of dignities, propagate error, and defend sinners; a great thing truly, and much to be desired, to be honoured by that evil world which dishonours God and His Son!

One additional caution I must add, about allowing ourselves the praise of others; not only must we desire the praise of none but good men, but we must not earnestly desire to be known even by many good men. The truth is, we cannot know, really know, many persons at all, and it is always dangerous to delight in the praises of strangers, even though we believe them to be good men, and much more to seek their praises, which is a kind of ambition. And further than this, it is more agreeable to the Christian temper to be satisfied rather to know and to be known by a few, and to grow day by day in their esteem and affection, than to desire one's name to be on the lips of many, though they profess religion, and associate us with religious objects. And it is our great privilege to have the real blessing in our power, while the fancied good alone is difficult to be gained. Few Christians can be great or can leave a name to posterity; but most Christians will, in the length of their lives, be able to secure the love and praise of one or two, who are to them the representatives of Him whom "having not seen they love," and in whose presence, or at least in whose memory, they may comfort their heart till He come. This doubtless has been the happiness of many saints who have not even left their names behind them. It was the privilege doubtless of St. Simon and St. Jude. They, indeed, were not simply unknown to the world in their lifetime, but even hated and persecuted by it. Upon them came our Saviour's prophecy, that "men should revile them . . . . and say all manner of evil against them falsely for His

[5] 2 Cor. i.4.   [6] Rom. i.8.   [7] Luke i.48.

sake."[8] Yet in the affection the Church bore them, in the love they bore to each other, and, above all, the praise of that Saviour whom they had followed on earth, and who named them in the number of those who had continued with Him in His temptations,[9] and were written in heaven, they had a real glory, not as the world giveth. Who can estimate, who can imagine the deep, the wonderful, the awful joy which the approbation of Christ would impart to them? When we consider how intimately they were allowed to associate with Him, how they were witnesses of His heavenly conversation through the days of His flesh, of His acts of mercy, of His Divine words, of the grace, the tenderness, the sanctity, the majesty, the calmness, which reigned within Him; of His knowledge, His wisdom, His perfect love of God, His zeal for God's service, His patient obedience,—and much more when they knew the dread secret of what He was before He came on earth, what He was even while on earth in presence,—to have had a smile, an encouraging word, from Him, was it not a privilege to treasure in memory beyond any thing else, a remembrance so bright that every thing else looked discoloured and dim? and would it not have amounted to a loss of reason in them to have even had the thought of seeking the praise of weak, ignorant, sinful mortals?

Let us seek this praise which cometh of God, though we shall not have that sensible experience of it which the Apostles were vouchsafed. Let us seek it, for it is to be obtained; it is given to those worthy of it. The poorest, the oldest, and most infirm among us, those who are living not merely in obscurity, but are despised and forgotten, who seem to answer no good purpose by living on, and whose death will not be felt even by their neighbours as a loss, these even may obtain our Saviour's approving look, and receive the future greeting, "Well done, good and faithful servant."

Go on, then, contentedly in the path of duty, seeking Christ in His house and in His ordinances, and He will be your glory at His coming. He will own you before His Father. Let the world record in history the names of heroes, statesmen, and conquerors, and reward courage, and ability, and skill, and perseverance, with its proud titles of honour. Verily, these have their reward. Your names will be written in Heaven, with those of St. Simon and St. Jude, and the other Apostles. You will have the favour of Him whose favour is life. "The secret of the Lord is with them that fear Him; and He will show them His covenant."[10]

---

[8] Matt. v.11.   [9] Luke xxii.28–30.   [10] Ps. xxv.14.

TRUTH HIDDEN
WHEN NOT SOUGHT AFTER

*"They shall turn away their ears from the truth, and shall be turned
unto fables."*—2 Tim. iv.4.

FROM these words of the blessed Apostle, written shortly before he suffered martyrdom, we learn, that there is such a
thing as religious truth, and therefore there is such a thing as
religious error. We learn that religious truth is *one*—and therefore that all views of religion *but* one are wrong. And we learn,
moreover, that so it was to be (for his words are a prophecy) that
professed Christians, forgetting this, should turn away their
ears from the one Truth, and should be turned, not to one, but
to many fables. All this is fulfilled before our eyes; our religious
creeds and professions at this day are many; but Truth is one:
therefore they cannot all be right, or rather almost all of them
must be wrong. That is, the multitude of men are wrong, so far
as they differ; and as they differ, not about trivial points, but
about great matters, it follows that the multitude of men,
whether by their own fault or not, are wrong even in the greater
matters of religion.

This is a most solemn thought, and a perplexing one. However, there is another which, though it ought not to be perplexing, is perplexing still, and perhaps has greater need to be
considered and explained; I mean that men of learning and
ability are so often wrong in religious matters also. It is a stumbling-block to many, when they find that those who seem the
legitimate guides furnished by God's providence, who are in
some sense the natural prophets and expounders of the truth,
that these too are on many sides, and therefore many of them
on the side of error also. There are persons who can despise
the opinions of the *many*, and feel that *they* are not right, but
that truth, if it be to be found, lies with the *few*; and since men
of ability *are* among the few, they think that truth lies with
men of ability, and when after all they are told that able men
are ranged on contrary sides in religious questions, they either

hastily deny the fact, or they are startled, and stagger in their faith.

But on the contrary, let us honestly confess what is certain, that not the ignorant, or weakminded, or dull, or enthusiastic, or extravagant only turn their ears from the Truth and are turned unto fables, but also men of powerful minds, keen perceptions, extended views, ample and various knowledge. Let us, I say, confess it; yet let us not believe in the Truth the less on account of it.

I say that in the number of the adversaries of the Truth, there are many men of highly endowed and highly cultivated minds. Why should we deny this? It is unfair to do so; and not only unfair, but very unnecessary. What is called ability and talent does not make a man a Christian; nay, often, as may be shown without difficulty, it is the occasion of his rejecting Christianity, or this or that part of it. Not only in the higher ranks of society do we see this; even in the humble and secluded village, it will commonly be found, that those who have greater gifts of mind than others around them, who have more natural quickness, shrewdness, and wit, are the very persons who are the most likely to turn out ill—who are least under the influence of religious principles—and neither obey nor even revere the Gospel of salvation which Christ has brought us.

Now if we consult St. Paul's Epistles to the Corinthians, we shall find the same state of things existing even in the first age of Christianity. Even the Apostle speaks of those who were blind, or to whom his Gospel was hid; and he elsewhere describes them, not as the uneducated and dull of understanding, but as the wise of this world, the scribe and the disputer. Even then, before the Apostle's prophecy in the text was fulfilled, there were many who erred from the truth even in the midst of light, and in spite of superior intellectual endowments and acquirements.

Does not our Saviour Himself say the same thing, when He thanks His Father, Lord of heaven and earth, that He hath hid these things from the wise and prudent, and revealed them unto babes?

Now it should not surprise us when men of acute and powerful understandings more or less reject the Gospel, for this reason, that the Christian revelation addresses itself to our hearts, to our love of truth and goodness, our fear of sinning, and our desire to gain God's favour; and quickness, sagacity, depth of thought, strength of mind, power of comprehension, perception of the beautiful, power of language, and the like, though they are excellent gifts, are clearly quite of a different kind from these spiritual excellences—a man may have the one without having the other. *This*, then, is the plain reason why able, or again why learned men are so often defective Christians, because there is no necessary connexion between faith and ability; because faith is one thing and ability is another; because ability of mind is a *gift*, and faith is a *grace*. Who would ever argue that a man could, like Samson, conquer lions or throw down the gates of a city, because he was able, or accomplished, or experienced in the business of life? Who would ever argue that a man could see because he could hear, or run with the swift because he had "the tongue of the learned"?[1] These gifts are different in kind. In like manner, powers of mind and religious principles and feelings are distinct gifts; and as all the highest spiritual excellence, humility, firmness, patience, would never enable a man to read an unknown tongue, or to enter into the depths of science, so all the most brilliant mental endowments, wit, or imagination, or penetration, or depth, will never of themselves make us wise in religion. And as we should fairly and justly deride the savage who wished to decide questions of science or literature by the sword, so may we justly look with amazement on the error of those who think that they can master the high mysteries of spiritual truth, and find their way to God, by what is commonly called reason, i.e. by the random and blind efforts of mere mental acuteness, and mere experience of the world.

That Truth, which St. Paul preached, addresses itself to our spiritual nature: it will be rightly understood, valued, accepted, by none but lovers of truth, virtue, purity, humility, and peace. Wisdom will be justified of her children. Those, indeed, who are thus endowed may and will go on to use their powers of mind, whatever they are, in the service of religion; none but they can use them aright. Those who reject revealed truth wilfully, are such as do not love moral and religious truth. It is bad men, proud men, men of hard hearts, and unhumbled tempers, and immoral lives, these are they who reject the Gospel. These are they of whom St. Paul speaks in another Epistle—"If our Gospel be hid, it is hid to them that are lost, in whom the god of this world hath blinded the minds of them which believe not." With this agree the instances of turning the ears from the truth which the New Testament affords us. Who were they who were the enemies of Christ and His Apostles? The infidel Sadducees,

[1] Is. l.4.

the immoral, hard-hearted, yet hypocritical Pharisees, Herod, who married his brother Philip's wife,[2] and Felix, who trembled when St. Paul reasoned of righteousness, temperance, and judgment to come.[3] On the other hand, men of holy and consistent lives, as Cornelius the Centurion, and those who were frequenters of religious ordinances, as Simeon and Anna, these became Christians. So it is now. If men turn unto fables of their own will, they do it on account of their pride, or their love of indolence and self-indulgence.

This should be kept in mind when Christians are alarmed, as they sometimes are, on hearing instances of infidelity or heresy among those who read, reflect, and inquire; whereas, however we may mourn over such instances, we have no reason to be surprised at them. It is quite enough for Christians to be able to show, as they well can, that belief in revealed religion is not inconsistent with the highest gifts and acquirements of mind, that men even of the strongest and highest intellect have been Christians; but they have as little reason to be perplexed at finding *other* men of ability not true believers, as at finding that certain *rich* men are not true believers, or certain *poor* men, or some in every rank and circumstance of life. A belief in Christianity has hardly more connexion with what is called talent, than it has with riches, station, power, or bodily strength.

Now let me explain what I have said by a further remark. Is it not plain that earnestness is necessary for gaining religious truth? On the other hand, is it not a natural effect of ability to save us trouble, and even to tempt us to dispense with it, and to lead us to be indolent? Do not we see this even in the case of children—the more clever are the more idle, because they rely on their own quickness and power of apprehension? Is indolence the way to gain knowledge from God? Yet this surely is continually forgotten in the world. It is forgotten in a measure even by the best of Christians, for no man on earth seeks to know God's will, and to do His duty with an earnestness suitable to the importance of the object. But not to speak thus rigorously, let us consider for an instant how eagerly men in general pursue objects of this world; now with what portion of this eagerness do they exert themselves to know the truth of God's word? Undeniable, then, as is the doctrine that God does not reveal Himself to those who do not seek Him, it is certain that its truth is not really felt by us, or we should seek Him more earnestly than we do.

[2] Matt. xiv.3.   [3] Acts xxiv.25.

Nothing is more common than to think that we shall gain religious knowledge as a thing of course without express trouble on our part. Though there is no art or business of this world which is learned without time and exertion, yet it is commonly conceived that the knowledge of God and our duty will come as if by accident or by a natural process. Men go by their feelings and likings; they take up what is popular, or what comes first to hand. They think it much if they now and then have serious thoughts, if they now and then open the Bible; and their minds recur with satisfaction to such seasons, as if they had done some very great thing, never remembering that to seek and gain religious truth is a long and systematic work. And others think that education will do every thing for them, and that if they learn to read, and use religious words, they understand religion itself. And others again go so far as to maintain that exertion is *not* necessary for discovering the truth. They say that religious truth is simple and easily acquired; that Scripture, being intended for all, is at once open to all, and that if it had difficulties, that very circumstance would be an objection to it. And others, again, maintain that there *are* difficulties in religion, and that this shows that it is an indifferent matter whether they seek or not as to those matters which are difficult.

In these and other ways do men deceive themselves into a carelessness about religious truth. And is not all this varied negligence sufficient to account for the varieties of religious opinion which we see all around us? Do not these two facts just illustrate each other; the discordance of our religious opinions needing some explanation; and our actual indolence and negligence in seeking the truth accounting for it? How many sects, all professing Christianity, but opposed to each other, dishonour this country! Doubtless if men sought the truth with one tenth part of the zeal with which they seek to acquire wealth or secular knowledge, their differences would diminish year by year. Doubtless if they gave a half or a quarter of the time to prayer for Divine guidance which they give to amusement or recreation, or which they give to dispute and contention, they would ever be approximating to each other. We differ in opinion; therefore we cannot all be right; many must be wrong; many must be turned from the truth; and why is this, but on account of that undeniable fact which we see before us, that we do not pray and seek for the Truth?

But this melancholy diversity is sometimes explained, as I just now hinted, in another way. Some men will tell us that this difference of opinion in religious matters which exists, is a proof, not that the Truth is withheld from us on account of our negligence in seeking it, but that religious truth is not worth seeking at all, or that it is not given us. The present confused and perplexed state of things, which is really a proof of God's anger at our negligence, these men say is a proof that religious truth cannot be obtained; that there is no such thing as religious truth; that there is no right or wrong in religion; that, provided we *think* ourselves right, one set of opinions is as good as another; that we shall all come right in the end if we do but mean well, or rather if we do not mean ill. That is, we create confusion by our negligence and disobedience, and then excuse our negligence by the existence of that confusion. It is no uncommon thing, I say, for men to say, "that in religious matters God has willed that men should differ," and to support their opinion by no better argument than the fact that they *do* differ; and they go on to conclude that *therefore* we need not perplex ourselves about matters of *faith*, about which, after all, we cannot be certain. Others, again, in a similar spirit, argue that forms and ordinances are of no account; that they are little matters; that it is uncertain what is right and what is wrong in them, and that to insist on them as important to religion is the mark of a narrow mind. And others, again, it is to be feared, go so far as to think that indulgence of the passions, or self-will, or selfishness, or avarice, is not wrong, because it is the way of the world and cannot be prevented.

To all such arguments against religious truth, it is sufficient to reply, that no one who does not seek the truth with all his heart and strength, can tell what is of importance and what is not; that to attempt carelessly to decide on points of faith or morals is a matter of serious presumption; that no one knows *whither* he will be carried *if* he seeks the Truth perseveringly, and therefore, that since he cannot see at first starting the course into which his inquiries will be divinely directed, he *cannot* possibly say beforehand whether they may not lead him on to certainty as to things which at present he thinks trifling or extravagant or irrational. "What I do," said our Lord to St. Peter, "thou knowest not now, but thou shalt know hereafter." "*Seek*, and ye shall find;" this is the Divine rule, "If thou *criest* after knowledge, and *liftest up* thy voice for understanding; if thou seekest her as silver, and searchest for her as *for hid* treasures; *then* shalt thou understand the fear of the Lord, and find the knowledge of God." [4]

---

[4] Prov. ii.3–5.

This is a subject which cannot too strongly be insisted on. Act up to your light, though in the midst of difficulties, and you will be carried on, you do not know how far. Abraham obeyed the call and journeyed, not knowing whither he went; so we, if we follow the voice of God, shall be brought on step by step into a new world, of which before we had no idea. This is His gracious way with us: He gives, not all at once, but by measure and season, wisely. To him that hath, more shall be given. But we must begin at the beginning. Each truth has its own order; we cannot join the way of life at any point of the course we please; we cannot learn advanced truths before we have learned primary ones. "Call upon Me," says the Divine Word, "and I will answer thee, and show thee great and mighty things which thou knowest not." [5] Religious men are always learning; but when men refuse to profit by light already granted, their light is turned to darkness. Observe our Lord's conduct with the Pharisees. They asked Him on what authority He acted. He gave them no direct answer, but referred them to the mission of John the Baptist—"The baptism of John, whence was it? from heaven or from men?" [6] They refused to say. Then He said, "Neither tell I you by what authority I do these things." That is, they would not profit by the knowledge they already had from St. John the Baptist, who spoke of Christ—therefore no more was given them.

All of us may learn a lesson here, for all of us are in danger of hastily finding fault with others, and condemning their opinions or practices; not considering, that unless we have faithfully obeyed our conscience and improved our talents, we are no fit judges of them at all. Christ and His Saints are alike destitute of form or comeliness in the eyes of the world, and it is only as we labour to change our nature, through God's help, and to serve Him truly, that we begin to discern the beauty of holiness. Then, at length, we find reason to suspect our own judgments of what is truly good, and perceive our own blindness; for by degrees we find that those whose opinions and conduct we hitherto despised or wondered at as extravagant or unaccountable or weak, really know more than ourselves, and are above us—and so, ever as we rise in knowledge and grow in spiritual illumination, they (to our amazement) rise also, while we look at them. The better we are, the more we understand their excellence; till at length we are taught something of their Divine Master's perfections also, which before were hid from us, and see why it is that, though the Gospel is set on a hill in the midst of the world, like a city which cannot be hid, yet to multitudes it is notwithstanding hid, since He taketh the wise in their own craftiness, and the pure in heart alone can see God.

How are the sheep of Christ's flock scattered abroad in the waste world! He came to gather them together in one; but they wander again and faint by the way, as having lost their Shepherd. What religious opinion can be named which some men or other have not at some time held? All are equally confident in the truth of their own doctrines, though the many must be mistaken. In this confusion let us, my brethren, look to ourselves, each to himself. There must be a right and a wrong, and no matter whether others agree with us or not, it is to us a solemn practical concern not to turn away our ears from the truth. Let not the diversity of opinion in the world dismay you, or deter you from seeking all your life long true wisdom. It is not a search for this day or that, but as you should ever grow in grace, so should you ever grow also in the knowledge of our Lord and Saviour Jesus Christ. Care not for the perplexing question which many will put to you, "How can you be sure that you are right more than others?" Others are nothing to you, if they are not holy and devout in their conversation—and we all know what is meant by being holy; we know whom we should call holy; to be holy is to be like an Apostle. Seek truth in the way of *obedience*; try to act up to your conscience, and let your opinions be the result, not of mere chance reasoning or fancy, but of an improved heart. This way, I say, carries with it an evidence to ourselves of its being the right way, if any way be right; and that there is a right and a wrong way conscience also tells us. God surely will listen to none but those who strive to obey Him. Those who thus proceed, watching, praying, taking all means given them of gaining the truth, studying the Scriptures, and doing their duty; in short, those who seek religious truth by principle and habit, as the main business of their lives, humbly not arrogantly, peaceably not contentiously, shall not be "turned unto fables." "The secret of the Lord is with them that fear Him;" but in proportion as we are conscious to ourselves that we are indolent, and transgress our own sense of right and wrong, in the same proportion we have cause to fear, not only that we are not in a safe state, but, further than this, that we do not know what is a safe state, and what an unsafe—what is light and what is darkness, what is truth and what is error; which way leads to heaven and which to hell.

"The way of the wicked is in darkness; they know not at what they stumble." [7]

I know we shall find it very hard to rouse ourselves, to break the force of habit, to resolve to serve God, and persevere in doing so. And assuredly we must expect, even at best, and with all our efforts, perhaps backslidings, and certainly much continual imperfection all through our lives, in all we do. But this should create in us a horror of disobedience, not a despair at overcoming ourselves. We are not under the law of nature, but under grace; we are not bid do a thing above our strength, because, though our hearts are naturally weak, we are not left to ourselves. According to the command, so is the gift. God's grace is sufficient for us. Why, then, should we fear? Rather, why should we not make any sacrifice, and give up all that is naturally pleasing to us, rather than that light and truth should have come into the world, yet we not find them? Let us be willing to endure toil and trouble; and should times of comparative quiet be given to us, should for a while temptation be withdrawn, or the Spirit of comfort poured upon us, let us not inconsiderately rest in these accidental blessings. While we thank God for them, let us remember that in its turn the time of labour and fear, and danger and anxiety, will come upon us; and that we must act our part well in it. We live here to struggle and to endure: the time of eternal rest will come hereafter.

"Blessed are the undefiled in the way, who walk in the law of the Lord. Blessed are they that keep His testimonies, and that seek Him with the whole heart." [8] "The path of the just is as the shining light, that shineth more and more unto the perfect day." [9]

---

[7] Prov. iv.19.   [8] Ps. cxix.1, 2.   [9] Prov. iv.18.

OBEDIENCE TO GOD THE WAY TO FAITH IN CHRIST

*"When Jesus saw that he answered discreetly, He said unto him,
Thou art not far from the kingdom of God."*—Mark xii.34.

THE answer of the scribe, which our blessed Lord here commends, was occasioned by Christ's setting before him the
two great commandments of the Law. When He had declared
the love of God and of man to comprehend our whole duty, the
scribe said, "Master, Thou hast said the truth: for there is one
God; and there is none other but He: and to love Him with all
the heart, and with all the understanding, and with all the soul,
and with all the strength, and to love his neighbour as himself,
is more than all whole burnt-offerings and sacrifices." Upon
this acknowledgment of the duty of general religious obedience, Christ replied, in the words of the text, "Thou art not far
from the kingdom of God," i.e. Thou art not far from being a
Christian.

In these words, then, we are taught, first, that the Christian's
faith and obedience are not the same religion as that of natural
conscience, as being some way beyond it; secondly, that this
way is "not far," not far in the case of those who try to act up to
their conscience; in other words, that obedience to conscience
leads to obedience to the Gospel, which, instead of being something different altogether, is but the completion and perfection
of that religion which natural conscience teaches.

Indeed, it would have been strange if the God of nature had
said one thing, and the God of grace another; if the truths which
our conscience taught us without the information of Scripture,
were contradicted by that information when obtained. But it is
not so; there are not two ways of pleasing God; what conscience
suggests, Christ has sanctioned and explained; to love God and
our neighbour are the great duties of the Gospel as well as of the
Law; he who endeavours to fulfil them by the light of nature is
in the way towards, is, as our Lord said, "not far from Christ's
kingdom;" for to him that hath more shall be given.

It is not in one or two places merely that this same doctrine is declared to us; indeed, all revelation is grounded on those simple truths which our own consciences teach us in a measure, though a poor measure, even without it. It is One God, and none other but He, who speaks first in our consciences, then in His Holy Word; and, lest we should be in any difficulty about the matter, He has most mercifully told us so in Scripture, wherein He refers again and again (as in the passage connected with the text) to the great Moral Law, as the foundation of the truth, which His Apostles and Prophets, and last of all His Son, have taught us: "Fear God, and keep His commandments; for this is the whole duty of man." [1]

Yet though this is so plain, both from our own moral sense, and the declarations of Scripture, still for many reasons it is necessary to insist upon it; chiefly, because, it being very hard to keep God's commandments, men would willingly persuade themselves, if they could, that strict obedience is not necessary under the Gospel, and that something else will be taken, for Christ's sake, in the stead of it. Instead of labouring, under God's grace, to change their wills, to purify their hearts, and so prepare themselves for the kingdom of God, they imagine that in that kingdom they may be saved by something short of this, by their baptism, or by their ceremonial observances (the burnt offerings and sacrifices which the scribe disparages), or by their correct knowledge of the truth, or by their knowledge of their own sinfulness, or by some past act of faith which is to last them during their lives, or by some strong habitual persuasion that they are safe; or, again, by the performance of some one part of their duty, though they neglect the rest, as if God said a thing to us in nature, and Christ unsaid it; and, when men wish a thing, it is not hard to find texts in Scripture which may be ingeniously perverted to suit their purpose. The error then being so common in practice, of believing that Christ came to gain for us easier terms of admittance into heaven than we had before (whereas, in fact, instead of making obedience less strict, He has enabled us to obey God more strictly; and instead of gaining *easier* terms of *admittance*, He has gained us *altogether* our admittance into heaven, which before was closed against us); this error, I say, being so common, it may be right to insist on the opposite truth, however obvious, that obedience to God is the way to know and believe in Christ.

[1] Eccles. xii.13.

1. Now, first, let us consider how plainly we are taught in Scripture that perfect obedience is the standard of Gospel holiness. By St. Paul: "Be not conformed to this world: but be ye transformed by the renewing of your mind, that ye may prove what is that good, and acceptable, and perfect, will of God." [2] "Circumcision is nothing, and uncircumcision is nothing, but the keeping of the commandments of God." [3] "Whatsoever things are true . . honest . . just . . pure . . lovely . . of good report: if there be any virtue, and if there be any praise, think on these things." [4] By St. James: "Whosoever shall keep the whole law, and yet offend in one point, he is guilty of all." [5] By St. Peter: "Giving all diligence, add to your faith virtue . . knowledge . . temperance . . patience . . godliness . . brotherly kindness . . charity." [6] By St. John: "Hereby do we know that we know Him, if we keep His commandments." Lastly, by our Lord Himself: "He that hath My commandments, and keepeth them, he it is that loveth Me: and he that loveth Me, shall be loved of My Father, and I will love him, and will manifest Myself to him." [7] And, above all, the following clear declaration in the Sermon on the Mount: "Whosoever . . shall break one of these least commandments, and shall teach men so, he shall be called the least in the kingdom of heaven: but whosoever shall do and teach them, the same shall be called great in the kingdom of heaven." [8]

These texts, and a multitude of others, show that the Gospel leaves us just where it found us, as regards the necessity of our obedience to God; that Christ has not obeyed instead of us, but that obedience is quite as imperative as if Christ had never come; nay, is pressed upon us with additional sanctions; the difference being, not that He relaxes the strict rule of keeping His commandments, but that He gives us spiritual aids, which we have not except through Him, to enable us to keep them. Accordingly Christ's service is represented in Scripture, not as different from that religious obedience which conscience teaches us naturally, but as the perfection of it, as I have already said. We are told again and again, that obedience to God leads on to faith in Christ; that it is the only recognized way to Christ; and that, therefore, to believe in Him, ordinarily implies that we are living in obedience to God. For instance: "Every man . . . that hath heard and hath learned of the Father, cometh unto Me;" [9] "He that doeth truth, cometh to the light," [10] i.e. to Christ;

---

[2] Rom. xii.2.   [3] 1 Cor. vii.19.   [4] Phil. iv.8.
[5] James ii.10.   [6] 2 Pet. i.5–7.   [7] John xiv.21.
[8] Matt. v.19.   [9] John vi.45.   [10] John iii.21.

"No man can come to Me, except the Father which hath sent Me, draw him;" "If any man will do the will of God, he shall know of the doctrine." [11] On the other hand: "He that hateth Me, hateth My Father also;" [12] "If ye had known Me, ye should have known My Father also;" [13] "Whosoever denieth the Son, the same hath not the Father;" [14] "Whosoever transgresseth, and abideth not in the doctrine of Christ, hath not God: he that abideth in the doctrine of Christ, he hath both the Father and the Son." [15]

In these and other passages of Scripture we learn, that though Christ came to be the light of the world, yet He is not and cannot be a light to all, but to those only who seek Him in the way of His commandments; and to all others He is hid, the god of this world "blinding the minds of them which believe not, lest the light of the glorious Gospel of Christ, who is the Image of God, should shine unto them." [16]

2. And if we look to the history of the first propagation of the Gospel, we find this view confirmed. As far as we can trace the history, we find the early Christian Church was principally composed of those who had long been in the habit of obeying their consciences carefully, and so preparing themselves for Christ's religion, that kingdom of God from which the text says they were not far. Zacharias and Elisabeth, to whom the approach of Christ's kingdom was first revealed, are described as "both righteous before God, walking in all the commandments and ordinances of the Lord, blameless." [17] Joseph, St. Mary's husband, is called "a just man;" [18] Simeon is spoken of as "a just and devout" [19] man; Nathaniel, as "an Israelite in whom was no guile;" [20] Joseph of Arimathea was "a good man and a just;" [21] Cornelius, the centurion, was a "religious man, and one that feared God with all his house, who gave much alms to the people, and prayed to God alway." [22] And in the book of Acts generally, we shall find (as far as we are told any thing) that those chiefly were addressed and converted by St. Paul, who had previously trained themselves in a religious life:—At Perga, St. Paul addressed the Israelites and those who feared God, not the mere thoughtless heathen; and many of these followed him. [23] At Thessalonica a great multitude of religious Greeks believed; [24] and at Athens the Apostle still dis-

---

[11] John vii.17.   [12] John xv.23.   [13] John viii.19.

[14] 1 John ii.23.   [15] 2 John 9.   [16] 2 Cor. iv.4.

[17] Luke i.6.   [18] Matt. i.19.   [19] Luke ii.25.

[20] John i.47.   [21] Luke xxiii.50.   [22] Acts x.2.

[23] Acts xiii.   [24] Acts xvii.

puted with the Jews, and with the professedly religious persons, though he also addressed the educated heathens who lived there. Here then is much evidence that Christ and His Apostles chiefly sought and found their first followers, not among open sinners, but among those who were endeavouring, however imperfectly, to obey God.

But it may be asked, Did Christ hold out no hope for those who had lived in sin? Doubtless He did, if they determined to forsake their sin. He came to save all, whatever their former life, who gave themselves up to Him as their Lord and Saviour; and in His Church He gathered together of every kind, those who had departed from God, as well as those who had ever served Him well. Open sinners must have a beginning of repentance, if they are to repent; and on this first beginning Christ invites them to Him at once, without delay, for pardon and for aid. But this is not the question; of course all who come to Him will be received; none will be cast out.[25] But the question is, not this, but whether they are likely to come, to hear His voice, and to follow Him; again, whether they will, generally speaking, prove as consistent and deeply-taught Christians as those who, compared with them, have never departed from God at all; and here all the advantage, doubtless, is on the side of those who (in the words of Scripture) have walked in the ordinances of the Lord blameless.[26] When sinners truly repent, then, indeed, they are altogether brothers in Christ's kingdom with those who have not in the same sense "need of repentance;" but that they should repent at all is (alas!) so far from being likely, that when the unexpected event takes place it causes such joy in heaven (from the marvellousness of it) as is not even excited by the ninety and nine just persons who need no such change of mind.[27] Of such changes some instances are given us in the Gospels for the encouragement of all penitents, such as that of the woman, mentioned by St. Luke, who "loved much." Christ most graciously went among sinners, if so be He might save them; and we know that even those open sinners, when they knew that they were sinners, were nearer salvation, and in a better state, than the covetous and irreligious Pharisees, who added to their other gross sins, hypocrisy, blindness, a contempt of others, and a haughty and superstitious reliance on the availing virtue of their religious privileges.

And, moreover, of these penitents of whom I speak—and whom, when they become penitents, we cannot love too dearly

[25] John iv.3, 7.   [26] Luke i.6.   [27] Luke xv.7.

(after our Saviour's pattern), nay, or reverence too highly, and whom the Apostles, after Christ's departure, brought into the Church in such vast multitudes—none, as far as we know, had any sudden change of mind from bad to good wrought in them; nor do we hear of any of them honoured with any important station in the Church. Great as St. Paul's sin was in persecuting Christ's followers, before his conversion, that sin was of a different kind; he was not transgressing, but obeying his conscience (however blinded it was); he was doing what he thought his duty, when he was arrested by the heavenly vision, which, when presented to him, he at once "obeyed;" he was not sinning *against light*, but *in* darkness. We know nothing of the precise state of his mind immediately before his conversion; but we do know thus much, that years elapsed after his conversion before he was employed as an Apostle in the Church of God.

I have confined myself to the time of Christ's coming; but not only then, but at all times and under all circumstances, as all parts of the Bible inform us, obedience to the light we possess is the way to gain more light. In the words of Wisdom, in the book of Proverbs, "I love them that love Me; and those that seek Me early shall find Me. . . . I lead in the way of righteousness, in the midst of the paths of judgment." [28] Or, in the still more authoritative words of Christ Himself, "He that is faithful in that which is least, is faithful also in much;" [29] and, "He that hath, to him shall be given." [30]

Now let us see some of the consequences which follow from this great Scripture truth.

1. First of all, we see the hopelessness of waiting for any sudden change of heart, if we are at present living in sin. Far more persons deceive themselves by some such vain expectation than at first sight may appear. That there are even many irreligious men, who, from hearing the false doctrines now so common, and receiving general impressions from them, look forward for a possible day when God will change their hearts by His own mere power, in spite of themselves, and who thus get rid of the troublesome thought that now they are in a state of fearful peril; who say they can do nothing till His time comes, while still they acknowledge themselves to be far from Him; even this I believe to be a fact, strange and gross as the self-deception may appear to be. And others, too, many more, doubtless, are there who, not thinking themselves far from Him, but, on the contrary, high in His favour, still, by a dreadful deceit of Satan, are

[28] Prov. viii.17, 20.   [29] Luke xvi.10.   [30] Mark iv.25.

led to be indolent and languid in their obedience to His commandments, from a pretence that they can do nothing of themselves, and must wait for the successive motions of God's grace to excite them to action. The utmost these persons do is to talk of religion, when they ought to be up and active, and waiting for the Blessed Spirit of Christ by obeying God's will. "Awake thou that sleepest, and arise from the dead, and Christ shall give thee light." [31] This is the exhortation. And doubtless to all those who live a self-indulgent life, however they veil their self-indulgence from themselves by a notion of their superior religious knowledge, and by their faculty of speaking fluently in Scripture language, to all such the word of life says, "Be not deceived; God is not mocked;" He tries the heart, and disdains the mere worship of the lips. He acknowledges no man as a believer in His Son, who does not anxiously struggle to obey His commandments to the utmost; to none of those who seek without striving, and who consider themselves safe, to none of these does He give "power to become sons of God." [32] Be not deceived; such have fallen from that state in which their baptism placed them and are "far from the kingdom of God." "Whatsoever a man soweth, that shall he also reap." [33] And if any one says that St. Paul was converted suddenly, and without his exerting himself, it is sufficient to reply, that, guilty as St. Paul was, his guilt was not that of indolence, and self-indulgence, and indifference. His sin was that of *neglecting the study of Scripture*; and thus, missing the great truth that Jesus was the Christ, he persecuted the Christians; but though his conscience was ill-informed, and that by his own fault, yet he obeyed it such as it was. He did what he did ignorantly. If then the case really be that St. Paul *was* suddenly converted, hence, it is true, some kind of vague hope may be said to be held out to furious, intolerant bigots, and bloodthirsty persecutors, if they are acting in consequence of their own notions of duty; none to the slothful and negligent and lukewarm; none *but* to those who can say, with St. Paul, that they have "lived in all good conscience before God until this day;" [34] and that not under an easy profession, but in a straitest religious sect, giving themselves up to their duty, and following the law of God, though in ignorance, yet with all their heart and soul.

2. But, after all, there are very many more than I have as yet mentioned, who wait for a time of repentance to come while at

---

[31] Eph. v.14.   [32] John i.12.
[33] Gal. vi.7.   [34] Acts xxiii.1.

present they live in sin. For instance, the young, who consider it will be time enough to think of God when they grow old; that religion will then come as a matter of course, and that they will then like it naturally, just as they now like their follies and sins. Or those who are much engaged in worldly business, who confess they do not give that attention to religion which they ought to give; who neglect the ordinances of the Church; who desecrate the Lord's day; who give little or no time to the study of God's word; who allow themselves in various small transgressions of their conscience, and resolutely harden themselves against the remorse which such transgressions are calculated to cause them; and all this they do under the idea that at length a convenient season will come when they may give themselves to religious duties. They determine on retiring at length from the world, and of making up for lost time by greater diligence then. All such persons, and how many they are! think that they will be able to seek Christ when they please, though they have lived all their lives with no true love either of God or man; i.e. they do not, in their hearts, believe our Lord's doctrine contained in the text, that to obey God is to be near Christ, and that to disobey is to be far from Him.

How will this truth be plain to us in that day when the secrets of all hearts shall be revealed! *Now* we do not believe that strict obedience is as necessary as it is. I say we do *not* believe it, though we say we do. No one, of course, believes it in its fulness, but most of us are deceived by words, and say we accept and believe, when we hardly do more than profess it. We say, indeed, that obedience is absolutely necessary, and are surprised to have our real belief in what we say questioned; but we do not give the truth that place in the scheme of our religion which this profession requires, and thus we cheat our consciences. We put something *before* it, in our doctrinal system, as *more* necessary than it; one man puts faith, another outward devotion, a third attention to his temporal calling, another zeal for the Church; that is, we put a part for the whole of our duty, and so run the risk of losing our souls. These are the burnt-offerings and sacrifices which even the scribe put aside before the weightier matters of the Law. Or again, we fancy that the means of gaining heaven are something stranger and rarer than the mere obvious duty of obedience to God; we are loth to seek Christ in the waters of Jordan rather than in Pharpar and Abana, rivers of Damascus; we prefer to seek Him in the height above, or to descend into the deep, rather than to believe that the word is nigh us, even in our mouth and in our heart.[35] Hence, in false religions some men have even tortured themselves and been cruel to their flesh, thereby to become as gods, and to mount aloft; and in our own, with a not less melancholy, though less self-denying, error, men fancy that certain strange effects on their minds—strong emotion, restlessness, and an unmanly excitement and extravagance of thought and feeling—are the tokens of that inscrutable Spirit, who is given us, not to make us something *other than* men, but to make us, what without His gracious aid we never shall be, upright, self-mastering men, humble and obedient children of our Lord and Saviour.

In that day of trial all these deceits will be laid aside; we shall stand in our own real form, whether it be of heaven or of earth, the wedding garment, or the old raiment of sin;[36] and then, how many (do we think) will be revealed as the heirs of light, who have followed Christ in His narrow way, and humbled themselves after His manner (though not in His perfection, and with nothing of His merit) to the daily duties of soberness, mercy, gentleness, self-denial, and the fear of God?

These, be they many or few, will then receive their prize from Him who died for them, who has made them what they are, and completes in heaven what first by conscience, then by His Spirit, He began here. Surely they were despised on the earth by the world; both by the open sinners, who thought their scrupulousness to be foolishness, and by such pretenders to God's favour as thought it ignorance. But, in reality, they had received from their Lord the treasures both of wisdom and of knowledge, though men knew it not; and they then will be acknowledged by Him before all creatures, as heirs of the glory prepared for them before the beginning of the world.

[35] Rom. x.8.   [36] Zech. iii.4.

SUDDEN CONVERSIONS

"By the grace of God I am what I am: and His grace which was bestowed upon me was not in vain."—1 Cor. xv. 10.

WE can hardly conceive that grace, such as that given to the great Apostle who speaks in the text, would have been given in vain; that is, we should not expect that it would have been given, had it been foreseen and designed by the Almighty Giver that it would have been in vain. By which I do not mean, of course, to deny that God's gifts are oftentimes abused and wasted by man, which they are; but, when we consider the wonderful mode of St. Paul's conversion, and the singular privilege granted him, the only one of men of whom is clearly recorded the privilege of seeing Christ with his bodily eyes after His ascension, as is alluded to shortly before the text; I say, considering these high and extraordinary favours vouchsafed to the Apostle, we should naturally suppose that some great objects in the history of the Church were contemplated by means of them, such as in the event were fulfilled. We cannot tell, indeed, why God works, or by what rule He chooses; we must always be sober and humble in our thoughts about His ways, which are infinitely above our ways; but what would be speculation, perhaps venturous speculation, before the event, at least becomes a profitable meditation after it. At least, now, when we read and dwell on St. Paul's history, we may discern and insist upon the suitableness of his character, before his conversion, for that display of free grace which was made in him. Not that he could merit such a great mercy—the idea is absurd as well as wicked; but that such a one as he was before God's grace, naturally grew by the aid of it into what he was afterwards as a Christian.

His, indeed, was a "wonderful conversion," as our Church in one place calls it, because it was so unexpected, and (as far as the appearance went) so sudden. Who of the suffering Christians, against whom he was raging so furiously, could have conceived that their enemy was to be the great preacher and champion of the despised Cross? Does God work miracles to reclaim His open malevolent adversaries, and not rather to encourage and lead forward those who timidly seek Him?

It may be useful, then, to mention one or two kinds of what may be called sudden conversions, to give some opinion on the character of each of them, and to inquire which of them really took place in St. Paul's case.

1. First; some men turn to religion all at once from some sudden impulse of mind, some powerful excitement, or some strong persuasion. It is a sudden resolve that comes upon them. Now such cases occur very frequently where religion has nothing to do with the matter, and then we think little about it, merely calling the persons who thus change all at once volatile and light-minded. Thus there are persons who all of a sudden give up some pursuit which they have been eagerly set upon, or change from one trade or calling to another, or change their opinions as regards the world's affairs. Every one knows the impression left upon the mind by such instances. The persons thus changing may be, and often are, amiable, kind, and pleasant, as companions; but we cannot depend on them; and we pity them, as believing they are doing harm both to their temporal interests and to their own minds. Others there are who almost profess to love change for change-sake; they think the pleasure of life consists in seeing first one thing, then another; variety is their chief good; and it is a sufficient objection in their minds to any pursuit or recreation, that it is old. These, too, pass suddenly and capriciously from one subject to another. So far in matters of daily life;—but when such a person exhibits a similar changeableness in his religious views, then men begin to be astonished, and look out with curiosity or anxiety to see what is the meaning of it; and particularly if the individual who thus suddenly changed, was very decided before in the particular course of life which he then followed. For instance, supposing he not merely professed no deep religious impressions, but actually was unbelieving or profligate; or, again, supposing he not merely professed himself of this creed or that, but was very warm, and even bitter in the enforcement of it; then, I say, men wonder, though they do not wonder at similar infirmities in matters of this world.

Nor can I say that they are wrong in being alive to such changes; we *ought* to feel differently with reference to religious subjects, and not be as unconcerned about them as we are about the events of time. Did a man suddenly inform us, with great appearance of earnestness, that he had seen an accident in the street, or did he say that he had seen a miracle, I confess it is

natural, nay, in the case of most men, certainly in the case of
the uneducated, far more religious, to feel differently towards
these two accounts; to feel shocked, indeed, but not awed, at
the first—to feel a certain solemn astonishment and pious reverence at the news of the miracle. For a religious mind is ever
looking towards God, and seeking His traces; referring all
events to Him, and desirous of His explanation of them; and
when to such a one information is brought that God has in
some extraordinary way showed Himself, he *will* at first sight
be tempted to believe it, and it is only the experience of the
number of deceits and false prophecies which are in the world,
his confidence in the Catholic Church which he sees before
him, and which is his guide into the truth, and (if he be educated) his enlightened views concerning the course and laws of
God's providence, which keep him steady and make him hard
to believe such stories. On the other hand, men destitute of
religion altogether, of course from the first ridicule such accounts, and, as the event shows, rightly; and yet, in spite of
this, they are not so worthy our regard as those who at first
were credulous, from having some religious principle without
enough religious knowledge. Therefore, I am not surprised
that such sudden conversions as I have been describing deceive
for a time even the better sort of people—whom I should
blame, if I were called on to do so, not so much for the mere
fact of their believing readily, but for their not believing the
Church; for believing private individuals who have no authority more than the Church, and for not recollecting St. Paul's
words, "If any man . . . though we, or an Angel from heaven,
preach any other Gospel unto you than that ye have received,
let him be accursed." [1]

2. In the cases of sudden conversion I have been speaking of,
when men change at once either from open sin, or again from
the zealous partizanship of a certain creed, to some novel form
of faith or worship, their light-mindedness is detected by their
frequent changing—their changing again and again, so that one
can never be certain of them. This is the test of their unsound-
ness;—having no root in themselves, their convictions and earnestness quickly wither away. But there is another kind of
sudden conversion, which I proceed to mention, in which a
man perseveres to the end, consistent in the new form he
adopts, and which may be right or wrong, as it happens, but
which *he* cannot be said to recommend or confirm to us by his

[1] Gal. i.8, 9.

own change. I mean when a man, for some reason or other, whether in religion or not, takes a great disgust to his present course of life, and suddenly abandons it for another. This is the case of those who rush from one to the other extreme, and it generally arises from strong and painful feeling, unsettling and, as it were, revolutionizing the mind. A story is told of a spend-thrift who, having ruined himself by his extravagances, went out of doors to meditate on his own folly and misery, and in the course of a few hours returned home a determined miser, and was for the rest of his life remarkable for covetousness and pe-nuriousness. This is not more extraordinary than the fickleness of mind just now described. In like manner, men sometimes will change suddenly from love to hatred, from over-daring to cowardice. These are no amiable changes, whether arising or not from bodily malady, as is sometimes the case; nor do they impart any credit or sanction to the particular secular course or habit of mind adopted on the change: neither do they in reli-gion therefore. A man who suddenly professes religion after a profligate life, merely because he is sick of his vices, or tor-mented by the thought of God's anger, which is the conse-quence of them, and without the love of God, does no honour to religion, for he might, if it so chanced, turn a miser or a mis-anthrope; and, therefore, though religion is not at all the less holy and true because he submits himself to it, and though doubtless it is a much better thing for *him* that he turns to reli-gion than that he should become a miser or a misanthrope, still, when he acts on such motives as I have described, he cannot be said to do any honour to the cause of religion by his conversion. Yet it is such persons who at various times have been thought great saints, and been reckoned to recommend and prove the truth of the Gospel to the world!

Now if any one asks what test there is that this kind of sudden conversion is not from God, as instability and frequent change are the test, on the other hand, in disproof of the divinity of the conversions just now mentioned, I answer,—its moroseness, inhumanity, and unfitness for this world. Men who change through strong passion and anguish become as hard and as rigid as stone or iron; they are not fit for life; they are only fit for the solitudes in which they sometimes bury themselves; they can only do one or two of their duties, and that only in one way; they do not indeed change their principles, as the fickle con-vert, but, on the other hand, they cannot apply, adapt, accom-modate, modify, diversify their principles to the existing state of things, which is the opposite fault. They do not aim at a perfect obedience in little things as well as great; and a most serious fault it is, looking at it merely as a matter of practice, and without any reference to the views and motives from which it proceeds; most opposed is it to the spirit of true religion, which is intended to fit us for all circumstances of life as they come, in order that we may be humble, docile, ready, patient, and cheerful,—in order that we may really show ourselves God's servants, who do all things for Him, coming when He calleth, going when He sendeth, doing this or that at His bidding. So much for the practice of such men; and when we go higher, and ask *why* they are thus formal and unbending in their mode of life, what are the principles that make them thus harsh and unserviceable, I fear we must trace it to some form of selfishness and pride; the same principles which, under other circumstances, would change the profligate into the covetous and parsimonious.

I think it will appear at once that St. Paul's conversion, however it was effected, and whatever was the process of it, resembled neither the one nor the other of these. That it was not the change of a fickle mind is shown by his firmness in keeping to his new faith—by his constancy unto death, a death of martyrdom. That it was not the change of a proud and disappointed mind, quitting with disgust what he once loved too well, is evidenced by the variety of his labours, his active services, and continued presence in the busy thoroughfares of the world; by the cheerfulness, alacrity, energy, dexterity, and perseverance, with which he pleaded the cause of God among sinners. He reminds us of his firmness, as well as gentleness, when he declares, "What mean ye to weep, and break my heart? for I am ready not to be bound only, but also to die at Jerusalem for the Name of the Lord Jesus;" and of his ready accommodation of himself to the will of God, in all its forms, when he says, "I am made all things to all men, that I might by all means save some." [2]

3. But there is another kind of sudden conversion, or rather what appears to be such, not uncommonly found, and which may be that to which St. Paul's conversion is to be referred, and which I proceed to describe.

When men change their religious opinions really and truly, it is not merely their opinions that they change, but their hearts; and this evidently is not done in a moment—it is a slow work; nevertheless, though gradual, the change is often not uniform,

[2] Acts xxi.13; 1 Cor. ix.22.

but proceeds, so to say, by fits and starts, being influenced by external events, and other circumstances. This we see in the growth of plants, for instance; it is slow, gradual, continual; yet one day by chance they grow more than another, they make a shoot, or at least we are attracted to their growth on that day by some accidental circumstance, and it remains on our memory. So with our souls: we all, by nature, are far from God; nay, and we have all characters to form, which is a work of time. All this must have a beginning; and those who are now leading religious lives have begun at different times. Baptism, indeed, is God's time, when He first gives us grace; but alas! through the perverseness of our will, we do not follow Him. There must be a time then for beginning. Many men do not at all recollect any one marked and definite time *when* they began to seek God. Others recollect a time, not, properly speaking, when they began, but when they made what may be called a shoot forward, the fact either being so, in consequence of external events, or at least for some reason or other their attention being called to it. Others, again, continue forming a religious character and religious opinions as the result of it, though holding at the same time some outward profession of faith inconsistent with them; as, for instance, suppose it has been their unhappy condition to be brought up as heathens, Jews, infidels, or heretics. They hold the notions they have been taught for a long while, not perceiving that the character forming within them is at variance with these, till at length the inward growth forces itself forward, forces on the opinions accompanying it, and the dead outward surface of error, which has no root in their minds, from some accidental occurrence, suddenly falls off; suddenly,—just as a building might suddenly fall, which had been going many years, and which falls at this moment rather than that, in consequence of some chance cause, as it is called, which we cannot detect.

Now in all these cases one point of time is often taken by religious men, as if the very time of conversion, and as if it were sudden, though really, as is plain, in none of them is there any suddenness in the matter. In the last of these instances, which might be in a measure, if we dare say it, St. Paul's case, the time when the formal outward profession of error fell off is taken as the time of conversion. Others recollect the first occasion when any deep serious thought came into their minds, and reckon this as the date of their inward change. Others, again, recollect some intermediate point of time when they first openly professed their faith, or dared do some noble deed for Christ's sake.

I might go on to show more particularly how what I have said applies to St. Paul; but as this would take too much time I will only observe generally, that there was much in St. Paul's character which was not changed on his conversion, but merely directed to other and higher objects, and purified; it was his creed that was changed, and his soul by regeneration; and though he was sinning most grievously and awfully when Christ appeared to him from heaven, he evidenced then, as afterwards, a most burning energetic zeal for God, a most scrupulous strictness of life, an abstinence from all self-indulgence, much more from all approach to sensuality or sloth, and an implicit obedience to what he considered God's will. It was pride which was his inward enemy—pride which needed an overthrow. He acted rather as a defender and protector, than a minister of what he considered the truth; he relied on his own views; he was positive and obstinate; he did not seek for light as a little child; he did not look out for a Saviour who was to come, and he missed Him when He came.

But how great was the change in these respects when he became a servant of Him whom he had persecuted! As he had been conspicuous for a proud confidence in self, on his privileges, on his knowledge, on his birth, on his observances, so he became conspicuous for his humility. What self-abasement, when he says, "I am the least of the Apostles, that am not meet to be called an Apostle, because I persecuted the Church of God; but by the grace of God I am what I am." What keen and bitter remembrance of the past, when he says, "Who was before a blasphemer, and a persecutor, and injurious; but I obtained mercy, because I did it ignorantly in unbelief."[3] Ah! what utter self-abandonment, what scorn and hatred of self, when he, who had been so pleased to be a Hebrew of Hebrews, and a Pharisee, bore to be called, nay gloried for Christ's sake in being called, an apostate, the most odious and miserable of titles!—bore to be spurned and spit upon as a renegade, a traitor, a false-hearted and perfidious, a fallen, a lost son of his Church; a shame to his mother, and a curse to his countrymen. Such was the light in which those furious zealots looked on the great Apostle, who bound themselves together by an oath that they would neither eat nor drink till they had killed him. It was their justification in their own eyes, that he was a "pestilent fellow," a "stirrer of seditions," and an abomination amid sacred institutions which God had given.

[3] 1 Tim. i.13.

And, lastly, what supported him in this great trial? that special mercy which converted him, which he, and he only, saw—the Face of Jesus Christ. That all-pitying, all-holy eye, which turned in love upon St. Peter when he denied Him, and thereby roused him to repentance, looked on St. Paul also, while he persecuted Him, and wrought in him a sudden conversion. "Last of all," he says, "He was seen of me also, as of one born out of due time." One sight of that Divine Countenance, so tender, so loving, so majestic, so calm, was enough, first to convert him, then to support him on his way amid the bitter hatred and fury which he was to excite in those who hitherto had loved him.

And if such be the effect of a momentary vision of the glorious Presence of Christ, what think you, my brethren, will be their bliss, to whom it shall be given, this life ended, to see that Face eternally?

THE SHEPHERD OF OUR SOULS

*"I am the good Shepherd: the good Shepherd giveth His life
for the sheep."*—John x.11.

OUR Lord here appropriates to Himself the title under
which He had been foretold by the Prophets. "David My
servant shall be king over them," says Almighty God by the
mouth of Ezekiel: "and they all shall have one Shepherd." And
in the book of Zechariah, "Awake, O sword, against My Shepherd, and against the man that is My fellow, saith the Lord of
Hosts; smite the Shepherd, and the sheep shall be scattered."
And in like manner St. Peter speaks of our returning "to the
Shepherd and Bishop of our souls." [1]

"The good Shepherd giveth His life for the sheep." In those
countries of the East where our Lord appeared, the office of a
shepherd is not only a lowly and simple office, and an office of
trust, as it is with us, but, moreover, an office of great hardship
and of peril. Our flocks are exposed to no enemies, such as our
Lord describes. The Shepherd here has no need to prove his fidelity to the sheep by encounters with fierce beasts of prey. The
hireling shepherd is not tried. But where our Lord dwelt in the
days of His flesh it was otherwise. There it was true that the
good Shepherd giveth His life for the sheep—"but he that is an
hireling, and whose own the sheep are not, seeth the wolf coming, and leaveth the sheep, and fleeth, and the wolf catcheth
them and scattereth the sheep. The hireling fleeth, because he is
an hireling, and careth not for the sheep."

Our Lord found the sheep scattered; or, as He had said
shortly before, "All that ever came before Me are thieves and
robbers;" and in consequence the sheep had no guide. Such
were the priests and rulers of the Jews when Christ came; so
that "when He saw the multitudes He was moved with compassion on them, because they fainted, and were scattered abroad
as sheep having no shepherd." [2] Such, in like manner, were the

---

[1] Ezek. xxxvii.24; Zech. xiii.7; 1 Pet. ii.25.
[2] Matt. ix.36.

rulers and prophets of Israel in the days of Ahab, when Micaiah, the Lord's Prophet, "saw all Israel scattered on the hills, as sheep that have not a shepherd, and the Lord said, These have no Master, let them return every man to his house in peace."[3] Such, too, were the shepherds in the time of Ezekiel, of whom the Prophet says, "Woe be to the shepherds of Israel that do feed themselves! should not the shepherd feed the flocks? . . . . They were scattered, because there is no shepherd: and they became meat to all the beasts of the field, when they were scattered:"[4] and in the time of the Prophet Zechariah, who says, "Woe to the idle shepherd that leaveth the flock!"[5]

So was it all over the world when Christ came in His infinite mercy "to gather in one the children of God that were scattered abroad." And though for a moment, when in the conflict with the enemy the good Shepherd had to lay down His life for the sheep, they were left without a guide (according to the prophecy already quoted, "Smite the Shepherd and the sheep shall be scattered"), yet He soon rose from death to live for ever, according to that other prophecy which said, "He that scattered Israel will gather him, as a shepherd doth his flock."[6] And as He says Himself in the parable before us, "He calleth His own sheep by name and leadeth them out, and goeth before them, and the sheep follow Him, for they know His voice," so, on His resurrection, while Mary wept, He did call her by her name,[7] and she turned herself and knew Him by the ear whom she had not known by the eye. So, too, He said, "Simon, son of Jonas, lovest thou Me?"[8] And He added, "Follow Me." And so again He and His Angel told the women, "Behold He goeth before you into Galilee . . . go tell My brethren, that they go into Galilee, and there shall they see Me."

From that time the good Shepherd who took the place of the sheep, and died that they might live for ever, has gone before them: and "they follow the Lamb whithersoever He goeth;"[9] going their way forth by the footsteps of the flock, and feeding their kids beside the shepherds' tents.[10]

No earthly images can come up to the awful and gracious truth, that God became the Son of man—that the Word became flesh, and was born of a woman. This ineffable mystery surpasses human words. No titles of earth can Christ give to Himself, ever so lowly or mean, which will fitly show us His condescension. His act and deed is too great even for His own

[3] 1 Kings xxii.17.   [4] Ezek. xxxiv.2, 5.   [5] Zech. xi.17.
[6] Jer. xxxi.10.   [7] John xx.16.   [8] John xxi.15.
[9] Rev. xiv.4.   [10] Cant. i.8.

lips to utter it. Yet He delights in the image contained in the text, as conveying to us, in such degree as we can receive it, some notion of the degradation, hardship, and pain, which He underwent for our sake.

Hence it was prophesied under this figure by the Prophet Isaiah, "Behold, the Lord God will come with strong hand, and His arm shall rule for Him . . . . He shall feed His flock like a shepherd: He shall gather the lambs with His arm, and carry them in His bosom, and shall gently lead those that are with young." [11] And, again, He promises by the mouth of Ezekiel, "Behold, I, even I, will both search My sheep, and seek them out. As a shepherd seeketh out his flock in the day that he is among his sheep that are scattered; so will I seek out My sheep, and will deliver them out of all places where they have been scattered in the cloudy and dark day." [12] And the Psalmist says of Him, "The Lord is my Shepherd, therefore can I lack nothing. He shall feed me in a green pasture, and lead me forth beside the waters of comfort." [13] And he addresses Him, "Hear, O thou Shepherd of Israel, Thou that leadest Joseph like a sheep, show Thyself also, Thou that sittest upon the Cherubims." [14] And He Himself says in a parable, speaking of Himself, "What man of you having a hundred sheep, if he lose one of them, doth not leave the ninety and nine in the wilderness, and go after that which is lost, until he find it? And when he hath found it, he layeth it on his shoulders, rejoicing." [15]

Observe, my brethren, it is here said that Christ, the Lord of Angels, condescends to lay the lost sheep on His shoulders: in a former passage of the Prophet Isaiah it was said that He should "gather them with His arm, and carry them in His bosom." By carrying them in His bosom is meant the love He bears them, and the fulness of His grace; by carrying them on His shoulders is signified the security of their dwelling-place; as of old time it was said of Benjamin, "the beloved of the Lord shall dwell in safety by Him . . . and the Lord shall cover him all the day long, and he shall dwell between His shoulders;" [16] and again, of Israel, "As an eagle stirreth up her nest, fluttereth over her young, spreadeth abroad her wings, taketh them, beareth them on her wings: so the Lord alone did lead him, and there was no strange god with him." And again, in the Prophet Isaiah, "Bel boweth down, Nebo stoopeth; their idols were upon the beasts and upon the cattle . . hearken unto Me, O house of Jacob . . which

[11] Is. xl.10, 11.   [12] Ezek. xxxiv.11, 12.   [13] Ps. xxiii.1, 2.
[14] Ps. lxxx.1.   [15] Luke xv.4, 5.   [16] Deut. xxxiii.12.

are carried *by Me* from the womb . . Even to your old age I am
He, and even to hoary hairs will I carry you; I have made and I
will bear, even I will carry, and will deliver you." [17] He alone,
who "bowed Himself and came down," He alone could do it;
He alone could bear a whole world's weight, the load of a guilty
world, the burden of man's sin, the accumulated debt, past,
present, and to come; the sufferings which we owed but could
not pay, the wrath of God on the children of Adam; "in His
own body on the tree," [18] "being made a curse for us," [19] "the
just for the unjust, that He might bring us unto God," "through
the Eternal Spirit offering Himself without spot to God, and
purging our conscience from dead works to serve the Living
God." [20] Such was the deed of Christ, laying down His life for
us: and therefore He is called the Good Shepherd.

And hence, in like manner, from the time of Adam to that of
Christ, a shepherd's work has been marked out with special
Divine favour, as being a shadow of the good Shepherd who
was to come. "Righteous Abel" was "a keeper of sheep," "and
in process of time" he "brought of the firstlings of his flock and
of the fat thereof. And the Lord had respect unto Abel and to
his offering." [21] And who were they to whom the Angels first
brought the news that a Saviour was born? "Shepherds abiding
in the field, keeping watch over their flock by night." [22] And
what is the description given of the chosen family when they
descended into Egypt? "Thy servants," they say, "are shepherds, both we and also our fathers;" [23] and what, in consequence, was their repute in Egypt, which surely is a figure of
the world? "Every shepherd is an abomination unto the Egyptians." [24]

But there are three favoured servants of God in particular,
special types of the Saviour to come, men raised from low estate
to great honour, in whom it was His will that His pastoral office
should be thus literally fulfilled. And the first is Jacob, the father of the patriarchs, who appeared before Pharaoh. He became, as Abraham before him, a father of many nations; he
"increased exceedingly, and had much cattle, and maid-servants, and men-servants, and camels, and asses," [25] and he was
visited by supernatural favours, and had a new name given
him—Israel for Jacob. But at the first he was, as his descendants

[17] Deut. xxxii.11; Is. xlvi.1–4.
[18] 1 Pet. ii.24.
[19] Gal. iii.13.
[20] 1 Pet. iii.18; Heb. ix.14.
[21] Gen. iv.2, 4.
[22] Luke ii.8.
[23] Gen. xlvii.3.
[24] Gen. xlvi.34.
[25] Gen. xxx.43.

solemnly confessed year by year, "a Syrian ready to perish;" and what was his employment? the care of sheep; and with what toil and suffering, and for how many years, we learn from his expostulation with his hard master and relative, Laban— "This twenty years have I been with thee," he says; "thy ewes and thy she-goats have not cast their young, and the rams of thy flock have I not eaten. That which was torn of beasts I brought not unto thee; I bare the loss of it; of my hand didst thou require it, whether stolen by day, or stolen by night. Thus I was; in the day the drought consumed me, and the frost by night; and my sleep departed from mine eyes. Thus have I been twenty years in thy house; . . . and thou hast changed my wages ten times." [26]

Who is more favoured than Jacob, who was exalted to be a Prince with God, and to prevail by intercession? Yet, you see, he is a shepherd, to image to us that mystical and true Shepherd and Bishop of souls who was to come. Yet there is a second and a third as highly favoured in various ways. The second is Moses, who drove away the rival shepherds and helped the daughters of the Priest of Midian to water their flock; and who, while he was keeping the flock of Jethro, his father-in-law, saw the Angel of the Lord in a flame of fire in a bush. And the third is David, the man after God's own heart. He was "the man who was raised up on high, the anointed of the God of Jacob, and the sweet Psalmist of Israel;" [27] but he was found among the sheep. "He took him away from the sheep-folds; as he was following the ewes great with young ones, He took him; that he might feed Jacob His people, and Israel His inheritance. So he fed them with a faithful and true heart, and ruled them prudently with all his power." [28] Samuel came to Jesse, and looked through his seven sons, one by one, but found not him whom God had chosen: "And Samuel said unto Jesse, Are here all thy children? And he said, There remaineth yet the youngest; and, behold, he keepeth the sheep." And when he came "he was ruddy, and withal of a beautiful countenance, and goodly to look to; and the Lord said, Arise, anoint him, for this is he." [29] And again, after he had been in Saul's court, he "went and returned from Saul, to feed his father's sheep at Bethlehem;" [30] and when he came to the army his brother reproached him for "leaving those his few sheep in the wilderness;" and when he was brought before Saul, he gave an account how a lion and a bear "took a lamb out of the flock,"

[26] Gen. xxxi.38–41.   [27] 2 Sam. xxiii.1.   [28] Ps. lxxviii.71–73.
[29] 1 Sam. xvi.11, 12.   [30] 1 Sam. xvii.15, 28, 35–37.

and he went after them, and slew them both, and delivered it. Such were the shepherds of old times, men at once of peace and of war; men of simplicity, indeed, "plain men living in tents," "the meekest of men," yet not easy, indolent men, sitting in green meadows, and by cool streams, but men of rough duties, who were under the necessity to suffer, while they had the opportunity to do exploits.

And if such were the figures, how much more was the Truth itself, the good Shepherd, when He came, both guileless and heroic? If shepherds are men of simple lives and obscure fortunes, uncorrupted and unknown in kings' courts and marts of commerce, how much more He who was "the carpenter's Son," who was "meek and lowly of heart," who "did not strive nor cry," who "went about doing good," who "when He was reviled, reviled not again," and who was "despised and rejected of men"? If, on the other hand, they are men of suffering and trial, how much more so He who was "a man of sorrows," and who "laid down His life for the sheep"?

"That which was torn of beasts I brought not unto thee," says Jacob; "I bare the loss of it; of my hand didst thou require it." And has not Christ undertaken the charge of our souls? Has He not made Himself answerable for us whom the devil had rent? Like the good Samaritan, "Take care of him," He says, "and whatsoever thou spendest more, when I come again I will repay thee."[31] Or, as in another parable, under another image: "Lord, let it alone this year also . . and if it bear fruit, well; and if not, then after that thou shalt cut it down."[32] "In the day the drought consumed me," says Jacob; and who was He who at midday sat down at that very Jacob's well, tired with His journey, and needing some of that water to quench His thirst, whereof "Jacob drank himself, and his children and his cattle"? Yet whereas He had a living water to impart, which the world knew not of, He preferred, as became the good Shepherd, to offer it to one of those lost sheep whom He came to seek and to save, rather than to take at her hand the water from the well, or to accept the offer of His disciples, when they came with meat from the city, and said, "Master, eat." "The frost" consumed me "by night," says Jacob, "and my sleep departed from mine eyes;" and read we not of One whose wont it was to rise a long while before day, and continue in prayer to God? who passed nights in the mountain, or on the sea? who dwelt forty days in the wilderness? who, in the evening and night of His passion,

[31] Luke x.35.   [32] Luke xiii.8, 9.

was forlorn in the bleak garden, or stripped and bleeding in the cold judgment hall?

Again: Moses, amid his sheep, saw the vision of God and was told of God's adorable Name; and Christ, the true Shepherd, lived a life of contemplation in the midst of His laborious ministry; He was transfigured on the mountain, and no man knew the Son but the Father, nor the Father but the Son.

Jacob endured, Moses meditated—and David wrought. Jacob endured the frost, and heat, and sleepless nights, and paid the price of the lost sheep; Moses was taken up into the mount for forty days; David fought with the foe, and recovered the prey—he rescued it from the mouth of the lion, and the paw of the bear, and killed the ravenous beasts. Christ, too, not only suffered with Jacob, and was in contemplation with Moses, but fought and conquered with David. David defended his father's sheep at Bethlehem; Christ, born and heralded to the shepherds at Bethlehem, suffered on the Cross in order to conquer. He came "from Edom, with dyed garments from Bozrah;"[33] but He was "glorious in His apparel," for He trod the people "in His anger, and trampled them in His fury, and their blood was sprinkled upon His garments, and He stained all His raiment." Jacob was not as David, nor David as Jacob, nor either of them as Moses; but Christ was all three, as fulfilling all types, the lowly Jacob, the wise Moses, the heroic David, all in one— Priest, Prophet, and King.

My brethren, we say daily, "We are His people, and the sheep of His pasture." Again, we say, "We have erred and strayed from Thy ways, like lost sheep:" let us never forget these truths; let us never forget, on the one hand, that we are sinners; let us never forget, on the other hand, that Christ is our Guide and Guardian. He is "the Way, the Truth, and the Life."[34] He is a light unto our ways, and a lanthorn unto our paths. He is our Shepherd, and the sheep know His voice. If we are His sheep, we shall hear it, recognize it, and obey it. Let us beware of not following when He goes before: "He goes before, and His sheep follow Him, for they know His voice." Let us beware of receiving His grace in vain. When God called Samuel, he answered, "Speak, Lord, for Thy servant heareth." When Christ called St. Paul, he "was not disobedient to the heavenly vision." Let us desire to know His voice; let us pray for the gift of watchful ears and a willing heart. He does not call all men in one way; He calls us each in His own way. To St. Peter He said, "Follow thou

[33] Is. lxiii.1–3.   [34] John xiv.6.

Me;" of St. John, "If I will that he tarry till I come, what is that to thee?" Nor is it always easy to know His voice. St. John knew it, and said, "It is the Lord," before St. Peter. Samuel did not know it till Eli told him. St. Paul asked, "Who art Thou, Lord?" We are bid, "try the spirits, whether they be of God." But whatever difficulty there be in knowing when Christ calls, and whither, yet at least let us look out for His call. Let us not be content with ourselves; let us not make our own hearts our home, or this world our home, or our friends our home; let us look out for a better country, that is, a heavenly. Let us look out for Him who alone can guide us to that better country; let us call heaven our home, and this life a pilgrimage; let us view ourselves, as sheep in the trackless desert, who, unless they follow the shepherd, will be sure to lose themselves, sure to fall in with the wolf. We are safe while we keep close to Him, and under His eye; but if we suffer Satan to gain an advantage over us, woe to us!

Blessed are they who give the flower of their days, and their strength of soul and body to Him; blessed are they who in their youth turn to Him who gave His life for them, and would fain give it to them and implant it in them, that they may live for ever. Blessed are they who resolve—come good, come evil, come sunshine, come tempest, come honour, come dishonour —that He shall be their Lord and Master, their King and God! They will come to a perfect end, and to peace at the last. They will, with Jacob, confess Him, ere they die, as "the God that fed them all their life long unto that day, the Angel which re-deemed them from all evil;" [35] with Moses, that "as is their day, so shall their strength be;" and with David, that in "the valley of the shadow of death, they fear no evil, for He is with them, and that His rod and His staff comfort them;" for "when they pass through the waters He will be with them, and through the rivers, they shall not overflow them; when they walk through the fire, they shall not be burnt, neither shall the flame kindle upon them, for He is the Lord their God, the Holy One of Is-rael, their Saviour."

[35] Gen. xlviii.15, 16.

RELIGIOUS JOY

"And the angel said unto them, Fear not: for, behold,
I bring you good tidings of great joy, which shall be to all people.
For unto you is born this day in the city of David a Saviour,
which is Christ the Lord."—Luke ii.10, 11.

THERE are two principal lessons which we are taught on the great Festival which we this day celebrate, lowliness and joy. This surely is a day, of all others, in which is set before us the heavenly excellence and the acceptableness in God's sight of that state which most men have, or may have, allotted to them, humble or private life, and cheerfulness in it. If we consult the writings of historians, philosophers, and poets of this world, we shall be led to think great men happy; we shall be led to fix our minds and hearts upon high or conspicuous stations, strange adventures, powerful talents to cope with them, memorable struggles, and great destinies. We shall consider that the highest course of life is the mere pursuit, not the enjoyment of good.

But when we think of this day's Festival, and what we commemorate upon it, a new and very different scene opens upon us. First, we are reminded that though this life must ever be a life of toil and effort, yet that, properly speaking, we have not to seek our highest good. It is found, it is brought near us, in the descent of the Son of God from His Father's bosom to this world. It is stored up among us on earth. No longer need men of ardent minds weary themselves in the pursuit of what they fancy may be chief goods; no longer have they to wander about and encounter peril in quest of that unknown blessedness to which their hearts naturally aspire, as they did in heathen times. The text speaks to them and to all, "Unto you," it says, "is born this day in the city of David a Saviour, which is Christ the Lord."

Nor, again, need we go in quest of any of those things which this vain world calls great and noble. Christ altogether dishonoured what the world esteems, when He took on Himself a

---

[1] For Christmas Day.

rank and station which the world despises. No lot could be more humble and more ordinary than that which the Son of God chose for Himself.

So that we have on the Feast of the Nativity these two lessons—instead of anxiety within and despondence without, instead of a weary search after great things,—to be cheerful and joyful; and, again, to be so in the midst of those obscure and ordinary circumstances of life which the world passes over and thinks scorn of.

Let us consider this more at length, as contained in the gracious narrative of which the text is part.

1. First, what do we read just before the text? that there were certain shepherds keeping watch over their flock by night, and Angels appeared to them. Why should the heavenly hosts appear to these shepherds? What was it in them which attracted the attention of the Angels and the Lord of Angels? Were these shepherds learned, distinguished, or powerful? Were they especially known for piety and gifts? Nothing is said to make us think so. Faith, we may safely say, they had, or some of them, for to him that hath more shall be given; but there is nothing to show that they were holier and more enlightened than other good men of the time, who waited for the consolation of Israel. Nay, there is no reason to suppose that they were better than the common run of men in their circumstances, simple, and fearing God, but without any great advances in piety, or any very formed habits of religion. Why then were they chosen? for their poverty's sake and obscurity. Almighty God looks with a sort of especial love, or (as we may term it) affection, upon the lowly. Perhaps it is that man, a fallen, dependent, and destitute creature, is more in his proper place when he is in lowly circumstances, and that power and riches, though unavoidable in the case of some, are unnatural appendages to man, as such. Just as there are trades and callings which are unbecoming, though requisite; and while we profit by them, and honour those the more who engage in them, yet we feel we are glad that they are not ours; as we feel grateful and respectful towards a soldier's profession, yet do not affect it; so in God's sight greatness is less acceptable than obscurity. It becomes us less.

The shepherds, then, were chosen on account of their lowliness, to be the first to hear of the Lord's nativity, a secret which none of the princes of this world knew.

And what a contrast is presented to us when we take into account who were our Lord's messengers to them! The Angels who excel in strength, these did His bidding towards the shep-

herds. Here the highest and the lowest of God's rational creatures are brought together. A set of poor men, engaged in a life
of hardship, exposed at that very time to the cold and darkness
of the night, watching their flocks, with the view of scaring
away beasts of prey or robbers; they—when they are thinking
of nothing but earthly things, counting over the tale of their
sheep, keeping their dogs by their side, and listening to the
noises over the plain, considering the weather and watching for
the day—suddenly are met by far other visitants than they
conceived. We know the contracted range of thought, the
minute and ordinary objects, or rather the one or two objects,
to and fro again and again without variety, which engage the
minds of men exposed to such a life of heat, cold, and wet, hunger and nakedness, hardship and servitude. They cease to care
much for any thing, but go on in a sort of mechanical way,
without heart, and still more without reflection.

To men so circumstanced the Angel appeared, to open their
minds, and to teach them not to be downcast and in bondage
because they were low in the world. He appeared as if to show
them that God had chosen the poor in this world to be heirs of
His kingdom, and so to do honour to their lot. "Fear not," he
said, "for behold I bring you good tidings of great joy, which
shall be to all people. For unto you is born this day in the city of
David a Saviour, which is Christ the Lord."

2. And now comes a second lesson, which I have said may be
gained from the Festival. The Angel honoured a humble lot by
his very appearing to the shepherds; next he taught it to be joyful by his message. He disclosed good tidings so much above
this world as to equalize high and low, rich and poor, one with
another. He said, "Fear not." This is a mode of address frequent in Scripture, as you may have observed, as if man needed
some such assurance to support him, especially in God's presence. The Angel said, "Fear not," when he saw the alarm
which his presence caused among the shepherds. Even a lesser
wonder would have reasonably startled them. Therefore the
Angel said, "Fear not." We are naturally afraid of any messenger from the other world, for we have an uneasy conscience
when left to ourselves, and think that his coming forebodes
evil. Besides, we so little realize the unseen world, that were
Angel or spirit to present himself before us we should be
startled by reason of our unbelief, a truth being brought home
to our minds which we never apprehended before. So for one
or other reason the shepherds were sore afraid when the glory
of the Lord shone around about them. And the Angel said,

"Fear not." A little religion makes us afraid; when a little light is poured in upon the conscience, there is a darkness visible; nothing but sights of woe and terror; the glory of God alarms while it shines around. His holiness, the range and difficulties of His commandments, the greatness of His power, the faithfulness of His word, frighten the sinner, and men seeing him afraid, think religion has made him so, whereas he is not yet religious at all. They call him religious, when he is merely conscience-stricken. But religion itself, far from inculcating alarm and terror, says, in the words of the Angel, "Fear not;" for such is His mercy, while Almighty God has poured about us His glory, yet it is a consolatory glory, for it is the light of His glory in the Face of Jesus Christ.[2] Thus the heavenly herald tempered the too dazzling brightness of the Gospel on that first Christmas. The glory of God at first alarmed the shepherds, so he added the tidings of good, to work in them a more wholesome and happy temper. Then they rejoiced.

"Fear not," said the Angel, "for behold I bring you good tidings of great joy, which shall be to all people. For unto you is born this day in the city of David a Saviour, which is Christ the Lord." And then, when he had finished his announcement, "suddenly there was with the Angel a multitude of the heavenly host, praising God and saying, Glory to God in the highest, and on earth peace, good will towards men." Such were the words which the blessed Spirits who minister to Christ and His Saints, spoke on that gracious night to the shepherds, to rouse them out of their cold and famished mood into great joy; to teach them that they were objects of God's love as much as the greatest of men on earth; nay more so, for to them first He had imparted the news of what that night was happening. His Son was then born into the world. Such events are told to friends and intimates, to those whom we love, to those who will sympathize with us, not to strangers. How could Almighty God be more gracious, and show His favour more impressively to the lowly and the friendless, than by hastening (if I may use the term) to confide the great, the joyful secret to the shepherds keeping watch over their sheep by night?

The Angel then gave the first lesson of mingled humility and joyfulness; but an infinitely greater one was behind in the event itself, to which he directed the shepherds, in that birth itself of the Holy Child Jesus. This he intimated in these words: "Ye shall find the babe wrapped in swaddling clothes, lying in a

[2] 2 Cor. iv.6.

manger." Doubtless, when they heard the Lord's Christ was born into the world, they would look for Him in kings' palaces. They would not be able to fancy that He had become one of themselves, or that they might approach Him; therefore the Angel thus warned them where to find Him, not only as a sign, but as a lesson also.

"The shepherds said one to another, Let us now go even unto Bethlehem, and see this thing which is come to pass, which the Lord hath made known to us." Let us too go with them, to contemplate that second and greater miracle to which the Angel directed them, the Nativity of Christ. St. Luke says of the Blessed Virgin, "She brought forth her first-born Son, and wrapped Him in swaddling clothes, and laid Him in a manger." What a wonderful sign is this to all the world, and therefore the Angel repeated it to the shepherds: "Ye shall find the babe wrapped in swaddling clothes, lying in a manger." The God of heaven and earth, the Divine Word, who had been in glory with the eternal Father from the beginning, He was at this time born into this world of sin as a little infant. He, as at this time, lay in His mother's arms, to all appearance helpless and power-less, and was wrapped by Mary in an infant's bands, and laid to sleep in a manger. The Son of God Most High, who created the worlds, became flesh, though remaining what He was before. He became flesh as truly as if He had ceased to be what He was, and had actually been changed into flesh. He submitted to be the offspring of Mary, to be taken up in the hands of a mortal, to have a mother's eye fixed upon Him, and to be cherished at a mother's bosom. A daughter of man became the Mother of God—to her, indeed, an unspeakable gift of grace; but in Him what condescension! What an emptying of His glory to be-come man! and not only a helpless infant, though that were humiliation enough, but to inherit all the infirmities and im-perfections of our nature which were possible to a sinless soul. What were His thoughts, if we may venture to use such lan-guage or admit such a reflection concerning the Infinite, when human feelings, human sorrows, human wants, first became His? What a mystery is there from first to last in the Son of God becoming man! Yet in proportion to the mystery is the grace and mercy of it; and as is the grace, so is the greatness of the fruit of it.

Let us steadily contemplate the mystery, and say whether any consequence is too great to follow from so marvellous a dispen-sation; any mystery so great, any grace so overpowering, as that which is already manifested in the incarnation and death of the

Eternal Son. Were we told that the effect of it would be to make us as Seraphim, that we were to ascend as high as He descended low—would that startle us after the Angel's news to the shepherds? And this indeed is the effect of it, so far as such words may be spoken without impiety. Men we remain, but not mere men, but gifted with a measure of all those perfections which Christ has in fulness, partaking each in his own degree of His Divine Nature so fully, that the only reason (so to speak) why His saints are not really like Him, is that it is impossible— that He is the Creator, and they His creatures; yet still so, that they are all but Divine, all that they can be made without violating the incommunicable majesty of the Most High. Surely in proportion to His glory is His power of glorifying; so that to say that through Him we shall be made *all but* gods—though it is to say, that we are infinitely below the adorable Creator—still is to say, and truly, that we shall be higher than every other being in the world; higher than Angels or Archangels, Cherubim or Seraphim—that is, not here, or in ourselves, but in heaven and in Christ:—Christ, already the first-fruits of our race, God and man, having ascended high above all creatures, and we through His grace tending to the same high blessedness, having the earnest of His glory given here, and (if we be found faithful) the fulness of it hereafter.

If all these things be so, surely the lesson of joy which the Incarnation gives us is as impressive as the lesson of humility. St. Paul gives us the one lesson in his epistle to the Philippians: "Let this mind be in you, which was also in Christ Jesus: who, being in the form of God, thought it not robbery to be equal with God: but made Himself of no reputation, and took upon Him the form of a servant, and was made in the likeness of men:"[3] and St. Peter gives us the lesson of joyfulness: "whom having not seen, ye love; in whom, though now ye see Him not, yet believing, ye rejoice with joy unspeakable, and full of glory: receiving the end of your faith, even the salvation of your souls."

Take these thoughts with you, my brethren, to your homes on this festive day; let them be with you in your family and social meetings. It is a day of joy: it is good to be joyful—it is wrong to be otherwise. For one day we may put off the burden of our polluted consciences, and rejoice in the perfections of our Saviour Christ, without thinking of ourselves, without thinking of our own miserable uncleanness: but contemplating

[3] Phil. ii.5–7; 1 Pet. i.8, 9.

His glory, His righteousness, His purity, His majesty, His over-flowing love. We may rejoice in the Lord, and in all His creatures see Him. We may enjoy His temporal bounty, and partake the pleasant things of earth with Him in our thoughts; we may rejoice in our friends for His sake, loving them most especially because He has loved them.

"God has not appointed us unto wrath, but to obtain salvation through our Lord Jesus Christ, who died for us, that whether we wake or sleep, we should live together with Him." Let us seek the grace of a cheerful heart, an even temper, sweetness, gentleness, and brightness of mind, as walking in His light, and by His grace. Let us pray Him to give us the spirit of ever-abundant, ever-springing love, which overpowers and sweeps away the vexations of life by its own richness and strength, and which above all things unites us to Him who is the fountain and the centre of all mercy, lovingkindness, and joy.

IGNORANCE OF EVIL

"And the Lord God said, Behold, the man is become as one of Us, to know good and evil."—Gen. iii.22.

IT is plain that the temptation under which man fell in paradise was this, an ambitious curiosity after knowledge which was not allowed him: next came the desire of the eyes and the flesh, but the forbidden tree was called the tree of *knowledge*; the Tempter *promised* knowledge; and after the fall Almighty God pronounced, as in the text, that man had gained it. "Behold, the man is become as one of Us, to *know* good and evil."

You see it is said, "man is become *as one of Us*, to know good and evil," because God does know evil as well as good. This is His wonderful incommunicable attribute; and man sought to share in what God was, but he could not without ceasing to be what God was also, holy and perfect. It is the incommunicable attribute of God to know evil without experiencing it. But man, when he would be as God, could only attain the shadow of a likeness which as yet he had not, by losing the substance which he had already. He shared in God's knowledge by losing His image. God knows evil and is pure from it—man plunged into evil and so knew it.

Our happiness as well as duty lies in not going beyond our measure—in being contented with what we are—with what God makes us. They who seek after forbidden knowledge, of whatever kind, will find they have lost their place in the scale of beings in so doing, and are cast out of the great circle of God's family.

It is, I say, God's incommunicable attribute, as He did not create, so not to experience sin—and as He permits it, so also to know it; to permit it without creating it, to know it without experiencing it—a wonderful and incomprehensible attribute truly, yet involved, perhaps, in the very circumstance that He permits it. For He is every where and in all, and nothing exists except in and through Him. Mysterious as it is, the very prison

---

[1] For Innocents' Day.

beneath the earth, its chains and fires and impenitent inmates, the very author of evil himself, is sustained in existence by God, and without God would fall into nothing. God is in hell as well as in heaven, a thought which almost distracts the mind to think of. The awful God! "Whither shall I go from Thy Spirit, or whither shall I go from Thy Presence? If I climb up into heaven, Thou art there; if I go down to hell, Thou art there also." Where life is, there is He; and though it be but the life of death—the living death of eternal torment—He is the principle of it. And being thus intimately present with the very springs of thought, and the first elements of all being, being the sustaining cause of all spirits, whether they be good or evil, he is intimately present *with* evil, being pure from it—and knows what it is, as being with and in the wretched atoms which originate it.

If there be this sort of connexion between God's knowledge and sufferance of evil, see what an ambition it was in our first parents to desire to know it without experiencing it; it was, indeed, to desire to be as gods,—to know the secrets of the prison-house, and to see the worm that dieth not, yet remain innocent and happy.

This they understood not; they desired something which they knew not that they could not have, remaining as they were; they did not see how knowledge and experience went together in the case of human nature; and Satan did not undeceive them. They ate of the tree which was to make them wise, and, alas! they saw clearly what sin was, what shame, what death, what hell, what despair. They lost God's presence, and they gained the knowledge of evil. They lost Eden, and they gained a conscience.

This, in fact, is the knowledge of good and evil. Lost spirits do not know good. Angels do not know evil. Beings like ourselves, fallen beings, fallen yet not cast away, know good and evil; evil not external to them, nor yet one with them; but in them, yet not simply of them. Such was the fruit of the forbidden tree, as it remains in us to this day.

We do not know in what the duty and happiness of other beings consist; but at least this seems to have been man's happiness in Paradise, not to think about himself or to be conscious of himself. Such, too, to recur to the parallel especially suggested on this day, seems to be the state of children. They do not reflect upon themselves. Such, too, seems to be the state of those orders of Angels whose life is said to consist in contemplation—for what is contemplation but a resting in the thought of God to the forgetfulness of self? Hence the Saints are described as "Virgins who *follow the Lamb whithersoever He goeth.*" But Adam, discontented with what he was, pined after a knowledge which he could not obtain from without—which he could only have from miserable experience within—from moral disorders within him, and from having his mind drawn to the contemplation of himself in consequence of those disorders. He obtained the wished for knowledge; and his first recorded act afterwards was one of reflection upon self, and he hid himself among the trees of the garden. He was no longer fitted for contemplating glories without him; his attention was arrested to the shame that was upon him.

What is so miserably seen in the history of our first parents has been the temptation and sin of their posterity ever since,—indulgence in forbidden, unlawful, hurtful, unprofitable knowledge; as some instances will show.

1. I ought to notice in the first place that evil curiosity which stimulates young persons to intrude into things of which it is their blessedness to be ignorant. Satan gains our souls step by step; and his first allurement is the knowledge of what is wrong. He first tempts them to the knowledge, and then to the commission of sin. Depend on it that our happiness and our glory, in these matters, is to be ignorant, as well as to be guiltless. St. Paul says that "it is a shame even to speak" of those things which are done by the sons of Belial in secret. Oh, thoughtless, and worse, oh, cruel to your own selves, all ye who read what ye should not read, and hear what ye should not hear! Oh, how will you repent of your folly afterwards! Oh, what bitter feelings, oh, what keen pangs, will shoot through your souls hereafter, at the memory, when you look back, of what has come of that baneful curiosity! Oh, how will you despise yourselves, oh, how weep at what you have brought on you! At this day surely there is a special need of this warning; for this is a day when nothing is not pried into, nothing is not published, nothing is not laid before all men.

2. In the next place I would observe, that the pursuit of science, which characterizes these times, is very likely to draw us aside into a sin of a particular kind, if we are not on our guard. We read, in the book of Acts, of many who used curious arts burning their books; that is, there are kinds of knowledge which are forbidden to the Christian. Now this seems strange to the world in this day. The only forbidden subjects which they can fancy, are such as are not *true*—fictions, impostures, superstitions, and the like. Falsehood they think wrong; false religions, for instance, *because* false. But they are perplexed when

told that there may be branches of real knowledge, yet forbidden. Yet it has ever been considered in the Church, as in Scripture, that soothsaying, consulting the stars, magic, and similar arts, are unlawful—unlawful, even though not false; and Scripture certainly speaks as if at least some of them were more than merely a pretended knowledge and a pretended power; whereas men now-a-days have got to think that they are wrong, merely because *frauds* and *impostures*; and if they found them not so, they would be very slow to understand how still they are unlawful. They have not mastered the idea that real knowledge may be forbidden us.

3. Next it is obvious to speak of those melancholy persons who boast themselves on what they call their knowledge of the world and of life. There are men, alas not a few, who look upon acquaintance with evil as if a part of their education. Instead of shunning vice and sin, they try it, if for no other reason, simply for this—that they may have knowledge of it. They mix with various classes of men, and they throw themselves into the manners and opinions of all in turn. They are ready-witted perhaps, prompt and versatile, and easily adapt themselves so as to please and get acquainted with those they fall in with. They have no scruples of conscience hindering them from complying with whatever is proposed; they are of any form of religion, have lax or correct morals, according to the occasion. They can revel with those that revel, and they can speak serious things when their society is serious. They travel up and down the country perhaps, or they are of professions or pursuits which introduce them to men of various languages, or which take them abroad, and they see persons of opposite creeds and principles, and whatever they fall in with they take as so many facts, merely as facts of human nature, not as things right or wrong according to a certain fixed standard independent of themselves. Now whatever of religion or truth remains in our fallen nature is not on the surface: these men, then, studying what is uppermost, are in fact but studying all that is evil in man, and in consequence they have very low notions of man. They are very sceptical about the existence of principle and virtue; they think all men equally swayed by worldly, selfish, or sensual motives, though some hide their motives better than others, or have feelings and likings of a more refined character. And having given in to sin themselves, they have no higher principle within them to counteract the effect of what they see without; all their notions of man's nature, capabilities, and destinies, are derived from, and are measured by, what goes on in the world, and ac-

cordingly they apply all their knowledge to bad purposes. They think they know, and they do know too truly on the whole, the motives and inducements which will prevail with men; and they use their knowledge to overreach, deceive, seduce, corrupt, or sway those with whom they have to do.

4. Another very different class of persons who study evil, and pride themselves upon it, and are degraded by it, are those who indulge themselves in contemplating and dwelling on the struggle between right and wrong in their own minds. There have been from time to time men of morbid imaginations, of any or no religious creed, who have so exercised themselves. Indeed there has been a large school of writers in very various departments, for years, I may say centuries past, though happily they are diminishing now, who delight in bringing out into open day all the weaknesses and inconsistencies of human nature; nay worse, take pains to describe bad men, and how they feel, and what they say; who interest the mind in bad men, nay in bad Angels, as if Satan might be thought of otherwise than with shuddering. And there are others, men of mistaken religious views, who think that religion consists in dwelling on and describing the struggle between grace and corrupt nature in the soul. Christ has brought us light and life, and would have us put off what we are, and follow Him, who knew no sin. But these men, far from rising even to the aspiration after perfection, do not advance in their notion of spiritual religion beyond the idea of declaring and lamenting their want of it. Confession is with them perfection; nay, it is almost the test of a Christian, to be able to discourse upon his inward corruption. It is well to confess sin in detail with shame as an act of penitence; it is a snare to speak of it vaguely and in public.

5. Lastly, even when used rightly, the knowledge of sin is not without its danger. As mediciners would not exist were there no illness or disease, so it is mental disease which gives rise to casuists. Pain leads us to think of our bodies, and sin of our souls. Were our souls in perfect harmony, they would act like an instrument in tune; we should with difficulty divide the sounds, even if we would; but it is the discordance, the jar within us, which leads us to a serious contemplation of what we are. The same remark obviously applies to a great deal of theological knowledge, on which men who have it are tempted to pride themselves; I mean exact knowledge of heresies and the like. The love of God alone can give such knowledge its right direction. There is the danger lest men so informed find themselves scrutinizing when they should be adoring, reasoning when

they should be believing, comparing when they should be choosing, and proving when they should be acting. We know two things of the Angels—that they cry Holy, Holy, Holy, and that they do God's bidding. Worship and service make up their blessedness; and such is our blessedness in proportion as we approach them. But all exercises of mind which lead us to reflect upon and ascertain our state; to know what worship is, and why we worship; what service is, and why we serve; what our feelings imply, and what our words mean, tend to divert our minds from the one thing needful, unless we are practised and expert in using them. All proofs of religion, evidences, proofs of particular doctrines, scripture proofs, and the like,—these certainly furnish scope for the exercise of great and admirable powers of mind, and it would be fanatical to disparage or disown them; but it requires a mind rooted and grounded in love not to be dissipated by them. As for truly religious minds, they, when so engaged, instead of mere disputing, are sure to turn inquiry into meditation, exhortation into worship, and argument into teaching.

Reflections such as these, followed up, show us how different is our state from that for which God made us. He meant us to be simple, and we are unreal; He meant us to think no evil, and a thousand associations, bad, trifling, or unworthy, attend our every thought. He meant us to be drawn on to the glories without us, and we are drawn back and (as it were) fascinated by the miseries within us. And hence it is that the whole structure of society is so artificial; no one trusts another, if he can help it; safeguards, checks, and securities are ever sought after. No one means exactly what he says, for our words have lost their natural meaning, and even an Angel could not use them naturally, for every mind being different from every other, they have no distinct meaning. What, indeed, is the very function of society, as it is at present, but a rude attempt to cover the degradation of the fall, and to make men feel respect for themselves, and enjoy it in the eyes of others, without returning to God. This is what we should especially guard against, because there is so much of it in the world. I mean, not an abandonment of evil, not a sweeping away and cleansing out of the corruption which sin has bred within us, but a smoothing it over, an outside delicacy and polish, an ornamenting the surface of things while "within are dead men's bones and all uncleanness;" making the garments, which at first were given for decency, a means of pride and vanity. Men give good names to what is evil, they sanctify bad principles and feelings; and, knowing that there is vice and error, selfishness, pride, and ambition, in the world, they attempt, not to root out these evils, not to withstand these errors;—that they think a dream, the dream of theorists who do not know the world;—but to cherish and form alliance with them, to use them, to make a science of selfishness, to flatter and indulge error, and to bribe vice with the promise of bearing with it, so that it does but keep in the shade.

But let us, finding ourselves in the state in which we are, take those means which alone are really left us, which alone become us. Adam, when he had sinned, and felt himself fallen, instead of honestly abandoning what he had become, would fain have hid himself. He went a step further. He did not give up what he now was, partly from dread of God, partly from dislike of what he had been. He had learnt to love sin and to fear God's justice. But Christ has purchased for us what we lost in Adam, our garment of innocence. He has bid us and enabled us to become as little children; He has purchased for us the grace of *simplicity*, which, though one of the highest, is very little thought about, is very little sought after. We have, indeed, a general idea what love is, and hope, and faith, and truth, and purity, though a poor idea; but we are almost blind to what is one of the first elements of Christian perfection, that simple-mindedness which springs from the heart's being *whole* with God, entire, undivided. And those who think they have an idea of it, commonly rise no higher than to mistake for it a mere weakness and softness of mind, which is but its counterfeit. To be simple is to be like the Apostles and first Christians. Our Saviour says, "Be ye harmless," or simple, "as doves." And St. Paul, "I would have you wise unto that which is good, and *simple concerning evil*." [2] Again, "That ye may be *blameless and harmless*, the sons of God, without rebuke, in the midst of a crooked and perverse nation." [3] And he speaks of the "testimony of" his own "conscience, that in *simplicity* and godly sincerity, not with fleshly wisdom, but by the grace of God," he had his conversation in the world and towards his disciples. Let us pray God to give us this great and precious gift; that we may blot out from our memory all that offends Him; unlearn all that knowledge which sin has taught us; rid ourselves of selfish motives, self-conceit, and vanity, littlenesses, envying, grudgings, meannesses; turn from all cowardly, low, miserable ways; and escape from servile fears, the fear of man, vague anxieties of

[2] Rom. xvi.19.   [3] Phil. ii.15

conscience, and superstitions. So that we may have the boldness and frankness of those who are as if they had no sin, from
having been cleansed from it; the uncontaminated hearts, open
countenances, and untroubled eyes of those who neither suspect, nor conceal, nor shun, nor are jealous; in a word, so that
we may have confidence in Him, that we may stay on Him, and
rest in the thoughts of Him, instead of plunging amid the
thickets of this world; that we may bear His eye and His voice,
and know no knowledge but the knowledge of Him and Jesus
Christ crucified, and desire no objects but what He has blessed
and bid us pursue.

INDEX OF BIBLICAL REFERENCES

Bold numbers refer to pages

ACTS OF THE APOSTLES

INDEX